Corporate Governance

Corporate Governance

Law, Theory and Policy

SECOND EDITION

Edited By

Thomas W. Joo
UNIVERSITY OF CALIFORNIA, DAVIS
SCHOOL OF LAW

CAROLINA ACADEMIC PRESS
Durham, North Carolina

Library of Congress Cataloging-in-Publication Data

Corporate governance : law, theory and policy / [edited by] Thomas W. Joo. -- 2nd ed.
    p. cm.
  ISBN 978-1-59460-739-4 (alk. paper)
  1. Corporate governance--Law and legislation--United States. 2. Corporate
governance--United States. I. Chu, U-il. II. Title.

  KF1422.C6728 2010
  346.73'0664--dc22

                                        2009042021

Carolina Academic Press
700 Kent Street
Durham, North Carolina 27701
Telephone (919) 489-7486
Fax (919) 493-5668
www.cap-press.com

Printed in the United States of America

Contents

Preface to the Second Edition

The first edition of this book was prepared in 2003, as the nation was sorting through the wreckage of Enron, WorldCom, and the other corporate disasters that accompanied the turn of the millennium. In that post-Enron moment, the Sarbanes-Oxley Act of 2002 seemed to mark an end to the deregulatory philosophy of the 1980s and 1990s. But a backlash of anti-regulatory sentiment soon followed, accompanied by a booming economy. I believe it was Professor Larry Ribstein who first dubbed that backlash the "post-post-Enron era." I had imagined this second edition would focus on that shift, but then came the financial meltdown of 2008 and the subsequent recession, which was the dominant economic narrative while this edition was being prepared. A re-regulatory post-post-post Enron era may be dawning as I write this Preface—but it may well have faded by the time it is published. Stay tuned for the third edition.

The obvious question today is why an epidemic of corporate failures recurred so soon after Enron and Sarbanes-Oxley. Perhaps there was insufficient regulatory reform; perhaps too much. Or perhaps the vagaries of the business cycle, and of human cognitive limitations and behavior, are simply beyond our control.

I thank Nina Bell, Xong Vang, and Glenda McGlashan for their help in preparing the manuscript and obtaining reprint permissions and to Adam Lunceford for providing research assistance. I would also like to thank Dean Kevin Johnson, the University of California, Davis, and the UC Davis School of Law for supporting my work on this edition. Finally, I thank Irene, Jason and Alicia Joo for their love and patience.

Preface to the First Edition

At the turn of the millennium, the collapse of the "dot.com" stock market and the rash of scandals involving Enron and other major corporations attracted renewed attention to corporate governance. Shareholders, employees, and society at large felt betrayed by the managers of America's large corporations. The challenges to corporate governance today involve many new economic and business factors, but are rooted in perennial issues of governing the publicly traded corporation.

In their classic 1932 book, *The Modern Corporation and Private Property,* Adolf Berle and Gardiner Means identified the separation between the ownership by shareholders and control by professional managers as a crucial characteristic of the public corporation. They argued that this separation makes public corporations fundamentally different from conventional forms of private property and justifies special legal treatment of the corporate form. Also in 1932, Berle and F. Merrick Dodd engaged in a famous scholarly debate over the question, "For Whom Are Corporate Managers Trustees?" In contrast to the Berle and Means focus on shareholder ownership rights, Dodd argued that other elements of society have an interest in the conduct of large corporations.

Despite their differences, these pioneering scholars agreed that despite its legal form, a corporation is not a monolithic entity, but a complex intersection of various interests seeking control over shared "corporate" resources. As this book shows, subsequent commentary continues to wrestle with the implications of this fundamental insight. Decades after Berle and Means, the separation of ownership and control remains a central concern of corporate governance. In addition, newer theoretical approaches consider the place of additional parties—employees, creditors, corporate acquirers, and others—in the competition and negotiation for control of corporate resources. Regulators—states, the federal government, and stock exchanges—also compete with corporate constituents and even with one another. Social interest groups also vie for control, using both politics and internal corporate governance mechanisms.

Underneath this ongoing competition is a debate over which parties have a legitimate claim to controlling the fate of the corporation. And underlying that debate are the fundamental normative questions about what criteria should determine social priorities, and what role the law should play in all of this.

This volume anthologizes previously published recent scholarship on the law of corporate governance in publicly traded corporations. The selections have been chosen to address current policy issues, as well as to present a wide range of both established and developing approaches to legal analysis, such as law and economics, corporate finance, public choice theory, expressive law, organizational behavior, and sociology.

This book's focus on recent works is not meant to slight the classic literature in the field, but to put the perennial legal and theoretical issues in a contemporary policy context. In addition to exposing the reader to a broad range of theoretical approaches, I hope to familiarize the reader with current policy debates and provide useful descriptive detail about fundamental legal and economic institutions such as the proxy process, takeover defenses, the stock exchanges, shareholder litigation, institutional investors, and the roles of auditors and corporate lawyers.

The discussion questions at the end of each chapter invite readers to compare and contrast the readings and to form their own opinions about the issues raised. Admittedly these questions tend toward the critical. Some issues raised in the questions are addressed by the author in other work or even in excised parts of the articles presented. The questions are intended to encourage critical reading and inspire further thought; they are not meant to pass judgment on any of the works presented.

For the sake of brevity and focus, I have had to excise a great deal of fascinating material from each article. (I have also taken the liberty of altering and renumbering footnotes and section headings in order to increase readability.) Moreover, there are of course many more important works of scholarship excluded from this volume than I could include in it. I encourage readers interested in learning more to seek out the original sources in their entirety, as well as to consult the other sources referred to in the notes and questions.

I would like to thank the authors and publishers of the original articles for their permission to include the edited versions in this book. I also thank Glenda McGlashan, Courtney Hennigan, and Linda Cooper for their invaluable help in preparing the manuscript and obtaining reprint permissions, Charles Yu for his tireless research assistance, my colleagues Bob Hillman and Dick Wydick for their insights, and Dean Rex Perschbacher, Associate Dean Kevin Johnson, and the UC Davis Martin Luther King, Jr. Hall School of Law for financial and moral support. I would also like to thank the King Hall students who have taken my Law of Corporate Governance seminar for helping to shape these materials. Finally, I could not have completed this project without the support and patience of Irene and Jason Joo.

Corporate Governance

Chapter 1

The Role of the Corporation

What is the role of the corporation in society—and what should it be? The orthodox view sees the corporation primarily as a relationship between investors and managers. The primary concern of corporate law policy and scholarship has been to address the divergence of shareholder and management interests. Contemporary economic terminology refers to this divergence with the term "agency costs"—that is, the costs a firm's "owners" (typically defined as shareholders) incur when, instead of operating the firm themselves, they have "agents" (professional directors and officers) operate the firm. Agency-cost analysis focuses on the cost of attempts to monitor and prevent selfish behavior on the part of agents, as well as any losses due to inability to fully control such behavior. Agency costs are not inherently bad, because there are corresponding benefits to having professional management, and these benefits cannot be obtained for free. The problem of agency costs, then, is not how to eliminate them, but how to keep them lower than the corresponding benefits by as much as possible. In the 1970s and 1980s, influenced by economic theories of the business firm, corporate law scholars formulated the hugely influential "contractual" or "contractarian" theory of the corporation. In this chapter, Henry Butler and Fred McChesney present one version of this theory. In their view, the corporation is a "contract," or voluntary economic relationship, between shareholders and management. This contract constitutes the parties' negotiated solution to the agency cost problem, a solution which, they argue, courts and legislatures should treat with deference.

While orthodox corporate law theory tends to focus on corporate managers' duties to shareholders, a competing view of the corporation holds that the large public corporation is more than a relationship between shareholders and managers. This debate can be traced back at least as far as a famous scholarly exchange between Adolf Berle and E. Merrick Dodd in 1932.[1] Dodd argued that corporate managers have duties to society at large as well as to shareholders. The contemporary version of Dodd's position, represented here by Lynne Dallas and Kent Greenfield, points out that large corporations have a profound influence on multiple constituencies in addition to shareholders: creditors, customers, employees, local communities, and the environment, for example. The law's focus on shareholder interests, they argue, is a political choice rather than an inevitability.

Corporations' pursuit of high stock prices may sometimes conflict with the interests of other corporate constituencies, but it would seem to benefit shareholders by definition. William Bratton's article, however, shows how the concept of shareholder value ironically came to betray shareholders as well as others at the turn of the millennium. The spectacular failure of Enron Corporation in 2001 exemplified this betrayal.

---

1. Adolf Berle, *Corporate Powers as Powers in Trust,* 44 HARV. L. REV. 1049 (1931); E. Merrick Dodd, *For Whom Are Corporate Managers Trustees?*, 45 HARV. L. REV. 1145 (1932).

As Cynthia Williams points out, most commentators agree that corporations should focus on shareholder wealth, but only within the bounds of laws enacted to protect other priorities, such as the environment or workers' welfare. This position simplifies the task of corporate social responsibility by reducing it to legal compliance. Williams argues, however, that this compliance theory imposes few constraints on corporate conduct in a globalizing economy.

[handwritten margin note: Cosp. philanthropy K theory]

Henry N. Butler & Fred S. McChesney, *Why They Give at the Office: Shareholder Welfare and Corporate Philanthropy in the Contractual Theory of the Corporation*[*]

… This paper explores the "problem of corporate philanthropy" from the standpoint of the contractual theory of the firm. That is, it considers corporate philanthropy within a framework of the types of contracts that shareholders generally would find desirable to govern relations among themselves and between shareholders and managers.…

… [T]o achieve the benefits of corporate philanthropy, investors who leave philanthropic decisions to firm management must countenance the possibility that management's own objectives, not those of shareholders, may motivate some philanthropy. This problem is no different, however, from any other agency cost that shareholders willingly confront when they choose to invest in firms that have a split between ownership and control.…

I. Agency Costs, Market Forces, and the (Limited) Role of Corporate Law in Controlling Managerial Discretion

[handwritten margin note: team prod.]

The logical starting point for both the economic and legal analysis of corporate philanthropy is the *raison d'être* of the corporate firm itself. The existence of firms reflects two distinct, if related, phenomena. First, firms exist because production is optimally undertaken by more than one individual, typically because of gains from specialization. These gains from specialization lead to team production among the various actors in the firm. In law firms, for instance, lawyers, paralegals, secretaries, and other workers each specialize in various sub-tasks that constitute the team production of legal services for clients.

[handwritten margin note: Cost of temps too high]

Second, firms exist because the transactions costs of organizing production through market transactions often make it desirable to take some activities from the market and perform them in the firm. This observation in fact complements the team-production theory: gains from team production are a necessary but not sufficient condition for the existence of firms. Team production can always be accomplished by hiring other team members in the market for specific tasks without combining them into a firm. For example, the lawyer can hire temporary paralegals and secretaries in the "spot" labor market as needed without creating a law firm. But the transactions costs of doing so, Ronald Coase has explained, are often so high that it is preferable to create a firm in which labor is typically available as production needs arise, avoiding frequent and thus costly trips into the spot labor market.[2] The nature of the firm, then, is the use of ongoing internal direction

---

* Originally published in 84 CORNELL LAW REVIEW 1195 (1999). Reprinted with permission.
2. R.H. Coase, *The Nature of the Firm*, 4 ECONOMICA 386–405 (1937).

by the firm's managers to control labor and other resources, rather than negotiating a series of external contracts in the marketplace as needs arise. When the costs of internal control rise relative to the use of spot contract markets, entrepreneurs will substitute external market (i.e., contract-based) direction of resources in place of internal direction by managers. Thus, there is a limit to the scope of firm production.

There is an important corollary to Coase's insight that firms exist as lower-transaction-cost alternatives to contracting in spot markets: firm owners will only commit their resources internally to firms to the extent that the firm can make better (i.e., more profitable) use of those resources than individuals themselves could.... Unless firms can achieve optimal portfolios more cheaply than can dispersed individuals, investors have no reason to entrust their funds to firms. So, for example, it would be unusual to find individuals investing in firms whose assets consist solely of treasury bills and which pay the interest as dividends to shareholders. Individuals who want treasury bills can just as easily buy them and collect the interest themselves.

The points above apply to all firms, not just corporations. Among firm types, corporations are distinct because those directing the use of resources internally (managers) may not be the ones who own the firm (shareholders). Thus arises the traditional concern, which Adolf Berle and Gardiner Means popularized, about the separation of ownership and control in the large publicly traded corporation. Non-owner managers may be tempted to maximize their own welfare rather than the profits of the firm that employs them, preferring themselves over the shareholders who own the firm. The literature on this topic is voluminous, the more recent literature referring to the separation of ownership and control as creating a "principal-agent" problem. Managers should act as agents of the firm, but they have some incentive to maximize their own utility at the expense of firm profits (and thus the welfare of the firm's owners).

This well-founded concern about manager-agents disregarding their shareholders' interests has resulted in disagreement among legal commentators about how to confront the problem. Berle and Means, of course, believed that changes in corporation law and securities regulations were necessary for the development of corporate democracy and the protection of shareholders. Many other commentators have followed in the Berle-Means tradition of addressing the principal-agent problem through legal solutions.

An alternative (and less legalistic) concept of the corporation is the contractual, or market, theory of the corporation. The contractual theory of the corporation also starts with the recognition of the principal-agent problem. This theory, as its name suggests, stresses that private contracts and anonymous market forces act as the primary restrictions on managerial discretion and thus on agency costs that reduce shareholder welfare. Legal restrictions on managerial discretion necessarily take a back seat because they are often unnecessary to resolve any problem.

In this view, the corporation is based on mutually beneficial exchange (that is, contract) among various suppliers of inputs to the firm. Although some of these exchanges are explicit, legally enforceable contracts, many are informal or implicit contracts that market mechanisms, such as repeat dealing and reputation, enforce. The gist of the contractual theory of the corporation is that market forces—not the threat of legal sanctions—give corporate management the incentives to act as if it has the shareholders' best interests at heart. The contractual theory of the corporation is rigorous and supported by numerous empirical studies.

Under the contractual theory of the corporation, the primary external force holding the publicly traded corporation together is the market for corporate control. This market forces managers to behave by threatening them with the loss of their jobs through hostile takeovers, proxy battles, board revolts, or mergers.... Additional market forces put pressure on managers to act in their shareholders' best interests. Capital markets, internal and external markets for managerial talent, product markets, and service markets give managers the incentive to maximize share value.

Corporation law does play an undeniable role in the contractual theory of the corporation. It provides a standard-form governance structure, including a set of legal remedies that are available to shareholders when managers get too far out of line. The law governing boards of directors illustrates this standard-form characterization of corporation law. Increasingly, shareholders are free under state corporation statutes to define the duties for which a director will be liable if they do not like the "off-the-shelf" definition the statutes provide—or in some instances, to dispense with a board of directors altogether.

The flexibility under the law for shareholders to shape directors' duties reflects the law's recognition that boards do matter and that shareholders who elect boards of directors expect them to function as agent-monitors over corporate affairs. Although some mistakenly view it as a formalistic, legally imposed requirement of a publicly traded corporation, the board plays an important economic role in the contractual theory of the corporation. The board of directors supplements the market for corporate control by providing an internal source of monitoring to force managers to act in their shareholders' best interests.

In the contractual theory of the corporation, the primary role of the board of directors is to assure shareholders that agency conflicts are under control. Eugene Fama and Michael Jensen have explained that when decision-making agents do not bear the wealth effects of their decisions (and thus do not necessarily have an incentive to act in their shareholders' best interests) the decision-making process will split between agents who manage and agents who control.[3] Thus, in the publicly traded corporation characterized by the separation of ownership and control, decision management (initiation and implementation) is the responsibility of senior management, and decision control (ratification and monitoring) is the responsibility of the board of directors.

The contractual theory of the corporation explains why boards of directors have the legal authority to define the perimeters of managerial decision making. In this view, the board of directors is a market-induced mechanism for monitoring management on behalf of shareholders. The relevant question then becomes whether directors—either individually or collectively—have the incentive to do their job. Corporate law provides standard-form fiduciary duties of care and loyalty, but it is widely recognized that directors easily satisfy and rarely violate the standard of care. On the other hand, market forces do provide directors with an incentive to monitor the performance of senior managers. Specifically, competitive markets for outside directors' services reward directors if the firms they monitor perform well. Also, directors know that they could lose their positions if the firm is taken over in a control transaction due to poor performance.

The contractual theory explicitly recognizes that in many in stances market constraints have a greater effect on managerial discretion than legal constraints. Corporate philanthropy provides a classic illustration of this point. For legal commentators steeped in the Berle-Means tradition of skepticism regarding managerial motives and behavior, calls for increased corporate social responsibility represent nothing more than yet another excuse

---

3. Eugene F. Fama & Michael C. Jensen, *Agency Problems and Residual Claims*, 26 J.L. & ECON. 327, 331 (1983).

for managers to abuse shareholders. By law, managers have a great deal of discretion, including the ability to give away corporate assets to various groups. Moreover, it is certainly easy to come up with profit-maximizing or value-maximizing rationales that deflect legal challenges to corporate giving. Thus, it is clear that corporations could give away more money than they currently give or traditionally have given without fear of shareholder actions.

II. Corporate Philanthropy in the Contractual Theory of the Corporation

A. *Good Philanthropy*

The contractual nature of the firm provides a useful framework for analyzing the "problem" of corporate philanthropy. First, it is clear that shareholders as individuals may well have a desire to commit philanthropic acts. Not only is this understood as a matter of formal economics, but it comports with common sense and everyday observation. Individuals give money to churches, schools, hospitals, and countless other institutions— not to mention family members and friends.

However, the issue is why individuals might prefer to make charitable contributions through the corporations of which they are shareholder-owners. The answer typically given is that corporate giving often benefits the firm by increasing its "goodwill"—the extent of future patronage by those who become familiar with the firm's name....

But the fact that giving by corporations is valuable, though undoubtedly true, does not explain why shareholders give through corporations. After all, General Motors (GM) shareholders could just give their own money, designating it a contribution of Smith, GM shareholder....

But it is not hard to see why in fact shareholders would prefer to give at the office, assuming that there is corporate goodwill to be captured by the philanthropy. By hypothesis, the firm already has the earnings (current or past) necessary for the philanthropy. Distributing the earnings as dividends which Smith can contribute individually simply imposes an additional transaction cost.

Second, and perhaps more importantly, dispersed share ownership creates a potentially important free-rider problem among shareholders. Assuming that there is value to be had in contributions propagating the firm's name, that value accrues to all shareholders in proportion to their share holdings. Shareholders would prefer to give at the office precisely because giving through the firm forces all others who will also benefit from giving at the office too....

For these reasons, the law wisely accords wide deference to managers' choices of both the amounts and the targets of corporate giving. Doing so recognizes that shareholders want the firm, rather than themselves, to take the lead in choosing the objects and amounts of corporate charity.

B. *Bad Philanthropy*

This recognition, of course, does not mean that managers never will abuse shareholders' trust in making charitable donations. Managers are human, and personal utility maximization, rather than shareholder wealth maximization, doubtless exerts some influence over some managerial action sometimes. It does not follow, however, that shareholders are worse off in a system in which managers, sometimes venal and corruptible, make firms' philanthropic decisions.

… [C]onsider again the contractual nature of the firm. What would shareholders want courts to do concerning a possibly tainted contribution—one that violates the manager's contractual obligation to advance the firm's welfare? It would depend upon courts' ability to distinguish good philanthropy from bad. Stricter legal controls on bogus philanthropy could impose substantial costs on shareholders by deterring the value-increasing, profit-maximizing philanthropy that, it seems agreed, ordinarily motivates charitable giving. In a world in which (1) corporate philanthropy usually makes good business sense, (2) transaction and information costs are positive, (3) judges have difficulty distinguishing profit-maximizing from utility-maximizing philanthropy, and (4) market forces constrain managerial discretion, fully informed shareholders ordinarily would choose legal rules that give managers a great deal of discretion….

If corporations changed their practices and began distributing cash in ways that resembled utility maximization more closely than profit maximization, then one would expect to see changes in economic and legal constraints. For example, the changes could be a catalyst for institutional investors to take a more active role in monitoring charitable contributions. Other possible actions to constrain managers' utility-maximizing donations might include shareholder resolutions, charter amendments, and changes in corporate law default rules.

Given the current array of market constraints, however, there is no reason to expect that either shareholders or interest groups want the law to change. Ultimately, the issue is an empirical one, but purely gratuitous corporate transfers without an expected benefit to the granting corporation seem rare. The economic explanation for this rarity turns on market constraints on management; legal constraints seem largely irrelevant to managerial decision making….

C. Much Ado About Little?

… [Like corporate philanthropy,] [s]upra-optimal office sizes, excessive use of company cars, and [similar] "problems" are just particular manifestations of the generic agency costs that afflict any team production enterprise. Profits await those who can solve these "problems" at lower cost than the available benefits. There is no specific literature on the problem of office sizes or company cars. Nor do scholars think that particular legal rules are necessary to govern managers' non-maximizing behavior concerning offices or cars. These matters are essentially for shareholders to figure out and resolve for themselves. The value of a separate literature and the need for separate legal rules concerning philanthropy are both far from evident….

III. Conclusion

Under the standard portrayal, corporate philanthropy can be either good (profit maximizing) for shareholders or good (utility maximizing) for management, which advances its own interests with shareholders' assets. But as illustrated here, that assertion is too Manichean a view of corporate philanthropy. In a (real) world in which shareholders gain by having management make decisions about corporate philanthropy, even personally-motivated management decisions still can work to shareholders' advantage overall, given the apparent advantages of giving at the office. When personally motivated decisions begin to outweigh the advantages of giving at the office, competitive markets will tend to penalize managers and corporations that engage in corporate philanthropy that hurts share value overall. Market forces act as the primary constraint on corporate management. Legal constraints on corporate philanthropy are largely irrelevant.

Of course, an omniscient judiciary would make the world a better place by separating good from bad philanthropy, punishing only the latter. But judges are not omniscient, and separating good from bad philanthropy would be virtually impossible to accomplish from outward appearances. Liability for philanthropy would often be meted out when in fact the motivation was firm profitability (Type I error). Avoiding that error by allowing managers wide discretion over philanthropy of course means that some bad philanthropy will go unpunished (Type II error). But given that there is no evidence that bad philanthropy is widespread and that shareholders have their own remedies for any defalcations, the law's relatively permissive attitude concerning philanthropy makes perfect sense.

The economics and law of the philanthropy "problem" see philanthropy as just one of any number of situations in which manager-agents can advance their own welfare at the expense of shareholders. Philanthropy is just one manifestation of a generic agency problem, but one that is easily analyzed in the contractarian model of the firm. Attempts to invent new explanations are unnecessary....

It is difficult to accept the logic of a theory of corporation law that distinguishes itself on the ground that it provides a rationale for managers to harm shareholders. The principal-agent model of the firm recognizes that managers are not altruists, and expects that shareholders will tolerate a certain amount of excess charity motivated by managers' personal utility. The law's general refusal to interfere with philanthropic decisions within the firm is tolerable as well, given the overall benefits of philanthropy to the firm, the general sense that profit maximization motivates most philanthropy, and the difficulty of distinguishing profit maximization from utility maximization. But tolerance of inevitable costs is not the same as applause for philanthropy not motivated by firm profitability.

Lynne L. Dallas, *Two Models of Corporate Governance: Beyond Berle and Means**

... The American Law Institute's Principles of Corporate Governance § 2.01 provides that the principal objective of the corporation is to enhance corporate profits and shareholder gain. This legal principle rests on the acceptance of the efficiency model. The efficiency model maintains that the most efficient governance structure of a corporation is one in which shareholder benefit (or profit) serves as the controlling factor in corporate decision making.

Various reasons have been examined for the adoption of this principle. Briefly, shareholders, according to the incentive-residual rights theory, have the incentive to utilize the resources of the corporation most efficiently, because they are the "owners" of those resources and receive only the profits that those resources can produce. Therefore, a corporation managed in a way that shareholders would approve emerges as the standard of efficiency. Under the agency cost approach, shareholder representation on the board

* Originally published in 22 UNIVERSITY OF MICHIGAN JOURNAL OF LAW REFORM 19 (1988). Copyright 1988 Lynne L. Dallas. Reprinted with permission.

is the most efficient governance arrangement for the firm. If it were not, market forces would cause a different arrangement to be utilized. Thus, efficiency is enhanced by having the interests of shareholders ultimately control decision making. Finally, according to the transaction cost approach, shareholders make asset-specific investments in the firm, which presumably can be obtained by the firm only by promising to shareholders that corporations be operated to maximize profits for shareholders. This contractual term then contributes to the viability of the firm and would not exist unless it were efficient.

In contrast, the power model maintains that corporations pursue numerous objectives, sometimes inconsistently. Indeed, this manner of operation is not necessarily "inefficient," but may contribute to the adaptability of the firm to its environment. Implicit in the power model is the notion that the struggles within the firm, and between internal and external coalitions, do not mainly revolve around whether efficient or inefficient methods of operating decisions, or arrangements should be adopted, but on the goals or values to be pursued by the organization. A political model of the corporation is involved in that what results from the political struggle may be rationalized on efficiency grounds, but more accurately reflects power considerations. If profit is adopted as the objective of the corporation, this conclusion is the result of a power struggle in which certain power coalitions have prevailed.

As noted above, profit maximization may not be synonymous with the best interests of society. In the real world, efficiency is not a neutral concept, as some efficiency theorists would have it, but is value-laden. This is particularly the case when third-party effects are not taken into account.... [F]irms that maximize profits are not necessarily those most likely to survive. Even if those firms were most likely to survive, the utility of "survival" is itself value-laden, depending on one's judgment of the value of the corporation's products, services, and methods of operation. In addition, the maximization of profits for shareholders does not necessarily translate into the enhancement of the value of underlying assets.

A principal justification for the adoption of the profit objective by corporate law scholars is that it supposedly provides "a single, objective, easily monitored [residual] goal." Nothing could be further from the truth. First, the pursuit of profit is not the pursuit of a single goal, but involves decisions and actions in furtherance of numerous goals. Second, it is not objective. What costs and benefits, for example, are to be included in the calculation of profits? If social costs are to be included, how are various social costs and benefits to be valued? How are potential future economic benefits and costs to be quantified given the uncertainty of future markets? Third, it is not an easily monitored goal. How can decision-makers be made accountable on the basis of profit when their decisions involve making predictions of future returns from uncertain markets? How are decisions to be monitored when various business alternatives may be chosen involving different degrees of profit potential, some long-term and others short-term? Finally, how are decisions to be judged when alternatives are available with equal profit prospects? I submit that the only way these decisions can be assessed is on the basis of values other than profit. Fourth, if profit is deemed to be a "single, objective, easily monitored goal," why wouldn't other goals, such as the maximization of employee wages, consumer prices, and survival, do equally as well?

The profit objective is to a large extent a fiction, which hides under the guise of objectivity the substantial amount of discretion managers have to make value choices. This is reflected in the [draft] commentaries to the American Law Institute's [Principles of Corporate Governance § 2.01], which recognizes how the selection of time horizons can justify a substantial range of choices by managers:

Activity that entails a short-run cost to achieve an appropriately greater long-run profit is therefore not a departure from the economic [profit] objective, and an orientation toward lawful, ethical, and public-spirited activity will normally fall within this description.... Although the corporate decisionmaker ... needs to meet a standard of care in making his decisions, that standard can be satisfied even when, as is often the case, a prospective profit cannot be particularized. Recurring cases of this sort include those in which the object of a corporate action is to maintain the confidence of business organizations with which the corporation deals, to foster the morale of employees, or to encourage favorable or forestall unfavorable government regulation—as by abstaining from conduct that would engender unfavorable public reaction against the corporation, providing lawful assistance in connection with lobbying or referenda activities, or voluntarily adopting a course of conduct so as to forestall legislation that would instead mandate such conduct.

Case law also reflects the substantial amount of discretion that the profit objective provides managers. Judgments rarely, for example, disturb a decision for which some plausible profit-oriented justification is given. Even charitable contributions have been permitted. The profit objective does not serve as a single, objective, easily monitored goal, but as a justification for managers to do essentially what they please. The "agenda" of those defending the profit objective is perhaps to maintain this state of affairs.

Supporters of the profit objective have criticized the corporate social responsibility proponents for the "insuperable problem of defining what the public interest is, and when the pursuit of profit maximization should be sacrificed for these ends."[4] Implicit in this position is the notion that it is known what the profit maximizing course of action is which must then be sacrificed. As previously explained, profit maximization does not produce a readily identifiable goal or course of action. Efficiency theorists also assume that a corporation can operate only on the basis of a single replacement goal. Indeed, some of those who have adopted the efficiency model have gone so far as to suggest that a corporation will self-destruct if it pursues inconsistent goals. Of course, that is not the case when the power model's conceptual lens is used. The corporation pursues numerous and often inconsistent goals which enable the corporation to adapt to its social, political, and economic environment. The social responsibility debate loses contact with reality when it becomes involved with the abstraction of a single end or objective for the corporation. The important focus must be instead on the procedures for making decisions on behalf of the corporation and on the identity of decision-makers.

The importance of the identity of those making decisions (which in turn affects the goals that the public corporation will pursue) becomes apparent when the breadth of the corporate decision-maker's discretion is made explicit. The Delaware Supreme Court ... for example, stated that the "board may have regard for various constituencies in discharging its responsibilities, provided there are rationally related benefits accruing to the stockholders."[5] This is not a restatement of the law, but it makes explicit that which has been, to a large extent, implicit in the law and obscured somewhat by the fiction of the profit objective. Even the ... Pennsylvania statutory provision[6] is not a large departure from what is currently permitted, given the substantial deference granted by courts to

4. Daniel R. Fischel, *The Corporate Governance Movement*, 35 VAND. L. REV. 1259, 1268–69 (1982).
5. Revlon v. MacAndrews & Forbes Holdings, 506 A. 2d 173 (1986).
6. Penn. Stat. Ann. Tit. 15, § 1715 (2003). *Excerpts from this statute are reprinted in the Discussion Questions section of Chapter 2. —Ed.*

the substantive decisions of corporate decision-makers. These developments, however, bring to the fore basic issues of whether directors are appropriately selected and qualified to make such decisions. These issues have been obscured by the fiction of the profit goal, which is held out as the single objective and easily monitored goal with respect to which managers have special expertise....

Kent Greenfield, *There's a Forest in Those Trees: Teaching About the Role of Corporations in Society*[*]

Corporate law is primarily about the relationships among shareholders, boards of directors, managers, and, occasionally, bondholders and other creditors; questions surrounding the role of corporations in society arise only at the periphery of the dominant narratives of corporate law, if at all. It is not surprising, therefore, that typical courses in corporate law, and the basic texts used to teach them, rarely pause for any meaningful length of time to consider, broadly, the position of the corporation within society at large, or narrowly, the relationship between the corporation and the workers. Inattention to these issues is curious. Not only is corporate law (like all law) understandably only within a social and political context, but, by any account, workers provide essential input to a corporation's productive activities and have much to do with the success or failure of the enterprise. Indeed, the theory of the firm — the theory explaining why corporations exist at all — depends centrally on certain notions about workers.

Ronald Coase theorized that the firm exists when it is more efficient to engage in intra-firm transactions (organized by direct authority) rather than market transactions.[7] Thus the theory of the firm depends on insights about when it is most efficient for people to work together within a firm rather than through individually negotiated contracts. Much literature about the economics of the firm turns on arguments about the consolidation of productive work....

In this Essay, I explain briefly why I believe it is important in the basic course to concentrate students' attention on the role of corporations in society, the responsibilities of the corporation to nonshareholder stakeholders, and the question of how corporate governance regimes affect those matters. This Essay will also offer a concrete suggestion, namely a case corporate law professors can add to the basic course to facilitate this discussion.

... The basic corporate law course ... should spend more time on the "forest" of corporate law, which I believe is the question of the role of corporations in society.

Without such coverage, our courses fail to address an obvious point: while the corporation is a hugely important and successful engine of wealth creation, it can also be an amoral behemoth that fouls the environment, worsens political and economic inequalities, and takes advantage of horrible injustices for its own financial gain. Without such coverage, we fail to challenge our students to consider whether the corporation is too powerful an institution. Without such coverage it is impossible to encourage our students to ask whether society as a whole would be better off if the law of the corporation or,

---

[*] Originally published in 34 GEORGIA LAW REVIEW 1011 (2000). Copyright 2000 Kent Greenfield. Reprinted with permission.

7. *See Profs. Butler and McChesney's article in this chapter for further discussion of Coase's model of the firm.* — Ed.

more fundamentally, the nature of the corporation itself was significantly, if not radically, changed.

These are some of the most pressing political and economic issues of our day. If these questions are not dealt with in the basic corporate law course, most of our students will graduate without facing them at all. And if we let that happen, what we have done, frankly, is to train our students to help rich people get richer. Or, at the very least, we have taught our students that corporate lawyers can ignore non-shareholder constituencies on the theory that they should either help themselves or get the government to do it for them.

One response to these points, of course, is that we do not have to worry about the concerns of nonshareholder constituencies in corporate law, and thus in the corporate law course, because what is good for the shareholders tends to be good for everyone else, and vice-versa. This makes sense in many cases. A profitable company is probably more likely to obey environmental laws and to provide good jobs than is a company surviving at the margin.

But even if the interests of shareholders and the interests of other stakeholders coalesce in certain circumstances and for certain activities, those interests are in basic conflict in another set of not-so-hypothetical cases. The conflict is real in the micro sense, in the decisions of individual firms. It is also true in the macro sense, in the tensions within the general economy.

[*The next few paragraphs describe American economic conditions as of 1999.*[8]] Corporate profits are at an all-time high, and wage rates for workers are falling. Corporations enjoyed double-digit profit increases for five years in a row from 1993 through 1997. Meanwhile, hourly wages fell for the bottom eight percent of workers over the last ten years. Indeed, the hourly earnings of the typical production worker, in constant dollars, was over one dollar less in 1997 than it was in 1973. [*By 2007, the average hourly wages of production workers (in manufacturing) and nonsupervisory workers (in other sectors) had risen by about 54 cents over 1973 levels.*]

... Worker productivity has risen about one percent per year over the last twenty years. But almost thirty percent of workers earn wages that do not lift them out of poverty. [*Between 1973 and 2007, productivity (the output of goods and services per hour worked) rose 83%, while the average compensation of all employees rose only 49%. Median compensation grew by far less, reflecting the disparity between higher- and lower-paid workers. In 2007, 26.5 percent of the workforce were "low wage workers," defined as those who earned an hourly wage below $10.20 an hour, the wage that would lift a family of four above the poverty level ($21,027), given full-time work. Forty-four percent of these workers had a household income of less than $25,000.*]

The difference between the salary for workers and management is growing as well. Twenty years ago, pay for corporate CEOs was less than thirty times that of the average worker. [*In 2000, the average CEO's total compensation was 299 times that of the average worker. This figure fell to a low of 149 times in the wake of the 2001 stock-market decline, but by 2007, the figure had risen to 275 times.*]

... The wealthiest one percent of the United States population has thirty-nine percent of the nation's personal wealth. This is more than the poorest ninety-five percent of

---

8. *Professor Greenfield's original article drew the statistics in these paragraphs from* LAWRENCE MISHEL, JARED BERNSTEIN & JOHN SCHMITT, THE STATE OF WORKING AMERICA 1998–1999 (1999). *Updated figures in brackets are from* LAWRENCE MISHEL, JARED BERNSTEIN & HEIDI SHIERHOLZ, THE STATE OF WORKING AMERICA 2008/2009 (2009). — *Ed.*

Americans combined. Since the early 1980s the richest one percent has seen its share grow from less than thirty-four percent of the nation's wealth to over thirty-nine percent. The poorest ninety-five percent has seen its share fall.... [*In 2007, the wealthiest one percent of U.S. households owned 34 percent of the nation's wealth (defined as net worth), more than the bottom 90%, which all together owned 29%.*]

These economic trends occur in a context in which Wall Street praises companies that cut jobs, because cuts are seen as evidence that the management is slashing unnecessary costs. The day Sears announced it was cutting fifty thousand jobs, its stock price climbed four percent; when Xerox said it would prune ten thousand jobs, its stock shot up seven percent. From the perspective of the shareholders and of Wall Street, these companies may well have been more valuable the day after these cuts were made than they were the day before; from the perspective of those who lost their jobs, however, they were probably not more valuable. Between 1991 and 1995, nearly 2.5 million Americans lost their jobs because of corporate restructuring, and even in a so-called boom economy, only about a third of those who [lost] their jobs [found] replacement work that pays as well.

These statistics reveal significant flaws in our economic system. It is not enough, however, to discuss these flaws in the context of undergraduate macroeconomics classes or law school poverty law seminars. Corporate law is a key part of an economic system. Corporate lawyers and corporate law professors should be participants in the discussion of how to remedy that system's flaws.

This participation would be important even if adjustments in corporate law were available only as remedies for the system's flaws; such participation is essential, however, when the laws governing corporations are arguably part of the cause of the system's flaws. Any discussion about the inequality between the rich and the poor in the United States is incomplete without recognizing that corporate law's emphasis on profit maximization requires companies, to the extent possible, to transfer surplus from labor to capital. Discussions about the decline of workers' wages are similarly incomplete without exploring how the more powerful party in employment negotiations (the employer) has the legal ability to use that power to exact concessions from the weaker party (the worker) under both the at-will employment rule and the discredited, though commonly abided, *Lochner*-ian[9] notion of a "freedom" to contract for wages. One cannot reasonably suggest that the major work of redistribution be done through progressive taxes and redistributive government programs without noting that much of what government now does is regressive—billions of dollars a year go into export subsidies, price supports, tax concessions, and other examples of "corporate welfare," which in effect redistribute wealth from the working and middle classes to the wealthy.

We could remind our students that they, and the polity generally, could choose differently. This is perhaps the most important but most difficult task. Frankly, what Justice Brandeis said about his own generation might be said of ours:

> The prevalence of the corporation in America has led men of this generation to act, at times, as if the privilege of doing business in corporate form were inherent in the citizen; and has led them to accept the evils attendant upon the free and unrestricted use of the corporate mechanism as if these evils were the inescapable price of civilized life and, hence, to be borne with resignation.[10]

Our students, then, could be reminded that the status quo itself is a choice. It is non-neutral; it represents a political and social decision. It is not the only model.

---

9. [*See* Lochner v. New York, 198 U.S. 45 (1905)].
10. Liggett Co. v. Lee, 288 U.S. 517, 548 (1933) (Brandeis, J., dissenting).

We could encourage our students to look at the other models available. Other advanced countries are more rigorous in regulating even the internal affairs of corporations, and it would be worthwhile to educate our students about, say, German codetermination.[11] Other countries have different ways of regulating the employer-employee dynamic, and it would be worthwhile to teach our students about, for example, the ways other countries are more protective of union organization. It would also be worthwhile to remind our students that other advanced countries do a better job than we do at reducing poverty and lessening inequality between the rich and the poor, and that other advanced countries pay their workers more and their CEOs less. [*According to a 2005 survey of advanced economies, CEOs in the U.S. earned two and a quarter times the average of CEOs in the 13 other countries surveyed. In a study conducted in 2000 comparing 19 industrialized countries belonging to the Organization for Economic Cooperation and Development (OECD), the U.S. had the highest total poverty rate (17.0%) and the highest child poverty rate (21.9%)*] ...

Other countries also do a better job of providing opportunities to move up the economic ladder. The "American Dream" is made real more often in France, Germany, Ireland, Holland, and Sweden than in the United States. That is, these countries do a better job of moving people out of poverty than the United States does. Significantly, these priorities are not driving these countries into an economic abyss. Belgium, France, Holland and the former West Germany all appear to have productivity levels that are about the same as, or better than, those of the United States.

Our students also might be reminded that we do not necessarily have to look toward other countries. We Americans could choose to consider our own national mythology and try to embody it more honestly. Maybe we would choose to focus less on gross national product growth or profit increases, and focus more on those ultimate goods that are supposedly gained with that wealth. Perhaps the time has come to spend some disposable income helping those who have been left behind, or to use our wealth "buying" necessities such as tranquility, community, and stability. In a society in which many people have nice cars but cannot find a place to park them safely, ought that society not spend less effort on producing cars more efficiently and more effort in trying to create a society that is stable and safe? In a country in which companies are very profitable but workers in those companies are barely making ends meet, should not the focus be less on increasing profitability of the companies and more on making it possible for those workers to provide for their families?

So the central question for corporate law scholars in the new century is this: Are there ways to make the economy more fair and just without ruining the great engine of commerce and wealth creation that is the corporation? Essentially, I believe that this is the debate we should be having as a polity and indeed as a world economy. Corporate law should be a key element of the discussion, and corporate law academics need to join it.

.... How does one teach about these conflicts? As I have suggested, there is much that could be changed, and should be changed, even in my own classroom. Pedagogy is notoriously entrenched, and not just in corporate law.

Perhaps the best contribution I can offer is a suggestion of a simple first step: teach *Local 1330, United Steel Workers v. United States Steel Corp.*,[12] the Youngstown Steel plant-closing case. Much has been written about this case, but my guess is that few of us teach it. Plant

---

11. *"Codetermination" refers to the practice of employee representation on the board of directors. See Marleen O'Connor's article in Chapter 2.* — Ed.

12. 631 F.2d 1264 (6th Cir. 1980).

closings are not the focus of much attention in the typical law school curriculum, much less in the corporate law course.

Local 1330 considered the closing of two United States Steel facilities in Youngstown, Ohio. The corporation had operated two large steel mills in Youngstown since the turn of the century, and in the fall of 1977, the workers became worried about rumors that the two factories were to be closed. United States Steel made a series of representations to its employees to reassure them. Specifically, the company noted that the plant was profitable and that the company would not close its plant as long as it stayed that way. This went on for a couple of years, until the company closed the plant.

The workers sued to enjoin the closure and asserted two claims. First, the employees argued that statements made by the company constituted an enforceable promise to keep the plants open as long as the plants were profitable. The claim ultimately failed because United States Steel argued successfully that, despite its earlier assurances to the contrary, the plants were not profitable. Neither the federal district court nor the Sixth Circuit was willing "to exchange its own view of the parameters of profitability for that of the corporation." Second, the workers raised a property claim, based on reliance interests, arguing that "a property right has arisen from the long-established relation between the community ... and Plaintiffs, on the one hand, and Defendant on the other." After some initial statements admitting sympathy with this claim, the district court decided that there was no precedent for such a property right and that it lacked power to create such a legal claim. The Sixth Circuit affirmed this holding.

This case is great to teach for a couple of reasons. First, the students' emotions tend to run in favor of the workers, but their legal intuition is that the court got it right on both fronts. Second, the court decided both employees' claims, in effect, on first principles— on beliefs about who owns the corporation and why the corporation exists.

The workers' promissory estoppel claim failed because the court was unwilling to hold the company liable for what amounted to material misstatements of fact. Although making similar misstatements to shareholders is a violation of federal law, lying to workers is not a violation. The difference in legal duty stems from the notion that shareholders own the corporation and are the beneficiaries of fiduciary duties. In *Local 1330*, whether the corporation had a duty not to mislead its employees in effect turned on who the "owner" of the corporation was. The second claim dealt with this same ownership issue, but more directly. The workers alleged that they had developed a property interest in their jobs over time, similar to how the users of land can develop rights to an easement through use over time. Again, the court held against the workers, and again, the reason was that it was the shareholders who owned the corporation, not the workers.

I try to point out in my class that if we are willing to rethink the fundamental questions surrounding shareholder supremacy and the corporation's duties to other stakeholders, one could imagine a different outcome on both of the employee claims. Why are shareholders deemed to be the sole "owners" of the corporation? To be sure, shareholders own their shares. But bondholders own their bonds, suppliers own their inventory, and workers own their labor. Each of these groups contributes what it owns to the corporate enterprise. As Margaret Blair and Lynn Stout write, "shareholders are not the only group that may provide specialized inputs into corporate production."[13] No one group among these contributors is making a charitable act; each expects to make some return on its contribution. And the input of each is essential to the success of the firm. To say that

---

13. *See their article in Chapter 2.* — *Ed.*

shareholders are the only "owners" is to say that there is something inherent in the act of contributing money to buy shares that distinguishes that act from the act of contributing money to buy bonds issued by the company, contributing raw materials to be refined by the company, or contributing labor to be used by the company.

Moreover, as Joseph Singer has pointed out, the law frequently deems property interests to have been created as the result of relationships and understandings on which people rely over time.[14] Examples include property rules surrounding "adverse possession, prescriptive easements, public rights of access to public property, tenants' rights, equitable division of property on divorce, [and] welfare rights." Singer argues that workers often develop reliance interests in their jobs that are analogous to these other kinds of reliance interests in property already recognized by the law.

Rather than seeing the corporation and the workers in isolation ... we can see the corporation and the workers as together having established and relied on long-standing relations with each other in creating a common enterprise. The rights of the members of the common enterprise cannot be fully articulated by reference to ownership rights defined a priori or by the explicit terms of written contracts. If workers are considered to be part of the corporation, rather than factors of production or hired hands, our analysis of property rights changes.

Thus, even if property rights are the touchstone for corporate law, workers could be seen as having cognizable property interests in the firm and in their jobs. The concept of an employment-based property interest is sufficiently unfamiliar to most students that I do not expect many converts to this view. And, I must admit, I do not win many. But I win a few. More importantly many of my students leave the class doubting some assumptions that they had never questioned before. And that I call success.

William W. Bratton, *Enron and the Dark Side of Shareholder Value*[*]

... Enron flew high. When its stock price peaked at close to ninety dollars in August 2000, it was America's seventh largest firm by market capitalization. In one category it even had the number one slot—Fortune Magazine hailed it as America's most innovative firm for five years running. Enron also came in number one when it fell. It went into Chapter 11 on December 2, 2001, as the largest bankruptcy reorganization in American history. Meanwhile, its stock had fallen to around sixty cents a share, victim to two more Enron superlatives—history's biggest financial fraud and its biggest audit failure....

Growing worries about other firms' financial reports finally caused a major market correction two months later. The residuum of insecurity will continue to raise risk premiums and depress stock prices. But the most visible victims are Enron's stockholders and employees, especially the employees who were shareholders. Even as 4000 were laid off around the time of the bankruptcy filing, all faced the grim realization that in the company's final weeks management had locked down their 401(k) plan, which had been sixty-percent invested in Enron stock.

---

14. Joseph W. Singer, *The Reliance Interest in Property*, 40 STAN. L. REV. 611, 622 (1988).

* Originally published in 76 TULANE LAW REVIEW 1275–1361 (2002). Reprinted with the permission of the Tulane Law Review Association, which holds the copyright.

Corporate failures as big and fast as this one tend to be held out as examples for future business regulation. Enron's failure is no exception, implicating a long list of regulatory topics well before completion of formal investigations into the company's management and the collapse's cause. On its face Enron raises issues for the future of energy deregulation, the mandatory disclosure system under the securities laws, the regulation of the accounting profession, and internal corporate governance systems....

The claims of regulatory failure have a sharp edge due to Enron's profile as one of corporate America's most aggressive political players. Deregulatory politics lay at the core of the company's business plan. Its primary business, energy trading, only came into existence in the wake of deregulation of electricity and natural gas production and supply....

Enron spent copiously on politics. For example, the $2.4 million of political contributions it paid in 2000 exceeded by 100% those of the next-most-generous energy company. In 2000, Enron also paid $2.1 million to a dozen or so Washington lobbying firms. Enron obtained good results from such investments, notably in connection with the passage in 2000 of the Commodity Futures Modernization Act.[15] Senator Phil Gramm, spouse of Wendy Gramm, one of Enron's outside directors and a member of its audit committee, assured that the legislation included the "Enron Point," a complete exclusion for energy trading companies from financial or disclosure requirements respecting portfolios of over-the-counter derivative securities. Enron thereby achieved something available to no other leading dealer in derivative contracts—complete exemption of its activities from federal supervision and oversight....

Two schools of thought show up prominently in discussions of the meaning of Enron's collapse. On one side stand supporters of deregulation, many of whom once touted Enron and now find it more than a little embarrassing. Its collapse, they tell us, should be taken as an exemplar of free market success. If Enron was a house of cards, it was free market actors who blew it down, with a free market administration keeping its hands off. Any violations of law will be brought to light through investigations by the Congress, the Securities and Exchange Commission (SEC), and the Justice Department, along with fact finding connected with a raft of pending lawsuits. Meanwhile, the histories of rogues and outliers like Enron never provide a sound basis for new regulatory initiatives.

On the opposite side stand those, including this Article's author, predisposed to draw regulatory inferences from business disasters. Enron, with its reputation as America's corporate shock troop for radical reliance on market discipline and concomitant dismantling of the New Deal regulatory legacy, provides an especially attractive basis for argument. These assertions encompass power supply, the deregulation of which, according to one recent commentator, "guaranteed that sharks such as Enron would emerge to cream profits by manipulating supply." They encompass campaign finance reform, in the eyes of many a necessary prerequisite to any other law reform triggered by Enron. And they encompass business law, in particular corporate and securities law's system of self-regulatory corporate governance.

This Article addresses the self-regulatory regime of corporate governance, to which Enron comes as a considerable shock. In the 1990s, corporate self-regulation had been widely thought to have reached a high plateau of evolutionary success due to proliferating good practices and sophisticated institutional monitoring. Yet the failure in this case stemmed not from business reversal, which often cannot be avoided, but from legerdemain, which usually can be controlled. The breaking stories defied explanation—$30 million of self-

---

15. Commodity Futures Modernization Act of 2000, Pub. L. No. 106-554, 114 Stat. 2763 (2000).

dealing by the chief financial officer, $700 million of net earnings going up in smoke, $1.2 billion of shareholders' equity disappearing as if by erasure of a blackboard, more than $4 billion in hidden liabilities—and all in a company theretofore viewed as an exemplar. How could this happen in a corporate governance and disclosure system held out as the envy of the world? Either deeply concealed skullduggery or some hidden regulatory defect requiring legislative correction must have been at work.

As the scandal deepens and the criminal justice system comes to bear, the concealed skullduggery characterization becomes more prominent. The principals emerge as rogues, to be roughly expelled by the respectable business community. There lies much truth in the characterization. But the rogue characterization serves a double function—it deflects attention from the respectable community's own business practices.

This Article aspires to counterbalance with a picture of Enron's collapse that deemphasizes the rogue to focus on the regular. It reviews the particulars of the case, emphasizing the points of continuity between Enron and respectable firms. It asserts that Enron in collapse was wrought into the fabric of our corporate governance system every bit as much as Jack Welch's General Electric (GE) was in success. Like GE under Jack Welch, Enron under Ken Lay and Jeff Skilling pursued maximum shareholder value. Like GE's managers, Enron's pursued a plausible and innovative business plan. The firm collapsed for the most mundane of reasons—its managers suffered the behavioral biases of successful entrepreneurs. They overemphasized the upside and lacked patience. They pursued heroic short-term growth numbers that their business plan could not deliver. That pursuit of immediate shareholder value caused them to become risk-prone, engaging in levered speculation, earnings manipulation, and concealment of critical information.

They were rogues to be sure, but the self-regulatory system nevertheless is deeply implicated in their company's failure. Enron's collapse reminds us that our corporate governance system takes some significant risks in the name of encouraging innovation and entrepreneurship and economizing on enforcement costs. Enron's principals abused the system in plain view, taking advantage of the considerable slack it extends to successful actors. Although they did not disclose everything, they disclosed more than enough to put the system's layers of monitors on notice that their earnings numbers were soft and their liabilities understated. Similarly aggressive accounting and soft numbers are commonplace in business today. They have become wrought into the practice of shareholder value maximization.

The theory of shareholder value maximization tells a different story, of course. Academics define shareholder value by reference to management practices that enhance productivity—corporate unbundling and concentration on core competencies, the return of free cash flow to shareholders, compensation schemes that align incentives, and prompt restructuring of dysfunctional operations. But in the transfer from theory to practice, the set of economic instructions diffuses into a norm. The norm is informed by the demands of shareholders themselves in addition to the official economics. As the norm becomes more capacious it takes on a dark side, a negative aspect quite apart from the pain it inflicts on millions of employees for whom the cost-cutting entailed in restructuring means termination. For equity investors in recent years, the practice of shareholder value maximization has not meant patient investment. Instead, it has meant obsession with short-term performance numbers. For managers, the shareholder value norm accordingly has come to mean more than astute investment and disinvestment. It also means aggressive management of reported figures responsive to the investment community's demands for immediate value. Enron stated its adherence to the norm in its Annual Report for 2000—it was a company "laser-focused on earnings per share."

Enron forces us to confront a discomfiting fact: even as academics have proclaimed rising governance standards, some standards have declined, particularly those addressed to the numerology of shareholder value. The decline has not been limited to companies subject to enforcement actions, like Cendant and Sunbeam. Investigations and criticisms touch reputable names like Xerox, Lucent, Qualcomm, American International, Coca-Cola, IBM and GE itself. The number of accounting restatements, cases in which companies lower previously reported earnings, averaged 49 per year from 1990 to 1997. By 2000, the annual number was up to 156. Clearly, the line between appropriate and inappropriate behavior has dissolved for many under real-world pressure to produce shareholder value. Exploitation and expansion of the gray area has become routine. The resulting loss of perspective facilitated Enron's step across the line to fraud. Special regulatory attention accordingly devolves on its auditor, the actor in the self-regulatory system whose primary function is to deter fraud.

This Article's inquiry into Enron's implications for corporate self-regulation (and the legal theory that supports it) begins with Enron's business plan. When Enron rode high, it aspired to embody and realize the ideal of a contractual firm rooted in the touchstone economics of Michael Jensen and the late William H. Meckling. Enron would transform itself into a "virtual" corporation, a center for market making and hedging by high-tech experts, rather than an asset-heavy energy producer. Thus viewing itself as a real-time nexus of contracts, Enron looked out at the field of traditional large, vertically integrated, asset-based companies and saw a great arbitrage opportunity. Those lumbering behemoths with low returns on assets were just waiting to be dismantled, their coordinative functions to be replaced by Enron's proprietary trading markets. The strategy was lionized in the business press in early 2001 as Skilling ascended Enron's throne. By the year's end it was derided. Paul Krugman has called it "death by guru"—little more than a "perfect PowerPoint presentation." It was so trendy that "few analysts were willing to fly in the face of fashion by questioning Enron's numbers." ...

Enron's top executives and board of directors bear the primary blame. Yet the directors went though the motions dictated by the book of good corporate practice. Negative implications accordingly arise for the monitoring model of the board of directors. But, despite the author's disposition to draw regulatory inferences from business disaster, there follows no plausible reform prescription. Secondary blame attaches to Enron's auditors, who manifestly should have refused to give a favorable opinion on Enron's financials. Here arise the case's strong regulatory implications. It is clear that Enron had captured its auditor, denuding the relationship of its necessary adversary aspect. Similar situations of capture are ubiquitous in America's corporate landscape. Secondary blame also attaches to members of the community of institutional investors. Our self-regulatory system assumes that these actors make a governance contribution when they monitor large companies like Enron. Here they failed to do so even though Enron's financials provided enough information about shady deals to give them cause to demand explanations. If actors with billions of other people's money invested do not require managers and boards to make a coherent informational account of themselves before disaster strikes, despite clear signs of trouble, then we must put a heavy qualification on our reliance on the monitoring system. In contrast, the legal system will work as intended in this case so far as concerns ex post enforcement, given multiple prima facie violations of the securities laws and an emerging picture of widespread culpability. The disturbing thing is that the system's standing army of civil and criminal enforcers had no deterrent effect.

Enron shows that the incentive structure that motivates actors in our self-regulatory governance system generates much less powerful checks against abuse than many observers have believed. This point does not by itself validate any particular regulatory corrective. The costs of any regulation can outweigh the compliance yield, particularly in a system committed to open a wide field for entrepreneurial risk taking. Such a system can no more break the iron law of risk and return than could Michael Milken and his junk bonds. If we seek high returns, we must discount for the risk that rationality and reputation will sometimes prove inadequate as constraints....

I. Enron and the Contractarian Ideal

In early 2001, Enron was in a process of transformation, determined to leave behind its original business, an asset-laden producer and transporter of natural gas, to become a pure financial intermediary.... To get a better look at Enron's intermediary operation, let us hypothesize Enron's entry as a trader into a new market, say pulp and paper. To effect entry as a seller, Enron first had to assure itself of sources of supply, whether through contracting or through direct ownership of the sources of the product, here timber tracts. Once it established itself as a seller, Enron would start bringing other sellers together with timber buyers. As Enron saw it, such a new market could grow spectacularly if many timber users had captive sources of supply. In this scenario, the vertically integrated forest products companies notice the Enron market and see that it has sufficient volume to supply their needs. They begin to draw on it for marginal supplies. It becomes clear that Enron's market offers timber at lower prices than do their captive timber sources. Ultimately, these companies unbundle themselves, selling off their forest tracts, pocketing the gain, and relying on Enron's market for future supplies....

Enron, in short, aspired to be better than a market. It was reducing the costs of finding, contracting with, and communicating with outside suppliers and customers—costs that formerly meant bringing disparate operations under a single corporate roof....

II. Accounting for Enron's Collapse

[*Various factors contributed to Enron's demise. One was the simple fact that its revenues began to decline as competitors entered energy trading, a field Enron had developed and dominated.*] ... [E]ven as Enron had opened more and more new trading territory, entrance barriers were low. As time went on, Enron had to deal with dozens of competitors who hired away its employees to compete in what had become its bread-and-butter business, undercutting its profit margins. According to one analyst, Enron's trading margins collapsed from 5.3% in early 1998, to 1.7% in the third quarter of 2001. Investor attention to the problem was deferred for a time because the California energy crisis and the attendant period of sky-high electricity prices led to extraordinary returns to all traders in that market. As California's prices dropped back to normal, Enron's shrinking trading returns became more apparent.

Enron's managers saw that rapid maturation of its new markets presented a problem for its growth numbers. Their strategy for dealing with it was to step up the process of market creation, moving into new commodities like pulp and paper, steel, and, most daringly, bandwidth. In addition, in 1999 they successfully launched EnronOnLine, an Internet-based commodity trading platform. But these initiatives did not make up for the shrinking returns in Enron's bigger volume energy trading business. And there was another problem. Good as they were at opening markets, Enron's managers were less adept at the old economy discipline of cost control. Indeed, extravagant spending was an everyday incident of life at the firm.

[*Bratton also attributes Enron's demise to other, more exotic, factors, including aggressive accounting practices that Enron used to inflate its apparent profits and reduce its apparent debt. For example, Enron created "equity affiliates" to disguise debt. If a parent firm owns the majority of another firm's stock, their financial reporting must be consolidated as if they were a single firm. However, if a firm owns less than half of another, they make separate financial reports. Despite its aspirations to become a "pure financial intermediary," Enron depended on debt-laden "bricks and mortar" assets, such as power plants, to generate cash. Enron made sure to own these assets through "equity affiliates"—firms in which it had less than a 50 percent equity stake. Thus the debt did not appear on Enron's financial statements. At the same time, accounting rules allowed Enron to count a pro rata portion of the affiliates' income as its own.*

Accounting rules do not permit the investor company to count transactions with an equity affiliate as revenue. But the rules do permit corporations to transfer assets to "special purpose entities" (SPEs) and perform transactions with them that may be counted as revenue. To prevent SPEs from being used for sham transactions that falsely increase revenues, an SPE cannot be a mere puppet of the transferor corporation. An outsider must own 3% of the SPE's equity and control its activities.

These accounting techniques are legitimate by themselves, but Enron apparently used them in conjunction with unethical or illegal behavior. For example, Enron apparently violated the requirement that SPEs have 3% outside equity. In the notorious "Chewco" example, Enron itself provided the "outside" equity and attempted to disguise this fact. In certain SPEs, the role of the "outsider" was filled by limited partnerships controlled by Enron's chief financial officer, Andrew Fastow. Thus Enron could have essentially conducted transactions with itself and counted them as corporate revenue.

A related controversy was the fact that Enron paid Fastow $30 million for his role in the SPEs. When these irregularities were discovered, Enron had to subtract hundreds of millions of dollars from its reported revenues (i.e., revenues improperly counted from "transactions" with the SPEs) and add hundreds of millions in unreported debt (i.e., from debt-laden assets that had been improperly "transferred" to the SPEs). Furthermore, the Fastow revelations triggered a crisis in confidence that hurt Enron's credit rating, stock price, and its ability to engage in its primary business, energy trading contracts, which are built on trust. Professor Bratton argues, however, that the market's reaction to news of Fastow's $30 million was excessive. The payments to Fastow did not violate state conflict-of-interest laws, since disinterested directors approved them after full disclosure. Furthermore, although it did not fully disclose the Fastow payments to shareholders, Enron had disclosed that Fastow stood to profit from the SPEs. Bratton theorizes that during good economic times, investors tolerate self-dealing as a management perk, but retaliate fiercely if the market takes a downturn.

Finally, although using "equity affiliates" to offload debt is an acceptable practice, Enron failed to disclose its own contingent liability on that debt. Enron raised a great deal of cash by leveraging (that is, borrowing against) the assets of the equity affiliates, but lenders were apparently unwilling to lend based solely on these "junk assets." To satisfy lenders, Enron guaranteed the affiliates' debts, and in certain cases, agreed to repay the loans on an accelerated basis if Enron's credit rating or stock price fell below certain levels. This exposed Enron to significant undisclosed risks.]

... If [Enron's] stock remained buoyant, the obligation to pay the debt came due only on the debt's maturity. At that time, the still-buoyant stock would provide a painless vehicle for paying off the debt should the value of the affiliate's assets fall short. If Enron's stock fell gradually and caused the trigger to go off, Enron could get out from under the debt by minting more stock. It would have a problem on only one scenario. If the triggering stock decline was a free fall, Enron would be unable to bail itself out with a new stock offering and the debt would be accelerated directly against it. It was the last scenario that actually occurred.

Here was high-leverage financing in a mode that the promoters of the leveraged buyouts of the 1980s never would have dared to imagine.... In the 1980s, a highly leveraged deal presupposed a projection that the company would generate earnings before interest and taxes sufficient to cover the debt. At Enron in the virtual 1990s, the value to back the deal came not from such an inside projection of what the firm could earn, but from the market stock price. Stock prices also result from future earnings projections—projections made by outside traders with limited information about the company. Sometimes, in runaway stock markets, the projections are dispensed with entirely as the traders chase trends.

Unfortunately, Enron took this gamble on its own stock price in such a bubble stock market. And so the gamble failed.... Enron's stock declined for independent reasons as 2001 unfolded [for example, increased competition in the energy trading business it had previously dominated]. This, together with the crisis in confidence triggered by the SPE disclosures, caused further price declines. Contract contingencies began to trigger obligations on billions of off-balance sheet debt. And, in a conjuring trick unimaginable to the principals of Drexel Burnham Lambert[16] in their most creative moments, Enron had incurred these contingent liabilities without bothering fully to disclose them in its financial statements, whether on the balance sheet or in the footnotes. Indeed, it delayed public disclosure until the last possible point—mid-November 2001. [*According to Bratton, the belated disclosure of the hidden contingent liabilities, which amounted to $4 billion, "trigger[ed] a credit downgrade, a liquidity crisis, and a ticket to Chapter 11."*]

... Two paragraphs above all in Enron's 2000 MD&A[17] stand out in light of hindsight. They disclosed the contingent affiliate liabilities and triggers:

> Enron is a party to certain financial contracts which contain provisions for early settlement in the event of a significant market price decline in which Enron's common stock falls below certain levels (prices ranging from $28.20 to $55.00 per share) or if the credit ratings for Enron's unsecured, senior long-term debt obligations fall below investment grade. The impact of this early settlement could include the issuance of additional shares of Enron common stock.

---

16. The investment bank Drexel Burnham Lambert was the leading financier of hostile takeovers in the 1980s. Its bankers included Michael Milken, who pioneered the practice of junk-bond financing and was eventually jailed for securities-law violations. After settling criminal and SEC charges, Drexel failed in 1990 following the collapse of the junk-bond market.

17. *"MD&A" (Management Discussion and Analysis) is Item 303 of the SEC's Regulation S-K. The SEC's Regulation S-K provides corporations with an integrated list of their mandatory disclosure requirements under the securities laws. Required disclosures under MD&A include the following:*

> *(a)(1) ... Identify any known trends or any known demands, commitments, events or uncertainties that will result in or that are reasonably likely to result in the registrant's liquidity increasing or decreasing in any material way.*

> *(a)(3)(ii) Describe any known trends or uncertainties that have had or that the registrant reasonably expects will have a material favorable or unfavorable impact on net sales or revenues or income....*

17 C.F.R. § 229.303.

For further discussion of MD&A, see Donald Langevoort's article in Chapter 4. —Ed.

… Enron's continued investment grade status is critical to the success of its wholesale businesses as well as its ability to maintain adequate liquidity. Enron's management believes it will be able to maintain its credit rating.

The paragraphs omit at least two material facts—that the "financial contracts" are affiliate debt contracts and derivative contracts unconsolidated on Enron's balance sheet and that Enron's contingent liabilities under the "provisions" amount to $4 billion. [*According to Bratton, this incomplete disclosure was almost certainly in violation of generally accepted accounting principles*].

… We can pare down the [above] account by coupling the crisis of confidence and the hidden $4 billion of obligations as primary causes. The coupling works well—both stories involve equity affiliate and SPE transactions incident to Skilling's "asset light" strategy and aggressive earnings management. Both stories also involve heavy use of Enron's common stock as a back-up currency importing stability to an otherwise shaky deal structure.

Viewed with the benefit of hindsight, the equity affiliate and SPE transactions appear foolish, reckless, or fraudulent. There arises a question as to just what the top officers of Enron thought they were doing.…

Enron's managers responded with a gamble and borrowed against their own stock price. This reflects a belief in their own business plan. They must have figured that the stock price eventually would become bulletproof once the firm was awash in earnings from broadband and other new initiatives.…

So, what now seems foolish, reckless, or fraudulent, does so only because the gamble failed. Of course, gambling is what high-risk high-return businesses are all about. Rarely, however, do we see managers of large firms stake so much (the whole company and their own liberty) on so little (concealment of off-balance sheet obligations and earnings manipulation).

Thus did Enron's managers cross the line from risk-averse to risk-prone behavior. Did they do so rationally? We have seen that they had their reasons. We should add compensation to the list. Like most managers today, Enron's managers received significant compensation in the form of stock options. Option holding dulls the actor's sensitivity to degrees of distress on the downside, and at the same time giving the actor an incentive to generate chances for upside gains of high magnitude. Thus directed, a group of managers certainly would be more disposed to high-risk strategies. It should be noted, however, that stock-option-based incentives tend to operate in the long term. To effect a tie between compensation and Enron's managers' obsession with short-term numbers, we need to look to Enron's performance-based bonus scheme. These awards grew as Enron's stock price performed better relative to the market as a whole and as managers met performance criteria in respect of factors like funds flow, return on equity, and earnings per share. Amounts paid in 2001 based on 2000's numbers were substantial: $9.6 million for Lay; $7.52 million for Skilling, $3.925 million for Jeffrey MacMahon; $3.036 million for Fastow; and $2.3 million for Kopper.

But option holding and bonus taking do not, taken alone, provide a plausible explanation for the Enron disaster. For one thing, option holding now is ubiquitous among American managers. If option holding explains the behavior of Enron's managers, we accordingly should be seeing their behavior pattern everywhere instead of the present handful of companies beset by scandal. As yet, however, these firms remain outliers. For another thing, the Enron officers gambled with more than other people's money. As they crossed the line to fraud, they staked their personal liberty. One senses such actions to lie outside the box of option pricing.

For an alternative rational expectations explanation of the behavior of Enron's managers, we can turn to the "end period problem."[18] In this scenario, an ordinarily risk-averse rational actor finds her firm in distress due to business reverses. Bankruptcy being the most negative outcome possible, the actor rationally becomes risk-prone, gambling everything in one last play to avoid destruction. Concealment comes with the territory. This explanation would make sense for Enron if … Enron's principals stumbled into distress and rationally started manufacturing income and concealing obligations as a way of buying time to turn things around and avert disaster.

If, on the other hand, Enron's business was sound but troubled, we need to tell a longer story. This was a firm where concealment became a way of life long before the start of the end period. Enron's principals did not just wake up to find themselves in trouble. They created much of the trouble themselves, voluntarily and unnecessarily driving the firm into an end period…. To tell a compelling causation story on this scenario, we must look to Enron's organizational culture as well as its principals' economic incentives.

Enron fell because it pursued winning to excess. At Enron, winning was everything and everything became a tournament. Its business plan took unbundling to its logical conclusion, projecting a competitive victory over not only other firms but vertical industrial organization itself. Enron's top managers wanted to be surrounded exclusively by winners. So they made their workplace a tournament without end. They created a space that, unlike the outside world of regulation protecting losers, valued above all winning and the risk taking which necessarily precedes it. Winning also meant stunning earnings numbers: Where the tournament is ongoing, what counts is the most recent score. So important was winning at Enron that it became conflated with value maximization….

… [A]s corporate cultures develop, tournament schemes can do more than encourage strenuous efforts and filter out losers. They tend to produce winners of a certain type. To be sure, such executives are ambitious, persistent, optimistic, and hard working. But persistence does not always guarantee success. Enron's managers pursued their business plan so persistently that they lost their flexibility. They continued to open new markets on an accelerated schedule, even though their need to maintain an investment grade credit rating made it impossible to do this and at the same time tell the truth about themselves to the capital markets. Nor is the relentless optimism of the tournament winner always a productive force. The optimistic entrepreneur labors under a cognitive bias, which underweights downside risk and overweights both the probability of upside gain and the entrepreneur's own abilities and contributions. That cognitive bias is inseparable from shareholder value maximization, for the big scores in the stock market come from firms run by entrepreneurs rather than by conventional managers. On the downside, however, it can lead to errant decision making….

III. Enron and Corporate Self-Regulation

… The preceding story supports a highly confident prediction that the federal securities laws' regime of ex post liability will come to bear on Enron's managers with considerable force. It only remains to complete the picture of who knew what and when…. Thus does the defense strategy emerge: Cite the complexity of the contractual arrangements in question, plead ignorance, and point the finger downward in the chain of command.

---

18. *See* Jennifer H. Arlen & William J. Carney, *Vicarious Liability for Fraud on Securities Markets: Theory and Evidence*, 1992 U. ILL. L. REV. 691. *Arlen and Carney use the term "last period." — Ed.*

... The Powers Report[19] rightly faults Enron's board for defective ongoing monitoring of the LJM transactions [i.e., the SPE transactions involving Fastow's limited partnerships]. But like all such reprimands, this one has the benefit of hindsight. And even as it finds fault, the report also shows us that Enron's board went by the book when it approved the LJM transaction structure. Favorable reports lay on the table at the board meeting in question. [Enron's outside auditor, Arthur Andersen] and Enron's outside counsel, Vinson & Elkins, had been involved every step of the way. Because of the transactions' self-dealing aspect, the Board required ongoing monitoring by managers representing Enron's interest. In addition, the [Board's] audit committee was to review the transactions annually. There also was active concealment of negative information by middle management. This occurred both with the sham transaction concocted to lend Chewco the appearance of an outside equity investor and with a series of patch-up arrangements concluded after the swaps went sour. At only one point does the Powers Report account hold out hope for a plaintiff contemplating a duty of care lawsuit against Enron's outside directors. The three committee reviews of the ongoing LJM-related transactions were conducted quickly, lasting no more than 10 or 15 minutes, without probing questions being asked. Between *Smith v. Van Gorkom*[20] and the duty of care cases respecting financial institutions, these facts give a plaintiff a basis for argument. But a strong defense can be anticipated—each of Andersen, Vinson & Elkins, and Enron's managers had reviewed the transactions and continued to endorse them. The audit committee met with the Andersen partners with Enron's managers out of the room to ask if there was anything about which to worry. Andersen kept silent.

Thus do the facts of the case send a strong but disturbing signal: Enron stumbled into its end period while following the book of good governance practice, at least nominally.... As a matter of policy, the finger points not to lower officers, as Skilling and Fastow would have it, but to Enron's outside directors and with them the monitoring model of corporate governance.

The monitoring model holds out an objective, process-based system. It importunes companies to put a majority of highly qualified outside directors on the board and to integrate the board into its decision-making structure as an active participant. At the level of mandate, however, it only requires that boards go through the motions of making considered business judgments respecting corporate transactions. It does not and cannot make the further subjective inquiry into the degree of attention and quality of judgment actually brought to bear. Corporate counsel are well-schooled in packaging documentation so that compliance is well evidenced. The system responds to breakdowns such as Enron's by adding layers of new processes, each a ritualized enactment of the substance of the good governance.

To see how little this can mean in terms of sustained and searching confrontation with problematic topics, consider the audit committee of the board of directors and its central place in the system.... For a pristine example of compliance with all the ... rules [governing audit committees], open Enron's 2001 proxy statement. Its audit committee of five met five times during 2000 with its outside auditors and its inside managers responsible for accounting and internal controls. The committee was chaired by a professor emeritus in accounting from Stanford University. And yet despite the review and the committee's

---

19. *This is an investigative report commissioned by Enron's new, post-bankruptcy board of directors.* — Ed.

20. 488 A.2d 858 (Del. 1985) *The case held that when faced with an important corporate decision, directors' fiduciary duty of care requires them to "inform themselves of all information reasonably available to them and relevant to their decision."* — Ed.

formal recommendation of the audited financials, the audit had failed and with it the committee process.

[One suggestion for audit committee reform] originated with [former SEC Chair] Arthur Levitt and follows the example of Delaware special negotiating committees, which hire their own legal and business advisors. By extension, audit committees should hire their independent auditor to lead and assist them in evaluating internal compliance systems and the accounting treatments applied by the company's managers and auditors. Such a contrarian voice might have raised difficult questions about Enron's accounting policies respecting SPEs and affiliates. Whether the process of questioning would have led to a different accounting result and full disclosure of SPE arrangements is another question. For one thing, audit committee members do not differ from other board members in their cooperative dispositions. For another thing, given a limited universe of what are now four big accounting firms, each under pressure to approve the same types of deals, one wonders how much lawyerly adversity can be imported into the system....

Meanwhile, if reliable boardroom "conscientiousness" is what is needed, the solution is an independently nominated outside director—an outside super monitor. This suggestion figured prominently in policy discussions a decade ago, when it was thought that newly emerging activist investment institutions could find it convenient to pool resources and nominate candidates to the boards of poorly performing, large capitalization firms. Unfortunately, no super monitors have appeared because the collective action problems, which prevent shareholders from coordinating on and investing in their own board candidates, persist despite concentration of holdings in institutional hands. We will not see super monitors absent massive federal intervention to change the structure of board election and proxy solicitation.

Enron, then, reminds us that the monitoring model assures us of little. It gives only a circumstantial guarantee of good governance because it only requires evidence of a "conscientious," well-informed business judgment. The conscientiousness itself is ill-suited to ex post verification. In the alternative, the substance of the business judgment could be reviewed. But we have avoided such strict scrutiny on the sound theory that ex post review of risk taking would have perverse deterrent effects. In the chasm separating the circumstantial guarantee from such an actual guarantee lie untold billions of lost investment dollars, and not only in respect of Enron. It is a cost of capitalism.

With that vision of billions in lost capital we finally encounter the self-regulatory corporate law scheme's last line of defense, the investors themselves. When we look at Enron's shareholders, in particular the institutional shareholders (and the market actors analysts who sell them services), we witness a failure as marked as the failure in Enron's boardroom. Institutional actors with significant capital stakes, whether debt or equity, have access to top executives. It is their job to ask questions when company disclosures fail to tell a coherent story. We have seen that in Enron's case a long list of questions needed to be asked. We also have seen that Enron's public disclosures, although presenting an inadequate picture of the company, provided a basis for asking every question that needed to be asked. Two stand out even without the benefit of hindsight: (1) Just how much contingent liability will be triggered if your stock falls? (2) What percentage of net income would disappear if your SPEs had to be consolidated? The questions' formulation did not require an advanced business degree. A diligent Accounting for Lawyers student who studied Enron's financials with care ought to be up to the task.

But the questions were not asked. Now, the usual villain at this point is the Wall Street analyst. These actors today are dismissed as mouthpieces for their own firms' investment bankers—because negative reports destabilize investment banking relationships, negative reports are more and more rarely given. Certainly, the analysts provided no early warnings in Enron's case; indeed, many stayed positive even as the collapse went into its late stages. But the analysts' reputational stock fell to the floor even before Enron's common stock. No experienced institutional investor was relying on them....

The point is neither that agents of investment institutions always invest foolishly nor that such agents never intervene constructively on the financial side. Rather, the point is that there are surprisingly tight constraints on their utility as a governance check. It seems that even substantial institutional block holding, at least at the five percent level, provides no basis for assuming that the tough questions have been asked and addressed. To find a shareholder who takes on the properties of a super monitor, we presumably need a holder of a bigger block—a twenty-five or thirty percent owner with an inside position or inside agents. One hopes that such an actor, very common in the capital structures of firms on the continent of Europe, would have prevented the fatal excesses of Enron's managers. But, then, if Enron teaches us anything, it is to question the reasonableness of reliance on any corporate monitor....

IV. Conclusion—Enron and the Way We Live Now

... There is nothing new about fraudulent financials, even from repeat players with no immediate plans to skip the jurisdiction. The operative motivations are well-known, and Enron conforms to the pattern: The firm becomes risk-prone, whether it stumbles into an end period or drives itself there in a cultural context in which it loses touch with objective controls. Concealment occurs as it buys time until an external cure relieves its distress.

Despite this, there is an aspect of the Enron story shaped by its time and place. Enron and associated actors reenacted these old pathologies on a stage set by the contemporary shareholder value maximization norm. The norm first made the transition from business commentary to business practice in the 1980s. At the time it still had a sharp edge of critique. In those days, managers did not pursue shareholder value maximization. Instead they behaved in risk-averse ways, seeking to make the company bigger and safer whether or not that meant more for the shareholders. Actors in the capital markets imposed the shareholder value norm on unwilling managers through the harsh medicine of the leveraged restructuring and the hostile takeover.

Things changed in the 1990s. Managers internalized the norm, building resumes as shareholder value maximizers. Stock options better aligned their incentives with those of the shareholders. They emerged in the risk-neutral posture counseled by financial economics. They unbundled conglomerates and concentrated on core competencies. They laid off excess workers. They took care to divert free cash flow to their shareholders through open market stock repurchases. They took on the challenge of global markets. And they emerged as winners as they did so. The high leverage thought by observers in the 1980s to be the key that unlocked the shareholder value treasure turned out to be unnecessary. Its disappearance seemed to remove a threat that pursuit of shareholder value could have perverse effects. Many observers in the 1980s warned that high leverage meant underinvestment in long-term projects. In the 1990s, with the leverage strategy abandoned, shareholder value maximizing management went forward with its only apparent costs falling on the firm's disempowered constituents, the employees let go due to relentless cost cutting. But such losers did not matter. Proponents of America's system of corporate governance took a victory lap on the world stage.

As the 1990s progressed, darker colors appeared in the picture. Some began to question whether the fabulous wealth generated through the combination of liberal stock option plans and rising stock prices had its own perverse effects. At the same time, real-world shareholder value maximization came to be acted out in a bubble stock market. The bubble expanded on projections, which, however wild, were built on the same components that imported content to the maximization norm. The norm became a big tent that encompassed both short-term gains in stock prices stemming from the antics of noise traders and the more sober fundamental value maximization precepts of economists, management scientists, and fundamental value investors.

Managers came under pressure to satisfy both shareholder value constituencies. But the greater pressure, of course, came from the short-term maximization voice of the marketplace. As managers struggled to make their numbers, they were assisted by the Big Five accounting firms, who aggressively peddled tax shelter and earnings management ruses, termed "products." Those who saw through the smoke and mirrors and suggested regulation, whether in the self-regulatory system, like the FASB [Financial Accounting Standards Board],[21] or in government, like Arthur Levitt,[22] were shouted down and subjected to threats by attack-dog congressmen.

It all came to a head with Enron, where pressure to maximize and a culture of winning combined to draw a huge firm into risk-prone decision making. But the story is exceptional in only two respects. First, comes the magnitude of the numbers. Second, comes the giant step Enron's managers took across the line that separates aggressive accounting from securities fraud. Every other critical detail, including aggressive treatments, auditor capture, and the cognitive biases that facilitated the fatal step to fraud, implicates a well known business pathology and a concomitant and well-worn regulatory discussion.

Meanwhile, three strong lessons emerge from the wreckage. First, Enron collapsed the same way banks routinely collapsed in the days before deposit insurance. It did so because it had largely succeeded in realizing Skilling's vision of becoming a financial institution. Huge financial institutions present special regulatory problems and are subject to special requirements. Enron remained free of such regulation, partly because of the speed of its transition and partly due to its own successful influence activities. Its collapse shows its exemption to have been unjustified. Emerging financial institutions should be brought into the system in the ordinary course.

Second, even as additional regulatory implications devolve largely on the auditor, avoiding the rest of the self-regulatory system, this case controverts the often asserted claim that existing regulatory mandates fail the cost-benefit test. Those who make that claim rely on market forces and the self-interest of inside actors who face market discipline to assure providers of outside capital against the existence of shabby shops. That the firm with the seventh largest market capitalization and also the firm that preached market discipline the most loudly turned out to be the shabbiest of shops with the cooperation of outside directors, outside auditors, and institutional investors, highlights the limits on what self-regulation and market incentives can achieve. Sovereign mandate and punishment remain capitalism's bedrock.

Third, a century and a half ago, conservatives steeped in the classical economic model of Adam Smith voiced suspicions about the accumulation of significant assets within

21. *The FASB's attempts to reform the SPE accounting rules had been thwarted by opposition from corporations and their accountants, including Andersen and Enron. — Ed.*

22. *Former SEC Chair Levitt had called for reform of the accounting industry since at least 1998. See William Bratton's article in Chapter 12. — Ed.*

corporate organizations. Only when human beings owned property, they said, could individual interest and moral responsibility work together to keep the use of the property consonant with the interests of society as whole. Corporate ownership subverted market control of private economic power and diluted responsibility amongst the members of a group.[23] We still hear many voices advocating market control. But we hear it in a fundamentally different context in which corporations, rather than individuals, own the producing assets. For that reason, market controls taken alone cannot possibly assure responsible use of economic power. For the same reason, we should treat with utmost skepticism actors who preach market discipline from positions of safety behind the shields of corporate entities.

Cynthia A. Williams, *Corporate Social Responsibility in an Era of Economic Globalization*[*]

... In this Article, I examine the predominant legal consensus on corporate responsibility in the United States in light of globalization of the world's economy. That consensus suggests that corporations have no specific social responsibilities beyond profit maximizing for the benefit of shareholders, but that such profit maximizing must occur within the confines of the law, without deception or collusion. In other words, the constraints of law, buttressed in some specific instances by contractual obligations, will be sufficient to address any and all concerns about the exercise of corporate power and in particular will be sufficient to ensure that companies fully internalize all of the social and environmental costs of their productive processes and labor relationships. As this Article concludes, however, the predominant view at least requires an ultimate sovereign, a condition that does not exist in the increasingly global economy. Thus, the predominant academic solution to these problems is incomplete in the current economic context. Something more is needed than optimistic reliance on the theory of shareholder wealth maximizing within the constraints of domestic law and private contractual arrangements.

The second in this series of Articles [will begin] to develop what that "something more" might be. It starts by developing a distinction between the concepts of "corporate accountability" and "corporate responsibility." The concept of corporate accountability asks what duties might exist for corporations to account to society for the implications of their actions; that is, what duties might require corporations to inform society about the social, political, economic, and environmental consequences of managers' and directors' exercise of their fiduciary responsibilities. This concept of corporate accountability does not imply that changes are required in how corporations operate, but it does suggest that companies might have a duty to provide society with more information about those operations. The concept of corporate responsibility implies more affirmative obligations concerning what constitutes proper corporate conduct and so necessarily suggests changes, in specified ways, in how companies operate....

23. *See* JAMES WILLARD HURST, THE LEGITIMACY OF THE BUSINESS CORPORATION IN THE LAW OF THE UNITED STATES 1780–1970, at 43, 45, 48, 55–57 (1970).

* This work, copyright 2002 by Cynthia A. Williams, was originally published in 35 U.C. DAVIS LAW REVIEW 705 (2002), copyright 2002 by the Regents of the University of California. Reprinted with permission.

I. Brief Overview of Transnational Economic Activity in the Globalizing Economy

According to the United Nations Commission on Trade and Development (UNCTAD), there are 53,000 companies with headquarters in more than three countries, which it defines as transnational corporations.[24] [*This number had grown to 79,000 by 2007.*] Transnational companies carry on two-thirds of world trade, nearly half of it within their own company networks. The regional distribution of foreign direct investment (FDI), which is a measure of international production, is "heavily skewed towards developed countries, reflecting the fact that, in the past, most FDI [nearly three-fifths of world inflows] originated and stayed in developed countries." Much of this FDI inflow and outflow in developed countries results from cross-border merger activities, which is estimated to account for more than 60% of FDI in Europe and the United Kingdom and 80% of FDI in the United States in 1998. (Inward investment into OECD countries [*i.e., relatively developed countries*] reached $465 billion in 1998, representing a 71% increase over 1997; outflows were $566 billion.) [*In 2006, inflows increased to $910 billion and outflows reached $1.12 trillion. Due to the financial crisis, these levels were expected to decline in 2009.*]

Although in absolute terms most FDI stays in developed countries, if relative indicators are used (such as FDI per $1,000 GDP), then the top 30 host countries for FDI are developing countries. Thus, in 1997, developing countries received about two-fifths of world FDI inflows or $149 billion; this is twice the level they received in 1993. [*By 2007, FDI inflows to developing countries had grown significantly, reaching a record $500 billion. However, outflows from developing countries also reached a record level of $253 billion. As might be expected, FDI inflows and outflows declined in 2009 due to the financial crisis.*] In the early 1990s, half of this inflow to developing countries was official development finance, such as from the World Bank; by 1997 that share was down to 15%, which is a function of the growing importance of private capital inflows into developing countries. Of this private capital inflow, one-half is foreign direct investment (i.e., investment in production); one-third is "portfolio investment," such as investment in currency trading or capital market investment; and the rest is commercial bank loans and private investment.

These, and myriad other statistics, indicate the growing economic interdependence of the world's economies. These statistics also suggest the growing importance of transnational companies' investments in developing countries, as private capital inflows begin to replace official development sources of money into developing countries. Given the growing financial significance of private investment, the social significance of private, corporate actors' conduct is concomitantly enhanced.

II. The Corporate Social Responsibility Dilemma

As a general matter, the field of corporate social responsibility asks what the social obligations of companies, as citizens, are to the societies in which they are embedded.

---

24. *Professor Williams's original article drew its FDI statistics from* UNCTAD, WORLD INVESTMENT REPORT (1995, 1998, and 1999), *and* ORGANIZATION FOR COOPERATION AND ECONOMIC DEVELOPMENT ("OECD"), RECENT TRENDS IN FOREIGN DIRECT INVESTMENT 1998 (1999). *The updated figures in brackets are from* UNCTAD, WORLD INVESTMENT REPORT (2008) *and Hans Christiansen, Andrea Goldstein and Ayse Bertrand*, Trends and Recent Developments in Foreign Direct Investment, in OECD, INTERNATIONAL INVESTMENT PERSPECTIVES: FREEDOM OF INVESTMENT IN A CHANGING WORLD (2007). — *Ed.*

The general corporate social responsibility concern tends to be a seemingly pessimistic preoccupation with the potential negative social and environmental effects that may be created by economic entities in their pursuit of economic returns. In particular, academics have sought to evaluate the conditions under which decisions presumed to be shareholder wealth-maximizing have had negative effects on employees, consumers, communities, or the environment....

III. The Limits of Law

Looking at the question as a matter of theory, there seems to be no reason that well-designed laws, that take account of all social costs from every type of industrial production and employment relationship and that correctly require companies to internalize all such costs, could not be sufficient constraints to solve the corporate responsibility problem. Certainly for these constraints to be sufficient, attention would need to be paid to organizational design within companies such that the requirements of law are effectively translated into actions at all levels of the organization. Moreover, the complex of liability regimes and enforcement would need to be well designed to motivate compliance by recalcitrant companies. Yet, none of these preconditions is theoretically impossible by any means, and indeed this seems to be the ideal state of law towards which much thinking and writing strives and towards which actual law stumbles, slouches, or slogs, depending on one's optimism. But, such well-designed laws, organizational designs, and liability and enforcement structures are the necessary theoretical precondition for the predominant view to be correct.

There have always been reasons to be concerned that, in reality, even in a purely domestic setting, laws will not be well designed in this ideal sense, and so they will not correctly structure all of the underlying relationships and reflect all of the negative externalities. But there are particular features of globalization of the economy that accentuate the difficulties of relying upon law as an external constraint to correctly structure the corporate social relationship. One of the defining features (and perhaps the defining feature) of globalization, as it is now understood, is that it undermines the ability of sovereign nations to impose substantive, proactive limits on economic actors such as transnational corporations and capital market participants. Moreover, because of the structure of globalization and because there is no international sovereign, the power of nations to tax corporate enterprises and spend money on social welfare benefits in order to address distributive concerns arising from globalization is waning, although it is far from fully diminished. Finally, in the increasingly common international context, when there are instances that can be understood as a breakdown in corporate social responsibility, law is often insufficient to provide redress. Each of these points, clearly, needs elaboration.

A. *The Undermining of Sovereignty: Problems in the Proactive Application of State Power*

As stated above, one distinctive feature of globalization of the economy is the effect it has on the ability of nations to exercise proactive, regulatory power on transnational companies. That is, globalization of the economy as an economic process undermines the practical ability of nation-states to regulate the totality of activities of transnational companies in a dispassionate, objective fashion. This process is occurring in a number of different ways, so I will focus on two of the more important ways it is occurring: through companies' ability to relocate production processes to countries whose regulatory structure is perceived to be most favorable and through companies' influence on the kinds of laws and regulations countries promulgate and enforce in the first instance.

1. Relocation as a Method of Choosing the Applicable Regulatory Structure

One of the major reasons that globalization undermines sovereigns' power to regulate corporate activity is that companies can, and do, move their productive processes to different countries or "outsource" to independent producers in other countries to take advantage of competitive opportunities, including favorable regulatory climates. This process has been responsible for raising the standard of living in some developing nations, and countries compete to encourage such foreign investment, indicating that it is perceived as a positive influence on economic development. The process "shrinks" sovereignty, however. I will elaborate upon that point with respect to two substantive areas of particular concern in discussions of globalization of the economy: environmental and labor law.

a. Environmental Law

The Environmental Protection Agency in the United States recently promulgated integrated regulations about the disposal of toxic and conventional pollutants in the pulp and paper industry, one of the most pollution-intensive industries in the United States, covering both air and water emissions. The technology standards in the regulations will "cut toxic air pollutant emissions by almost 60 percent … and virtually eliminate all dioxin discharged from pulp, paper and paperboard mills into rivers and other surface waters." If U.S. companies move their paper production facilities to other countries with less stringent environmental laws; however, such as Mexico, then the environmental impact of these regulations will be substantially undermined. While the paper and pulp industry may be less "mobile" than many (given the economics of transporting the raw materials such as wood to the production facilities), other industries, such as the furniture-making, automobile manufacturing, electronics, and semiconductor industries, have made just such moves.

Avoiding environmental regulations by moving production abroad may not actually be a typical decision, however. First, some kinds of production likely to have serious environmental impacts — particularly electrical power generation and transportation — cannot be moved. Likewise, while mining and the extractive industries generally are of serious environmental concern, oil, gas, coal, and other minerals can only be extracted where there are such deposits. Second, studies by the World Trade Organization ("WTO") indicate that complying with environmental regulations in the United States accounts for 0.6% of production costs for most industries, rising to between 1.5% and 2% of the costs of production for the most pollution-intensive industries (petroleum and coal products, chemicals and allied products, metal industries, and paper and allied products). Companies seem unlikely to move production facilities to save 1–2 percent of their costs of production (unless it is an industry subject to extreme international competition), particularly because any actual cost savings would be offset by increased shipping costs. Indeed, the data do not show migration of polluting industries from developed countries to developing countries (perhaps because most polluting industries also tend to be capital intensive and so tend to move to other developed countries), while the data do show migration of labor-intensive industries to developing countries.

Moreover, not every company that moves production facilities abroad takes advantage of the host country's laws. A number of studies have shown that transnational companies tend to use standardized technologies throughout their productive facilities. Indeed, this makes good economic sense. Where companies have developed stringent environmental management systems, they are financially better off using those systems in all of their production facilities, notwithstanding the local laws and indeed have higher firm values than firms without stringent environmental management systems. Presumably many companies are aware of this, and thus the synchronicity between doing good and doing well promotes compliance with stricter environmental regulation than would be required in the international context.

This is not to suggest that there are no adverse environmental impacts from globalization, of course. Once production facilities are moved offshore to take advantage of lower labor costs, the lower environmental standards of host countries may become quite relevant within factories, as they have in the apparel and footwear industries. In addition, part of the impetus for increasing global economic integration is a reduction on tariffs and liberalization of the rules concerning foreign investment, both of which fuel economic development, which itself entails environmental consequences. There have also been concerns expressed that some domestic environmental regulations may be undermined in the process of complying with international trade regulations under the auspices of the [WTO] or international trade regimes such as the North American Free Trade Agreement (NAFTA).

Moreover, even the [WTO], which obviously supports expanding the processes of globalization, recognizes that there is a perception that environmental regulations are expensive and thus that countries which adopt stringent environmental requirements will be at a competitive disadvantage in attracting foreign investment. Companies have used this perception to lobby against new environmental laws, with some success. Thus, the process of globalization, and the competition by countries for capital investments, has led to what the WTO terms a "regulatory chill" with respect to countries enacting protective environmental laws, with the effect that global environmental regulation may not cause companies to fully internalize the costs of negative environmental externalities. While the effects of globalization on environmental regulation cannot necessarily be accurately described simply by using the familiar rubric of an environmental "race to the bottom;" therefore, it is at the same time clear that domestic regulators are not able effectively to address all of the environmental problems industrial production entails, given the mobility of capital and of production and given the "intellectual leverage" such mobility creates.

b. Labor Law

The potential effect of globalization on the labor relationships between transnational corporations and people throughout the world is another area of growing corporate social responsibility concern. Here, as in the environmental area, globalization has undermined the ability of any one country to regulate the full panoply of activities of transnational companies, casting doubt on the assumption that corporate social responsibility concerns can be fully addressed by reliance upon existing law. American, Japanese, and European companies do move production offshore to take advantage of lower wages, and the generally less stringent labor, health, and safety regulations associated with those lower wages. Part of the phenomenon of globalization is the increasing irrelevance of geography to the means of production, given new technologies for the global shipment of goods, the advent of the computer, and in particular the Internet. So, of course, it is possible for U.S. and European banks, credit card companies, or insurance companies to have their "back office" operations located in India, Thailand, or Indonesia. Some industries, such as the textiles, apparel, and footwear industries, have moved almost all of their production away from the United States and the European Union to developing nations to take advantage of lower wages.

And yet this mobility implicates serious corporate social responsibility issues, primarily about wages and the conditions of labor. With respect to the conditions of labor, as Harvard economics Professor Dani Rodrik has pointed out, U.S. law prevents U.S. manufacturers from competing with each other by requiring workers to agree to work twelve hour days, without overtime, by paying workers below the minimum wage, or by requiring workers to agree to be fired if they join a union.[25] And yet globalization facilitates exactly that sort of competition, undermining the effective power of domestic governments to regulate labor conditions and what constitutes "fair" competition within its borders and affecting the range of social policy choices perceived to be available to governments domestically.

With respect to wages, some evidence suggests that globalization may be leading to downward pressures on wages in developed countries, at least among people who are "unskilled" and "semi-skilled" according to traditional labor definitions, because their labor can be substituted by trade with or outsourcing to countries with lower wages. Indeed, although the comparative advantage used by many developing countries in their efforts to attract foreign investment has been lower wages, there is now some evidence suggesting that efforts to compete for investment on the basis of low wages is causing wages to remain depressed in some developing countries as well. Because increasing globalization has occurred at the same time as increasing economic inequality in the world, both within nations and between the industrialized nations and the developing nations, if wage stagnation or wage depression is affected by globalization, that is cause for a serious examination of what role, if any, transnational corporations might play in creating the underlying problems and what corporate accountability or even responsibility may be required under those circumstances to start to solve these problems.

The relationships between increased global trade, economic growth, and economic inequality are obviously complex, however; and I have no expertise to add in resolving the conundrum of growing economic inequality in the world, which has perplexed economists. [*Global income inequality is severe, but there is some dispute as to whether it has been improving or worsening in recent years, and, whatever the direction, whether it is the result of globalization.*[26]] ... [I]f wages in many developing countries are remaining depressed as a result of the global competition for capital, that, I submit, is part of the complex of corporate social responsibility issues. Indeed, world business leaders have recognized as much.

By the above brief discussion, I am not meaning to imply that companies relocating production in response to comparative regulatory advantage can be quickly and confidently labeled a "bad thing," or irresponsible, however. The corporate social responsibility area

---

25. DANI RODRIK, HAS GLOBALIZATION GONE TOO FAR? 36 (1999).
26. *See, e.g.,* G. Firebaugh & B. Goesling, Accounting for the Recent Decline in Global Income Inequality, 110 AM. J. SOCIOLOGY 283 (2004); R. Wade, Is Globalization Reducing Poverty and Inequality? 32 WORLD DEVELOPMENT 567 (2004).—*Ed.*

of inquiry does not admit of simple solutions. Globalization is obviously a structural phenomenon, and it is creating competitive wage and price pressures in many industries that managers of transnational companies are not free to ignore. I doubt that any divisional manager of any transnational company wakes up in the morning with a zeal to figure out which workers in which country she can squeeze that day, but probably many a divisional manager of many a transnational company wakes up with the anxious certainty that she needs to cut costs or her division or her job will be in jeopardy, given the brutal reality of global competition. Producers are under pressure from retailers to cut costs, and retailers are under pressure from the global competition with other retailers to cut costs; and all of them are under pressure from the capital markets to show continuing profit improvement. What I do suggest, though, is that given these competitive dynamics, the constraints of domestic law will be necessary but not sufficient to address the social implications of globalizing production. Rather, the structural pressures brought about by globalization demand structural solutions, or at least demand the development of structural counter-pressures....

IV. Conclusion

The primary implication of the above analysis is that the predominant academic position on corporate social responsibility must be amended in light of globalization. While the constraints of domestic law are clearly necessary and important to structure the relationship between the corporation and society, they are not sufficient fully to address the corporate social responsibility complex of issues as the economy becomes increasingly global; neither will purely contractual solutions fill the gap. Rather, the competitive pressures on countries to attract foreign investment are too severe, and the regulatory chill that competition creates is too pervasive. This is true not only for the American "hot button" sectors of law that have been implicated in human rights litigation, such as environmental protection and labor law but also for the bedrock issues of social structuring, such as taxation and social spending. As this Article asserted initially, something more is needed as a theory of corporate social responsibility than companies acting simply to maximize shareholder wealth within the constraints of various countries' domestic law.

Admittedly, that conclusion can be seen as doing nothing more than posing the traditional corporate social responsibility question in perhaps starker relief: what exactly, then, is that "something more" and how should corporate board members and managers know that they should do it if it is not legally required? Over the past decades, as various corporate law scholars in the United States have sought to advance discussions of different theories of corporate social responsibility, they have been met with two, seemingly intractable problems. First, it has been difficult to define what one means, in any fully specified way, by the concept of corporate social responsibility, and thus it has been difficult to discuss except at a high level of generality. While many advocates of more corporate social responsibility share a concern that managing global corporations to maximize shareholder wealth has the potential to lead to harmful social effects, including exacerbating persistent income inequalities, there is much less agreement about how to suggest reforming corporate law to address that concern.

Second, to the extent that very general definitions of corporate social responsibility have been developed, they tend to be ... multifiduciary or stakeholder models.... under which corporate managers and directors can be understood to owe consideration (and perhaps even fiduciary obligation) to a wider range of constituents than to the shareholders, including obligations to employees, consumers, communities, suppliers, and other constituents of the corporate contract, broadly construed.[27]

And yet this notion of corporate managers and directors being responsible to multiple constituencies has been deeply problematic from the standpoint of traditional corporate theory in the United States, precisely because it undermines one of the key values of corporate law—accountability. Central aspects of corporate law doctrine, such as the concepts of fiduciary duties of loyalty and care, exist to ensure that managers and directors are ultimately accountable to the corporation and its shareholders. Market mechanisms, such as the existence of a highly developed stock market and a robust market for corporate control, are also understood to promote accountability to stockholders' interests. If managers are accountable to various other constituents in theory, they are likely to be accountable to no one but themselves in fact or so the traditional corporate law response has suggested. So, for instance, managers may profess concern with the effects of a takeover on employees and the communities in which they operate, while their actual motivations in resisting a takeover are self-interest and concerns about their own positions (entrenchment). Moreover, if corporate managers and the board are responsible to a broad range of constituents rather than being responsible solely to the shareholders and the corporation, we lose a seemingly clear metric by which to judge the efficacy and fidelity of management's actions. Under the shareholder view of the corporation, whether management has done a good job is evaluated by determining whether management has increased the value of the firm over the period in question. While it may be, in fact, difficult to determine whether management has increased the value of a firm over the period in question, the shareholder view of the corporation typically assumes that this question can be answered simply by looking to increases in share prices. Under a multiple constituency model, an evaluation of a broader range of social and financial facts is necessary to judge how well managers and the board are doing and thus to hold them accountable to their multiple constituencies. Thus, ironically, in a number of ways calls for increased corporate social responsibility have floundered on the shoals of corporate accountability.

It is for that reason that I am so intrigued by distinguishing the concept of "social accountability" from that of "social responsibility" ... and further intrigued by examining the arguments for an expanded duty of corporate social accountability as one solution to the corporate social responsibility dilemma. Such accountability, as described in the introduction to this Article, would derive from companies producing more information to be publicly disseminated about the social, political, economic, and environmental consequences of managers' and directors' exercise of their fiduciary responsibilities. As such, it would not require any changes in how directors or managers exercise their fiduciary responsibilities, and it would leave to managers and directors decisions about how, precisely, to balance the competing demands of various constituents, including shareholders, exactly as corporate law and practice do today. Yet, the production and dissemination of such information would produce greater corporate social transparency, actuating the goal of enhanced corporate social accountability without directly undermining the traditional corporate law goal of shareholder accountability. That social accountability may, in turn, help to produce structural pressures to inculcate humanistic concerns into otherwise brutal global competition. That, at least, is one premise worthy of serious examination.

Thus, I submit, expanded corporate social transparency is one important candidate for the "something more" that must be incorporated into the prevailing theory of corporate

---

27. *This concept is discussed further in Chapter 2.* —Ed.

social responsibilities to make that theory sufficient in light of the challenges of globalization....

Discussion Questions

1. The shareholder-centered, contractarian model Butler and McChesney describe has dominated corporate law and theory for decades. Proceeding from a similar model, economist Milton Friedman famously concluded that the law should prohibit corporate philanthropy because it constitutes unchecked management misuse of shareholder property. *See The Social Responsibility of Business Is To Increase Its Profits,* N.Y. Times Magazine, Sept. 13, 1970; *see also* FRIEDMAN, CAPITALISM AND FREEDOM (1962). In contrast, Butler and McChesney conclude that the model militates *against* legal regulation of corporate philanthropy.

Assuming the validity of the shareholder-centered contract model, which conclusion do you find more convincing? Why? What assumptions underlie each conclusion? More generally, does the shareholder-centered model give support to the existing corporate law regime, to an increase in regulation, or to deregulation?

2. Butler and McChesney argue that "competitive markets will tend to penalize managers and corporations that engage in corporate philanthropy that hurts share value overall." Through what mechanisms will "markets" inflict this penalty? What form will the penalty take? What kinds of preconditions are necessary for the market to work in this way?

3. In reviewing shareholder challenges to corporate philanthropy, courts tend to follow the approach Butler & McChesney advocate. Delaware, for example, applies the business judgment rule, under which courts defer to corporate directors' business decisions. *See Kahn v. Sullivan,* 594 A.2d 48 (1991). Does this seem appropriate? Are corporations' charitable contributions business decisions or altruistic acts? Should courts defer to boards' characterizations of decisions as "business decisions" or inquire into whether they truly are business-related? Do you agree with Butler and McChesney's assertion that corporate philanthropy should be viewed through the same agency-cost lens as other managerial behavior?

4. Berkshire Hathaway Inc. (the corporation run by the famous investor Warren Buffett) used to allocate a specific aggregate amount of money for contribution to charity. Each shareholder had the power to designate which charitable organizations would receive a portion of the money, in proportion to the number of shares the shareholder owned. What advantages and disadvantages does this approach have in relation to management-controlled giving? Assuming this approach to giving is a good one, should it be mandated by law, as some states have considered doing? Why do you suppose Berkshire Hathaway discontinued the program?

Consider also other alternatives to the existing system of corporate philanthropy, such as a tax on corporations that would be used to fund private or government social programs, or increased tax incentives for individual contributions.

5. As the agency cost perspective indicates, corporate governance is typically portrayed as a power struggle to keep management true to the purpose of the firm—defined as the maximization of corporate profit for shareholder benefit. Dallas argues, however, that "[i]f profit is adopted as the objective of the corporation, this conclusion is [itself] the result of a power struggle in which certain power coalitions have prevailed." Should the purpose

of each corporation be left to a power struggle within that corporation, or should the purpose be defined for corporations generally by the law (involving a broader power struggle in the political arena)? What are the advantages and disadvantages to each approach?

6. In response to arguments that corporate social responsibility is too vague to meaningfully constrain directors, Dallas argues that the orthodox concept of a duty to enhance shareholder wealth is similarly indeterminate. But if neither concept imposes a meaningful constraint on corporate directors, why does she favor the former? Indeed, if neither one provides an enforceable constraint, does it even matter which one the law professes to apply?

7. Can the law clearly and meaningfully define the duties of directors, the rights of shareholders, and the purpose of a business corporation? Should it attempt to do so? Why or why not? If so, how? If not, how is it that shareholder-based capitalism works at all?

8. As Dallas points out, despite the rhetoric of shareholder wealth maximization, corporate directors in reality make many decisions based on factors other than profit. Chapter 2 discusses this idea in depth. Dallas argues that corporate directors have no special competence to make such decisions. Should board composition be changed? If so, how? Should directors' discretion be reined in? If so, how? We will return to this issue in Chapter 9.

9. Many commentators argue that corporate law is to blame for corporations' indifference to social, economic, and environmental justice because the law requires corporate managers to maximize shareholder wealth. But does the law really contain a legally enforceable rule to that effect? If so, where is it? Moreover, in the absence of a legally enforceable duty to maximize shareholder wealth, do you think corporations would become more sensitive to issues of social justice? Why or why not?

10. As Dallas points out, almost any non-wasteful business decision can be defended as maximizing firm value in the long term. Thus, even assuming the primacy of shareholder interests, "wealth maximization" does not serve as much of a constraint on directors' discretion. A more narrow definition of corporate purpose is the maximization of *short-term share value*. Is this a preferable way to make managers accountable to shareholders?

If Dallas is correct and there is no enforceable legal rule of wealth maximization, what accounts for Enron's self-destructive focus on short-term share value as described by Bratton?

11. Even after the Enron debacle, few commentators have questioned state courts' traditional deference to directors' decisions under the business judgment rule. Even Bratton, who believes strongly in "sovereign mandate and punishment" and acknowledges that the rule can shelter poor decision making, defends the rule as an inevitable "cost of capitalism." Why? Do you agree?

12. Explain Bratton's concept of the "super monitor." How would such a monitor differ from an outside director under the current system? Do you agree that super monitors could improve corporate governance?

13. As Bratton points out, many of Enron's alleged accounting manipulations were clearly illegal. But some were closer calls. Is the distinction between "proper" wealth maximization and "earnings management" as simple as Bratton suggests? Can legal rules clearly define the distinction in advance for directors, officers, and auditors? If not, does the law's failure to do so excuse those corporate players accused of fraud for exploiting loopholes and vagueness in the accounting rules?

If confusing but legally permissible accounting practices make it possible to enhance apparent revenues, can a corporation be faulted for taking advantage of them? Indeed, isn't such behavior consistent with (if not demanded by) the conventional understanding that directors have a duty to serve shareholders?

14. As Greenfield points out, both real corporate activity and the economic theory of the business firm depend on the role of workers. Why, then, do corporations law and theory focus primarily on management and shareholders? What is the difference between shareholders' commonly accepted "property" interest in the corporation and the "property" interest of workers that Greenfield suggests? What is the difference between workers' contract rights and shareholders' "contract" interests that Butler and McChesney discuss?

15. How could the corporate "transparency" Williams advocates be achieved in the absence of an international sovereign to mandate it?

16. Would increased transparency result in increased corporate sensitivity to social justice issues? If so, by what mechanisms?

17. Large corporations have undeniable effects on society. But is this public role of corporations central or merely incidental? Can it be reconciled with the contractarian model of the corporation? Consider the public and private roles of corporations in light of the government's decision to bail out (some) troubled banks, other financial firms, and automobile companies in 2008 (and earlier, in the savings and loan crisis of the 1980s and the Chrysler bailout of 1979). This issue will be addressed further in the articles by Block and Silvers & Slavkin later in this volume.

Chapter 2

Balancing Interests in the Corporation

Although it is often argued that directors *should* owe duties only to shareholders, as Butler and McChesney did in Chapter 1, in practice directors often consider the interests of multiple constituencies. Corporate law recognizes this reality in varying degrees: for example, some states have broad and explicit "other constituencies" statutes,[1] while others espouse a more limited version of the concept.[2] The readings in this chapter present various approaches to the issues of how directors balance these competing interests and, moreover, how they *should* balance them.

While Butler and McChesney view the corporation as a "contract" between shareholders and managers, Jonathan Macey broadens the focus of the "contractual" model to encompass other relationships that make up a corporation. Thus, he argues, fiduciary duty to shareholders determines management's duties only to the extent that management has not made agreements to the contrary with non-shareholder corporate constituencies (such as creditors). In their article, Margaret Blair and Lynn Stout also argue that directors' duty is not to any one constituency. Rather than identifying the explicit contractual rights of various constituencies, however, they argue that the role of directors is to balance the interests of all so as to maximize the joint product of the corporate "team."

Marleen O'Connor looks at labor's attempts to influence management priorities, an example of the political competition over corporate purposes that Dallas outlined in Chapter 1. Finally, Stephen Bainbridge takes a skeptical view of the law's involvement in balancing corporate interests. He questions the idea that the law can make corporations into virtuous social actors and calls for greater candor about the usually hidden normative underpinnings of corporate law.

Jonathan R. Macey, *Fiduciary Duties as Residual Claims: Obligations to Non-Shareholder Constituencies from a Theory of the Firm Perspective**

This Article intends to reconcile two competing paradigms within the law and economics model of corporate governance. The first paradigm, which has its intellectual origins in

---

1. See, e.g., *Penn. Stat. Ann. Tit. 15, §1715, reprinted in the Discussion Questions section of this chapter.*
2. *See, e.g., Revlon v. MacAndrews & Forbes Holdings*, 506 A.2d 173, 176 (Del. 1986). The court held that directors considering whether to resist a hostile takeover may weigh the interests of nonshareholder constituencies, as long as there is also "some rationally related benefit accruing to the shareholders."

* Originally published in 84 Cornell Law Review 1266 (1999). Reprinted with permission.

the work of Ronald Coase, holds that the modern, publicly held corporation is a nexus of contracts among the company's various contributors.[3] The term "nexus of contracts" has become a revolutionary banner that has "transformed not only our understanding of the law, but the law itself."[4]

The nexus-of-contracts approach to corporate law offers a simple lesson: one should not view corporations as particularized forms of trusts or as fictitious creatures of state law. Rather, according to the law and economics perspective that the nexus-of-contracts approach to corporate law exemplifies, one should view the corporation as a "complex set of explicit and implicit contracts," and corporate law as enabling "the participants to select the optimal arrangement for the many different sets of risks and opportunities that are available in a large economy." In other words, one should view the corporation as nothing more than a set of contractual arrangements among the various claimants to the products and earnings generated by the business. The group of claimants includes not only shareholders, but also creditors, employee managers, the local communities in which the firm operates, suppliers, and, of course, customers.

The core insight of this nexus-of-contracts paradigm is that contract defines each participant's rights, benefits, duties, and obligations in the corporate endeavor. This insight, in turn, implies that one should not give any class of claimants preference over any other. Instead, each claimant or a group of claimants deserves to receive only the exact benefits of the particular bargain that it has struck with the firm, no more and no less. What claimants have bargained for, however, may differ enormously from firm to firm, depending on a complex set of exigencies.

The nexus-of-contracts approach to the corporation appears to be strongly at odds with the second paradigm of corporate governance. The second paradigm represents both the standard law and economics view and the view reflected in traditional state and corporate law rules; it posits that corporations and their directors "owe fiduciary duties to shareholders and to shareholders alone." Commentators advance a variety of arguments to support this second paradigm. For example, some argue that needless complexity would result if corporations were required to serve the interests of groups other than shareholders. Specifically, corporate practitioners often argue that if directors must serve constituencies other than shareholders,

> the confusion of … trying to … require directors to balance the interests of various constituencies without according primacy to shareholder interests[ ] would be profoundly troubling. Even under existing law, particularly where directors must act quickly, it is often difficult for directors acting in good faith to divine what is in the best interests of shareholders and the corporation. If directors are required to consider other interests as well, the decision-making process will become a balancing act or search for compromise. When directors must not only decide what their duty of loyalty mandates, but also to whom their duty of loyalty runs (and in what proportions), poorer decisions can be expected.[5]

Scholars who approach this issue from a law and economics perspective reach the same result as the corporate bar. Those scholars argue that corporations should maximize value for shareholders and shareholders alone because shareholders, as residual claimants, have

---

3. *See Butler & McChesney's article in Chapter 1 for a discussion of Coase's model of the firm.*

4. Lewis A. Kornhauser, *The Nexus of Contracts Approach to Corporations: A Comment on Easterbrook and Fischel*, 89 Colum. L. Rev. 1449, 1449 (1989).

5. ABA Comm. On Corporate Laws, *Other Constituencies Statutes: Potential for Confusion*, 45 Bus. Law. 2253, 2269 (1990).

the greatest incentive to maximize the value of the firm. As Frank H. Easterbrook and Daniel R. Fischel observed:

> As the residual claimants, the shareholders are the group with the appropriate incentives ... to make discretionary decisions. The firm should invest in new products, plants, etc., until the gains and costs are identical at the margin. Yet all of the actors, except the shareholders, lack the appropriate incentives. Those with fixed claims on the income stream may receive only a tiny benefit (in increased security) from the undertaking of a new project. The shareholders receive most of the marginal gains and incur most of the marginal costs. They therefore have the right incentives to exercise discretion.[6]

Thus, one seemingly cannot reconcile the two paradigms. The nexus-of-contracts approach to corporate law posits that one can decompose the corporation into a complex set of contractual relationships. Consequently, under this approach, everything is up for grabs or, at least, subject to negotiation. Constituencies such as workers, bondholders or other creditors, customers, suppliers, and managers ought to be able to contract for the right to be the exclusive (or, at the very least, the partial) beneficiaries of corporate fiduciary duties. After all, if a corporation is simply a complex web of contracts, the various participants to the corporate venture should be able to contract among themselves to obligate the directors to serve broad societal interests, the interests of the firm's workers, or the interests of any other non-shareholder constituency.

By contrast, everything is not up for grabs with respect to fiduciary duties. There is a single one-size-fits-all solution; the parties should write the corporate contract such that the shareholders always win. The notion that shareholders are the exclusive beneficiaries of a corporation's fiduciary duties is fundamentally at odds with the idea that a corporation is merely a nexus of contracts, with no set of claimants having any a priori rights in relation to any other.

This Article seeks to reconcile these two competing corporate law paradigms. My thesis is quite radical. Simply put, fiduciary duties are not all that they appear to be. They can be (and frequently are) modified by contract. Thus, contrary to popular wisdom, the notion that shareholders are the exclusive beneficiaries of fiduciary duties is the default rule rather than the mandatory rule. One can reconcile the tension between the shareholder-primacy paradigm and the nexus-of-contracts paradigm if one recognizes that the shareholders can consent to waive the shareholder-primacy paradigm. Because shareholders are at the top of the contract heap, the nexus-of-contracts paradigm subsumes the shareholder-primacy paradigm.

I also will argue that this issue has generated confusion because no shareholders rarely find it in their interest to contract with shareholders to vary the shareholder-primacy default rule. However, in certain contexts, such as bankruptcy, circumstances change, and the interests of shareholders are subordinated to the interests of other constituencies....

I. The Nexus-of-Contracts Approach

The nexus-of-contracts approach to the modern, publicly held corporation produces three important and related insights about corporate law. The first is that shareholders' rights and duties are (or should be) defined by contract. The second is that corporate law should be "enabling" rather than mandatory. The third is that no particular set of outcomes

---

6. Frank H. Easterbrook & Daniel R. Fischel, *Voting in Corporate Law*, 26 J.L. & ECON. 395, 403 (1983).

is best for all firms. Rather, each firm must find the specific set of contractual obligations that best suits its shareholders.

As Oliver Hart observed, each type of business organization, including the corporation, "represents nothing more than a particular 'standard form' contract."[7] Indeed, the very justification for having different types of business organizations is to permit investors, entrepreneurs, and other participants in the corporate enterprise to select the basic organizational design they prefer from a menu of standard-form contracts. It is possible (though difficult) to imagine a legal system in which the various initial constituencies of a business venture (equity claimants, fixed claimants, managers, entrepreneurs) create new contracts that establish the core features of their business (limited liability, legal "personhood," indefinite life, freely transferable shares) *ex nihilo* each time they form a new corporation. The virtue of the standard-form arrangement characteristic of modern corporate law is that it is "convenient"; it reduces transaction costs by allowing the participants in the corporate enterprise to take advantage of an arrangement that suits the needs of investors and entrepreneurs in a wide variety of situations.

Corporate law should be enabling rather than mandatory because there are limits to the cookie-cutter approach reflected in the standard-form rules that constitute state corporate law. Specifically, different firms have different needs, and different firms conduct their businesses in a very wide variety of contexts. If corporate law were not enabling, the various claimants to the cash flows could not customize the standard-form rules to meet their particular needs.

Significantly, this analysis implies that no particular set of contractual outcomes is ideal for every firm. Perhaps the best way of illustrating this implication is with reference to the core characteristics of the modern corporation. As noted above, at its most elemental level, the standard-form contract for corporations consists of four features: limited liability, legal personhood, indefinite life, and freely transferable shares. It is possible, however, and even common in certain contexts for firms to dispense with these key features to suit their interests.

For example, with respect to limited liability, shareholders in closely held firms commonly sign personal guarantees of indebtedness to give their firms access to bank credit. Their willingness to guarantee demonstrates that even the "core feature" of limited liability can be waived by contract....

... [T]he core feature of free transferability of shares can be contracted around as well. The Model Business Corporation Act makes free transferability a default rule by stipulating that "the articles of incorporation, bylaws, an agreement among shareholders, or an agreement between shareholders and the corporation may impose restrictions on the transfer or registration of transfer of shares of the corporation." Thus, all of the core features that characterize the corporation fit easily into the nexus-of-contracts paradigm because one can easily vary or waive each by contract. Certain other corporate law rules, however, are mandatory, and it is not obvious that one can waive these rules by agreement. However, as Roberta Romano observed in a penetrating analysis of ostensibly mandatory rules, "the rules that are identified as 'mandatory' in practice have very little in common with the ordinary understanding of that term. They are either easily—and legally—side stepped, or they pose nonbinding constraints because there is no burning demand to

---

7. Oliver Hart, *An Economist's Perspective on the Theory of the Firm*, 89 Colum. L. Rev. 1757, 1764 (1989).

deviate from them."[8] Rules in this category include the provision for annual election of directors, the prohibition on delegating to committees the decision to approve a merger, the limitation on dividend payouts, the demand requirement in derivative suits, the requirement that shareholders vote on mergers, and the existence of shareholder appraisal rights. As Romano showed, these rules are far more malleable than has been suggested.

Moreover, the enabling elements of corporate law permit a firm to structure a transaction in a certain way to avoid liability or reincorporate in more permissive states to reach a desired outcome. By reincorporating, firms opt out of one set of corporate laws and opt into another. Likewise, firms can change their organizational form to achieve a desired outcome or to avoid a legal provision they find undesirable. Firms can go private or public, change from mutual to stock form, or become a limited liability company or a partnership if they feel one of these organizational forms provides a better result for the participants in the corporate venture.

Another striking example of the power of the nexus-of-contracts paradigm is reflected in state law statutes that permit corporations to limit or eliminate personal liability of directors for monetary damages arising from a breach of their fiduciary duty of care.[9] As Robert Clark pointed out, "to this limited extent, a corporation will be allowed to ask its shareholders to vote to 'opt out' of the otherwise applicable judge-made rules of fiduciary duty."[10]

Thus, the nexus-of-contracts approach provides a powerful analytical device for conceptualizing the modern corporation. Not surprisingly, the "theory now dominates the thinking of most economists and most economically oriented corporate law scholars who focus at all on the theory of the corporation."

It is also important to recognize, however, that the nexus-of-contracts paradigm is purely descriptive. It is a positive, not a normative, tool. To say that the firm is a nexus of contracts is only the beginning of the analysis because this paradigm tells us nothing about the substance of these contracts. The theory provides no information about either what provisions are (or should be) contained in the standard-form contracts or what provisions are (or should be) waived and by whom. As Jensen and Meckling observed in their seminal article on the subject of capital structure, "the 'behavior' of the firm is like the behavior of a market; i.e., the outcome of a complex equilibrium process."[11] Stated another way, from a nexus-of-contracts perspective, because firms consist of a complex web of contractual relationships, firm behavior depends critically on what those contracts provide. In turn, the contract provisions themselves depend on the outcome of the bargaining process that takes place between the contracting parties.

There are two possible ways to reconcile the nexus-of-contracts paradigm with the rival paradigm positing that corporations owe fiduciary duties to shareholders and to shareholders alone. The first possibility is the existence of a "corner solution." A corner solution is one in which the solution to every problem is the same. Thus, one might reconcile the nexus-of-contracts paradigm with the shareholder-primacy paradigm because in every single situation, shareholders and the other participants in the corporate enterprise

---

8. Roberta Romano, *Answering the Wrong Question: The Tenuous Case for Mandatory Corporate Laws*, 89 COLUM. L. REV. 1599, 1599 (1989).

9. *See* Model Bus. Corp. Act 2.02(b)(4); Del. Gen. Corp. L. § 102 (b)(7).

10. Robert C. Clark, *Contracts, Elites, and Traditions in the Making of Corporate Law*, 89 COLUM. L. REV. 1703, 1704 (1989).

11. Michael C. Jensen & William H. Meckling, *Theory of the Firm: Managerial Behavior, Agency Costs, and Ownership Structure*, 3 J. FIN. ECON. 305, 311 (1976).

mutually agree that the interests of the non-shareholder constituencies should be subordinated to the interests of the shareholders.

The second possibility is that the ideal of shareholder primacy is a myth. Under this reconciliation, the nexus-of-contracts paradigm reigns supreme because the idea of shareholder primacy, like the other elements of corporate law described above, is merely a default rule that the parties can, and frequently do, vary to suit their particularized needs. The following section considers each of these possibilities in turn and concludes that no corner solution exists and that the default rule of shareholder primacy can be varied by contractual arrangement. In fact, under a wide variety of situations, shareholders and non-shareholder constituencies mutually agree that shareholder claims should be subordinated to the claims of non-shareholders. Therefore, I conclude that even fiduciary duties are, at their core, contractual in nature.

II. Fiduciary Duties to Shareholders

Commentators extensively have discussed the question of why shareholders are the exclusive beneficiaries of directors' fiduciary duties. The economic justification for having fiduciary duties at all is that "fiduciary duties are the mechanism invented by the legal system for filling in the unspecified terms of shareholders' contingent [contracts]." However, one cannot jump from the fact that fiduciary duties serve a gap-filling function in the law to the conclusion that shareholders should be the exclusive beneficiaries of such duties. One needs an additional step.

Easterbrook and Fischel maintain that one can justify making shareholders the exclusive beneficiaries of directors' fiduciary duties because of the shareholders' unique status as residual claimants. Because shareholders are residual claimants, they receive the benefits— and incur the costs—associated with marginal, or discretionary, corporate decisions. Thus, according to Easterbrook and Fischel, unlike shareholders who are residual claimants, non-shareholder constituencies, as fixed claimants, are indifferent to most corporate decisions. Corporations still will be able to meet their contractual obligations to the other constituencies regardless of whether corporate decisions turn out well or not. In other words, every decision a corporation makes affects shareholders' wealth, but far fewer decisions will affect, for example, the ability of the firm to meet its payroll or its obligations to bondholders.

Thus, the essence of the corner-solution argument is that fiduciary duties flow to shareholders because shareholders are the corporate constituency that values those duties most highly. The problem with this argument is that one can easily imagine situations in which non-shareholder constituencies will be concerned as much as, if not more than, shareholders about the outcomes associated with a particular corporate decision. Take, for example, a large publicly held company with many highly diversified, small-stakes shareholders. Suppose further that this company has a workforce comprised of people with undiversified, firm-specific skills. A firm-specific skill is a job skill that is specific to a particular job. Firm-specific skills, by definition, cannot easily be transported from one job to another because these skills are of value only to the firm with which they are associated. Under this set of assumptions, one easily can imagine that workers who possess only firm-specific skills would be harmed far more than shareholders by layoffs, plant closings, and other corporate decisions that would cause the workers to forfeit the value of their investments in firm-specific human capital.

Thus, while Easterbrook and Fischel are correct that for a wide range of issues corporate decisions concern shareholders alone, this observation will not be true with respect to all issues. For many issues, workers and local communities, not to mention customers, suppliers, and managers, will care much more deeply about the decision than shareholders. Thus, the corner-solution argument, which posits that fiduciary duties flow exclusively to shareholders because they value them most highly and therefore will always contract for them, seems clearly wrong.

III. Contracts Versus Fiduciary Duties

One should view the arguments made above about firm-specific human capital investment from the perspective of the nexus-of-contracts paradigm. Clearly, workers care deeply about issues such as job security. A theory that argues that workers value job security and high wages less than shareholders value competitive returns on their equity investments is highly implausible. It stands to reason that workers should be able to contract ex ante for job security and competitive wages. Of course, the fiduciary duties owed to shareholders do not prevent workers from bargaining for and obtaining an agreement with respect to these and other employment issues.

The point here is that one can contract away fiduciary duties to shareholders. Consequently, despite the appearance of intractability, fiduciary duties are simply another default rule that shareholders and non-shareholder constituencies can customize as they please. Fiduciary duties only operate in the shadow of the express contractual arrangements that non-shareholder constituencies have with the firm. For example, banks, bondholders, and other fixed claimants commonly negotiate contractual protections for themselves. These provisions seriously impair the ability of shareholders to use the cash flows generated by a firm in a manner in which the shareholders can benefit at the expense of fixed claimants.

Corporations in search of capital routinely agree to restrict their ability to make investments, loans, or other extensions of credit as a condition to receiving funds from lenders. Additionally, when shareholders grant secured credit, they voluntarily agree to subordinate their claims to specific assets to certain creditors. Similarly, firms routinely restrict their ability to make dividend payments to shareholders to obtain access to bond markets.

Thus, as with contracts with workers, contracts between shareholders and firms routinely subordinate the claims of shareholders to those of non-shareholder constituencies. These contracts clearly impede the freedom of directors and managers to maximize shareholder wealth. One response to this argument is that these restrictions on the ability of corporations to maximize shareholder value are consistent with the shareholder-primacy paradigm because all of these contracts benefit shareholders in the end. Shareholders are willing to bargain with workers to give them job security and better wages because doing so allows them to attract and retain better workers, and thereby increases profitability. Presumably, shareholders only would approve wage packages and job security commitments to the extent that the benefits of these agreements in the form of higher worker productivity equal or exceed the costs in the form of higher operating costs.

Similar logic applies to other fixed claimants such as bondholders and lenders. For example, corporations often provide fixed claimants with security interests in corporate assets or agree to restrictions on dividend payments or investments. These agreements benefit shareholders by increasing the availability of credit and lowering the cost of borrowing. In other words, shareholders price the promises they make to non-shareholder constituencies. Shareholders will make such promises only to the extent that the benefits of making these promises outweigh the costs. The same argument applies to fiduciary duties themselves. Just as shareholders must weigh the costs and benefits of making promises to non-shareholder constituencies, so too must non-shareholder constituencies weigh the costs and benefits of fiduciary duties.

A simple example illustrates this point. Imagine two firms, X and Y. The firms are identical in every way, except that firm X grants shareholders the benefits of the fiduciary duties of care and loyalty, while firm Y operates in a legal system in which it owes fiduciary duties to the employees rather than to the shareholders. Both the workers and the shareholders in firm X would be better off than the workers and the shareholders in firm Y if the shareholders in firm X are willing to pay the workers a sum that is greater than the value of these fiduciary duties to the workers in order to obtain the benefits of these fiduciary duties. Consistent with the nexus-of-contracts perspective, in which the firm's bargains result from a complex equilibrium process, shareholders will enjoy the benefits of fiduciary duties to the extent that they value the benefits associated with these fiduciary duties more than other corporate constituencies.

One can illustrate this point with reference to what Professor Coffee accurately has described as "extraordinary departures" from typical patterns of corporate behavior.[12] For example, in *Union Trust Co. of Maryland v. Carter*,[13] the court approved a charter provision that deprived shareholders of voting rights for the first six years of the corporation's life and prevented the shareholders from removing the directors named in the original articles of incorporation from office.

One also can conceptualize these arguments in terms of the shareholders' ability to contract away their fiduciary duties.... Take, for example, the classic case of *Meinhard v. Salmon*.[14] In that case, the court held that Salmon breached his fiduciary duty to Meinhard by pursuing a business project (the development of a valuable parcel of real estate in midtown Manhattan) without first offering his business partner Salmon the opportunity to participate in the venture. The case is controversial because, as the dissent points out, Meinhard and Salmon were not all-purpose partners, but rather joint venture partners in a real estate development covering some of the same space. Furthermore, the subsequent venture did not begin until after the joint venture between Meinhard and Salmon had terminated. According to the dissent, Salmon's duties to Meinhard should have ended when the joint venture ended.

Writing for the majority, Justice Cardozo maintained that, at a minimum, Salmon should have disclosed the new opportunity to Meinhard so that Meinhard could have had the opportunity to make his own offer. The majority's approach seems justified on the ground that the business opportunity in dispute had been extended to Salmon in his capacity as a joint venturer. Moreover, the opportunity arose while Salmon had an ongoing fiduciary duty to Meinhard.

From the perspective of this paper, the interesting question in *Meinhard v. Salmon* is whether the case would have turned out differently if the parties had a pre-existing agreement with respect to the disclosure of new opportunities. Suppose, for example, that Meinhard and Salmon's joint venture contract specified that their business relationship was to terminate at the end of the joint venture period and that Salmon was under no obligation to extend future business opportunities of any kind to Meinhard or even to

---

12. John C. Coffee, Jr., *The Mandatory/Enabling Balance in Corporate Law: An Essay on the Judicial Role*, 89 Colum. L. Rev. 1618, 1630 (1989).
13. 139 F. 717 (W.Va. 1905).
14. 164 N.E. 545 (N.Y. 1928).

inform Meinhard of such opportunities. Under these hypothetical facts, the case would have come out differently because the agreement would have defined the contours of the duties that Salmon owed to Meinhard. In other words, the fiduciary duty of loyalty that Salmon owed to his partner Meinhard was not intractable. He could have altered it by contractual agreement.

This is a startling claim. Commentators routinely assert that, regardless of whatever one may say about the duty of care, the duty of loyalty is nonwaivable. As Mel Eisenberg pointed out, virtually all statutes that permit corporations to limit or eliminate personal liability of directors for simple duty-of-care violations contain provisions that explicitly exclude from their coverage duty-of-loyalty violations by either directors or officers.[15]

However, the corporate opportunities doctrine

> ... is the law's attempt to regulate circumstances in which a corporate officer or director may usurp new business prospects for her own account without first offering them to the firm. The doctrine—a subspecies of the fiduciary duty of loyalty—has been a mainstay in the corporations law of virtually every state for well over a century.[16]

Even law and economics scholars routinely characterize the corporate opportunities doctrine as a mandatory rule rather than a default rule. For example, Ian Ayres and Rob Gertner claim that firms can contract to increase the scope of their fiduciary duties, but not to limit the scope of such duties. It does seem, though, that parties can "craft[ ] an express definition of a 'corporate opportunity'" by agreeing in advance to permit a director or other fiduciary to pursue a particular activity.[17] Moreover, even if the corporation and the fiduciary have not agreed in advance (for example, at the time the corporation hires the fiduciary) to permit the fiduciary to pursue a particular opportunity, the fiduciary may still avail herself of that opportunity by disclosing the opportunity to the firm and obtaining the firm's permission to pursue the opportunity. If the fiduciary fails to obtain permission prior to exploiting the opportunity, however, "any authorization, approval, or ratification by the firm is voidable, and an appropriation of the project by the agent constitutes a breach of fiduciary duty." In other words, the corporate opportunities doctrine, which is a component of the fiduciary duty of loyalty, "is, fundamentally, little more than a default mechanism for allocating property rights between a corporation and those who manage it."

The same analysis holds true for rules related to another important component of the duty of loyalty: the rules related to directors' conflict-of-interest transactions. Historically, transactions between corporations and their directors were automatically voidable at the wish of the corporation. This legal rule proved incompatible with the needs of many corporations, however, because countless situations arose in which transactions between directors and the corporation were in the best interests of the corporation. For example, cash-strapped businesses sometimes turn to directors for loans. Directors would be unwilling to make such loans if the corporation could void the terms of the accompanying loan agreements after credit had been extended.

The current law solves the problem of director conflict-of-interest transactions by establishing a default rule against these contracts, but permitting such transactions to go

---

15. Melvin Aron Eisenberg, *The Structure of Corporation Law*, 89 COLUM. L. REV. 1461, 1470 n.43 (1989).

16. Eric Talley, *Turning Servile Opportunities into Gold: A Strategic Analysis of Corporate Opportunities Doctrine*, 108 YALE L.J. 729, 743 (1998).

17. . Ian Ayres & Robert Gertner, *Strategic Contractual Inefficiency and the Optimal Choice of Legal Rules*, 101 YALE L.J. 729, 743 (1992).

forward if disinterested directors (or shareholders) approve them after full disclosure of both the existence of the conflict of interest and the specifics of the transaction being contemplated. Thus, as with the corporate opportunities doctrine, the law regarding directors' conflict-of-interest transactions is enabling and permissive rather than mandatory and inflexible.

Nevertheless, do all corporate law rules really fit so easily under the nexus-of-contracts umbrella? Are there certain corporate actions, such as stealing, that are clearly outside the realm of contract? The answer to these questions lies in understanding what is meant by the term "stealing." Stealing necessarily involves wrongful conduct. However, if one obtains the permission of the owner, there can be no theft. Consequently, a corporation cannot "permit" a fiduciary to steal things.

Somewhat more formally, the analytical confusion on this issue stems from an inability to distinguish between ex ante and ex post waivers of the duty of loyalty. The law does not permit ex post waivers because such waivers would constitute a breach of contract or worse; however, the law does permit ex ante waivers of fiduciary duties.

This analysis has interesting implications for the way that we view the relationship between shareholders and non-shareholder constituencies. Over a wide range of issues, of course, the interests of shareholders do not conflict at all with other stakeholders. In those areas where conflicts do arise, bargaining results. Non-shareholder constituencies can bargain for and obtain virtually anything they want ex ante, that is to say, at the time they enter their relationship with the company. Later, however, the non-shareholders are more or less at the mercy of the shareholders because only the shareholders as residual claimants can avail themselves of net earnings not already earmarked for other groups.

In other words, and this is the point to which the Article has been building, fiduciary duties are themselves a form of residual claim. Extending fiduciary duties to shareholders simply creates a legal environment in which non-shareholder constituencies are free to contract with the company as they wish ex ante. However, after these non-shareholder constituencies have secured whatever contractual protections for themselves that they can procure (e.g., bond covenants, restrictions on dividend payments, wage concessions, or long-term employment agreements), the shareholders are entitled to the residual. Critically, in this context, the residual does not mean residual cash flows. Instead, the concept of the residual claim captures the idea of residual legal rights. Just as the standard default terms of corporate law provide that shareholders are entitled to the firm's residual cash flows after they have paid the fixed claimants, so too are shareholders entitled to the residual legal rights that remain after the non-shareholder constituencies have reached their own agreements with the corporation....

Margaret M. Blair & Lynn A. Stout, *A Team Production Theory of Corporate Law**

... Who owns a corporation? Most economists and legal scholars today seem inclined to answer: Its shareholders do. Contemporary discussions of corporate governance have come to be dominated by the view that public corporations are little more than bundles

* Originally published in 85 Virginia Law Review 247 (1999). Reprinted with permission.

of assets collectively owned by shareholders (principals) who hire directors and officers (agents) to manage those assets on their behalf. This principal-agent model, in turn, has given rise to two recurring themes in the literature: First, that the central economic problem addressed by corporation law is reducing "agency costs" by keeping directors and managers faithful to shareholders' interests; and second, that the primary goal of the public corporation is—or ought to be—maximizing shareholders' wealth.

In this Article we take issue with both the prevailing principal-agent model of the public corporation and the shareholder wealth maximization goal that underlies it.... We explore an alternative approach that we believe may go much further in explaining both the distinctive legal doctrines that apply to public corporations and the unique role these business entities have come to play in American economic life: the team production approach.

In the economic literature, team production problems are said to arise in situations where a productive activity requires the combined investment and coordinated effort of two or more individuals or groups....

I. Economic Theories of the Corporation

A. *Conventional Economic Analyses of the Firm*

1. *Principal-Agent Analysis*

Principal-agent analysis deals with bilateral relationships of a particular kind: Typically, a "principal" who wants to accomplish some project she cannot do by herself hires an "agent" to do that project on her behalf. Agency relationships of this sort can pose efficiency problems if the principal cannot monitor the agent easily or well (as when the principal cannot accurately judge the quality of the agent's work) or when there is a significant component of chance in the link between what the agent does and how well the project turns out. The problem, then, is how the principal can write a contract that motivates the agent to do his best to accomplish the principal's goals.

Although principal-agent analysis has been very useful in analyzing certain kinds of contractual relationships, it ignores several problems we think are often important to production within corporations. Principal-agent analysis generally assumes that the problem of interest is getting the agent to do what the principal wants. But the mathematical models used to study this problem typically do not address the opposite possibility— that the agent might have trouble getting the principal to perform her end of the deal. Nor do they address situations in which part of the agent's job is to figure out what needs to be done (a situation we suspect is the norm rather than the exception in most public corporations). A related point is that the principal-agent model assumes that it is clear who the principal is, and who the agent is in the particular relationship or transaction under study. Yet many of the most important relationships inside corporations may be more ambiguous, in the sense that both parties may be contributing productive inputs and neither may have authority over the other. In fact, as we argue below, this fundamental ambiguity underlies the basic structure of corporate law and provides the foundation for a more useful theory of public corporations.

2. *Property Rights Analysis*

A second interesting organizational problem arises when parties deal with each other over the course of a long-term productive relationship. Writing "complete" contracts that explicitly provide for all contingencies can often be costly or even impossible. Hence, economic and legal theorists have shifted their attention in recent years to the study of "incomplete" contracts, and particularly to how parties in a working relationship can fill in the gaps in their understandings about who does what and who gets what in the course of a long-term productive relationship. One mechanism that has been identified is assigning property rights to one of the parties to the contract that give that party a residual right of control over the assets used in the joint enterprise.

Building on this idea, some economists define the firm as a bundle of assets under common ownership (and therefore, common control). When applied to public corporations, this way of thinking about firms sets up a sharp dichotomy between the "owners" of a firm — generally presumed to be the shareholders — and all other input providers, who are "hired." In this view, the degree of control and the share of joint output granted to contributors of hired inputs is understood to be clearly delineated ex ante by explicit contracts, while the "owner" is understood to retain all residual rights of control and to receive all the residual output after contractual obligations have been met.

The property rights view of the firm provides a powerful insight and may be a reasonable description of the way many proprietorships, partnerships, and closely held firms are organized. But it is not a theory of corporations: Corporate law is clearly not needed to achieve common ownership of assets. More importantly, the property rights view seriously misstates the nature of shareholders' interest in public corporations. If "control" is the economically important feature of "ownership," then to build a theory of corporations on the premise that ownership (and, hence, control) lies with shareholders grossly mischaracterizes the legal realities of most public corporations. Viewing the firm as a bundle of assets owned by shareholders also seems odd once we recognize that one of the key assets a corporation uses in production is "intellectual capital" — that is, the knowledge and experience residing in the minds of its employees, rather than the hands of its shareholders.

3. Combining the Principal-Agent and Property Rights Approaches: A Theory of Hierarchy (But Not of Public Corporations)

In introducing the principal-agent and property rights approaches to the theory of the firm, we have tried to suggest some concerns that caution against relying upon them as foundations for a theory of public corporations. Nevertheless, these models have been used, sometimes explicitly and sometimes implicitly, to bolster a conventional view of the corporation that looks something like the model depicted in Figure 1.

… Individuals at the upper levels of the hierarchy may delegate control over some assets to individuals below, but all ultimately work for (are "agents" of) the principal at the top. Thus the principal is understood to be the owner of the firm, as well as the residual claimant who receives all profits — that is, economic rents — left over after her contractual obligations to all the agents below her have been met.

In the rest of this Article, we refer to this conventional model of the firm as the "grand-design principal-agent model." With one small modification — substituting a body of shareholders for a single owner at the top — this model has been the basis for most theoretical discussions about public corporations in recent years. And because the shareholder/owners at the top of the pyramid have been understood to be the residual claimants to all profits left over after all the corporations' contractual obligations have

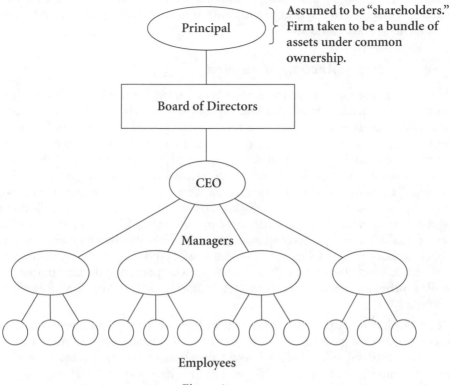

Figure 1.

been met, the model has been used to argue that directors should run the firm for the sole purpose of maximizing the shareholders' interests.

It should be noted that the grand-design principal-agent model incorporates a form of hierarchy. Economic theorists have only begun to study the many functions of hierarchy in detail, but much of what has been done generally supports the principal-agent interpretation of hierarchy's role. Thus hierarchy has been described as benefiting the principal at the top of the pyramid, for example by providing a mechanism by which information can be gathered by large numbers of people in the lower ranks of the hierarchy, aggregated and summarized and passed upward to those individuals at the higher levels who can best understand the big picture and make optimal decisions. Similarly, in the corporate context, shareholder delegation of decisionmaking authority to the board of directors has been defended as in the shareholders' best interests on the grounds that it allows for more efficient processing of information and decisionmaking....

Our break with previous work is to stress the importance of the coordination that happens not from the top down, but in the lateral interaction among team members. Hierarchical governance may still be needed in this context, but the role such governance serves is to mediate horizontal disputes among team members that may arise along the way. Thus when theorists simply substitute a body of undifferentiated shareholders for the single owner at the top of the grand-design principal-agent model, they gloss over some of the most interesting and vexing problems of organizing team production. Closer analysis of corporate law reveals that it accomplishes something much richer and more interesting than merely chopping up the role of the principal at the top of the pyramid into smaller pieces. In particular, the law of public corporations appears to actually eliminate the role of the principal, imposing in its place an internal governance structure—the mediating hierarchy—designed to respond to problems of horizontal coordination inherent in certain forms of team production.

B. *Team Production Analysis of the Firm*

One of the first serious attempts by economists to explore the problem of organizing joint production in teams can be found in a 1972 paper by Armen Alchian and Harold Demsetz.[18] In that paper, the authors defined team production as "production in which 1) several types of resources are used ... 2) the product is not a sum of separable outputs of each cooperating resource ... [and] 3) not all resources used in team production belong to one person." Consider, for example, a group of expert researchers working on developing a new drug. Each makes a different contribution: identifying the active ingredient in some compound and the mechanism by which it affects human physiology; designing the production method; developing a purification process; testing for undesirable side effects. All expect to share in the benefits of what they hope will ultimately be a profitable enterprise. Yet because the outcome of their efforts—a successful product—is nonseparable, it may be impossible to determine who is "responsible" for what portion of the final output. Who is to say which team member's contribution was more valuable, when all were essential to the venture?

Team production of this sort poses a difficult problem when it comes to designing efficient incentives. If the team members agree in advance to allocate any profits according to some fixed sharing rule, obvious free-rider problems arise: Each team member will have an incentive to shirk, since he will get the same share of the total whether or not he works hard. On the other hand, if the team members have no fixed sharing rule but simply agree to allocate rewards after the fact, when the time comes to divvy up the surplus all have incentives to indulge in wasteful rent-seeking, squandering time and effort haggling and trying to grab a larger share of the total output. The result in either case is suboptimal....

... Because shirking and rent-seeking can erode or even destroy the gains that can be had from team production, it is also in the collective interest of the team members to minimize such behavior if the terms of the relationship among the team members call for them to share in any rents. How can the team members save themselves from their own opportunistic instincts? We believe that when the potential for shirking and rent-seeking is especially pronounced, team members as a group might prefer to relinquish control over both the team's assets and output to a third party—a "mediating hierarch"—whose primary function is to exercise that control in a fashion that maximizes the joint welfare of the team as a whole....

... [T]he public corporation is not so much a "nexus of contracts" (explicit or implicit) as a "nexus of firm-specific investments," in which several different groups contribute unique and essential resources to the corporate enterprise, and who each find it difficult to protect their contribution through explicit contracts.

In this scenario, a number of individuals come together to undertake a team production project that requires all to make some form of enterprise-specific investment. Perhaps one individual brings critical technical skills to the table, while another has a talent for management, and a third provides marketing insights. They may lack financial

---

18. Armen Alchian & Harold Demsetz, *Production, Information Costs, and Economic Organization*, 62 AM. ECON. REV. 777 (1972).

capital, however, so they seek out wealthy friends or family members to put up initial funding. Thus, a team is born. Undertaking team production, however, requires each of the members to make irrevocable investments that leave them vulnerable to opportunistic exploitation by other team members. The marketing specialist, for example, must develop specialized knowledge and personal contacts (firm-specific human capital) whose value is vulnerable to actions and decisions of the team as a whole — likewise for the technical specialist. And while the cash contributions of financial investors may initially be generic and fungible, once those funds have been used to purchase specialized assets or to pay wages, they effectively become sunk in the firm.

Despite their mutual vulnerabilities, the team members expect for the most part to be able to get along with each other and figure out how to allocate tasks and divide up rewards as they go. When disputes arise, however, they want a decisionmaking procedure in place that all believe will be fair. The solution? They form a public corporation.

C. *The Public Corporation as a Mediating Hierarchy*

Let us see how forming a public corporation can be understood as creating a mediating hierarchy. When a productive team incorporates, one of the first tasks the law demands of the team is to select a board of directors to be given authority to make decisions for the corporation. This board may include several team members or their representatives, but it may also include (and in public corporations almost invariably does) several outsiders. The board enjoys ultimate decisionmaking authority to select future corporate officers and directors, to determine the use of corporate assets, and to serve as an internal "court of appeals" to resolve disputes that may arise among the team members. The net result is that, by forming a corporation, the original team members all agree to give up control rights over the output from the enterprise and over their firm-specific inputs. Providers of financial capital — shareholders and even, potentially, some creditors — are, by this agreement, just as "stuck" in the firm as are providers of specialized human capital.

The act of forming a corporation thus means that no one team member is a "principal" who enjoys a right of control over the team. To the contrary, once they have formed a corporation and selected a board, the team members have created a new and separate entity that takes on a life of its own and could, potentially, act against their interests, leading them to lose what they have invested in the enterprise. Knowing that incorporating means losing influence over the corporation's future and over the division of the rents the corporation generates, why would any of the team members do this?

The answer is that team members understand they would be far less likely to elicit the full cooperation and firm-specific investment of other members if they did not give up control rights. Thus, ex ante, they judge their chances of capturing some of the significant rents that can flow from team production to be greater if they give up control to a decisionmaking hierarchy, than if they attempted to write detailed contracts with the other participants. This analysis suggests that hierarchy can perform a third function in addition to the two economists have identified (streamlining information-gathering and decisionmaking, and controlling shirking through the cascade of sequential principal-agent contracts). This third function is encouraging firm-specific investment in team production by mediating disputes among team members about the allocation of duties and rewards.

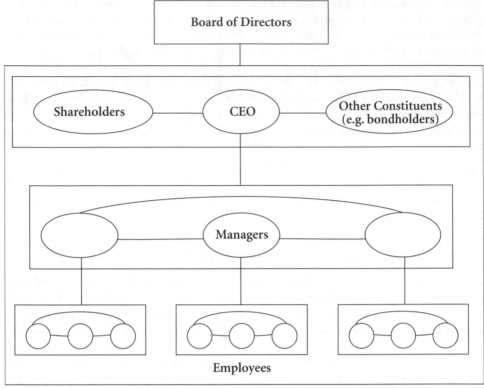

Figure 2.

Our argument suggests that it is misleading to view a public corporation as merely a bundle of assets under common ownership. Rather, a public corporation is a team of people who enter into a complex agreement to work together for their mutual gain. Participants—including shareholders, employees, and perhaps other stakeholders such as creditors or the local community ... yield control over outputs and key inputs (time, intellectual skills, or financial capital) to the hierarchy. They enter into this mutual agreement in an effort to reduce wasteful shirking and rent-seeking by relegating to the internal hierarchy the right to determine the division of duties and resources in the joint enterprise. They thus agree not to specific terms or outcomes (as in a traditional "contract"), but to participation in a process of internal goal setting and dispute resolution. Hence the mediating hierarchy of a corporation can be viewed as a substitute for explicit contracting that is especially useful in situations where team production requires several different team members to make various kinds of enterprise-specific investments in projects that are complex, ongoing, and unpredictable.

The net result is a corporation whose structure looks much more like Figure 2, than the grand-design principal-agent structure illustrated in Figure 1. Within the firm, there are several layers of hierarchy, and in each layer the relevant hierarch (the "boss") has authority to resolve disputes among members at lower levels. The peak of the pyramid is occupied not by some owner/principal, but by a board of directors whose job includes serving as the final arbiter in disputes that cannot be resolved at lower levels. At any point in time, members at lower levels who are unhappy about a boss's decision—whether the board's or some lower manager's—can choose to leave the firm. If they leave, however, they lose the value of their firm-specific investments and can no longer share in the residual rents generated by the enterprise. Similarly, if the hierarchy so decides, dissenting team members can be forced out of the coalition and cut off from sharing in future rents. Thus if they choose to stay, team members must abide by the decisions of the hierarchy about the division of duties and rewards.

When the mediating function is added to the story of what hierarchy accomplishes, it is no longer obvious that employees should be viewed as agents of the hierarchs to whom they report, as the grand-design principal-agent model suggests. Instead, it can be argued that hierarchs work for team members (including employees) who "hire" them to control shirking and rent-seeking among team members. This is true at each level in the organization, from first level managers up to the board. Thus, the primary job of the board of directors of a public corporation is not to act as agents who ruthlessly pursue shareholders' interests at the expense of employees, creditors, or other team members. Rather, the directors are trustees for the corporation itself—mediating hierarchs whose job is to balance team members' competing interests in a fashion that keeps everyone happy enough that the productive coalition stays together....

... [T]he model applies primarily to public—not private—corporations.... [D]irectors of public corporations with widely dispersed share ownership are remarkably free from the direct control of any of the groups that make up the corporate "team," including shareholders, executives, and employees. Although directors have incentives to accommodate the interests of all these groups, they are under the command of none. In contrast, in a closely held firm, stock ownership is usually concentrated in the hands of a small number of investors who not only select and exercise tight control over the board, but also are themselves involved in managing the firm as officers and directors. Thus the typical private corporation adheres more closely to the grand-design principal-agent model of the firm than to the mediating hierarchy model....

... In arguing that a mediating hierarchy can be an efficient response to problems of contracting over team production, we do not intend to suggest that it is a perfect solution. Most obviously, placing ultimate control of a business enterprise in the hands of a board of directors whose members have little or no direct stake in the firm exacerbates principal-agent problems. Nevertheless, ... if the likely economic losses to a productive team from unconstrained shirking and rent-seeking are great enough to outweigh the likely economic losses from turning over decisionmaking power to a less-than-perfectly-faithful hierarch, mediating hierarchy becomes an efficient second-best solution to problems of team production.

This sort of second-best solution, moreover, is surprisingly common. Corporate boards of directors are only one of many institutions in our society that rely upon some form of disinterested hierarch to resolve disputes between parties for whom resolution through explicit contracting is too costly. Other examples include the referee in a football game; the trustee who administers a trust for multiple, competing beneficiaries; and the judge who renders a decision in litigation between parties. This observation raises a final question about applying the mediating hierarchy model to public corporations—namely, why should we put the board of directors (instead of, say, a judge) at the top of the hierarchical corporate pyramid?

... Internal mediation has great advantages over courts and other external dispute resolution mechanisms, particularly in situations that involve repeated interactions among the contending parties and between the contending parties and the mediator. For example, internal decisions are made by people who know more about the special circumstances of any dispute, and who generally have a stake in seeing that the resolution truly settles the dispute and reduces the tensions created by the dispute. Internal decisionmaking processes and decisions can be less formal, more flexible, and better able to deal with subtleties. Whereas court decisions tend to be zero-sum, internal decisionmakers can use tradeoffs that avoid or side-step zero-sum games ("I can't give you the raise this month, but I'll go ahead and give you the larger office now, and in the next fiscal year, I can probably give you the raise."). Or they can pressure team members to work it out among themselves, under the threat that either or both could be "fired" (or reassigned or otherwise punished) if they fail to work it out....

II. A Team Production Analysis of the Law of Corporations

... Because only shareholders normally enjoy voting rights and derivative standing, it seems natural to infer that corporate law intends directors to be subject only to shareholders' control and to serve only shareholders' interests. We argue below, however, that a more careful inspection of American corporate doctrine reveals compelling reasons to question this description of the relationship. Corporate law does not treat directors as shareholders' agents but as something quite different: independent hierarchs who are charged not with serving shareholders' interests alone, but with serving the interests of the legal entity known as the "corporation." The interests of the corporation, in turn, can be understood as a joint welfare function of all the individuals who make firm-specific investments and agree to participate in the extracontractual, internal mediation process within the firm. For most public corporations, these are primarily executives, rank-and-file employees, and equity investors, but in particular cases the corporate team may also include other stakeholders such as creditors, or even the local community if the firm has strong geographic ties....

We conclude that—unlike the grand-design principal-agent model, which seems at odds with much of American corporate law—the mediating hierarchy approach provides a solid theoretical foundation for the basic structure of public corporation law. This conclusion, moreover, contains both positive and normative components. From a positivist perspective, the way corporate law actually works in practice is consistent with the notion that directors are independent hierarchs whose fiduciary obligations run to the corporate entity itself and only instrumentally to any of its participants. From a normative basis, a team production analysis suggests that this is how the law ought to work. By preserving directors' independence and imposing on them fiduciary obligations that run to the firm as a whole and not to any particular team member, corporate law reinforces and supports an essential economic role played by hierarchy in general, and by corporate boards of directors in particular.

A. Directors' Legal Role: Trustees More than Agents

In exploring the relative advantages of the mediating hierarchy model of the public corporation, we begin by examining one of the greatest weaknesses of the prevailing grand-design principal-agent approach: its assumption that directors are agents of the firm's shareholders. The notion that directors are shareholders' agents has exerted enormous influence in the theoretical literature....

[However,] corporate directors are not agents in a legal sense. The rules of agency provide that an agent owes her principal a "duty of obedience"—in other words, the principal enjoys control over, and has the power to direct the actions of, the agent.

Corporate directors depart radically from this model. As the ultimate decisionmaking body within the firm, they are not subject to direct control or supervision by anyone, including the firm's shareholders. Moreover, this fundamental principle of directorial discretion cannot be explained away as a legal response to the practical difficulties associated with shareholder voting. Even if a firm's shareholders were to pass a unanimous resolution directing the board to pursue some course of action—say, declaring a dividend, or firing a particular executive—the board has no legal obligation to comply. Shareholders can elect directors and, under some circumstances, remove them—but they cannot tell them what to do....

If directors are to act as hierarchs, it is essential for them to hold the ultimate decisionmaking authority within the firm and to be allowed full discretion to represent competing interests. If the board were instead subject to the direct command and control of one or more of the corporation's constituencies, that constituency could use its power over the board to seek rents opportunistically from other members of the productive team, thus discouraging team-specific investment. Accordingly, giving directors ultimate control over the corporation's assets serves economic efficiency by allowing coalitions that hope to benefit from team production but fear that their gains will be squandered in rent-seeking squabbling to "tie their own hands" for their mutual advantage.

B. Corporate Personality and the Rules of Derivative Procedure

... Although [directors'] duty to "the corporation" can perhaps be interpreted to mean a duty exclusively to the shareholders of the corporation, we agree with those who argue directors should be viewed as owing fiduciary duties to the corporation as a separate legal entity.... Several procedural aspects of derivative suits support this view. Most states, for example, require shareholders seeking to sue derivatively to first "demand" that the firm's board of directors take legal action on the firm's behalf; this demand requirement is excused only when the board is subject to conflicts of interest that are both obvious and substantial. Moreover, even when demand is excused, a board may be able to take control of, and terminate, a shareholder-led derivative suit if an independent investigating committee of directors who are not subject to conflicts of interest so recommends. Such procedural hurdles make it extremely difficult for shareholders to sue derivatively. They also insulate directors from shareholder challenge and control, in keeping with the mediating hierarchy model.

The law treats derivative suits filed on behalf of the corporation differently from shareholder suits claiming direct harm in other respects as well. Most importantly, if a derivative suit is successful, any damages recovered must go into the corporation's coffers. This requirement that damages be paid directly to the firm and not to the suing shareholders seems difficult to explain under the norm of shareholder primacy. Once we are willing to view the corporation as a coalition of shareholders and other stakeholders who have made firm-specific investments, however, the requirement makes sense....

C. The Substance of Directors' Fiduciary Duties

... Once we move beyond procedure to look at the substance of derivative suits—the rules that define the fiduciary duties derivative suits seek to enforce—it becomes even more clear that these suits serve "the firm" rather than its shareholders....

1. The Duty of Loyalty

… [C]ase law on the duty of loyalty appears consistent with the mediating hierarchy model we are espousing. This is because the duty of loyalty, as conventionally and narrowly defined, protects employees, creditors, and other stakeholders just as much as it protects shareholders. After all, when directors use their corporate position to steal money from the firm, every member of the coalition suffers. Allowing shareholders to sue derivatively in loyalty cases thus conforms to the mediating hierarchy model by benefiting all who make up the corporate "team."

2. The Duty of Care, the Business Judgment Rule, and the Best Interests of "The Corporation"

In addition to the duty of loyalty, corporate directors, in theory, owe their firms a duty of care. We say "in theory" because, while the idea of a duty to be careful at first appears to impose significant constraints on directors, in practice the duty of care is all but eviscerated by a legal doctrine known as the "business judgment rule." Because this doctrine seriously undermines directors' accountability to shareholders by virtually insulating directors from claims of lack of care, it seems inconsistent with the view that directors are shareholders' agents. The mediating hierarchy model we propose, however, suggests that the business judgment rule may serve an important economic function. In particular, the rule may help prevent coalition members (and especially shareholders) from using lawsuits as strategic devices to extract rents from the coalition. This is because the business judgment rule works to ensure that directors can only be found liable for breach of the duty of care in circumstances where a finding of liability serves the collective interests of all the firm's members.

To earn the protection of the business judgment rule, directors must show that a challenged decision satisfied three requirements: (1) The decision was made "on an informed basis"; (2) the directors acted "in good faith"; and (3) the directors acted "in the honest belief that the action taken was in the best interests of the company."[19] Although a requirement that directors inform themselves before taking action obviously benefits shareholders, it also seems likely to benefit employees, creditors, and other stakeholders. Similarly, while case law provides little guidance on what if anything the requirement of "good faith" adds to the existing duty of loyalty, "bad faith" seems likely to pose a threat to all who contribute to the coalition known as the firm.

Most importantly, however, the business judgment rule also requires directors to demonstrate that they honestly believed they were acting in the best interests of "the company." It is this third prong that most clearly suggests that American law views the corporation as an entity with interests of its own, and not just a proxy for shareholders' interests. This is because case law generally interprets the "best interest of the company" to include non-shareholder interests, including those of employees, creditors, and the community.…

… Thus judges have sanctioned directors' decisions to use corporate funds for charitable purposes; to reject business strategies that would increase profits at the expense of the local community; to avoid risky undertakings that would benefit shareholders at creditors' expense; and to fend off a hostile takeover bid at a premium price in order to protect the

---

19. *Aronson v. Lewis*, 473 A.2d 805, 812 (Del. 1984).

interests of employees or the community. As these examples illustrate, modern corporate law does not adhere to the norm of shareholder primacy....

Some legal commentators and some cases explain this approach as being in shareholders' interests in the "long run." This explanation makes little sense, however, under a grand-design principal-agent model that views shareholders' interests as meaning the interests of the shareholders of the particular firm whose directors are at that moment favoring other constituencies. Consider, for example, the common scenario in which a court upholds a board's discretion to reject a takeover bid at a substantial premium in order to protect the interests of the firm's employees or the community. How can rejecting a premium offer benefit the long-run interests of the present pool of shareholders if—as modern financial theory holds—today's lower market price reflects the best possible estimate of those shareholders' future returns under current management? ...

... Opportunistically exploiting the firm-specific investments of corporate stakeholders (say, violating employees' expectations of job security by moving the firm's manufacturing plants to Mexico) may well benefit, in both the short and the long run, those individuals who happen to hold shares in the corporation at the time the decision to move is made. If the firm's employees anticipated this sort of conduct ex ante, however, they might well have demanded higher wages—or been more reluctant to invest in firm-specific human capital—in earlier years.

The mediating hierarchy model thus lends intellectual content to the argument that treating directors as trustees charged with serving interests above and beyond those of shareholders in fact can be in shareholders' "long-run interests," because a shareholder decision to yield control rights over the firm to directors ex ante—that is, when the corporate coalition is first formed—can induce other participants in the team production process to make the kind of firm-specific investments necessary to reap a surplus from team production in the first place. Thus, a broad interpretation of the business judgment rule that permits directors to sacrifice shareholders' interests to those of other corporate constituencies "ties the hands" of shareholders in public corporations in a fashion that ultimately serves their interests as a class, as well as those of the other members of the corporate coalition.

3. Director Adoption of Takeover Defenses and Other "Mixed Motive" Cases

Because the duty of loyalty limits obvious self-dealing or takings of corporate opportunities, corporate law makes it difficult for directors to extract any monetary gain from their position with the firm beyond their agreed-upon compensation. However, this narrow interpretation of the duty of loyalty ignores the obvious reality that directors often can use their corporate powers to provide themselves with non-monetary benefits, such as an increase in their own authority, security of position, and quality of life....

Courts generally decline to treat these sorts of cases as loyalty issues and instead apply the liberal business judgment rule to such actions. This judicial tolerance is hard to reconcile with a shareholder primacy norm. The mediating hierarchy model, however, helps explain why corporate law declines to intervene in directors' decisions, even in these mixed motive cases. The reason is that the pursuit of directors' non-monetary interests in mixed motive situations often benefits other stakeholders in the firm, even as it harms shareholders.

Consider the example of a board's decision to reduce the volatility of a firm's earnings by acquiring an unrelated business or by using derivatives for hedging. Modern portfolio theory teaches that reducing such firm-specific or unique risk does not benefit diversified shareholders. Reducing unique risk does, however, benefit directors by decreasing the likelihood that their firm will become insolvent and they themselves might lose their positions. Yet, in addition to benefiting directors, reducing unique risk also benefits other corporate constituents—including managers, rank-and-file employees, and creditors—who have a stronger interest than the shareholders do in ensuring that the firm remains solvent.

A second example arises where a board chooses "the quiet life" by granting concessions to labor unions or creditors. While such a strategy obviously is contrary to shareholders' interests, it just as obviously benefits other members of the coalition that make up the firm. Thus, a broad interpretation of the business judgment rule that permits directors to sacrifice shareholder wealth in this fashion again may serve the interests of the corporate coalition even though it allows directors to serve their own non-monetary interests. The evident unwillingness of judges to second-guess directors' decisions even in such cases is strong evidence that corporate law protects directors' discretion to favor non-shareholder constituencies, even when directors may abuse this discretion to serve themselves.

Perhaps the most interesting example of the law's tolerance for director actions with mixed motives can be found in case law applying the business judgment rule to a board's decision to fight off a hostile takeover bid at a premium price. A board's decision to resist a hostile offer often can protect the expectations of the firm's employees, creditors, managers, or other team members who have made firm-specific investments, especially when the bidder appears poised to alter the structure of the firm by downsizing, recapitalizing, or simply replacing existing management. At the same time, because a takeover also threatens the principal benefit directors reap from being directors (their positions on the board), this situation presents the potential for conflict not only between the board and the shareholders, but between the board and other stakeholders as well.

Interestingly, Delaware courts have modified the business judgment rule in takeover situations, in recognition of this threat of directorial self-interest. In the landmark 1985 case of *Unocal Corp. v. Mesa Petroleum Co.*,[20] the Delaware Supreme Court held that directors of public corporations who wish to resist a hostile takeover bid cannot claim the protection of the business judgment rule unless they first demonstrate that the proposed takeover poses a threat to the "corporation." The *Unocal* decision also made clear, however, that in deciding whether there is a threat to the corporate entity, the directors of the corporation are invited to consider "the impact on ... creditors, customers, employees, and perhaps even the community generally." In other words, Unocal squarely rejects shareholder primacy in favor of the view that the interests of the "corporation" include the interests of non-shareholder constituencies.

Unocal's reformulation of the business judgment rule in the takeover context is itself subject to an exemption that provides intriguing—if tentative—evidence in favor of the mediating hierarchy model. Less than a year after deciding *Unocal*, the Delaware Supreme Court was again called upon to apply the business judgment rule in a takeover context in the case of *Revlon, Inc. v. MacAndrews & Forbes Holdings*.[21] In that case, the directors of Revlon Corporation adopted defensive strategies that favored a friendly bidder over a hostile bidder, citing in part a desire to protect the interests of certain creditors of the firm. The Delaware Supreme Court held that the directors had violated the business judgment rule because when "break-up of the company was inevitable ... the duty of the board ... changed from the preservation of Revlon as a corporate entity to the maximization

---

20. 493 A.2d 946 (Del. 1985).
21. 506 A.2d 173 (Del. 1986).

of the company's value at a sale for the stockholders' benefit." Thus, the court held that "the directors' role changed from defenders of the corporate bastion to auctioneers charged with getting the best price for the stockholders at a sale of the company."

On first inspection, this language appears to support shareholder primacy. Closer analysis suggests, however, that *Revlon* may in fact support the mediating hierarchy model. Although the *Revlon* opinion did not clarify what it meant to say that a company's "break-up" was "inevitable," in subsequent cases *Revlon* has been interpreted to apply "when a majority of a corporation's voting shares are [to be] acquired by a single person or entity, or by a cohesive group acting together." In other words, *Revlon* applies when a formerly publicly held corporation is about to become essentially a privately held firm. As noted earlier, in closely held firms subject to the control of a single shareholder or group of shareholders, directors enjoy relatively little independence and can no longer function effectively as mediating hierarchs. Thus the *Revlon* exception to the general rule may reflect an intuitive judicial recognition that when a firm "goes private," it abandons the mediating hierarchy approach in favor of a grand-design principal-agent structure dominated by a controlling shareholder.

D. Reexamining Shareholders' Voting Rights

Shareholders in public corporations enjoy voting rights in two areas. First, shareholders have the right to elect (and sometimes remove) the members of the board of directors. Second, shareholders also enjoy the right to vote on certain "fundamental" corporate changes. On first inspection, these rights seem to grant shareholders a much greater measure of control over how the firm is run than other members of the coalition enjoy.... In the vast majority of cases, [however,] shareholders' voting rights give them little or no control over directors, who remain free to balance the interests of, and allocate rewards among, the various groups that constitute the firm.

Let us first consider shareholders' right to elect and remove directors. In small, closely held firms, or in firms where a single stockholder or group of stockholders controls the majority of shares, voting may give a majority stockholder significant power to select the members of the board and to exercise influence over them while they are in office. In a typical publicly held firm with widely dispersed share ownership, however, legal and practical obstacles to shareholder action render voting rights almost meaningless. Most obviously, and as was first pointed out by Berle and Means, free-rider problems tend to inspire "rational apathy" among shareholders that leads them to "vote for whomever and whatever management recommends." This tendency for shareholders to follow management's lead is amplified by legal rules that grant directors authority to set the date for certain elections, nominate candidates for the board, and use corporate funds to solicit proxy votes from shareholders who do not plan to attend the shareholders' meeting (usually the overwhelming majority). The net result is that shareholders in public corporations do not in any realistic sense elect boards. Rather, boards elect themselves. Once elected, moreover, directors almost always get to serve a full term free of shareholder control. Although shareholders can sometimes try to remove directors, the removal process is difficult at best, and subject to the same proxy rules and collective action problems.

Shareholders' rights to vote on "fundamental" corporate changes also appear to be something of a fig leaf. Most states define very narrowly the categories of transactions on which shareholders are entitled to vote, including only statutory mergers, charter and bylaw amendments, and sales of substantially all assets. With the exception of shareholders' right to vote to change bylaws, these voting rights are essentially veto rights: Shareholders cannot initiate fundamental changes, but can only vote "yes" or "no" if the board proposes them. Thus, because there is usually more than one way to skin the corporate cat, directors often can restructure transactions to achieve their desired end without triggering a shareholder vote. Moreover, even when shareholders are entitled to vote, as in the case of director elections, the board still controls the proxy process, and shareholders still face collective action problems. The net result is that it is always extremely difficult, and often impossible, for shareholders to use their rights to vote on fundamental changes to oppose a transaction or policy the board favors....

E. *How Corporate Law Keeps Directors Faithful*

Our discussion thus far has focused on the many features of corporate law that can be explained by the mediating hierarchy model. These features allow directors to freely balance and make tradeoffs among the competing interests of the different constituents who, we argue, comprise the firm. Yet to say that directors are free to maximize the joint welfare function of all the firm's members is not the same thing as saying they will. If directors are despots, why should they be benevolent?

Although an extended discussion of director benevolence lies beyond the scope of this Article, at least three aspects of corporate law and culture are likely to encourage directors to serve their firm's interests, however imperfectly. First, directors have an interest in serving their corporate constituents well if (as seems plausible) they enjoy and want to keep their positions. To keep their jobs, directors must meet at least the minimum demands of all of the corporations' important constituencies. Otherwise some will leave, and the coalition will fall apart. Directors may also have reputational interests in being perceived as "good" directors if they hope to be invited to serve on additional boards.

Second, corporate law encourages directors to serve their firms' interests by severely limiting their abilities to serve their own. Our analysis of the duty of loyalty and the business judgment rule suggests that corporate law in practice places only one significant substantive limit on director action—to wit, no self-dealing. Directors can bring home their agreed upon (and publicly reported) compensation, which may be quite substantial, but beyond this compensation they cannot use their corporate positions to expropriate assets or returns that belong to the firm. Thus corporate law seems to presume that so long as directors are limited in their ability to use their positions to benefit themselves, they may instead choose to use their positions to benefit others by promoting the joint welfare of all the stakeholders who together comprise the corporation....

Finally, a third force that may work to encourage directors to serve their firms is, quite simply, corporate cultural norms of fairness and trust. Corporate law views directors as more than mere "agents." Rather, they are a unique form of fiduciary who more closely resemble trustees and whose duties are imbued with a similar moral weight. Trustees are expected to serve their beneficiaries' interests unswervingly and to settle conflicts between beneficiaries with competing interests fairly and impartially. Although this idea of faithful service appears to clash with an economic analysis premised on calculations of rational self-interest, trust is one of the most fundamental concepts in law, and it lies at the heart of a wide variety of legal relationships. These relationships include not only fiduciaries such as corporate directors, legal guardians, and trustees, but the judiciary itself. After all, the need for a benevolent and trusted mediator is implicit in all of contract theory—some sort of court system and police power are always assumed to be present in the background to enforce contracts....

Still, we believe that for a mediating hierarchy to work well, more may be needed. Hierarchs are only likely to be trusted if they have reputations for integrity, independence, and service, together with a desire to protect and enhance these reputations. Moreover, we believe that these reputational considerations must be reinforced by powerful social norms. This last notion is the one with which economists are most uncomfortable. Williamson argues, for example, that the only form of trust that is important in economic relationships is a carefully calculated estimate of the probability that the other party will not behave opportunistically.[22] We think there is more to it than this. Norms, such as trustworthiness, may come into existence because they have efficiency advantages, but the way they operate is to commit people ex ante to behavior that might not be welfare maximizing for those people ex post. In other words, to be effective, "trust" and "integrity" must prevent hierarchs (like directors) from behaving in opportunistic ways even when a careful calculation suggests that the benefits of betrayal outweigh the costs. Although much work remains to be done on this sort of "irrational" behavior, it suggests that a mediating hierarchy solution to problems of explicit contracting can be reinforced by the careful selection of trustworthy individuals who are supported by appropriate social norms. Thus, for example, [Henry] Hansmann stresses the importance of norms in controlling the behavior of directors of nonprofit organizations, and also notes that by self-selection, directors of nonprofits will tend to be people who value their reputations and share social views about what is appropriate behavior in their role as directors.[23] We believe some of the same mechanisms may operate among directors of for-profit corporations....

III. Conclusion

... When the central contracting problem investors face is the principal-agent problem, they do not need public corporations. Instead, they can organize and manage their businesses using explicit contracts and alternative organizational forms—including partnerships, limited liability companies, and privately-held corporations—that permit them to retain far more control over managers and employees. The fact that the lion's share of our nation's largest firms have opted to do business as public corporations rather than private companies or partnerships thus suggests there may be significant economic advantages to the public corporation form in spite of (or, as we suggest, because of) the requirement of ceding control to an independent board of directors. Of course, this argument assumes that the public corporation has thrived because corporation law offers unique advantages in organizing economic production. One could tell a different kind of story in which the public corporation has achieved dominance because political or historical factors (say, tax rules or the early development of a liquid stock market) have made the corporate form attractive for business despite legal rules that are less than optimal. But if the rise of the public corporation can be traced in whole or in part to efficiency advantages of corporate law, the prevalence of public corporations suggests that team production problems are far more pervasive—and the contracting problems associated with them far more endemic and costly—than is generally recognized. Hence we hope that both economists and legal scholars will give more attention in the future to these contracting problems.

A second lesson to draw from team production theory concerns the fundamentally political nature of the corporation.... [F]uture scholarship should explore in greater detail

---

22. Oliver E. Williamson, *Calculativeness, Trust, and Economic Organization*, 36 J.L. ECON. 453 (1993).

23. Henry B. Hansmann, *The Role of Nonprofit Enterprise*, 89 YALE L.J. 835, 875–76 (1980).

the internal and external political and economic pressures that affect the decisionmaking process in firms. Just as a burgeoning "public choice" literature now studies the politics of decisionmaking within legislatures and government agencies, corporate scholars need to develop a literature that approaches the study of corporate governance with attention to the use of political tools (including vote trading, coalition formation, public relations campaigns, organizing to reduce obstacles to collective action, and appeals to regulatory agencies and congressional investigative committees), and to the role of cultural norms in reducing and resolving conflict. They also need a richer literature on the ways in which economic pressures can shift the balance of power within corporations.

This brings us to our final lesson. It is widely perceived that during the late 1960s and 1970s, the performance of U.S. firms deteriorated markedly, and some have argued that boards of directors of American companies may have been both overly generous to employees and top management and insensitive to the wishes of the shareholders. Corporate America became fat and lazy, and returns from share ownership declined. Eventually (according to the conventional wisdom), these "inefficiencies" became so great that they sparked the 1980s takeover movement and a decade and a half of corporate restructurings and downsizings. This restructuring process has produced "leaner and meaner" corporations that are more attentive than ever to shareholders' desires, and returns from share ownership have correspondingly increased. At the same time, directors' new focus on shareholders' interests has adversely affected other corporate constituencies — especially rank-and-file employees — whose relative returns from participating in the corporate enterprise seem to have shrunk even as shareholders have prospered.

How should corporate scholars interpret, and lawmakers respond to, these events? The mediating hierarchy approach suggests two intriguing possibilities. First, corporate directors as mediating hierarchs enjoy considerable discretion in deciding which members of the corporate coalition receive what portion of the economic surplus resulting from team production. Although the board must meet the minimum demands of each team member to keep the coalition together, beyond that threshold any number of possible allocations among groups is possible. Thus, the returns to any particular corporate stakeholder from participating in the corporation will be determined not only by market forces, but by political forces. This analysis in turn suggests that the rise in the 1980s of institutional shareholders such as investment companies and pension funds (which control sizeable blocks of shares in many firms) has tipped the political balance of power toward shareholders by reducing obstacles to collective investor action. It further suggests that the decline of labor unions during the same period has made it more difficult for labor to protect its stake in the corporate enterprise. The net result is that shareholders as a class have acquired additional political power that allows them to capture a larger share of the rents from the corporate enterprise, and have thus grown richer, while employees as a class have lost political power, and have thus grown relatively poorer.

Yet the mediating hierarchy model also suggests a second possible interpretation of this redirection of corporate wealth from employees to shareholders. In particular, the shift can be explained as a response to changing market forces which have altered various team members' opportunity costs and thus, the minimum rewards they must receive to have an incentive to remain in the team. Technological change and an increasingly globalized economy have exerted downward pressure on U.S. workers' wages while increasing investors' opportunities to seek higher returns abroad. Recognizing this reality, corporate boards have also recognized that they must redirect some of the surplus produced by corporate team production from employees to shareholders in order to prevent the flight of capital and keep the coalition together. In other words, corporate boards' recent focus on shareholder wealth may be an appropriate and economically efficient response to changes in the underlying markets for capital and labor.

In either case, we do not think it is an accident that the idea of shareholder primacy has become increasingly popular among academics during this period. Our theory suggests that the shift in the balance of power in boardrooms toward shareholders is the result not of directors' sudden recognition that shareholders are in fact "owners" of the corporation, however, but of changing economic and political forces that have improved shareholders' relative bargaining power *vis-à-vis* other coalition members. If the driving forces are political, whether shareholders or employees receive a greater share of the rewards of the corporate enterprise may be a matter that raises primarily distributional concerns. If the shift reflects economic factors, however, it represents an efficient readjustment essential to continued team production. Thus, at a normative level our story cautions against attempts to "reform" corporate law either by contractarians who want to enhance shareholders' power over directors, or progressives who want to give other stakeholders greater control rights. Strikingly, corporate law itself has proven remarkably immune to both sorts of proposals, and continues to preserve directors' discretion to act as mediators among all relevant corporate constituents.

Thus we are not, so far, concerned about the direction that the law has taken. Nonetheless, we are somewhat concerned about the shift in rhetoric and in corporate culture that has taken place in recent years. We would not want the legal community, and especially the judiciary, to take the shareholder primacy rhetoric too seriously, lose sight of the important economic function played by boards that are free to mediate among competing interests, and begin to alter the law in ways that would compromise the independence of directors. For this reason, we believe that the emphasis placed on principal-agent problems in the corporate literature during the last two decades has been both excessive and misleading. We are convinced that future debates about corporate governance will be more fruitful if they start from a better model that more accurately captures the fundamental contracting problem corporation law attempts to resolve. The mediating hierarchy model is a first step toward that better view.

Marleen O'Connor, *Labor's Role in the American Corporate Governance Structure*[*]

... A preliminary examination of the topic of the role of employees in corporate governance reveals that Germany provides for codetermination,[24] Japan implicitly allows directors to balance the competing interests of employers with shareholders and the United States does not provide for participation for workers. The United States has a shareholder primacy model of the law, defining the interests of workers through contract and

---

[*] Originally published in 22 COMPARATIVE LABOR LAW & POLICY JOURNAL 97 (2000). Copyright Marleen O'Connor. Reprinted with permission.

24. *"Codetermination" refers to the practice of employee representation on the board of directors. Under German law, large corporations have a "supervisory board" whose role is roughly analogous to that of the American board of directors, and a "managing board" whose role is analogous to that of American executive officers. Depending on how many employees the corporation has, the law reserves one third to one half of the seats on the supervisory board for representatives of employees and unions. Austria, Luxembourg, and the Netherlands have similar requirements. See Mark J. Loewenstein,* Stakeholder Protection in Germany and Japan, *76 TUL. L. REV. 1673 (2002).—Ed.*

governmental regulation. This article explores why American workers do not have corporate governance rights. The absence of employee voice in corporate governance demonstrates a great deal about American corporate culture, as well as the American national political economy. The free market position states that employees do not play a role in corporate governance because they are protected by contractual mechanisms, such as collective bargaining. In contrast, this author has argued that corporate governance rights for workers are necessary because private contracts are inadequate; practical and legal hurdles prevent employees from negotiating against corporate opportunism.

In contrast to the absence of a role for American workers in corporate governance, American pension funds have a significant position in corporate governance matters as shareholders. Specifically, union pension funds are harnessing labor's pension power to exert much influence in the institutional shareholder movement. For the most part, union influence is limited to promoting so-called good corporate governance practices that promote shareholder value....

The employees' role in corporate governance can be analyzed at three different levels. First, at the shop floor, workers have access to much information about product production that would benefit managers. Second, at the collective bargaining level, workers do not have the right to bargaining over plant closings and relocations. Finally, at the strategic decision making level, the boardroom culture still resists efforts to include human capital perspectives. Relying on literature from human resources scholarship, this author has emphasized that these three levels interrelate. Specifically, a fundamental paradox has arisen: Downsizing has weakened the traditional ties of job security and loyalty that bind employees to firms; at the same time, decentralized decision making and cross-functional teams increase a firm's dependence upon human capital. This paradox suggests the need to reshape American corporate governance structures so as to reallocate decision making in a manner that would encourage investments in human capital....

Comparative corporate governance scholarship emphasizes that single parts of corporate governance systems cannot be transplanted because they operate within a complex system of laws and norms that develop over time. Employees' role in corporate governance, or lack thereof, needs to be analyzed within a broader framework that includes financial capital, labor unions, governmental regulation, welfare support, family structure, political systems and technological constraints. In the end, defining the proper role of employees in corporate governance raises important political questions. This article aims to establish a framework to explore these issues by reviewing proposals to include employees under the protection of corporate law. This article emphasizes that the proper role of employees in American corporate governance deserves more attention in light of the complex issues surrounding global corporate governance structures that we face in the future.

... This article concludes that although union pension funds face many barriers in promoting worker-shareholder interests, the union strategy is one of the most politically feasible and effective methods to provide workers with a voice in the new world of global corporate governance....

I. Proposals to Reform American Corporate Governance to Promote Worker Participation

A. Codetermination in the United States

Historically, unions in the United States did not support reform proposals for German-style codetermination because labor was reluctant to challenge the "system" that established managers as "thinkers" and workers as "doers." That is, under "job-conscious unionism," workers kept bargaining subjects restricted to wages and working conditions and allowed managers to maintain control over strategic decisions.

During the late 1980s, when the German economy appeared to be performing better than the U.S. economy, corporate law scholars began to reexamine the employees' role in the German system of codetermination. A few mainstream corporate scholars agreed that labor board representation might be an efficient measure to facilitate the tradeoff between worker commitment and firm adaptability in a world of rapid technological change. More frequently, however, mainstream scholars asserted that American workers are simply too heterogeneous for codetermination to operate efficiently in the United States....

... As the American economy slows down, arguments for employee participation on American boards may gain momentum.

B. Recognizing Directorial Fiduciary Duty to Displaced Workers

During the hostile takeover era of the 1980s, an important paradigm shift occurred in corporate law. Many states rushed to enact "stakeholder statutes" to allow managers to take into account interests of non-shareholder constituents, such as employees, customers, suppliers and the local community. Legislatures enacted these statutes to block hostile tender offers that would benefit shareholders, but the statutes were worded broadly to encompass any business decision.[25] It should be noted that policy makers enacted these statutes under the argument that hostile takeovers cause job loss, even though the scholarly evidence does not support this notion.

The stakeholder statutes prompted much commentary from the academic community because their logic ran parallel to the "nexus of contracts" model of the firm. This author argued that the stakeholder statutes and general fiduciary principles could be used to provide a precedential basis to give legal recognition to employees' implicit contracts with firms. The stakeholder statutes alone are inadequate to protect workers because managers will only side with employees when it is in the managers' interest to do so. Specifically, the permissive nature of the stakeholder statutes creates two problems. First, the stakeholder statutes may function only as a screen for directors because the statutes fail to reconcile the tension between corporate social responsibility and accountability to shareholders. Instead of following the shareholder wealth maximization standard, directors may hide behind vague duties to conflicting groups to serve their own interests. Second, the permissive nature of these statutes loses much in terms of shareholder accountability without gaining much in terms of protecting non-shareholder constituents. These statutes merely offer employees limited, indirect relief. For corporate law to achieve the goal of protecting employees while holding directors accountable, it must recognize that directors have enforceable fiduciary duties to employees.

Margaret Blair and Lynn Stout argue that the current legal regime, if understood properly, adequately accommodates the workers' role in the corporate structure.[26] The authors maintain that both employees and shareholders delegate authority to the board of directors to act as an impartial arbitrator to allocate resources necessary for team production. The Blair-Stout approach views the role of the board as a stewardship function to reconcile the competing interests of corporate stakeholders. They suggest that

---

25. *See, e.g., Penn. Stat. Ann. Tit. 15, §1715, reprinted in the Discussion Questions section of this chapter.* — Ed.

26. *See Blair and Stout's article in this chapter.* — Ed.

the current legal regime has the flexibility to accommodate directors in this role of impartial arbitrator. In addition, Blair and Stout suggest that this leeway allows directors to make necessary investments in human capital rather than seek shareholder value in the short-term. For these reasons, Blair and Stout conclude that there is no need to change the law.

auth's opinion

This author disagrees with the Blair-Stout analysis. Blair and Stout admit that shareholders benefit more than workers under the current regime because shareholders' political power increased in the 1980s and 1990s, whereas workers' political power has steadily declined. Blair and Stout respond by merely pointing to the need for more scholarly research to understand these changing political dynamics. This author agrees that corporate law theoretically allows for directors to protect workers' human capital investments, but reality suggests that the increase in shareholder power pushes managers to expropriate worker investments—to renege on implicit contracts—so as to increase shareholder value. This author suggests that we need to change corporate law to address this situation and not settle for theoretical possibilities.

General fiduciary principles support extending directorial fiduciary obligations to employees in recognition of the significant investments of human capital that employees make in the corporation. Although such a fiduciary duty would represent a substantial shift in the law, an overview of general fiduciary principles suggests that precedent for such a duty exists. In making this argument, it is necessary to recognize that fiduciary obligations arise as a matter of law in a wide variety of contexts because the status of the parties is sufficient to prove that a fiduciary relationship exists. Familiar examples are attorney to client, trustee to beneficiary and agent to principal. Outside these established categories, courts examine the facts to determine whether a so-called "unconventional fiduciary duty" exists. Based on their resemblance to the traditional fiduciary relationships, many courts apply fiduciary duties in such long-term commercial settings as franchises, distributorships, insurance and banking.

Unconventional fiduciary relationships provide precedential support for recognizing directorial fiduciary obligations to workers. An examination of the law reveals that courts impose such unconventional fiduciary obligations to defend the weaker party in various long-term contractual circumstances. In determining whether to use fiduciary duty to restrict the stronger party on the weaker party's behalf, courts first question whether the association involves mutual trust, loyalty and confidence and second, whether the stronger party has betrayed the weaker party's trust. Under these circumstances, courts use fiduciary law to restrict overreaching in long-term relationships when contract or market mechanisms are inadequate to deter the more powerful party from engaging in opportunistic conduct.

Fiduciary law has three advantages over contract law as a means for recognizing that employees have legitimate claims in the firm. First, implicit employment agreements are not legally recognized as implied contracts because the terms of these agreements are not sufficiently defined for conventional contract theory. Unlike contract law, fiduciary law does not stress the existence of a promise in protecting expectations. Second, fiduciary duties can be used to override express contractual provisions, such as the at-will employment term. Finally, fiduciary law contains a strong moral element not found in contract law.

Such a fiduciary duty could protect displaced workers by requiring directors to mitigate the harms of downsizing through severance payments and job retraining. Although courts have not had the opportunity to consider using fiduciary principles to protect workers, two cases demonstrate that fiduciary law could be used as a basis for recognizing employee rights in the corporation. First, in *Local 1330, United Steel Workers v. United States Steel*

Corporation,[27] the Sixth Circuit Court considered whether property law principles could be extended to protect employees' interests in their jobs. United States Steel had operated two steel plants in Youngstown, Ohio for over seventy years. When the plants became obsolete, U.S. Steel proposed to demolish them. In an effort to save its members' jobs and their community, the union tried to purchase the plants from U.S. Steel. The corporation refused to negotiate with the workers in an attempt to avoid competition. The union brought suit to force U.S. Steel to sell. The workers argued that a property right had evolved from the community's long-term reliance upon the continued operation of the plants. Although the court was sympathetic to the workers' plight, it ultimately decided that a change in property law should come from legislators. In creating new fiduciary rights, however, courts do not look to the legislature for permission. Courts have a long history of judicial activism in creating fiduciary duties in business settings, such as shareholders' fiduciary duties in close corporations and majority shareholders fiduciary duties to minority shareholders. This process of creating new fiduciary duties is necessary to allow judges to formulate standards over time through an evolutionary process not available to legislatures.

The second example where fiduciary law could be used to protect workers from the opportunistic breach of implicit employment agreements is *Ypsilanti v. General Motors Corp.*[28] In this case, the Township of Ypsilanti gave General Motors tax abatements of over $1.3 billion on investments in two plants over a fifteen-year period. In applying for these abatements, a General Motors spokesperson stated: "Upon completion of this project and favorable market demand, it will allow Willow Run to continue production and maintain profitable employment for our employees." Despite continuous market demand, General Motors announced its closing of the Willow Run plant to transfer production to another facility. The lower court used the contract doctrine of promissory estoppel to require General Motors to keep the Willow Run plant open. On appeal, the decision was reversed because the court held that the statement was not the type that workers should construe as a clear and definite contractual promise. Rather, the court construed the statement as mere puffery, that is, an expression of General Motors' hopes or expectations. In contrast, however, the court could have used fiduciary law to find a remedy for the workers because fiduciary law provides redress for acts of reliance performed in the absence of an express or implied promise. That is, fiduciary law serves to protect noncontractual expectations arising from tacit understandings such as the one that developed between Yspilanti and General Motors.

At this point, it is appropriate to ask how much protection workers would gain under fiduciary law. After all, fiduciary law does not provide much protection to shareholders because courts are reluctant to second-guess business decisions under the business judgment rule. Even if workers have standing to sue to enforce such obligations, courts are likely to continue to shy away from engaging in substantive review of business decisions. Despite these limitations, workers would benefit from recognizing a fiduciary duty in three ways. First, the most significant aspect of employment law is symbolic and pedagogic because, in many instances, the threat of formal sanctions is remote. Thus, legally recognizing the employees' role in corporate governance may promote greater labor-management cooperation. Second, the hallmark of fiduciary law is disclosure. Under this new fiduciary duty, workers would gain more rights to disclosure about corporate affairs that affect their investments in human capital. Third, recognizing fiduciary duty to workers would

---

27. 631 F.2d 1264 (6th Cir. 1980).
28. 506 N.W.2d 556 (Mich. Ct. App. 1993).

entail substantial benefits if combined with other changes in the law designed to encourage worker participation in strategic corporate decision making. The next section explores these benefits by examining a proposal for a new model of corporate governance that this author refers to as the "Neutral Referee Model."

C. *The Neutral Referee Model of Corporate Governance*

In exploring the notion of recognizing a directorial fiduciary duty to workers, this author has tried to translate Masahiko Aoki's economic model of the Japanese firm into the language of the law by developing a proposal for a Neutral Referee Model of corporate governance.[29] This Neutral Referee Model resembles the German system of codetermination by granting participation rights to workers in recognition of the employees' investments in human capital. Rather than provide direct representation on the board as under the German system, directors' fiduciary obligations would be altered so that directors would have the duty to balance the competing considerations of workers and shareholders in an equitable manner.

The Neutral Referee Model requires directors to inform employees about issues traditionally categorized as managerial prerogatives. Specifically, directors should be required to provide employees with regular and detailed information about the firm's personnel policies and the broader financial condition of the firm. Workers would also have the right to demand any additional information necessary to evaluate issues pertaining to working conditions and job security. Fiduciary disclosure obligations would reflect the need for managers and workers to develop openness and honesty with one another, rather than attitudes of skepticism and distrust that currently prevail in the workplace.

In order to obtain the efficiency benefits from enhanced communication within the firm, the neutral referee model relies on Employee Participation Committees that could evaluate this information and consult with managers about strategic policies of the firm. These strategic decisions would focus primarily upon employment issues such as compensation, hiring and training, technological innovation, work assignments, and layoffs and work reassignments. These representative bodies would permit managers to take full advantage of the knowledge and skills of the workforce by allowing discussion of problems as they unfold. In addition, through continual communication and negotiation, representatives of labor and management may come to trust and cooperate with each other to a much greater degree. Indeed, Works Councils in Germany have demonstrated the capacity to reduce substantially the conflicts that arise during industrial transition. Because fiduciary law would provide judicial recourse for employees and firms would try to avoid litigation, there is reason to believe that this consultation would be effective. That is, directors are not likely to make any important strategic decisions without first considering the possible reactions of the Employee Participation Committee.

The Neutral Referee Model not only accomplishes the same goals as the German system of codetermination, it also may offer two advantages. First, codetermination involves a potential threat that industrial conflict at the board level could seriously impede the process of directorial decision making. In contrast, the Neutral Referee Model may provide a more efficient institutional device to resolve the competing claims of employees and shareholders. The Neutral Referee Model reduces the potential for adversarial behavior because the board can make rational group decisions, rather than allowing the outcome to depend on the self-interested decisions of the two competing groups.

29. Masahiko Aoki, *The Participatory Generation of Information Rents and the Theory of the Firm*, in THE FIRM AS A NEXUS OF TREATIES 26 (Masahiko Aoki et al. eds., 1990).

Second, the Neutral Referee Model is more politically acceptable than reform proposals for codetermination. First, codetermination is not easily transferable to the United States because different norms of labor-management relations prevail. As discussed previously, the strong aversion of employers to worker participation in basic entrepreneurial decisions precluded discussion about codetermination in the past. In contrast, the neutral referee proposal draws upon existing managerial customs and conventions in the United States. Second, the neutral referee model builds upon recent legal changes in directorial fiduciary responsibilities of the takeover era. Third, given the anti-union sentiment that pervades the business community and given the growing interest in employee involvement committees, this proposal may be more favorably received than attempts to reform collective bargaining.

Although proposals to promote worker rights in corporate governance have not made much headway, workers have had greater success in using their rights as shareholders....

II. Labor's Shareholder Strategies Benefit Pensioners and Workers

A paradoxical development has occurred in the employees' role in American corporate governance. In the past, the traditional question posed by unions was: "which side are you on?"—representing a clear divide between labor and capital. As membership and bargaining power fell, however, unions began asserting their rights as shareholders to influence corporate decisionmaking outside the conventional labor law framework. For the past several years, organized labor has been one of the most active players in the shareholder revolution that seeks to pressure managers to single-mindedly focus upon creating shareholder value. Unions have devised innovative strategies to use shareholder rights to exercise unprecedented power over managers. While labor-shareholder activists have scored important victories for both shareholders and workers, the potential of "labor's capital" is just beginning to be realized. The AFL-CIO has begun to coordinate the voting practices of union pension funds; if these efforts succeed, labor unions would constitute one of the largest blocks of organized shareholders in the United States.

Corporate governance rights may eventually trump labor law in importance and, even if this does not occur, shareholder rights will constitute a new focal point for labor relations in the United States in the 21st century. Unions are using their rights as shareholders to influence corporate decision making outside the conventional labor law framework for two reasons. First, because the National Labor Relations Act does not adequately protect workers' rights against managers, unions are able to redress this by using their rights as shareholders to exert power over managers. Second, unions are using their shareholder rights to take advantage of the evolution in the balance of corporate power between workers and shareholders. The media recognizes that the clamor for higher profits often comes from pension fund managers and suggests that the latter are "cannibalistically" driving the downsizing phenomenon. Recognizing the significance of these events, AFL-CIO Secretary-Treasurer, Richard L. Trumka asserts: "There is no more important strategy for the Labor Movement than harnessing our pension funds and developing capital strategies so we can stop our money from cutting our own throats." ...

Institutional investors have become the dominant owners in corporate America. The one thousand largest companies in the United States have average institutional ownership in excess of 60%. However, only a small minority of institutions engages in shareholder activism. Unlike public employee pension funds, corporate management appoints private pension fund trustees. For this reason, private trustees do not usually challenge other corporate managers, even by engaging in mild proxy activity. The leading agents of the shareholder movement are public employee pension funds and union pension funds. The unions using this strategy most actively include the Teamsters, the Service Employees ["SEIU"], the Union of Needle Trades, Industrial & Textile Employees (UNITE) and the United Brotherhood of Carpenters and Joiners of America (Carpenters)....

For the most part, unions have not devised new measures beyond the so-called "good corporate governance practices," such as promoting more independent directors, redeeming poison pills, eliminating staggered boards and separating the CEO position from the chairperson on the board of directors. Unions push these practices because they receive widespread support from a large number of public pension funds. By targeting a company with a proposal that will receive a high vote, unions maximize their potential to gain management's attention....

When labor-shareholder activism is used as a method for creating bargaining power with management concerning employment matters, a conflict may arise between the interests of labor-shareholders and those of other shareholders. The next section explores the restraints on labor's use of shareholder activism in corporate campaigns.

A. *Constraints on Labor's Use of Its Pension Power*

Schwab and Thomas argue that legal restraints are not necessary to limit union's pension power in corporate campaigns because their use of shareholder proposals is subject to significant political constraints.[30] Most importantly, unions need the support of other institutional shareholders for their proposals to pass. For the most part, labor-shareholders have gained a great deal of credibility in the institutional shareholder community as legitimate players.... This leads Schwab and Thomas to conclude: "Our overall message is that these union-led techniques should not be viewed as ploys to enhance labor's share of the corporate pie, but rather as techniques that generally increased incentives of management to improve firm efficiency."

Viewing the matter in a different light, Reinier Kraakman asserts that even if unions gain a larger slice of the pie for themselves, "they are still supplying a public good—capable and innovative shareholder leadership to other institutional investors."[31] Kraakman concludes:

> If unions gain a private advantage from their efforts, their governance role need not be less important for that reason. Because shareholders face a collective problem when ownership is splintered, they are likely to under-invest in monitoring unless they can obtain an offsetting benefit. When unions obtain such a benefit, they simply join the back of a long line headed by controlling shareholders, leverage buyout firms, and hostile acquirers—all of which can monitor on behalf of equity interests and extract private benefits for doing so.

... For the most part, the gains of labor-shareholder activism so far have been political rather than economic. Specifically, this activism has had four important political consequences: First, labor-shareholders' innovative corporate governance reforms receive favorable media coverage that portrays organized labor as a potent force confronting

---

30. Stewart J. Schwab & Randall Thomas, *Realigning Corporate Governance: Shareholder Activism by Labor Unions*, 96 MICH. L. REV. 1018, 1030 (1998).

31. Reinier Kraakman, *The Mystery of Unions' Shareholder Activism: Commentary on Schwab and Thomas*, in EMPLOYEE REPRESENTATION IN THE EMERGING WORKPLACE, PROCEEDINGS OF NEW YORK UNIVERSITY 50TH ANNUAL CONFERENCE ON LABOR (Sam Estreicher ed., 1997).

managerial power. Second, labor-shareholder activism has important symbolic value in highlighting that pension money should not be used to hurt incumbent workers. Third, labor-shareholder activism destroys the perception created under Taylorism that workers are not competent to make strategic business decisions. Finally, labor-shareholder activism builds support for labor from a broad range of political groups because exercise of labor's shareholder rights is consistent with both shareholder supremacy and democracy in corporate governance.

These political achievements of labor-shareholder activism have led American scholars to compare American unions' use of their pension power with the role of employees in the German system of codetermination. For example, Schwab and Thomas have heralded labor-shareholder activism as a means to protect workers' firm-specific investments because unions can gain access to "behind-the-scenes" meetings with managers to discuss corporate governance as well as labor issues. Similarly, Henry Hansmann and Reinier Kraakman state: "In particular, the conventional conflict between the interests of labor and capital is beginning to break down.... Convergence of the interests of labor with those of shareholders has begun to take place on the level of ownership rather than, as earlier, via the direct participation of either workers or the state in corporate governance."[32]

... Unfortunately, labor-shareholder activism has two unintended negative consequences for workers. First, labor-shareholders may unwittingly hurt workers by defining the corporation solely in terms of the manager-shareholder relationship. Second, policymakers may use labor-shareholder activism as a means to divert attention from other methods of providing workers with a voice in corporate governance, such as codetermination.

Thus, American unions face a difficult balancing act in pushing stakeholder values through shareholder activism because such activism lends credence to the shareholder value credo, a credo that delegitimizes the stakeholder approach. The next and final part describes how unions can better promote a worker-shareholder vision of the firm by promoting the measurement and disclosure of human resource values.

III. Promoting Sustainable Shareholder Value Through Disclosure of Human Capital Values

The American system of corporate disclosure does not reveal sufficient information about firms' most important assets: their employees. Employees show up as payroll expenses rather than being a source of value for firms. In addition, under the federal securities laws, firms are required only to report the number of employees. Yet, because of the growing importance of intellectual capital to modern corporations, some of them—in the United States and abroad—are moving beyond traditional financial indicators and developing techniques to measure investments in human capital and innovative workplace practices, as well as measures of customer satisfaction, supplier relations and product quality.[33] This Intellectual Capital Project (IC Project) focuses on much of the same information that social activists in the past sought to disclose, including measures of training, turnover, health and safety, pay for performance and employee stock ownership. Thus, the IC Project has the capacity to promote stakeholder interests by measuring the contributions of stakeholders to shareholder value....

---

32. Henry Hansmann & Reinier Kraakman, *The End of History for Corporate Law*, 89 GEO. L.J. 439, 441 (2001).

33. For recent publications discussing intellectual capital, see LEIF EDVINSSON & MICHAEL MALONE, INTELLECTUAL CAPITAL (1997); THOMAS STEWART, INTELLECTUAL CAPITAL (1997)....

Under the theory that "you manage what you measure," a change in the rules concerning financial disclosure about workplace practices could lead to different corporate and societal perceptions about the contribution of human resources to firm performance. That is, the IC Project has the potential to educate business leaders and the public and hence shaping the public's collective preferences in favor of human capital investments.

Leaders of the IC Project suggest that pressure for development of new disclosure practices in the United States will likely intensify, producing dramatic change during the next ten to fifteen years. There are at least four reasons for this optimism. First, reform of disclosure practices is more politically acceptable than substantive regulation of business because the United States has strong cultural norms that favor transparency, that is, disclosure of corporate practices. Indeed, the recent global financial crisis underscores how important transparency and accountability have become to global investors; under the new world order, disclosure is preferred to substantive regulation. Second, the SEC sponsored a conference on the issue in 1996, focusing policymakers' attention on the possible need for new disclosure practices. Third, the Brookings Institution recently formed a task force to "initiate a national discussion about better ways of measuring, monitoring and reporting" human resource values. The fourth and most encouraging fact is that most of the research on disclosure is being conducted by the [leading] accounting firms, who hope to garner a larger share of the new market for human resource accounting.

Adoption of voluntary disclosure guidelines for workplace practices is a crucial step in the process of creating pressure for mandatory regulation. The environmental movement has had much success in using shareholder proposals to encourage companies to follow voluntary disclosure guidelines. Several organizations concerned with environmental issues track these disclosures to benchmark the quality and quantity of the disclosures over time. This process encourages experimentation and publicizes examples of best practices so that generally accepted practices will evolve over time. At this point, no organization systematically tracks corporate disclosures concerning human resource practices.

Labor-shareholders' use of shareholder proposals to request information about workplace practices would attract media attention and facilitate the debate over the scope and structure of disclosure and whether it should be voluntary or mandatory.

... [I]n the future, shareholders need to tailor their resolutions to request specific quantifiable measures about human resource policies, such as labor turnover and training expenses per employee. The SEC should allow shareholders to request this information, given the current environment of sophisticated institutional investors.

In the future, economic factors may converge with political forces to push institutional investors to promote new performance measures involving workplace practices. On the economic front, the distinctive feature of the new economy is human or intellectual capital, providing labor and shareholders with more common ground than they have had in the past. On the political side, organized labor is taking a lead role in educating pension fund beneficiaries about growing wage inequality, job insecurity and pension fund governance. In these ways, labor-shareholders advance the interests of workers by capitalizing on investors' interest in finding better corporate performance measures and their growing unease about the perceived legitimacy of the publicly held corporation. Using these strategies, labor-shareholder activism may become a significant countervailing force to promote stakeholder capitalism in the new world of global corporate governance....

Stephen M. Bainbridge, *Community and Statism: A Conservative Contractarian Critique of Progressive Corporate Law Scholarship*[*]

Although most corporate law scholars, including most in the law and economics camp, purport to embrace an apolitical objectivity, my disagreement with progressive corporate law scholars is explicitly political.[34] This Essay continues and refines our on-going dialogue by candidly articulating a conservative version of the law and economics account of corporate law....

According to Millon, communitarians argue that relationships within the corporation are not arm's-length market relationships, but rather are based on trust and mutual interdependence.[35] In their view, this requires corporate decision makers to be sensitive to the needs of all the corporation's constituencies; fair dealing requires that intracorporate relationships not be unilaterally abrogated to benefit shareholders....

Corporate law is concerned almost solely with the rights and interests of shareholders and, to a far lesser extent, creditors. The issue here is whether the regulatory purview of corporate law should be expanded to include the corporation's relationships with other corporate constituencies. Should directors be empowered, or even required, to consider the effect of their decisions on constituencies other than shareholders? Contractarians believe that non-shareholder constituencies are adequately protected through contract and/or general welfare law. Accordingly, corporate law should not be called upon to provide these constituencies with extra protections. Stakeholderists emphatically reject this claim....

The communitarian model's lack of predictive power is especially apparent when one begins to evaluate progressive proposals for expanding corporate law's regulatory jurisdiction to include the rights of non-shareholder constituencies. Marleen O'Connor, for one, argues in favor of a multifiduciary duty running from directors to workers[36].... It suffices to note David Millon's observation that multifiduciary duties of this sort are inherently indeterminate.[37]

I. Communitarians to the Left; Communitarians to the Right

At this point it is necessary to define the term "conservative contractarian." I intend the phrase to embrace only those corporate law scholars who accept the nexus-of-contracts model (and Economic Man) as the operational theory of the firm. But how does the conservative contractarian differ from mainstream contractarians? The answer lies in the scholar's political world view. Most contractarians, at least insofar as corporate law is concerned, are liberals in the classical sense. The link between contractarianism and classical liberalism arguably derives from the essentially atomistic perspective of the nexus-

---

[*] Originally published in 82 Cornell Law Review 856 (1997). Reprinted with permission.

34. *This article is a review of* Progressive Corporate Law *(Lawrence E. Mitchell ed., 1995), a collection of essays by legal scholars critical of the traditional shareholder-centered model of the firm.* — Ed.

35. *See* David Millon, *Communitarianism in Corporate Law: Foundations and Law Reform Strategies,* in Progressive Corporate Law, *supra.*

36. *See, e.g.,* O'Connor's *article in this chapter.* — Ed.

37. *See also Jonathan Macey's article in this chapter, citing the ABA Committee on Corporate Laws, and the conclusion of Cynthia Williams's article in Chapter 1.* — Ed.

of-contracts model. Contractarianism regards the corporation as a legal fiction created by the bargains struck between consenting individuals. The fact that the autonomous individual is the basic analytical unit of both world views makes it quite natural for those who embrace one to accept the other.

In contrast, the conservative contractarian is informed by the Burkean tradition that rejects the cult of the autonomous individual. Tory conservatism envisions a community of the spirit, bound together by chains of custom, prescription, loyalty, and honor.[38] Conservatives believe that only someone "bemused by reductions and abstractions" would doubt that "within a (largely) market economy there are going to be all sorts of non-economic groupings and activities that exercise a powerful influence on life as it is actually lived." In all aspects of life, including intracorporate relations, there always occur relationships of trust, unspoken understandings, settled expectations, and commitments that must be honored. It is precisely for this reason that I reject[ ] ... any suggestion that either the nexus-of-contracts model or Economic Man represent[s] a fully realized social construct. The conservative contractarian accepts these models as first approximations, useful for predicting the behavior of large masses of people, but nothing more. More importantly, the conservative contractarian further concedes that economic efficiency must sometimes give way to virtue.

In evaluating a legal regime, the conservative contractarian is thus concerned not only with efficiency, but also with social order and individual virtue. The conservative contractarian does not inquire only into the Pareto optimality of a given regime, but also asks of it such questions as: Does this regime empower people to lead more virtuous lives? Does this regime promote ordered liberty, tyranny, or license?

At first blush, it may seem that the conservative contractarian has much in common with ["progressive" or "communitarian" corporate law scholars] and, indeed, there is a subtle and perhaps amusing irony at work here. In at least some rhetorical respects, there is a surprising degree of similarity between progressive communitarianism and the philosophical underpinnings of modern social conservatism. For example, there is a particularly strong communitarian impulse among religious conservatives, who place great importance upon local communities and other mediating institutions as buffers against the encroaching powers of the central state and the debased elites who set the moral tone of secular society.

The communitarian themes in the progressive critique also bear a striking resemblance to the renewed social conservative interest in virtue. Virtue expressly comprises a willingness to act against personal interest, something Economic Man never does. Because Economic Man is both an autonomous individual and a purely rational calculator, the model of human behavior it provides leaves conservatives unsatisfied, precisely because it fails to account either for important social intermediating institutions or for virtue.

The communitarian movement holds an obvious attraction for social conservatives. In their world view, intermediating institutions such as churches, schools, and social clubs develop citizens holding a shared set of values: virtue, trust, responsibility, and the like. Inculcation of these values often runs afoul of the state-sanctioned cult of the autonomous individual. Conservative communitarians deplore the rise of this rights-based "culture which 'dignifies with high moral purpose what often amounts to low private interests or desires.'" It is ironic that the progressives represented in Progressive Corporate Law should embrace a set of communitarian ideals in the economic sphere that could easily lead to results in the social sphere they would presumably abhor.

38. RUSSELL KIRK, THE CONSERVATIVE MIND: FROM BURKE TO ELIOT 483–88 (7th rev. ed. 1995).

On close examination, of course, the parallels between progressive and conservative communitarianism break down. Despite some superficial rhetorical similarities between the two camps, conservatives and progressives embrace different, largely incompatible values. Where Tories worry about virtue, progressives worry about self-actualization. Where Tories worry about private property rights, progressives worry about the impact of humans on the environment. As we shall see, these differences come to a head in contrasting attitudes towards the proper role of state, which is precisely why the mainstream contractarian, not the progressive communitarian, turns out to be the natural ally of the conservative contractarian.

Here then is the essential conservative contractarian: one who seeks to reconcile conservative principle and economic theory by duplicating Russell Kirk's ability "consistently to favor free markets, private property, competition, and at the same time to champion virtue." That this path is not always easy, nor always generative of clear answers, does not reduce its import to conservative contractarianism.

A. Finding Statist Snakes in the Communitarian Grass

While the conservative contractarian does not deny the importance of trust between, say, worker and firm for the effective internal functioning of corporations, he notes that trust arises from shared values. Consider an almost wholly ignored bit of evidence from the stakeholderism debate. As we have seen, progressive communitarians focus extensively on the role of trust in the employment relationship. Yet they fail to acknowledge evidence that worker participation in corporate decisionmaking is most effective in homogeneous work forces. This evidence is consistent with the work of economic and political theorists who opine that trust is most likely to arise within homogeneous groups. If we may assume that most ["progressive" corporate law scholars] support ... the Left's diversity agenda, the progressive communitarian agenda would seem to suffer from a serious internal weakness.

Even within a homogeneous group, of course, individual interests are likely to be varied and in conflict. If nothing else, the basic economic principle of scarcity suggests a certain amount of intragroup competition for scarce resources. These conflicts are inevitably more pronounced in the absence of familial or tribal ties. If contractarians fail to give due weight to the value of trust, perhaps it is because progressives have failed to offer a plausible account of why a corporation's various constituencies should trust one another. Put another way, trust is a virtue with significant social benefits. Most people probably benefit from behaving in a trustworthy manner most of the time, which means trust also has considerable survival value. Precisely because trust is a virtue, however, the question arises: Can we assume virtuous behavior on the part of the unwashed masses of a secular society? ...

No realistic social order can assume "heroic or even consistently virtuous behavior" by its citizens. All men have sinned. Everybody puts self-interest ahead of altruism some of the time. Hence, trust is a commodity that is not easily bought. Or, as Ronald Reagan famously opined, "trust, but verify."

A realistic social order must be designed around principles that fall short of ideal virtues. Effective legal rules and reliable predictions about human behavior must be based upon the fallen state of human beings, which is precisely what economic analysis does and progressive communitarianism fails to do. Communitarianism demands a standard of behavior that most members of an unredeemed society are unable or unwilling to meet most of the time. Hence it is not surprising that failed communitarian utopias abound in world history.

The basic bone of contention between conservative and progressive scholars thus remains the old problem of the perfectibility of human nature. Conservatives blame human misery on causes which lurk naturally within the souls of men: pride, vanity, jealousy, greed, and insatiable or unruly desires. Conservatives are skeptical about the prospect of human perfectibility and suspicious of utopian projects, mostly because they must be "conducted by imperfect ... human beings, [who are] always dangerously unfit to remake the world." In contrast, progressives "believe that education, positive legislation, and alteration of environment can produce men like gods; they deny that humanity has a natural proclivity toward violence and sin."

If we conservatives are right, the progressive communitarian agenda for corporate law cannot be attained without invoking the state's monopoly on coercive force. As we shall see, many ["progressive" corporate law scholars] propose defining a set of honorable or trustworthy conduct to which corporate actors will be expected to adhere. Who would get to define the standard of conduct? What should we do about inevitable breaches of that standard? The answers to these questions reveal the essentially statist nature of the progressive agenda in *Progressive Corporate Law*. Because this is a serious charge, let us consider the evidence author by author.

According to David Millon, communitarians posit that corporations have obligations to employees and other non-shareholder constituencies that extend beyond mere contractual obligation. By taking this position, Millon's communitarians must be willing to use the state's coercive power to enforce such obligations against nonconsenting shareholders and their managerial representatives. Indeed, Millon acknowledges that communitarians "would be eager to entertain arguments for law reform aimed at addressing bargaining outcomes that are substantively unfair." In other words, they are willing to use the state's judicial arm to rework voluntary arrangements created through bargains that they find to be oppressive.

William Bratton cogently anticipates the argument that trust is a fragile commodity, which leads inexorably to the need for a "coercive backstop."[39] Or, as Bratton explains, "Doubts about the prevalence of honor in the population can be mitigated by a backstop regime of legal protection that enforces honor." In effect, Bratton proposes empowering the state to define what constitutes honorable behavior, and bringing the state's monopoly on the use of coercive force to bear on those who deviate from the state-imposed code.

Lawrence Mitchell unabashedly asserts that "at this point in our history, the dominant institution is the state," thereby relegating to insignificance the host of intermediary institutions that protect individual liberty against state encroachment.[40] This does not seem to trouble Mitchell, so long as the state uses its monopoly on coercive force to achieve the chosen progressive ends of trust and community. According to Mitchell, the state currently privileges individual autonomy over "the values of community built upon the foundation of trust." But what is the alternative? Authoritarian enforcement of community values? Apparently so, for Mitchell, acknowledging the vulnerability of trust to self-interest, proposes legal changes designed to reinforce trust. Despite his disclaimers of loyalty to liberal principles, Mitchell's position is inevitably statist. As does Bratton, Mitchell essentially proposes to define a code of conduct deemed trustworthy and to empower the state to require adherence to that standard.

Marleen O'Connor expects firms to recognize that "employee participation in workplace governance is valuable because it achieves human values by enhancing worker dignity."[41]

39. William W. Bratton, *Game Theory and the Restoration of Honor to Corporate Law's Duty of Loyalty,* in Progressive Corporate Law, *supra.*
40. Lawrence E. Mitchell, *Trust. Contract. Process.*, in Progressive Corporate Law, *supra.*
41. Marleen A. O'Connor, *Promoting Economic Justice in Plant Closings: Exploring the Fiduciary/Contract Law Distinction to Enforce Implicit Employment Agreements,* in Progressive Corporate Law, *supra.*

As such, her argument resembles "New Left visions of participatory democracy, in which, as the critical legal scholar Karl Klare has put it, 'the struggle [is] to make the workplace a realm of free self-activity and expression.'" Despite its democratic rhetoric, this view of worker empowerment contains within it the seeds of statism. Consider O'Connor's proposal to use fiduciary law's "socializing power to promote and reinforce trust and honesty in business transactions." As is the case with Bratton and Mitchell, O'Connor wants the state to define an acceptable code of corporate conduct and enforce obedience thereto.

To be fair, one cannot charge these modern progressives with precisely the same statist faults associated with the old Left. Instead of nationalization, the stakeholderists among them advocate regulation designed to protect non-shareholder constituencies and, in particular, to encourage their participation in corporate governance. But the difference is only in degree, not in kind. Instead of the state directly regulating corporate decisionmaking, as old-time leftists urged, these progressives seek to provide state-sponsored constituency groups (such as labor unions or environmentalists) the power to exercise some yet to be defined degree of control over corporate decisions....

Stakeholderism is in some respects even more invidious than traditional socialism. Instead of economic power being exercised directly by the central government, state control would be dispersed throughout the economy. This amounts to "the nationalization of people instead of companies, as individuals are subsumed by their officially designated communities."

B. Ordered Liberty and Corporate Law

… The great difficulty with the progressive variant of communitarianism is that, if taken to its extreme, it views individuals as little more than cells of a larger organism. Just as doctors kill cells to prevent cancer from spreading, communitarianism readily justifies state intrusion into the private sphere in the name of some communal good. As I explain below, this is precisely why conservatives have always balanced the communitarian elements of conservative philosophy with a strong commitment to ordered liberty. For conservative contractarians, the state's role is limited to that of a facilitator of private gain-seeking through provision of default rules. Hence, conservatives reject the progressive claim that the corporation is a creature of the state subject to regulation in the "public interest."

1. On Being Anti-Statist Without Being Anti-Community

It may be argued that I overstate the statist elements of progressive communitarian thought. After all, it may be said, law by definition sets a standard that is enforced by the state. Yet this objection simply illustrates the extent to which the nanny state has lulled us into allowing state mandates to displace private ordering.

The difference between conservative and progressive communitarians is captured by the distinction between virtue and principle ethics. Principle ethics are practiced by those who tend to propose rules as solutions to problems. In a principle-dominated ethical system, leading a moral life consists mainly of complying with society's mandated code of conduct. In contrast, virtue ethics reject codes of conduct in favor of context-based individual judgment. In a virtue-based ethical system, leading a moral life consists mainly of the habitual private exercise of truthfulness, courage, justice, mercy, and the other virtues.

Principle ethics seem especially attractive to progressive communitarians, who cannot envision a society in which trust and other virtues are solely a matter of private morality.

Recall Professor Mitchell's preference for "a society emphasizing cooperation and cohesion" over "one that breeds conflict and enmity." Why assume that these are the only conceivable states of society? Can we not imagine a society free of enmity or conflict, but which also values freedom from cohesion enforced by positive law? Can we not imagine a society of rugged individualists in which conflict is precluded by wary mutual respect? In other words, can we not imagine a society that resembles the American West (or, perhaps more accurately, John Ford's vision thereof)? Even if Mitchell's two alternatives are the only possible states of society, why must we assume that state-coerced cooperation and cohesion is preferable to the risk of conflict that comes from leaving morality to private virtues?

Principle ethics pose a double threat to ordered liberty, as they displace not only private ordering of economic relationships, but personal virtue as well. In principle-based ethical systems, individuals are not allowed to define for themselves what constitutes trustworthy or honorable behavior, but instead must comply with judges' and/or bureaucrats' definitions of honor.

Conservative contractarians claim it is possible to embrace communitarian values without having to embrace the statist baggage progressive communitarianism brings with it. American culture once partook of a dynamic interaction between individualistic and communitarian tendencies that produced a rich associational life.... The conservative pessimism about human nature thus does not lead to statism, but instead to promoting intermediating institutions that build "a citizenry regulating itself from within according to a shared public 'language of good and evil.'"

Conservatives believe that religious communities are critical to the creation of such a virtuous citizenry. Virtue is an adaptive response to the instinctive human recognition of, and need for, a transcendent moral order codified in a body of natural law. People are most likely to act virtuously when they believe in an external power, higher and more permanent than the state, who is aware of their shortcomings and will punish them in the next life even if they escape retribution in this life.

Civic virtue is also created by secular communities. As James Q. Wilson observes, "Something in us makes it all but impossible to justify our acts as mere self-interest whenever those acts are seen by others as violating a moral principle."[42] Rather, "we want our actions to be seen by others—and by ourselves—as arising out of appropriate motives." Voluntary communities strengthen this instinct in two ways. First, they provide a network of reputational and other social sanctions that shape incentives. Virtuous communities will rely upon such sanctions to encourage virtue among their members. Second, because people care more about how they are perceived by those close to them, communal life provides a cloud of witnesses about whom we care and whose good opinion we value, thus encouraging us to strive to comport ourselves in accordance with communal norms....

... [W]hile the state cannot make its citizens virtuous, it can destroy the intermediary institutions that do inculcate virtue: "Communities can be destroyed from without; but they cannot be created from without; they must be built from within."

I am not arguing for a libertarian utopia in which the state has no role in regulating corporate governance. Contractarian scholars endorse the state's role in providing necessary and appropriate default rules. As Edmund Burke once observed, moreover, there is "a limit at which forbearance ceases to be a virtue."[43] At that limit, the state properly steps in.

---

42. James Q. Wilson, *What is Moral, and How Do We Know It?*, COMMENTARY, June 1993, at 37, 39.

43. Edmund Burke, *Observations on a Late Publication, intituled "The Present State of the Nation"* (1769).

The differences in attitude about state regulation between contractarians and progressives thus are more accurately characterized as ones of degree, not of kind. Yet, they are nonetheless critical. As we have seen, progressive communitarians favor an activist role for the state in enforcing mandatory codes of honorable or trustworthy conduct. The stakeholderists among them favor a drastic expansion of corporate law's regulatory jurisdiction to encompass mandatory rules governing the relationships between the corporation and its various non-shareholder constituencies. Conservative contractarians simply argue for a far less ambitious state role.

It is difficult to imagine a state-sanctioned honor code that both rises above the lowest common moral denominator and can be maintained without an oppressively high level of state coercion. Assume arguendo the validity of the communitarian claim that law has a socializing effect, such that a legal regime designed to promote mutual interdependence and trust actually causes people to behave more virtuously. As the number of honorable and trustworthy people rises, the gains from cheating also rise. If most people are trustworthy most of the time, transactions will be premised on trust, which makes dishonorable behavior profitable precisely because it permits the dishonest to take advantage of their naively trusting business associates. Accordingly, the state must step in to provide Bratton's "coercive backstop."

This point is illustrated by Marleen O'Connor's discussion of *Charter Township of Ypsilanti v. General Motors Corp.* In that case, General Motors reneged on certain commitments made to a town in which one of its plants had been located. O'Connor approvingly cites the lower court's statement that "my conscience will not allow this injustice to happen." By doing so, this judicial agent of the state tried to impose his personal definition of trust and honor on a voluntary arrangement, invoking the state's monopoly on the use of coercive force to mandate compliance by others with his personal code of ethics. He made no serious effort to link his conscience with moral norms having demonstrably substantial support in the community, as our common law system requires, or to wrestle with the very serious policy concerns his action raises.

My opposition to this sort of lawmaking is premised on the principle of sphere sovereignty. Social institutions—including both the state and the corporation—are organized horizontally, none subordinated to the others, each having a sphere of authority governed by its own ordering principles. Expansion of any social institution beyond its proper sphere necessarily results in social disorder and opens the door to tyranny. The trouble with the state thus is not its existence, but its expansion beyond those functions prescribed by custom and convention, which were legitimized by ancient usage, into the pervasive nanny state perpetually grasping at new aspects of social life to drag into its slavering maw.

From a perspective founded on sphere sovereignty, the progressive project's basic flaw is its willingness to invoke the coercive power of the state in ways that deny the rights of mankind acting individually, or collectively through voluntary associations, to order society. Although the conservative contractarian is unwilling to sacrifice virtue at the altar of efficiency, he is equally unwilling to sacrifice ordered liberty at the altar of community. A conservative properly insists that individuals be left free to define for themselves what conduct shall be deemed trustworthy or honorable, rather than being forced to comply with, say, Professor Mitchell's code of ethics. Liberty is best preserved if the state's monopoly on the use of coercive force is invoked only rarely and, as a general rule, only to deal with serious moral questions. Otherwise, the state should confine itself to creating a public square where the virtuous can act honorably, while keeping a wary eye on the rest of society. This is precisely what the contractarian approach to corporate law promotes: a state that regulates corporate governance largely by providing default rules subject to contractual opt-outs.

2. *The Corporation v. Leviathan*

The preceding Part focused on the relationship between statism and virtue in rather general terms. Let us now turn our attention to the specific: how does state regulation of corporate governance affect the social institutions that inculcate virtue in free citizens? This question decomposes into two subsidiary issues. First, is the corporation itself an intermediary institution with virtue-inculcating functions? Second, if the corporation itself does not inculcate virtue, can the corporation help protect other voluntary communities that do fulfill that function?

We have seen that it is difficult to describe the large public corporation as a community of shared values. Such corporations in fact resemble the nanny state—a large, impersonal bureaucracy with the power to terrorize, but no ability to nurture. Yet, even so, the corporation may harbor within it sub-groups that amount to communities of shared values. Granted, a corporation's shareholders, creditors, and customers almost by definition cannot form communities. The host of familiar collective action problems that prevent shareholders from participating in corporate decisionmaking, for example, precludes them from developing any sense of community. Instead, true communities are most likely to arise among those who work for the corporation.... One's co-workers thus provide precisely the cloud of witnesses so essential to the inculcation of civic virtue.

To concede the existence of workplace communities, of course, does not necessitate that we accept the progressive argument for legal change designed to promote a utopian vision of industrial relations. To the contrary, if the corporation harbors within it communities that inculcate virtue in the firm's workers, then any state interference with the corporation's internal governance that tends to interfere with these communities' virtue-instilling functions becomes indistinguishable from, and no less tolerable than, state interference with any other virtue-inculcating institution.

Let us assume, however, that the modern public corporation has no power whatsoever to inculcate virtue in those who are employed by it. Even so, minimizing state regulation of corporate governance is essential to the preservation of a free, yet virtuous society. Viewed from a sphere sovereignty perspective, subordination of economic institutions to the state poses a grave threat to personal liberty. Society includes a host of communities with the potential to inculcate virtue and other communal values: churches, schools, fraternal organizations, and the like. Although it may be unrealistic to think of a large multinational corporation as constituting such a community, it is perfectly plausible to think of the corporation as an intermediary institution standing between the individual and Leviathan. In other words, although the development of virtuous citizens is arguably best performed by smaller institutions with roots in the local community, the corporation can still act as a vital countervailing force against the state. Resistance to expanding the realm of mandatory corporate law rules thus responds to the "notion that the prevailing moral threat in our era may not be the power of the corporations but the growing power and irresponsibility of the state."...

As a societal decisionmaking norm, the economic freedom to pursue wealth does more than just expand the economic pie. A legal system that pursues wealth maximization necessarily allows individuals freedom to pursue the accumulation of wealth. Economic liberty, in turn, is a necessary concomitant of personal liberty; the two have almost always marched hand-in-hand. Moreover, the pursuit of wealth has been a major factor in destroying arbitrary class distinctions by enhancing personal and social mobility. At the same time, the manifest failure of socialist systems to deliver reasonable standards of living has undermined their viability as an alternative to democratic capitalist societies in which wealth maximization is a paramount societal goal. Accordingly, it seems fair to argue that the economic liberty to pursue wealth is an effective means for achieving a variety of moral ends.

In turn, the modern public corporation has become a powerful engine for focusing the efforts of individuals to maintain the requisite sphere of economic liberty. Those whose livelihood depends on corporate enterprise cannot be neutral about political systems. Only democratic capitalist societies permit voluntary formation of private corporations and maintain a sphere of economic liberty within which they may function. This gives those who value such enterprises a powerful incentive to resist both statism and socialism. Because tyranny is far more likely to come from the public sector than the private, those who for selfish reasons strive to maintain both a democratic capitalist society and, of particular relevance to the present argument, a substantial sphere of economic liberty therein, serve the public interest. As Michael Novak observes, private property and freedom of contract were "indispensable if private business corporations were to come into existence."[44] In turn, the corporation gives "liberty economic substance over and against the state."

3. Public Choice Perspective

… Public choice's basic tenet is that well-defined, politically influential interest groups use their power to obtain legal rules that benefit themselves at the expense of larger, more diffuse groups. In other words, legislative decisions are not driven by distributive justice, but by interest group pressures.

I emphatically do not claim that all legislative choices are driven solely by interest group pressures…. I am merely claiming that we need to be suspicious of legislators who claim to be acting in the name of distributive justice. Ideology and morality often serve as cover for self-interest….

II. Conclusion

Progressive legal thought historically has contained two features of present import. First, progressives believe that government regulation allocates resources more fairly (and even more efficiently) than do markets. Second, progressives reject populist democracy in favor of bureaucratic direction. In the progressives' ideal world, public policy is set by government bureaucrats who are guided by academic experts in law, economics, and the social sciences….

The core issues of concern to this new generation are hardly original. Just as sunspots come in cycles, so too does the corporate social responsibility debate. In the 1930s, we had the Berle-Dodd debate. In the 1950s, Berle and others revisited the issue. In the 1970s, there was a major fracas over corporate social responsibility. Finally, today we have the non-shareholder constituency debate. The twenty-year spacing is particularly interesting, because it accounts for just about one academic generation. Each generation of new scholars seems compelled to rehash the same set of problems. To be sure, each iteration adopts a new terminology, focuses on a slightly different facet of the problem, and develops some new ideas. But, all-in-all, we have been here before. The central issue remains

---

44. MICHAEL NOVAK, TOWARD A THEOLOGY OF THE CORPORATION 45 (2d ed. 1990).

whether corporation law is a species of public or private law. As an intellectual matter, the debate is unlikely to ever be finally resolved. To the contrary, I can predict with confidence another outbreak sometime around the year 2015.

This is not to suggest that the debate is bootless. George Weigel wisely observes that both democracy and free markets are learned behaviors: "The institutions of a free polity and a free economy can indeed endure for generations—but only if the people become democrats and democratic capitalists, over and over again."[45] By prompting us to relearn the lessons of the past, the stakeholderists thus perhaps unwittingly promote a renewal of commitment to the idea of free markets.

Discussion Questions

1. According to the "contractarian" theory of corporate law, as Macey explains, corporate law consists of malleable default rules that corporate constituents can "contract around." Thus, although the law may appear to favor shareholders over other corporate constituents, in fact it does not because the law is only a "default" set of rights, which can be altered by bargaining. Workers, for example, could bargain with shareholders and management for a greater role in corporate governance (they would, of course, have to offer something in exchange—lower wages or longer hours, for instance).

The contractarian argument derives from the famous "Coase Theorem," authored by the same Professor Coase whose theory of the firm is referred to many times in this book. According to the Coase Theorem, no matter who is assigned a legal entitlement, the parties will bargain to the most efficient allocation of that entitlement—assuming the bargaining entails no significant transaction costs. That is, regardless of whether the default legal rule were to make shareholders or other constituents (say, workers) the beneficiaries of management's fiduciary duties, the constituent group that valued those rights most would end up with them—assuming that the bargaining is a costless transaction.

Under the actual default legal rule as conventionally understood, shareholders are the beneficiaries of management duties. Influenced by the Coase theorem, Macey is in effect arguing that if workers really want to be the beneficiaries of those duties more than shareholders do, they will "pay" shareholders (for example, by agreeing to lower wages) and obtain that entitlement. To the extent that shareholders retain that entitlement, we should assume that they value it more highly than workers do.

Through what actual mechanisms would such bargaining take place? What kinds of transaction costs might prevent entitlements from changing hands smoothly? *See* R.H. COASE, THE FIRM, THE MARKET, AND THE LAW 174 (1988); David Millon, *Communitarianism in Corporate Law: Foundations and Law Reform Strategies,* in PROGRESSIVE CORPORATE LAW (Lawrence E. Mitchell, ed. 1995); Russell Korobkin, *Inertia and Preference in Contract Negotiation: The Psychological Power of Default Rules and Form Terms,* 51 VAND. L. REV. 1583 (1998).

2. Butler and McChesney's version of the "contractual" theory of the firm (see Chapter 1) focuses on the principal-agent problem between shareholders and managers: they argue that "the primary role of the board of directors is to assure shareholders that agency costs

---

45. George Weigel, *Capitalism for Humans,* COMMENTARY, Oct. 1995, at 34, 37.

are under control." Macey, however, argues that the contractual theory argues against the primacy of shareholders in the firm: "one should not give any class of claimants preference over the other." How do you explain these divergent characterizations of the "contractual" model? Which one is more convincing, and why?

3. The conventional approach to corporate law assumes that shareholders are the corporation's "owners." What is the basis for this assumption? Do you agree with Blair and Stout's contention that this assumption is incorrect? Why or why not?

4. According to Dallas's "power model" (see Chapter 1), the corporation's purpose is determined by the relative power of corporate constituents. According to Blair and Stout's "team production model," the directors consider this bargaining power, but play an *independent* role in balancing constituents' claims. What principles should directors use in balancing competing claims? Should directors allocate corporate resources according to constituents' relative power, or should they consider other factors? If the latter, what factors?

As Blair and Stout note, similar issues arise in the political decision making process. How do the relevant considerations in corporate decision making resemble or differ from those in political decision making?

5. Even if Blair and Stout are correct that shareholders do not and should not occupy the top of the corporate hierarchy, why should directors occupy it (as opposed to, say, executive officers, workers, creditors, or the government)?

6. To support their argument against shareholder primacy, Blair and Stout point out that shareholders' nominal power to vote is in fact very limited. Why, then, does the law give shareholders a vote at all?

7. If voting power is indeed a meaningful check on management, why does the law give it only to shareholders, and not to other team members? In a portion of their article omitted from this volume, Blair and Stout suggest two possible answers to this question. First, shareholder voting may approximate, albeit imperfectly, the interests of all team members. Second, it may be a fair concession to give the vote exclusively to shareholders because they, unlike employees, creditors, and other team members, have no way to bargain directly with management for explicit contracts. Do you find either of these explanations compelling? Why or why not?

8. According to Blair and Stout, directors' discretion allows them to balance the interests of various corporate constituencies so as to maximize their joint output, or "team product." Are directors "referees" or members of the corporate team? If they are team members, shouldn't their interests be one factor to be weighed in making decisions that maximize the joint team product?

If they are referees, what does this suggest about the kind of people who should be directors? What gives them incentive to remain neutral and maximize the team product instead of their own wealth and power? How are we to verify whether directors are indeed using their power properly? We will return to this issue in Chapter 9.

9. As O'Connor points out, many states have "stakeholder statutes" designed to make the interests of non-shareholder constituents relevant to corporate governance decisions. For example, a Pennsylvania statute enacted in 1990 reads as follows:

(a) **General Rule.** — In discharging the duties of their respective positions, the board of directors, committees of the board and individual directors of a business corporation may, in considering the best interests of the corporation, consider to the extent they deem appropriate:

(1) The effects of any action upon any or all groups affected by such action, including shareholders, employees, suppliers, customers and creditors of the corporation, and upon communities in which offices or other establishments of the corporation are located.

(2) The short-term and long-term interests of the corporation, including benefits that may accrue to the corporation from its long-term plans and the possibility that these interests may be best served by the continued independence of the corporation.

(3) The resources, intent and conduct (past, stated and potential) of any person seeking to acquire control of the corporation.

(4) All other pertinent factors.

(b) **Consideration of interests and factors.**—The board of directors, committees of the board and individual directors shall not be required, in considering the best interests of the corporation or the effects of any action, to regard any corporate interest or the interests of any particular group affected by such action as a dominant or controlling interest or factor....

PENN. STAT. ANN. Tit. 15, § 1715 (2009).

Why does O'Connor think such statutes are inadequate to protect non-shareholder constituents? How do directors' duties and employee rights under O'Connor's "Neutral Referee Model" differ from their duties under these statutes? How does the Neutral Referee Model differ from the team production model of Blair and Stout?

10. O'Connor favors enforcing workers' rights under fiduciary duty law rather than contract or related doctrines (such as the promissory estoppel doctrine invoked by the trial court in *Ypsilanti*). She argues that fiduciary law has certain advantages over contract law for this purpose. Does fiduciary law have any *disadvantages* relative to contract law?

O'Connor also calls for the creation of fiduciary duties through judicial activism rather than through legislative enactment. What are the relative advantages and disadvantages of each method of law reform in this context and in corporate law generally?

11. American corporate governance tends to focus on improving management by aligning managers' interests with those of shareholders—for example, by compensating directors and officers with company stock. By contrast, Germany requires boards to include a labor representative precisely so that the board will consider *non*-shareholder interests. What are the pros and cons of these approaches? Should boards think like shareholders? Should labor (or creditors, or customers, or environmentalists) be represented on the board?

12. Assuming that the default rules of corporate law favor shareholders over other corporate constituents, as O'Connor argues, what is the normative justification for shifting the balance toward workers? What is the normative justification for keeping the status quo?

13. Consider and evaluate the following three statements about activism by labor unions' pension funds:

a. Shareholder activism by union-controlled pension funds is a threat to other shareholders. Unions will seek to raise wages and avoid layoffs for the benefit of unionized workers, even though lower wages and job cuts often increase shareholder wealth.

b. Shareholder activism by union-controlled pension funds is a threat to workers. Pension fund managers will feel pressure to maximize the size of the pension fund. Thus they will use their power to push corporations on traditional corporate governance issues intended to increase share price instead of demanding fair wages and job preservation.

c. Union-controlled pension funds have the same basic interests as other shareholders: good corporate governance and greater long-term firm value.

14. A central issue in the law of corporate governance is the extent to which corporate managers can be trusted with their immense economic power. Several of the authors in this book argue that directors should be allowed to decide the best course for the corporation after considering the interests of non-shareholder corporate constituents as well as those of shareholders.

Bainbridge warns, however, that directors are fallible individuals who may not deserve to be trusted with such broad discretion. How should this insight be incorporated into the design of corporate law? Should corporate law be based our aspirations of individual virtue or on our knowledge of individual fallibility? More concretely, what does this choice say about whether corporate law should give directors more discretion or give shareholders and other corporate constituents more actionable legal rights? *See* Lawrence E. Mitchell, *Trust. Process. Contract.*, in Progressive Corporate Law (Mitchell, ed. 1995).

15. Bainbridge calls his approach to corporate law "explicitly political." Is it possible to provide a politically or morally neutral body of corporate law? If not, should corporate law articulate its political and moral assumptions? Where does corporate law (or law generally) find its moral basis in a society that is culturally heterogeneous and observes a separation of church and state?

16. Is the law's power limited to coercing good behavior from corporate players, as Bainbridge suggests, or can it also play a part in moral suasion and education? See the articles by Rock, Coffee, Cox and Langevoort later in this book. Should the state be involved in defining and teaching virtue at all, or should that be left to the individual and to non-governmental community bodies? Is it possible for the law to *avoid* expressing normative concepts of virtue? In this respect, is "virtue" in the corporate context different from virtue in other contexts, such as violence, theft, drug use, or sexual behavior?

17. Although non-shareholder constituents have little explicit role in corporate law, their concerns are addressed by other bodies of law, such as labor/employment law, civil rights law, pension law, and environmental law. Would non-shareholder constituents be better advised to seek protection under these other bodies of law or to seek a more prominent place within corporate law? Why?

18. There are at least four possible kinds of legal approaches to corporate social responsibility:

a. limiting the duties of directors and officers to maximizing shareholder wealth;

b. giving directors *incentives* to choose socially responsible policies (e.g., tax benefits for charitable contributions);

c. giving directors an enforceable *duty* to be socially responsible (e.g., environmental standards); or

d. giving directors *discretion* to be socially responsible (e.g., the Pennsylvania statute above).

Discuss the advantages and disadvantages of each approach. Which approach or combination of approaches is most desirable? Why?

In the wake of the financial meltdown of 2008, some critics argued that troubled financial institutions had acted selfishly by endangering the world financial system in aggressive pursuit of profits, and again by taking advantage of subsequent government bailout programs. Which of the four approaches to social responsibility seems most appropriate in this context?

19. In light of their oft-cited duty to maximize shareholder wealth, how do directors get away with considering the interests of other corporate constituents? If directors are going to consider the interest of other constituents, should the law spell out directors' duties to those constituents? Why or why not? If law does not determine how directors balance these constituents' interests, what does? And what prevents directors from simply serving their own interests?

Chapter 3

State Corporate Law

Corporations are chartered under state law, and state law governs their "internal affairs." Although every state has a corporations code, every state relies heavily on its judiciary to apply that code, and some of the fundamental principles applied by courts, such as fiduciary duty and the business judgment rule, have little or no explicit statutory basis. What are the consequences of the decentralized and largely judge-made nature of corporate law?

The chapter begins with two articles explaining (and praising) Delaware's corporate governance law. Chancellor Leo Strine of the Delaware Court of Chancery emphasizes that Delaware law is enabling rather than mandatory. That is, it does not prescribe a one-size-fits-all governance regime, but allows managers and shareholders of each corporation to craft appropriate governance terms by contract. As Edward Rock points out, judicial sanctions on corporate management are extremely rare and thus unlikely to serve as a significant deterrent. Rock argues that Delaware court decisions are nonetheless significant for their "expressive" role in generating narratives that transmit normative standards to the business community.

The remaining two articles in this chapter discuss the concept of "regulatory competition" in state law. Corporate law commentators have long debated the effect of state-level chartering. If states are viewed as competing to attract incorporations, the question arises why the tiny state of Delaware has been the most successful: has Delaware won a "race to the bottom" (that is, provided a body of law that favors management) or a "race to the top" (provided law that favors shareholders)?[1] Roberta Romano is a strong advocate of the latter position, and argues here that extending interstate regulatory competition to securities law will result in an improvement over the existing federal "monopoly" over securities regulation. In contrast, Ehud Kamar is critical of the regulatory competition thesis and of Delaware's dominance. He argues that the "market" for charters does not yield optimal legal regimes: Delaware's commanding market position has allowed it to engage in anticompetitive practices to protect its market share. Kamar sees the flexible, open-textured nature of Delaware case law as such a practice, in contrast to Rock's positive view of Delaware's judicial narratives.

---

1. See William L. Cary, *Federalism and Corporate Law: Reflections Upon Delaware*, 88 Yale L.J. 663 (1974) (taking the former position); Ralph K. Winter, Jr., *State Law, Shareholder Protection, and the Theory of the Corporation*, 6 J. Leg. Stud. 251 (1977) (taking the latter position).

Leo E. Strine, Jr., *The Delaware Way: How We Do Corporate Law and Some of the New Challenges We (and Europe) Face*[*]

I. Introduction

....

... I intend to take some of the mystery out of Delaware's role in the governance of American public corporations. To accomplish that, I will describe for you the central principles that animate our corporate law. I will then explain a bit about how our corporate law is made. In particular, I will focus on an underappreciated fact about Delaware's small [size] — indeed, some have called "pygmy-sized." Our petite territory is not coincidental to the supple and balanced nature of our corporate law; rather, our size is a useful force in maintaining our corporation law's contractarian nature. Indeed, it is arguable that the United States' system of federalism, which permits corporations to govern their internal affairs through the laws of a state of their choosing, has enabled the evolution of a "national["] corporate law — i.e., that of Delaware — that better facilitates wealth creation than would the type of corporation law that Congress would likely produce.

....

II. The Delaware Model of Corporation Law

I start with the narrow and mundane: a basic description of Delaware's corporation law. Delaware's corporation law is not what, in a European context, might be called a broad-based company law. Aspects of company law like competition law, labor law, trade, and requirements for the filing of regular disclosures to public investors, are not part of Delaware's corporation law. Instead, those matters are primarily governed at the national level by regulatory regimes originating in congressional enactments and administered through agencies of our federal government, like the Federal Trade Commission and the Securities and Exchange Commission (SEC).

Delaware corporation law governs only the internal affairs of the corporation. In that sense, our law is a specialized form of contract law that governs the relationship between corporate managers — the directors and officers — of corporations, and the stockholders. Consistent with a contractarian vision, our statute is, by design, a broad enabling one that permits and facilitates company-specific procedures. In other words, our statute is much different than one might find in a civil law nation, which would more likely have a prescriptive corporation law chock full of mandatory terms specifying exactly how corporations must conduct their business.

By contrast, the Delaware approach to corporate law keeps statutory mandates to a minimum. And even some of the mandatory terms are subject to being overridden through charter and bylaw provisions. In particular, our law gives corporate planners tremendous power to use the charter — the equivalent of the corporate constitution — to vary otherwise mandatory terms. The charter, which is formally known as the certificate of incorporation, can only be amended upon recommendation by the board of directors and with stockholder approval. Because the charter reflects a contract that is agreed upon by both the managers

---

    * Originally published in 30 DELAWARE JOURNAL OF CORPORATE LAW 673 (2005). Reprinted with permission. The author is a Vice Chancellor (judge) of the Delaware Court of Chancery.

and the stockholders, our statute permits that more specific manifestation of contractual assent to override most of the statutory default terms.

The Delaware statute is flexible in another way. It provides transactional planners with multiple routes to accomplish identical ends. Under the doctrine of independent legal significance, a board of directors is permitted to effect a transaction through whatever means it chooses in good faith. Thus, if one method would require a stockholder vote, and another would not, the board may choose the less complicated and more certain transactional method.

In emphasizing the enabling nature of the Delaware statute, it is important to make two related points. First, and too often ignored, is that efficiency and flexibility are values that do not just serve the interests of corporate managers, they are also vital to stockholders. It is useful for stockholders to have the freedom to craft charter provisions that address their company-specific needs. But there is an even more important reason why stockholders are benefitted by a broad, enabling statute.

The central idea of Delaware's approach to corporate law is the social utility of an active, engaged central management. That idea is expressed by our statute, which states the fundamental principle that the "business and affairs of the corporation are managed by or under the direction of a board of directors." It is managerial ingenuity that creates stockholder wealth through the invention and exploitation of new products, the development and more efficient provision of services, and sound financial management. Delaware corporate law recognizes that reality by investing central management with wide discretion to make business decisions and a wide choice of means to effect those decisions. Those investments facilitate creativity and risk-taking.

The so-called business judgment rule, which requires that the judiciary not second-guess business decisions made in good faith and with due care, even if they turn out badly, is also designed to protect the economic value served by centralized management. The rule does so by insulating managers from fear that pursuit of an attractive, but risky, business venture will leave them liable to the stockholders if the venture fails.

But Delaware's broad grant of power to management leads to a second point, which also deserves emphasis. Delaware corporate lawmakers recognize that managers can abuse their clout, and have therefore deployed means to prevent and remedy disloyalty. The statutory means are several, and include the requirement that stockholders meet annually to elect directors. Although the analogy can be pushed too far, elections in the corporate republic have the same purpose as in real polities: they are designed to promote before-the-fact responsiveness and guarantee after-the-fact accountability to the electorate.

In the Delaware corporate republic, stockholders also get other ballot box opportunities that promote managerial fidelity. Our statute identifies certain transactions that may not be implemented by the directors without stockholder approval. These include sales of substantially all the assets of the corporation, mergers, and charter amendments. The requirement of stockholder approval permits stockholders to decide for themselves whether an important initiative of central management deserves support. The obvious goal is to provide, by the requirement of a stockholder vote, a before-the-fact incentive for management only to present transactions that management believes to be in the best interests of the corporation.

The other major check on managerial abuse is where Delaware's Court of Chancery and its Supreme Court comes in. Delaware's broad investiture of legal—i.e., statutory and contractual—authority in corporate management is policed by courts of equity, who review claims by stockholders that corporate fiduciaries have breached their fiduciary duties of loyalty and care. The intensity of that review varies in a sensible way correlated with the probability that the managers' business decisions might have been impermissibly influenced by self-interest, rather than a proper concern for the corporation's interests.

For example, when a corporate board decides to approve next year's natural gas supply contract, and none of the directors has an ownership interest in any of the competitors bidding to be the supplier, there is virtually no chance that a stockholder would be able to prove a claim that the directors breached their fiduciary duties by striking a bad deal. Because there was no conflict of interest, the business judgment of the board is sacrosanct, unless, at the extreme, no person of rational mind could think the deal fair to the corporation.

But, assume a different scenario, when a board is responding to an unsolicited takeover bid. Assume further that the board is comprised of a majority of independent directors. Unlike the situation in the United Kingdom,[2] the directors of a Delaware corporation may thwart even an all-shares, all-cash bid if they believe that the offer is not in the best interests of the corporation and its stockholders. But when the directors decide to take a defensive stance, our law scrutinizes their actions closely.

Under our law, the concern that the directors might be influenced by their desire to keep their positions, and to keep the company independent, justifies a tightened form of equitable review. Therefore, the court may overturn the defensive actions of the board if those actions are not reasonably proportionate to any threat the bid poses to proper corporate interests. In our jurisprudential lexicon, a "reasonableness" standard legitimates far more searching judicial scrutiny than exists under the business judgment rule. Yet, even here, our law does something that is consistent with the business judgment rule. In assessing the reasonableness of a board's defensive reactions to a takeover, we give more credit to a board that is comprised of a majority of independent directors.

Why? Because we intuit that the independent directors, although not immune from a desire to protect their positions, will be more likely than inside directors to impartially decide whether a bid is in the stockholders' best interest. The inside managers, in the ordinary course, have more at stake, both financially and reputationally. Therefore, our law encourages board processes that give a strong hand to the independent directors in responding to takeover bids and, even more generally, in handling M&A transactions, such as mergers of equals.

In other words, we do not wish to maximize judicial rulings finding board actions unreasonable; we wish to provide an incentive for boards to use good processes that can be trusted to reduce the role of self-interest and promote a focus on what is in the best interests of the stockholders. Notably, the heightened scrutiny the directors face in this context does not work in isolation; the voting rights I earlier described often come into play in M & A deals, requiring directors to face not only heightened judicial scrutiny, but also the need to convince the stockholders to ratify their actions. This combined pressure has led, in general, to boards who are far more willing to consider unsolicited bids and to abandon friendly mergers, if demonstrably preferable alternatives come along. As a result, most M & A battles are decided in boardrooms, and not by judicial injunctions.

Delaware reserves the most intrusive form of scrutiny for actual conflict of interest transactions. These transactions occur when a fiduciary—a director, a manager, or a controlling stockholder—is on the other side of the deal from the corporation. When a conflict transaction is effected, the burden is on the proponents to demonstrate that

---

2. [*The management of a U.K. firm is prohibited from taking "frustrating action" against a takeover bid unless shareholders approve. See City Code on Takeovers and Mergers, Rule 21 (8th ed. 2006).* — Ed.]

the deal is entirely fair to the corporation. In the absence of such proof, the fiduciary interested in the transaction—i.e., the one on the other side of the deal—must disgorge any profits or pay whatever damages are necessary to make the corporation whole. The interested fiduciary must do that regardless of whether or not she acted with the intention to take unfair advantage of the corporation; in other words, even if she acted in utmost good faith.

Even here, however, Delaware tries to respect the business judgment of disinterested directors and stockholders. How? By invoking the protection of the business judgment rule if an interested transaction is approved by a majority of the independent directors or by a majority of the disinterested stockholders, after full disclosure. The idea, of course, is that the investment of ultimate power over the transaction in impartial directors or stockholders suffices to police the conflict. By this instrumental means, Delaware law can protect the resulting business decision without any loss of integrity, because the decision was made or ratified by persons whose interests were aligned with those of the corporation and its stockholders.

Consistent with the nuance that infuses our common law, Delaware is more suspicious when the fiduciary who is interested is a controlling stockholder. When that is so, there is an obvious fear that even putatively independent directors may owe or feel a more-than-wholesome allegiance to the interests of the controller, rather than to the corporation and its public stockholders. For that reason, when a controlling stockholder is on the other side of the deal from the corporation, our law has required that the transaction be reviewed for substantive fairness even if the transaction was negotiated by independent directors or approved by the minority stockholders. To encourage the use of these protections, however, when these protections are deployed, the burden of proving that the transaction is fair falls not on the controlling stockholder or the corporation, but on the stockholders who sue, who must show that the transaction is unfair.

As this surface level overview shows, Delaware's scrutiny of managerial conduct gets tighter the more we have rational reason to suspect that a conflict of interest exists. Similarly, because Delaware gives great deference to decisions made by the stockholders' elected representatives, our law is extremely vigilant about policing abuse of the director election process. The heightened scrutiny given to defensive actions is applied even more intensively when the court suspects that incumbents are taking actions that have the effect of preventing a fair election.

III. How Delaware Makes Corporate Law and Why We Are Well Positioned to Construct a Fair and Efficient Corporation Law

That brisk tour of our law leads to the next logical topic, which is how Delaware breathes life into its corporate law. As we shall later see, by historical happenstance, our English heritage plays an important continuing role in that ongoing process.

Delaware's statutory law is made, of course, by our elected legislature, subject to veto by our Governor. Because of the special importance of our corporation law, amendments to the corporate code must pass with a super-majority vote. In practice, our legislature and governor defer in the making of statutory law to the corporate law council of the Delaware State Bar Association. That council consists of corporate lawyers of all kinds, not just the transactional lawyers who represent corporate managers, but also plaintiffs' lawyers who represent stockholder interests. The council is comprised entirely of Delawareans, but it regularly seeks out and receives national input from the only two constituencies involved in shaping Delaware's corporation law—corporate managers and stockholders.

I say they are the only two constituencies because that is what I mean. And that is where our small size comes in as, in my view, an important part of the story. Delaware is a state of fewer than one million residents. We have important industries headquartered here, such as chemicals (you might have heard of that little company called DuPont), pharmaceuticals (Astra Zeneca's U.S. headquarters, e.g.), banking (like MBNA), and agriculture (think chickens, corn, and soybeans). But the corporate law industry is as important, or more important, than any of those industries. For a state of our size, the corporate franchise taxes and legal jobs that our corporate law advantage brings in are a substantial reason why Delaware is among the most prosperous of the fifty states.

For other states, the integrity of their corporation law is of far less moment than the fate of a particular corporation facing a takeover bid or a major claim for damages. From sea to shining sea, we have witnessed examples of this phenomenon. For example, when Wachovia bank faced a takeover battle within the last five years, the North Carolina legislature passed a bill changing the state's corporation law precisely in order to help its home-based Wachovia avoid accepting a hostile bid from SunTrust. The legislatures of Massachusetts and Ohio have acted similarly, intervening to make changes in their corporate codes to address specific corporate feuds that they believed threatened the independence of corporations headquartered in their states. For these state legislators, the jobs and collateral community benefits that would be lost if a home-state headquartered firm was taken over far outweighed any concern about having a responsible corporation law that facilitates long-term wealth creation. The political calculus for them was not difficult. Their states receive a trivial portion of their revenue from corporate franchise taxes or their equivalent. Indeed, even if Delaware's advantage was wholly dissipated and all of our corporation business was distributed over the fifty states, the other states would barely notice.

But for us, a small state, it is vital that we remain the leader in corporation law. That leadership produces thousands of Delaware jobs and nearly a quarter of our state's budget revenues.

For that reason, our state will not tilt its corporation law to favor a corporation that happens to have its headquarters here. We cannot afford to do so. Even if the DuPont Company faced a hostile bid, we could not change the rules of the game to favor DuPont. The cost to our integrity and our ability to preserve our advantage in the corporation law field would be too high.

Because of that reality, corporation law in Delaware is influenced by only the two constituencies whose views are most important in determining where entities incorporate: managers and stockholders. Over time the relative power of these constituencies has changed, and it is now fair to say that both groups have a lot of clout, and that Delaware corporate lawmakers seriously consider each group's perspective on all key issues. Given the increasing flow of capital from individual investors into institutional investors, this rough equality of voice is likely to be preserved, and may at some point tilt heavily towards stockholder interests.

For now, the key takeaway point is that Delaware's financial self-interest in legal excellence leads to a productive dynamic for the creation and maintenance of an efficient and fair corporation law. That law is essentially a specialized body of contract law that governs the relations between the managers and stockholders of firms incorporated in Delaware. That is not to say that Delaware itself does not have laws protecting the environment, ensuring the fair treatment of workers, and guarding consumers against fraud. We do have such laws, but they only govern actual business operations that are conducted within our borders.

The corporation law itself does not address these issues. It only governs the internal affairs of the corporation. Within that domain, our law emphasizes that the goal of the corporation is to advance the interests of the stockholders. But we do not require boards to measure their success against the moment-to-moment impulses of the stock market. Rather, our law gives central management a strong hand to chart a course for the corporation that it believes will, in the end, produce the greatest increase in stockholder wealth. A good faith business judgment that does not maximize current payoffs to stockholders—such as a decision to grant pay increases to the workers, increase the corporation's involvement in charitable giving, or to sacrifice current dividend payments in order to make capital investments—will be respected if it is rationally related to a plan to enhance the corporation's long-term profitability.

Furthermore, our statutory corporation lawmaking process is not only careful, it is continuous. We do not look at the corporation law every five or ten or fifteen years as Congress might do with our national securities laws. Our corporation council meets regularly and the General Assembly makes modest adjustments at its instance annually to make sure our law remains as efficient as possible.

IV. The Role of Delaware's English Heritage

Because our statute is an enabling statute, the enforcement of the managers' fiduciary duties is arguably the most important check Delaware imposes on managerial abuse. When a stockholder believes a fiduciary breach has occurred, he can bring suit in the Delaware Court of Chancery, the court on which I am privileged to serve.

....

... Because our state is small, we could devote a Chancellor, and now four Vice Chancellors as well, substantially to the expert resolution of corporation law cases and other exclusively civil matters. Because corporation law became materially important to our state, the chancery and supreme court judges who handle corporate cases take them very seriously and are motivated to produce a law that fairly balances the interests of managers and stockholders. Each generation of corporate law judges truly feels invested with a sacred trust, and behaves accordingly.

And because most corporate cases involve corporations that are chartered, but not headquartered, in Delaware, our courts are not subject to hometown bias. To put a point on that, in most takeover battles filed in our court, one Delaware corporation headquartered somewhere else is seeking to take over another Delaware corporation headquartered elsewhere, not atypically because that second Delaware corporation has signed a friendly merger agreement with yet a third Delaware corporation also headquartered outside of Delaware.

The use of a specialized court that issues written rulings has other advantages. By its very nature, equitable review is situationally-specific and proceeds in the common law fashion. The case at hand is decided and the law is thereby evolved incrementally. Although that can lead to what some scholars like to call indeterminacy—i.e., some residual uncertainty—it also allows space for the judiciary to pull back in future cases if a prior decision turns out, in the wake of experience, to have been unwise. And the overall body of case law coherently fills in a map that guides transactional and corporate governance advisors in charting a course for their clients that is relatively risk free.

Although the Delaware system is not perfect, the value it generates for the United States is considerable and would be difficult for the federal government to replicate. Unlike Congress, our legislature attends to the corporation law every year and does so thoughtfully. Unlike what would be the case in Congress, our corporation law is solely focused on the relations between stockholders and managers, and is not heavily influenced by other constituencies. And unlike the federal judiciary, consisting of over one thousand judges, ten Delaware chancellors and supreme court justices devote a considerable amount of time to fashioning sensible, fair corporate law decisions in a timely way. Also unlike the federal judiciary, the Delaware judiciary is, by the state's Constitution, evenly balanced between the major political parties, resulting in a centrist group of jurists committed to the sound and faithful application of the law.

Through this means, the United States realizes the benefits of a virtual national company law, but more efficiently. Even for firms not chartered in Delaware, the teachings of Delaware courts are likely to be more important than their own state's law, as a practical matter. Delaware law is, in essence, American corporation law for most purposes. The balanced approach it embraces facilitates managerial innovation and creativity, while preventing managerial self-dealing and entrenchment.

....

V. Will the Federal Government Stay in its Lane?

....

After the first wave of corporate scandals involving, among others, Enron, the stock exchanges and Congress began to consider whether reforms at their level were advisable. For their part, the exchanges began considering extensive new listing standards that had the practical effect of mandating numerous board committees and specific duties that had to be staffed and carried out by independent directors. The exchanges had hoped that these new standards might head off the need for Congress to adopt onerous new mandates of its own, once the initial heat from the Enron debacle cooled. But after the exchanges were too far along to abandon their initiatives, the WorldCom mess floated to the surface of public and, therefore, congressional consciousness.

Soon, the sour scent of hypocrisy wafted from some important congressional chambers. Federal legislators who had played a leadership role in stymieing efforts at increasing the integrity of public accounting standards during the late Clinton years began to support rapid congressional action. Several of these legislators were no doubt hoping that their current drive for new federal regulation would cover for their prior efforts to hamper the SEC's initiatives to prevent improper overstatements of corporate earnings.

For others, the moment was one they had long been anticipating. These members of Congress genuinely desired a stronger federal role in corporate governance, and sensed an opening to advance their ideas.

What resulted was what might be fairly called an odd tasting "jumbalaya" of ideas, which came to be known as Sarbanes-Oxley. That strange stew coupled sensible ideas — like the idea of a strengthened independent body to enforce genuinely meaningful accounting standards — with narrow provisions of dubious value — such as an outright ban on the making of loans to managers by public corporations. When combined with the new stock exchange rules, Sarbanes-Oxley had the effect of requiring corporate boards—and particularly independent directors—to spend a huge portion of their time fulfilling regulatory mandates. Characteristic of the bachelor's fridge of ingredients that make up the jumble, many of these mandates were unrelated to the core problems that gave rise to a legitimately perceived need for reform.

Those core problems primarily involved financial fraud, and the incentive systems that led gatekeepers like independent directors, public accountants, and corporate lawyers to fail to stop it, and, on occasion, sadly, even to actively facilitate accounting chicanery. Instead of a focused initiative addressing the financial integrity of publicly listed firms—which in fairness parts of Sarbanes-Oxley do speak to in useful ways that deserve credit—Congress and the exchanges generated an unwieldy set of mandates that have the perverse effect of impinging on the time that independent directors have to spend on monitoring their corporation's legal compliance.

For today, the issue to consider is what it might mean for the U.S. system if this sort of creeping intrusion continues. For all their costs, the new exchange rules and Sarbanes-Oxley are survivable, and, indeed, may be modestly beneficial, so long as the responsible regulators are flexible about giving boards leeway to implement the new mandates in a cost-effective manner.

What will be more troubling is if the federal government continues to veer out of its traditional lane in the American corporate governance system. Whether Congress likes it or not—and in its heart of hearts Congress does secretly like it—Delaware has a well-thought out perspective on corporation law. We do not tie down all boards with a prescriptive set of procedural mandates. We do not create a thousand boxes to check. Instead, we give managers broad flexibility to chart the course that they believe is best for their corporations, using the stockholder franchise and the potency of fiduciary duty review to ensure managerial fidelity.

I freely admit that Delaware's system of corporate law relies heavily on the federal government for its overall integrity. We need the federal government to vigorously enforce national laws mandating accurate and sound accounting of corporate health, and the routine disclosure of material information to stockholders. When the federal government plays that role well, and when Delaware enforces fiduciary duties expertly, investors are well served.

What investors do not need, however, is for the federal government to undercut the valuable space for innovation and flexibility that Delaware's approach to corporation law creates. Delaware's approach recognizes that what works for one corporation might not be optimal for another. This approach recognizes that boards might perform more effectively if they contain a mix of not only independent directors, but also of directors who might have industry-specific knowledge that would actually be useful in crafting a business strategy.

Already, the new federal reforms are making it difficult for boards to include a blend of inside and outside expertise, as the multiple tasks required of independent directors generates a need for more of them. Meanwhile, the labeling by the exchanges of any director having company affiliations as "non-independent" has led potential "outside, inside directors" to rethink whether continued board service makes sense for them personally. The emerging model is a board comprised of one insider—the CEO, who knows everything about the corporation and has a keen interest in its future—and ten independent directors selected precisely because they have no affiliation with, or any historical or current interest in, the corporation's business or its fate. That is an odd group to help develop a business strategy, and seems likely to function largely as a monitor, with strategy being left to be decided by the CEO and her subordinates outside of the board's presence.

The present rules are not so deeply planted as to prevent some rethinking of this new model, thus enabling the creation of boards that combine strong independent majorities with several inside directors who have the acumen and experience to help fashion an innovating and successful strategy, too. The risk I highlight is that even more so-called "federal reforms" could emerge with costs that far outweigh their protective benefits.

The goal of corporations, after all, is to create societal wealth. That means creating new products and services, and delivering them in efficient ways. Corporate governance is a means, not an end.

Going forward, Congress needs to be mindful of these considerations and avoid stifling the wealth-creating potential of corporations through costly mandates that not only do little to protect investors, but also distract boards from their fundamental duties to develop and oversee the implementation of an effective corporate strategy, to select excellent managers, and to monitor the corporation's compliance with its legal and ethical responsibilities.

....

VI. Beyond Stockholders and Managers — The Challenge of Globalization: Can the Blessings of a Humane Capitalist System Be Preserved While Spreading Prosperity to the Developing World?

As I close, I want to widen the lens even further. In Delaware, those who know me recognize that corporation law is not my primary public passion. Rather, what primarily animates my commitment to public service, now as a Vice Chancellor and even more directly in my prior role as Counsel and Policy Director to Delaware Governor Thomas R. Carper, is the continued worthiness of the liberal vision of a just society. That vision, as I understand it, recognizes the need for a large sphere of life that is immunized from government intrusion. Importantly, for present purposes, that sphere includes the realm of commerce, which should largely be free to be conducted through the voluntary operation of markets.

The liberal vision is not an irrationally rosy one, that pretends that the unfettered pursuit of private advantage inevitably leads to optimal outcomes. Instead, that practical, realistic vision recognizes that there is no such thing as a free market in the state of nature, and that the unrestrained operation of markets does not maximize either societal wealth or happiness. Without appropriate regulation by the citizenry's duly elected representatives, the least ethical of businessmen will trash the environment, exploit workers, and steal from investors — thereby creating inexorable pressures for others to follow suit in order to survive. Just as the existence of government without a larger realm of private ordering leads to tyranny and oppression, so does private ordering without restraint lead to poverty, sharp class inequalities, and poor stewardship of our natural resources.

Much of what is most admirable about Europe, Canada, Japan, and the United States — what we might call the advanced, liberal democracies — rests in the balance we have struck between the need to allow market forces to operate with due freedom so as to generate innovation and wealth, with a commitment to protecting other, even more important, human values. We all went through a phase of economic development when smokestacks and open pipes fouled the air and water, when workers were grossly underpaid and overworked, when we exploited children for labor, and when there was no protection for those, who by misfortune or market cycles, found themselves unable to provide a dignified living for themselves. Despite our cultural diversity, all of our societies eventually came to the consensus view that those conditions had to be ameliorated through appropriate government action....

If these measures fall short of the ideal, they have, over time, helped produce societies that, by any human measure, are remarkably decent. The many, and not the few, enjoy comfortable lives. There is a great deal of personal freedom and liberty.

But these achievements are now under threat. Many of those protections were adopted with the expectation that our domestically chartered corporations would largely compete with each other. Or, at most, that our home chartered corporations would compete with corporations in other nations operating under similar, humanitarian restraints....

....

How, you might ask, does this relate to corporation law? Well, let me return to first principles. Our nations did not charter corporations to benefit solely investors. We chartered corporations for the interests of our societies as a whole.

The corporations our nations now charter increasingly face competition that plays by rules of the game that we, as a result of our enlightenment, no longer tolerate domestically — e.g., rules that tolerate manufacturers who pay substandard wages and immunize them from the need to protect the environment or their workers' safety. In the face of this pressure, corporations chartered in our lands are increasingly choosing to move jobs from places that require protections of these kinds to places that do not. More and more, our corporations lack any sense of commitment to their nations of origin.

In this respect, American corporations are probably on the leading edge of being emotionally and ethically untethered from their home nation.

America's sharper focus on the best interests of stockholders helps explain this. If the way to become more profitable is to shift production from an environmentally sound plant paying relatively low wages in the United States to an unsafe plant, paying extremely low wages in China, American corporate boards will increasingly support that decision on the grounds that it is in the stockholders' best interest. If their companies want to sell to Wal-Mart, they might have no choice other than to do so.

In twenty years, when these companies have little domestic production left, the obvious question will arise as to why they need a U.S. CEO, U.S. lawyers, U.S. investment bankers, or even a U.S. charter. Already, many of the leading brand names in the United States are owned by non-U.S. firms. That is no doubt true in Europe, as well. As more and more corporations lose their special ties to particular nations and communities — through shifts in their regions of production and multiple mergers — the practicability of the advanced liberal democracies to demand that the corporations they have chartered adhere to evolved standards of corporate responsibility may wither.

The big picture economic returns in the United States over the last few decades already show cause for alarm. Returns to capital and CEOs have grown enormously, a reality reflected in the growing percentage of American wealth held by the wealthiest one percent of our nation's populace. Meanwhile, median family income has grown in a trifling way, and has probably fallen on a per worker basis, when the huge increase in two wage-earner households is considered. Overall, economic inequality is growing.

... Can the liberal democracies combine together to create a rational economic structure that protects our hard-fought achievements, while facilitating the increasing inclusion of other nations in our markets? I have no doubt that none of our nations will be better off operating behind closed economic walls — I am no protectionist — but I also have little doubt that it is not in our best interests to sacrifice our humanitarian principles in the pursuit of cheap consumer goods.

....

What current sacrifices are we prepared to make to secure the prosperity of all of our children? Are the liberal democracies (particularly, the United States) prepared to reduce our use of the world's resources by operating more efficiently, in exchange for the enforcement of real labor and environmental standards that enable our workers to remain competitive, while being paid good wages? Are we willing to relent on our protectionist ways in areas like agriculture, in order to facilitate the adoption of more enlightened standards by our trading partners? Should there be escalating tiers of trading blocks, access to the markets of which requires a progressively more rigorous adherence to enlightened labor and environmental standards? Are there other, non-protectionist means by which the advanced liberal democracies can exert concerted leverage to spread the bedrock labor and environmental standards we all have independently determined are a necessary component of a humane capitalist economy to the nations that want access to our markets?

These are the real fundamental issues on which the vibrancy of the liberal vision's future rests.

....

Edward B. Rock, *Saints and Sinners: How Does Delaware Corporate Law Work?*[*]

... How is it that most managers do a good job most of the time? How is it that most managers most of the time are worthy of the trust of investors? The traditional corporate law answers to these core questions fall into three types. First, there are the legal constraints: The courts, through the enforcement of specific legal prohibitions (like laws outlawing theft, embezzlement, insider trading, and the like), and through the enforcement of more vague legal constraints (the duty of care and the duty of loyalty), sometimes catch errant managers. Second, institutional structures such as the board of directors, outside directors, shareholder voting, proxy contests, and derivative suits may keep managers in line. Third, pressure from the various markets that impinge on the corporation and managers (the product markets, the managerial labor market, capital markets, and the market for corporate control) may keep managers in line.

But on examination, none of these checks, with the exception of competitive product markets, when they exist, seems to provide a very robust check on managers. Each seems to help a little some of the time, and only occasionally seems to help a lot. At the end of a term in which I teach the basic Corporations course or a seminar on Corporate Governance, after weeks of exploring the weaknesses of each of the checks on managers, I find myself most impressed by the apparent impotence of the constraints.

But, more importantly, the standard answers tell us little of the mechanism by which these checks constrain managers. Implicitly, the various answers seem to assume a crudely behaviorist model of managerial behavior, a "stick-and-carrot" approach. The implicit

* Originally published in 44 UCLA LAW REVIEW 1009 (1997). Copyright The Regents of the University of California 1997. Reprinted with permission.

assumption seems to be that the sanction imposed, discounted by the likelihood of detection and punishment, outweighs the benefit to the agent of sloth or theft. To take but one familiar example, in the standard 1980s story, if managers mismanage, the stock price will drop and a takeover entrepreneur will buy up the shares to gain control, replacing bad managers with good managers. The threat of such a takeover, the story asserts, will lead all managers to manage better.

In the corporate context, however, the assumption of "direct deterrence" is particularly implausible: There are hundreds of corporations, the directors and officers of which have comprehensive liability insurance; damage liability is extremely rare; and, after the enactment by Delaware of section 102(b)(7) of the General Corporation Law, which allows Delaware corporations to opt out of director liability for breach of the duty of care, damage liability has become even rarer. If the principal sanction is not directly financial but reputational, then one must explain how this sanction works, an account entirely absent from the standard account.

And yet, the system seems to work. The triplet of restraints—legal, institutional, and market—seems to constrain managers generally to act for shareholders, despite their manifest looseness (if not impotence). How is it that they do so? What is the mechanism that connects these constraints with managerial behavior? In this Article, I do not claim that the traditional constraints do not "work," that is, do not generally constrain managers to act for shareholders. Rather, I assume that they do work, and I try to figure out how. The theory outlined in the following pages is incomplete, perhaps at times implausible, and certainly only partially verified. But it is a theory of how corporate law works, and, in evaluating it, it is worth keeping in mind the old Chicago School maxim: It takes a theory to beat a theory. In part, my aim here is to highlight the absence of any developed theory to explain how corporate law works.

This leads me back to my original question: How is it that managers at least try to do a good job most of the time? This is, of course, part of a more general question: How is it that most people most of the time try to do a pretty good job, even though the likelihood of sanctions is objectively slight? How is it that most tenured law professors (at least at Penn) try to teach well, even though we all know that we will not be fired if we do not?

The beginning of a thicker answer is that all of us internalize rules and standards of conduct with which we generally try to comply. We do this not only because we may fear some sanction, formal or informal, but also because doing so is important to our sense of self-worth, because we believe that doing a good job is the right thing to do. How are these rules and standards, which are the rails along which so much of our lives run, generated and maintained? For most employees of the firm, the set of formal and informal systems of socialization, detection, and sanction are sufficient. Thus, for the typical middle manager, the example of other managers, the gossip around the coffee machine, and the possibility of discharge by a more senior manager can provide an adequate set of instructions and sanctions.

The problem faced by such a "norm-based" account of managerial behavior is that senior managers and directors are, by design, the chief criticizers and the chief sanctioners. As such, they are less constrained by gossip around the coffee machine. What replaces gossip and other sanctions for this critically important group? How are the rules and standards that govern the behavior of senior managers and directors generated and maintained? A claim of this Article is that the Delaware courts provide a supplemental source of gossip, criticism, and sanction for this set of actors who are beyond the reach of the firm's normal systems of social control.

The subjects of the study of U.S. corporate governance—the senior managers and directors of large, publicly held corporations, and the lawyers who advise them—form a surprisingly small and close-knit community. The directors of large, publicly held corporations number roughly four to five thousand. A small group of lawyers, centered in New York and Wilmington, with others in Chicago and Los Angeles, specialize in Delaware corporate law. The community has its own court, the Delaware Chancery Court, with review by the Delaware Supreme Court. It has its own newspapers: the *Wall Street Journal* and, for the lawyers, the *New York Law Journal*. People know each other and, as we will see below, apparently care about their reputation in the community. The story I tell in this Article is very much the story of how a small community imposes formal and informal, legal and nonlegal, sanctions on its members.

From this perspective, three questions immediately present themselves: First, how is the content of corporate law rules and standards determined? Second, how are they generated? And third, how are they communicated to officers and directors? In this Article, I ignore the first question, which goes to the substance of corporate law, and has been the subject of much scholarship. Instead, I focus on the second and third questions, which go to the mechanisms of corporate law and have been almost entirely ignored.

There is a persistent tendency to acknowledge that Delaware corporate law largely involves standards, but then to try to reduce it to a set of rules. Take, for example, the following description: "Under Delaware law, when a potential acquirer makes a serious bid for a target, the target's Board of Directors is required to act as would 'auctioneers charged with getting the best price for the stock-holders at a sale of the company.'" This description views Delaware law as largely substantive: When a potential acquirer makes a serious bid for control, the target board must act as a neutral auctioneer, regardless of what sort of process it might follow in coming to the conclusion that it should not act as an auctioneer. Likewise, on this view, the Delaware cases established a rule for the conduct of target managers: If a potential acquirer makes a serious bid for control, then target management must act as a neutral auctioneer.

I mean to contrast this view—a view which naturally emerges from teaching Corporations and trying to help students synthesize cases into useful principles or algorithms—with a fundamentally different view that provides a much better description of Delaware fiduciary duty law. In the 1960s, when Delaware was revising its corporation law, Samuel Arsht, a leading figure of the Delaware corporate bar, is said to have proposed that the law be simplified to the following principle: Directors of Delaware corporations can do anything they want, as long as it is not illegal, and as long as they act in good faith. This principle—which is, in my view, a completely accurate description of Delaware fiduciary duty law—conceptualizes Delaware fiduciary duty law in process terms (boards can do whatever they want as long as they follow the right process) and as setting standards as opposed to rules (boards must act in good faith). Most importantly, the formulation is largely empty until the concept of good faith is defined. As I describe more fully below, in what is a central claim of this Article, the Delaware courts fill out the concept of "good faith" through fact-intensive, normatively saturated descriptions of manager, director, and lawyer conduct, and of process—descriptions that are not reducible to rules of the sort described above. Indeed, most such rules, like the one above, turn out to be manifestly incorrect descriptions of Delaware law.

To put my point differently, in this Article I seek to take the standard-like quality of Delaware fiduciary duty law seriously. At the core of my analysis is a claim that standards work very differently than rules, that standards are typically generated and articulated through a distinctively narrative process, leading to a set of stories that is typically not reducible to a rule.

My claim here—which is a descriptive claim—is that the Delaware courts generate in the first instance the legal standards of conduct (which influence the development of the social norms of directors, officers, and lawyers) largely through what can best be thought of as "corporate law sermons." These richly detailed and judgmental factual recitations, combined with explicitly judgmental conclusions, sometimes impose legal sanctions but surprisingly often do not. Taken as a whole, the Delaware opinions can be understood as providing a set of parables—instructive tales—of good managers and bad managers, of good lawyers and bad lawyers, that, in combination, fill out the normative job description of these critical players. My intuition is that we come much closer to understanding the role of courts in corporate law if we think of judges more as preachers than as policemen.

My claim is not that Delaware law is unpredictable and indefinite. In fact, as we will see below, despite the fact-specific, narrative quality of Delaware opinions, over time they yield reasonably determinate guidelines. My claim is, rather, that the process that leads to reasonably precise standards proceeds through the elaboration of the concepts of independence, good faith, and due care through richly detailed narratives of good and bad behavior, of positive and negative examples, that are not reducible to rules or algorithms.

The second part of my claim is a causal claim that I can only begin to defend here: That these standards of conduct are communicated to managers by corporate counsel, and that the judgments of the courts play an important role in the evolution of (nonlegal) norms of conduct. As I will try to show below, these claims, if true, have fundamental implications for how we think about corporate law.

To sketch out this picture of corporate law, I examine the emergence during the 1980s of new corporate law standards—or, equivalently, the elaboration of the same old standards in a new factual context—to govern management buyouts of large, publicly held corporations (MBOs). I focus on the situation in which managers who do not hold a controlling equity interest rely on outside financing ultimately secured by the assets of the corporation to buy the corporation from the public shareholders. This situation must be distinguished, on the one hand, from management buyouts of divisions (when the selling company can fully protect the interests of its shareholders), and from parent-subsidiary freeze-out mergers, when the parent company already has control. Although each of these other situations is important, neither poses the same dramatic conflict between managers' self interest (which is to buy the company for the lowest possible price) and their duty to shareholders (which is to sell for the highest possible price) in the context of widely dispersed public shareholders. As such, MBOs pose particularly hard questions of duty for the officers and directors that cannot be answered by reference to general social norms.

As many of the cases discussed here demonstrate, the "kindergarten" norms, like loyalty and cooperation, provide limited guidance when directors are faced with a conflict between loyalty to and cooperation with senior managers, with whom they have worked for years, and loyalty to the much more abstract "shareholders." This conflict is muddied further by the notion that directors owe their duties of loyalty and care to the "corporation," where "corporation" is left undefined, but, in practice at least, is often thought not to be identical with the shareholders. As we see below in many of the management buyout cases, when some "outsider" comes along and "threatens" one's friends, the managers for whom one has the greatest respect, the directors' "right" response, at least on the unreflective application of general social norms, may appear to be the support of management. It is in situations such as these—when general social norms provide insufficient guidance or may be in conflict with the goals or fundamental principles of corporate governance—that the generation and promulgation of role-specific standards for managers and directors become so critical. On this view, the Delaware decisions can be viewed as part of the definition and description of the "roles" that managers and directors are expected to fill.

Because MBOs of significant publicly held companies suddenly assumed prominence in the 1980s, they provide a case study in which we can watch Delaware corporate law in action: The development and articulation of standards of conduct and the communication of those standards to officers, directors, and lawyers. The evolution of the standards of conduct relating to MBOs is a sufficiently narrow example so that I can focus on the mechanics of their generation—on the language of the opinions—in sufficient detail to make the claim plausible. Finally, MBOs provide a useful context to consider the ebb and flow of corporate law: How quickly cases appear, how many cases there are relative to the number of transactions, and how much it costs (at least in terms of plaintiffs' attorneys' fees) to develop new norms....

These opinions illustrate a striking feature of the Delaware fiduciary duty cases, specifically, the multivalent character of the outcomes. In these cases ... the courts avail themselves of one of three options: Denying the request for an injunction and blessing the behavior; denying the motion for an injunction and criticizing defendants' behavior; or granting the injunction. The intermediate position plays three roles. First, it provides guidance applicable to future cases, that is, what kind of behavior the courts are likely to find to be a breach of fiduciary duty. Second, in these intermediate cases, although the court denies plaintiffs' motion for a preliminary injunction, it also typically denies defendants' motion to dismiss, leaving defendants with some substantial damages exposure. Finally, and perhaps most importantly—and certainly least noticed—it tells directors, who we may suppose are generally trying to do a good job, what they should do....

I. When Managers Try to Buy the Company: A Case Study in the Emergence of Corporate Norms

A. The Defining Trilogy: Macmillan, Fort Howard, and RJR Nabisco

... [This section discusses] the critical trilogy of 1988 and 1989: *Macmillan, Fort Howard*, and, finally, the biggest deal of all time, *RJR Nabisco*. These cases ... give us detailed and dramatic accounts with a vivid set of heroes and villains....

1. The Battle for Macmillan[3]

In the wake of takeover bids in the publishing industry, the management of Macmillan, Inc., a prominent publishing company, became concerned that the firm might become a target. Management's response to this concern led to two chancery court opinions and one supreme court opinion providing vivid and sharply critical descriptions of managerial corruption, of director passivity, and of investment banker manipulation. Together the opinions provide Exhibit A for how not to behave in an MBO.

Macmillan's two "inside" directors, Edward Evans ("Evans"), the chairman and CEO, and William F. Reilly ("Reilly"), the president and chief operating officer, turned out to be the principal villains in what even the courts thought of as a "drama."

[Evans and Reilly convinced the board to grant them shares and consider a restructuring of the corporation that would have given them control of the corporation without investing

---

3. Mills Acquisition Co. v. Macmillan, Inc., 559 A.2d 1261 (Del. 1989).

any new capital of their own. They also advised the board to reject a hostile takeover bid and told the board the bidder (the "Bass Group") was a "greenmailer."]

... [M]anagement decided to form a special committee of the board to evaluate its restructuring proposal. The court details the steps that Evans and Reilly took to corrupt the process from its inception, by extensively interviewing and eventually selecting the special committees' investment banker without ever disclosing these contacts to the committee eventually appointed. [The special committee recommended undertaking the proposed restructuring and rejecting the Bass group's hostile bid.]

... Rejecting defendants' claim that the Bass Group represented a threat to Macmillan because of their supposed reputation as "greenmailers" as unsupported by the record, the court condemned both the special committee and management [and enjoined the proposed restructuring.] ...

Three months later, ... we see Evans and Reilly continuing to undermine the integrity of the process.... On the very day that the restructuring plan was enjoined, Macmillan's management began looking for a (management-) friendly bidder. After Kohlberg, Kravis and Roberts ("KKR") contacted Macmillan, the two firms had extensive discussions "concerning a possible leveraged buyout of all of Macmillan's stockholders, in which Macmillan senior management would participate." At around the same time, Robert Maxwell, through Maxwell Communications Corp. ("MCC"), also indicated an interest in acquiring Macmillan. In its opinion, the court details the extent to which management aided KKR while discouraging Maxwell....

[Evans and Reilly favored KKR by giving it confidential corporate information not provided to MCC. They did not inform the other directors of what they had done.] In the final round of bidding, after a further conversation with each bidder in which Bruce Wasserstein, the investment banker for the management group, who inexplicably also ran the auction, again gave KKR more information than MCC, KKR came out on top....

... [T]he Delaware Supreme Court touched on each of the highlights: The central goal of making sure that Evans and Reilly ended up in control without investing new capital; the domination of the allegedly "independent" board by the financially interested members of management; the "directors' evident passivity in the face of their fiduciary duties"; the "rather grim and uncomplimentary [way in which management portrayed the Bass Group to the Board]" ... including the inaccurate claim that it was a "greenmailer"; the increases in nonemployee director compensation and the creation of a nonemployee director retirement plan. Like the chancery court, the supreme court focused on the corruption of the special committee process by Evans and Reilly....

[T]he supreme court (without addressing the question of whether Evans' and Reilly's breaches of fiduciary duty likely resulted in a lower price for shareholders) ... [used] harsh language to describe the behavior of the various participants:

> The board was torpid, if not supine, in its efforts to establish a truly independent auction, free of Evans' interference and access to confidential data. By placing the entire process in the hands of Evans, through his own chosen financial advisors, with little or no board oversight, the board materially contributed to the unprincipled conduct of those upon whom it looked with a blind eye....

When grouped together, these three opinions in Macmillan establish Evans and Reilly as among the villains of Delaware corporate law.... The very language of the opinions proclaims its identity as a morality play: "management's pejorative characterizations of the Bass group, even if honestly believed, served more to propagandize the Board than to enlighten it"; "little more than a charade"; "they chose to close their eyes"; "studied avoidance of a reasonable investigation, in order to rely upon self-serving conclusions without basis in fact"; "offending qualities that exacerbate its unreasonableness"; "domination of the allegedly 'independent' board by the financially interested members of management, coupled with the directors' evident passivity"; "tainted process"....

Consider how Evans, Reilly, or Wasserstein felt when reading these opinions. Consider how the members of the special committee, identified by name in the opinion, must have felt to be characterized as "torpid, if not supine" by the Delaware Supreme Court, combined with the equally strong terms used by the chancery court. Consider what it must be like to live with such a public shaming, to see in acquaintances' eyes the unasked question, "How could you have stood by and allowed this to happen?" Imagine how other managers and directors, when they read or heard about these opinions, felt about the prospect of being similarly pilloried. Anecdotal evidence confirms what we all would expect: No one, including directors and officers of Delaware corporations, Wall Street investment bankers, and Wall Street lawyers, enjoys being held up to this sort of public condemnation....

2. Fort Howard[4]

... In the spring of 1988, Fort Howard's management, concerned that a temporarily depressed stock price (post-October 1987) might lead it to be the target of an unfairly low and perhaps coercive takeover attempt, began to meet with an investment bank, Morgan Stanley, to discuss ways to elevate its stock price. Shortly thereafter, Morgan Stanley presented various options, recommending a leveraged buyout and indicating its interest in participating with senior management in such a transaction. Subsequently, Fort Howard's CEO informed Morgan Stanley that he and others of the senior management were interested in pursuing such a transaction. That same day, he met with a friendly, veteran director. The CEO informed the director, a law school classmate, that a special committee of the board would have to be formed to consider the buyout proposal and that the CEO wanted that director to serve as its chairman. They discussed other possible members of a special committee and agreed on two others.

At the next board meeting, the CEO presented his "proposal to make a proposal" to the board, and informed the board that Morgan Stanley and the three management directors were interested in exploring an LBO of Fort Howard. The management directors then left the meeting, and outside legal counsel guided the remaining directors through the adoption of the necessary resolutions to appoint a special committee and to select outside legal counsel and a financial adviser. The membership of the special committee was exactly as the CEO had suggested.

At its first meeting, the special committee made a determination to keep the developments confidential. Peter Atkins, a partner at Skadden, Arps, Slate, Meagher and Flom, and the committee's outside legal counsel, advised that disclosure was not legally required at that time. In the absence of advice that there was a legal obligation to disclose, the special committee ... elected secrecy....

Again, the question of disclosure was raised. The special committee concluded that a press release should be issued, which Atkins drafted. But after telephone discussions with

---

4. In re Fort Howard Corp. Shareholders Litigation, No. CIV.A.9991, 1988 WL 83147 (Del. Ch. Aug. 8, 1988).

the management group, which did not want any press release, the special committee again agreed not to proceed. The next day, after a telephone inquiry to the company about a rumored management LBO in the works, Fort Howard finally issued a press release.

The special committee met over the next several days, and ultimately accepted an offer from the management group without having actively solicited competing bids. The special committee did, however, make clear in the initial press releases that the company had the right to and would entertain alternative proposals, and, furthermore, would cooperate with any such person in the development of a competing bid. Within days of the press release, eight inquiries were received.... [B]ut, ultimately, no other bidders entered the fray.

Without doubt, the Fort Howard Special Committee performed more effectively than the *Macmillan* committee. But, although the court did not enjoin the transaction, it still found fault with the special committee's performance:

> There are aspects [of the Special Committee's performance] that supply a suspicious mind with fuel to feed its flame.
>
> It cannot, for example, be the best practice to have the interested CEO in effect handpick the members of the Special Committee as was, I am satisfied, done here. Nor can it be the best procedure for him to, in effect, choose special counsel for the committee as it appears was done here. It is obvious that no role is more critical with respect to protection of shareholder interests in these matters than that of the expert lawyers who guide sometimes inexperienced directors through the process. A suspicious mind is made uneasy contemplating the possibilities when the interested CEO is so active in choosing his adversary. The June 7 decision to keep the management interest secret, in a sense, represents a decision to sell the Company to management if it would pay a fair price, but not to inquire whether another would pay a fair price if management would not do so. It implies a bias.... So there is ground for suspicion with respect to the good faith of the Special Committee, but, on balance, not such that seem at this stage persuasive.

In refusing to draw any inference of bad faith, the court relied heavily on the effectiveness of the limited market test in probing the market for alternative possible transactions, and the wholehearted response to the eight inquiries received.

What is most striking, here as before, is the way the court, without enjoining the transaction, nonetheless makes clear that the behavior of the special committee fell below the appropriate standard. Although the Fort Howard committee did not behave as badly as the "torpid, if not supine" committee in *Macmillan*, and although Fort Howard's management acted better than Evans and Reilly did (by, for example, leaving the meeting after announcing their interest in pursuing an LBO, and not tipping confidential information during the bidding), the relationship between management and the special committee, and between their supposedly independent investment bankers, was nonetheless too cozy. The opinion made clear to the planners of all future deals that the court expects a higher standard of behavior.

Why might this be influential? If the court does not punish at time one, why should people feel that there is a higher standard at time two? First, such an opinion puts actors on notice that higher standards are liable to be applied to future deals, perhaps because of a notion that the court let the present deal go through because of insufficient precedent. Second, to the extent that actors internalize the articulated standard, they may well change their behavior irrespective of whether or not they face personal liability. Third, the criticism signals that the court will not subsequently grant a defendant's motion to dismiss, thereby substantially increasing the settlement value of a case.

3. *RJR Nabisco*[5]

The lessons of *Fort Howard*, it appears, were immediately taken to heart in the next big deal, the biggest LBO of all time, the buyout of RJR Nabisco. Luck, and a very small community, resulted in Peter Atkins again representing the special committee, and this time the committee performed in an exemplary fashion. We will never know whether he did so because of a desire to avoid criticism, to ensure that the deal withstood scrutiny, or a bit of both.

On October 19, 1988, at an RJR board meeting, F. Ross Johnson, RJR's president and CEO, informed the board that he and a management group were seeking to develop a transaction to take the company private in a leveraged buyout, and suggested a price of $75 per share. Charles Hugel, chairman of RJR's board but not an officer of the company, had some advance notice that this subject would be brought up, and had invited Peter Atkins to be present. On October 20, the very next day, the board issued a press release announcing the proposed transaction and the appointment of a special committee, with Hugel as chairman. The special committee immediately retained two financial advisors, Dillon Read (the company's regular investment banker) and Lazard Frères, as well as Mr. Atkins' firm, Skadden, Arps, Slate, Meagher and Flom.

The contrast between *Fort Howard* and *RJR Nabisco* is sharp. In *Fort Howard*, the management group handpicked the special committee and its advisors. Here, the chairman of the board, apparently on his own initiative, brought in outside counsel at the first indication of a management buyout. In *Fort Howard*, the special committee deferred to the management group's desire for secrecy and did not make any disclosure, ... until a rumor of a management buyout left them no choice. By contrast, here full disclosure of the possible management buyout was made the very next day, effectively broadcasting the message that the company was for sale.

Within four days, KKR informed the special committee that it was planning to make an offer to acquire RJR at $90 per share in cash and securities, and, on October 27, commenced a tender offer. Thereafter, the special committee acted as auctioneer, issuing a press release announcing that it was interested in receiving proposals to acquire the company. Again there is a stark contrast with *Fort Howard*, in which the committee did not take any steps to solicit competing bids until after it had reached an agreement with the management group.

Ultimately, three bids were made by the deadline, and, in the ensuing auction rounds, the price escalated from Johnson's initial suggestion of $75 per share, past KKR's opening bid of $90 per share, to KKR's ultimately successful bid of around $110 per share in cash and securities. The special committee was so independent of the management group that, in the shareholders' class action that was brought, plaintiffs were put in the position of arguing that the special committee was "inappropriately motivated to repudiate, and more importantly, to be seen publicly as repudiating the Company's management." To avoid being tarred by the public criticism directed at the management group, it was essential to the special committee that KKR win, or so the plaintiffs argued.

The court focused on the special committee's conduct of the auction—applying the supreme court's *Macmillan* holding—and concluded that the committee acted in good faith and with due care in ending the auction when it did, without returning to the bidders

---

5. In re RJR Nabisco, Inc. Shareholders Litigation, No. CIV.A.10389, 1989 Del. Ch. LEXIS 9 (Feb. 14, 1989).

for one more round of bids as plaintiffs argued they should have done. But the core of the case seems to lie in the independence of the committee from the start. Unlike the committees in *Macmillan* or *Fort Howard*, this was not a committee that could supply a suspicious mind with fuel to feed its flame.

When *RJR Nabisco* is placed next to *Macmillan* and *Fort Howard*, we see several things. First, we see a detailed example of how an effective special committee behaves in a management buyout transaction. Second, we see graphic evidence of how conduct seems to be shaped by Delaware opinions, even when the plaintiffs "lose," as they did in the *Fort Howard* preliminary injunction motion. Peter Atkins' performance in *Fort Howard* received a negative review from the most important of the critics, the Delaware Chancery Court. He had an opportunity to try again two months after his bad review, and he took that opportunity, leading one reviewer of [Bryan Burrough's 1990 book,] *Barbarians at the Gate: The Fall of RJR Nabisco* to characterize Atkins as one of the book's few heroes. Finally, when you put together the strongly negative portrayal of managers and directors in *Macmillan*, the somewhat less negative, but still negative, portrayal in *Fort Howard*, and the very positive portrayal in *RJR Nabisco*, you have a pretty clear set of guideposts for how managers and directors in management buyout transactions should behave.

In retrospect, the lessons may seem obvious. But at the time, the norms were substantially less clear. What led the directors astray in *Macmillan* and *Fort Howard* was a lack of clarity with respect to their roles. Were they to represent the interests of shareholders actively? Were they to facilitate the managers' buyout so long as the price was within the "range of fairness"? Were they to protect managers and perhaps shareholders from a hostile tender offer in the event that managers could not finance a buyout at a price within the range of fairness? Up until the *Macmillan*, *Fort Howard*, *RJR Nabisco* trilogy, there were relatively few and relatively vague guideposts. After these cases, the norms became fairly clear, sufficiently so that managers and directors who, by and large, were trying to do the right thing had sufficient guidance to figure out what the right thing was....

B. *What Is the Delaware Standard Governing MBOs?*

Can the Delaware MBO cases be reduced to a reasonably predictable standard or rule? Can one provide an algorithm to figure out what the courts will do? If so, what does it look like? This Article argues that, collectively, the cases do provide such guidance, but in a distinctive way that differs fundamentally from the rule-based view.

Consider a plausible substantive candidate for a rule governing MBOs: Managers may buy the company if and only if independent directors have auctioned the company and managers submit the highest bid. Although a plausible rule, this is clearly not Delaware law. It is clear, for example, that the special committee need not auction the company before selling the company to management; a post-agreement "market test" is sometimes enough. Moreover, directors may sometimes sell the company for less than the highest bid, if other factors make the lower bid more attractive (e.g., less uncertainty). Moreover, directors may, under certain circumstances, decide not to sell the company at all. In other words, the submission by managers of the highest bid in an auction of the company is neither a necessary nor a sufficient condition for buying the company.

Now consider the standard as articulated by Vice Chancellor Jacobs in the relatively late case of *In re Formica Corp.*:

> In any transaction where corporate management seeks to acquire the equity interest owned by the public shareholders, a conflict of interest is inherent.

> Management's personal motivation as a potential buyer is to pay as little as possible. Management's duty as a fiduciary is to obtain the highest available value for the stockholders[....] Because of that inherent conflict, the responsibility to represent the shareholders' interests adequately falls upon the independent directors, who must exercise the utmost good faith and the appropriate degree of care to assure "the most scrupulous adherence to ordinary principles of fairness in the conduct of an auction for the sale of the corporate enterprise."[6]

This summary, while on its face vague, is reasonably clear to those who have read the underlying cases, including those specifically cited. In conjunction with those cases, it provides substantial guidance on how to structure a management buyout transaction. A special committee should be established to negotiate with management and third parties. The special committee should retain its own investment bankers and legal counsel. In establishing the special committee, counsel should make sure that the managers do not appoint the members or their investment banker. The special committee should issue a press release announcing that management has made a bid and should be forthcoming in providing information to prospective bidders for control. If third parties enter the contest, the special committee should behave in an evenhanded manner and should not favor the management group. In any event, the special committee should test the market, although it need not conduct an auction, to see if competing offers are reasonably likely to be available.

Jacobs' summary is a summary, not a standard. The narratives are not the scaffolding—the investigative process—by which the norm is constructed, which can then be jettisoned once the standard is formed and articulated. On the contrary, the articulated "standard" does nothing more than stand in for the cases: The narratives it summarizes are the content of the norm. In the application of the standard—at least by a court, if not by the actor himself—the narratives become critical in characterizing the new fact pattern and extending the legal norm to a new situation.

Indeed, this interpretation is the only way to explain the coexistence of the typically open-textured and extremely vague statement of the legal norm under Delaware law (in an MBO, "independent directors, ... must exercise the utmost good faith and the appropriate degree of care to assure 'the most scrupulous adherence to ordinary principles of fairness in the conduct of an auction for the sale of the corporate enterprise'") and the reasonable predictability of Delaware outcomes that is essential to business planners. It is only if the statement is a summary that stands in for the set of cases that constitute the norm—with the guidance being provided by those cases, with all their factual specificity—that there could be sufficient certainty.

Confusion emerges in several situations: First, when there are too few cases from which to triangulate the norm; second, when a player confuses the summary with the constitutive narratives; third, when a player interprets the cases as establishing a substantive safe harbor, rather than explicating a conduct norm.

C. Summary

The preceding study of the Delaware MBO cases shows that the standards governing MBOs evolved through the incremental description of good and bad performances by managers. The overall doctrinal structure was unchanged throughout: From the beginning to the end, cases were analyzed either under the rubric of the "business judgment rule"

---

6. In Re Formica Corp. Shareholders Litigation, 1989 Del. Ch. LEXIS 27, 32–33. [*The Vice Chancellor is quoting Macmillan.—Ed.*]

or the "entire fairness standard," with an occasional reference to the intermediate Unocal test. At no point does the court ever say: "This is how you must do MBOs." Nor does the court ever say, "If you do MBOs this way, then we will leave you alone."

It is arguable that this fact-intensive, heavily normative narrative style is characteristic of all common law adjudication. It is likewise arguable that this style is, at least, characteristic of all standards. At the least, this seems to be the characteristic style of Delaware fiduciary duty case law.

This descriptive claim raises further questions. First, how do the narratives reach their ultimate audience, and in what form do they do so? This is the subject of the next Part. Second, if I am right as a descriptive matter, what are the implications for corporate law? That is the subject of [the final part of this article].

II. Traces of the Transmission of Norms: The Case of MBOs

The central hypothesis of this Article is that a large part of what the Delaware courts do is tell stories as a way of articulating and expressing norms, as a way of giving content to the amorphous and highly contextual concepts of "good faith," "independence," "due care," and "fair dealing." If this is correct, then one would predict that these stories would make their way out into the relevant community. There are two primary hypotheses for how the norms might be transmitted. First, the stories themselves might be transmitted directly to the target audience (directors and officers), either in detail or in summary form. Second, the stories may be digested by an intermediary, Delaware corporate lawyers, who then apply the norms without actually telling the stories to the clients....

A. Newspaper Accounts

As one would expect, Delaware cases are covered by the major business press. With regard to the MBO cases, one finds that although the early and minor cases receive no more than passing mention, the major, high-profile cases generate substantial coverage that focuses on what one would expect a priori, the dramatic clash of egos and the emergence of heroes and especially villains. In these articles, one finds the broadcasting of the stories told by the Delaware opinions, pitched at a somewhat higher rhetorical level and with supplemental reporting....

... [W]hen the [*Wall Street Journal*] does get interested, as in the *Macmillan* or *RJR Nabisco* cases, its prominence and additional reporting amplify the volume of criticism from the Delaware court. As one experienced Wall Street transactional lawyer put it in private conversation, "We're not afraid of what the Delaware courts say. We're afraid of what the press says."

B. Extrajudicial Utterances

Some Delaware judges give speeches and appear on panels. This provides an additional platform from which to summarize and promulgate standards of conduct for members of the corporate bar and their clients....

C. "A Memorandum to Our Clients"

If my hypothesis is correct, one would predict that the stories of the Delaware courts would find their way into the communications between lawyers and their clients. The best evidence of this would be the actual advice that lawyers give their clients, but such evidence is generally not available.

An indirect record of such communication is the relatively well-known, but little-studied legal genre, the "memorandum to our clients," that prominent firms use to keep their clients apprised of changes in the law (and, of course, to market their services)....

From an academic perspective, reading these memos is very hard going. Although the discussions of legal doctrine are extremely sophisticated, the memoranda are filled with enormous factual detail about the cases. Compared to more academic discussions, the case discussions seem only partly digested: One finds only summaries of the factual background without the synthesis that makes such case-by-case presentation unnecessary.

But the fact that the most sophisticated practitioners writing for sophisticated clients and practitioners present Delaware law in this way reflects a recognition — intuitively obvious to practicing lawyers, perhaps less obvious to those of us who spend our time responding to student requests for the "rule" — that the guidance resides in those specific factual accounts, and that summarizing the factual discussion is close to the limit of how far one can go to reduce the cases to a "rule." Clients are no less insistent than students in demanding clarity. The difference is that practitioners suffer a greater penalty than academics for giving in to the desire to provide clarity at the sacrifice of accuracy....

D. *Shareholder Litigation*

Shareholder litigation has come under mounting criticism of late. The conflicts of interest inherent in the relationship between class counsel and shareholder plaintiffs have been analyzed in detail....

Roberta Romano, in the most careful empirical study to date, could find little direct benefit to shareholders from shareholder litigation.[7] *Plaintiffs had abysmal success in litigated cases....*

... [In light of the fact that cases on MBOs were few and far between, while the pace of MBO activity was rapid,] *the "preachiness" of Delaware MBO opinions, the pattern of criticizing conduct even when no injunction is issued, and judges' extrajudicial utterances can all be read as attempts to be heard on a critical matter in the absence of a case raising just the right issue and in the absence of the articulation (or articulability) of a governing rule. Such utterances are, in a literal sense, advisory opinions.*

As such, these judicial comments share both the vices and virtues of advisory opinions. They are useful insofar as they help lawyers and parties plan transactions. They are problematic, however, precisely when they are "issued" without a full factual record. Given the fact-specific quality of Delaware opinions, this may make them particularly problematic. At the same time, the disproportion between the number of cases and transactions may make them especially necessary.

The lack of law also pushes transactional lawyers into a central and critical position. The MBO cases show that in a world of vaguely defined norms and rapidly evolving transactional forms, what the business lawyer tells the client — rather than what the judge announces to the world — is the "law." We see traces in the "memoranda to our clients" genre, but the core of this body of law resides in the firms and in the advice given to

---

7. Roberta Romano, *The Shareholder Suit: Litigation Without Foundation?*, 7 J.L. ECON. & ORG. 55, 85 (1991)

clients in confidence. This advice necessarily is given in the shadow of ex post judicial review, with, as we have seen in the Delaware cases, the possibility, albeit somewhat remote, of upsetting the deal. In only two [MBO] cases ... did the court enjoin a transaction, the ultimate failure for a business lawyer.[8] Although in other cases criticism may have signaled a refusal to grant a defendant's motion to dismiss, and may have led to a subsequent monetary settlement, such settlements can be budgeted for and do not destroy a deal.

One particularly striking manifestation of the tension in the production of law between the judges and the lawyers can be found in the competing attempts to put a "spin" on new opinions. If, for example, one compares Chancellor Allen's takeover opinions with, for example, Theodore Mirvis's columns in the New York Law Journal, one immediately feels that tension. In part, one observes competing attempts to convince the Delaware Supreme Court. But one also observes attempts to shape accepted practice in the transactional community.

MBOs again provide a good illustration. A per se ban on MBOs is conceivable. Serious and important commentators made just that argument in the 1970s. When MBOs started to arrive in significant numbers in the early 1980s, the law was clearly unsettled. Lawyers did these deals and, by the time the Delaware courts had an opportunity to articulate standards, that is, by the latter half of the 1980s, hundreds of deals had already been done. It was too late in the day to hold MBOs illegal per se. By doing these sorts of deals, in the absence of controlling case law, law office practice at least influenced and probably constrained judicial decisionmaking....

[Even critics of litigation concede that it can be a public good when it leads to case law that provides legal guidance. But some commentators criticize shareholder litigation because few reported cases produce a legal rule.]. If I am correct that fiduciary duty law evolves primarily at the level of norms rather than the level of rules, then to focus on the [*small*] number of cases that "produce a legal rule" ... is to miss a significant part of the benefit. In the MBO cases, it would be a fair reading of the cases to say that none of the cases individually "produces a legal rule." In none of the cases does the court overrule any prior cases or explicitly adopt any legal rule at all. Instead, all the discussions are couched as elaborations of the duty of care and the duty of loyalty. Indeed, one does not find any new legal "rule" even looking back on the cases as a group. Rather, what we see is the elaboration of the norms of conduct appropriate to management buyouts (all under the guise of applying the standard analysis of the duties of loyalty and care). From this perspective, each of the cases individually told something significant about legal norms governing management buyouts....

E. The Delaware Way: Could It Be Efficient?

... The earlier case study of the Delaware MBO cases provides a picture of the Delaware approach as regulating at least one difficult problem of managerial conduct. In this section, I speculate on how the system might work....

... First, why might such a system be superior to potential alternatives, such as a system in which the courts (or the legislature) articulate rules ex ante that make it clearer what sort of transactions are permitted and what sort of transactions are forbidden?

Second, if I am right that the system seems to rely on the possibility of public shaming to constrain behavior, how is it that such a system works? One might suspect, *ex ante,*

---

8. *The two cases were* Macmillan (see above) and EAC Industries, Inc. v. Frantz Manufacturing Co. No. CIV.A.8003, 1985 WL 3200 (Del. Ch. June 28, 1985), aff'd, 501 A.2d 401 (Del. 1985).—*Ed.*

"that being a successful businessman requires having a very thick skin, even enjoying the reputation of someone who skates close to the edge, even being something of an outlaw." How is it that such a person would be deterred by the possibility of being criticized by a Delaware civil servant who wears black robes, much less incorporate such criticism into his or her personal code of conduct? Third, might there be an alternative explanation for the distinctive Delaware style?

I will try to address these questions separately.

1. *The Mushiness of Delaware Fiduciary Duty Case Law*

Why might it be that Delaware corporate law shies away from using "laws" to deter bad behavior and leans, instead, towards morality tales? One can try to answer this question from several directions.

One can gain ... insight from a comparative perspective. Corporate law can be divided into two alternative and rather incompatible models. On one side there is the civil code, Germanic approach which, with some significant parody, can be described as "anything not explicitly permitted is prohibited." The second approach is the "enabling" approach that characterizes Delaware law: Anything not explicitly prohibited is permitted, and the law mainly serves to save transaction costs by providing low-cost standard form contracts. Tracking this difference in character is a difference in judicial role: In Germany, the free-ranging, fact-specific, fiduciary duty analysis of Delaware is absent and utterly foreign to the corporate law sensibility.

These contrasts in national styles suggest that the peculiar quality of Delaware cases may be linked to, and is perhaps a necessary consequence of or supplement to, the open-textured quality of the law. The virtues of the enabling approach to corporate law have been celebrated. But because the possibilities are (intentionally) open-ended, the Delaware legislature and courts cannot promulgate ex ante the standards to govern new situations until they see a variety of cases and figure out how well or badly people behaved. To put it differently, in an open-textured regulatory structure, many important norms can only be generated ex post, and with endless possibilities, safe harbors are particularly risky.

Because of the enormous discretion exercised by Delaware Chancery and Supreme Court judges, the personnel are critical. If one is to depend on the courts to fill out the details of proper behavior in the corporate community, the judges must be respected by the community. Delaware accomplishes this in two ways. First, a substantial number of the judges are drawn from the very world at issue, that is, they are experienced and respected practitioners of Delaware corporate law. Second, the Delaware courts have traditionally been characterized by a very high degree of collegiality among the judges, so that even those judges who did not practice in the area are socialized into the peculiar practices after joining the court.

But, if most law-following is self-induced, then a system of enabling rules with ex post judicial review, like Delaware's, faces an additional problem: It is notably lacking in mandatory rules that themselves provide the guidance that individual law followers need to follow the rules. Moreover, in such a system, the type of law-following required goes more to process and motive than to substantive outcome. In such circumstances, the articulation of substantive rules does not provide the sort of guidance required. On the contrary, the particular sort of guidance demanded seems to be better provided by narrative than by rule. Martha Nussbaum has argued that narratives, especially moralistic novels like those of Henry James, provide the kind of moral guidance one needs to be a moral person, and, in their thick descriptions, provide a better guide—that is, more useful, relevant, and interesting—than the kind of principles discussed in traditional moral theory.[9] The suggestion here is similar.

2. But How Could Shame Constrain the Shameless?

It is fine to claim that Delaware fiduciary duty law relies, in large measure, on the possibility of public shaming or praise to constrain managers, but, as was pointed out before, would one not expect that successful businessmen might have sufficiently thick skins to be immune to such influence?

Here, it seems to me, the answers are particularly interesting. The short answer is "yes," one would expect some particularly successful businessmen to be immune to such influence, and here the effect of Delaware corporate law seems particularly subtle.

Consider what I have claimed is a characteristic style of Delaware law: The denial of a preliminary injunction motion coupled with strong criticism. In the next deal, the "thick-skinned" businessman wants to skate close to the edge. Will he be constrained by the possibility that he will go down in history as a villain of Delaware corporate law? Probably not. But his lawyer is likely to advise him that such behavior will make it more likely that the deal will be enjoined, or that he will be left unprotected against maneuvers by his opponents. In other words, even the corporate actor who is immune to the social sanctions of Delaware corporate law will be constrained to some degree by Delaware "law." ...

And what about the others? Will the nonlegal sanctions have bite, separate from the possibility that the deal might not go through? To put it differently, under what circumstances are Delaware norms likely to be internalized?

Here we come to what one might call the silver lining in the agency cost cloud. The prototypical Delaware corporation is a large, publicly held corporation in which ownership is separated from control. In such corporations, the principal actors are agents. For them, the financial gains from allowing the corporations they manage to skate close to the edge are likely to be small. Moreover, the culture of such an organization is typically more bureaucratic than entrepreneurial, with directors of such corporations serving as much a ritual function as a managerial function. A system that relies on public shaming is perfectly suited to such contexts: The cost to the actor—the disdain in the eyes of one's acquaintances, the loss of directorships, the harm to one's reputation—may often be sufficiently great to deter behavior, even without anything more.

Consider how this dynamic played out in the MBO context. MBOs, overnight, provided the opportunity for the senior managers to become very rich, to go from being bureaucrats to entrepreneurs. Under such circumstances, one can expect that some managers might rather quickly become indifferent to the criticism of the judges. The possibility of becoming seriously rich sometimes has that effect.

How did the courts respond? In the MBO cases, one sees a subtle shift of attention from the managers to the special committee. Although the potential gains to managers in MBOs might lead them to develop resistance to the deterrent effect of public shaming, the members of the special committee had no such prospects. They were not getting rich. They were simply trying to do their best as outside directors. One would predict that

---

9. Martha C. Nussbaum, Love's Knowledge: Essays On Philosophy And Literature 125–47 (1990).

such actors are likely to be far more susceptible to the kind of influence that Delaware opinions exert than the managers. The Delaware courts, perhaps sensing this, focused much of their attention — both in the opinions and in extrajudicial utterances — on influencing the conduct of the special committees.

Note, now, a surprising implication of this analysis. If the success of Delaware's method for constraining or encouraging managers to act on behalf of shareholders depends critically on a separation of ownership and control, with the greater susceptibility to reputational effects that agents have in comparison to principals, then the system is likely to be less suitable for corporations not characterized by this separation, such as closely held corporations. The Delaware style may well have evolved in response to the particular needs and properties of the large, publicly held corporation. The same mixture of flexibility and court scrutiny may be less effective when the objects are less susceptible to shaming....

Roberta Romano, *Empowering Investors: A Market Approach to Securities Regulation**

... The U.S. securities laws have repeatedly been assailed as burdensome or ineffective. Reform efforts have conversely been attacked for undermining an effective mechanism by which shareholders can discipline management. Moreover, even reformers have been dissatisfied with the effectiveness of their product. For example, after enacting the Private Securities Litigation Reform Act of 1995, members of Congress became concerned that their efforts to rein in frivolous private lawsuits under the federal securities laws were being circumvented by state court filings and introduced legislation to preempt such action. There is some validity to their concern: In a report to President Clinton on the impact of the 1995 Act, the Securities and Exchange Commission (SEC) cited preliminary studies indicating a decrease in federal court filings and an increase in state court filings.

This Article contends that the current legislative approach to securities regulation is mistaken and that preemption is not the solution to frivolous lawsuits. It advocates instead a market-oriented approach of competitive federalism that would expand, not reduce, the role of the states in securities regulation. It thereby would fundamentally reconceptualize our regulatory approach and is at odds with both sides of the debate over the 1995 Act, each of which has sought to use national laws as a weapon to beat down its opponent's position by monopolizing the regulatory field.

The market approach to securities regulation advocated in this Article takes as its paradigm the successful experience of the U.S. states in corporate law, in which the fifty states and the District of Columbia compete for the business of corporate charters. There is a substantial literature on this particular manifestation of U.S. federalism indicating that shareholders have benefited from the federal system of corporate law by its production of corporate codes that, for the most part, maximize share value. This Article proposes extending the competition among states for corporate charters to two of the three principal components of federal securities regulation: the registration of securities and the related continuous disclosure regime for issuers; and the antifraud provisions that police that system. The third component, the regulation of market professionals, is not included in

---

* Originally published in 107 YALE LAW JOURNAL 2359 (1998). Reprinted by permission of The Yale Law Journal Company and William S. Hein Company from The Yale Law Journal, Vol. 107, pages 2359–2430.

the proposed reform. The proposed market approach can be implemented by modifying the federal securities laws in favor of a menu approach to securities regulation under which firms elect whether to be covered by federal law or by the securities law of a specified state, such as their state of incorporation.

Under a system of competitive federalism for securities regulation, only one sovereign would have jurisdiction over all transactions in the securities of a corporation that involve the issuer or its agents and investors. The aim is to replicate for the securities setting the benefits produced by state competition for corporate charters—a responsive legal regime that has tended to maximize share value—and thereby eliminate the frustration experienced at efforts to reform the national regime. As a competitive legal market supplants a monopolist federal agency in the fashioning of regulation, it would produce rules more aligned with the preferences of investors, whose decisions drive the capital market.

Competitive federalism for U.S. securities regulation also has important implications for international securities regulation. The jurisdictional principle applicable to domestic securities transactions is equally applicable to international securities transactions: Foreign issuers selling shares in the United States could opt out of the federal securities laws and choose those of another nation, such as their country of incorporation, or those of a U.S. state, to govern transactions in their securities in the United States. The federal securities laws would also, of course, not apply to transactions by U.S. investors abroad in the shares of firms that opt for a non-U.S. securities domicile. Under this approach, U.S. law would apply only to corporations affirmatively opting to be covered by U.S. law, whether they be U.S.—or non-U.S.—based firms. It therefore would put an end to the ever-expanding extraterritorial reach of U.S. securities regulation, which currently extends to transactions abroad involving foreign firms, as long as there are any U.S. shareholders or U.S. effects.

Stemming the trend of extraterritorial application of U.S. law will not harm U.S. investors because they have, in fact, often been disadvantaged by the expansion of U.S. securities jurisdiction. For example, to avoid the application of U.S. law, foreign firms have frequently explicitly excluded U.S. investors from takeover offers, and such investors have thus missed out on bid premiums.

In addition, adoption of the market approach would facilitate foreign firms' access to capital, as they would be able to issue securities in the United States without complying with U.S. disclosure and accounting rules that differ substantially from their home rules, a requirement that has been a significant deterrent to listings. This consequence of the proposed modification of U.S. law would also benefit U.S. investors, who would no longer incur the higher transaction costs of purchasing shares abroad in order to make direct investments in foreign firms....

There may be an understandable desire to discount the need for the proposal because of the vibrancy of U.S. capital markets and the calls for piecemeal reform rather than comprehensive revamping of the current regime by issuers and investors. This would be a mistake. While U.S. capital markets are the largest and most liquid in the world, it is incorrect to attribute this fact to the federal regime. U.S. capital markets were the largest and most liquid global markets at the turn of the century, before the federal regime was established, and their share of global capitalization has declined markedly over the past two decades, facts at odds with the contention that the current federal regime is the reason for the depth of U.S. capital markets. The absence of calls for comprehensive reform is a function of a lack of imagination, rather than evidence that the current regulatory apparatus does not produce deadweight losses. Blind adherence to the securities regulation status quo imposes real costs on investors and firms, and there is a better solution.

Some may conclude that the proposal does not go far enough, and that all government interference in capital markets, whether federal or state, should be abolished. I believe that the intermediate position advocated in this Article is a more sensible public policy than eliminating all government involvement. This is because state competition does not foreclose the possibility of deregulation should that be desired by investors: A state could adopt a securities regime that delegates regulatory authority over issuers to stock exchanges, just as the current federal regime delegates regulatory authority for market professionals to the stock exchanges and National Association of Securities Dealers (NASD). State competition permits experimentation with purely private regulatory arrangements, while retaining a mechanism to reverse course easily—migration to states that do not adopt such an approach—which is not present in a purely private regime. On a more pragmatic level, there is a more immediate point to the Article: To caution against the current impetus to extend the federal government's monopoly over securities regulation. Instead of supplanting state securities regulation, Congress should rationalize it by legislatively altering the multijurisdictional, transactional basis of state regulatory authority to an issuer-domicile basis....

I. Competitive Federalism: A Market Approach to Securities Regulation

Although both the states and the federal government regulate securities transactions, the current regulatory arrangements are a far cry from competitive federalism. The federal securities regime, consisting of the Securities Act of 1933 and the Securities Exchange Act of 1934, applies to all publicly traded firms and is a mandatory system of disclosure regulation, bolstered by antifraud provisions. While the federal laws do not preempt all state regulation, states cannot lower the regulatory standards applicable to firms covered by the federal regime because its requirements are mandatory. They have also been prevented from raising regulatory standards on some occasions. As a consequence, the states have essentially abandoned the regulation of public firms to the SEC. In the proposed system of competitive federalism, state and federal regulators would stand on an equal regulatory footing, and firms would be able to choose the applicable regulatory regime.

A. The Essence of Competitive Federalism

A market approach to U.S. securities regulation requires two significant departures from current law. First, a public corporation's coverage under the national securities laws must be optional rather than mandatory. Second, the securities transactions of a corporation that elects not to be covered by the federal securities laws are to be regulated by the corporation's selected domicile for securities regulation. This approach is premised on the idea that competition among sovereigns—here the fifty states, the District of Columbia, and the federal government (represented primarily by the SEC)—in the production of securities laws would benefit investors in public corporations by facilitating the adoption of regulation aligned with investors' preferences, as has been true of the competitive production of corporation codes. The motivation for the proposal is that no government entity can know better than market participants what regulations are in their interest, particularly as firms' requirements are continually changing with shifting financial market conditions. Competing regulators would make fewer policy mistakes than a monopolistic regulator as competition harnesses the incentives of the market to regulatory institutions.

Regulatory competition is desirable because when the choice of investments includes variation in legal regimes, promoters of firms will find that they can obtain a lower cost of capital by choosing the regime that investors prefer. For example, as long as investors are informed of the governing legal regime, if promoters choose a regime that exculpates them from fraud, investors will either not invest in the firm at all or will require a higher return on the investment (that is, pay less for the security), just as bondholders charge higher interest rates to firms bearing greater risk of principal nonrepayment. Investors set the price because financial capital is highly mobile and financial markets are highly competitive; the set of investment opportunities is extensive, and with the use of derivatives, virtually limitless. It is plausible to assume that investors are informed about liability rules given the sophistication of the institutional investors who comprise the majority of stock market investors and whose actions determine market prices on which uninformed investors can rely. Promoters thus will bear the cost of operating under a legal regime inimical to investor interests, and they will therefore select the regime that maximizes the joint welfare of promoters and investors.

The analytical point concerning the ability of capital markets to assess legal regimes and consequently the beneficial effect of competition is confirmed by empirical research in the bond indenture and corporate law contexts: Creditor protection provisions in bond indentures are positively priced, and firms experience statistically significant positive changes in stock prices upon changing their incorporation state. The entrepreneurial motivation to reduce capital costs that operates in a competitive legal system mitigates the otherwise core problem for a government regulator of identifying what regulation will benefit investors in capital markets.

Federal intervention in capital markets in the 1930s was justified by a contention that securities markets operate poorly on two dimensions: First, they fail to protect investors from stock price manipulation and fraud; and second, they produce an inadequate level of corporate disclosure because the benefits of information concerning a firm cannot be appropriated solely by the firm that bears the cost of the information's production (that is, corporate information is a public good). Analytically, a demonstration that there are information externalities necessitating government intervention depends on the mix of informed and uninformed investors. But a theoretical need for government regulation to prevent a market failure is not equivalent to a need for a monopolist regulator. The premise of competitive federalism is that if, for example, corporate information would be underproduced to investors' detriment in an unregulated market, then there would be a demand for, matched by a supply of, mandated disclosure regulation in a regime of state competition for securities regulation, just as in the monopolist SEC system.

A third rationale more recently offered for federal intervention is a refinement of the public good rationale. This rationale identifies the information problem as involving information that would benefit an issuer's competitors as well as investors. According to this theory, because competitors can use such information to compete more effectively with the issuer and thereby diminish the issuer's profitability, investors as well as firms would not wish to reveal such information, even though it would improve investors' ability to evaluate firms. Such an externality would render mandatory disclosure rules necessary. It can be shown analytically, however, that even in the case of such third-party externalities, mandatory disclosure is not always optimal compared to voluntary disclosure, and it would in all likelihood be extremely difficult for a regulator to determine when mandatory disclosure is optimal. But putting aside the theoretical uncertainty of the need for a mandatory regime, even this third-party externality argument does not require an exclusive federal regulator. The majority of investors hold portfolios, not single shares of stock, and therefore, unlike the issuer, they will internalize the externality if they make the disclosure decision. That is, they will desire a regime requiring the information's disclosure because, by definition of a positive externality, the expected gain on their shares in competitors will offset the loss on their shares in the issuer.

Because the antifraud rationale does not depend on the presence of an externality for government action, it presents even less of an objection to a system of competitive federalism than the mandatory disclosure rationale: It is silly to contend that investors will choose regimes that encourage fraud. Joel Seligman states that a federal antifraud law was needed in the 1930s because state securities laws did not reach out-of-state sellers.[10] Whatever the merit of the argument at that time, it is not applicable to modern jurisdictional doctrines and is therefore not relevant to today's policy discussions. Moreover, if there was concern in the 1930s over the states' capacities to handle securities fraud cases, this is no longer a serious issue. Given the overlapping nature of the current antifraud regime, the states have developed active securities law enforcement divisions and coordinating capacities to deal with interstate fraud....

B. Is Abandoning a Mandatory Federal Securities Law Justified?

... Even today, little empirical evidence suggests that the federal regime has affirmatively benefited investors. To develop an educated prediction of what the counterfactual (a competitive securities regime) would produce, this section then reviews the empirical evidence on investor welfare of the next best thing—state competition for corporate charters. It compares favorably.

The difficulty of discerning an affirmative impact on investors from the federal regime detailed in this section supports abandoning its exclusivity. While it does not prove the counterfactual— that state competition would be better—the near total absence of measurable benefits from the federal regulatory apparatus surely undermines blind adherence to the status quo. Under regulatory competition, lawmakers have incentives to replace regimes that do not measurably support their objectives with those that do. In a competitive regulatory system, undesirable mandatory policies cannot be maintained over time, because they are not enforceable: Firms will migrate to the regulatory regime that does not impose such mandates.

The competitively produced state corporation codes, in contrast to the federal securities laws, consist primarily of enabling provisions that reduce the cost of business by providing firms and investors with a standardized contractual form to govern their relationships. Thus, to the extent the empirical literature suggests that federal securities laws have been fashioned from a set of misguided premises, adoption of the market approach to securities regulation will weed out inefficiencies in the federal regime, by permitting capital market participants to establish a new regulatory equilibrium with a mix of enabling and mandatory provisions, if that is what investors prefer.

1. Empirical Evidence on the Rationales for Federal Securities Regulation

a. Mandatory Disclosure

There is little tangible proof of the claim that corporate information is "underproduced" in the absence of mandatory disclosure, or that the benefits to investors from information that firms would not produce in the absence of mandatory disclosure actually outweigh their costs. For instance, before the enactment of the federal securities laws in the 1930s, public corporations voluntarily disclosed financial statements, typically under a stock

---

10. Joel Seligman, *The Historical Need for a Mandatory Disclosure System*, 9 J. CORP. L. 1 (1983).

exchange listing requirement, that contained substantially all of the information subsequently required under the federal laws. In an important and still underappreciated study, George Benston found that the only major mandated item that was not reported by a significant set of firms prior to the 1934 legislation was sales.[11] Comparing the pre- and post-legislation stock returns of the firms for which the legislation was relevant (firms that had not previously reported their sales, which were 38% of New York Stock Exchange (NYSE)-listed corporations) with those for which it was not (the remaining 62% of NYSE corporations that had disclosed sales information), he found no significant price effect from the new mandated disclosure.

Benston's finding, upon reflection, should not be surprising: Because firms need capital and investors need information, firms have powerful incentives to disclose information if they are to compete successfully for funds against alternative investment opportunities....

... [C]apital markets have changed dramatically since the securities laws were adopted. The institutional investors who dominate today's markets have far greater ability, as well as financial incentives, to process information and price securities than does the SEC staff. Institutional investors' pricing determinations better protect unsophisticated investors than any of the SEC's mandated disclosure requirements because, given the efficiency of U.S. capital markets in information aggregation, and the fact that securities sell for one price, institutional investors cannot use their superior information-processing ability to extract wealth systematically from uninformed investors, particularly those long-term investors who follow a buy-and-hold strategy. The federal regime has not adapted well to this changed context. The interests of sophisticated and unsophisticated investors in the choice of securities regime will not diverge for the issuer-investor relations that come under the regime of competitive federalism proposed by this Article, and will, in fact, be better served by the new regulatory arrangement.

One particularly egregious example of the SEC's problematic disclosure policies will serve to underscore the point that it would be a profound mistake to presume that the SEC gets things right. The SEC prohibited for decades the disclosure of projected earnings. Such information, however, is far more valuable to investors than the accounting information the SEC required, because stock value is a function of future cash flows not historical data. The SEC modified its position in 1979 to permit the disclosure of projections within a safe harbor rule, but even today the agency's approach is still quite guarded when it comes to such disclosures. For instance, when Congress recently legislated a safe harbor from civil liability for forecasts [in the 1995 Private Securities Litigation Reform Act], the SEC was responsible for the extended list of transactions excluded from the safe harbor provision.

The SEC's historic concern was that projections were more susceptible to abuse than accounting data. This concern was premised on a bizarre view of investor decisionmaking, that investors believe all figures are "written on stone" and do not discount managers' optimism and therefore have to be protected from all but "verifiable" information (namely, historical cost). This approach has made SEC disclosure documents of limited value for investment decisionmaking and was the subject of sustained criticisms throughout the 1970s. Ironically, the SEC's approach particularly disadvantaged public investors by closing off their ability to obtain information on projected earnings, as firms would not make

---

11. George J. Benston, *Required Disclosure and the Stock Market: An Evaluation of the Securities Exchange Act of 1934*, 63 AM. ECON. REV. 132, 144–45 (1973); *see also* George Benston, *An Appraisal of the Costs and Benefits of Government-Required Disclosure: SEC and FTC Requirements*, LAW & CONTEMP. PROBS., Summer 1977, at 30, 51–52.

public earnings forecasts for fear of liability, although they would provide them to analysts and other professionals.

The 1979 modification did not substantially increase public forecasts, given firms' liability concerns, and was clearly outmoded for modern markets populated by institutional investors. Congress therefore sought to increase the disclosure of forecasts in the 1995 securities reform legislation by explicitly creating a safe harbor from civil liability for the release of forecasts. Whether the legislation will have the intended effect is not yet ascertainable, but some early indications suggest that the new law is having minimal impact on the disclosure of projections. The restrictions on the applicability of the safe harbor so vigorously advanced by the SEC surely enhance the likelihood that the statute's impact will be limited, and they serve as a useful reminder of how difficult it is for a monopolist government agency to alter course and implement significant policy changes.

This illustration of utterly misguided SEC disclosure mandates makes plain that an SEC disclosure initiatives does not itself provide evidence that the market is inadequately producing relevant information and, consequently, should not be privileged by assuming that the agency is always (or even more often than not) right. It indicates quite the opposite, that the SEC may not possess even a rudimentary understanding of, much less a superior capacity over anyone else to identify, what information investors require for decisionmaking. Such regulatory mistakes would be far less likely with competition: Investors would be able to reveal their preference for particular information by bidding up the price of firms subject to a regime in which they could make forecasts, compared to firms subject to one that prohibits such disclosures....

b. Antifraud Provisions

The federal antifraud laws have not been a focus of as much empirical research as the federal disclosure regime. But even here there is little evidence indicating that federal, as opposed to state, securities laws are necessary to protect investors from fraud and manipulation. In truth, the data that would be probative of the efficacy of the federal antifraud regime have not been compiled. Because all states had antifraud statutes prior to the adoption of the federal securities laws, and only Nevada did not have an administrative entity to investigate securities fraud at that time, an investigation of whether reported instances of investor fraud decreased after the enactment of federal securities laws would be a useful step in determining the efficacy of the federal regime. The difficulty, however, of establishing a pre-enactment baseline rate (given differences in enforcement regimes across states, for example), probably would make the task infeasible. Other probative research would examine whether securities issued outside of the SEC's jurisdiction (intrastate issues of small firms, state and local government securities, or foreign issues) have higher frequencies of fraud and price manipulation than SEC-registered securities, although, again, developing good estimates of comparative base-rate frequencies would be quite difficult.

Seligman cites SEC testimony to Congress in the 1940s and a 1963 SEC study as part of the agency's twenty-year effort to expand its jurisdiction over small firms, indicating that the SEC initiated more fraud investigations against issues exempt from federal registration requirements than against those that were registered. These data are of little import. First, we do not know whether the SEC allocated more resources to investigating exempt issues than to investigating registered issues, an altogether plausible possibility given the SEC's agenda at the time, the extension of its disclosure requirements to small firms exempt from its regulation. Such an enforcement policy would make it impossible to draw any conclusion concerning relative rates of fraud from the data. And, of course, the initiation of an investigation does not mean that fraud actually occurred. Second, it is important to ascertain the level of state antifraud activity against such issuers to determine whether federal intervention was necessary. Third, even if one accepted Seligman's contention that massive securities frauds went undeterred by the states and necessitated the enactment of the federal laws, it is important to determine whether fraud occurred more frequently in small rather than large firms. Such a finding would indicate that the lower rate of fraud investigations for firms covered by the 1933 Act would not be a function of the mandatory disclosure regime, but of the population's lower underlying occurrence rate.

But the evidence supporting the contention that rampant fraud necessitated the federal laws is itself quite thin. After reviewing the legislative record and other sources, Benston concludes, in contrast to Seligman, that there is scant evidence of fraudulent financial statements prior to the 1934 Act. Harold Bierman has also reviewed the evidence concerning stock market fraud and manipulation prior to the 1929 crash, scrutinizing in particular the sensational charges raised against several prominent financiers in the Pecora hearings that led to the federal securities legislation.[12] He concludes that the hearings and the attempted prosecutions in their aftermath did not uncover fraudulent or dishonest behavior on Wall Street and that the amount of manipulation in the 1920s was "surprisingly small." More important, a recent empirical study of the operation of stock pools that were a principal focus of the congressional investigation leading to the enactment of the federal securities laws found no evidence that the pools manipulated stock prices.

In short, a fair reading of the empirical literature on the effects of the federal securities laws points to an expansive regulatory apparatus with no empirical validation for its most fundamental objectives. The SEC appears to be a regulatory edifice without foundation. A competitive regulatory system would put such a characterization to the test, as firms would be able to seek out the securities regime that investors prefer.

2. Empirical Evidence on Corporate Charter Competition

... To find fault with a market approach one must maintain that a competitive regulatory setting will do a worse job than the federal monopolist in achieving the investor-protection goals of securities regulation. For such a contention to be correct, a further assumption is required, that the states will engage in a "race for the bottom" and enact rules that favor promoter-issuers over investors. This assumption cannot be directly tested because there is at present no competitive regime for securities laws; besides the national mandates, the governing regime is fixed by the investor's residence or place of sale. But there is a competitive regime for corporate charters. The most important data bearing on the question whether the federal securities regime should be eliminated is, consequently, the research on the impact on shareholder welfare of state competition for charters. This research indicates convincingly, in my judgment, that investors are at a minimum not harmed from the competition and, in all likelihood, benefit from changes in corporate domicile to states such as Delaware, the leading incorporation state.

There have been six event studies of the effect of state competition on shareholder wealth. The wealth effect is measured by the stock price reaction to a domicile change. Measured over a variety of time periods and sample firms, these studies find either a

---

12. HAROLD BIERMAN, JR., THE GREAT MYTHS OF 1929 AND THE LESSONS TO BE LEARNED 133–45 (1991).

significant positive stock price effect or no significant price effect upon reincorporation. No study observes a negative stock price effect. The empirical research on state competition undermines the race-for-the-bottom argument against eliminating the federal securities monopoly by demonstrating that choice of jurisdiction does not leave investors defenseless against unscrupulous promoters.

The race-for-the-bottom view of state competition is no longer the consensus view of scholars in the debate over the efficacy of state competition for corporate charters precisely because its advocates cannot provide tangible proof that competition is, in general, harmful to investors. There is no reason to expect state competition to operate differently for securities law than it does for corporate law. The informational efficiency of capital markets and the dominant presence of institutional investors in such markets ensure that the content of legal regimes will be impounded in the cost of capital, whether they concern only corporate governance or include securities transactions. Accordingly, if mandatory securities rules benefit shareholders, notwithstanding the absence of empirical support in their favor, then competitive federalism will produce mandatory rules as well.

This is not to say that state competition is perfect. In the 1980s, when hostile takeovers emerged as a mechanism for changing control and, correlatively, for replacing incumbent management, the vast majority of states enacted laws that attempted to lower the probability of a hostile takeover. Because shareholders receive substantial premiums in hostile takeovers, most commentators hypothesized that the objective of these statutes was not to enhance shareholder welfare, but to entrench management. Indeed, some antitakeover statutes made explicit their non-shareholder-wealth-maximization objectives. Such laws, referred to as "other constituency statutes," permit management to consider interests other than those of shareholders (that is, factors besides the offered price) in deciding whether to oppose a bid.

Consistent with the view that restricting hostile takeovers is not beneficial to shareholders, the enactment of antitakeover laws produced negative or statistically insignificant stock price reactions. Delaware, with the largest stake in the chartering business, stands out, however, as an anomaly in the takeover statute legislative process. In contrast to its position as an innovator in corporation code provisions, in the takeover context Delaware was a laggard behind other states, and its regulation is considerably less restrictive of bids. More important, charter competition limits the extent to which states can restrict takeovers: When Pennsylvania enacted what was considered to be a draconian statute, a majority of firms opted out of its coverage because of demands made by their investors, who raised the prospect of selling their shares and reinvesting in firms incorporated in states with no statutes or less restrictive statutes, such as California and Delaware. Consequently, other states did not adopt the Pennsylvania statute.

There is also no evidence that a monopolist-regulator enforcing one national corporation law would produce better takeover regulation than the states. Quite to the contrary, in all likelihood a monopolist regulator would make the situation worse. The political dynamics of takeover regulation at the state level would be unchanged at the national level. The groups that are influential in state politics outside of Delaware—local firm managers— are as influential in Washington. They provide, for instance, the bulk of the witnesses testifying for takeover regulation. In addition, members of Congress whose districts included hostile takeover targets were the principal advocates for antitakeover legislation, just as states with hostile targets were the enactors of similar protective legislation. Moreover, the congressional legislation on takeovers enacted under the securities laws, the Williams Act, paralleling the state statutes, favors incumbent managers over bidders by delaying bids, and the overwhelming majority of bills introduced concerning federal takeover regulation since the Williams Act have sought to make hostile bids more difficult.

With only a national law, there would be no safety valve offered by a competing jurisdiction (such as California and Delaware in the current federal system of corporate law) to constrain takeover legislation, and a legislative or judicial mistake would be more difficult to reverse, as Congress moves considerably more slowly than state legislatures. As the experience with state takeover laws indicates, although in the short run there will be deviations from the optimum in a federal system, in the longer run competitive pressure is exerted when states make mistakes, as in the example of firms opting out of Pennsylvania's takeover statute. Such pressure is absent in an exclusive one-regulator system.

The empirical literature concerning the efficacy of state competition for corporate charters has been my focus of analysis, not only because an assessment of the efficacy of charter competition underlies the arguments for and against the market approach to securities regulation, but also because economic theory provides limited guidance concerning whether a monopolist will provide the optimal degree of product quality, variety, or innovation, issues of importance in the regulatory context. Whether a monopolist's choice of quality is socially optimal depends on the difference between the marginal and average consumers' willingness to pay for quality, as is true of price-taking competitors; whether the monopolist will undersupply quality compared to the competitive market depends on the elasticity of demand. There is a similar ambiguity concerning whether a monopolist will produce too few or too many products; the answer again depends on the elasticities of demand and whether the goods in question are substitutes....

II. Which State Should Be the Securities Domicile?

There are three plausible candidates for the single state whose rules govern a firm's securities transactions in place of the SEC: (1) a state chosen specifically for securities regulation by the issuer; (2) the issuer's incorporation state; and (3) the issuer's principal place of business. The first approach would be implemented through a choice-of-law clause in the corporation's charter (and noticed on the security). It would create, in effect, a statutory domicile for securities law. Under a choice-of-law clause approach, the choice of securities domicile could vary across a firm's financial instruments, as well as differ from the firm's statutory domicile (its incorporation state). The other two approaches operate automatically by the firm's choice of statutory domicile or headquarters site and hence would not require independent action by the corporation to effect a securities domicile choice, unless that choice were the SEC.

The least desirable securities domicile approach is to choose the state of principal place of business. This is because a physical presence requirement introduces friction into state competition. When physical and human capital must be relocated in order to effect a change in legal regime, a firm's decision to move to a more preferable securities domicile is considerably, if not prohibitively, more expensive than when such a relocation can be accomplished by means of a paper filing. Few firms would change domicile to take advantage of incremental legal improvements under such a domicile approach compared to the other two approaches and, correspondingly, the incentives of states to provide securities codes responsive to investor preferences would be sharply diminished. The difference between the domicile choice of incorporation state (statutory domicile) and state of physical presence (referred to as the "*siège réel*," the corporation's real or effective seat, in some European nations) in corporate law is, in fact, a principal reason for the absence of charter competition across the nations of the European Union compared to U.S. states.

Whether the most desirable approach for fostering competition over securities regulation is the choice-of-law clause or the incorporation state approach depends, in large part, on whether there are synergies from one state's administering both the corporate and securities law regimes. This is because the incorporation state approach harnesses the in-place apparatus of charter competition to the securities context. In general, such synergies should be substantial because corporate law expertise readily transfers to securities law. For instance, with one state's law adjudicating both corporate and securities issues, the standard for directors' and officers' fiduciary duties, including disclosure obligations, would be harmonized. More specifically, all litigation relating to conduct during hostile takeovers would be governed by one state's law. In addition, all legal issues concerning shareholder meetings would be subject to the same legal regime, eliminating the considerable confusion surrounding the SEC's rules regulating shareholder proxy proposals, which simultaneously look to state corporate law's allocation of authority between shareholders and managers and effectively ignore it. Where the synergies of an incorporation state securities domicile include the expertise of the judiciary, a firm could adopt a forum clause to ensure that securities claims are filed in the incorporation state.

But even if the substantive law synergies were limited in number, there is a further benefit associated with the incorporation state approach. Litigation costs would be reduced because the significance of line-drawing over whether a dispute implicates securities or corporate law is reduced, as the same sovereign's rules would apply in either scenario.

Although the arguments supporting the choice of incorporation state as the securities domicile appear to be compelling, there are countervailing considerations that militate against mandating such an approach rather than leaving the choice of domicile up to the issuer (the choice-of-law clause approach). First and most important, the choice-of-law clause approach obviates the need to guess whether the potential synergies of one regime for corporate and securities law are substantial—market participants' domicile choices would provide the information. It is therefore most consistent with the market approach to securities regulation. Second, given the variety of securities issued by firms, it is possible that states would specialize in different securities, and consequently, that firms could benefit from being able to select different domiciles for different issues. This is particularly relevant for debt securities, where there are no regulatory synergies with the incorporation state because corporate law deals solely with manager-shareholder relations. Third, permitting a self-standing securities domicile might enhance state competition, as a state could decide to compete more vigorously for securities issues than for corporate charters and thus prevent Delaware from being able to slouch on the securities regime it offers because of its success in obtaining incorporations....

III. Conclusion

This Article has advocated fundamental reform of the current strategy toward securities regulation by implementing a regulatory approach of competitive federalism, under which firms select their securities regulator from among the fifty states and the District of Columbia, the SEC, or other nations. Competitive federalism harnesses the high-powered incentives of markets to the regulatory state in order to produce regulatory arrangements compatible with investors' preferences. This is because firms will locate in the domicile whose regime investors prefer in order to reduce their cost of capital, and states have financial incentives (such as incorporation and registration fees) to adapt their securities regimes to firms' locational decisions. This prediction of securities market participants' and regulators' responses to competition is well-grounded: There is a substantial literature examining the workings of competitive federalism in the corporate charter setting that indicates that such regulatory competition does not harm, and in all likelihood benefits, investors.

To establish competitive federalism in the securities law context, the current choice-of-law rule for securities transactions must be altered to follow the issuer's securities domicile rather than the securities' site of sale. In addition, two procedural safeguards would be required of firms opting out of federal regulation: domicile disclosure upon securities purchases and a security-holder vote to effectuate a domicile change. These requirements ensure that informed investor preferences drive the regulatory competition. When competition is introduced, SEC rules and regulations that are not cost-effective or are otherwise detrimental to investors will be replaced by competing regulators with rules investors prefer, as the domicile choices of capital market participants establish a new regulatory equilibrium.

The mandatory federal securities regime has been in place for over sixty years, but the theoretical support for it is thin, and there is no empirical evidence indicating that it is effective in achieving its stated objectives. In fact, there is a developing literature pointing in the opposite direction. At a minimum, this literature suggests that the securities status quo should no longer be privileged, and that it should instead be opened up to market forces by means of competitive federalism. Corporation codes have benefited from precisely such competition. Although the current legislative trend in Congress, supported by both the proponents and opponents of the existing regulatory regime, is to seek to monopolize even further securities regulation at the federal level, this Article maintains that it would be far better public policy to expand, not restrain, state regulatory involvement. As long as only one state's law, chosen by the issuer, controls the regulation of a firm's securities transactions, regulatory competition will emerge, and there are compelling reasons to prefer such a regulatory arrangement to the mandatory federal regime.

Ehud Kamar, *A Regulatory Competition Theory of Indeterminacy in Corporate Law*[*]

... Federalism in American corporate law is widely thought to have bred a system of regulatory competition in which states formulate law to attract incorporation. While commentators disagree about the desirability of this regulatory competition—with race-to-the-bottom theorists arguing that it spawns overly pro-managerial laws, and race-to-the-top theorists arguing that it results in laws beneficial to shareholders—they agree that it induces states to play to corporate decisionmakers. They also agree that Delaware has emerged as a clear winner in this system, attracting over half of the large, publicly traded corporations.

Yet state competition theories fail to explain the well-documented indeterminacy of Delaware corporate law, which is evident in the state's ample use of vague standards that make prediction of legal outcomes difficult. While Delaware law offers relatively clear rules that govern technical aspects of corporate governance, the fiduciary duties at its core are open-ended. They define only crudely the guidelines for managerial behavior, and rely heavily on ad hoc judicial interpretation. Indeterminacy poses a challenge to

---

[*] Originally published in 98 COLUMBIA LAW REVIEW 1908 (1998). Reprinted with permission.

both race-to-the-bottom and race-to-the-top theories because it obstructs business planning and thereby harms managers and shareholders alike.

This Article suggests an explanation for Delaware's legal indeterminacy based on a view of state competition as imperfect competition. While current theories assume perfect competition among states and hence optimal law (either for shareholders or for managers), this Article claims that Delaware has market power that allows it to engage in anticompetitive behavior. Specifically, I argue that Delaware law may be less determinate than is optimal and yet still stimulate demand. Although indeterminacy diminishes the value to corporations of Delaware law, it diminishes the value of rival laws to a greater extent by stymieing their compatibility with Delaware law.

I. The Indeterminacy of Delaware Corporate Law

Delaware has been praised for its elaborate body of corporate case law, which is argued to be the reason why many firms choose to incorporate there. According to this view, the mass of corporate litigation channeled to Delaware has culminated in a comprehensive set of precedents that facilitates business planning. Nevertheless, a multiplicity of precedents does not necessarily result in optimal predictability. In the case of Delaware corporate law, court decisions merely reiterate and apply to different fact patterns a small number of fit-all legal standards, leaving much uncertainty to be resolved. To be sure, the large conglomerate of precedents in Delaware may well lend a higher degree of predictability to the law than that achieved by other states with fewer precedents. Corporate actors in Delaware do have an idea of which practices increase the risk of liability, and which reduce it. Compliance with the recommended practices, however, only reduces the risk, and never eliminates it. While the existence of a large stock of precedents makes Delaware law more predictable and hence more conducive to business planning than the laws of other states, the law is less predictable than it could be. The discussion below will elaborate on these points. After illustrating the open-ended nature of Delaware law, it will argue that, in light of the importance of certainty in corporate law, Delaware law seems too indeterminate.

A. Fact-Intensive Standards

Legal norms can be sorted along a continuum, with the two poles being rules and standards. Rules delineate the law ex ante. Their application in court requires determination only of whether their pre-set conditions were met. Standards do not provide a clear pronouncement of the law ex ante. Rather, they lay out general principles to be applied by judges to particular sets of facts. The more judicial discretion a law permits, the closer it is to a standard; the more it constrains judicial discretion, the closer it is to a rule.

Delaware law is at one end of this continuum. It relies extensively on broad legal standards that grant courts wide discretion in deciding corporate disputes. Delaware courts are reluctant to provide corporate actors with bright-line rules distinguishing legitimate from illegitimate actions. Instead, their decisions involve loosely defined legal tests whose precise meaning depends on the particular facts of each case. It is difficult to generalize from these tests. Their meaning is revealed only when they are applied by the court to specific scenarios.

The following three examples of fact-intensive legal standards illustrate this point. Consider first the proportionality test governing antitakeover defensive measures. It requires showing that the board had "reasonable grounds for believing that a danger to corporate policy and effectiveness existed," and that the defensive action was "reasonable in relation to the threat posed." The law does not define what constitutes a cognizable threat in this regard, nor does it clarify what defensive measures are reasonable. Instead, it lists a host of considerations that may be relevant: "inadequacy of the price offered, nature and timing of the offer, questions of illegality, the impact on 'constituencies' other than shareholders (i.e., creditors, customers, employees, and perhaps even the community generally), the risk of nonconsummation, and the quality of securities being offered in the exchange," as well as the "basic stockholder interests at stake, including those of short term speculators, whose actions may have fueled the coercive aspect of the offer at the expense of the long term investor." At a certain stage during the evolution of the proportionality test, Court of Chancery decisions did seem to clarify what would amount to a cognizable threat by distinguishing between coercive and noncoercive takeover bids. The Delaware Supreme Court, however, overturned these decisions as unduly restrictive of the flexible proportionality test. To the dismay of many, the proportionality test is as indeterminate today as when the court first articulated it in 1985.

Consider next the doctrine of corporate opportunity. To determine whether a business opportunity belongs to the corporation and cannot be usurped by officers or directors, the court examines whether the corporation is financially able to exploit the opportunity, whether the opportunity is in the corporation's line of business and is of practical advantage to it, whether the corporation has an interest or reasonable expectancy in the opportunity, and whether seizing the opportunity will bring the interest of the officer or director into conflict with that of the corporation. These tests, however, only "provide guidelines to be considered by a reviewing court in balancing the equities of an individual case. No one factor is dispositive and all factors must be taken into account insofar as they are applicable." In the opinion of prominent commentators, such tests are intolerably ambiguous and uncertain in application.

Consider last the test used by the court for reviewing a decision of a special board committee to seek a derivative suit's dismissal. Under Delaware law, the court will apply a two-step test to the motion to dismiss the suit. First, the court will "inquire into the independence and good faith of the committee and the bases supporting its conclusions." If the court is satisfied "that the committee was independent and showed reasonable bases for good faith findings and recommendations," the court "may proceed, in its discretion," to the next step of determining, by "applying its own independent business judgment, whether the motion should be granted." This second step "is intended to thwart instances where corporate actions meet the criteria of step one, but the result does not appear to satisfy its spirit, or where corporate actions would simply prematurely terminate a stockholder grievance deserving of further consideration in the corporation's interest." The court must "carefully consider and weigh how compelling the corporate interest in dismissal is when faced with a non-frivolous lawsuit." When doing so, the court may give consideration to such broad matters as "law and public policy in addition to the corporation's best interests." In other words, the court is entrusted not only with applying open-ended standards to the case at bar, but also with determining which standards it will apply. In both decisions, the court is guided by little more than experience and common sense.

These examples illustrate the general trend in Delaware corporate law. One can never be confident that a certain corporate action will be upheld in court, given that a litany of factors, which are neither conclusive, nor cumulative, nor prioritized, can come into play. Even understanding past decisions in and of themselves can be puzzling, since fact-specific decisions often do not square with each other. Determinative facts in one case may be less consequential in another, creating the impression of inconsistency.

A brief look at two landmark takeover cases, *Paramount v. Time*[13] and *Paramount v. QVC*,[14] demonstrates this point. Both cases involved corporations that were close to consummating a negotiated merger and rejected a last-minute tender offer that attempted to derail the merger. In the first case, the court approved the rejection. In the second case, it reached the opposite conclusion. The key to explaining the different outcomes, without dismissing them as inconsistent, is a close reading of factual nuances that color management's behavior differently in the two cases. This, however, can only be done in hindsight. Predicting the second decision on the basis of the first was much more difficult. This example is not unique, but rather illustrates a common pattern in Delaware case law. In many cases, the impression of inconsistency can be avoided only if the holdings are read together with their underlying facts. Such a reading, however, is of limited value in business planning, as it does not always predict what facts will be deemed material by the next court.

B. Suboptimal Indeterminacy

It is hard to prove that Delaware's legal indeterminacy is suboptimal. Theoretically, it is possible that Delaware law does strike an optimal balance between determinacy and flexibility. In the following paragraphs I address this difficulty. My argument is that, while some indeterminacy in corporate law may be inevitable, the degree of indeterminacy in Delaware law appears too high. Optimal determinacy is a function of the legal context in question. In corporate law, business planning needs render legal determinacy vital. Since legal standards are indeterminate in comparison to legal rules, an optimal law would limit their role, and when they were unavoidable, use them in a way that minimized uncertainty. The observed structure of Delaware law is very different from this model. It relies heavily on open-ended legal standards that admit myriad factual criteria as relevant.

Business planners often stress the importance of being able to carry out transactions with minimal risk of liability. Yet open-ended standards lead to greater legal exposure. Instead of delineating what can and what cannot be done, they leave this question open to ex post judicial determination. Such indeterminacy imposes high costs on individuals who try to plan their behavior so that it will meet legal requirements. As the law becomes more uncertain, they face higher costs of legal advice, and a greater risk of litigation.

Corporate managers and directors fall squarely into this category. Having invested their entire human capital in the firm, they are highly averse to the risk of being sued by shareholders. While litigation is unlikely to cost them their jobs, liability can damage their reputations and future careers. In addition to reputational effects, legal exposure also entails a risk of personal liability for damages in amounts that far exceed their personal wealth. All these costs of legal indeterminacy are passed on to the firm, which may pay dearly for legal services, liability insurance, and missed business opportunities.

The obvious way of avoiding the indeterminacy associated with open-ended standards is the employment of rules. Not all rules are so rigid as to preclude their use in the relational context of corporate law. For instance, procedural and structural rules that stipulate how

---

13. 571 A.2d 1140 (Del. 1990).
14. 637 A.2d 34 (Del. 1994).

decisions should be made in the firm without dictating their content can be both determinate and flexible. The same is true of rules that limit directorial ability to interfere with shareholder choice in defined situations. Such rules may stipulate, for instance, that boards must allow shareholders to decide whether to accept or reject noncoercive takeover bids. Even rules that prescribe a binding course of action for a firm may be desirable, despite their rigidity, if their benefits outweigh their costs. An example of such a rule is the proposal to ban full-time executives in public corporations from taking any other active business positions.

Notwithstanding the preference for bright-line rules, some issues in corporate law are best governed by flexible standards. This does not imply, however, that a high level of indeterminacy must follow. Standards can reduce indeterminacy by limiting and prioritizing the criteria relevant to their application, adopting presumptions, or ruling certain options in or out. Delaware law makes little use of such techniques. Rather, as the courts often hold, many factors can bear on the outcome of a case. No single factor is dispositive, and factors other than those enumerated by the court may prove to be relevant in other circumstances. Delaware law also fails to employ presumptions to reduce uncertainty. For instance, it subjects to fiduciary duties any shareholder that holds at least half of the voting power in a firm or otherwise exercises actual control over its business decisions. What amounts to actual control is never defined. But it could be. The proposal advanced [in the American Law Institute's Principles of Corporate Governance § 1.10(b)], for example, provides more determinacy without compromising flexibility. It adopts a presumption that holding one quarter of the voting power confers control over the firm. Finally, Delaware law offers no safe harbors, compliance with which would preclude judicial review and reduce uncertainty. It is instructive in this regard to compare Delaware law with federal securities law, which, in addition to being rule-based, makes use of safe harbors to accompany standards where rules cannot readily be devised.

The preceding paragraphs do not prove that the level of legal indeterminacy in Delaware is excessive. It is doubtful that such a claim could be proved at all. Nonetheless, by contrasting the importance of legal determinacy to business planning with the low level of determinacy in Delaware law, they present strong circumstantial evidence pointing in that direction. Some indeterminacy in corporate law is probably inescapable, but Delaware's extensive reliance on loosely defined standards seems to go far beyond what is necessary. This conclusion is consistent with similar sentiments expressed by academics and practitioners alike. To the practical mind, the existence of such sentiments may be the ultimate proof of the claim.

The tension between the primacy of legal certainty in business planning and the high level of indeterminacy in the leading incorporation state presents a puzzle. How can Delaware offer overly indeterminate law without being dethroned by another state offering a better alternative? This Article argues that the observed structure of the market for corporate chartering provides little assurance that Delaware leads by selling an optimal product, either to shareholders or to managers. The disproportionate market share that Delaware has held for a prolonged period of time suggests that the chartering market is not perfectly competitive. Delaware enjoys various competitive advantages that protect its market share and allow it to engage in uncompetitive behavior without losing business. Delaware can take advantage of its competitive position by charging a higher franchise tax than other states, as well as by offering corporate law that is overly indeterminate, but that still enhances its competitive position in the market.

Since even suboptimal indeterminacy may assist Delaware in maintaining its lead, there is no reason to interpret the survival of indeterminacy as proof of its optimality. The frequently voiced criticism of excessive indeterminacy in Delaware law may thus be well-founded. On the other hand, showing that suboptimal indeterminacy can benefit Delaware does not prove that Delaware's indeterminate law is in fact suboptimal. This Article therefore does not definitively conclude that Delaware law is suboptimally indeterminate. Rather, it argues that Delaware law may well be so.

II. Delaware's Competitive Advantages

The debate over the desirability of interstate competition in corporate chartering has become a staple of corporate legal scholarship in the United States. It centers on whether Delaware law, the clear winner in the competition, attracts firms by protecting investors or by protecting managers. But any such favoritism cannot in itself explain the preeminence of Delaware. Other states clearly could adopt laws that protect either shareholders or managers, just as Delaware does. Nevada, for instance, followed the Delaware model closely, and yet failed to lure significant incorporation. Something other than the tilt of Delaware law must therefore account for its lead. Below I analyze three competitive advantages that commentators recognize as supporting Delaware's lead. These advantages include the ease of using an already popular law; the proficiency of the Delaware judiciary in corporate adjudication; and the state's commitment to corporate needs that results from its dependence on chartering. All of these are first-mover advantages. Ever since Delaware established its dominant position in the market for corporate law, these advantages have made competition with Delaware difficult.

A. Network and Learning Externalities

One advantage that Delaware has over its rivals is the lure of network and learning externalities that accrue to firms incorporated in the state. Network externalities are the increasing returns to users of a product as the total number of users grows. The telephone is a classic example. The greater the number of telephone users, the more extensive the telephone network becomes, and the higher its value for each user. The car is another example. As the number of car owners increases, the supply of roads, gas stations, and garages increases, and the more valuable each car becomes.

Corporate law can also be viewed as a product whose value increases with the number of corporations using it.[15] First, as more corporations are governed by the same law, court decisions begin to accumulate that apply that law to various factual settings and increase legal certainty. Moreover, the law sometimes refers to a common practice as a benchmark for appropriate conduct. The more firms that are subject to the same law, the more common is the practice, and the more certain is the benchmark. Second, a commonly used law is likely to be better serviced by lawyers. As the number of firms needing legal counseling and representation in connection with a certain law increases, lawyers gain expertise in providing these services. Lawyers can also refer to the legal commentary, reference tools, and professional symposia that proliferate around a commonly used law. Legal services

---

15. The discussion below is based on [Marcel Kahan & Michael Klausner, *Standardization and Innovation in Corporate Contracting (or "The Economics of Boilerplate")*, 83 VA. L. REV. 713, 718–29 (1997)] and [Michael Klausner, *Corporations, Corporate Law, and Networks of Contracts*, 81 VA. L. REV. 757, 772–89 (1995)].

improve in quality and timeliness, while legal costs fall. Third, the marketability of securities improves as the network grows. Legal uniformity facilitates securities pricing by making comparison with other securities on the market easier. When a security is subject to the same legal regime as many other securities, it can be priced more accurately and cheaply.

Network externalities are forward-looking. They reflect the value added by the wide use of the product at present. In corporate law, this means that contemporaneous use of a law by many firms adds to its value, because this use will produce the benefits discussed above in the future. A product may also have an added value because of its wide use in the past, which mirrors these network externalities. For example, past use may have generated comprehensive case law and first-rate legal services. These benefits, termed "learning externalities," are different from network externalities, as they do not depend on the number of firms using the law at present. They are nonetheless related to network externalities, in that a product widely used in the past is often still widely used in the present.

Delaware law, being the most widely used corporate law, offers greater network and learning externalities to corporations than do rival laws. It boasts comprehensive case law, superb legal services, and improved marketability of securities, resulting from its extensive present use, as well as similar benefits resulting from its past use. In order to lure corporations away from Delaware, rival laws must be sufficiently superior to offset these benefits.

B. Judicial Proficiency

Another important source of Delaware's attractiveness is its experienced judiciary.[16] The preeminence of the Delaware judiciary stems from its unique history. Delaware initially replaced New Jersey as the leader in corporate chartering early in this century, following changes in New Jersey law that were unfavorable to business. Delaware has never lost its lead, and its courts, particularly the Court of Chancery, have gained experience in corporate adjudication and earned a reputation for proficiency. The courts were ideally suited to do so due to their small size, low caseload, selected judges, and a concentration of corporate cases. Once established, their qualitative advantage became self-perpetuating, as it attracted still more high-stake corporate cases, prominent corporate lawyers, and talented judges.

The advantage of Delaware's courts is twofold. First, they are experienced in deciding corporate matters. Over the years, Delaware courts have adapted to this task in a way that is difficult for other courts to emulate. Delaware judges possess experience as a group that would take time to amass. Moreover, they continuously hone their superior skills through hearing cases. Frequent exposure to corporate disputes is a key element in the quality of corporate adjudicators. Not only does it keep judges current, but it also enables them to compare cases they hear and distinguish the meritorious from the frivolous. Even if other states were to recruit experienced corporate jurists to their courts, those courts would subsequently lose their initial advantage if few cases were filed in them.

Second, over the years, Delaware courts have earned a unique reputation for quality adjudication. This reputation is particularly meaningful since the quality of courts can be

---

16. [See Bernard S. Black, *Is Corporate Law Trivial? A Political and Economic Analysis*, 84 Nw. U. L. Rev. 542, 589–90 (1990); Roberta Romano, *Law as a Product: Some Pieces of the Incorporation Puzzle*, 1 J.L. Econ. & Org. 225, 280 (1985)].

ascertained only through the use of their services. Even if a rival state recruited judges proficient in corporate law—a difficult task in itself, when that state's judiciary has no prior reputation—the market would react slowly to this new recruitment.

The significance of the judicial advantage is not merely theoretical. It is demonstrated by the fact that the bulk of suits pursuant to Delaware corporate law are filed in the Delaware Court of Chancery, although they could be brought in federal or other state courts. A likely explanation is that plaintiffs consider Delaware's judiciary to be better than those of other states.

C. Credible Commitment

A third advantage supporting Delaware is its credible commitment to the needs of corporations. Delaware is the only state that has grown dependent on income generated by corporate chartering, and is therefore the only state that must constantly ensure that its law meets corporate needs. In a direct sense, Delaware depends on revenues from its franchise tax. More indirectly, its sunk investments in legal capital are valuable only if it can retain the chartering business. This legal capital includes comprehensive case law, judicial expertise in corporation law, administrative expertise in the processing of corporate filings, and a specialized bar.[17]

This advantage for Delaware is a disadvantage for other states. Since only Delaware is credibly committed to corporate needs, investors discount any other state law by the risk of adverse future changes in that law. A rival state may not be able to monger chartering business away from Delaware simply by offering better law. Charging a lower franchise tax to attract incorporation may not help either, because it will make the rival's own commitment to corporations even less credible compared to Delaware's commitment.

III. Enhancement of Competitiveness Through Indeterminacy

This Part suggests an explanation for the indeterminacy of Delaware law. Indeterminate law enhances Delaware's competitive advantages—network externalities, judicial advantage, and credible commitment—and thus reinforces its market power. Indeterminacy makes Delaware law incompatible with other laws, thereby excluding non-Delaware firms from network benefits. As long as this exclusion reduces the value of rival laws by more than indeterminacy reduces the value of Delaware law, the competitive edge that Delaware has over its rivals is heightened. The differential effect of indeterminacy on the respective values of Delaware law and rival laws is bolstered by two additional effects that mitigate, only for Delaware, the costs of legal indeterminacy. First, the centrality of courts under indeterminate law accentuates the judicial advantage that Delaware enjoys over other states. Second, legal indeterminacy strengthens Delaware's commitment to corporate needs by making its versatile system of corporate adjudication more valuable for the state. Finally, incompatibility with other states' laws raises the cost to Delaware corporations of reincorporating elsewhere, cementing Delaware's large market share. To secure these competitive advantages, it is worthwhile for Delaware to adopt even overly indeterminate law.

Previous scholarship has recognized that legal indeterminacy may benefit the Delaware bar by generating demand for legal services. This scholarship acknowledges that Delaware's

---

17. [See ROBERTA ROMANO, THE GENIUS OF AMERICAN CORPORATE LAW 39 (1993)].

competitive advantages allow it to raise the cost of incorporation in Delaware above the cost of incorporation elsewhere. A straightforward way to exploit this advantage is to charge a higher franchise tax. While Delaware does in fact charge a higher franchise tax than other states, the tax is lower than it could be because the state's indeterminate law invites excessive litigation. Firms regard the high exposure to litigation as part of the price they pay for incorporation in Delaware and reduce the amount of franchise tax they are willing to pay accordingly. Delaware accepts the loss of potential tax revenue because its lawmaking apparatus is captured by the bar. The explanation I advance below for legal indeterminacy in Delaware is not at odds with the claim that indeterminacy benefits the corporate bar. But, I argue, indeterminacy may also benefit the state as a whole by enhancing its competitive position in the market for corporate law and entrenching its lead.

A. Network Externalities

Under imperfect competition, a producer can gain by taking anticompetitive measures that increase its competitive advantage over other market participants. In particular, a producer whose product confers network benefits on consumers gains if it can exclude rival products from the network. As long as rival products are incompatible, they cannot offer similar network benefits, and both old and new consumers will prefer the dominant product in order to avoid being stranded from the network.

Legal indeterminacy allows Delaware to exclude other states from its unparalleled network externalities. To be sure, if Delaware had determinate law, it would still offer network externalities to chartered corporations. But other states would quickly emulate this law in order to link up with the network and offer comparable externalities. The value of Delaware law would increase by the value of determinacy. The value of other states' laws, however, would increase not only by the value of determinacy but also by the value of Delaware's otherwise exclusive network externalities. The loss of its competitive advantage would cost Delaware more than its gain from product improvement.

When Delaware law is indeterminate, its content cannot be captured in a firm set of rules, and the courts must give it meaning piecemeal. Other states may well adopt Delaware's current law wholesale. But states cannot adopt future Delaware law as well. Blindly committing themselves to future statutes and court decisions of another state is politically unthinkable and fraught with practical difficulties.

In fact, even if importation of future Delaware law were feasible, it would not be enough to secure compatibility with the Delaware practice. The importing state would also need to have Delaware judges apply the law. Other judges, no matter how skilled and experienced, could not divine how a Delaware judge would decide a given case. While Delaware cases would automatically be binding in other jurisdictions, non-Delaware cases would not be binding in Delaware, and the laws of Delaware and other states would gradually diverge. Thus, for example, a lawyer specializing in Delaware law could not advise a non-Delaware corporation without first consulting the case law of the relevant state, and investors comparing that firm to Delaware firms could not assume that they are subject to the same law. To the extent that such network externalities are valuable, the only way for firms to benefit from them would be by incorporating in Delaware.

The exclusion of other states from network externalities can benefit Delaware even if this advantage is achieved through the adoption of an overly indeterminate law. While such law is worth less than determinate law to corporations, it forestalls compatibility and secures exclusive network externalities to Delaware. As long as exclusion from network externalities reduces the value of rival laws by more than indeterminacy reduces that of

Delaware law, the demand for Delaware law will increase. The reason for this is that corporations compare the value of Delaware law to that of rival laws. Since the value of Delaware law relative to rival laws is higher when Delaware law is indeterminate, the demand for Delaware law will increase notwithstanding any decline in its absolute value....

B. *Judicial Proficiency*

In addition to excluding rival states from network externalities, legal indeterminacy accentuates Delaware's judicial advantage over other states. It does so by inducing litigation, and at the same time leaving more discretion to the courts in applying the law. The value of determinate law may also increase when it is applied by a proficient court, but the increase in the value of indeterminate law is greater still. Compare, for example, New York law and Delaware law concerning judicial review of a litigation committee's motion to dismiss a derivative suit. New York law requires that the court examine only the disinterestedness of the committee members and the adequacy of the investigative procedures they pursued. Delaware law requires that the court, in addition to conducting this examination, also use its own business judgment to assess the committee's decision on its merits. While both laws can benefit from application by proficient courts, it is clear that a court applying Delaware law has a greater impact on the outcome.

Corporate law is transferable, as the convergence of other states' laws to the Delaware model demonstrates. Judicial quality, by contrast, is relatively fixed. If Delaware courts formulate tests that are most valuable when applied by them, legal plagiarism becomes infeasible. By adopting indeterminate law, Delaware may be reducing the intrinsic value of its law, but this reduction is partially offset by a more pronounced judicial advantage. By contrast, states with less proficient judiciaries are not similarly compensated for adopting indeterminate law. In fact, by expanding the role of their less proficient judiciaries, they increase their disadvantage.

The previous Section demonstrated how Delaware can gain from reducing the value of rival laws even at the cost of reducing the value of its own law. Firms incorporate in Delaware based on the value of Delaware law relative to that of rival laws. While excessive indeterminacy reduces the value of Delaware law, it also reduces the value of rival laws by excluding them from network externalities. Delaware's proficient judiciary mitigates the reduction in the value of Delaware law, thereby further increasing its value relative to rival laws.

C. *Credible Commitment*

Indeterminacy, in addition to excluding other states from network externalities and allowing Delaware full exploitation of its judicial advantage, may also benefit Delaware by reinforcing its commitment to corporate needs. Delaware is said to have made a credible commitment to maintain the quality of its law by making itself economically dependent on corporate chartering. To the extent that this dependence results from reliance on franchise tax revenues, it is not affected by Delaware's adoption of either determinate or indeterminate law. Reliance on revenues from the franchise tax adds the same value to Delaware law when it is determinate as when it is indeterminate.

But Delaware's commitment is based on more than its reliance on revenues from the franchise tax. It is also based on sunk investments that Delaware has made in expert judges, comprehensive case law, and administrative expertise in processing corporate litigation. Moreover, Delaware has established local legal services as well as office and accommodation facilities to support litigation activity to an extent unusual for a state of its size. All these legal assets are closely linked to the indeterminate and litigation-oriented nature of Delaware law. It was legal indeterminacy that historically required Delaware to invest in these assets, and it continues to make them valuable today. Legal indeterminacy may thus strengthen Delaware's commitment to leadership in corporate chartering and render this commitment more valuable. This effect is similar to that of the enhancement of the judicial advantage discussed earlier. The benefit that Delaware derives from increasing the value of its credible commitment may not in itself be enough to induce legal indeterminacy, but may mitigate the reduction in the value of Delaware law due to indeterminacy, thus making the exclusion of rival states from network externalities more profitable.

D. Switching Costs

There is no consensus in legal scholarship on the magnitude of the costs that firms incur when migrating between states. Some commentators believe that these costs influence migration decisions; others downplay their significance. Whatever the costs of migration, indeterminacy raises them by making Delaware law incompatible with other laws, thus further benefiting Delaware.

When laws are incompatible, reincorporation in a new state requires learning and adapting to a new law. This is clear with respect to the learning and adaptation that would be necessary for in-house counsel, directors, and officers, all of whom remain with the firm after reincorporation. But such switching costs also apply to any learning and adaptation done by outside counsel. While a migrating firm can replace its outside counsel with a new one specializing in the new law, that firm still incurs switching costs associated with the time and effort needed to establish a working relationship with its new counsel.

The incompatibility of Delaware law with other laws as a result of its indeterminacy increases the costs of immigration just as it increases the costs of emigration. In both cases, the migrating firm must adjust to the law of the destination state, a need that would be obviated if the laws were compatible. The symmetric increase in the costs of both types of migration is worthwhile for Delaware, however, because it dominates the market, and would stand to lose more firms than other states if their laws were compatible....

IV. The Political Economy of Delaware's Indeterminacy

While indeterminacy may enhance the competitive position of Delaware, it is unlikely that anyone designed Delaware law to this end. To be sure, interpreting legal indeterminacy as a strategy would be in line with state competition commentary, which assumes strategic formulation of Delaware law to attract corporations. Nonetheless, as this Part will argue, a more plausible explanation links the indeterminacy of Delaware law to the influence of the corporate bar, judicial preferences, and a court-centered legal culture. Although these forces had little to do with a calculated plan to use indeterminacy to secure market power, they were able to bring about this result. Thus, the competitive advantage that Delaware derives from legal indeterminacy may have shaped its law indirectly. It was the absence of constraining market forces that allowed Delaware to develop indeterminate law while retaining its preeminence. Had it not been profitable, Delaware would have been less likely to yield to the influences that made its law indeterminate; and if it had yielded, its dominance would have been eroded.

A. Lawyers as an Interest Group

Interest-group theorists describe the corporate bar, and particularly the Delaware corporate bar, as an influential interest group that, through its involvement in legislation and judicial appointments, has made Delaware law indeterminate and litigation-oriented in order to generate demand for legal services.[18] According to this view, firms view exposure to litigation as a cost they incur along with a state's franchise tax. Delaware could raise its franchise tax if it reduced firms' exposure to litigation by making its law more determinate. It does not do so because of the bar's political clout.

This Article suggests that indeterminate and litigation-oriented law is not necessarily inimical to the interests of Delaware, and indeed may enhance its competitiveness. Relations between the bar and the state may therefore be symbiotic rather than confrontational. This alignment of interest sheds new light on the interest group theory of Delaware law. First, greater indeterminacy is possible when it supports, rather than merely exploits, market power. Second, less political clout is needed than was previously believed to induce Delaware lawmakers to develop indeterminate law. This is not to say that the bar's interest in legal indeterminacy is irrelevant. Rather, the bar has been one of the visible driving forces that have made Delaware law indeterminate. This confluence of forces is important, since it is implausible that legal indeterminacy was intentionally designed as an anticompetitive strategy.

B. Judicial Preferences

Delaware's judges may also be inclined toward legal indeterminacy as a consequence of their own preference for wide judicial discretion. Judges generally give up a successful and lucrative legal career to assume a judgeship. In doing so, they are motivated mainly by nonpecuniary rewards, such as prestige, challenge, and a sense of serving society. The intangible rewards of judging are most pronounced under indeterminate corporate law, which places judges at the center of the business arena. This incentive is particularly powerful when the usual judicial aversion to increased workload is absent. Since dockets in Delaware are not congested, and judges are already specialized in corporate law when appointed, they may encourage corporate litigation and develop intricate corporate jurisprudence. Indeterminacy in Delaware law may thus feed on itself by inviting more litigation, which may in turn produce more indeterminacy.

V. Implications

The theory presented above offers an alternative account of Delaware's uninterrupted lead in corporate chartering. It shifts the focus away from the substance of Delaware law toward its form as an explanation for Delaware's success. While substance can be emulated by other states, an indeterminate form is more difficult to copy and serves to accentuate the advantages that Delaware has over its rivals. Several implications follow

---

18. Douglas M. Branson, *Indeterminacy: The Final Ingredient in an Interest Group Analysis of Corporate Law*, 43 VAND. L. REV. 85, 111 (1990); Jonathan Macey and Geoffrey Miller, *Toward an Interest-Group Theory of Delaware Corporate Law*, 65 TEX. L. REV. 469, 505 (1987).

from this theory. One clear implication is that, whether Delaware law favors managers or shareholders, it may harm both by being too indeterminate. Another implication is that competition among regulators, in the market for corporate law as well as in other markets, is susceptible to anticompetitive behavior that may not breed the law most desired by consumers. Such an outcome is conceivable, for example, in a market for securities law, should such a market be formed. Last, the centrality of adjudication under indeterminate law helps to explain investor fragmentation and passivity in the United States.

A. Social Welfare

An unfavorable picture emerges on calculation of the possible inefficiencies of Delaware's indeterminate law. First, legal indeterminacy is costly. It obstructs business planning by corporate managers and invites expensive litigation. Delaware firms that wish to avoid these costs have no real alternative. By incorporating elsewhere, they would forgo the benefits of network externalities and a proficient judiciary, and might well not benefit from a clearer law. Second, legal indeterminacy isolates firms incorporated in other states from the Delaware network. The excluded firms then miss the network benefits offered by Delaware law. Delaware firms also lose, because their network remains smaller than it could be, and so their network benefits are not maximized. The unrealized potential of a larger network is a cost to them just as it is to firms in other states. Third, Delaware's indeterminacy increases the cost of switching between states, thereby artificially differentiating the market without the benefit of wider product choice. If other states were able to attain compatibility with Delaware, this needless friction would be spared.

B. Theories of the Market for Corporate Law

At this stage, it is useful to relate the thesis of this Article to the state competition debate. Two diametrically opposed views define the boundaries of that debate. Race-to-the-top adherents contend that incorporation decisions prioritize investor interests, and consequently improve the quality of states' corporate laws. Race-to-the-bottom adherents believe that incorporation decisions prioritize management interests, and consequently lower the quality of states' corporate laws. An intermediate position is that some managerial decisions are made with a view to shareholder interests, while other decisions serve the interests of managers themselves. State competition is productive with respect to the former decisions and destructive with respect to the latter. This Article is consistent with all of these views.

That this Article is consistent with a race-to-the-top theory is clear from the fact that all the advantages accentuated by indeterminacy—network externalities, judicial advantage, and credible commitment—benefit investors and managers alike. The argument that Delaware increases its market power by accentuating these advantages is thus consistent with an alignment between management and shareholders. The argument is also consistent, however, with a lack of such alignment. The race-to-the-bottom theory holds that investor interests are subordinated to management interests only when they are in direct conflict. There is no such conflict with regard to indeterminacy. Exposure to legal risk is undesirable from the standpoint of investors as well as managers. Delaware law attracts firms despite its riskiness because indeterminacy accentuates the competitive advantages that both investors and managers appreciate.

In sum, strategic indeterminacy is consistent with both the race-to-the-top and the race-to-the-bottom theories. In the former case, it undercuts the argument that corporate law is efficient. In the latter case, it adds another level of inefficiency. In both cases, it is detrimental to social welfare.

C. Agenda for Future Research

The theory of regulatory competition has been known for more than four decades, and its precursors in the context of corporate law are even older. Throughout this time, the theory limited itself to using only a few of the tools provided by industrial organization economics. Traditional theory treats regulatory rivalry as perfect competition in a market for laws, which necessarily yields the law most appealing to consumers. In corporate law, managers are the immediate consumers — through their central role in making incorporation decisions — and their incentives determine the direction of the competition.

The disagreement between proponents and opponents of state competition is not about whether the market is competitive, but whether managers make socially optimal choices. Opponents of state competition argue that managers are not aligned with shareholders. The outcome of state competition, they argue, is indeed the law most desired by managers, which is precisely what makes it socially suboptimal. They therefore advocate federal corporate law, which avoids undesirable competition. Unfortunately, federal law may result in monopolistic regulatory behavior, as has arguably happened to federal securities regulation. Monopolistic regulators may charge supracompetitive prices, provide low-quality law, and be captured by interest groups.

This Article suggests imperfect competition as a plausible intermediate regulatory structure between perfect competition and monopoly. Under imperfect competition, regulators may employ various strategies to enhance their market position, even if these strategies are detrimental to consumers of the law. Previous commentary has recognized that regulatory markets are often imperfectly competitive, allowing dominant regulators to price their law higher than the competitive price. This Article extends the literature by arguing that imperfect competition lends itself to other forms of uncompetitive behavior as well, and in particular to a preference by the dominant regulator for indeterminate and judge-oriented corporate law. By no means does this exhaust the panoply of strategies that regulators may employ to enhance their competitive position and exploit it to maximize profits. Future research may explore other strategies and other legal contexts....

VI. Conclusion

Participants in the state competition controversy agree that, to date, Delaware is the undisputed winner. They part company only on why. Whereas race-to-the-bottom adherents argue that Delaware attracts corporate managers to the detriment of investors, race-to-the-top adherents argue that the interests of investors and managers are aligned, rendering Delaware's law advantageous to both. What has thus far received little attention is that, no matter where the race is headed, it may not be a race among equals. That Delaware has commanded the market for corporate chartering for close to a century raises the suspicion that the market for corporate law is not perfectly competitive. What has been missing from the debate is the possibility that Delaware utilizes its market power to enhance its competitive position.

This Article attempts to fill this gap in the state competition story. According to the amended story, Delaware's preeminence is reinforced by the indeterminate nature of its law, which makes it impractical to copy. Although indeterminacy may not be optimal, it secures barriers to entry—such as network externalities, judicial advantage, and credible commitment—that protect Delaware. This strategy need not have been premeditated. Judicial tendencies, the interests of the bar, investor apathy, and the general legal culture may have serendipitously combined to encourage it.

This leads to a more general reflection on the nature of corporate law. The centrality of the courts is a unique feature of American corporate law. The sophistication and reliability of American courts do not explain the stark difference between the American system and those of other developed countries. It has been commonplace to compare corporate governance in the United States with that in other industrialized countries such as Germany, Britain, and Japan. Yet in none of those countries do courts play a role in corporate law similar to that played by courts in the United States. It is implausible that courts in those countries are inherently less equipped than their American counterparts to handle corporate disputes. If corporate governance by courts were optimal, then a comparable role for the judiciary might have developed in at least one of those countries as well. That it has not suggests that the American model may not be optimal, but rather an outcome of the peculiar evolution of American corporate law.

If there were no reason to question the efficiency of the American model, its uniqueness could be dismissed as an efficient adaptation to the idiosyncratic conditions of this country. This Article offers such reasons, by explaining the centrality of adjudication in American corporate law as a product of state competition. Rather than being a virtue, judicial predominance is what allows one state to maintain its dominance in the market for corporate law. By being judge-oriented, Delaware corporate law becomes a proprietary product of Delaware, one that other states find difficult to match.

Discussion Questions

1. Does Delaware's judge-made corporate law provide "reasonable predictability," as Rock argues, "practical" and "efficient" results, as Strine argues, or impose excessive "indeterminacy," as Kamar argues?

2. Strine states that the legal requirement of shareholder voting for some transactions is useful in disciplining management. Yet he praises Delaware law's flexibility in allowing management to select the form of a transaction for the purpose of avoiding shareholder voting. Can these positions be reconciled?

3. As Strine notes, Delaware law guards against conflicts, but not against poor decisionmaking. Are conflicts of interest the main danger to shareholders? What assumptions underlie the business judgment rule's deference to directors? Consider these questions with respect to bank directors' performance in the wake of the subprime meltdown.

4. Strine describes Delaware as a "corporate republic." How does its responsiveness to shareholders and managers compare with the American political republic's responsiveness to voters?

5. Can Strine's call for enlightened regulation of business be reconciled with his defense of the business judgment rule and the maximization of shareholder wealth? Can state corporate law do more to advance human values? Should it?

6. Rock's article examines Delaware courts' response to the then-new phenomenon of MBOs. What are the relative advantages and disadvantages of *ex ante* substantive rules and *ex post* "narratives" in providing norms of conduct in the rapidly developing world of business transactions?

7. What does Rock mean when he states that the "law" is "what the business lawyer tells the client—rather than what the judge announces to the world"? (See the section of his article entitled "Shareholder Litigation.") What are the ethical duties of the lawyer with respect to this power?

8. Event study methodology is designed to measure an event's immediate effect on stock price. In the studies Romano cites, the event was a corporation's reincorporation in a new state. An event study compares a stock price's performance relative to the market immediately after the event with its relative performance immediately before the event. (Event study methodology is described in more detail in the article by Professors Johnson, Nelson and Pritchard in Chapter 5.) What kinds of assumptions underlie the use of this method to determine the effect of an event on shareholder wealth?

9. The event studies Romano cites study the effect of reincorporation on stock price and suggest that the corporation's choice to reincorporate in a new state is to the benefit of shareholders. Does this support the proposition that a business's initial choice of state of incorporation (which for large public corporations is usually Delaware) is to the benefit of shareholders? Why or why not?

10. In 2007, North Dakota adopted the Publicly Traded Corporations Act, a new "shareholder friendly" corporations code. N.D. CENTURY CODE, Chapter 10–35. The code, which applies only to publicly-traded firms incorporated in North Dakota that elect to be governed under it, incorporates many shareholder-empowerment rules currently favored by shareholder advocates but seen in few corporate codes, such as requiring director elections by majority (as opposed to plurality) vote, one-year terms for directors, shareholder access to the corporate proxy to nominate director candidates, and advisory shareholder voting on executive pay. Do you expect to see many corporations change their state of incorporation to North Dakota? Why or why not? Besides reincorporation, what effect might the Act have on non-North Dakotan corporations and their shareholders? Would making the Act mandatory make it more useful?

11. The SEC as regulatory "monopolist" might do a less than ideal job of securities regulation, as Romano argues. But even assuming that interstate competition would improve securities regulation, do you think the states would engage in such competition? Why or why not?

12. Although Romano is a staunch advocate of state regulatory competition, her proposal would provide corporations with the option of federal securities law as well as the states' laws. Other than the federal government's already entrenched position as the "monopolistic" regulator, what factors justify the federal government's participation in the competition for securities registrations? Are there factors militating against it?

Note that the federal government does not compete with states for corporate charters. Should it? Is this competition any different from Romano's proposed securities regulation competition?

13. Although the federal government does not offer a chartering regime, the federal securities laws, which preempt state law, regulate a great deal of corporate governance, as we shall see in the next chapter. What effect might this have on the "race" among the states? *See* Mark J. Roe, *Delaware's Competition*, HARV. L. REV.(2003).

14. Romano suggests that the United States should allow foreign corporations selling their securities in the U.S. to opt out of U.S. securities law and choose to be governed by the securities laws of another country. [This is already true to a very limited extent, as a stock exchange can grant a foreign corporation a waiver from an exchange listing requirement. See Roberta Karmel's article in the next chapter.] Should this opt-out right extend to U.S. corporations as well?

15. What implications does Kamar's theory of Delaware corporate law have for Romano's argument that the states should offer competing securities regulation regimes?

16. Romano argues that a corporation's principal place of business is the "least desirable" state of domicile for purposes of the internal affairs rule and for her proposed system of competitive securities regulation regimes. Why?

Kamar and Marcel Kahan have argued elsewhere that there is no evidence that states are actually competing for corporate charters at the present time. Most significantly, only Delaware has incentive to attract and keep charters because only Delaware has a franchise tax structure that generates significant revenues from charters. The authors hypothesize that other states do not compete because the cost of entering the competition is too high: a state would need not just a code, but also the costly judicial infrastructure Kamar describes in this chapter. *The Myth of State Competition in Corporate Law*, 55 STAN. L. REV. 679 (2002).

Assuming that state competition is desirable, what does Kahan and Kamar's argument suggest about the choice of domicile for internal affairs and securities regulation purposes? What factors other than competition for charters might affect states' corporate laws?

17. The primary academic debate over state competition for corporate charters focuses on whether states "race to the top" by offering regulatory regimes that favor shareholder wealth or "race to the bottom" by offering regimes that favor management power. It does not ask the effect of regulatory competition on other corporate constituents. What is the likely effect? Does Professor Williams's article from Chapter 1 provide any insights into this issue?

18. While the rules of corporate law are said to provide many of the terms of the corporate "contract," those rules are often unclear *ex ante* (at the time a shareholder purchases shares), and are determined by judges *ex post* (in an appellate opinion rendered after litigation). One commentator goes so far as to argue: "What is most mandatory in corporate law is not the specific substantive content of any rule, but the institution of judicial oversight.... In drafting the corporate contract ... the parties contract in the shadow of the law, knowing that courts will not seek simply to enforce the contract as written, but will to some uncertain extent serve as an arbiter to determine how the powers granted to management by the corporate charter may be exercised under unforeseen circumstances." John C. Coffee, *The Mandatory/Enabling Balance in Corporate Law: An Essay on the Judicial Role*, 89 COLUM. L. REV. 1618 (1989).

Is the ultimate "hierarch" in corporate governance the board (as Blair & Stout would have it) or the judge? Blair and Stout argue that directors should be guided by the goal of maximizing team production. To the extent that the judge is the "hierarch," what principles should guide the judge?

19. Given that corporate law is made by both legislatures and judges (not to mention administrative agencies), does it make sense to conceive of "states" as entities that consciously compete with one another? While a legislature as a group might have incentive to attract incorporations to increase revenues, no individual legislator would necessarily feel pressure

to focus on that particular issue. Moreover, judges are unlikely to feel direct pressure to attract incorporations.

Judges and legislatures may find themselves at cross-purposes. For example, the Delaware Supreme Court arguably made Delaware an unattractive state of incorporation when it expanded director liability under the duty of care in *Smith v. Van Gorkom*, 488 A.2d 858 (1985). The state legislature quickly mitigated *Van Gorkom* by adding section 102(b)(7) to the Delaware General Corporation Law, which permitted corporations to insert charter provisions protecting directors from such liability. Then the Delaware Court of Chancery restricted the reach of this statute by holding that it did not shield directors from liability for breaches of due care that involve "bad faith." Ultimately, however, the Court of Chancery and the Delaware Supreme Court backed away from that holding by limiting the meaning of "bad faith." See *In re Walt Disney Company Derivative Litigation*, reprinted in this volume.

Chapter 4

Federal Corporate Law

Although corporations are chartered at the state level, the federal government plays a major role in regulating corporations under the rubric of securities regulation. Federal securities law is built largely around the concept of providing information to investors by placing extensive financial disclosure requirements on securities issuers. In response to Enron and various other corporate scandals at the turn of the millennium, Congress made major additions to federal securities law in the Sarbanes-Oxley Act of 2002. The financial meltdown of 2008 inspired calls for further federal regulation. But even before 2008, the Act had been criticized both for regulating too much and for not regulating enough, as this chapter and subsequent chapters will show. The debate over Sarbanes-Oxley continues, and is instructive as the nation considers further reform of federal securities law.

In this chapter, Robert Thompson and Hillary Sale argue that federal law, including Sarbanes-Oxley, uses the traditional securities law tool of disclosure requirements to regulate corporate governance matters traditionally covered by state law. Donald Langevoort examines how the federal regulatory regime shapes the expectations of investors. While the SEC's primary goal is the protection of investors, it must also portray the markets as relatively safe lest it appear to have failed in its main goal. This creates the risk of raising investor expectations to unrealistic levels, thereby undermining investor protection. In his critique of Sarbanes-Oxley, Larry Ribstein argues that excessive regulation can interfere with the proper functioning of securities markets and shares Roberta Romano's preference for state-level regulatory competition over federal-level regulation.

A significant but under-examined aspect of the federal securities regime is its self-regulatory aspect. The interstate commerce clause gives Congress the power to regulate securities, which Congress delegates to the SEC. The SEC in turn delegates a large portion of its authority to the stock exchanges and other self-regulatory organizations (SROs), which regulate certain corporate governance features through their listing standards. Roberta Karmel's article addresses the issues raised by this regime, in which private business organizations work with the SEC to perform significant quasi-governmental functions.

Robert B. Thompson & Hillary A. Sale, *Securities Fraud as Corporate Governance: Reflections upon Federalism**

State law gives corporate managers extremely broad power to direct increasingly large pools of collective business assets. Not surprisingly, economic incentives, norms, markets,

---

* Originally published in 56 Vanderbilt Law Review 859 (2003). Reprinted with permission.

and law all work to constrain the breadth of the power and the potential for abuse of what is other people's money. State corporate law has occupied the center stage in the legal portion of this landscape, with federal securities law playing a supporting role — at least in the academic presentation of the debate. The New Deal's securities legislation eschewed a general federal corporations statute in favor of a more focused federal role emphasizing disclosure and antifraud protections for those who purchase and sell securities. The Supreme Court has made clear that "fraud" as proscribed in federal law was not to be defined in a way that annexed corporate governance. And, in [the Private Securities Litigation Reform Act of] 1995, Congress expressed a clear desire to limit the use of federal securities fraud lawsuits, at least insofar as those lawsuits were perceived to be frivolous.

Yet, as this Article demonstrates, federal securities law and enforcement via securities fraud class actions today have become the most visible means of regulating corporate governance.[1] Securities fraud law is ostensibly directed at buyers and sellers of securities, but in the context of class actions, this purchaser-seller connection acts more like the minimalist jurisdictional hook of the interstate commerce requirement than a real constraint on the use of securities law to regulate corporate governance....

The Sarbanes-Oxley Act of 2002, passed by Congress in the wake of numerous corporate accountability scandals, provides new evidence of the expanded role of federal law. The move to federal corporate governance, however, is broader than that law and has a longer history than the current scandals. The ascendancy of federal law in corporate governance reflects at least three factors. First, disclosure has become the most important method to regulate corporate managers, and disclosure has been predominantly a federal, rather than a state, methodology. Second, state law has focused largely on the duties and liabilities of directors, and not those of officers. Yet, officers have become the fulcrum of governance in today's corporations, and federal law has increasingly occupied the space defining the duties and liabilities of officers. Third, federal shareholder litigation based on securities fraud has several practical advantages over state shareholder litigation based on fiduciary duty that have contributed to the greater use of the federal forum. As a result of these trends, federal law now occupies the largest part of the legal corporate governance infrastructure in the twenty-first century. The outpouring of suggested reforms that have followed in the wake of the Enron and WorldCom scandals have focused on federal law and on the conduct of officers and directors, rather than on state law, which in practice focuses mainly on directors. Indeed, the discussions about reforms have excluded state law almost entirely....

I. State Law — Combating Agency Costs When Managers Control Other People's Money

At the core of corporations law is what we discuss here as corporate governance, the relative allocation of power in the collective entity among three groups of participants named by the statute: shareholders, directors, and officers. This allocation of power defines the nature of the relationship between these participants and their role in determining the direction, strategy, and policy of the corporate entity and, ultimately, its performance. The term "corporate governance," then, incorporates all of these relationships and issues....

---

1. *This excerpt discusses disclosure regulations under federal securities law. Securities fraud class actions are discussed in a further excerpt from this article in Chapter 5. — Ed.*

II. Federal Law

... The government response to the excesses of the 1920s and to the pain of the Great Depression again led to calls for federal corporations law, but the New Deal Congress that passed securities legislation in 1933 and 1934 chose less intrusive means.

A. *The Original Focus: Disclosure in the Purchase or Sale of Securities and Sporadic Shareholder Governance Actions*

The [Securities Act of 1933] focuses on the issuance of securities and, particularly, the initial pubic offering. Initial public offerings present the most significant form of informational asymmetry that the New Deal legislation attempts to address. Issuers are selling securities to noninsiders who may know little or nothing about the company.... To address this informational imbalance and to prevent the sale of bad securities, or even securities in companies that do not exist, the 1933 Act requires that all offering documents conform to specific requirements and that all disclosures be true and accurate....

In contrast, the [Securities Exchange Act of 1934] focuses on disclosures that take place after the company's stock is publicly traded. Here, the approach is ... focused ... on ensuring that when a public company speaks, it does so truthfully. Disclosure, again, is the primary focus. Statutorily, the most significant and direct extension into the corporate governance realm occurs when managers or others solicit proxies to gain shareholder votes as may be required by state law. State and federal law interact in the proxy context, jointly regulating the means and ends of management-to-shareholder communications....

B. *The Expanded Federal Focus: Continuous Disclosure and Corporate Governance*

Other sections of the 1934 Act provide the foundation for a more expansive federal role in corporate governance. The two most prominent mechanisms are the periodic disclosure requirements under section 13 and the antifraud provisions and concomitant liability under section 10(b) and Rule 10b-5. We use the term disclosure here as broadly as the regulations and the case law have provided, referring to all types: mandatory, voluntary, and, in some cases, silence.

These disclosure mechanisms have also expanded since 1934, and, thereby, again expanded the role of federal law in corporate governance....

1. *The Dramatic Increase in Mandatory Disclosure*

... In 1982, the [SEC] promulgated an integrated disclosure package using Regulation S-K.[2] In doing so, the Commission systematized the disclosure package that public companies must provide. As a result, in addition to the timing of the disclosures, the Commission regulates the actual content of disclosures. The regulations are extensive and provide for disclosures arguably designed to enforce what are basic state law fiduciary duties. The required disclosures aid directors in performing their governance functions. The disclosure also aids other monitors, including accountants, whose work is required by the stock exchanges and the Commission. As recent corporate announcements about

---

2. 17 C.F.R. § 229.

restated financial statements reveal, these mandated disclosures are detailed and are therefore potential sources of manipulation and fraud. These mandated disclosures are also considerably more substantive in nature than the proxy provisions. They now include more than sixty items and occupy more than one hundred pages of the federal rulebook.

For example, under Regulation S-K, Item 303 (Management's Discussion and Analysis ["MD&A"]), the Commission requires registrants' annual reports to include descriptions of the company financial conditions, changes in those conditions, and results of operations. The specific categories of required financial information include explanations of liquidity, capital resources, and operational results.

Without going into mind-numbing detail, it is worth considering one passage of Item 303 to see specifically how the Commission is using a description of liquidity to enforce, at least indirectly, management care. To comply with Item 303, the registrant must identify "known trends or any known demands, commitments, events, or uncertainties that will result" in material increases or decreases in liquidity. Managers who are fulfilling their duty of care should be concerned about liquidity and the events related to those changes. Through a requirement that such changes be disclosed, the Commission is enforcing the substantive duty.

Further, once management identifies the trend, it must "indicate the course of action that [it] has taken or proposes to take to remedy the deficiency." Again, managers acting to fulfill their duty of care would presumably resolve to remedy any such deficiency. But, by forcing managers to disclose the trend and describe how they plan to remedy it, the Commission is regulating the conduct, not just what management says about the conduct. Through disclosure can come substance—here, the duty of care....

Finally, the Commission has also adopted various mandatory disclosure items that arguably regulate the duty of loyalty. For example, managers must tell shareholders what they are paying themselves. And the Commission dedicates fifteen pages of the rulebook to telling management how to do so, providing specific categories of compensation and exact formulations for the charts in which management must present the information. Here, again, disclosure is presumably forcing substance in contexts in which conflicted loyalty might be at issue....

Officers already had to sign the 10-K [*the annual report required by the SEC*], for which personal liability was a possibility. [Section 302 of the Sarbanes-Oxley Act directs the SEC to pass regulations requiring CEOs and CFOs to] sign a statement declaring that they have reviewed the requisite reports and, where appropriate, discussed them with the audit committee or board, before determining that the reports are in fact correct. [3] [Sarbanes-

---

3. [*Under § 302 (15 U.S.C. § 7241) the CEO and CFO must certify that:*
* *they have reviewed the report;*
* *the report does not contain any untrue statements of material fact or material omissions;*
* *the report fairly presents the corporation's financial condition;*
* *the signing officers are responsible for internal informational controls ensuring that they are informed of material information;*
* *the signing officers have disclosed to the corporation's auditors and the board's audit committee all significant deficiencies in the internal controls and any fraud involving employees who play a significant role in internal controls;*
* *the report discloses any significant changes in internal controls, including corrective actions with regard to deficiencies.*
—Ed.]

Oxley §906 makes it a criminal offense for CEOs or CFOs to knowingly certify false reports.]

This provision directly imposes a duty of care on company managers. It not only makes them agree to a particular disclosure, but it also tells them what they must do before signing the disclosure statement. State law has long addressed this issue, as illustrated in the well-known recent case, *In re Caremark International, Inc. Derivative Litigation.*[4] The executive officer declaration is, however, a direct intrusion of federal legislation into what has traditionally been the province of state law corporate governance.

Note the emphasis here — on officers, not directors. As Alan Greenspan recently observed, "the state of corporate governance to a very large extent reflects the character of the CEO." And, in recognition of where the locus of today's governance is, federal law imposes obligations directly on officers, bypassing the intermediaries of the board. A telling example of the federalization of corporate governance is the section of the Sarbanes-Oxley Act that regulates the fiduciary duty of loyalty by banning corporate loans to executive officers and directors. Such a ban was historically part of state corporate law. In many states the earlier prohibition has been watered down to a requirement for director approval, and the Model Business Corporation Act deleted the provision entirely in its 1988 revision. The federal government has now mandated a contrary view.

The Sarbanes-Oxley Act [§302] also requires an annual report to be accompanied by a statement that management is responsible for creating and maintaining adequate internal controls and that officers making the required certification have evaluated the effectiveness of those controls within ninety days. Even more directly, it requires the companies' chief executive and financial officers to disgorge any incentive — or equity — based compensation within twelve months of reports that lead to an accounting restatement.[5] The new federal act also intervenes in corporate governance by requiring the SEC to promulgate rules requiring attorneys to report to the chief legal officer and then the chief executive officer any evidence of a material violation of the federal securities laws or breaches of a fiduciary duty.[6] Here, then, the federal government has gone over the directors' heads, rejecting the deference to their prerogative that characterizes Delaware law. Instead, it has specified officer-level governance at a level exceeding the state law mechanisms and applied it not just to securities fraud but to fiduciary duty as well. In doing so, Congress has explicitly recognized the now-connected nature of federal securities law and fiduciary duty that we describe in this Article.

2. *The Increase in Disclosure Obligations Beyond Mandatory Disclosure*

... Generally speaking, misleading statements and omissions in corporate disclosure statements, whether voluntary or mandatory, give rise to federal securities fraud liability claims. The location, so to speak, of the alleged misstatements or omissions can be the required quarterly and annual reports, but it can also be a press release, conference call, or any other oral or written statement made by the company....

---

4. [698 A.2d (Del. Ct. Ch. 1996) (discussing directors' duty to monitor corporate operations).]
5. [Sarbanes-Oxley Act §304, 15 U.S.C. §7243.]
6. [Sarbanes-Oxley Act §307, 15 U.S.C. §7245.]

Donald C. Langevoort, *Managing the "Expectations Gap" in Investor Protection: The SEC and the Post-Enron Reform Agenda**

As far as we know, the Enron story is one of artfully managed expectations. Company executives created high expectations among investors regarding the company's growth potential and their unique skill-set to reach it, producing for a time an extraordinarily high stock market valuation. Meanwhile, the economic reality was turning out to be more sobering. Increasingly aggressive, apparently fraudulent, steps were taken to report financial results and conditions that would not deflate investors' expectations in a way that would put the managers' jobs, compensation and perquisites—not to mention social status and self-esteem—immediately at risk. One can tell similar stories about other of this past year's financial reporting scandals, like WorldCom and Global Crossing....

Issuers of securities are not the only possible creators of "expectations gaps." In the disclosure area, the term was coined to describe the difficulties the accounting profession faces with investor expectations that the audit process "assures" accurate reporting on the one hand, and the reality that audits are far from fail-safe on the other. But it applies more broadly to all of securities regulation. The rhetoric of securities regulation—much of it generated by the Securities and Exchange Commission (SEC)—trumpets our commitment and success in creating strong marketplace integrity, inviting deep investor trust in the transparency of the corporate system. The reality is also different here, as Enron and similar cases show. There is still far too much obfuscation and concealment—and hence rent extraction—on the part of corporate managers, creating harmful stock price distortions with disturbing regularity....

The expectations gap is real: securities regulation is far from any assurance of corporate transparency, delivering neither as much protection as many investors assume nor as much as is optimal. Marketplace mechanisms, as Enron painfully shows, do not always offer reliable correctives. My story, however, is not one of a failure of administrative imagination or will. The United States has under-funded the hard work of investor protection, holding back from the system the resources it would take to substantially lessen the expectations gap, even if it can never be eliminated. Although no other country invests more, either comparatively or in absolute terms, we still leave many opportunities for the creation of investment illusions, which managers guilefully exploit.

In theory, then, the remedy should be easy, and one could argue that the recent Sarbanes-Oxley Act is exactly the right medicine. The Act calls for investing in a far higher level of monitoring of corporate candor so that the probability of identification and detection of corporate fraud rises to a cost-efficient level, and it imposes serious penalties when wrongdoing is found. The Act's mandates seek to eliminate the rents made available to corporate managers from being able to hide accurate economic performance.

Sarbanes-Oxley's increased funding and new criminal threats are indeed an important step forward, but in broader terms, probably not enough to deliver anything approximating an optimal assurance of the credibility of issuer financial reporting. The SEC has lived nearly all its life in a world of chronically inadequate resources, for reasons that are complex but I suspect at least include the business community's unwillingness to let go of the underlying rents. Perhaps the niggardly funding also reflects a reasonable suspicion that the bureaucracy has never expended its resources in an economically efficient fashion anyway and thus

* Originally published in 48 VILLANOVA LAW REVIEW 1139 (2003). Reprinted with permission.

would not spend a major funding increase efficiently either. That question touches on what is the most contentious academic debate in securities regulation, one well beyond the scope of this paper. Suffice it to say that, for any number of reasons, there will be no increase in SEC funding large enough to substantially eliminate the expectations gap. Sarbanes-Oxley only makes things marginally better.

This paper attends to both the politics and the substance of the post-Enron debate about appropriate investor expectations, with main attention to the role of the SEC. For substance, my goal is to shed some light on certain of the policy choices away from the distortion that occurs when these choices are viewed—as they have been for the last year—through a politically refracted lens.

We will never, however, get too far away from politics, and so let me make my main political point at the outset. The SEC's role in investor protection inevitably brings it up against the affect-laden, socially constructed question of how much managerial autonomy, power and status a capitalist society ought to allow. The conservative view, of course, is that it should allow quite a lot. Over-regulation is a threat to entrepreneurship and the bundle of rights that in their view legitimately attaches to economic success. To promote this vision and maintain a lean regulatory environment, conservatives must react aggressively to corporate scandals like Enron when they erupt. Denial is dangerous, so the best thing is the "bad apple" account. According to this story, only a very small number of managers act in so dysfunctional a way; the system remains socially benign. Hence, the right response to scandal is tough enforcement. Hang the bad guys high, but otherwise permit business as usual....

The progressive voice in securities regulation is different. It wants to focus attention on the concentration and abuse of economic power and is comfortable drawing starker lines of conflict between managerial and investor interests and in recognizing that those two interests do not themselves coincide with the public interest. Disclosure has a social virtue in spreading disinfectant on the world of wealth and power, not just an informational role. This view chafes at the artificial distinction long drawn between federal and state spheres of authority, wishing to extend the federal presence to a full range of matters touching on managerial accountability and corporate governance. To the progressive, Enron is a story about arrogance and abuse, and a call for wide-ranging reforms designed to reduce the rents from corporate stewardship. Individual enforcement cases, though certainly important, are hardly enough, and too easily distract from deeper needs.

The foregoing explains much about the post-Enron reform efforts. The initial Republican agenda was hardly real institutional reform at all, except timidly in the accounting area. As typical, it relied on the fire and brimstone of enforcement to respond to the increased level of social discontent, until it subsided. The Democratic agenda more willingly tapped into that discontent, but still faced a difficult implementation problem. In fact, there are relatively few moderate, cost-efficient strategies, especially in a world of chronic under-investment in securities enforcement, that are likely to make a compelling difference with respect to abuses of managerial power. Real reform is either fairly radical (attacking matters like conflicts of interest and excessive executive compensation directly), very expensive (extraordinary funding increases for monitoring and enforcement, empowering aggressive private securities litigation, etc.), or both. Given the current political and budgetary landscape, neither is practicable. To me, the Democratic reform proposals came closer to touching on some of the real problems in the world of corporate behavior, but in ways that by themselves still will not change all that much. They are best seen as a shot across the bow, perhaps saving the heavier ammunition for a time when they hold a stronger political hand. Sarbanes-Oxley did some very good things, especially in the accounting and auditing area, but in the end—and notwithstanding the Sturm und Drang rhetoric—it is still fairly moderate legislation.

My primary focus here, however, is on the SEC's place in the reform efforts. The investor protection mission of the Commission naturally tilts it slightly in the progressive direction; it is hard to devote so much time and attention to instances of investor harm without perceiving the fairly widespread presence of managerial arrogance and selfishness. Republican SEC chairmen are inclined to moderate this, but I suspect that even they usually leave office with a stronger, if unspoken, sense of the venality of large segments of the business community than they had when they took office.

To understand the SEC's behavior in carrying out its dramaturgical role, it is important to return to the expectations gap. The SEC is in an awkward position *vis-à-vis* the investing public. On one hand, it has to underscore its own importance as "the investor's champion," and for that there has to be a visible enemy—typically, self-serving managers who lie or cheat. At the same time, it cannot portray the risk of investing as so severe that investors actually become discouraged and drop out of the markets. Any significant reduction in the depth and liquidity of the markets would both reduce the scope of the Commission's stature and authority (if not eliminate much of its reason for being) and invite the inference that it was to blame for not doing its job beforehand. Hence, the risks of investing must always be portrayed as moderate and, with serious bureaucratic intervention, manageable. In the end, in other words, the Commission must promote the viability and attractiveness of broad individual participation in the stock markets, the ultimate capitalist tool. This is a strong check on too much drift in the progressive direction. Only if the SEC stays in the middle ground—which may require some artful management of investor expectations of its own—is it in a position to bargain effectively for the additional scarce resources in a not-terribly-friendly political environment necessarily to do its job better.

My sense is that most SEC chairmen, commissioners and senior staff in recent memory have had a high level of commitment to this mission. They have invested their professional identities in the task. They may disagree about matters of ideology and style, but whatever their specific objectives, they have all confronted the resource problem and hence faced the core negotiation dilemma. To gain those resources, there are a limited number of strategies. One is to appeal for support aggressively to investors (or even the non-investing public) to counter the more organized and focused efforts of the business community. While essential to some degree, this has natural difficulties: investors are diffusely organized, especially individual ones, and are fickle in their preferences. During bull markets, their demand for investor protection is limited. Institutional investors are a more powerful group, but politically difficult. They pose threats to individual investors in many respects (e.g., the agency cost problems embedded in mutual fund structures) and will refuse to ally themselves politically with the Commission in other areas if the Commission is too aggressive in their domain. So, too, with other organized groups who have self-interests in promoting high expectations of investor protection, such as the broker-dealer industry, the accountants and the securities bar.

In sum, whatever the ideological leanings of the sitting commissioners, the SEC has to make substantial regulatory compromises in order to protect or enhance its claim for resources. It frequently avoids debilitating opposition either by muting its regulation or offering a trade of concession in one area for aggressiveness in another. To me, what has occasionally been described as the agency's "captive" behavior is not surrender but pragmatic negotiation … to cement political alliances in aid of the SEC's core objectives.

If that is right, then the prevailing strategies of securities regulation will often be politically driven rather than substantively ideal, even putting aside the problem of scarce resources. In turn, the scholar's task becomes one of separating substance from politics and critiquing the prevailing regulatory regime on its merits alone (i.e., the net of real costs and benefits to the public). In Enron's aftermath, our search will be primarily for places where the current law might have been unduly weak for reasons having to do with political compromise rather than simple lack of enforcement or surveillance resources. Obviously, weakness is not the only possibility. Over-regulation is also possible at the behest of a particular interest group (particularly lawyers) or because of bureaucratic inertia. But if our search is for regulatory deficiencies apart from a gross lack of enforcement resources that might have contributed to Enron and related scandals, that should be our focus.

I. Identifying the Underlying Problem

A. *Motive and Rationalization*

... Two extraordinary developments of the last two decades are (a) the explosive growth in executive compensation, especially in the form of incentive compensation and (b) the more frequent turnover of senior management personnel, including the CEO, for failing to satisfy investor expectations. Together, this means CEOs and their closest associates can expect incredible rewards for each year control is maintained, but that control is very much at risk if expectations drop in the face of reality. The motive, then, is to make the large promises necessary to gain the job and excite investors, and then delay any appreciation of the truth once adversity is encountered so that the period of wealth can be extended, if only by a matter of a year or two (or even a few months) before any adverse reckoning.

I do not mean to suggest that CEOs or other senior officials who succumb to pressure are always deliberate in their obfuscation. Their hubris and capacity for rationalization enable them to perceive as justified what is often just enriching. Indeed, I suspect that this brings us to an unappreciated aspect of the scandals. Return to the mid and late 1990s, when the economy and the stock market were vibrant....

In the minds of many new age business people back then, the conventions of accounting were under a thick cloud of doubt with respect both to their accuracy and relevance. Accounting is a practice built on an ethic of conservatism to provide standardized treatment of the financial performance of a business. Its principles were formed in an era of bricks and mortar industry, when discrete inventory moved off shelves and into customers' possession for simple cash or credit. As every beginning accounting student is taught, this never, even then, quite captured economic reality and always requires a good bit of subjective judgment. But for a long time, it worked well enough within the norms and mores of the American economy.

The high-tech and knowledge-sector booms of the 1980s and 90s helped change that view. Orthodox accounting does not apply well at all to intangibles like human and intellectual capital, or to new style methods of creating and selling products and services. It paints an unrealistic picture in many ways, understating the value of those companies that cannot demonstrate the tangibles in terms of assets and recognizable revenue compared to those that can. That frustrated the innovators. They were convinced that their business models held the real economic value in America's future, but conventional accounting ignored that truth and shackled their ability to attract more and more capital. After all, investors still seemed to obsess on announcements of steadily ascending quarterly earnings per share, which are nothing but accounting artifacts.

What was an enlightened financial executive to think then? If old-style accounting was unfair, then "aggressive" accounting—taking the judgment calls to their limits—was a legitimate way of fighting back. If a few rules actually got broken, it was not so bad either. The shackles needed to come off. It is hard to consider what you are doing fraudulent if you do not think that following the rules conveys much truth either.

It worked.... And nearly everyone was getting away with it, which did two things. First, the absence of any serious crackdown bolstered the impression the system was willing to tolerate their philosophy—the opposite of the expressive function that aggressive enforcement of the law can play. That encouraged further rationalization, which when coupled with the positive feedback (higher stock prices) from the practices, emboldened them to become even more aggressive. Second, the evolving norm pressured even those competitors not caught up in the postmodern spirit to follow suit.

They had help, of course. A new wave of leaders in the accounting profession, seeking new sources of revenue so that they could be wealthy too, developed strategies for pushing the limits of the old rules, first as tax avoidance, then importing the same tactics into financial cosmetics. They were pleased to be part of the creative destruction of their own faith. Investment bankers had deals to sell, especially complex synthetic financing techniques by which assets, liabilities and risk could be moved in, out and around the company in a blur. They, too, were willing converts to new age accounting, as were many lawyers who benefited from the work that came with the financial frenzy.

In this setting, restraint crumbled, and therein came the problem. By now, the norm in many places was that if the financial, legal and accounting people could "get comfortable" with some rationalization of the rules (that is, not cringe or laugh), do it. Investors will thank you eventually. Transparency dimmed even more. With the dimming of transparency, in turn, came a loss of accountability—the executives were now free to take bigger risks selected from an ever more sophisticated menu of financial engineering techniques than could be hidden from investors' view. Their egos and their greed got the better of them.

Accounting may be treated as *passé*, but economics is not, and the executives' self-defined, socially constructed brilliance was not quite up to tougher market conditions. The real economic returns were in doubt, and the executives were locked into inflated expectations. In some of these instances, what may have started as postmodern accounting turned into real fraud as insiders acted like most human beings caught in traps of their own making, trying desperately to hide the truth for a little while longer, waiting for some last-minute stroke of fortune. For most, it never came.

This process of rationalization and self-serving inference is not purely an individual one by any means. Corporate cultures exacerbate certain biases, especially ones built on optimism or illusions of control. Enron was in many ways the organizational embodiment of a belief system that rationalized to the extreme, made all the worse by the flattery and adulation the press, other business people and investors lavished on it for so long.

B. *Opportunity*

Motive alone is not enough; deception requires opportunity as well. Some of what follows addresses that question—compromises in the aggressiveness of auditors, deficiencies in antifraud enforcement and private litigation, etc. To that we must assign a good bit of responsibility to investors who demand unreasonable levels of earnings growth and then believe management's numbers too readily notwithstanding the obvious motive to cheat, abetted by the investment professionals and journalists inclined to celebrate management's self-serving stories rather than doubt them. Indeed, investors' irrational obsession with short-term performance metrics serves to give the rationalizing manager further excuse to mislead them in the name of protecting their strategic vision for underlying business from the vagaries of exuberance. And the more some executives fall prey to temptation, others will follow simply because the first group has set a norm that would be risky for any competitor to ignore.

Opportunity also is enhanced by financial innovation. Complicated derivatives and hedging strategies create the ability to shift risk in ways that are not apparent to investors. The same is true of off-books "special purpose entities." All of these are perfectly legitimate tools in most contexts, but increase the range of creative possibility for obscuring economic reality. (Many of these techniques were learned and honed, I suspect, as tax avoidance strategies and then imported into the world of financial reporting—a point that will be taken up below). I will venture a guess that one commonality among many of the financial frauds recently exposed was a fairly charismatic outward-oriented CEO with at best a dim understanding of complex financial engineering, who delegated more and more power to a CFO with the implicit understanding of "don't ask, don't tell" about how the numbers needed to satisfy the CEO's "vision" were being produced. A Faustian bargain results: the CFO with more arrogance and brains than good judgment begins to take risks, encouraged by skilled salespeople from the investment banks. When the risks go bad, he faces either being honest and losing all the power and status, or taking even more risks, including stepping outside the law, in the hope that good fortune will return. Frankly, it is human nature to do the latter.

While regulation has to respond to any given form of innovation, the pace can be pernicious. We know that regulation—whether in the form of disclosure rules from the SEC or accounting principles issued by the Financial Accounting Standards Board—is slow to develop, and can be the subject of political interference. In the meantime, the dimly understood and often elastic interim principles leave ample room for opportunism without any compelling appreciation of impropriety—exactly the circumstance that creates all the more opportunity for deception....

II. Post-Enron Reform: Substance or Window Dressing?

....

A. *The Disclosure Regime*

One of the curious sleights of hand that has occurred since Enron has been the SEC's promotion of "real-time disclosure" as a response to the scandals. In fact, real-time disclosure—that is, accelerating the timetable for disclosure of key information—was already in the works as a key re-regulatory objective.... However, with a few exceptions such as the reporting of conflict of interest transactions with the issuer (e.g., Kenneth Lay's stock transactions[7]), we have to admit that there are few places where the simple acceleration of disclosure would have made much of a difference in these recent scandals.

This might be different were the SEC to employ a more aggressive strategy than just a "prompt" disclosure after the fact, focusing instead on disclosure of plans and intentions

---

7. *Lay, Enron's then-CEO and Chair, was accused of selling his stock shortly before the company's stock price collapsed, even as he publicly denied rumors of the company's troubles and the company prohibited employees from selling Enron stock from their 401(k) retirement accounts. — Ed.*

to engage in certain kinds of activities before they occur. For instance, it would be of substantial benefit to investors to know that an executive intends to buy or sell company stock before that transaction takes place; so, too, with significant conflict of interest transactions.... The legal standard authorizes the SEC to require reports designed to "keep reasonably current" the initial disclosure mandated upon attaining public company status. It is well within the realm of reasonableness to say that a proposed transaction is the kind of information needed to update the file; if so, there is leeway here.... This is an idea the SEC probably ought to pursue.

Turning to the substance of disclosure, we should remember the two separate, if related, purposes to the mandatory disclosure regime. One is to allow investors to make informed valuation decisions—in other words, what are the securities worth compared to their current price? The other is an agency cost idea: disclosure designed to reduce the opportunities of insiders to extract rents at investor expense. These are inseparable insofar as a valuation decision is impossible without an assessment of the risk that incumbent management will divert to itself the otherwise expected stream of earnings. Here we see clearly why, so long as it is disclosure that we are talking about, there is no persuasive federalism-based reason to keep the SEC away from corporate governance matters. Management integrity, or fear of mismanagement, is a legitimate concern that is part and parcel of the valuation process as well as the shareholder franchise protected by the proxy rules.

Are the mandatory disclosures found in Regulation S-K up to this task? ...

The main focus of disclosure is the issuer's business and prospects, rather than management's stewardship per se. Here again, the question is what additional forms of disclosure might have been helpful to investors in Enron-like situations. My sense, based on the available facts, is that there were ample violations of the current legal rules, which naturally leads to the possibility that no reforms would be efficacious—the issuer bent on violating the current rules would surely have violated any new ones as well. While that is certainly well taken, the response is two-fold. First, disclosure requirements that are too vague or open-ended invite, as noted earlier, "violation by rationalization"—seeing if a possible argument can be devised to justify noncompliance, which quickly can lead down a slippery slope. The clearer the rules are, the less room there is for this. Second, more focused disclosure requirements may lead to more careful attention by persons not directly involved in the wrongdoing, the so-called gatekeepers.

The primary issue here, in the abstract at least, is the divergence between reported results on the balance sheet, income statement and cash flow statement and "economic reality." While I have no doubt that many GAAP [Generally Accepted Accounting Principles] rules deserve refinement or change in order to produce more reliable numbers, I recognize that the very nature of accounting makes capturing economic reality with precision impracticable. The reasons are familiar ones. Accounting looks backwards, while investment analysis is forward looking. Accounting rests on principles of conservatism and the need to quantify, while economic reality often involves non-quantifiable risks and opportunities. And as noted earlier, the rules of accounting can never quite change as fast as the pace of financial innovation.

If so, can investors be apprised of material differences known to the company? That, of course, is what the Management Discussion and Analysis (MD&A) portion of mandatory disclosure is supposed to be about.[8] I think the SEC is correct in the points made in a

8. *"MD&A" is Item 303 of Regulation S-K (also discussed in Thompson and Sale's article). Its disclosure requirements include the following:*

(a)(1) ... Identify any known trends or any known demands, commitments, events or uncertainties that will result in or that are reasonably likely to result in the registrant's liquidity increasing or

series of interpretive releases this past year that nearly all of the kinds of concealment that Enron did violated the current MD&A requirements, whether or not GAAP was technically complied with in the underlying reporting. In other words, a fair reading of the requirements regarding known trends and uncertainties would suggest, for example, that Enron's use of its own stock as a guarantee of certain contingent liabilities should have been disclosed in the MD&A regardless of the proper accounting treatment or footnote disclosure.

However, one cannot read the current MD&A instructions without a sense that they miss the point in a number of respects, failing on grounds of obscurity if not misdirection. The underlying issue is a profound one: to what extent does the issuer have a duty to disclose forward-looking information in its possession that would lead investors to see that reported results are not a good indicator of even the near-term future, if not longer-term prospects? Carefully trying to avoid an overbroad duty, the MD&A fails to make sufficiently principled distinctions and hence collapses into a muddle. Although there are many flaws in the execution, the primary one is the emphasis on "known" trends and uncertainties. What does that mean, in distinction to all forward-looking information material to the financial condition of the issuer? In 1989, the Commission tried to answer that question by saying that the requirement applies only to events "reasonably likely" to occur (though it gave no helpful guidance even on what that particular phrase means). And there we see the difficulty in terms of "rationalized nondisclosure." Management can take big risks (e.g., the use of Enron stock as a contingent guarantee) and hide them on the assumption—which it may actually believe, aided by a bit of self-deception—that the downside is not "reasonably likely" to happen.

My sense is that the MD&A needs a complete overhaul, beginning with a jettisoning of the "reasonably likely" locution in favor of the more traditional materiality standard. As a result of Sarbanes-Oxley, this is happening piecemeal; what I am suggesting is a more coherent re-conceptualization. The fear here, of course, is that this opens the floodgates to disclosure of the full range speculative possibilities about the issuer's prospects, making the MD&A unwieldy and useless. In response, I would refine the focus of the MD&A. To me, what investors really want and need is a warning of material future risks—not just their possibility (as boilerplate risk disclosure tends to do), but a discussion of their probability and magnitude from management's perspective as well. They deserve a flashing yellow light when future risks edge into the realm of materiality. Thus, in the end I would prefer to restyle the MD&A into a "risk discussion and analysis" requirement based simply on materiality, which in turn I would make—as Congress suggested in Sarbanes-Oxley— part of the "real time," not just periodic, disclosure requirement. This would make it far harder to hide risks, as Enron seemingly did, on the grounds that even if the magnitude of the impact might potentially be severe, the possibility was unlikely to occur.

B. Targeting Insiders: Officer and Director Responsibilities

While much of the inadequate deterrence in the financial reporting area stems from the under-funding of the SEC, there are a few ways in which the Commission contributed to the problem. One, historically at least, was through a combination of settling its

decreasing in any material way ...

(a)(3)(ii) Describe any known trends or uncertainties that have had or that the registrant reasonably expects will have a material favorable or unfavorable impact on net sales or revenues or income ...

17 C.F.R. § 229.303.

—*Ed. (emphasis added).*

enforcement cases with relatively low penalties and allowing most, if not all, of the costs of settlement or judgment to be borne by the issuer (and hence its innocent shareholders) rather than the insiders who engineered the wrongdoing. This, of course, gave insiders the impression that they had relatively little to lose in personal wealth from risking a securities law violation. To me, the most important change in the past year has been a refocusing of attention on deterring the insiders most likely responsible for financial fraud.

The SEC's main innovation — codified and expanded, somewhat confusingly, in two different places in Sarbanes-Oxley — is the requirement that both the CEO and CFO "certify" that the 10-K and 10-Q are accurate in all material respects as of the date of filing and "fairly present" the financial condition and operations of the issuer. Technically, this is not much of a departure given the previous signature requirements.... While the new certification requirement is beneficial, one should not advertise certification in and of itself as a revolutionary change.

One thing the certification requirement clearly does is place more emphasis than ever on what it means to say that the financial statements "fairly present" the financial condition and operations of the issuer. We shall turn to this question later in discussing the responsibilities of auditors, where similar language has long been employed. My sense is that "accounting reality" and "economic reality" are two distinct concepts, posing a profound intellectual challenge to the executive forced to certify. To me, the right bridge here is to turn the MD&A into a narrative that comprehensively discusses the differences known to management, which as noted above would require some revisions to the instructions to that line-item. Until then, awkwardness will remain.

Significantly, the certification requirements avoid imposing an explicit duty to investigate. Hence, the predictable organizational response may simply be to increase the incentive to isolate the CEO and CFO from the wrongdoing in the firm — the familiar "plausible deniability" or "don't ask, don't tell" scenarios. Where the CEO lacks knowledge or awareness of the improprieties, the SEC's task is much more difficult — and certification by itself does no good. The open questions are two-fold. First, how elastic is the state of mind standard? One of the to-be-explored connections here is how similar certification language that has long been in place in health care and government contract regulation has been interpreted, and whether this analogy will stick as imported into securities law. The second is whether adding to the requirement a certification that goes to the quality of the "disclosure controls and procedures" in place will actually improve information flow sufficiently to overcome the organizational tendency to suppress bad news. It is simply too early to predict the answers.

If liability in an SEC proceeding is clear enough, then the remaining issue is one of the severities of the civil sanctions. In 1990, Congress gave the SEC deterrence power via the introduction of civil penalty liability for all securities law violations, and by making it possible for the SEC to seek a bar order preventing any person from further service as an officer or director of a publicly traded corporation. Unfortunately, each of these remedies had serious limitations. The civil penalty amounts are smaller than they should be compared to the gravity of many financial frauds. And the Second Circuit has held that the officer-director bar is available only in "recidivist" kinds of cases. This is an area where Sarbanes-Oxley made a useful contribution.[9] My sense is that the new statutory

---

9. *Section 1105 of the Sarbanes-Oxley Act, 15 U.S.C. §78u-3(f), allows the SEC to bar individuals if it finds them "unfit" to serve as officers or directors; the prior standard was one of "substantial unfitness." —* Ed.

language should be read in a way that presumes the propriety of a bar order from any finding of serious, intentional securities fraud.

Much credit goes to the SEC for its willingness to expand the scope of disgorgement sought in serious financial fraud cases, another step clarified in Sarbanes-Oxley. In some ways, it is surprising that the Commission had not long ago taken the position—amply justifiable even then—that executives complicit in financial fraud forfeit their right to any special compensation they made during the time in question that might reasonably be tied to the wrongdoing. Given that incentive compensation and bonuses tied to stock price performance is commonplace, the money at stake here should be large. And happily, disgorgement is not the kind of thing normally protected by insurance or indemnification.

C. Outside Directors and Audit Committees

As noted earlier, each of the recent scandals falls into one familiar pattern: the outside directors inevitably claim that they were as much the victims of deceit as investors.... [The Powers Report, an independent investigation commissioned by Enron's new post-bankruptcy board of directors, found that Enron's outside directors had been unaware of its frauds. In contrast, the Senate Committee on Governmental Affairs concluded, after holding hearings, that all of Enron's directors should have recognized numerous warning signs.]

The natural response is to ask whether something more should be done to make directors more diligent in their monitoring. For reasons I have explained elsewhere, I am skeptical that increasing the threat of liability for outside directors is a wise idea—it too easily misconceives the role of the outside director and introduces a chill that redirects attention away from the handful of things outsiders do well. I share the view of Ed Rock and Michael Wachter, among others, who argue that norms rather than law ought to be the main drivers of directorial diligence.[10]

My inclination is instead to refocus on information flow to the board as a precursor to good disclosure to investors. I do not think it accidental that bad disclosure and board ignorance are positively correlated. The prevailing assumption in much of the academic literature and business press is that CEOs see the board as a group whose expectations have to be managed as much as those of investors and other stakeholders.... ... [T]hey are given only the information senior management wants them to have. The underlying image is an arms-length type negotiation between the managers and the board, with an imbalance of bargaining power.

Maybe so. But it is at least worth noting that this kind of posture by senior management, however commonplace, is a breach of fiduciary duty. Though underdeveloped, the common law is quite clear that agents and other fiduciaries owe a duty of utmost candor to their superiors, a duty not only to tell the whole truth but also to volunteer all information needed for the superior to make informed decisions. And the board is the superior in any corporation. While I think the case is easy to make under current law that any executive who fails to inform the board of the truth about the company at least aids and abets any resulting misreporting, I am concerned that the working norms and assumptions in too many companies about candor with the board still miss this point. To make the point clearer, the SEC could adopt a rule (or revise Rule 13b2-2) to provide that any executive

---

10. Edward B. Rock & Michael Wachter, *Islands of Conscious Power: Law, Norms and the Self-Governing Corporation*, 149 U. Pa. L. Rev. 1619, 1622 (2001). *See also Prof. Rock's article in Chapter 3.*—Ed.

officer who is aware that the issuer's financial reports are or are likely to be materially false or misleading has an affirmative duty to notify the board of that fact.

One of the most interesting steps taken in Sarbanes-Oxley is the requirement that the audit committee of the board take control over the retention and compensation of the company's auditors.[11] That this was not already ordinary practice is a testament to a breakdown of corporate governance norms—if a primary purpose of an audit was to look over the shoulders of the company's financial managers, it is foolish to put those managers in charge of choosing the auditor. Of course it should be the audit committee. It is tempting at first to applaud this step, but then the problem immediately comes to mind: if the board was not willing on its own to claim this responsibility, will compliance with the new law simply be an empty formality, with the audit committee still taking direction from the managers? Here, I am somewhat optimistic. If one believes that norms are what drive most of director behavior, then the fact that, prior to Sarbanes-Oxley, it was normal to put control over the audit in the CFO's hands was a strong constraint. Any board that defected from the norm risked sending a signal that it did not trust the CFO or that it suspected some serious problem. Now, the new law provides cover to any such step, making it possible that we will see a shift in norms to the more rational posture.

This solution will fail, however, if either of two conditions occurs. One, obviously, is that the board lacks any desire to operate independently and gives de facto control back to the managers. The other is that the managers deprive the newly emboldened auditors of access to enough information to make judgments.... The insiders' fiduciary obligation of candor should extend not only to the board but those who work for the board—i.e., the auditors. Sarbanes-Oxley gives the SEC the authority to adopt rules on managerial interaction with auditors, rules that should say not only that it is unlawful to mislead the auditors, but that managers have an affirmative duty to provide auditors with all material facts necessary and appropriate to the conduct of the audit.

III. Conclusion

One of the standard media questions after Sarbanes-Oxley and the flurry of certifications to the SEC and criminal indictments is whether investing is now "safe" from misconduct (or even more foolishly, whether we can now expect the stock market to go back up). That brings us back to the expectations gap. New rules that are not enforced effectively become part of the problem—they exacerbate the gap, rather than help reduce it. Sarbanes-Oxley's funding increase will surely lead to some step-up in the level of enforcement by the SEC, but it is unlikely that we will have reached an optimal level even once the skilled enforcers are hired and trained (which will take a while). In other words, I still have doubts about whether we will see sufficiently sustained, aggressive enforcement, especially of the hard-to-prove requirements, at the level necessary to cause executives to perceive

---

11. *Section 301 of the Act added, among other things, the following provision to § 10A of the 1934 Securities Exchange Act:*

> The audit committee of each issuer, in its capacity as a committee of the board of directors, shall be directly responsible for the appointment, compensation, and oversight of the work of any registered public accounting firm employed by that issuer (including resolution of disagreements between management and the auditor regarding financial reporting) for the purpose of preparing or issuing an audit report or related work, and each such registered public accounting firm shall report directly to the audit committee.
> 17 U.S.C. § 78j-1(m)(2).

—*Ed.*

that a securities law violation is not a risk worth taking, no matter how much money or status is involved. That is especially so if you think that executives have a tendency to rationalize in the face of greed or fear and fail to perceive risk accurately as a result. I am especially skeptical that we will see enough criminal enforcement for the *in terrorem* effect to be real, at least once this round of political attention subsides.

Thus, the ultimate response to the residual risk of managerial opportunism in financial reporting remains in private hands. Realizing that a considerable risk remains does not mean investors should not invest: it does, however, argue for careful diversification and reduced expectations. As has been suggested repeatedly over the past few months, it argues for realism about growth stocks. On average, stocks grow at a pace with the economy and increases in productivity. Any company that promises that it can grow faster than that bears a heavy burden of proof about how and why. Intellectual property and a unique internal skill-set may provide an answer, but we should be suspicious of that—job market mobility means that companies have little assurance that whatever special talents they may have for a time will still be there next year. Enron gives us the perfect objective lesson that what may seem to be extraordinary talent may really be some combination of luck and cheating. Growth by serial acquisitions should be equally suspect, given the evidence of the last decade. In sum, investors need to ratchet down their investment expectations— a message Wall Street's retail side hardly wants to embrace, and investors themselves resist.

As Henry Hu has shown, the SEC is in a difficult position with respect to investor education in the face of all this.[12] The underlying message—if stated accurately—is that stocks are more risky than many investors expect for reasons that include (but are hardly limited to) managerial abuse and that investors by and large lack the time, skill, data and judgment to evaluate risk and return on individual stocks. They should therefore diversify broadly and passively, or leave investment analysis to professionals—who, unfortunately, charge dearly for their services and too often deliver disappointing results. Those cautionary messages are inconsistent, however, with the overarching theme of individual investor empowerment on which the Commission's own political fortunes largely rest. The SEC wants to persuade successive generations of retail investors that everything is controllable (and largely under control), because that is why it gets its funding and power. It is tempted to rationalize, too, and so we cannot seem to escape the expectations gap. Post-Enron reforms or not, the SEC will long be trying to muddle through the delicate task of trying to persuade investors that the issuers are honest enough to justify broad and confident public participation without committing its own version of a fraud on the market.

Larry E. Ribstein, *Market vs. Regulatory Responses to Corporate Fraud: A Critique of the Sarbanes-Oxley Act of 2002*[*]

... This Article argues that, despite all the appearances of market failure, the recent corporate frauds do not justify a new era of corporate regulation. Indeed, the fact that the frauds occurred after seventy years of securities regulation shows that more regulation is not the answer. Rather, with all their imperfections, contract and market-based approaches are more likely than regulation to reach efficient results. Post-Enron reforms, including

12. Henry T.C. Hu, *Faith and Magic: Investor Beliefs and Government Neutrality,* 78 Tex. L. Rev. 777, 778 (2000).

* Originally published in 28 Journal of Corporation Law 1 (2002). Reprinted with permission.

Sarbanes-Oxley, rely on increased monitoring by independent directors, auditors, and regulators who have both weak incentives and low-level access to information.[13] This monitoring has not been, and cannot be, an effective way to deal with fraud by highly motivated insiders. Moreover, the laws are likely to have significant costs, including perverse incentives of managers, increasing distrust and bureaucracy in firms, and impeding information flows. The only effective antidotes to fraud are active and vigilant markets and professionals with strong incentives to investigate corporate managers and dig up corporate information....

Whatever the cause, the costs of corporate fraud potentially go beyond owners, employees, and others associated with defrauding firms. If the market cannot distinguish efficient from inefficient firms, investors may, at least at first, put too many resources in the inefficient firms, and ultimately may stay out of the market because they cannot spot the "lemons," with the result that the economy becomes less productive. This suggests that if markets have failed, government must step in.

I. Regulatory Responses to Corporate Fraud

Highly publicized corporate frauds engendered a blizzard of reform proposals, mostly in Congress. Although current federal securities law does not permit direct federal regulation of corporate governance, Congress can change those laws. Moreover, even under the current general disclosure-oriented approach, Congress, and the SEC on its own, can regulate corporate governance indirectly through disclosure laws. The securities exchanges also can regulate corporate governance through their listing requirements....

II. Problems with the Regulatory Approach

A. Effectiveness of Regulatory Proposals

....

1. Increased Disclosure

The recent corporate frauds were attributable less to firms' silence or misleading than to the falsity of their disclosures. Thus, it is not clear how much difference the Sarbanes-Oxley requirements concerning disclosure of off-balance-sheet transactions, pro forma earnings, and material changes in financial condition will make in preventing future fraud. To be sure, burying information in financial statements can make it difficult for

---

13. *Section 301 of Sarbanes-Oxley, mentioned in the previous article, also added the following provision to § 10A of the 1934 Securities Exchange Act:*

(3)(A) Each member of the audit committee of the issuer shall be a member of the board of directors of the issuer, and shall otherwise be independent.

(B) In order to be considered to be independent for purposes of this paragraph, a member of an audit committee of an issuer may not, other than in his or her capacity as a member of the audit committee, the board of directors, or any other board committee—

(i) accept any consulting, advisory, or other compensatory fee from the issuer; or

(ii) be an affiliated person of the issuer or any subsidiary thereof.

17 U.S.C. § 78j-1(m)(3).

Sections 201–209 of the Act amend § 10A of the 1934 Act to add auditor independence requirements. 17 U.S.C. § 78j-1(g).

—Ed.

individual investors to determine a firm's financial condition. But misleading legions of analysts, reporters, and others in an active market requires greater opacity. In any event, these provisions deal with yesterday's problem. Recent events have cast so much light on these specific matters that additional wattage is unlikely to make any difference in these particular areas. The next great fraud probably will occur elsewhere.

2. The Marginal Deterrent Effects of Liability

... [T]he marginal deterrent effect of pre-PSLRA rules or post-Enron reforms on corporate actors' conduct, as compared with corporate actors' incentives under current law, is unlikely to be significant.

First, there is no indication that the above law changes significantly reduced federal securities law liability. To begin with, both the number of suits and the size of settlements have increased since the enactment of the PSLRA. This is consistent with the incremental nature of the law's changes. The PSLRA clarified the standard for pleading scienter by requiring the complaint to "state with particularity [the] facts giving rise to a strong inference that the defendant acted with the required state of mind." These pleading standards did not affect liability for fraud, were the same as that previously adopted by the Second Circuit, and nowhere significantly affected plaintiffs' ability to bring claims in the cases of blatant misstatements that have attracted recent attention....

Second, any effects of reducing securities liability must be considered in the context of the whole set of incentives and constraints facing corporate actors. Even without securities liability, accountants and corporate insiders still face state law liability for fraud and breach of contract. Although state law privity rules may block direct investor suits against auditors, a corporation or bankruptcy trustee can sue a corporation's auditors for failing to spot or report a corporate fraud....

To be sure, some may question the wisdom of leaving sanctions to state law or extra-legal devices. In particular, some commentators are skeptical of the power of reputational sanctions, and the threat of such sanctions obviously did not prevent the recent corporate frauds. But it is important to keep in mind that the issue under consideration is not whether federal liability for securities violations should be reduced, but whether it should be increased from present levels. The recent corporate frauds do not demonstrate that more penalties are appropriate. Rather, they demonstrate that corporate insiders are willing to proceed in the face of potential reputational or other injury because they are driven by strong impulses of loyalty, greed, or fear, and failed realistically to assess the risks of their conduct. It is unclear how more liability would have succeeded where other constraints failed....

The requirement of executive certification of issuers' reports in section 302 of [Sarbanes-Oxley],[14] which probably has received more publicity than any other provision, seems to provide an important incentive given its potential effect in triggering civil liability for misstatements made with the requisite scienter. But even under prior law, chief executives and chief financial officers had to sign the annual 10-K and the latter had to sign the quarterly 10-Q, with potential direct liability based on scienter. Thus, the rule's main innovation is requiring certification of, and therefore creating a basis of liability for, not only financial information, but also the firm's internal controls and the executives' candor with the firm's auditors and audit committee....

---

14. *Section 302 is described in further detail in Thompson and Sale's article in this chapter. — Ed.*

B. Costs of Increased Liability and Regulation

1. Agency Costs

Contracts in firms are designed to a significant extent to maximize the benefits and minimize the costs of hiring nonowner agents. In order to operate efficiently, large firms must separate capital raising and control functions. The tradeoff is that nonowner agents who control property have incentives to use their control to benefit themselves rather than the owners. This generates what have been referred to as "agency costs," which include the owner's costs of monitoring the agent, the agent's cost of posting a bond to protect the owner, and residual losses that agents impose on owners despite monitoring and bonding. Optimal contracting in the firm involves minimizing these costs without unduly reducing the benefits of using nonowner agents....

... Optimal agency contract design involves encouraging the agent to take the owners' interests into account, but not forcing the agent to bear so much of the firm's risks that she is more cautious than the owners would want her to be.

This general discussion suggests a potential problem with Sarbanes-Oxley provisions that encourage executives to police their firm's fraud, including section 302, which forces chief executives to vouch for their firms' financial statements and internal controls, and section 304, which requires reimbursement of compensation and stock profits following accounting misstatements. The former provision may permit liability on the basis of a court's ex post judgment that the executive certified controls that proved to be inadequate. The latter explicitly provides for liability up to the amount of compensation or stock profits for misconduct by others in the organization regardless of scienter, and, indeed, even if the executives exercised all reasonable care in monitoring and instituting controls. The provisions therefore require executives to bear some of the risk of fraud formerly borne more cheaply by diversified investors. This may increase rather than reduce agency costs in the sense of causing agents to act more conservatively than owners would prefer....

... First, they may manage the firm to reduce the potential for liability. One possible approach is to reduce the variance in its expected returns, thereby reducing the chance of an earnings "surprise" that could trigger massive liability.... Second, liability may perversely affect the disclosure policies executives set for the firm. The general agency problem is that, while executives do not get the benefits of minimizing disclosure costs or of extra clarity of disclosure, they bear the costs of failing to disclose fraud. For example, executives may under-report earnings on the theory that they are less likely to be held liable for overly conservative than for exaggerated earnings reports, cover themselves by inundating investors with information, or surround disclosures with obfuscating hedges and qualifiers. These options would not necessarily better serve investors' interests than managerial inattention to fraud....

The perverse effects of increased agent liability are exacerbated by regulation of agent compensation. Stock-based compensation may have the beneficial effect of aligning agents' and shareholders' incentives, as indicated by researchers' finding positive share-price effects associated with the adoption of stock-based compensation. Conversely, regulating such compensation could cause corporate executives to behave more like bureaucrats and less like entrepreneurs by reducing their benefits from risky decisions that pay off for the firm and their incentive to work hard to produce profits. This is particularly a problem regarding outside directors, who must take on new governance responsibilities while facing new restrictions on compensation....

2. Information Costs

Post-Enron regulation has two kinds of effects on information costs. On the one hand, the regulation directly increases firms' costs in part by requiring them to spend more to get information. In particular, new auditor regulation significantly increases firms' audit fees as well as their costs of dealing with and producing information for auditors. Although firms may get more and better information, the question is whether the increased benefits outweigh the costs.

The regulation also may indirectly increase firms' costs of obtaining the same quantity and quality of information.... The moves toward auditor and outside director independence are intended to reduce job-preservation incentives for fraud by severing other links between monitors and the monitored firm, such as by prohibiting consulting work by auditors or revolving doors between auditing and client firms, requiring periodic change of auditors, or forbidding independent directors from having other associations with or receiving other benefits from the company.[15] The problem is that monitors' other links with firms increase their access to information. If the fully independent monitor can duplicate the connected monitor's information, requiring greater independence just increases the firm's cost of obtaining information....

There may be similar effects at the director level. The closer the relationship between the director and the particular firm or industry, the more insight the director is likely to have into the firm's problems and the quality of the information the board is receiving. This relates to the board's ability not only to advise managers, but also to uncover fraud. For example, directors with inside knowledge of the company may be better able than outside directors to see through ambiguous, opaque, or misleading financial statements because they have enough background to understand the kinds of tricks insiders might be playing.

The costs and benefits of independence may vary from one situation to another. First, some types of independence may have higher net benefits than others. Monitors may have better or cheaper access to information if they perform other tasks for the company, but not if they simply receive more compensation. Second, the amount of information provided by monitors' other links with firms may vary according to the complexity or uniqueness of the firm's business. Third, the cost-benefit tradeoff may depend on how many levels of monitors the firm has. For example, it may make sense to require complete independence at the auditor or director level, but the total costs of independence may exceed the benefits if it is required at both levels. Thus, a fully independent audit committee might provide the optimal mix of independence and access without prohibiting nonaudit services. These variables and uncertainties support a flexible and contractual approach to regulation, including requiring disclosure of, but not otherwise regulating, auditor independence.

3. Distrust

The level of trust among those working in a firm can significantly affect the firm's operating costs by, among other things, increasing the flow of information among personnel and the extent to which people in the firm are willing to rely on informal assurances of reciprocal fair play, rather than insisting on costly regulatory and contractual protection. As discussed above, high levels of trust may disarm monitors. Conversely, mandating

---

15. [Sarbanes Oxley Act §§ 201, 203 & 301, 17 U.S.C. §§ 78j-1(g),(j) & (m).]

complete independence of monitors risks creating an adversarial relationship between insiders and outsiders that may reduce both the efficiency of day-to-day management and the monitors' access to information....

C. Politics of Reform

Sarbanes-Oxley emerged under circumstances that virtually ensure against the sensitive cost-benefit tradeoff that the above analysis shows is necessary. First, those who see corporate fraud as a wedge to push a broader regulatory agenda applied significant pressure in favor of regulation. Corporate fraud helped Democrats by discrediting Republican deregulatory and antitax policies and the probusiness Bush administration on the eve of the November 2002 Congressional elections. Republicans, for their part, risked compromising their broader agenda by appearing to side with corporate criminals.

Second, the political parties' general goals mesh to some extent with those of specific interest groups. For example, large, established issuers and law and accounting firms will tend to find it easier to comply with new regulations than smaller or newer firms. Some parties gain from corporate frauds, including the "monitoring" industry of large law firms and others who are hired to investigate corporate frauds and defend the accused and trial lawyers, demand for whose work will be increased by new duties and increased penalties.

Third, public perceptions contribute to this political environment. Revelations of corporate fraud coincided with public anxiety over the economy and populist sentiments condemning the insiders who took great wealth out of now-fallen companies. More importantly, just as judgment biases supposedly can make investors tend to underestimate risks in a rising or bubble market, so too can they lead investors and the public generally to overestimate risks and the need for regulation in a falling market....

Finally, the hasty adoption of the Sarbanes-Oxley Act in the midst of a stock market crash was even less conducive to careful weighing of costs and benefits than the circumstances surrounding typical legislation. By contrast, the law Sarbanes-Oxley amends, the Securities and Exchange Act of 1934, was enacted years after the 1929 Crash, following extensive hearings. The Sarbanes-Oxley Act, among other things, reversed decisions made in more deliberative settings on such important issues as auditor independence and attorney reporting of fraud.

III. Market Responses to Corporate Fraud

... [B]efore adopting regulatory solutions it is necessary to consider the feasibility of market-based responses.... Indeed, it was markets and not regulators that uncovered the problems and adjusted the share prices of offending companies, while years of regulation of securities disclosures and membership of boards of directors failed to prevent the frauds. In other words, dishonest insiders were able to outrun the kinds of monitors that regulators favor, but not, ultimately, the markets.

If markets can react, there are significant benefits to allowing them to do so. Market actors are likely to be better informed and motivated than regulators. Markets also lead to a variety of competing solutions. As long as these solutions are evaluated in liquid securities markets, the most efficient solutions are likely to dominate, and firms can pick the approaches that best suit their particular circumstances. A political or regulatory approach will pick a particular solution that may not be the most efficient overall..., and may be unsuitable for many firms.

Although market responses are likely to be imperfect, it is necessary to compare market with regulatory imperfections, rather than unrealistically assuming that only markets are flawed. Moreover, it is important to keep in mind that markets have been constrained by past regulation, particularly regulation of takeovers and of insider trading. Although repeal of this regulation may be politically infeasible amid calls for more regulation of the securities markets, it is worth reflecting on the contribution of past regulation to current problems when considering whether additional regulation is appropriate....

A. Market Scrutiny

Most of the corporate frauds that have been exposed so far left tracks in the public record that observant market watchers noticed before they caught the public's eye.... Fundamental risks of Enron's business, particularly including its susceptibility to competition in the various markets it was entering and the implausibility of the assumptions underlying its market valuation, were obvious to astute observers. Moreover, footnotes to financial statements disclosed the basic facts, if not the details, of Enron's potential exposure to debts incurred by special purpose entities.

This discussion indicates that the market can significantly reduce its vulnerability to fraud simply by paying closer attention to warning signs.... Market skepticism is more likely now that investor biases have moved from overoptimism to excessive pessimism....

Although market scrutiny of corporate conduct can increase without changes in the law, the level of market scrutiny is affected by past regulation. Regulation's perverse effects in this regard counsel caution about the desirability of additional regulation. An example is Regulation FD, which the SEC promulgated in August 2000, which requires firms that disclose material nonpublic information to securities analysts to publicly disclose the same information simultaneously or promptly....

The actual effect of Regulation FD, however, may be to reduce analysts' ability to uncover fraud. Regulation FD gave insiders a legitimate excuse for avoiding analysts, thereby making it easier for firms to hide accounting and other problems. Regulation FD was promulgated in August 2000, just as the bull market was ending and firms started to have strong incentives to manipulate their accounting in order to maintain their earnings increases and the high stock prices that depended on those increases. Thirty years ago, Ray Dirks broke the notorious Equity Funding scandal with information he obtained from a corporate insider because of Dirks' position as a leading insurance company analyst — a disclosure that the Supreme Court ultimately decided did not violate the securities laws,[16] but that may now violate Regulation FD....

Finally, it is important to be wary of regulation based on the need to restore investor "confidence." In the short run, this claim seems to be supported mainly by the apparent panic at the time of the passage of the Sarbanes-Oxley Act. Yet this panic itself might have had a political origin. More importantly, over the longer run, the investor confidence rationale depends on complex judgments about perceived, as compared to actual, market risk, the effect of various regulatory approaches, the benefits of additional investor confidence, and the costs of the law's requirements and liabilities.

Moreover, even if lack of confidence is keeping investors out of the market, it is not clear that regulation should bring them back in unless it actually justifies greater confidence. The Sarbanes-Oxley Act may justify little confidence because it makes only incremental

---

16. *See* Dirks v. SEC, 463 U.S. 646 (1983).

changes in prior law. Corporate frauds arguably were facilitated because there was too much investor confidence, as indicated by investors' willingness to ignore what the market knew about questionable accounting and to not question firms' extravagant claims about unproven business plans. Overselling regulation might perpetuate this misjudgment and mislead investors back into the same complacency that contributed to the recent frauds.

By contrast, a new stress on market risks and investor education could encourage the development of a more sophisticated market. Rather than betting their savings and retirement funds on single stocks, particularly including their employers in which they have already invested their careers, investors are better off diversifying their investments, as they seem increasingly to be doing. The market crash also might encourage investors to seek investment advice in various forms, including managed mutual funds, rather than speculating based on fads or the pronouncements of the latest hot analysts. A more sophisticated market will provide less fertile ground for future corporate frauds.

B. Signaling

.. Issuers have strong incentives to demonstrate to investors, consumers, creditors, potential employees, and others that they are not like Enron and WorldCom. This is particularly the case for firms using now-suspect devices such as derivatives and special purpose entities. Firms can signal, among other ways, by maintaining a high level of voluntary disclosure, including meetings with, and disclosures to, securities analysts and the media, or by voluntarily adopting reforms such as expensing stock options, as several companies have done.

The potential for signaling may not only reduce the benefits of regulation, but also may increase its cost. Mandatory governance rules reduce firms' ability to signal quality by choosing governance forms, auditors, disclosure methods, and so forth. The benefits of signaling may exceed those of regulation.

C. Shareholder Monitoring and Takeovers

Firms are subject to scrutiny not only by various capital and other markets, but also by their own shareholders. Shareholders do not need to wait for corporate managers or regulators to decide that firms need protection from fraud. First, institutional shareholders can press for these changes through direct communication with managers, as TIAA-CREF [Teachers Insurance and Annuity Association-College Retirement Equity Fund] has done regarding expensing of stock options, and through shareholder proposals that enable shareholders to gather support from other shareholders. Even if private institutions do not gain enough from such moves to invest significant resources in them, managers of public funds have political incentives to do so. In light of the political salience of the issue, firms' managers likely would respond positively to high-visibility institutional holders like TIAA-CREF and to shareholder proposals receiving significant, even if minority, votes. The proposals could serve as firm-by-firm referenda testing the level of shareholder acceptance of various alternatives, by contrast with federal laws or SEC rules imposed on all firms.

Second, and more importantly, there is a theoretical potential for monitoring by outside bidders for control. Bidders have the sort of high-powered, profit-driven incentives that independent directors, auditors, and analysts may lack. Even insiders in firms that are never subject to hostile bids may be less likely to take excessive compensation or to engage in fraud if they know potential hostile bidders are watching them. Among other things, bidders for control could buy firms that have hired low-quality auditors, directors, or managers, fire the monitors and hire new ones, and pocket the resulting difference in the share price.

A problem with relying on hostile takeovers for monitoring is that takeover regulation has eased the threat of such takeovers. Indeed, this regulation may help account for the recent corporate frauds. Extensive takeover regulation began in 1968 with the Williams Act, which imposed disclosure requirements on bidders and required them to structure their bids to give incumbent directors time to defend. This reduced potential gains from risky hostile bids, and therefore takeovers' effectiveness as a monitoring device. Despite the Williams Act, there was a takeover boom in the 1980s facilitated by Michael Milken's ability to quickly assemble massive financing and to count on the support of arbitrageurs, notably including Ivan Boesky. Formation of these networks may have depended to some extent on Milken's being able to share information about his moves with others. This detour around the Williams Act was closed with the prosecution of Milken for a technical violation of the Williams Act and with the adoption of SEC Rule 14e-3, which covered disclosures of information about impending acquisitions. State regulation of takeovers further limited their effectiveness, mainly by authorizing directors to adopt very effective poison pill-type defenses without shareholder approval.

Takeover regulation therefore has substantially diluted firms' agency-cost-control arsenal, forcing them to resort to second-best incentive devices and control mechanisms. The greater efficiencies created by, among other things, corporate downsizing and the increasing use of technology together with the hype of the dot.com boom, initially produced enough profits, or at least high enough stock prices, to cover any weakened discipline. But as the boom ended, the effects of weakened discipline started to show through.

The cure would seem to be to resurrect takeovers as a viable monitoring mechanism. While this is probably politically infeasible in the current environment, this discussion teaches a lesson about regulating corporate governance that suggests caution in responding to the recent corporate frauds. Takeover regulation was supposed to be the solution to the last problem of excessive job insecurity for managers and workers. But tinkering with corporate governance in response to this problem may have helped create the conditions for the next crisis of corporate fraud. The lesson is that additional market regulation may have unforeseeable perverse effects and should be approached with caution rather than embraced in panic.

D. Market for Regulation

Even if regulation may be appropriate notwithstanding regulatory costs and the availability of market-based remedies, there is a further question concerning the level at which this regulation should be imposed. Capital markets provide a mechanism for competition among various bodies of regulation as well as among corporations and individual corporate contracts. A firm's decision to be subject to a particular body of regulation is subject to capital market evaluation as part of its general bundle of governance terms.

These "contractual" approaches currently dominate regulation of corporate governance. The governance of U.S. corporations is largely determined by the law of the state in which each firm has chosen to incorporate. State legislatures can mandate particular forms of governance, such as independent directors, and state courts can impose standards of conduct, as in *Smith v. Van Gorkom*[17] and *In re Caremark International Inc. Derivative*

---

17. 488 A.2d 858 (Del. 1985).

Litigation.[18] Governance provisions in stock exchange listing agreements also can be considered a form of contract given firms' ability to choose the exchange or exchanges on which they are listed. The NYSE, for example, has an incentive in competing with Nasdaq and other exchanges to encourage firms to pay higher listing fees in exchange for a lower cost of capital by assuring investors in those firms that the NYSE is actively monitoring them. The same principle could apply to competition among professional associations of auditors.

The Sarbanes-Oxley Act changes course from this contractual approach to corporate regulation. Its provisions relating to, among other things, the composition of board audit committees, the activities of corporate counsel, protecting whistleblowers, regulating loans to officers, requiring reimbursement of bonuses and stock profits, mandating disclosures regarding particular types of transactions and of the issuer's code of ethics for senior financial officers, fixing responsibility on officers for corporate disclosures, and increasing the SEC's power to bar people from serving as officers and directors, all involve insertions of federal regulators into corporate governance. The Act thus sides with corporate reformers who argue for a federal corporation law on the ground that corporate managers' ability to influence the firm's incorporating decision disables state law as a constraint on insider misconduct.

Federalizing corporate governance should be approached with caution. The state-based system of regulating corporate governance can be considered one of the main strengths of the U.S. capital markets. Moreover, there is significant evidence supporting the view that firms' incorporation decisions are efficient. The occurrence of recent corporate frauds is as much an indictment of the effectiveness of existing federal regulation of disclosure as of state regulation of governance. Even if some reform is appropriate ... any reform involves complex cost-benefit tradeoffs. Moreover, governance rules should be designed to suit the particular circumstances of each firm, as indicated by the evidence that there is no optimal level of board independence. These considerations suggest that these issues are best resolved in a market for regulation that would permit experimentation and flexibility.

Nor do the recent corporate frauds indicate a specific problem with Delaware law, which currently dominates state competition. Interestingly, at least two of the main culprits, Enron and WorldCom, were not Delaware corporations, but rather incorporated in Oregon and Georgia, respectively. These firms' choice of state law may have been based on an expectation of favorable regulatory treatment or better protection against takeovers than in Delaware. The recent corporate frauds may encourage firms to consider more carefully how well the incorporating state protects shareholders against managerial agency costs and may encourage Delaware to sharpen its corporation law to compete in this altered market. In other words, Delaware is more likely to be part of the solution than to have been part of the problem.

One possible qualification of the pro-state-law position concerns state antitakeover law. It has been argued that state competition is inefficient to the extent that it involves the rules managers care most about, namely protection against takeovers. This argument is significant given takeovers' role as a potential market-based constraint on managerial agency costs. Nevertheless, it is not clear that state takeover defenses either are effective or reduce shareholder wealth. Thus, even if firms tend to be attracted to states that have stronger antitakeover laws, this may either not harm shareholders or may increase shareholder wealth because the benefits of such protections for particular types of firms

---

18. 698 A.2d 959 (Del. Ct. Ch. 1996).

(for example, in encouraging managers to make firm-specific investments of human capital in their firms) outweigh any increase in other agency costs. Moreover, it is significant that the leading incorporation state (Delaware) has a relatively weak antitakeover statute. As suggested above, the new focus on agency costs in the wake of the recent corporate frauds may increase the benefits of takeovers, and thus may cause firms to move from very protective states to Delaware. A federal corporation law would eliminate such choices. Indeed, federal antitakeover law may be more of a problem than state law, in part because the former applies equally to all firms regardless of firm-specific characteristics.

Not only are there arguments against federalizing corporate governance law, but there are strong arguments favoring extending jurisdictional competition from internal governance rules into the area of disclosure rules. Some commentators propose permitting issuers to choose their disclosure regime. Even under current law, firms can to some extent choose their disclosure regime. Foreign issuers have significant ability to avoid U.S. regulation and have provoked exemptions and rule changes in the United States aimed at encouraging foreign issuers to raise capital here. Securities exchanges can be effective in promoting jurisdictional competition. Despite some commentators' fears of a race-to-the-bottom in securities regulation, there is substantial evidence that issuers have chosen to bond their integrity by deliberately choosing regimes with more rigorous regulation.

For present purposes, it is unnecessary to go all the way to competition of disclosure rules. The question at hand is simply whether to increase regulation in the light of recent corporate frauds, including reducing the amount of jurisdictional competition that already exists, assuming this would be feasible. The serious questions about the costs and benefits of proposed regulation support subjecting these proposals to the discipline of jurisdictional competition.

Roberta S. Karmel, *The Future of Corporate Governance Listing Requirements**

...

I. The Development and Legal Status of Listing Standards

A. *The History of Stock Exchange Listing Standards*

1. *The NYSE [New York Stock Exchange]*

[*"Listing standards"* are criteria, set by a stock exchange and approved by the SEC, which a securities issuer must meet in order for its securities to be traded on that exchange. — Ed.] The first NYSE listing standards were not considered a set policy by the exchange but instead were flexible terms inserted in listing agreements negotiated between each issuer and the exchange. The contractual flexibility of listing agreements meant that listing standards were not uniformly enforced and were subject to change. Also, because such standards were not retroactively applied, nonconforming issuers who had obtained listings prior to a new rule were not delisted. Thus, the NYSE employed no uniform set policy

---

* Originally published in 54 SOUTHERN METHODIST UNIVERSITY LAW REVIEW 325 (2001), Vol. 54, No. 1 of the SMU Law Review. Reprinted with permission of the SMU Law Review and the Southern Methodist University Dedman School of Law.

which applied to all listed companies. Nevertheless, this flexibility allowed the NYSE to change its listing agreements according to its economic needs....

Historically, listing standards were seen as a substitute for government regulation. The NYSE argued that if its listing standards for securities offered for sale adequately protected the investing public, then government regulation would be unnecessary. Former President of the NYSE, Richard Whitney, stated in a memorandum submitted to the Committee on Banking and Currency of the United States in 1932 the following in support of furthering self-regulation of securities exchanges:

> New forms of securities are frequently evolved, and changes in the corporations acts of the states, together with changes in economic conditions, give rise to frequent new problems as to forms of charters, accounting methods, and business practices. The attitude of the exchange is one of constant watchfulness to prevent the admission to its list of securities of corporations the nature of whose business and character of whose charters, or whose business and accounting practices, do not appear to adapt such securities to widely disseminated public ownership.[19]

Initially, the NYSE was concerned with financial disclosure, but this emphasis precipitated several corporate governance listing standards. An annual stockholder's meeting, the first corporate governance standard, was imposed as a term within the listing agreement and was eventually linked to annual reporting requirements. By 1900, listing agreements required companies to distribute annual reports to [their] stockholders. By 1909, those reports had to be distributed prior to the stockholders' annual meeting. By 1914, agreements provided that a listed company notify the exchange of any change in the rights of stockholders or in the redemption of preferred stock. By 1917, agreements provided for the disclosure of a semiannual income statement and balance sheet. In 1926, the NYSE adopted a one-share, one-vote listing standard. The history of this standard and its demise will be discussed [below]....

By 1932, independent audits became mandatory for all new listed companies. Also by 1932, companies agreed to report their earnings quarterly. Finally, with the enactment of the Exchange Act, the policies of the NYSE regarding independent audits became a matter of federal law. The value of the NYSE's listing requirements was demonstrated by the fact that "Congress closely tracked the NYSE disclosure requirements when it drafted the Exchange Act." ...

Even after the promulgation of the Exchange Act, the NYSE was still concerned with the practices of its listed companies. However, the impetus for these changes may have been "the NYSE's focus during that time on bolstering trading volume." The NYSE believed that by appealing to the needs of the individual investor and improving corporate governance practices, it could attract additional investors for already listed shares....

Today, the NYSE's listing standards include policies and requirements regarding "independent audit committees, ownership interests of corporate directors and officers, shareholders' voting rights, and other matters affecting shareholders' ownership interests and the maintenance of fair and orderly markets in listed securities," including the election of independent directors, holding annual shareholders' meetings, and the solicitation of proxies. It has been argued that the NYSE's incentives were disingenuous concerning investor protection, since its primary goal was to successfully compete in the marketplace for listings among the exchanges. Notwithstanding those accusations, history illustrates

---

19. Hearings on S. 84, 72nd Cong., 1st Sess., Part I, at 285–56 (1932), *cited in* Max Lowenthal, *The Stock Exchange and Protective Committee Securities,* 33 Colum. L. Rev. 1293, 1298 (1933).

that the NYSE, since its inception, was dedicated to ensuring the integrity of the securities markets and used listing standards as a device to protect investors and the market in general. If the NYSE believed that better listing standards gave it a competitive edge, this does not mean investor protection was an unimportant goal. Stock exchange listing standards are deeply rooted in NYSE history and may not be as easily compromised by competition and demutualization as critics of the NYSE assume. Nevertheless, competition among exchanges and demutualization may reduce the NYSE's bargaining leverage in pushing for higher standards. These issues will be further discussed [below].

2. The American Stock Exchange

Compared to the NYSE, the American Stock Exchange ("AMEX") adopted significantly more lenient listing standards and initiated them at a much later date in history. One possible explanation for this inaction is because throughout AMEX's entire history, it competed with the NYSE for listings....

During the 1960s, reforms swept through the AMEX. In 1962, following the exposure of several scandals, the SEC issued a report criticizing almost every aspect of the AMEX's operations, including its board, methods of stock listing and retention, and trading methods. The [Securities and Exchange Commission] SEC concluded that the AMEX failed at achieving any type of self-regulation. Only then, the AMEX began to initiate several reforms regarding its organization and listing standards.... [*AMEX was acquired by the NYSE's parent company in 2008 and was renamed NYSE Amex Equities in 2009.*]

3. Nasdaq

The history of Nasdaq listing requirements is rooted in state blue sky merit regulation. Every state, the District of Columbia, and Puerto Rico has a securities regulation statute. Some state blue sky regulation is merit regulation. A merit regulator has the authority to prevent an issuer from selling securities in the state because the offering or the issuer's capital structure is "substantively unfair or presents excessive risk" to investors. Although the blue sky laws vary from state to state, they all contain a requirement for registration of securities to be sold in the state. However, most state securities laws traditionally provided an exemption from their securities registration requirements to issuers which were listed on a national securities exchange....

In 1985, the Nasdaq initiated its first corporate governance listing standard in an effort to secure blue sky exemptions in a greater number of states. These standards included the submission of annual and periodic reports to shareholders, appointment of independent directors, an independent audit committee, required shareholder participation in certain corporate transactions, and execution of a listing agreement. This was part of a campaign for broader exemptions from state registration so that securities listed on Nasdaq or designated as "National Market System Securities" would be exempt from state blue sky registration requirements.

This controversy concerning the merit of Nasdaq listing standards in contrast to the standards of national securities exchanges was settled by the National Securities Markets Improvement Act of 1996, which preempted state regulation of the securities registration and offering process for "covered securities." This means merit review is not applicable to nationally traded securities, including Nasdaq listed securities. As a result, competition was eliminated between the NYSE, AMEX, and Nasdaq for better listing standards where this competition was an effort to exempt issuers from state blue sky merit review.

4. Foreign Issuers

Foreign issuers can obtain a waiver from many NYSE corporate governance requirements if an independent counsel licensed in the issuer's home country opines that its practices are not prohibited by the issuer's domicile. This means, in effect, that if the laws in the issuer's home country are silent or do not explicitly require the standard, the foreign issuer will be able to obtain a waiver. Under the AMEX and Nasdaq listing rules, similar exemptions are available. [*An SEC rule change in 1987 empowered exchanges to grant these exceptions.*][20] ...

A critic of the foreign issuer listing standards has argued that the rule change was an SEC response "to the needs of its constituencies, the U.S. stock exchanges and their investment banking members to develop a U.S. market for foreign securities."[21] Differences among the corporate governance practices of foreign issues would unduly inhibit those companies from listing on American exchanges unless foreign issuers were afforded special treatment.

The SEC concluded that the foreign issuer listing rule would not have a "detrimental competitive impact on domestic companies." The SEC stated that it was "appropriate to permit differentiations from the requirements imposed on domestic companies in order to permit the exchanges to be more competitive on an international basis and to provide access to U.S. investors to investment opportunities in a large number of foreign securities." Nevertheless, there is some concern that domestic issuers will eventually campaign for a reduction in listings requirements under the same justifications cited for foreign issuers, an argument for equal treatment of all issuers....

Excusing foreign issuers from listing standards can be justified on the ground that corporate governance is generally a matter of home state regulation, but it can also be viewed as a means to attract foreign issuer listings in a competitive global market. Thus, the competition for listings can result in races to the top or races to the bottom, depending upon how an exchange perceives its competitive edge with regard to particular listing standards.

B. The SEC's Authority over Corporate Governance

Corporate governance is primarily a matter of state corporation law. This was expressed by the United States Supreme Court in a non-securities law case as follows:

> Corporations are creatures of state law, and investors commit their funds to corporate directors on the understanding that, except where federal law expressly requires certain responsibilities of directors with respect to stockholders, state law will govern the internal affairs of the corporation.[22]

Thereafter, in *Santa Fe Indus., Inc. v. Green*,[23] the Court applied this principle in a case arising under the federal securities laws involving a short form merger. Under Delaware law owners of at least ninety percent of a subsidiary's stock may merge with that subsidiary

---

20. *Self-Regulatory Organizations, Order Approving Proposed Rule Changes by the American Stock Exchange, Inc. and New York Stock Exchange, Inc. to Amend the Exchanges' Listing Standards for Foreign Companies,* Exchange Act Release No. 24,634, 52 Fed. Reg. 24,230 (June 23, 1987).

21. James A. Fanto, *The Absence of Cross-Cultural Communications: SEC Mandatory Disclosures and Foreign Corporate Governance,* 17 Nw. J. Int'l L. & Bus. 119 , 177 (1996).

22. Cort v. Ash, 422 U.S. 66, 84 (1975).

23. 430 U.S. 462 (1977).

without requesting the consent of minority shareholders—who, in turn, must receive fair value for their shares. The plaintiff, the minority shareholders in Santa Fe, did not allege any material misrepresentation or omission. Rather, they argued that the antifraud provisions of the federal securities laws were applicable to a breach of corporate fiduciary duty, in that the majority shareholders were not pursuing a legitimate corporate purpose. The Court, however, refused to apply Rule 10b-5 to allegations of internal corporate mismanagement. It stated: "Absent a clear indication of congressional intent, we are reluctant to federalize the substantial portion of the law of corporations that deals with transactions in securities, particularly where established state policies of corporate regulation would be overridden." ...

The more common view is that the Securities Act is a full disclosure, rather than a merit, statute and the SEC does not have the power to regulate corporate governance....

Nevertheless, the SEC has had a tendency to use disclosure requirements for their prophylactic effect of regulating corporate conduct. In addition, various provisions of the Exchange Act can and have been used by the SEC to effect corporate conduct. These include regulatory authority over proxy solicitations and regulatory authority over tender offers. Further a catch-all antifraud provision and broad rulemaking authority gave the SEC the ability to utilize enforcement cases and disclosure rules to impose its notions about corporate governance on public companies. In a wide variety of management fraud cases and disclosure rules concerning management remuneration the SEC succeeded in regulating corporate governance....

II. The SEC's Authority over Stock Exchange Rulemaking

A. Statutory Provisions

Until 1975, exchange listing standards were clearly the subject of private or contract law between an exchange and its listed companies. However, in 1975, Congress laid the foundation for the establishment of a national market system in amendments to the Exchange Act. Without mandating specific components of the national market system or even defining the term, Congress vested the SEC with broad flexible authority to design, implement, and regulate the trading markets. Further, important new powers over stock exchanges and the NASD were given to the SEC. Sections 19(b) and (c) of the Exchange Act gave the SEC a new power to approve, disapprove, abrogate, add to, or delete from rules adopted by exchanges. Any amendments to any exchange rules mandated by the SEC remain rules of the exchange and do not become SEC rules. Nevertheless, the SEC's authority under section 19(c) is limited to actions in "furtherance of the purposes" of the Exchange Act....

B. Audit Committee Requirements

As early as 1940, the SEC recommended that corporations form audit committees composed of independent directors. The SEC did not have an opportunity to force such a requirement on public companies, however, until the 1970s. In connection with widespread scandals concerning questionable or illegal payments by many public corporations to domestic and foreign government officials, the SEC discovered inadequate or improper corporate books and records that concealed the existence of these payments. This was very disturbing since the integrity of corporate books and records is essential to the entire reporting system administered by the SEC. Among other things, the SEC pointed to the importance of audit committees in uncovering falsification of corporate records and the use of "slush" funds and endorsed audit committees as appropriate models of corporate conduct....

The NYSE thereafter developed such a proposal. On March 9, 1977, the SEC then approved the NYSE rule requiring all listed domestic companies to establish by June 30, 1978, and maintain thereafter, an audit committee comprised solely of directors independent of management and free from any relationship that "would interfere with the exercise of independent judgment as a committee member." ...

The voluntariness of the NYSE's adoption of this rule was debatable. So was the extent of the SEC's power to compel the NYSE to change its listing requirements. Although the SEC might have invoked its power to modify exchange listing requirements, since it is questionable that the SEC could compel issuers to form audit committees, it could have been argued that the SEC's power to mandate listing requirements to this effect was not in furtherance of the purposes of the Exchange Act. Such an analysis would have been in keeping with the Court's demarcation between federal and state power in Santa Fe. On the other hand, the SEC has fairly broad powers to define auditor independence. Further, the SEC has the power to mandate disclosure about corporate governance matters, and about this same time it exercised its authority by requiring a description of the structure of certain board committees, including the audit committee....

The NYSE listing standards therefore now provide that each listed company must have a qualified audit committee that meets certain standards. The audit committee must have a formal written charter specifying the scope of the committee's responsibilities and how they are implemented, including the accountability of the outside auditor to the board and audit committee and that the committee satisfies itself that the outside auditor is independent. In addition, the audit committee must have at least three directors who have no relationship to the company that may interfere with their independence, and each member must be financially literate; one member must have accounting or related financial management expertise. The new AMEX and NASD rules are essentially the same, but have slightly different definitions of "independence" and financial literacy. [*The Sarbanes-Oxley Act of 2002 made the independent audit committee a universal and uniform requirement.*]

In this more recent round of rulemaking on audit committees there were almost no voices raised questioning the SEC's authority to pressure exchanges into revising their listing requirements, even though the D.C. Circuit Court had in the interim between 1977 and 1999 struck down the SEC's efforts to impose a one-share, one-vote standard on exchanges, as will be explained below. Whether this was because of general agreement on the advisability of the tightened standard, or the exchange's seeming voluntary initiatives with regard to improving its audit committee requirements, is unclear. As a practical matter, the SEC has enormous leverage over exchanges and so they are unlikely to resist SEC "suggestions" that are not controversial or perceived by an exchange to be contrary to its interests.

C. The One-Share, One-Vote Listing Requirement

An important shareholder protection listing standard that was in effect at the NYSE from 1926 until the late 1980s was the principle that all shares of common stock of a listed company should have one vote. During the hostile takeover boom of the 1980s, however, some companies engaged in defensive recapitalizations whereby company insiders obtained shares with greater voting rights than public shareholders. Some well known

AMEX listed companies, for example Wang, had a weighted capitalization of ten to one in favor of insiders and ... such unequal voting shares were permitted by the AMEX and Nasdaq. The NYSE proved unable to resist this competition, especially after General Motors Corporation ("GM") issued a class of lesser-weighted voting shares in connection with its acquisition of Electronic Data Systems, Inc. ("EDS")....

... [I]n 1984, when GM acquired EDS, it refused to comply with the NYSE rule and threatened to list with competitor exchanges AMEX or Nasdaq. Because of the importance of GM as a listed company, the NYSE ignored its rule and did not delist GM.... Finally, in 1986, the NYSE officially modified its "longstanding rule mandating a one-share, one-vote for all common stocks listed on the NYSE." Several factors influenced the NYSE to reconsider the rule:

> the growing competition for listings with the AMEX and NASD, the desire of NYSE-listed companies to adopt disparate voting rights plans as takeover defenses, the belief that corporate issues should have flexibility in raising capital and adopting corporate structures, and the belief that regulatory changes, such as improvements in corporate disclosure, had made the shareholder protection provided by the one-share, one-vote rule less important.[24]

The NYSE abandonment of its one-share, one-vote rule illustrates the political organization of the exchanges and the limits of exchange regulation. Competition among the exchanges was the primary cause leading to revision of the rule. The NYSE folded after feeling pressured by listed corporations to abandon its policy.... Indeed, the NYSE's abandonment of the one-share, one-vote rule has been used as a critique of exchange regulation, raising questions about the exchanges' credibility in enforcing investor protections.

After attempts to persuade the exchanges to adopt a uniform voting rights rule failed, in 1988 the SEC adopted its own rule to the Exchange Act prohibiting listed companies from changing the voting rights of common stockholders. Recognizing that the abandonment of the NYSE rule would have far reaching consequences, the SEC adopted Rule 19c-4 that required the exchanges to bar the listing of a domestic corporation's securities if that company acted disparately to reduce the per share voting rights of existing stockholders. The rule prohibited an issuer from issuing securities, or taking other corporate action, which would either nullify, restrict, or disparately reduce the per share voting rights of common stockholders. Nevertheless, disparate voting rights were permitted if they served a bona fide business purpose. The rule was intended to achieve several contradictory goals: ensure management accountability; limit hostile tender offer situations and adverse changes in corporate control; maintain the rights of public shareholders; limit competition among SROs [self-regulatory organizations; i.e., the stock exchanges]; and preserve the integrity of U.S. securities markets.

However, in 1990, in *Business Roundtable v. SEC*[25] the D.C. Court of Appeals abrogated Rule 19c-4 on the grounds that the rule directly controlled the substantive allocation of powers among classes of shareholders and therefore was in excess of the SEC's authority under section 19 of the Exchange Act. In the court's view, the rule was not in furtherance of any purpose of the Exchange Act, and could not be justified under the proxy rules, the SEC's plenary power over exchanges, including its power to approve or add to exchange

---

24. *Voting Rights Standards; Disenfranchisement Rule*, Exchange Act Release No. 25,891, 53 Fed. Reg. 26,376, 26,377 (Jul. 12, 1999)
25. 905 F.2d 406 (D.C. Cir. 1990).

rules, or its powers to facilitate the establishment of a national market system and designate securities qualified for trading in such a system. This is because permitting the SEC to adopt corporate governance standards through the back door by mandating uniform listing standards would disrupt state jurisdiction over corporate governance and shareholder voting rights. Although an exchange could adopt a voting rights listing standard, such a standard was not a rule under the authority of the Exchange Act. This was not viewed as the exercise of governmental power regulating an issuer.

The *Business Roundtable* case did not put an end to the voting rights rule story. After much negotiation with the SEC, the NYSE and Nasdaq adopted a uniform rule that was essentially a modified version of former SEC Rule 19c-4. The policy prohibited any restriction or disparate reduction in the voting rights of the common stock of public shareholders through any corporate action. In view of changes in the marketplace, the NYSE emphasized the "flexibility" of the new policy: "The Exchange's interpretations under the Policy will be flexible, recognizing that both the capital markets and the circumstances and needs of listed companies change over time." The rule was intended to eliminate a race to the bottom in shareholder voting rights. It was the NYSE's stated aim to permit those corporate actions previously permitted under Rule 19c-4. As such, the policy does permit disparate voting rights and the listing of non-voting common stock as long the stockholders are afforded certain safeguards, which seek to align (as much as possible) the rights of non-voting shareholders with voting shareholders. Minimum voting rights are also required for preferred stockholders.

Several commentators have suggested that the primary motivator for the NYSE's decision to maintain a voting rights rule was a "concern with public opinion." However, the NYSE has emphatically stated that its policy is based upon a desire to "encourage high standards of corporate democracy." It would appear that in the case of the voting rights rule, as in the case of exchange rules concerning audit committees, the SEC accomplished what the D.C. Circuit Court said it could not do—establish a federal voting rights standard through the back door of exchange listing standards. Yet, the legal basis for such initiatives is unclear and the tenuous nature of the SEC's power in the corporate governance area weakens the ability of exchanges to establish and enforce listing standards that issuers find objectionable.

III. The Current Status and Future of Listing Standards

A. *Stock Exchange Demutualization*

When the Exchange Act was passed in 1934 and when it was amended in 1975 to establish a framework for SEC regulation of exchanges, stock exchanges all operated in the form of non-profit mutual or membership organizations under state law. To the extent market power was not curtailed by competition or regulation, mutual governance gave specialist or market maker members of an exchange control of the price, quality, and range of services produced by the exchange. Exchange profits were returned to broker and dealer members in the form of lower access fees or trading profits. Further, exchanges have long operated as self-regulatory organizations ("SROs") with members contributing their time to governance and self-regulation to make exchanges more effective and more profitable. Self-regulation gave exchanges more credibility as quasi-public institutions and also protected their monopoly type powers....

In addition to having to compete with new markets, the world's exchanges are demutualizing [*that is, converting from non-profit mutual or membership organizations to for-profit corporations*], and this is leading to new challenges. The first exchange to demutualize was the Stockholm Stock Exchange in 1993, followed by the Helsinki Stock Exchange in 1995, the Copenhagen Stock Exchange in 1996, the Amsterdam Stock Exchange and the Borsa Italiana in 1997, and the Australian Stock Exchange in 1998. By the end of 2000, many more exchanges will have joined this group, including the Paris Bourse, the Toronto Stock Exchange, the London Stock Exchange, and Nasdaq.... [*The NYSE demutualized and became a for-profit, publicly traded company in 2006. Its current parent company, NYSE Euronext, is itself traded on the NYSE.*][T]he Stockholm and Australian Stock Exchanges have [also] gone public and listed on their own boards.

When the federal securities laws were passed, stock exchanges were required to register with the SEC. The SEC thus obtained oversight authority over stock exchanges, but the stock exchanges continued to have rulemaking and regulatory authority with respect to their members, their trading markets, and their listed companies. Although the efficacy of self-regulation was called into question by stock market abuses reported in the 1963 SEC Special Study, that study concluded that self-regulation should be maintained and strengthened. Nevertheless, in 1964 the SEC obtained greater direct authority over the continuous disclosures made by public companies. Previously, the SEC was given power to regulate financial disclosure by issuers making initial public offerings, but after 1964 the SEC also was given responsibility for regulating annual and periodic reports.

The 1975 [amendments to the Exchange Act] further strengthened the SEC's oversight role over the stock exchanges and NASD by, among other things, giving the SEC the power to initiate and approve SRO rulemaking, thus expanding the SEC's role in SRO enforcement and discipline by allowing the SEC to play an active role in structuring the market. For the first time, the statute set forth requirements with respect to the composition of exchange and association boards of directors. The 1975 Act sought to preserve and reinforce the concept of industry self-regulation with SEC oversight. However, by directing the SEC to facilitate the creation of a national market system, injecting competition as a statutory goal and giving the SEC greater authority over SRO rulemaking, disciplinary activities and other matters, the SEC became able to exert more leverage over exchange self-regulation and corporate governance than in the past....

One of the more contentious questions under discussion concerning exchange demutualization is the future of self-regulation. There are several issues that have been raised. First, some have argued that there would be conflicts of interests between shareholders and members in a demutualized exchange environment that would diminish the ability of exchanges to engage in effective self-regulation. A potentially more serious conflict is the regulation of an [alternative trading market (e.g., a regional exchange, such as the Pacific Stock Exchange)] by the NYSE or NASD. Second, securities firms are concerned about the costs of multiple SROs, especially if several alternative trading markets become exchanges and begin to engage in self-regulation. Therefore, some industry members are arguing in favor of a single SRO for exchanges and member firms.

Exchanges engage in self-regulation in four areas: listed company governance and disclosure; surveillance and discipline of their markets and specialists, floor brokers and market makers; member firm financial and operational compliance; and fair and equitable treatment of customers. Of particular relevance to the future of listing standards is what conflicts will be encountered if and when Nasdaq or the NYSE become public companies.... By what authority could a for-profit public company regulate other companies?

[*As noted above, both Nasdaq and the NYSE are now for-profit, publicly traded companies. The enforcement of NYSE listing standards is now handled by an independent, not-for-profit company, NYSE Regulation, Inc. Self-regulation in the post-demutualization era nonetheless remains a cloudy and contentious issue.*[26]]

IV. Conclusion

In a future marketplace of demutualized for-profit exchanges it is difficult to predict whether listing standards will be used as a differentiating marketing device for selling higher quality trading products, or whether listing standards will be abandoned in a competitive race to list issuers. It is likely that the ability of exchanges to adhere to and enforce listing standards that become unpopular with listed companies will be more difficult for exchanges that are themselves listed companies. Whether the SEC would be able to compel exchanges to maintain and improve such listing standards is entirely a matter of politics. Very little tinkering with section 19(c) of the Exchange Act would be required for Congress to overturn the result of the *Business Roundtable* case. Also, the case could be distinguished or overruled in subsequent cases.

Other private section solutions are also possible. The securities industry has employed self-regulation in a wide variety of ways to avoid direct government regulation. It can be anticipated that even if stock exchanges become unable to effectively raise and police the corporate governance standards of their listed companies, some self-regulatory solutions to resulting problems will be proposed as preferable to direct SEC regulation of corporate governance.

Discussion Questions

1. Langevoort points out two broad types of legal response to widespread corporate scandals and failures: punishing specific wrongdoers and making systemic changes. Which approach should the government emphasize and why? By what mechanism does each approach hope to improve the situation? What assumptions does each approach make about markets, politics, and human behavior?

2. While protecting investors and encouraging investment can be complementary, they can also conflict, as Professor Langevoort points out. He argues that this tension causes the SEC to take the middle ground. Is this result a desirable one? How should corporate governance law and policy manage the tension between investor protection and investor confidence? Is it justifiable to promote investor confidence at the cost of understating the risks of investing? Is it justifiable to frighten off investors in order to protect them from the possibility of loss?

3. In Chapter 1, Bratton argued that Enron and its contemporaneous debacles illustrate the failure of markets and the need for greater regulation. Ribstein argues, however, that the disasters may indicate the failure of economic *regulation* as it existed prior to Enron. At any time, the "free market" is in large part the product of regulations, so market problems may indicate over-regulation as well as under-regulation. Ribstein argues that

---

26. *Karmel discusses the issue further in* Should Securities Industry Self-Regulatory Organizations Be Considered Government Agencies? 14 Stan. J.L. Bus. & Fin. 151 (2008).

Enron and related debacles show that the prevailing "monitoring model" of corporate governance is incapable of preventing fraud by "highly motivated insiders." Do you agree? Can the "monitoring model" be reformed, as post-Enron reforms attempt to do, or should it be cast aside? If the latter, do you agree with Ribstein that contract and market solutions are a suitable replacement?

4. Is federal securities regulation's traditional focus on disclosure appropriate? Or should it increase its involvement in matters of directors' duties and governance structure, as it has in Sarbanes-Oxley?

Langevoort favors many of the Sarbanes-Oxley reforms that Ribstein criticizes as federal intrusion into corporate governance matters that are traditionally left to the states. Where should the line be drawn between federal and state authority over corporate matters? Is it sufficient to give the federal government authority over "securities regulation" and the states authority over "corporate governance"? What does this line-drawing problem say about regulatory competition in corporate chartering and Roberta Romano's proposal to expand it to securities regulation?

5. Langevoort and Ribstein agree that future Enrons might be prevented if investors reduced risk by lowering their expectations and broadly diversifying their investments. On the one hand, this advice reflects the conventional wisdom familiar to everyone: "there's no such thing as a free lunch" and "don't put all your eggs in one basket." On the other hand, however, investors have ignored this sage advice for centuries.

One commentator has argued:

> If history is permitted to be a guide, emotions will beat governance every time. Put forensically, the market exuberance of the late 1990s and early 2000s did not arrive out of the blue, but constituted repetition of a pattern seen repeatedly in world financial history. The cause of schemes such as Global Crossing or Enron is more likely rationality breakdown than regulatory breakdown.

Lawrence A. Cunningham, *The Sarbanes-Oxley Yawn: Heavy Rhetoric, Light Reform (And It Just Might Work)*, 35 CONN. L. REV. 915, 979 (2003).

If investors periodically descend into irrationality, how should the law respond to that fact? Should regulators protect investors from their own irrationality? If so, how? Should regulators take a hands-off approach and let irrational investors suffer losses in hopes that they will eventually learn their lesson? Can market irrationality be corrected with better investor education and information, as Ribstein suggests? If so, who should take the lead in providing education? *See* James A. Fanto, *We're All Capitalists Now: The Importance, Nature, Provision and Regulation of Investor Education*, 49 CASE W. RES. L. REV. 105 (1998).

6. Langevoort argues that MD&A should require a narrative that candidly explains risks as well as any differences between "accounting reality" and "economic reality." What are the benefits and limitations of his proposed reforms?

Are investors better off under a mandatory disclosure regime (which may contribute to an "expectations gap") or under a voluntary disclosure regime (under which the buyer is required to beware)? What kinds of expectations and assumptions about human behavior justify each regime?

7. Langevoort and Ribstein, like Bratton in Chapter 1, argue that investors should recognize some degree of management fraud as another type of investment risk. Do you agree with this assessment? How does the risk of fraud differ from other kinds of risk? How does the legal treatment of fraud differ from the legal treatment of other kinds of risk?

Should federal securities law move toward treating fraud like other forms of risk or continue to treat fraud differently?

8. What do you make of Ribstein's proposal for improving corporate governance through reduced takeover regulation instead of increased securities regulation? We will return to the topic of takeovers in Chapter 11.

9. Can stock exchanges, through their listing standards, provide a kind of regulatory competition among securities regulation regimes like that Roberta Romano (in the previous chapter) proposed that the states provide? How do the exchanges as regulators differ from states as regulators?

10. To what extent do stock exchange listing standards constitute "federal law"? As Karmel points out, the nature of the SEC's power over listing standards is unclear. Consider the convoluted history of the "one share, one vote" requirement. Does it illustrate the strength or the weakness of the existing regime? How does the adoption of "one share, one vote" as a uniform listing standard differ from having the same requirement in the SEC Rules? What are the pros and cons of each approach?

Is it appropriate for the SEC to pressure exchanges to adopt listing standards that are beyond the SEC's power to impose in the form of regulations, as it arguably did in the "one share, one vote" episode?

Should the SEC's relationship to the exchanges change now that the major stock exchanges are for-profit, publicly traded companies? Why or why not?

11. When the Enron Corporation failed in 2001, early public attention focused on the plight of Enron employees who had lost their jobs and their 401(k) retirement savings. As rumors of the company's troubles began to surface, employees, whose 401(k) accounts were heavily invested in Enron stock, questioned management about the condition of the company. Kenneth Lay, Enron's chair and CEO, assured employees that the company was sound. Meanwhile, Enron prevented employees from trading in their 401(k) accounts while Lay and other managers sold their stock. Soon thereafter, the stock price crashed and Enron went into bankruptcy.

Other corporate scandals around the same time had similar effects on employees. Job losses had negative ripple effects on the national and local economies. The scandals also caused huge financial losses for bondholders and other creditors.

Despite the harm done to non-shareholder interests, the Sarbanes-Oxley Act and other post-Enron reforms focus on making management more responsive to shareholders rather than to employees or other constituents. Why? Do you agree with that emphasis?

12. In Chapter 3, Prof. Kamar questioned whether Delaware corporate law is subject to competitive pressures from other states. Other commentators have argued that the primary pressure on Delaware comes not from other states, but from the federal government. Delaware legislators and courts make corporate law with the knowledge that federal securities authorities (including Congress, the SEC, and the federal courts, as well as the securities exchanges) can preempt Delaware law that displeases them. Mark Roe, *Delaware's Competition*, 116 HARV. L. REV. 588 (2003); *see also* Renee Jones, *Rethinking Corporate Federalism in the Era of Corporate Reform* 29 J. CORP. L.625(2004).

Roe points out that in the first year after the passage of the Sarbanes-Oxley Act, all of the Delaware Supreme Court's decisions went, often surprisingly, against managers (as did a major Chancery Court decision, *In re Walt Disney Co. Derivative Litigation*). He suggests that after the federal government's new wave of post-Enron reform, Delaware courts' reaction was to "get tough" with management out of fear of federal preemption. What do you think of this explanation?

As Enron faded from public memory and the stock market recovered, the same Chancellor who had issued a pro-plaintiff decision in the *Walt Disney* case held against the shareholder-plaintiffs at trial, and the Delaware Supreme Court upheld that verdict. The Supreme Court's opinion appears later in this volume.

13. Given states' traditional place in corporate governance law, why do you suppose the legislative response to Enron and its contemporaneous scandals came almost entirely at the federal level? Does the regulatory competition discussion from the previous chapter shed any light on this question?

14. The Sarbanes-Oxley Act has been criticized for mandating practices (such as independent audit committees of corporate boards and the prohibition of non-audit services by corporate auditors) whose efficacy is not supported by empirical evidence. *See* Roberta Romano, *The Sarbanes-Oxley Act and the Making of Quack Corporate Governance,* 119 YALE L. J. 1521 (2005). The Act's critics are split over whether the Act has been excessively burdensome on corporations, too lenient toward management, or mostly harmless. But critics of all stripes tend to agree that the Act was driven by politics rather than an understanding of corporate governance problems. What political forces are at play in corporate and securities law reform? In light of the effect of politics, what interests would you expect legislation to favor?

15. The years following Sarbanes-Oxley saw many publicly held corporations "go private"—that is, acquirers bought out their public shareholders.[27] Some of the Act's detractors argued that companies were going private because the Act had imposed excessively burdensome reporting requirements on public corporations. But one commentator has argued that Sarbanes-Oxley cannot fully explain the going-private phenomenon, because most large corporations that go private *do not* escape Sarbanes-Oxley reporting. Most large going-private transactions in the post-Sarbanes-Oxley period have been financed by borrowing—that is, by issuing bonds. To avoid legal limitations on their resale, these bonds are usually registered with the SEC, triggering reporting requirements, including those under Sarbanes-Oxley. *See* Robert P. Bartlett III, *Going Private But Staying Public: Reexamining the Effect of Sarbanes-Oxley on Firms' Going-Private Decisions,* 76 U. CHI. L. REV. 7 (2009).

Small- and medium-sized public corporations that go private, however, tend to use other methods of financing that do not require Sarbanes-Oxley reporting. *See id.* What does this disparity suggest about the costs and benefits of Sarbanes-Oxley? Does it suggest smaller companies should be exempt from the Act?

---

27. The management buyouts (MBOs) discussed in Edward Rock's article in this volume were a type of going-private transaction, as were many of the hostile takeovers of the 1970s and 1980s discussed Chapter 11 and elsewhere in this book.

Chapter 5

Shareholder Litigation

Corporate and securities laws are enforced through private litigation more than through government civil or criminal actions. As in other civil litigation contexts, the perennial question is how to balance the beneficial aspects of private law enforcement against the dangers of excessive, frivolous lawsuits. In 1995, Congress addressed this issue with the Private Securities Litigation Reform Act (PSLRA), which attempted to restrict federal securities lawsuits. Steven Ramirez questions the PSLRA's restrictions and argues that a better balance could be struck if securities fraud claims were moved out of the courts and into a specialized arbitration forum. Marilyn Johnson, Karen Nelson, and A.C. Pritchard argue that strict judicial interpretation of the PSLRA has benefited shareholders. Their article addresses fundamental questions about the normative goals of securities regulation and the use of empirical studies in policy making.

As with other forms of litigation, the value of shareholder suits lies not only in the immediate resolution of disputes, but also in their potential to deter future misconduct. Like Professor Rock in Chapter 3, James Cox believes that law performs not only a coercive role, but also an "expressive" role as the communicator of social values. Thus Cox hypothesizes that the deterrent effect of federal securities lawsuits and state derivative litigation derives not only from the likelihood of an adverse judgment, but also from the perceived legitimacy of the shareholder lawsuit as an institution.

Given that corporations are chartered at the state level and state law traditionally defines the shareholder-management relationship, federal shareholder litigation implicates the federalism themes of the previous two chapters. Robert Thompson and Hillary Sale look at corporate federalism through the lens of federal securities litigation. Arguing that shareholder claims traditionally brought in state fiduciary litigation are increasingly being brought in the guise of federal securities fraud, they highlight the uneasy distinction between state "corporate" and federal "securities" law and raise questions about the purpose of federal securities regulation.

Steven A. Ramirez, *Arbitration and Reform in Private Securities Litigation: Dealing with the Meritorious as Well as the Frivolous*[*]

... An important debate is raging regarding the federal regulatory role in the securities markets. On one side of this debate are those arguing that private securities litigation is dominated by greedy attorneys who use protracted litigation to extort large settlements

---

[*] Originally published in 40 WILLIAM AND MARY LAW REVIEW 1055 (1999). Copyright 1999 The William and Mary Law Review. Reprinted with permission.

from legitimate business, imposing a pernicious "litigation tax" upon the cost of capital in America and flooding our courts; on the other side are those arguing that private litigation is the only realistic means of enforcing federal regulation, that the American financial markets are widely perceived to be the fairest and most efficient in the world, and that there is little, if any, evidence that the system has been abused. The stakes in this debate are huge. American fortunes ride upon the success of our financial markets as never before because of increased international economic competition and important demographic trends. Unfair financial markets are a breeding ground for panic. Inefficient markets, like those that impose arbitrary costs upon capital, stunt economic growth. Most importantly, the public must have confidence in the integrity of our financial markets in order to insure a stable and inexpensive source of capital for American business growth.

... [T]hose arguing in favor of restricting private enforcement of the federal securities laws have scored near-fatal restrictions in the scope of private remedies available under the federal securities laws. In late 1995, Congress enacted the Private Securities Litigation Reform Act of 1995 (PSLRA), which restricted private claims generally and class actions in particular. Congress enacted this legislation for the purpose of restricting "strike suits." Congress viewed these suits as a threat to the ability of financial markets to finance start-up companies and generate jobs. One notable effect of these "reforms" is that securities litigation has shifted to state courts. Consequently, Congress [in the Securities Litigation Uniform Standards Act of 1998 (SLUSA)] preempted state law claims when raised in class action suits involving publicly-held companies. Perhaps the most critical effect of the PSLRA, however, is that it leaves private enforcement of the federal securities laws in near terminal condition. This Article proposes an approach to resolving the tension between weeding out frivolous securities claims and permitting meritorious claims to proceed that neither side in this debate is likely to embrace. Specifically, this Article proposes that private securities claims relating to public companies be arbitrated to the maximum extent possible. Arbitration has a long and successful history in the securities broker-dealer industry, in which it is the dominant form of dispute resolution....

I. The PSLRA: Wrong Reform in the Wrong Industry at the Wrong Time

Any discussion of the proper method of resolving private securities claims must begin with the historical basis of such litigation. Private securities litigation under federal securities laws is only a part of the overall enforcement of the federal regulatory regime. This regulatory regime includes the imposition of registration requirements designed to achieve full disclosure of material facts to the financial markets, the regulation of the securities brokerage industry, and the prohibition of fraudulent conduct through the broad antifraud provisions of the federal securities laws.

Enforcement mechanisms consist of SEC civil enforcement proceedings and penalties, including administrative sanctions, criminal sanctions, and the extension of private remedies to injured investors. The broadest private remedy and antifraud provision is Rule 10b-5, which the SEC promulgated pursuant to statutory authority under the Securities Exchange Act of 1934 ("Exchange Act"). Although Congress has tightened this regulatory regime periodically, Congress had left its basic structure largely intact until it enacted the PSLRA. Before that, this regulatory scheme had functioned successfully for over sixty years.

A. A Short History of Private Securities Litigation

The federal role in securities regulation has its roots in the ultimate financial catastrophe—The Great Depression. Shortly after taking office, as one of the earliest New Deal initiatives, President Franklin Roosevelt proposed legislation that ultimately became the Securities Act of 1933 ("Securities Act"). The Securities Act required the registration (and accompanying full disclosure) of initial distributions of securities. The Securities Act focused only upon initial offerings of securities; therefore Congress enacted the Exchange Act, which provided for regulation of the securities industry and required periodic disclosure for publicly-held companies. Roosevelt made clear that these acts were designed to heighten fiduciary obligations in securities transactions in order to restore public confidence in the nation's financial markets. Congress joined the President in emphasizing the importance of investor confidence within a modern economic system.

The courts initially embraced the remedial nature of the federal securities laws and broadly interpreted their provisions to achieve those ends. Further, the courts, as well as the SEC, recognized the crucial role of private securities enforcement proceedings as an essential supplement to the SEC's limited enforcement resources. Indeed, in 1946, the federal courts began to imply private rights of action under the federal securities laws. Since then, the Supreme Court has determined the existence of a private action under Rule 10b-5 to be "beyond peradventure," and has proceeded to define this implied private right of action in a series of opinions. The Court, with the support of the SEC, allowed the private remedy under Rule 10b-5 to thrive, and no Justice has ever seriously questioned the propriety of recognizing such a remedy.

After many decades of remarkable success, and with fading memories of the cataclysm of the Great Depression, the judicial view of private securities litigation "evolved" from a "necessary enforcement supplement" to a positively vexatious tool. In an era of pervasive demonization of attorneys, the private securities lawyer became the caricature of the greedy, self-serving destroyer of upstanding captains of industry. Courts began to take a more restrictive approach to private securities claims.

By the 1990s, the Supreme Court in particular seemed determined to reign in private securities claims. In *Lampf, Pleva, Lipkind, Prupis & Petigrow v. Gilbertson*,[1] the Court dramatically shortened the statute of limitations applicable to private claims under Rule 10b-5. In *Central Bank of Denver v. First Interstate Bank of Denver*,[2] the Court eliminated aiding and abetting liability in private actions under Rule 10b-5. In *Gustafson v. Alloyd*,[3] the Court restricted the availability of rescission claims under the Securities Act by engrafting a requirement that a plaintiff in such an action be a purchaser in a public offering. These are only the most recent judicial retrenchments. Some commentators have noted that the Court has been scaling back investor protections under the federal securities laws for twenty years.

The lower federal courts, taking a cue from the Supreme Court, have developed broad doctrinal rules that have resulted in an increasing number of early dismissals or summary judgments in private securities cases. For example, the federal courts used Federal Rule of Civil Procedure 9(b) as a means of terminating private securities claims, often in ways that turned that rule on its head. Similarly, the lower courts developed doctrines that effectively robbed juries of the ability to determine if the given conduct constituted fraud

---

1. 501 U.S. 305 (1991).
2. 511 U.S. 164 (1994).
3. 513 U.S. 561 (1995).

by granting judicial discretion over the issue, which invariably resulted in claim termination. Securities claims were blamed for much of the flood of litigation allegedly swamping the federal courts. The tone of many judicial opinions changed as well, from open sympathy for the purposes of the federal securities laws to open hostility toward private claims. Securities plaintiffs, beginning in the 1980s, began facing the frequent imposition of sanctions. Although the Court has continued to interpret the federal securities laws broadly in areas dominated by public enforcement action, it recently has expressed little support for private enforcement of the federal securities laws.

In 1995, Congress significantly curtailed the availability of private securities claims under federal law by enacting the PSLRA. The PSLRA modifies the sanctions available against private securities claimants in a manner approaching a "loser pays" regime. Under Federal Rule of Civil Procedure 11, federal courts are granted discretion to impose sanctions against those pleading claims that are not legally warranted, supported by evidence, or pursued for a proper purpose. Under the special sanctions provisions now applicable to securities claims, courts must scrutinize pleadings for compliance with Rule 11 at the end of a case and must assess sanctions if a violation is found. The PSLRA also creates a presumption that the appropriate sanction for a complaint that violates Rule 11(c) is an award of all attorneys' fees and costs incurred by the defendants during the entire action. There is no similar provision for answers that violate Rule 11(c).

Ironically, Congress amended Rule 11 in 1993 specifically because it had led to abusive "satellite" litigation....

The PSLRA imposes heightened pleading standards in actions under the Exchange Act's antifraud provisions that are a dramatic departure from the notice pleading standards generally imposed under the Federal Rules of Civil Procedure. Under the Federal Rules of Civil Procedure, allegations as to a defendant's state of mind may be alleged generally, at least if one takes a plain meaning approach to the statute. Now, for private claims under the federal securities laws, a plaintiff must plead facts "giving rise to a strong inference" of scienter. Judicial interpretations of this new pleading requirement have raised the question of whether it can be satisfied at all, short of explicit admissions of an intent to defraud. For example, courts have held that pleading a mere motive and opportunity to commit fraud fails this heightened pleading standard. Even before the PSLRA, courts had used Rule 9(b) to terminate claims that seemed improbable to them; now it seems courts are eager to use the PSLRA as a basis for even wider terminations.

This heightened pleading standard endangers important securities law principles, such as the "group-published" information doctrine, which had operated to preclude defendants with joint drafting responsibility for documents from shifting the responsibility to some other drafter. Under the PSLRA, a court could conceivably hold that a plaintiff must allege facts giving rise to a strong inference of scienter against each defendant. The PSLRA also denies a plaintiff discovery until this pleading standard is satisfied. Thus, not only must a plaintiff allege facts "giving rise to a strong inference" of fraud, the plaintiff also is denied discovery in aid of uncovering such facts.

The PSLRA creates a safe harbor for certain fraudulent misstatements in "forward looking statements." Specifically, the PSLRA protects specified persons from liability for such statements if the statement is accompanied by "meaningful cautionary statements" that identify important factors that could cause actual results to diverge from projections, even if the statements are made with a fraudulent intent. Persons who enjoy this insulation from liability include issuers, underwriters, and reviewers of information provided by issuers. The PSLRA provides various exemptions from the applicability of the safe harbor and limits the application of the safe harbor to statements relating to issuers that are required to register under the Exchange Act.

The PSLRA statutorily prescribes causation standards that may be interpreted to support broad pretrial terminations of securities actions. It requires that plaintiffs plead loss causation in all claims brought under the Exchange Act. Similarly, defendants now may avoid rescission liability under section 12(2) of the Securities Act if they can prove an absence of loss causation. Loss causation is a form of proximate cause that requires a plaintiff to allege and prove that, but for the defendant's wrongdoing, the plaintiff would not have incurred the damages that form the basis of the suit. Thus, if a plaintiff invested because a securities promoter did not disclose his criminal background, but the plaintiff suffers damages because of a crash in oil prices, the plaintiff can show only transaction causation and not loss causation.

This provision of the PSLRA directly overruled many federal decisions that required only "but for" causation or "substantial factor" causation for claims under the federal securities laws. For example, under the proxy rules, courts have long held that materiality satisfied causation requirements for private litigants. Loss causation generally is a form of proximate cause that cuts off claims for injuries that are deemed too remote from the alleged misconduct. As a result of the PSLRA, courts will now dismiss more claims of securities fraud for failure to demonstrate causation. State courts generally have been far more lenient in dealing with causation in the securities area, leaving the issue to the jury.[4]

Prior to the PSLRA, securities violators were jointly and severally liable. Under the PSLRA, only defendants who knowingly commit violations of the Exchange Act are jointly and severally liable. Other defendants are liable only for the proportion of damages for which the trier of fact finds them responsible. Thus, under the PSLRA, the trier of fact must determine each defendant's liability. The PSLRA includes certain exceptions to the operation of the modified system of proportionate liability it imposes, such as preserving joint and several liability against those who commit knowing violations of law. This "reform," which essentially shifts the risk of an insolvent or judgment-proof defendant to the plaintiff, specifically operates only with respect to meritorious claims.

The PSLRA also takes aim at private class actions brought under the federal securities laws. Class actions frequently have been the subject of scholarly analysis and have been criticized for creating divergent interests between class members and class counsel. The PSLRA presents a multi-pronged attack upon private securities class actions. First, individuals are restricted from acting as lead plaintiffs in such actions without certifying that they meet certain eligibility requirements and have received no payments for serving as class representatives. Congress intended these eligibility requirements to eliminate "professional plaintiffs." Second, the incentives for initiating class actions are diminished because control over such actions now generally vests in a lead plaintiff, who is presumed to be the person with the greatest economic stake in the litigation. Congress intended this provision to encourage institutional investors, or other significant investors, to control class counsel and to assure that the litigation is pursued for the benefit of the class. Third, class settlements of securities claims must be supported by far more extensive disclosures than those required for other claims. This provision serves to assure settlements are fair to investors. These provisions have a common thread: Congress wanted a check on the power of class counsel to manage the litigation in their own interest. Along these lines, Congress also required that attorneys' fees awarded pursuant to any class settlement not exceed a reasonable percentage of the damages awarded the class....

---

4. *The Supreme Court emphasized the importance of the PSLRA's loss causation requirement in* Dura v. Broudo, 544 U.S. 336 (2005). — *Ed.*

B. An Assessment of the PSLRA

One effect of the PSLRA is that many plaintiffs have pursued securities claims in state court. Thus, the "reforms" wrought by the Court and Congress have resulted in the de facto de-federalization of private securities claims. Another result is sure to be weaker enforcement of the federal securities laws and, therefore, less incentive for compliance. Despite its likely effects, the PSLRA was passed with little debate of the risks of returning to a pre-Depression regime of investors being relegated to state law remedies, or the dangers of deregulation in the financial services industry.

With federal regulation emasculated, discussion of the prospects for a "race to the bottom" among the states in securities regulation takes on a new importance. Every state would want to encourage business development within its borders, especially if the costs of doing so can be shifted to out-of-state investors. In fact, Arizona already has passed legislation modeled on the PSLRA.

One also must question whether Congress really is prepared to increase the resources allocated to the SEC or to rely on the states to increase regulation to compensate for decreased private enforcement. Indeed, [in the SLUSA], Congress ... preempted state law remedies in certain cases, and now forces plaintiffs to run the gauntlet in federal court in some cases involving publicly-traded companies. This is a further move toward the risky strategy of financial deregulation. The original conception of federal securities regulation— that the nation needed federal regulation to create more stringent standards of conduct than those prevailing under state law—seems to have been lost in the shuffle.

Additionally, to the extent that Congress has now joined the Court in a bias away from private enforcement, such a bias seems fundamentally misguided. First, virtually all experts working in securities law enforcement recognize the crucial role private enforcement plays in assuring compliance with the federal securities laws. Second, private enforcement, unlike public enforcement, is fundamentally remedial in nature, reflecting one of the basic goals of the federal securities laws—to provide remedies to injured investors. Third, the compensatory nature of the federal securities laws is fundamental to investor confidence. Investors are most sensitive to their pocketbooks and only private enforcement truly protects this interest. Moreover, stacking the deck against securities plaintiffs is a sure-fire way of destroying the confidence of investors in the fairness of financial markets. The preservation of investor confidence is another foundational goal of the federal securities laws.

The system that worked so well appears to have been taken for granted. Indeed, Congress appears never to have really considered issues of investor confidence, de-federalization, enforcement costs, and remediation of investors' losses. In sum, federal law, originally promulgated to enhance the rights of investors relative to state law now serves only to diminish the rights of investors. The recent "reforms" of private securities litigation are a betrayal of several fundamental goals of the federal securities laws and expose our financial system to risks that are not fully appreciated. A more reactionary cycle could hardly have been imagined by the promulgators of the federal securities laws in the early 1930s.

The federal securities laws have been a success. For six decades after their promulgation, panics largely have disappeared and American capital markets have successfully fueled the demand for start-up capital, thereby aiding the economy's ability to generate continued growth through innovation. The market disruptions that have occurred have not damaged the economy and have been temporary in nature. America's financial system has served as a model for the world.

With such a successful record, any argument for a substantial structural change should be supported by compelling evidence....

The putative problem [justifying reforms like the PSLRA] is that federal securities laws are abused by "entrepreneurial" attorneys bent upon extracting extortionate settlements from innocent issuers and associated persons. The leverage for these sharp practices is the large costs of defending such claims through endless pleading and discovery squabbles to trial. Supposedly the merits of these claims do not matter, and settlement is achieved based upon the costs of the litigation. Stock price volatility invariably leads to claims of fraud. Thus was born the "litigation explosion" that impaired American capital formation, discouraged risk taking, and enriched lawyers at the expense of American workers. The story currently makes excellent politics, but there is little or no evidence to support it. Scholars have shown an utter absence of a "litigation explosion," have demonstrated that any evidence that capital formation has been stunted is weak, and have opined that the merits matter very much to the price paid for settlement of claims.[5] Indeed, this was abundantly clear at the time the PSLRA became law. The growing perception is that the PSLRA is not about "merits" at all, but rather is simply about money and influence peddling. This is a dangerous perception.

Moreover, there is even less evidence that the putative solution to the putative problem will work. The solution embodied in the PSLRA simply makes it much more difficult and expensive for plaintiffs to prevail and, ironically, makes a merits-based adjudication even more difficult to obtain. For example, PSLRA's class action reforms will lead to even more litigation regarding who will serve as "lead plaintiff." The PSLRA has the obvious side-effect of throwing out the meritorious with the frivolous. This is problematic inasmuch as it sacrifices justice in order to chill the pursuit of weak claims. Worse yet, it appears that the "reforms" fail to curb the supposed abuses. Each of the primary "reforms" suffers from an inherent flaw in logic: increasing the risks of sanctions for claims that fail is useless against frivolous claims that settle and fails to recognize that discovery often is needed even to assess the merits of claims. Similarly, the PSLRA safe harbor has failed to encourage more meaningful forward-looking disclosures. Increasing the pleading standards of claims certainly will prevent many claims from proceeding, but there is no assurance that only the weak claims will fail to clear this hurdle....

Any argument in favor of the PSLRA garners no support from the record of the securities industry over the past ten or fifteen years. Although empirical evidence on this score is hard to come by, most commentators agree that the business of issuing, selling, or buying securities has not advanced to such an ethical and fair level that traditional regulatory strictures should be relaxed. In fact, many believe the contrary to be the case.

Indeed, the 1980s and early 1990s were a sordid time for financial markets in the United States. Regulators uncovered massive insider trading scams. Outlaws built a new market for a new kind of security—junk bonds—on a foundation of fraud and manipulation.[6] This, in turn, extended to corporate take-over artists the necessary financial firepower to run roughshod over, dismantle and dismember long-established businesses. Rogue divisions

---

5. *See* 141 CONG. REC. S19,057 (daily ed. Dec. 21, 1995) (statement of Sen. Bryan) (summarizing the empirical evidence showing no securities litigation explosion and healthy increases in capital formation).

6. *"Junk bond" is a name for a type of bond that offers a high interest rate, but also runs a high risk of nonpayment (which accounts for the derogatory nickname). Issuing junk bonds was (and still is) often used to finance corporate takeovers. While there is nothing inherently fraudulent about junk bonds, they were associated with scandals in the 1980s: the pioneering 1980s junk-bond financier Michael Milken ended up in prison for securities-law violations. —Ed.*

of previously respected broker-dealers systematically channeled retirees and IRA funds into reckless limited partnership investments in blatant breach of all standards of law and the securities profession. Prestigious Wall Street firms bilked savings and loans, banks, insurance companies, and even municipalities on a scale previously thought impossible. No market was safe from such skullduggery, as one pillar of Wall Street even manipulated the market for U.S. Treasury obligations. This pervasive run of fraud, theft, and malfeasance imposed astounding costs upon our economy; trillions were lost, much of which is still being paid off. Such frauds militate strongly against relaxing any sanctions available under the federal securities laws.

Other economic developments support the argument against imposing restrictions upon investor remedies. In fact, public participation in, and reliance upon, the financial markets is greater than ever. When the baby-boom generation begins to retire at the end of the next decade, the capital markets will be expected largely to finance this huge claim on capital. This could well begin an unstable economic era that will test investors' confidence in the financial system. When Congress was debating the PSLRA, this issue caused concern among some members. Consequently, the PSLRA included a provision directing the SEC to study the impact of the PSLRA upon the investments of senior citizens. Ironically, that study concluded that, while seniors may be susceptible to fraud and abuse, it was "too soon" to determine the impact of the PSLRA upon this important group of investors. This is, however, an issue that cannot be left to chance. These investors must have the highest degree of confidence in the fairness of our financial markets because they will control a large source of capital. Even now, investors over sixty-five own, directly or indirectly, one-third of all shares; by 2020, there will be more than twenty million new seniors. The aging population also means that there is no crisis in the securities industry, as profits are at record levels....

C. Why the Merits of the PSLRA Matter

This Article does not argue that frivolous lawsuits do not exist, or that such lawsuits do not cause injuries to innocent defendants, investors, the marketplace, and the economy generally. Discouraging frivolous lawsuits is a laudable goal. Allowing investors to have greater control over class actions also is laudable and the PSLRA includes innovative provisions for achieving this goal. Although empirical evidentiary support for an explosion of frivolous litigation is weak, the anecdotal evidence that there are some abuses is strong. Expert after expert testified to serious problems emerging in the private securities litigation arena. A parade of SEC commissioners attested to strong indications that the private securities enforcement system was not operating correctly. In fact, President Clinton did not oppose the goals of the PSLRA, only certain provisions that he thought would "have the effect of closing the courthouse door on investors who have legitimate claims." The PSLRA simply goes too far given the scope of the problem....

Moreover, perceptions are important for issuers of securities as well as for investors. If the perception is that "going public" is accompanied by an arbitrary litigation tax, more costly sources of capital may be utilized and inefficiencies created. Similarly, if the perception is that there is an "innovation tax," some companies, especially new or smaller companies, may be more risk averse than is necessary. To the extent that the PSLRA addresses these concerns, it is difficult to argue that the Act has no merit. Quite simply, it is a salutary goal to eliminate frivolous litigation, and the securities business, because of its complexity and economic importance, may justify special litigation rules to quell such suits.

The issue therefore, becomes one of balance. The benefits of private enforcement must be balanced against the dangers of "strike suits." Any special litigation rules for securities claims must be tested against this balance, and the set of special rules that achieves the most promising balance should be implemented. The next section of this Article will demonstrate that arbitration is the special litigation procedure that achieves the best balance. Arbitration can thrust the merits onto center stage and slash defense costs— these benefits are fatal to strike suits and can restore fairness and efficiency to capital markets.

II. Arbitration: The Road Not Taken

... The system of securities arbitration for broker-customer disputes has been under intense scrutiny for many years. The General Accounting Office (GAO) has studied the fairness of the system and has concluded that it is not inherently biased in favor of the industry. Other scholarly studies of the fairness of arbitration in the SRO for a generally have concluded that investors are given "fair" treatment....

A. *The Advantages and Disadvantages of Broadening the Role of Securities Arbitration*

... This Article proposes the implementation of a system of arbitration modeled on the arbitration systems governing broker-customer disputes. This kind of arbitration is characterized by: the use of small panels of adjudicators with legal and nonlegal expertise in the securities industry; informal procedural rules providing for expedited discovery and adjudication; limited appeal rights; elimination of juries; the restriction of extended motion practice; standardized discovery provisions; and minimal technical requirements, such as particularity in pleading. Under such a system of arbitration, the emphasis shifts from technical legal analysis to doing that which is just. Arbitrators may not ignore the law, but they are not bound by it either.

1. *Potential Pitfalls of Wider Securities Arbitration*

... [E]xpansion of securities arbitration to all securities disputes involving publicly-traded companies is a specific area of law in which the benefits of ADR [alternative dispute resolution] easily outweigh the detriments. This Article demonstrates that the criticisms leveled at ADR generally do not apply with full force to the kind of securities arbitration proposed herein.

One of the most persuasive criticisms of arbitration, and of the Supreme Court's willingness to enforce almost all arbitration agreements, is that it allows powerful interests to use superior resources and bargaining power to impose unfair restrictions on the legal rights of the weak.... Indeed, the courts have been quite reluctant to void arbitration agreements on grounds of unconscionability or unfairness. Instead, courts have allowed parties to impose unfair conditions on remedies such as the ability to select arbitrators, restrict the statute of limitations, and eliminate punitive damages, all under the guise of arbitration agreements.

This Article does not propose an unregulated arbitration regime. Indeed, the Court has approved of securities arbitration only because of the SEC's oversight. This Article proposes a highly regulated arbitration process in which the SEC and Congress ultimately would determine how arbitrators are selected, which procedures apply, which methods of discovery are available, and which remedies are authorized. The SEC and Congress already have been successful in regulating securities industry arbitration. The proposed arbitration system simply would allow the SEC (with congressional oversight) to expand its supervisory role and to apply arbitration procedures to a larger universe of securities disputes. Given the SEC's reputation as a tough but fair regulator and an effective pro-investor advocate, as well as its track record in regulating industry arbitration procedures, there simply is no reason to suspect that the evils of unregulated arbitration would infect wider securities arbitration under the auspices of the SEC. The proposed expansion of securities arbitration also must be tested against the currently existing system (i.e., the system under the PSLRA), which has undergone a severe restriction of investor remedies, instead of against a historical ideal securities adjudication system. Viewed in that light, arbitration hardly disempowers investors, who currently have few rights under federal law. If the SEC can provide a fair forum, investors will benefit greatly from arbitration because it would provide a quick, nonappealable remedy. Consequently, the proposed arbitration would empower, not disempower, consumers of securities.

Delegalization is another criticism that persistently has been leveled against ADR. The idea of delegalization raises two concerns: first, that movement to ADR retards the ability of the law to evolve creatively to meet new problems or to craft new solutions on behalf of society, and second, that the movement of disputes from the courts to ADR has the effect of denying legal rights because arbitrators are not bound by law. Although the Court no longer views the second point as valid, it is sound in theory. Specifically, it is true that because arbitrators are not bound by law they may deny relief in circumstances in which legal remedies otherwise may exist. It is just as true, however, that there may be circumstances in which the law denies remedies and arbitration extends them. Arbitrators are charged to do what is just and fair; this is, after all, the end game of law. If arbitrators ignore law to achieve justice, has the purpose of law been frustrated? This Article takes the position that choosing justice over formalistic law is the superior result.

With respect to the first concern identified above, securities arbitration supervised by the SEC need not lead to any atrophied area of law. First, the expansion of arbitration advocated in this Article would have no impact on the development of the antifraud provisions of the federal securities laws in the criminal context, in the context of SEC enforcement actions, or in securities disputes not involving public companies. In many ways, the criminal and enforcement context is the context in which the SEC's regulatory influence is most prominent. For example, a criminal action recently enabled the SEC to expand liability for insider trading to persons who are not classic "insiders." The antifraud provisions could continue to develop in these contexts and be applied to SEC-sponsored arbitration proceedings. Second, all other areas of law that could be subject to the proposed arbitration jurisdiction would continue to develop in state proceedings not involving publicly held companies. Again, these developments could be applied to SEC arbitration proceedings. Third, the antifraud provisions are committed to the discretion of the SEC. The SEC therefore is in a position to redefine the antifraud provisions administratively in response to new frauds. Similarly, if the SEC sees fit to modify existing obligations in light of new circumstances, there is no sound reason why it should not be able to do so. Finally, the SEC could require written opinions, and publish those of widespread importance or those addressing novel issues....

2. Advantages of Wider Securities Arbitration

Certain types of disputes are more amenable to arbitration than others, and securities disputes appear to be ideally suited to arbitration. First, this is an area where expert adjudicators have the ability to extend a higher quality of justice because of the complexity and specialized nature of these disputes. Courts have recognized the shortcomings of juries in the context of sophisticated business litigation. One court even held that in certain cases due process could be denied if a case is of sufficient complexity as to be beyond the ken of a typical jury. Securities litigation often may qualify as such a case. It often demands knowledge of sophisticated business techniques and financial analysis, as well as how such factors may affect a company's securities. Highly qualified experts with advanced business degrees may be called upon to testify. Depending upon the business involved, a case may require expertise in biotechnology, computer engineering, or the oil industry. Arbitration seeks to substitute expert fact finders for lay fact finders. This may not only enhance the quality of justice available but also lower the cost of adjudications. Using experts in this way does not in any way call into question the abilities of jurors. In fact, specialized arbitrators also may be preferable to judges. An arbitrator who is an accountant is likely to know what motivates accountants better than a judge without an accounting background. In any event, comparisons between juries and arbitrators are misplaced. Under the PSLRA, juries only rarely hear securities claims. Arbitration of these disputes thus is more democratic than the current dispute resolution regime.

Second, this is an area that can limit litigation costs by requiring standardized discovery. Transactions involving the securities of publicly-traded companies produce predictable sources of documentary evidence. For example, investment bankers and other professionals usually are involved in material transactions and compile extensive "due diligence" files containing the findings of their investigations. Similarly, attorneys and accountants maintain detailed files containing relevant, nonprivileged information. These documents can be produced at the outset of every securities dispute, thereby greatly reducing discovery squabbles, lowering expenses, and increasing efficiency.

Third, speedy adjudications would provide unique benefits to the parties to these kinds of disputes. Business risks and uncertainties would remain unresolved for less time. For companies that have engaged in no wrongdoing, quick adjudication and lower defense costs eliminate pressure to settle otherwise meritless claims. If a defendant is faced with a weak claim that can be economically and quickly resolved, the leverage of an "extortionate" settlement evaporates. Granting arbitrators the express power to sanction parties for pursuing frivolous claims or maintaining frivolous positions can strengthen this aspect of arbitration. As an additional tool to deter frivolous litigation, courts have recognized that arbitrators retain discretion to award attorneys' fees to prevailing parties. Even in the absence of a provision within the agreement commanding arbitration or a rule of the arbitration forum, courts have upheld awards of attorneys' fees. In short, arbitration can eradicate the ills that formed the basis for enacting the PSLRA.

In this respect, the experience of securities arbitration in the broker-customer dispute arena is instructive. For example, during 1994, the NASD was able to achieve an average resolution time of 10.4 months for securities disputes referred to it. Arbitration of securities claims costs only one-third of the cost of adjudication of securities claims. In addition, NASD arbitrators in these disputes have imposed sanctions in appropriate circumstances, even absent explicit authority in the rule governing industry arbitration.

On the other hand, requiring the arbitration of disputes should not close the doors of justice to meritorious claims. In fact, because awards must be paid thirty days after decisions, investors with meritorious claims receive compensation swiftly. Even though arbitrations in the broker-customer context are sponsored by industry-controlled self-regulatory organizations [SROs], each study of the fairness of arbitration has concluded that there is no evidence of systematic unfairness to investors. Similarly, although plaintiffs originally were suspicious of industry-sponsored arbitration, many prominent plaintiffs' counsel now have embraced arbitration. The SROs that sponsor arbitration in the securities industry have strived to maintain the perception of impartiality and fairness. Over the years, they appear to have achieved just that.

If the SEC were responsible for overseeing the arbitration of investor claims involving publicly-traded companies, it would begin with some key advantages. The SEC is widely perceived to be a tough, fair, and efficient industry watchdog. The SEC has established itself generally as a pro-investor agency over the years. The SEC already has a long history in supervising arbitration in a balanced fashion. With this reputation, any SEC-operated arbitration forum would start out as presumptively fair. The SEC also has a specific mandate from Congress to use its expertise to stem fraud in the securities markets: Rule 10b-5. If the SEC concluded that the best policy to pursue in such efforts is arbitration, it is not likely that any court would interfere with that exercise of discretion.

In all, arbitration can provide a means for a fair and efficient resolution of private securities claims involving publicly-held companies. Speed and low cost can eliminate frivolous claims. The SEC, because of its reputation, expertise, administrative powers, and experience, is uniquely qualified to administer and regulate this system of dispute resolution.

Marilyn F. Johnson, Karen K. Nelson & A.C. Pritchard, In re Silicon Graphics Inc.: *Shareholder Wealth Effects Resulting from the Interpretation of the Private Securities Litigation Reform Act's Pleading Standard**

I. Introduction

... This Article presents an empirical study of changes in shareholder wealth resulting from the Ninth Circuit Court of Appeals decision in *In re Silicon Graphics Inc. Securities Litigation*,[7] which interpreted the pleading provision established in the Private Securities Litigation Reform Act of 1995 (the "Reform Act"). Congress passed the Reform Act as part of an ongoing effort to protect corporations from abusive suits alleging "fraud by hindsight." In such suits, plaintiffs claimed that a sudden drop in a company's stock price was evidence that the issuer and its management covered up the bad news that led to the price drop. The Reform Act discourages such suits by requiring complaints alleging fraud to "state with particularity facts giving rise to a strong inference that the defendant acted with the required state of mind." Courts have interpreted the Reform Act's pleading standard in diverse ways. The Ninth Circuit's interpretation in *Silicon Graphics* is the most stringent, requiring plaintiffs to allege facts that would show the defendants were "deliberately reckless" in making the misrepresentation that gave rise to the fraud claim. This pleading standard allows courts to dismiss fraud suits at an early stage if the court deems they lack merit, but it also increases the risk courts will dismiss meritorious suits as well.

In this Article, we examine the effects of the stringent *Silicon Graphics* standard using event study methodology to provide empirical evidence regarding investors' perception

* Originally published in 73 SOUTHERN CALIFORNIA LAW REVIEW 773 (2000). Reprinted with permission.
7. 183 F. 3d 970 (9th Cir. 1999).

of the Ninth Circuit's interpretation of the pleading standard. Event study methodology previously has been used to assess the effect of state corporate law on shareholder wealth. Our study differs from that prior work because it tests the market reaction to a decision before the United States Supreme Court has conclusively decided the question. Given the clear split in the circuit courts over the interpretation of the pleading standard, the Supreme Court is likely to eventually grant certiorari to resolve the issue.[8] In the face of textual ambiguity in the statute and confusion in the legislative history, shareholder wealth provides one potential normative criterion the Supreme Court could consider to determine the "correct" interpretation of the Reform Act's pleading standard. In this case, social science has the potential to directly influence the path of the law.

We recognize that the use of wealth maximization as a normative criterion for judicial decisionmaking is controversial. But wealth maximization for shareholders may be more acceptable as an appropriate norm in the context of securities laws because investors unquestionably purchase securities in an effort to increase their wealth. In particular, we believe shareholder wealth provides the appropriate baseline for interpreting the Reform Act because it best serves Congress' purposes in adopting the law, and it best reflects the interests of investors, who are the principal beneficiaries of the securities laws. At a minimum, courts should consider the effect that securities law decisions have on shareholder wealth when empirical evidence is available, as it is here, and Congress has not clearly expressed a contrary intent.

Two competing hypotheses may explain the effect of *Silicon Graphics'* rigorous pleading standard on shareholder wealth: (1) the high standard primarily discourages suits that, regardless of their merits, are not cost-justified in terms of deterring fraud, thereby enhancing shareholder wealth on average; or (2) the high standard chills suits that are both meritorious and cost-justified in addition to non-cost justified suits, thus undermining deterrence and diminishing shareholder wealth. To determine the effect of the *Silicon Graphics* decision on the wealth of shareholders, we look at the stock prices of a sample of high technology companies from the computer hardware, computer software, and pharmaceutical industries, and a sub-sample of those companies headquartered in the Ninth Circuit. A positive stock price reaction would support the first hypothesis, while a negative reaction would support the second.

The *Silicon Graphics* decision has implications beyond the law of any particular circuit. It offers a unique opportunity to evaluate the wealth effects of the varying interpretations of the Reform Act's pleading standard for three reasons. First, the *Silicon Graphics* "deliberate recklessness" standard for pleading scienter is generally regarded as the most difficult interpretation for plaintiffs to satisfy. The Securities and Exchange Commission and other critics of the "deliberate recklessness" standard have warned that the Ninth Circuit's interpretation will harm investors because it will discourage the filing of meritorious suits. Since the plaintiff cannot use discovery to determine what the defendants knew when they were making the allegedly fraudulent statements, the case will be dismissed unless

---

8. *Unfortunately, this sensible prediction had not yet been borne out as of 2009. In 2007, the Supreme Court interpreted the PSLRA's "strong inference" requirement to toughen pleading standards in two ways. First, it held that no particular types of factual allegations could dispositively prove scienter. Second, it held that the factual pleadings must support an inference of scienter that is "more than merely plausible or reasonable — it must be cogent and at least as compelling as any opposing inference of nonfraudulent intent." Tellabs v. Makor, 551 U.S. 308 (2007). But the Court did not address the circuit split described in this article: whether the required level of scienter is the "deliberate recklessness" required by the Ninth Circuit, or the less demanding "severe recklessness" or mere "recklessness" required by other circuits. — Ed.*

the defendant can find evidence in public sources of the defendants' fraudulent intent. If cases of genuine fraud were dismissed or never filed, deterrence would be undermined.

Second, the decision was unexpected. Given that the Ninth Circuit previously had the least stringent requirements for pleading fraud, its decision to adopt the most stringent interpretation under the Reform Act caught many securities lawyers by surprise. Accordingly, the decision was unlikely to have been anticipated by stock market participants and reflected in stock prices prior to its announcement. Finally, the Ninth Circuit encompasses Silicon Valley, so the *Silicon Graphics* decision governs a substantial number of companies commonly targeted by attorneys bringing securities fraud class actions. Thus, the decision is likely to be of economic significance....

II. Securities Fraud, Class Actions, and Shareholder Wealth

An analysis of the effects of the Reform Act's pleading standard on shareholder wealth requires a balancing of the benefits from deterring securities fraud through class actions against the costs of such suits. Securities fraud class actions are a beneficial enforcement device only if the deterrence they produce is greater than the deadweight losses they impose. In this Part, we analyze the costs of securities fraud, as well as the benefits and costs of using class actions to deter that fraud.

The leading securities law treatise states, "there is no science yet known for quantifying the dollar value of fraud avoided; so in a sense, policy judgments in this area are based on often widely varying guesses as to whether increased fraud avoidance can be justified."[9] We disagree with the premise that the "dollar value of fraud avoided" cannot be quantified and we believe policymakers can do better than "guess" when making policy in this area. The presence of fraud has the potential to seriously depress stock prices by impairing managerial accountability, distorting capital allocation, and reducing liquidity. Insofar as securities fraud class actions provide an efficient enforcement device, stock prices generally should reflect the effectiveness of those suits in deterring fraud....

Class actions are a central component of the federal securities laws' anti-fraud regime. The SEC considers private class actions a "necessary supplement" to its own efforts in policing fraud. In fraud on the market class actions, plaintiffs' attorneys sue the corporation and its officers under Rule 10b-5 of the Securities Exchange Act. The plaintiffs are classes of investors who have paid too much for their shares or (less frequently) sold their shares for too little because of price distortion caused by the misstatements.

In the typical case, the corporation being sued neither bought nor sold its securities and, accordingly, did not gain from the fraud. Nonetheless, fraud on the market suits allow investors to recover their losses from the corporation based on its managers' misstatements. Given the trading volume in secondary markets, the potential recoverable damages in such suits can be a substantial percentage of the corporation's total capitalization, easily reaching hundreds of millions of dollars. Thus, class actions are a potential punitive sanction that should provide a substantial deterrent to fraud.

The effectiveness of that deterrence will be determined by how closely class action suits correlate with the actual incidence of fraud. Congress passed the Reform Act because it believed that the targeting of class actions was not very precise. Plaintiffs' lawyers were filing suits "citing a laundry list of cookie-cutter complaints" against companies "within hours

---

9. LOUIS LOSS & JOEL SELIGMAN, SECURITIES REGULATION 701 (3d ed. Supp. 1999).

or days" of a substantial drop in the company's stock price. Moreover, plaintiffs' lawyers had incentives to "file frivolous lawsuits in order to conduct discovery in the hopes of finding a sustainable claim not alleged in the complaint."

Sorting fraud from mere business reversals is difficult. The external observer may not know whether a drop in a company's stock price is due to a prior misstatement about its prospects—fraud—or a result of risky business decisions that did not pan out—bad luck. Unable to distinguish the two, plaintiffs' lawyers are forced to rely on the limited publicly available objective indicia when deciding to sue. Thus, a substantial drop in stock price following previous optimistic statements may well lead to a lawsuit.

The scienter standard establishes the defendants' requisite knowledge of falsity at the time of the misstatement and is the primary means by which courts sort fraud from non-fraud. But the standard is notoriously amorphous. It is somewhat more stringent than negligence, but even in theory it is difficult to say how much more, and it is nearly impossible in practice. Knowingly false statements and unfortunate business decisions both create a risk of liability and, thus, provide a basis for filing suit. An uncertain standard for liability therefore makes filing a diverse portfolio of cases a reasonable strategy for plaintiffs' lawyers.

Filing numerous cases is profitable for plaintiffs' attorneys because of the incentives that defendants face. If plaintiffs can withstand a motion to dismiss, defendants generally will find settlement cheaper than litigation....

III. The Reform Act's Pleading Standard

Congress attempted to improve the screening process for securities class actions when it enacted the Private Securities Litigation Reform Act. The Reform Act adopted a series of procedural obstacles to securities fraud class actions designed to weed out nonmeritorious actions at an early stage. Early dismissal greatly reduces the expense to corporations forced to defend such suits, thereby limiting the settlement value of weak cases.

The pleading standard established by the Reform Act gives the judge a more significant role in deciding the merits of the lawsuit than is typical under the Federal Rules of Civil Procedure. Under the Reform Act's pleading standard, plaintiffs must specify in their complaint each statement alleged to have been misleading and the reasons why the statement is misleading. In addition, if an "allegation is made on information and belief, the plaintiff shall state with particularity all facts on which the belief is formed." Finally, the pleading standard requires plaintiffs to state with particularity facts giving rise to a "strong inference" that the defendant acted with "the required state of mind." By requiring plaintiffs to plead facts demonstrating scienter, the motion to dismiss becomes a substantive challenge to the merits of the lawsuit, a substantial departure from the "notice pleading" ordinarily required by the Federal Rules. The significance of this departure is enhanced by the fact that plaintiffs are left without the usual access to discovery to bolster their complaint....

An ultimate decision by the Supreme Court [establishing a uniform interpretation of the pleading standard] will have significant policy consequences. If the Court adopts a strict interpretation of the pleading standard, fraud claims that are not plausible on the face of the complaint will be dismissed. If such an interpretation discouraged only meritless suits, it could reduce the enormous transaction costs imposed by those suits, thereby producing deterrence at a lower cost. On the other hand, if the bar for pleading an adequate complaint is set too high, it may screen out a large number of meritorious suits, as well as the frivolous, thus undermining deterrence. In the next Part, we attempt to shed some empirical light on how the Court should strike that balance.

IV. Data and Findings

Event study methodology is a well-established means for measuring investors' perception of the effect of an economic event on shareholder wealth, and it is widely used in the context of the securities laws. Indeed, the event study methodology used here relies on the Efficient Capital Markets Hypothesis—which is also the fundamental premise of the fraud on the market class action. The Efficient Capital Markets Hypothesis postulates that stock prices rapidly incorporate publicly available information regarding the value of those shares. In *Basic, Inc. v. Levinson*, the Supreme Court endorsed the use of stock price effects to establish that the market relied on misstatements.[10] Courts have also relied on the event study methodology employed here in other contexts concerning the federal securities laws, including the measurement of damages in open-market fraud cases and to demonstrate the materiality of misstatements.

A. *The Sample and Methodology*

To test the effects of the *Silicon Graphics* decision on shareholder wealth, we select a sample of firms that historically have been vulnerable to class action securities litigation. These firms are therefore the ones most likely to be affected by the interpretation of the Reform Act's pleading standard. Compared to firms in other industries, high technology companies are involved in a disproportionately large number of securities lawsuits. We use companies from three high technology industries—pharmaceuticals, computer hardware, and computer software....

The Ninth Circuit handed down its *Silicon Graphics* decision on the morning of July 2, 1999. That same morning, the decision was posted on the court's web site, and the clerk's office notified by telephone the lawyers for the parties to the appeal. The lawyers notified their clients and interested journalists that day. The decision also was announced at a securities litigation conference in Colorado that afternoon. Later that evening, the Associated Press ran the story on its newswire at 6:53 P.M. The AP story is the first news account of the decision that we have found. Stories reporting the decision ran in three major California papers—the *San Jose Mercury News*, the *San Francisco Chronicle*, and the *Los Angeles Times*—on July 3, 1999, a Saturday. Because the following Monday—July 5—was a holiday, the story did not run in the Wall Street Journal until July 6. Given court rules regarding confidentiality, we assume that the news of the decision was not available to traders before July 2. Additionally, we conclude from the widespread media coverage that virtually any securities analyst following companies in the three high technology industries we examine was likely to be aware of the decision on July 6. Accordingly, we examine stock return data from July 2 through July 6, which includes only two trading days, the second and the sixth.

The event study methodology requires a measure of abnormal returns. The abnormal return is the actual stock return over the event period minus the return expected if the event did not take place. The expected return is obtained by estimating the relation between a given security's return and the market return for a period prior to the event in question. This relation provides a benchmark for determining the expected return of a firm's stock during the event period, given the market return. We calculated the abnormal return for each firm in the sample for the two trading days indicated above, and added these daily abnormal returns to obtain cumulative abnormal returns (the "CARs") for

---

10. 485 U.S. 224 (1988).

the event period for each firm. The overall CAR is an average of the individual firm CARs. If investors viewed the *Silicon Graphics* decision as beneficial to their interests, we would expect to observe a positive average CAR. Conversely, if investors believed that the decision harmed their interests, we would expect a negative average CAR....

B. Results

We find that there was a significant positive market reaction to the *Silicon Graphics* decision, which is consistent with the hypothesis that investors believed that the Ninth Circuit's stringent interpretation of the Reform Act's pleading standard, on average, enhanced shareholder wealth.... [T]here was a cumulative positive mean abnormal return of 1.78% over the two days following announcement of the decision. This result is statistically significant at the 99% level of confidence, meaning that there is less than a 1% chance that the result would occur purely by chance....

The average CAR for those firms most directly affected by the decision—the Ninth Circuit firms—is 2.79%, compared to only 1.27% for the other firms in the sample. Both of these results are significant at the 99% level of confidence. It is not surprising that the non-Ninth Circuit firms should have a positive price reaction—before the Ninth Circuit ruling, no appellate court had accepted the stringent "deliberate recklessness" standard. The Ninth Circuit's decision made it more likely that other appellate courts, and more importantly, the Supreme Court might accept the stringent standard....

To put these results in more concrete terms, the average change in market value for our sample companies was $12,429,000. Once again, the increase was substantially greater for firms headquartered in the Ninth Circuit, despite the fact that these firms were considerably smaller, on average, than the non-Ninth Circuit firms. The average change in market value for Ninth Circuit firms was $18,459,000, compared to $9,381,000 for the non-Ninth Circuit firms in our sample. Thus, the Silicon Graphics decision had a substantial impact, whether measured in percentage of value or dollar terms.

V. Conclusion: The Use of Event Studies in Statutory Interpretation

How should courts interpret ambiguous statutes? A variety of answers to this question have been offered, with the range seemingly limited only by the imagination of law professors. For those more focused on the real world, however, Jane Schacter argues that the actual practice of the Supreme Court reflects a "common law originalism."[11] In her view, the Court's approach is "'originalist' in that it uses statutory language as an interpretive anchor and focal point," but it also reflects "the common law form because it draws from an array of judicially-created sources to delineate the ranges of plausible textual meanings and then to select from among them." Among these sources are a variety of policy norms such as federalism. These norms provide "value-laden interpretive baselines against which the meaning of the disputed language is measured and assessed." Reliance on these policy norms affords judges a substantial role in determining the content of legal rules.

It is not our purpose in this Article to assess whether judges should rely on such contestable policy norms when interpreting statutes. Instead, our proposal is more modest: If judges are going to rely on policy norms when faced with statutory ambiguity, the

---

11. Jane S. Schacter, *The Confounding Common Law Originalism in Recent Supreme Court Statutory Interpretation: Implications for the Legislative History Debate and Beyond*, 51 STAN. L. REV. 1, 5 (1998).

appropriate baseline norm for interpreting the Reform Act should be shareholder wealth maximization. We reach that conclusion for two reasons. First, we believe that norm best reflects Congress' purposes in adopting the Reform Act. Second, shareholder wealth maximization is the background norm that best serves the interests of the parties governed by the securities laws.

Courts have not, to date, used event studies of shareholder wealth effects as a guide to the interpretation of the federal securities laws—that is, they have not relied upon shareholder wealth maximization in determining the substance of the law. One obvious obstacle to the use of shareholder wealth maximization as an interpretive tool is the Supreme Court's decision in *Basic, Inc. v. Levinson* defining the scope of the securities laws' antifraud prohibitions. In that case, the Court clearly rejected investor wealth in favor of investor protection, suggesting that it was for Congress, not the courts, to implement such a shift in the focus of the securities laws.

But this decision predates Congress' enactment of the Reform Act, which may represent just such a shift. Congress' purposes in adopting the Private Securities Litigation Reform Act make shareholder wealth maximization a more appropriate reading of congressional intent in this context. According to the Statement of Managers that accompanied the final version of the Reform Act, the Act was designed to achieve a balance between investor protection and the deterrence of frivolous suits. Congress claimed that it was seeking to protect the welfare of investors in striking this balance:

> The overriding purpose of our Nation's securities laws is to protect investors and to maintain confidence in the securities markets, so that our national savings, capital formation and investment may grow for the benefit of all Americans....

> Private securities litigation is an indispensable tool with which defrauded investors can recover their losses without having to rely upon government action. Such private lawsuits promote public and global confidence in our capital markets and help to deter wrongdoing and to guarantee that corporate officers, auditors, directors, lawyers and others properly perform their jobs. This legislation seeks to return the securities litigation system to that high standard....

> When an issuer must pay lawyers' fees, make settlement payments, and expend management and employee resources in defending a meritless suit, the issuers' own investors suffer. Investors always are the ultimate losers when extortionate "settlements" are extracted from issuers.

> This Conference Report seeks to protect investors, issuers, and all who are associated with our capital markets from abusive securities litigation. This legislation implements needed procedural protections to discourage frivolous litigation.[12]

This passage supports the view that Congress was seeking to maximize shareholder wealth when it adopted the Reform Act's pleading standard. Congress clearly recognized that securities fraud class actions have costs as well as benefits and expressed its intention to balance those costs and benefits for the benefit of shareholders.

Further evidence of Congress' preference for the consideration of economic efficiency in interpreting the securities laws can be found in the National Securities Market Improvement Act (the "NSMIA"). Passed in 1996, NSMIA directs the SEC to "consider,

---

12. *Conference Report on The Private Securities Litigation Reform Act of 1995,* H.R. Conf. Rep. No. 104-369, at 31–32 (1995), *reprinted in* 1995 U.S.C.C.A.N. 730, 731.

in addition to the protection of investors, whether the action will promote efficiency, competition, and capital formation" when it is engaged in rulemaking. While this law is directed toward the SEC, not the courts, it does suggest a change in Congress' attitude toward the securities laws from the paternalistic attitude of the 1930s. It seems unlikely that today's Congress would want courts to ignore efficiency concerns in interpreting the Reform Act, even if the text of the statute does not specify that goal as NSMIA does.

In addition to reflecting congressional intent, shareholder wealth maximization provides a normatively justifiable basis for balancing the costs and benefits of securities fraud class actions. Shareholders presumably invest in securities in an effort to maximize their wealth, and, therefore, they prefer governing rules tailored to that purpose. To be sure, our study's results do not establish that the *Silicon Graphics* interpretation of the Reform Act's pleading standard benefits all corporations. Our sample consists of only high technology companies, and our results would not necessarily extend to other industry sectors. Additionally, for those companies that were most likely to commit fraud, the abnormal returns were statistically indistinguishable from zero, but notably were not negative. For the shareholders of some companies, raising the bar for securities fraud class actions may be neither wealth-enhancing nor wealth-diminishing. The result for the firms most likely to commit fraud suggests another policy prescription that might be drawn from our study: Abolishing the fraud on the market class action altogether might well impose such a significant loss of deterrence that it would produce a negative stock price reaction.

Our results do, however, provide evidence that market participants believe that the hurdle imposed to securities fraud class actions created by the *Silicon Graphics* rule is likely to enhance wealth on average—the price reaction was positive for the sample as a whole. While these market participants may be wrong in their assessment of the effects of the *Silicon Graphics* decision, investors have powerful incentives to value these effects correctly. Because the stock price effect was positive even for firms that are unlikely to face litigation, it seems probable that companies operating in sectors where securities fraud litigation is less common would not experience negative stock returns from the decision. Thus, shareholders on average are likely to benefit from the Ninth Circuit's interpretation. And most shareholders are likely to be average shareholders because they hold a reasonably diverse portfolio, either by purchasing a number of different stocks or by purchasing automatic diversification through a mutual fund.

In a world where most shareholders hold diversified portfolios, policymakers designing rules for shareholders' benefit will succeed if the rules adopted are beneficial on average. Other stakeholders in the corporate enterprise—managers, employees, creditors— presumably benefit from rules that maximize shareholder wealth as well because such rules reduce the corporation's cost of capital, thereby giving the corporation greater resources with which to compensate its managers and employees and greater ability to repay its debts.

In passing the Reform Act, Congress sought to maintain investor protection while minimizing the costs imposed by securities fraud class actions. Any interpretation of the Reform Act's pleading standard necessarily entails a trade-off between those two goals. The tools of statutory interpretation most frequently relied upon by courts—text and legislative history—do little in this context to tell us where that balance should be struck. Congress studiously avoided resolving the question in the text of the statute, and the legislative history is hopelessly conflicted. The Supreme Court will have to look elsewhere when it eventually resolves the dispute over the proper interpretation of the pleading standard. The empirical evidence presented in this Article suggests that the *Silicon Graphics* interpretation of the pleading standard enhances shareholder wealth. In the absence of a more compelling basis for picking among the competing interpretations, we believe that evidence provides a strong basis for the Supreme Court to accept the stringent interpretation adopted by the Ninth Circuit in *Silicon Graphics....*

James D. Cox, *The Social Meaning of Shareholder Suits*[*]

Private enforcement of the proxy rules provides a necessary supplement to Commission action. As in antitrust treble damage litigation, the possibility of civil damages or injunctive relief serves as a most effective weapon in the enforcement of the proxy requirements.

—*J.I. Case Co. v. Borak*[13]

There has been widespread recognition that litigation under Rule 10b-5 presents a danger of vexatiousness different in degree and in kind from that which accompanies litigation in general.... A complaint which by objective standards may have very little chance of success at trial has a settlement value to the plaintiff out of any proportion to its prospect of success at trial....

—*Blue Chip Stamps v. Manor Drug Stores*[14]

The two above quotes express very different judgments of the social value of the representative shareholder suit. In *Borak*, the Supreme Court embraced the shareholder suit as an important medium for achieving compliance with the securities laws. *Blue Chip Stamps* warned of the abuses that accompany such suits. Although their difference may well be attributed to the gulf that separates the Warren Court from the more conservative Burger Court, the opinions are also a reflection of contemporary America. *Borak* was decided at the height of the most dramatic social revolution in America's history—a time when the courts, and more particularly private litigation, were engines for establishing, even redistributing, legal rights within the country. In contrast, *Blue Chip Stamps* reflects the social pendulum's swing in the other direction. By the mid 1970s, economic growth, not social change, had become the dominant ideology in American politics.

This article examines the public image, or expressive value, of the shareholder suit. My purpose is to determine if many features common to the conduct of class actions and derivative suits enhance or detract from shareholder litigation being understood as a positive social force. The premise driving this inquiry is my belief that the higher the public esteem of the shareholder suit, the greater will be its deterrent value....

In this article, I ask whether shareholder litigation itself is viewed as a responsible actor so that ... the suit's existence deters misconduct by others. The continued existence of the shareholder suit is easier to justify if it has such an effect. Simply stated, we customarily consider the deterrent value of private litigation in terms of the sanctions they provide. Here I add a new consideration, namely, the social opprobrium that attaches to the suits' defendants as a consequence of being pursued in a shareholder suit. In this respect, I consider to what extent certain procedural and substantive features of shareholder suits contribute positively or negatively to their social meaning. Finally, I suggest reform

---

[*] Originally published in 65 BROOKLYN LAW REVIEW 3 (1999). Copyright 1999 James D. Cox. Reprinted with permission.
13. 377 U.S. 426, 432 (1964).
14. 421 U.S. 723, 737–38 (1975).

measures that will enhance the status of shareholder suits and hence improve their likely deterrence of misconduct.

I. Construction and Deconstruction

Whether and to what extent shareholder suits harbor reputational impacts upon their defendants is proportional to the expressive value enjoyed by all shareholder suits. That is, the message of the individual derivative suit or securities class action is affected by the company it keeps with other shareholder suits....

Even though a suit's substantive charges have reputational impacts that depend on the nature of the complaint, the charges are weakened if the medium through which they are asserted itself lacks a credible reputation.... Much like the shepherd who cries wolf too frequently, shareholder suits, if commonly understood to be frivolous, will not in their commencement, prosecution and settlement affirm the social norms the suit's defendants allegedly violated. Their defendants will instead be seen as the objects of bad luck, not derision. Thus, the procedural context in which corporate and securities norms are developed and affirmed are of the utmost significance if those norms are to discipline managers.

Corporate law is about norm management. The powers of corporations to repurchase their shares, to issue securities, and to combine with one another, as well as the fiduciary standards of their managers and related disclosure obligations, reflect contemporary judgments of how best to arrange relations among owners, managers and capital markets in order to maximize wealth. The existence of shareholder suits, and their procedural requirements, are highly visible components of norm management for corporate law. Most of the content of the fiduciary obligations of officers, directors and controlling shareholders, as well as much of the substantive disclosure obligations of the securities laws, is established through shareholder suits. This section examines to what extent features of shareholder suits are consistent with the process of establishing and affirming norms for business organizations. As discussed below, some features of shareholder suits are destructive to their role in managing norms for corporate law, whereas other features contribute positively toward that role and in turn enhance the suit's social meaning.

The inspiration for organizing the following analysis is Professor Lawrence Lessig's insights on techniques for constructing social meaning.[15] Even though he focuses on how the social meaning of events is changed—or more positively, constructed—the importance of his contribution to this article is his isolation of the ways the expressive value of an event, such as a sanction's imposition, can be influenced. The four ways he poses, and around which the following discussion is organized, are ambiguation, tying, inhibition and ritual.

A. *Ambiguation of the Suits' Mission*

Compensation of the injured and deterrence of misconduct commonly are the joint missions of representative suits. Neither mission conflicts with the other since to hold one accountable to those harmed by his misdeeds provides a powerful disincentive for others to similarly conduct themselves. The private shareholder suit, as recognized in *Borak*, serves a public function as well as a private one. However, in the corporate setting, shareholder suits are consistently dismissed when they fail to serve a compensatory end,

---

15. *See* Lawrence Lessig, *The Regulation of Social Meaning*, 62 U. Chi. L. Rev. 943 (1995).

even though the goal of deterrence would be advanced by the suit's successful prosecution. Simply stated, compensation is the prevailing objective of shareholder suits and deterrence, its valuable byproduct.

The most dramatic illustration of this state of affairs is the "net loss" requirement that applies when the knowing violation of a criminal statute underlies the derivative suit. When directors or officers have knowingly engaged in an illegal act, they no longer are entitled to the presumption of propriety that normally accompanies the disinterested decisions of managers. Nevertheless, the directors who knowingly violate the law are not without a defense. Absent proof that the corporation suffered a net loss through their illegal act, the suit must be dismissed. Therefore, if the plaintiff fails to establish that the harm suffered by the corporation as a consequence of the misconduct exceeded the benefits it received by their misconduct, the defendant escapes any sanction by a derivative suit.

A further illustration that compensation is the sine qua non of the corporate suit is ... the contemporaneous ownership requirement for derivative suits, which requires the suit's plaintiff to have owned the shares at the time of the defendant's misconduct. The prevalence of the contemporaneous ownership rule stems from the reasoning that if the derivative suit could be maintained by a plaintiff who did not own her shares when the defendant's breach occurred, the plaintiff could recover for misconduct that did not harm her.

The divide between compensation and deterrence also exists in substantive areas of corporate law. The most dramatic illustrations of this are the different approaches courts have taken in determining whether corporate insiders have breached their fiduciary duty to their corporate employer when they trade in its securities on the basis of material nonpublic information acquired by virtue of their positions. Whereas Florida conditions the breach on proof of actual injury to the corporation as a result of the insider's private use of confidential corporate information, New York and Delaware require the fiduciary to disgorge any ill-gotten gains without proof of harm to the corporation.

The courts' preoccupation with the compensatory rather than punitive aspects of shareholder suits ambiguates the suits' expression of social values. Few shareholder actions entail breaches of a private contract between the plaintiffs and the suit's defendants. Suits are based on breaches of fiduciary obligations or disclosure requirements embodied in common law or state or federal statutes. In all shareholder suits, the norm invoked has a substantial, if not exclusive, public source. In theory, therefore, these suits provide a public link to the norm by requiring resolution in state-funded courts, where potentially a public voice, the courts, will address each case's facts through the lens of the applicable norm. Because compensating the injured is a private matter, whereas deterrence is of public concern, the more squarely the courts place the objectives of shareholder suits in the compensatory sphere, the weaker the public perception will be that such suits are reflections of society's condemnation of the misconduct underlying the suit's charges. To the extent that suits are perceived as addressing purely private injuries, instead of being understood to address violations of the public interest in ways that cause private harms, the public perception will be that derivative suits are but a subset of the standard commercial dispute between two warring financial interests.

Settlements also play a role in ambiguating the public character of shareholder suits. The vast preponderance of shareholder suits that survive pretrial motions result in settlements, not judgments on the merits. Settlement breaks the shareholder suit's link to the state. Whereas the authority to impose a judgment arises from the law, and by extension society, settlements are private contractual matters. Professor Owen Fiss, in a classic article, questions the increasing role of settlement and alternative dispute resolution mechanisms because of their harmful effects on the public norms that underlie the suit:

> The purpose of adjudication should be understood in broader terms. Adjudication uses public resources and employs not strangers chosen by the parties but public officials chosen by a process in which the public participates. These officials, like members of the legislative and executive branches, possess a power that has been defined and conferred by public law, not by private agreement. Their job is not to maximize the ends of private parties nor simply to secure the peace, but to explicate and give force to the values embodied in authoritative texts such as the Constitution and statutes: to interpret those values and to bring reality to accord with them. This duty is not discharged when the parties settle.... [16]

B. Tying Suits to a Failed Objective

Social scientists have long stressed the importance of "framing" in evaluative decisions. The anchor point that is set forth significantly impacts the judgment made about a proposition. The anchor not only fixes the point at which inquiry begins, but it is also frequently the standard for judging the merits of an idea, argument, or social institution.

The public perception of shareholder litigation and its social meaning has been affected by framing. Complementing the courts' view that shareholder suits are private suits intended to compensate injured investors, the academic and political debate surrounding shareholder suits continues to judge their social value in terms of whether they result in financial awards consistent with this compensatory mission. By finding, as they do, that shareholder suits fail in their compensatory mission, the studies support a negative view of their social value. Against the benchmark of compensation, both the derivative suit and the class action have fared badly in the public contest for political support. Indeed, some studies openly suggest that many such suits are, at best, misguided because they produce small awards to their plaintiffs, and are, at worst, frivolous claims designed to extort an award of attorneys' fees.

The derivative suit is more vulnerable than the class action to assaults on whether it fulfills its compensatory mission. Two leading studies each conclude that derivative suits yield no significant wealth effects. Within Professor Romano's sample of 139 shareholder suits, 41 resulted in monetary recoveries, with the average monetary recovery in derivative suit being $6 million ($11 million for class action awards).[17] The standard recovery represents a very small proportion of the firm's assets or translates into a small recovery on a per share basis; in such comparisons, the derivative suit recoveries are consistently smaller than for class actions. In a larger sample of derivative suits, Professors Bradley and Fischel found that the successful derivative suit yields only a slight positive effect for the firm's stockholders.[18] They conclude that "derivative suits are not an important monitoring device to curb managerial malfeasance." Additionally, Professor Romano, on examining stock price reactions to announcements of the commencement and termination of class actions and derivative suits, found that stock price changes "do not provide compelling support for the proposition that shareholders experience significant wealth effects

---

16. Owen Fiss, *Against Settlement*, 93 YALE L. J. 1073 (1984).
17. Roberta Romano, *The Shareholder Suit: Litigation Without Foundation?*, 7 J.L. ECON. & ORG. 55 (1991).
18. Daniel R. Fischel & Michael Bradley, *The Role of Liability Rules and the Derivative Suit in Corporate Law: A Theoretical and Empirical Analysis*, 71 CORNELL L. REV. 261 (1986).

from litigation." Her condemnation is strongest for the derivative suit: "To the extent that derivative suits consistently return less to shareholders than class actions, there is a greater likelihood that more of these suits are frivolous...." Thus, she concludes that the primary beneficiaries of shareholder suits are attorneys.

The findings of Professors Bradley, Fischel and Romano frame the arguments over which most of the skirmishes leading up to the Private Securities Litigation Reform Act of 1995 were fought. This legislation introduced procedural and substantive changes for the securities class action, with the goal of reducing the incidence of lawyer-driven frivolous class actions. The legislative history of the Reform Act is replete with empirical reports examining the amounts recovered by class action members as compared to the damages that were allegedly in dispute. Those championing the cause of the class action marshaled data to demonstrate that class members receive a significant portion of their losses in settlements, whereas those arguing that class actions are simply strike suits emphasized the large number of suits settled within the policy limits of applicable D&O insurance,[19] and more generally noted that securities class actions produce small rewards to class members when compared to their alleged damages.

One may well conclude that the passage of the Private Securities Litigation Reform Act is the most visible symbol of the expressive value of the securities class action. Judged by the standard of compensation, the securities class action was seen as so wanting that Congress constrained their use by enacting restrictive procedures that applied only to securities litigation. Existing class action procedures were not believed to assure that the suit's defendants had violated the securities laws. Simply stated, procedural rules existing prior to the Reform Act were seen as confirming the belief that being a defendant in a securities class action was nothing more than legalized bad luck. And worse, this phenomenon was labeled by the Congress as impeding capital formation and entrepreneurial activities.

Tying the measure of the shareholder suit's social value to its compensatory functions most certainly will condemn it to failure. Certainly this is the case for derivative suits. Consider the characteristics common to derivative suits. Amounts involved in derivative suits typically are quite small in terms of the firm's overall value. The domain of the derivative suit are charges for which a demand on the board of directors can be excused. Such cases overwhelmingly involve self-dealing behavior—wasteful executive compensation, misappropriating corporate opportunities, or gaining on dealings with the corporation— which by their nature tend to involve small sums of money relative to the overall value of the firm. To be sure, managers who thwart a lucrative hostile bid pose potentially large value suits based on their alleged self-interest, but the derivative or class action suit in such cases customarily results in equitable relief and not a financial recovery.

The public image of the securities class actions is no better than that of the derivative suit. As seen earlier, securities class actions are understood by many to be lawyer-driven suits where most recoveries fall within the limits of the company's D&O insurance policy. Suits are brought only when the amount involved is expected to be sufficiently rewarding for the class action lawyer. Thus, it is not surprising that there is significant under enforcement of fraudulent offerings of small issuers. Moreover, the fact that a significant percentage of cases involve settlements of less than $2 million feeds the view that nuisance, rather than actual harm, prompts many suits to be initiated. This image is further reinforced for both derivative suits and class actions when the sole benefit garnered by the suit is a nonpecuniary award to the shareholders but cash for their lawyers.

---

19. *"D&O insurance" is liability insurance for directors and officers, usually provided by the corporation.* — Ed.

The image of the securities class action may well be different if there were more complete data on its effects. Many securities class actions yield not only substantial amounts to the class, but significant amounts for many of the individual class members. To be sure, small recoveries, especially those within the coverage limits of any available insurance policy, are consistent with the strike suit thesis, which holds that baseless actions are brought by unscrupulous attorneys seeking a fee award as the price for the suit's dismissal. On the other hand, a recovery limited to the amount of any available insurance policy is also consistent with the idea that the defendants have no other available funds to contribute toward a larger settlement or possible judgment. Even the latter view projects a disturbing image of the securities class action. Can a suit that recovers only from the neutral D&O carrier be seen as being compensatory, when the amount recovered is so small in relation to the harm suffered by the class? Even less appealing is the view that such suits deter misconduct because the recovery comes from a innocent insurance carrier rather than the wrongdoers themselves.

The data regarding the role of insurance in settlements and the frequency of dismissals of shareholder suits can lead to a more positive view of shareholder suits if the anchor point of the analysis is the inherent indeterminacy of rights that can only be determined through litigation. Consider, for example, that the disclosure demands of the antifraud provisions are continually evolving case-by-case through private and SEC enforcement actions. Standards such as what are material omissions or misstatements, as well as what constitutes their reckless commission, are inherently vague, thereby inviting ad hoc determinations. The opaqueness of the antifraud rule most certainly invites many long shot suits, so that what some see as abuses within this process can also be understood as the evolution of federal common law around inherently vague norms. Therefore, the prevalence of settlement within the bounds of available insurance, or even the frequency of dismissal of shareholder suits, are predictable consequences of the fact that, in most corporate disputes, the contesting rights are inherently indeterminate. It is interesting to speculate why this perspective has not gained as much force as the more negative view described above. The prevailing view, however, is one that lends itself to measures of costs and benefits. To the extent that objectivity is associated with measurement and each is a desideratum within society, the preoccupation with the compensation provided by shareholder suits is understandable since compensation is measurable but deterrence is not. Shareholder suits are thus tied to a metric, i.e., the compensation they provide, that most surely measures their failure, not their success.

C. Applying the Right Inhibitions

The social meaning of an act can be shaped by the inhibitions imposed around it. By inhibiting certain behavior, the occurrence of which would otherwise create or reinforce a disfavored social meaning, we shape our perception of the act itself....

The most important inhibition that can be used to nurture positive deterrent effects flowing from shareholder suits are pretrial procedures that lead to the dismissal of baseless suits.... To the extent that pretrial procedures bias results so that meritorious cases tend to survive, a suit's continued prosecution or settlement can be expected to have a greater deterrent value than if there were no pretrial procedures so that on average there would be a lower likelihood that any suit's complaint addressed actual misconduct. Because the class action aggregates a large number of claims such that the amount in controversy is of great significance to the defendant, courts have long appreciated the class action's power to extort sizeable settlements even if the suit's merits were questionable....

Pursuant to the heightened pleading requirement introduced by the Private Securities Litigation Reform Act in 1995, private securities suits can now be subject to a preliminary assessment of their merits as part of the court's response to the defendant's motion to dismiss. Under the Reform Act, the complaint must specify not only each statement alleged to have been misleading and the reasons the statement is misleading, but it must also state with particularity facts giving rise to a strong inference that the defendant acted with scienter. The Reform Act therefore rejected notice pleading that has been a fixture of federal civil procedure since 1938 and replaced it with pleading standards that invite the court to undertake a much closer scrutiny of the plaintiff's allegations and their factual support in ruling on the defendant's motion to dismiss.

The degree to which district court judges will scrutinize the complaint under the Reform Act's heightened pleading requirements varies widely among judges and reflects, among other things, their own perceptions of contingency fee litigation, and especially securities class actions. Overall, the Reform Act's heightened pleading requirement will lead to suits that survive a motion to dismiss on average having more merit than suits possessed under the pre-Reform Act notice pleading requirement. This in turn should lead to the private securities action enjoying a higher status than existed prior to the Reform Act. Moreover, the Reform Act's bar to any discovery while the defendant's motion is pending further enhances the suit's image. The filing of a securities suit is no longer seen as the medium for the plaintiff to gain access to the defendant's records so that the plaintiff can determine if there is a basis to allege the defendant violated the securities laws. Thus, whatever impact the Reform Act has had on preventing meritorious securities claims from being redressed, there is every reason to believe its provisions have also inhibited many questionable suits, so that those suits that do survive the defendant's motion to dismiss convey more credible claims of misbehavior....

[The demand requirement in state law litigation serves a similar screening purpose.] Screening the suit's merits provides an important bulwark against the continuation of strike suits past the demand stage. Upon satisfying the demand requirement, the derivative suit can more easily be understood to reflect a public condemnation of the conduct that is the subject of the suit. The court's early involvement in the facts supporting the derivative suit complaint provides an important pre-trial screening mechanism. Both the Reform Act's pleading requirements and the derivative suit's demand requirement have positive winnowing effects so that shareholder suits that meet these pretrial demands enjoy greater merit than if these requirements did not exist.

The conditions for availability of insurance and indemnification merit consideration as to whether their limitations provide the right inhibitions. Overall, there is something of a mixed message that one derives from the standard source—insurance—for the funds obtained through settlements or judgments of shareholder suits. In these suits, insurance plays as important a role as it does in other types of litigation. Testimony that preceded the enactment of the Private Securities Litigation Reform Act estimated that 96 percent of securities class action settlements were for amounts within the limits of available insurance coverage. One implication of this is that those individuals who are actually responsible for violation rarely are required to recompense those they have harmed from their own funds. Even when there is no insurance, the employing corporation's vicarious liability for the misstatements of its officers or directors produces a joint liability between the active wrongdoing officers or directors and their passive employer. Because the employing corporation is more likely to have greater resources to contribute toward the suit's settlement or judgment, the active wrongdoers rarely contribute toward the suit's settlement.

There are some distinctive inhibitions within the law that nevertheless prevent the complete insulation of officers and directors from accountability for their misconduct.

The scope of the standard D&O insurance policy and state indemnification statutes assure that any award arising from an officer's or director's knowing or willful misbehavior will not be paid by the insurer or indemnified by the employer. Among the numerous exclusions to the standard D&O policy are those for dishonesty, a breach in which the director or officer has reaped a personal gain, and intentional wrongdoing. Similar restrictions are likely under contemporary indemnification statutes, which typically condition indemnification on the officer's or director's having acted in "good faith." Thus, in *Waltuch v. Conticommodity Services, Inc.*, the Second Circuit barred an officer who knowingly engaged in a series of manipulative acts from obtaining indemnification rights under the broad indemnification provision of the company's articles of incorporation.[20] The court reasoned that the Delaware indemnification statute conditioned permissive indemnification on the agent acting in good faith.

Both the standard insurance exclusions and the "good faith" requirement of state indemnification statutes, therefore, reinforce the view that those who intentionally misbehave are personally accountable for the harm they cause, even though as a practical matter the misbehaving officer or director may lack the funds to fully compensate the plaintiffs. More importantly, the D&O policy's exclusions and state indemnification statutes' conditions reflect a public judgment that certain types of conduct are beyond the pale of legitimate business practices and should be condemned. Thus, suits to redress such officer and director misconduct are more sharply seen as vindicating public not private values....

D. Beyond Ritual: The Private Nature of Public Settlements

... The most visible and important ritual for the shareholder suit is the procedural requirements that accompany the suits' initiation and settlement.

The public character of the shareholder suit is heightened by some important recent procedural developments. In the case of securities class actions, under the Reform Act courts must follow a process that can lead to the appointment of a lead plaintiff whose powers include selecting and retaining class counsel. The Reform Act provides a rebuttable presumption that the member of the class with the largest financial stake in the relief sought is the "most adequate plaintiff." ...

There can be little doubt that the lead plaintiff provision has shaken the quiet life of the class counsel. More significantly, the lead plaintiff provision alters the perception of the securities class action as being a lawyer-driven suit. The lead plaintiff provision replaces the tainted image of the plaintiff as figurehead with that of the plaintiff as a true functioning representative of the class with statutory powers over the suit's attorney. The lead plaintiff's large financial stake provides much needed incentives with respect to the suit's diligent prosecution, tempers the award of attorney's fees, and curbs the continued prosecution of unmeritorious suits, since the harm of such suits to the corporation is also harmful to the interests of the lead plaintiff. Moreover, the court's appointment of the lead plaintiff removes the self-selecting, even professional, image of the suit's plaintiff. By virtue of the court's power to appoint the suit's representative, the suit gains an important public connection. As a result, the selection of a lead plaintiff not only enhances the legitimacy of the suit's basis but also raises its overall public character.

---

20. 88 F.3d 87 (2d Cir. 1996).

In contrast to the securities class action, derivative suit plaintiffs remain self-selecting and derivative suit procedures do not systematically invite other shareholders to become the suit's plaintiff. As seen earlier, only through satisfying or excusing the demand requirement does the plaintiff earn the right to prosecute the action. The derivative suit exists because the real plaintiff, the corporation, is disabled by its board of directors' self-interest to terminate the derivative suit.... Overall, the derivative suit lacks the same legitimizing of the plaintiff as occurs with the securities class action's lead plaintiff. The demand requirement does not require an inquiry into whether the derivative suit plaintiff has a substantial economic interest in the firm such that he will diligently oversee the suit's progress or, most importantly, its settlement.

Both the class action and the derivative suit, however, may easily lose their public character through weaknesses in the settlement process. Though the lead plaintiff provision in the securities class action and the demand requirement confer a public status on their suit's plaintiff, weaknesses in the settlement ritual prevent the shareholder suit from securing a position as a mechanism for vindicating public norms.

The weak incentives for the attorneys and their clients to aggressively pursue the representative suit to trial are well recognized. With the exception of the lead plaintiff provision for securities class action, there is no legal requirement that the representative suit plaintiff have a substantial financial interest in the suit's successful prosecution. Lacking such an interest, the plaintiff bears little of the consequences if the suit produces either adverse consequences to the corporation or yields insubstantial awards to its intended beneficiaries, namely, fellow class members or the derivative suit corporation. A further financial firewall between the suit's plaintiff and its adverse effects is the contingent fee arrangement that holds the plaintiff harmless for the litigation costs of a misguided suit. Because of the contingent fee arrangement, any possible adverse impact of an ill-advised suit is not likely to rein in the maverick plaintiff. Moreover, the presence of a contingency fee arrangement separates the plaintiff from the suit's counsel. Further, the plaintiff's counsel enjoys a strategic advantage *vis-à-vis* the suit's defendants in aggressively pursuing risky claims. While the defendant's focus is upon the risk posed by a single suit, the plaintiff's attorney assesses a particular suit in light of a portfolio of suits being prosecuted by its office. Tipping the strategic balance further in favor of the plaintiff's counsel is that while the defendant assesses outcomes in terms of its overall liability exposure, the plaintiff's counsel's assessment is the much smaller incremental cost of pursuing the suit and negotiations to the next level.

The defendants are not, however, without their own advantages. First, to the extent their litigation costs fall within available D&O coverage, and perhaps even liberal indemnification under applicable state law or provisions of their employment contracts, defendants are somewhat above the financial consequences of the fray. This reality does, however, introduce a new actor into the scenario, namely, the insurer. The natural temptations of the defendants to clear their names and see justice done may well be tempered by the terms of the D&O policy. The control of the issuers is even greater when the policy includes a so-called "hammer clause" whereby insurer's obligations to its insured can be limited to the settlement offered by the plaintiff that was acceptable to the insurer but which was rejected by the insured. Furthermore, the possibility of a judgment beyond the policy coverage has the same salient impact on the defendant as the "wasting asset" feature common to D&O policies has on the plaintiff. Plaintiffs may gain nothing by pursuing a suit beyond a settlement offer supported by the insurer if the insurer's responsibility under the policy is limited to that offer. Moreover, the plaintiff's counsel has little interest in prolonging the suit; most insurance policies are in the nature of a wasting asset whereby their coverage limits are eroded by defense costs so that any sums from the insurance policy for the award of plaintiff's counsel fees is what remains after the plaintiff's adversaries have been compensated. This is a point missed by neither the plaintiff nor the insurer, especially when the corporation and other named defendants have insufficient funds to cover any resulting settlement or judgment. Finally, both the plaintiff's counsel and the insurer are well aware of the law of diminishing returns; an early settlement for a known amount is valued more highly than a potentially larger judgment discounted by the time and riskiness of a trial.

No one had the pulse of the settlement process better than the late Judge Henry Friendly, whose insights are helpful in assessing the settlement ritual:

> There can be no blinking at the fact that the interests of the plaintiff in a stockholder's derivative suit and of his attorney are by no means congruent.... The plaintiff's financial interest is in his share of the total recovery less what may be awarded to counsel, simpliciter; counsel's financial interest is in the amount of the award to him less the time and effort needed to produce it. A relatively small settlement may well produce an allowance bearing a higher ratio to the cost of the work than a much larger recovery obtained only after extensive discovery, a long trial and an appeal. The risks in proceeding to trial vary even more essentially. For the plaintiff, a defendant's judgment may mean simply the defeat of an expectation, often of relatively small amount; for his lawyer it can mean the loss of years of costly effort by himself and his staff.[21]

In the face of such weak incentives to pursue the complaint or defense aggressively, it is natural that settlements are the predominant outcome of those shareholder suits that survive pretrial motions....

Judge Friendly's observations enshroud the shareholder suit in a cynical veil. They project, perhaps aptly, that representative suits at the settlement stage succumb to their attorneys' utility curves so that neither compensatory nor deterrent objectives guide their resolution. Stated differently, settlements are lawyer and insurance driven. They do not reflect the broader private interest of the class or corporation, or, for that matter, the public objective of deterrence. Against this background, we can surmise that whatever opprobrium or public condemnation the shareholder suit directs toward the suit's defendants is undermined by the hollowness of the condemnation embodied in the suit's settlement. Was this a baseless action to extort an insurance-funded settlement or was it a meritorious suit quickly settled before the wasting asset, qua insurance policy, was depleted by defense costs? Adding to our malaise is the realization that few settlements are rejected by the courts and that there is little evidence of settlements where the officer and directors who have misbehaved contribute substantially personally toward the settlement fund in substantial amounts.

We also should appreciate the overall reluctance of the court to disturb the settlement before it.... Lacking true adversaries at the moment of settlement, how is a court to assess the adequacy and overall fairness of the settlement before it? With the pressures of its docket, the limited resources a court can employ to retain masters to review a settlement, and the absence of adversaries, not only do courts rarely reject settlements but often they do not closely review the settlement's terms in light of the suit's merits. Perhaps the following statement regarding shareholder suits reflects accurately the position of most

21. Saylor v. Lindsley, 456 F.2d 896, 900–01 (2d. Cir. 1972).

courts called upon to review a settlement: "The court starts from the familiar axiom that a bad settlement is almost always better than a good trial." ...

II. Enhancing the Social Meaning of Shareholder Suits

Ambiguation, tying, and ritual currently weaken the social influence of the shareholder suit. On the other hand, the above review found important strengthening inhibitions for shareholder suits in their procedural requirements that fostered court screening of the suit's merits, as well as inhibitions that prevail in D&O policies and state indemnity provisions. This section considers strategies that can be pursued to reverse the negative effects of those forces that weaken the social meaning of shareholder suits so that the shareholder suit is more likely to be viewed as an instrument that affirms desirable norms in the corporate setting.

A. *Reorienting the Judiciary's Focus*

The most apparent error courts make is elevating compensation over deterrence in defining the mission of the derivative suit. This concern also arises with respect to class actions where the preoccupation in approving settlements is the extent the settlement makes the class members whole. Courts instead should reverse their orientation so that their examination of the shareholder's standing to initiate a derivative suit and their approval of settlements emphasizes the public character of the norms raised by the suit.

Useful guidance in understanding the purpose of this new emphasis is provided by Pennsylvania, which liberalized the contemporaneous ownership requirement to confer standing to bring a derivative suit when necessary to avoid the injustice of a serious wrong to the corporation going unredressed. Other departures from the strict contemporaneous ownership requirement condition such liberalization on there being no public disclosure of the wrongdoing before the plaintiff acquired his shares. This, however, carries forward the concern of avoiding unjust enrichment to the plaintiff rather than preventing the defendant from being unjustly enriched by retaining her ill-gotten gains. Certainly, the present retention of the contemporaneous ownership requirement is an important commitment to the compensatory orientation of the derivative suit and obscures the deeper concern of why such suits exist at all and who the most adequate representative is for the suit. In contrast, an approach such as that taken in Pennsylvania invites early consideration of the important public character of derivative suits.

Though standing for class actions does not pose the same problem as it does for derivative suits, there continues to be a need to underscore the deterrence features of the class actions. As seen earlier, few settlements of securities class actions call upon the defendants to contribute to the award to the class; settlements are paid by the employer or, where recklessness is alleged, fall within an available insurance policy. This is not an important weakness in derivative suits if the award arises from willful or self-dealing behavior, but it is a problem when the misconduct falls under the more benign charges of inattention or wastefulness. Deterrence is poorly served and the suit is robbed of its public character when its defendants are not called upon to make a significant contribution to the settlement. At a minimum, settlement procedures should regularly require as part of the court's approval an affirmative finding as to why the individual actors were not required to contribute toward the settlement. Here the courts should consider the insights provided by the American Law Institute in its corporate governance project, which embraced a liability ceiling for directors and officers equal to the defendant's annual compensation from the corporation.[22] The courts could include within their finding why the directors or officers were not called upon to contribute to the suit's settlement by an amount at least equal to their most recent year's compensation from the corporation. To be sure, such a new dimension to settlement procedures is likely to prolong suits without increasing the amount of the overall settlement. Complaints along these lines can easily be seen as merely documenting the unfortunate set of incentives that predominate for shareholder suits that rob the suits of their public and deterrent effects. In this regard, courts should address these weak incentives by increasing the fees to be awarded plaintiff's counsel when the defendants have made a non-trivial contribution to the overall settlement. Correlatively, settlements that, without convincing explanation, fail to extract non-trivial contributions from the defendants and do not adequately protect against the defendant's recouping her contribution through insurance, indemnity or other arrangements should include a visible penalty in the court's determination of the attorneys' fees it will award.

B. Confirming the Public Nature of Shareholder Suits

Prosecuting shareholder suits is a risky business for which the plaintiff's attorney must receive large rewards in order to avoid poor or under-representation. Though incentives, as suggested above, can be tweaked to accomplish fairly targeted objectives, such as extracting from the individual defendant some contribution toward the settlement, it remains likely that the overall incentives of shareholder suits will continue to cause them to be lawyer-driven. Assuming this is the case, then the role of the law should be to direct the suits in such a way as to increase their stature.

The easiest step for more closely harnessing the derivative suit to the corporate interest it represents is for the courts to invigorate the long dormant requirement that the suit's representative be an adequate one. Borrowing from the lead plaintiff provision introduced by the 1995 Reform Act, the derivative suit court should actively seek one or more shareholders to serve as advisors to the court on matters related to the selection and retention of class counsel. This change, however, must confront the legitimate fear that a lead plaintiff is armed with the power to substitute counsel for those that initiated the suit. The concern here is that if counsel could easily be supplanted, the attorney will be reluctant to invest his time and money in the many activities that are necessary to file a complaint. Thus, the lead plaintiff provision may have the unintended consequence of reducing the deterrent effects of derivative suits by reducing the incentives for attorneys to pursue events that suggest misbehavior by company executives. Similarly, the lead plaintiff provision may cause the complaint's allegations to be poorly supported because the attorney is unwilling to invest heavily in a preliminary investigation of the facts until finally chosen as the suit's attorney. Courts could pursue several strategies to address these concerns. For example, the court should, in its consideration of who should represent the action, give substantial attention to the overall quality of the filing attorney's efforts in preparing and pleading the case. Thus, any recommendation by the lead plaintiff that another attorney should be selected to represent the action should address the quality of representation the attorney will provide. Here the court should be very reluctant to substitute counsel if it has been satisfied with the thoroughness of the preparation and pleadings submitted to date by the filing counsel. Even if it believes new counsel should be appointed, it can call for *quantum meruit* compensation for the suit's filing attorney

---

22. AMERICAN LAW INSTITUTE, PRINCIPLES OF CORPORATE GOVERNANCE: ANALYSIS AND RECOMMENDATIONS § 7.19 (1992).

if the suit is successfully concluded by new counsel. The important objective is to more closely link the suit's prosecution to the public norm that is to be vindicated on behalf of the derivative suit corporation. If the court fails to do this, then much like the passive plaintiff in securities class actions, the court will merely be confirming that the true combatants are the attorneys and not the public interest that underlies the corporation's or investor's rights that give rise to the suit.

A further reform that would raise the public stature of the shareholder suit is to accord to non-intervening shareholders or class members greater rights to review settlements. The standing of non-intervenors to pursue appeals in both derivative and class actions is a matter over which the circuits are badly divided. It is not uncommon for shareholders or class members to seek review of a settlement, even though they have not formally intervened in the shareholder suit. Not surprisingly, the charge they raise on appeal is that the class or derivative suit's lawyers have failed to achieve a settlement that is in the best interest of their client. Sometimes these disputes reflect the competing turf war of rival law firms....

Intervention into a shareholder suit is not without its procedural difficulties. We ought not to deny to non-intervenors standing to appeal on the ground that they could have easily qualified themselves to pursue an appeal.

According standing to appeal the settlement of a shareholder suit to non-intervenors who had raised their objections to the settlement before the trial court would recognize the substantial public nature of the shareholder suit. Indeed, such a rule would likely encourage objectors to step forward so as to establish their standing to seek an appeal of an arguably unfair settlement. Moreover, according such non-intervenors standing to appeal would provide a useful inhibition to the suit's attorney proposing settlements that would not benefit the interests of the class or derivative suit shareholders....

Robert B. Thompson & Hillary A. Sale, *Securities Fraud as Corporate Governance: Reflections upon Federalism*[*]

I. The Dramatic Expansion in the Scope of Federal Liability Relating to Disclosure

Even more dramatic than the expansion of mandatory disclosure and the ancillary liability for half-truths and silence is the broadened scope of liability once a misstatement is established. A simple comparison to common law fraud makes the point. At common law, the basic liability for misstatements extended only to those in privity with the fraud feasor who could prove actual reliance on the fraud.

... [T]he cause of action responsible for most of the litigation under the securities laws is court-created, an implied right of action pursuant to Rule 10b-5. Liability under this implied right of action is more expansive than common law liability in at least three ways that are relevant to its use in the corporate governance context. First, any person who purchases or sells securities in connection with a material misstatement or omission may sue if they are damaged thereby. The case law makes clear that courts interpret this cause of action broadly such that fraud feasors can be liable for the losses not just of the person with whom they trade, but also for the losses of anyone who traded in reliance on

---
[*] Originally published in 56 VANDERBILT LAW REVIEW 859 (2003). Reprinted with permission.

the misleading statement. In a 10b-5 context, the plaintiffs might, for example, claim that they lost money in a trade. Someone else presumably made money, but that offsetting trader is probably not the defendant.... The defendants are exposed to all of the plaintiffs' trading losses even though the defendants did not necessarily have an offsetting trading benefit. Of course, the defendants may have indirectly benefited—for example, through a compensation package tied to short-run market performance. Either way, the connection between the fraud and the harm is indirect and through the market, with a potentially severe impact on the defendants.

Second, the Supreme Court's acceptance of the fraud on the market doctrine to establish reliance has facilitated plaintiffs' litigation in a governance context. Under this doctrine, plaintiffs who did not, for example, read a public document containing a misstatement or omission, can utilize a rebuttable presumption allowing them to plead and prove that they traded in an active and efficient market like the New York Stock Exchange. If they succeed in doing so, their reliance on the market incorporating the alleged misstatement or omission is presumed. This doctrine makes class actions by plaintiffs more attractive and, thus, expands the potential for lawsuits focused on governance issues.

Third, damages for 10b-5 claims brought in a developed market can be large and the means for determining them seem, at least at first glance, to be accessible to judges and litigants. In a typical securities fraud suit, the damages depend on the size of the class period and the magnitude of the change in the stock price. The longer the class period and the more dramatic the price change in the stock after the "truth" is revealed, the larger the size of the total potential recovery....

When securities litigation is used to regulate the relative rights of shareholders, directors, and officers in corporate governance, the federalism doctrine also acts to restrain the litigation. This tension between the fraud-based mechanism and corporate governance is revealed, in part, in the refrain in securities fraud opinions that the cause of action is not properly used to target mismanagement. The Supreme Court addressed the role of federal litigation and regulation in the traditional state law context in *Santa Fe Industries, Inc. v. Green*.[23] In *Santa Fe*, the Court focused on whether federal judges were allowing securities fraud claims to determine when directors' actions were unfair to minority shareholders. This corporate governance issue, concerning the relative rights of directors and shareholders, had been established at state law. The Court was unwilling to federalize it absent explicit congressional action. Indeed, in *Santa Fe* the Court clearly attempted to cabin the role of federal law in corporate governance and management contexts.

Despite the principles articulated in *Santa Fe*, this Article describes a dramatic growth in the role of federal law in regulating officers and directors. The growth arguably runs afoul of the principles expressed in *Santa Fe*, because, after all, state law gives directors free rein to determine how much or how little officers can do. When federal law increases the role of officers it also diminishes the corporate authority of directors to determine the governance structure of the business. Simultaneously, this action increases the role of shareholders by permitting them (rather than the directors) to hold officers accountable.

There is, however, room to fit this expanding federal role within the parameters set forth in *Santa Fe*. In that case, the Court expressed its federalism concern that absent a clear indication of congressional intent, it would not override "established state policies of corporate regulation." State law actually says very little affirmatively about what officers are supposed to do (in contrast to the relatively well-developed roles of directors and shareholders)....

---

23. [430 U.S. 462 (1977).]

II. Data on Corporate Governance Litigation

A. *The Different Faces of Shareholder Litigation*

State-Law Fiduciary Duty Derivative Cases Raising, Principally, Loyalty Allegations. The classic shareholder litigation case is one based on breach of fiduciary duty brought by a shareholder against an insider who has engaged in a transaction with the corporation that benefits the insider more than the corporation.... In a recent study of Delaware complaints[24] there were about fifty derivative cases a year brought against public corporations in Delaware courts. Almost two-thirds of those alleged conflict of interest or other loyalty claims. About 20% of the complaints alleged improper financial reporting or a failure to supervise....

State-Law Fiduciary Duty Cases in Acquisitions. By far the largest number of state shareholder litigation claims against publicly held companies are fiduciary duty claims brought as class actions arising out of acquisitions. The Thompson and Thomas Study shows that such class actions dwarf derivative suits in terms of the number of suits filed, with about four hundred cases a year, or about eight times the number of derivative suits filed against public corporations.... The most common count in the complaints states that the directors have breached their duty to maximize share value. The desired result, then, is a higher price for the transaction.... Most cases are dismissed within a year of filing, without damages or other relief.

Securities Fraud Class Actions. The securities fraud class actions brought in recent years follow a typical pattern. These cases are brought under the federal securities laws, generally following a company's correction of a prior earnings misstatement. Of course, the company's stock price falls when the new earnings numbers are released....

Further, these earnings management cases combine elements of both loyalty and care claims and might have been made in state court. As discussed above, the theory of these cases is that the managers have caused the corporation to do something that has made the corporation's shares less valuable and, thereby, harmed the shareholders. Unlike the traditional state court conflict of interest case, the insider is not on the other side of the transaction from the corporation and its shareholders. However, the insider may receive some indirect benefit from the action, perhaps related to additional consideration....

B. *Characteristics of the Securities Fraud Class Actions*

We have undertaken a detailed examination of securities fraud class action complaints filed in 1999 for the purpose of examining to what extent these cases seek to redress claims that relate to corporate governance. We created our data set from the list of securities class action filings for 1999 ... We limited our examination of complaints to those filed in district courts within the Second, Third, and Ninth Circuits. We defined our sample to include the courts within the Second and Ninth Circuits, because these circuits are widely recognized to be the most prominent courts today in securities litigation. The Third Circuit includes Delaware, the site for the state law database to which we make comparisons in this discussion. The total cases filed in those three circuits make up approximately half of all cases filed in that year.

---

24. Robert B. Thompson and Randall S. Thomas, *The New Look of Shareholder Litigation: Acquisition-Oriented Class Actions,* 57 VAND. L. REV. 133 (2004).

1. The Companies Sued

Most of the companies named in these suits were incorporated in Delaware....

California was the headquarters for half of the companies in the sample; companies sued were more likely to be listed on Nasdaq than the NYSE; and more companies were in high-tech industries than traditional manufacturing.... If, as we posit, securities litigation is playing largely a care-based corporate governance role, it is possible that these young companies lack some of the internal governance structures of their more established counterparts. If securities fraud claims are working to address some of those issues, then the lawsuits against those companies may be playing an ex post deterrence role. Or it may be, as many have claimed, that start-up, high-tech companies are disproportionately and inappropriately sued....

2. Securities Fraud Class Actions and the Perils of Representative Litigation

... Our analysis of the federal complaints reveals that complaints are often premised on allegations of fraud related either to a significant drop in earnings or other accounting allegations. The majority of complaints in our sample identify a precipitous drop that precedes the suit.... These types of claims are consistent with today's major corporate scandals, like Enron and WorldCom. They are also consistent with the climate of earnings management.

3. Claims Made in Securities Fraud Class Actions

Securities fraud claims are directed against individuals in their capacity as officers, not directors. State law fiduciary duty complaints are brought against directors, but federal claims are made against officers. Often, of course, the same individuals serve in both positions, but the position in which they are sued is telling with respect to the function that each law seeks to serve.... Of the eighty-two complaints that identify individual defendants, eighty-one name the chief executive officer ("CEO") as a defendant, and sixty name the chief financial officer ("CFO")....

Securities fraud claims address officer behavior in managing the company and in their duty of care. Notably, the subject matter of the alleged misrepresentations encompasses the duty of care/duty to monitor governance aspects of traditional corporate law and reflects the care-based concerns expressed in the debates about recent corporate scandals. The majority of the alleged misrepresentations focus on accounting misrepresentations. These misrepresentations arguably represent the earnings-management phenomenon that others have documented in today's public companies.... Fuller and Jensen posit that analysts' focus on predictions, short-term numbers, and earnings data, thus, influences managerial decisions, resulting in changes in management focus that may impact operational decisions and harm long-term corporate profitability.[25]

Securities fraud claims arise out of statements made in periodic reports and other statements reflecting management's stewardship of the business. In the majority of the cases, the specific claims are framed in terms of allegations of misleading statements or omissions occurring in the ongoing operation of business, like regularly filed reports, press releases, and

---

25. Joseph Fuller & Michael C. Jensen, *Just Say No to Wall Street: Putting a Stop to the Earnings Game,* 14 J. APPLIED CORP. FIN. 41, 41 (2002).

conference calls.... More than three-fourths of the complaints refer to misstatements appearing in press releases and to other voluntary disclosures. These claims arise in the regular course of business, conversations with the media and required reports, or situations implicating day-to-day decisionmaking and, largely, the duty of care. Thus, most of the cases involve corporate governance-type allegations....

Securities fraud complaints often allege that a misrepresentation occurred for insider benefit. As a result, they often appear to contain loyalty-type claims. For example, some complaints rely on the trades of insiders in company stock to support these allegations. Others focus on executive compensation. Consistent with our care/governance findings, these allegations are merely hooks, not substantive claims. Insider trades, for example, serve as proxies for scienter—an alleged motive for managers to commit fraud—rather than evidence of the fraud itself....

The small per share award in most securities fraud class actions suggests a deterrence function that is more consistent with corporate governance than with compensating a class of purchasers or sellers. A significant percentage of the relief in securities class actions, 20 to 30%, goes to attorneys, and the remaining relief is increasingly small relative to the alleged loss in corporate value....

III. Shareholder Litigation's Role in Corporate Governance

... As the federal disclosure obligations have increased, they have begun to provide the basis to enforce duty of care obligations that in the past might have been enforced under state law. In either jurisdiction the allegation would be that the managers' actions have harmed shareholders by decreasing the corporation's value. Federal law, of course, allows only those shareholders who bought and sold to recover for this loss, but that limit seems to reflect concern for vexatious litigation more than a substantive belief about the culpability of managers. In theory, state law duty of care litigation continues to afford relief to these shareholders, but as disclosure and securities fraud litigation have expanded, and as Delaware has raised the bar for care claims, the balance has shifted to a larger federal role.

Fiduciary duty and securities fraud litigation have much in common. Both occur after the fact and through a lawsuit brought by a self-appointed individual, ostensibly a shareholder but in reality an attorney acting as a private attorney general, motivated by the fees to be earned in successful suits. Further, litigation in the two settings works with roughly the same set of incentives. No one shareholder has sufficient interest to make litigation worthwhile. Collectively, however, the damage is sufficient to warrant recovery. The attorney's job is both to create and file the complaint and to help the class plaintiffs understand and follow the litigation.

It is not surprising that the lawyers may have mixed incentives in both settings. Those delegated to act as class plaintiffs must represent both the class and themselves, at least in the context of fees. And, both sets of claims suffer from parallel litigation agency cost problems to the extent that the economic incentives of the attorney for the plaintiffs are not closely aligned with the economic incentives of the class as a whole.

The overlap between the governance motives in both sets of litigation is striking. Today's federal securities fraud claims are largely efforts to recover from what could be care claims at state law. To be sure, elements of the duty of loyalty appear in the context of, for example, insider trading by a defendant or efforts to increase executive compensation. But the main story line of these complaints is focused not on recovery of a wrongful benefit received by the insider, as in the Delaware cases, but on recovery of the entire loss that can arguably be said to flow from the managerial mistake, overvaluation, or misrepresentation.

Arguably, then, these federal cases are working to fill the hole in Delaware law brought about by the lack of liability for, and concomitant inability to sustain, suits for breaches of the fiduciary duty of care. Unlike their loyalty-focused, state law counterparts, the federal cases detail shareholders' complaints that the officers' stewardship of the business has not been what the owners would like it to be. The question raised is the one currently in the news every day—what did the CEOs at WorldCom, Enron, Qwest, Xerox, and others actually know about their respective company's financial situation and when did they know it? And, if as some claim, they did not know, then why not? The latter question raises the same issues as the duty of care/duty to monitor, with the duty of loyalty in the background.

To the extent that federal securities fraud and state fiduciary litigation are both constraints on possible abuses of managers' positions, it is worth comparing the relative manner in which the two types of litigation function. The increased growth in the role of federal law in corporate governance can be explained by several advantages that federal litigation has relative to state litigation. First, the disclosure basis for federal securities law provides other ancillary benefits beyond shareholder litigation that contribute to its use as the preferred response when problems like those in 2002 occur in corporate governance. Disclosure can aid several parties in the corporate monitoring context. In addition to assisting shareholders, disclosure aids directors in their monitoring function and can be an important support for accountants as they undertake the monitoring role that is a key component of corporate governance....

Second, the federal focus on the behavior of officers is much more in line with the reality of modern corporate America. As our business enterprises have become larger and more complex, increased power has passed to chief executive officers and the line hierarchy that flows from that person....

For Delaware to expand its focus on officer conduct it would have to amend its jurisdictional statute to include officers rather than just directors. In 1977, the U.S. Supreme Court rejected Delaware's use of *quasi in rem* jurisdiction to reach corporate directors and officers.... The Delaware legislature responded by passing a statute stating that the corporation's registered agent serves as the directors' agent, thereby creating a form of implied jurisdiction. The statute, however, does not apply to officers. This statutory gap may explain the lack of lawsuits naming officers, but it does not explain the legislature's choice not to include officers as corporate fiduciaries who ought to be subject to litigation in the Delaware court system to enforce their corporate governance functions....

Third, disclosure questions, the focus of federal law, can be more easily handled under the current legal regime than questions alleging a duty to supervise and monitor, which are the basis of care review under state law. Delaware's implementation of section 102(b)(7) [which allows corporate charters to exempt directors from personal liability for breaches of the duty of care] and judicial focus on the failure to supervise has made it very difficult for it to be a presence in determining the care portion of corporate governance. When infectious greed overwhelmed our historical guardians, Delaware was at a relative disadvantage in acting. Federal law has been stepping into that vacuum for years, and recent legislation expands the federal corporate governance role—most strikingly in the care context. State law continues to have the core role for duty of loyalty issues, but it now explicitly shares corporate governance with the federal government....

The underexamined aspect of [federal] litigation is the expanding role of disclosure. Over time, mandatory and voluntary disclosure pursuant to the federal securities laws has increased dramatically. As the quantity of disclosure has increased, so has the litigation over its quality. The original premise for requiring disclosure was to decrease informational asymmetries and thereby to improve market efficiency through accurate information, while stopping short of creating a body of federal corporate law. State law was to remain the monitor of the shareholders' relationship with corporate management and only marginally be the focus of disclosure discussions. In reality, federal law now occupies the space originally reserved for the states—monitoring corporate managers through disclosure.

Although, in general terms, disclosure is a good thing, it is not necessarily entirely good or a good regulatory mechanism for corporate governance claims. First, disclosure is an indirect way to regulate managerial behavior. As discussed above, disclosure is, at best, a monitor of what managers say, not what they do. The two may be linked only at the margin. Second, disclosure can, as the recent cycle reveals, create pressure for more disclosure—truthful or not. Disclosure then is a double-edged sword. Truthful disclosures work to decrease informational asymmetries. Fraud increases them. More disclosure can lead to pressure for more disclosure. In a world where analysts and others depend on releases of company information, the expectation and appetite for more disclosure grows with each new disclosure. In addition, the pressure to meet the predictions and make the disclosures accurate increases. Yet, the current corporate climate reveals that, short of a major market turnaround, it is not clear that the pressure will produce accurate disclosures. In that world, then, the disclosures are of little value except as ex post litigation links. And, third, if managers are truthful about their shortcomings, the securities laws presumably offer no protection for breaches of the duty of care, no matter how egregious. The remaining question for further discussion, then, is whether the disclosure approach is sufficiently efficacious, and if not, whether we should recognize the strong role of federal law in monitoring corporate governance and reformulate it to do so in a more direct fashion.

Discussion Questions

1. Ramirez argues that arbitration is superior to the litigation system under the PSLRA. But assuming his criticisms of the PSLRA are accurate, would an attempt to shift to arbitration be preferable to an attempt to repair the litigation system by reforming or repealing the PSLRA? Why or why not?

2. Ramirez argues that industry-sponsored securities arbitration, with a layer of SEC regulation, will be fair and more streamlined than litigation. But other commentators have questioned the fairness of the existing system of arbitrating disputes between broker-dealers and their customers, and note that it has come to involve cumbersome procedures much like those of formal litigation. *See* Barbara Black and Jill I. Gross, *Making It Up as They Go Along: The Role of Law in Securities Arbitration,* 23 CARDOZO L. REV. 991 (2002).

In Ramirez's proposed system, how could the SEC guarantee fairness without sacrificing the informal character of arbitration? Who would supply the arbitrators, pay their salaries, and write the applicable rules? What are the advantages and disadvantages of the fact that arbitrators would not be strictly bound to apply the federal securities laws?

3. Should the resolution of civil disputes focus on redress or deterrence? With respect to this issue, are there factors that distinguish securities law from civil law generally? Under the current securities law regime, the federal courts supply much of the substance of the securities laws. Ramirez contends that a shift to arbitration would not lead to "delegalization." Do you agree?

4. The number of federal securities fraud suits filed decreased in the first year after the passage of the PSLRA, but soon rose to historic highs. What might explain this? Note also Thompson and Sale's argument that federal securities litigation has certain advantages over state litigation from the point of view of shareholder plaintiffs.

Does all this suggest that the PSLRA has been a failure? Does it necessarily mean that Ramirez's criticism of the Act turns out to have been unwarranted?

5. Lawsuits handled by the nation's dominant plaintiff-side securities firm, Milberg Weiss Bershad Hynes & Lerach LLP, are often said to have inspired the PSLRA. Ironically, that firm saw its already-large share of securities suits rise dramatically after the passage of the PSLRA. *See* Randall Thomas, Stuart Schwab, & Robert Hansen, *Megafirms*, 80 N.C. L. Rev. 115, 194 (2001). Can you think of reasons for the increase in this large firm's market share after 1995? Might this development constitute a policy concern?

6. Consider the distinction that Johnson, Nelson and Pritchard draw between "investor protection" and "investor wealth"; they argue that securities law should focus on the latter. Do you agree? Compare this view with Cox's argument that securities law should focus on deterrence.

7. As Johnson, Nelson and Pritchard point out, the corporate defendant in the typical fraud-on-the-market case did not directly benefit from the alleged fraud because it did not trade in its own securities. Contemporaneous traders can, nonetheless, recover from the corporation based on statements made by its managers.

If the corporation does not stand to gain, why do managers make false statements? *See* Jennifer H. Arlen & William J. Carney, *Vicarious Liability for Fraud on Securities Markets: Theory and Evidence*, 1992 U. Ill. L. Rev. 691 (cited by William Bratton in Chapter 1); Donald Langevoort, *Organized Illusions, A Behavioral Theory of Why Corporations Mislead Stock Market Investors (And Cause Other Social Harms)*, 146 U. Pa. L. Rev. 101 (1997).

If managers' false statements are not motivated by gain to the corporation, will corporate liability deter managers from making such statements? Is deterrence the only justification for holding the corporation liable? See also Chapter 6, debating the role of deterrence in criminal law.

8. Johnson, Nelson and Pritchard argue that it is possible to "quantify the dollar value of fraud avoided." Although the authors present many theories as to the cost of fraud, have they quantified it or explained how to do so? Assuming that deterrent value can be quantified, should the law discourage suits whose deterrent effects are not cost-justified, even if they are substantively meritorious?

9. According to Johnson, Nelson and Pritchard, "Two competing hypotheses may explain the effect of *Silicon Graphics'* rigorous pleading standard on shareholder wealth: (1) the high standard primarily discourages suits that, regardless of their merits, are not cost-justified in terms of deterring fraud, thereby enhancing shareholder wealth on average; or (2) the high standard chills suits that are both meritorious and cost-justified in addition to non-cost justified suits, thus undermining deterrence and diminishing shareholder wealth."

Their evidence suggests that the decision had an immediate positive effect on share prices. Thus they conclude that the evidence supports the first hypothesis. What assumptions are required to draw this conclusion? Are there other possible explanations for the rise in price?

10. In recent years, academic studies of corporate law and other areas of law have come to rely increasingly on empirical research as opposed to traditional legal research

and argument. As Johnson, Nelson and Pritchard note, event studies have been used in court as evidence in specific instances of fraud, but have not yet been used for the broader purpose of formulating general rules. Do you agree that empirical research such as event studies should guide legal policies such as the pleading standard for securities fraud? What are the pros and cons of lawmakers focusing primarily on the quantifiable and directly measurable effects of laws?

11. Does it matter *who* receives the benefits from securities litigation reform or other aspects of corporate law? Johnson, Nelson and Pritchard on the one hand and Cox on the other argue (for different reasons) that rules restricting lawsuits are justified by the benefits they create, even if they also frustrate some meritorious suits. Do you agree that these putative benefits justify blocking some meritorious suits against the corporation?

Most observers today agree with Ramirez's argument that although the PSLRA sought to contain an "explosion" of frivolous litigation, no such crisis has been documented. Assuming this to be true, but assuming also that restrictions on securities litigation, such as the *Silicon Graphics* ruling, increase share price, is it good policy to restrict litigation?

12. As Johnson, Nelson and Pritchard point out, Congress passed the PSLRA in part based on the belief that shareholders were filing "cookie-cutter" securities-fraud complaints in immediate response to fluctuations in stock prices, without attempting to ascertain first whether fraud caused the fluctuation. Note, however, that where information is difficult to obtain, filing a complaint gives the plaintiff access to civil discovery. While discovery requests may be used to harass an adversary, they can also be made in a good faith effort to obtain information that would otherwise have been unavailable. The heightened pleading requirements of the PSLRA make it more difficult for shareholders to get access to discovery procedures. Unlike other civil plaintiffs, however, shareholders have a special tool to obtain information even in the absence of civil discovery: their state-law right to inspect the books and records of the corporation. *See, e.g.,* Del. Gen. Corp. L. § 220; *Brehm v. Eisner,* 746 A.2d 244 (Del. 2000). Is this tool sufficient to alleviate the information problem caused by the PSLRA's heightened pleading requirements? What advantages and limitations does it have, for shareholder plaintiffs, management, and the courts?

13. As the editor's footnote in the Johnson, Nelson and Pritchard case points out, there remains, as of 2009, a circuit split over the level of scienter required in 10b-5 cases. The PSLRA raised the pleading requirements for scienter, but did not specify what the required *level* of scienter is. In *Tellabs v. Makor,* the Court interpreted the "strong inference" language of the PSLRA, but stated that the level of scienter was not before the Court. With respect to scienter (and other aspects of the 10b-5 civil and criminal actions), should the courts or Congress provide the definitions? Why?

14. Cox contends that a focus on compensation rather than deterrence diminishes the social meaning of shareholder suits by making them appear to be purely financial squabbles as opposed to matters of public interest. As Cox also notes, however, compensation is easily measured, while deterrence is not. Would replacing compensatory awards with injunctive relief aimed at preventing the recurrence of misconduct increase the social standing of shareholder litigation? What effect would it have on the amount of shareholder litigation? Would it deter future corporate misconduct more effectively than compensatory awards?

15. Do you agree with Cox's argument that the PSLRA's aggressive attempts to screen out frivolous litigation will help enhance the positive social meaning of shareholder suits? Is it possible that this focus might have a *negative* effect on the social meaning of suits?

16. One commentator argues that the restriction of shareholder lawsuits by the PSLRA and other recent legislation sends a "message" that is "inconsistent with and thus undercuts the effectiveness of parallel criminal laws." *See* Geraldine Szott Moohr, *An Enron Lesson: The Modest Role of Criminal Law in Preventing Corporate Crime*, 55 FLA. L. REV. 937 (2003). Do you agree? Are there ways in which the restriction of civil suits might make criminal laws *more* effective?

17. Lawrence Mitchell and others have argued that placing legally enforceable duties on management is useful because it enhances shareholders' and workers' "trust" in management. *See Trust. Contract. Process.* in PROGRESSIVE CORPORATE LAW (Lawrence E. Mitchell, ed. 1995). Larry Ribstein has argued, however, that legal duties do not enhance "trust," but serve as a "substitute" for trust:

> To be sure, corporate managers may need to demonstrate the firm's benign attitude to shareholders and workers in order to induce the latter to reciprocate.... Rules that punish managers for breaches [, however,] actually prevent them from demonstrating their genuine commitment to the workers and their innate trustworthiness. Although law may usefully provide a substitute constraint that induces shareholders or workers to rely on managers, this has nothing to do with trust.

Larry Ribstein, *Law v. Trust*, 81 B.U. L. REV. 553, 575 (2001). See also Stephen Bainbridge's discussion of trust in Chapter 2.

With whom do you agree? On the one hand, can management demonstrate a "genuine commitment" to act in the interests of shareholders, workers or other constituents without submitting to legal liability to them? On the other hand, can a relationship truly be based on "trust" if it is also founded on the threat of legal liability?

Then again, why does it matter whether corporate relationships are based on liability or trust? What are the advantages and disadvantages of trust and liability as the basis for a relationship with respect to shareholders, employees, creditors, and customers? How do corporate relationships differ from relationships outside the corporate context?

18. Thompson and Sale characterize many federal securities fraud suits as actually intended to deter bad corporate governance. Is the distinction between "securities fraud" and "corporate governance" is a useful one? Why or why not? If so, how would you define the distinction?

19. Thompson and Sale are skeptical of what they see as the trend toward the use of federal disclosure litigation to indirectly regulate corporate governance. At the end of their article, they suggest a more direct federal approach to corporate governance regulation. What form might a direct approach take? What are the advantages to such an approach? Can you see any advantages to the current "indirect" approach?

Chapter 6

Criminal and Regulatory Law

The prototypical legal subject is the human individual, and the law sometimes treats the corporation as if it were a kind of individual. But a corporation has no single mind or soul; it is a complex organization that acts through various individuals whose interests and motives often diverge from those of the corporation as an organization. As we have seen, much of corporate governance analysis is based on the proposition that this internal complexity imposes agency costs on shareholders. The readings in this chapter consider the questions corporate complexity raises for the government's criminal and civil regulation of corporate behavior. These questions include how incentives and punishments in the organizational context should differ from those applied to individual conduct, whether the law should focus on corporations or individual corporate agents, and whether criminal or civil penalties are appropriate. Underlying all these inquiries are fundamental questions about the role of the corporation, the role of government regulation, and the purpose of criminal law.

Jennifer Arlen points out that the internal complexity of the corporation complicates the deterrent effect of criminal punishment. Both corporations and society have an interest in corporations policing their own agents. Arlen argues, however, that exposing corporations to criminal liability for the actions of their agents can create a perverse incentive for corporations to refrain from such internal policing, because such measures may bring hidden criminal conduct to the attention of the government and invite sanctions.

While corporate agents who break the law are often "rogues" within the corporation, the turn-of-the-millennium corporate scandals at firms like Enron, WorldCom Inc. and Tyco International Ltd. focused attention on illegal activity that was allegedly sanctioned at the highest levels of the corporation or even constitutes corporate policy. Pamela Bucy argues that in such situations, corporate criminal liability may be justified on a theory of moral culpability. In such situations, individual employees and officers need incentives to report corporate misconduct even when to do so would conflict with the corporation's immediate interests. Leonard Baynes discusses this phenomenon and critiques the Sarbanes-Oxley Act's attempts to provide incentives to "blow the whistle."

Bucy argues that corporate-level criminal liability undermines the law's moral authority. John Coffee sees a similar effect in the criminalization of "technical" regulatory violations, particularly as applied to individual corporate officers. Coffee contends that this direction in regulatory law threatens the moral and policy distinctions between criminal and tort law.

In addition to imposing penalties, the law also attempts to influence corporate conduct by offering positive incentives. Timothy Malloy's examination of this phenomenon highlights an aspect of corporate complexity that both incentive and penalty structures often overlook: the bureaucratic compartmentalization of the corporation. Building on the basic insight that the law must consider the divergent interests of individual agents within the firm, Malloy analyzes the effect of bureaucratization on corporate agents' responses to legal incentives.

Deregulation of industry was a common theme of economic policy beginning in the 1980s. The financial collapse of 2008, however, has caused some observers to blame deregulation for economic inequality and volatility. Damon Silvers and Heather Slavkin present this point of view in the final selection of the chapter. They describe the complex regulation of the banking and financial sector and how that regulation was largely dismantled in recent decades.

Jennifer Arlen, *The Potentially Perverse Effects of Corporate Criminal Liability*[*]

Both the maximum allowable criminal fines for corporate crime and the fines actually imposed on corporations have increased dramatically.... Moreover, courts and legislatures have considerably expanded the scope of criminal liability. These reforms appear to be premised on the idea that imposing vicarious criminal liability on corporations necessarily reduces corporate crime, with higher sanctions leading to lower amounts of corporate crime. Many seeking to evaluate these reforms have looked for guidance to the economic analysis of corporate crime. The standard economic approach to corporate criminal liability supports the view that imposing strict vicarious criminal liability on corporations invariably reduces corporate crime, with higher sanctions leading to less crime. A more thorough analysis of strict vicarious liability as it is currently applied reveals that this conclusion is not necessarily correct.

The simplest economic approach treats the corporation as a person capable of committing crime. In this view of corporate crime, corporate criminal liability operates as a direct sanction on the actual wrongdoer—the corporation—with higher sanctions leading to lower amounts of crime. Crime is deterred efficiently, this view holds, if the corporation is held strictly liable for all its crimes, subject to a fine equal to the social cost of crime divided by the probability of detection (H/p), because this forces the corporation to internalize the social cost of its criminal activity. As corporate criminal fines historically have been far less than the social cost of the crime, this analysis appears to support both the current use of strict vicarious liability and the current trend toward higher corporate fines.

Devising efficient corporate criminal sanctions is substantially more complicated than this analysis indicates, however. Corporate crime is not analogous to individual crime. Corporate crimes are not committed by corporations; they are committed by agents of the corporation. These agents are rational self-interested utility maximizers who commit crimes in order to benefit themselves. In pursuit of his own self-interest an agent may commit a crime that incidentally benefits the corporation, but this is not its purpose. In addition, an agent who commits a crime risks direct individual criminal liability for his actions.

Some scholars, recognizing the agency cost nature of corporate crime, argue that corporate criminal liability is best analyzed as a substitute for direct criminal liability of the agent. In this view, corporate liability is simply an indirect means of sanctioning wrongful agents, on the assumption that corporations subject to criminal liability will in turn sanction the wrongful agents, either by seeking indemnification or by reducing the

---

[*] Originally published in 23 JOURNAL OF LEGAL STUDIES 833 (1994). Reprinted with permission of the publisher, the University of Chicago Press. Copyright 1994 by The University of Chicago. All rights reserved.

agents' wages. Corporate criminal liability accordingly is warranted when corporations are better able to sanction agents than is the state. Should this be the case, this view holds that a corporation should be strictly liable for its agents' crimes and subject to a fine equal to H/p. The corporation will in turn impose this liability on the wrongful agent in each case, producing efficient deterrence. Corporate criminal liability is not justifiable, however, when the state is as capable as the corporation of sanctioning the wrongful agent directly— as often is the case.

Corporate criminal liability may indeed sometimes deter crime by inducing corporations to sanction their agents for wrongful acts. But corporate liability also has another effect. Many corporate crimes—such as securities fraud, government procurement fraud, and some environmental crimes—cannot be readily detected by the government. Corporations often are better positioned to detect such crimes and determine which agents committed them. In these circumstances, corporate criminal liability may affect corporate expenditures on detecting and investigating crimes committed by their employees, here described as "enforcement costs." Should vicarious criminal liability increase corporate enforcement expenditures, it magnifies the deterrent effect of direct agent liability by increasing the probability that wrongful agents will be detected and sanctioned. Should it have the opposite effect, however, corporate crime will increase. The deterrent effect of vicarious criminal liability therefore depends on the effect of vicarious liability on corporate enforcement expenditures.

Recognizing the influence of corporate enforcement expenditures ... dramatically changes the analysis of corporate criminal liability. Previous analysis suggests that increased corporate liability necessarily reduces crime. Introducing corporate enforcement costs, however, reveals that increased corporate liability does not necessarily reduce corporate crime and, indeed, may result in increased crime. The existing legal regime governing many crimes is best approximated as a rule of "pure strict vicarious liability," under which the fine imposed for a particular crime is fixed, in that it does not vary precisely with the level of corporate enforcement expenditures. This regime of strict vicarious liability presents corporations contemplating enforcement expenditures with conflicting, potentially perverse, incentives. On the one hand, increased enforcement expenditures reduce the number of agents who commit crimes by increasing the probability of detection and thus each agent's expected cost of crime. On the other hand, these expenditures also increase the probability that the government will detect those crimes that are committed, thereby increasing the corporation's expected criminal liability for those crimes. If the expected cost to the corporation of the resulting increase in its expected criminal liability exceeds the expected benefit to the corporation of the reduction in the number of crimes, a corporation subject to strict vicarious liability will not respond by increasing its enforcement expenditures because additional enforcement would only increase the firm's expected criminal liability. In fact, in some circumstances a corporation subject to vicarious liability may spend less on enforcement than it would absent vicarious liability. Moreover, even when strict vicarious liability can induce efficient enforcement, the conflicting incentives it creates affect the efficient fine: to induce efficient enforcement, the fixed fine must exceed the net social cost of crime divided by the efficient probability of detection. These results call into question both the current trend toward increased corporate criminal liability and much of the accepted wisdom regarding strict vicarious criminal liability. This analysis also may be relevant to administrative sanctions against corporations and to vicarious civil liability, including employer liability for sexual harassment under Title VII.

In theory, the perverse incentives created by strict vicarious criminal liability can be eliminated by employing a variable fine equal to the net social cost of crime divided by the actual probability of detection (given the corporation's expenditures on enforcement). This rule would eliminate the perverse incentives otherwise present under strict vicarious liability because any increase in the probability of detection occasioned by corporate enforcement expenditures would result in an equivalent decrease in the fine imposed. Implementing this rule, however, would require a dramatic change in the current law. In particular, it would require us to abandon the goal of imposing relatively fixed fines for each type of crime—a goal that permeates the U.S. Sentencing Guidelines—in favor of a rule under which the corporate criminal fine could not be determined until after the crime was committed and investigated since only then could the corporation's precise expenditures on enforcement be determined. Perhaps more important, the precise calculations required for this rule—if feasible—would be very costly.

Accordingly, alternative rules to strict vicarious criminal liability warrant consideration. Three such rules are considered briefly in the present analysis: (1) mitigation rules, under which the fine is reduced (but not eliminated) if the firm's enforcement is efficient; (2) a "negligence" rule, under which the firm bears no liability if it incurs efficient enforcement; and (3) a modified "evidentiary privilege" (akin to use immunity) under which any information disclosed by the corporation can be used to prosecute the wrongful agents but cannot be used against the corporation in criminal or civil litigation....

Although vicarious corporate criminal liability tends to be broad in scope, until recently the penalties imposed on corporations were not particularly large. Prior to 1984, there were no specific guidelines governing corporate criminal sanctions; corporations, therefore, were subject to the same penalties as individual defendants. Because the maximum fines generally were set with individual defendants in mind, they were relatively low—both in absolute terms and relative to the harm caused. One empirical study found that the median corporate fine imposed by federal courts was 13 percent of the harm caused.

In 1984 and 1987, Congress enacted statutes designed to increase corporate criminal sanctions.... The trend toward increased corporate criminal sanctions for federal crimes continued in the 1990s. Acting at the behest of Congress, in 1991 the U.S. Sentencing Commission promulgated guidelines to govern the sentencing of organizations in federal court.[1] Under the guidelines, corporate criminal fines are based on the greatest of (i) the pecuniary gain to the organization from the offense, (ii) the pecuniary loss to others from the offense (to the extent the loss was caused intentionally, knowingly, or recklessly), or (iii) an amount determined by a table presented in the guidelines corresponding to the offense level of the crime. To determine the actual fine, the guidelines provide that the court must adjust this base fine by a multiplier which reflects the corporation's level of culpability; unless the firm can get relief under the guideline's mitigation provisions, the multiplier generally will exceed 1 and may be as high as 4. Given that previously corporate fines generally did not equal the harm caused, much less exceed it, the guidelines should dramatically increase corporate criminal fines, particularly for crimes that impose substantial harm on others.

In addition to increasing and standardizing organizational sanctions, the federal sentencing guidelines introduced an additional innovation: explicit provisions regarding fine mitigation for corporations that have "effective" monitoring programs and that report violations promptly to the government. These provisions represent an important departure from state law governing corporate criminal liability, which generally does not include

---

1. *The Supreme Court has ruled that the Guidelines do not impose mandatory restrictions on courts' sentencing decisions. See United States v. Booker, 543 U.S. 220 (2005). The Guidelines nonetheless remain an important advisory source for determining sentences.—Ed.*

explicit mitigation provisions. Nevertheless, they may be less significant than might at first appear. The federal mitigation provisions stop substantially short of effectuating a negligence rule: under the guidelines corporations with effective monitoring programs may nevertheless be subject to substantial criminal liability. Moreover, and more important, the mitigation provisions generally will not be applicable to many important crimes. The guidelines provide that a corporation generally is not eligible for fine mitigation based on its monitoring program if the crime was committed by a more senior employee with managerial authority. Fine mitigation accordingly generally will not be available for crimes such as antitrust violations, securities fraud, or government procurement fraud, which are likely to be committed by employees with managerial authority. Accordingly, in this situation the fine imposed on the corporation is essentially fixed, invariant to corporate enforcement expenditures....

Some corporate managers have responded to concerns about the effects of strict vicarious liability by arguing that corporations should be granted a privilege for information obtained through internal audits. One possible approach would be to adopt a modified "evidentiary privilege" rule—akin to use immunity—which prohibits prosecutors from using voluntarily prepared corporate records against the corporations, while allowing such records to be used to prosecute wrongful agents.[2] Such a privilege would remove the distortions created by pure strict vicarious liability because increased corporate enforcement expenditures would not increase the corporation's probability of being found liable.... [Furthermore,] unlike negligence and mitigation approaches, this solution does not require courts to calculate efficient enforcement....

Pamela H. Bucy, *Organizational Sentencing Guidelines: The Cart Before the Horse**

I. Assessing the Current Standards of Corporate Criminal Liability

American jurisprudence currently employs two major standards to determine organizational criminal liability. Both standards impose vicarious liability by imputing the criminal acts and intent of corporate agents to the corporation. The "traditional" or "respondeat superior" standard is a common-law rule developed primarily in the federal courts and adopted by some state courts. Derived from agency principles in tort law, this standard provides that a corporation "may be held criminally liable for the acts of any of its agents who (1) commit a crime (2) within the scope of employment (3) with the intent to benefit the corporation." As construed by most courts, the latter two requirements are almost meaningless. Courts deem an agent's criminal conduct to be "within the scope of employment" even when corporate policy specifically forbids such conduct and the corporation has made a good-faith effort to discourage such behavior. Similarly, courts deem criminal conduct by an agent to be "with the intent to benefit the corporation" even when the corporation received no actual benefit from the offense and no one else within the corporation knew of the criminal conduct at the time it occurred. With these latter

---

2. *This approach is employed by many state statutes that immunize corporations from liability based on information revealed in corporate environmental audit reports. See. e.g., Ill. Ann. Stat. ch. 415, ¶¶ 5/52.2 (1996). See also David Dana*, The Perverse Incentives of Environmental Audit Immunity, 81 Iowa L. Rev. 969 (1996).—*Ed.*

* Originally published in 71 Washington University Law Quarterly 329 (1993). Copyright 1992 Pamela H. Bucy. Reprinted with permission.

two requirements thus weakened, a court may hold a corporation criminally liable whenever one of its agents (even an independent contractor in some circumstances) commits a crime related in almost any way to the agent's employment.

The American Law Institute's Model Penal Code ("MPC") provides the major alternative standard for assessing an organization's criminal liability. Developed in the 1950s, the MPC provides three standards for such liability. The type of criminal offense charged determines which standard applies. For the majority of corporate crimes, the MPC provides that a corporation may be held criminally liable if the criminal conduct was "authorized, requested, commanded, performed or recklessly tolerated by the board of directors or by a high managerial agent acting in behalf of the corporation within the scope of his office or employment." This standard is still based upon a respondeat superior model, but in a limited fashion—a corporation is criminally liable for the conduct of only some of its agents (directors, officers, or other higher echelon employees).

The critical weakness in both the traditional respondeat superior and MPC standards is that by automatically imputing the agent's criminal liability to the corporation, they fail to consider the culpability of the corporation itself. Two Fourth Circuit cases, *United States v. Hilton Hotels Corp.*[3] and *United States v. Basic Construction Co.*,[4] aptly demonstrate this. In *United States v. Hilton Hotels Corp.*, the purchasing agent at a Hilton Hotel in Portland, Oregon threatened a supplier of goods with the loss of the hotel's business if the supplier did not contribute to an association created to attract conventions to Portland. Hilton Hotel's president testified that such action was contrary to corporate policy. Moreover, the manager and assistant manager of the Portland Hilton Hotel testified that they specifically told the purchasing agent not to threaten suppliers. Nevertheless, the court convicted Hilton Hotels of antitrust violations under the respondeat superior standard of liability.

In *United States v. Basic Construction Co.*, the court found the defendant corporation liable for bid rigging on state road paving contracts. The bid rigging was conducted by "two relatively minor officials, ... was done without the knowledge of high level corporate officers," and was in violation of the company's "longstanding, well known, and strictly enforced policy against bid rigging." Basic objected to the trial court's instruction informing the jury that a "corporation may be responsible for the action of its agents ... even though the conduct of the agents may be contrary to the corporation's actual instructions, or contrary to the corporation's stated position." Basic argued that this instruction allowed the jury to "fix absolute criminal liability on a corporation for acts done by its employees" and that this relieved the government from proving that the corporation "had an intent separate from that of its lower level employees to violate the antitrust laws." The Fourth Circuit rejected Basic's argument by noting that the law allowed exactly what Basic complained of—absolute criminal liability of corporations for acts committed by corporate agents.

The failure of the traditional respondeat superior and the MPC standards to focus on corporate intent is antithetical to the criminal law. The mens rea requirement is essential to a fair application of criminal justice. It serves at least three functions: it enhances social stability; it promotes more consistent and more appropriate exercise of prosecutorial discretion; and it facilitates planning by potential defendants—including efforts by potential defendants to comply with the law.

---

3. 467 F.2d 1000 (9th Cir. 1972), cert. denied, 409 U.S. 1125 (1973).
4. 711 F.2d 570 (4th Cir.), cert. denied, 464 U.S. 956, 1008 (1983).

Requiring proof of criminal intent as a prerequisite for criminal liability enhances social stability by promoting voluntary compliance with the law. For laws to succeed in promoting social stability, the vast majority of citizens must comply with them. Resources are not available, nor should they be, to fuel the large law enforcement machine that universal lawlessness would require. Voluntary compliance will wane, however, if the law is viewed as unjust, unfair, or arbitrary. The law will be so perceived if it punishes A for acts that occur despite A's best effort to avoid such conduct (strict liability), or it punishes A for what B did even when A had no knowledge of B's behavior (vicarious liability). The criminal intent requirement avoids both of these possibilities by narrowing liability to voluntary acts committed by a defendant.

Realistically, a few exceptions of strict or vicarious liability will not so greatly taint the public's perception of the criminal justice system so as to substantially curtail voluntary compliance. Extending these exceptions to most offenses, however, creates such a risk. Because vicarious liability currently is the universal rule of liability seen by the group of people most directly affected by corporate criminal liability, namely, corporate executives, these individuals may view the criminal justice system as unreasonable and unfair—and choose to disregard it.

Requiring proof of criminal intent before imposing criminal liability serves a second function: it enhances consistent enforcement of the law. The current, broad, vicarious liability standards for charging organizations with crimes offer prosecutors little guidance as to which of the many corporations that fall within the literal terms of these standards should be charged. Between 1984 and 1987, an average of 320 corporations per year were convicted of crimes. Surely there were more corporations than this which broke the law and are liable under the current standards of corporate criminal liability. What this statistic really represents is the wide discretion prosecutors exercise when deciding which corporations to charge.

Because resources do not exist to prosecute every offending corporation that meets our current standards of organizational criminal liability, prosecutors must pick and choose which organizations to prosecute. Assuming, *arguendo*, that prosecutors responsibly attempt to make the decision whether to charge an organization, individual prosecutors must resort to their personal, and therefore variable, views on whether to indict a corporation. Forcing prosecutors to select cases based on corporate criminal intent, however, curtails this broad discretion and decreases the potential for abuse and arbitrariness. Furthermore, focusing corporate criminal prosecutions on organizations with criminal intent wisely utilizes scarce prosecutorial resources.

The third major function served by the criminal intent requirement is that it allows potential defendants to better predict and plan their futures. Under the broad vicarious liability standards of respondeat superior and the MPC, a corporation has no way of predicting whether an individual prosecutor will seek criminal charges against it for any given crime. However, when a corporation knows that criminal liability depends upon its own voluntary acts, it can better plan and predict its future by choosing whether to engage in activities that limit or expand its exposure to criminal liability. Thus, by standardizing prosecutorial decisions, the criminal intent requirement allows corporate executives to assess more accurately the costs of engaging in unlawful behavior.

In summary, because corporations are and historically have been convicted of criminal offenses without an assessment of intent, those most affected by this standard of liability, corporate executives, see the criminal law at its worst. They see the criminal law used arbitrarily, with no guidance for prosecutors, no direction for businesses that wish to plan ahead, and no incentive for corporations to engage in law-abiding behavior.

II. A Proposed Standard of Corporate Criminal Liability

A focus on the individual actor pervades our jurisprudence on intent. To date, our approach to corporate criminal liability has been to impute an individual actor's criminal intent to the corporation. This approach is not only inadequate, but also harmful to the integrity and power of the criminal law. With the rising prominence of corporate actors, courts and legislatures must develop the concept of intent beyond the context of individual actors to focus on corporate intent. Such a focus should begin by acknowledging that each organization has an identifiable character or "ethos." Before convicting an organization, the government should be required to prove that the organization's "ethos" encouraged the corporation's agents to commit the criminal act.

In a sense, this standard takes its cue from notions of intent developed in the context of individual liability. When considering whether an individual should be held criminally liable, we ask whether the person committed the act accidentally or purposely. If the individual committed the act purposely, we consider it to be a crime, while if the individual committed the act accidentally, we do not. Similarly, the corporate ethos standard imposes criminal liability on a corporation only if the corporation encouraged the criminal conduct at issue. If it did, the criminal conduct is not an accident or the unpredictable act of a maverick employee. Instead, the criminal conduct is predictable and consistent with corporate goals, policies, and ethos. In the context of a fictional entity, this translates into intention.

If the corporate ethos standard represents a more jurisprudentially sound use of the criminal law, one may wonder why courts or legislatures have not adopted such a standard. At least three possible explanations exist. The first is precedent. American jurisprudence has never employed anything but strict, vicarious liability in assessing an organization's criminal liability. Yet an examination of precedent reveals that courts adopted and perpetuated this standard with little analysis of its jurisprudential soundness. As O.W. Mueller noted, "many weeds have grown on the acre of jurisprudence which has been allotted to the criminal law. Among these ... is corporate criminal liability.... Nobody bred it, nobody cultivated it, nobody planted it. It just grew."[5]

The Supreme Court's opinion in *New York Central & Hudson River Railroad v. United States*[6] sheds light on this growth. Not only is *New York Central* the premier decision establishing criminal liability for corporations in American law, but its flawed and outdated reasoning exemplifies subsequent courts' analysis of corporate criminal liability. The New York Central Railroad employed an assistant traffic manager who gave "rebates" on railroad rates to certain railroad users. As a result, the effective shipping rate for these users was less than the mandated rates. The federal trial court held New York Central Railroad criminally liable under bribery statutes for the acts of its assistant traffic manager. Noting that the principle of respondeat superior was well established in civil tort law, the Supreme Court stated that "every reason in public policy" justified "going only a step farther" and applying respondeat superior to criminal law. Based upon this rationale, the Court established the traditional respondeat superior standard of criminal liability for corporations.

The Court's reasoning in *New York Central* contains three major flaws which subsequent courts have perpetuated and exacerbated. First, the Court failed to appreciate the difference between civil and criminal law. The only indication that the Court recognized such a difference was when it disregarded it, stating "we see no good reason"

---

5. Gerhard O.W. Mueller, *Mens Rea and the Corporation: A Study of the Model Penal Code Position on Corporate Criminal Liability*, 19 U. Pitt. L. Rev. 21 (1957).
6. 212 U.S. 481 (1909).

for not applying the civil concept of respondeat superior to criminal corporate liability. Lower courts have followed the Supreme Court's lead. For example, the United States Court of Appeals for the Eighth Circuit, in affirming the conviction of a utilities corporation, stated that "if the act was ... done by a corporate employee it will be imputed to the corporation.... There is no longer any distinction in essence between the civil and criminal liability of corporations, based upon the element of intent or wrongful purpose."

The second flaw in the *New York Central* reasoning is its failure to consider civil alternatives to corporate criminal liability. The Court stated that failure to impose criminal liability on corporations would "virtually take away the only means of effectually controlling the subject matter and correcting the abuses aimed at." This conclusion ignores the two major options to imposing criminal liability upon corporations: (1) criminal liability of the responsible individuals within the corporation, and (2) civil remedies against the corporation, both of which are probably more viable methods of controlling behavior today than they were in 1909 when the Court decided *New York Central*. Nevertheless, without assessing the development, success, or greater propriety of these alternatives, subsequent courts have continued to rely on this rationale in imposing criminal liability on corporate entities. For example, the United States Court of Appeals for the Second Circuit, in affirming the conviction of a corporate wholesaler of fruits and vegetables for evading price regulations, noted that not to impose criminal liability in this case was "to immunize the offender."

The third flaw in the *New York Central* reasoning is its failure to consider the conceptual alternatives to respondeat superior as the standard for corporate criminal liability. The Supreme Court assumed it had only two options for imposing criminal liability on corporations: respondeat superior or no criminal liability. Such a rigid view of its available options is understandable given the posture of the case (the Court was dealing with a strict liability statute) and the historical setting of this opinion. Courts have extended the rationale of *New York Central* beyond the context of strict liability statutes, however, and almost a full century has passed since it was decided. During this time, there has been considerable experience with and substantial scholarship on the nature of organizations. The *New York Central* Court's simplistic choice between two options, while understandable, ignores the subtleties of organizational behavior that today's courts are better able to identify and appreciate. Thus, in this early effort to impose criminal liability on fictional entities, the Supreme Court gave as precedent a sledgehammer when a scalpel is needed. As in other areas where sophisticated tools have replaced primitive ones, the criminal law needs a more sophisticated and refined mechanism for imposing corporate criminal liability.

Another possible reason that our standards for assessing an organization's criminal liability have not evolved to include an assessment of corporate mens rea is the perception that such an assessment is not possible. Yet it is, theoretically and practically. The strongest evidence of the workability of such a standard for assessing corporate criminal liability is the willingness of the United States Sentencing Commission to focus on organizational culpability and its demonstration of how to do so. In requiring that any criminal fine assessed against an organization be based, in part, on the organization's "culpability," the Guidelines demonstrate the viability of identifying corporate intent. By directing courts to examine factors such as involvement in or tolerance of criminal activity, commission of prior criminal offenses, cooperation with the government in its investigation of the criminal conduct, and existence of effective internal programs to prevent and detect violations of the law, the Guidelines point the way to identifying corporate intent.

The Guidelines are not the first effort to identify corporate intent. During the past twenty years or so, as organizations increasingly have been targets of criminal and civil lawsuits, jurists and scholars have demonstrated their willingness to identify the intent, or ethos, of fictional entities. For example, in assessing municipal liability under 42 U.S.C. 1983, which provides that persons, including fictional persons, who deprive citizens of certain rights are liable to the injured person, courts repeatedly focus on the intent of municipal organizations as manifested by their policies. In *Monell v. New York City Department of Social Services,*[7] the Supreme Court held that section 1983 clearly envisions liability of municipal corporations "only where the municipality itself causes the constitutional violation at issue." Rather than employing traditional respondeat superior theory, whereby a corporation would be found liable for an employee's isolated act, section 1983, like the corporate ethos standard for corporate criminal liability, provides for a "fault-based analysis for imposing ... liability." Such an analysis requires courts to focus on the municipal "custom" or "policy" which is the "moving force" of the constitutional deprivation. Under section 1983, liability is imposed only if the evidence shows that "some official policy" "'causes' an employee to violate another's constitutional rights." Thus, since at least the *Monell* decision in 1978, courts and juries have worked with and applied the notion that a fictional entity assumes responsibility for acts of its agents only when it employs an internal custom or policy that encourages such violations.

Perhaps the most direct example of courts' willingness to consider corporate intent is the use of the concept of "collective intent." *United States v. Bank of New England*[8] exemplifies this concept. The Bank of New England was convicted on thirty-one counts of violating 31 U.S.C. 5313 and 5322 for failing to file Currency Transaction Reports ("CTRs") on cash transactions of more than $10,000. On thirty-one occasions, James McDonough, a bank customer, withdrew more than $10,000 in cash from a single account by simultaneously presenting multiple checks in sums less than $10,000 to a single bank teller.

Acknowledging that under applicable law a corporation's criminal intent is imputed from an agent's intent, the bank argued that it was not liable because no one bank employee had sufficient criminal intent of McDonough's transactions. In other words, according to the bank, the teller who conducted the McDonough transactions did not know that the law required the filing of CTRs when a customer withdraws $10,000 from a single account using multiple checks all of which are less than $10,000, and the bank employee who knew of the CTR requirement did not know of the McDonough transactions. Thus, according to the bank, there was no single bank employee with sufficient mens rea to impute to the corporation. The court rejected the bank's argument, and gave an instruction to the jury describing "collective intent":

> You have to look at the bank as an institution. As such, its knowledge is the sum
> of the knowledge of all of the employees. That is, the bank's knowledge is the totality
> of what all of the employees know within the scope of their employment.

By employing the notion of "collective intent," courts are, in effect, recognizing the existence of an organizational identity that exceeds the sum of its parts and exists independently of the individuals who work for it.

Law developing in other countries has begun to require a finding of corporate intent before holding corporations criminally liable. In several instances Dutch courts, for

---

7. 436 U.S. 658 (1978).
8. 821 F.2d 844 (1st Cir.), cert. denied, 484 U.S. 943 (1987).

example, have held a corporation criminally liable if, but only if, the organization itself has demonstrated culpability. To assess culpability, the Dutch courts have looked to the corporation's efforts, or lack of efforts, to remedy the situation that led to the criminal conduct. In a 1981 case, *Kabeljauw*,[9] a Dutch court acquitted a corporate shipowner on criminal charges that it had violated shipping regulations when one of its vessels caught prohibited species of animals. Both the trial and appellate courts based their decisions of acquittal on the fact that the corporation had taken affirmative steps to prohibit such unlawful fishing by equipping its ships with nets specially designed for fishing only permitted species. Likewise, in 1987, a Dutch appellate court affirmed the first conviction of a corporation for manslaughter based upon a finding of numerous instances of poor monitoring by a hospital of its equipment and employees, which led to the death of a patient.

Australian law currently follows the MPC approach of imposing criminal liability on corporations if the conduct was committed by higher echelon corporate agents. The Attorneys General of Australia, however, have suggested legislation that would amend this standard to also hold criminally liable any organization that "expressly, tacitly or impliedly authorized or permitted the commission of the offense." Such authorization or permission could be proven by showing that a "corporate culture existed within the body corporate that directed, encouraged, tolerated or led to non-compliance with the relevant provision or that the body corporate failed to create and maintain a corporate culture that required compliance with the relevant provision." The proposed legislation defines corporate culture as "an attitude, policy, rule, course of conduct or practice existing within the body corporate."

In explaining the rationale for moving from the current standard which focuses only on vicarious liability to one that also focuses on an organization's culpability, the Attorneys General found that the strict liability approach was "no longer appropriate" and indicated that it was striving to deal with organizational blameworthiness by developing "rules which fairly adapt the general principles of criminal responsibility to the complexities of the corporate form."

Assessment of corporate intent is not only theoretically sound, but making such an assessment is practicable, workable, and provable from concrete information already available in grand jury investigations of corporate crime. To ascertain the ethos of a corporation, and to determine whether this ethos encouraged the criminal conduct at issue, the factfinder would examine the following corporate policies and procedures: (1) the corporate hierarchy; (2) the corporation's goals and policies; (3) the corporation's historical treatment of prior offenses; (4) the corporation's efforts to educate and monitor employees' compliance with the law; and (5) the corporation's compensation scheme, especially its policy on indemnification of corporate employees.

Not only is access to these facts obtainable through a grand jury investigation of corporate activity, but such facts are subject to proof in court. For example, inquiry into corporate hierarchy would begin with the board of directors' role. Does the board operate as a figurehead or does it monitor the corporation's efforts to comply with the law? If the board or any board member allegedly performs this function, does the board or the member have effective access and resources? In addition to examining the board of directors' role, the factfinder should also examine management's organizational structure.

---

9. Hoge Raad, July 1, 1981, N.J. 1982, 80, *summarized in* Stewart Field & Nico Jorg, *Corporate Liability and Manslaughter: Should We be Going Dutch?*, 1991 CRIM. L. REV. 156, 164.

As Professor Braithwaite has stated: "The key to understanding so much organizational crime … is the way that organizational complexity can be used to protect people from … exposure to criminal liability."[10] The factfinder should focus on whether management left unmonitored or inaccessible positions within the corporation where illegal behavior could have occurred easily. If positions were left unattended, the factfinder should scrutinize the reason: was the oversight an honest error in judgment or was it a callous recognition that if corporate employees commit illegal activity, it is best done outside the usual channels of supervision? Intentional gaps in the corporate hierarchy that allowed the criminal conduct to occur would weigh in favor of finding a corporation criminally liable. On the other hand, a finding that a corporation's organizational structure provides for effective supervision of all aspects of the organization weighs against finding a corporation criminally liable, even though corporate agents committed the criminal act.

When considering the corporate goals, the factfinder should examine whether the goals set for the relevant division, subsidiary, or employee promote lawful behavior or implicitly encourage illegal behavior. As the American Law Institute noted in devising the Model Penal Code's standard of corporate criminal liability, "the economic pressures within the corporate body may be sufficiently potent to tempt individuals to hazard personal liability for the sake of company gain."

In some corporations, employees have the opportunity to disobey or to comply with the law many times each day. These corporations have a greater duty to educate their employees about legal requirements than do corporations where employees do not have such opportunities. Likewise, a corporation's duty to educate its employees about legal requirements varies with the type of employee involved. For example, few would disagree that a banking corporation has a duty to educate all of its tellers about reporting requirements for cash transactions, but that it has no duty to so educate its janitorial employees. The factfinder, therefore, should consider whether the corporation has made reasonable efforts to educate its employees about legal requirements. Relevant inquiries in assessing these efforts include: (1) Whether the corporation informed the appropriate employees of regulatory changes that affect their duties; (2) Whether the corporation explained new regulations in a comprehensible manner; (3) Whether middle management executives held regular meetings to discuss problems of compliance; (4) Whether the corporation made its legal staff available for discussions on compliance; and (5) Whether middle management attended or held specific training programs on ethics and government regulation.

In a study of corporations conducted by Marshall Clinard, middle level managers cited effective employee monitoring as one of the practices important in cultivating an ethical corporation.[11] A factfinder applying the corporate ethos standard should determine how effectively the corporation monitors employee compliance with applicable legal requirements. To determine effectiveness, the factfinder should ask: (1) Does the company conduct internal audits? (2) Does the corporation maintain open channels of communication throughout the management hierarchy? (3) Does the corporation require employees to sign an annual statement indicating that they are familiar with pertinent government regulations and acknowledging that they realize such violations will result in dismissal? (4) Does the corporation have an ombudsman?

The factfinder also should determine who committed the criminal violation, who contributed to its success, and which (if any) higher echelon officials "recklessly tolerated"

---

10. JOHN BRAITHWAITE, CRIME, SHAME AND REINTEGRATION 147 (1989).
11. MARSHALL B. CLINARD, CORPORATE ETHICS AND CRIME 159 (1983).

the offense. At this point, the corporate ethos standard deviates from current vicarious liability standards for corporate criminal liability. Under traditional respondeat superior doctrine, if a corporate agent intentionally commits a criminal offense while acting within the scope of her duties and for the benefit of the corporation, a court will find the corporation itself guilty. Under the MPC standard, if higher echelon officials participate in or recklessly tolerate the offense, corporate liability results. Under the corporate ethos standard, however, such facts do not conclusively establish criminal liability. The government must go further to demonstrate that the corporation encouraged such conduct. Admittedly, the chance of finding a corporate ethos that encouraged the criminal conduct increases if higher echelon officials are involved, but such officials' participation or acquiescence is not decisive. Rather, the conduct of higher level officials is simply more relevant and indicative of corporate intent than is the action of lower level officials.

According to Marshall Clinard's study, a corporation's reaction to a prior violation of the law may be one of the more important factors encouraging ethical patterns in the corporation: "Prior enforcement actions ... not only affected compliance in the particular area in which they were brought, but also had tended to affect compliance with government regulations generally." The factfinder should consider the corporation's prior treatment of employees who violated the law. Relevant inquiries include: (1) Did the corporation discipline, or promote, the violators? (2) Did the corporation reimburse the violators for criminal or civil fines assessed in their individual capacity or pay their attorneys' fees? (3) What steps did the corporation take to prevent such action from occurring again? (4) Did the corporation make efforts to rectify the situation that led to the violations, or did it attempt to conceal the violations? If a corporation conscientiously and in good faith attempted to remove the cause of the prior violation, it is unlikely that an ethos existed within that corporation that encouraged the criminal conduct. However, if a corporation took few or no steps to remedy the situation that encouraged a violation, or if it attempted to conceal misconduct, a corporate ethos which promotes illegal behavior likely exists and should subject the corporation to criminal liability.

One must concede to the critics of a "corporate intent" standard for assessing criminal liability that we cannot fully, completely, and accurately ascertain a corporate ethos. This is true, it is not possible. But if we are candid we will admit the criminal law's requirement of proof of mens rea has long imposed a factually impossible burden on the government. We are accustomed to this burden, however, and so do not easily realize that direct proof of intent is impossible and that we have simply become comfortable with approximations that do not overcome the impossibility of our task. However, our inability to prove directly an individual's intent does not cause us to reject the entire concept or, given sufficient circumstantial evidence, to question whether the factfinders have accurately deduced an individual's intent. So it is with corporate ethos. When the government presents sufficient circumstantial evidence, we can and should feel confident in the factfinders' deduction of a corporation's ethos.

The third major hurdle in adopting a standard of corporate criminal liability that hinges upon finding corporate intent is the perception by some that such a standard is "soft" on corporate crime. Certainly it is expected that under such a standard, some corporations that are criminally liable under the current standards would not be liable, yet this is because our current standards hold all corporations criminally liable for crimes committed by their agents or, with the MPC, some of their agents. To exempt from criminal liability law-abiding corporations that make every effort to ensure that their employees follow the law is not being "soft" on crime. It is using the criminal law wisely. Under a standard of criminal liability that focuses on corporate intent, the corporations that will be convicted are culpable and deserve punishment. Our criminal justice resources will be saved for these corporations rather than spent on corporations that have objectively and in good faith performed as good corporate citizens.

Leonard M. Baynes, *Just Pucker and Blow? An Analysis of Corporate Whistleblowers, the Duty of Care, the Duty of Loyalty, and the Sarbanes-Oxley Act*[*]

.... [Sherron] Watkins was a Vice-President at Enron Corp. She earned a master's degree in professional accounting from the University of Texas at Austin. In 1982, she began her career as an auditor with the accounting firm Arthur Andersen, spending eight years at its Houston and New York offices. In 1983, she became a certified public accountant. Enron Vice-President Andrew Fastow hired Ms. Watkins to manage Enron's partnership with the California Public Employee Retirement System. From June to August 2001, Ms. Watkins worked directly for Mr. Fastow. During this time, Ms. Watkins learned that Enron was engaging in accounting improprieties with certain affiliated entities. She believed that Enron was using its own stock to generate gains and losses on its income statement. Ms. Watkins testified before the House Subcommittee on Oversight and Investigations that she failed to receive satisfactory explanations regarding these accounting transactions from Enron executives. Ms. Watkins admitted that she was troubled by the accounting practices but was uncomfortable reporting them to either Mr. Fastow or former Enron President Jeff Skilling, fearing termination if she approached them directly. On August 15, 2001, Ms. Watkins sent to Kenneth Lay, the CEO of Enron, a seven-page anonymous letter. In the letter, Ms. Watkins asked, "Has Enron become a risky place to work?" She also more specifically described the accounting improprieties and stated that "to the layman on the street [it will look like] we are hiding losses in a related company and will compensate that company with Enron stock in the future." She shared her prescient fears that Enron might "implode in a wave of accounting scandals." On August 22, 2001, Ms. Watkins met with Mr. Lay and outlined her concerns about the accounting improprieties, and requested a transfer from working for Mr. Fastow. In late August she was reassigned to the human resources group. Ms. Watkins reported that Mr. Lay assured her that he would investigate the irregularities. Ms. Watkins never reported her concerns to the SEC, the Department of Treasury, or any other governmental official.

Upon Ms. Watkins's disclosure, Mr. Lay passed Ms. Watkins's letter to Enron's general counsel, James V. Derrick, who hired Enron's attorneys, Vinson & Elkins, to investigate, even though the law firm was involved in some of the transactions that Ms. Watkins criticized. The Vinson & Elkins report indicates that Mr. Derrick acknowledged the "downside of hiring Vinson & Elkins because it had been involved." Mr. Derrick concluded that the decision to hire Vinson & Elkins was permissible because the investigation was to be a "preliminary one." Vinson & Elkins (along with Arthur Andersen) investigated Ms. Watkins's allegations, but used no independent accountant. This investigation reported only limited cosmetic problems and no illegal activities. Vinson & Elkins' investigation, however, "was largely predetermined by the scope and nature of the investigation and the process employed."

In October 2001, before Enron announced a huge third quarter loss, Arthur Andersen auditors, in a memo, warned Enron officials that its public explanation for the loss "was

---

[*]   Originally published in 76 St. John's Law Review 875 (2002). Reprinted with permission.

potentially misleading and illegal." On October 16, 2001, Enron announced a $618 million third quarter loss. Two weeks later, the SEC announced that it was investigating Enron. In early November, Enron announced that, since 1997, it had overstated its earnings by $586 million. On December 2, 2001, Enron filed for bankruptcy. On January 23, 2002, Ken Lay resigned as CEO of Enron, stating "we need someone at the helm who can focus 100 percent of his efforts on reorganizing the company." ...

Prior to the Sarbanes-Oxley Act, the protections for private corporate whistleblowers varied depending upon state law. Because of these varied protections, senior officers and managers had to worry about the fact that, in some states, they held their jobs at-will. Therefore, they could be fired at any time for no reason. Forty-two states and the District of Columbia, however, now recognize a cause of action for retaliatory discharge. These statutes and rulings protect at-will employees who "blow the whistle" on important public policy issues. Therefore, an employee who is terminated for refusing to violate the law or for reporting a violation of the law can bring an action for wrongful discharge against her employer. Upon successful litigation of her suit, the "wronged" employee can get damages and reinstatement to her job. The interpretations of what constitutes protected whistleblowing varies depending on the state. One of the goals of the Act was to afford a whistleblowing employee the same protection irrespective of her state of residence. Most state claims for wrongful retaliation revolved around claims for wrongful discharge based on the employee's termination for refusing to violate a law, rule, or regulation or for reporting such violation. The employee could, however, be fired if the reported behavior did not actually violate an existing law....

Most states seem to protect employees who report issues of safety or who are required to report safety violations. Those employees who were merely reporting failures to follow company procedure were least protected. In addition, several states deny protection for those whistleblowers who make unfounded claims or who fail to sufficiently investigate their claims. These states merely require that the employee's allegation be made in "good faith."

The Sarbanes-Oxley Act prohibits any public company from discriminating against any employee who lawfully provides information or otherwise assists in an investigation of conduct that the employee "reasonably believes" constitutes a violation of the federal securities laws.[12] This provision was designed from the lessons learned from Sherron Watkins's testimony [in Senate hearings on the Enron collapse]. As Senator Patrick Leahy stated, " 'We learned from Sherron Watkins of Enron that these corporate insiders are the key witnesses that need to be encouraged to report fraud and help prove it in court.' " The legislation protects an employee from retaliation by an employer for testifying before Congress or a federal regulatory agency, or giving evidence to law enforcement of possible securities fraud violations. To secure this protection, the employee must have assisted in an investigation, which was conducted by Congress, a federal agency, the employee's supervisor, or anyone else authorized by the employer to conduct an investigation. Under the Act, within ninety days of the discriminatory act, the employee must file an administrative claim with the Secretary of Labor. If the Secretary of Labor fails to issue a final decision within 180 days of filing of the complaint, the employee can bring a private cause of action at law or equity for de novo review in federal district court. Relief available under this statute shall include compensatory damages, such as reinstatement with the same level of seniority, back pay with interest, and any special damages, that is, litigation costs, expert witness fees, and reasonable attorney fees. In addition, every public company is required

---

12. [Sarbanes-Oxley Act § 806, 18 U.S.C. § 1514A].

to establish mechanisms to allow the employees to provide information anonymously to the corporation's board of directors.

The Sarbanes-Oxley Act was designed to promote investor confidence by ensuring that the public receives more information about possible corporate fraud. Such disclosures would ensure that the markets have perfect information so that investors could make informed investment choices. Senator Leahy reported that the Act is designed to "include all good faith and reasonable reporting of fraud, and there should be no presumption that reporting is otherwise, absent specific evidence." This reasonable person standard would include the usual standard used in a variety of contexts. In fact, Senator Leahy stated that the type of action taken by the corporation or the agency would be "strong indicia that it could support such a reasonable belief." In addition, Senator Leahy explained that the whistleblowing provision would exclude unlawful actions such as the "improper public disclosure of trade secret information."

Undoubtedly, the Sarbanes-Oxley Act provides an extra level of protection for employees. Despite this added protection and the increased prominence of whistleblowers, we must be cognizant that federal whistleblowers have low success rates in their suits before government agencies. [Tom Devine] reports that "the rate of success for winning a reprisal lawsuit on the merits in administrative hearings for federal whistleblower laws has risen to between 25 and 33 percent in recent years."[13] Under the Act, the corporate senior executive or employee is likely to confront some of the same dilemmas, which the Act does not quite address, and is likely to also have a low rate of success under its whistleblowing provisions. First, the statute only affords protection against retaliations based on securities fraud [and mail or wire fraud]. Whistleblowing of other kinds of wrongdoing remain unprotected under this Act. [Except for a few other narrow areas where federal statutes specifically protect whistleblowers], whistleblowers ... must rely on the vagaries of state law, which generally give preference to those allegations dealing with public safety....

Second, low-level employees are ... relatively unprotected. They probably are unaware of these new protections. They may feel particularly oppressed by the many layers of management that may exist in some corporations. Some may be unsophisticated and may not know whether certain actions violate the law. Many of the wrongful or illegal activities that they observe may not rise to the level of securities fraud. For example, an employee at McDonald's may notice that large numbers of pre-packaged hamburgers disappear shortly after delivery. The disappearance may be the result of conversion by the store manager. The McDonald's employee might be in the best position to ascertain whether this wrongdoing is occurring, but she is unprotected by the Sarbanes-Oxley Act because this conversion does not involve securities fraud. She will have to rely on the vagaries of state law. In addition, many of these employees rely very heavily on their paychecks; a high turnover rate exists in these jobs. Students and those re-entering the workforce hold many of these jobs. These individuals may be particularly reluctant to "rock the boat" and report wrongdoing unless they are guaranteed that their job is protected. The Act does nothing to address this population of whistleblowers.

Third, for both senior executives and low-level employees, the Sarbanes-Oxley Act gives little guidance as to the circumstances under which an employee is to disclose allegations of wrongdoing to her supervisor as opposed to law enforcement authorities.... [I]f the whistleblowing employee reports the evidence of wrongdoing immediately to law enforcement authorities, she may be violating her duty of loyalty to the corporation,

---

13. Tom Devine, The Whistleblower's Survival Guide: Courage Without Martyrdom (1997).

especially if her allegations are unfounded.... She has an obligation to protect certain proprietary and confidential corporate information. Also by going to the law enforcement authorities right away, she may be depriving the corporation of the opportunity to resolve the matter or, in the case of wrongdoing, get the best deal for the corporation. In addition, the employee who jumps the gun and goes to law enforcement authorities may be putting herself in a difficult political situation at her corporation. Even though the terms of her position and employment may remain the same, she will always, to her detriment, be remembered for making that report.

Fourth, the Sarbanes-Oxley Act gives no guidance concerning whether the whistleblowing employee should disclose the information to her direct supervisor or her supervisor's supervisor. Who is the principal of senior executives? Is it the corporation? Is it the board of directors? Is it the senior executive's boss? To some extent, this decision may be a judgment call by the whistleblowing employee.... [T]he employee who "jumps the gun" and goes to her supervisor's supervisor may be putting herself in a difficult political situation at her corporation in that her direct supervisor may never trust her....

[Fifth], the Sarbanes-Oxley Act prohibits a corporation from "discharging, demoting, suspending, threatening, harassing, or in any other manner discriminating against an employee in the terms and conditions of employment" because she blew the whistle.... A deft supervisor, however, could "set up" the whistleblowing employee for failure. For instance, the employer may place the whistleblower in a job unsuitable to her skill level to ensure her failure. The employer could then document the employee's poor performance. The Act provides protections for whistleblowing employees except in cases where valid business reasons exist for their termination like inferior work performance. In addition, even if the employer refrains from discriminating against the whistleblowing employee in the terms and conditions of her employment, the employer is unlikely to give that employee any opportunities for advancement. By blowing the whistle, she may have "tapped out" her career trajectory. For instance, Sherron Watkins's present job and terms of employment are probably very secure, but can we really imagine her ever advancing from her present position at Enron? Her future supervisors will probably always worry that she is not a "team player" who may go over their heads when she suspects they are doing something wrong.

Despite the recent positive press concerning corporate whistleblowers, it is fraught with grave dangers. The whistleblower is under simultaneous duties of loyalty and care. By reporting suspicious activities, the whistleblower may violate her duty of loyalty to the corporation by misusing corporate proprietary information, but at the same time the failure to report such activities may be a violation of the duty of care. The Sarbanes-Oxley Act provides the whistleblower with some federal protection against retaliation but does not ease the tension between the whistleblower's duty of care and loyalty. In addition, there are several matters that the Act fails to address or provide sufficient protection, i.e., (1) non-securities fraud matters are not covered; (2) low-level employees may not be aware of the protections; (3) no guidance is given as to when to report wrongdoing to outside authorities or to a supervisor; (4) no guidance is given as to when the whistleblower should go over his or her supervisor's head to senior management; and (5) no protection is given to undercover retaliations that do not quite manifest themselves as a "discharge, demotion, suspension, threat, or other manner of discrimination." In promulgating its rules in implementing this matter, the SEC, to the extent possible, should take some of these limitations of the Act into account. As a consequence, the corporate whistleblower cannot just pucker and blow. She has to use a great deal of thought to whether and how she may want to blow the whistle.

John C. Coffee, Jr., *Does "Unlawful" Mean "Criminal"?:* *Reflections on the Disappearing Tort/Crime Distinction in American Law**

> *What sense does it make to insist upon procedural safeguards in criminal prosecutions if anything whatever can be made a crime in the first place?*
>
> —Professor Henry M. Hart, Jr.[14]

My thesis is simple and can be reduced to four assertions. First, the dominant development in substantive federal criminal law over the last decade has been the disappearance of any clearly definable line between civil and criminal law. Second, this blurring of the border between tort and crime predictably will result in injustice, and ultimately will weaken the efficacy of the criminal law as an instrument of social control. Third, to define the proper sphere of the criminal law, one must explain how its purposes and methods differ from those of tort law. Although it is easy to identify distinguishing characteristics of the criminal law— e.g., the greater role of intent in the criminal law, the relative unimportance of actual harm to the victim, the special character of incarceration as a sanction, and the criminal law's greater reliance on public enforcement—none of these is ultimately decisive. Rather, the factor that most distinguishes the criminal law is its operation as a system of moral education and socialization. The criminal law is obeyed not simply because there is a legal threat underlying it, but because the public perceives its norms to be legitimate and deserving of compliance. Far more than tort law, the criminal law is a system for public communication of values. As a result, the criminal law often and necessarily displays a deliberate disdain for the utility of the criminalized conduct to the defendant. Thus, while tort law seeks to balance private benefits and public costs, criminal law does not (or does so only by way of special affirmative defenses), possibly because balancing would undercut the moral rhetoric of the criminal law. Characteristically, tort law prices, while criminal law prohibits.

The fourth and final assertion of this Article is that implementation of the crime/tort distinction is today feasible only at the sentencing stage. Neither legislative action nor constitutional challenge is likely to reverse the encroachment of the criminal law upon areas previously thought civil in character. But, at the sentencing stage, courts can draw a line between the enforcement of norms that were intended to price and those intended to prohibit. Indeed, because a sensible implementation of the crime/tort distinction requires a close retrospective evaluation of the defendant's conduct, sentencing may be the only juncture where the distinction can be feasibly preserved....

Fundamental as the distinction between pricing and prohibiting misbehavior may be, there are still cases that fall on the borderline. Chief among these is the problem of corporate criminal liability. Essentially, corporate criminal liability (at least as recognized in the United States) is a species of vicarious criminal liability; that is, the principal is held liable for the acts of its agent—even when the principal makes a substantial good faith attempt to monitor the agent and prevent the illegality. Conceptually, vicarious criminal liability for failing to prevent the agent from acting illegally seems a form of behavior that should be priced, rather than prohibited. This is because society must make a judgment about the appropriate amount of behavior (i.e., preventive monitoring) to

---

* Originally published in 71 BOSTON UNIVERSITY LAW REVIEW 193 (1991). Reprinted with permission.
    14. Henry M. Hart., Jr., *The Aims of the Criminal Law,* 23 L. & CONTEMP. PROBS. 401, 431 (1958).

demand and cannot take a simple all-or-nothing position. Once it is conceded that some level of monitoring could be excessive, then the cost to the corporation must be compared to the benefit to society. Essentially, a pricing policy does this, focusing presumably on the gravity of the social harm involved.

This observation does not deny that in other cases corporations might have "intended" the crime (at least to the extent that senior officials encouraged, tolerated, or ratified it). Nonetheless, the point remains that to the extent that the role of corporate criminal liability is to encourage the principal to monitor its agents, the criminal law is inevitably caught up in the problem of pricing. To be sure, the law is not pricing the value of the illegal benefit to the defendant, but rather the cost of preventing the crime to the principal. Still, the analysis is much the same because private costs (i.e., monitoring expenditures) and public benefits (i.e., the deterrent benefits of crime suppression) are subject to a trade-off.

The bottom line is that the criminal law seems to be expanding into a variety of areas where it is infeasible or even irrational to ignore the costs of law compliance. Yet, both Congress and state legislatures have shown little interest in slowing this trend; nor is there much possibility that the Supreme Court will place constitutional limits on crime definition (as Professor Hart had hoped). As a result, the only decisionmakers who can attempt in a coherent way to determine when the criminal law should price and when it should prohibit are those who make sentencing policy and judgments. Uniquely, the sentencing stage affords a perspective from which nuances too subtle or fact-specific to be defined in advance by legislation can be examined retrospectively and in detail. In the case of the corporation, for example, it becomes possible to consider whether the corporate defendant simply failed to monitor a reckless agent adequately or whether it pressured its agents into criminal misconduct....

Three trends, in particular, stand out. First, the federal law of "white collar" crime now seems to be judge-made to an unprecedented degree, with courts deciding on a case-by-case, retrospective basis whether conduct falls within often vaguely defined legislative prohibitions. Second, a trend is evident toward the diminution of the mental element (or "*mens rea*") in crime, particularly in many regulatory offenses. Third, although the criminal law has long compromised its adherence to the "method" of the criminal law by also recognizing a special category of subcriminal offenses—often called "public welfare offenses"—in which strict liability could be combined with modest penalties, the last decade has witnessed the unraveling of this uneasy compromise, because the traditional public welfare offenses—now set forth in administrative regulations—have been upgraded to felony status. This Article will refer to this last trend as the "technicalization" of crime and will combine departures from most of the above-described elements that characterize the criminal law's "method."

The upshot of these trends is that the criminal law seems much closer to being used interchangeably with civil remedies. Sometimes, identically phrased statutes are applicable to the same conduct—one authorizing civil penalties, the other authorizing criminal sanctions. More often, the criminal law is extended to reach behavior previously thought only civilly actionable ...

In overview, the two principal claims made by this Article exist in some obvious tension. If true, the first claim—that the criminal law is more a system of socialization than of pricing—makes the second predictable: namely, that the criminal sanction is increasingly being used by regulators as a preferred enforcement tool without regard to the traditional limitations on its use. Almost by definition, a system for socialization will be put to new uses, as authorities attempt to harness its educational power. Thus, the very success of the criminal law as a socializing force implies the erosion of the traditional point at which the tenuous crime/tort distinction had been maintained. Indeed, traditional libertarians—such as Hart, [Sanford] Kadish, and [Herbert] Packer—have been criticized on this ground by sociologists, who have argued that the social standards of blameworthiness necessarily evolve over time along with other social attitudes. These critics have found the "over-criminalization" thesis to be empty of content, because of its failure to recognize the interactive, reciprocal relationship between the content of the criminal law and the public's perception of what conduct is blameworthy. In their view, the public learns what is blameworthy in large part from what is punished.

Undoubtedly, there is some merit in this argument. Obviously, new problems may arise for which the criminal law is the most effective instrument, but which involve behavior not historically considered blameworthy. Modern technology, the growth of an information-based economy, and the rise of the regulatory state make it increasingly difficult to maintain that only the common law's traditional crimes merit the criminal sanction. In fact, historically, the criminal law has never been static or frozen within a common law mold, but has constantly evolved. This has been especially true within the field of "white collar" crime. Even the first modern "white collar" offenses to be criminally prosecuted—price-fixing, tax fraud, securities fraud, and, later, foreign bribery—were "regulatory" crimes in the sense that they had not been traditionally considered blameworthy. In short, the line between *malum in se* and *malum prohibitum* has been crossed many times and largely discredited. Today, to rule out worker safety, toxic dumping, or environmental pollution as necessarily beyond the scope of the criminal law requires one to defend an antiquarian definition of blameworthiness.

But where does this leave us? Those following in the footsteps of Hart, Kadish and Packer have a powerful rejoinder: if the criminal law is overused, it will lose its distinctive stigma. While conceding that the criminal law is a system of socialization, they would reply that for precisely that reason it must be used parsimoniously. Once everything wrongful is made criminal, society's ability to reserve special condemnation for some forms of misconduct is either lost or simply reduced to a matter of prosecutorial discretion. Still, valid as this response is, it does not answer fully the criticism that the traditional criminal law scholar's focus on blameworthiness is anachronistic because it freezes the criminal law's necessary evolution, like a fly in amber.

If so, what alternative is left? What substitute bulwark can prevent the criminal law from sprawling over the landscape of the civil law? One answer is to update the notion of blameworthiness, looking not only to historical notions of culpability, but to well-established industry and professional standards whose violation has been associated with culpability within that narrower community. Another answer is to focus on the temporal relationship of the civil and criminal law. At some point, a civil standard can become so deeply rooted and internalized within an industry or professional community that its violation becomes blameworthy, even if it was not originally so. Insider trading may supply such an example, where the norm has long since become internalized within the industry. The relationship of the civil and criminal law here is sequentially interactive: the civil law experiments with a standard, but at some point it may "harden" into a community standard that the criminal law can enforce. At that point, it may be appropriate to prohibit, rather than price, at least if society believes that the defendant's conduct lacks any colorable social utility.

I. The Blurring of the Border

Three distinct subarguments will be made in this section. First, the criminal sanction has been applied broadly, and sometimes thoughtlessly, to a broad range of essentially civil obligations, some of which were intended as aspirational standards and others which are inherently open-ended and evolving in character. Second, there has also been a retreat from the traditional "method" of the criminal law, as the role of *mens rea* has been diminished and that of vicarious liability expanded. Third, a transition is evident in the characteristic "white collar" prosecution. Prosecutions increasingly tend to be less for violations of a statutory standard than for failures to comply with administrative regulations. Characteristically, these regulations resemble what an earlier era called "public welfare offenses," but with two differences: (1) substantial criminal sentences are authorized, and (2) the sheer volume of regulations that are now potentially enforceable through criminal prosecution means that the criminal sanction has penetrated much further into everyday life.

A. Criminalizing the Civil Law

Short of a doctrinal treatise or a major empirical study, no article could hope to demonstrate the degree to which the criminal law has encroached upon formerly "civil" areas of the law. What can be done, however, is to illustrate this trend by examining changes in some areas that had seemed quintessentially civil in character. For example, few legal categories seem inherently less "criminal" in character than the civil law applicable to fiduciary duties or to the use of economic duress in negotiations. Yet, both areas have, to an uncertain extent, been subjected to the reach of the criminal law. This section will use these two areas as case studies to illustrate how overlaying the criminal law on the civil law may distort the latter.

1. The Criminalization of Fiduciary Duties

The federal mail and wire fraud statutes supply the most obvious example of the criminal law being overlaid on civil law standards. By the mid-1960s, federal courts had accepted the principle that the term "scheme to defraud" (which is the critical element in both the mail and wire fraud statutes) required neither that there be any pecuniary or property loss to the victim nor that the purpose of the scheme be contrary to state or federal law.... In 1988, Congress enacted a statutory definition of the critical term, "scheme to defraud." [18 U.S.C. § 1346, as amended,] defines this term to include any "scheme or artifice to defraud another of the intangible right of honest services." At a stroke, this language may criminalize any violation of fiduciary duties or the law of agency. The expansion of section 1346 then supplies a paradigm of the criminal law being overlaid unthinkingly on top of the civil law, without serious consideration being given to whether the civil law standard in question should be backed by the special threat of the criminal law....

What is wrong with such an approach? As a matter of civil law, the short answer is relatively little. Courts constantly create or discover new torts. However, as a matter of criminal law, this approach should be unacceptable, for several reasons. First, in traditional constitutional terms, it denies fair notice, invites arbitrary and discriminatory enforcement, and violates the separation of powers principle that has traditionally denied federal courts the power to make common law crimes. However, in terms of this Article's concerns, the vocabulary of constitutional law does not adequately express the full dimensions of the problems inherent in broadly criminalizing civil law standards. The basic problem is that tort law standards often display a soft-edged quality that is consistent with their evolutionary and often aspirational character. For example, Cardozo wrote: "A trustee is held to something stricter than the morals of the marketplace. Not honesty alone, but the punctilio of an honor the most sensitive, is then the standard of behavior." And often this should be the standard expected of the fiduciary. But, precisely because such a standard can neither be realized fully nor even be defined with specificity in advance, it should not be criminalized. Aspirational standards imply that there will be shortfalls in performance, and this in turn means that to criminalize such a standard is to ignore the prudential constraint that criminal laws should be capable of even and general enforceability....

B. The Diminution of Mens Rea

American criminal law scholarship has always placed the issue of *mens rea* at center stage. Its greatest achievement—the Model Penal Code—creates a presumption that *mens rea* applies to every material element in the crime, unless the statute clearly indicates otherwise....

[I]n *Liparota v. United States,*[15] the Court reaffirmed this presumption, at least with respect to those elements in the crime that establish moral blameworthiness. Simultaneously, however, *Liparota* acknowledged that an exception to this generalization existed for "public welfare offenses." Reviewing its prior decisions on *mens rea,* the Court explained that in those cases in which it had upheld the omission of a mental element, the statute "rendered criminal a type of conduct that a reasonable person should know is subject to stringent public regulation and may seriously threaten the community's health or safety."

This language frames a central question: what is the scope of this exception for public welfare offenses? Lower courts have read the *Liparota* exception as limited to cases in which the risks created by the defendants' conduct "may be presumed to be regulated because of their inherent danger." ...

If public safety is the deciding test, the possibility arises that many environmental statutes, which commonly require permits before various conduct (e.g., the disposal of waste, the filling-in of wetlands, etc.) may be engaged in, will fall on the strict liability side of the line....

C. Vicarious Responsibility

Generally, in American criminal law, individuals are criminally liable only for conduct that: (1) they direct or participate in; (2) they otherwise aid or abet; or (3) with respect to which they conspire. Corporate officers, however, now appear to face an additional form of vicarious liability. In *United States v. Park,*[16] the Supreme Court upheld the imposition of criminal liability upon "corporate employees who have 'a responsible share in the furtherance of the transaction,'" even when the corporate officer took action to prevent the violation. Lower federal courts have extended this principle to apply, even when it has appeared that subordinate employees had purposely failed to follow the superior's orders or that the officer took significant corrective action that could not be implemented in time because of a labor strike.

Park's "responsible share" theory was announced in the context of a strict liability statute, whose uncompromising harshness the Court actually relaxed marginally by recognizing an "objective impossibility" defense. Both legislation and subsequent decisions

---

15. 471 U.S. 419 (1985).
16. 421 U.S. 658 (1975).

seem to be extending *Park's* standard of vicarious liability both to other "public welfare" statutes and, more questionably, to statutes requiring higher *mens rea* levels. This expansion of the *Park* doctrine has particular significance in light of new and proposed "reckless endangerment" statutes. Under one environmental statute, a defendant can receive fifteen years in prison for "knowing endangerment" that creates a risk of "serious bodily injury." Although the *mens rea* level here of "knowing" is certainly adequate to satisfy traditional civil libertarian concerns, *Park's* "responsible share" concept broadens the scope of potential defendants so as arguably to make anyone within the corporate hierarchy with power to correct or mitigate the risk liable if they have knowledge of it. Is, for example, a vice president for public relations liable where he or she has knowledge and might conceivably have influenced the chief executive officer to change a practice? ... Although the statutory focus is on the employer, *Park* could be read to expand the class of persons liable so as to reach all "responsible" managers within the firm....

D. The "Technicalization" of Crime

Regulatory violations that involve no mental element and pose strict liability have long been known to the criminal law.... Professor Francis Sayre catalogued the occasions on which legislatures and courts had dispensed with *mens rea*, naming this special class of criminal prosecutions "public welfare offenses."[17] Tracing the history of such offenses back before the Civil War in the United States and even earlier in England, he found their common denominator to be an attempt to protect the public health and safety by attaching light penalties (usually small fines) to police regulations. Typically, the offenses so criminalized involved the sale of adulterated food or alcohol and narcotics violations where mere possession was deemed sufficient to establish liability. Although Sayre approved of the creation of such a special category of offenses involving no showing of personal culpability, he was emphatic that the doctrine neither should be extended to "true crimes" nor should justify more than *de minimis* levels of punishment, because "to do so would sap the vitality of the criminal law."

Since the mid-1980s, American law has experienced a little noticed explosion in the use of public welfare offenses. By one estimate, there are over 300,000 federal regulations that may be enforced criminally....

Obviously, environmental crime is important, and knowing violations — such as falsification of records or willful endangerment — are serious offenses that do not merit leniency. But, the typical environmental offense involves the mishandling of toxic substances, and recent decisions have reduced or eliminated the role of *mens rea* in these statutes, while also applying *Park's* doctrine that corporate officers who have a "responsible relation" to the performance of the statutory obligations are liable under them. As a result, the traditional public welfare offense has now been coupled with felony level penalties. While the defendant in *Park* was only fined, corporate executives in an equivalent position in the future may face years in prison.

This process is only beginning.... [In 1989, for example] the SEC [made] criminal referrals in stock parking cases, which at bottom involve record-keeping and reporting violations having little, if any, relationship to the public health or safety.[18] [In 1990,] Exxon [was] indicted in connection with the Valdez oil spill for entrusting control of a vessel

---

17. Francis Sayre, *Public Welfare Offenses,* 33 Colum. L. Rev. 55 (1933).

18. *See* United States v. Regan, Fed. Sec. L. Rep. (CCH) P 94,481 (S.D.N.Y. 1989) (prosecution of Princeton Newport partners), *aff'd in part and rev'd in part,* 937 F.2d 823 (2d Cir. 1991). The conviction

to a person that it allegedly knew or should have known to have been an alcoholic. Finally, the [1990] indictment of Eastern Airlines and several of its employees for failure to follow correct maintenance and safety procedures, as required by Federal Aviation Administration regulations, opens a vast horizon of potential criminal prosecutions. As with stock parking prosecutions, the actual behavior involves falsification of the company's own business records. At this point, there are few, if any, federal regulations that could not potentially support a federal criminal prosecution under one theory or another.

In fairness, the federal government's attempt to use criminal sanctions in traditionally civil areas — such as stock parking — has met with some judicial resistance.... Still, these decisions lack any clear rationale and tend to depend on specific ad hoc judicial theories....

E. An Initial Summary: The Uncertain Cost/Benefit Calculus

Public concern about a newly perceived social problem — the environment, worker safety, child neglect, etc. — seems to trigger a recurring social response: namely, an almost reflexive resort to criminal prosecution, either through the enactment of new legislation or the use of old standby theories that have great elasticity. Increasingly, criminal liability may be imposed based only on negligence or even on a strict liability basis. The premise appears to be that if a problem is important enough, the partial elimination of *mens rea* and the use of vicarious responsibility are justified. No doubt, the criminal sanction does provide additional deterrence, but what are the costs of resorting to strict liability and vicarious responsibility as instruments of social control? This will be a theme of Part II, but one aspect of this problem deserves special mention in view of the apparent escalation of public welfare offenses into felonies.

If the disposal of toxic wastes, securities fraud, the filling-in of wetlands, the failure to conduct aircraft maintenance, and the causing of workplace injuries become crimes that can be regularly indicted on the basis of negligence or less, society as a whole may be made safer, but a substantial population of the American workforce (both at white collar and blue collar levels) becomes potentially entangled with the criminal law. Today, most individuals can plan their affairs so as to avoid any realistic risk of coming within a zone where criminal sanctions might apply to their conduct. Few individuals have reason to fear prosecution for murder, robbery, rape, extortion or any of the other traditional common law crimes. Even the more contemporary, white collar crimes — price fixing, bribery, insider trading, etc. — can be easily avoided by those who wish to minimize their risk of criminal liability. At most, these statutes pose problems for individuals who wish to approach the line but who find that no bright line exists. In contrast, modern industrial society inevitably creates toxic wastes that must be disposed of by someone. Similarly, workplace injuries are, to a degree, inevitable. As a result, some individuals must engage in legitimate professional activities that are regulated by criminal sanctions; to this extent, they become unavoidably "entangled" with the criminal law. That is, they cannot plan their affairs so as to be free from the risk that a retrospective evaluation of their conduct, often under the uncertain standard of negligence, will find that they fell short of the legally mandated standard. Ultimately, if the new trend toward greater use of public welfare offenses continues, it will mean a more pervasive use of the criminal sanction, a use that intrudes further into the mainstream of American life and into the everyday life of its citizens than has ever been attempted before.

---

for conspiracy to commit securities fraud was upheld, while the convictions on the tax counts were reversed....

Several replies are predictable to this claim that there is a social loss in defining the criminal law so that individuals cannot safely avoid its application. Liberals may claim that the traditionally limited use of the criminal sanction was class-biased and that a more pervasive use of it simply corrects that imbalance. Economists may argue that the affected individuals will only demand a "risk premium" in the labor market and, having received one, cannot later complain when the risk for which they were compensated arises. Others may conclude that the anxiety imposed on such employees, while regrettable, is necessary, because it is small in comparison to the lives saved, injuries averted, and other social benefits realized from generating greater deterrence. This may be true, but the cost/benefit calculus is a complex and indeterminate one that depends upon a comparison of marginal gain (in terms of injuries averted) in comparison to other law enforcement strategies (such as greater use of corporate liability or civil penalties) that have not yet been utilized fully. Moreover, on the cost side of the ledger, one must consider not simply the consequences to those actually prosecuted, but the anxiety created within the potential class of criminal defendants. To the extent that liability is imposed for omissions (i.e., failure to detect and correct dangerous conditions), such fear will affect a broad class of employees, most of whom will never be prosecuted or even threatened with prosecution. In addition, there is a cost to civil libertarian values, because statutes that apply broadly can never be enforced evenly. Hence, some instances of "targeting" or selective prosecutions (based on whatever criteria influence the individual prosecutor) become predictable. These costs would be more tolerable if the conduct involved were inherently blameworthy, but negligence, like death and taxes, is inevitable.

Ultimately, much depends on how we define the purposes of the criminal law. If its purpose is simply to prevent crime, the costs of the broad use of the criminal sanction against corporate managers to deter pollution, negligence-caused injuries, or other social harms may be justified. But if we define the criminal law's purposes more broadly—for example, as to "liberate" society from fear, or to enable the realization of human potential—these broader goals may be seriously compromised by a pervasive use of the criminal sanction against individuals who cannot escape its potential threat. Pursued single-mindedly, a purely negative definition of the criminal law's purposes that asserts that the criminal law's only goal is the prevention of crime ultimately ends up, as Herbert Packer wrote, "creating an environment in which all are safe but none is free."[19]

II. The Rationale for the Tort/Crime Distinction

Generalizations about the difference between crimes and torts usually oversimplify. The standard "black letter" law distinction is a good illustration of this tendency. It holds that crimes represent injuries to society generally, while torts involve only private interests. Although this public/private distinction dates back at least to Blackstone, it is a distinction without a difference. Roscoe Pound stated the most important objection: events that cause private injuries also cause public ones, because public injuries are usually only private injuries writ large. For example, an individual's private interest in the enforcement of a contract can also be described as the collective, public interest in the security of transactions. The problem with the public/private distinction, then, is that private and public injuries are correlative, with the result, as Henry Hart said, "that society is interested also in the due fulfillment of contracts and the avoidance of traffic accidents and most of the other stuff of civil litigation"....

---

19. HERBERT PACKER, THE LIMITS OF THE CRIMINAL SANCTION 65 (1968).

... [T]he criminal law has a unique "educational role," within which it is one of the primary socializing forces within society. More recently, this view has been rediscovered and articulated in economic terms as a claim that the criminal law is, ultimately, a social instrument for shaping preferences as much as opportunities. Provocative as this view is, one must be careful here not to overstate the criminal law's capacity. Whether it can truly shape preferences is debatable; crimes of theft, violence, and sexual exploitation have been with us for millennia. Similarly, despite decades of criminal prosecutions for income tax evasion, few have learned to "prefer" paying taxes, although most have learned that the consequences of deliberate evasion can include prison.... Thus, it seems more accurate to speak of the "educational" role of the criminal law, to say that one learns what the public morality is, even if one does not fully internalize it. Here, empirical evidence is available to support the proposition that the criminal law is very effective at teaching citizens what the contours of the public morality are....

... [H]enry Hart ... had little difficulty in describing the criminal law's defining character: "What distinguishes a criminal from a civil sanction and all that distinguishes it ... is the judgment of community condemnation which accompanies and justifies its imposition." Crime then, in this view, is conduct that, once proven, "will incur a formal and solemn pronouncement of the moral condemnation of the community." Accordingly, it followed from this first step that the scope of the criminal law should include only behavior that the community as a whole would consider "blameworthy." ...

[H]art's themes were directly applied to the context of economic regulations by an intellectual descendent, Professor Sanford Kadish. Writing shortly after the 1960s price-fixing cases in which executives of major corporations were sent to prison for the first time, Kadish warned that the use of criminal law simply to place a tax on disfavored behavior would rob the criminal law of its distinctive force.[20]

The central theme in both Hart's and Kadish's critiques was that the criminal law would be devalued if it were to be used to express not society's moral revulsion, but merely its utilitarian preferences. This argument drew a sharp retort from those who favored the increased use of the criminal law against high-status offenders. Drawing on sociological studies, Professors Ball and Friedman challenged the idea that the criminal law would lose its unique status in the public's mind simply because it was employed to penalize behavior not historically thought to be "criminal" in nature.[21] They argued that the relationship between the criminal law and the public morality was interactive and reciprocal. Each affected the other, and, to a degree, the public learned what was immoral from what was made criminal.

Although Ball and Friedman had only a limited data base upon which to generalize at the time they wrote, subsequent events seem to confirm their position. Each of the major "white collar" scandals of recent decades—the price-fixing scandals in the electrical equipment industry of the 1960s, the foreign payments scandal of the 1970s and the insider trading revelations of the 1980s—shocked and aroused the American public. In general, the public has shown little apprehension about the use of the criminal sanction in these cases, but rather has applauded its use. No one who has followed the media coverage of the Ivan Boesky or Michael Milken prosecutions can doubt the attitude of the American public: it has wanted prison sentences imposed—substantial ones. In part,

---

20. Sanford Kadish, *Some Observations on the Use of Criminal Sanctions in Enforcing Economic Regulations*, 30 U. Chi. L. Rev. 423, 424 (1963).

21. Harry V. Ball & Lawrence M. Friedman, *The Use of Criminal Sanctions in the Enforcement of Economic Legislation: A Sociological View*, 17 Stan L. Rev. 197, 206–07 (1965).

this may simply reflect the public's enjoyment of the spectacle of the once mighty made humble, but the possibility at least exists that those commentators who predicted an erosion in respect for the criminal law if it was used to enforce economic regulations have either overestimated the legal sophistication of the American public or underestimated its appetite for bread and circuses. Possibly, the public is more concerned about being victimized by the underlying offenses, or possibly it simply does not believe that it will be at risk from such prosecutions. Whatever the reason, the public may not share the legal profession's unease with strict liability offenses....

Even if a general decline in the community's respect for law does not result from increased use of the criminal sanction, this should not end the debate about overcriminalization. One flaw in Hart's conceptualization of the law's educational role is his reification of the community as a single, indivisible body of public opinion. American society is too large, diverse, and specialized for such a concept to be generally meaningful. Moreover, the "technicalization" of crime discussed earlier means that the broad mass of public opinion will never quite understand what the law required or why the behavior was illegal. However, it is not necessary to educate or socialize all of society. What Hart should have recognized is that the educational and socializing role of the criminal law focuses principally on specialized audiences within the broader society. While all of society cannot be educated as to the specialized requirements of the SEC, EPA, or OSHA, a relevant business or professional community can be. Sometimes this specialized community can be induced to internalize new community standards. For example, both price-fixing and insider trading represent crimes that, in my judgment, are today accepted as criminal by the relevant affected community. Conversely, when strict liability criminal statutes are used, it is less likely that the prohibited behavior will be internalized, and some possibility exists that it will generate hostility and resistance. Thus, even if there is not a general erosion in public respect for law and even if there is increased general deterrence, the criminal law may fail in its principal socializing mission—making law compliance habitual within the relevant population of potential offenders.

Another way to express much the same point is to say that stigma is a scarce resource. Society does not have an unlimited capacity to express condemnation or to feel revulsion. A little noticed fact about the major modern episodes of "white collar" criminal prosecutions has been their presentation to the public as newly developed crises: a crisis of price-fixing in the 1960s, of illegal payments in the 1970s, and of insider trading in the 1980s. In fact, the behavior in question in each case was not particularly new. What the public was actually witnessing is more accurately described not as a crime wave, but as a prosecution wave. Nonetheless, from the public's perspective, there was an urgency to these cases that justified the resort to the criminal sanction. In contrast, when the criminal law is applied to more mundane crimes on a continuing basis, the public may grow indifferent to whether the prosecution is civil or criminal in nature. At this point, Professor Hart's fears will have been realized: the criminal law will have lost its distinctive character.

III. Separating Tort from Crime: Toward Implementation

... [T]here is no immutable line between crime and tort. Rather, this Article has suggested that the line depends primarily on whether society is willing to recognize social utility in the value that the criminal derives from the criminal behavior. If it does, the strategy should be to price, rather than to prohibit, in order to minimize the external costs. Conversely, when society wishes to prohibit the behavior, it cannot permit the offender to derive any benefits from the activity without undercutting the educational and socializing impact of the criminal law. Generally, society seeks to prohibit (rather than price) those activities that violate fundamental community standards. Yet, over time, society can and does decide that some activities, which formerly were only priced, should be prohibited. Unlawful toxic dumping seems a clear example of a form of conduct where society's attitude has changed. Once this might have been seen as simply a regulatory matter—a *malum prohibitum* offense in the language of an earlier era—but today it is more likely to be viewed as behavior that knowingly endangers human life. Community standards have changed, and they will continue to do so.

Admittedly, substantial problems of implementation surround any attempt to operationalize a distinction between pricing and prohibiting. Two stand out: (1) the "real world" continuum of criminal behavior, ranging from the trivial to the egregious, has few, if any, obvious partitions; thus, an abrupt shift from a "pricing" policy of incremental cost increases to a "prohibitory" policy of sharp, discontinuous jumps in penalty levels may seem unjustified; and (2) the competence of juries to judge issues of social utility seems highly questionable. Nonetheless, to shift from pricing to prohibiting without framing some role for the jury as fact-finder might be thought to trivialize the constitutional safeguards surrounding the trial stage.

The most feasible answers to both these problems dovetail. Put simply, the existence or non-existence of criminal intent supplies a traditional jury issue that also furnishes the most practical breakpoint at which to shift from pricing to prohibiting. To illustrate the kind of criminal intent on which the jury should be asked to focus, it is useful to [consider] *United States v. Sellers*.[22] In *Sellers*, the court refused to give a jury instruction that required the jury to find that the defendant realized that his disposal of waste substances "could be harmful to others or the environment." To be sure, such a level of *mens rea* is not constitutionally required, but this focus on harm to others supplies a practical test, readily comprehensible to a jury, for determining when the defendant's conduct knowingly lacks any claim to social utility (and hence should be subject to "sanctions," rather than "prices" in Professor Cooter's terminology[23]). Ideally, criminal legislation might therefore distinguish two grades of the crime of toxic dumping: the higher grade requiring a subjective perception by the defendant of the serious risk of harm to others, and the lower grade not. The former might be "prohibited," and the latter "priced."

Such an approach might be ideal, but it is also constitutionally permissible for the court to engage in this same inquiry at sentencing.... Sentencing guidelines could respond in the following general ways:

1. *Strict Liability.* In principle, strict liability offenses should not result in incarceration or high financial penalties, unless the prosecution can show at sentencing that the individual acted with at least the minimum level of *mens rea* that American criminal law defines as "recklessness." Although regulatory authorities maintain with some truth that they prosecute only defendants, who, they believe, acted with actual knowledge, this issue is seldom resolved at trial, at least if the statute dispenses with *mens rea* toward the element in question. Absent legislation that appropriately frames this issue, it should still be resolved at sentencing (albeit with lesser formality and a lower burden of proof) before punishment above that appropriate for traditional public welfare offenses could be imposed.

22. 926 F.2d 410 (5th Cir. 1991).
23. Robert Cooter, *Prices and Sanctions*, 84 COLUM. L. REV. 1523 (1984).

2. *Fear.* Nozick's basic claim—that the criminal law is primarily justified by the noncompensable fear that some unlawful actions impose on others[24]—deserves explicit recognition in any morally sophisticated system of sentencing. Its role should be that of an aggravating factor. Obviously, such a criteria distinguishes crimes, such as insider trading, from homicide. But what kinds of fear count? Community values probably answer this question and imply that fear of a financial loss is not the same as fear of injury or illness. Note, however, that the fear need not be directly attributable to a personal assault. Toxic dumping crimes, for example, may subject an even larger proportion of the citizenry to fears that they are drinking contaminated water. Similarly, crimes involving concealed exposure of workers to dangerous substances (e.g., asbestos) could fall under this same heading.

3. *Industry Standards and Agency Rules.* Hart's approach can be faulted as backward-looking and anachronistic because it looks only to traditional moral standards. Perhaps unintentionally, it thus implicitly revives the discredited *malum in se* versus *malum prohibitum* distinction. Often, however, the regulatory rules imposed by an agency will have simply codified standards long recognized within an industry or other professional community. Significant departures from these standards may involve the same degree of culpability within that specialized group as departures from prevailing moral standards recognized universally within the larger community. In short, if the conduct would be seen as wholly unjustified by those within the field (who best understand it), it should be prohibited, not priced. Egregious departures from professional norms should not be excused simply because the rules involved were technical. In this light, consider again the pending indictment of Eastern Airlines for failure to conduct adequate maintenance on its planes. The gravity of such a crime can range from the trivial to the very serious. How should a court appraise it? While industry standards are never dispositive, they provide the most useful benchmark for measuring the culpability of such an offense. When well-established industry standards are violated, the court's response should be the same as if the conduct violated fundamental community standards.

4. *Corporate Crime.* Corporate crime can be distinctive in several respects, but two respects bear special mention here. First, sometimes the corporation has failed to comply with a standard toward which it was making substantial progress, and, second, sometimes (but probably less often) the crime can be the consequence of a "rogue" employee acting contrary to specific instructions or corporate policy. [*United States v. Y. Hata & Co.*[25]], in which a strike prevented the corporate officer from installing the necessary bird cage around an open-air food storage warehouse, illustrates the first scenario. The court's view that the business could have been shut down if compliance were otherwise physically impossible seems extreme, because it denies that there is any social value in the continued operation of the plant pending full compliance. While one can easily criticize the court's decision, the more difficult question arrives at sentencing. Having rejected the defense, can the court still consider this same factor as a mitigating factor that reduces the fine? This Article's answer would be yes, at least when the crime is essentially a public welfare offense that should be priced, not prohibited. This conclusion rests, however, on the defendant's good faith in attempting to correct the problem. Once again, behavior that has social utility should be priced, not prohibited. Deliberate defiance, however, lacks such utility and should be prohibited because it undercuts the socializing role of the criminal law.

The second recurring element in corporate crime is the claim that a "rogue" employee was responsible. Often, this claim is overstated, because the so-called rogue may be

---

24. ROBERT NOZICK, ANARCHY, STATE AND UTOPIA 65–71 (1974).
25. 535 F.2d 508 (9th Cir. 1976).

responding to subtle (or not so subtle) intraorganization signals and pressures that place profit above law compliance. Indeed, middle managers are often almost fungible, with the result that the corporation can replace those employees who are caught with little harm to itself—if the fine will be modest so long as senior corporate personnel are not implicated. Nonetheless, it cannot be denied that cases arise in which a rogue employee does appear to have frustrated a good faith corporate attempt to comply with the law. In these cases, the corporation's culpability seems low, and a pricing approach would be appropriate, whose intent would be to induce the corporation to install improved monitoring controls.

The problem with this answer is that any corporation can adopt a compliance plan and it may be difficult for the prosecution to prove, except in the most egregious case, that it was cosmetically manipulated. When internal monitoring amounts to a sham, the conclusion seems obvious that it lacks social utility, and a prohibitory approach becomes appropriate. Thus, a sharp, discontinuous jump in corporate penalties is appropriate when there is evidence that senior corporate officials knew of, or "recklessly" tolerated, the criminal behavior or sought to outflank monitoring controls.

But how does one draft guidelines that distinguish "true" from "cosmetic" monitoring? One approach would be to grant a provisional sentencing credit for seemingly adequate monitoring controls, but then treat this credit as a suspended sentence which is forfeited if there is any repetition of the behavior (as evidenced by either subsequent civil or criminal findings during a period of corporate probation). Such an approach takes much of the burden off the court by assuming that cosmetic monitoring will ultimately result in future violations, and the time to be punitive is at that future moment. Above all, corporate recidivism merits prohibition, not pricing.

IV. Conclusion

Ultimately, appropriate sentencing policy is a function of one's theory of the criminal law. Those who view the criminal law as a "pricing" system can make a coherent case for their view that Sentencing Commission guidelines for corporate offenders are too high and that courts should reduce the sentences currently imposed on corporations by recognizing any of a variety of offsets or mitigating factors. In contrast, those who believe that the criminal law is intended to prohibit and not price can view high fines with equanimity and argue that if they are too severe corporations have only to obey the law to avoid them.

Although this Article has argued that the criminal law should normally prohibit, and not price, it has also recognized that the expansion of the criminal law into formerly civil areas of law and the increasing departures from the traditional "method" of the criminal law make it difficult to state this policy as an iron rule. An either/or choice is also unnecessary. Rather, pricing is appropriate precisely in those areas where the criminal law has relaxed its usual requirement of *mens rea* or has abandoned its normal hostility to vicarious responsibility. Clearly, corporate criminal responsibility straddles this line, and thus distinctions must be drawn that the current federal law of corporate criminal liability does not make.

How can these distinctions best be drawn? The sentencing determination today represents the only point in our criminal justice system where it remains feasible to preserve the distinction between "true" crimes and public welfare offenses. To say that this can be done is not to claim that such distinctions are today being drawn or will be in the near future. Procedural reform, clearer sentencing guidelines that are more focused on culpability factors, and numerous other steps would be desirable. Still, if the criminal law is not to be corrupted into simply a utilitarian instrument for administering legal threats, reform at the sentencing stage is the last, best hope.

Timothy F. Malloy, *Regulating by Incentives: Myths, Models, and Micromarkets**

Environmental regulation is all about using incentives to control behavior. Under direct "command and control" regulation, the government creates specific obligations and generally relies upon the negative incentives of civil and criminal penalties to motivate individuals or organizations to comply with those obligations. Alternatively, the new generation of "market-based" or "incentive-based" regulations typically create an opportunity rather than (or in addition to) an obligation, offering the positive incentive of increased profits (or reduced costs) in the hope of eliciting the desired behavior. A regulator using either of these two regulatory approaches must identify the appropriate type and level of incentive—be it positive or negative—needed to produce the "correct" response from the target. In crafting and evaluating regulatory incentives, a regulator necessarily relies upon some basic model of how the target makes decisions. If that model is flawed, then the incentive will miss the mark, and the desired behavior may never occur.

Given the importance of accurately predicting responses to regulation, one might expect that regulators and legal scholars alike would carefully select the decision-making models they use. Yet surprisingly little attention is paid to how businesses make choices in the face of government regulation. Many regulators and scholars rely upon a "black-box" model in developing and evaluating environmental regulatory incentives directed at businesses. Although no single, authoritative description of the black-box model exists, most formulations include three major components. First, the model assumes that the organization is a monolithic entity that essentially makes decisions as a natural individual would. Thus, the collective nature of the firm and its internal features are largely ignored. Second, the model assumes that the unitary firm makes decisions rationally. For these purposes, a "rational" person makes decisions by collecting all relevant information, identifying and evaluating all alternatives and their likely outcomes, and selecting the alternative most likely to achieve the person's goals. Third, the traditional formulation of the black-box model assumes that the firm has one dominant goal: maximizing profits....

... [S]cholars and regulators from both [the direct and incentive-based schools] use the black-box model, albeit in subtly different ways. Proponents of direct regulation often justify the need for government intervention by pointing to the myopic, profit-driven nature of industry, and they design regulation and its enforcement accordingly. Supporters of incentive-based regulation view the profit motive as a tool rather than an obstacle. Government's role is largely limited to establishing clear economic incentives for the regulated community and getting out of the way.

This Article argues that the black-box model is a precarious foundation on which to build social regulation directed at larger business organizations. The Article proposes the "resource-allocation" model, an alternative that peers inside the opaque walls of the business firm. Inside, the model identifies internal features that cause a profit-seeking firm's behavior to diverge from the black-box predictions. The resource-allocation model

* Originally published in 80 TEXAS LAW REVIEW 531 (2002). Copyright 2002 Texas Law Review Association. Reprinted with permission.

treats the firm as a system for allocating and coordinating organizational resources, such as capital, information, and personnel time and expertise. It likewise characterizes a firm's response to a regulatory incentive—whether a regulatory obligation or opportunity—as a decision by the firm about how to allocate its limited resources....

The central point of the resource-allocation model is straightforward: a firm's organization and internal processes affect its reaction to regulation in predictable ways. Thus, for example, differences among firms in how freely information moves between divisions causes the firms to respond quite differently to identical regulatory opportunities....

From the public policy perspective, the conclusions suggest that existing regulations should be supplemented—or in some cases replaced—with regulation that either anticipates internal firm barriers or attempts to alter those barriers....

I. Encouraging Innovation: The Case of Chemco

A. *Innovation and Regulation*

The ability to encourage innovation is widely recognized as the pre-eminent test of an environmental regulatory tool's mettle.... From an engineering standpoint, existing technologies are unlikely to be able to deal with the broadening scope and diversity of pollution and other environmental impacts, requiring constant innovation to keep pace with continued growth.... [F]rom an economic and political perspective, cost-reducing innovations can shrink the perceived divide between environmental quality and economic impact, easing the way for broader environmental improvements....

Given the importance of innovation, it is not surprising that virtually every comparison of direct regulation and incentive-based regulation includes some discussion of the subject. Much of the discussion focuses on the role that emissions trading can play in encouraging continuous innovation by industry. In a typical emissions-trading system, the regulator establishes default emission limits for all regulated firms. However, a firm with low control costs may "overcontrol" its emissions and sell those extra reductions to another regulated firm, presumably at a price below the second firm's marginal cost of control. Thus, the argument goes, the trading program creates a market for voluntary emission reductions, providing firms with a clear profit incentive to search for and implement innovative pollution-management strategies. In theory, the possibility of profit is ever present, and therefore the incentive to innovate is continuous.

Black-box assumptions are ubiquitous in the relevant literature concerning innovation gains from emissions trading....

The legal literature on this point overwhelmingly favors incentive-based regulation in general, and emissions trading in particular, as the best route to innovation. Like the mainstream environmental economics literature, the legal literature relies upon the assumption that the drive for profit will lead to innovation.... [The legal literature argues that] incentive-based programs such as emissions fees and emissions trading will provide continuous, positive incentives for innovation because of the constant opportunity to generate profits or reduce costs as a result of innovation. With limited exceptions, the role that organizational features and bounded rationality of individuals within the firm could play on the adoption of innovative technologies is typically ignored or minimized.

Proponents of direct regulation also rely upon a black-box conception of the firm, viewing regulation as a force for innovation. In their view, the firm's drive to reduce costs is the catalyst for innovation.... Environmental regulation can have the same effect as an increase in the price of a factor because such regulation essentially increases the firm's cost of emitting pollution. Under direct regulation, innovation would occur in cases in which the regulator imposes strict performance standards, such as emission limits, but gives the firm wide discretion over how to achieve the performance standard. The black-box model tells us that, when faced with mandatory regulation, the firm will identify and evaluate all viable alternatives, ultimately selecting the one that minimizes its compliance costs. Numerous federal regulations use performance standards, with the express purposes, at least in part, of providing firms with flexibility and encouraging innovation....

... [T]here is surprisingly little empirical support for the proposition that either emissions trading or direct regulation actually leads to continuous and systematic innovation....

... The remarkable influence of the myth of the unitary, rational firm in this area invites a closer look at the black-box model that spawned it. That closer examination is best done in the context of a specific example, which is presented in the next section.

B. The Chemco Scenario

The following scenario asks how a hypothetical company named Chemco—a sort of industrial "everyman"—would respond to the profit incentive offered by an emissions-trading program. The scenario posits that Chemco's synthetic organic chemicals division could make a physical alteration to the production process for MDE, a chemical sold by Chemco to the plastics industry. The process change would reduce Chemco's use of a particularly toxic raw material, resulting in a significant reduction in air emissions of the material. The reduction would be entirely voluntary; Chemco is already in compliance with all existing regulations concerning its emissions. However, the alterations would be quite expensive, involving capital costs and other indirect costs totaling $400,000. The resulting emission-reduction credit could be sold for $500,000, a respectable return of twenty-five percent. There is a problem, though. The fact that such a physical alteration could be made is not obvious. Identifying the opportunity would require fairly sophisticated knowledge of the process chemistry and the production equipment. Moreover, even someone with that knowledge would have to spend time evaluating the process in order to recognize the opportunity.

In evaluating whether the regulatory investment of $400,000 would be made, the resource-allocation model looks to the internal structure and processes of the firm. Therefore, it is useful to understand a bit about Chemco's structure and processes before discussing the model in detail. "Structure" refers to the formal organizational design of the firm—the hierarchy and formal lines of communication." Processes" refer to the firm's standard operating procedures and routines, including the management-accounting system and budgeting process, as well as informal information channels throughout the firm.

Chemco is a large chemical manufacturer with eight plants located across the United States. Like many large companies competing in national and international markets, Chemco is organized as a traditional, hierarchical multidivisional firm. It consists of a corporate headquarters overseeing four operating divisions with each division in charge of a separate product line: synthetic organic chemicals, inorganic chemicals, lubricants, and petrochemicals. Corporate headquarters is responsible for charting the firm's overall strategy (with input from the divisions), allocating firm resources within and among divisions, and serving an advisory and coordinating role for the divisions. Each division has a quasi-independent governance structure: a series of departments report to a divisional vice president who in turn reports to the corporate headquarters. Each department is responsible for a separate divisional function, such as marketing; production; research and development; and environmental, health, and safety (the "environmental department"). The divisional departments each have a corresponding corporate-level office that serves an oversight and advisory function.

As a major industrial actor, Chemco faces extensive environmental regulation at each of its eight facilities, including source-specific requirements; obligations relating to permitting, reporting, and disclosure; and remediation obligations. At Chemco, the laboring oar of the environmental function is pulled by the respective divisional environmental departments. When a new regulation becomes effective, it is the divisional environmental department that identifies the recommended compliance strategy and implements the final strategy. The divisional environmental department is responsible for responding to spills of hazardous materials and for dealing with agency inspections, notices of violations, and—in conjunction with the corporate legal department—formal enforcement actions. The manager of each divisional environmental department reports formally to the divisional vice president, who sets the compensation and evaluates the performance of the environmental department manager. The environmental department manager also reports informally to the corporate environmental office.

The scenario focuses on Chemco's synthetic organic chemicals division ("OC"), which is the company's smallest (in terms of revenue and size) and least profitable division. The division has two main product lines, plastics and industrial materials, produced by separate production departments. In the division's environmental department, staff assignments are broken down according to "environmental media," meaning that some staff deal with air emissions, some with wastewater issues, others with solid waste, and so on. In OC, Carol McCain, a professional engineer with an advanced degree in environmental engineering, is the divisional environmental staff person charged with managing the firm's obligations under federal, state, and regional air-pollution regulation. She is the gatekeeper in this scenario.

II. Application of the Resource-Allocation Model

A. The Gatekeeper and the Firm's Agenda

The gatekeeper function incorporates a threshold issue that invariably arises in the real world, but is rarely addressed in the black-box world: the question of organizational agenda.... The capacity of any organism, be it human or social, to process information and stimuli is necessarily limited; attention itself is a scarce resource that is directed and allocated.... In other words, a regulatory obligation or opportunity is not relevant to the firm until it becomes a part of the firm's agenda. The gate-keeper is the first step in the process of reaching the agenda.

Theoretical studies of how firms respond to regulatory incentives typically fail to consider the role of attention. Instead, they assume at the outset that all stimuli are created equal in terms of their ability to garner firm attention. The literature on innovation and emissions trading is an excellent example of this inattention to attention. The typical analysis selects two or more types of regulation, such as direct regulation, emissions trading, and emissions taxes, and compares the financial impact of the same innovation under each type of regulation in various scenarios. The regulation that provides the greatest return in a particular scenario is proclaimed the one most likely to lead to innovation in those circumstances, without consideration of whether the firm would even consider making the innovation in the first place. The resource-allocation model instead begins with the question of whether the firm would "notice" the opportunity to innovate. Drawing upon the theoretical and empirical work of organizational theorists and sociologists, the model identifies two significant obstacles to regulatory opportunities striving to reach the multidivisional firm's agenda: the use of organizational subgoals and the impaired flow of information within the firm.

1. The Role of Subgoals

In the Chemco scenario, it is fair to assume that Carol, one of Chemco's environmental managers, is generally aware of the fact that an emissions-trading program exists. As the environmental manager in charge of "air issues," she is expected to keep up on current developments in her field.... Thus, she has also been exposed to the strategy of using process changes for emission reduction. However, general awareness of a program is quite different from active attention to a specific opportunity arising under the program. In order to take advantage of the program, Carol would have to search for and identify a specific opportunity, such as the changes to the MDE production process. Such a search would require Carol to devote significant resources to a project, which, at least initially, would have a very uncertain payoff. The impacted resources include her own time, time of subordinate staff, time of staff in other departments, and any costs paid to consultants or other vendors from her operating budget to assist her in the search for a viable emission reduction....

In the Chemco scenario, the rational black-box entrepreneur would quantify the likely cost of the search for the necessary information and the probable net value of the potential innovation, and determine whether pursuing the search is efficient....

... Under the resource-allocation model, [however], the gatekeeper does not channel resources solely in accordance with explicit or even implicit calculations. Rather, she directs her attention and resources in accordance with principles imbedded in the firm's incentive and communication structures. In other words, Carol will only attend to those matters that fit her perception of what the firm expects from her, which in turn is largely controlled by how her performance as a manager is evaluated and what information is supplied to her by other members of the firm. For Carol, the relevant issue is not whether the search for a profitable project would be efficient, but whether the firm expects her to search for profit in the first place.

The critical point here is that even a perfectly efficient, profit-maximizing firm will not consist of a group of profit-maximizing employees and managers. The sheer size and complexity of the modern firm virtually precludes it from using profit-maximization as the driving goal for every firm participant. Delegation of specialized tasks to different subunits and participants within the firm increases efficiency, but it also requires some form of central coordination through which the individual efforts of firm participants collectively result in optimal profit for the firm. Mere exhortations to increase profits provide little direction to the departments and individuals in the lower levels of the firm. Instead, their goals must be more clearly articulated in specific, operational terms. Consequently, just as labor and production are broken down into smaller and smaller pieces, so too is the general goal of profit maximization.

Thus, for example, at a manufacturing firm, the production manager's goals may be to maintain product quality and minimize costs, while the engineering manager may focus on devising process improvements and increasing capacity. The subunit, or more specifically the individuals within it, is expected to focus on pursuing the subgoals without regard to the underlying primary goals of the organization....

Empirical research suggests that in many traditional, hierarchical firms, the mission of the environmental department is clear: keep the firm in compliance as cheaply as possible.... As one executive described it, "Our job at that time was to get permits and don't screw up".... [R]ecent surveys of business firms ... identify compliance and cost-reduction as dominant environmental department goals.

In our Chemco scenario, then, the subgoals of the environmental department will revolve around increasing or maintaining compliance and reducing costs. The subgoals are created and signaled to Carol in a number of ways, some express and some implicit in firm routines or policies. The subgoals will be most clearly articulated in the environmental manager's job description and embedded in the format of any performance evaluations. Likewise, formal operating procedures and written policies often identify the firm's expectations for various positions within the firm....

... [A]s Carol identifies and responds to regulatory stimuli, she will be guided in large part by the goal of maintaining compliance subject to the constraint of minimizing cost. In the emissions-trading example, Carol is faced with a fairly stark question: whether to investigate voluntary emissions reductions in order to generate a profit. The opportunity does not fit very well with Carol's subgoals: it does nothing to assist with compliance nor does it directly reduce compliance costs. Because the MDE project falls outside of Carol's perception of "what the company expects from me," she is likely to ignore or significantly undervalue it.

In fact, absent a clear signal from firm management that the pursuit of profit is a sanctioned subgoal, allocation of resources to the potential MDE process change would be against Carol's own self-interest. Presumably, her compensation and position in the firm are affected by her performance in achieving the existing subgoals. At an industrial facility, maintaining compliance is typically a difficult task, given the breadth and dynamic nature of the relevant state and federal regulation. The demands of the compliance task will leave little time or resources for use in evaluating voluntary profit opportunities. Diversion of her limited resources to the MDE process change would be personally risky for Carol as it may detract from her performance in her core functions. Given an incentive system in which her compensation is tied not to profit but to cost-effective compliance, that risk brings little payoff for her. Therefore, in a world in which the gatekeeper for environmental issues is focused on compliance and costs, the profit opportunities offered by the emissions-trading program will likely be unnoticed or even ignored....

2. The Role of Information Flows

.... Specialization of tasks within a firm often leads to the uneven distribution of information concerning firm activities and technologies. Because not everyone in the firm will need or even want access to all the information available to the firm, an efficient firm will have processes for distributing items of information to those participants who need the items. If information needed by the gatekeeper to identify and consider a cost-minimizing investment is located in another part of the firm, then the ease with which information flows within the firm will have a significant impact on how the potential investment fares with the gatekeeper. Application of the resource-allocation model demonstrates that the environmental gate-keeper may face significant barriers in obtaining information from other firm participants. We can explore this phenomenon by altering the Chemco scenario.

Recall that in the initial profit scenario, Chemco was faced with the issue of whether to make a voluntary reduction in emissions from the MDE production process. In this revised scenario, the regulations require Chemco to control emissions from the MDE process. The issue in this "cost-reduction" scenario is not whether Chemco will control emissions, but rather how. In the cost-reduction scenario, federal regulations limit emissions from MDE production processes to no more than 10 pounds of emissions for every 1000 pounds of MDE produced. Chemco uses a standard "add-on" pollution-control device to keep emissions below the limit. The standard equipment cost $200,000 to install two years ago. Chemco will incur $500,000 (in present value terms) in operation and maintenance costs over the remaining fifteen-year life of the equipment. Alternatively, the innovative change in the MDE process (previously described in the profit scenario) would also reduce emissions to below the limit, obviating the need for continued use of the add-on control. The physical alterations needed to make the process change cost $400,000, resulting in compliance-cost savings of $100,000.

The black-box model, at least as it is applied by supporters of direct regulation, predicts that Carol will seek funding for the process changes. Under the resource-allocation model, Carol's choice will be contingent on how well information flows through the firm. As noted in the profit scenario description, identification and evaluation of the MDE process change requires in-depth knowledge of the process chemistry, as well as the as-built workings of the process unit. Although Carol may be generally aware of the MDE process, she is unlikely to have the level of knowledge needed to develop and evaluate the process change. The requisite information will rest with other departments within the division, such as the plastics-production department, sales department, and engineering department. Therefore, whether Carol will propose the cost-minimizing regulatory investment depends on how difficult it will be to obtain the necessary information and technical support from those departments....

As the discussion of subgoals noted, the specialization of tasks generally increases the firm's efficiency, but at some cost. One of those costs is the creation of barriers to communication of information and expertise across departmental boundaries. Task specialization can impede the free flow of information for at least the following two reasons: misalignment of departmental subgoals and ossification of interdepartmental communication routines.

First, because a department or other subunit is typically focused on attaining its own subgoals, it will make only limited efforts to assist in the pursuit of the subgoals of other departments. In our cost-reduction scenario, neither the engineering nor the sales departments is likely to be concerned with the reduction of environmental-compliance costs.... In fact, the departments may even view the regulatory investment as a direct threat to the attainment of their own subgoals: the project will cause production slowdowns and may affect the quality of the product....

... [T]he MDE production manager will not be interested in reducing all firm costs, but rather only those that are allocated to the MDE process as production costs. If Chemco's management-accounting procedures allocate the operation and maintenance costs of the existing control equipment to the MDE process, then the MDE production manager will be inclined to cooperate with Carol in her quest to reduce those costs. However, if the operation and maintenance costs are allocated to a general overhead account or elsewhere within the firm, the production manager will be significantly less enthusiastic about assisting Carol....

... [M]ost companies do not allocate environmental-compliance costs to the production activities that gave rise to them ... [but rather] to overhead accounts. The survey is consistent with previously reported anecdotal accounts of environmental-cost-accounting practices....

Commentators typically argue that the failure to assign the costs to the process "hides" the costs, making it difficult for environmental managers and production managers to identify and develop likely candidates for cost-reduction efforts. Yet the practice may have a more basic impact. When compliance costs are separated from the production process and consequently from the compensation system, identifying and developing cost-reduction strategies is pointless and even counterproductive for the production manager. In that case, the production manager and staff would be unlikely to devote their limited resources to assisting the environmental manager.

However, even where compliance costs are severed from the process, the resulting dilution of the production manager's incentive to reduce costs may be mitigated ... [E]ven though the overhead account may not be directly associated with the MDE process, it may be associated with the production department at large. In that case, although the MDE-production manager will not view the compliance costs as relevant, the department's manager will have an interest in reducing the costs....

Beyond problems of information flow caused by inconsistent subgoals, effective communication between specialized departments may be difficult as a practical matter. Individuals within a particular department develop a common language and a common understanding of what information and activities are important. This shared departmental culture makes communication with members of other departments more difficult. Together, these factors of disparate subgoals and distinctive subcultures can isolate departments and other subunits from one another.

B. The Allocation Function

The prior subpart of this Article described barriers to the identification and development of regulatory investments, using the potential MDE process change as an example. Of course, even in the traditional hierarchical firm, some regulatory investments will overcome those barriers and secure the attention and sponsorship of the environmental manager. However, that success does not guarantee that the regulatory investments will be made. Rather, the environmental department must now obtain the necessary resources from the firm's internal capital market. In this instance, therefore, we assume that Carol has secured the tacit cooperation, although not the enthusiastic support, of the division's plastics-production department. Armed with financial analysis and a feasibility study, Carol's supervisor, the environmental-department manager, will pursue funding for the regulatory investment in the firm's resource-allocation process. This subpart argues that the project (in its original incarnation as a profit-making investment) is unlikely to survive the competition for capital. This subpart also describes why the project would fare better in the micro-market when cast as a cost-minimizing—rather than a profit-generating— investment.

In a world without constraints on capital investment, microeconomic and finance theory tell us that the profit-maximizing firm should invest in any capital project having revenues or benefits that exceed its costs. In such a world, the firm would either fund projects from internal cash flow, or through new debt or equity. The resource-allocation model assumes that managers in many multidivisional firms live not in that world, but rather in a world in which limited capital is available to subunits for investment. The scarcity of capital results from intentional "rationing" of capital by the firm. For our purposes, rationing has two important consequences. First, the scarcity created by rationing creates competition for funds in the firm's "internal capital market." Second, as a result of this capital rationing, the firm will pass up some potentially profitable capital investments. This subpart argues that regulatory investments face systemic, significant disadvantages in the competition for capital, disadvantages that could result in the disproportionate rejection of ostensibly profitable regulatory investments.

Rationing of capital can take many forms. Corporate management may set a cap on the amount of capital available to each division, thus forcing divisional managers to be more selective in proposing projects to headquarters. Managers may also use stringent hurdle rates to limit capital spending. It appears that rationing is a fairly common practice. Empirical studies over the last thirty years have consistently demonstrated the wide use of capital rationing....

Capital rationing, which is difficult to explain when the firm is viewed as a unitary actor, is a predictable phenomenon when one considers the internal organizational problems caused by asymmetrical information. Division managers, lower level managers, and employees typically have better information than corporate managers regarding the expected return and necessary level of funding for any given project. This disparity in information allows division managers and others to exaggerate the value of a project and/or the level of investment needed to complete the project. The manager may engage in this practice of distorting the value or size of the project so as to divert excess funds (also known as "slack") to the manager's personal benefit. The benefits could take the form of perquisites such as nicer working areas, increased administrative support, or other amenities. Alternatively, the benefit may simply be the expansion of the manager's division, a form of empire building. Absent some method of monitoring or deterring this practice, the firm may consistently over-invest in some projects and under-invest in others. By creating a competition for capital, the firm headquarters can force managers to be more selective in the projects they propose. In other words, all other things being equal, a manager will tend to prefer higher value projects when forced to choose.

Recall that in the profit scenario, Chemco can create emissions credits by making changes to the MDE process and then selling those credits for a significant profit. To obtain funding for the changes, the MDE process-change project will have to move up through the environmental department for initial approval, after which it and other projects from that department will compete at the divisional and finally the corporate level. The MDE project faces its most telling competition at the divisional level. The divisional manager has a limited amount of funds for capital investment, so the environmental department's projects must compete directly for funds against projects from other operating departments in the division. The empirical and theoretical literature on capital allocation identifies several common factors that influence capital allocation decisions by divisional and corporate managers in many large firms: return on investment, nexus to corporate strategy, and influence of sponsoring department. The discussion below argues that in many cases these factors tend to significantly and systematically disadvantage profit-oriented regulatory investments.

1. Return on Investment

The first factor, return on investment, is perhaps the most obvious.... When funds are limited, the rational manager will choose the most valuable projects and reject less profitable ones. In the Chemco case, the success of the MDE project in attracting funding will depend not on whether it is profitable, but whether it is more profitable than competing projects from other departments in the division....

The case study of the Dow Chemical Company (Dow) facility in La Porte, Texas is a stark example of the role of return on investment. In 1996, the Natural Resources Defense Council (NRDC) and Dow ... showed that certain process changes could have eliminated approximately 500,000 pounds of hazardous waste, redirected the remaining waste to other treatment or recycling options, and freed the plant to shut down its hazardous waste incinerator. The changes would have saved the company over one million dollars per year. Dow participants calculated that the project's rate of return ranged from 20% to 70% with a payback period of 15 months to 5 years, depending upon the assumptions used.

Thus, the Dow project had the trappings of the archetypical "win-win" environmental project. Nonetheless, when it moved from the plant-management level to the polyurethane-business-group management for capital funding, it was rejected—twice.... Dow's corporate management allocates a limited amount of capital to each of its fifteen global business units. Accordingly, in 1996 the polyurethane business group established an 86% hurdle rate for new capital projects, a level significantly higher than the 70% expected return for the project....

At the divisional level, many firms break proposed investment projects into categories for purposes of evaluation, such as business expansion, business and asset maintenance, cost reduction, and mandatory regulatory compliance. Projects in the first three categories must compete against one another on financial and other grounds. However, regulatory-compliance projects do not typically compete against the other projects on the basis of financial return. As long as the relevant department has determined that the expenditure is necessary, regulatory-compliance projects will generally be approved. The creation of a separate category for compliance investments is consistent with the view that capital rationing is a self-imposed protective measure rather than a market-imposed restriction on available debt or equity funding. To the extent that some types of investments are viewed as "mandatory" by corporate management, one would expect such investments to be excluded from an essentially discretionary system of investment controls. Thus, if a project can be fit within the mandatory category, it will receive preferential treatment in the micro-market, at least with respect to the return-on-investment factor....

In the Chemco cost-reduction scenario, although the process change would reduce the costs of complying with a law, it is not truly a mandatory project. Chemco was already in compliance with existing regulations. The project simply changes the compliance method in order to reduce compliance costs. This project falls within the "cost-reduction" project category, and would have to compete financially with other non-environmental projects....

2. Influence of the Sponsoring Subunit

In theory, the return-on-investment factor is a bureaucratic decision rule. It provides an ostensibly objective, rational basis for distinguishing between competing projects. There is also a political aspect to the capital-allocation process, sometimes referred to as the "dark side" of internal-capital markets, in which subunits battle on the basis of their relative influence with the decision-maker. Simply put, some departments and divisions are better than others at capturing capital within the micro-market, not because of the relative value of their projects but because of their influence within the firm....

In the Chemco scenario, the power of the environmental department ... depends in large part on the strategic importance of the department as perceived by division managers. The major role of the environmental department in many firms continues to be ensuring compliance with the law and obtaining necessary approvals and permits for the firm's activities. Clearly, these are important activities; lack of an adequate permit can jeopardize the firm's ability to operate at all, and noncompliance exposes the firm to significant fines and remediation costs. However, information from a number of empirical studies suggests that in most firms, neither environmental concerns nor the environmental department are viewed as playing a substantial strategic role in the firm. Despite the operational importance of permitting and compliance, they are often viewed as constraints to be overcome rather than as integral parts of the planning, production, or marketing functions....

3. Nexus to Corporate Strategy

In evaluating a regulatory investment, the division will not limit its evaluation to financial analysis. It will also evaluate how well the project fits the strategic goals of the division and the firm.... As part of the budget process, firms typically attempt to operationalize the concept of profit maximization through business or strategic planning which identifies short-term and long-term goals for the firm, its divisions, and its departments. For these purposes, strategic planning refers to such functions as targeting new businesses or markets; defining competitive strategy; identifying existing businesses to be sold, liquidated, or let run down; and the like. These strategic plans reflect the formal priorities of corporate management and signal to the division managers what is expected of them. In evaluating potential investments, the division managers will generally favor those investments that advance the identified strategic goals, and are more likely to reject or postpone those that are more tangential....

A preference for strategically oriented projects could tend to consistently disadvantage regulatory projects. For example, the generation of profits through emissions trading does little to enhance the strategic goals of the typical industrial firm. Strategic goals generally focus attention and resources on the expansion of existing markets, the development of new businesses, and disentanglement from failing product lines or businesses....

C. Resolving the "Efficiency Paradox"

Application of the resource-allocation model to the traditional hierarchical firm demonstrates that such firms are likely to pass up profitable or cost-reducing projects on a fairly regular basis....

The development and modification of firm routines is path dependent; that is, the scope and nature of a routine is strongly influenced by the historical context in which it began and flourished. The path-dependent nature of firm routines helps to explain the existence and persistence of seemingly inefficient structures and procedures that allow the firm to pass up ostensibly valuable regulatory opportunities. The routines that define the relationship of the environmental function with other firm departments are particularly relevant. Prior to the emergence of broad federal environmental laws in the early 1970s, most companies had no formal environmental function. The emergence of a series of comprehensive environmental statutes and regulations, coupled with significant enforcement activity by the newly created EPA, created a new challenge to industry. In response, firms created internal environmental positions and ultimately entire subunits charged with regulatory compliance. The environmental-management departments were grafted onto the existing organizational structure not for a business purpose, but solely as a result of external regulatory mandates. Other departments typically paid little attention to the environmental department, viewing it as a necessary evil....

Over time, the relationship between the environmental department and operating departments ossified, and the firm routines (such as the accounting practices for compliance costs) became deeply embedded in the firm. Two decades later, when there are ample profit and cost-minimizing opportunities, the established routines and relationships between departments are no longer efficient in an abstract sense. The separation of the environmental function from other departments and the management-accounting practices prevent firms from exploiting those opportunities. Yet changing routines and policies is costly, disruptive, and time-consuming. To the extent that the cost of changing routines is greater than the benefits flowing from the new opportunities, retention of the existing routines would be an efficient response....

Embedded routines are notoriously hard to alter in large organizations absent a crisis or a resulting substantial benefit. For example, altering the management-accounting system to allocate compliance costs to specific processes could affect the resources, status, and compensation of various actors within the firm. New accounting procedures and data-reporting requirements will likely be seen as an unwelcome burden by many accounting managers and line managers. More significantly, shifting costs from pooled overhead accounts to specific processes will alter the bottom line for those processes, creating resistance to the change by those who benefited from the "artificially" high profits under the existing system....

III. The Implications of Opening the Black Box

...

A. *Integrating Regulatory Design and Organizational Research*

If internal features of firms have a significant impact on firm response, then the systematic study of firm organization becomes an essential element of regulatory design. Integration of an organizational perspective into the rule-making process will require evaluation of the specific industry sectors being regulated. For example, in designing a new regulation, the agency would identify the industrial sectors affected and the typical firm structures dominant in the identified sectors. For the last few decades, the literature on environmental regulatory policy has focused largely on the regulations themselves — their failings and strengths — rather than on the regulated entities. Even where analyses of the regulated firms have been conducted, those studies tend to examine the firms' technological processes, financial capabilities, and other features having little to do with the firms' decision-making process. Consequently, there is little empirical information concerning the internal features of the firms — such as information flow, subgoal formation, and resource allocation — relevant to the environmental function. Likewise, regulators have virtually no information about how those features may vary with industry sector, firm size, firm age, and other factors. Although there have been some isolated efforts by researchers to collect empirical data concerning internal firm decision-making processes in the environmental area, regulators have yet to integrate the resulting information or approach into mainstream regulatory policy.

The resource-allocation model can serve as a starting point for a program of research on firm organization and behavior in the environmental-policy context. The model concentrates on the roles that attention, sub-goal formation, information flow, and resource allocation play in shaping firm responses. The Chemco scenarios provide a glimpse of how those internal features could affect responses to regulation in a particular type of firm—the multidivisional, hierarchical firm with centralized corporate management. Although that firm type appears to be the dominant one in this country (at least for the moment), it is by no means the only type. More importantly, even within the general category of "hierarchical firm," there will be variations of structure and process that could affect the response to regulation. Having identified the relevant internal features, future research might attempt to identify how common organizational variations affect firm response and to correlate those variations with particular industry sectors or other identifiable categories of firms.

Organizational research will likely uncover types of firms in which information barriers are less potent. For example, some firms with traditional, functionally organized departments may use cross-departmental teams or other coordination devices to integrate firm activities. In such firms, the lateral flow of information across departments and divisions will likely be more fluid and thus more conducive to interactions between environmental and other departments. Thus, we might expect to see more environmental innovation from "high-tech" Silicon Valley firms because of their shallow hierarchical structure and highly developed cross-functional communication and coordination processes.

Likewise, organizational research may demonstrate that in certain types of firms the environmental department plays a central role with respect to critical workflows within the firm, thus increasing the relative power of the environmental department within the firm....

Organizational theorists have developed a number of firm typologies or classification systems for different purposes. They range from simple systems that classify organizations according to the societal "sector" they serve (for example educational, agricultural, or governmental) to more complex taxonomies that classify organizations on the basis of their structural characteristics, including standardization of routines, concentration of authority, and control of workflow.... A similar approach can be used to construct a general typology of firms based upon the internal features that drive the response to regulation.

Obviously, resource constraints and the sheer number and variability of firms preclude a comprehensive typology in every case.... Nonetheless, even a crude classification of firms on the basis of internal features such as information flow, subgoals, and the like would allow regulators to target incentives more effectively through "tailored regulation." The next subpart defines tailored regulation and describes its potential use in the context of the traditional hierarchical firm.

B. Resource Allocation, Incentives, and Tailored Regulation

Tailored regulation identifies internal barriers to the desired behavior within the firm and attempts to modify the barriers or design around them to achieve the targeted response. Some forms of tailored regulation are already in use within environmental law. The federal Clean Air Act programs contain several structural provisions intended to create or alter systems within firms. In some instances, the regulations require the creation of a new system or process within the firm to ensure that the environmental personnel attend to specific issues. For example, some regulations require that firms develop and implement standard procedures for the operating and maintaining of air-pollution-control equipment or for responding to emergencies. The procedures often require identification of specific individuals, by position, within the firm who are responsible for performing various actions. However, in the past, tailored regulation has been used sporadically.

A tailored approach to regulation could be used in at least two ways. First, tailored regulation may be used as a supplement to a direct regulation or incentive-based regulation in order to remove or minimize barriers to the full implementation of the underlying regulation. Second, a tailored approach may affect the basic choice between types of regulation—that is, selecting between direct regulation and incentive-based regulation.

1. Tailoring Regulation to Firm Structures or Processes

In some circumstances, an internal structure or process will impair the firm's ability to adopt an innovation. For example, in the Chemco cost-minimizing scenario, the firm could have reduced its compliance costs by adopting an innovative production-process change. However, Carol was unable to obtain the necessary information from the production department because the firm's management-accounting practices and compensation system established no incentive for the production engineers to cooperate. The production department would only attend to opportunities that could reduce the costs allocated to that department by the firm's management-accounting system. Tailored regulation could breach this barrier by directly altering the firm's management-accounting process, thus forcing operating personnel to identify production processes and other activities generating high compliance costs. Alternatively, tailored regulation could work around the barrier, creating a new information channel through which the necessary process information could reach Carol.

Although most firms allocate environmental-compliance costs to general overhead accounts, in the last decade, some firms have begun to use "environmental-cost-accounting" methods to allocate such costs to the specific firm activity or product that generates the costs....

Regulators could remove information barriers within firms on a broader scale and more quickly by requiring the use of environmental cost accounting. Alternatively, regulators could establish the use of environmental-management accounting as a prerequisite for participation in desirable regulatory programs. One must recognize, however, that the development and implementation of a new management-accounting system can be expensive and disruptive. Before requiring such a measure for any particular industry or group of firms, regulators should confirm that impaired information flow from the use of overhead accounts is a significant barrier to innovation within that sector or group. This illustrates the usefulness of a framework or typology of firms, which could be used to assist in making that judgment.

Alternatively, tailored regulation could address the issue of impaired information flow by designing around the barrier to create a new information channel within the firm.... Tailored regulation can be used to require interaction between the environmental and operating departments in particular circumstances. For example, as a regular part of permit renewals for emission sources, the firm could be required to perform a technology review and a process evaluation to identify alternative pollution-management strategies. To ensure involvement by the operating staff, the regulation could require certification of the evaluation report by an individual with management responsibility over the process. The ultimate choice of the pollution-management strategy would remain with the firm, but the search and evaluation would be mandatory. Such regulation is consistent with the call by regulatory reformers in industry, government, and academia for performance-based regulation, but adds the search requirement to ensure that innovative approaches are considered. By making the search and evaluation mandatory, the regulation not only "nudges" the environmental manager — it also provides her with additional leverage within the firm in attempting to obtain information from other operating departments.

2. Tailoring and the Choice of Regulatory Tool

In some cases, regulators may be unwilling to impose changes to the internal systems or processes of firms in a particular sector. This may occur where structural changes would create costs for the firms or the regulators that exceed the expected benefits of the regulation. For example, suppose that a new, commercially viable low-emission printing technology is available, but has not been widely adopted by the printing industry. Smaller firms with severely limited financial and personnel resources may simply be unable to attend to regulatory incentives such as tax benefits or emissions credits intended to promote diffusion of the technology. Yet, these same constraints may render the adoption of cost accounting or other systems impractical or even inefficient. Likewise, even in larger, more financially stable printing firms with adequate information flow, the profit opportunities presented by incentives such as tax benefits or emissions trading may not attract internal investment because business strategies direct investment elsewhere.

In both cases, the internal barriers prevent the adoption of the new technology and therefore must be addressed in order to elicit the desired behavior. In either case, the regulators may determine direct regulation requiring use of the new technology is the most effective catalyst for innovation. In the case of the smaller firm, the mandatory nature of the regulation and the associated risk of penalty for noncompliance may garner significantly more attention than a tax credit. Likewise, in the larger firm, the potential regulatory investment would likely overcome the bias in capital allocation towards more strategic projects. The Chemco example, and the capital allocation research on which it is based, demonstrate that investments mandated by regulation are granted preferential treatment in the internal competition for capital.

IV. Conclusion

The resource-allocation model accepts the reality that what goes on within the firm matters. In the case of the innovation debate, the organizational perspective warns that reliance upon profit as a regulatory incentive is a dangerous thing. Although direct regulation relying on cost-minimization is on slightly stronger organizational ground, it still faces significant barriers within the firm. These points suggest a new orientation for regulatory initiatives, one that focuses on internal structure and processes in evaluating and designing regulation.

This Article takes only one step towards integrating organizational analysis into regulatory policy. More work must be done to accomplish that integration. Clearly Chemco is a stylized firm, and the internal environments of actual firms no doubt are considerably messier than Chemco's. Moreover, Chemco reflects the structure and processes of only one, simplified organizational form. Despite these limitations, an organizational analysis of the Chemco scenarios sheds new light on how a firm's internal features could impact the firm's response to regulation in a number of areas, including the selection of regulatory tools, the encouragement of innovation, and the maintenance of compliance. Implementing an organizational prospective more broadly will require significant empirical research across a number of industry sectors in order to develop a typology of firms. That research and the resulting typology then can be used to develop tailored regulation that takes organizational features into account.

Damon Silvers & Heather Slavkin, *The Legacy of Deregulation and the Financial Crisis — Linkages Between Deregulation in Labor Markets, Housing Finance Markets, and the Broader Financial Markets**

This article examines deregulation's contribution to the financial crisis that began in the spring of 2007. We begin with the view that the financial crisis was not an unpredictable, unforeseeable event that landed on the global economy from nowhere. Rather, it was the all too foreseeable consequence of a series of policy decisions made over decades that weakened a carefully constructed economic regulatory structure designed in part to guard the U.S. economy against the consequences of radical instability in the financial markets....

The underlying theory of the article is that weak labor market regulation led to stagnant real wages, growing inequality and falling savings rates even as aggregate wealth and productivity grew dramatically. These trends weakened consumer demand, and led to a variety of pressures to make credit provision easier as a method of bolstering consumer spending and protecting households from the full consequences of stagnant wages. As these trends intensified, financial transactions contributed a larger and larger share of U.S. economic activity, and financial firms contributed more and more disproportionately to overall U.S. corporate profits. In this environment, the political pressures for further financial deregulation were irresistible.

... Our aim is not a comprehensive history, but rather a kind of map of how the deregulatory impulse fed upon itself, and in ways that might not be immediately obvious, made our economy and our society more dependent on unsustainable financial practices, and more vulnerable to the inevitable denouement that followed on the heels of the growth of those practices.

I. Deregulation of Labor Markets

The New Deal and World War II produced a fairly high degree of regulation in both labor and capital markets, augmented by a progressive income tax system. This regulatory structure was designed to prevent the reoccurrence of the Great Depression by ensuring stable, widespread consumer demand through regulated labor markets, and in parallel capital market regulation aimed at meeting the demand for both expensive consumer goods (homes and cars) and for business financing with a minimum amount of instability.

In the area of labor market regulation, the key elements were a legally established system of private sector collective bargaining, a system of wage and hour regulation including the minimum wage and the forty hour week, enforced by the Federal Department

---

* Originally published in 4 JOURNAL OF BUSINESS & TECHNOLOGY LAW 301 (2009). Reprinted with permission.

of Labor, and finally, a progressive tax system. [*The authors argue that all these elements have been significantly eroded by deregulation.*—*Ed.*]

While proving causal connections between legal developments and economic outcomes is treacherous, the weakening of labor market regulation over the past 30 years has been associated in time with labor market outcomes that set the stage for the financial crisis. The past thirty years has been a period of stagnant real wages, with the attendant consequence that increases in household consumption have had to be based on either more intensive participation in labor markets by household members, lower taxes or lower savings, or all three....

Finally, of course, all these developments combined to cause a steady, and ultimately quite significant increase in consumer spending as a percentage of GDP. This increase has been fed by unregulated consumer credit, provided through increasingly opaque capital market structures. Both developments are discussed in the next two sections of this paper. This section has shown how labor market deregulation contributed to an environment of stagnating wages and endangered benefits where policymakers in both parties were interested in finding ways to prop up consumer spending in what was fast becoming a low wage economy.

II. Deregulation of the Residential Mortgage Markets

A. History of U.S. Mortgage Regulation

Congress passed a series of emergency acts in the early 1930s intended to prevent the banking crisis from doing unnecessary damage to the nation's financial infrastructure and spreading further into the real economy. Simultaneously, the federal government began the longer process of regulating the banking, securities and home mortgage markets....

Events in the housing markets in the years leading up to the Great Depression exhibited many of the same qualities as today's markets—the real estate markets were responsible for a disproportionate amount of economic activity, homeownership generally required either very large down payments or the willingness to take on interest only mortgages requiring balloon payments, lenders commonly made loans to borrowers with little regard for their abilities to repay, and speculative borrowers and irresponsible lenders stoked a real estate bubble....

... Congress passed the National Housing Act of 1934, which created the Federal Housing Administration (FHA). In order to stimulate the housing markets, FHA provided mortgage insurance to protect private lenders from losses if the insured mortgage ended up in foreclosure, provided that the loans met criteria defined by federal regulators. In order to qualify for FHA insurance, the mortgage had to meet specific criteria including a 5% interest rate cap and the loans were required to be fully amortizing, so balloon payments and interest only products were prohibited. Four years later, the Federal National Mortgage Association (Fannie Mae), a government-sponsored enterprise (GSE), was created to finance home mortgages in the secondary market....

B. Deregulation of Mortgage Markets

The New Deal system of housing finance lasted until the economic turmoil of the 1970s. Rising interest rates in the late 1970s and early 1980s put pressure on banks and savings and loans (S&Ls), which had long been major providers of real estate loans to U.S. borrowers. Banks and S&Ls were being forced to pay higher interest rates to finance their lending activities but caps on the interest rates they were permitted to charge borrowers made it nearly impossible to operate profitably.

Throughout U.S. history, state usury laws capped interest rates lenders were permitted to charge consumer borrowers, but that changed when Congress passed the Depository Institutions Deregulation and Monetary Control Act of 1980 (DIDMCA), which preempted interest rate caps imposed by states. By preempting state usury laws and in other ways discussed later in this article, DIDMCA began the gradual erosion of regulations that both prevented systemic risk in the financial services industry and protected consumers from predatory creditors.

Two years later, the Alternative Mortgage Transactions Parity Act of 1982 (AMTPA) lifted restrictions on lenders' ability to offer adjustable rate mortgages. The Act gave the primary federal banking regulators exclusive authority to regulate the "alternative mortgage transaction[s]" undertaken by entities under their respective jurisdictions.

According to McCoy and Renuart,

> Federal deregulation permitted lenders to charge a risk premium to less creditworthy borrowers in the form of higher interest rates and fees. Equally importantly, deregulation allowed lenders to market new and more complex types of mortgage products, including adjustable-rate mortgages and loans with balloon payments and negative amortization, which expanded the pool of eligible borrowers and helped lenders control for interest-rate risk.[26]

. . .

C. GSEs—Privatizing Public Institutions

After Fannie Mae was founded in 1938, its success in providing liquidity to the mortgage markets led the government to create additional government-sponsored enterprises (GSEs) to provide mortgage financing, including Ginnie Mae and Freddie Mac. Fannie Mae operated as a government agency during its first 30 years and was only permitted to purchase FHA-insured mortgages. In 1968, Fannie Mae was split into two separate entities—Ginnie Mae and Fannie Mae. Ginnie Mae remained a government agency and was directed to provide mortgage financing for special government projects. Fannie Mae, however, became a "government-sponsored private corporation," owned by public stockholders and run like a public company. The 1968 Charter Act transformed Fannie Mae into a profit-seeking, shareholder owned company, tasked with creating a secondary market for mortgages made to low- and moderate-income borrowers....

The combination of the conversion of the GSEs into for-profit enterprises with the competition they faced from deregulated competitors proved to be an irresistible temptation for the GSEs. Although the GSEs were neither the primary actors in the subprime fiasco nor the cause of the financial crisis, as some conservative commentators have asserted, they did become fatally infected with the disease of overleverage and indifference to risk in the pursuit of unsustainable returns....

---

26. Patricia A. McCoy and Elizabeth Renuart, *The Legal Infrastructure of Subprime and Nontraditional Home Mortgages, in* Borrowing to Live: Consumer and Mortgage Credit Revisited 110 (Nicolas P. Retsinas & Eric S. Belsky, eds., 2008).

D. The Explosion of Subprime Lending

This long-term decline in the regulation of the mortgage industry, and in particular, the boom in unregulated non-GSE financed lending after 2001, set the stage for an explosion of high cost, exotic mortgage products offered to subprime borrowers. In 2001, subprime lending represented 7.2% of mortgage originations but exploded over the next five years until they reached 20% of mortgage originations in 2006. The breakdown of subprime mortgage by type illustrates the prevalence of risky mortgages being offered to less creditworthy borrowers: only 16% were fixed-rate mortgages, 40% were 30-year ARMs, 17% were interest-only loans, 19% were 40-year ARMs, and 8% were balloon loans. In addition, between 2000 and 2005, the number of subprime loans made without full documentation of the borrowers' income, assets or employment climbed from 26% of subprime mortgages in 2000 and by 2005 the portion had grown to 44%.

Subprime mortgages were targeted at communities of color. At the height of the subprime lending activity in 2006, white borrowers took on 71% of new mortgages and 56% of all subprime mortgages, African-American borrowers were responsible for 10% of new mortgage originations and 19% of new subprime mortgages and Hispanic people represented 14% of new borrowers and 20% of new subprime mortgage originations....

E. Conclusions

Deregulation was offered as a solution to the strains placed on regulated mortgage markets by instability in the larger financial system in the 1970s. Despite efforts to rebuild the regulatory system surrounding the mortgage finance system through FIRREA after the S&L crisis, it is clear that the long-run trend since the 1970s has been to weaken mortgage regulation. This long-term weakening accelerated dramatically after 2003 in an environment of very cheap credit and a federal government uninterested in consumer protection regulation. For a time, the mortgage bubble that resulted substituted for a healthy labor market as a source of increasing aggregate demand in the U.S. economy. However, mortgage markets did not exist during this period in isolation. Mortgage markets grew at an enormous pace due to their being able to access capital flows available due to a broader deregulatory trend in the capital markets writ large. But that very deregulatory trend had in it the seeds of a further crisis of opacity that returned to haunt both the mortgage markets and the larger economy in the crisis of 2007–08.

III. Financial Market Deregulation and the Creation of the Shadow Financial System

A. Early Stages of Deregulation

Deregulation affected nearly all areas of the financial markets during the period from the 1980s through 2008. While it is outside the scope of this article to discuss all areas of deregulation, several areas particularly facilitated the flow of funds into mortgage-related assets and led to opacity throughout the financial system.

The histories of the weakening of mortgage regulation and the emergence of the shadow financial system begin at the same point—with the passage of DIDMCA, whose mortgage-related implications were discussed above. DIDMCA established the Depository Institutions Deregulation Committee to phase out interest rate controls on non-checking account bank deposits over a six-year period.

The purposes of DIDMCA included making the cost of capital more equal among depository institutions, leveling the playing field among bank and non-bank financial services providers and allowing consumers access to higher interest savings, and improving public access to financial services and encouraging competition among financial services providers. One of the deregulatory measures used to accomplish this was the removal of caps on interest rates banks could pay on deposits.

Since the late 1970s and early 1980s, there has been a marked flow of funds away from checking and savings accounts, traditionally the only FDIC-insured accounts, and into riskier, higher yielding parts of the financial markets. This began with the rapid rise of interest rates in the 1970s when individuals began moving their savings into higher yielding money market mutual funds.

Traditionally, banks have served as the providers of capital for companies that could not access the public equity and debt markets. The commercial paper market, however, began to erode banks' prevalence in the corporate loan market in the 1970s. From 1970 to 1995 the commercial paper market grew from one-twentieth the size of the commercial bank loan market to one-fifth of the size.

When interest rates began to rise in the late 1970s and early 1980s, depositors took money out of savings accounts and invested in money market funds, which are mutual funds that invest in short-term bonds and provide significant liquidity to investors. Investors viewed money market funds as a high-yield alternative to a savings account.

B. Securitization

Securitization was pioneered by Freddie Mac as a way to increase capital available to finance fixed rate mortgages in the secondary market and provide investors with a moderate-yield, home mortgage backed bond. It later became the tool utilized by lending institutions to access seemingly limitless amounts of capital to finance loans that were too risky for regulated institutions to hold on their balance sheets. [*The term "securitization" refers to the process by which interests in assets (such as loans) are converted into, and sold as, securities. In a mortgage securitization, the owner of many mortgage loans assembles them in a single pool and divides that pool into securities (bonds) which it sells to investors. Historically Freddie Mac purchased loans from banks and securitized them. By purchasing the loans from banks, Freddie Mac provided the banks with capital to make additional home loans. By selling the mortgage-backed securities to investors, Freddie Mac obtained capital that allowed it to purchase more bank loans, perpetuating the cycle. As the article states, when deregulation allowed banks to invest in mortgage-backed securities, it encouraged private institutions to enter the securitization business. This freed up enormous amounts of capital for lending purposes. Widespread securitization of mortgages and other loans has also been blamed for reducing lenders' incentive to police the quality of borrowers, because securitization meant lenders did not hold the loans they originated; instead, they passed the risk of nonpayment on to investors.—Ed.*]

The GSEs pioneered securitization as a means of improving liquidity of mortgage assets and increasing the flow of capital into the markets. Until 1984, however, private financiers were largely prevented from purchasing or owning mortgage-related securities. Congress passed the Secondary Mortgage Market Enhancement Act of 1984 (SMMEA) to allow private financial institutions to invest in MBS. SMMEA included provisions that preempted state laws that would have prevented state regulated banks from investing in privately issued MBS and prohibiting states from regulating private MBS issuances. This set the stage for a dramatic increase in both the supply and demand for securitized debt.

In the mid-1980s, private issuers began securitizing non-mortgage assets to create securities backed by car loans, credit card receivables, corporate loans and other types of assets.

Most securitizations meet the definition of an "investment company" under the Investment Company Act of 1940 and would be regulated like mutual funds if they did not find ways to operate under exceptions to the Act. The Investment Company Act of 1940 ("1940 Act") was enacted to address the differences between direct investments in public companies and participation in pooled investment vehicles. The 1940 Act requires that these pooled investment vehicles be subject to enhanced regulation.

In order to facilitate the issuance of securitized debt, the SEC issued a rule in connection with SMMEA that relaxed the registration requirements applicable to these issuances, generically called asset-backed securities (ABS). In 1992, the SEC expanded its 1984 rulemaking and relaxed registration requirements for non-mortgage ABS and exempted many ABS transactions from 1940 Act registration. ABS are also exempt from anti-fraud provisions of Sarbanes-Oxley that require chief executive officers and chief financial officers of public companies to file attestations with the commission certifying the accuracy of their financial reports. The Commission also issued no-action letters exempting large portions of the securitization market from registration requirements and issued a rule in 2005 codifying these decisions.

The market for securitized debt stimulated the U.S. bond market to nearly double in the last eight years, from $17.20 trillion at the end of 2000 to $33.18 trillion in the third quarter of 2008. The types of debt pooled and sold to investors has expanded to include auto loans, credit card receivables, student loans, commercial real estate loans, and corporate loans. While growth in the debt markets between 2000 and 2008 was led by mortgage-related debt, which exploded by more than 250% during this period, corporate debt was not far behind, having grown 182%.

Securitization of loans to companies purchased in leveraged buyouts provided the necessary capital to finance a boom in leveraged buyouts that coincided roughly with the boom in the subprime mortgage market. U.S. and European leveraged buyout funds, or "private equity", raised $250 billion in 2005 alone, five times LBO fund raising 10 years earlier. According to some estimates, in 2006 new LBO transactions valued at around $500 billion were completed.

As securitization evolved to include riskier types of loans, the structure of securitizations changed with the intent of continuing to provide highly rated securities that institutional investors, especially money market funds and pension funds, would purchase as well as riskier, higher yielding securities to appeal to investors with more appetite for risk. This was accomplished by creating multi-tiered capital structures so that investors that owned interests in different tiers of the structure had different rights to cash flows generated by the pool. In most circumstances, this meant that the highest level or tranche had the senior-most interest in the pool and was paid the lowest interest rate and the junior-most interest holder was paid the highest interest rate.

The end result was that investors owned varying interests in diverse pools of corporate and personal loans that made it difficult, if not impossible, for even the most sophisticated investors to perform proper due diligence. Rating agencies claimed to provide the due diligence necessary to give investors comfort that the securities were safe and secure and the ratings allowed investors, chasing higher yielding assets for their money market funds or pension funds, to buy trillions of dollars of the senior-most tranches of these securities. [*Recall that a mortgage-backed security is an interest in a pool of mortgage loans. In a given pool, the senior-most tranches of securities were to be paid out of the pool first. Theoretically, this meant they faced little risk of nonpayment in the event that some borrowers defaulted on their loans; the riskier, junior tranches would absorb those losses (the higher interest rates paid to junior tranches were compensation for this greater risk). But when the housing bubble burst in 2008, default rates were extremely high, such that many pools could not repay even their supposedly safe senior tranches. Frank Partnoy's article later in this volume further discusses securitization and the role of credit rating agencies.—Ed.]*

C. Shadow Financial Markets

In order for financiers to continue to sell these securities en masse there had to be a market for the most junior tranches. Hedge funds—opaque and unregulated investment pools only saleable to wealthy investors—provided this market.

One of the ways that owners of more junior interests in securitized debt attempt to shield themselves from the risk that the borrowers whose loans are held in the securitized pool will default is through the purchase of unregulated insurance contracts called "credit default swaps" (CDS). According to data from Bank of America published in March 2007, banks and brokers are the largest participants in the CDS market, accounting for 33% of buyers and 39% of sellers. Hedge funds are the second most active participants and account for an estimated 31% of CDS purchasers and 28% of CDS sellers.

Until Congress passed the Commodity Futures Modernization Act (CFMA) in 2000, CDS and other derivatives contracts were subject to the Commodities Exchange Act and regulated by the Commodities Futures Trading Commission. CFMA, however, removed CDS from regulators' purview, allowing the market to grow to as large as $58 trillion by some estimates. The CDS markets became the unseen glue that linked the world's financial institutions to one another and, according to some reports it was Bear Stearns' activities in the CDS markets that led regulators to believe it was too interconnected to fail. [*The same has been said of AIG, a major beneficiary of government bailout assistance.—Ed.*]

All of these factors have contributed to the creation of a huge system of lending, borrowing, securities underwriting, and insurance underwriting that exists completely outside the purview of regulators. The lending, mostly done by unregulated mortgage brokers, the borrowers themselves, the pooling, the entities that bought these assets, and the insurers are, to a large extent, opaque. Neither regulators nor the public have access to sufficient information to assess the risk within these assets or counterparty exposure arising from participating in these opaque markets....

D. The End of Glass-Steagall

Meanwhile, the Federal Reserve had begun chipping away at the Glass-Steagall Act's separation of banking and securities activities in 1987. Over 10 years, the Fed issued a series of regulations that allowed bank subsidiaries to underwrite and deal corporate debt and equity securities. In 1987, bank subsidiaries were limited to transactions in commercial paper and a small range of securities as long as these activities did not account for more than 5% of the subsidiary's gross revenues. By 1997, however, the Fed had broadened the types of securities transactions that could be undertaken by bank subsidiaries, the revenue limit was increased to 25% of the subsidiaries' gross revenues and rules had been lifted that barred banks from marketing the securities services provided by their subsidiaries. This allowed regulated commercial banks to enter the securitization markets in a substantial way and also exposed regulated financial institutions to these unregulated loan pools.

The final nail in the coffin for the Glass-Steagall Act's prohibition of providing banking and securities services within a single entity came in 1998 when the Federal Reserve authorized the merger of Citicorp, a commercial bank, with Travelers Group, Inc., an insurance company that had securities firm Salomon Smith Barney as a subsidiary, to form Citigroup, the first universal bank in the U.S. Citigroup has become the bank that has received the largest amount of TARP bailout funds including $45 billion in preferred stock purchases and a $300 billion asset guarantee.

In 1999, Congress passed the Gramm-Leach-Bliley Act (GLBA), which repealed restrictions on financial institutions' business operations that had been in place since 1933 when Congress passed the Glass-Steagall Act. Glass-Steagall was intended to address conflicts of interest and systemic risk issues that arose from the operation of commercial and investment banking within the same firm. GLBA dismantled the barriers between commercial and investment banking, insurance, and mortgage lending. Once commercial banks were permitted to enter the riskier and more lucrative businesses previously reserved for investment banks, which did not take FDIC-insured consumer deposits, bank holding companies shifted away from consumer lending. As a result, unregulated mortgage brokers moved into the home mortgage business.

IV. Conclusion

This article has attempted to survey the history of deregulation since 1970 in the areas of labor markets, housing finance, and the broader capital markets. We have sought to suggest how weakened labor market regulation creates an environment of downward pressure on aggregate demand. In such an environment, where credit is very cheap, asset-based lending becomes an attractive source of alternative consumer demand. Such a strategy cannot work in a world of financial transparency and comprehensive regulation of leverage and credit quality. Thus another set of pressures comes into being, pressures to create regulatory-free spaces where leverage can be incurred and real risks taken without the expensive backup of capital reserves or the necessity of market actors telling anyone else what they are actually doing. Of course, in a downturn, these shadow markets act as procyclical accelerants to an economic downturn.

The challenge facing policymakers and regulators is how to rebuild an overall system of economic regulation in a global context that can once again channel capital to productive uses without the levels of volatility characteristic of recent years.

Discussion Questions

1. In 2003, the SEC brought a civil action against Merrill Lynch based on various fraudulent transactions involving Enron Corporation. Merrill paid the SEC an $80 million fine to settle the matter. The SEC then filed criminal charges against three Merrill executives. Assuming the $80 million settlement against the Merrill firm reflected the social cost of the firm's conduct divided by the probability of detection (what Arlen refers to as H/p), was it a proper penalty? Why docs Arlen caution that it may not be?

Are individual criminal charges against the firm's executives justified if the firm has already paid a penalty? Would individual charges be justified if the firm had not paid a penalty? Should Arlen's "enforcement costs" theory treat top executives differently from other corporate agents?

2. As Arlen explains, "Under the [federal sentencing] guidelines, corporate criminal fines are based on the greatest of (i) the pecuniary gain to the organization from the offense, (ii) the pecuniary loss to others from the offense (to the extent the loss was caused intentionally, knowingly, or recklessly), or (iii) an amount determined by a table presented in the guidelines."

Why isn't the fine limited to the second measure—the loss caused to others? Why is the loss caused to others measured solely in terms of *pecuniary* losses, as opposed to nonpecuniary harms, and less concrete social harms (such as environmental damage)? Why does the rule require scienter with respect to causing the loss (as opposed scienter with respect to committing the misconduct)?

3. As William Bratton pointed out in Chapter 1, corporate executives tend to be risk-preferring individuals with unusual faith in their own abilities and luck. What does this suggest about how to set the efficient levels of criminal penalties for executives and corporations?

4. The costs of corporate-level criminal fines are ultimately borne by the corporation's shareholders and other stakeholders (such as customers, who may pay higher prices, and workers, who may face pay cuts or job losses). Does this fact make corporate criminal liability unfair if it lacks a *mens rea* element? Does it disable its deterrent power?

5. Arlen criticizes the traditional strict vicarious liability approach to corporate criminality. Because corporate crime is committed by agents, she argues, corporate responses to criminal fines are more complex than those of individuals. Malloy argues that the bureaucratic fragmentation of a large corporation further complicates the way it responds to economic incentives. What implications does Malloy's theory have for Arlen's suggested approaches to incentivizing internal corporate monitoring?

6. Is a corporation's "knowledge" (and "intent") greater or less than the sum of its agents' knowledge (and intent)? Bucy acknowledges that "we cannot fully, completely, and accurately ascertain a corporate ethos." But she also points out that the same can be said of *mens rea* generally—it is impossible to directly prove an individual's state of mind.

Is Bucy's description of a corporation's "collective intent" convincing? Can it be reconciled with Malloy's portrayal of the corporation as a bureaucratically fractured organization? If collective corporate intent cannot be identified, should criminal law reject corporate liability or reject the intent requirement?

7. The "corporate ethos" theory looks at whether corporate policies contributed to the crime. Is "corporate ethos" thus properly viewed as a type of *mens rea*, or is it more akin to a duty of care in creating effective compliance policies—that is, a kind of negligence standard? If the latter, should it be sufficient to support a corporation's *criminal* liability for the acts of its agents?

Even assuming a corporation has an "ethos" or "culture" with responsibility for the illegal acts of individual agents, don't individuals create the "ethos"? Are there reasons to punish the corporate entity instead of (or in addition to) the individuals responsible for the "ethos"?

8. Consider the following hypothetical situation.

In the years immediately after passage of the Sarbanes-Oxley Act, the CEO of GlobalCon Inc. repeatedly made extremely optimistic earnings projections to Wall Street. She demanded that her managers and employees meet those targets. When the corporation's division managers and internal accountants told her the targets were unrealistic, she berated them and called them "lazy," "losers," and "disloyal." She also told them that if they could not meet the earnings projections, the stock price would suffer. "I don't want to hear that it can't be done. I took half my compensation in options to show I mean business," she told the division managers. "If you can't meet the projections, my options will be worthless. That will cost me millions, and it will cost you your jobs."

Several division managers began to tacitly encourage employees to manipulate earnings data. As the practices became widespread, the corporation's reported profits and stock price increased. The managers did not inform the CEO of these practices. In accordance with Sarbanes-Oxley, the CEO certified that the corporation's financial statements were accurate to the best of her knowledge.

GlobalCon's internal and outside auditors did not discover the accounting manipulations until they a GlobalCon officer "blew the whistle" to the SEC two years later. After the revelations, GlobalCon adjusted its earnings reports to show massive losses. The stock lost half its value in a matter of days, its credit rating declined, and it filed for bankruptcy.

Is the CEO responsible for the accounting manipulation? What kind of legal response would best address this kind of CEO behavior? Should criminal liability for securities fraud (or aiding and abetting) extend to her conduct? Why or why not?

Should the corporation be held criminally liable? Does GlobalCon satisfy Bucy's requirement of a criminal "corporate ethos"?

9. The goals of criminal law are commonly said to include deterrence, retribution, and the expression of social condemnation. Which goal is most important? Do you agree with the argument, cited by Coffee, that excessive use of deterrence-based criminal law may lead to a society where "all are safe, but none are free"? Does your answer depend on:

    a. whether the defendant is a corporation or an individual?

    b. whether the crime is a "white collar" crime or a "street" crime?

10. Do you agree with Bucy's argument that strict liability and vicarious liability in the corporate context will be seen as unfair and undermine public faith in government?

11. Suppose a corporation's managers discovered that if they committed certain illegal acts on behalf of the corporation, the corporation would be liable for criminal fines equal to H/p, but would enjoy profits greater than those fines. The managers would be subject to individual criminal penalties, but they would enjoy stock price appreciation and bonuses greater than those fines. Would it be proper for the managers to authorize the illegal acts if they were willing to pay the corporate and personal fines? The orthodox answer is no. Why?

If the managers authorized the illegal acts but were not caught, should they confess and voluntarily pay the fines? Should such a confession and payment be considered a breach of duty to the corporation and its shareholders? Would it make a difference if the violations were:

    a. acts that endangered workers or customers?

    b. toxic dumping?

    c. insider trading that benefited the corporation (and not individual managers)?

12. In large bureaucratic organizations, individual accountability tends to disappear, and individuals thus tend to follow orders rather than take moral responsibility. One set of commentators argues that this can be alleviated by greater "transparency":

> Demanding that corporations disclose their decision making processes, that responsibility be clearly assigned within the organization, that justifications for

corporate acts be explicit and traceable to those making the decisions, could go some way toward ensuring greater individual accountability and, hence, moral responsibility.... if individuals were held to account and knew that they would be, they would be more likely to act within the moral frameworks they bring to the corporations rather than be transformed by it.

Lawrence E. Mitchell & Theresa A. Gabaldon, *If Only I Had a Heart: Or, How Can We Identify a Corporate Morality?* 76 TUL. L. REV. 1645, 1656 (2002). How might this insight be implemented in practice?

13. Bucy and Coffee argue that corporate and "white collar" criminal liability lack coherent logical and moral foundations. If so, are government civil enforcement actions a desirable alternative?

In 2003, the SEC filed civil charges alleging insider trading against Martha Stewart, media personality and CEO of Martha Stewart Living Omnimedia, Inc., and her stockbroker, Peter Bacanovic. Civil and criminal insider trading involve essentially the same conduct. Why do you suppose no criminal charge of insider trading was filed in the Stewart case? (Stewart was ultimately convicted on criminal counts of obstruction of justice and making false statements to investigators. After serving a prison term on those counts, she settled the SEC's civil insider trading action for $195,000 without admitting guilt.)

In what ways do criminal prosecutions, private lawsuits, and government civil enforcement actions differ? What are the relative merits of each approach? When the same conduct violates both criminal law and civil law, what reasons might the government have to pursue civil rather than criminal charges? *See* V.S. Khanna, *Corporate Criminal Liability: What Purpose Does it Serve?* 109 HARV. L. REV. 1477, 1512–20 (1996).

14. In *Bohatch v. Butler & Binion,* 977 S.W.2d 543 (Tex. 1998), the Texas Supreme Court held that a law firm partnership was justified in expelling a partner for accusing another partner of overbilling a client. According to the court, such accusations "whether true or not, may have a profound effect on the personal confidence and trust essential to the partner relationship."

Do Sarbanes-Oxley's whistleblower protections concern themselves too much with uncovering potential misconduct at the expense of confidence and trust within the firm? Or is it proper to strike this balance differently with respect to employees of large corporations than with respect to professionals in a partnership?

15. Baynes argues that although Sarbanes-Oxley purports to protect whistleblowers from retaliation, those protections are insufficient to protect employees against all the potential negative consequences of whistleblowing. Is it possible to do so? Should the law provide positive incentives, such as rewards, to whistleblowers?

Sarbanes-Oxley extends whistleblower protections to employees who "reasonably believe" that a violation of law has occurred. Note that this protection extends not only to those who report suspected securities law violations, but also to those who report suspected violations of mail and wire fraud laws. See Sarbanes-Oxley Act § 806, 18 U.S.C. § 1514A. Consider this in light of Coffee's discussion of the mail and wire fraud laws. What are the benefits and costs of extending whistleblower protection to those who reasonably believe that mail or wire fraud has occurred?

16. The following excerpt from *United States v. Pennington,* 168 F.3d 1060 (8th Cir. 1999), illustrates some of the issues raised in Coffee's article.

In the early 1990s, Donald Pennington was President of Harvest Foods, a grocery store chain. He received secret payments or kickbacks from consultant John Oldner ... based on monies [Oldner] received from Harvest Foods and its suppliers.... A jury convicted Pennington and Oldner of aiding and abetting mail fraud.... Both defendants appeal their convictions.... We affirm both judgments.

In February 1990, Harvest Foods began paying $10,000 per month to Oldner's consulting company.... Shortly after Oldner received each monthly payment, he sent [half of it] to ... a consulting company owned by Pennington ...

In the spring of 1990, another Harvest Foods employee, Scott McPherson, decided to award a supply contract to SAJ, Inc. Pennington intervened, telling McPherson to get Oldner involved because any commission or bonus Oldner received from SAJ could be split among the three of them. Oldner then entered into a consulting agreement with SAJ under which he received a $90,000 bonus [which he split with McPherson and Pennington].... SAJ increased its prices to Harvest Foods by one percent to cover the bonus paid to Oldner.... SAJ's president testified that Harvest Foods paid too much for its purchases under this arrangement.

... To sustain a conviction for aiding and abetting mail fraud, the government must prove defendants knowingly aided and abetted a scheme to defraud in which use of the mails was reasonably foreseeable.... In this case, the government's mail fraud theory was that defendants' kickback schemes deprived Harvest Foods of its intangible right to the honest services of CEO Pennington.

... As a Harvest Foods corporate officer, Pennington owed Harvest Foods a fiduciary duty of loyalty, including the duty to disclose all material information. Yet he never disclosed [the kickbacks he received] to anyone at Harvest Foods; indeed, he concealed the payments by use of a sham corporation, Capitol City Marketing.... [A] mere breach of fiduciary or employee duty may not be sufficient to deprive a client or corporation of "honest services" ... — to be guilty of mail fraud, defendants must also cause or intend to cause actual harm or injury, and in most business contexts, that means financial or economic harm.... However, proof of intent to harm may be inferred from the willful non-disclosure by a fiduciary, such as a corporate officer, of material information he has a duty to disclose.... Here, a reasonable jury could find that the scheme was intended to and did defraud Harvest Foods by depriving it of Pennington's honest services in obtaining the most advantageous supply, brokerage, and consulting contracts that could be negotiated.

Oldner argues he should be acquitted of aiding and abetting a scheme to defraud because there was no proof he knew of Pennington's duty to Harvest Foods. We disagree. The jury could reasonably find that Oldner, an experienced businessman, knew the secret kickbacks to Capitol City Marketing violated Pennington's duty to disclose material information to his employer.

... Pennington ... argues the district court erred in denying him a downward departure because Harvest Foods received a $6,000,000 judgment in its civil fraud action against him for the conduct at issue in the criminal case. The district court concluded that an adverse judgment in a prior civil case involving the same fraudulent conduct is not a permissible basis to reduce the prison sentence for the criminal fraud. We agree....

Is it appropriate that Pennington's conduct was subject to criminal penalties? Is imprisonment appropriate? Is civil liability based on corporate law sufficient to deal with conduct like Pennington's? Why or why not?

Does the same analysis apply to Oldner?

Is it accurate to conclude that criminal liability in this case derives from a breach of fiduciary duty? "Mail fraud" is often criticized as too vague a category of criminal conduct. Would it be more appropriate to explicitly declare breach of corporate fiduciary duty a criminal offense?

17. How does an officer or director's defrauding of a corporation differ from one stranger defrauding another? The latter has long been subject to criminal penalties; is criminal sanction more or less appropriate (or no different) in the corporate setting? Why?

Is a *federal* criminal sanction more or less desirable than allowing the states to have their own regimes?

18. How does corporate criminal liability differ from corporate civil liability? Coffee argues that tort law prices, while criminal law prohibits. How does individual criminal liability "prohibit"? Does *corporate* criminal liability similarly prohibit? If not, how might it do so? *See* Robert Benson, Challenging Corporate Rule: The Petition to Revoke Unocal's Charter as a Guide to Citizen Action (1999).

19. According to Malloy's model of bureaucratic corporate structure, middle- and lower-level decisionmaking in a large business firm is determined by concerns other than maximizing the value of the firm as a whole. Does this model of firm behavior complement or contradict Arlen's "enforcement cost" approach to criminal penalty design?

20. Most selections in this volume focus on the legal characteristics of corporations. Note that Malloy's model turns on the organizational aspects of large business firms, regardless of whether they take the legal form of corporations. Should the law of firm governance be geared to a firm's legal form or to its organizational structure?

As Malloy argues at the end of his article, the differing bureaucratic structures among firms suggest that regulation would be more effective if it were "tailored" to suit different firms. What are the benefits and drawbacks of adopting a tailored approach to regulation? Should traditional aspects of corporate governance law, such as fiduciary duties and securities regulation, be tailored to suit individual firms?

21. To what extent should corporate governance law take into account the differing organizational characteristics of large and small firms? To what extent does the law of corporate governance determine the organizational characteristics of firms? To what extent is the opposite true? Note that within the law of "corporations," there are some significant differences between the law of public corporations and the law of closely held corporations. See Thomas Joo's article in Chapter 7.

22. Criminal liability can implicate the federalism concerns raised in Chapters 3 and 4. In 2001 and 2002, for example, the New York state attorney general initiated prosecutions under state securities-fraud law in several high-profile Wall Street controversies before federal authorities had taken action. In 2003, Oklahoma state authorities were the first to bring criminal charges against Bernard Ebbers, the former CEO of the failed WorldCom corporation. Federal prosecutors and SEC officials complained that the states were acting precipitously and jeopardizing federal investigations. In 2007–2009, New York used its state securities law to force energy companies to make disclosures (not required under federal law) about greenhouse-gas emissions, and to subpoena corporations about subprime lending, executive compensation, and other issues in the absence of action by federal

regulators. Does the theory of "regulatory competition" apply in the context of criminal liability and prosecutorial decisions? Why or why not?

23. The millennial corporate scandals resulted in several criminal prosecutions of top officers, including CEOs. But these were unusual cases in which CEOs were accused of close involvement in the misconduct. In most cases, top officers are too remote from the actual misconduct to justify their prosecution. Recall Professor Rock's argument, in Chapter 3, that Delaware case law probably influences managerial behavior through shaming more than through the actual fear of liability.

One commentator has taken the shaming approach a giant step further, arguing that when criminal liability is imposed on a corporation, the law should require the CEO to appear in court to receive the corporation's sentence. (The federal sentencing guidelines currently permit a judge order such an appearance, but do not require it.) *See* Jayne W. Barnard, *Reintegrative Shaming in Corporate Sentencing,* 72 S.CAL. L.REV. 959 (1999). Does this approach seem useful? Is it justified if the CEO has not been personally charged or convicted? What are the pros and cons of this approach as a method of deterrence and of punishment?

24. Silvers and Slavkin document the intricate regulation of the banking industry which was largely undone beginning in the 1980s. What justifies intrusive regulation of an industry? Is corporate governance law a form of industry regulation? Is industry regulation a form of corporate governance law? Silvers and Slavkin identify stagnant wages, themselves the result of labor-market deregulation, as a major cause of the deregulation of the financial sector. Is labor market regulation also an aspect of corporate governance law?

Can you define corporate governance law to exclude industry and labor regulation, as well as environmental, tax, tort, and other areas of law?

25. Malloy argues that profit incentives alone are insufficient to cause emissions trading to spur innovations in pollution control. According to his theory, the organizational characteristics of corporations might cause them to ignore the profit opportunities of emissions trading. When this book went to press in 2009, the U.S. House of Representatives had passed a bill that would establish an emissions-trading regime for greenhouse gases. If the U.S. adopts an emissions trading regime for greenhouse gases, do you think Malloy's skepticism would apply?

Chapter 7

Shareholder Voice

Orthodox scholarship identifies the "separation of ownership and control" as the central problem of large corporations in the U.S. Shareholders have little ability to monitor or discipline the conduct of the professional managers who control the corporate assets. In many other countries, the separation of ownership and control is largely absent because large corporations tend to have a shareholder (usually a financial institution) whose stake is large enough to give it significant control over the corporation. Mark Roe's article in this chapter argues that the pronounced separation of ownership and control in American corporations is the result of political forces in U.S. history rather than local economic conditions.

Bernard Black argues that large institutional shareholders may be able to mitigate the separation of ownership and control in American corporations. While retaining the traditional American skepticism of institutions as controlling investors, Black argues that institutional investors, unlike individuals, have the potential to monitor corporate management, even if they hold less than a controlling stake.

Some academic commentators question the standard characterization of the separation of ownership and control as a "problem." Rather, they see it as a *solution* to the problem of managing a large organization with a multitude of owners: centralized, professional management can do a better job if it is free from the interference of non-expert shareholders. Roberta Romano represents that view here. In contrast to Black, she argues that the rise of institutional investor voice does not solve the agency cost problem, but rather presents new problems. Institutional shareholder participation in corporate governance should not be expanded but restricted, she argues, because it imposes costs on the corporation without increasing corporate value.

Leo Strine is skeptical of monitoring by institutional intermediaries for different reasons. He argues that the main categories of institutional investors—mutual funds and pension funds—have peculiar incentives that conflict with those of their investor beneficiaries.

The next two selections in this chapter examine the effect of shareholders' weak voice on corporations' reflection of values other than shareholder wealth. Daniel Greenwood challenges the view that corporate wealth alone defines shareholders' interest in the corporation. This view, he argues, ignores the fact that shareholders are real human individuals who hold other values as well. As Professor Dallas argued in Chapter 1, corporate constituents engage in a political struggle over the priorities of the corporation. As Greenwood points out, however, the corporate governance regime prevents shareholders from making corporate conduct reflect values other than wealth. Thomas Joo's discussion of corporate campaign finance argues that a corporation can be the streamlined engine of wealth that Romano favors, or the participatory and expressive organization that Greenwood favors, but it cannot be both. Large public corporations invariably choose to be the former. Joo argues that this makes their participation in campaign finance fundamentally different from individual participation for First Amendment purposes.

In the debate over whether the separation of ownership and control is a problem or a solution, both sides tend to assume the public corporation exists to serve its shareholders. Ronald Gilson and Charles Whitehead bring this chapter to a close with a contrary view: corporations may be outgrowing their need for public shareholders. Reversing the traditional shareholder-centered perspective, they argue that business enterprises needed public shareholders to bear general undefined risks of enterprise. As developments in financial technology (derivative instruments, in particular) enable firms to sell more specifically defined risks, they argue, public shareholders have become less necessary to corporate finance and thus to corporate governance.

Mark J. Roe, *A Political Theory of American Corporate Finance*[*]

... Why is the public corporation—with its fragmented shareholders buying and selling on the stock exchange—the dominant form of enterprise in the United States? Since Berle and Means, the conventional corporate law story begins with technology dictating large enterprises with capital needs so great that even a few wealthy individuals cannot provide enough. These enterprises consequently must draw capital from many dispersed shareholders. Shareholders diversify their own holdings, further fragmenting ownership. This combination of a huge enterprise, concentrated management, and dispersed, diversified stockholders shifts corporate control from shareholders to managers. Managers can pursue their own agenda, at times to the detriment of the enterprise.

In the classic story, the large public firm survived because it best balanced the problems of managerial control, risk sharing, and capital needs. In a Darwinian evolution, the large public firm mitigated the managerial agency problems with a board of directors of outsiders, with a managerial headquarters of strategic planners overseeing the operating divisions, and with managerial incentive compensation. Hostile takeovers, proxy contests, and the threat of each further disciplined managers. Fragmented ownership survived because public firms adapted. They solved enough of the governance problems created by the large unwieldy structures needed to meet the huge capital needs of a modern technology. In the conventional story, the large public firm evolved as the efficient response to the economics of organization.

I argue here that the public corporation is as much a political adaptation as an economic or technological necessity. The size and technology story fails to completely explain the corporate patterns we observe. There are organizational alternatives to the fragmented ownership of the large public corporation; the most prominent alternative is concentrated institutional ownership, a result prevalent in other countries. But American law and politics deliberately diminished the power of financial institutions to hold the large equity blocks that would foster serious oversight of managers, making the modern American corporation adapt to the political terrain. The modern corporation's origin lies in technology, economics, *and* politics.

Shareholder control of managers arises when the owner holds a large block of stock. Individuals rarely have enough money to buy big blocks. Institutional investors do. But law creates barriers to the institutions' taking big blocks. Banks, the institution with the most money, cannot own stock. Mutual funds generally cannot own control blocks of stock. Insurance companies can put only a fragment of their investment portfolio into the

---

[*] Originally published in 91 Columbia Law Review 10 (1991). Reprinted with permission.

stock of any one company. Pension funds own stock, but they also face restrictions. More importantly, corporate managers control private pension funds, not the other way around.

And we have just exhausted the major financial institutions in America; none can readily and without legal restraint control an industrial company. That is the first step of my argument: law prohibits or raises the cost of institutional influence in industrial companies.

The second step is to examine the politics of corporate financial structure. Many legal restraints had public-spirited backers; some rules would be those that wise regulators, unburdened by politics, would reach. But many important rules do not fit into this public-spirited mold. Examining financial regulation through the lens of the new public choice literature reveals a complex and new political story, of law repeatedly foreclosing alternatives to the Berle-Means corporation.

Opinion polls show Americans mistrust large financial institutions with accumulated power and have always been wary of Wall Street controlling industry. Politicians responded to that distrust by enacting rules restricting private accumulations of power by financial institutions. Various interest groups also benefited from fragmentation; Congress and the administrative agencies also responded to them....

An inquiry into the interplay of political ideology and financial institutions follows. We shall examine the ideas of opinion leaders and political actors, and the content of major political investigations, leading us to speculate on a political explanation for corporate structure: Main Street America did not want a powerful Wall Street. Laws discouraging and prohibiting control resulted.

I. Berle and Means

Berle and Means' vision is central to corporate law scholarship. Their story is straightforward: "[T]he central mass of the twentieth-century American economic revolution [is a] ... massive collectivization of property devoted to production, with [an] accompanying decline of individual decision-making and control [, and a] massive dissociation of wealth from active management." This restructuring turns corporate law on its head: stockholders, the owners, become powerless. The stockholder's vote "is of diminishing importance as the number of shareholders in each corporation increases— diminishing in fact to negligible importance as the corporations become giants. As the number of stockholders increases, the capacity of each to express opinions is extremely limited." As a result, corporate wealth is held by shareholders as a "passive" investment while managers control the corporation.

The problem is not solely the separation of shareholders from managers or, as Berle and Means put it, the "massive dissociation of wealth from active management." The problem is atomization. Most public companies are held by thousands of shareholders, each with only a small stake....

Modern writers blame corporate mismanagement on shareholders, who they say value short-run profits excessively, to the detriment of the nation. They claim that managers would take the long-view but are stymied by Wall Street's short-run goals; companies shun long-term investment, and industry underinvests in research and development.

The long/short controversy posits a market failure. After all, institutions should know how to discount long-term value to present value. While no one has *demonstrated* that the long/short phenomenon exists, consider the effect of fragmentation. Fragmentation diminishes the value to a single shareholder of assessing long-run soft information not reflected in the hard numbers of current financial statements. To assess long-term research and development plans often requires staff or consultants with specialized expertise. If there are scale economies in evaluation, then a fragmented shareholder may rationally decline to incur the cost....

Imploring an owner of $10 million of the stock of a $10 billion industrial firm to be an active shareholder is useless. The shareholder can capture only 1/1,000 of the corporation's gain. The shareholder should rationally decline to invest $100,000 of his or her time and wealth, even if that $100,000 would yield a $100 million gain *for the corporation.*

But a 25% shareholder could invest millions of dollars in monitoring and in costly evaluation of soft research and development information....

Moreover, management would more willingly reveal proprietary information to the large long-term shareholder, who has the incentive to maintain secrecy. The large shareholder would protect secrets *and* protect managers from outsiders who would second guess truly profitable long-run investments. If an owner could take 25% stock positions in a few firms, it might find it worthwhile to assemble a staff with the expertise to monitor effectively. Finally, managerial motivation to pursue wealth-maximizing operating policies could change for the better if managers knew that a 25% block was already assembled, even if the owner was inactive day-to-day; managers would realize that deviation from long-run profitability could activate the large-block holder, or activate an outsider who would find it easy to buy the control block. Financial economists argue that large block shareholding improves corporate operations.

Few of the largest public firms are controlled by a holder of a substantial block of shares. Few individuals have the wealth to take that large a position. Although banks, insurance companies, mutual funds, and pension funds have enough money, they do not take large positions.

Possibly financial institutions do not because they believe they would fail to be effective. But examples from the past offer tantalizing prospects. General Motors—the largest American industrial corporation—today has no controlling shareholder. But once it had one. Du Pont owned 25% of GM until the courts ordered antitrust divestiture. In the 1920s, an ineptly managed GM neared bankruptcy. Its management was reinvigorated by neither a proxy fight, nor a hostile takeover, nor a leveraged buyout in reaction to the prospect of a takeover, but by the intervention of its large shareholder. Pierre du Pont moved to Detroit, reorganized the company, and installed new managers. Similarly, the J. P. Morgan investment bank monitored many of the country's railroads when reorganizing them at the turn-of-the-century.

II. The Financial Institutions: Who Has the Money and What Can They Do with It?

Four types of financial institutions dominate: commercial banks, mutual funds, insurance companies, and pension funds. They have assets, respectively, of $3.2 trillion, $548 billion, $1.8 trillion, and $1.9 trillion.

Clearly these financial institutions have enough assets to influence large corporations. But portfolio rules, anti-networking rules, and other fragmenting rules disable them from systematically taking control blocks. Demonstrating this requires regulatory detail, but the rules can be summarized quickly for those who do not want the detail: Banks and bank holding companies were repeatedly prohibited from owning control blocks of stock or from affiliation with investment banks that did. Insurance companies were for quite some time prohibited from owning any stock, and portfolio rules still restrict their ability to take control. Mutual funds cannot deploy more than a fraction of their portfolio in a concentrated position; buying more than 5% of a company triggers onerous rules. Pension funds are less restricted, but they are fragmented; rules make it difficult for them to operate jointly to assert control. Private pension funds are under management control; they are not constructed for a palace revolution in which they would assert control over their managerial bosses.

... Politics never allowed financial institutions to become powerful enough to control operating companies. American politics destroyed the most prominent alternative to the Berle-Means corporation: concentrated institutional ownership....

The conclusion of all this is that legal decisions deeply influenced corporate structure. Some influence was direct: prohibitions on banks and bank holding companies—the institutional players with half of the money—from owning and controlling, prohibitions on insurance companies from owning stock for a half-century and now limiting their ownership, and tax penalties on mutual funds owning control blocks. And some influence was indirect: (1) fragmented investors talking to one another must act through the SEC's proxy machinery; (2) schedules have to be filed with the SEC; (3) groups that own 10% or more of an industrial company's stock risk imposition of 16(b) liability, forcing disgorgement of any short-swing profits; and (4) an institution wishing to obtain influence and control will be subject to enhanced duties and liabilities.

Just as important as these prohibitions and costs are social constraints and *fear*: fear that a successful effort at control [by financial institutions] will trigger a political reaction. If the political system will turn on the controllers anyway—and worse yet, if control would risk overregulation in response—then those who might overcome the legal obstacles could decline the added risk of political reaction. Social constraints—the view that control by institutional investors is improper—also have a role. These social constraints may themselves be the result of political and legal conditioning.

Furthermore, when the Glass-Steagall Act and the [Investment Company Act] severed financial institutions from one another, the law eliminated an easy coordinating link.[1] Influence on operating companies could have come through internal coordination in a financial institution that would (1) underwrite the industrial company's securities, (2) own a big block of its stock directly, (3) own a big block of stock indirectly through an affiliated commercial bank's trust department, (4) own stock through a sponsored mutual fund, (5) own stock through an affiliated life insurance company, and (6) also own stock in a pool of pension fund assets managed by the financial institution. Such financial supermarkets are impossible to build in the United States.[2]

---

1. *The Banking Act of 1933 (commonly known as the Glass-Steagall Act) prohibited a financial institution from performing both commercial banking services (such as taking deposits and making loans) and investment banking services (such as underwriting and dealing in securities). The Investment Company Act of 1940 required separation between mutual funds' management and the management of the companies in which the funds invest. —Ed.*

2. *Since 1991, when this article was written, a great deal of banking deregulation has occurred through administrative actions, judicial interpretations, and legislation. In particular, the Financial Services Modernization Act of 1999 (the "Gramm-Leach-Bliley Act"), repealed parts of the Glass-Steagall Act, eroding the enforced separation between commercial and investment banking. See the article by Silvers*

That nexus of relationships does exist in Japan and Germany; elements of that nexus appeared in the banking networks of J. P. Morgan, Chase, and National City during the beginning of this century. Indeed, an internal network might function better than an external network of several financial institutions talking to one another, or acting jointly through a leveraged buyout fund. Monitoring requires staff and specialized expertise; when the institutions fragment, they lose scale economies of staff and expertise.

Whether these internal networks are good or bad is worthy of discussion: the networks could siphon resources for banker profit and still fail to monitor managers effectively. Or, the networks could represent politically intolerable concentrations of economic power. But the point here is not to evaluate the networks. The point is that politics either makes them costly or prohibits them.

Hence, the first step in my argument is that portfolio rules guide the uneasy relationship between financial institutions and industrial companies: financial institutions can shuttle capital in and out of industrial companies, but rarely can they exercise controlling influence.

III. Elements of a Political Theory

The second step in my argument is that these portfolio rules are not solely the result of political drift or public-spirited laws; behind them lies an array of political forces that helped determine and maintain them. Public choice theory helps explain the ownership structure of the public corporation. There were winners in fragmenting financial institutions. These winners had a large voice in Congress and their goals matched public opinion.

Public choice is about politicians making decisions. Politicians advance their careers, their ideologies, their chance to win the next election by the decisions they make. Popular ideology made it easy for politicians to fragment financial institutions; if the politician believed that was the best result, the voters would impose no penalty. Interest groups also pressured politicians to fragment financial institutions.

The simplified political picture I shall use is of politics as the interplay between selfish economic interests and ideology on the playing field of the nation's institutions. Policy choices depend on ideology and interest group power, each of which is impeded or enhanced by existing political institutions. American federalism magnified the power of fragmented financial institutions; fragmented financial institutions did not want to compete with large, powerful financial institutions; politics helped small financial institutions maintain themselves as winners. Neither interest group power nor ideology alone appears strong enough to have fragmented ownership patterns. Together they achieved financial fragmentation....

A. *The Political Story: Ideology*

1. Populism

... Anger at large institutions that seem to control the average person's life is one element of the political story. In recent decades anger against large institutions has been directed at government, particularly government in Washington. Earlier it was directed

---

& Slavkin in this volume. Nonetheless, deregulation has not progressed so far as to allow the creation of "financial supermarkets" as comprehensive as those found in Germany. — Ed.

at financiers, particularly Wall Street financiers, and big business. At the end of the nineteenth century the populist movement, which had farmers at its core, gave the impetus to passage of the Sherman Antitrust Act, formed its own political party, and captured the Democratic Party. It reflected deep, widespread sentiments....

By populism, I mean more than the 1890s political movement. I mean to refer to a widespread attitude that large institutions and central accumulations of economic power are inherently undesirable and should be reduced, even if the concentration serves a useful productive function. That notion of populism is familiar to students of antitrust, and has been an important American ideology from nearly a century before the populists—first called Jeffersonians—to today....

2. Political Investigations

The [Pujo investigation, an] eight-month 1912 Congressional investigation [of Wall Street's financial workings] was said to have "frightened the nation with its awesome, if inconclusive statistics on the power of Wall Street over the nation's economy. [T]he nation was suitably frightened into realizing that reform of the banking system was urgent—presumably to bring Wall Street under control." Counsel to the committee attacked J. P. Morgan for his bank's representation on corporate boards and for its hand in selecting managers.

... The New Deal began with a seventeen-month investigation of banking and securities practices on Wall Street.... Ferdinand Pecora, counsel to the Senate Banking Committee for the hearings, ... reflected the national mood: "[T]he terrific concentration of power in [bankers'] hands from many sources [was] threatening.... The bankers were neither [just] a national asset nor [just] a national danger—they were both." Investment bankers' control over industrial companies was again denounced; representation of banking interests on the boards of industrial companies perniciously magnified banker power.

The Pecora hearings were a conduit for populist sentiment to punish Wall Street, presumably with legislation such as the Glass-Steagall Act and the Investment Company Act of 1940 ...

3. Ideological Leaders and a Conceptual Framework for Political Restraints: Brandeis, Wilson, and Douglas

The Pujo investigation gathered data and concluded that a Wall Street money trust dominated industrial America. But historians believe that the investigation might not have influenced later legislation had Louis Brandeis not picked through the data and quickly published popular magazine articles and a book, providing both an ideology and a plan for action. Brandeis wrote: "The dominant element in our financial oligarchy is the investment banker. Associated banks, trust companies and life insurance companies are his tools."[3] Return bankers to their proper role as middlemen and eliminate the interlocking of financial institutions; that would end the evils of the oligarchy.

Woodrow Wilson believed small groups of people in large corporations made autocratic decisions, concentrating in their own hands the "resources, the choices, the opportunities, in brief, the power of thousands".... "If there are men in this country big enough to own the government of the United States, they are going to own it"....

---

3. LOUIS BRANDEIS, OTHER PEOPLE'S MONEY—AND HOW THE BANKERS USE IT 3 (1914).

William O. Douglas had a pivotal role in the regulation of financial institutions, as commissioner and chair of the SEC in the 1930s. During his days as commissioner, the SEC proposed the Investment Company Act and formulated rules limiting joint action. Undoubtedly reflecting the concepts and prejudices of many during that crucial time, Douglas *wanted* to destroy any Wall Street control of Main Street:

> [T]he banker *will* [be] restricted to ... either underwriting or selling. Insofar as management [and] formulation of industrial policies ... are concerned, it is my belief that *the banker will be superseded.* The financial power which he has exercised in the past over such processes will pass into other hands.

... In short, bankers should provide and direct the flow of capital, but not control the enterprise after the capital has flowed to it. Douglas was not alone in this view among the key players at the 1930s SEC; its first chair, Joseph Kennedy, agreed. And this view is not just historical. In 1980, the Senate Government Affairs Committee's staff examined corporate ownership and reported that "Congress [has been] concerned that the tremendous growth in securities held ... by the larger banks, insurance companies, pension funds, and investment advisors might result in a concentration of economic power by a few institutional traders ... *over the managements of the companies whose stock they held, and indeed over American industry itself.*"

4. Ideology: Public-Regarding Goals

Neither populist ideology nor interest group power explains everything; fragmentation had public-regarding justifications.... Keeping banks out of risky assets such as common stocks seemed to reduce the riskiness of their investments, thereby reducing the chance of bank failure. Similar considerations of policyholder protection and ease of government supervision justify limiting insurance company investment in stocks....

Elimination of the potential for conflicts of interest was another public-spirited justification for fragmentation. Banks with nonbanking affiliates would be difficult to examine, and problem assets could be shunted between bank and operating company. Conflicts of interest and monopoly power could be reduced by restricting the activities of bank affiliates....

... [In addition,] some politicians and the general public believed that monopoly capital restricted new ventures, and that the best way to open the bottlenecks was to eliminate banker control of industry. A handful of investment bankers controlled the spigots of finance....

A prominent historical view is that at crucial times in American history, business interests became so powerful that a political counterweight had to arise. Before business could crush others in the economic system, politicians saved the nation from injustice by checking the business interests. The genius of American politics was, in this view, that business interests were checked, but not destroyed. First, it is said, Andrew Jackson rose to destroy the Second Bank of the United States, checking the crushing weight of eastern finance on the average American. Then, Woodrow Wilson created a Federal Reserve System, taking power away from Morgan who had become the nation's de facto central banker. And then, in the Great Depression, Franklin Roosevelt built an administrative structure as a counterweight to financial interests that were said to have brought on the Depression....

Thus, one can see the historical bargain between the policy and financial institutions as this: unleashed capital, with disciplined control of the enterprise had to have a political counterweight. Either government would ultimately have to own companies directly or it would place strict public controls on them....

... I emphasize that I am not arguing that the American fragmentation result is necessarily wrongheaded; the sharp point is precisely that through politics America chose, perhaps wisely, to fragment financial institutions. That fragmentation induced, partly unintentionally, a shift in operating power from financial institutions to the managers of the largest corporations. Other countries have chosen (or accidentally evolved) to have power shared in the boardroom or to have severe restrictions on the range of acceptable actions by managers. The essential point is that the Berle-Means corporation is a product of American politics, not just American economics.

B. The Political Story: Interest Groups

I first sketched populist antibank sentiment for a reason. It is the backdrop to the interest group pressures for fragmentation. Popular opinion might not have been strong enough to generate and preserve fragmenting rules, but policy makers could see that fragmentation would foster plausibly public-spirited goals and interest groups could press their advantage. A politician who sought fragmentation, whether to implement public goals or to deliver to an interest group, would not meet public resistance.

Interest group pressures were critical. Small financial institutions were the most important interest group militating for fragmenting finance. Small banks wanted to fragment large money-center institutions. Small businesses also wanted fragmentation, believing that small banks served them better than large ones. These groups have had great weight in Congress....

... [O]nce fragmenting legislation passed, even if it passed without managers as necessary supporters, the *subsequent* stability of fragmentation probably has been due to managers as an interest group. Decades after passage, managers would oppose changes in fragmenting laws and would throw their weight in the way of change. When large financial institutions clash with managers, managers call upon politicians for aid, as they did when proxy contests heated up in the 1950s. Managers appealed to politicians to raise the costs of proxy contests, the Senate held hearings, and the SEC responded by promulgating rules that pulled informal joint discussions among institutions into the proxy ambit. News reports showed managers' complaints getting a sympathetic response from journalists and politicians. Modern political inquiry suggests that managers, sometimes allied with labor, are moving forces behind many antitakeover statutes....

One can see a historical sweep to this. Once a position is obtained, whether by the beneficiaries' own doing or as the incidental beneficiary of other political forces, the occupants of those positions seek through politics to maintain and extend that position. So one could expect to see managers and labor seeking to loosen the disciplinary restraints that capital would impose upon them. Or, more subtly and more realistically, laws that would loosen the control capital would have on managers and labor have survival properties; their repeal would be unpopular, and would lose the politician votes. Those laws remain stable, shielding managers and workers from the raw and unpleasant consequences of an unrestrained market....

C. The Political Story: The Preexisting Institutions of Federalism, Congress, and the Bureaucracies

American politics created elements of its fragmented financial system unintentionally. Federalism fragmented banks; and federalism and the structure of Congress enhanced the political power of those that would further fragment finance. The ideological forces and the interest groups pressures played out in a political system that already had fragmented the banks.

1. Federalism

America's fragmented federal political system induced a fragmented banking system. Each state regulates its own state banks; national banks are regulated under the National Bank Act of 1863. Until the 1980s, most states protected local bankers from out-of-state entry. So when large enterprise emerged in the nineteenth century, few banks then had the resources to finance large enterprises. Thus, fragmented politics induced fragmented banking, making far-flung stockholders and not banks the best source of risk capital at the turn of the century. Law then reduced the chances of consolidation in financial institutions that might provide concentrated risk capital. Moreover, the fragmented banking system created interest groups—local bankers with money in their pockets and political influence—who wanted to maintain the status quo.

Similarly, the federal structure favored the political forces that wanted fragmentation. Farmers and small-town bankers have been disproportionately represented in the Senate. Their economic interests and ideology made them favor financial fragmentation....

2. Bureaucracy

A political elite in Washington, of agency bureaucrats and some members of Congress, might have wished to fragment business elites. If Wall Street could not control industrial enterprises, political elites in Washington would have more room to maneuver. Politicians might have recognized that a financial-industrial coalition would have been powerful. If at crucial moments political actors had the upper hand and could permanently change the rules and sever finance capital from industry by making financial control difficult or impossible, financial-industrial coalitions would be weaker....

3. Inertia

Social phenomena can occur without an apparent *intentional* causative agent. A rule must be chosen, so this rule is chosen. The exact contrary also could have been chosen. For example, Senator Carter Glass changed his mind a few years after the Glass-Steagall Act severed investment from commercial banking. Investment banks, he then thought, could not satisfy industry's capital needs without an affiliated commercial bank. Evidence suggests that populists and the forces of small-town bankers in Congress in 1933 really wanted federal deposit insurance, not severance. In the hope of defeating deposit insurance, various money-center bankers and politicians supported severance, not because they really wanted it but because they hoped to head off deposit insurance. What if Carter Glass had changed his mind before Glass-Steagall passed, or the deposit insurance negotiations had taken a different path?

Many argue that the initial severing of American banks from commerce was copied without reflection from English precedent.... Legal elites lack imagination to create and prefer to borrow legal frameworks.... But the long-run consequence of separating banks from commerce was apparent neither in England in 1694 nor when copied and recopied in America, because the large firm had yet to emerge....

IV. An Evaluation

A. *The Mechanisms of Monitoring*

I should briefly sketch how institutional monitoring might work. After all, the monitoring financial institutions of which we speak are themselves Berle-Means corporations. Why should they not succumb to the same agency problems that affect the Berle-Means industrial corporation?

Realistically, they often will succumb. But as long as their agency difficulties do not correlate with those difficulties afflicting the industrial companies in which they own stock, beneficial monitoring could occur....

Even if the monitoring institution would usually be *worse* than the industrial company in making corporate decisions, monitoring still could improve performance, if the monitor specialized, only intervening when it was likely to be better than the operating firm managers. I categorize three potentially beneficial forms of monitoring: hierarchal, collegial, and probabilistic.

Hierarchal monitoring could occur if specialized units of financial institutions have industry expertise. The managerial literature suggests that managers overbuild enterprises for prestige and power. But financial institutions controlling an oil company, for example, might well be less susceptible to continuing to drill for oil when it was no longer profitable. The financial institutions could be concerned more directly than the oil company managers with the cash flowing out of the enterprise; the oil company managers might be more concerned with the power and size of their company. If the managers at the financial institution did not themselves become infected by the day-to-day excitement of the oil business, they might then make more objective decisions that would reduce the operating managers' wastefulness.

Collegial monitoring is different. No financial institution commands the operating company; instead, operating managers and financing managers seek consensus. The financing monitor does not need to have superior information, or less bias when evaluating the available information....

Collegial monitoring seems to occur in Japanese conglomerates, where banks and industrial companies own one another and meet regularly to exchange ideas to reach consensus.... A single large shareholder would find it more worthwhile to understand the value of the portfolio company's investments than do the stock market's scattered shareholders.

Probabilistic monitoring is generally nonintrusive. Day-to-day the financial institution does nothing. When operating results are poor, the monitor judges whether managerial misfeasance has caused the poor results. If so, the monitors would obtain the early retirement of the responsible managers. For probabilistic monitoring to be worthwhile, the monitors need not fully understand the industry. They must only be able to identify poor results and understand whether poor management probably caused the poor results. The replacement mechanism might be direct—a conversation with senior managers, in which the financial institution suggests early retirement—or indirect through a takeover. Takeovers to replace management are easier when a large block is preassembled and the offering company can negotiate with large blockholders over the terms of transfer.

Institutional monitoring can be useful even if it would not improve the management of all corporations. Many companies would find institutions insufficiently entrepreneurial; institutions could be worse managers on average, as I suspect they would be. But as long as institutional monitoring would *sometimes* be superior, its prohibition and regulation is costly. Corporations and monitors should sort themselves out: those corporations that would benefit from institutional monitoring would tend to be monitored by institutions; those needing entrepreneurial leaders should tend not to be institutionally controlled.

B. Weaknesses in the Securities Markets

Thus far I have treated the operating firm as the weak link, and raised the prospect that strong financial institutions might beneficially monitor the firm. But the efficiency issues are not solely those of monitoring. The *securities markets* might be the weak link. The fragmentation of institutions and their portfolios may weaken the securities markets and their debilities might be transmitted to operating firms, weakening them.

I have already given one possibility [above]. Scale economies in securities research could plausibly debilitate securities markets from accurately assessing operating firm's long-term outlook. If expertise and staff are needed, a large holding might be necessary over which the costs of research would be spread. But if portfolio rules put a ceiling on the size of holdings, that staff may never be assembled. Large blocks would facilitate the flow of soft, technological information from the company to the large blockholder. If the securities markets undervalue long-term research and development because they cannot understand it, for example, then so will many managers who fear a takeover. Rules that prohibit or make costly the long-term positioning of large blocks of stock make it difficult for institutional shareholders and their companies to develop stable relations; shareholders become homeless.

C. The Conglomerate

Has the owner as monitor already been tried, and did it fail? Was the conglomerate movement of the 1960s and 1970s now largely discredited—functionally the same as institutional block ownership? In large part, yes. The managers of the conglomerate were said to run a mini-capital market, pulling cash away from the managers of subsidiaries no longer in growing industries, sending that cash into the companies in growing industries, and monitoring managers of all the subsidiaries.

But the structures do *appear* to be different. The conglomerate typically owned *100%* of many companies. The institutional owner would typically have a large block, but would lack complete ownership. Does more than form distinguish the two?

Let's begin with the simplest monitoring paradigm. The monitor does *nothing* until it receives a signal of substandard performance, then it tries to identify whether managerial missteps caused the poor results. If those missteps are likely to continue, the monitor requires early retirement of the senior managers and promotion of the next rung of managers.

Where does the conglomerate monitor get the signal of faulty performance in its subsidiary? Principally from accounting data. The outside blockholder could also get that signal. But the blockholder could get *other* signals. Before the accounting numbers show a decline, the stock price set by traders should register *the market's expectations* of future trouble. A steep decline in stock price or underperformance of the stock compared to industry averages could trigger blockholder action. Financial economists argue that internal managerial changes are more likely when *stock* price lags industry averages. A financial monitor could be beneficial even if it did no more than filter out poor market signals and force managers to listen to a few of the good ones; conglomerates owning 100% of a subsidiary lack the benefit of market signals. Firms with outside large shareholders who *lack* vise-like control perform well, according to data from the financial economists....

Some monitors will be better than others; markets for monitors could develop. But the conglomerate would tend to stifle monitoring markets. Public information about a conglomerate's divisions and wholly-owned subsidiaries is not readily available, making unsolicited offers difficult and reducing the ability of the conglomerate managers to sell, since the buyer has to contend with a risky informational base. This debility would be less prominent for financial institutions owning a large fraction of a public company's stock. With information readily available for public companies, some monitors will offer to buy the block from other, less able monitors. Similarly, there is now evidence that takeovers are easier when there are prepositioned large blocks than when the stock is in scattered hands....

And perhaps conglomerates were not so bad after all. But as often happens with anything new and initially successful, success turned to excess. Conglomerates got too big, too many operating managers tried to diversify their company unwisely. Maybe conglomerates are still a good managerial tool, but in their place, only so much, only in related industries, and only if disciplined by a corporate control market. Nevertheless, we cannot yet reject the possibility that institutional monitoring would systematically fail, as the conglomerates did.

D. National Comparisons: Germany and Japan

Banks are more heavily involved in commerce in other nations than in the United States. Despite the American military occupation's suppression of the Japanese zaibatsu, major Japanese firms have a quarter of their stock controlled by large shareholders, typically life insurance companies and banks; major American companies have only one-twelfth of their stock controlled by large shareholders, which more so than in Japan tend to be individuals.

German banks also influence industrial companies, by block voting of shares they own directly, shares they hold as custodian, and shares they manage for pensions. Bankers sit on the boards of portfolio companies. Although passive in day-to-day affairs, they intervene when there is trouble. Banker control is quite concentrated; three banks control 40% of the stock. Government in Germany and in several other continental nations is said to have *wanted* banks to become engines of development, gathering long-term capital and influencing the industries and managers to which that capital was allocated....

Stock in large blocks makes a portfolio more risky and less saleable; even without mandated diversification, many institutions would want some. The question remains whether financial institutions, if permitted to take influential positions in the United States, would do so. Foreign experience provides strong evidence that they would.

American financial institutions have sought transactional end-runs around and amendment of the prohibitions and restrictions. This also suggests that the legal limits are real constraints....

To be sure, they might not take stock to monitor, but to force controlled companies to take loans or do deals. Or they might take stock because it yields higher returns than do other investments. And even if we were sure that foreign financial systems are efficient— which we are not—that would not necessarily recommend importation. If American financiers are more opportunistic, heightening the chance of scandal and abuse, or if government regulation is needed to stabilize financial power, and American government cannot regulate effectively, then foreign finance cannot be successfully grafted. And, if what we really want in America is fragmentation of power, then powerful financial institutions will give us less of what we really want.

E. A Research Agenda

I obviously want to open up a large new area for research. First, more detailed studies of the legislation are needed. While we now have studies of the Glass-Steagall Act's passage and effects on underwriting competition, little has been done to examine its effects on monitoring, and there are few studies of the forces behind passage of ERISA, the 1940 Act, or the Bank Holding Company Act. We also need to know more about how financial institutions can enhance or weaken managerial performance.

The political explanations can be deepened. The history available suggests that federalism, small financial institutions as interest groups, and populism largely explain fragmentation. Confirming studies can be made.

We should also want comparative studies to learn when the close ties between banks and industry in Japan and Germany are beneficial and when they are detrimental. Public choice studies of Japan and Germany would also be useful....

Development of a monitoring financial institution might not now be easy. Conditioned by legal restrictions, Wall Street's culture of financial speculation may be too deeply embedded to change readily. People go to business school, are trained, and become partners in investment banks or officers of commercial banks without understanding how to operate an industrial concern or, more to the point, how to check those operating an industrial firm. Carl Icahn, Kohlberg Kravis Roberts, and others began as financial players who became monitors; we do not know how quickly financial institutions could be transformed.

We do not even know *whether* they could be transformed: small investment partnerships that reap large gains may monitor better than large institutions where gains are diffusely distributed. Portfolio managers might have to be compensated differently.

The political perspective offers pessimism even if powerful financial institutions could improve corporate performance. If the alternatives are imperfect substitutes, then we have put ourselves at a national disadvantage by foregoing an institutional arrangement that other nations tolerate. History shows that this nation would have difficulty reconciling itself with such concentrations of financial power, *even if* legal reforms would properly enhance the role of institutional investors. Managers would prefer not to see financial institutions with significant ownership, popular attitudes would support managers, and tradition would make reforms seem abnormal, resulting in inertial drag. Other goals— generally of avoiding conflicts of interest—would be disrupted. In the political balance, the operational question of *whether* reforms would really enhance corporate performance would be lost. For now, I would expect politics will continue to restrain institutional action. If more institutions act, as a few now are, a confrontation may ensue.

Bernard S. Black, *Agents Watching Agents: The Promise of Institutional Investor Voice**

... [T]he manager-controlled corporation is not the only way to amass large amounts of capital. Politics killed a competing model, in which large financial institutions are

---

* Originally published in 39 UCLA Law Review 811 (1992). Reprinted with permission.

major shareholders and monitor the actions of corporate managers.[4] ... In a different legal environment, financial intermediaries could monitor the actions of corporate managers. In other countries, they do.

The ... "political" model also relies on other factors to explain institutional passivity. Many institutional investors depend on corporate managers for business. They face conflicts of interest if they monitor corporate managers. Managers also, for the most part, control the shareholder voting agenda. That agenda control can affect substantive outcomes. Legal rules *could* control promanager conflicts of interest, at least in part, and *could* give the shareholders more control over their own voting agenda. Today they mostly don't. Cultural factors may also be at work. Until recently, money managers didn't think they were supposed to be corporate monitors. Most still don't. If the legal environment changed, money manager culture might change as well.

Recent evidence supports this new view. Despite the impact of legal rules, conflicts of interest, and manager agenda control, institutional investors are no longer entirely passive. Proxy fights are still rare, but many institutions vote against manager proposals on some governance issues. A few institutions offer their own governance proposals, and occasionally succeed. Under a less obstructive, more facilitating legal regime, the institutions might do much more.

If institutional oversight is *possible,* the next question, and the subject of this Article, is whether it is *desirable.* Is institutional monitoring likely to improve corporate performance? What limits should there be on institutional power? Answering these questions is especially important now that politics has also gone far toward killing hostile takeovers as a constraint on managerial discretion.

The case for institutional oversight, broadly speaking, is that product, capital, labor, and corporate control market constraints on managerial discretion are imperfect, corporate managers need to be watched by someone, and the institutions are the only watchers available. The concerns about institutional oversight arise for two main reasons. First, controlling shareholders may divert funds to themselves at the expense of noncontrolling shareholders. Second, the institutions are themselves managed by money managers who need (and often don't get) watching and appropriate incentives. Mutual fund investors, for example, have little information about the corporate governance actions of mutual fund managers, little reason to care, and no power to do anything except sell their shares and invest in another fund. Public pension fund managers are watched as much by state politicians and the press as by fund beneficiaries.

Pure theory can't tell us whether we'd be better off if imperfectly watched money managers did more watching of corporate managers. Institutional detail matters. A complicating factor is that there are many different types of institutions: corporate pension plans; public pension plans; mutual funds; commercial banks; insurers; investment banks; foundations and endowments. Each has its own incentives, conflicts of interest, culture, history, and regulatory scheme. Some can take the lead in corporate governance initiatives. Conflicts of interest make others likely to be only followers.

Regulation is pervasive. It governs what the institutions, as currently constituted, can do. But it also determines, in substantial part, what the institutions are. Banks, mutual funds, insurers, and pension funds are in significant part *defined* by a web of regulation. Each could be defined differently, if we so choose. Regulatory detail matters.

---

4. *See Professor Roe's article in this chapter.*— Ed.

The benefits and costs of institutional oversight defy easy summary. Taking them as a whole, I believe that there is a strong case for measured reform that will facilitate joint shareholder action *not directed at control,* and reduce obstacles to particular institutions owning stakes *not large enough to confer working control.* Such reform will let six or ten institutions collectively have a significant say in corporate affairs, while limiting the power of any one institution to act on its own. I will call this limited role *institutional voice.* Institutional voice means a world in which particular institutions can easily own 5–10% stakes in particular companies, but can't easily own much more than 10%; in which institutions can readily talk to each other and select a minority of a company's board of directors, but can't easily exercise day-to-day control or select a majority of the board.

Institutional voice should be distinguished from *institutional control,* from a world where Citibank or Prudential could control General Motors in the way that Deutsche Bank controls Daimler-Benz.[5] The far-reaching reform needed for concentrated control has large potential benefits, because with control can come strong oversight. But strong oversight is inevitably accompanied by strong potential for abuse of control. Moreover, the extensive legal reform needed for institutional control involves redefining our institutions, at least in part. It's hard to predict how the newly recreated institutions would behave. Thus, the relative costs and benefits of institutional control are unclear.

The line that divides voice from control is admittedly fuzzy. We can see institutional power as lying along a rough continuum, with passivity at one end, voice in the middle, and control at the other end. Today, legal rules, agenda control, conflicts of interest, cultural factors, and historical accident combine to keep financial institutions far over toward the passivity end of the continuum. I believe that legal reform should allow — and where necessary encourage — the institutions to move toward the middle of the continuum. Such reform has little downside risk and holds substantial promise of improved corporate performance. We can't know today how much of that promise will be realized. But as long as the costs are small, institutional voice is worth a try. In economic terms, the *expected* benefit outweighs the *expected* cost.

The necessary reform will be partly deregulatory. We need to reduce the legal barriers that discourage institutions from offering shareholder voting proposals, communicating with each other on corporate governance issues, owning large stakes in particular companies, and exercising the influence that those stakes could convey. But deregulation is not enough. We also need rules that encourage monitoring. We could, for example, spread some monitoring costs over all shareholders by expanding the range of proposals that shareholders can include in company proxy statements. We may also need new conflict-of-interest rules, plus more aggressive enforcement of the existing rules, to ensure that money managers act in their beneficiaries' interests; agenda rules that increase shareholder influence over the shareholder voting agenda; and rules that limit manager ability to manipulate election outcomes.

The central theme of this Article — Agents Watching Agents — affects institutional monitoring in several ways. First, and most obviously, institutional voice means asking one set of agents (money managers) to watch another set of agents (corporate managers). Money managers have limited incentives to monitor because they keep only a fraction of the portfolio gains. But money managers also won't take the legal chances that an individual shareholder might, because they face personal risk if they breach their fiduciary duty or break other legal rules. The institution, however, realizes most of the gains from such misdeeds. That limits the downside risk from institutional voice.

---

5. *In 1998, Daimler-Benz acquired Chrysler and became DaimlerChrysler. At the time, Deutsche Bank remained the corporation's largest shareholder. — Ed.*

Second, institutional voice requires a number of institutions, including different *types* of institutions, to join forces to exercise influence. That further limits the downside risk from institutional power, because money managers can monitor each others' actions to some extent. Reputation is a central element in this second form of watching. Diversified institutions interact over and over, at many different companies, over a span of years. Institutions that earn good reputations will elicit cooperation from other institutions; institutions that cheat will invite retaliation.

Third, corporate managers can watch their watchers. Corporate managers indirectly control the largest category of institutional investor, the corporate pension fund. Also, if other institutions abuse their power, corporate managers can complain—loudly and often—to state and federal lawmakers. If the costs to other shareholders, including smaller institutions, of abuse of power by the largest institutions exceed the other shareholders' gains from better monitoring, those shareholders will support corporate managers' efforts to clip the large institutions' wings. Political outcomes are hard to predict, but financial institutions have lost political battles before. Money managers know that, which limits their incentive to misbehave in the first place.

Moreover, much of the promise of shareholder monitoring lies in *informal* shareholder efforts to monitor corporate managers or to express a desire for change in a company's management or policies. That enhances corporate managers' ability to police money manager behavior. Corporate managers can cooperate only with those money managers who earn a reputation for promoting long-term company value.

A second central theme of this Article is diversification. Diversification creates the opportunity for economies of scale in monitoring. Scale economies, in turn, affect the issues that the institutions will care about. Institutions are likely to devote more attention to process and structure issues, which promise scale economies, than to company-specific concerns. Process and structure issues include the value of confidential voting, the desirability of poison pills and other antitakeover devices, the composition and structure of the board of directors, the process by which directors are nominated, whether a company should have a nonexecutive chairman, and the form of management compensation.

Diversification also means that money managers interact repeatedly at different companies. That makes it easier for money managers to watch each other and makes reputation an important constraint on money manager behavior. Diversification also limits the risk that money managers will divert funds to themselves. Insider trading, for example, won't materially affect portfolio performance if done only occasionally. And a money manager who frequently trades on inside information runs a high risk of being caught.

Partly because institutional incentives push against direct, company-specific monitoring, a central reform goal should be to facilitate indirect monitoring through the board of directors. If the institutions can more easily select directors, at least for a minority of board seats, they can hire directors to watch companies on their behalf. Currently, directors are often more loyal to corporate officers than to the shareholders whom the directors nominally serve. Shareholder-nominated directors will owe more loyalty to shareholders, and may be more willing to ask tough questions when a company's performance lags, or when its CEO has dreams of grandeur.

Reform should focus on the *process* of voting, rather than substantive governance rules. For example, corporate boards may perform better if they include some directors who are nominated by large institutions. But we shouldn't legislate that result. Instead, we should empower the institutions to make their own decisions about optimal governance structures. They have incentives to make good choices—or at least better choices than lawmakers would make. Moreover, procedural reform won't force oversight or impose large regulatory costs on companies or shareholders. Oversight will take place only where the institutions conclude that the benefits of monitoring outweigh the costs.

Critics worry that the institutions will botch the job of monitoring corporate managers. There will undoubtedly be mistakes and false starts. Institutional shareholders won't develop monitoring skills overnight. But we should let them learn from their mistakes, like other actors in our market economy. In practice, legal change will occur gradually. That will make the inevitable mistakes less costly, and allow time to adjust the reforms if the initial efforts have unforeseen consequences. Given the level of congressional inertia, reform should, where possible, rely on federal agency action rather than legislative command.

The promise of institutional voice is substantial. In a companion article, I collect evidence of a number of systematic shortfalls in corporate performance. These include the functioning of corporate boards, corporate diversification strategies, takeover decisions, proincumbent governance rules, dividend policy, and manager compensation. Unshackled institutions *could* take steps to remedy these shortfalls. There is also limited direct evidence that some institutions already do valuable monitoring. The direct evidence isn't conclusive, but that isn't surprising, since the institutions don't currently do much monitoring. Importantly, there is little evidence that greater shareholder oversight will be harmful....

... The case for rule-by-rule reform turns on a number of questions that I don't address here, including: What purposes unrelated to shareholder voting do particular rules serve? Can the rules be altered without sacrificing those other purposes? When can reform cut across institutions, and when must rules be tailored to particular institutions? How will different reforms interact? Which rules should be mandatory, and which should be default rules, waivable by shareholder vote?

I. The Possibility of Shareholder Monitoring

This Part reviews the implications of collective action theory and economies of scale for shareholder action (section A), and explains why shareholder passivity may result as much from legal obstacles to shareholder action (section B), manager agenda control (section C), and institutional investor conflicts of interest (section D), as from the logic of collective action.... The discussion is framed in terms of formal shareholder voting proposals, but much of it applies to informal oversight as well. I assume throughout this Article a company without voting control by insiders. I also work within a conventional model of the corporation, in which managers are expected to maximize long-term company value and owe fiduciary duties to shareholders and *only* to shareholders. Corporate social responsibility and duties to constituencies other than shareholders are outside the scope of this Article....

A. *Collective Action Problems*

The standard explanation for shareholder passivity relies on the collective action problems faced by shareholders who each own a fraction of a company's stock. There are two related problems. First, control contests aside, a shareholder proponent bears most of the cost of a proxy campaign, but receives only a pro rata share of the gains from success, while other shareholders can free ride on her efforts. Second, any one shareholder's vote is unlikely to affect whether a proposal wins or loses. Many shareholders therefore choose rational apathy—they don't carefully evaluate particular proposals, and instead adopt a crude rule of thumb like "vote with management."

Collective action problems can lead shareholders to remain passive in situations where a sole owner would monitor. But shareholders will still act if their private gain from monitoring exceeds their private cost. A shareholder who owns a large percentage stake is more likely to engage in monitoring than a shareholder who owns a smaller stake. Thus, legal rules that prevent shareholders from owning large stakes or acting jointly increase incentives to remain passive. Moreover, the higher the cost of making a shareholder proposal, the greater the incentive to remain silent. Thus, rules that increase the cost of a proxy campaign or prevent cost-sharing among shareholders discourage shareholder action. Conversely, rules that shift costs to the company encourage shareholder action.

Moreover, the standard model overstates the case for passivity. When the voting outcome is in doubt, apathy becomes much less rational as shareholdings grow. Both a shareholder's gains from the voting outcome she favors and the likelihood that her vote will be decisive increase with the number of shares owned. A shareholder who owns 1,000 shares is 1,000 times more likely to cast a decisive vote than a shareholder who owns a single share, and realizes 1,000 times the net gain if her vote is decisive. Thus, the incentive to cast an informed vote increases *exponentially* as shareholdings grow. A 1,000 share holder has 1,000,000 times more incentive to become informed than someone who owns a single share!

Diversification also enhances incentives to monitor by creating the potential for economies of scale in monitoring. Many process and structural issues arise in similar form at many companies. A shareholder who offers the same proposal at a number of companies can reduce her per-company solicitation cost, while preserving the per-company benefit from success. Similarly, a shareholder who votes on the same proposal many times has reason to invest more time and attention in casting an informed vote.

B. Legal Obstacles to Shareholder Action

A broad array of state and federal rules makes it hard for a single shareholder to own a large percentage stake in a single company. Other rules encumber joint action by a number of shareholders and increase the cost of a proxy campaign. This section sketches the principal rules.

For an active shareholder or a shareholder group, owning a 5% stake triggers filing requirements under section 13(d) of the Securities Exchange Act and related SEC rules. Owning a 10% stake can trigger short-swing profit forfeiture under Exchange Act section 16(b) and related SEC rules. A large shareholder or group also risks being considered a control person, with adverse consequences under securities, bankruptcy, and other laws. And a shareholder or group can't cross the trigger percentage for the company poison pill, often only 10 to 15%, without manager approval. Banks, insurers, and mutual funds face additional legal limits on their ability to hold large stakes. Corporate crossholdings are discouraged by an extra layer of taxation, and by unfavorable accounting treatment for stakes under 20%....

Legal obstacles are especially great if shareholders want to choose some directors instead of rubberstamping the incumbents' choices. The SEC's proxy rules help shareholders on some matters, but mostly create obstacles for director elections. The sponsoring institution(s) risk being deemed to be a control person, or to have "deputized" the director (which would create short-swing profit forfeiture liability under section 16(b)). Choosing directors also creates a risk of insider trading liability under Exchange Act section 10(b), because the director will have access to inside information.

Legal rules also raise the costs of a proxy campaign or other shareholder action.... [6]

Often, the law is uncertain. This creates legal risk, which is especially troublesome for institutional fiduciaries. They face personal risk on the downside, while their beneficiaries get most of the upside. For many money managers, the adverse publicity from a lawsuit is a major deterrent without more. Legal uncertainty also encourages company managers to sue shareholders, because the managers can impose costs on shareholders even if they lose the suit.

Moreover, corporate managers begin a proxy contest with various advantages. They can spend the shareholders' money to support their own proposals or fight a shareholder proposal. They can issue large blocks of stock to employees (who will predictably vote promanager) through a leveraged employee stock ownership plan ("ESOP"). Managers can also control, in various ways, the voting of some shares that they don't own.

No single legal rule forecloses shareholder action. But the obstacles are many, and their cumulative effect is large. A shareholder who remains quiet is safe. A shareholder who buys a large stake, especially a shareholder who becomes active on governance issues, pays a price. That price, for a shareholder whose stake is kept small by legal rules, is often enough to make passivity the preferred course.

C. *Agenda Control by Corporate Managers*

Agenda control can sometimes determine the outcome of a shareholder vote. Except for the occasional full-scale proxy fight and subjects on which shareholders can put proposals in the company proxy statement, corporate managers control what the shareholders vote on, when they vote, and when the shareholders learn what's on the agenda....

D. *Institutional Investor Conflicts of Interest*

Many institutional money managers face conflicts of interest. Money managers who vote against a company's proposals are likely to lose any business that they conduct with the company. Money managers who develop an antimanager reputation may lose corporate business, or find it harder to gain new business. These conflicts lead some institutions to vote promanager even when doing so is likely to decrease company value....

The single phrase "institutional investor" obscures important differences between institutions in the strength of their conflicts. Banks and insurers have strong conflicts because of their extensive business dealings with corporate managers. Corporate pension funds, even when they hire outside money managers, are still controlled by corporate managers. Public pension funds don't solicit corporate business, but respond to political pressure. No institution is completely beholden to corporate managers; no institution is conflict-free....

II. The Promise of Institutional Voice

Much of the value of institutional oversight will come through informal manager response to the wishes of large shareholders and through negotiated compromises....

---

6. *See Thomas Joo's article in Chapter 9. — Ed.*

There is reason to think that negotiated compromises will become common. Corporate and money managers often talk about the need for dialogue between shareholders and managers. The money managers, who are outside the walled citadel and want in, recognize the limited value of shooting arrows over the walls. The managers want the infidels to go away, but when pushed, often prefer compromise to a public fight. To date, many shareholder successes have come through negotiations with managers, in which the managers "voluntarily" adopt all or part of a shareholder proposal.

Informal shareholder pressure may already be having an effect beyond the limited number of explicit shareholder proposals. Boards of directors, though far from perfect, are more independent and vigilant today than in the past and more likely to question or fire an underperforming CEO. Shareholder pressure surely contributed to this shift....

Despite the importance of informal action, formal shareholder power is still essential. Compromises, after all, developed only after managers realized that they might lose if they pushed matters to a vote. Formal shareholder action at some companies also serves as a warning to other corporate managers whose companies haven't been targeted for shareholder action....

III. Problems with Expanded Institutional Power

... This Part responds to the central concerns with institutional power and argues that the risks from institutional *voice* are limited....

We can't have both effective oversight of corporate managers and bulletproof protection against money manager abuses. Instead, we must seek a rough optimum in which there is some institutional oversight, some risk of institutional abuse of power, and some continued corporate manager abuse of discretion. The downside risks from institutional *voice* are modest, and outweighed by the potential gains. In contrast, institutional *control* has both large potential benefits and large potential costs. We are on safer ground if one institution can't do too much by itself.

A. Agents Watching Agents

Institutional voice involves principals (whom I will call "investors" or "beneficiaries") hiring a first-tier set of agents (money managers) to watch a second-tier set of agents (corporate managers). The first-tier agents are often themselves organizations with principal-agent problems. Some money management firms are publicly held, with fiduciary obligations both to investors and to their own shareholders. To complicate matters further, a number of money managers will be watching each company....

Institutional voice will not merely recreate our current agency problems at a different level. Investors weakly watching money managers who watch corporate managers is more promising than today's world, where most of the time no one watches corporate managers. First, monitoring is easier than managing. Money managers can assess whether manager A is running steel company X as well as his industry peers, or choose directors to perform that assessment, without being able to run a steel company themselves. They can assess whether Kodak should buy Sterling Drug—to cite one of many misguided acquisitions— without being able to run either Kodak or Sterling Drug. They can use stock price and accounting evidence to assess whether a company is performing worse than its peers, without knowing exactly where the problem lies.

Moreover, money managers will be more closely watched *as monitors* than corporate managers are today. Money managers can watch each other in a way that corporate managers cannot. Also, stronger oversight of public companies will include stronger oversight of publicly-held financial institutions. For instance, Berkshire Hathaway, an insurer, could respond to a crisis at Salomon Brothers, an investment bank, because Berkshire owned a large stake in Salomon and had representatives on the Salomon board.

It's also easier for investors to watch money managers than corporate managers. Money manager performance is more readily quantifiable. For most institutions, if performance lags, investors or pension sponsors can change money managers. In contrast, shareholders can't withdraw equity capital from companies. Thus, they must act jointly to affect corporate managers, with attendant collective action problems. And history gives money managers more reason than corporate managers to fear political reprisal if they misuse their influence.

Institutional voice can be distinguished from the conglomerate firm, for which one claimed virtue was oversight of division managers by top managers. In the conglomerate, no one watches the top managers. Conglomerate CEOs often turned out to be empire-builders instead of good monitors, and the conglomerate form kept them highly insulated from product market and capital market constraints. Money managers can be watched more easily, and have no comparable way to build an empire.

B. *Money Manager Competence*

If we empower money managers to monitor corporate managers, will they botch the job? To date, the institutions haven't done much monitoring. Their people aren't trained to do it, and might not do it well. The response to this concern depends on the institution and the type of issue. Many institutions already have some monitoring skills. Others lack those skills, but could develop them if they had reason to. Still others won't be good monitors, but can recognize their own limits and hire others—institutional directors, for example—to monitor for them.

To begin with, the institutions are likely to devote more attention to process and structure issues than to company-specific oversight. That reduces the risk of misdirected meddling in a company's business. Specialized knowledge is needed to assess whether a company should build a new plant, but isn't needed to decide whether the company should redeem its poison pill. Institutional directors, if valuable at all, are likely to be valuable across many industries. Indeed, diversification makes money managers better situated than corporate managers to assess some issues. The money managers can see how a structural rule works across a number of companies. Corporate managers lack a comparable perspective.

It's also hard for shareholders to intervene in ordinary business decisions even if they want to. Such decisions don't require a shareholder vote. Thus, shareholder influence must be indirect and informal. Often, the need for speed and secrecy means that shareholders learn of decisions only after the fact....

To date, the institutions have seemed to recognize the limits of their expertise. They disclaim any interest in the day-to-day operation of portfolio companies. These disclaimers are consistent with the limited attention that a diversified institution can give to any one company, and with institutional behavior in Germany and Japan. German and Japanese banks have the power to micromanage, but don't. Instead, they intervene only for major decisions, or when companies are in trouble. Indeed, there is an air of unreality about concerns that institutions will micromanage corporate actions. By far the larger risk is that the institutions will continue to monitor too little, not that they will make a drastic turn and monitor too much....

C. Institutional Myopia

A concern related to institutional competence involves the institutions' time horizon. If the institutions are myopically concerned with short-term gains, then institutional voice might be harmful in the long run. Some institutions may indeed be interested mostly in a quick profit. Institutional myopia, however, looms larger in public perception than in reality, and institutional voice should reduce whatever myopia may exist.

To begin with, the available evidence strongly suggests that institutional investors are not *systematically* myopic. Research and development is a quintessential long-term investment. Yet: (i) stock prices react favorably, on average, to increased R&D spending; (ii) if investors undervalue R&D, R&D-intensive firms should be more vulnerable to takeovers, but such firms are *less* likely to be acquired than other firms; and (iii) if institutional investors are more myopic than other investors, they should own lower percentages of R&D-intensive firms, but institutions hold *higher* stakes in such firms. Similarly, stock prices react favorably to increased capital expenditures....

Indeed, a credible argument can be made that institutions pay *too much* attention to long-term promise and ignore the rocky road that often separates today's promise from tomorrow's performance. That could explain the "Nifty Fifty" bubble of the early 1970s, and the astronomical valuations of biotechnology companies in the mid-1980s. Antimyopia would be consistent with evidence that stock prices underreact to earnings surprises.

Second, short-sighted institutions won't do much monitoring, because the payoff from oversight is long-term. Pension funds should be especially long-term oriented. That's where their liabilities are. The active institutions certainly claim to be long-term investors. Many are heavily indexed, which is consistent with a long-term horizon.

Third, institutional investors have little ability to reap short-term gains at the expense of long-term value. In a reasonably efficient capital market, even an investor who plans to sell next month must care about long-term value, because buyers will have a longer horizon. Some commentators worry that shareholders can extract wealth from employees or bondholders. But diversified institutions won't care much about such one-time gains because they won't significantly affect a diversified portfolio. For transfers from debtholders to shareholders, few large institutions will be interested in the first place because most own both debt and equity. *Particular money managers* may specialize in equity but most *institutions* own both. Most mutual fund groups, for example, offer both debt and equity funds.

In the long run, shareholders can't systematically exploit other "stakeholders" in the corporate enterprise. The price of labor or debt capital will reflect the risk of shareholder opportunism, or employees and lenders will insist on contractual protection. If layoffs become more likely, employees will demand higher wages or severance pay. If leverage increases become common, lenders will demand higher interest rates or stronger covenants. The institutions should also realize that there are long-run costs from trying to exploit employees or bondholders. If implicit contracts are broken too often, they will be replaced by explicit contracts, even if informal arrangements are more efficient. Moreover, wealth transfers are only that—transfers. Capital structure changes may be largely a wash as far as social wealth is concerned. Bankruptcy and workout costs are a deadweight loss, but *ex ante,* the price of debt and equity should reflect those costs, which provides incentives for capital structures that limit bankruptcy risk.

Finally, part of the promise of institutional voice is that it may *reduce* shareholder and creditor myopia. Enhanced voice may improve information flow, and thus enable shareholders to rely less on short-term earnings as a signal of long-term value. Greater ability to engage in monitoring may also make institutions more willing to be long-term investors. Weak institutions have little choice but to vote with their feet for a takeover bid at a reasonable premium to market. Influential institutions could talk and reject bids where they think the target's management is doing a good job. Creditors who also own a sizeable equity stake will be less risk-averse. One does not hear complaints that Japanese and German banks, who can exercise effective voice, do so myopically. In Albert Hirschman's terminology, voice can be an alternative to a quick exit.[7]

D. *Managerial Myopia*

Even if institutional shareholders aren't systematically myopic, corporate managers may be, or may think that shareholders are. Greater institutional voice could lead managers to behave myopically, in the misguided belief that doing so will placate institutional hunger for a quick buck.

Managerial myopia is a serious concern. Often, the CEO is only a few years from retirement and wants to leave on a high note, or cares less about long-term projects for which others will take the credit. That may explain why R&D spending drops in the year before a CEO retires. Executive compensation also often depends heavily on short-term accounting results, which are notoriously easy to manipulate. Even for stock-based compensation, asymmetric information models predict that managers can boost short-term stock prices by underinvesting in long-term projects, or investing in unprofitable projects.

Institutional voice, though, is more likely to reduce than to increase the scope of the problem. Shareholder voice should reduce miscommunication between shareholders and managers. The institutions can convince managers that they value long-term investments. If major shareholders are better informed, managers will be less likely to try to fool shareholders about corporate values. The institutions can also endorse compensation systems that reward far-sighted investments and give less weight to near-term profits. And keeping managers insulated from shareholder oversight isn't the answer: companies, on average, *decrease* R&D intensity after adopting antitakeover amendments.

E. *The Risks of Concentrated Institutional Power*

United States culture has long resisted concentration of economic power. Will financial institutions grow too powerful if we move toward institutional voice? Skeptics worry that money managers may embrace fads en masse or deny capital to new ideas. Some have an inchoate concern that concentrated power is dangerous in and of itself.

The institutions have embraced market fads before, and may do so again. If money managers who defy convention suffer greater reputational loss from portfolio declines than those who fail with the crowd, that could contribute to herd behavior.

---

7. Albert O. Hirschman, Exit, Voice and Loyalty: Responses to Decline in Firms, Organizations, and States (1970).

We can't prevent money managers from making mistakes. But several factors limit the risk of large errors. First, legal change to enhance institutional power will occur slowly. Culture will probably change slowly as well. That will give money managers time to make some early mistakes on a few companies instead of a few hundred. Money managers should also realize the limits of their own knowledge. They can stay out of areas where their expertise is thin, or enter slowly. For example, they can experiment with performance incentives at a few companies instead of trying them everywhere at once.

The need for institutions to join forces to exert influence will also reduce mistakes. The institutions are highly diverse. On any issue, some will be leaders, while others will be skeptics. There is no consensus today about investment styles or the value of governance initiatives, even within a single type of institution. Some mutual fund groups are active on governance issues; others are not. Some public pension funds are vocal; others urge caution. Some corporate pension funds buy and hold; others trade frantically. Yet it will take consensus to produce action. Moreover, while committees don't always make better decisions than individual actors, they do make slower decisions. A camel may indeed be, as a wag suggested, a horse designed by committee, but one suspects that the committee designed only a few camels before someone realized that they weren't working as planned.

Moreover, corporate managers can argue with money managers if they think the money managers are making a mistake. The money managers might listen, or move more cautiously, against the risk that the corporate managers are right. Private pension fund managers *must* listen—they are hired by corporate managers. Corporate managers also can (and gleefully will) use the institutions' mistakes against them in the political arena, to limit institutional power. Banks, insurers, and mutual funds have lost political battles before. Fear of losing again will lead them to move cautiously, which limits the scale of the inevitable mistakes.

In addition, corporate managers embrace fads today. Many jumped on the conglomerate bandwagon in the 1960s and continued to diversify even after investors had recognized the problems with diversification. Corporate managers also bear some blame for the overleverage of the late 1980s. Mixing corporate and money manager cultures could produce *fewer* fads than corporate managers would embrace on their own.

There is also little reason to worry that new ventures will starve for lack of capital. Venture capital funds, today often funded by institutions, won't disappear. Nor will banks and insurers abandon their traditional role as lenders to small and midsized companies. On the contrary, financial institutions should be *more* willing to make risky loans if they can hold sizeable equity stakes, which increase the upside from a risky investment and enhance influence if a business heads downhill. If existing institutions don't pursue profitable lending opportunities, new firms should do so. Money is the ultimate fungible commodity, and entry barriers are low.

Inchoate concerns about concentrated economic power are hard to rebut because the asserted harms are vague. Still, there is little reason to fear institutional power in a regime of institutional voice. Large companies are far more powerful today than financial institutions. Institutional voice may provide a counterweight to industrial power, and thus reduce the overall concentration of private power—if we can even measure such a thing. Moreover, most financial institutions operate in highly competitive environments. That limits their ability to use their influence in non-profit-maximizing ways. Many are themselves publicly traded, which subjects them to oversight by their own shareholders. The institutions also know that power, if used, risks a political response. And power that can be taken away if used isn't much power in the first place.

Public pension funds raise special concerns because they are partly accountable to politicians. There would be reason to worry if public funds could control particular companies. But public funds are not yet large enough to merit serious concern. In 1990, all public funds together owned only about 8% of U.S. equities. And concerns about public fund power would call for institution-specific regulation, not constraints on all institutions....

Legal rules *could* explain institutional passivity. Skeptics contend, however, that even without legal barriers, most money managers won't do much monitoring....

Given the diversity among institutions, it's likely that *some* institutions will monitor. Institutions that aren't active monitors will often have sufficient incentives to cast informed votes on proposals made by others. We must also distinguish the possibility that money managers will do too little from the risk that they will take actions adverse to long-term company values. As long as money managers do more monitoring, something will have been gained, even if they do less than we might have hoped....

IV. Conclusion

... Reform should focus on procedure, not substantive governance rules. We shouldn't *mandate* oversight. Procedural reform can facilitate shareholder action, but oversight will occur only if the costs of monitoring are less than the benefits from reducing the agency costs that flow from the separation of ownership and control in our large companies.

Institutional voice creates some risk that the institutions will abuse their power, but that risk is modest if particular institutions can't control particular companies. If a half-dozen institutions must act jointly to exercise effective voice, the institutions can watch each other at the same time that they're watching corporate managers. The risks of institutional power counsel measured reform, through administrative rule rather than statute when possible, so that it will be easier to reverse course if the benefits prove smaller and the costs larger than expected. They counsel reform to encourage institutional voice, not institutional control.

We will be asking one set of agents to watch another set of agents. That complexity pervades this Article; it limits both the upside and the downside from institutional voice. Money managers have imperfect incentives to watch well. Some may not watch at all because promanager conflicts of interest are too strong. But money managers are also less likely than individual investors to divert corporate income or to break the bans on insider trading or collusion between competitors.

The judgment here is that the upside from institutional voice is substantial and the downside is limited. Perhaps institutional shareholders can become skilled monitors of corporate managers. And perhaps not. But the current system leaves much to be desired, and we'll never know if there's a better system unless we try.

Roberta Romano, *Less Is More: Making Institutional Investor Activism a Valuable Mechanism of Corporate Governance*[*]

Institutional investors have, in the past decade, increasingly engaged in corporate governance activities, introducing proposals under rule 14a-8, the Securities and Exchange

* Originally published in 18 YALE JOURNAL ON REGULATION 174 (2001). Reprinted with permission.

Commission's proxy proposal rule, and privately negotiating with management of targeted firms with the stated goal of improving corporate performance. For example, since the mid-1980s, institutions have submitted to hundreds of firms shareholder proposals on corporate governance consisting principally of proposals to eliminate defensive tactics to takeovers, to adopt confidential proxy voting, to enhance board independence, and to restrict executive compensation. Before 1986, only a small set of individual investors engaged in such activism: from 1979–83, religious groups and six or seven individuals, depending on the year, submitted more than half of all proposals, which ranged in the hundreds every year. From 1986 until the early 1990s, five institutions (four public pension funds and the pension fund of university teachers and administrators) accounted for almost 20% of all proposals. Since 1994, unions have overtaken public pension funds as the most active corporate governance proposal sponsors. More than a dozen unions and union pension funds, including both national and local-level organizations, have used the proxy mechanism to sponsor such proposals....

This Article reviews the corporate finance literature on corporate governance activism involving shareholder proposals and uses it to inform normative recommendations concerning the proposal process. The finance literature presents an apparent paradox: notwithstanding commentators' generally positive assessment of the development of such shareholder activism, the empirical studies suggest that it has an insignificant effect on targeted firms' performance. Very few studies find evidence of a positive impact, and some even find a significant negative stock price effect from activism....

... [F]inancial economists have not been able to identify a positive performance effect of shareholder activism because much of that activism is, in fact, misdirected. I reach this conclusion by relating the studies of shareholder activism to the studies of the underlying corporate governance devices that are the object of that activity. A review of that literature makes evident that, for a very large proportion of the governance structures that are the focus of shareholder activism, such as independent boards of directors, limits on executive compensation, and confidential proxy voting, there is a paucity or utter absence of data that demonstrate that such devices improve performance. Hence, it should not be surprising that shareholder activism directed at reforming those governance structures does not produce positive results, and that this result would persist regardless of proposals' expected voting support....

The wide gulf between the prior perceptions of commentators and pension fund managers and the reality conveyed by the data presents a perplexing picture: why are time and effort being devoted to fruitless or marginal activities? This Article does not answer this question directly, although there is a plausible explanation relating to pursuit of personal benefits (such as political ambitions or collective bargaining goals) rather than portfolio firm value-maximization by proposal proponents, who are not private sector fund managers. There are also data substantiating this conjecture: the New York City public pension fund manager emphasized her activism in seeking election to higher office, and union funds have targeted firms where there were ongoing contract negotiations. This Article takes problematic motivational issues as a given and seeks instead to recommend devices to provide fund boards in charge of oversight, as well as fund managers, with more information and incentives to minimize the effect of agency problems on portfolio performance.

The Article takes a two-pronged approach to the problem of ineffective shareholder activism. First, the Article recommends adoption of a mechanism of internal control, something akin to a good management practice, whereby funds would engage in periodic comprehensive review of their shareholder-activism programs to identify the most fruitful governance objectives....

The Article further advocates changing the SEC proxy proposal rules to reduce the current subsidy of proposal sponsorship unless a proposal achieves substantial voting success, or to permit firms to opt out, in whole or in part, of the current subsidized proposal regime....

I. Internal Controls: Refocusing Activist Programs

One means of reducing the likelihood that shareholder activism is a non-value-maximizing activity is to improve the quality of decision-making by institutional investors by encouraging implementation of comprehensive, formal internal reviews of corporate governance programs. Such reviews should include an evaluation of the empirical research relating to the objective of contemplated proposals or private negotiations, as well as the voting outcome of previously submitted proposals. The review should be forwarded to the fund board and not simply the officers or employees supervising activism programs. This would enable a fund board to identify better what activity is worthwhile, facilitating the fulfillment of their fiduciary obligations to fund beneficiaries. A formal mechanism of reporting on a fund's activities and their effectiveness would put fund trustees and fund managers on a more equal footing and thus lessen the possibility that better-informed managers could rationalize an agenda to a board in terms of good corporate governance practices that consists, in fact, of non-value-enhancing proposals.

The formal review of corporate governance activities should also be incorporated in the fund's annual report or statement sent to beneficiaries or holders of fund shares. As a publicly available document, it will be of use to fund participants willing to expend the effort to monitor fund managers' efforts at enhancing the value of their portfolio. In addition, legislators and taxpayers who finance public pensions will also be better able to identify inappropriate expenditures that could affect the funding of plan assets for which they are legally liable.

What should be a fund's response to the proposed review? At minimum, proxy proposals that have a negative impact upon performance given the literature on corporate governance devices, such as those involving executive compensation limits, ought to be scrapped in favor of those whose effect is at least arguably ambiguous, such as proposals to relax takeover defenses. Such a policy will also require the fund's staff to develop firm-specific knowledge to engage in activism: just as the empirical literature finds that the stock price effect of takeover defenses varies with firm characteristics, such as board composition and firm size, proposals to eliminate those defenses would, accordingly, be more beneficial for some firms than others. If a fund does not possess adequate firm-specific knowledge, proposals whose impact is highly firm-dependent, such as takeover defense rescissions, ought to be discouraged. In fact, some institutional investors are aware of this problem and have adapted their governance activities accordingly. For instance, Del Guercio and Hawkins note that the heavily-indexed New York City pension fund does not sponsor poison pill proposals because they "require too much company-specific knowledge."[8]

Similarly, proxy proposals that receive little support from other investors (which not surprisingly invariably are those whose substantive objectives produce the least positive impact on firm value) should be reevaluated, with an eye to their elimination. The

---

8. Diane Del Guercio & Jennifer Hawkins, *The Motivation and Impact of Pension Fund Activism*, 52 J. FIN. ECON. 293, 322–26, tbl. 8 (1999). *"Poison pills" are corporate defenses against hostile takeovers. They are discussed further in Chapter 11.*—Ed.

reasoning for such a criterion is that support levels are an excellent proxy for the judgment of other informed investors that the proposal is in their interest. Hence, proposals that obtain a higher level of voting support have a higher probability of being those that maximize share value. Only if shareholders' beliefs are biased concerning the value of a specific type of proposal, would the level of voting support not be an accurate proxy for the proposal's impact on performance.

Given the large number and diversity of institutional investors and their information sources, however, systematic errors across investors over proposal valuation effects is simply not a plausible scenario. The more plausible assumption is that shareholder mistakes on the value of a particular governance device are randomly distributed. In such a scenario, with a large number of voting shareholders, investor errors will cancel out and the proportion of yes votes is the best estimate of the proposal's value....

Pension fund boards should find implementation of the proposed review process sufficiently desirable to do so voluntarily as a good management practice. But it might well be difficult for boards to evaluate their programs' efficacy, as they are not likely to possess the requisite expertise. Inability to evaluate an activism program effectively, in turn, might lead to hesitancy in adopting the proposed formal review process or implementing it effectively.

A potentially more important problem for implementation is a fund board that is subject to political pressure itself: board members are often political appointees or elected officials, who may support an activist agenda favored by constituents, and be led to place less weight on concerns over portfolio value than would be other fiduciaries. Politicization of a fund board would greatly attenuate the incentive to undertake the proposed review. In such cases, implementing the review procedure may well be in the interest of the fund managers, for it could provide political cover for a manager focused on maximizing the value of portfolio firms from a politicized board whose members are instead interested in implementing political and social investment objectives.

Politicization has been a problem, for instance, for the CalPERS staff. Politicians on the fund's board recently advanced an investment policy opposed by the staff for financial reasons, tobacco stock divestment, and the staff recommended amending proposed divestiture legislation supported by the State Treasurer, a fund board member, to include indemnification for "board members, money managers and others connected with the fund from potential liabilities" from implementing the policy if the bill were enacted. Indeed, the political composition of the CalPERS board is considered to affect "every single activity" of the fund, "from the benefits side to investment policy to corporate governance." To the extent that the source of non-value-maximizing activism is fund boards and not fund managers, it would be in the managers' self-interest to implement the proposed review procedure that provides external evaluations to the fund board, as it would be a shield against potential fiduciary liability....

II. External Controls: Shifting the Financial Burden of Shareholder Proposals

... [B]ecause the most active funds are public pension funds that are defined benefit plans, their beneficiaries' payouts are independent of the funds' endowment. Hence fund managers will not have powerful incentives to adopt comprehensive evaluations even if some funds would for fear of adverse signaling, since their beneficiaries are not as actively monitoring fund performance as are shareholders of mutual funds. Politicians are also not likely to target fund activism out of concern about taxpayer expense as the expenditures on such activities are relatively small and some non-value-maximizing forms of activism may actually provide political benefits: limiting executive compensation, for instance, has been a perennial focus of Congressional attention. Consequently, another mechanism is necessary to incentivize public pension fund managers.

One means of providing an incentive to fund managers to engage in more cost-effective forms of activism is to eliminate the subsidy of losing proposals under the SEC's proxy proposal rules. If funds incur the cost of a losing proposal, then the fund managers will have to scrutinize, on a continuing basis, the fund's corporate governance program, to determine which proposals are most likely to attract voting support, because their cash position will be affected if they do not. Admittedly, the incentive created by this proposal is low-powered, as fund beneficiaries are not likely to be able to monitor fund outflows or budget reallocations due to a poorly performing corporate governance program. But over time the expenses from losing proposal reimbursements will affect fund performance, and the fund board will have increased incentives to intervene. It is in the interest of fund managers to avoid such board action, as it could have adverse employment repercussions beyond the immediate curtailment of discretion upon the intervention, and managers anticipating the possibility of such action will adjust their behavior regarding shareholder proposals from the outset.

A. Should Proxy Proposals Be Subsidized?

It is textbook economics that parties bearing the full cost of their actions make better decisions than those that do not. When a party does not bear the full cost of its activity, it will engage in more of the activity, for in equating the marginal benefits and costs of the enterprise, a lower level of benefit from the activity suffices to meet the reduced cost. But under the shareholder proposal regime, this analysis is generally thought to be overridden by collective action concerns. Namely, if the cost of action by an individual shareholder is greater than the shareholder's pro rata benefit, albeit less than the aggregate gain to all shareholders, the activity will be under-, rather than over-supplied. The proxy proposal regime assumes that this is the proper calculation of the costs and benefits of shareholder proposals.

But where there are private benefits from the shareholder's action, that is, benefits that accrue solely to the proposal sponsor and that are not proportionately shared by all shareholders, as is the case with an increase in firm value, then matching pro-rated costs and benefits will not produce the optimal level of activity. This is because when costs are allocated across all shareholders, small private benefits will induce individual action that does not benefit the shareholders in the aggregate.

It is quite probable that private benefits accrue to some investors from sponsoring at least some shareholder proposals. The disparity in identity of sponsors—the predominance of public and union funds, which, in contrast to private sector funds, are not in competition for investor dollars—is strongly suggestive of their presence. Examples of potential benefits which would be disproportionately of interest to proposal sponsors are progress on labor rights desired by union fund managers and enhanced political reputations for public pension fund managers, as well as advancements in personal employment, the "revolving door" issue for government employees, whose salaries are considerably lower than the private sector. It is possible that engaging in activism will enhance an individual's subsequent job opportunities, analogous to suggestions that prosecutors bring high profile criminal cases either to further political careers or partnerships in top criminal defense firms, a charge directed at the white collar crime prosecutions brought by Rudolph Giuliani, a

U.S. attorney who later became Mayor of New York, and others in his office who went on to prominent law firms. For example, a top official involved in CalPERS's corporate governance program, Richard Koppes, left the fund and joined a law firm that advises management on takeover defenses after leaving the fund. Because such career concerns—enhancement of political reputations or subsequent employment opportunities—do not provide a commensurate benefit to private fund managers, we do not find them engaging in investor activism.

The private benefits implicated in career concerns also have a higher likelihood of being present in certain classes of proposals than others. For example, proposals to limit executive compensation and increase board diversity, appealing to populist sentiment or the political preferences of some constituents, are more likely to enhance political reputations for fund managers than confidential voting or takeover defense rescission proposals. There is far greater media publicity surrounding executive compensation and minority representation issues, and these proposals implicate the kinds of social issues on which political reputations can be advanced, in contrast to more mundane corporate governance devices. This conjecture has plausibility given the far lower level of voting support for executive compensation and board proposals compared to confidential voting and defensive tactic proposals by those who have a financial stake in firms.

A broader set of proposals—all those making managers' lives more uncomfortable—may provide private benefits to union fund managers seeking a more accommodating management; these include proposals rescinding takeover tactics as well as proposals to limit executive pay and enhance board independence. But these proposals may also be offered strategically, to gain support and good will from other investors that is hoped will carry over to future issues of greater importance to labor. Although such a carryover is a "private" benefit to the union, it is not a "private" benefit in the strict sense because any gain from the specific proposal, such as an increase in stock value from rescission of a poison pill, is a pro rata gain.

Although it may have had relevance historically, the rationale advanced for the shareholder proposal rule's subsidization of sponsors' costs, a collective action problem, has little relevance for contemporary capital markets, in which a majority of shares is held by institutional investors. Institutional investors own large blocks of stock and often cannot sell shares in a poorly-managed firm because their fund is indexed to a portfolio including that firm. Consequently, they experience far less of a free rider problem than the individual shareholder whose hypothesized dilemma motivated adoption of a cost-subsidization regime.

In addition, there are a number of organizations, such as the CII [*Council of Institutional Investors*], ... [*RiskMetrics Group, and Glass, Lewis & Co.*] that collect and disseminate information to institutional investors concerning corporate governance issues, which further reduces the need for a regulatory solution to a hypothesized collective action problem. The AFL-CIO has also published a detailed set of voting guidelines for union funds and the possibilities of inexpensive and widespread dissemination of information through the internet are already present and potentially enormous. Besides the websites of the AFL-CIO, CalPERS, CII and other organizations that detail their corporate governance activities, some small activist funds are posting on their websites how they have voted their proxies and are encouraging use of their sites to facilitate individual shareholder participation in an activist agenda.

B. *Proposed Reform of the Proposal Process*

Subsidization is not necessary for active use of the proxy process by investors and, in fact, it has created perverse incentives for institutional investors, as the best available data suggest that fund managers are not using the proposal process in furtherance of the best interest of their beneficiaries. This Article accordingly advocates revising the present proxy proposal regime to reduce such incentives. It presents three alternative approaches that would all have the salutary effect of changing funds' incentives by reducing the subsidy: (i) adoption of a vote cutoff below which the sponsor must fully reimburse the firm for the cost of submitting the proposal; (ii) use of a sliding scale of reimbursement depending on the level of votes obtained; and (iii) shareholder selection of the extent of subsidization of proposals. The third option is my preferred approach, but in contrast to the other two proposals, it is at odds with the mandatory approach of the SEC rules.

The proposition that shareholders should finance their proposals is not a novel idea. Commentators writing in the 1980s critiqued the shareholder proposal subsidy, contending that the mismatched incentives for individual shareholders arising from the subsidy were greater than the benefits from reducing free rider problems. Specifically, these commentators emphasized the extremely low voting support for the proposals and the small number of "professional gadfly" individual sponsors. Although the critique of the regime necessarily differed in the 1980s' context of individual sponsors and low support levels, the policy position is equally apt today in the quite different landscape of institutions' higher-support-generating proposals.

In particular, the essential incentive mismatch of the rule identified by earlier critiques is as relevant for institutional as it is for individual investors, given the opportunity for fund managers to obtain private benefits from proposal sponsorship. If institutional sponsors obtain private benefits, then not only is there even less cause for other shareholders to subsidize such activity, but also, special cause for concern: such benefits accrue to the fund manager and not the fund beneficiaries, who are in a similar position to that of the other shareholders, as they benefit solely from proposals producing performance improvements. Moreover, the free rider problem justifying subsidization of individual investor action is mitigated for institutions given their larger ownership positions and their participation in trade organizations that assemble detailed information on governance issues. Finally, the corporate finance literature, which was not available to 1980s commentators, strongly bolsters the case for altering the policy of subsidized access to the proxy machinery because it indicates persuasively that proposal sponsors are frequently not pursuing a value-maximizing agenda....

Some might contend that because the cost [of subsidizing shareholder proposals is] quite modest compared to the market value of publicly-traded firms, it is unnecessary to rein in the subsidy as the problem is self-correcting: informed funds can be expected to revise their activist strategies in the face of the new learning of the finance literature. In this view, it is better for shareholders to bear the relatively low cost of the subsidy during an adjustment period in which institutions reassess their activist programs, than for them to operate under a reformed regime that reduced the subsidy. There are two rationales that could be advanced in support of this position. First, a reduction in the subsidy could undermine whatever deterrent effect is provided by shareholder proposals, and second, it could decrease the extent of governance innovations that arise from institutional investors' experimentation with governance reforms through proposal sponsorship, as they would no longer be able to offer, at no cost to themselves, proposals that take several years of submission before they achieve substantial support.

These objections to the need for reform are not, however, persuasive. A significant deterrent effect is improbable because of the lack of any performance effect from, and the infrequency of top management turnover after, proposal submissions. In addition, the experimentation aspect of shareholder proposals is attenuated: the governance proposals offered by institutional investors have not been directed at novel devices for which there have been no empirical research on performance effects. For example, the drive to propose independent directors in the 1990s occurred after most firms' boards had a majority of outside directors and substantial research had been undertaken regarding their impact, and the defensive tactics that were the object of the initiation of shareholder proposals had been the subject of prior empirical study, although the performance effect of defenses has been found to differ over time, which has changed the calculus concerning the efficacy of shareholder targeting of them. But experimentation over governance reforms will not be eliminated by a reduction in the subsidy—it will instead require a higher threshold for action.

Most important, the premise of the contention, that activist institutions will significantly alter their governance programs as the results of the finance literature are publicized, is dubious. The disparity in proposal sponsorship across public and private fund managers strongly suggests that there is an agency problem, so that the regime will not, in fact, be subject to self-correction. The current regime provides no incentive to mitigate an agency problem in institutional proposal sponsorship. Instead, it encourages the submission of proposals that have private benefits and hence may not be value-maximizing, by allocating proposal costs across all shareholders. Accordingly, the more compelling response to the current regime's relatively low annual cost compared to market capitalization is to recognize that the low cost is a contributing factor to the tolerance of a wasteful regime.

Although the case is exceedingly strong for reducing, if not for eliminating, the subsidization of shareholder proposals, in all likelihood, such a reform of the proxy proposal process will be politically difficult to implement. It is improbable that politically well-connected institutions (public pension funds and unions) which have been obtaining access to the proxy process for free will voluntarily agree to begin paying for it. Indeed, institutional investors have opposed even minor changes that could limit their free access to the proxy process, such as an increase in the minimum threshold of votes required for a proposal's resubmission in a subsequent year. It is, however, hoped that this Article's marshaling of the evidence and analysis of the dismal ineffectiveness of the institutional investor activism agenda will alter the view of those investors (or at least of nonactivist institutional investors) of the proposal process such that they will acknowledge, and support, the need for meaningful reform....

Leo E. Strine, Jr., *The Delaware Way: How We Do Corporate Law and Some of the New Challenges We (and Europe) Face*[*]

....

... What Does It Mean to Be a Stockholder?: The Rapidly Accelerating "Separation of Capital from Capital"

Compounding these regulatory pressures is the next issue I'll highlight: what I call the "separation of capital from capital." This separation is well-developed in the United States

---

[*] Originally published in 30 DELAWARE JOURNAL OF CORPORATE LAW 673 (2005). Reprinted with permission. The author is a Vice Chancellor (judge) of the Delaware Court of Chancery.

and is rapidly emerging in Europe, as well. Those of us who are corporate law junkies are of course familiar with the phrase the "separation of capital from management," which encapsulates the key idea behind the public corporation. But, it has become increasingly common for individual investors to not directly own stock in operating corporations. They instead own shares in mutual or pension funds, which in turn own shares in the operating companies.

These institutional intermediaries have interests that are not perfectly aligned, to state it mildly, with those of their own stockholders. Mutual funds make money through fees, and do not have a profit motive to undertake efforts at shareholder activism at the operating company level. A mutual fund family knows that whatever benefits its activism generates for the operating company will not be exclusively or even primarily theirs, but will be spread among the operating company's diverse investor base, including the mutual fund's own industry competitors. For that reason, the huge institutions that manage an enormous amount of equity for many Americans—like Vanguard, Fidelity, and Barclay's—have been relatively docile stockholders in the United States.

In relative contrast, pension funds under the control of elected state officials and affiliated with labor unions have been more vociferous, but these institutions have their own agency costs. The agendas of these institutions have often seemed quixotic and not rationally designed to promote the long-term creation of wealth. These institutions focus almost obsessively on corporate takeover policy. Meanwhile, they were for too long tolerant of accounting and disclosure practices that masked real corporate rot.

More recently, institutions of these kinds have been looking to increase the competitiveness of the corporate election system. They desire access to the company's proxy card in seeking votes and corporate reimbursement for their campaign expenses if their preferred candidates attain a substantial, but not winning, show of support from the electorate. But, many investors, and most managers, fear that these institutions have less-than-optimal incentives and expertise to select corporate directors who have the experience and wisdom to guide corporations towards sound business strategies.

The purpose is not to single this class of institutional investors out for undue criticism. By comparison to the mutual funds, these institutions were at least not inert.

To address institutional inertia, the U.S. Department of Labor, which governs pension funds for many purposes, now requires institutional investors who manage pension money to vote their shares in an informed manner. And the SEC is now forcing mutual funds to disclose how they vote. But these are not panaceas leading to rational voting behavior.

Many institutional investors have, as I mentioned, little desire to do any thinking of their own, particularly about investments that they often hold for nanoseconds. Into this opportunistic breach has stepped an organization called Institutional Shareholders Services (ISS), which provides institutions with recommendations as to how to vote on corporate governance issues. [*ISS was acquired by RiskMetrics Group in 2007, and is now known by that name.*] Following ISS constitutes a form of insurance against regulatory criticism, and results in ISS having a large sway in the affairs of American corporations.

Moreover, powerful CEOs come on bended knee to Rockville, Maryland, where ISS resides, to persuade the managers of ISS of the merits of their views about issues like proposed mergers, executive compensation, and poison pills. They do so because the CEOs recognize that some institutional investors will simply follow ISS's advice rather than do any thinking of their own. ISS has been so successful that it now has a California rival, Glass Lewis.

Institutional investors now hold over half the stock in most American corporations. They are duty bound to vote it. But they often have interests that diverge from those of a hypothetical investor who has entrusted his capital to an operating firm in exchange for shares.

As a result, we face a world in which stockholders of operating companies are both more active and more conflicted. Those institutions most inclined to help set the corporate governance agenda — public and union affiliated pension funds — are probably least suited to evaluate what ideas make the most business sense. Those institutions better positioned to act on sound business logic — mutual funds — are the least inclined to be active stockholders. Mutual funds have a profit motive to be torpid, and also have business reasons to not upset corporate managers, even if upsetting managers is best for their own clients. Most frustratingly, those mutual funds whose stockholders have the most to gain from an overall increase in corporate integrity — index funds — are often the ones with the most interest in avoiding activism, in order to keep their management fees down.

Not only that, but institutional investors face incentives that can lead them to act in a way that is bad in the long-run for a particular operating company whose shares they hold if that act would benefit their overall portfolio. If a takeover bid for a healthy operating company involves only a twenty-five percent premium, instead of a forty percent premium, an institution whose overall portfolio for the quarter is suffering will often be willing to accept a low-ball bid rather than supporting the board's demand for independence until a full-priced bid comes along. Why? Because the profits from the underpriced bid will help mask the overall weakness of the portfolio's performance in the quarter. Likewise, when considering between alternative strategic stock-for-stock merger bids for a target, institutions are often more focused on which offers the highest immediate premium, rather than on which combination is more likely to produce stockholder wealth in the long run.

Short-term thinking of that kind should come as no surprise to any of you who own an actively managed mutual fund. Just what does it mean to be an investor when mutual fund portfolio turns over 300% or more of its holdings in a year? Is that rational? And what sort of monitoring does such an "investor" perform and to what end?

An increasingly popular form of investment fund is putting even more confounding pressure on corporations. So-called "hedge funds" now sometimes hold voting rights in corporations in which they hold net short positions. Rather than having an incentive to vote their shares in the manner that will increase the value of those corporations, these hedge funds often have an economic incentive to vote in a manner that will impair corporate value.

These and other related factors are making it difficult for corporate law makers to avoid a fundamental look at the system. Questions of the following kind are surfacing: Should mutual fund boards face the same kind of fiduciary duty review that operating boards do? And just precisely what are the duties that institutional investors owe to their beneficiaries? Must they be intelligent and active monitors of the operating companies in which they invest? What mechanisms should, or feasibly can, be implemented to prevent the casting of votes designed to injure, rather than help, the corporation? Are there means by which the influence of long-term stockholders with a demonstrated commitment to particular operating firms can be enhanced, while the ability of transient, short-term profit seekers to disrupt sound corporate planning is limited?

I have grave doubt that corporate law alone can engender greater rationality. Without tax and other policy changes designed to reform the incentives of these institutions and to check their agency costs, it is unlikely their behavior will change. For example, most of us think the market's preoccupation with quarter-to-quarter profits is stupid. Anyone who is honest will admit that this obsession contributed to wrongdoing at corporations like Enron and HealthSouth. But, as presently constituted, the institutions who most shape the market's movements and focus are not designed with the goal of patient, fundamentally sound wealth creation in mind. These institutions respond to, and thus behave in ways that further fuel, short-term pressures for immediate payoffs. Meanwhile, these institutions suffer little—compared to their clients, corporate workers, and society as a whole—if that myopia contributes to corporate debacles, which have deep roots in hypersensitivity to the production of so-called "accounting profits." The divergence in interests between institutions, particularly mutual funds, and their stockholders (i.e., individual investors) is likely to become even starker. As more and more "mom and pops" (individual investors) are forced to depend on equity investments as a means to finance a secure retirement, the chasm between the institutions' incentives to focus on the very short-term and their typical stockholders' need and desire for responsible, durable portfolio growth will widen further.

That said, corporate law bears its share of responsibility. It must continue to provide space for well-intentioned boards to conceive and execute long-term strategies. Where it can, corporate law should facilitate a greater voice for true long-term investors, willing to put patient capital at risk in pursuit of plans to produce wealth, not through accounting gimmickry, but through the provision of new products and services.

In Europe, the phenomena I have described are probably in a somewhat more nascent state, but seem to be evolving rapidly in the same directions we have experienced. But watch out—the outbursts of institutional investor pressure [European] companies now occasionally face are likely to become more commonplace than unusual.

. . . .

Daniel J.H. Greenwood, *Fictional Shareholders: For Whom are Corporate Managers Trustees, Revisited*[*]

It is a commonplace of American law that corporations are fictional. The U.S. Supreme Court said so, in the first important corporate law case to come before it, *Bank of the United States v. Deveaux*,[9] and repeated it in the next, the famous contract case of *Dartmouth College v. Woodward*:[10] The corporation is simply a convenient, though misleading, way to refer to its shareholders or members. Many modern theorists agree that the corporation is a metaphor, though they have different visions of what it "really" is.

But despite this ancient and sophisticated discourse regarding the corporation, the literature and cases have relatively little discussion of the shareholders. This omission is particularly glaring in light of the dominant paradigm of corporate law, which holds that the central task of corporate law is to lessen or eliminate the potential conflict between shareholders and corporate managers—the so-called problem of separation of ownership

---

    * Originally published in 69 Southern California Law Review 1021 (1996). Copyright 1996 Daniel J.H. Greenwood. Reprinted with permission.
    9. 9 U.S. (5 Cranch) 61 (1809).
    10. 17 U.S. (4 Wheat.) 518 (1819).

and control identified in Berle and Means' seminal work and put into its modern form by Jensen and Meckling.[11]

Modern cases and theory, like the older ones, assume that shareholders, unlike corporations, are not problematic. Corporations may be legal fictions, mere metaphors for underlying—and quite different—realities. But shareholders, it is generally assumed, are not problematic at all. They are widows in Iowa, profit-maximizing investors or—more recently—institutional investors, and little further discussion is needed. After all, whatever else shareholders may or may not want, every shareholder wants to make a profit and that is all that is really important for the operation of corporate law and, indeed, the corporation itself.

Virtually all the major groups of corporate law scholars today agree on the centrality of the shareholder to corporate law; all but the communitarians agree that virtually the sole task of corporate law is to ensure that managers act as agents for the shareholder owners. This Article directly challenges the almost universally held assumption that shareholders, in the form understood by the law, are a group of human beings entitled to respect and consideration and having interests that exist independent of corporate law. I contend, rather, that corporate law theorists have missed the critical point that an agency (or trust) relationship has quite a different significance when the "principal" (or beneficiary) is a set of legally defined interests that are not under the control of any individual or group of individual human beings who could choose to redefine or act in opposition to those interests.

This Article, then, is an attempt at a careful look at the role of shareholders in corporate legal theory. Shareholders, I contend, are a legal fiction, and in many ways a far more problematic fiction than the corporation itself. Indeed, since corporate law and the market alike drive corporations to act in the interests of these fictional shareholders, the shareholder is the most important fiction of corporate law: The legally imputed characteristics of corporate shareholders are the power behind the throne of managerial autonomy, the driving force that determines the structure and functioning of our corporate system. For this reason, we need to examine the nature of our fictional shareholders more carefully: Both the successes and the failures of our system ultimately reflect the characteristics of the shareholder we have created.

Specifically, I contend that the fictional shareholder is fundamentally different from the human beings who ultimately stand behind the fiction. The law and the legally created structure of corporation and market filter out all the complexity of conflicted, committed, particularly situated, deeply embedded and multi-faceted human beings, leaving only simple, one-sided monomaniacs. Human beings have short lives, spent in particular places with particular relationships to other human beings; they constantly confront the problems of finitude and commitment. Shareholders, in contrast, are in significant senses immortal, uncommitted and universal: They are indifferent as to time and place, language and religion. They are indifferent between projects and personalities. They are understood to care deeply about one important and vital human aim—profit maximization—but not at all about numerous others. While the ultimate owners of the shares are specific, situated, conflicted and committed human beings, shareholders in most instances may be thought of more appropriately as a "large, fluid, changeable and changing market."

These differences between fictional shareholders and human beings can be grouped into two broad categories, each with a distinctive impact on the society and economy we

---

11. Michael C. Jensen & William H. Meckling, *Theory of the Firm: Managerial Behavior, Agency Costs and Ownership Structures*, 3 J. FIN. ECON. 305 (1976).

use them to create. First, like classical utilitarians and the market itself, shareholders do not take the distinction between persons seriously. That is, in many important situations they are indifferent to distributional issues that are critical to ordinary human beings. Second, they are fundamentally inhuman because they have only one goal, profit maximization—and, thus, need not make the compromises among conflicting goals that are the essence of human politics and life.

The consequences for corporate law are also twofold: First, in the eyes of the law and corporate management, shareholders are all the same. As a result, managers are given relatively clear direction without any need to pierce the cacophony of inconsistent demands from conflicted and conflicting individuals. Corporate management is therefore far easier than political management. This simplicity, however, is based on an illusion—the conflicts do not disappear merely because the law presumes that shareholders are above them.

Second, the actual owners of the shares are irrelevant to corporate law: Neither the interests nor the desires of the people behind the shares count. Because managers manage on behalf of a fictional principle rather than a human principal, corporations are a strange, driven kind of institution—neither managers nor anyone else has the ultimate authority to stop the institution from acting out its logic to the fullest.

This Article proceeds as follows. First, I explain what I mean by calling shareholders fictional and outline in more detail the basic characteristics of the legally determined fictional entity. Second, I illustrate some ways in which the fictional shareholder imposes its will on the corporation—here, I follow the current consensus that the conflict between managers and shareholders has been resolved in favor of shareholder control, but with a twist, since I view the corporations not as controlled by human owners but rather as run in the largely legally defined interests of fictional creations. Neither those legally defined interests nor their fictional holders can be mapped in any simple way onto an underlying group of human beings. Finally, I explore the consequences of having our largest institutions run in the interests of a legal fiction and offer some preliminary suggestions regarding areas in which an institution run in the interests of fictional shareholders will be similar to, or different from, one run by or in the interests of human beings.

Berle and Means' classical corporate theory and their leading contemporary critics agree that corporate law should strive to organize corporations so that managers act in the interests of shareholders. In the modern jargon, corporate law should seek to reduce the agency costs inherent in the separation of ownership and control. In contrast, this Article's analysis suggests that the agency metaphor is deeply misleading. Since shareholders are a legal fiction rather than living, breathing human beings in their full richness, they are not principals in any ordinary sense. The corporation, then, is not usefully understood as a more or less perfect agent acting more or less responsibly on behalf of its principal. Rather, corporate law creates a corporate entity that may behave distinctly differently from the ways in which any (or all) of the human participants would behave were they free from legal constraint.

For corporate theory, this shift in perspective is of enormous importance. If the corporation's shareholders cannot be identified with human citizens of the political community, then even the most sophisticated proof that the "genius" of American law forces corporations to act in shareholder interests cannot demonstrate that corporate actions reflect the will or interest of any citizen or group of citizens. Rather, the corporation becomes an independent actor in our polity and economy. Because the fictional shareholder is fundamentally different from any human being—even human beings who own shares—a corporation acting in shareholder interests will act quite differently from the way its supposed principals would have it act....

The corporate system we have created generates a conflict that is not reducible to either of the classic conceptions: It is not a class conflict, as that term is understood in either the Marxist or sociological traditions, and it is not the agency conflict with which so much of corporate law is concerned. It is, instead, more closely related to the problem of government as understood by the classic liberal theorists: a human institution which may often and in predictable ways cease to serve the limited (if essential) purposes for which it was formed.

In short, we have created an institution for a specific purpose and put it on a sort of automatic pilot, so that it continues to pursue the preset goals whether or not they continue to be useful. Corporate law succeeds because it is single-minded, and fails because it lacks a principle of moderation or any significant countervailing power.

I. Understanding Shareholders: The Theory of the Fictional Shareholder

A. *Distinguishing People Who Own Shares from Shareholders*

... Shareholders are a legal fiction in a very precise sense. The law demands that corporate directors and managers manage the corporation in the interests of the shareholders and the corporation. But by "shareholder interests" the law does not mean the interests—let alone the will—of the actual people who are the beneficial owners of the shares (or, in our increasingly institutional stock market, the people who are the ultimate beneficiaries of the legal entities that own the shares). The actual people are not consulted; they have only primitive, indirect and ineffective means of letting their perceived interests or actual will be known. No owner of shares ever negotiates a contract with or submits instructions to the directors or managers. Nor does the board act like a sort of Benthamite neutral observer examining the life situations of the actual people out there and determining that, whether they know it or not, their interests require some action or other.

Rather, the law creates a simplified and fundamentally inaccurate image of a hypothetical shareholder and then requires that the interests of this nonexistent person be the focus of corporate efforts. It is the interests of a fictional person whose sole interest is the shares it owns that is the focus of legal and corporate efforts to promote "shareholder" interests—in effect, the shareholder is reduced to the shares.

I call this shareholder fictional because it is a coherent story, an essentially complete and unified being, lacking the complexity and contrasting commitments of real, human, people. When corporations are seen as owned by the fictional shareholder, the struggles of the corporate world seem to be a simple novel about a central character with one driving force, one story to tell and—although this has not often enough been remarked—one fatal flaw.

The fictional shareholder is also fictional because of a specific falsehood: the ideological belief that shareholders, as they are understood in the law and the marketplace, can be identified with specific individual human beings, and therefore, that defending shareholder rights is the same as defending human rights....

I do not mean to suggest that the shareholder is fictional in the sense of nonexistent. On the contrary, shareholders are legally created entities that exist in the strong sense that they determine much of our lives....

Nor do I mean to suggest that the motivations of fictional shareholders are entirely different from those of the underlying owners. After all, presumably most owners of shares would prefer that their shares be worth more rather than less, ceteris paribus. This Article is concerned with those instances where ceteris is not paribus. The problem is not that fictional shareholders always or even often make the wrong decision, but that they make no decision at all: The fiction of the one-sided shareholder hides the tradeoffs that must be made in life from the view of those who must make them....

B. The Owners of the Shares

The facts about the ownership of publicly traded stock in the United States are fairly well known. About half the publicly held stock is held institutionally—principally by pension funds, insurance companies, mutual funds, bank trust funds and endowment funds. Most of this institutional ownership is, in turn, on behalf of identifiable individual human beings: the beneficiaries of pension funds, the policy holders of mutual insurance companies, the stockholders of mutual funds. Some of it is more difficult to see as held on behalf of specific people: Who is, for example, the ultimate beneficiary of Harvard University's endowment?

The indirect ownership of this institutionally owned stock is fairly broad. Virtually all American households own a car and carry automobile insurance. A large percentage of Americans own their own homes and carry homeowners insurance. Many Americans hold life insurance. Virtually all of these people—clearly the ones who hold their insurance through mutual companies, and arguably the rest as well—are indirect beneficiaries of insurance company stock holdings. In addition, a significant number of Americans have pension plans or 401(k) plans; all of the former and most of the latter group are also indirect holders of stocks. Finally, about twenty percent of American households hold stock mutual funds. Thus, it seems safe to assert that a significant proportion of Americans are indirect stockholders or closely related to such stockholders....

C. Fictional Shareholders

1. The Puzzle of the Uniform Shareholder

Here is the puzzle. If shares are held directly or indirectly by half the American population, and corporations act as agents of their shareholders, then we should expect two things: First, that corporate America would reflect the full diversity of human America, and second, that shareholder elections and other methods of determining what exactly it is that the shareholders are directing their agents to do would reflect in some fashion the wide range of human American politics.

We should see publicly held corporations that are as deeply dedicated to particular projects, or products, or places, or ideologies, or religions, or ways of working and lifestyles as many Americans are. We should see Berle and Means corporations that decide that profits are not the most important thing—just as many Americans put other values ahead of wealth maximization, some corporations should reduce their income in order to better serve needs of children, family, art, leisure time, status or religion. We should see Democratic corporations, Republican corporations, stamp collector corporations and the like.

We do not. Instead, public corporations have a rather narrow range of styles and interests. Few of them even claim to have Time Inc.'s dedication to a particular corporate culture, and even those that do seem able to throw it off—generally in the direction of corporate normality—as easily as IBM abandoned lifetime employment or the American Can Company abandoned the can business.

There are some importantly idiosyncratic corporations out there. But by and large the idiosyncratic ones are the ones that do not fit the Berle and Means model. Either they are privately held, and thus able to vary all the basic structures of corporate law, or they are dominated by founders who exploit the looseness of corporate law to treat a public company as if it were still private. We do not see public companies dropping their blandness to reflect the diversity of America.

Similarly, we do not see the hotly contested shareholder elections one might expect if corporations were reflecting a diverse shareholder body....

2. The Puzzle of the Missing Agency Rights

Another set of oddities seems to challenge the very notion of shareholders as principals of the corporation: Shareholders have few or none of the rights that agency law grants to principals. This is no secret; why, then, do courts and scholars continue to use the agency metaphor?

The Restatement [of Agency] states that an agency relationship is characterized by two special traits. The agent, who acts on behalf of the principal, is subject to the principal's control. And the principal has an unlimited right to terminate the agent at any time.[12]

In sharp contrast, Delaware courts never tire of repeating that the board of a Delaware corporation has original, undelegated power to manage the corporation. The board may make virtually every decision on its own authority; only a few decisions must be ratified by the shareholders. Even in those relatively unusual circumstances where shareholder approval is required, shareholders generally have no right to initiate action. They can vote only at specified times for specified purposes; subject to a few exceptions, the board controls their agenda. Shareholders, to be sure, have the right to present proper proposals at the annual meeting. But state law generally bars most proposals ordering the directors to take particular actions: That would be a breach of the directors' fiduciary duty to act in the best interests of all shareholders. Federal law has been even more restrictive, denying even to purely advisory proposals access to the proxy machinery necessary to make proposals meaningful if, inter alia, the "proposal deals with a matter relating to the conduct of the ordinary business operations of the registrant"; this rule has been applied—though not consistently—to bar shareholders from expressing to management their opinions regarding employee health benefits, compensation policies, workplace management, racial discrimination, hiring and firing practices, labor relations, conditions of employment, EEO compliance, affirmative action, a company policy discriminating against homosexuals and so on.

Even the most important decision from a shareholder perspective—whether to sell the corporation as a whole—must be made in the first instance by the board. Merger agreements, sales of all assets, dissolution of the corporation and even amendments to its articles of incorporation must all be initiated and approved by the board prior to shareholder action....

3. A Different Kind of Principal

We have seen, then, that shareholders do not have the kinds of disputes one would expect if they were a diverse group of Americans engaged in a struggle to make corporations

---

12. RESTATEMENT (SECOND) OF AGENCY §§ 1, 14, 118 & cmt. b (1984).

in their images, and that as a matter of law, shareholders, even taken as a collectivity, lack the control over directors that characterizes an ordinary agency relationship. The facts are no surprise: Every reader of the Wall Street Journal knows that corporate elections are generally won by margins not seen in democratic politics....

One might conclude from this that the agency metaphor is simply wrong; that in fact directors are not agents of the shareholders and the shareholders are not the principals, or owners, of the firm. Directors, after all, are explicitly authorized by statute in over half the states and by case law in Delaware to consider the interests of corporate participants other than the shareholders. Thus, the law of directors defies even the remaining aspect of agency law, that the agent acts on behalf of the principal. Taking these "constituency statutes" and the agency metaphor seriously, one might come to view the corporation as a coalition of bargaining groups with the shareholders as one among equals, or as a quasi-state that has (presumptively wrongfully) limited the franchise to but one subsection of the governed, or as a more amorphous kind of community.

The persistence of the notion that the directors are agents for shareholders, in the face of well-known facts and law to the contrary, however, suggests that the metaphor should not be dismissed so easily. The fictional shareholder solves the puzzle and rescues the agency metaphor from otherwise hopeless obscurity.

The key to the puzzle, in my view, is that in a sense directors often do view themselves as acting on behalf of shareholders, and the shareholders do control the corporation, despite the law and appearances to the contrary. But the shareholders on behalf of which the directors act and the shareholders that control the corporation are not the owners of the shares. Rather, they are a kind of personification of the shares themselves, almost imaginary creatures driven by only one goal: to maximize the value of their shares.

I claim, then, that the agency picture of the corporation is right in this sense: The people who make corporate decisions—directors and managers—do so and are required to view themselves as doing so in an agency role. Their job, as they see it, is to put aside their own interests and views and act on behalf of someone else's views and interests. In that strong sense, they are agents, regardless of whether the law gives that someone else the technical rights of a principal under agency law. But the someone whom the corporate agents represent, in whose behalf they must act, is not a full human being in all its complexity, much less a collection of half the citizens of the United States of America. Rather, it is the fictional simplification we call a shareholder.

4. *Hypothetical Politics of Imagined Monads: Hobbes Meets the Fictional Shareholder*

The fictional principal solves many of the puzzles of the agency metaphor. First, it explains the startling absence of intra-shareholder conflict and actual agency rules in corporate law noted in the prior two sections. Second, it justifies an extraordinary level of deference to the professional managers of the corporation.

Fictional shareholders, unlike real ones, do not have strong conflicts in their attachments or ideologies. They are not Democrats and Republicans, religious and atheist, committed to New York or Iowa, tied to a job or a family or encumbered by the life stages of a real human being. They do not have a multiplicity of plans for a too-short life: They have one, to maximize the value of their shares. As a result, they are all the same (or almost all the same, as we shall see in a moment).

Now, timeless, ageless, familyless, unencumbered imaginary people with unified goals getting together and deciding what to do are a familiar image to students of Western political philosophy. That is a crude, one-sentence description of persons in the state of nature of the liberal political theory tradition of John Locke and Thomas Hobbes....

Consent, especially consent under fair conditions, is notoriously difficult to obtain. Those who premise justice on obtaining actual agreement tend to conclude that all existing societies are unjust and the possibility of creating a future just society is slim indeed, as do Robert P. Wolff, Robert Nozick and John Jacques Rousseau.[13] Furthermore, their work can easily become a justification for creating agreements by force—by killing or expelling those who disagree, as in the nationalist and revolutionary reinterpretations of Rousseau.

In contrast, if we could imagine an agreement that all rational people would agree to under fair conditions, some philosophers have argued that there would then be no need to reach an actual agreement. Real people might well refuse to agree—but their refusal may be disregarded, since it must (by hypothesis) stem either from irrationality or from an unfair bargaining situation.

Hobbes thus argued that all people, whatever else they want and whatever their goals in life, wish to stay alive; accordingly, under fair bargaining conditions they would all agree to create a government that will keep them alive.[14] From this foundation, he constructed the Leviathan—a massive defense of a rather unfree politics based on a hypothetical unanimous agreement. The power of his argument is that if we were persuaded that all rational people would, after reflection, agree to the society he describes, then such a political arrangement would be legitimate regardless of its history or origin: No investigation of real history, no questioning of real people, no actual debates or politics in this world are necessary to show the legitimacy or illegitimacy of the existing government. Hypothetical politics replaces the real form....

The exciting thing is that once the philosopher has identified a common goal—life, or maximization of primary goods, or whatever—the philosopher can then derive the agreement that such individuals would reach if they were in a fair starting point. No actual discussions with actual people are necessary: We can figure out what they would want by applied logic....

In our corporate law, this liberal model of a hypothetical politics is taken to its fullest, Hobbesian, extreme. Fictional shareholders all want to maximize the value of their shares. They exist without context or history. Since the value of their shares is nothing more than the discounted value of the future income stream represented by the dividends, they are time indifferent. Since dividend streams are fully fungible, they are as uncommitted as persons in the state of nature. Since fictional shareholders function in a free market, they are individualist and self-interested. And like the persons in the state of nature or behind the veil of ignorance, they are fully equal and able to enter into a fair bargain.

Fictional shareholders, then, meet all the requirements of hypothetical politics. Here, as in the Hobbesian model, something very exciting happens: Once we agree that all the shareholders share this common goal, actual politics becomes an unnecessary distraction. We can calculate what rational and equal shareholders want by mere reason. Discussion is unnecessary; expertise can replace persuasion and voting.

---

13. *See* ROBERT P. WOLFF, IN DEFENSE OF ANARCHISM (1970); ROBERT NOZICK, ANARCHY, STATE AND UTOPIA (1974) John Jacques Rousseau, *The Social Contract*, in POLITICAL WRITINGS (Frederick Watkins trans. & ed., 1986).

14. THOMAS HOBBES, LEVIATHAN (1651).

... [F]ictional shareholders, whatever else the people behind them may want, all want to maximize the value of their shares. And as follows from the basic teachings of Adam Smith regarding the division of labor, rational share-value-maximizers would agree to delegate management of the company to professionals. Maximizing the value of the shares is a job for technical experts; there is no reason to think that the average (or indeed any) shareholder is particularly good at it.

It follows, then, that the separation of ownership and control is not a vaguely illegitimate deprivation of the rightful prerogatives of ownership, but rather a supremely sensible application of the division of labor. Companies need professional managers; the shareholding system allows competent managers to be chosen without regard for whether they also have the wealth to be shareholders....

Finally, the fictional shareholder model explains the strikingly primitive understanding of agency problems in the corporate law agency cost literature. Corporate law agency theory concerns itself almost exclusively with corruption costs — the problem of agents who deliberately refuse to do the job they are hired to do, or who ignore their duties, intentionally putting their own interests ahead of their principals'.

Compare this thin view of the difficulties of the role of the professional agent to, for example, the elaborate discussions of how best to represent another that arise entirely within good faith models of professionalism in other fields: lawyers and doctors struggling to understand how to pursue their clients' interests and goals in a world where those interests and goals may be nonexistent, underdeveloped or incoherent. These issues drop out of corporate law because the fictional shareholder — unlike the human clients of doctors and other professionals — is seen as having only a single, consistent and clear goal....

II. The Conflict Between the Fictional Shareholder and Living Humans

....

We have seen that the shareholder of corporate law is a fictional stripped-down being interested in only one thing. Corporations acting in good faith consider only the needs and interests of the stripped-down fiction, not the desires or wishes of the underlying complex humans. At the same time, institutional investors seeking to advance the interests of their own fictional shareholders push the corporations whose shares they own to act in ways they deem beneficial to their portfolio (and therefore to their fictional shareholders).

Many of the difficult issues in modern corporate law can be understood in terms of the conflict between these two visions of the shareholder. Unlike the corporate law shareholder, the portfolio shareholder does not take seriously the distinction among companies: The institutional integrity of a particular corporation is of no interest to it. For the portfolio shareholder, dismantling a company is of no special significance; all that matters is the total value of the portfolio and the particular security's contribution to that value. Similarly, prevailing against a publicly traded competitor may not even seem a desirable goal to the portfolio shareholder.

Some rational portfolio shareholders, then, should oppose a series of investment and competitive decisions — including all those aimed at shifting wealth from one set of securitized interests to another — that less diversified fictional investors would support. Because of their different perspective, portfolio investors drive companies to take actions that are likely to seem inappropriate to managers deeply invested (literally and figuratively) in the particular institution.

These conflicts between the portfolio shareholder view and managerial perspectives may drive managers to seek to free themselves from shareholder control—through poison pills, anti-takeover laws and other takeover defenses that effectively reduce the portfolio shareholder's ability to use the right to sell the company to force it to adopt portfolio perspectives, or through constituency statutes that essentially remove any threat of judicial enforcement of a fiduciary duty that might remain even after the business judgment rule. Alternatively, the conflict between portfolio and corporate law shareholder perspectives may create a space in which corporate leaders may feel conflicting duties without a clear guide explaining which to follow (or may be able to appeal to conflicting norms to justify actions adopted for other reasons).

At least equally important as the ongoing conflict of the fictions, however, is a set of conflicts largely ignored by modern corporate law and the associated scholarship. Both the diversified and the undiversified fictional shareholder agree on far more than they disagree. If only the portfolio investor fails to take the distinction among companies seriously, both fail to take the distinctions within companies seriously. That is, fictional shareholders of all varieties are supremely inhuman in their indifference to particularity within the corporation.

The fictional shareholder takes the position that a dollar is a dollar. It does not matter if it is earned in the company's traditional field of business or a new acquisition (unless, of course, experience allows the company to be more profitable). It does not matter if it is earned in the Rust Belt or the Sun Belt or the Third World. So long as the dollar results are the same, it does not matter if it is earned with highly paid, highly motivated labor or with low-paid child labor abroad. It does not matter if it is earned in a high-risk operation with a high potential for putting many people out of work or a more stable operation. All that matters is the risk-adjusted present discounted value of the future income flows....

The fictional shareholder focuses our corporate managers' minds admirably. But sometimes we need a little less focus and a little more breadth. The old task of corporate law has been to tie the managers to the shareholders; the new task must be to align the fictional shareholder more closely with us.

Thomas W. Joo, *The Modern Corporation and Campaign Finance: Incorporating Corporate Governance Analysis into First Amendment Jurisprudence**

... The Supreme Court has ... fail[ed] to consider the institutional peculiarities of business corporations when applying constitutional law to them. The Court has pursued the opposite extremes of awarding corporations rights as if they were human beings and insisting that the state has power to regulate corporations by fiat. The former approach completely ignores the institutional nature of corporations. The latter assigns too much importance to the legal category of "corporation" without explaining why the legal distinction should make a constitutional difference. In pursuing each of these approaches, the Court has relied on outdated, metaphysical concepts of the corporation and has failed

* Originally published in 79 Washington University Law Quarterly 1 (2001). Copyright 2001 Thomas W. Joo. Reprinted with permission.

to consider the ways in which corporations actually operate as organizations. Using the example of campaign finance jurisprudence, this Article argues that courts applying constitutional law to publicly traded business corporations should take into account the effects of the corporate governance regime on the corporate decision making process....

I. Supreme Court Case Law on the Regulation of Election-Related Spending

[In *First National Bank of Boston v. Bellotti*,[15] the Supreme Court struck down a Massachusetts law restricting corporations' ability to spend money to influence voter initiative and referendum campaigns.] The *Bellotti* Court struck down the statute on the ground that the public interest in hearing debate on governmental affairs justified protecting the spending from regulation under the First Amendment.... Because the constitutional protection derived from the public interest in hearing the speech, the Court stated that it was unnecessary to address whether corporations, as speakers, have the same First Amendment rights as individuals....

Nonetheless, the Court also strongly suggested that corporations have the same constitutional right as individuals to participate in public discourse. For example, the Court stated that the government may not "dictate the subjects about which persons may speak and the speakers who may address a public issue." Furthermore, the Court cited the *Buckley*[16] principle that the state may not "restrict the speech of some elements of our society in order to enhance the relative voice of others." The individual is the paradigmatic "element of society" with a right to participate in political discourse; this passage suggests that corporations are equivalent elements of society.

In defense of the statute, [the Massachusetts Attorney General argued that it] protected shareholders by "preventing the use of corporate resources in furtherance of views with which some shareholders may disagree." The Court identified the protection of shareholders as both a legitimate state interest and one traditionally within the province of state law. The Court assumed, without deciding, that this interest may be sufficiently compelling to justify burdens on speech. The Court found, however, that corporate election-related spending did not implicate that interest because shareholders themselves control corporate spending "through the procedures of corporate democracy."

... [I]n *Austin v. Michigan State Chamber of Commerce*[17] [the Supreme Court] upheld a restriction on independent expenditures by corporations, despite the fact that *Bellotti* suggested that corporate expenditures deserve the same strict First Amendment protection that individual expenditures enjoy. The Ninth Circuit has held that this conflict can be explained on the ground that *Bellotti* struck down the regulation of corporate spending on ballot questions, while *Austin*'s more permissive stance toward regulation involved the financing of candidate elections.... The *Austin* Court [however] did not credit this distinction with making a difference. [The Court justified its holding in *Austin* on the likelihood that concentrated corporate wealth might sway the outcome of elections. That argument, however, conflicts with the rule from *Buckley* cited in the *Bellotti* case, above. Thus, although federal law restricts corporate political expenditures, Supreme Court jurisprudence offers no clear justification for the constitutionality of these restrictions. This

---

15. 435 U.S. 765 (1978).
16. *Buckley v. Valeo*, 424 U.S. 1 (1976).
17. 494 U.S. 652 (1990).

Article argues that, with respect to large publicly traded corporations, the corporate governance structure provides a justification.]

II. Recognizing the Realities of Corporate Governance

Constitutional analysis should not simply assume that the acts of a corporation represent the expression of its constituent individuals, as the *Bellotti* Court did. Dissenting in *Bellotti*, Justice White asserted that corporate spending does not express the preferences of shareholders, but he did not directly counter the majority's assertion that shareholders control decisions through "corporate democracy." Justice White's assertion that corporate spending does not represent shareholder interests was as conclusory as the majority's insistence that it does.

Instead of jumping to either of these conclusions, constitutional law should use the insights of corporate law to ask whether corporate spending implicates individuals' expressive rights. Neither the majority nor the dissent examined the actual institutional characteristics of the appellant corporations in *Bellotti*. The justices simply analyzed them as generic corporations. The opinion neither considers nor mentions whether they were small enterprises or large, publicly traded corporations. In fact, they were among the nation's largest business corporations and banks: First National Bank of Boston, New England Merchants National Bank, Gillette Co., Digital Equipment Corp., and Wyman-Gordon Co. In addition, both Justice White and the majority considered only the interests of shareholders, and not those of other corporate constituents, who are completely disenfranchised by "corporate democracy."

Rather than relying on the easy assumption that a corporation's acts express its constituents' preferences as the *Bellotti* Court did, a court could undertake another approach and employ an intense factual inquiry for each given speech act by each given organization. A court would have to determine both how the organization in question actually reached a given decision to make a political expenditure, and to what extent it considered its members' concerns in that decision. While this idea may work in principle because it requires the speech to truly reflect the will of individuals, the required fact-finding would be terribly cumbersome in practice. Courts should therefore stake out a middle ground between conclusory assumptions on the one hand, and an unmanageable individualized empirical approach on the other.

Large business corporations share significant and similar organizational characteristics because of the common default form of their internal management. State corporate laws and federal securities laws prescribe default governance norms for publicly traded business corporations. These default norms tend to favor wealth creation over individuals' participation and thus justify presumptions that corporate spending does not reflect the expression of individual shareholders.... So-called "corporate democracy" does not give shareholders meaningful input into such decisions, much less control over them. The default corporate governance regime gives shareholder voting very limited power. Even to the extent that shareholders can challenge management's decisions, federal and state law fail to guarantee shareholder access to information about such decisions. Meaningful opposition to management decisions requires the owners of large numbers of shares to band together. Collective action problems, such as the limited opportunities for shareholders to communicate with one another, limit successful shareholder organization. Finally, while dissatisfied shareholders may dissociate from a corporation by the sale of shares, there are constraints on their ability to exercise this option.

... As Melvin Eisenberg notes, publicly traded corporations and closely held corporations are "two types of business associations which may have little in common but their form."[18] In the simplest case, a corporation may be owned, managed, and operated by a single individual. In such a case, the corporation's election-related spending may, quite literally, be that individual's expressive act. Shareholders may also participate more actively, and with less severe collective action problems, in corporations with a small number of shareholders. While shareholders of a public corporation are atomized and generally have no interactions with one another, the few shareholders of a closely held corporation are often "closely associated persons." Thus, they are more likely to have the opportunities to communicate directly with management and other shareholders and to bargain explicitly for participatory rights, simply by virtue of the small size of the organization....

In the large, public corporation, however, collective action problems created by the sheer number of shareholders can impose insurmountable transaction costs to contracting around default rules that discourage participation. Thus, courts should presume that speech does not constitute the expression of individuals with publicly traded corporations but should presume the opposite with closely held corporations....

A. Shareholder Access to Corporate Information

... [T]he power of the shareholder vote is inherently limited. [*See the remainder of this chapter, as well as Chapter 9. — Ed.*] Corporate law further constrains shareholders' ability to use their votes meaningfully and to participate in corporate decision making because it limits shareholders' access to information about the corporation's political expenditures. Large gaps in the scope of required disclosure in this area mean that management need not even inform shareholders of many kinds of corporate political activity. The rational apathy of the diversified portfolio investor makes it unlikely that she will go to the lengths necessary to seek out such information....

Some mistakenly believe that the materiality standards surrounding corporate disclosure [under the federal securities laws] protect shareholders by requiring corporations to disclose all "material" information. There is, however, no general obligation to disclose all information that might be of interest to shareholders or potential investors. To the contrary, a disclosure obligation must have a specific, independent legal foundation — corporations must disclose information that the SEC requests and only that information. In the present context, such obligations usually arise from the express disclosure requirements of Regulation S-K. Because Regulation S-K does not currently call for disclosure of information about election-related spending, corporations do not routinely provide this information. Even regulations that call for specific information are sometimes limited by explicit, quantitative materiality standards, generally in the range of five to ten percent of the corporation's assets or earnings. While five to ten percent of a corporation's assets or earnings may sound like a small figure, it translates into enormous dollar amounts. For example, for the year 2000, the fifty largest American corporations, based on assets, ranged in size from Bank of New York Co. with over $77 billion to Citigroup with over $902 billion.

The specific information required by securities regulations is "further 'filtered' through the screen of materiality."[19] According to the Supreme Court, the general test of materiality "is an objective one, involving the significance of an omitted or misrepresented fact to a

---

18. MELVIN A. EISENBERG, THE STRUCTURE OF THE CORPORATION: A LEGAL ANALYSIS 5 (1976).
19. Cynthia A. Williams, *Corporate Social Transparency*, 112 HARV. L. REV. 1197 (1999).

reasonable investor."[20] According to the SEC, however, this hypothetical reasonable investor is interested only in investment return. An SEC Advisory Committee on Corporate Disclosure reviewed SEC and judicial standards of materiality and recommended that the SEC consider "social and environmental information" material "only when it reflects significantly on the economic and financial performance" of a corporation....

Shareholders' primary role in corporate governance is the election of directors. Surprisingly, however, shareholders may not use the [corporation's] proxy statement to advocate for or against the election of particular directors.[21] The apparent justification for this odd exception is the potential drain on corporate resources if shareholders were to have such access. This Rule is yet another indication that corporate law is meant to further efficient wealth creation and not shareholders' participation or expression.

In *Bellotti*, the Court stated that even if protecting shareholders from management abuse of corporate property constitutes a compelling state interest, the statute at issue was overinclusive with respect to that goal. According to the Court, the statute would prohibit expenditures on referenda "even if [the corporation's] ... shareholders unanimously authorized the contribution or expenditure." The statute would indeed have prohibited such an expenditure, but the Court failed to recognize that a unanimously authorized act by a large publicly traded corporation is a creature of fantasy. [Moreover,] corporate law does not require management to consult shareholders at all before making such expenditures, much less acquire their unanimous approval. Political expenditures specifically authorized by shareholders simply do not occur in large corporations. Management is not required to disclose such expenditures to the shareholders, so they are unable to protest. Even if a shareholder discovered the expenditures and wanted to launch a shareholder protest, the shareholder would have difficulty obtaining access to lists and proxy statements to inform other shareholders and organize them to protest.

B. "Voting with Your Feet": Divestment as an Unsatisfactory Remedy

The "Wall Street Rule" teaches that if a shareholder disagrees with management, it is more efficient for her to sell her stock than to attempt to change management. This course of action is a poor remedy, however. A shareholder will know she has reason to sell only after she discovers that management is using corporate resources for political purposes with which she disagrees. First, the limitations on required disclosure impair her ability to obtain this information. Second, even if the shareholder learns of objectionable election-related spending, "voting with her feet" allows the shareholder only to escape continued unauthorized use of corporate resources. It does not put a stop to the activity generally or provide any remedy for the unauthorized use that has already occurred.

Moreover, selling shares because of the corporation's election-related spending is unlikely to have a disciplining effect on management. A sell-off in sufficient volume or threat of such sell-off can discipline management indirectly by depressing share prices and threatening their jobs. A divestiture, however, will not depress share prices unless an extremely large group of shareholders sells at roughly the same time. Even if divestiture causes stock price to fall, management may be unaware of the reason, as the corporate governance structure does not offer a method of communicating to management that

---

20. TSC Industries v. Northway, 426 U.S. 438, 445 (1976).
21. *At the time this book went to press in 2009, the SEC was considering new rules that would allow large shareholders to place director candidates on the corporate proxy. See Thomas Joo's article in Chapter 9. —Ed.*

political spending prompted the sell-off. Furthermore, orchestrating a concerted shareholder threat of sell-off is extremely difficult because of the obstacles to communicating and coordinating with other shareholders. Even if these obstacles are overcome, the exit option will not necessarily cause the market to provide the governance terms that investors prefer. Indeed, the availability of exit may actually reduce corporations' incentive to satisfy investor preferences by leading investors to sell and to search quixotically for ideal terms rather than staying invested in the firm and agitating for change from within.

In addition, while it is literally true that "the shareholder ... is free to withdraw his investment at any time and for any reason," selling shares does not serve to punish the corporation by depleting its capital. An exiting shareholder does not "reclaim" his capital investment from the corporation but merely sells his investment to a new shareholder. Moreover, shareholders' "freedom" to exit is limited by the fact that exit can entail significant costs. If the share price is depressed at the time the shareholder disagrees with management, the shareholder will pay a price to exit. If the share price has appreciated, exit by liquidation of stock constitutes a taxable event which may impose costs on the exit. Furthermore, notwithstanding the current boom in day-trading and other high-turnover strategies, economists generally agree that a long-term buy-and-hold strategy is the most reliably profitable method of equity investing. Thus exit may impose costs even absent a depressed stock price or a tax penalty.

C. *Wealth Maximization: A Flawed Model of Shareholder Interests*

Even though shareholders do not participate directly in election-related spending decisions, it may be argued that corporate governance law ensures that corporate actions indirectly represent shareholders' interests. The standard fiduciary and contractarian models of corporate law both hold that management must use its control over corporate powers to enrich shareholders. This shareholder wealth maximization is both the main source of management power and the principal limitation upon it. The *Bellotti* Court failed to understand the wealth maximization principle's intended role as a limit on management activity. It stated that the government violates the First Amendment if it requires business corporations to "stick to business" in their election-related spending. In fact, "stick to business" is corporate law's prime directive to managers.

Although not explicitly mentioned in state corporate codes, the wealth maximization principle is generally accepted as "the most basic principle of corporate law." Under the fiduciary model, managers' fiduciary duty to shareholders, the owners of the corporate assets, is often reduced to a single duty: namely, to maximize the value of those assets. In contractarian terms, the duty may be described as a term of the contractual relationship between shareholders and management. In areas where management's powers and duties are not expressly provided for in background law or governance documents, the wealth maximization principle fills the gap.

While the wealth maximization rule is a useful approximation of shareholder interests in most corporate governance disputes about the duties of directors, it has two major shortcomings as a justification of the legitimacy of management control over election-related spending. First, it fails to ask whether corporate election-related spending implicates shareholder interests other than wealth. Second, the business judgment rule renders the wealth maximization principle's constraints on management largely illusory. Wealth maximizing action is not easily defined. No law actually requires management to prove compliance with the wealth maximization principle. Instead, the business judgment rule imposes a presumption of compliance that shields all but the most egregious management misconduct.

1. Nonpecuniary Interests of Shareholders

... The corporate governance regime does not provide a system to resolve conflicts among shareholder preferences about the purpose of their ownership of the corporation. Instead, it privileges one type of preference—wealth maximization—and refuses to recognize others. Indeed, corporate law does not allow shareholders to use the corporation to pursue purposes other than wealth creation, even if they demonstrate that wealth maximization is not their actual preference. The principle does not operate as an approximate description of shareholder preferences but, rather, as a normative directive by the state. In corporate governance, the wealth of shareholders is worthy of legal protection, and other concerns are not.

Any legal rule unavoidably embodies some particular conception of the good. The law not only reflects but also communicates and shapes normative values. Despite its pretenses to political neutrality, this is as true of corporate law as it is of other areas of the law. Wealth creation is a worthy societal goal. Centralizing power in management can contribute to achieving that goal, despite the risks of management abuse. Meaningful, multidimensional shareholder participation in corporate governance conflicts with that goal. No politically neutral reason exists, however, why this conflict should always be resolved in favor of efficient wealth creation. The resolution does not depend only on individuals' actual priorities (which, in any event, cannot be satisfactorily determined), but also on what priorities society should encourage individuals to hold.

Constitutional law does not and should not share corporate law's single-minded devotion to the maximization of wealth. Because corporate law justifies shareholder nonparticipation in election-related spending decisions based on the wealth maximization principle, the law presumes that all shareholders hold that view. Such a presumption amounts to the state's implicit endorsement of the idea that citizens should abandon their nonpecuniary political priorities in pursuit of wealth. The state's choice of what values to endorse can contribute to the formation of norms that will guide managerial and shareholder behavior. Certainly, shareholders have the right to hold and to support that mercenary view, but the law should not endorse such views that do not comport with the values of a self-governing polity. The law should communicate society's disapproval of the mercenary view by rejecting the presumption that shareholders always value wealth above their political preferences.

2. Enforcement and the Business Judgment Rule

The wealth maximization principle also fails to constrain management discretion because of enforcement difficulties. In theory, the wealth maximization principle is enforced by shareholders' rights to file suit on behalf of the corporation against the managers who violate it. The *Bellotti* Court cited derivative actions as evidence that corporate governance law enables shareholders to control corporate election-related spending. A shareholder derivative suit, however, is a drastic and costly course of action likely to be worthwhile only in cases of massive abuse of funds. The inability of shareholders to organize compounds the difficulty of bringing suit. Moreover, even if shareholders bring suit, the business judgment rule renders management's business decisions largely immune to judicial review. Under the rule, it is irrelevant whether management's conduct substantively benefits shareholders, as long as management acted "on an informed basis, in good faith and in the honest belief that the action was taken in the best interests of the company."[22] The rule presumes that management behaved in this manner and places a

---

22. Aronson v. Lewis, 473 A.2d 805, 812 (Del. 1984).

heavy burden on shareholders attempting to prove otherwise. In effect, if a managerial decision falls under the rule, neither courts nor shareholders may disturb that decision.

The limited case law available suggests that managerial decisions regarding election-related spending fall within the business judgment rule. In other words, courts presume that election-related spending is intended in good faith to serve shareholder interests. For example, in *Marsili v. Pacific Gas & Electric Co.*,[23] the California Court of Appeals used the rule to reject a shareholder challenge to a utility corporation's contribution to a group supporting a municipal ballot measure. Neither state law nor the corporate charter expressly authorized or prohibited the political expenditure. The measure would have required voter approval for the construction of any building over seventy-two feet tall in San Francisco. While fighting the measure could possibly have benefited the corporation, the court did not require management to show any such benefit. The court even indicated that it would be insufficient for shareholders to prove a lack of benefit. Citing the business judgment rule, the court stated that in the absence of allegations of bad faith, the contribution was immune to a shareholder challenge "unless it is held, as a matter of law, that the contribution could not be construed as incidental or expedient for the attainment of corporate purposes."

The ostensible purpose of the business judgment rule is the institutional competency concern that, unlike professional managers, "the judges are not business experts." Business judgment deference to management's political decisions, however, is inconsistent with this purpose. Managers are business experts, not political experts, and decisions regarding political expenditures are not manifestly business decisions. A shareholder suit challenging a political expenditure by management does not merely question the wisdom of a business-related decision by management. It also raises the question of whether election-related spending is a business-related decision. Remarkably, *Marsili* allows managers themselves to answer this question. The opinion defines "business decision" as any decision that might benefit the corporation. As if this standard were not permissive enough, the court also defers to management's judgment as to whether any benefit exists.

Such a toothless definition of "business decision" transforms the business judgment rule from one that requires courts to defer to managerial business expertise into a rule mandating deference to managerial decisions in all matters. It remains to be seen whether other courts will follow *Marsili*'s lead. However, the application of business judgment rule deference to the review of charitable contributions suggests that they may. In *Kahn v. Sullivan*,[24] the Supreme Court of Delaware extended the business judgment rule to shareholder suits challenging charitable corporate contributions. Like *Marsili*, the court relied on case law applying the rule to business decisions but failed to explain why the rule should be imported into the charitable corporate contributions context. Because Delaware is the leading corporate law jurisdiction, *Kahn* is likely to be an influential case in many jurisdictions.

... Leaving both political and business decisions to the sole discretion of management suggests that there is no distinction at all; all decisions are business decisions, and political or ideological content is irrelevant. As with the presumption that shareholders always prefer wealth maximization, the extension of business judgment discretion to political decisions expresses norms inconsistent with our self-governing polity. Most shareholders presumably have neither expertise nor interest in making the corporation's routine business decisions and understandably assign them to professional managers. However, to presume

---

23. 51 Cal. App. 3d 313 (1975).
24. 594 A.2d 48, 59–61 (1991).

that shareholders have neither expertise nor interest in matters involving political preference contradicts the basic assumptions of self-government and thereby perverts the meaning of the First Amendment.

Management enjoys a presumption that corporate spending in favor of a candidate is intended as a worthwhile investment for the corporation, but managers are not required to articulate what that benefit is. If pressed, management would likely argue that spending is simply intended to secure the election of the candidate whose positions are the best for the corporation's interests. Even corporate donors themselves, however, admit that their spending is intended to purchase influence with, or at least access to, decision makers. This intention is of course precisely the kind of quid pro quo corruption the [Supreme] Court [has] recognized as a justification for regulating contributions to [political candidates'] election campaigns.[25]

... Unlike individuals, corporate managers acting in good faith do not have authority to engage in election-related spending for purely ideological or expressive purposes. Rather, the central principle of corporate governance requires management to seek material benefit in exchange for election-related spending. Even corporate codes that specifically permit corporations to engage in election-related spending do not purport to relieve management of its duty to maximize wealth. Thus corporate election-related spending in compliance with the corporate governance regime is more likely than individual spending to cause corruption or the appearance of corruption. This is true of both corporate election-related contributions and expenditures, though it applies with more force to contributions.

In short, both the wealth maximization rule and the competitive marketplace pressure managers to engage in corrupt spending. Under the business judgment rule, management need not explain to courts or shareholder plaintiffs the corrupt purpose behind such spending. The state has an interest in using campaign finance law to blunt the effect of these perverse incentives and protections created by the corporate governance regime.

D. Accounting for Nonshareholder Interests

... Corporate [election-related spending] cannot constitute the expression of nonshareholder corporate constituents, because they have even less input into corporate decisions than shareholders do. These corporate stakeholders—such as creditors, employees, customers, the neighboring community, and the environment—do not have even the shareholders' limited opportunities for formal participation in corporate decision making. In addition, their ability to use informal pressure to affect corporate political decisions is weakened because they do not have the information rights of shareholders either. On one level, this amplifies the complaint that corporate governance and campaign finance law regimes give managers disproportionate control over the corporation's "speech." The argument that management acts are legitimated by shareholders via corporate democracy is not only inaccurate but irrelevant. Even if shareholders have consented to give management control of election-related spending, other constituents with equally legitimate interests in the corporation have not. On a deeper level, the powerlessness of nonshareholders suggests an even more devastating critique of corporate "expression": the problem is not that one constituent group (shareholders) is disenfranchised, but that it is impossible even to identify, much less empower, all the corporation's relevant constituents. The constituents comprising the corporation are so diverse, decentralized,

---

25. *Buckley v. Valeo*, 424 U.S. 1, 26–30 (1976).

and amorphous that there can be no meaningful participatory process by which they can support or oppose the political positions management presents as representative of the corporation's interests.

III. Conclusion

There are of course important policy reasons for the existing concentration of power in top management. As the team production theory argues, the concentration of control in upper management is certainly more efficient than participatory corporate governance when shareholders and other constituents are numerous and widely dispersed.[26] Under a participatory governance system, corporate political spending would more likely constitute a form of individuals' expression. Such a system of corporate governance would, however, be cumbersome, slow, and costly, thereby reducing corporate profitability. This Article does not mean to argue that publicly traded business corporations should adopt more participatory forms of governance. The point is, rather, that corporate governance can be centralized and efficient, or it can be participatory and expressive, but it cannot be both. Law and markets have created a corporate law regime that favors the efficient over the expressive and, thus, have created organizations that deserve less First Amendment protection than individuals do....

Ronald J. Gilson & Charles K. Whitehead, *Deconstructing Equity: Public Ownership, Agency Costs, and Complete Capital Markets*[*]

Introduction

Public shareholders and agency costs are two sides of the same coin. If companies need residual risk capital, and if public investors who can diversify their shareholdings are the cheapest risk bearers, then we get agency costs. The capital provided by these cheap risk bearers necessarily is managed by someone else, whose interests are not perfectly aligned with those of investors, a divergence famously framed by Adolph Berle and Gardiner Means a little over seventy-five years ago. As a result, for at least the last thirty years, modern corporate governance scholarship has focused on finding a means to bridge the agency gap between diversified risk bearers and managers. Proxy fights, hostile takeovers, independent directors, institutional investors, and, most recently, hedge funds and activist shareholders have all held the mantle of favored agency-cost-reducer at one time or another.

The traditional law and finance focus on agency costs presumes, without acknowledgment, that the agency cost framework's bedrock premise—that diversified shareholders are the cheapest risk bearers—is immutable. In this Essay, we confront the possibility that the continued development of increasingly complete capital markets, in which working capital can be separated from risk capital and discrete slices of risk can be

---

26. *See Blair and Stout's article in Chapter 2. —Ed.*

* Originally published in 108 Columbia Law Review 231 (2008). Copyright 2008 by Columbia Law Review Association, Inc. Reproduced with permission of Columbia Law Review Association, Inc. via Copyright Clearance Center.

separately transferred, pooled, and shared among market participants, has called the premise into question. From this perspective, the traditional need for residual shareholders, whose risk exposure spanned the marketplace, reflected the absence of low-cost means to transfer—and market participants who could be paid to bear—only a portion of that risk. In complete capital markets, private owners can purchase risk bearing and liquidity in discrete slices. And if risk management and liquidity are available by the slice—if, for example, the owners of a private company can separate and transfer the risk of commodity prices, or catastrophic acts of nature, or even a business cycle, rather than transfer bundled risk through the issuance of common stock—then much of what has constituted the corporate governance debate may require reexamination.

We write at a remarkable moment in the history of the capital markets. Over the last few years, there has been a large movement of public companies into private ownership through leveraged acquisitions by private equity firms. This recalls, of course, Michael Jensen's then premature announcement in the late 1980s, in the face of an earlier private equity wave, of the "eclipse of the public corporation" by a more efficient organization form: the leveraged buyout (LBO) association. At that time, Alfred Rappaport argued that the concept of the LBO was self-limiting, and in particular, that most public firms failed to meet the criteria necessary to go private—strong and predictable cash flows, readily saleable assets or businesses, strong market positions or brands, status as a low-cost producer, and limited sensitivity to cyclical swings. Now, some eighteen years after the Jensen-Rappaport debate, as the size and range of public companies being taken private has expanded dramatically, the capital market phenomena that concern us here again raise questions regarding the future of the public corporation and corporate governance in stark terms. Those questions arise notwithstanding the turmoil in the debt market, which appeared during the summer of 2007, raising concerns over the capacity of private equity buyers to finance current as well as future private equity deals. We do not mean to downplay the extent of the uncertainty in the debt market or the ability of buyers and lenders to use those events to renegotiate the terms of pending transactions. Our timeframe here, however, is much longer than the recent private equity wave or the credit market uncertainty that is slowing it down. Our goal is to highlight what we argue is a secular trend, driven by economic forces that will survive current perturbations.

... To ground some of our speculations, we offer the example of Agricore United (AU), a publicly traded corporation listed on the Toronto Stock Exchange since 1993, as evidence of the kind of risk management that is possible. The potential impact of increasingly complete capital markets on corporate governance and ownership structure is driven by these possibilities.

AU provides handling and delivery services to the grain farmers of western Canada. Historically, its main source of unmanaged risk was related to weather—grain crops in western Canada are affected by regional temperature and precipitation during June and July, in turn affecting seasonal yields, the amount of grain transported through AU, and ultimately, AU's profitability. Weather variation, in fact, resulted in wide and unpredictable swings in AU's annual profits, forcing AU to borrow funds in order to make needed capital investments and to rely on equity capital as a cushion against unexpected drops in revenue.

AU decided to remove the direct effects of weather on its profits by transferring its weather exposure outside the firm. It did so by entering into an insurance contract with Swiss Re, the world's largest reinsurer and a leading expert in capital and risk management. Under the terms of that contract, Swiss Re agreed to pay AU whenever actual industry-wide grain production fell below average volumes over the prior five years (subject to limits and deductibles). The resulting insurance solution was both over-and underinclusive: over-inclusive because it extended coverage to any reduction in grain volumes, not simply shortfalls resulting from weather, and could result in payments that were greater than AU's actual losses; and under-inclusive because actual losses might exceed payments received under the policy (collectively referred to as "basis risk"). The policy, however, had a direct impact on AU's capital structure—allowing it to increase its debt financing levels, separate a portion of its working capital needs from its risk capital, substitute its new insurance for existing equity, and lower its overall cost of capital.

As AU's experience illustrates, in today's capital markets, the more a firm is able to identify and hedge its risk exposure, the less equity it may need to support its operations. The ability to identify and transfer risk outside the firm means that firms no longer must rely on equity capital as a catch-all for residual risk, and so the associated agency costs of equity become increasingly optional. Derivatives, sophisticated insurance contracts, and other risk transfer instruments can begin to substitute for equity's traditional risk-bearing function, with the result that a firm's decisions on risk management must increasingly become part of its decisions on capital.

... Do more complete capital markets mean that the predicted eclipse of the public corporation has finally caught up with us? Our prediction is that going public will continue to be meaningful for many firms, but that the equilibrium between agency costs and the benefits of public ownership may begin to shift in the direction of private ownership....

I. Incomplete Capital Markets and the Traditional Role of Equity

Our analysis builds on the observation that a basic premise of the traditional model of the corporation—that diversified investors holding common stock are the cheapest risk bearers, resulting in the separation of ownership and management—is being called into question by advances in risk management and increasingly complete capital markets. We argue that these changes warrant a reconsideration of the role of common stock in corporate governance and the agency cost framework that results from diversified shareholders as residual risk bearers.

A little over seventy-five years ago, Berle and Means identified the growing independence of management in the public corporation. That independence arose from the separation of ownership and control as widely dispersed public shareholders effectively became passive providers of equity capital with little or no control over corporate managers. A key to that thesis was the relationship between corporate structure and the public capital markets, no doubt triggered by their growth over two extended bull markets during the thirty years leading up to the Great Depression. As usually presented, the separation of ownership and control is the natural outcome of the specialization needed for the corporate form to respond to increases in efficient scale and scope that resulted from the development of a continent-wide market. Public shareholders, with the ability to diversify away unsystematic risk, could specialize in risk bearing; and professional managers, necessary to run organizations of the new scale and scope, could specialize in management.

This focus on shareholders as broadband risk bearers resulted in part from the dearth of alternative risk-bearing instruments. The capital markets of the 1930s were relatively incomplete, with few financial instruments available to firms or investors beyond stocks, bonds, and bank loans. Insurance was limited to traditional products, such as life, property, and casualty coverage. It would be another forty years before a new wave of risk transfer instruments would be introduced, and twenty more years after that before the new risk management of the 1990s began to fundamentally change how firms manage and transfer risk. Consequently, while the Berle and Means framework recognized a basic relationship between corporate structure and the capital markets, it was premised on the underdeveloped markets of the period—presuming, as a result, that a firm's shareholders would bear most of the residual economic risk of managerial decisions.

More recent scholarship has deconstructed the corporation into a "nexus of contracts," rejecting a characterization of the shareholder as "owner" in favor of one in which the corporation is an equilibrium among actors, including shareholders, creditors, and managers, who bargain within a complex set of relationships with the corporate entity at the center. In the contractarian framing, investors rely on the liquidity of the public markets to inexpensively manage risk by diversifying their holdings across a spectrum of firms; and as residual claimants, shareholders bargain for ownership-type benefits, such as voting rights and fiduciary duties, to constrain the resulting agency costs. Diversified risk bearing at the shareholder level was presumed to be the least costly means to manage firm risk, even after taking account of those costs. At the same time, while limiting residual claims to a small group of investors might lower agency costs, the contractarian model predicted that doing so would increase the costs of risk bearing and make concentrated ownership less attractive.

So there we have a snapshot of the capital markets and corporate governance in the mid-1970s, when Jensen and Meckling framed the agency cost perspective on corporate structure and governance.[27] Firms financed by their managers eliminate the drag of agency costs associated with public investment but sacrifice scale economies and new opportunities because of their own limited capital. For Jensen and Meckling, a firm's scale and scope turned on the tradeoff between the gains from expansion and the agency costs of debt and equity, the outcome of which was conditioned on the instruments made available by the capital markets and the existing techniques to constrain the agency costs of outside investment. In the 1970s, this tradeoff still dictated the predominance of equity held by diversified shareholders.

To be sure, the contractarian model left open the possibility that the development of more complete capital markets, with new investment vehicles, could change the tradeoff between the level of agency costs associated with public investment and gains from new investment. For example, Jensen and Meckling identified the conversion feature in convertible bonds, a derivative of sorts, as a less costly means to reduce management and shareholder incentives to transfer wealth from bondholders to shareholders (for example, by increasing riskiness) compared to other, more costly means of control, such as ongoing monitoring in support of contractual covenants. They also acknowledged the likelihood that new corporate instruments would appear as the cost-benefit balance of creating and maintaining a market for them changed over time.

In the next Part, we describe important changes since the early 1970s that have begun to erode the traditional model's reliance on public equity—in particular, the creation of new risk management tools and the development of liquid markets to transfer risk. Financial innovation over the last thirty years gave rise to an explosive growth in new instruments to facilitate a private owner's purchase of risk bearing and liquidity in discrete slices. In short, these are not your father's capital markets.

---

27. Michael C. Jensen & William H. Meckling, *Theory of the Firm: Managerial Behavior, Agency Costs, and Ownership Structure*, 3 J. FIN. ECON. 305 (1976).

II. The Risk Revolution and Capital Structure

A. *The Rise of Risk Management*

For our purposes, "risk management" is a firm-level management discipline that identifies and measures risks that may affect firm value, assists in choosing which risks to retain and which to transfer, and then implements and monitors strategies to execute those decisions. Derivatives are important risk transfer tools but comprise only one facet of risk management.

Managing risk, of course, is nothing new. For years, business people have managed risk by purchasing insurance, diversifying business lines to reduce cash flow volatility, pursuing projects with greater certainty but lower returns, and restricting leverage. However, corporate risk management—which identifies, manages, and transfers risk on a consolidated, entity-wide basis—is a fairly recent development, having only emerged as businesses have confronted a range of new risks and uncertainties.

Those risks have differed in magnitude (if not always in kind) from the risks faced by prior generations, ranging from a succession of financial system crises, to natural disasters, and even to acts of terrorism. The end of Bretton Woods and the start of the OPEC oil embargo in 1973 subjected peacetime businesses to new, and potentially catastrophic, exchange rate and energy cost volatility.[28] Businesses that failed to take those risks into account did so at their peril, often with disastrous consequences. Traditional insurance policies offered little or no protection, and so managers began to search for alternatives to minimize or transfer their new exposures.

The capital markets quickly responded. Financial intermediaries, including banks, broker-dealers, and insurance companies, saw an opportunity to profit from the creation and trading of new financial instruments that responded to client demands to improve risk sharing. Those instruments pooled and transferred discrete slices of financial risk from corporate counterparties to those (in many instances, the financial intermediaries themselves) who, through diversification or otherwise, were in a better position to manage them. Over time, the growing demand for those instruments resulted in greater liquidity, in turn lowering their cost and expanding the scope of what risks could be transferred through the capital markets. Exchange-traded currency and oil price derivatives, for example, overtook less liquid and more costly private instruments that were popular just a few years earlier. Greater liquidity in the risk markets, and the introduction of new risk management technologies, also permitted financial intermediaries to provide a growing array of private, over-the-counter (OTC) hedging solutions that were closely tailored to their clients' specific risks.

Today, the spectrum of risk transfer instruments has expanded beyond financial and commodities futures to include now-standard interest rate, currency, and credit derivatives. Weather derivatives, such as those underlying AU's insurance contract, can be more finely sliced into risks associated with temperatures in an identified region or group of cities, levels of snowfall and frost, and even the occurrence of hurricanes. Through "catastrophe bonds," investors can now take on risks as diverse as earthquakes in Southeast Asia, flooding in Great Britain, and windstorms in Japan. At the cutting edge, economic derivatives permit financial intermediaries to precisely hedge their exposures to a growing array of macroeconomic risks, as evidenced by macroeconomic data releases—ranging from

---

28. *From 1944 until 1971, the Bretton Woods agreement required most major economies to take actions to maintain international exchange rates roughly constant.*—Ed.

changes in U.S. employment rates to U.S. retail sales, industrial production, consumer prices, and economic growth—on which the value of those instruments is based.

Of course, in a frictionless world, if a firm chooses to transfer risk, we would expect the premium it pays to mirror the risk-related costs the firm would otherwise incur in raising capital—a zero-sum game, since the risk would now be borne by the transferee's [e.g., an insurer's] shareholders, who should demand the same returns as the transferor's shareholders. If the [transferee], however, is better able to manage risk at lower cost—through increasingly complete capital markets that enable the transferee to diversify its risks across a portfolio of companies—then, over time, we would expect the premium to fall below the cost the transferor would otherwise bear if the risk was retained. The implications are significant: As markets develop for the transfer of risk, risk transfer instruments may become a lower cost substitute for public equity, permitting managers to supplement, and even replace, traditional capital and capital-related costs....

III. The Evolving Model of the Corporation

Increasingly complete capital markets may begin to offer a less costly means than public equity for firms to manage risk, with risk transfer instruments over time taking on the risk-bearing role of traditional equity. By diversifying risk at the firm level, those instruments may also allow for a greater concentration in equity ownership among owner-managers with important consequences for the future of public corporations and corporate governance. If risk management can begin to substitute for risk capital, and if the risks of concentrated ownership can be diversified at the firm level, then a central reason for an owner to take a company public in the first place disappears and the agency costs of public equity become increasingly optional. In effect, the traditional balance between agency costs and the benefits of public ownership may begin to shift toward a new equilibrium, which we discuss below, as firms assess their ability to manage risk relative to the marketplace, retaining those risks where they are at a competitive advantage and transferring the rest.

The realistic option of remaining private envisions a corporate structure that resembles the LBO association that Michael Jensen described almost twenty years ago—with working capital funded primarily by debt, and private equity ownership aligning management and shareholder incentives. The characteristic LBO target in the 1980s private equity wave about which Jensen wrote was a market leader in a mature industry—a firm with low capital needs and high, consistent cash flow—where debt could largely substitute for equity, thereby reducing equity levels. The residual equity, held by the LBO firm and management, was reduced essentially to an incentive contract. In that setting, the agency cost of equity was eliminated and the agency cost of debt was addressed by contract, resulting in a corporate form that more efficiently reduced agency costs than the public corporation. Jensen, like most economists a good Darwinian, predicted the public corporation's eclipse.

The intuition we address in this Essay is that more complete capital markets, resulting from the demand for more efficient risk-bearing instruments, now make the governance structure Jensen extolled available to a much wider range of companies. A company will use risk management instruments to transfer those risks that counterparties can manage at lower cost and retain only those risks over which management has a comparative advantage relative to the capital markets. Again, equity approaches a management incentive contract. A riskier company that would not have matched the 1980s private equity profile —due to significant systematic risk that made it unsuitable for debt to replace equity, such as for an airline—can lay off that systematic risk slice by slice, thereby supporting a far higher level of debt and, it follows, Jensen's more efficient governance structure. Thus, companies for whom the costs of an LBO in the 1980s would have been prohibitive may now manage and reduce those costs through the transfer of risk. Moreover, as a borrower's systematic risk is reduced through risk management techniques, lenders may be willing to increase the size of their loans over longer periods and so increase the size of companies that undertake an LBO. As we will consider later in this Part, the story— that is, LBOs of a wider range of companies and of a much larger size than the 1980s preferred profile—at least superficially fits the most recent private equity wave.

More complete capital markets may also affect the public corporation in another way. Private equity acts on corporations that are already public. But what about the decision to go public in the first place? Here, we suggest that risk management's ability to reduce systematic risk through increasingly complete capital markets provides an alternative to an initial public offering (IPO), both of which respond to an owner's need to secure liquidity to diversify her own portfolio. Some historical evidence supports this conjecture. Tradable derivatives [i.e., commodities futures] were developed quite early for agricultural products to facilitate risk management by farmers and by companies for which farm commodities were a central input. The hypothesis—that private ownership should be more likely among large businesses for which the price and availability of commodities are a central determinant of profitability—appears to have been the case in the agricultural market. For those companies, the capital markets were complete at a much earlier time.

... To this point, we have told a fairly straightforward story. Increasingly complete capital markets, developed in response to the demand for risk management techniques that could increase firm value, also turn out to change the most efficient way to manage the agency costs of public investment. The ability to lay off systematic risk by the slice rather than through the broadband risk bearing of common stock allows a wider range of public companies to be the subject of an LBO and, we believe, has the potential to permit a broader range of companies to remain private. In short, the story is one in which changes in financial technology change the border between public and private companies....

... In more complete capital markets, firms can accept or reject the agency costs of public ownership, choosing instead to manage risk using alternative risk transfer instruments; working capital can be funded with debt. A firm's decision to go (or remain) public, therefore, may increasingly be less a function of the need to raise risk capital or diversify risk, as in the traditional construct, and more a balance between the incremental costs of going public (compared to a reliance on risk transfer instruments) and the incremental benefits of being a public company (beyond the receipt of broadband risk capital).

What will be the impact of private equity funds—LBO associations in Jensen's 1980s terminology—on the future of public ownership? The recent LBO wave has been both broader and deeper than the 1980s wave, with larger and more diverse companies being acquired by private equity funds. Has the increasing completeness of the capital markets eliminated the barrier that prevented the eclipse of the public corporation when it was first predicted?

We think not, or at least not yet. Most important, the structure of the private equity market now, as in the 1980s, requires a liquidity event (such as an IPO or a sale of the acquired business) within the usual ten-year life of the private equity fund in order to return capital to investors. In the absence of taking the portfolio company public again, from where does the private equity fund secure liquidity? One might sell the portfolio company to another company in its industry. For venture capital funds, there are cycles in which a sale is preferred to a public offering as a liquidity event. However, venture capital portfolio companies are typically much smaller than the companies being taken private in the most recent LBO wave. For these larger companies, there may be barriers to an acquisition-funded liquidity event.

In recent years, another form of liquidity event has arisen: the sale of a portfolio company by one private equity fund to another. The puzzle is the underlying logic of this pattern. One source of value creation from an LBO is what Steven Kaplan has called "shock-therapy"—the quick fix of operating and investment problems at the acquired company. If that is the primary value of an LBO, then what value is added by the second, post-shock therapy private equity fund, and from what source will the returns to its investors come?

A second source of value from the purchase of the portfolio company by a second private equity fund has more promise, but also promises lower returns. A private equity fund simply may provide better governance—that is, a more cost effective reduction of agency costs—than is possible in a public corporation. From this perspective, even the best part-time independent directors are not the equivalent of full-time, highly incentivized private equity managers. Thus, the portfolio company is worth more in the hands of a private equity fund than with diversified public ownership. After shock therapy is completed, the first fund will sell to a second fund because the first fund requires liquidity and because the company is worth more in private hands. The second fund will earn less than the first —the difference being the return on shock therapy—but will still earn more than investors in public companies due to the superior governance structure it provides.

This analysis leads to an interesting speculation. If the benefit of the second private equity fund is the reduced agency costs resulting from the quasi-public ownership of a limited partnership with outside investors, then would fully private ownership provide an even better governance structure? We are then back to the question, why go public in the first place?; or in the context of our example, why not sell the company to its managers with the addition of debt supported by risk transfer instruments entered into by the company or its lenders? Given transaction costs, would private ownership be more efficient than the serial monogamy of successive sales to private equity firms? To be sure, even private owners have liquidity needs, but they are certainly of lesser magnitude than the need to reduce to cash the entire value of the corporation every ten years. To reframe Jensen's provocative question of twenty years ago, can we foresee the eclipse of the quasi-public corporation?

To this point in our assessment of how different ownership structures reduce agency costs, we have ignored the potential for those costs to arise in connection with the risk transfer instruments that support the transformation of common stock from an all-purpose risk bearer to an incentive contract. Will owner-managers alter the company's business strategy to the detriment of the risk counterparties? The Black-Scholes option pricing model assumes that when the parties are shifting risks whose probability distribution cannot be influenced by either side, the transfer is a fair game. However, if one of the parties can influence the probability distribution ex post, the game is no longer fair. Put more concretely, suppose a manager-owned airline has transferred 100% of its exposure to oil prices to a counterparty. Will the airline then have the same incentive to reduce the risk of oil price increases through changes in its operations?

At present, the response to this agency cost problem has been to define the transferred risks by reference to measures beyond the transferor's ability to influence, in order to minimize the potential for moral hazard. In the case of AU's insurance policy, for example, the risk was defined by reference to an industry measure over which AU had little influence. Doing so limited AU's managers' capacity to adjust AU's behavior to manipulate the measure. The result, however, was a mismatch—between an optimal transfer of those risks where the firm was competitively disadvantaged and a second-best solution where a portion of that risk remained with the firm—that reflected the residual agency costs that remained.

The deconstruction of equity is still too preliminary for the shape of the responses to moral hazard in risk transfer to have taken shape. AU illustrates one approach—reduce the possibility of hidden action by making the measure both transparent and outside the risk transferor's control. The cost was basis risk, a partial mismatch between the underlying risk and its contractual measure. But just as the demand for instruments that allowed risk to be transferred by the slice led to innovation on the supply side that made the capital markets more complete, so too will the demand for techniques that constrain agency costs associated with risk transfer give rise to responsive structural and contractual innovations. The landscape of corporate ownership—the distribution of public, quasi-public, and private ownership across different industries—at any given time depends on the comparative capacity to reduce agency costs in each ownership arrangement.

Conclusion

In this Essay, we have argued that the premise that public shareholders are the cheapest risk bearers, which forms the foundation for the focus of modern corporate governance on agency costs, may no longer be accurate. Changes in the capital markets have led to new risk management techniques and instruments, which enable firms and private owners to transfer risk in discrete slices. Risk management at the firm level, therefore, may be more efficient than risk bearing by diversified shareholders, providing real benefits that shareholders cannot duplicate for themselves. These innovations suggest that equity as a broadband risk bearer may no longer be a standard feature of the large corporation, and so the agency costs associated with that structure may also become voluntary. If so, then the traditional balance between agency costs and the benefits of public ownership may begin to shift lurchingly toward a new equilibrium, for the time being reflecting a balance between the incremental costs of going public (compared to a reliance on risk transfer instruments) and the incremental benefits of being a public company (beyond the receipt of broadband risk capital)—a balance that was decidedly second-order in the traditional analysis.

We also considered the extent to which the recent private equity wave, both broader and deeper than that of the 1980s, ultimately may be a precursor of change in the traditional construct of the corporation—raising again the possibility of the eclipse of the public corporation, but with more complete capital markets now making the LBO structure anticipated by Michael Jensen available to (and sustainable by) a much wider range of companies. In doing so, we distinguished between private ownership and what we have called the quasi-public ownership of large corporations by a series of private equity funds —an ownership pattern of serial monogamy driven by the institutional structure and liquidity needs of private equity funds.

Our goal has been to be provocative—to view a snapshot of today's corporate ownership landscape through the prism of more complete capital markets, as a means to think about where it is all going. As with any effort of this sort, continued capital markets innovation may cause our predictions to be wrong. However, we have accomplished our goal if our account successfully frames the issues that corporate planners and financial intermediaries must confront going forward.

An appropriate place to conclude is with what we have not considered. A shift to private ownership or even quasi-public ownership, fueled by discrete as opposed to broadband risk transfer, will return capital to current investors in public equity. But that capital still will be necessary to fund future risk transfers of the character that gave rise to its return, and the investors still will need a destination for that capital. We have not considered here the institutional structure and financial instruments by which investors then will invest their capital in the market for risk transfer. We expect that the deconstruction of equity on the supply side that we have considered here will be mirrored on the demand side by a deconstruction of investment instruments. Institutions and the public may then build portfolios by investing in slices of different risks offered by intermediaries just as they now do in common stock, but speculating on the shape of those arrangements is a project for another day.

Discussion Questions

1. Roe points out that other economies allow financial institutions to control corporations through large blocks of stock, and that the practice is not found in the U.S. due to political reasons. As Black points out, giving institutional investors enough voice to control corporations creates the danger that they will abuse that control. In the absence of institutional investors with the power to control, however, who enjoys control? Are they more or less likely than institutional investors to abuse it?

2. In 2002, institutional investors were criticized for failing to notice warning signs presaging the failures of Enron and other fraud-ridden corporations. In 2003, the mutual fund industry was plagued by its own scandals involving the favorable treatment of large investors at the expense of smaller investors. Institutional investors were also burned by disastrous investments in mortgage-backed securities and other risky derivative instruments that crashed with the housing bubble in 2008. Are institutional investors still credible as potential monitors? Black suggests some forces that may discipline institutional investors even if the legal regime increases their power — do these seem sufficient? Are there other methods of monitoring the monitors?

3. Black argues that diversification reduces institutional investors' incentives to focus on company-specific issues, but creates economies of scale that increase incentives to monitor issues of corporate process and structure. To what extent should an investor develop and act on positions with respect to corporate process and structure independently of company-specific information?

4. Why does Romano refer to the federal proxy rules as creating "subsidies" for shareholder proposals? Do you agree with this characterization?

5. Most of the corporate finance literature supports Romano's contention that shareholder proposals do not increase firm value. Can shareholder activism and the "subsidization" of proposals be justified on other grounds?

6. Berle and Means famously argued that the separation of ownership and control is the central problem of governing large corporations. Some commentators defend the limits on shareholder participation, however: "Investor involvement in corporate decisionmaking threatens to disrupt the very mechanism that makes the public corporation

practicable; namely, the centralization of essentially nonreviewable decisionmaking authority in the board of directors." Stephen Bainbridge, *Director Primacy in Corporate Takeovers: Preliminary Reflections*, 55 STAN. L. REV. 791, 807 (2002). See also Blair & Stout's article in Chapter 2. Is centralized director power the problem or the solution? On what assumptions does the characterization depend?

Would your answer differ with respect to different kinds of corporate decisions? Consider, for example: a) setting the prices for products; b) laying off workers; c) contracting with a supplier from a country that tolerates exploitative labor practices; d) making philanthropic or political contributions; e) setting executive compensation; f) nominating candidates for directorships; g) responding to a hostile takeover offer.

7. Although SEC Rule 14a-8 governs management's ability to exclude shareholder proposals, particular exclusions are in practice governed largely by SEC discretion. In close cases, management seeks SEC no-action review before it excludes a shareholder proposal from the corporation's proxy material under Rule 14a-8. That is, management explains to the SEC why it wishes to exclude a proposal. The SEC then informs management whether it will or will not recommend enforcement action if the proposal is excluded. These determinations are not always accompanied by detailed explanations but are rarely challenged in court.

Is the SEC no-action process the appropriate method of determining whether the substance of a shareholder proposal is appropriate for shareholder voting? Should this determination be made by internal corporate procedures, a more formal SEC process, federal courts, or state courts? On the one hand, the no-action process is quick and convenient, and the SEC has a deep understanding of corporate governance. On the other, the relatively informal no-action process performs a judge-like function, can be unpredictable, and lacks accountability. *See* Alan R. Palmiter, *The Shareholder Proposal Rule: A Failed Experiment in Merit Regulation*, 45 ALA. L. REV. 879 (1994); Donna M. Nagy, *Judicial Reliance on Regulatory Interpretation in SEC No-Action Letters: Current Problems and a Proposed Framework*, 83 CORNELL L. REV. 921 (1998).

8. Corporate and securities law focus on the shareholder's interface with firms, primarily through elections and disclosure. The entire concept of mandatory disclosure is based on information about individual firms. Mandatory disclosure does not inform investors that picking stocks based on such information is rarely more profitable than random trading. Modern portfolio theory holds that investors should be more concerned with diversification than with information about any particular firm—not just social and political information, but even information about a firm's financial performance. According to one commentator,

> [The existing mandatory disclosure system] provides huge amounts of firm-specific data, which is singularly useful for constructing irrational trading strategies. The current system is more analogous to making the casino disclose which slot machines have paid off, in which order, in the last month—this does not improve the gambler's odds at all, but it may encourage those gamblers who profess to see a "pattern" in the slot machine payoffs.

Paul G. Mahoney, *Is There A Cure For "Excessive" Trading?*, 81 VA. L. REV. 713, 744 (1995).

Should corporate and securities law concern themselves with shareholders' voice and information in relation to individual firms, or should it focus on helping investors to maximize their portfolios through diversification in relation to the market?

9. Greenwood argues that corporate management should be required to more closely reflect the preferences of real individuals. In light of the immense complexity and

contradictory preferences of individuals, can this be done? If so, how? If not, is the "fictional shareholder" a satisfactory second-best solution? What other solutions might be appropriate?

10. In contrast to Greenwood's position, Romano argues that the law should limit shareholder participation in governance. Joo argues that large corporations must choose whether to be relatively inefficient, participatory organizations with constitutional speech rights or centralized and economically efficient organizations without such rights. With which of the three positions do you agree? Why? What are the normative assumptions behind each position?

11. Joo and Greenwood argue that corporate decisions do not reflect shareholder preferences because shareholders have no direct input into the decisionmaking process of a large organization. Note that the members of large, bureaucratic nonprofit organizations also lack the ability to directly influence the organization's decisions. Does this suggest that the limitation of speech rights that Joo advocates for large business corporations should also apply to large nonprofits? *See FEC v. Massachusetts Citizens for Life, Inc.*, 479 U.S. 238 (1986).

12. Joo argues that the political speech of large corporations should be regulated more closely than that of individuals or closely held businesses. But if traditional constitutional analysis does not apply to large corporations' political contributions, is there *any* basis for limiting government regulation of such activity? Does it follow from his analysis that government may freely regulate corporate speech other than political contributions?

13. Consider again Berkshire Hathaway Inc.'s former process for "shareholder-designated" charitable contributions (described in the Chapter 1 Discussion Questions). Would a similar model be appropriate for corporate political contributions? Would it address the concerns raised in Joo's article?

14. According to one commentator,

> The Japanese and German systems of corporate governance share certain characteristics absent from the Anglo-American systems: significant involvement of labor in corporate decision making; cross-shareholding with suppliers and customers; bank influence (direct in Germany and indirect in Japan); an absence of hostile takeovers; and limited shareholder litigation. The aggregate effect of these factors in both countries is to isolate the board of directors from the kind of pressures the typical U.S. director receives from outside shareholders. In theory, the combination of employee influence and director isolation in Germany and Japan should facilitate the ability of directors in those countries to respond to the concerns of other stakeholders. Whether this is indeed the case is difficult to determine, and empirical work in this area is nonexistent.

Mark J. Loewenstein, *Stakeholder Protection in Germany and Japan*, 76 TUL. L. REV. 1673 (2002).

Would diminishing U.S. directors' accountability to shareholders necessarily make directors more responsive to concerns other than shareholder wealth? What other factors are required to yield such results? Is there some way to increase director responsiveness to other constituents other than broadening directors' discretion to consider multiple factors?

15. Chancellor Strine is skeptical of the ability of mutual funds to monitor corporate management. What do you think of these arguments? Other than Strine's arguments, are there alternative explanations for the apparent docility of funds with respect to corporate

governance reform? Do you think fund docility is a problem? If so, can you suggest reforms to make funds more active?

16. Do you believe capital markets are becoming "complete" in the way Gilson and Whitehead predict? What developments will be necessary to further market completeness? Consider Bratton's description in Chapter 1 of Enron's attempts to "slice up" and manage risk. Consider also mortgage-backed securities, collateralized debt obligations, and other attempts to slice up the risks of lending. (Frank Partnoy discusses these devices in Chapter 12.)

17. Gilson and Whitehead argue that shareholders' traditional role as "broadband risk bearers" can be distributed among other kinds of investors or insurers. Corporations rely much more heavily on debt and retained earnings than stock issues to finance their activities. See the article by Armour, Cheffins and Skeel in this volume; Lawrence A. Mitchell, *Who Needs the Stock Market? Part I: The Empirical Evidence* (October 30, 2008), *available at* http://papers.ssrn.com/sol3/papers.cfm?abstract_id=1292403. Are shareholders necessary? Other than financing corporate activity, what purposes might public share ownership serve?

Chapter 8

Creditors, Bankruptcy, and Corporate Governance

Although corporate governance law and theory tend to focus on shareholders, U.S. firms in fact obtain most of their financing not by selling shares, but by drawing on their earnings and by borrowing. Large corporations conduct long-term borrowing primarily by issuing bonds.[1] This chapter opens with *Metropolitan Life v. RJR Nabisco*, a case exemplifying the law's treatment of bonds as contracts. The court's opinion distinguishes bondholders' contractual rights from the fiduciary duties owed to shareholders.

According to Jonathan Macey's article in Chapter 2, contractual rights and fiduciary duties are intimately related in that fiduciary duties merely give shareholders the residual legal rights left over after contracts have been made. Thus nonshareholder constituents could in theory obtain, through bargaining, any of the rights we normally think of as belonging to shareholders. In this chapter, Thomas Smith and Frederick Tung further debate the proper relationship between contractual rights of creditors and management's fiduciary duty to shareholders. Smith argues that management should have greater mandatory duty to creditors. He points out that the specific contractual rights of bondholders can be threatened by corporations' general orientation toward maximizing share value, which entails risks that tend not to benefit creditors. Tung, however, argues that fiduciary duty should be owed only to shareholders because creditors can—and do—protect themselves by contract.

It is generally agreed that directors' duties shift from enriching shareholders to protecting creditors' interests if and when a corporation becomes insolvent. Bankruptcy and firm failure are typically considered separately from corporate governance. In their article in this chapter, however, John Armour, Brian Cheffins and David Skeel argue that bankruptcy law influences how corporations operate even outside of insolvency, because every corporation is constantly exposed to the possibility of bankruptcy.

The issue of how law and policy should treat failing corporations came up repeatedly in the wake of the Enron-era failures and again during the 2008–09 financial crisis, as many firms failed and a select few were rescued by government intervention. Douglas Baird and Robert Rasmussen argue that bankruptcy law should not presume that a failing corporation is worth saving: in some cases, a firm should be allowed to fail and its parts sold on the market. Most observers would agree, however, that at least some potential

---

1. To be more precise, corporation use three main types of long-term debt instruments: bonds, debentures, and notes. As a general matter, bonds have the longest maturities and notes the shortest, and bonds are typically secured by collateral. But there are no hard-and-fast definitions, and in practice the term "bond" is often used to refer to all three types. Thus this general discussion will simply use the term "bond." Like a public offering of shares, a public bond issue is an issuance of securities that must be registered with the SEC.

corporate failures should be avoided. Cheryl Block analyzes how to identify when the government should intervene to prevent failure, a question that came to prominence recently in light of the massive bailouts of 2008–09.

U.S. District Court, Southern District of New York, *Metropolitan Life Insurance Company v. RJR Nabisco, Inc.* *

Jon M. Walker, United States District Judge:

I. Introduction

The corporate parties to this action are among the country's most sophisticated financial institutions, as familiar with the Wall Street investment community and the securities market as American consumers are with the Oreo cookies and Winston cigarettes made by defendant RJR Nabisco, Inc. (sometimes "the company" or "RJR Nabisco"). The present action traces its origins to October 20, 1988, when F. Ross Johnson, then the Chief Executive Officer of RJR Nabisco, proposed a $17 billion leveraged buy-out ("LBO") of the company's shareholders, at $75 per share.[2] Within a few days, a bidding war developed among the investment group led by Johnson and the investment firm of Kohlberg Kravis Roberts & Co. ("KKR"), and others. On December 1, 1988, a special committee of RJR Nabisco directors, established by the company specifically to consider the competing proposals, recommended that the company accept the KKR proposal, a $24 billion LBO that called for the purchase of the company's outstanding stock at roughly $109 per share.

The flurry of activity late last year that accompanied the bidding war for RJR Nabisco spawned at least eight lawsuits, filed before this Court, charging the company and its former CEO with a variety of securities and common law violations. The Court agreed to hear the present action—filed even before the company accepted the KKR proposal—on an expedited basis, with an eye toward March 1, 1989, when RJR Nabisco was expected to merge with the KKR holding entities created to facilitate the LBO. On that date, RJR Nabisco was also scheduled to assume roughly $19 billion of new debt. After a delay unrelated to the present action, the merger was ultimately completed during the week of April 24, 1989.

Plaintiffs now allege, in short, that RJR Nabisco's actions have drastically impaired the value of bonds previously issued to plaintiffs by, in effect, misappropriating the value of those bonds to help finance the LBO and to distribute an enormous windfall to the company's shareholders. As a result, plaintiffs argue, they have unfairly suffered a multimillion dollar loss in the value of their bonds....

At the heart of the present motions lies plaintiffs' claim that RJR Nabisco violated a restrictive covenant—not an explicit covenant found within the four corners of the

---

* 716 F. Supp. 1504 (S.D.N.Y. 1989).

2. A leveraged buy-out occurs when a group of investors, usually including members of a company's management team, buy the company under financial arrangements that include little equity and significant new debt. The necessary debt financing typically includes mortgages or high risk/high yield bonds, popularly known as "junk bonds." Additionally, a portion of this debt is generally secured by the company's assets. Some of the acquired company's assets are usually sold after the transaction is completed in order to reduce the debt incurred in the acquisition.

relevant bond indentures,[3] but rather an *implied* covenant of good faith and fair dealing—not to incur the debt necessary to facilitate the LBO and thereby betray what plaintiffs claim was the fundamental basis of their bargain with the company. The company, plaintiffs assert, consistently reassured its bondholders that it had a "mandate" from its Board of Directors to maintain RJR Nabisco's preferred credit rating. Plaintiffs ask this Court first to imply a covenant of good faith and fair dealing that would prevent the recent transaction, then to hold that this covenant has been breached, and finally to require RJR Nabisco to redeem their bonds.

RJR Nabisco defends the LBO by pointing to express provisions in the bond indentures that, *inter alia*, permit mergers and the assumption of additional debt. These provisions, as well as others that could have been included but were not, were known to the market and to plaintiffs, sophisticated investors who freely bought the bonds and were equally free to sell them at any time. Any attempt by this Court to create contractual terms *post hoc*, defendants contend, not only finds no basis in the controlling law and undisputed facts of this case, but also would constitute an impermissible invasion into the free and open operation of the marketplace.

For the reasons set forth below, this Court agrees with defendants. There being no express covenant between the parties that would restrict the incurrence of new debt, and no perceived direction to that end from covenants that are express, this Court will not imply a covenant to prevent the recent LBO and thereby create an indenture term that, while bargained for in other contexts, was not bargained for here and was not even within the mutual contemplation of the parties.

II. Background

. . . .

A. *The Parties*

Metropolitan Life Insurance Co. ("MetLife"), incorporated in New York, is a life insurance company that provides pension benefits for 42 million individuals. According to its most recent annual report, MetLife's assets exceed $88 billion and its debt securities holdings exceed $49 billion. MetLife is a mutual company and therefore has no stockholders and is instead operated for the benefit of its policyholders. MetLife alleges that it owns $340,542,000 in principal amount of six separate RJR Nabisco debt issues, bonds allegedly purchased between July 1975 and July 1988. Some bonds become due as early as this year; others will not become due until 2017. The bonds bear interest rates of anywhere from 8 to 10.25 percent. MetLife also owned 186,000 shares of RJR Nabisco common stock at the time this suit was filed.

Jefferson-Pilot Life Insurance Co. ("Jefferson-Pilot") is a North Carolina company that has more than $3 billion in total assets, $1.5 billion of which are invested in debt securities. Jefferson-Pilot alleges that it owns $9.34 million in principal amount of three separate RJR Nabisco debt issues, allegedly purchased between June 1978 and June 1988. Those bonds,

---

3. [*The rights of bondholders are governed by a contract known as a bond indenture. Note that the bondholders are not parties to this contract. Rather, the indenture is a contract between the issuing corporation and an "indenture trustee." The trustee, typically a bank, is the agent of the bondholders and the bondholders are third-party beneficiaries of the indenture contract.* — Ed.]

bearing interest rates of anywhere from 8.45 to 10.75 percent, become due in 1993 and 1998.

RJR Nabisco, a Delaware corporation, is a consumer products holding company that owns some of the country's best known product lines, including LifeSavers candy, Oreo cookies, and Winston cigarettes. The company was formed in 1985, when R.J. Reynolds Industries, Inc. ("R.J. Reynolds") merged with Nabisco Brands, Inc. ("Nabisco Brands"). In 1979, and thus before the R.J. Reynolds-Nabisco Brands merger, R.J. Reynolds acquired the Del Monte Corporation ("Del Monte"), which distributes canned fruits and vegetables. From January 1987 until February 1989, co-defendant Johnson served as the company's CEO. KKR, a private investment firm, organizes funds through which investors provide pools of equity to finance LBOs.

B. The Indentures

The bonds[4] implicated by this suit are governed by long, detailed indentures, which in turn are governed by New York contract law.[5] No one disputes that the holders of public bond issues, like plaintiffs here, often enter the market after the indentures have been negotiated and memorialized. Thus, those indentures are often not the product of face-to-face negotiations between the ultimate holders and the issuing company. What remains equally true, however, is that underwriters ordinarily negotiate the terms of the indentures with the issuers. Since the underwriters must then sell or place the bonds, they necessarily negotiate in part with the interests of the buyers in mind. Moreover, these indentures were not secret agreements foisted upon unwitting participants in the bond market. No successive holder is required to accept or to continue to hold the bonds, governed by their accompanying indentures; indeed, plaintiffs readily admit that they could have sold their bonds right up until the announcement of the LBO. Instead, sophisticated investors like plaintiffs are well aware of the indenture terms and, presumably, review them carefully before lending hundreds of millions of dollars to any company.

Indeed, the prospectuses for the indentures contain a statement relevant to this action:

> The Indenture contains no restrictions on the creation of unsecured short-term debt by [RJR Nabisco] or its subsidiaries, no restriction on the creation of unsecured Funded Debt by [RJR Nabisco] or its subsidiaries which are not Restricted Subsidiaries, and no restriction on the payment of dividends by [RJR Nabisco].

Further, as plaintiffs themselves note, the contracts at issue "[do] not impose debt limits, since debt is assumed to be used for productive purposes."

1. The Relevant Articles

A typical RJR Nabisco indenture contains thirteen Articles. At least four of them are relevant to the present motions and thus merit a brief review.

---

4. For the purposes of this Opinion, the terms "bonds," "debentures," and "notes" will be used interchangeably. Any distinctions among these terms are not relevant to the present motions.

5. Both sides agree that New York law controls this Court's interpretation of the indentures, which contain explicit designations to that effect. The indentures themselves provide that they "shall be deemed to be a contract under the laws of the State of New York, and for all purposes should be construed in accordance with the laws of said State, except as may otherwise be required by mandatory provisions of law."

Article Three delineates the covenants of the issuer. Most important, it first provides for payment of principal and interest. It then addresses various mechanical provisions regarding such matters as payment terms and trustee vacancies. The Article also contains "negative pledge" and related provisions, which restrict mortgages or other liens on the assets of RJR Nabisco or its subsidiaries and seek to protect the bondholders from being subordinated to other debt.

Article Five describes various procedures to remedy defaults and the responsibilities of the Trustee....

Article Nine governs the adoption of supplemental indentures. It provides, *inter alia*, that the Issuer and the Trustee can

> add to the covenants of the Issuer such further covenants, restrictions, conditions or provisions as its Board of Directors by Board Resolution and the Trustee shall consider to be for the protection of the holders of Securities, and to make the occurrence, or the occurrence and continuance, of a default in any such additional covenants, restrictions, conditions or provisions an Event of Default permitting the enforcement of all or any of the several remedies provided in this Indenture as herein set forth ...

Article Ten addresses a potential "Consolidation, Merger, Sale or Conveyance," and explicitly sets forth the conditions under which the company can consolidate or merge into or with any other corporation. It provides explicitly that RJR Nabisco "may consolidate with, or sell or convey, all or substantially all of its assets to, or merge into or with any other corporation," so long as the new entity is a United States corporation, and so long as it assumes RJR Nabisco's debt....

3. The Recognition and Effect of the LBO Trend

... A ... comprehensive memorandum, prepared [by MetLife] in late 1985, evaluated and explained several aspects of the corporate world's increasing use of mergers, takeovers and other debt-financed transactions. That memorandum first reviewed the available protection for lenders such as MetLife:

> Covenants are incorporated into loan documents to ensure that after a lender makes a loan, the creditworthiness of the borrower and the lender's ability to reach the borrower's assets do not deteriorate substantially. *Restrictions on the incurrence of debt*, sale of assets, mergers, dividends, restricted payments and loans and advances to affiliates *are some of the traditional negative covenants that can help protect lenders in the event their obligors become involved in undesirable merger/takeover situations.*

> Because almost any industrial company is apt to engineer a takeover or be taken over itself, *Business Week* says that investors are beginning to view debt securities of high grade industrial corporations as Wall Street's riskiest investments. In addition, *because public bondholders do not enjoy the protection of any restrictive covenants*, owners of high grade [*corporate bonds*] face substantial losses from takeover situations, if not immediately, then when the bond market finally adjusts.... There have been 10–15 merger/takeover/LBO situations where, *due to the lack of covenant protection, [MetLife] has had no choice but to remain a lender to a less creditworthy obligor....* The fact that the quality of our investment portfolio is greater than the other large insurance companies ... may indicate that we have negotiated better covenant protection than other institutions, thus

generally being able to require prepayment when situations become too risky ... [However,] a problem exists. And *because the current merger craze is not likely to decelerate* and because there exist vehicles to circumvent traditional covenants, the problem will probably continue. Therefore, *perhaps it is time to institute appropriate language designed to protect Metropolitan from the negative implications of mergers and takeovers.*

Indeed, MetLife does not dispute that, as a member of a bondholders' association, it received and discussed a proposed model indenture, which included a "comprehensive covenant" entitled "Limitations on Shareholders' Payments." As becomes clear from reading the proposed—but never adopted—provision, it was "intend[ed] to provide protection against all of the types of situations in which shareholders profit at the expense of bondholders." The provision dictated that the "corporation will not, and will not permit any subsidiary to, directly or indirectly, make any shareholder payment unless ... (1) the aggregate amount of all shareholder payment during the period [at issue] ... shall not exceed [figure left blank]." The term "shareholder payments" is defined to include "restructuring distributions, stock repurchases, debt incurred or guaranteed to finance merger payments to shareholders, etc."

Apparently, that provision—or provisions with similar intentions—never went beyond the discussion stage at MetLife. That fact is easily understood; indeed, MetLife's own documents articulate several reasonable, undisputed explanations:

> While it would be possible to broaden the change in ownership covenant to cover any acquisition-oriented transaction, *we might well encounter significant resistance in implementation with larger public companies* ... With respect to implementation, we would be faced with the task of imposing a non-standard limitation on potential borrowers, *which could be a difficult task in today's highly competitive marketplace. Competitive pressures notwithstanding, it would seem that management of larger public companies would be particularly opposed to such a covenant since its effect would be to increase the cost of an acquisition* (due to an assumed debt repayment), a factor that could well lower the price of any tender offer (thereby impacting shareholders).

(emphasis added). The November 1985 memorandum explained that

> obviously, our ability to implement methods of takeover protection will vary between the public and private market. In that public securities do not contain any meaningful covenants, it would be very difficult for [MetLife] to demand takeover protection in public bonds. Such a requirement would effectively take us out of the public industrial market. A recent *Business Week* article does suggest, however, that there is increasing talk among lending institutions about requiring blue chip companies to compensate them for the growing risk of downgradings. *This talk, regarding such protection as restrictions on future debt financings, is met with skepticism by the investment banking community which feels that CFO's are not about to give up the option of adding debt and do not really care if their companies' credit ratings drop a notch or two.*

(emphasis added).

The Court quotes these documents at such length not because they represent an "admission" or "waiver" from MetLife, or an "assumption of risk" in any tort sense, or its "consent" to any particular course of conduct—all terms discussed at even greater length in the parties' submissions. Rather, the documents set forth the background to the present action, and highlight the risks inherent in the market itself, for any investor. Investors as sophisticated as MetLife and Jefferson-Pilot would be hard-pressed to plead ignorance of these market risks. Indeed, MetLife has not disputed the facts asserted in its own internal documents. Nor has Jefferson-Pilot—presumably an institution no less sophisticated than MetLife—offered any reason to believe that its understanding of the securities market differed in any material respect from the description and analysis set forth in the MetLife documents. Those documents, after all, were not born in a vacuum. They are descriptions of, and responses to, the market in which investors like MetLife and Jefferson-Pilot knowingly participated.

III. Discussion

... The indentures at issue clearly address the eventuality of a merger. They impose certain related restrictions not at issue in this suit, but no restriction that would prevent the recent RJR Nabisco merger transaction. The indentures also explicitly set forth provisions for the adoption of new covenants, if such a course is deemed appropriate....

Under certain circumstances, however, courts will, as plaintiffs note, consider extrinsic evidence to evaluate the scope of an implied covenant of good faith. However, the Second Circuit has established a different rule for customary, or boilerplate, provisions of detailed indentures used and relied upon throughout the securities market, such as those at issue. Thus, in *Sharon Steel Corporation v. Chase Manhattan Bank, N.A.*, 691 F.2d 1039 (2d Cir. 1982), Judge Winter concluded that

> boilerplate provisions are ... not the consequences of the relationship of particular borrowers and lenders and do not depend upon particularized intentions of the parties to an indenture. There are no adjudicative facts relating to the parties to the litigation for a jury to find and the meaning of boilerplate provisions is, therefore, a matter of law rather than fact. Moreover, uniformity in interpretation is important to the efficiency of capital markets ... Whereas participants in the capital market can adjust their affairs according to a uniform interpretation, whether it be correct or not as an initial proposition, the creation of enduring uncertainties as to the meaning of boilerplate provisions would decrease the value of all debenture issues and greatly impair the efficient working of capital markets ... Just such uncertainties would be created if interpretation of boilerplate provisions were submitted to juries sitting in every judicial district in the nation.

A. *Plaintiffs' Case Against the RJR Nabisco LBO*

1. *Count One: The Implied Covenant*

In their first count, plaintiffs assert that defendant RJR Nabisco owes a continuing duty of good faith and fair dealing in connection with the contract [i.e., the indentures] through which it borrowed money from MetLife, Jefferson-Pilot and other holders of its debt, including a duty not to frustrate the purpose of the contracts to the debtholders or to deprive the debtholders of the intended object of the contracts—purchase of investment-grade securities.

> In the "buy-out," the company breaches the duty [or implied covenant] of good faith and fair dealing by, *inter alia*, destroying the investment grade quality of the debt and transferring that value to the "buy-out" proponents and to the shareholders.

In effect, plaintiffs contend that express covenants were not necessary because an *implied* covenant would prevent what defendants have now done.

A plaintiff always can allege a violation of an express covenant. If there has been such a violation, of course, the court need not reach the question of whether or not an *implied* covenant has been violated. That inquiry surfaces where, while the express terms may not have been technically breached, one party has nonetheless effectively deprived the other of those express, explicitly bargained-for benefits. In such a case, a court will read an implied covenant of good faith and fair dealing into a contract to ensure that neither party deprives the other of "the fruits of the agreement." ... Such a covenant is implied only where the implied term "is consistent with other mutually agreed upon terms in the contract." ... Viewed another way, the implied covenant of good faith is breached only when one party seeks to prevent the contract's performance or to withhold benefits....

Thus, in cases like *Van Gemert v. Boeing Co.*, 520 F.2d 1373 (2d Cir.), *cert. denied*, 423 U.S. 947, 46 L. Ed. 2d 282, 96 S. Ct. 364 (1975) (*"Van Gemert I"*), and *Pittsburgh Terminal Corp. v. Baltimore & Ohio Ry. Co.*, 680 F.2d 933 (3d Cir.), *cert. denied*, 459 U.S. 1056, 74 L. Ed. 2d 621, 103 S. Ct. 475, (1982)—both relied upon by plaintiffs—the courts used the implied covenant of good faith and fair dealing to ensure that the bondholders received the benefit of their bargain as determined from the face of the contracts at issue. In *Van Gemert I*, the plaintiff bondholders alleged inadequate notice to them of defendant's intention to redeem the debentures in question and hence an inability to exercise their conversion rights before the applicable deadline. The contract itself provided that notice would be given in the first place.... Faced with those provisions, defendants in that case unsurprisingly admitted that the indentures specifically required the company to provide the bondholders with notice.... While defendant there issued a press release that mentioned the possible redemption of outstanding convertible debentures, that limited release did not "mention even the tentative dates for redemption and expiration of the conversion rights of debenture holders." ... Moreover, defendant did not issue any general publicity or news release. Through an implied covenant, then, the court fleshed out the full extent of the more skeletal right that appeared in the contract itself, and thus protected plaintiff's bargained-for right of conversion. As the court observed,

> What one buys when purchasing a convertible debenture in addition to the debt obligation of the company ... is principally the expectation that the stock will increase sufficiently in value that the conversion right will make the debenture worth more than the debt ... *Any loss occurring to him from failure to convert, as here, is not from a risk inherent in his investment but rather from unsatisfactory notification procedures.*

I also note, in passing, that *Van Gemert I* presented the Second Circuit with "less sophisticated investors." ... Similarly, the court in *Pittsburgh Terminal* applied an implied covenant to the indentures at issue because defendants there "took steps to prevent the Bondholders from receiving information which they needed *in order to receive the fruits of their conversion option should they choose to exercise it.*" ...

The appropriate analysis, then, is first to examine the indentures to determine "the fruits of the agreement" between the parties, and then to decide whether those "fruits" have been spoiled-which is to say, whether plaintiffs' contractual rights have been violated by defendants.

The American Bar Foundation's *Commentaries on Indentures* (1971) ("the *Commentaries*"), relied upon and respected by both plaintiffs and defendants, describes the rights and risks generally found in bond indentures like those at issue:

> The most obvious and important characteristic of long-term debt financing is that the holder ordinarily has not bargained for and does not expect any substantial gain in the value of the security to compensate for the risk of loss ... The significant fact, *which accounts in part for the detailed protective provisions of the typical long-term debt financing instrument*, is that *the lender (the purchaser*

of the debt security) can expect only interest at the prescribed rate plus the eventual return of the principal. Except for possible increases in the market value of the debt security because of changes in interest rates, the debt security will seldom be worth more than the lender paid for it … It may, of course, become worth much less. Accordingly, the typical investor in a long-term debt security is primarily interested in every reasonable assurance that the principal and interest will be paid when due…. Short of bankruptcy, *the debt security holder can do nothing to protect himself against actions of the borrower which jeopardize its ability to pay the debt unless he … establishes his rights through contractual provisions set forth in the debt agreement or indenture.*

A review of the parties' submissions and the indentures themselves satisfies the Court that the substantive "fruits" guaranteed by those contracts and relevant to the present motions include the periodic and regular payment of interest and the eventual repayment of principal…. ("The Issuer covenants … that it will duly and punctually pay … the principal of, and interest on, each of the Securities … at the respective times and in the manner provided in such Securities …")…. Plaintiffs' Amended Complaint nowhere alleges that RJR Nabisco has breached these contractual obligations; interest payments continue and there is no reason to believe that the principal will not be paid when due.

It is not necessary to decide that indentures like those at issue could never support a finding of additional benefits, under different circumstances with different parties. Rather, for present purposes, it is sufficient to conclude what obligation is *not* covered, either explicitly or implicitly, by these contracts held by these plaintiffs. Accordingly, this Court holds that the "fruits" of these indentures do not include an implied restrictive covenant that would prevent the incurrence of new debt to facilitate the recent LBO. To hold otherwise would permit these plaintiffs to straightjacket the company in order to guarantee their investment. These plaintiffs do not invoke an implied covenant of good faith to protect a legitimate, mutually contemplated benefit of the indentures; rather, they seek to have this Court create an additional benefit for which they did not bargain.

Plaintiffs argue in the most general terms that the fundamental basis of all these indentures was that an LBO along the lines of the recent RJR Nabisco transaction would never be undertaken, that indeed *no* action would be taken, intentionally or not, that would significantly deplete the company's assets…. But as Judge Knapp aptly concluded in *Gardner*, "Defendants … were under a duty to carry out the terms of the contract, but not to make sure that plaintiffs had made a good investment. The former they have done; the latter we have no jurisdiction over." [*Gardner & Florence Call Cowles Foundation v. Empire, Inc., 589 F. Supp. 669, 674 (S.D.N.Y. 1984)*] Plaintiffs' submissions and MetLife's previous undisputed internal memoranda remind the Court that a "fundamental basis" or a "fruit of an agreement" is often in the eye of the beholder, whose vision may well change along with the market, and who may, with hindsight, imagine a different bargain than the one he actually and initially accepted with open eyes.

The sort of unbounded and one-sided elasticity urged by plaintiffs would interfere with and destabilize the market. And this Court, like the parties to these contracts, cannot ignore or disavow the marketplace in which the contract is performed. Nor can it ignore the expectations of that market—expectations, for instance, that the terms of an indenture will be upheld, and that a court will not, *sua sponte*, add new substantive terms to that indenture as it sees fit. The Court has no reason to believe that the market, in evaluating bonds such as those at issue here, did not discount for the possibility that any company, even one the size of RJR Nabisco, might engage in an LBO heavily financed by debt. That the bonds did not lose any of their value until the October 20, 1988 announcement of a possible RJR Nabisco LBO only suggests that the market had theretofore evaluated the risks of such a transaction as slight.

The Court recognizes that the market is not a static entity, but instead involves what plaintiffs call "evolving understanding[s]." Just as the growing prevalence of LBO's has helped change certain ground rules and expectations in the field of mergers and acquisitions, so too it has obviously affected the bond market, a fact no one disputes....

To respond to changed market forces, new indenture provisions can be negotiated ... New provisions could include special debt restrictions or change-of-control covenants. There is no guarantee, of course, that companies like RJR Nabisco would accept such new covenants; parties retain the freedom to enter into contracts as they choose. But presumably, multi-billion dollar investors like plaintiffs have some say in the terms of the investments they make and continue to hold. And, presumably, companies like RJR Nabisco need the infusions of capital such investors are capable of providing.

Whatever else may be true about this case, it certainly does not present an example of the classic sort of form contract or contract of adhesion often frowned upon by courts. In those cases, what motivates a court is the strikingly inequitable nature of the parties' respective bargaining positions. *See generally*, Rakoff, *Contracts of Adhesion: An Essay in Reconstruction*, 96 Harv. L. Rev. 1173 (1982). Plaintiffs here entered this "liquid trading market," with their eyes open and were free to leave at any time. Instead they remained there notwithstanding its well understood risks....

In the final analysis, plaintiffs offer no objective or reasonable standard for a court to use in its effort to define the sort of actions their "implied covenant" would permit a corporation to take, and those it would not. Plaintiffs say only that investors like themselves rely upon the "skill" and "good faith" of a company's board and management, and that their covenant would prevent the company from "destroy[ing] ... the legitimate expectations of its long-term bondholders." As is clear from the preceding discussion, however, plaintiffs have failed to convince the Court that by upholding the explicit, bargained-for terms of the indenture, RJR Nabisco has either exhibited bad faith or destroyed plaintiffs' *legitimate*, protected expectations....

2. Count Five: In Equity

... In their papers, plaintiffs variously attempt to justify Count V as being based on unjust enrichment, frustration of purpose, an alleged breach of something approaching a fiduciary duty, or a general claim of unconscionability. Each claim fails. First, as even plaintiffs recognize, an unjust enrichment claim requires a court first to find that "the circumstances [are] such that in equity and good conscience the defendant should make restitution." Plaintiffs have not alleged a violation of a single explicit term of the indentures at issue, and on the facts alleged this Court has determined that an implicit covenant of good faith and fair dealing has not been violated. Under these circumstances, this Court concludes that defendants need not, "in equity and good conscience," make restitution.

Second, in support of their motions plaintiffs claim frustration of purpose. Yet even resolving all ambiguities and drawing all reasonable inferences in plaintiffs' favor, their claim cannot stand. A claim of frustration of purpose has three elements:

> First, the purpose that is frustrated must have been a principal purpose of that party in making the contract.... The object must be so completely the basis of the contract that, as both parties understand, without it the transaction would make

little sense. Second, the frustration must be substantial. It is not enough that the transaction has become less profitable for the affected party or even that he will sustain a loss. The frustration must be so severe that it is not fairly to be regarded as within the risks that he assumed under the contract. Third, the non-occurrence of the frustrating event must have been a basic assumption on which the contract was made.

Restatement (Second) of Contracts § 265, comment *a* (1981).... [T]here is no indication here that an alleged refusal to incur debt to facilitate an LBO was the "essence" or "principal purpose" of the indentures, and no mention of such an alleged restriction is made in the agreements. Further, while plaintiffs' bonds may have lost some of their value, "discharge under this doctrine has been limited to instances where a virtually cataclysmic, wholly unforeseeable event *renders the contract valueless to one party*." ... That is not the case here. Moreover, "the frustration of purpose defense is not available where, as here, the event which allegedly frustrated the purpose of the contract ... was clearly foreseeable." ... Faced with MetLife's internal memoranda, plaintiffs cannot but admit that "MetLife has been concerned about 'buy-outs' for several years." Nor do plaintiffs provide any reasonable basis for believing that a party as sophisticated as Jefferson-Pilot was any less cognizant of the market around it.

Equally important, plaintiffs' position on this issue — that "A Company May Not Deliberately Deplete its Assets to the Injury of its Debtholders," — provides no reasonable or workable limits, and is thus reminiscent of their implied covenant of good faith. Indeed, many indisputably legitimate corporate transactions would not survive plaintiffs' theory. With no workable limits, plaintiffs' envisioned duty would extend equally to trade creditors, employees, and every other person to whom the defendants are liable in any way. Of all such parties, these informed plaintiffs least require a Court's equitable protection; not only are they willing participants in a largely impersonal market, but they also possess the financial sophistication and size to secure their own protection.

Finally, plaintiffs cannot seriously allege unconscionability, given their sophistication and, at least judging from this action, the sophistication of their legal counsel as well. Under the undisputed facts of this case, this Court finds no actionable unconscionability.

III. Conclusion

For the reasons set forth above, the Court grants defendants summary judgment on Counts I and V, judgment on the pleadings for certain of the securities at issue in Count III, and dismisses for want of requisite particularity Counts II, III, and IX. All remaining motions made by the parties are denied in all respects ...

Thomas A. Smith, *The Efficient Norm for Corporate Law: A Neotraditional Interpretation of Fiduciary Duty*[*]

To economically oriented corporate law professors, distinguishing between directors' fiduciary duty to shareholders and a duty to the corporation itself smacks of reification — treating the fictional corporate entity as if it were a real thing. Now the orthodox view

[*] Originally published in 98 MICH. L. REV. 214 (1999). Copyright 1999 by Thomas A. Smith. Reprinted with permission.

among corporate law scholars is that the corporate fiduciary duty is a norm that requires firm managers to "maximize shareholder value." Giving the corporation itself any serious role in the analysis of fiduciary duty, the thinking goes, obscures scientific insight with bad legal metaphysics.

Some recent scholarship and legislation, such as constituency statutes, have challenged this "shareholder primacy" view. Contestants on both sides of the debate over corporate fiduciary duty assume, however, that economic analysis inevitably favors shareholder primacy. Critics of shareholder value maximization encourage this assumption by making their case turn, in part, on criticisms of economic methodology itself and on invocations of moral and political values most economists would find controversial at best.

Nevertheless, the economic approach to corporate law does not foreordain the maximization of shareholder value as the primary norm of corporate law. The economic case for shareholder value maximization is, in fact, initially puzzling and ultimately unconvincing. If economic efficiency is the normative guidepost for substantive law, the principal norm of corporate law cannot be the maximization of shareholder value.

It is easy to see why this must be so. The corporate fiduciary duty, according to the leading economic analysis of corporate law, is a principle that fills gaps in the "corporate contract." The "corporate contract" is the metaphorical contract consisting of the sum of the voluntary arrangements among the various parties who contribute resources to the corporate enterprise and have claims against it. Discovering the correct gap-filling principles for the corporate contract involves hypothetical bargain analysis—asking what contractual terms rational parties would have agreed to had they addressed ex ante the matter that falls into a contractual gap. For corporate contracts, the prevailing view is that this gap-filling principle should be "maximize shareholder value." According to this view, that is the substance of the corporate fiduciary duty.

One can adopt the contractual approach to corporate law and agree that the fiduciary duty is essentially a principle for filling gaps in corporate contracts. Nevertheless, the next step in the argument for the prevailing view, that the substance of this gap-filling principle should be shareholder value maximization, does not follow. Rational corporate investors in a hypothetical bargain setting would not agree to shareholder value maximization as their gap-filling rule. The main point of this Article is to explain why they would not and to explain what they would choose instead.

Rational corporate investors would not choose shareholder wealth maximization as their gap-filling rule because of what investor rationality entails. In economic analysis of corporate law, it is standard to treat shareholders as rational in the sense described in basic finance theory, in particular, the Capital Assets Pricing Model ("CAPM"). Investors who are rational in the CAPM sense would hypothetically agree to a gap-filling principle, but it would not be "maximize shareholder value." Under CAPM, rational investors will diversify among all classes of capital assets, including both corporate stocks and bonds. In fact, they will hold the "market portfolio," that is, a portfolio that is a microcosm of all capital assets, in which each type of capital asset has the same place proportionally in the rational investor's portfolio as it does in the capital market as a whole. Thus it would be irrational for investors to agree to a principle that required the value of their shares to be maximized if it meant reducing the value of their bonds (or of any other nonresiduary class of capital assets they might hold) by more than the increase in the value of their stock. The shareholder value maximization norm allows, and under plausible assumptions even requires, managers to make inefficient decisions which hypothetical rational investors would not permit ex ante. Rational investors would therefore not agree to it.

To what corporate law norm would rational investors hypothetically agree? They would agree to a norm that told managers to maximize the value of the diversified portfolios that CAPM says rational investors would hold. As a gap-filling principle, this would require firm managers to make the choices that would maximize the value of the sum of financial claims against the corporation, because these claims will be held proportionally by rational CAPM investors holding the market portfolio. If a public corporation were financed half by stock and half by bonds, a rational investor holding the market portfolio would have his investment in that corporation divided evenly between its stock and its bonds. He would obviously not agree to a rule that allowed managers to make choices that diminished the value of his bonds by more than they increased the value of his stock. He would insist on a rule that required managers to maximize the value of the sum of the two classes of claims against that corporation. This rule would be the gap filler which rational investors would agree managers should follow if the corporate contract did not provide otherwise. This would be the content of the fiduciary duty rational investors would accept ex ante.

Articulating this duty has interesting consequences. A fiduciary duty running to the corporation itself would be most consistent with the gap-filling rule that emerges from hypothetical bargain analysis. This rule would require corporate managers (absent explicit contractual terms to the contrary) to take whatever actions maximized the value of "the corporation"—maximized, that is, the sum of the value of financial claims against the corporation—whether doing so primarily benefited shareholders or some other class of corporate claimants. Far from mysteriously reifying the corporation, this approach requires nothing more conceptually murky than addition. This reformulation of the duty is notably inconsistent, however, with treating one class of corporate claimants, such as common shareholders, as the exclusive and direct beneficiaries of the fiduciary duty, as is now standard in economic analysis of corporate law. It is also inconsistent, however, with making all or several classes of claimants against the corporation direct and simultaneous beneficiaries of the fiduciary duty, as seems to be suggested by some advocates of bondholder rights. The "neotraditional" conception of fiduciary duty I propose, a duty running to the corporation itself, would require actions of managers that would sometimes benefit one class of claimants and sometimes another, depending on the circumstances. Once one dispenses with misguided fears of reification, there is nothing particularly troubling about this approach....

I. The Inefficiency of the Shareholder Value Maximization Norm

Corporate law scholars generally assume that efficiency arguments inevitably lead to the conclusion that maximizing shareholder value should be the primary norm of corporate law. This conclusion, however, is unwarranted. In fact, the shareholder value maximization norm, if strictly applied, would require firm managers to make socially inefficient choices. This analysis follows from the familiar corporate law problem of the firm in the "vicinity of insolvency."

A. Shareholder Value Maximization Mandates Inefficiency

In this Part, I use a numerical example to show how a norm to maximize shareholder value mandates inefficiency and then explore some implications.

1. An Inefficient Risky Investment

Consider the choice faced by the managers of XYZ corporation. They must choose between only two investment opportunities. Investment 1 is relatively safe; Investment 2, risky. XYZ corporation is solvent. It has assets worth $20 million and liabilities of $15 million, all of which is owed to bondholders.

Investment 1 requires an outlay of $10 million and has a 90 percent probability of being worth $12 million, and a 10 percent probability of being worth $8 million, after one period. Thus Investment 1 has an expected value of $11.6 million, and net of the initial outlay of $10 million, a value of $1.6 million.[6] Put another way, shareholders have a 90 percent chance of a $2 million gain, and a 10 percent chance of a $2 million loss, for an expected gain to shareholders from Investment 1 of $1.6 million.

All of the expected gain from Investment 1 would go to the shareholders because the claim of bondholders is fixed at $15 million. Whether Investment 1 pays off at $12 million or $8 million, XYZ will have enough value left in it to pay the bondholders all of the $15 million that is owed to them.

Investment 2, on the other hand, is much more risky. It also requires an outlay of $10 million, but it has a 10 percent probability of paying off grandly at $200 million. But it has a 90 percent probability of wiping the company out by generating losses of $20 million, equal to all of the assets of the company. Investment 2 has an expected value of only $2 million, and, net of the required initial outlay of $10 million, a value of negative $8 million.[7] From the perspective of social wealth, it is obviously a bad investment—it has a negative net expected value.

Shareholders, however, will not view it as so bad. If Investment 2 pays off at $200 million, shareholders will get all of it. If the bet pays off at negative $20 million, on the other hand, shareholders will not lose the entire $20 million, because they enjoy limited liability. Instead, they will lose their equity in XYZ, which is only $5 million. Thus the expected value of Investment 2 to shareholders is 10 percent of $200 million plus 90 percent of negative $5 million, for a total expected gain to shareholders of $16.5 million. Net of the $10 million initial outlay, Investment 2 has an expected value to shareholders of $6.5 million.

Bondholders, of course, would bear the brunt of the risk of Investment 2. If Investment 2 pays off big, they will be no better off than before; they will still be paid only their fixed claim of $15 million. If Investment 2 fails, however, they will lose their investment, which was worth $15 million before the risky bet was made. With the former event having a 10 percent chance of happening, and the latter a 90 percent chance, bondholders face an expected loss of $13.5 million from Investment 2.

Faced with the choice between Investment 1 and Investment 2, corporate managers exclusively loyal to the shareholders should choose Investment 2, even though it has a net expected value of less than Investment 1. That is, managers loyal to shareholders will choose Investment 2, even though it is inefficient. In terms of normative economic theory, this is an absurd result. There must be something wrong with the simple formulation of corporate fiduciary duty as a duty to "maximize shareholder value."

---

6. [(90% x $10 million) + (10% x $8 million) - $10 million = $1.6 million.—Ed.]
7. [(10% x $200 million) + (90% x -$20 million) - $10 million = -$8 million.—Ed.]

2. In the "Vicinity of Insolvency"

Corporate law scholars will recognize that the illustration above is similar to those used to illustrate the "vicinity of insolvency," the region in which managers are said to have incentives to make excessively risky investments. Because of this problem, Delaware corporate law recognizes an exception to the rule that managers owe their fiduciary duty exclusively to shareholders. In the Credit Lyonnais case, Chancellor William Allen opined that "in the vicinity of insolvency," the fiduciary duty "shifts" from being owed to shareholders to being owed to creditors.

One could argue that the illustration above is merely an instance of a firm operating in the vicinity of insolvency. It is already well known, one could say, that in this vicinity, managers have incentives to make inefficient choices, and corporate law recognizes an exception in this region to the general rule that managers have a duty to maximize share value. For this objection to have any force, however, there must be some region which is outside the vicinity of insolvency: it must be the case that, except in unusual settings, the norm of shareholder value maximization does yield efficient choices.

In fact, however, this is not the case. Rather, firms are always in the vicinity of insolvency because all it takes for any firm, no matter how solvent, to become insolvent is to lose a sufficiently risky bet. One can construct for any firm, no matter how solvent (so long as it has debt and limited liability), a bet sufficiently risky that it would increase the value of its shares, while it decreased the total value of the company—a bet, that is, that would be socially inefficient for the firm to make. For example, take very solvent firm ABC, which has assets of $100 million and liabilities of $10 million. By making a highly leveraged bet in, say, the derivatives market, it would have, let us suppose, a one in one hundred chance of gaining $10 billion, and a 99 percent chance of losing the firm's entire value. This bet would have a present value of $10.9 million to shareholders, while it would have an expected value to the corporation of only $1 million. The price of this lottery-ticket-like bet is, let us suppose, $10 million. Thus it has a net expected value to the corporation of negative $9 million—obviously a bad bet for the firm. Yet managers maximizing shareholder value would still choose this investment over any similarly priced bet that had an expected value of less than $10.9 million for the shareholders, even though other bets would be better for the corporation.

That, however, has to do with the firm being in the vicinity of insolvency only in a trivial sense. It is just that the closer to insolvency a firm is, the less risky a bet has to be for its loss to push the firm into bankruptcy. If managers really are duty bound to maximize the value of shares, then they are duty bound to make inefficient choices like the one just illustrated as long as these choices are available, and they will be. The conflict of interest between shareholders and bondholders, therefore, does not merely result in inefficient incentives when the firm is in the vicinity of insolvency. It exists whenever there are inefficient risky bets available that would increase share value but decrease firm value. In theory, and increasingly in reality, this is all the time.

A possible reaction to my argument above would be to dismiss it as invoking excessively unlikely events. This reaction, however, would be inappropriate. It may seem that opportunities to bet the company on a long shot are rare and therefore that my argument does not raise a serious problem with the shareholder value maximization norm. This and other practically minded objections to my argument are likely based on misunderstandings of how a corporate law norm should function, as I discuss below.

3. Complete Capital Markets

It may seem that managers rarely make bets like those illustrated above, unless their company is about to fail. If these occurrences are very rare, the problems they create for fiduciary duty theory, one might argue, are of academic interest only. This objection, however, misses the point. These occurrences may be rare, but not because managers lack opportunities to make long-shot bets. Indeed, modern finance theory typically assumes (with increasing realism) the near completeness of capital markets. In complete capital markets, it is possible to bet on nearly any possible future world state, including low probability ones. Managers can, in theory, bet the company on very risky opportunities, and there is no reason to suppose that these opportunities are rare. There are an infinite number of possible investments that, while inefficient, would increase the value of a given company's stock. The claim that share-value-increasing but inefficient bets are not available would fly in the face of capital-market completeness, a fundamental assumption of modern finance theory.

The abundance of these opportunities for the firm becomes more obvious if one considers that bets that must be expected to lose money for the firm as a whole cannot be scarce as long as there are people willing to take the firm's money. Any risk neutral party should be willing to be the counter-party of a bet that has a negative expected value for the firm but a positive expected value for the other party. If firms were willing to pay an unfair price for bets, so long as they were risky enough, and so long as they increased share value, there could be no shortage of parties willing to relieve firms of their money. This sort of bet would amount to a collusion between equity holders and third parties to impose costs on the fixed claimants of the firm and split the benefits among themselves. This sort of behavior is hardly universal among managers, but not for lack of opportunity —and not because it would be disloyal to shareholders.

The assumption of complete capital markets is increasingly realistic. The emergence of financial derivative markets means practically unlimited opportunities exist for firms to bet, where they are so inclined, on possible but low probability future states of the world. [*The financial meltdown of 2008 was caused at least in part by financial institutions making such risky bets (although many institutions claim to have been unaware of the risks). Had those bets paid off (which they did, for a time), shareholders might have made great gains.—Ed.*] ...

B. Agency Costs

If managers of solvent corporations do not lack the opportunity to make inefficient bets that would increase shareholder value, then why do managers rarely bet the company on long shots? It is not because they are loyally serving the interests of the diversified shareholders who figure so prominently in the conventional economic analysis of corporations. Managers loyal to shareholders would make such bets. In practice, managers apparently make these bets only when firm insolvency looms. When the firm is on the brink of bankruptcy, managers' interests are aligned too well with those of shareholders. Managers want to avoid the stigma of bankruptcy and the loss of their firm-specific human capital. For managers, there is little solace in managing their firm only slightly into bankruptcy. To avoid it, they will take desperate chances. When the firm is comfortably solvent, the conventional wisdom is that managers will be more risk averse than relatively risk neutral shareholders would prefer. Unlike diversified shareholders, managers typically have specialized much of their personal wealth in one firm. Also unlike shareholders, managers typically do not participate fully in the upside potential of the firm. Diversified shareholders, it is often observed, would prefer managers to make all investments with a positive net discounted present value to shareholders, even if they are very risky. Managers, however, will not do this, being far more exposed than the shareholders to firm-specific risk. In fact, if investors owned only the common stock of the firm, they would prefer that managers undertake even riskier projects that had negative discounted present values, so long as the expected result would increase the value of their stock.

The divergence of the attitudes toward risk of shareholders and managers gives rise to agency costs in the conventional view of corporations. Manager agents will not take risks shareholder principals would prefer they take. This standard view goes wrong, however, by implicitly overvaluing the interests of shareholders. This over-weighting stems from the assumption that managers should be analyzed as agents of diversified shareholders. But why should this be so? Shareholders are a legal category, not a natural category of economics. By analyzing firms in terms of the "shareholders," it is the conventionalists who are indulging in reification. Legal scholars have adjusted their thinking to the imperative of diversification that comes from modern finance theory, but only as far as they may without leaving the legal category of the "shareholders" behind. The result is a hybrid that does not quite make economic sense.

Legal scholars have not fully appreciated the extent to which modern finance has left the analysis of Berle and Means's [*The Modern Corporation and Private Property*] outmoded. That influential book still weighs heavily on corporate law scholarship. Berle and Means stressed that the shareholder in the modern corporation, with his mere atom of property, has no power to control management. Ownership and control are split, in their vision, producing a radioactive alienation that threatens to poison economic life. The remedy, they thought, was to recharacterize firms as virtual public utilities with public duties. The rational investor of modern capital asset pricing models, viewed through the lens of Berle and Means, looks like an aggravated version of what they feared. Thus the mythology of the lost age of the active shareholder owner lives on into contemporary corporate scholarship. The diversified investor of modern finance theory, however, is not a particularly frightening version of Berle and Means's shareholder. It (usually an institution) is not a "shareholder" as we have been taught to think of shareholders at all. The rational investor is diversified across all classes of capital assets and consequently is, in spite of much academic cheerleading to the contrary,[8] largely passive. If this rational investor is the starting point, what agency costs should matter?

The agency costs that matter are properly seen as the divergence between what self-interested managers do and what rational investors would have them do. Rational investors will have a stake in that part of the firm's capital that trades on the debt market, just as they will have a stake in that part of the firm's capital that trades in the stock market. Thus when managers fail to be as risk neutral as diversified shareholders would have them be, this does not necessarily mean they are more averse to risk than rational investors who own a proportional stake in the firm's debt would have them be. This does not mean that the agency costs are trivial, but it does suggest that the conventional picture of managers as agents of "the shareholders" exaggerates agency costs. Rational investors will not be as risk-loving as would be investors holding only equity.

If the bulk of a firm's capital comes from rational investors, investors heavily positioned in the firm's equity might nevertheless yield a disproportionate influence over managers. In this case, the firm-specific investments of managers might mitigate the pressure toward excessive risk-taking that risk-preferring shareholders might put on managers. Public choice theory suggests that smaller groups with narrower interests tend to wield more influence than do larger groups with diffuse interests. Narrow special interest lobbies are

---

8. *See Bernard Black's article in this volume.—Ed.*

able routinely to exercise more influence in the legislative process than diffuse groups such as taxpayers can. There is a danger that something similar may occur in the context of corporate governance. Consider a public corporation that has two groups of shareholders, one of which is fully diversified according to the CAPM mandate and another that has specialized in the corporation's common stock. The tendency of economic analysis of corporate law is to view this allocation of ownership as benign, because it reduces monitoring costs. Mark Roe and others have argued, for example, that restrictions on ownership by financial intermediaries of large stakes in public corporations should be lifted, because strong owners would make good monitors of firm managers, who otherwise tend to shirk, self-deal, and otherwise generate excessive agency costs.[9]

Having a strong "interest group" focused specifically on the value of the firm's stock, to the exclusion of the other financial claims against it, however, will not necessarily be efficient. Especially if the firm is highly leveraged, the specialized-equity interest group may have an incentive to use its influence, through the corporate governance system, to get managers to take excessive risks. This would harm rationally diversified investors in the firm....

C. Contracts with Shareholders and Creditors and Duties to Bondholders

... Contractarians argue that the corporation is best understood as a nexus of contracts and that the relationship of shareholders to the firm is essentially contractual. They also argue that shareholders are beneficiaries of a fiduciary duty, while bondholders have only a contractual relationship with the firm. But what does this mean? If the corporation is a nexus of contracts, is not everyone's relationship within the nexus contractual? Contractarians must be using the term contract in two different senses, one literal and one more metaphorical.

Corporate-law contractarians argue that those who provide the firm with inputs agree to certain terms specified by provisions of statutory corporate law, the firm's articles of incorporation and bylaws, and other rules that govern the claims of the various input providers. These rules are not part of a literal contract, but a contract is still a good model of the voluntary, self-interested arrangement that constitutes a joint business venture among many different parties. "Contract" is used here as a metaphor or analogy that captures the essence of the actual web of voluntary arrangements. The idea is similar to, but not nearly as fanciful as, the classic description of fundamental social relations as a "social contract."

It would be impractical for any input provider to specify this "contract" in complete detail. The costs of trying to make the corporate "contract" complete would be greater than the benefits. Instead of attempting to spell out completely all of the duties managers owe shareholders, the standard contractualist now holds that corporate law subjects managers to a broad fiduciary duty. According to Easterbrook and Fischel, leading proponents of the contractual view of the corporation, the fiduciary relationship is characterized by its open-endedness. Bondholders, Easterbrook and Fischel would agree, are also participants in the corporate "contract." They are among the parties who pool their resources in the firm. Unlike shareholders, however, bondholders do have a literal, detailed contract with the firm. Gaps in the bondholders' contract are smaller and fewer than those in the shareholders' "contract" because the costs of specifying the former contract are lower. This difference in cost is partly due to the difference in the nature of

---

9. *See Mark Roe's article in this volume.—Ed.*

their claims. The fixed claims of creditors must be protected against a relatively known and describable set of threats such as fraudulent transfers and subordination to other creditors. Creditors typically get certain "boilerplate" proscriptions built into their contracts that limit the risk that the firm will fail to fulfill its obligations. Because the relationship between the firm and bondholders is not so open-ended, bondholders do not need or get the benefits of a fiduciary duty owed to them, in the standard view. Maximizing the value of equity, on the other hand, involves entrepreneurs seeing opportunities others do not see and making the most of them. This duty is unavoidably much more vague.

The corporate "contract" with shareholders thus has great need of a gap-filling principle provided by the fiduciary duty, while the contract with fixed claimants on the firm needs it much less. This point, stressed by many corporate scholars, is well taken, but tends to be exaggerated. It does not imply that contracts with creditors do not also need a gap-filling principle. All contracts have gaps. Contractors cannot anticipate all future contingencies. While the nature of bondholder claims is profoundly different from that of equity, both variable and fixed corporate claimants will have need of principles to fill the gaps in their incompletely specified voluntary arrangements....

D. *Fiduciary Duty and Gapless Contracts with Creditors*

... It is natural to suppose that if creditors such as bondholders have essentially an express contractual relationship with the firm, then there is little gap filling for any fiduciary principle to do in the creditors' contracts with the firm, and the fiduciary principle should be thought of mainly as a principle that completes the shareholders' contract with the firm. In a sense, this is correct, but it is also misleading. Even if it is the case that bondholder contracts with the firm are gapless, it is still a mistake to imagine that the hypothetical contract from which we derive corporate fiduciary duty arises from negotiations between or among "the shareholders" and anybody else. It is a logical mistake to infer from the completeness of bond contracts, and the idleness of fiduciary duty as a gap filler in that context, that shareholders, rather than rational investors more generally, are the only parties to the hypothetical corporate contract. Ironically, this logical mistake, which I believe subtly animates much of corporate contractualist analysis of fiduciary duty, is an instance of reification. It is as if contractualists imagine there are shareholders and bondholders in the hall where the corporate contract is being negotiated. Because contracting costs are lower for bond-holders, they finish negotiating their contracts first and leave. The shareholders remain and have to settle on the broad fiduciary duty because to specify their contracts completely would be too costly. Thinking of shareholders in this way, however, reifies them as a separate class. Sixty years of Berle-and-Means-influenced thinking makes it difficult not to do so. Nevertheless, reifying shareholders this way has no warrant in modern finance theory. Shareholders as a separate class, the Berle and Means "owners," represent a nostalgic longing for a political economy that never existed. In any event, modern finance theory has little room for them. Rational investors are not exclusively shareholders, but are widely diversified across asset classes. The diversified investors who hypothetically negotiate the corporate contract will internalize the costs and benefits of different fiduciary rules to the bonds they hold whether or not there are gaps in bond contracts. They will only agree to a fiduciary rule that calls for gaps to be filled in the corporate "contract" with the principle of the maximization of firm value, not shareholder value, even if we imagine bond contracts were gapless....

II. The Hypothetical Bargain Among Rational Corporate Investors

In their influential book on corporate law,[10] Easterbrook and Fischel express the standard view that "the holders of [residual claims]," who "bear the marginal risks of the firm[,] ... have the best incentives to make the optimal investment and management decisions [for the firm] — not perfect, just best." In fact, this standard view is quite wrong, and the confident assumption of this proposition as economic truth is the source of perhaps subtle, but deep and persistent, confusion in corporate law scholarship. In fact, as the examples above show, the incentives of residual claimants are too risk-preferring to be efficient. They would have managers increase the value of residual claims even if it decreased the total value of financial claims against the firm, and they would always have these incentives, not just in unusual cases. So who does have the best incentives to make optimal investment and management decisions for the firm? It turns out this question has a pleasing answer. It is rational investors. Since they are proportionally invested in all the financial claims on the firm, just as CAPM mandates, they have these optimal incentives. Thus the diversified portfolio that CAPM mandates is also the portfolio which, when held by rational investors, gives them precisely the correct incentives to make, or to influence management to make, "the optimal investment and management decisions" for the firm. Rational investors, not shareholders, have the best incentives.

Why do Easterbrook and Fischel miss this point? Were one to ask them, "best of whose incentives to make optimal decisions?" their answer would presumably be, "best among shareholders, preferred shareholders, junior creditors, senior creditors, and so on — best of the various classes in the capital structure of the firm." But these categories are imposed by law, not finance. Easterbrook and Fischel, for all their economic sophistication, remain trapped in the antique world of Berle and Means. To maximize the value of its portfolio, a rational investor must be shareholder, senior bondholder, and everything in between, all at once. To have the right incentives to maximize the value of the firm, the rational investor must have the correct incentives respecting investment and management decisions of the firm. And the rational investor will have those incentives as a natural consequence of diversifying its portfolio to maximize value. Thus diversification theory, management's incentives to maximize the value of investment in the firm, and the normative content of corporate law are all tightly linked, but not in the way economic corporate law scholarship has heretofore explained. It is not "the shareholders," but rational investors, by virtue of diversifying to maximize the value of their portfolios, who have the best (indeed, with the usual strong assumptions, perfect) incentives to maximize the value of the firm.

Once this point is grasped, a socially efficient corporate law norm is not difficult to formulate. It is simply that managers should make the decision, such as the investment choice, that maximizes the value of the firm. This does not necessarily entail maximizing the value of the residual claims, such as common stock, of the firm but rather entails maximizing the total value of all financial claims on the firm. In the example in Part I above, managers would be violating this rule by choosing Investment 2 over Investment 1, even if Investment 2 were better for shareholders....

---

10. FRANK H. EASTERBROOK & DANIEL R. FISCHEL, THE ECONOMIC STRUCTURE OF CORPORATE LAW (1991).

III. The Indifference of Public Corporation Law to Distributional Issues

Conceiving of the corporate law norm as maximizing the value of the corporation has some interesting consequences. The fiduciary gap-filling rule that flows from hypothetical bargain analysis mandates maximization of firm value, but the rule is indifferent among equally efficient distributions among different asset classes of public corporations. When one considers the permissive attitude corporate law takes in the public corporation context toward gap-filling decisions with distributional consequences, this formulation of fiduciary duty seems descriptive of, or at least consistent with, some actual practice. I briefly consider below three areas where this thesis is borne out: leveraged buyouts (LBOs), targeted share repurchases, and recapitalizations affecting preferred stock. The doctrines that produce the judicial results found in these areas differ, but one could regard the principle as the same. Unless express terms of the corporate contract provide otherwise, managers may take steps to maximize firm value regardless of the horizontal or distributional effects on particular assets classes.

A. LBOs, Bondholders, and Fiduciary Duties

In the late 1980s, the RJR/Nabisco transaction and other large LBOs generated considerable controversy. One debated feature of LBOs was the losses they could cause to the market value of bonds outstanding when acquirers bought the target firm. Acquirers often financed LBOs partly through the issuance of new debt by the target firm. Even if existing debt of the target was senior to the new debt, the market value of the old debt could fall, partly because in practice absolute priority is usually not strictly observed in bankruptcy. Thus the new debt, even though junior, could effectively dilute the claims of senior bondholders.

This effect was particularly stark in the RJR/Nabisco deal, where bondholders reportedly lost approximately $40 million in market value from the pretransaction value of their bonds. Bondholders of RJR/Nabisco sued their issuer, claiming that by approving the LBO, the target board had violated a fiduciary or similar duty that they owed bondholders. While bondholders lost this case, they won the support of some academic commentators. David Millon, for example, has argued that bondholders in cases like RJR/Nabisco ought to benefit from fiduciary protection. Managers should be regarded, he argues, as having a duty to treat shareholders and bondholders according to a rule of Pareto-optimality. That is, managers should not be able to make an investment decision, such as to approve an LBO, even if it would make shareholders better off, if it would make bondholders worse off.

To test Millon's claim, it might seem we should ask whether Pareto-optimality is the rule to which hypothetical shareholders and bondholders would agree as a gap-filling principle for the corporate contract. As I noted above, the main response of economic analysts to arguments of Millon and other bondholder advocates has been to insist that bondholders have in effect contracted out of any fiduciary protection in the hypothetical bargain. In this view, bondholders have agreed to shareholder value maximization as the gap-filling rule, or contracts with bondholders are assumed to be effectively gapless. In either event, bondholders do not enjoy fiduciary protection. This response, however, is weak. The argument that bond contracts need no gap filling, which I criticize above, seems especially disingenuous in the LBO context, when one considers the surprise with which bondholders and bond markets greeted the financial innovations spawned by LBOs. One could also argue that the emergence of event risk covenants, devices intended to protect existing bondholders from losses caused by LBOs, is evidence that creditors had not anticipated bond losses by LBOs. If one grants that bond contracts do require a gap-filling principle, then the question of what it should be remains.

If one envisions the appropriate gap-filling principle as emerging from a hypothetical contract negotiation between bondholders and shareholders, then Millon's proposal might seem correct. Bondholders, one might argue, would have little reason to agree to anything less than Pareto-optimality, since such a rule would not allow managers to favor shareholders at their expense. Yet proponents of shareholder wealth maximization might equally well contest this point. They might argue that bondholders would agree to a rule that shareholder value be maximized, subject only to the express constraints in bond contracts. Bondholders would prefer to have no open-ended protection, they could argue, because the cost of this protection to them in terms of lower interest rates would be too high.

The important thing to notice about this disagreement between bondholder advocates and proponents of shareholder value maximization is its intractability. They disagree essentially over what preferences should be ascribed to bondholders. The mere ascription of preferences, however, is a notoriously weak foundation for economic explanation. Consider first the claim of proponents of shareholder value maximization. Their argument against any duty to bondholders rests on the claim that bondholders and shareholders would agree ex ante to terms that put the risk of loss from financial innovation on bondholders, because shareholders would demand a price higher for protection from such loss than bondholders would be willing to pay. This argument amounts to no more than an assertion about what prices, as a result of underlying preferences, would be. We cannot, however, know what relative preferences and therefore prices will be between bondholders and shareholders respecting financial innovation risk by looking at any deals shareholders and bondholders have actually struck. In practice, bondholders cannot contract into fiduciary or similar protection as a gap-filling rule that is superior to what shareholders get, whether or not they wanted to do so. Bondholders could not get a contractual term that says, "for all matters not addressed in this contract, the interests of bondholders are to be treated by corporate directors as equal to (or superior to) those of common shareholders." As interpreted by modern courts and academic commentators, such a provision would violate managers' fiduciary duty to shareholders. If bondholders and shareholders were so free, then their failure to agree on such benefits for bondholders might be evidence that from their perspective the costs of this protection would outweigh the benefits. But as long as the governing rule is that shareholders benefit exclusively from a fiduciary duty and bondholders can get only express contractual protections, a contract term purporting to provide bondholders with something like gap-filling fiduciary protection would be unenforceable. Nothing consequently can be inferred from the present allocation of risks, not even underlying preferences.

Critics of shareholder value maximization, however, are in an equally untenable position. Millon imagines, in effect, a hypothetical bargain between bondholders and shareholders, resulting in a Pareto-optimality rule protecting bondholders; however, this result is based, as much as the argument above is based, on ungrounded assumptions about what bondholders would prefer. It simply assumes bondholders would value this protection by more than shareholders would charge for it. Millon on one side, and Easterbrook and Fischel on the other, are arguing over what is inside a black box.

Yet the exercise is useful because it makes one realize that once one has imaginatively put bondholders and shareholders across the table to negotiate gap-filling rules, there is no determinate outcome, be it Pareto-optimality, or shareholder wealth maximization, or anything else (unless one begs the question by asserting that the parties' preferences will lead to one's preferred result). Framed as a hypothetical contract between shareholders and bondholders, the problem of settling on a gap-filling rule is intractable. This is a clue that the problem is incorrectly formulated. As I have argued in this Article, however, there is a way out. That way is to take the gap-filling rule as the result not of a hypothetical bargain among shareholders and bondholders (and other layers of the corporate capital structure), but as the result of a hypothetical bargain among the rational investors in the firm. They would settle on the maximization of firm value as the filler of gaps in the corporate contract. Cast this way, the problem is anything but intractable.

We can apply this gap-filling principle to cases in which bondholders have invoked a purported fiduciary duty owed to them. In [*MetLife v. RJR Nabisco, excerpted in this chapter*] and other cases, the courts ruled that bondholders could not recover losses they suffered as a result of leveraged transactions that did not violate express contract terms. This result would be consistent with the rule rational investors would select as a gap-filling rule, but only if the transaction in question increased the value of stock by more than it decreased the value of the bonds. There is some evidence that LBOs by and large did have this firm-value-increasing effect. Rationally diversified investors would approve transactions that increased firm value and would be indifferent toward distributional issues, for example the losses to bondholders. This principle would, of course, only be a gap-filling rule. If firms would be worth more with stronger or weaker bondholder protections than those implicit in this gap-filling rule, they should be able to provide for that by contract. Absent such express provisions, however, if an LBO were to decrease total firm value by reducing the value of bonds by more than it increased the value of stock, a court applying the fiduciary duty principle I propose should rule that the transaction breached a fiduciary duty that the managers [*of the target corporation*] owed not to bondholders, but to the target corporation.

[*Assuming the LBO in question does increase the overall value of the target corporation,*] [c]ases such as Metropolitan would thus probably come out the same way under the neotraditional version of the fiduciary duty I propose as they did under the analysis courts actually employed. This convergence may constitute some weak support for my view, in the sense that it is consistent with these judicial results. LBO cases might also be taken as support for the general view that courts applying fiduciary duty analysis to public corporations accord little weight to purely distributional concerns in filling gaps in the public corporate contract. This emphasis on maximizing firm value is consistent with the neotraditional approach....

Conclusion

The efficient norm for corporate law is simply: Maximize the value of the corporation, that is, the sum of the values of all the claims the corporation has issued on its value. This is just a default rule, around which one would expect much contracting, especially as contracting costs diminish over time. But it is the rule to which rationally diversified investors would agree ex ante, and a rule that can survive the disaggregation of traditional equity that seems likely as financial markets continue to evolve. Until that time, to say the primary corporate norm is to "maximize shareholder value" perhaps will do, as long as we are sure not to mean exactly what we say.

To shareholder value maximization, this Article offers an alternative—a duty to the corporation to maximize firm value. Firm value maximization is the efficient default rule. Hypothetical investors, modeled according to the most highly developed relevant theory of rational choice, would choose it. The proposed rule avoids problems that are theoretically clear now and will become increasingly pressing in practice.

More compelling as a theoretical matter is the convergence of rational portfolio theory and a theory of an efficient version of the corporate law norm. For reasons independent of corporate law norms, rational investors will hold a certain portfolio. This portfolio also gives these investors the correct incentives to maximize the value of the firm. The default rule chosen by investors of this sort will be the efficient default rule for filling gaps in the corporate contract. This bridge between the neotraditional corporate law norm and efficient portfolio theory strongly recommends my approach.

Frederick Tung, *The New Death of Contract: Creeping Corporate Fiduciary Duties for Creditors*[*]

… Across seemingly unrelated issue areas, courts and scholars have lost faith in private corporate bargains. They propose expanded duties, inviting judicial intervention into private contract. Interventionists generally fear the traditional shareholder-centered focus of corporate fiduciary duty. Unswerving loyalty to shareholders might cause corporate managers to pursue inefficient investments to benefit shareholders at other claimants' expense. Potential victims include banks and bondholders, all parties owed contractual performance by the firm, startup-company founders and early-stage investors, and investors in derivatives and hybrid securities, among others. Their contracts with the firm are assumed to be deficient in constraining managerial opportunism. New duties are required.

Despite their sundry applications, proposals for expanded fiduciary duty—what I refer to as "Expanded Duty"—share a common approach, a commonality that has so far gone unnoticed. They spot a conflict between classes of corporate claimants—typically common shareholders versus some other class. Noting the possibility of perverse investment incentives for shareholder-focused managers when interclass conflict becomes acute, proponents prescribe inclusion of both classes as joint beneficiaries of managerial fiduciary duties. Under these duties, managers are forbidden from favoring either class unless the benefit to the one exceeds the harm to the other.… Managers' behavior is subjected to ex post standards-based judicial assessment, second-guessing private contract.

This betokened death of contract in corporate law runs counter to the contractarian theory of the corporation that has come to dominate corporate law thinking over the past two decades. In this conception, the shareholder contract is but one among many, and duties to shareholders are conceived in contractarian terms. The duties merely fill the gaps in the incompletely specified relationship between shareholders and firm managers. Given the myriad complex decisions that firm managers must make to run the company, an explicit contract between shareholders and firm management to govern their relationship would be hopelessly incomplete. Instead, corporate fiduciary duty supplies a general gap-filling standard: firm managers should run the firm for shareholders' benefit. This traditional shareholder primacy norm has long been dominant among courts and commentators. But Expanded Duty revisits the fundamental question: for whom should corporate managers manage?

…. In this Article, I focus on Expanded Duty specifically in the context of shareholder-creditor conflict, perhaps the most important corporate conflict for assessing Expanded Duty. This debt-equity conflict has absorbed the attention of corporate and finance

---

[*] Originally published in 57 EMORY LAW JOURNAL 809 (2008). Reprinted with permission.

scholars for at least three decades, and expanded fiduciary duty for creditors is the original Expanded Duty. Longstanding doctrine already operates to curb shareholder primacy when conflict is thought to be at its most severe—when the firm is insolvent. At that point, fiduciary duties shift from shareholders to creditors. Courts and scholars have offered extensions of this insolvency-triggered duty-shifting doctrine....

As a putative hypothetical bargain, Creditor Duty suffers from both substantive and process objections. The general substantive objection is that the content of any putative Creditor Duty bargain is implausible. Efficiency-demanding duties are neat in theory and facially unobjectionable, but parties negotiate over distribution, not joint efficiency. The absence of explicit efficiency requirements in any of the actual contracts that Creditor Duty implicates is telling. Moreover, creditors have varying contract rights and risk preferences. Those that enjoy extensive contract protections are unlikely to favor duties for weaker creditors that might affect relative distributions. Creditor Duty ignores intercreditor conflict. It paints all creditors as one undifferentiated unitary mass of unsecured creditors. Only with this blind eye can an imagined Creditor Duty bargain be conjured. But once intercreditor conflict is acknowledged, a hypothetical Creditor Duty bargain becomes farfetched....

With [many] contracts, plausible tradeoffs may exist between bargain and duty. Given the vast array of contexts in which contract law must operate, standards-based ex post judicial intervention may elucidate parties' intent in a way that bargain formalism cannot. Corporate credit contracts, however, are different. Parties' relative sophistication and delegated monitoring among creditors suggest the incongruity of a general license for courts to rewrite corporate credit contracts ex post. While the threat of shareholder-primacy-induced managerial opportunism exists, private contracting provides a tailored response to the problem.

Run-of-the-mill credit contracts limit managers' discretion to favor shareholders. In addition, a creditor may effectively contract for its own primacy, displacing common shareholders as managers' favored constituency. This contractual revision to shareholder primacy goes against the conventional wisdom that the duty of loyalty is mandatory and non-contractible. Yet, as I show, courts have approved such private arrangements for creditors. In so doing, however, courts have been tethered to existing duty-shifting doctrine requiring the firm's insolvency in order to sanction creditor primacy by contract. Moreover, even if no such contract exists, duty shifting occurs upon insolvency by law. The doctrine therefore turns out to be overinclusive and underinclusive. It offers rights to creditors who have not contracted for them, and it may impede a creditor from exercising rights for which it has contracted. I argue against the doctrine and in favor of contract.

Under this approach—what I call contract primacy—shareholder primacy should remain the default rule. Private contracting alone should be effective to shift managers' loyalties in favor of creditors. Additional legal constraints are both unnecessary and costly. Contracting for creditor primacy has gone unrecognized as such in the literature. Identifying this development reinforces the disutility of mandated duties. Creditors can attain primacy without courts....

I. Expanding Fiduciary Duties

A. Fiduciary Duties for Incomplete Shareholder Contracting

Shareholder primacy demands that managers run the firm with a view to maximizing shareholder wealth. In general, this rule is efficient. The economic justification is straightforward. Common shareholders are ordinarily the firm's residual claimants—they own the claim on the corporation's residual value after all other obligations have been paid. As residual claimants, shareholders suffer the firm's marginal losses and enjoy its marginal gains, so every decision by the firm's management directly affects shareholder wealth. Shareholders therefore value the benefit of managerial fiduciary duties more highly than other corporate constituents. Maximizing shareholder value also generally maximizes firm value, which is socially beneficial. So managers should manage the firm with a view to maximizing shareholder value. This shareholder primacy norm harnesses the zest for private wealth maximization to serve the broader goal of social wealth maximization.

According to the standard contractualist view of the corporation, corporate fiduciary duties merely fill the gaps in the incompletely specified relationship between shareholders and firm managers. Given the range of complex decisions that firm managers must make—and the broad discretion they must exercise—in order to run the business, an explicit contract between shareholders and firm management to govern their relationship would be hopelessly incomplete. Instead, corporate fiduciary duty supplies a general gap-filling standard: firm managers should run the firm for shareholders' benefit.

B. The Conventional Case for Including Creditors

When a firm is insolvent, creditors, rather than shareholders, by definition become the firm's primary residual risk-bearers. Shareholders have essentially lost their bet on the company, and now creditors suffer the firm's marginal losses. Post-insolvency investments by the firm are in effect gambles with the creditors' money. Managers' fiduciary duties should shift to creditors. Instead of maximizing shareholder wealth, managers should instead look after the interests of creditors when the firm is insolvent. This insolvency-based duty-shifting approach is fairly settled law in Delaware and other jurisdictions.

With the firm's insolvency, managers would face perverse incentives under a shareholder primacy rule. Limited liability for shareholders means that shareholders enjoy the potentially unlimited upside from a spectacularly risky investment, but downside risk is borne by creditors. Firm managers faithfully pursuing shareholder wealth maximization, therefore, may be tempted to make very risky investments, since spectacular returns—however unlikely—would inure to the benefit of shareholders, while losses would be borne by creditors. Even investments with negative expected value for the firm would be pursued, as long as there was positive expected value to shareholders. This is the problem of overinvestment. The social objection is not that creditors would lose value, but that these projects destroy firm value. Creditors stand to lose more than shareholders stand to gain.

Courts have recognized that these perverse incentives for managers may operate not only at insolvency, but even as the firm nears insolvency. The closer the firm is to insolvency, the greater the incentive for managers—now likely to be gambling at least in part with creditors' money—to choose risky and possibly even negative expected value investments to maximize shareholder returns. It may be, therefore, that shareholders' primacy should begin to fade even before the firm reaches the point of insolvency....

C. The Case for Further Expansion of Fiduciary Duties to Creditors

Scholars have advocated expanding on the insolvency-based duty shifting embodied in existing case law. They point out that shareholder-creditor conflicts are in fact broader than existing doctrine recognizes. Fiduciary duty should be correspondingly expanded.

Tom Smith has argued that the "zone of insolvency" notion may not be a coherent construct. For Smith, managers governed by shareholder primacy have perverse incentives to make inefficient investments all the time, regardless of the firm's nearness to insolvency. Big risky bets are increasingly available to firm managers. Bet-the-company projects are not hard to find. What this means is that managers do not have far to search for projects that will maximize shareholder value if successful but will leave the company insolvent if unsuccessful. In other words, the firm's "nearness" to insolvency—the value of its equity, in conventional balance sheet terms—does not affect managers' latitude to make negative expected value bets that are good for shareholders. The only difference between a firm "near" insolvency in the conventional sense and one that is not is the size of the bet that would push the firm into insolvency. From this perspective, every firm is always in the zone of insolvency, and shareholder primacy always leaves managers free to overinvest to the benefit of shareholders.

Rather than setting and shifting fiduciary duties based on the firm's solvency, Smith argues that managers should always strive to maximize the value of all financial claims on the firm....

II. Hypothetical Bargains for Creditors

... A crucial difference between shareholders and creditors is that creditor interests are not unitary and may often conflict. By the time the firm is in distress, creditors are competitors, not allies. They understand that when the firm goes into distress, they will be fighting one another over an undersized and shrinking pie. While shareholders ordinarily share pro rata, one creditor's gain is typically another's loss when the firm is at or near insolvency. By contrast, Creditor Duty relies on a highly stylized model of the debt-equity conflict, treating all debt as undifferentiated and unitary unsecured debt. Conflict among creditors is ignored. Creditor Duty reduces a complex multiparty conflict into a seeming bilateral bargain. Hypothetical consensus appears easily proclaimed.

This multiparty consensus among conflicting creditors—our second assumption above —seems dubious, however. Creditor Duty imagines that each creditor would agree to empower every other creditor to challenge the firm's course of action as a breach of duty. But creditors have varying risk preferences and varying contract protections. Those with superior contract protection will prefer their actual contract rights to any generalized judicially-imposed hypothetical creditor-shareholder bargain that serves only to empower creditors with inferior contract rights. Not all creditors would agree to this....

A. Creditor Heterogeneity

...

1. Security Interests and Residual Claimant Status

Whether a creditor enjoys a security interest has a crucial effect on its risk preferences. At the limit, an oversecured creditor may be indifferent as to the firm's performance. Assuming the value of its collateral is stable, that creditor will be paid in full whether the firm recovers from its reverses or not. If the collateral value is unstable, that creditor may prefer early liquidation of the firm's assets, to the detriment of not only equity holders but also unsecured creditors. Depending on the context, the secured creditor may be more or less willing than unsecured creditors to endorse managers' preference for risky investments when the firm is marginally solvent.

More generally, unsecured creditors' fates are much more closely tied to the fortunes of the firm than is the case with secured creditors. The former therefore have a much stronger claim to residual status. To the extent that one accepts the traditional notion that fiduciary duties should run to the firm's residual claimants—and should "shift" when the identity of the firm's residual claimants changes—unsecured creditors seem far more deserving than secured creditors.

To date, even this simple distinction has eluded courts and commentators. None have suggested that Creditor Duty should distinguish secured from unsecured creditors. Outside of the Creditor Duty context, however, the conflicts between secured and unsecured creditors of an insolvent firm are well understood. Secured and unsecured creditors will likely have irreconcilable differences over investment policy, similar to the classic conflict between unsecured creditors and equity holders. Moreover, secured creditors' rights to collateral generally give them better leverage over firm management than unsecured creditors enjoy.

2. Nonfinancial Interests

Even among unsecured creditors, variation exists. Financial creditors are different from trade creditors. A trade creditor—a supplier of goods or services to the firm—makes its money primarily from the sale of its goods or services. Extensions of credit merely facilitate the trade creditor's primary business of selling its product. Its profits typically come predominantly from sales, not financing. By contrast, the financial creditor's profit comes almost exclusively from interest and fees charged to its borrowers.

Because their businesses differ, financial creditors and trade creditors will often differ in their preferences over the borrower firm's fate. Liquidation may maximize a financial creditor's recovery, but it eliminates a customer for the trade creditor, who often has a greater stake in the firm's survival than does the financial creditor. Similarly, employee pension funds—often major creditors of distressed public companies—will care about a firm's survival as an employer, so that the decision whether to push for liquidation will involve more than the short-term financial calculation another creditor might make.

3. Contract Protections and Renegotiation Prospects

Related to the distinction between financial creditors and trade creditors, certain creditors typically enjoy better-defined contract protections than others. Contracts will vary in their initial covenants and default triggers, which are largely targeted at constraining borrower risk-taking. Financial creditors generally enjoy more elaborate contract protections than trade creditors—not surprising given the relative importance of financing revenues to the financial creditor's business. Trade credit is often arranged quite informally, with any agreement running only a few pages in length. Bank and bond debt, by contrast, is elaborately contracted, with documents running into the hundreds and perhaps thousands of pages.

These contracting differences are understandable given the differing magnitudes of exposure and differing noncontractual enforcement devices available. Trade credit, for example, is typically granted in small increments, with future shipments dependent on repayment of outstanding credit. The trade creditor's exposure is therefore limited, and its implicit threat to withhold future shipments may often serve as a powerful nonlegal inducement to the borrower's repayment. Moreover, because the trade creditor's primary objective is to sell its wares to the borrower, it may be more focused on maintaining the quality and competitiveness of its products than on the detailed terms of its financing arrangements. On the other hand, banks are in the business of lending money, and the money they lend may be advanced in large tranches. The bank's exposure might be quite large relative to the borrower firm's cash flows and assets. Understandably, then, bank debt contracts are typically quite elaborate in terms of covenants and defaults.

Similarly, creditors' varying institutional constraints will affect their capacity to renegotiate their credit contracts, which also affects initial contract terms. These differences exist even among financial creditors. For example, banks generally enjoy tighter covenants than public bondholders. Moreover, the initial bank credit agreement is structured specifically with renegotiation in mind. This difference in initial terms is due largely to the fact that banks can more readily monitor their borrowers and renegotiate if necessary. While large loans are typically syndicated—a group of banks shares the loan exposure in specified percentages—collective action problems are avoided through intercreditor agreements among syndicate banks. A lead bank is typically empowered to make many enforcement decisions on behalf of the syndicate. Banks therefore have some capacity to anticipate problems with their borrower and work with the borrower to resolve problems. Bondholders, by contrast, enjoy no similar arrangements, and collective action is more costly. Bondholders are likely to be relatively widely dispersed, and unlike syndicated bank loans, the agent for bondholders—the indenture trustee—has relatively weak powers to act on behalf of the bondholders. Modification of bond terms typically requires a consent solicitation. Modification of principal or interest provisions requires the approval of each affected bondholder. Changing other terms typically requires approval by a majority or two-thirds of the face amount of the bonds. Because of the hurdles to collective action, bond covenants must be looser than bank debt covenants. Bond indentures contain no simple device to work out problems with the borrower.

While renegotiation possibilities affect initial contract terms, actual renegotiation of course enables the parties to adjust their contracts for new circumstances. Because renegotiation may be more readily available for some credit contracts than others, credit contracts will vary in the protections and remedies the creditor enjoys by the time the firm is in distress. Bank debt, for example, will typically be renegotiated when a firm is in distress. Once the debtor defaults, the bank enjoys enormous leverage to negotiate additional protections it desires. A properly drafted credit agreement ordinarily offers default triggers and remedies that would allow the creditor to destroy the business. In exchange for forbearance, the lender generally gets what it wants in workout. Serial renegotiation of a loan is not unusual. Bank and borrower may make fine adjustments to reflect the changing circumstances of the borrower's business. The bank's protections may therefore be very finely tuned by the time the borrower is in distress....

III. Contract Primacy

    ....

A. *Contracting for Primacy*

Conventional wisdom holds that managers' fiduciary duty of loyalty to shareholders is mandatory and nonwaivable. While there is some truth to this conventional view—managers cannot simply contract away their duty of loyalty wholesale—they can, do, and must in piecemeal fashion. Managers make all sorts of commitments for their firms that circumscribe their later discretion to favor shareholders. Only what is left of managerial discretion remains to be exercised for shareholders' benefit. In that sense, and contrary to the conventional wisdom, managerial fiduciary duties are contractible. Every contract commitment "contracts away" fiduciary duties insofar as it constrains managers' subsequent discretion to pursue shareholder value.

Creditors often contract with managers for arrangements that impinge on shareholder primacy. For example, bank loan agreements often restrict firm investment policy with restrictions on capital expenditures. Such a restriction may later operate to preclude a project that shareholders would otherwise have preferred. When managers originally decided to accede to this restriction, of course, they presumably considered the various tradeoffs involved—tighter covenants versus higher interest rate, for example—and concluded that the terms were in shareholders' best interest. The arrangement may turn out to have been less than optimal ex post, but every contract carries that risk. Through these contract terms, creditors enjoy direct influence over fundamental management decisions—influence that corporate law denies to shareholders. Managers explicitly subordinate their duty of loyalty to shareholders to the rights of contracting parties. Managers' latitude to pursue shareholder interests in the future is constrained.

Sometimes, these contract constraints include more than simple limits on managers' discretion. For example, non-shareholder constituents may contract for representation inside the firm's management structure, even to the point of taking control of the firm. Banks often contract for the right to appoint a representative to sit on a borrower's board of directors. The purpose for the bank designee is presumably not to protect shareholders' interests, but the bank's. Less modestly, creditors have negotiated for appointment of their own designees to manage borrower firms. Creditor-appointed managers have made decisions favoring creditors over shareholders, and courts have approved these decisions. In the famous Credit Lyonnais case, which I discuss in the next section, bank and borrower negotiated a comprehensive Corporate Governance Arrangement that, among other things, appointed the bank's designee as CEO. Douglas Baird and Bob Rasmussen also describe in detail the rise of the chief restructuring officer (CRO), the bank's designee to run the distressed borrower firm if existing management fails to turn the company around. The CRO appointment is now common practice, as the culmination of the process of banks' gradual easing of the reins from the management of defaulted borrowers.

Even contracts giving creditors control of the firm may be in the best interests of the common shareholders. If the alternative is immediate liquidation, the common are likely better off allowing creditors to control the firm in an attempt to salvage value. In principle, these contracts are not qualitatively different from firms' run-of-the-mill contracts commitments, which also circumscribe managers' latitude to pursue shareholder value.

Courts have validated these arrangements in a qualified way. They have upheld management decisions favoring creditors at shareholders' expense, but have insisted on the firm's insolvency, according to existing duty-shifting doctrine. To these cases we turn.

B. Actual Contracts

This section presents two examples of contracts for creditor primacy. Courts have approved these arrangements favoring creditors over equity holders, laboring somewhat to adhere to the existing duty-shifting framework. The decisions suggest, however, that parties' expectations—derived from the content of their specific arrangements—drive decisions. I discuss only two cases—one of which involves not a corporate borrower, but a Delaware limited liability company. My goal is not to show the universality of contract solutions when shareholder primacy is or may become inefficient, but more modestly to demonstrate that contracting for creditor primacy does occur, despite the conventional view of shareholder primacy's mandatory nature.

1. The Corporate Governance Arrangement in Credit Lyonnais

From an incomplete contracts perspective, it is ironic that Credit Lyonnais should be the touchstone case for any Creditor Duty discussion. Credit Lyonnais was not a case crying out for judicial gap filling. Quite the opposite. By the time the case descended into litigation, the parties had completed their own contract with a tailor-made governance arrangement placing the dominant bank creditor in control.

The case involved a workout between sophisticated parties—an international bank and a publicly traded borrower. The parties devised a comprehensive management arrangement to govern for the duration of their workout. Credit Lyonnais (the "Bank") was a major lender to both MGM-Pathe Communications (MGM) and its publicly traded parent Pathe Communications Corporation (PCC). The Bank's loans were secured by a controlling block of MGM stock. When MGM was forced into bankruptcy by its trade creditors, the Bank agreed to finance MGM's exit from bankruptcy, but with conditions. The Bank agreed to forbear from foreclosing on its stock pledge and taking explicit control of MGM, and the parties negotiated a Corporate Governance Agreement (CGA). It set out a comprehensive scheme for management of MGM, including appointment of Alan Ladd—the Bank's choice—for chairman and CEO. The CGA also called for the formation of an executive committee, comprised of Ladd and his choice of COO—"to which all corporate powers and duties permitted by law ... to be delegated ... shall be delegated exclusively."

To insure compliance with the CGA, the Bank obtained the right to vote its controlling block of MGM stock pursuant to a voting trust. The Voting Trust Agreement was placed in escrow, and the Bank was given sole discretion to break the escrow to render the voting trust effective. PCC's controlling shareholder Giancarlo Parretti acceded to these arrangements.

Ultimately, Parretti breached the CGA by attempting to wrest control from the CGA-created management structure. The Bank terminated the escrow on the voting trust and exercised its voting power to remove Parretti and his confederates from the board of directors. The Bank followed with a suit for a judicial determination that its elected board was the rightful board of MGM.

In this suit, Parretti claimed that CEO Ladd and his executive committee breached their fiduciary duty to MGM's shareholder-parent PCC by failing to facilitate asset sales that Parretti sought in order to raise capital to pay off the Bank and regain control of MGM. The court rightly gave short shrift to this argument, finding that Ladd's management team had acted properly. The opinion is not surprisingly couched in Creditor Duty language. Chancellor Allen explicitly extended existing insolvency-based duty shifting into the "vicinity" of insolvency. In that area, he asserted, the board was not merely an agent for shareholders, "but owes its duty to the corporate enterprise" and to the corporate "community of interests" that includes creditors. Management acted appropriately under this standard. It could reasonably suspect that under the circumstances, Parretti might accept fire-sale prices for the firm's asset.

The vicinity-of-insolvency analysis seems largely superfluous—if not pernicious—given the actual terms of the contractual arrangement between the Bank and MGM. The Bank retained veto rights over significant asset sales in any event—a standard term in credit agreements, and one that gets tightened as a matter of routine in workout. Even absent a Bank veto, Parretti could hardly have expected that Ladd or the management structure created at the Bank's behest would do his bidding or fail to consider the Bank's wishes and interests, especially given the Bank's grip on the controlling shares of MGM. Parretti had relinquished control over MGM. He had also relinquished any expectation that MGM would be run for his benefit or the benefit of other pre-default shareholders. Moreover, Chancellor Allen's "vicinity of insolvency" innovation—while conceptually but perhaps not practically defensible—had no basis in precedent, and none was cited. The Delaware Supreme Court recently rejected Credit Lyonnais' vicinity-of-insolvency Creditor Duty.

Here, the actual terms of the parties' agreement supply sufficient basis for concluding that Ladd's primary duty was to the Bank. None of the parties could have expected otherwise, whether the firm was near insolvency or not. An extracontractual insolvency requirement merely increases the creditor's cost of enforcing its contract. The actual bargain obviated any need for Creditor Duty. With the CGA, no gaps remained to fill.

2. Blackmore Partners

Blackmore Partners, L.P. v. Link Energy LLC involved not a corporation but a Delaware limited liability company. Despite this, the court applied corporate precedents without comment, suggesting that Delaware may take a common approach to these limited liability entities, at least with respect to fiduciary duties. The transaction at issue, along with the Delaware Chancery Court's two-stage resolution of the litigation, nicely illustrates the two main features of contract primacy: the default rule that managers owe primary loyalty to their equity holders and the prospect that equity holders may contract away their default protection to creditors. On its face, the challenged transaction raises an eyebrow. The managers of Link Energy sold the firm's assets in a transaction that paid certain creditors—a group of note holders—$25 million more than the amount of their claims against the firm, but left equity holders with nothing. The day the details of the deal were announced, the market price of Link equity units dropped from over $5 to $1. Plaintiff Blackmore Partners, a holder of equity units whose interest was wiped out in the sale, brought a putative class action against the firm and its board of directors, alleging the board had breached its primary duty to equity holders.

Defendants lost their motion to dismiss in the first reported decision. Though the complaint failed to allege a conflict of interest or lack of independence of the board, the court held that it was sufficient to allege that the directors approved a transaction that disadvantaged the equity holders. "No transaction could have been worse for the unit holders." The court found it "reasonable to infer ... that a properly motivated board of directors would not have agreed to a proposal that wiped out the value of the common equity and surrendered all of that value to the company's creditors." Under the circumstances, simply alleging that the directors "approved a sale of substantially all of Link's assets and a resultant distribution of proceeds that went exclusively to the company's creditors raises a reasonable inference of disloyalty or intentional misconduct."

Ultimately, however, in a second decision, the Chancery Court granted summary judgment to the defendants. The transaction looks bad on its face, no doubt, overpaying creditors with sale proceeds that should have gone to equity holders. However, a closer examination suggests that the board satisfied whatever duties it owed to equity. The parties had specifically negotiated the relatively unusual governance mechanisms that were in effect at the time the deal, such that board approval of a transaction of the type at issue was plausibly contemplated by the parties.

Link Energy had emerged as the reorganized debtor from the bankruptcy reorganization of EOTT Energy Partners, L.P. The note holders, prebankruptcy creditors of EOTT, had received their notes as part of the reorganization. With their acceptance of the notes, the note holders took a huge reduction in principal as well as a lower interest rate compared to the terms of their prebankruptcy debt claims against EOTT. They also received 95% of Link's equity units newly issued under the reorganization plan. To protect themselves going forward, the note holders obtained two important conditions regarding future asset sales. First, the terms of their notes required any purchaser of substantially all of Link's assets to assume the notes. Second, Link's operating agreement authorized its board to approve such a sale without requiring a vote of the equity. In addition, six of Link's seven directors were appointed by the note holders pursuant to the reorganization plan. In short, the note holders obtained control of the board, the right to demand assumption of their notes by any asset purchaser, and freedom to sell all of the assets without approval of the equity holders.

The court recognized the import of these arrangements. It held that no enhanced scrutiny of the board's decision was required, since no extraordinary corporate power was being used against the equity class. Under the circumstances, approval of the transaction was routine: "Crucially, the Unit holders, by charter, did not even retain the right to vote on the sale of substantially all of Link's assets. Thus, no extraordinary efforts were needed to secure approval, or to stop a vote, for no such approval or vote was necessary." The court found the board sufficiently disinterested that the business judgment rule applied to insulate the board decision from further scrutiny.

The court also tracked the conventional duty-shifting analysis, thinking it crucial to emphasize the firm's insolvency, which triggered directors' fiduciary duties to creditors. Despite this homage to the doctrine, it is hard to see what an insolvency requirement adds, except potential litigation costs. Blackmore can be understood as simply a vindication of the parties' agreed corporate governance arrangement, which was far from conventional. Directors were not appointed by the conventional means of equity voting. Equity holders were not afforded their customary right to vote on the sale of the company. Instead, creditor appointees dominated the board, while equity holders were shut out of the sale process. Creditor-appointed directors could be expected to favor their patron's interests. Otherwise, there would be no point to this nonstandard arrangement. Equity holders presumably accounted for these various features in their negotiations over the reorganization plan. The court's refusal to revisit the board's decision respects the parties' deal.

C. Bargain Should Trump Duty: Abolishing Duty-Shifting Doctrine

The preceding cases illustrate parties' ability to tailor firms' governance arrangements by contract. The duty-shifting doctrine, however, imposes an additional condition to the parties' bargain. The firm's insolvency is seemingly required before managers may honor their arrangement to favor a creditor over shareholders. But why should this be so? Presumably, the firm's distress is what leads to these governance concessions to the creditor. In any event, the creditor and the firm's management each understand their own interests. The duty-shifting doctrine adds nothing on that score. An insolvency requirement merely increases litigation costs.

To be fair, an insolvency-based doctrine might perform [a] useful function.... [It] may preclude managers from selling out to creditors too soon, to the disadvantage of shareholders. That is, an insolvency requirement may reduce agency costs of equity. But the business judgment rule offers the right framework for handling this agency cost. Assuming no management conflict of interest, it is hard to see why managers would give in to creditor demands unless survival of the business required it, and why this decision would not merit deference as a business judgment. The exigencies of the situation might be useful evidence on managers' motivations. But insolvency makes little sense as a mandatory condition to contract enforcement.

More generally, this issue seems not to be qualitatively different from the generic agency cost question with every transaction: did managers give away too much? That the deal may involve governance features or some measure of managerial control does not change the fundamental question. As noted earlier, every contract commitment of the firm gives away some managerial discretion to pursue future shareholder value. The framework for evaluating managers' decisions and constraining agency costs of equity should not be different for governance contracts.

Duty-shifting doctrine turns out to be both overinclusive and underinclusive. It offers rights to creditors who have not contracted for them, and it impedes creditors exercising rights for which they have contracted. In both cases, the doctrine is costly. Depending on actual contracts promotes more certainty of application than courts' attempting after the fact to discern the firm's solvency or whether managers failed to act in creditors' best interests. Actual contracts offer arrangements tailored to specific firm conditions. Duty-shifting doctrine should be eliminated....

Actual contracts are superior to imagined contracts. Shareholder interests sometimes conflict with those of other corporate constituencies, and managers bent on maximizing shareholder value may sometimes pursue inefficient projects that benefit shareholders but harm other claimants and the firm generally. Expanding managerial fiduciary duties to protect those other claimants, however, is ill-advised. For sophisticated parties, especially those institutionally equipped to monitor the firm, private contract is sufficient to constrain manager opportunism. Expanding fiduciary duty beyond its traditional shareholder-centered focus has no contractual basis and is costly.

... While private contracts may not perfectly constrain managerial opportunism, the cure is likely to be worse than the disease. The costs of that opportunism are likely dwarfed by the costs of bestowing a shared fiduciary duty among conflicting parties. Private bargains should be respected. Parties should be permitted to constrain or modify shareholder primacy by contract. They have sufficient incentive on their own to design careful limits on managerial opportunism....

John Armour, Brian R. Cheffins & David A. Skeel, Jr., *Corporate Ownership Structure and the Evolution of Bankruptcy Law: Lessons from the United Kingdom**

I. Introduction

The corporate world today subdivides into rival systems of dispersed and concentrated ownership, each characterized by different corporate governance structures. The United States falls into the former category, whereas major industrial rivals such as Japan and

---

* Originally published in 55 VANDERBILT LAW REVIEW 1699 (2002). Reprinted with permission.

Germany are members of the latter. The past decade has seen intense academic debate over possible explanations for the different systems of ownership and control in key developed economies. Anecdotal evidence suggesting that market forces may be serving to destabilize traditional business structures and foster some form of convergence in a U.S. direction has given the controversy powerful current relevance.

... Corporate bankruptcy, it has been said, is the "crucial missing piece in understanding corporate governance." According to this thesis—an "evolutionary" account of corporate governance—a country's system of bankruptcy law is either "manager-driven" or "manager-displacing," with the former offering the executives of a financially troubled firm substantial scope to launch a rescue effort and the latter having a strong bias in favor of liquidation. The thinking, in very basic terms, is that a manager-driven bankruptcy regime complements dispersed share ownership, while its manager-displacing counterpart aligns with a governance regime where concentrated ownership prevails....

II. The Complementarity of Bankruptcy Regulation, Corporate Law, and Corporate Governance: An Evolutionary Hypothesis

A. *Debt as the Missing Piece of the Corporate Governance Puzzle*

One feature that links the various theories [about why corporate governance regimes differ across countries] is an equity bias. Each seeks to address the same primary question: Why do share ownership patterns differ?[11] To be sure, bank-oriented finance has attracted attention, but this popularity is the result of its treatment as the logical corollary of underdeveloped equity markets. The analytical bias in favor of shares means that in the comparative corporate governance literature, a potentially important piece of the puzzle is missing: a systematic appraisal of corporate borrowing. This bias is not restricted to the cross-border analysis of financial systems. Instead, on a more general level, the typical model of corporate governance views issues through the lens of equity interests.

The analytical bias in favor of share ownership patterns seems odd when aggregate patterns of corporate finance are taken into account. The available data indicates that in major industrialized nations debt is a more important source of corporate funding than is the issuance of shares ... [T]his is even the case in the U.S. and the U.K., even though both have a "shareholder economy."

Regardless of the precise balance between equity and debt as a source of finance, corporate governance is best seen as an "interactive" process involving shareholders and creditors. Often, the interests of these two constituencies will be congruent. For instance, a lender's monitoring of a corporate borrower can benefit shareholders since the disciplinary aspect will help constrain managerial misconduct. Moreover, a lender's strong reaction to changing circumstances can provide signals for those owning equity to intervene and vice versa.

The relationship between debt and equity can, however, also have its frictions. These frictions, which we will refer to as the "agency costs of debt" or "financial agency costs," can take several forms. The first arises because managers may take actions that are calculated to benefit shareholders at the expense of creditors. An example is where a corporation takes on a substantial debt load, thereby increasing the risk of default, in order to finance high-risk ventures with a potentially lucrative "upside."

---

11. *This is the focus of Mark Roe's article in this volume.*—*Ed.*

Conflicts of interest between shareholders and creditors can also run in the opposite direction. Take the case of a corporation that obtains financing primarily from one lender. Management may, in response to an implicit threat of exit by the lender, implement decisions benefiting that party at the expense of shareholders. Biasing the borrower's investment decisions in favor of projects with low risk would be one example of this type of "creditor rent extraction." Others would include arranging fresh borrowing on terms highly favorable to the lender and charging excessive fees for the supply of additional services (e.g., management consulting or underwriting).

There is an additional reason why debt finance deserves consideration from a corporate governance perspective. When a company defaults on its debts, its creditors become entitled—more or less—to take over the rights previously enjoyed by its shareholders. The transition essentially occurs when bankruptcy proceedings are commenced. At this point, it is the creditors, rather than the shareholders, who become the firm's residual claimants.

It should now be evident that a fully developed account of the configuration of the corporate economy in major industrialized nations needs to account for the role of debt in corporate governance....

B. *The Evolutionary Theory of Corporate Governance and Corporate Bankruptcy: A Précis*

For the purposes of [David Skeel's] evolutionary theory, national bankruptcy regimes can be divided into two categories. These are "manager-driven," where those in charge of a financially troubled firm have substantial scope to launch a rescue effort, and "manager-displacing," where there is a strong bias in favor of liquidation. The intuition underlying the evolutionary theory is that corporate executives are aware of the bankruptcy law they face and adjust their behavior accordingly. At the same time, though, the way managers conduct themselves may help to dictate how a country's bankruptcy system is configured. By virtue of this sort of feedback loop, the result should be a complementary relationship between a country's system of ownership and control on one hand and its regulation of corporate financial distress on the other.

To appreciate the connections, let us start with arrangements in the United States. As we have seen, the U.S. has an outsider/arm's-length system of ownership and control, which means that investors engage in, at most, only intermittent oversight of the managers of a publicly quoted company. Corporate executives do not, however, have unfettered discretion. Instead, various constraints make managers fearful of poor share price performance and give them incentives to boost earnings.

One consideration is the managerial labor market. Executives, mindful that other jobs might be more challenging and lucrative, will want to perform well in their current positions in order to increase their marketability with possible future employers. At the same time, they will know that the board of directors might orchestrate a managerial shake-up in the event that earnings are stagnant or declining....

Also pertinent will be executive compensation. During the past two decades, managerial remuneration has become much more strongly "incentivized" in the U.S. Between 1980 and the late 1990s, the percentage of chief executives of publicly quoted corporations who were awarded stock options increased from 30% to more than 70%. Indeed, by 1997, a typical CEO received more pay in the form of option grants than salary (42% of total remuneration as compared with 29%).

A distinctive feature of stock options is that they operate somewhat like a "one-way" bet for management. To elaborate, while shareholders and an executive entitled to exercise options both benefit when a company's share price rises, if there is a decline the shareholders suffer genuine losses whereas the executive simply must forgo a potential profit opportunity. Correspondingly, a management team that has a large number of options will tend to discount adverse outcomes when evaluating business opportunities to exploit. Hence, as the [Enron-era] wave of U.S. corporate scandals seems to illustrate, when stock options are a pivotal part of CEO compensation, those running public companies have a financial incentive to proceed with projects that shareholders might like but creditors will fear: those that might yield spectacular returns but which encompass "downstream" risks that could cause default in the event of a mishap.

The market for corporate control is an additional factor that can influence managerial decisionmaking and thereby motivate executives to pursue strategies that could leave their corporation vulnerable if things go wrong. The theory involved is well known. If there is a substantial disparity between a corporation's actual and potential performance, a bidder may calculate that it is worthwhile to make a tender offer to the shareholders with a view to installing new managers. The bidder will presume that with new direction the target company will generate enough additional profit to compensate for the costs and risks associated with making the offer.

Executives fear takeover bids since they usually lose their jobs after a successful offer. This anxiety, however, has a beneficial by-product: managers, with their jobs potentially on the line, have an incentive to deploy corporate assets to best advantage. On the other hand, apprehension about a possible bid can cause managers to respond in a way that wreaks havoc on the capital structures of their companies. For instance, target managers may engage in a leveraged recapitalization[12] to consolidate control of the firm, thus adding a large layer of new debt to the firm's balance sheet. More generally, executives might seek to make their corporation less attractive as a takeover target by borrowing large sums since potential bidders will not be able to finance an acquisition of the corporation as easily if it is heavily leveraged.[13]

As Marcel Kahan and Ed Rock have argued, in the U.S. the relative potency of the disciplinary mechanisms just described has been reconfigured [between the 1980s and the early 2000s].[14] Partly due to the prevalence of poison pills, there has been a transition from tender offers opposed by those running the target company ("hostile" bids) to proposals supported by management ("friendly" bids). Though defining whether a takeover bid is hostile or friendly can be difficult, this switch implies a shift from acquisition activity that is explicitly disciplinary in orientation to deals motivated by the desire to increase market share or generate synergies. This does not mean, however, that the disciplinary pressures faced by U.S. executives have abated. Instead, the markets for managerial talent and

---

12. *In a "leveraged recapitalization," a corporation borrows large amounts of money in order to pay its shareholders a large dividend or to repurchase their shares. The additional debt is likely to make the corporation less attractive to a would-be hostile acquirer. If the leveraged recapitalization involves the repurchase of shares, it can further impede a takeover by increasing management's concentration of share ownership. Unocal employed this type of leveraged recapitalization as a defense against takeover in* Unocal v. Mesa Petroleum Corporation, *493 A.2d 946 (Del. 1985).—Ed.*

13. *See, for example,* Paramount v. Time, *571 A.2d 1140 (Del. 1990), in which Time management sought to impede a hostile takeover by Paramount by borrowing large sums of money to purchase shares of Time's preferred merger partner, Warner Communications.—Ed.*

14. Marcel Kahan and Edward Rock, *How I Learned to Stop Worrying and Love the Pill: Adaptive Responses to Takeover Law,* 69 U. Chi. L. Rev. 871 (2002).

executive compensation have functioned as "adaptive devices." As we have seen, the incentives they create for managers to focus on shareholder value have become stronger in recent years.

Now that we have a sense of the disciplinary mechanisms that can motivate the executives of America's publicly quoted corporations to focus closely on share prices, we can explore the ramifications with respect to bankruptcy. Consider a scenario that the literature on financially distressed companies suggests is highly plausible. A publicly quoted firm has a positive operating income but also has a substantial debt load because those in charge have been pursuing costly but worthwhile ventures predicted to earn excellent returns for shareholders over time. Conditions outside the control of those in charge subsequently render the company unable to service its debts. This highly leveraged but otherwise sound and viable company will end up facing financial distress that could result in liquidation.

The evolutionary theory of corporate governance and corporate bankruptcy comes in at this point. It suggests that if a country has a system of ownership and control like America's, it will function more effectively if there is a framework in place designed to preclude the outcome just described. Matters fit together smoothly if the managers of a troubled but viable business have the option to continue running the firm, at least initially, rather than losing their jobs as soon as formal bankruptcy proceedings are commenced. Consider the advantages this arrangement offers from the managerial perspective. If bankruptcy means immediate ouster, executives would face, ex ante, an unpleasant combination of possible results. On the one hand, if they adopt a "safety first" mentality they will fail to reap the rewards available under their managerial services contracts, and they could face dismissal at the hands of outside directors or a takeover bidder. On the other hand, if they pursue promising but risky ventures that require substantial corporate borrowing, they will be displaced if factors beyond their control lead to the launch of bankruptcy proceedings.

One way that managers facing this sort of "lose-lose" situation could respond would be to orchestrate a reconfiguration of the pattern of ownership and control by seeking out large, stable, relational shareholders. These shareholders, under the new arrangement, would take a "hands-on" role within the firm, thus muting the need for discipline via incentive-oriented executive pay, vigilant outside directors, and hostile takeover bids. A widely held view is that in the U.S., legal constraints deter the sort of "relationship investing" just described.[15] If the law imposes this sort of obstacle, a second move would be to attenuate the unforgiving nature of corporate bankruptcy law. The idea would be to pursue legislative changes or to use the existing regime creatively to ensure that managers of financially distressed companies remain at the controls at the outset of a restructuring.

The latter outcome, as the evolutionary theory predicts, is what prevails in the United States. Chapter 11 of the Bankruptcy Code essentially provides a distressed company's incumbent executives with a mechanism to orchestrate a turnaround while remaining at the helm. With Chapter 11 proceedings, there is no requirement that a firm entering reorganization be insolvent. Correspondingly, the executives in charge have substantial discretion to direct the timing of entry into bankruptcy. Moreover, matters subsequently function on a "debtor-in-possession" ("DIP") basis, which means the incumbent directors remain in control and continue to run the business.

Chapter 11 offers other forms of assistance to the executives in charge of a financially troubled corporation. Crucially, management has extensive powers to arrange new financing, including the power in some circumstances to grant priority over all preexisting

---

15. *See Mark Roe's article in this volume.—Ed.*

security interests. Also, a corporate debtor acquires valuable breathing space because creditors, secured and unsecured alike, are stayed from enforcing their claims. In due course, the creditors must vote on a plan of reorganization. Their ability to do so gives them some leverage against management, but no creditor may propose an alternative plan for at least the first 120 days after the case commences, which is routinely extended by courts to 180 days and beyond. Correspondingly, if creditors do not approve management's proposed plan of reorganization, this may result in the proceedings being substantially prolonged. Creditors will also be induced to approve what the incumbent management team suggests, because doing so can serve to avoid a costly hearing during which the corporate debtor seeks to "cram down" nonconsenting classes of debt.

In recent years, creditors have sought to counteract the influence of incumbent managers relying on Chapter 11. Perhaps most importantly, DIP lenders are increasingly imposing stringent requirements as a condition to their agreement to provide financing. A condition that might be attached is that the corporate debtor must sell important assets if a positive cash flow is not being generated within a specified period of time. Also, creditors are now beginning to negotiate "pay-to-stay" deals with key executives in a Chapter 11 company that provide a substantial bonus if the assets are sold or the reorganization is completed quickly. Such developments have put managers on a tighter leash in bankruptcy than in the past. Still, it remains fair to say that U.S. managers have much more influence over the corporate rescue process than their counterparts in most other bankruptcy regimes.

A related point should be made about executive tenure. Chapter 11 is not always as manager-friendly as the analysis thus far may suggest, because executives are frequently fired during, or immediately before, such proceedings. Such an outcome is potentially devastating for those affected, since they are unlikely to return to top managerial posts for a number of years, if ever. The fact remains, though, that Chapter 11 gives executives of financially distressed companies the option to take control of the agenda in a way that is unavailable when a country's bankruptcy law is more manager-displacing in character.

Let us turn now to insider/control-oriented corporate governance systems. As we have seen, the received wisdom in Germany and Japan is that banks constitute the focal point of the insider financial systems that prevail in the two countries. With respect to corporate bankruptcy, neither country can be said to have a manager-driven regime. Instead, managers are routinely displaced at the outset of bankruptcy, and corporate bankruptcy filings in both Germany and Japan will, in the vast majority of cases, result in liquidation. To be sure, the two countries do have procedures available under bankruptcy law for reorganizing a financially troubled company. Yet the German provisions do not contemplate a debtor-in-possession rescue. In Japan this option is possible, but there is no automatic stay[16]in the event that such a rescue is commenced, and the relevant procedure has been largely moribund because of procedural complexities. The upshot is that in both countries the executives of distressed companies cannot count on arranging a second chance under corporate bankruptcy law.

To fit Germany and Japan within the context of the evolutionary theory, assume for a moment that they offered a manager-driven bankruptcy regime like that in the U.S. This sort of arrangement could seriously undermine the leverage of a company's main bank. The problem would be that the managers of a troubled company could file for bankruptcy and attempt to pilot the restructuring process themselves. To be sure, the prospects for

---

16. *The "automatic stay" in U.S. bankruptcy law temporarily suspends all debt collection, judgments, foreclosures, and repossessions against a debtor who files for bankruptcy under Chapter 11. 11 USC 362(a). The provision is meant to give the debtor time to renegotiate with its creditors.—Ed.*

successful reorganization would be dim unless the bank was eventually persuaded to sign on. Still, bankruptcy would provide a mechanism that executives could use to keep a pivotal monitor of their corporation's affairs at bay.

By contrast, a manager-displacing bankruptcy regime powerfully reinforces the leverage of lenders. If the executives of a financially troubled company know that they will immediately lose their jobs if the company's main bank launches formal bankruptcy proceedings, they will listen closely to what representatives from the bank have to say. Manager-displacing bankruptcy law is thus a natural component of insider governance, and this combination is what we see in Germany and Japan.

As mentioned, in recent years, key features of insider/control-oriented financial systems have come under stress as part of a possible transition to an "outsider" bias. Since the evolutionary theory contemplates a feedback loop between corporate governance and bankruptcy law, it follows that the equilibrium which currently exists in Germany and Japan could be unstable. More precisely, the theory implies that if and when the control blocks held by "core" shareholders are unwound, a reconfiguration of bankruptcy law along manager-friendly lines could be in the cards.

Consistent with the implications of the evolutionary theory, there are hints of a transition towards a manager-driven bankruptcy regime in Germany and Japan. German companies were given a more robust reorganization option under the country's bankruptcy laws in the late 1990s, though the new procedure still lacks the "debtor-in-possession" feature that characterizes Chapter 11 in the U.S. In Japan, steps are currently being taken to streamline the cumbersome debtor-in-possession reorganization option that now exists. If outsider governance truly takes hold in these countries, the evolutionary theory predicts further changes in favor of manager-friendly bankruptcy law. . . .

Douglas G. Baird & Robert K. Rasmussen, *Four (or Five) Easy Lessons from Enron*[*]

. . . Temptation. It lies at the heart of financial swindles. The promise of 50% returns in three months can lure thousands of investors—so too can a stock that soars 500% in three years. But those who are tempted are often skeptical. Before they invest, they want to know how one can enjoy such supracompetitive returns. The answer usually is a facially plausible story, though with a bit of mystery attached. The mystery is often touted as the reason that the investment opportunity is exclusive to the entrepreneur who discovered it. It is what ensures that the gains are not competed away.

The classic case remains that of Charles Ponzi. While not a very adept con artist—he was caught several times—in a six-month period in 1920, Ponzi convinced ten thousand investors to part with an aggregate of $9.5 million. He promised amazing returns—50% in ninety days. As a testament to his financial wizardry, Ponzi often paid off his investors in half the time he had initially promised. How could he work such financial magic? Allegedly, Ponzi had discovered a lucrative arbitrage opportunity in postal reply coupons. Postal reply coupons allowed the sender of a letter to ensure that the recipient in another country would be able to obtain sufficient postage to respond. For example, a letter writer

---

[*] Originally published in 55 VANDERBILT. LAW REVIEW 1787 (2002). Reprinted with permission.

in America would purchase a reply coupon here and send it along with a letter to a relative in another country, say, Spain. The Spanish relative could then redeem the coupon for Spanish stamps sufficient to send a reply.

Ponzi noticed a pricing discrepancy in the postal reply coupons. One could buy a coupon in one country for, say, one penny, and redeem it in another for six cents worth of stamps. This opportunity existed because ... [t]he Great War changed the relative value of many currencies, but the rates for postal exchange coupons remained fixed....

But transaction costs limit any opportunity to profit from arbitrage. Consider the steps necessary to exploit this state of affairs. Money would be gathered in the United States. This money then had to be converted into a foreign currency and put in the hands of an agent in the appropriate foreign country. The agent would have to buy the postal reply coupons in large quantity, although there were limits on the number of coupons that could be bought at one time. The agent then had to send the coupons back to the United States. Another agent would have to redeem them. Given these elaborate requirements, it is hard to imagine how anyone could purchase a sufficient number of reply coupons to support the millions of dollars that Ponzi collected.

When pressed by potential investors on how he could overcome these costs, Ponzi resorted to a favorite theme of the con artist—that such information was a trade secret that could not be disclosed. After all, letting the cat out of the bag would allow his competitors to come in and seize the opportunity he had discovered. A 50% return based on a somewhat plausible story coupled with the allure of a trade secret proved irresistible to over ten thousand investors who willingly gave their money to Ponzi. At its high point, the "Ponzi Plan" as he called it, was taking in $200,000 a day.

Of course, Ponzi's real trade secret was to never incur transaction costs at all. He was able to avoid them because he never bought a significant amount of postal reply coupons. Rather, Ponzi was running a simple pyramid scheme, with the money from later investors being used to pay off earlier ones. When the pyramid collapsed, panic ensued as investors' dreams of fantastic riches turned to fears of losing all that they had entrusted to Ponzi. Ponzi, of course, lacked sufficient funds to return the money to those who were the last to invest, let alone make good on his promised return. Ultimately, it fell to the bankruptcy court to sort out the mess. All were clear, however, on what was and what was not at stake in the court's proceedings. The court's job was to apportion the loss among the disappointed investors in Ponzi's operations. It had to determine what assets were available and who had claims against these assets....

One thing the bankruptcy court did not have to do, however, was make any decision about how this group of assets should be deployed in the general economy. There was no firm to rescue. There was simply a pile of cash with too many claims against it. This particular aspect of Ponzi's failure would seem to distinguish it from current corporate bankruptcy practice. Chapter 11 today is often viewed as a forum where a decision has to be made as to how the assets of a financially distressed firm should be used. These are real firms with real assets. The goal of bankruptcy in this view is to preserve the firm's going-concern value. In contrast, there were no assets in the Ponzi case other than the remaining cash the court could collect. The major issue was whether earlier investors who had been paid off should be forced to return their proceeds to the kitty and settle for a pro rata share of the money they had originally turned over to Ponzi. There was no contention that the money was worth more if kept together rather than distributed to other parties. As such, it would be tempting to conclude that Ponzi is a colorful figure who reminds us of our tendency to be blinded by the prospect of easy money, but offers little by way of analogy to today's bankruptcy proceedings of publicly held firms.

As the quotation at the outset of this Article illustrates, the recent collapse of Enron has revived the memory of Charles Ponzi. It is easy to see why. Early investors in Enron who cashed out became rich. Enron told its investors that it would continue to enjoy above-market returns indefinitely and that it was a firm that would live up to the promise embedded in its high stock valuation relative to its reported earnings. At its peak, it traded at a price-earnings ratio of fifty-five to one. Similar energy and trading firms had a PE ratio of a quarter of this amount.

This situation should have raised questions—the same questions raised by Ponzi's promise to increase an investor's money by half in a three-month period. Like Ponzi, Enron had answers. Enron presented itself to the world as a market-maker, a firm that excelled at creating new markets. Market-makers, however, rarely enjoy spectacular returns in the long run. To be sure, the enterprise of creating new markets is a worthwhile endeavor. By organizing markets, one enables buyers and sellers to find each other at low cost, eliminating wasted resources through a reduction in transaction costs. The entrepreneur who creates such a market can capture as profit a fair portion of the benefit the initial buyers and sellers enjoy by finding each other. Creating a market for the first time offers the promise of a big one-time profit—the proverbial home run. Enron was no Charles Ponzi; it actually made markets. Indeed, in at least the energy markets where Enron first operated, they seem to have made a good deal of money. Billions of dollars changed hands across the various markets that Enron created.

Over the long term, however, market-makers must be satisfied with making a small profit on each trade. One cannot create a market and keep it secret. Once the entrepreneur creates the market, others can follow the example at little cost. As soon as buyers and sellers can choose among a number of different market-makers, profits are competed away. Despite this, Enron was able to convince investors that it was special. It did not maintain that it would increase its returns in the energy markets that it developed. After all, basic economic principles suggest that, if anything, Enron could expect decreasing returns in this aspect of its business. Rather, Enron sold investors on the notion that it could translate its success to international energy markets and to all commodities alike. After colonizing one market, Enron believed it could transport its expertise to other, undeveloped markets. What worked in North America would work in Europe, Asia, and South America. What worked in natural gas and electricity should work in water, broadband, newsprint, metals, coal, crude oil, and steel. The firms that had worked in these areas for years simply had not seen the money that they were leaving on the table.

This concept, while plausible in theory, did not work in practice. Enron, however, endeavored to hide this truth from investors, and perhaps even from itself. As a result, Enron is currently best known as a company that cooked its books. In early October 2001, before disclosing its bookkeeping improprieties, Enron's stock sold for more than $30 a share. Less than two months after these shenanigans came to light, Enron filed for bankruptcy.

When Ponzi failed, there was no business to carry on. The only issue was allocating the few remaining assets. Enron presents a different sort of case. Unlike Ponzi's feigned use of postal reply coupons, Enron ran a real business. Indeed, it was an innovator in energy trading, a business that provided a valuable service and has spawned many imitators.

It might seem that the job of the bankruptcy judge is to preserve Enron's ongoing operations. Just as we would not tear apart a railroad that had dishonest managers, we would not want to allow Enron to be torn apart either. Enron offers what would appear to be a paradigmatic case for an old-fashioned Chapter 11 case. In this Article, we show that this view is mistaken. In the end, what the bankruptcy court can do for Enron (and indeed other firms in Chapter 11) is not much different from what it could do with the mess left by Charles Ponzi. The bankruptcy court is well suited to the task of penetrating the accounting miasma that enshrouds Enron. It may take years, but eventually the court will clear away the obfuscation created by Chewco, JEDI, the Raptors, and the other creatures of accounting imagination that encircled Enron. Other decisions, such as what to do with the assets that once comprised the nation's seventh largest company, are best left to others. Some of Enron's assets left the company prior to bankruptcy, others shortly after, and most of the rest will soon be gone. It will be the new owners, not the bankruptcy court, nor Enron's erstwhile managers, who decide the future use of these assets. The market will decide what happens to Enron's business, not the bankruptcy judge.

I. Enron's Business Plan and the Idea of the Going-Concern Surplus

Enron was nothing if not dynamic. Enron began in the mid-1980s as a gas pipeline company owning the largest gas pipeline in the United States. It was formed by the merger of two natural gas pipeline companies, Houston Natural Gas and InterNorth. This merger left Enron with $4.2 billion in debt. Using additional debt financing, Enron soon acquired other energy-related assets, including power plants. In 1989, after deregulation of the gas industry, it opened GasBank, an energy trading operation that allowed consumers of natural gas to secure reliable sources of supply at a predictable price. Five years later, it created a market for electricity. These two markets operated at the wholesale level. By the late 1990s, most of Enron's earnings came from businesses in which it had not engaged ten years earlier. In a decade and a half, Enron evolved from an old-economy firm centered on hard assets to a new-economy enterprise centered on a scalable strategy of creating markets where none had existed previously. In the year before its stunning collapse, Enron touted that its most valuable asset was its people and their ability to apply Enron's business strategy far and wide.

In both the natural gas and electricity markets, Enron hit it big. Deregulation allowed the natural gas industry to change both the way in which natural gas was delivered and the structure of the contracts among the various market participants. Enron was well positioned to take advantage of these changes. It knew where overcapacity existed and where it did not. Its computer system and highly skilled traders allowed it to identify and enter favorable transactions.... By the mid-1990s, Enron dominated the domestic wholesale markets in natural gas and electricity. There were few other players in this field at the outset, and none possessed Enron's knowledge of the marketplace.

... [As competitors emerged, however, Enron's profits declined.] Trading firms in mature markets simply do not receive the returns that Enron did when it first developed the electricity and natural gas markets. At this point, Enron could have simply accepted this steady flow of less spectacular profits.

Enron's managers, however, were not content with standing pat. The lesson that they took from their success in energy markets was not that they were in the right place at the right time, but that they had discovered a strategy for reducing risks that could be transplanted to other areas. Enron sought to expand in two ways. It attempted to expand internationally....

More provocatively, Enron believed that its success in wholesale energy could be replicated in other domestic markets, many of which were unrelated to energy. Enron's managers believed that what they had done for the wholesale energy market they could do for the retail market. In late 1996 they created Enron Energy Services to provide energy management services to business customers. To illustrate the potential demand for this service, consider a department store chain. It competes with other chains based on selection and price of its merchandise. It does not want to have its success turn on its energy costs. Enron's trading operations would allow the chain to enter into a long-term contract for up to ten years where its supply of electricity was secured and its costs fixed.

Enron's vision was to expand this model across all commodities and other risks that a firm must manage. Simply put, Enron decided to lead the way in solving a problem that entrepreneurs have faced for as long as commerce has existed: how to contend with fluctuating commodity prices and other risks over which they have no control. Retailers have to contend with fluctuating energy needs; farmers can do nothing about the weather; airlines can do nothing to change the price of jet fuel; and importers can do nothing about exchange rates....

To be sure, all entrepreneurs must take risks. As Chaucer observed: "Nothing ventured, nothing gained." But entrepreneurs want to choose their risks and bear the ones they believe they can control. They want to focus on areas where they believe they have a comparative advantage. For example, Ford Motor Company lost a billion dollars in the market for palladium. While Ford needed palladium to make cars, Ford had no comparative advantage in timing the market for this rare metal. Enron's dream was to prevent situations like this. Enron would make it possible for companies to eliminate such risks by supplying commodities, making markets in them, and strategically investing in the firms and resources needed to provide them. Ultimately, Enron might promise to protect the retail chain that wanted to fix its energy costs not merely if energy prices went up, but also if unusual weather increased its demand for energy. Weather derivatives and other exotic financial instruments allow an intermediary like Enron to make these promises and transfer risk to others.

In creating these various markets, Enron attempted to mimic the strategy that it had used in the wholesale energy business. The first step was to acquire assets. Just as they could assure liquidity in their energy contracts by buying power plants, they could acquire other hard assets to reinforce the other derivative contracts they created. Enron became the seventh largest producer of newsprint. It built fiber-optic networks, acquired firms that dealt in precious metals, and bought a water company. It made strategic investments in start-up ventures built around these commodities. The fiber-optic cable created a demand for routers and other pieces of hardware. Enron invested in these items, and invested big. Similarly, the new capacity created a new outlet for movies. Enron took advantage of this opportunity to invest in a start-up venture that would supply movies on demand on the fiber-optic cables that it was building and that its trading operations were making accessible....

As an example of Enron's vision, consider the following. During the summer of 2000, Enron helped a zinc producer in the Northwest shut down its operations for six weeks and sell the power it would otherwise have used to a buyer who needed it more. Enron then provided a financial derivative to lock in the sale at a fixed price. Enron also provided zinc from its metals subsidiary so that the zinc producer could meet preexisting obligations. Such transactions make everyone better off and put resources to their highest valued use. Enron created value in situations such as these....

Enron identified its business model as a "network" where the trading operations allowed it to "leverage" its investments in assets. Enron believed that others could not compete with it because it was the only competitor able to combine trading operations with hard assets. Yet its own experience suggested that combining these two components was becoming less important. For example, Enron's annual report boasted that over time it would become less reliant on its own assets in servicing its customers. But rather than a source of pride, this goal should have sounded an alarm. To the extent that owning the hard assets is less necessary, the less value Enron has as a going concern and the more plausible it becomes that others can compete with it in the market. There is no reason to believe that Enron had access to contracts with third parties that could not be replicated by others.

If transaction costs go down, a firm can stabilize its costs by entering into different contracts with a number of firms. It no longer needs a single firm such as Enron. Even if it wants to deal with one firm, a single intermediary who is neither a market-maker nor a supplier can bundle the appropriate contracts and sell them. The technological advance that Enron relied upon to create its markets was a dramatic decline in transaction costs, but such a decline also reduces any advantage Enron had over competitors. The easier it is for others to compete with Enron, the less value Enron has above and beyond the value of its assets. The same force that made Enron possible also capped its value as a going concern.

When Enron filed for bankruptcy, it owned thousands of miles of gas pipelines and fiber-optic cable. It was one of the largest wholesalers of coal and the seventh largest producer of newsprint. It owned power plants all over the world, some completed, some still under development. Even if it had made astute investments in all these areas (and there is much to suggest that it did not), there seems to have been little synergy between these assets. There is no reason to think that these assets have a greater value in Enron's hands than in the hands of some other party. The ability to enter into contracts for any of these commodities and the ability to form networks through contracts made it less valuable to have a collection of physical assets under the control of any particular firm.

We come then to the first easy lesson of Enron. It is all too easy, inside of bankruptcy and out, to assume that any particular business has an enormous going-concern surplus. Much is lost if a firm is shut down and its assets are sold off piecemeal. But the extent to which a firm as a whole has value above and beyond the sum of the highest value of its discrete assets is easy to overestimate. In a world in which transaction costs are rapidly declining, the value created by simply bringing assets into the firm is likely to decrease over time. Enron may provide an especially vivid illustration. Indeed, as we have noted above, Enron's business plan was to make money by reducing transaction costs. Enron made it continuously cheaper for others to buy and sell all the things for which it was a market-maker. But as these costs declined, Enron's own ability to profit as a market-maker declined as well. The benefits that arise when transaction costs decline and markets come into being are commonly called "consumer surplus." The name is no accident. When markets work correctly, it is the buyers who enjoy the benefits rather than the intermediaries that made the trade possible. The huge valuations the stock market placed upon Enron (and other similar intermediaries who brought us the "new economy") may reflect a failure to acknowledge this basic principle....

II. Market Sales and the Enron Assets

We come now to one more lesson of Enron. Modern Chapter 11 practice, unlike that of twenty years ago, relies on the market. Even where dedicated assets exist and control rights are in disarray, modern bankruptcy judges often maintain control of the assets and take the necessary steps to preserve their value for only as long as it takes to find a buyer. For example, bankruptcy judges today have the ability to approve short-term contracts to keep a business together and the ability to sell the assets as soon as buyers can be found. In Enron's case, the bankruptcy judge approved the retention of the traders and others for a period of weeks even though they were only coming to work to play poker with each other. As those in control searched for a reliable counterparty to run the trading operation, Enron's traders needed to be kept on board.

A trading operation in a rapidly changing economy cannot remain dormant for long. The fate of the trading operation could not wait until Enron's financial affairs were sorted out. Within a few weeks of the bankruptcy petition, the bankruptcy judge conducted an auction in which the winning bidder promised to pay only a portion of the profits of the operation for some period of years. In a different world, where the firm was not clouded by improprieties, a prevailing bidder would have been required to produce some amount of hard cash. But Enron no longer possessed the credibility needed to be a market-maker and could not engage in any transactions at all, rendering it considerably less valuable as an acquisition. Moreover, the sudden shutdown of the trading system made it unclear how many customers would return when the power went back on. In such a world, a bankruptcy judge must simply do the best she can. It is a testimony to the flexibility and creativity of the modern bankruptcy bench that the judges administering the Enron case were able to orchestrate such sales and ensure that they took place within a few weeks....

Enron is the twenty-first century's parallel to the late-nineteenth-century railroads. They too had their share of fraud and corruption. They also had capital structures that took years to unravel. Much of the railroad reorganization business, however, required judicial oversight of the railroad's operations and their restructuring. This aspect of the equity receivership was necessary only because the capital markets of the time were insufficient to allow marketplace sales of the assets. Today, however, firms can muster the billions needed to buy Enron's hard assets or serve as a reliable counterparty for its trading operations.

The fourth lesson of Enron is again a simple one. Markets for the assets of large firms exist in a way they did not at the time the law of corporate reorganization came into being. Shortly before it filed for Chapter 11, Enron controlled 25% of a trading volume that measured many billions of dollars. Its working capital itself ran in the billions. But it could cease its trading operations without creating even a ripple in the marketplace. When the trading operation that had purportedly generated billions in profits was put up for sale, no cash bidders appeared. The absence of a cash bid for its trading operations did not raise concern about the liquidity of markets, but rather new doubts about the underlying value of Enron's operation. With respect to large firms in reorganization, liquidity constraints and the inability to raise sufficient capital can no longer justify a law of corporate reorganizations.

Conclusion

Enron was not a Ponzi scheme. Money from late-arriving investors was not used to pay off those who arrived earlier. But Enron and Ponzi do have two features in common. First, the bankruptcy itself was precipitated by the failure of investors to understand that extraordinary profits from financial intermediation, to the extent they exist, disappear in competition. Second, the primary business of bankruptcy is not to save or rehabilitate firms, but to allocate losses after the assets are sold. The business of making such decisions, especially in the presence of fraud, is a hard business, but it is one in which our bankruptcy judges are especially skilled.

Enron's story has cast a shadow over nearly everyone associated with it, from politicians to accountants, but the bankruptcy bench and the modern Chapter 11 process may be a striking exception. Judges in Delaware and elsewhere have transformed Chapter 11 just as judges in the nineteenth century transformed the then-arcane equity receivership. Bankruptcy judges no longer pretend to possess the wisdom to chart the destiny of great corporations. Nor does Chapter 11 provide a chance for investors to sit down and spend years pondering the fate of a large firm. But the new face of large-firm bankruptcy practice, one that began only a few years ago in Delaware, may give us something to celebrate. Judges and markets work hand in glove, each doing their work in the arena in which they operate best. This observation is another, and perhaps the most reassuring, lesson from Enron.

Cheryl D. Block, *Overt and Covert Bailouts: Developing a Public Bailout Policy**

...

I. Definitions and Classification Models

A. *What Is a Bailout?*

...

1. *Bailout as a Form of Government Subsidy*

Bailouts and general government subsidies are members of the same conceptual family and have some overlapping characteristics, but they differ largely as a matter of degree. Bailouts may include fewer beneficiaries than do general government subsidies. For example, bailout assistance to a particular firm provides benefits to a more concentrated group than general subsidies to assist small businesses. More significantly, though, bailouts differ from other government subsidies in focus. Whereas general subsidies tend to encourage a particular desired or favored activity, bailouts are designed to prevent enterprise failure. The focus of bailout is on saving a particular private enterprise or industry from collapse ...

2. *A Proposed Definition*

a. General Definition

... As a first step toward a definition, I propose the following: Bailout is a form of government assistance or intervention specifically designed or intended to assist enterprises facing financial distress and to prevent enterprise failure. This definition does not require

---

* Originally published in 67 INDIANA LAW JOURNAL 951 (1992). Reprinted with permission.

that the bailout be successful; the business or industry may fail despite government assistance. The crucial element is that the attempt be a form of *government* intervention. Although individuals or other private entities may provide assistance to a failing enterprise, this Article focuses on *governmental* action....

b. The Concept of Financial Distress

One challenge presented by the bailout definition will be to establish precisely when an enterprise is facing financial distress or failure. One useful place to look for a definition is the "failing firm defense" to alleged violations of antitrust law. The Justice Department's Merger Guidelines, state that it is

> unlikely to challenge an anticompetitive merger in which one of the merging firms is allegedly failing when: 1) The allegedly failing firm probably would be unable to meet its financial obligations in the near future; 2) it probably would not be able to reorganize successfully under Chapter 11 of the Bankruptcy Act; and 3) it has made unsuccessful good faith efforts to elicit reasonable alternative offers of acquisition of the failing firm.

> ...

B. A Taxonomy of Bailouts

If one adopts the broad definition of bailout as a form of government intervention designed to prevent enterprise failure, a wide array of government activity will fit the definition. Use of such a broad definition will prove to be an asset in assessing the appropriate public policy approach to economic failure. As a matter of public policy, a consistent, well-developed, and thoughtful approach to economic failure is called for. Hidden bailouts should be exposed and subject to the same kinds of scrutiny and attention given to the more obvious arrangements referred to as bailouts by the popular press. The sections that immediately follow develop a taxonomy or classification of different types of bailouts.

1. Overt v. Covert Bailouts

... Hidden or covert bailouts can be provided in a number of different ways. Assistance may be provided to a troubled enterprise through special tax breaks. Covert bailouts may also be provided in the form of relief from compliance with burdensome regulation. Finally, covert bailouts may be provided through trade restrictions, tariffs, and quotas on foreign imports. Such measures reduce competition and provide domestic producers with a greater share of the market and the power to increase prices.

In the general regulatory setting, tax advantages and subsidies often provide incentives for taxpayers to engage in desired behavior. Although they fit within the general subsidy family, tax subsidies designed as incentives differ slightly from bailouts. In the case of a bailout, the entity may not be in a position to alter behavior in response to incentives. The tax break or subsidy operates not as a carrot, but as a lifeline assisting the troubled entity in its struggle to regain financial strength. In the early stages of the savings and loan crisis, for example, Congress provided special tax breaks to encourage the merger of failing thrifts into healthier ones. These special provisions were later repealed and a far more substantial bailout was undertaken....

Troubled companies often attribute some portion of their financial problems to the cost of compliance with government regulations.... Relief is often provided to a particular industry by a regulatory statute itself. For example, Congress in 1981 created specific exemptions for steel industry compliance with Clean Air Act emissions standards based upon economic distress within the industry. In other cases, particular industries or firms obtain relief at the regulatory level. For example, the Environmental Protection Agency sets particular effluent and emissions standards on an industry-wide basis, often providing unique standards for industrial subclassifications. By carving out a narrow industry subclassification and promulgating lower standards for that subclass, the agency can provide a form of bailout relief to a firm in economic distress.

Another significant indirect form of bailout is the "failing firm defense" to compliance with the antitrust laws.... To the extent that the failing firm defense does significantly immunize anticompetitive mergers that would otherwise be challenged by the Justice Department, the defense can be regarded as a bailout....

As another example of potentially hidden bailouts, established procedures under United States international trade law are available through which a domestic industry faced with serious economic injury can apply for import relief. The "escape clause" procedure permits relief when "an article is being imported into the United States in such increased quantities as to be a substantial cause of serious injury, or the threat thereof, to the domestic industry producing an article like or directly competitive with the imported article."[17]

... The "escape clause" mechanism may operate as a bailout of domestic private industry. Although the relief granted generally is industry-wide, narrow conceptions of the relevant industry can result in a firm-specific bailout. For example, the Reagan Administration in 1983, at the request of Harley-Davidson, temporarily imposed quotas and increased tariffs on imports of foreign motorcycles with "engines with total piston displacement over 700 cubic centimeters." Although the firm's name appears nowhere in the presidential proclamation, Harley-Davidson was the only U.S. company at the time manufacturing engines of the type described.

2. Prospective v. Retrospective Bailouts

Most of the bailouts that receive widespread public attention are after-the-fact public rescues of firms or industries already in financial distress. Less obvious, perhaps, are ways in which government may provide bailout prospectively. The most obvious examples of prospective bailouts are federal insurance programs, which set aside reserves to provide assistance in times of future financial distress. Although many federal insurance programs were designed primarily to protect customers, they generally were implemented at times of financial crisis and were designed to prevent financial collapse of industries faced with economic hardship. The mission of the FDIC was not only to insure deposits, but also to "reduce the economic disruptions caused by bank failures." Although the customer is the direct beneficiary of many federal insurance programs, the firms or industries saved from financial collapse are surely indirect beneficiaries. More important, perhaps, the presence of federal insurance instills consumer confidence and provides direct and immediate benefits to the industries whose customers are willing to leave higher deposits or invest more funds than they would if uninsured. To the extent that insurance programs provide such benefits to private enterprise managers and owners otherwise threatened with financial difficulty, they should be considered bailouts.

---

17. 19 U.S.C. §2251.

The Federal Crop Insurance Program is more directly focused on preventing enterprise failure. Established by the Agricultural Adjustment Act of 1938, the program was designed "to promote the national welfare by alleviating the economic distress caused by wheat-crop failures due to drought and other causes, by maintaining the purchasing power of farmers, and by providing stable supplies of wheat for domestic consumption and the orderly flow thereof in interstate commerce." The primary beneficiary was the farming enterprise, while the consumer was intended to be a secondary beneficiary.

Most federal insurance programs are funded through contributions made by industry members themselves and thus fall into the category of "special fund" prospective bailouts. For example, the Bank Insurance Fund and the Savings Association Fund, both administered by the FDIC, are funded through annual assessments on insured depository institutions based upon a percentage of estimated insured deposits. In contrast, premiums for some insurance programs are funded only partially through industry contributions with the remainder coming from general revenues. Given the hardship of extremely high premiums, farmer expenses for federal crop insurance are supplemented with a federal premium subsidy, making this prospective program a "combination bailout." However, even insurance pools funded entirely by industry premiums may be inadequate to cover large losses, thus requiring ultimate resort to general revenues. A recent report on deposit insurance observed that "the potential for losses to the taxpayers exists in part because the deposit insurance funds were never intended to be funded at a level that would create reserves sufficient to cover heavy losses from large numbers of bank failures."

II. The Public Policy Debate: To Bail Out or Not to Bail Out?

A. *Alternative Methods for Allocating Risk of Loss*

Bailout decisions involve allocating risk of economic loss. General revenue bailouts, for example, allocate losses to the general taxpaying public. Special fund bailouts allocate losses more narrowly to those contributing to the bailout fund. Before turning to bailout policy, one must consider whether bailout is in fact the appropriate response to the threat of loss. Accordingly, one should consider the available alternative loss allocation possibilities.

1. *No Shifting of Loss*

One obvious alternative response to threatened enterprise failure is simply to let firms fail. The burden or cost of enterprise failure will then be imposed upon the investors, managers, employees, and others with relationships to the firm or industry. Losses are left to fall where they may without any shifting of costs. In a capitalist, free-market economy such as ours, this approach to loss is the general rule.

2. *Allocation of Loss Through the Tort Regime*

An alternative mechanism for imposing costs from losses is through the common law tort system, under which losses resulting from wrongful acts are borne by the wrongdoer....

Injured individuals typically sue privately to recover losses in a civil lawsuit. Where enterprise failure results from fraud or corruption and the class of injured parties is large, it may be appropriate to provide government agencies with authority to prosecute and collect reimbursement for losses on behalf of the consumer. Banking regulators, for example, have authority to prosecute for bank fraud and impose civil and criminal penalties. In such cases, the government's role is limited and does not involve direct or indirect bailout of the failing enterprise itself....

3. The Insurance Alternative

A third alternative risk-of-loss approach is the insurance model. Under insurance principles, the allocation of financial loss is determined by private contract. The private insurer acts as an administrator, managing a resource pool contributed by the many insured. This fund is used to reimburse those among the group who suffer losses. Those with lower than average losses will bear some of the cost of those with higher than average losses. Thus, the insurance alternative permits loss spreading....

By definition though, most cases of enterprise failure considered for bailout relief by government decision makers involve uninsurable losses. For example, when considering federal crop insurance, the President's Committee on Crop Insurance reported that "[p]rivate companies have tried all-risk crop insurance, but after repeated losses have practically retired from the field. Crop insurance on a large scale would probably be a larger enterprise than any one company or group of companies would now desire to underwrite." Similarly, Congress adopted deposit insurance after numerous early failures of private industry co-insurance clearing houses and state insurance plans. Private deposit insurance simply was not considered viable.

When a firm's or industry's failure can be attributed to its own errors in judgment, serious questions arise as to whether federal bailout is appropriate. Costs of wrongdoing generally should be internalized to take advantage of general deterrence effects. At some point, however, the consequences of enterprise failure may be so extreme that bailout is necessary regardless of blame....

Numerous proposals for deposit insurance were rejected by Congress between 1886 and 1933. The controversy in part stemmed from concerns with enormous potential costs in the event of widespread bank failures, loss of market discipline resulting from high levels of bank risk taking, and interference with market interest rates that depositors would demand without insurance protection. There appears, then, to be controversy on several fronts. First, one minority view holds that deposit insurance would be unnecessary for sufficiently "narrow banks" whose investments were limited to certain safe and liquid assets. Another minority view holds that the market, left on its own, will provide sufficient protection for depositors and the overall economy. Second, even if deposit insurance is necessary, some economists and banking experts recently have argued that privately capitalized insurance, or at least a partially private bank insurance system, would not only be viable, but also would be preferable to federal insurance in reducing the moral hazard problems and other distortions generated by a federal insurance regime.

This Article will not attempt to address this particular debate in the banking world except to suggest that possibilities for privatization of deposit insurance should be seriously considered....

4. The Bankruptcy Alternative

Modern bankruptcy law provides an opportunity to reorganize a troubled enterprise rather than liquidate it. Successful reorganization in bankruptcy eliminates the need for a public bailout. Thus, any well-considered bailout policy must address the bankruptcy alternative.

The purpose and use of bankruptcy laws has been the focus of much recent controversy. One side of the debate argues that bankruptcy law serves only a narrow debt collection function. Dean Thomas Jackson argues that bankruptcy law has the distinct purpose of allocating a debtor's limited common pool of resources among its creditors....

Thus, while "[b]ankruptcy law can and should help a firm stay in business when it is worth more to its owners alive than dead[,] ... [n]ot all businesses are worth more to their owners—or to society—alive than dead."

The other side of the debate suggests that bankruptcy law can play a more expansive role. Professor Warren, for example, points out that

> [c]ongressional comments on the Bankruptcy Code are liberally sprinkled with discussions of policies to "protect the investing public, protect jobs, and help save troubled businesses," of concern about the community impact of bankruptcy, and of the "public interest" beyond the interests of the disputing parties. These comments serve as reminders that Congress intended bankruptcy law to address concerns broader than the immediate problems of debtors and their identified creditors; they indicate clear recognition of the larger implications of a debtor's widespread default and the consequences of permitting a few creditors to force a business to close.

...

B. The Free Market Presumption Against Bailout

... Many policy makers undoubtedly view bailout as a solution for only the most extreme cases. At the same time, however, early bailouts set a stage that makes subsequent requests for assistance more difficult to resist. When Congress authorized loan guarantees to the Lockheed Aircraft Corporation in 1971, it set a precedent for later similar guarantees to Chrysler [in 1979] and New York City [in 1975].... A formal bailout policy should not leave the impression that bailouts will be easy to come by. To the contrary, a presumption against bailouts should be the first principle in any formal enterprise failure policy.

The first justification for the presumption against bailout is that government intervention to protect private industry violates the free-market principles that generally govern our economy. According to these principles, economic markets operate reasonably efficiently without government intervention. Under ideal competitive conditions, voluntary exchanges of goods and services will achieve efficient outcomes, and prices will reach equilibrium. Conditions are rarely ideal, however. Markets may fail for numerous reasons, including inadequate flow of information, nonexistence of a market for certain goods, concentration of power in the form of monopolies, high transaction costs for certain exchanges, and spillover or externality effects of individual behavior that the market does not take into account. Government regulation or intervention is frequently necessary to correct for these structural market failures.

In a bailout, government intervention generally is *not* a response to a structural market failure, but rather a response to the economic failure of the enterprise. From a market perspective, leaving the enterprise to fail may well be the most efficient outcome....

One reason for caution is the moral hazard problem[:].... A policy of freely provided bailouts would encourage greater levels of risk taking by management than would be societally optimal. Investors in the business enterprise who harbor expectations of a bailout in the event of business failure will have little incentive to monitor risky management activities. Rescue of a failed firm protects these investors at the expense of the larger community bearing the bailout costs.

Another reason to be especially cautious with bailouts is the risk of rent-seeking behavior on the part of firms seeking assistance. A general revenue bailout involves expenditures of tax revenues that are reasonably concentrated and inure to the benefit of management, employees, investors, and others with some relationship to the firm being rescued. These groups will have greater incentives to organize and lobby for the bailout. The taxpaying public that will incur the costs is more dispersed and will have difficulty organizing to oppose the bailout....

C. Overcoming the Presumption Against Bailout

1. The Public Interest v. Pluralist Approaches

a. The Public Interest Approach

... Virtually all legislative histories include some discussion of the public interest or general welfare. Bailout legislation is no exception. For example, the history of the Emergency Loan Guarantee Act expresses concern for the economy and the potential costs "in terms of jobs destroyed, confidence impaired, income lost, and goods not produced." Similarly, the House Banking, Finance and Urban Affairs Committee reported in connection with the [1979] Chrysler bailout that "a Chrysler failure would create consequences of an entirely different order of magnitude from the normal experience. There is, therefore, a presumption that such widespread human suffering should be avoided if that is reasonably possible." In its Declaration of Policy for the Regional Rail Reorganization Act of 1973, Congress declared that "public convenience and necessity require adequate and efficient rail service in this region and throughout the Nation to meet the needs of commerce, the national defense, the environment, and the service requirements of passengers, United States mail, shippers, States and their political subdivisions, and consumers." The declaration also concluded the "preservation and maintenance of adequate and efficient rail service is in the national interest."

... Statements of the sort found in the bailout legislative histories have significant rhetorical force. At the same time, we are all aware that legislators and their staffs are quite adept at composing such "public interest" language for political purposes. Some substantive and procedural standards will be necessary to more genuinely identify the public interest to be served by any bailout.

b. The Pluralist Approach

Many political scientists, economists, and legal scholars have argued that there is no such thing as a "social will" or "public interest." These pluralists, or "interest group" [or "public choice] theorists, view politics as the clash and ultimate compromise among individuals or interest groups, each seeking his or her own presumably rational self-interest....

Public choice theorists would argue that the real explanation for bailout legislation lies in the economic bargain struck by the relevant players. In the case of a bailout, the individual firm or industry and its customers, creditors, and employees usually benefit. Public interest rhetoric may be scattered throughout the Chrysler bailout legislative history, but a public choice analysis would conclude that the bailout simply was a deal struck between the Chrysler Corporation and Congress. Although one of the major "public interest" arguments for the Chrysler bailout was preservation of jobs, the number of employees at Chrysler was reduced dramatically as a result of plant closings and other cost-cutting measures imposed as conditions for the bailout assistance. The shareholders were the true beneficiaries of the efforts of Chrysler's powerful lobbyists....

2. The Distributive Justice Approach

Much empirical work regarding the distributional effects of bailouts remains to be done. The outcome of this analysis of course will vary depending upon the industry and the structure of the bailout plan. In any given bailout, it may be difficult to measure the amount, and perhaps even the direction, of redistribution. One suspects, however, that most bailouts are redistributive rather than allocative. Because a bailout should not be measured by efficiency alone, a closer look will be necessary to determine who the winners and losers from redistribution are or how gains from allocations are distributed.

The discretion provided to banking regulators in addressing bank failures is another more subtle example of redistribution and thus of more subtle analytical problems. The Federal Deposit Insurance Corporation is obligated only to insure depositors up to the amount of $100,000. Nevertheless, the FDIC, Federal Reserve Board, and Office of Comptroller of the Currency have protected depositors beyond this insurance obligation and, in the cases of certain large banks, also protected bank investors along the way. In a recent controversial set of cases, federal regulators followed a too-big-to-fail policy in deciding to bail out some banks and not others. When the Bank of New England failed in January, 1991, federal regulators "protected all depositors because it was the judgment of [the FDIC] board that financial conditions in the area required stabilization and one of the ways to stabilize them was to provide insurance for all depositors, not only depositors insured to $100,000." The FDIC solicited bids from buyers and arranged to keep the bank in operation. In contrast, when the Freedom National Bank of Harlem failed in November, 1990, the same regulators allowed the bank to close its doors and did not protect uninsured depositors. "In the case of Freedom Bank," FDIC Chairman Seidman testified, "we had no basis to make a finding that the conditions in New York where that bank was located were such that it required us to protect uninsured depositors in that *small* bank."

Choices such as those made in the Bank of New England and Freedom National Bank episodes involve redistributions of wealth. Wealth is distributed to depositors and indirectly to others connected with large banks and away from depositors in smaller banks. Assessing the redistributional effects of these decisions will require further exploration. First, information about those with deposits in excess of $100,000 will be necessary. One's initial instincts may not be sympathetic to wealth transfers among depositors who are so well-endowed that they have exceeded the $100,000 insurable amount. Upon closer examination, though, serious redistributive issues emerge. In the case of Freedom National Bank, for example, many of the large uninsured depositors were nonprofit organizations providing services to the community. Uninsured depositors in smaller banks may also be small businesses with lower income employees. In short, decisions to bail out in some circumstances and not in others involve serious equitable and redistributive issues. In the banking context, these choices are made by the FDIC Board with little or no congressional oversight or other procedural safeguards....

III. Developing a Substantive and Procedural Bailout Policy

A. *Developing a Substantive Standard*

1. *Preconditions to Bailout*

... Bailouts are extraordinary events and should not be lightly undertaken. Four basic preconditions should be met as a first step toward overcoming the presumption.

First, any firm seeking bailout relief should be required to attempt an informal workout or a chapter 11 reorganization in bankruptcy or at least establish that such an effort would not be viable. In other words, "private bailout" should be attempted before resorting to "public bailout." From a public policy perspective, one advantage of the reorganization in bankruptcy is that it distributes bailout costs among those more intimately connected with the enterprise and those who have the most to gain from the success of the enterprise. Such an approach appears most equitable in the interest of distributive justice....

Second, except in extreme circumstances, an enterprise seeking bailout assistance should be required to establish that the threat of collapse is due to circumstances beyond its control. Sometimes, the cause of failure will be economic or other extreme conditions outside the control of the enterprise seeking assistance. At other times, however, threatened failure may be due to fraud, mismanagement, or other internal reasons. Freely provided bailout under the latter circumstances may increase the moral hazard problem.

The no-fault requirement is merely a precondition, not an argument in favor of bailout. Chrysler, for example, argued that a significant part of its financial trouble could be attributed to costs imposed by environmental and safety regulations imposed on the automobile manufacturing industry—circumstances beyond its control. As the smallest of the "Big Three" automobile manufacturers, Chrysler argued that it was most vulnerable to financial distress resulting from compliance with burdensome regulations. Even if all of Chrysler's problems could have been attributed to the burdens of environmental regulation, it is not clear that bailout relief should have been provided. Such regulation is promulgated to protect consumers and the environment. Firms that are unable to meet such burdens perhaps should collapse. Nevertheless, establishing that the threatened collapse is due to outside factors should be an important precondition to serious consideration of bailout relief.

As a third precondition, the firm seeking relief should establish that private insurance was unavailable to distribute costs among those in the industry. Although others in the same industry are not as intimately connected with the enterprise as parties to a chapter 11 bankruptcy proceeding, they have a strong interest in survival of the industry. Before broadly distributing bailout costs to the general public, efforts should be made to concentrate costs within a more appropriate group of beneficiaries.

Finally, before bailout relief can be considered, it should be reasonably clear that the enterprise in fact would collapse without the relief. Although the threatened collapse ordinarily should be clear and imminent, the fourth precondition does not *require* that the threatened collapse be imminent. As a practical matter, this precondition has the benefit of sparing unnecessary expenditure of government resources. Moreover, it is necessitated by the operating definition of bailout itself—that bailout is a form of government assistance or intervention designed to prevent enterprise failure. Government assistance in the absence of reasonable evidence that the firm would fail without relief is not a bailout but a different form of government subsidy.

Each of the four preconditions to bailout should apply except under extraordinary circumstances. In extreme cases, the preconditions might be relaxed to some extent. When the potential "community catastrophe" from financial collapse is extreme, earlier bailout intervention may be necessary....

Similarly, the no-fault precondition may be relaxed under extreme circumstances. Ordinarily, an enterprise seeking bailout assistance should establish that the threatened failure is due to circumstances beyond its control. Nonetheless, there may be cases where, despite the fault of the enterprise, the public interest is so great as to require bailout in any event. Certain bank bailouts arguably fall into this category. These should be rare and extraordinary cases.

2. Substantive Policy Assessment

a. Assessing the Impact of a Failure to Intervene

Even after the preconditions are met, the presumption against bailout should continue. A strong public interest should be established to overcome this presumption. Too often, however, the public interest is described in vague, ambiguous, and flowery terms. No doubt, this is what has led some pluralists to claim that there is no such thing as the "public interest." Despite these protestations, the "public interest" may be just slightly more identifiable in the bailout setting.

One mechanism for deciding when to intervene is to consider the cost to the government of nonintervention. Failure of an enterprise or industry will result in lost tax revenues, as well as increased government costs for unemployment coverage, welfare, and other programs. In his report on guidelines for rescuing large failing firms, the Comptroller General suggested that "Congress should compare the costs, benefits, and consequences expected to occur if assistance is offered with expectations of what would occur if market forces and established legal procedures are allowed to operate." Where the government cost of a decision not to intervene exceeds the cost of government assistance that would be necessary to rescue the troubled enterprise, bailout would appear the financially prudent and—at least in the short-run—the wise thing to do.

On the other hand, Congress also must consider the long-run implications. Even if the anticipated costs of nonintervention are higher than anticipated bailout costs, concern for equity or legislative integrity may caution against the bailout....

Another similar measure of the public interest is the economic impact that would result from allowing the enterprise to fail. Economists can assist in designing tests to measure the impact or ripple effects of market failures....

... Within the same industry, failure of one firm may impose ripple effects on other firms. Banking regulators have long been concerned that, given interrelationships among some members of the banking community, the collapse of a large bank would cause ripple effects among many other banks and lead to a banking crisis. Thus, the FDIC adopted a too-big-to-fail policy....

This discussion ... does not suggest that interindustry analysis is the only appropriate measure. One concern with major financial failures, from the public interest perspective, is the extent to which poverty levels would increase if government intervention is rejected.... Nevertheless, it should be possible to develop some objective measures to determine the impact of a failure to provide government assistance.

b. Public Goods Analysis

... One is tempted to argue that bailout of an entire industry is ... more likely to be a public good than bailout of an individual firm. But even in the case of failure or threatened failure of an entire industry, the degree of [public benefit] may be so low that government intervention will not be considered. For example, if the kite-manufacturing industry were to disappear altogether, few would consider government intervention to assist the industry appropriate. On the other hand, if the entire airline industry were threatened with economic collapse, government intervention would be considered quite seriously....

Failures in other industries will present much closer questions. The textile and electronics industries are examples. If market failure arises largely from foreign competition, is bailout a public good? What should the response be to a failure of the private university system? It will be a useful exercise to develop a list and rank of those industries the strength of which is an indivisible public good. To determine whether the collapse of a particular industry would be a public bad calling for the corrective public good bailout, one must examine the degree of exclusivity. How integral is the industry to the overall economy? How many customers, employees, and other participants does the industry affect, directly or indirectly? ...

c. Noneconomic Considerations

Even if the impact of collapse of an enterprise would be extreme and bailout relief appears appropriate on economic grounds, equitable considerations must be taken into account. For example, the too-big-to-fail policy in connection with bank bailouts protects investors and uninsured depositors in large banks but does not provide similar protection to investors in smaller banks and to depositors who happen to have accounts in smaller banks. Assuming that the bailout is necessary, should the government, in the interest of equity, go further and provide similar relief to small bank investors and uninsured depositors as well? [See the Freedom National Bank example above.]

Other cases may involve lower levels of potential economic harm that would ordinarily not be sufficient to overcome the presumption against bailout. Nonetheless, there may be other compelling policy considerations. For example, the Newspaper Preservation Act[18] provides bailout relief of a sort to failing newspapers. Here the overriding policy concern was for an independent free press that would strengthen and support the first amendment free speech rights so fundamental to our constitutional framework. As another illustration, even though failure of a particular enterprise would have a reasonably small economic impact, it might be appropriate to provide relief in the interest of community diversity. Thus, assistance to the sole minority-owned business in a community may be considered to be in the "public interest."

A word of caution is important here, however. If other policy considerations are the primary driving force behind a direct or indirect bailout, one should critically examine whether or not other alternatives might be a more appropriate way to effectuate the policy. If first amendment concerns are indeed paramount, careful consideration of alternatives to promote such freedoms should be undertaken *before* resorting to bailout.

The point here is that economic principles can provide only a threshold level of analysis in connection with bailouts. One cannot escape the ontological question: What is in the public interest? Although some substantive standards for reviewing requests for bailout relief can be identified, the policy choices remain difficult, and there is no obvious bright-line substantive test by which to measure the wisdom of any given bailout.

---

18. 15 U.S.C. § 1801. The law provides an exception to antitrust laws that allows economically distressed newspapers to enter into joint operating agreements to avoid failure.

B. Developing Procedural Standards

Given the lack of a substantive bright-line test for deciding when bailout serves the public interest, the procedures used to make that decision become all the more important. While process-oriented reforms to improve the extent and quality of deliberation prior to enactment of legislation may be a good idea generally, the call for bailout often arises when time for deliberation is short. This setting, as well as the fact that bailout decisions require a reasonably unique form of economic analysis, implicate the need for special bailout procedures. The suggestions that follow are designed to increase the deliberativeness of the decision-making process while at the same time recognizing the need for speedy action in many bailout scenarios. They are also designed to increase the number of participants in the process so that the voice, or at least the interest, of more diffuse groups can be heard along with the voices of well-organized interests.

1. Need for a Central Monitoring Agency

Detailed economic information is critical in making any decision regarding bailouts. To wait to gather this information until a firm or industry is on the brink of collapse is unwise, however. In the bailout setting, firms or industries in *potential* distress should be monitored. On the eve of its bankruptcy, the Drexel Burnham Lambert Group withdrew substantial amounts of cash from its broker-dealer and government securities subsidiaries without notifying the Securities and Exchange Commission (SEC) or the New York Stock Exchange (NYSE). The SEC, working with other federal government regulators, was able to stave off disaster in the securities markets by "facilitat[ing] an orderly liquidation of the broker-dealer's positions and a speedy transfer of customer accounts to other financial institutions." At the same time, SEC Chairman Breeden argued that "[t]he events surrounding the Drexel insolvency underscore the need for the SEC to have regular and unquestioned access to information regarding the financial position of a broker-dealer's holding company and its other affiliates." In his testimony, Chairman Breeden urged passage of the Market Reform Act [of 1990] to provide for SEC access to such data.

Financial problems needing government attention are not limited to those industries subject to securities regulation; early monitoring should be more generally available. Such monitoring could be done through a nonprogrammatic agency with authority to monitor the financial situation of industries in trouble and to make recommendations to Congress or the appropriate regulatory agency at a stage prior to crisis. Such an agency might be called upon to provide revenue estimates and other economic information. Unlike most agencies that are established to administer already existing legislation, such an agency would not have enforcement authority.

Perhaps one lesson of the savings and loan crisis is that it may be difficult for an agency responsible for industry regulation to admit its defeat at an early enough stage to take proper corrective action. Insolvent banks were permitted to operate long after evidence of their insolvency was apparent. Some have argued that moral hazards caused banking regulators to pursue this policy of forbearance rather than close insolvent banks. Closing a significant number of banks would have severely strained the deposit insurance system. "When confronted with a correlated wave of insolvencies and the prospect of putting numerous institutions out of business, it often seems to be expedient to forego immediate action and hope that things may get better." Regulators knew that if the bank failures became extreme enough Congress would provide a bailout. Some of this problem might be eliminated if the financial monitoring function was performed by a nonprogrammatic agency. Moreover, a nonprogrammatic agency would be less susceptible to "capture" by a regulated industry....

In addition to collecting information and monitoring financial conditions in various industries, a separate division of the agency that I envision would be asked to provide sophisticated economic cost-benefit assessment and analysis of redistributive implications of proposed bailouts....

While recommending that such analysis should be applied to legislative bailout proposals, I am mindful of the limitations of cost-benefit analysis.

First, the obligation to perform such analysis can be burdensome and those responsible may do a perfunctory job. Second, cost-benefit analysis is far from a precise science and information can be manipulated to engineer a particular outcome. Cost-benefit analysis was an important component of conservative deregulation efforts and has been correctly criticized for "compressing the issue of social regulation into an artificial set of restrictive guidelines." Because benefits such as life, good health, and clean air were difficult to value, they were often trivialized or ignored. Cost factors that were easier to quantify often won out in the balance. The use of economics in public policy decisions arguably has a dehumanizing effect....

b. Greater Oversight of Major Regulatory Bailouts

Many regulatory bailouts are provided overtly under explicit legislative authority. Congress has given banking regulators discretionary authority to bail out banks with no oversight, reporting requirements, or procedural safeguards.... Serious tensions surely accompany issues of agency discretion and congressional oversight. On the one hand, agencies are thought to be better able to deal with complex policy problems given their high levels of expertise. Another argument in favor of delegating substantial authority to agencies is the depoliticization of the policy review process. On the other hand, agencies insulated from legislative and judicial oversight arguably are prone to capture by special interests and just as inclined to politics as other government branches. Providing significant discretion to agencies insulated from congressional and public review is antidemocratic and displays a serious mistrust of the democratic process. A strong case can be made that Congress should reassert its control and revive the nondelegation approach. This is not to suggest that Congress needs to concern itself with every detail of designing and implementing public policy. Congress should be more involved, however, in making fundamental policy choices. Major bailouts represent fundamental policy decisions in which Congress should play a greater role.

In the bailout setting, I am mindful of the need for quick response to emergency situations. Irvine Sprague, past Chairman and member of the FDIC Board forcefully argues that banking regulators are the experts best suited to deal with complex bank failures. The FDIC, he argues, needs authority to act quickly under emergency circumstances, and greater congressional involvement in the process would hinder effective responses to bank failure. Even in emergency situations, however, there should be a formal requirement for the FDIC, the Federal Reserve, and the Treasury Department to report their actions and the reasons for those actions to the appropriate congressional committees.

IV. Structuring and Funding the Bailout

Given the presumption against bailouts and the high standard required to overcome it, bailouts should be reasonably infrequent. However, once other private assistance methods have failed and Congress or other government officials decide to intervene, the bailout arrangement itself must be structured. It should already be clear that many alternative methods for achieving a bailout are available. As argued earlier, covert forms of bailout pose special dangers and should be avoided. Once the decision is made to provide a more *overt* bailout, numerous options still are available. Given the different types of bailouts and the possible variations in terms within each of the types, difficult policy decisions remain at this next step in the process. This Part will first consider the choice of the proper bailout technique and, second, the proper method of funding and distributing bailout costs in those cases where the decision is made to provide a public bailout.

A. Structuring the Bailout

1. Government Involvement in Management

The most extreme form of overt bailout and government intervention in management is creation of a public enterprise or nationalization. While such extreme government intervention has been common elsewhere in the world, nationalization has not been used with great frequency in the United States. Nevertheless, numerous examples of "public enterprise" can be found in the United States. The collapse of the Penn Central railroad and subsequent railroad reorganization forming Conrail can be viewed as a bailout through nationalization or creation of a public enterprise. An earlier illustration is the Tennessee Valley Authority established during the Depression. In the bailout setting, government agencies may take over supervision and management to such an extent that the operation can be viewed, at least temporarily, as a public enterprise. For example, in the rescue of Continental Bank of Illinois, the FDIC took an eighty percent ownership interest in the bank and chose its new managers. In the recent bailout of the savings and loan industry, the Office of Thrift Supervision is so extensively involved in the operation and closing of certain banks that the banks can be said to be public enterprises as well. In addition, throughout the period that federal loan guarantees on Chrysler debt remained outstanding, the corporation was required to submit periodic reports on its activities and meet conditions set by the Chrysler Corporation Loan Guarantee Board. Failure to meet conditions set by the Board could have resulted in a declaration that the debt was due and payable in full. As a result, the government was involved in substantial oversight of Chrysler operations. Moreover, in order to protect its interest, the government received an equity interest in Chrysler in the form of warrants to acquire Chrysler stock.

While extreme forms of nationalization should be used only rarely, government involvement in management appears wise. When a private firm or industry seeks public bailout assistance and a policy decision is made to grant such assistance, the government has a strong interest in the success of the bailout. This is certainly true in the case of general revenue bailouts, where the taxpaying public in effect becomes an investor in the private enterprise. In a public bailout, the government in effect plays the role of bankruptcy trustee and should be entitled to have the same substantial input in overseeing management decisions that is provided in the private bailout setting.

2. Structuring the Loan or Loan Guaranty

Many instances of past bailout activity took the form of direct federal loans or guaranteed loans to particular firms or municipalities threatened with failure. Concerned with the ad hoc response of Congress in each of these instances, the Comptroller General's Office urged the President and Congress to develop policies for federal assistance to failing firms and municipalities. Early in his report, the Comptroller argued that one of the overriding considerations in any assistance package should be protection of the government's financial interest. To this end "reliance on the principles and practices followed by commercial lenders is not only possible but crucial."

... The borrower seeking government assistance generally finds itself in financial crisis. Thus, the commercial principles to be applied are those that would be used in a commercial workout for a borrower in financial trouble. Applying commercial workout lending notions in the government assistance context involves four basic elements. First, concessions may be required from the borrower in order to reduce the amount of assistance needed. This may include concessions from creditors, stockholders, bondholders, management, labor, suppliers, customers, state and local governments, and foreign beneficiaries. Second, the lender should be empowered to exercise some management control over major contracts and financial and operating plans. Third, adequate collateral should be required. Finally, the lender should receive adequate risk compensation. A commercial lender will charge higher rates of interest depending upon the level of risk involved with the loan. Where the government assistance is in the form of loan guarantees, as opposed to direct loans, this option is not available. Thus, in loan guarantee settings, the government's risk compensation should be in the form of guarantee fees or equity participation in the firm requiring assistance.

3. Federal Insurance Programs

As noted earlier, federal insurance programs themselves reflect bailouts of a sort. Just as the government as lender or loan guarantor can rely to a large extent on the principles and practices of commercial lenders, the government as insurer can use many of the principles and practices of commercial insurers. Some of these were discussed previously. Most important, the private insurance industry has developed numerous mechanisms to minimize the moral hazards to which insureds may fall prey. Among the most significant of these mechanisms is risk-based assessment of premiums. Higher premiums imposed on high-risk activity will create disincentives to engage in such activity and thus reduce moral hazard problems.... Statutory changes directing the FDIC to establish a risk-based assessment system for insured depository institutions certainly reflect a step in the right direction. [Banks' FDIC premiums became risk-based beginning in 1993.] In addition, those insured through federal programs should be required to meet rigid safety standards to be eligible for coverage.

B. Funding and Distributing Bailout Cost

... Costs that take the form of direct outlays can be covered by special funds, general revenues, or a combination of sources. Where possible, costs for a bailout should be imposed more precisely on the group that benefits from the bailout. Thus, special fund bailouts generally should be preferred to general revenue bailouts. We have already seen one illustration of the special fund approach in the case of bailouts in the form of insurance funds. Most government insurance programs are funded through fees imposed upon those protected by or benefitting from the program.

... Clearly, the costs of providing a pure public good, such as the national defense, should be covered by general revenue from all taxpayers. As one moves away from the pure public good end of the continuum, one increasingly finds goods from which some segment of the population is excluded. Nevertheless, the group of beneficiaries of the good may have difficulty forming voluntary associations or clubs to provide the good privately. Reorganization in bankruptcy is an illustration of a mechanism designed to bring together a group of potential beneficiaries to negotiate an acceptable arrangement for the payment of creditors and rehabilitation of the firm. Survival of the firm may be viewed as a public good, at least with respect to those creditors with an ongoing relationship to the firm. Although some government involvement may be necessary to manage the bailout, the cost should be borne, to the extent that it can be identified, by the beneficiaries.

One practical problem with such an approach is that by designating an identifiable group to bear the costs one has set up an interest group that will lobby heavily against bearing the charge. The larger group that is not bearing the charge will perhaps be too diffuse to organize on the other side.... To the extent that one can identify a discrete class of bailout beneficiaries, a strong case can be made for spreading costs among that group through some form of special fund bailout. I do not advocate using this approach for social programs. Many social programs are designed to provide benefits to those most in need. It is counterproductive to impose the cost of the programs on their beneficiaries. The cost for food stamp programs should not be borne by those receiving food stamps.

Conclusion

One thing should be clear from this Article. There is no consistent public policy regarding enterprise failure. An examination of the history of domestic bailouts shows that Congress and government regulators respond to threatened private industry failure, if at all, in ad hoc fashion....

Bailout decision makers should be required to study the distributional consequences of bailout action in a systematic way. To whom are the benefits flowing and from whom will the costs be extracted? Many of these questions are not limited to bailouts. Whenever firms engage in what economists refer to as rent-seeking activity, rents extracted from others are transferred to the rent seeker. Many of the observations and suggestions made throughout this Article might be used to achieve more general legislative reforms. One might even argue that economically healthy rent-seeking enterprises that are simply lining their pockets with economic surplus raise more serious public policy issues than the private enterprise seeking assistance for survival....

Discussion Questions

1. Relative to bondholders, shareholders are more receptive to risky corporate management styles because there is no limit on their potential gain from risks that pay off. Bondholders get paid a fixed return even if the firm's profits increase, so they prefer stability over risk-taking. In the Enron era and again in the recent bubble years, we have seen risky and ultimately disastrous corporate management behavior. William Bratton and other commentators attribute such risky behavior to an excessive focus on share value. Does excessive corporate risk-taking suggest that the law should orient management duties toward bondholders?

2. Do you agree with the result in *Metropolitan Life* (consider in particular its doctrinal contract analysis)? If so, why: for the reasons given in the case, for the reason Smith gives, or for some other reason? If not, why not?

3. As we have seen, the contractarian model of the corporation holds that all corporate relationships are contracts, including shareholders' relationship with the corporation.

As the *Metropolitan Life* case demonstrates, however, courts distinguish bonds from shares on the ground that bonds, unlike shares, are contracts. Is there a difference? What is the difference between fiduciary duty and the implied covenant of good faith and fair dealing in contracts?

4. As pointed out in the editor's footnote in *Metropolitan Life*, bondholders are third-party beneficiaries of the bond indenture, not parties to it. In bond indentures, "limitations on the bringing of a suit are standard in indenture agreements and have been generally upheld by the courts." *Simons v. Cogan*, 549 A.2d 300 (Del. 1988). *Simons* quoted an example of such a provision:

> No holder of any Debenture shall have any right to institute any action, suit or proceeding at law or in equity for the execution of any trust hereunder or for the appointment of a receiver or for any other remedy hereunder, unless (i) such holder previously shall have given to the Trustee written notice of the happening and continuing of one or more of the Events of Default herein specified, (ii) the holders of 35 percent in principal amount of the Debentures then outstanding shall have requested the Trustee in writing to take action in respect of the matter complained of, and shall have afforded to it a reasonable opportunity either to proceed to exercise the powers herein granted or to institute such action, suit or proceeding in its own name....

Such provisions are intended "to deter individual debenture-holders from bringing independent law suits for unworthy or unjustifiable reasons, causing expense to the Company and diminishing its assets." American Bar Foundation, *Commentaries on Model Debenture Indenture Provisions* §5–7, at 232 (1971), quoted in *Simons*.

Do such provisions, or bondholders' third-party status generally, affect the argument that bondholders are, and should be, viewed solely as contractual claimants?

5. In what other ways are the bonds in *Metropolitan Life* like and unlike typical form contracts?

6. Smith's argument is based on theory that the *hypothetical* rational investor holds a diversified investment portfolio. Should the validity of Smith's argument depend on whether *actual* investors are rationally diversified?

7. The debate represented here by the Tung and Smith articles assumes that fiduciary duty rules have a significant effect on the kinds of business risks corporate directors and managers will take. How accurate do you think this assumption is? What other factors might affect such decisions?

8. Compare Smith's view of fiduciary duty to Dallas's "power model" and Blair & Stout's "team production model." How are they similar? How do they differ?

9. Smith and Tung addresses the controversy over whether directors should maximize shareholder value, creditor value or overall firm value. It is generally undisputed that duties shift to creditors in insolvency. Why? Should duties shift in the zone of insolvency? Do you agree with Smith's even more radical position that directors should have a legal duty to maximize overall firm value? In practice, how do you think these duties are actually enforced? Do you think managers' behavior in this respect responds more to legal duties or market pressures?

10. Which position—Smith's or Tung's—seems more consistent with the contractarian notion of the corporation? Why?

11. Smith argues that directors should consider the claims of creditors as well as the claims of shareholders. Why stop there? Should managers be required to also serve the interests of other claimants, or other considerations? Why or why not?

12. As noted in the Chapter 4 discussion questions, the high-yield notes used for financing going-private transactions are registered with the SEC, which triggers Sarbanes-Oxley reporting requirements. Because these notes are not widely held, however, securities law exempts them from reporting requirements after one year. But the bond indentures typically require the issuer to continue reporting *voluntarily* under the Exchange Act, despite the exemption. *See* Robert P. Bartlett III, *Going Private But Staying Public: Reexamining the Effect of Sarbanes-Oxley on Firms' Going-Private Decisions*, 76 U. CHI. L. REV. 7 (2009). What does this fact suggest about the role of contract in protecting investors?

It is sometimes said that corporate governance law has relatively little to say about bonds because the nature of a bond is determined by the terms of the bond indenture and by contract law more than by corporations or securities law. What do you think of the argument that corporate governance in general depends more on "contract" than on "law"?

13. As Armour, Cheffins and Skeel point out, corporations raise more capital by issuing bonds (i.e., borrowing) than by issuing shares (equity). Why then do you think corporate governance law and theory focus overwhelmingly on the role of shareholders?

14. According to Armour, Cheffins and Skeel, why is a "manager-driven" bankruptcy regime is better suited to U.S. corporations than a "manager displacing" regime would be?

15. In their article, Baird and Rasmussen identify the following prevailing view: "Chapter 11 today is often viewed as a forum where a decision has to be made as to how the assets of a financially distressed firm should be used. These are real firms with real assets. The goal of bankruptcy in this view is to preserve the firm's going-concern value." Baird and Rasmussen, however, reject this view, arguing instead that "The primary business of bankruptcy [law] is not to save or rehabilitate firms but to allocate losses after the assets are sold." Note the contrast between this view and that of Armour, Cheffins and Skeel. Why do they prefer this approach?

16. Baird and Rasmussen argue that many, if not most, bankrupt firms are worth no more than the sum of their parts. Does this conclusion follow from the theory that a firm is merely a set of contracts? Put another way, does firm structure or corporate structure add value to the contracts that constitute a firm? If so, how?

17. During the financial crisis of 2008–09, the government rescued and subsidized many troubled banks instead of allowing them to fail. There was no market for many of the "toxic assets" of troubled banks, so the government and government-subsidized buyers of those assets gave the banks financial support and bought stock in them. Do "lessons of Enron" apply here? Are there distinguishing factors? Do you think the bank bailouts satisfied Block's criteria? Why or why not? Do you agree with Block's criteria?

18. Block begins with a presumption in favor of markets and against bailouts. She acknowledges, however, that failures, even if dictated by the market, may sometimes be intolerable from a public-interest standpoint. But how can we determine when the "public interest" is significant enough to justify a bailout? What can be done to minimize the chances of performing unnecessary bailouts or failing to perform necessary bailouts?

19. In Chapter 6, Silvers and Slatkin criticized the deregulation of the financial industry. Are Block's reasons for bailing out an industry also reasons that would justify regulating

an industry? Assuming an industry has high public value, what are the relative merits of a policy of prospective bailout, *ex ante* regulation, or *ex post* bailout?

20. What goals should the law pursue when a corporation becomes insolvent? The articles in this chapter present different views on this subject. What are their underlying assumptions? Whom do they benefit? With whom do you agree and why?

Chapter 9

Corporate Boards and Executives

State corporate law gives the board primary authority to manage the corporation, as well as the power to appoint executive officers, whom the board has a duty to monitor. The current orthodox policy view assumes that boards largely delegate management authority to officers and emphasizes the board's role in mitigating agency costs by monitoring officers on behalf of shareholders. It is commonly held that boards will best perform this function if they have a significant contingent of "outside" directors who are independent of the corporation's management. In this chapter, Charles Elson represents this point of view and argues that compensating outside directors with equity will enhance their independence from management.

Jill Fisch and Donald Langevoort question the orthodox preference for independent directors and the focus on monitoring over management. While including outside perspectives can improve the quality of decisionmaking, it can also impose costs. According to Fisch, the optimal balance between the board's monitoring and management functions may vary from corporation to corporation and thus the law should not mandate independence for all corporate boards. Langevoort argues that "inside" board members can represent the legitimate interests of upper and middle management. Furthermore, too much focus on monitoring can create an unproductive adversarial relationship on the board and between the board and management.

Cheryl Wade's article suggests that boards and management need more diverse membership in order to identify issues that benefit shareholders and society. Specifically, she argues that corporate directors and managers, who are overwhelmingly white and male, fail to pay appropriate attention to compliance with antidiscrimination law because they are unable to empathize with the concerns of people of color in their workforce. The resultant violations of law not only harm society, but also have economic costs for the corporation and its shareholders.

How are directors nominated and elected? The orthodox view is that shareholders choose the best-qualified directors through a competitive election process. As Professors Blair and Stout argued in Chapter 2, however, "shareholders in public corporations do not in any realistic sense elect boards. Rather, boards elect themselves." While federal proxy regulation is nominally limited to regulating voting procedures, in practice it has significant effect on the substantive distribution of power between shareholders and management. Thomas Joo's article describes proxy rules regarding shareholder nomination of directors and recounts the convoluted recent history of rule changes and proposals for further changes.

Lawrence Mitchell explains how the Sarbanes-Oxley Act departs from traditional corporate governance law in two ways. First, while corporate law generally says little about the specific governance structures and procedures boards must follow, Sarbanes-Oxley specifically mandates an independent audit committee of the board. Second, while state codes barely even recognize the existence of executives, much less their central role in decisionmaking, Sarbanes-Oxley puts specific substantive requirements on the CEO and CFO. In a second article, Mitchell expands on the role of executives, suggesting that CEOs be elected by a vote of shareholders, creditors, and employees.

Charles M. Elson, *Director Compensation and the Management-Captured Board: The History of a Symptom and a Cure*[*]

The most significant problem facing corporate America today is the management-dominated, passive board of directors. A common occurrence in many of our largest corporations is that passive boards are responsible for excessive executive compensation and, more importantly, poor corporate performance. The board, created to monitor management in order to ensure effective decision-making, has evolved into a body that, in its most extreme form, simply "rubber stamps" executive prerogative. Management, no longer checked, freely engages in conduct that is slothful, ill directed, or self-dealing— all to the corporation's detriment. Shareholders, mindful of recent disasters ... are keenly aware of this problem. But is there a solution?

Corporate governance scholars have debated potential solutions for years. Numerous legal reforms have been proposed, often involving such acts as the creation of the professional "independent" director, the development of strengthened board fiduciary duties, or the stimulation of effective institutional shareholder activism. All, it seems, have yielded little success because the passive board still flourishes. Yet the solution may be simple and obvious. Just as compensation is used to motivate employees to do their best, directors' compensation must induce directors to think more like shareholders. A shareholding mind-set will stimulate the outside directors to engage in the kind of active management oversight that so many boards now fail to exercise.

To create this perspective, companies should compensate their outside directors primarily in company stock that is restricted as to resale during their term in office. Each director will thus possess a powerful personal financial incentive to examine questionable management initiatives with the vigorous, independent, and challenging eye of an owner. All other forms of director compensation, which I believe promote board passivity and a pro-management bias, should be discontinued in favor of this equity-based approach.

In order to understand why stock-based compensation will solve the problem of board passivity, we must first examine its origins and the history of board compensation. This passivity problem is not a new one, but dates back over seventy years with the rise of the large-scale public corporation. Adolf Berle and Gardiner Means, in their 1932 landmark work, *The Modern Corporation and Private Property*, were the first to identify the force that was to lead to passive boards—the rise of management domination of the large corporation through the separation of ownership from control. Traditionally, corporate directors were major shareholders and received no compensation for their services. Early corporate legal doctrine clearly stated that directors were not entitled to remuneration for their activities as board members. However, with the tremendous expansion of the American economy

---

occurring throughout the early part of the twentieth century, corporations became vast financial entities. With this growth in the size of the modern corporation, shareholdings in these enterprises became proportionally smaller and smaller, with no one shareholder or shareholding group possessing enough stock to exercise effective control over the entity. Consequently, professional management filled this control vacuum. Directors, rather than being selected from among shareholder ranks, instead were nominated by management. Their connection with the enterprise generally resulted from a prior relationship with management (in fact, many directors were themselves members of management), not the shareholding owners, and they often had little or no shareholding stake in the company. However, as the shareholders' legal fiduciaries, directors were expected to expend independent time and effort in their roles, and, consequently, it was recognized that they must now be compensated for their activities. By the mid-1950s, the legal [presumption] against director compensation was crumbling, and directors increasingly were receiving cash compensation for their services.

Because directors primarily were appointees of management and subject to management approval in relation to retention, the interests of the directors naturally became more aligned with the group that selected and retained them than with the stockholders. This was the real origin of the board passivity *vis-à-vis* management oversight with which we grapple today. If a director owed his or her position (and continuance in that seat) to management largesse and that position entailed considerable compensation and prestige, the director had little personal incentive to actively challenge the appointing party. This trend became increasingly more pronounced throughout the 1980s with changes in board compensation practices. In addition to simple cash retainers (which were becoming increasingly more generous—amounting to $40,000 or more at many companies), directors began to receive numerous and substantial other benefits for board service. The typical director of a large, publicly traded corporation was now provided, among other things, with a substantial pension for board service following retirement, company-sponsored health and life insurance, and significant charitable donations to organizations of the director's choosing. Perhaps the most generous benefit of all, provided to selected directors, was a rich consulting contract, at rates far exceeding those for regular board service.

All of these special forms of compensation, it has been argued, were necessary to retain the services of top-flight director talent. Unfortunately they also compromised outside director independence from management, thus further fueling the board passivity that resulted in minimal management oversight and poor corporate performance. Today, board compensation treats the outside director as an employee of management, rather than a fiduciary of the shareholders. The nonmanagement board member's stake in the enterprise does not reflect the performance-based concerns of ownership, but instead reflects the interests of a highly salaried company employee. Outside directors, whose compensation is unrelated to corporate performance, have little personal incentive to challenge their management benefactors. Eager not to "bite the hand that feeds them," it is little wonder that boards became so passive and subject to management domination.

As board compensation practices may have acted to compound the problem of board passivity, these practices may also form the basis for its solution. To break management's grip on the board and stimulate real oversight, an appeal must be made to the director's same sense of personal self-interest that initially created the problem. There is nothing inherently wrong with a management-appointed board. The problem arises when a management-sponsored director fails to exercise appropriate oversight because of loyalty to the appointing party. The outside directors must be motivated to view management not from the perspective of a loyal employee, fearful of discharge, but from the viewpoint of an owner, concerned with overall profitability. To ensure that directors will examine executive initiatives in the best interest of the business, the outside directors must become substantial shareholders. To facilitate this, directors' fees must be paid primarily in company stock that is restricted as to resale during their term in office. No other form of compensation which acts to compromise their independence from management should be permitted. The goal is to create within each director a personal motivation to actively monitor management in the best interest of corporate productivity and to counteract the oversight-inhibiting environment that management appointment and cash-based fees create.

In June 1995, in what business commentators termed a major development in American corporate governance, the National Association of Corporate Directors' Commission on Director Compensation released a report calling for a radical overhaul of the compensation system for U.S. public company directors. Focusing on greater board equity ownership, the Commission made a series of recommendations designed to improve corporate governance by changing board pay practices to more closely align director and shareholder interests. Of greatest importance, the panel called upon companies to pay their directors primarily in stock, set substantial stock ownership targets for directors, and abolish all benefit programs, including pension plans, for board members.

Since the report's release, a substantial number of companies have adopted the Commission's recommendations on director stock ownership and elimination of directors' pensions, including some of the nation's largest and most respected corporate institutions. That trend accelerated considerably with the approach of the 1996 proxy season, as the Investor Rights Association of America (IRAA), a small-shareholder advocacy group, announced that it was proposing over 120 shareholder resolutions calling for the discontinuation of director pension plans and the adoption of outside director stock-based compensation. With the widespread coverage of the IRAA's efforts by the national financial press along with the group's success in previous years in attracting substantial shareholder support for their efforts, a number of companies voluntarily adopted the director compensation changes requested by the organization in exchange for the withdrawal of its shareholder proposals. If current trends continue, within a short time equity-based director compensation will have become the norm for most of America's largest corporations.

This development has significance far beyond the change it represents in director compensation structure. It promises to fundamentally alter a decades-old norm of corporate governance—the separation of ownership and control and resulting management-created board passivity. Oddly enough, while director compensation was an outgrowth of the split between ownership and control, it may also result in their reunification. By changing the form of compensation to include primarily equity, we will make the directors substantial owners of the corporation once again and perhaps will have finally found the solution to the conundrum Berle and Means identified over sixty years ago. With board control in the hands of owner-directors once again, boards should become more active management monitors and the oversight-driven problems resulting from board passivity will become much less prevalent....

The primary consequences of board passivity created by management capture is decreased management monitoring. But why does management control over board appointments necessarily create board passivity? Why would nonmanagement, outside directors on such captured boards, be unwilling to challenge management prerogative and engage in active oversight? There are three problems with a management-appointed board that lead to ineffective oversight. First, personal and psychic ties to the individuals who are responsible for one's appointment to a board make it difficult to engage in necessary confrontation. It is always tough to challenge a friend, particularly when the challenging party may one day, as an officer of another enterprise, end up in the same position. Second, conflict with a manager who is also a member of one's own board may lead to future retribution on one's own turf, thus reducing the incentive to act. Third, and most important, when one owes one's own board position to the largesse of management, any action taken that is inimical to management may result in a failure to be renominated to the board, which—given the large fees paid to directors (and the great reputational advantage of board membership)—may function as an effective club to stifle dissension. This is why the development of substantial director compensation, a consequence of management control, has acted to stifle board oversight of management and has, in fact, enhanced management domination. But it is not the fact of compensation in and of itself that created the problem, it is the form that compensation now takes.

Today's director compensation with its emphasis on substantial cash payments and employee-type benefits, including insurance and retirement programs, acts to align the interests of the outside directors with current management rather than with the shareholders, making necessary management oversight an almost impossible task. Why? Because the outside directors are compensated in a way that makes them, in effect, salaried employees of the corporation—or, in reality, the management—rather than the representatives and fiduciaries of the corporation's owners, the stockholders. Most board members receive substantial annual salaries for their services and large fees based simply on meeting attendance. Even though part-timers, they are entitled to the kinds of benefit programs rank-employees receive, including insurance programs and generous pensions upon retirement. Pensions are particularly problematic because they reward board longevity, controlled by management, rather than the quality of service. The message of this benefit to the director would seem to be not to rock the boat, so as to remain aboard long enough to be entitled to his or her pension—a great reward for what is essentially part-time employment.

This situation is only made worse by the prevalent use of director consulting and employment arrangements, and charitable contribution programs whereby the company makes substantial donations to the director's favorite charity, both of which are created and administered by management. They serve no real purpose other than to further link the directors' fortunes to management, rather than the company's overall productivity. It is management who decides who gets to consult and for how much, and it is management who decides how much to give to the director's charity of choice and when to give it. These arrangements seem to function more as side-bribes than legitimate furtherances of the corporate purpose. Appointed to the board by management, subject to easy termination because of management control of the proxy process, and compensated in a manner determined by, or at the least, under the influence of management, the outside director has become a mere retainer rather than watchful fiduciary....

Jill E. Fisch, *Taking Boards Seriously**

Today's corporate world is taking corporate governance and, in particular, the role of the board of directors, very seriously.... These efforts are supported by regulatory

* Originally published in 19 CARDOZO LAW REVIEW 265 (1997). Reprinted with permission.

developments that place a growing emphasis on the use of independent boards or board committees in corporate decision making.

Corporations are criticized for allowing their directors to serve on too many boards or for utilizing "trophy directors" who fail to provide value. To alleviate this problem, corporate attention has been focused upon obtaining qualified directors. Corporations are also striving to strengthen director participation in corporate governance, both by structuring boards and board committees to facilitate independent action and by creating compensation plans that increase the alignment of director and shareholder interests. Courts have embraced the model of an activist board and are indicating their willingness to impose liability on directors who fail to research, investigate, and ask challenging questions. No longer can independent directors rubber-stamp management recommendations without mastering the financial details of proposed transactions.

With the growing attention to improving corporate boards, it becomes important to evaluate the merits of the reform proposals. Toward that end, a number of recent empirical studies have attempted to explore the relationship between board structure and corporate performance. To date, this work has failed to provide clear direction about the value of restructuring the corporate board. Accordingly, studies have not resolved the debate between those who advocate the independent board as the answer to all business ills and those who criticize the enterprise.

Examination of the empirical work reveals an analytic shortcoming in the reform movement — the failure of many reformers fully to consider the appropriate scope of board function. In particular, the focus on independence as a criterion for evaluating board structure may place undue emphasis on the monitoring role of the corporate board while ignoring its management function. Although director independence may enhance the board's ability to monitor effectively, this gain may come at the expense of a decline in the board's management capacity. This analysis suggests that the normative vision of independence currently embraced by the corporate governance movement is a vision that imposes costs as well as benefits upon corporations that respond to the reform pressure.

Recognizing that corporate boards can perform a range of monitoring and managing functions may explain the failure of market forces, despite pressure from institutional activists and regulators, to produce a single model of the corporate board corresponding to the reformers' "flavor of the month." Moreover, the relative value of the managing and monitoring functions of the corporate board need not be uniform across the corporate spectrum. Although it may be possible to develop general predictions, the importance of managing versus monitoring is more likely a function of firm-specific characteristics....

I. The Development of the Monitoring Board

The separation of ownership and control in the modern public corporation creates agency costs that interfere with efficient corporate decision making. In an effort to reduce these agency costs, corporate law has developed a number of mechanisms to align the interests of non-owner management with the interests of shareholders. Most recently, these efforts have focused upon the board of directors. By empowering shareholders to elect the board and imposing fiduciary duties upon board members, corporate law creates a structure responsive to shareholder interests. Corporate law grants the board the power to make various decisions on behalf of the corporation, including the power to choose the corporate officers, set executive compensation, and review certain types of transactions.

Recent developments in corporate practice have emphasized the monitoring aspects of the board's role. The audit committee, for example, now a staple of the public corporation, is focused upon monitoring the internal affairs of the corporation and its compliance with financial reporting requirements. Corporation statutes provide increasing deference to corporate decisions that are subjected to independent board scrutiny—even transactions traditionally viewed with skepticism such as those involving conflicts of interest or the decision to dismiss a shareholder derivative suit. Courts have emphasized that modern directors have an affirmative obligation to monitor a corporation's compliance efforts and can be subject to liability for their failure to do so.

In an effort to enhance the board's ability to monitor effectively, commentators have identified two goals for improving board structure and function: greater director participation and greater director independence. Proposals to increase the use of board committees, limit the number of boards on which a director can serve, and structure director compensation in a manner that rewards directors for improved firm performance, all attempt to increase director participation. Similarly, proposals that the board adopt formal mechanisms for evaluating the CEO and other board members are designed to eliminate board passivity.

The goal of greater board independence is more difficult. Traditionally directors were classified either as employee directors or independent directors. Categorizing all non-employee directors as independent has proven problematic, however. Although most public corporations no longer staff their boards with mostly insiders, many non-employee directors have substantial professional or personal ties to the corporation or its CEO. These ties may interfere with a director's ability to monitor aggressively due to fears of retaliation by the CEO. Consequently, the perceived unwillingness of many non-employee directors to act independently has focused increased attention on the definition of director independence.

Recent efforts to improve board monitoring have included revising director qualification standards to encourage greater use of directors without relationships that could interfere with independent action. Stricter definitions of independence range from barring all business relationships between the director and the company to focusing on personal as well as business ties. Michigan, the one state thus far to enact a statutory definition of independent director, has one of the strictest standards. Under the Michigan statute, directors who have served on a firm's board for more than an aggregate of three years, as well as those with family or business relationships with the firm or firm employees, are not considered independent.

Corporations are also seeking to enhance director independence through the use of board committees.[1] Committees are particularly useful for effecting board monitoring because they allow independent directors to make decisions free from the risk of domination by insiders. Thus corporations are placing responsibility for reviewing executive compensation shareholder derivative suits in the hands of independent board committees. Finally, proposals such as separating the positions of CEO and Chairman of the Board or creating a lead director position attempt to direct greater control over board agenda and deliberations into the hands of outsiders.

The end product of these efforts is a board capable of exercising independent oversight. Restructuring board composition and procedures reduces both the presence of corporate

---

1. *The Sarbanes-Oxley Act 301 requires audit committees, requires that they be independent, and defines independence. See Ribstein's article in Chapter 4 and Mitchell's first article in this chapter. — Ed.*

insiders and their ability to influence board decision-making. This movement to take corporate boards seriously has identified monitoring management decisions as the primary governance role of the board of directors, in order to reduce the agency costs created by management decision-making.

II. The Competing Conception — The Managerial Board

Board function need not be viewed solely in terms of monitoring management. Traditionally, the board of directors was the ultimate managerial authority in the corporation. Early statutes expressly granted the board, not management, the power to run the corporation. Even at the time that Berle and Means wrote their classic expose of the separation of ownership and control, directors were defined as part of the management structure rather than shareholder representatives. This definition is significant because it recognizes the distinct managing function of the board.

The duties of the managing board include advising the CEO, participating in strategic planning, and reviewing the structure of significant corporate transactions. These functions were originally carried out by a board composed predominantly of corporate executives. Insider directors had both the intimate familiarity with the corporation and the time to devote to effective management of corporate affairs. Although no bright line separates the board's managing and monitoring functions, the obligations of the modern board continue to contain a management component.

The board's statutory obligations have typically emphasized the board's management responsibilities over its monitoring role. Corporation law statutes require board approval before a company issues stock or pays dividends, even when these transactions involve no element of management self-dealing. The board is responsible for reviewing and approving mergers and other changes to the corporate structure. Finally, the board is responsible for maintaining and revising the corporate charter.

Although, as described above, recent judicial decisions have characterized the board's role as that of monitor, courts also recognize the management role of the board. Accordingly, courts have consistently imposed the duties of managers on outside directors. This is most apparent in the merger context, in which the courts have required active participation by the board and have held independent directors accountable for their failure to make sufficient efforts to maximize shareholder value. Particularly when independent directors serve on special committees, courts appear to take for granted active participation extending well beyond the monitoring function.

The developments in modern corporate governance that emphasize greater director participation contemplate a board that manages as well as monitors. Commentators, activists, and even courts have begun to advocate greater director responsibility for firm performance. For example, reformers have demanded that the board of directors develop a long-term strategic plan for the corporation. Strategic planning is clearly a managing function. Choosing the corporation's executive officers and setting their compensation is also, at least in part, a management task.

Independence is not the only relevant qualification for an effective managing board. In order to formulate a strategic plan, determine whether a merger will provide long-term value, or select an executive capable of running the business, directors need a detailed familiarity with and appreciation for the nature of the corporation they oversee. Corporate insiders such as present and former employees are likely to be more familiar with the corporation than outsiders who attend twelve meetings a year. Directors in related industries, or those who have business relationships with the company, can serve as resources, contributing valuable expertise in addition to general management talent.

Corporate ties also serve to motivate directors to participate more actively. An insider, whose career and compensation depend on corporate performance, has a greater stake in the firm's success than an outsider, who receives $50,000 per year regardless of whether the company does well. Although Warren Buffet's holdings of Berkshire Hathaway stock are an extreme example, many corporate executives also have large equity holdings in their companies which give them an incentive to be attentive to stock price.

Recent reform efforts have attempted to address the rational apathy of outside directors by encouraging stock ownership requirements and/or equity-based compensation. Studies suggest, however, that few outside directors are motivated by financial rewards. Indeed, most outside directors are CEOs of other major corporations and receive sufficient compensation to render trivial their compensation for serving as outside directors. Moreover, with the increasing availability and sophistication of derivative instruments, a director need not retain the undesirable firm-specific risk associated with an equity position in a company on whose board he or she sits.

III. Empirical Analysis of Board Composition

As the foregoing analysis suggests, the choice between a managing and a monitoring board has clear implications for board structure. To determine optimal board structure and thereby evaluate current proposals to increase board independence, it would be helpful to ascertain the relative importance of managing and monitoring on profitability. Recent empirical work has examined board structure to determine whether increased director independence can improve firm performance. To date, the conclusions of these studies provide little support for the monitoring board. Although the studies provide some support for the proposition that independent boards are more effective monitors, evidence demonstrating a relationship between independence and profitability is in short supply....

A variety of empirical studies explore the relationship between board structure and monitoring. For example, Michael S. Weisbach finds that firms with outsider-dominated boards are more likely to remove a CEO when the firm is performing poorly than firms with insider-dominated boards. Hamid Mehran shows that firms with outsider-dominated boards pay executives with a higher percentage of equity-based compensation—a structure generally perceived to reduce agency costs and tie compensation more closely to firm performance. Laura Lin summarizes several studies that address the manner in which outside directors employ anti-takeover devices and that conclude that outsider-dominated boards are more likely to use anti-takeover devices to increase shareholder returns than to entrench management.[2]

... Despite these findings, studies have failed to establish an empirical link between board independence and profitability. In one of the most recent studies, Bhagat and Black conduct a large scale survey of board composition and firm performance over a ten year period and [conclude that "the conventional wisdom favoring highly independent boards

2. Michael S. Weisbach, *Outside Directors and CEO Turnover*, 20 J. FIN. ECON. 431, 433 (1988); Hamid Mehran, *Executive Compensation Structure, Ownership, and Firm Performance,*38 J. FIN. ECON. 163, 165–66 (1995); Laura Lin, *The Effectiveness of Outside Directors As a Corporate Governance Mechanism: Theories and Evidence*, 90 NW. U. L. REV. 898, 930–37 (1996).

lacks a solid empirical foundation."[3]] One study by Anup Agrawal and Charles Knoeber
even identifies a negative relationship between corporate performance and greater outsider
representation on the board.[4] Additionally, a few studies have found that insider
representation on corporate boards enhances the board's managerial function. April
Klein's study of board committees, for example, finds a correlation between the percentage
of insiders who serve on board productivity committees—defined to include strategy,
investment, or finance committees—and firm productivity.[5] Another study finds a positive
relationship between insider representation and corporate research and development
spending. Finally, the process of simply adding independent directors to a board to
enhance board independence may be counterproductive, as studies have identified a
negative correlation between profitability and board size.

There are several possible explanations for these findings. One possible explanation is
that board structure does not matter because corporate governance in general or board
structure, in particular is trivial. Alternatively, empirical studies may not be sufficiently
sensitive to capture the relevant differences in board structure.

Defining independence appropriately for purposes of these studies is particularly
difficult. Many studies rely on relatively superficial criteria in classifying directors as
independent—treating employee-directors as insiders, for example, and non-employees
as independent—rather than attempting the massive task of scrutinizing personal ties
and business relationships. Given the concern that employment status alone is an insufficient
indication of a director's capacity for independent action, the failure of studies to scrutinize
independence more carefully may explain their findings.

Classifying directors appropriately in terms of independence is also complicated by
the issue of whether the relevant criterion is independence from the company or
independence from the CEO. If the board is viewed as a check on the power of the CEO
in particular, instead of as a general management decisionmaker, then seemingly minor
personal ties between otherwise independent business people and the CEO may hamper
the board's effectiveness. The board at Disney, for example, drew criticism recently because
it included a number of directors who, although they lacked business relationships with
the company, had financial or personal ties to Disney's CEO, Michael Eisner. Director
independence from the CEO, as opposed to independence from the company, is
considerably more difficult to analyze because most existing reporting requirements do
not provide meaningful data on relationships with the CEO. Personal ties, in particular,
are virtually impossible to uncover with any assurance of accuracy.

An alternative possibility, consistent with the findings of studies linking board composition
to board function, is that board structure affects board effectiveness, but the relationship
between director independence and firm performance is more complex than a linear
correspondence. As the preceding analysis suggested, board function includes aspects of
managing as well as monitoring. Although greater independence may enhance the board's
ability to monitor, independence may also reduce the board's managerial effectiveness.
Accordingly, the modern move to increased board and director independence analyzed in
these studies may result in a cost/benefit trade-off that cannot be fully captured in a study
that measures overall performance. If both monitoring and managing are important

3. [Sanjai Bhagat and Bernard Black, *The Non-Correlation between Board Independence and Long-Term Firm Performance*, 27 J. CORP. L. 231 (2002).]

4. Anup Agrawal & Charles R. Knoeber, *Firm Performance and Mechanisms to Control Agency Problems Between Managers and Shareholders*, 31 J. FIN. & QUANT. ANAL. 377, 379 (1996).

5. *Firm Productivity and Board Committee Structure*, [41 J. L. & ECON. 275 (1998)].

components of board function, a study may fail to identify systematic gains from greater board independence because of the corresponding costs attributable to that independence.

IV. The Costs of the Monitoring Board

This Article suggests that the complexity of the relationship between board independence and firm performance may be explained by costs associated with the monitoring board, costs for which reform efforts fail adequately to account. When all other factors are equal, greater board independence enhances the board's ability to monitor; therefore increasing independence adds value. The problem, however, is that if corporate governance reform increases the relative importance of board monitoring, all other factors are not held equal.

As Professor Brudney warned more than ten years ago, there is a natural inconsistency between the board's monitoring and managing functions.[6] As a board participates actively in corporate decision-making, it sacrifices the capacity to monitor those decisions independently. A board that has negotiated the structure of a merger is unable to evaluate the transaction neutrally. The board that works closely to advise the CEO and other top executives sacrifices the distance necessary to assess executive performance critically. Moreover, to the extent that the board undertakes an affirmative role in strategic planning, the performance that the board evaluates is partially its own. Should a board judge a CEO deficient who adheres to the board's strategic plan for the corporation when that plan produces poor results?

Alternatively, a board that maintains a greater distance may risk inadequately understanding the company it is attempting to monitor. Although reform proposals stress the problem of board passivity and the failure to take effective corrective action, it is also dangerous for a board to engage in excessive or inappropriate efforts to override management. The policy reasons behind judicial adoption of the business judgment rule — including deference to the expertise of specialized management and providing management with the freedom to take risks — counsel against allowing the board to second guess management as well. Too much involvement by a monitoring board can squelch management initiative.

This problem is exacerbated by institutional investor pressure for less board passivity and greater accountability. An independent board may well be responsive to calls for change by the press or dissatisfied institutional investors. Investors' dissatisfaction with corporate performance is not necessarily an indication that board action is warranted, however, and investor pressure may cause a board inappropriately to replace a CEO or change corporate strategy.

Another cost associated with the monitoring board is the sacrifice of substantial value offered by the availability of the board of directors as a management resource. Through the mechanism of the board of directors, corporations are able to obtain the services of talented executives at an amazingly low price....

V. Rediscovering Board Function

The costs associated with strengthening the monitoring function of the board suggest that reformers and commentators need to take board function more seriously. This does

---

6. Victor Brudney, *The Independent Director — Heavenly City or Potemkin Village?*, 95 HARV. L. REV. 597 (1982).

not require rejection of the monitoring board. Many companies can benefit from increased monitoring. Corporations such as W.R. Grace, Morrison Knudsen, and Archer Daniels Midland reveal a frequent correlation between consistently under-performing companies and boards that lack sufficient independence to exercise meaningful oversight. These examples also demonstrate that increased board independence can have a meaningful impact in reducing executive excesses or improving profitability. Following the successful modernization of governance standards at W.R. Grace, including the installation of an activist independent board and a CEO unrelated to the Grace family, earnings and stock price at the company skyrocketed.

Current reform efforts frequently focus on cosmetic improvements to board structure rather than the relationship of that structure to firm performance. Reformers fail to recognize that managing and monitoring are distinct components of board function, thus ignoring the trade-off between monitoring and managing effectiveness. Consequently, reformers, particularly institutional investors, seek to require greater director independence and increased board monitoring in all corporations, regardless of the anticipated benefits of that monitoring or the cost imposed by sacrificing board management services.

Recent protests by institutional investors about the lack of independence of the Disney board of directors, despite Disney's phenomenal performance, illustrate this concern. Investors have claimed that ten members of the sixteen member board have financial ties to the company or the CEO that compromise their independence. Investors also criticize the board's approval of CEO Michael Eisner's compensation package even though experts acknowledge that Eisner can justifiably command the high pay based on his success in taking Disney's earnings and stock price to record highs.

The preceding analysis of the managing and monitoring aspects of board function does not purport to provide a complete normative vision of the role of the board of directors. This Article does, however, take the position that efforts to construct an ideal board are unwarranted. Ideal board structure, as explained above, depends on board function. Contrasting examples such as W.R. Grace with Berkshire Hathaway, suggests that companies can have very different needs from their boards of directors, and that a universal model board may be incapable of meeting those needs.

Firm-specific characteristics may cause some corporations to require more extensive monitoring from their boards of directors. In other firms, alternative monitoring mechanisms operate as substitutes for board monitoring. Ownership structure, for example, can provide an alternative monitoring device. Firms with a controlling stockholder appear to require less monitoring by directors, and creditors may substitute for monitoring by equity-holders. Institutional investors or banks may monitor management behavior directly. Similarly, the influence exerted by the markets in which the firm competes—the product, capital, management, and takeover markets—varies the need for board monitoring.

The nature of a corporation's business may also affect its need for board monitoring. Some industries present greater opportunities for management self-dealing. A firm with large free cash reserves, for example, or one in which direct market oversight of management decision-making is difficult, needs an enhanced internal monitoring structure. In contrast, firms in regulated industries may require less monitoring by virtue of the transactional controls mandated by regulation.

Some firm-specific characteristics call for greater use of the managing board. Immature or rapidly growing firms that face extensive strategic planning decisions waste a valuable resource if they do not utilize the business expertise of their board members in management decisions. Troubled firms, those in transition, or those with an inexperienced CEO may need to rely heavily upon the expertise of directors for managerial functions such as advising management. Engaging directors in firm management is efficient for firms that require managerial support, particularly in comparison to the cost of obtaining similar services through outside consultants.

Increased business complexity further demands that corporations involve directors in strategic planning and other management decisions. Boards that include directors with technical expertise, industry background, or experience in comparable business issues, provide a CEO with a team of experts. Their input can enhance corporate decision-making and prevent costly mistakes. Firms seeking to expand their international operations, for example, can benefit from the participation of outside directors with experience in the idiosyncrasies of foreign markets.

These factors illustrate how the relative importance of board managing and monitoring can vary from firm to firm. Board structure should be tailored to the needs of a particular firm. For a growth company in a developing field, faced with a variety of strategic decisions and an inexperienced CEO, the board's role as manager may be an essential component of firm success. That role may require board members with developed industry expertise, business relationships with the firm, or even insiders. Alternatively, for an established company with large cash reserves and a dispersed shareholder body, monitoring may be more important, and the board may need board members sufficiently independent of both personal and professional relationships with management to ask tough questions. Similarly, if institutions are able to target under-performing companies in which inside directors have not managed effectively, replacing these directors with outsiders may increase monitoring capability at little cost. Furthermore, a firm's needs may change, requiring corresponding adjustments to board structure.

The historical evolution of the board supports the conclusion that managing is an important component of board function and that, absent regulatory pressure, firms will use a governance structure compatible with this function. This intuition is supported by "race to the top" arguments about state corporation statutes. If managing functions were an insignificant aspect of modern board function, state statutes would presumably evolve away from requiring boards to manage and toward a greater emphasis on directors' monitoring obligations. This evolution has not occurred. The flexibility provided by state corporation law suggests that it may be efficient to allow corporations to tailor board structure to the functions most important to each individual corporation.

Donald C. Langevoort, *The Human Nature of Corporate Boards: Law, Norms, and the Unintended Consequences of Independence and Accountability**

Studies of corporate boards of directors often observe team-like traits. Invitations to the board are based heavily on matters like compatibility and "fit." The work of the board prizes consensus, not conflict. Absent some sort of crisis, outside members see their value

---

* Originally published in 89 Georgetown Law Journal 797 (2001). Reprinted with the permission of the publisher, Georgetown Law Journal, copyright 2001.

largely in terms of constructive advice, giving insiders the benefit of an expert external perspective on the company's uncertain world.

This portrait of cooperation is subject to two interpretations. The dominant view in corporate governance theory today is that heavy emphasis on teamwork and conflict-avoidance marks a board that has been captured by its CEO, an illusion of a governing body that acts largely as an elite private club with a rubber stamp. Much of the work in corporate governance over the last twenty-five years in academic circles and in the lobbying efforts of shareholder activists has been to extinguish this kind of board. Their goal is to replace it with the new-style "monitoring" board, where independence, skepticism, and a rigorous loyalty to shareholder interests are the dominating norms. By most accounts, this effort has had some noteworthy successes. In the United States, independent boards have become common for larger corporations—in fact, a majority of such companies have reduced insider presence to a small fraction—and these boards do seem to be more activist. Many other countries are mimicking this emphasis on director independence as they seek to make their systems of corporate governance more attractive to investors....

The other plausible interpretation of board cohesion is that it rests on a sound intuition: that the most productive boards are the ones where insiders and outsiders work cooperatively, not at odds with each other. If this is so, the monitoring model misses something important. To this end, some scholars, including Bhagat and Black,[7] have suggested that a positive case can be made for a judicious mix of inside and outside directors as the optimal board structure. Some independence is essential on boards, they agree, but there can be too much of a good thing....

Before beginning, one note of caution. My use of the term "independent" director is exceedingly subjective; that is, as suggested above, an independent director is one who actually takes the monitoring task for the benefit of the shareholders and/or other constituencies seriously. This leads to an important caveat. While we can document empirically the trend toward greater outsider presence on corporate boards, we cannot prove by demographic evidence alone that there is, in fact, greater independence. That can come only from a hard inside look at the people who make up any given board. There is ample anecdotal and indirect evidence of a power shift toward greater de facto independence, and this Article will assume that there is a positive aggregate correlation between the observed trend toward more outsiders and an inclination on their part to monitor more aggressively. For any given company, however, outsider domination may simply create a carefully calculated illusion of board independence.

I. The Debate over Board Composition

A. *The Standard Typology: The Three Well-Recognized Board Functions*

The literature on boards of directors identifies three basic functions that boards perform. The first is the monitoring role, which is itself divided into two parts. One is that board members select, compensate, and make implicit or explicit decisions regarding the retention of the chief executive officer (CEO) and (occasionally) other members of the senior management team. They also, albeit less frequently, review and cleanse conflict of interest transactions between senior managers and the company. The second part of the monitoring function involves overseeing the process of accounting, financial reporting, auditing, and disclosure—the mechanisms by which investors and other stakeholders are able to make

---

7. *See their article cited in note 2 above.—Ed.*

assessments about the performance of the company and its management. These two monitoring functions are the heart of what the agency cost model of the firm identifies as the central role for the board, necessary in light of managers' temptations toward shirking or more overt forms of self-interested behavior. In the absence of an effective monitoring board, we would expect a diminished willingness of investors to invest in companies under conditions of widely dispersed share ownership. This is precisely, according to many comparative corporate law scholars, what we observe in countries without independent boards of directors and the legal apparatus to assure a reasonably high level of accountability to shareholders. There we find a much higher incidence of controlling blockholders, whose own monitoring of company managers substitutes for independent boards and legal constraints.

The second board function, with a long tradition in the sociology of organizational behavior, is to assist the company in claiming and protecting its shares of external resources. Carefully chosen board members help make the company more legitimate in the eyes of key resource providers such as governments, customers, labor, and so on. Their connections can be of substantial use to the firm.

The third function, something of a catch-all, is the so-called service role. Boards do help to formulate corporate strategy, acting as a sounding board for the chief executive and senior management team and providing external input into the strategic process. This role is the one often cited by board members as their most valuable and satisfying one. On occasion—as in a significant merger or acquisition transaction—the board may actually take control of a strategic decision, displacing the management team as the primary actors in the drama.

But the service/strategic function is somewhat curious if seen as a completely distinct role from that of monitoring. Why should the provision of advice, perspective, and external expertise be a job for the board? After all, managers who sense the need for these inputs can readily hire consultants, investment bankers, lawyers, and others for exactly the same good outside judgment. Maybe the service function is better seen as just a different form of monitoring, to compensate for the cognitive *biases*—as opposed to the deliberate self-interest—of the managers and their organizational culture. A sizable body of research in cognitive psychology indicates that, left to their own, managers tend to develop biased constructions of the firm's strategic position. Moreover, they will be overconfident and heavily invested in those beliefs, and hence disinclined to seek out information that would suggest that they might be wrong. Only by giving formal power to a more objective group of outsiders (that is, making them directors) can the insiders be forced both to expose their biases and to take dissonant viewpoints seriously. The rules encouraging independent director control over particular decisions may also be a form of support for the monitoring function; those decisions that require independent director involvement are ones when management's self-interest and biases are most clearly at stake.

The resource-gathering function may or may not be subject to the same recharacterization. To be sure, management can hire lobbyists, public relations advisers, lawyers, and the like to increase the probability that key resource providers will look with favor on the firm. Why, then, would it be necessary for board members to play this role? There are two intuitive answers here. One is that competition for the best external resource providers is sufficiently intense that they can be attracted to the firm most readily by conferring status (placing the person at the top of the hierarchy with an elite set of others) as well as compensation. Gaining such status triggers a reciprocal sense of responsibility, which may be a useful motivator, by making the person more committed as the company's champion in the hyper-competitive market for resources and legitimacy. But another explanation is also possible. To the extent that, say, banking officials are pleased to find a given person on a financial institution's board, it is because they believe that the person will use her board power and influence in a particular way. In this sense, the director's reputation is put forward as a form of commitment that the company will be sensitive to the external interests in question. Of course, the commitment may not be sincere, and even if intended sincerely when the director is elected, there is no guarantee those interests will be respected by the full board later on. The hostage [i.e., the director's reputation] may be sacrificed. But at least potentially, the director's reputation is on the line, and the director can be expected to work vigorously to protect it....

B. *The Positive Case for a Balanced Board*

If we are searching for a case against board independence, we are now far off course. The foregoing would simply seem to strengthen the case for independent boards. Independence is essential to good monitoring, and as we have just seen, the service- and resource-oriented functions probably are best performed by outsiders as well. Yet we seldom observe complete domination by outsiders, and the empirical work noted at the outset of this Article suggests that such clear-cut domination may be costly in terms of profitability and productivity. The search, then, is for a good set of reasons why.

The most conventional justification for a critical mass of insiders is the idea that insiders bring a special and detailed knowledge of the company—its history, personnel, prospects, and the like—that is essential to at least the service work of the board. But for the same reasons suggested above, this is far from necessary. One can readily have insider participation in board deliberations on a regular and invited basis without conferring the attendance and voting rights that are the essence of director status. A fully independent board can make use of whatever inside talent it wants, including inviting full participation in deliberations, before moving (privately or not) to a vote.

Another claim in the literature carries more weight. Perhaps insiders bring a higher level of *motivation* to the task of monitoring and strategic decision-making. They are heavily invested in the corporation, whereas the typical outsider is not. Adding insiders may have a positive influence on the work habits of the board. While I do not doubt this explanation, it can readily be met with an alternative remedy that does not involve compromising board independence: creating more high-powered incentives for outside directors, largely through stock ownership requirements and compensation plans.

So the search for a justification for full insider status for a significant portion of the board should proceed further. Two additional lines of inquiry strike me as promising.

1. *The Stakeholder Argument Flipped: Senior and Middle Managers as Key Constituents, and the Problem of "Outsider Bias"*

In the last section, we considered the possibility that a segment of the board might be chosen as a way of holding those directors' reputations hostage *vis-à-vis* some constituency besides investors. The examples used there were labor-, community-, and government-oriented directors. The most obvious explanation for the value of adding insiders to the board simply extends this logic to the firm's managers as a constituency. After all, it is the company's management that makes the largest investment of firm-specific capital, throwing their lot both in terms of reputation and financial well-being to the company as a collective (or at least the performance of identifiable subgroups within). Naturally, they want some measure not only of influence but control, and the choice of a critical mass of directors whose jobs and reputations depend on taking due account of managerial interests would be one way of gaining such control. How much power senior management gets in this setting will vary over time as its bargaining power changes with good or bad firm performance.

While this could simply be characterized as a political bargain, there is probably a good bit more to it. Recall earlier that we said the presence of outsiders is important to counter the myopic biases of the senior managers. Conversely, we might ask whether the presence of insiders might serve as a counterweight to predictable *outsider* biases. Outsiders lack detailed knowledge of the firm's inner workings and are likely to use fairly heuristic forms of thought tied to readily observable data (for example, stock prices). If they are nonetheless overconfident in their inferences about the firm—a common human tendency, especially among the highly successful—they will not draw on insider expertise to the extent that would be prudent. Give them complete control and these egotistical group biases will be unchecked. Making them share control with managers, by contrast, forces them to reckon with the better informed, if sometimes unreflective, insight that management naturally has. The idea of a balanced board as a *symmetrical* debiasing mechanism has not yet been explored in the literature, but deserves consideration.

If some form of the control-bargain story is plausible, the interesting question becomes how we define the relevant managerial constituency. The initial temptation is to think solely in terms of the senior management team currently in place. They have an immense amount at stake, and—like coaches of professional sports teams who insist on control over player personnel decisions—we can readily understand their desire to insist on a place on the board, not just an expectation that they will be listened to.

However, my sense is that the key managerial constituency is not limited to the senior team. After all, the top managers have strong bargaining power, and can use explicit contracting (especially severance protection and performance-based compensation) as a trade-off against control. By contrast, as some scholars have begun to see, one of the underestimated elements in the study of corporate governance is the role of middle management. Many managerialist accounts locate the real day-to-day control over the firm not in its senior management team, but more diffusely among the many executives whose line responsibilities both carry out the often abstract strategy announced at the top and provide the information flow from which future top-level strategic decisions derive.

These individuals are the line and staff managers, who are almost always hired at-will, and inhabit an intensely political, hierarchical world of "teams" that support the firm's business activity. Just as important, they—especially the younger, more mobile ones—compete in a tournament of successive assignments of two or three-year duration, after which the successful, *vis-à-vis* their peers, move up to the next level and begin the competition anew. Although year-by-year compensation can be based somewhat on team performance, the more high-powered incentive here is the right to move on toward the place of delayed but exorbitant pecuniary, power, and status rewards: a spot on the senior management team.

I suspect that many inside directors put their reputations at stake implicitly to vouch for the value of the tournament to younger generations within the firm. Just as in the other stakeholder contexts, that does not mean the same thing as guarantee; these inside directors may lose a battle or sell out their reputations for some other form of gain. But the presence on the board of a critical mass of persons whose agenda includes "tournament protection" is meaningful, practically and symbolically, to the mobile segment of middle and upper-middle managers. Having such a block on the board is likely to give voice to a bias for promoting from within when possible. Moreover, the very presence of multiple "inside" seats gives insiders a special opportunity to perform visibly for other board members and to create social ties that enhance the possibility of selection as the "CEO in waiting."

This implicit directorial role, if powerful enough, has some important consequences. One obvious one is pressure toward both the growth and autonomy of the company. When another acquires their firm, the acquirer takes over control of the tournament and hence can be expected to bias it in favor of its own upwardly mobile middle managers. The decline in opportunities for acquiree managers, even if they do not actually lose their existing jobs, is painful. By contrast, firms that remain independent at least have a chance at preserving their tournament, and those that assume the preferred role of acquirer get to enlarge the size and quality of their own tournament. I have long suspected that a portion of what is often described as an unprofitable "acquisition bias" among American corporations is in fact driven by senior managers' desire—conscious or not—to benefit the talented subordinate executives in the firm. As they ascend, these middle managers face the inevitable risk of a slow-down in the pace of their careers as the pyramid narrows, unless the size of the pyramid increases.

As an aside, I also suspect that directors who see middle and upper-middle managers as their key constituency have a related agenda that conflicts with their shareholder protection role. If the key is encouraging talented middle managers to keep playing aggressively in the tournament, then it becomes essential to foster a sense of optimism about the firm's prospects. Organizational optimism promotes trust, delayed gratification, and a host of other cooperative forms of behavior by middle managers. In contrast, pessimism triggers selfish, last-period behaviors. Directors committed to the efficacy of the tournament can be expected to adopt a perspective that the firm has better control over its environment than some more dispassionate observers might consider reasonable. While this posture might occasionally be a manufactured form of corporate "spin," there is strong reason to suspect that those who passionately feel such optimism may be the most likely winners of their own tournaments and most credibly communicate it to others once they reach the top. In performing this role, they essentially disqualify themselves from acting as useful monitors of the candor of corporate disclosures.

By pushing expansion plans and eschewing candor, insiders may impose a cost on firm performance. But this is nothing new. All that the foregoing goes to show is that insider presence poses a *mix* of costs and benefits. Arguably, these might be managed best by having a significant insider presence on the board that is nonetheless balanced by a strong outsider presence.

2. Intra-group Dynamics, and the Role of Trust

a. Diversity Versus Collegiality

Boards of directors are small groups. As such, they are subject to the same social and psychological influences as small groups generally. To the extent that boards are expected to work at some task—be it monitoring, resource gathering, or service—it is worth considering what impact the structural balance on the board is likely to have on how well that task will be performed. In other words, we should relate structure to the effectiveness of the board as a work group.

Getting groups to make good decisions is always a challenge. Intuitively, the likelihood of multiple viewpoints and different sets of information should be a positive factor in the deliberative process, and sometimes it is. But a variety of forces conspire to blunt the quality of group decisions. The time-consuming and often unpleasant task of coming to consensus is aversive absent high-powered incentives to succeed—studies show that the more dissension there is in a group, the less committed members become to it. Highly "diverse" groups are negatively associated with good performance. As one article relating this to board behavior says, "When a board's meetings are dominated by prolonged debates between two individuals, cognitive conflict may actually inhibit the use of members' knowledge and skills."[8] In contrast, highly collegial groups create a better environment for productive work. Unfortunately, they are subject to different flaws: most famously, the notion of "groupthink."[9] That phrase, invented by Irving Janis, refers to the tendency of cohesive groups implicitly (indeed, subconsciously) to censor nonpreferred points of view and any information inconsistent with what is preferred. Such implicit censorship is a stress-reducing mechanism that preserves group solidarity. The key, then, seems to be moderation. The most productive boards are ones that have enough diversity to encourage the sharing of information and active consideration of alternatives, but enough collegiality to sustain mutual commitment and make consensus-reaching practicable within the tight time frames in which boards must operate.

That is a tricky balance to achieve and maintain. For a variety of reasons, the natural gravitational pull is away from diversity and toward collegiality. Boards self-select, often with strong input from the chief executive officer. The natural inclination, as we have seen, is to choose those who will "fit" well with existing members. The invitation itself creates a strong pressure: the norm of reciprocity, strongly felt in American culture, inclines people to support those who have favored them in the past. And once on the board, social ties build so that, as Cox and Munsinger demonstrated in their study of board structural bias, those members committed to the group gradually develop a sense of "in-group" bias that colors how they evaluate claims by others (such as derivative lawsuits brought by shareholders) that threaten one or more group members.[10] To this one might add another strong tendency: to be overcommitted to decisions once made, and resist evidence that a mistake has been made. A board that selects or decides to retain a chief executive officer is likely to see subsequent events in a light most favorable to the CEO, for otherwise, they bear some of the blame. One reason for having a sizable number of independent directors on the board is to create a critical mass of mutual support for resisting the centripetal pressures of cognitive conformity. But as we are about to see, too much independence also has some unexpected costs.

b. Enter the CEO

The dynamics of board behavior become more complicated when we consider the presence of the company's insiders. Consistent with almost universal practice, assume that the company's chief executive officer is a member of the board. Assume also that the board has a large number of outsiders. If, for any of the reasons just discussed, the CEO sees the other board members as weak monitors, then the chief executive can largely turn her attention to other priorities. This does not mean that the CEO will be free to shirk. Other incentives, such as her compensation package or market forces affecting the firm,

---

8. Daniel P. Forbes & Frances J. Milliken, *Cognition and Corporate Governance: Understanding Boards of Directors as Strategic Decision-Making Groups*, 24 ACAD. MGMT. REV. 489, 497 (1999).

9. *See* IRVING JANIS, VICTIMS OF GROUPTHINK(1982).

10. James D. Cox & Harry L. Munsinger, *Bias in the Boardroom: Psychological Foundations and Legal Implications of Corporate Cohesion*, 48 LAW & CONTEMP. PROBS. 83 (1985).

might still be strong constraints. But at least the chief executive's sense of "in-house" autonomy grows. On the other hand, to the extent that the CEO expects the outsiders to take their monitoring task seriously, there is a serious dilemma in terms of strategic interaction with the board. Such aggressive monitoring might come from external forces (a powerful shareholder block), some increase in the directors' own equity holdings, or an attitude shift. On the latter point, there is an interesting research study that suggests that directors who are CEOs of other companies become, for psychological reasons, more assertive externally after outside directors at their own companies seek internally to assert more control over them. Such assertiveness can then become contagious, creating a norm.

A strategic dilemma for the CEO comes in terms of communication of information to the board. The senior management team has a large stock of private information about how the company is being run, the day-to-day strategic decisions being made, and, especially, likely future performance. Although this stock of information is by no means perfect—senior management teams are themselves informationally at the mercy of their subordinates, with strategies for encouraging optimal information flow that will succeed only some of the time—it is far superior to what the board can elicit on its own, given the limits of time, attention, and staff.

In the face of serious monitoring, the CEO will be very careful in what she does or does not tell the outsiders. This is especially so if the CEO anticipates that the outsiders use very heuristic modes of evaluation, overweighting highly salient numbers and measures. The goal is to maximize the perceived reputation of the CEO and her team in the context of bargaining over compensation and tenure, rather than painting an accurate portrait of the firm's prospects. This does not mean deceit, necessarily, because the outsiders may eventually learn much about the historical performance of the firm by way of audited financial reports and other sources of data. If they feel misled, the CEO's reputation sinks and her job is in jeopardy. Still, if the chief executive senses that full disclosure will have a large enough adverse impact on her compensation package or prospects for continued employment, there is a strong last-period temptation to manipulate the information given to the board.

There are two kinds of problems that can arise within the boardroom from the information disparity between the CEO and the board. First, the CEO's incentive to distort information and engage in other influence activities makes the task of monitoring far more difficult, costly, and unpleasant. If the outsiders sense the CEO's temptation and respond with increased skepticism, the board implicitly subdivides into two separate coalitions, resulting in a growing, perhaps even exaggerated, level of mistrust between the two groups that further chills effective communication. As a consequence, the board becomes less productive as a unit.

This, in turn, severely limits the usefulness of the board's strategic advisory function. If the strategic function were unimportant, there would be little cause for concern. But as we have seen, the strategic function may be significant, especially as a form of corporate "debiasing." One prominent researcher who has done work on intraboard relationships, James Westphal, has made the case for a positive correlation between levels of trust between the CEO and the board and various measures of firm profitability.[11] His hypothesis is that, absent relatively strong social ties between the CEO and the board, the CEO will be reluctant to seek advice freely from board members who are her only real peers in terms of status and experience. Such advice seeking runs the risk that she will be viewed as weak

---

11. James Westphal, *Collaboration in the Boardroom: Behavioral and Performance Consequences of CEO-Board Social Ties*, 42 ACAD. MGMT. J. 7 (1999).

or dependent, and requires relinquishing the informational advantage that she has *vis-à-vis* the board. On the other hand, social ties create a more trusting environment in which such fears can better be put aside. Westphal's empirical study finds—contrary to the conventional view that board friendships are dangerous to shareholder interests because they compromise board independence—a statistically significant relationship between measures of social ties and subsequent financial performance. This is especially so if the CEO has other strong incentives (such as a high-powered, performance-based compensation package) to pursue the shareholders' interests. Indeed, he concludes that "board effectiveness and ultimately, firm performance, may be enhanced by close, trusting CEO-board relationships combined with moderate to high levels of CEO incentive alignment."

In sum, there are at least three potential costs to worry about once a board is divided between serious monitors and senior managers. The first is a decrease in the smooth functioning of the group as a result of identifying two separate factions with separate roles. As such diversity increases, productivity will slow. The second is a loss of valuable information by the outsiders that would otherwise be provided in a more trusting environment. The third potential cost is the increase in the time and attention the CEO devotes to influencing activities instead of more productive tasks. None of this implies that such diversity should necessarily be abandoned entirely to eliminate these costs: such an abandonment might come at an even higher cost in terms of lower quality monitoring and excessive cognitive conformity. But we now see why excessive independence can compromise board effectiveness to some degree. There is a distinct trade-off between aggressive monitoring and other tasks that board members perform.

3. Steps in the Direction of Compromise: The Search for Mediating Directors

One message from all this is that the ideal board structure may be firm-specific, or in some cases, industry-specific. As Westphal notes, if shareholders can have some confidence in the quality of the senior management team's incentive compensation packages, or in market constraints imposed by product competition, high leveraging, and the like, there may be a case for diminished independence, especially where the strategic and resource roles for the board are particularly valuable. On the other hand, there are industries where the case for independence is compelling. The best example here is the mutual fund industry, where conflicts of interest are commonplace and traditional checks on managerial overreaching, such as vigorous shareholder voting and hostile tender offers, do not exist. Conversely, the nature of fund managers' work is such that the strategic dimension of board deliberations, while hardly absent, is far less pressing.

This insight, however, is not helpful for resolving the dilemma faced by the typical corporation in finding the most desirable board structure (or those setting regulatory or self-regulatory guidelines for such a process). If over-independence is not necessarily the wise course, too little independence is even more dangerous. This suggests that we give more careful thought to the virtues of a board of directors that is made up of a roughly equal number of persons who are either managers themselves or have management's trust and those who will be diligent monitors.

At first glance, this seems like an unappealing solution. There is literature suggesting that parity is most likely to factionalize, if not paralyze, the board, creating an environment of contentiousness, frustration, and diminished satisfaction with board service. Neither group senses enough control, and too much time is spent negotiating divergent perspectives rather than working. This is one of the frequent criticisms of "constituency" boards of directors, such as the German system of codetermination by the so-called supervisory board. According to some scholars, the principal effect has been to diminish the efficacy and importance of the supervisory board as information flow and real political power move away from that location towards other more private and cohesive settings.

This danger is apt if we are in fact talking about two distinct factions. But there may be an implicit form of compromise that occurs in many well-functioning boards, whatever the formal insider/outsider mix may be. Whenever there are competing interests within a group, there needs to be one or more "mediators" whose main function is to bridge the chasm between them. This is not necessarily a formally identified person or persons, but rather those with the skills and desire to be shuttle diplomats and smooth out the difficult negotiations that arise between the monitors and the managers. To qualify, a person must have the trust of both sides and be formally beholden to neither. Most of the communications that will occur in this mediation will be private, taking place outside the formal board meeting itself. If successful, this should diminish the gamesmanship that the managers might otherwise feel inclined to display, and increase the confidence of the monitors that their perception of the company is firmly grounded.

Who best plays such a mediating role? One candidate is the CEO of another company, albeit one who has achieved success by virtue of his consensus-building skills rather than charismatic (often narcissistic) vision. Such persons may not, for reasons often emphasized in the literature, be the best external monitors. But they may well make up for this shortcoming as advisers to management and as emissaries to the true outsiders on the board. The same may be true of the so-called "gray" directors. Lawyers and investment bankers may derive, indirectly at least, a higher level of compensation from the company than other directors, creating a stronger connection to the senior management team than would be desirable for the perfect monitor. For that reason, they are often criticized as directors. But again, whatever their limits as monitors, their knowledge of, and ties to, the senior managers put them in a good position to earn trust inside. They can then build on this trust to work with the outsiders to reduce the level of cognitive diversity and allow the board to function more efficiently. If this is an important role for gray directors, we probably should be less critical.

There is, of course, a risk in seeing the board in terms of three implicit groups. It does seem to reduce the influence of the true monitors, at least in numbers, thereby threatening whatever confidence investors might draw from greater numerical superiority. Two responses are possible. First, this three-part structure could be accomplished while ensuring that a majority of the board are true monitors (although this might diminish the confidence of other constituents, like the middle and upper-middle managers). It is paramount that there be a critical mass for each of the groups, not necessarily parity. Alternatively, one could have approximate parity, but then give complete control of key *committees*—most notably the audit committee—to the real monitors. In this light, the recent SEC and self-regulatory organization rule revisions designed to enhance the independence of the audit committee, as opposed to the full board, make some sense.

C. Summary

We have now put forward two sets of less conventional reasons why firms with "mixed" boards may be more productive than super-independent ones. The first is that giving insiders a significant political presence on the board may help both debias the outsiders and bolster the perceived quality and stability of the internal promotion tournament in which the great bulk of the company's middle and upper middle managers compete. The second reason is that overloading the board with true monitors may create too stark a dilemma for the senior managers, forcing them to engage in impression management tactics at the expense of seeking needed advice and assistance in strategy formulation and resource gathering. The resulting diminution in collegiality makes the board less efficient as a working group, and less attractive as a body to which members (especially busy outsiders) develop long-term commitments.

When this is coupled with the more conventional accounts and the empirical data that suggests a danger to over-independence, we have a clear caution signal. To the extent that legal policy has sought to prompt increased independence—which in fact it has done only mildly—the message is that structural matters are probably better left to norms rather than law. Many commentators have concluded that changing norms have been a more important influence on the structural evolution of board dynamics than law anyway. This is a reflection of the increased power of the investor constituency and the vivid financial success of this investor-oriented model of corporate governance *vis-à-vis* foreign competitors over the last two decades. Norms have the virtue of greater flexibility than law. We could expect that as the case for balance becomes better grounded, the political pressure to balance the board might ease. The institutional investor community would simply become more sophisticated at identifying the nuances in board structures that create shareholder value. If all this sounds too harsh of an indictment of independence, that is certainly not what I intend. The growth in board independence has been an important and positive step in contemporary corporate governance. I am simply suggesting that the extralegal social forces that prompted it be left free to pull back as well, if that is what seems best for any given firm. Indeed, it strikes me that from a legal perspective, accepting the multiple functions of the board generally—and the costs as well as the benefits of independence—may if anything prompt courts to be *more* skeptical in making judgments about one context where independence truly counts: controlling conflict of interest situations. Once we see the board as a complex social unit that implicitly and variably balances monitoring efficacy against other functions, it is harder to sustain the fiction that formal indicia of independence can be equated with good monitoring incentives. If that leads to more rigorous judicial scrutiny of independence, thoroughness, and reasonableness in matters such as setting executive compensation, terminating derivative suits, erecting takeover defenses, and the like, so much the better....

Cheryl L. Wade, *Corporate Governance as Corporate Social Responsibility: Empathy and Race Discrimination*[*]

... In the 1990s, African-American employees filed class action litigation against several large companies. Most notably, Texaco and Coca-Cola paid $176.1 and $192.5 million, respectively, to settle racial discrimination litigation. Also part of the settlement was an agreement by both companies to change the way they treated employees of color. In this Essay, I note that the changes agreed to by Texaco and Coca-Cola were merely steps that should have been taken long before the racial discrimination litigation was filed. Both companies agreed to establish systems that would adequately monitor and respond to discrimination allegations. In other words, the companies agreed to take the kind of action that should have been taken all along to satisfy the fiduciary duty of care that

[*] Originally published in 76 TULANE LAW REVIEW 1461–1482 (2002). Reprinted with the permission of the Tulane Law Review Association, which holds the copyright.

directors and managers owe to ensure that shareholder profits are not reduced as a result of noncompliance with applicable law.

In this Essay, I consider the reasons why racial discrimination persists in large publicly held companies, in spite of antidiscrimination law. I see the problem as a corporate governance issue. I explore the role of empathy in corporate governance, concluding that lack of empathy for employees of color, and too much empathy for privileged groups, precludes adequate monitoring and investigation of racial discrimination in the workplace. This results in litigation and large settlements, or excessive arbitration, and the attendant negative publicity, all of which are antithetical to shareholder wealth maximization. The empathy imbalance is a matter of internal corporate social irresponsibility, which precludes the potentially positive effect that workplace racial integration could have on American society....

Because they employ, purchase from, and provide goods and services to so many, it makes sense to consider the impact of large publicly held companies on society. Not only do these companies affect the lives of their employees, suppliers, and consumers, they have huge import for the communities in which they do business, as well as the entire nation. Because the workplace is where racial groups are most likely to come together, corporate governance of the workplace has some modest potential for favorably influencing the nation's race relations. The discourse on race, however, within large corporations among corporate officers and directors is superficial or nonexistent. If corporate managers, directors, employees, and shareholders were to elevate the workplace and boardroom discussions of race beyond the superficial discussions that now occur, the societal discourse on race may also improve.

The initial reaction of Texaco's corporate managers to employees' complaints of racial discrimination typifies the inadequacy of the discourse on race in the corporate context. When African-American employees at Texaco met with the vice president in charge of human resources to discuss racial discrimination at Texaco, they suggested that the company take some of the steps taken by other businesses to avoid discriminatory employment practices. Texaco's vice president exploded. "He slammed his hand on the table ... and bellowed: "You people must have lost your minds! I think you're a bunch of militants! I've been here for thirty-three years and I can tell you right now that Texaco will not even consider any of these crazy proposals! ... The next thing you know we'll have Black Panthers running down the halls or ... in front of the building!" The "crazy" proposals included suggestions such as "basing managers' bonuses in part on how well they implemented diversity, or starting a black employees association, or beefing up recruiting from black colleges."[12]

The twenty-first-century workplace has undergone dramatic changes, but at the same time, very little has changed with respect to race discrimination in the workplace. Antidiscrimination law has not remedied the racially toxic corporate cultures of many large companies. Because Title VII of the 1964 Civil Rights Act has no "generalized code of workplace civility," it does little to ameliorate workplace racial harassment. For this reason, a new approach to corporate governance as it relates to race discrimination is required. In order for the opportunity for racial interaction in the workplace to have any positive effect on societal race reality, socially responsible corporate governance is necessary.

Continued race discrimination and harassment within large companies impose huge social costs because of the significant societal impact of these companies. Continued

---

12. Bari-Ellen Roberts & Jack E. White, Roberts v. Texaco 146–48 (1998).

workplace discrimination is an obvious issue of corporate social irresponsibility. This is a corporate governance issue also because racism imposes huge costs on shareholders, diminishing, instead of maximizing, shareholder wealth.

In this Essay, I distinguish the typical discussion of corporate social responsibility that looks to businesses to achieve social good even when not required by law, from corporate responsibility that is required under the law. Corporate charitable donations fall under the former category. Under the latter, I place diligent and adequate corporate compliance with the law. I consider compliance with the laws that prohibit discrimination a matter of corporate social responsibility. It can be accomplished only to the extent that corporate boards and managers scrupulously adhere to already existing corporate governance principles. In other words, better compliance with antidiscrimination law may be ensured through the observance of corporate governance principles, specifically by satisfying the fiduciary duty of care that officers and directors owe shareholders. Corporate officers and directors should diligently monitor corporate compliance with antidiscrimination law....

I. Race and the Corporate Culture's Impact on Society

Commentators have acknowledged the critical importance of workplace realities on society in general. Professor Vicki Schultz describes the workplace as "one of the few arenas in which diverse groups of citizens can come together and develop respect for each other due to shared experience."[13] Professor Cynthia L. Estlund describes the workplace as "an important component of civil society" because "it has the capacity to serve, and to some degree does serve, as a vanguard institution in the movement for greater equality and integration on the basis of race and ethnicity in the society as a whole." For Estlund, the importance of the workplace in fostering improved race relations derives from the fact that, because we live in a racially segregated society, the workplace is one of the few opportunities for interaction among disparate racial groups. Even though Estlund concedes that racial minorities continue to endure discriminatory hiring and promotion decisions, she remains optimistic about the ability of the law to change workplace racial reality and that "those changes [may] have a significant impact on peoples' lives and have ripple effects outside the workplace."[14]

Estlund admits to being "optimistic, if not heroic" in assuming that workplace interaction among various racial groups will have positive influences on race relations in American society. Considering the racial segregation that continues to exist within the workplace, Estlund's assumptions are beyond optimistic, or even heroic. They may be impossible. Many large companies are reminiscent of the plantation life of the Old South, where enslaved Africans worked the fields and their overseers, the whites who enslaved them, went about the business of running the plantation. In today's companies, there are few or no people of color on boards or among the ranks of senior executives. The overwhelming majority of corporate employees of color continue to do the "field work" of middle management in mail rooms, or toil among the ranks of workers providing janitorial or secretarial services, or performing other menial tasks.

The workplace's potential for altering social discrimination exists only to the extent that companies move beyond racial discrimination and tokenism. As long as corporate

---

13. Vicki Schultz, *Life's Work*, 100 Colum. L. Rev. 1881, 1885 (2000).
14. Cynthia L. Estlund, *The Changing Workplace as a Locus of Integration in a Diverse Society*, 2000 Colum. Bus. Rev. 331, 332.

racial hierarchies persist, and as long as boards and managers ignore them, societal racism will be entrenched. There is clear evidence that racially toxic corporate cultures abound. In April 1999, Coca-Cola's African-American employees alleged discrimination in "pay, promotion, and job-performance evaluations" and received a $192.5 million settlement months after the suit was filed. In the 1990s, other huge settlements were paid by large companies to victims of racial discrimination. Texaco settled a racial discrimination class action in 1997 for $176.1 million. Shoney's settled in 1993 for $132 million; Winn-Dixie Stores settled in 1999 for approximately $28.1 million; and CSX Transportation settled in 1999 for $25 million. Denny's Restaurants, AT&T Corp., and Boeing Co. have also paid significant amounts to settle racial discrimination litigation in recent years. The class actions filed against Texaco and Coca-Cola included allegations of racial harassment. Companies have also paid significant amounts to individual employees for racial harassment. For example, one African American was awarded $4 million in a jury trial after having been "subjected to a hangman's noose, ransacking of his locker and racial slurs."

II. The Role of Empathy in Corporate Governance Processes

Even before companies such as Texaco and Coca-Cola paid huge amounts to settle racial discrimination suits, Professor Charles D. Watts, Jr. linked "unique aspects of [American] society" to the persisting and long-standing problem of "racial discrimination in employment." Watts observed that some economists conclude "that the market will, in fact, eliminate racial discrimination in the long run" because it is not profitable. "Have we not had a long run experience with racial discrimination? When will this lengthy intermediate period come to an end?"[15]....

While some academic scholars have considered the intractability of racism in large publicly held companies, books on corporate governance are silent on race issues. These are the books most likely to be consulted by corporate boards and managers, because they offer practical consideration of appropriate directorial and managerial behavior. The books cover good times and times of crisis, but they do not offer advice about how to avoid debacles such as those that occurred at Texaco, Coca-Cola, and other companies, which culminated in huge financial settlements paid to racial discrimination victims. Considering the evidence of continued racial discrimination and harassment, it seems that corporate officers and directors are not thinking or talking about race and racism within their corporations other than in the most superficial ways.

Professor Ian F. Haney Lopez has written about the pervasive importance of race in all areas of the law. "Race suffuses all bodies of law ... even 'the purest of corporate law questions'.... No body of law exists untainted by the powerful astringent of race in our society." Lopez emphasizes the structural nature of racism in the United States and argues against the predominant belief that racism is a disease that primarily affects individuals. He describes the factual reality of institutional racism, writing that the failure to acknowledge racism in America's institutions "not only fails to challenge but reinforces a crucial cultural and political myth, that every element in U.S. society is committed to equality and social justice for racial minorities."[16]

---

15. Charles D. Watts, Jr., *In Critique of a Reductivist Conception and Examination of "The Just Organization,"* 50 WASH. & LEE L. REV. 1515, 1518–21 (1993).

16. Ian F. Haney Lopez, *The Social Construction of Race: Some Observations on Illusion, Fabrication, and Choice,* 29 HARV. C.R.-C.L. L. REV. 1, 4, 24 (1994).

If race "suffuses all bodies of law," why aren't corporate lawyers, managers, officers, and those who advise them writing and talking more about race? Why aren't boards and officers creating and implementing the types of effective monitoring systems that may more capably confront workplace racism until they are forced to do so after racial discrimination litigation is filed? What can convince corporate directors and managers to live up to the fiduciary duty of care they owe shareholders to monitor compliance with antidiscrimination law in a way that would better achieve internal corporate social responsibility that may have external or societal impact? My initial consideration of these questions led me to an intuitive conclusion that empathy may be a prerequisite for real corporate social responsibility.

Empathy, as used in this Essay, is defined as the "identification with and understanding of another's situation, feelings, and motives." "Empathy ... is more than an intellectual predisposition, or belief; it is a readiness to be engaged in the experience of others." "Empathy has been variously described as a ... process, ... a mode of observation, and an information-gathering activity." Initially, I thought that understanding the situation in which many people of color find themselves in companies with racially toxic cultures, would lead to effective monitoring of discrimination. I was drawn to definitions of empathy that described it as a "process" and an "information-gathering activity" because satisfaction of the duty of care is itself a process of information gathering. Perhaps, I thought, empathy for people of color would inspire adequate monitoring of corporate compliance with antidiscrimination law, and such monitoring would foster further understanding of the discrimination faced by people of color. In other words, empathy may inspire satisfaction of the duty to monitor, and the monitoring may foster further empathy.

The role that empathic consideration plays in legal decision making has been examined in a variety of contexts. Professor Estlund has explored the possibility of empathy in the workplace, writing, "Through informal social interactions, employees often learn about each others' lives and develop feelings of mutual understanding ... [and] empathy." Even while acknowledging the inevitability of empathy, or its potential value in legal decision making, however, scholars have recognized empathy's shortcomings and limitations.

First, one component of empathy is finding similarities with the object of empathic understanding, or analogizing the other's situation to that of the one who empathizes. The comparisons that inspire empathy, however, obscure important distinctions and reduce the possibility for true understanding of another's circumstances. Second, some scholars conclude that "we think we—and others—have much more empathy for the downtrodden than we, in fact, do" and that this kind of "false empathy is worse than indifference.... It encourages the possessor to believe he is beyond reproach." Third, "unequal power arrangements can block any instinct toward empathy." Fourth, a single decision or situation may give rise to competing claims for empathy. In a criminal case, for example, one can empathize with the victim or the defendant, depending on the circumstances that gave rise to the defendant's conduct. Finally, "empathy does not guarantee that our emotions will lead us to act in an ethical or just way."

Understanding empathy's shortcomings may begin to explain the entrenchment of racism in the workplaces of large publicly held corporations. White managers and directors, successful themselves, are not likely to understand the impediments to success faced by many people of color. Much of the racial discrimination that occurs in the workplace is unconscious. The privileges enjoyed by whites in the workplace remain unnoticed by the beneficiaries, masked by discussions of meritocracy. Any unfairness faced by a white male in the workplace may be used by him in an attempt to understand the unfair treatment of people of color. The comparison between his own situation to that of minority employees will produce, at best, a superficial understanding of racial inequities faced by employees of color. His attempt to understand, to empathize, will place him beyond reproach, leaving him unable to recognize any unconscious bias in employment decision making.

Inequities in power arrangements within a company may also preclude white managers from empathizing with employees of color. Moreover, the manager must grapple with several competing claims for empathy. He is required to "empathize" with shareholders, and must also attempt, in some instances, an understanding of situations faced by nonshareholder constituencies. Finally, even if managers and directors find a way to understand workplace racial realities adequately, they may not be moved to make changes.

Because empathic understanding of people who are different from the one who empathizes is difficult, or perhaps impossible, as some have argued, taking action to enhance empathy for people of color is not the solution for persistent workplace racial inequities. Empathy is not the solution, empathy is the problem. "Empathetic feelings toward members of one's own racial group ... explain indifference or even hostility toward members of other racial groups." Empathy for others who are similarly situated is not difficult, and in the workplace, this may mean that corporate managers and directors, almost all of whom are white and male, will easily empathize with corporate constituents who are most like them.

Enhancing empathy for people of color is not a viable resolution of the persistent problem of racial discrimination. Ubiquitous empathic understanding on the part of corporate boards and managers for other white males, however, may begin to explain why racism persists in large companies. White men are hired more easily, promoted more frequently, and paid more than people of color and women because they are most similar to the white men who make these corporate decisions. Senior executives and directors may fail to investigate and monitor compliance with antidiscrimination law because they empathize with the white men who are hired, promoted, and paid more. At the same time, they may not be able to empathize with their employees of color.

A. *Barriers to Empathic Consideration for Employees of Color*

An examination of the relationship between the African-American community and the segment of society to which an overwhelming majority of corporate managers belong (most corporate directors and managers are white and male) illustrates the barriers that preclude empathic consideration for racial minorities. While the observations I make in this Essay apply to all racial minorities affected by corporate activity, I use the social realities relating to African Americans as a vivid example of empathic barriers. One force that helped create these barriers to empathy is the alarming fact that people of African descent are the subjects of almost daily news items relating to criminal activity. While it is indisputable that African Americans engage in criminal activity, these frequent portrayals of African-American criminality, coupled with the social reality of racial isolation and de facto segregation, may make it difficult for some white Americans and, most relevant to the thesis in this Essay, corporate managers, to empathize with African-American victims of racial discrimination....

Negative societal messages about African Americans abound. These messages are internalized by many, and this affects even the professional reputation of African Americans. The fact that most negative beliefs about African Americans are held unconsciously does not lessen the harm to the collective reputation of Americans of African descent. African Americans are implicitly and explicitly stereotyped as criminal and unintelligent. These are characteristics that are obviously antithetical to corporate success, and, to the extent such stereotypes are unconsciously held by corporate managers, empathy for people of color who confront discriminatory employment practices is impossible.

The best example of the positive value of empathy for victims of discrimination is found by considering the woman's place in corporate life. This nation's legal and social discourse on sexual discrimination and harassment has been far more extensive and meaningful than that which has taken place regarding racial discrimination. Formal discussions of, and prohibitions against, racial discrimination lack the detail and clarity found in legal and corporate prohibitions against sexual harassment and discrimination. For example, in a treatise on the law relating to civil rights and employment discrimination, there is a section entitled "Sexual and Racial Harassment," describing problems in the workplace. Only a small part of the extensive discussion is devoted to racial discrimination. Almost every one of the cases cited relates to sexual discrimination or harassment. Only one of the cited cases clearly covers the problem of racial discrimination. Moreover, the Equal Employment Opportunity Commission (EEOC) has published several policy guides relating to the problem of sexual harassment in the workplace. I found no EEOC-published guidance on the problem of racial discrimination.

Corporate officers, directors, legislators, administrators, and even judges may more easily understand, and be able to empathize with, women professionals who allege gender discrimination. The stories told by women who are victims of discrimination may be similar to the stories of unfair treatment that these jurists and executives, most of whom are white, have heard told by their wives, sisters, daughters, and even mothers. Generally, jurists and corporate managers who are white will have fewer opportunities to hear personal accounts of discrimination told by people of color because they have no familial or other close personal relationship with people of color. Empathy for racial minorities, with whom there is no close personal relationship, is less likely. This may explain why sexual harassment policies in particular, and sexual discrimination law in general, are far more developed than policies and law relating to racial discrimination and harassment.

B. Empathy: Women of Color in Corporate America

All of the accounts of the Texaco debacle ignore the significance of the fact that the litigation was filed initially by an African-American woman who remained the named plaintiff in the class action. Nothing is said about the discrimination that she and other women suffered because they were women of color. Even in a book authored by [Bari-Ellen Roberts, lead plaintiff in the discrimination suit against Texaco,] giving her personal account of Texaco's toxic racial culture, nothing is said about differences in the way women of color were treated when compared to minority men. For example, one pregnant woman was the target of a degrading "joke" that was attributed to the racism of the "joker," rather than his sexism, even though the "joke" was about her pregnancy.

In the immediately preceding Part, I hypothesized that corporate directors and managers are more likely to empathize with white women who are victims of discrimination than with minority victims of discrimination. Close personal relationships with white women who share personal narratives of discrimination inspire corporate managers to develop policies against sexual harassment and discrimination. Corporate policies prohibiting racial discrimination are not as clearly stated, and conduct that breaches these policies is infrequently monitored. Because close personal relationships between corporate managers, most of whom are white and male, and people of color are more rare than their relationships with white women, directorates and management respond more effectively to sexual discrimination and harassment than to racial discrimination allegations. I compare empathic understanding of women and racial minorities, not to compare or compete about who has suffered the most, but simply to make an observation about the way companies are governed and the role that empathy plays in their governance.

It is even more unlikely that corporate decision makers would have the kinds of personal relationships that would foster empathy with women of color. Stereotypes and personal experience with women of African descent, in particular, lead to conceptions of women of color that are completely antithetical to the paradigm of corporate success. The personal relationships with women of color, which are experienced by most who belong to the class of persons to which corporate officers and directors belong, revolve around the provision of childcare, elder care, or domestic work.

C. Empathic Approaches in Corporate Governance

The power and importance of empathic understanding is demonstrated by the observation that empathy may be the basis of some fundamental corporate governance principles. Certain corporate governance rules may have emerged because of the role empathy plays in the processes of corporate decision making. I offer several examples.

First, the Delaware Supreme Court explicitly acknowledged the role empathy plays when special committees of the board of directors are formed in order to determine whether derivative litigation alleging directorial or managerial wrongdoing that harmed the corporation should go forward.[17] The Court held that substantive review of a special litigation committee decision to prevent such litigation is necessary, because committee members will empathize with the directors or officers whose conduct is challenged. "We must be mindful that directors are passing judgment on fellow directors in the same corporation.... The question naturally arises whether a 'there but for the grace of God go I' empathy might not play a role." Professor Donald Langevoort describes what I have labeled empathy as an "'in-group' bias that colors how [directors] evaluate claims by others (such as derivative lawsuits brought by shareholders) that threaten one or more group members."[18] Second, empathy may preclude board members, even outside directors who are not employed by the company, from adequately monitoring the conduct of chief executives because they too are senior officers.

Third, judicial justifications of the business judgment rule tacitly describe empathic understanding of the difficulties of corporate decision making. Courts explain that they defer to the business decisions made by corporate boards under the business judgment rule, because they cannot reproduce the exigencies of boardroom decision making in the courtroom. This illustrates unexpressed empathy for corporate officers and directors. Moreover, the very basis for the creation of the business judgment rule is to resolve the problem in large publicly held companies that those who own the company, the shareholders, are not the ones who manage the company. In other words, the business judgment rule is necessary because directors and managers cannot be expected to empathize sufficiently with shareholders.

Another example of corporate governance rules implicitly aimed at inspiring empathy is found in the Securities Act of 1933. [Section 11 of the Act (15 U.S.C. 77k)] imposes liability for materially misleading statements or omissions in registration statements. The section also provides what is called the "due diligence" defense, which is available to any defendant

---

17. *See* Zapata Corp. v. Maldonado, 430 A.2d 779, 786–87, 789 (Del. 1981).
18. *See Langevoort's article in this chapter. —Ed.*

who conducted a reasonable investigation about the truthfulness of registration statement materials. The Act defines reasonable investigation as requiring a level of reasonableness that "a prudent man" would apply "in the management of his own property." This standard inspires empathy for shareholders, or potential shareholders, who may rely on a registration statement by requiring defendants to manage shareholders' affairs in the same way they would manage their own.

Even the most mundane corporate governance issues implicitly recognize the importance of empathy, or aligning the interests of the decision maker with the interests of the group for whom decisions are made, as a way to resolve the separation of ownership and control problem. For example, some companies provide corporate managers with stock options. This aligns the manager's personal wealth with that of shareholders. It fosters a manager's identification with the company....

III. Conclusion

Professor Lawrence E. Mitchell writes:

> Corporations will be unlikely to achieve any level of social responsibility as long as their purposes and goals are narrowly limited by the state. In other words, the law requiring a limited focus on profit maximization together with the law directing management's concerns solely to the corporation's stockholders leads management to behave much like the young child under adult constraint — following rules simply because they are given as rules, with no concern or feeling of responsibility for the consequences of their actions on others.[19]

In this Essay, I suggest another reason for the corporate social irresponsibility of large publicly held companies that continue to discriminate against employees, suppliers, and consumers of color—lack of empathy for victims of racial discrimination, and too much empathy for privileged whites. This empathy imbalance precludes directorial and managerial satisfaction of the fiduciary duty of care owed shareholders. The imbalance prevents boards and managers from establishing or implementing adequate monitoring and investigation systems aimed at racist employment practices that would prevent some of the significant financial losses suffered recently by companies that have settled discrimination litigation.

At least in the context of racial discrimination, I don't see the shareholder primacy model as unduly constraining and preclusive of corporate responsibility. The best way to maximize shareholder wealth is to avoid arbitration and litigation of racial discrimination allegations that waste corporate resources in time and money paid to settle claims. Shareholder wealth is also maximized by avoiding negative publicity that may harm shareholder value. Empathic understanding of the discrimination victim's situation is unlikely to inspire a change in the way companies are managed. Adherence to shareholder wealth maximization principles, however, may cause managers and boards to be more diligent about their duties to monitor and investigate race discrimination allegations.

White males may be hired and promoted more frequently and paid more than employees of color because the corporate managers who make these decisions, the overwhelming majority of whom are white and male, empathize with them. My goal in this Essay is not to make a futile attempt to inspire more empathy for employees of color and less empathy

---

19. Lawrence E. Mitchell, *Cooperation and Constraint in the Modern Corporation: An Inquiry into the Causes of Corporate Immorality*, 73 Tex. L. Rev. 477, 480 (1995).

for white males. My objective is to encourage corporate managers and directors and the attorneys who advise them to consider the role that empathy plays in corporate governance processes. These empathic feelings are subtle. It is even more likely that this kind of empathic sentiment is unconscious, and therefore almost undetectable and indestructible. The modest goal of this Essay is to offer the insight that too much empathy for white males, and too little empathy for employees of color may prevent corporate officers and directors from adequately investigating and monitoring allegations of racial discrimination. It is my hope that this insight will encourage a more effective satisfaction of the directorial and managerial duty of care as it relates to ensuring compliance with antidiscrimination law.

Thomas W. Joo, *Proxy Access and Director Elections*[*]

After a great deal of fanfare about proxy reform and shareholder empowerment, the federal proxy rules were amended in 2007 to limit shareholder power to nominate directors through the proxy process. The story of the amendment illustrates the roles of corporations' internal rules, institutional investor activism, SEC interpretations, no-action letters, and rulemaking, and politics in corporate governance.

In large corporations, most shareholders vote through the proxy process. This system resembles voting by absentee ballot in political elections but with some significant differences. Before elections take place, the incumbent corporate board produces and mails to shareholders a package including the annual report, the board's partisan description of the offices and issues to be voted upon, and a proxy card. The vast majority of shareholders will not personally attend the shareholder meeting at which the election will take place. By providing a shareholder with a proxy card, the board asks that a shareholder give the board the power to cast her votes. Critically for present purposes, this includes a request for permission to vote in favor of the board's nominees for board seats.

Thus, contacting shareholders to solicit their proxies is crucial to success in a corporate election. Shareholders are often scattered around the world. The board of directors has easy access to the corporation's lists of shareholder names and addresses and uses the corporation's funds to print and send the official corporate proxy mailing. SEC rules give shareholders some opportunity to air their concerns throughout the corporate proxy mailing process. Under SEC Rule 14a-8, the corporation must include certain types of shareholder proposals in its proxy mailings. This rule significantly reduces shareholders' costs in communicating with other shareholders and thus facilitates putting policy proposals to a shareholder vote.

Unfortunately for activist shareholders, Rule 14a-8 is qualified with significant limitations on the shareholders' right to proxy access. The corporation may invoke one or more of those limitations as grounds to exclude a proposal from the corporate proxy. Some of these limitations are formal and procedural. For example, at the time she submits a proposal, a shareholder must have owned at least $2000 worth of voting stock in the corporation, or 1% of the voting stock, for at least one year. Other limitations go to the

---

    * Portions of this selection were originally published in different form as part of *A Trip Through the Maze of "Corporate Democracy": Shareholder Voice and Management Composition,* in 77 St. John's Law Review 735 (2003). This revised version reflects recent changes in the law. Copyright 2003, 2009 Thomas W. Joo.

substance of the proposal. For example, 14a-8(i)(1) states that a corporation may exclude a proposal that "is not a proper subject for action by shareholders" under the laws of the state of incorporation. This rule underscores the fact that, despite the federal rule of shareholder proxy access, state laws limit shareholders' powers to set corporate policy. Under state law, the directors, not the shareholders, run the corporation. The SEC has inserted a note, after the text of the rule, warning that shareholder proposals that intend to have a binding effect on the corporation may be improper under state law and further recommends that shareholders should phrase their proposals as "recommendations or suggestions." Thus, in order to remove any doubt as to whether the subject of a proposal is proper, shareholder proposals submitted to a vote usually take this precatory form. (Even assuming such a non-binding proposal were placed on the proxy and approved by shareholders, directors would be legally entitled to ignore it, although they might feel some market pressure to respond.) Shareholders may propose binding changes to the bylaws, as long as they concern "proper subjects" and do not fall under any other 14a-8 exclusions.

If shareholders nominate alternative candidates for election to the board, Rule 14a-8(i)(8) allows the corporation to exclude those nominations from the corporation's proxy mailing. (As will be explained below, a change to this rule was under consideration when this book went to press in 2009.) Thus insurgent shareholders can only challenge incumbent directors and their nominees through difficult and costly independent proxy campaigns. Giving shareholders access to the proxy to make nominations of director candidates would increase activist shareholders' ability to put dissident candidates before the shareholders.

Since 1976, SEC Rule 14a-8(i)(8) has allowed a company to exclude from its proxy any shareholder proposal that "relates to a nomination or an election for membership on the company's board of directors or analogous governing body." Despite the broad language of this Rule, the SEC originally interpreted this "Election Exclusion" to allow exclusion of proposals relating to the election of a specific director (such as a nomination), but not the exclusion of proposals relating to election procedures. Around 1990, however, the SEC began to allow exclusion of procedural proposals if they would tend to result in "contested elections," such as proposals to amend a company's bylaws to require the inclusion of shareholder nominations on the company proxy.

In October 2003, the SEC proposed amendments to the proxy rules that would have required a corporation to list shareholder nominees in the corporate proxy materials (the "Proxy Access Requirement"), subject to a number of significant conditions.[20] Most significantly, the amendment would have applied only to nominations made by a shareholder or group of shareholders holding 5% or more of the company's stock. Shareholder activists and academics tended to loudly support the plan, while industry was equally vociferous in its opposition. The SEC eventually withdrew the proposed Proxy Access Requirement without action. SEC Chair William Donaldson was soon removed as SEC Chair, a development many observers attributed to his support of the Proxy Access Requirement.

Despite the death of the Proxy Access Requirement proposal, activist shareholders continued to pursue proxy access. The American Federation of State, County and Municipal Employees (AFSCME) Pension Plan (the "Pension Plan") had begun a shareholder-proposal campaign in 2002. In 2005, it proposed that the bylaws of American International

---

20. *Proposed Rule: Security Holder Nominations*, SEC Release No. 34-48626, 68 Fed. Reg. 60783 (Oct. 23, 2003).

Group, Inc. (AIG) be amended to require the corporation's proxies to include the names of shareholder-nominated director candidates under certain circumstances. AIG planned to exclude the proposal under the "contested election" interpretation of the Election Exclusion. AFSCME sued to prevent the exclusion, and the Second Circuit ultimately held, in 2006, that the Election Exclusion Rule did not permit the exclusion of the bylaw-amendment proposal. According to the court, excluding the proposal would contravene the SEC's expressed interpretation of the Election Exclusion at the time it was adopted in 1976; the SEC had not issued any formal change in interpretation since then.[21]

In July 2007, the SEC presented for public comment two conflicting proposed revisions of Rule 14a-8-(i)(8). The first would have followed the Second Circuit's *AFSCME* opinion and prohibited the exclusion of "a proposal to establish a procedure by which shareholder nominees for election of director would be included in the company's proxy materials," if the proposal were made by a shareholder or group of shareholders owning five percent or more of the company's voting stock. The second proposed revision, which ultimately prevailed, amended Rule 14a-(8)(i)(8) to allow exclusion "If the proposal relates to a nomination or an election for membership on the company's board of directors or analogous governing body *or a procedure for such nomination or election.*" (The amendment added the underlined language to the existing Rule.)

As noted above, prior to the amendment, the Division had developed the position that the Election Exclusion allows exclusion of proposals to change voting procedures when they would result in contested elections. The new wording on its face seems to go even further, allowing exclusion of *any* proposals relating to elections. But in a release accompanying the amendment, the SEC insisted that the amendment was meant to "clarify" the SEC's "contested election" interpretation and not to expand it.[22] The release was clearly meant to formally replace the 1976 interpretation of the Election Exclusion, which the Second Circuit had relied upon in *AFSCME v. AIG*, with the "contested election" interpretation. Christopher Cox, Donaldson's replacement as SEC Chair, voted for *both* proposed revisions. The SEC adopted the second proposed revision in December 2007.

The SEC's position toward shareholder participation in elections changed under the Obama Administration. In 2009, the Commission advanced a proposal that would empower shareholders in two ways.[23] First, it would revise Rule 14a-8(i)(8) to explicitly allow only the exclusion of election-related proposals that would interfere with an upcoming election; this change would reverse the "contested election" interpretation of the current Rule and return to the 1976 interpretation. Second, the proposal would revive the Proxy Access Requirement proposed in 2003. The proposal would add a new Rule 14a-11 requiring a corporate proxy to include certain shareholder nominations of director candidates. This proposed nomination power would apply only to a shareholder or group of shareholders holding from one to five percent of the corporation's shares, depending on the size of the corporation. The 2009 proposal remained open for public comment as of the time this book went to press in fall of 2009.

Recall that the AFSCME Pension Plan had not originally sought an SEC rule change. It sought to make changes to the *internal rules* of a corporation of which it was a shareholder. The Division acknowledged that under the Pension Plan's preferred interpretation of Rule 14a-8's Election Exclusion, proposals could "be drafted individually to reflect the makeup

21. AFSCME Employees Pension Plan v. AIG, 462 F.3d 121 (2d Cir. 2006).

22. SEC Release No. 34-56914 (Jan. 10, 2008).

23. See SEC Release Nos. 33-9046, 34-60089, "Facilitating Shareholder Director Nominations," 74 F.R. 29024 (June 18, 2009).

of a particular company as opposed to a 'one size fits all' access rule that applies to all companies." Nonetheless, the Division expressed preference for a uniform rule over custom-tailored rules for each company. This uniform approach, reflected in the 2007 amendment to Rule 14a-8(i)(8) and the 2009 14a-11 proposal, seems inconsistent with the prevailing view of corporate law as "enabling" shareholders and management to create optimal governance arrangements.[24]

In contrast to the one-size-fits-all approach, state laws have followed an enabling approach. In 2009, Delaware General Corporation Law section 112 was amended to permit (but not to require) corporations to adopt bylaws giving shareholders access to the corporate proxy in order to nominate directors, and to place conditions on such access. (The American Bar Association proposed a similar revision to the Model Business Corporations Act in 2009.) Also in 2009, Delaware General Corporation Law section 113 was amended to permit bylaws requiring a corporation to reimburse shareholders for expenses incurred in soliciting proxies in connection with a director election, and to place conditions on such a reimbursement right. In 2007, North Dakota passed the Publicly Traded Corporations Act, which allows corporations to elect to be governed by certain shareholder-friendly provisions, including a provision mandating proxy access to shareholders or shareholder groups that own over five percent of the corporation's voting stock.[25]

Lawrence E. Mitchell, *The Sarbanes-Oxley Act and the Reinvention of Corporate Governance?*[26]

....

Accountants and the Federalization of Corporate Governance

The [Sarbanes-Oxley Act of 2002] connects auditors with the board and management in a way that brings them inside the corporate box. [*See Chapter 12 for further discussion of the role of auditors and other outside "gatekeepers"*] Title II of the Act [*sections 201–209*] gives the corporation's audit committee a substantial role in monitoring auditor independence and avoiding conflicts of interest. But most interesting for the link between accounting reform and the federalization of corporate governance is the manner in which Title III, the Corporate Responsibility portion of the Act [*sections 301–308*], links accounting reform with the internal affairs of the corporation. [*These provisions are further discussed in Chapter 4.*] A simple listing of those provisions would make this clear, but I shall indulge in somewhat more detailed discussion.

The real action lies in the way the Act specifies the duties of a corporation's board of directors. In the first place, every listed corporation is required either to have an audit committee composed solely of independent directors or to treat the board as a whole as the audit committee. Two things about the corporate governance aspect of this requirement are notable. First, the Act specifies not only the composition of the audit committee but also the procedures by which the audit committee is to operate, requiring each corporation to provide "appropriate funding" for its audit committee and requiring that the audit

---

24. *See Macey's article in Chapter 2 and Romano's article in Chapter 3.*—*Ed.*
25. N.D. Century Code 10-35-08 (2007).
26. Originally published in 48 VILLANOVA LAW REVIEW 1189 (2003). Reprinted with permission.

committee establish procedures for "the receipt, retention, and treatment of complaints received by the issuer regarding accounting, internal accounting controls, or auditing matters; and the confidential, anonymous submission by employees of the issuer of concerns regarding questionable accounting or auditing matters." [*As noted in Chapter 4, §301 of the Act also requires the audit committee to "be directly responsible for the appointment, compensation, and oversight" of the corporation's auditors.*] While the Act does not specify the exact procedures the audit committee is to adopt, the fact that it specifies the nature of the procedures, including the very substantive one of establishing whistle-blowing chains, goes far toward setting a standard of care that seems already to be substantially in excess of that required generally by state corporate law.

Moreover, the Act not only requires that the audit committee consist of independent directors, but it also defines the meaning of independence, a definition heretofore left to state law, and in a more rigorous way than does, for example, Delaware or New York. The Act defines "independent" as a director who may not "accept any consulting, advisory, or other compensatory fee from the issuer; or be an affiliated person of the issuer or any subsidiary thereof." Both Delaware and New York, at least for some purposes (derivative suit dismissal, for example) have less stringent requirements for independence. In this respect, the Act can be said to have established a higher duty of loyalty for public corporations than currently exists under state law. At a minimum, it federalizes the definition of independent director for general purposes.

The regulations go further than does the Act. Section 407 of the Act directs the Commission to adopt disclosure rules defining the term "audit committee financial expert" and requiring an issuer to disclose whether its audit committee includes a financial expert. Not only does the regulation require this disclosure, but it imposes on the board the obligation to specifically identify that person or persons it has determined to meet the definition and fill the role of "audit committee financial expert." In addition, the regulation goes beyond the Act in requiring disclosure of whether the audit committee financial expert is independent.

The Commission's regulations have the potential to have significant impacts on corporate governance. In addition to the board and its committees, we will now have the ability to identify a new kind of director, an "audit committee financial expert" who is far more likely than not to be independent in light of the Commission's requirement that this fact be disclosed. And while the Commission is explicit in noting that the financial expert is not, by that designation alone, subject to a "higher degree of individual responsibility or obligation as a member of the audit committee," nor does such a designation constitute the financial expert an "expert" for liability purposes under Section 11 of the Securities Act of 1933, it undoubtedly is the case that the designation of a director as a financial expert will, as a psychological matter, impose upon that director a greater sense of responsibility for the corporation's financial affairs than would be the case in the absence of such designation. The financial expert will undoubtedly spend far more time with the corporation's accountants as well, further bringing them inside the gate.

Finally, the fact that an identifiable person is disclosed to be the corporation's financial expert will allow investors to demand specific accountability from a member of the board (even if the regulations do not impose greater duties on that person). This is likely to have the salubrious effect of diminishing the fractured accountability (or the ability of a director to hide in the group) that currently characterizes our corporate governance structure. This exposure is likely to lead the financial expert to be vigilant in a manner that is unusual for the average director, and will most likely (because of the financial expert's public exposure) give her greater authority on the board. To the extent that the corporation and its accountants engage in financial shenanigans, the financial expert is the person left hanging out to dry. The effect of the Act and the proposed regulations is likely to be a substantially greater presence of accountants in the boardroom.

In addition, the highly publicized certification of the financial statements required of the chief executive officer and chief financial officer[27] serves an important function. This provision accomplishes three things in terms of reforming internal corporate governance. In the first place, it makes the audit central to the nature of care in corporate governance, linking the public auditor to the two most important officers of the corporation. Going forward, CEOs and CFOs have no choice but to work directly with auditors in evaluating financial statements and thus defining the determinants of corporate performance.

Second, it makes these non-statutory (as a state law matter) corporate actors statutorily required (as a federal matter) for publicly held corporations. In so doing, it expands upon state requirements of corporate governance as a legal matter (even if such officers already have a central place as a practical matter) and thus directs corporate governance scholars to focus more sharply on the role of these corporate actors in a way that, while familiar to management scholars, is less so to lawyers. It forces us to look inside the box we have defined as the parameters of corporate governance and, having opened that box, will almost certainly lead us to explore, in far greater detail than is yet common in the literature, the relationship among these officers, the board, and officers lower down the executive chain. One might even go so far as to say (although it is premature to say so in a strong way) that it ought to diminish our obsession with the board as the central focus of corporate governance and instead lead us to spend more time examining where the real power (and now where meaningful federal regulation) lies, the corporation's executives.

Third, Title III, by linking accounting reform with the internal affairs of a corporation, imposes on officers a substantial duty of care with respect to the corporation's financial statements which, on its face and without the benefit of judicial interpretation, seems to be significantly more stringent than that required of the board (and certainly of the officers) under state corporate law. Not only does the Act require certification of the financials, which already goes beyond state law, but it also makes these officers "responsible for establishing and maintaining internal controls ... designing such internal controls to ensure that material information relating to the issuer and its consolidated subsidiaries is made known to such officers; ... [and] evaluating the effectiveness of the issuer's internal controls...." Moreover, it requires these officers to disclose to the audit committee "all significant deficiencies" in the design and operation of internal controls, as well as to report any material or immaterial fraud that involves employees who have responsibilities for internal controls.

....

Lawrence E. Mitchell, *On the Direct Election of CEOs**

I. Introduction

American legal and scholarly interest in the board of directors as an institution of corporate governance largely was nonexistent until the 1970s. At that time, due to a confluence of

27. [*This provision, in Section 302 of the Act, is further described and discussed in Chapter 4.—Ed.*]
  * Originally published in 32 OHIO NORTHERN UNIVERSITY LAW REVIEW 261 (2006). Reprinted with permission.

factors, lawyers and business people turned to the institution of the board as an instrument of corporate reform. The result was the monitoring board, the model currently dominant and most recently reaffirmed in the Delaware Chancery Court's opinion in *Disney*.[28]

The monitoring board doesn't work. It was designed to work, but it was hijacked by business interests and developed not to govern but to protect corporate directors from liability. While there have been numerous scholarly and popular calls for board reform in the post-Enron era, most suggestions tinker around the edges of a dysfunctional institution. The purpose of this paper is to engage in a thought experiment to examine an alternative that may or may not be feasible but puts more squarely on the table than board reform proposals the issues of management, monitoring, and corporate democracy. This alternative is the direct election of CEOs.

The history of the board in America raises the question of the utility of the board as an institution of corporate governance. Prior to the 1970s reforms, boards generally were, and were recognized to be, tools of their corporation's CEOs. While this presented a number of problems, including a strong degree of insularity from social issues and perhaps some conflict with shareholder interests, it nonetheless reigned throughout the power years of the American century when American industry indisputably was the envy of the world. It may not have done much, but neither did it interfere with the management of American business. Since the advent of the monitoring board, while American industry has prospered, it also has been struggling, at some substantial cost, with the role and purpose of the board of directors, even as the real seat of corporate power remains in the CEO. Our history with boards may lead to the conclusion that the board is an irrelevant institution.

If one concludes that the board is an irrelevant institution, or at least may be more trouble than it's worth (an empirical question I am not equipped to analyze), the question arises as to what the central organ of corporate governance should be. Since at least the death of J.P. Morgan, corporate power has been vested largely in the CEO and top executive officers of the corporation. One could reasonably conclude that there are good reasons for power to be centralized in this officer. It is, after all, centralized management that is the touchstone of corporate efficiency, not centralized monitoring. If that is the case, perhaps we should look directly to the CEO as the principle organ of corporate governance.

The question of monitoring that so bothers academics and reformers is a question of the latter third of the twentieth century. It is a question that sharpened dramatically with the rise of neo-classical law and economics, with its deconstruction of the corporation, its emphasis on each actor's maximization of wealth, and its perfection of the corporate ethic of stockholder-centrism, which both gave the board a central focus and highlighted the issue of agency costs. But monitoring, except for actual conflict of interest transactions, was no meaningful part of board functions before the 1970s. And monitoring to enhance shareholder wealth, the product of the reforms of the '70s and '80s, has, as I noted earlier, produced questionable results.

Absolute power corrupts absolutely. It would probably be a bad idea, and completely inconsistent with the structures legitimating the modern corporation, to permit CEOs to run corporations unchecked. But one of the legitimating ideas underlying the modern American corporation is that the corporation is to be run for shareholders and, perhaps, stakeholders, and that shareholders have some say in who runs the corporation. Fiduciary obligation, for example, has the potential to tie managers as much to shareholder interests

---

28. *The author refers to the lower-court opinion affirmed by Delaware's Supreme Court in* In Re The Walt Disney Company Derivative Litigation, *reprinted in Chapter 10 of this volume. — Ed.*

as elections of directors and could be treated as legitimating in the same way. And the market for corporate control always exists as a failsafe device.

This leads to the idea that I would like to discuss in this paper, the idea of the direct election of CEOs by three corporate stakeholder groups: stockholders, debtholders, and employees, each voting as a class....

There is nothing about the corporation or corporate law that mandates the existence of a board. It does, however, appear inherent in the corporate concept that there must be a central manager or managers. And it appears equally inherent in the concept of the business corporation that there must be those who provide capital and those who work for the enterprise.

Consequently, reconfiguring these groups within a legitimated institutional framework seems, at a minimum, like an intellectual exercise that potentially could help produce meaningful corporate reform within the current rubric. It could perhaps even result in a different view of the nature of the corporation itself in ways that would benefit corporate governance and performance. To explore that possibility is the purpose of this exercise.

II. A Very Brief History of Boards

Neither scholars nor reformers paid much attention to the board prior to the 1970s.... Matters changed in the 1970s for a variety of reasons. The early 1970s brought recession and a poorly performing stock market after the go-go years of the 1960s. A number of substantial bankruptcies or near-bankruptcies were occurring, including the spectacular failure of the Penn Central.[29] The Watergate investigation brought revelations of illegal corporate campaign contributions which led to an SEC investigation uncovering corporate briberies overseas. The SEC was at the high point of its attempt to federalize corporate law through the securities laws and calls for federal corporate law were increasing. Congress was investigating the role of shareholders in corporations and the appropriate means of corporate regulation. Activist groups were using Rule 14a-8 of the 1934 Act to politicize corporate action, especially with regard to the Vietnam War. And agitation for reform of the board for the sake of social and political goals was rife.

It was in this atmosphere that business and legal consensus began to coalesce around the idea of a board of directors, composed principally of outsiders, to monitor management. The American Bar Association, The Conference Board, the American Society of Corporate Secretaries, and the Business Roundtable all accepted the monitoring board, most likely as the least dangerous reform alternative. Business people and practitioners also began to see that the monitoring board, which is structural in concept and minimal in substance, could provide an effective shield against legal liability for directors. More legitimating justifications for the monitoring board ranged from enhanced corporate efficiency to greater corporate social responsibility....

The corporate trade groups and stock exchanges quickly integrated the virtues of the independent board into their statements of best practices and listing requirements. Somewhat more precisely at first, with auditing committees, nominating committees, and compensation committees to be composed of a majority of independents, independent dominated boards became even more universally the standard rule after the corporate

---

29. *The failure of this sprawling conglomerate, which encompassed railroads, real estate, and other disparate industries, was the largest bankruptcy up to that time. It was seen as an indictment both of large conglomerates and of excessive borrowing.*—Ed.

collapses of the early century and the enactment of Sarbanes-Oxley. That statute itself more or less federally legislated independent audit committees and, taken as a whole, recognized the significance of independent boards.[30]

Whatever the status of board reform in the 1970s and 1980s, it became a cottage industry after the corporate scandals of 2002. The idea of the monitoring board captured the Delaware courts during the 1980s when the boom in takeovers presented perhaps the most sharply drawn conflict between shareholders and directors in modern corporate history. The threat to managerial hegemony posed by takeovers created a legitimate presumption in every case that the board and executives had an irreducible conflict between short-term stock price maximization and maintaining their jobs. Perhaps no better context could have been presented to catalyze the idea of the monitoring board into legal fact, and the tests developed by the Delaware courts to evaluate defensive corporate behavior in the face of hostile threats relied upon this model of the board.

III. The Benefits of Boards

There are good and responsible boards. But the question remains as to whether their monitoring role, even when well-performed, is worth the costs. Moreover, the legal model of the board is dysfunctional. If the Disney board's conduct was sufficient to shield it from liability, then certainly we are entitled to (and ought to) ask the question as to why we have boards at all.

Today, the independent monitoring board has all but become the standard model. Boards that fail to conform do so at their peril. But what are the benefits? From the shareholders' standpoint, the benefits are questionable. A number of studies examine the effect of independent boards on corporate financial performance and conflict rather radically in their conclusions as to whether corporations with independent boards return more value to their shareholders than insider dominated boards. And there is a strong theoretical case to be made that, at least in terms of this metric, insider boards might even be better than outside boards. So at least in terms of shareholder value creation, the jury is still out.

There has been an increase in boards' willingness to remove CEOs of underperforming companies. . . . This increased board willingness to terminate CEOs of underperforming companies has been celebrated by shareholder activists. But what does it prove? It proves exactly what we've known all along: corporations are managed by their executives, not by their boards. This realization doesn't diminish the possible benefits created by monitoring boards. Even if corporations whose CEOs have been removed don't perform better under new CEOs, the very fact that a CEO knows that he or she can be fired is a powerful incentive to work harder. But to what end? Of the corporations whose CEOs have been removed by the board, falling share prices often precede CEO removal. How many would have been removed if share prices simply had remained stable? We can't know for sure, but studies suggest that stock prices do tend to decline before CEOs depart the company. A flat stock price is unlikely to provoke the kind of investor outrage that falling share prices do. Moreover, a board that removes a CEO it appointed is a board that is forced to admit failure, a

---

30. *See Sarbanes-Oxley Act § 301. In addition, since 2003, the New York Stock Exchange and Nasdaq have required listed companies to have majority-independent boards. — Ed.*

circumstance in which few boards like to find themselves. CEO removal, probably appropriately, still remains an extreme solution.

But the incentives that the existence and increased use of this solution creates for CEOs is hardly clear. The measure of modern corporate success is increased share price. Financial incentives and market pressures are often enough to stimulate CEOs to this goal. But stock options notwithstanding, the only honest way to keep your stock price increasing is to take risks. The inevitable fact about risk taking is that you could win or you could lose. Stock price could go up. It could go down. Even the most measured and carefully thought-out risks present this threat.

So what's a CEO to do? Well, if you're unlikely to be fired simply for keeping share prices where they are, the safest strategy is to do just that. Don't take the risks that may result in celebrity and a big pay day or that might result in your looking for a job. Stay the course. Such a strategy certainly doesn't appear to have affected CEO compensation. And so one possible result of increased monitoring board activity in firing CEOs is to return to the state of satisfying that characterized the managerialist era. Keep the corporation on course, grow it carefully, don't make waves, and retire a wealthy and happy leader. The active monitoring board might well restore the very business world that gave managerialism a bad name.

It could have a different, and perhaps more pernicious, effect. As is well known, it has increasingly come to be the case that the size of a CEO's payday bears an important and direct relationship to her corporation's stock price. Indeed, as much as sixty-six percent of a Fortune 1000 CEO's compensation can come in the form of stock options. Thus, the more adventurous CEO may be quite willing to take the risk of poor performance against the chance of a significantly higher paycheck and stockholder acclaim. I noted above that the only honest way to keep stock prices rising is to take risks. But that's not entirely true, at least in the short-term and perhaps in the middle term as well. Layoffs are a guaranteed way to increase stock price. So are measures like cutting R & D budgets, environmental compliance budgets, and the like, which may create serious long-term damage to the corporation itself but will benefit the CEO and the board, perhaps through a reasonably long tenure. Thus, the pressure placed by an independent monitoring board on a CEO might result in something more unfortunate than steady if not lackluster corporate performance. It could result in long-term corporate damage.

Logic, as well as empiricism, challenges the virtues of the new board model. The old hands-off board of the managerialist era may not have done much, but it probably did little harm. After all, the age in which it ruled was that in which the United States rose to world financial dominance, a position it has rapidly been losing in the new age to a variety of challengers both in developing and industrial nations. But even if it did no harm, it functioned more or less like tonsils. Perhaps the board simply is more trouble than it is worth.

IV. A New Model of Corporate Governance

How many investors can name a corporation's board of directors? How many can name its CEO? I don't know the answer and couldn't find it. But my guess is that far more shareholders can name the CEOs of corporations in which they invest than can name any member of the board (except of course the CEO). From the CEO folk hero days of the 1990s to the Snidely Whiplash era of the new century, and well back into corporate history, CEOs are center stage. The financial and business press rarely report on directors except in the most unusual circumstances, whereas any given day can bring statements from or stories on corporate CEOs.

This simple fact suggests a conclusion which even in the monitoring age appears obvious. CEOs, not boards, run corporations. This conclusion has significant consequences for the proper structure of corporate governance.

Start with the idea of responsibility and accountability. Psychology tells us that we hold accountable those people whom we can see to make decisions. The CEO, unlike the board, is a focal point of decisionmaking. And the CEO, unlike the board, is easily identifiable.

Some have argued persuasively that group decisionmaking is generally better than individual decisionmaking, and that justifies the continuation of the board. But it has been recognized from at least the age of managerialism that the CEO engages in group decisionmaking as well, certainly in consultation with senior corporate executives and sometimes with the board. Nothing about the virtues of group decisionmaking implies the need for a board. The same virtues are present when the CEO manages the corporation as part of a consultative process. And given the size and complexity of modern corporations, no CEO would manage without it.

The kind of institutionalized group thinking presented by the board is not without its problems.... Groups may be better sometimes, but as psychology, not to mention history, suggests, the dangers of group identification are real and serious.

It has also been argued that the modern public corporation demands a hierarchical structure with authority at the top.... But ... there is nothing inconsistent with the notion of hierarchical authority in recognizing the CEO as the ultimate hierarch. While others have argued that the board serves in a way that the CEO might not, as a mediating hierarch among competing corporate factions,[31] the reality of modern stockholder-centrism, as well as the structural pressures on the board to favor shareholders, makes this account practically implausible despite its long-standing pedigree and theoretical elegance....

Even though these justifications for a board have their merits, identification of the board as the locus of corporate responsibility, whether to the shareholders or others, presents serious problems of responsibility and accountability. The board model of governance, whatever the function of the board, presents issues of fractured accountability and diffuse responsibility. Moral theory and social psychology, as well as plain common sense, suggest that when a group makes a decision, nobody makes a decision. This is particularly the case when the group is relatively unknown. So while the members of a board may be embarrassed by poor corporate performance, they retain a great deal of anonymity in their decisionmaking, except perhaps in the relatively insular community of directors.

Moreover, when the board fails, it fails as an institution and not as individuals. The board itself may be held accountable, but the individuals who comprise it are relatively immune. Even when a board is sued for violation of its duty of care or good faith, it is the board that is held liable (if at all) rather than the individual members. As a mechanism for ensuring responsibility and accountability, the board is a weak creation.

The CEO presents a different story. The CEO is an identifiable, known individual. The CEO is someone to hold accountable and blame when things go wrong, just as we celebrate the CEO when things go well. Since the CEO is in fact the principal corporate

---

31. *See Margaret Blair and Lynn Stout's article in this volume.*—*Ed.*

decisionmaker, such blame is appropriate. Moreover, identifying the CEO as the figure to bear the brunt of corporate accountability will instill in the CEO the kind of sense of responsibility that will help to ensure the best kind of corporate decisionmaking—far more than simple certification of financial statements mandated by Sarbanes-Oxley. Unlike the board, not only is the CEO responsible, but he is nakedly responsible. There is no group in which to hide.

Recognizing all of this and still accepting the reality of managerialism, it may yet be possible to make the board responsible and accountable, at least for the performance of the CEO, in a way that it has not yet been. We could, for example, amend the SEC rules to require detailed biographical information on each board member in proxy statements and 10Ks. Such information would reveal not only each board member's business history but some of his or her family or social history as well. It could require an annual statement by each director of how and why that director voted on major corporate decisions, as well as a statement of each director's business philosophy. Such information not only would make directors real and identifiable people, destroying the concealing curtain that is the board, but require each director to stand accountable for his or her own decisionmaking for the corporation. Thus, each individual director could be held accountable in a manner that would also give each director an incentive to behave with a level of responsibility that he does not presently have.

This reform, while it still does not actually answer the question of what the board does, at least would go a long way towards minimizing the problems of board governance. It would create a world of real people making real decisions in a clear and identifiable way that would allow for true corporate and public accountability.

... Those who are afraid to make themselves accountable should not assume positions of responsibility in the first place. Finally, there remains the question of whether the board has any significant utility at all. If we cannot get people to serve, perhaps the institution is not one worth having.

The institution of the board has been a notable failure. Perhaps it is time to try something different.

V. Corporate Democracy — Direct Election of the CEO

... [I]t is worth noting that most state corporations codes anticipate the possibility that shareholders of a given corporation might opt for a governance structure that eliminates the board and permits them to create a different governance structure in the corporation's charter.... While the virtual universality of this statutory permissiveness suggests a solution, and at the same time affirms the conceptual integrity of a corporation without a board, this is not the basis for my suggestions.

Rather, having identified the problem both as a function of board cost arguably in excess of any benefit the board might provide, a historical pattern of uncertainty as to what the board should do, and the inevitable reality of CEO management, the solution identifies itself. State corporations codes should permit direct election of the CEO.

At first blush, the concept of electing an unmonitored autocrat, not to mention the mechanisms for achieving this, might appear not only strange but frightening. But a description of the proposal will illustrate that direct election of the CEO could not only empower the CEO to fulfill some of the functions attributed to the board but could also create a real and responsible democratic corporate regime that would ensure both responsible and efficient business. Moreover, monitoring, while it can be improved both by the election process and by increasing the role of the auditor, would remain where it has been most effective—the market....

There are sufficient reasons to think that direct elections of CEOs would be something unlikely to develop even if it produced a more efficient and responsible corporate regime. Such a shift would require either political or shareholder pressure, coordinated perhaps by enlightened institutions that had sufficient power to overcome collective action problems. For this reason, it is a shift unlikely to take place. But the idea is instructive, and perhaps at the least suggests some different ways of thinking about appropriate corporate governance mechanisms.

The idea is also highly suggestive with respect to ways of achieving a goal to which lip service, and little more, often is paid—the goal of ensuring corporate democracy. It does seem passingly odd that perhaps the most powerful institution in our democratic society is the most autocratic, the most socialistic in its command and control structure. While moderated a bit in the increasingly common horizontally managed corporation, it remains unchanged in its basic premise of authority and fiat; the difference is simply that there are more participants in the elite ruling group. It has been noted that workers who spend much of their time in this kind of institution receive a citizenship education far different from the civic education necessary for full participation in political democracy, as it has also been noted that their opportunities for self-expression and fulfillment, at least at work, are stifled by the structure.[32] Similarly, shareholders who only play at the game of corporate democracy could hardly be blamed if they developed the same kind of cynical attitude toward political democracy that we have institutionalized with respect to corporate democracy. These reasons alone are probably insufficient to justify a regime of direct CEO election. But added to the problematic board, and the possibility of diminished agency costs created by boards and perhaps greater managerial efficiency, they give the suggestion even greater weight.

In order fully to develop the proposal, then, let me begin with a description of the electorate. While the stockholders elect the board of directors, it is not obvious that they are the appropriate, or at least the sole appropriate, electorate for the CEO. The election of a CEO is a far more complicated process than the election of directors. While directors are generalists, notwithstanding the Sarbanes-Oxley requirements for the audit committee, CEOs are specialists. I do not mean by this to suggest that CEO skills are not transferable between corporations; at least in the same or similar industries, but rather that the personal and professional qualities that go into making a good CEO are far more specialized and subtle than those that go into making a good director.

Shareholders are poorly suited for this task. The American investment tradition of diversified small holdings has led to the often-described rational apathy of shareholders who lack the time and incentives to study proxy statements and engage in informed decisionmaking....

One could argue that CEO elections would finally bring about the promise of institutional investor governance. Certainly the institutions are, or have the potential to be, far better informed than the individual shareholder about CEO quality and qualities. But there is a question as to whether this golden age of institutions would be realized. After all, despite some institutional activism on governance, institutional investors as a class have been almost as passive as the stereotypical small shareholder. Even if the

---

32. *See Marleen O'Connor's article in this volume. —Ed.*

institutions awoke and took active roles in CEO selection, the danger of unified interests from concentrated capital may be serious. If, for example, institutions acting with bounded rationality chose short-term management for stock price over long-term management consistent with good business practice, a real possibility given compensation patterns of institutional money managers, the institutionally-elected CEO might be under pressure to run the business in a way that might not align with her good judgment or the corporation's long-term interests....

The weakness of shareholders as a voting class and their presumed narrow interest in the corporation, are not enough to disenfranchise them, but they are significant enough to counsel against their status as the sole voting class in CEO elections. So the question of ensuring an informed, motivated, and responsible electorate remains. The answer is to have the CEO elected by shareholders, long-term debtholders, and employees, each voting as a class, with the winning CEO to receive a majority of the votes of two of the three classes.

The debtholders are a relatively easy choice. In the first place they, like shareholders, contribute significant capital to the corporation and in many ways resemble the shareholders in their vulnerability to corporate management. The major problem consistently raised when suggestions of creditors' rights come up is that their incentives are somewhat different from those of the shareholders. Creditors are said to prefer stability to risk, steady earnings to large profits. And this is undoubtedly true.

But this argument proves too much. In the first place, while we distinguish the creditor class from the shareholder class in discussions about these matters, it is simply the fact that most investors are neither complete creditors nor complete shareholders but a mix of the two. While relatively few individuals may own corporate bonds, there is no question as to heavy institutional ownership of corporate bonds. While this fact doesn't justify lumping stock and bonds together (and I haven't since I argue for class voting), it does suggest that the interests of investors are more nuanced than ordinary academic debate allows. Add to this the fact that the average creditor, at least one holding privately placed debt, is probably significantly better informed than the average shareholder about the corporation's characteristics and performance. Finally, the balance of the creditor's long-term view with the shareholders' greater preference for risk ought to produce decisions that are better for the business as a whole....

The final voting class should be the corporation's full time employees. There are a number of reasons for this. First, nobody knows the business of the corporation and its demands better than the employees as a class. Faculties, not students or alumni, select their deans, or at least the very small group of candidates from which the president chooses. Like the other groups, not all employees will know everything that goes into identifying the right CEO for the job. Yet, as a class they surely will, and there is no more reason to doubt the powers of persuasion of senior and respected members of each group of workers than there is to doubt the collective wisdom of the American electorate in choosing a president (my own political views notwithstanding). It is also increasingly the case that through pensions and stock options, workers have a significant vested interest in the long-term well-being of the corporation and the relative immobility of their human capital, at least relative to shareholders and bondholders. While it is often claimed in academic debates that workers tend to have risk profiles similar to debtholders, contemporary compensation structures should tend to increase the amounts of risk that workers are willing to take. Moreover, their interest in the long-run well-being of the corporation should lead them to understand that innovation and risk taking are essential for the corporation's success and thus their continued employment. The arguments for workers as risk-averse may be considerably overstated.

What I have thus far said about workers goes only to their role in ensuring good business performance for the corporation in their choice of CEO. However, including workers in the election process could enhance morale, job satisfaction, and productivity. These reasons, although nonetheless real and deserving of serious attention, are beyond the scope of this article. Worker voting is likely to have all of the benefits cited in favor of worker participation on boards of directors without the drawbacks that boards composed of interest group representatives have. Workers would have to be guaranteed secrecy in balloting to protect against retaliation for negative votes by a re-elected incumbent CEO.

While arguments against bondholder and employee voting may have some validity, they are outweighed by the benefits. But what I have thus far argued should suggest that it would be unlikely that voters would vote on straight class lines any more than the determining swing vote group in the American electorate votes consistently on party lines. Moreover, the establishment of class voting by these stakeholders should not obscure the fact that they are unlikely to vote in isolation. Nothing would prevent representatives of shareholder interests, debtholder interests, and employee interests from campaigning to persuade the other groups of the virtues of their candidate. Direct class election of corporate CEOs should produce vigorous campaigning and debate, and perhaps create for the first time in American history a meaningful corporate democracy....

Monitoring the CEO is a bit more of a problem.... One way of ferreting out executive self-dealing might be to increase the role of the auditor. Boards, even with good information systems, historically are unable to discover concealed misconduct by the CEO, at least absent a corporate crisis. It would naturally fit the auditor's function to request it to engage in a conflicts audit of the CEO and senior executives. One might object that the auditing firm would be tied to the CEO even more strongly than auditing firms may be tied to their clients now. But this problem seems almost unavoidable, especially in light of the oligopoly in the auditing industry. Perhaps the solution to auditor independence will continue to be, as Sarbanes-Oxley recognizes, external regulation rather than corporate governance rules.

The CEO's fiduciary duty to the corporation should be strengthened and members of all three voting constituencies should be given the opportunity to bring suit against her for breaches of duty to the corporation. The cost and disruption of a new CEO search would serve as a disincentive to promiscuous lawsuits. In addition, there is no reason to think that market-based monitoring in the stock market, the debt market, the analyst and institutional communities, and the credit rating agencies would be any less effective than it currently is in monitoring boards of directors, CEOs, and corporations themselves....

One question that certainly should be raised is whether this would be a mandatory or optional change and, if so, who would choose the latter? ...

As to the first question, it seems to me necessary that the choice be optional. Corporate law has always done well by its flexibility of form. Moreover, to argue that a shift like that from board-governed corporations to directly elected CEOs be mandated would consign this proposal to complete failure....

Who would opt in? I admit that it is not likely that most directors would give up their board seats, nor would most CEOs expose themselves to the potentially enhanced liabilities (or greater exposure leading perhaps to more asserted liabilities) that my proposal implies. But if I am correct about the dysfunctionality of the board, as well as the need for centralized management as contrasted with centralized monitoring, it is relatively easy to think that newly forming corporations might choose this option.

... Direct election of CEOs seems to place the governance emphasis on where true power lies. It is at least worth thinking about.

Discussion Questions

1. The fact that independent directors are free from conflicts does not guarantee they will do a good job, even if they have the most impeccable credentials. Directorship is typically a part-time job held by prominent, busy people with other important responsibilities. What are the pros and cons of Elson's proposal to incentivize performance by compensation reform? What other incentives do independent directors have to perform their jobs well? How can those incentives be heightened?

2. Assuming Elson is correct about the beneficial effect of director compensation reform, what should be done about it? Should the law mandate or incentivize Elson's preferred form of compensation? Or should it be left to the market to adopt? What forces militate for and against market adaptation of his proposed reform?

3. Fisch and Langevoort offer reasons why insider-dominated boards may be preferable to independent boards. What are the implications for Blair and Stout's model of directors as "mediating hierarchs" who balance the interests of all corporate constituents?

4. According to Fisch, the relative importance of the board's monitoring and managerial functions may vary among different corporations or industries. To what extent should the law mandate aspects of board structure? What factors determine whether a given corporation would benefit from a monitoring-oriented board or a managerial-oriented board? If boards' structural characteristics are left up to individual corporations, by what processes will they be determined and what forces will affect the outcomes?

5. In theory, directors must monitor managers' actions as to whether they involve conflicts of interest and as to whether they are good for business. Independent outside directors have special qualifications to perform the first function, but insiders are usually best suited to perform the second. Is it possible to design a governance structure that is ideally suited to perform both functions? One suggestion is to require two boards — a conflict-review board and a business-review board, of which only the former need be independent. *See* Lynne Dallas, *The Multiple Roles of Corporate Boards of Directors*, 40 San Diego L. Rev. 781, (2003). What do you make of this suggestion?

6. As Langevoort points out at the end of his article, "formal indicia of independence" do not guarantee effective monitoring by boards. He suggests that rather than enhanced director independence, enhanced judicial scrutiny is the best way of monitoring corporate decisions that may involve conflicts of interests. Do you agree?

7. Langevoort argues that inside directors can represent the legitimate interests of middle and upper management. To what extent are managers corporate constituents who need representation on the board? Should they participate in electing directors? What other mechanisms protect their interests as corporate constituents? In this context, how do they resemble, and differ from, employees more generally?

8. Assuming that increased board independence will contribute to improving corporate governance, how might it be achieved? Conflict-of-interest doctrine under traditional state law involves context-specific judicial review of directors' conduct. By contrast, the Sarbanes-Oxley Act and stock exchange listing standards impose definitions of independence. What are the relative merits of these two approaches?

9. Do purely procedural and structural requirements on board decisionmaking mandate wasteful busywork? As Bratton pointed out in Chapter 1, Enron's directors "went through the motions dictated by the book of good corporate practice." The board of another

prominent corporate failure, WorldCom, was roundly criticized for its hasty, poorly informed approval of transactions initiated by its CEO. In 2000, for example, it made a $6 billion acquisition of Intermedia, Inc., the corporate parent of web-hosting firm Digex Inc., with only two hours' notice and 35 minutes of discussion.

After WorldCom's sudden and dramatic bankruptcy, a new board took control. In 2003, the new board, having conducted due diligence and following formal and deliberate decisionmaking procedures, decided to acquire the remaining shares of Digex. While the latter transaction may have been substantively superior to the former, it is also possible that both were equally bad (or good) in substance. Do legal mandates of procedural care guarantee that board decisions will be better, or just that they will be more expensive and time-consuming?

If procedural regulation has limited effect, can it be improved upon? Should courts engage in substantive evaluation of business decisions? How could that have been done with respect to the second Digex acquisition?

10. Wade argues that directors and executives tend to lack empathy for employees of color. How might Wade's empathy theory be formally assimilated into corporate law? Might it have applications outside of the racial discrimination context? How does it interact with Fisch and Langevoort's theories about board composition?

11. While directors of color may be more able to empathize with minority employees as *minorities*, can they empathize with them as *employees*?

As Marleen O'Connor notes in Chapter 2, Germany requires corporate boards to include representatives of labor. What are the pros and cons of this approach to making corporate boards "empathize" with employees? *See* Mark Roe, *Political Preconditions to Separating Ownership from Control*, 53 Stan. L. Rev. 539, 554, 567–68 (2000).

12. One recent empirical study found a correlation between greater racial and gender diversity among a corporation's directors and higher firm value. *See* David A. Carter et al., *Corporate Governance, Board Diversity, and Firm Value*, 38 Fin. Rev. 33, 50–51 (2003). However, another commentator questions whether it is possible to measure the effect of women directors and directors of color, "because most corporate boards, which contain twelve members on average, usually have only one female or minority member who is unlikely to be able to influence significantly board decision making." Lynne L. Dallas, *The New Managerialism and Diversity on Corporate Boards of Directors*, 76 Tul. L. Rev. 1363, 1403 n.181 (2002). What does this suggest about the relationship between board composition and empathy?

13. In the same article quoted above, Dallas notes:

> One study of 240 nonprofit YMCA boards found that gender diversity was positively associated with an organization's ability to fulfill its social agency mission and had no relationship with the organization's operating efficiency. The study found a negative association between higher percentages of female directors and fundraising by the YMCA, which suggests, according to the researcher, that "women may not have access to needed economic, social and political resources, which may have influenced their success in the fundraising arena."

[The study referred to is Julie I. Siciliano, *The Relationship of Board Member Diversity to Organizational Performance*, 15 J. Bus. Ethics 1313, 1317 (1996).] Is the "resource-gathering function" identified by Langevoort analogous to nonprofit fundraising? If so what lessons does this study of nonprofits suggest for business corporations?

14. It is often assumed that corporations must choose between profitability and social responsibility. Wade's article, however, maintains that corporations can "do well by doing good." Can corporate social responsibility be reconceived as consistent with shareholder welfare instead of competing with it? What are the advantages and limitations of that approach?

If vigilant compliance with antidiscrimination laws benefits the corporation as well as society, as Wade argues, won't corporate directors and managers engage in such compliance measures out of self-interest? Why does effective compliance require racial empathy as well?

15. According to Wade, corporations should have systems to monitor and respond to allegations of employment discrimination in order "to satisfy the fiduciary duty of care that directors and managers owe to ensure that shareholder profits are not reduced as a result of noncompliance with applicable law." If the lack of monitoring systems puts corporate profits at risk, directors would have an incentive to implement such systems. But would a failure to implement such systems constitute a breach of the duty of care?

16. Consider John Coffee's argument from Chapter 6 that tort law prices, while criminal law prohibits. What does the fact that employment discrimination is a civil, not criminal, offense suggest about corporations' responsibility to comply with antidiscrimination law?

17. In Chapter 5, Johnson, Nelson and Pritchard argued that the PSLRA's effect on stock price may vary from firm to firm. In Chapter 6, Timothy Malloy argued that regulations should be "tailored" to fit the different bureaucratic characteristics of different firms. In this chapter, Langevoort and Fisch argue that optimal board composition will vary from firm to firm. Why then do you suppose the SEC has mandated a "one size fits all" rule for the exclusion of election proposals? What are the pros and cons of mandatory and enabling approaches to proxy access?

18. Would the SEC's 2009 14a-11 proposal (described in Joo's article) constitute a "subsidy" of shareholder proposals, as Romano uses the term in Chapter 7? Is there any justification for disfavoring contested elections other than favoritism for incumbents?

19. Why do you suppose the SEC amended 14a-8 in 2007 with such facially broad language, and narrowed the scope of that language by an interpretive release? Why not put the "contested election" interpretation into the Rule itself?

20. Should corporate law prescribe more specific corporate governance procedures and structures, as the Sarbanes-Oxley Act does? If so, should those prescriptions be made at the federal or state level?

21. On what basis does Mitchell conclude that the board of directors, and the monitoring board in particular, has been a failure? Do you agree?

22. Mitchell argues that a board that actively monitors CEO performance might encourage excessive caution or excessive risk. Should CEOs be made less accountable to boards? What effect might Mitchell's proposal for CEO elections have on CEOs' incentives to take risks?

23. Assuming that the CEO holds the real power in a corporation, does it follow that the office should be an elected one? Why do you suppose CEOs are appointed by boards, while boards are elected? Might this arrangement have advantages over the direct election of CEOs?

Chapter 10

Executive Compensation

Executive compensation implicates two major issues related to the separation of ownership and control. First, managers have incentives to neglect the effective management of corporate resources insofar as those resources belong not to them, but to shareholders. Executive compensation packages may be able to mitigate this problem if they can align managerial incentives with those of shareholders; Charles Elson applied this concept to directors in Chapter 9. Second, the design of managerial compensation is in the hands of another set of agents: directors. As discussed in Chapter 9, some observers believe that directors' relationships with executives may lead directors to favor executives' interests over those of shareholders.

In the 1990s, bonus payments, stock options, and equity compensation proliferated on the belief that such compensation packages linked executives' pay to their performance and thus aligned their interests with those of shareholders. In this chapter, Charles Yablon argues that performance-based pay cannot completely align management and shareholder interests due to intractable conflicts of interest in the corporate governance structure. The conflicts can be ameliorated, however, if directors are held more accountable for executive pay and performance-based pay is reformed to make executives bear greater risks for poor performance. Mark Loewenstein is skeptical of the prevailing arguments that executives receive "excessive" compensation and that CEOs effectively determine their own pay. He also critiques the effectiveness of legal tools currently employed to limit executive pay.

Troy Paredes examines the significance of executive compensation from a different perspective, examining its effect on CEO behavior. This approach reflects a growing interest in psychological analysis both in corporate governance and in policy debates in general.

This chapter then presents an important recent Delaware Supreme Court opinion regarding the role of directors in overseeing executive compensation. After nearly a decade of litigation, the court affirmed a trial verdict rejecting shareholders' claim that directors violated their fiduciary duty of care in approving an executive pay package.

Finally, Omari Simmons offers a contrarian view of the topic. He questions whether executive-pay reform, and the very issue of executive pay, are truly important matters, or merely serve to distract attention from more significant economic issues.

Charles M. Yablon, *Bonus Questions: Executive Compensation in the Era of Pay for Performance**

... Executive compensation traditionally has been a matter of concern to corporate law policy makers. It has long been recognized that the intimate ties between top executives

---

* Originally published in 75 NOTRE DAME LAW REVIEW 271 (1999). Volume 75, No. 1, Notre Dame

and the directors who set their salaries create an inherent conflict of interest, a tendency toward overgenerosity exacerbated, in the case of publicly held companies, by the fact that the money the directors are paying the CEOs is not their own. However, given judicial reluctance to second guess corporate decision making or judge any particular level of executive pay to be unreasonable, the problem was also understood to be pretty much insoluble through traditional legal means.

... In the good old days, circa 1990 or so, the problem of executive compensation was that greedy CEOs were receiving outrageous levels of compensation they did not deserve. These days, the problem is that greedy CEOs are receiving even more outrageous levels of compensation, which they may very well deserve. The trend towards performance-based pay means that some (although far from all) of the highest paid CEOs are those that have obtained extremely good results for their shareholders, making their multi-million dollar bonuses seem like justifiable rewards for a job well done and making plausible (although hardly proving) the proposition that such CEOs are being appropriately compensated for their unique managerial skills.

But it would really be rather surprising if these highly skilled corporate executives, whose talents, after all, consist primarily of their ability to utilize corporate resources in the manner most likely to maximize the value of the firm, would not use those same talents to utilize the corporate governance mechanisms in the manner most likely to maximize the value of their own compensation packages. That is precisely what many have done. Far from erasing the fiduciary problems inherent in executive compensation, the pay for performance trend has opened new potential conflicts between shareholders, the compensation-setting boards that shareholders increasingly view as their surrogates, and the CEOs.

The theory of pay for performance is that shareholders benefit when management compensation is significantly at risk, so that a high level of compensation is dependent on a high level of corporate performance. What most pay for performance fans tend to forget, however, is that it is not in management's interest to have a substantial portion of their potential remuneration at risk. All other things being equal, a CEO would much rather have the same levels of compensation at little or no risk. Accordingly, while CEOs and their compensation consultants often use the rhetoric of pay for performance to justify higher amounts of compensation, they may also seek to reduce the risk attached by increasing the number of options granted, setting easy performance goals, or repricing underwater options.

... The broader point of this Essay ... is that neither performance-based pay nor any other change in the form of executive compensation can fully align the interests of management with shareholders. Conflicts between agents and principals are built into the structure of the public corporation. Compensation is one area where they most directly conflict, and can only be ameliorated, never solved. The elements most likely to restrain the perennial executive push for more money are (1) full public disclosure concerning the compensation of top executives; (2) institutional shareholder concern and pressure for reform, at least in the most egregious cases of abuse; (3) serious directorial attention and responsibility for justifying both the form and amount of compensation they approve; and (4) a willingness on the part of the executives themselves to accept greater risk as a price for potentially greater compensation.

Law Review (October 1999), pages 271–308. Reprinted with permission. Copyright by Notre Dame Law Review, University of Notre Dame. The publisher bears responsibility for any errors that may have occurred during reprinting or editing.

As the following Essay shows, the first two elements are already largely, though not entirely, in place. The latter two, however, which are equally critical in restraining compensation abuses, still need quite a bit of work....

I. A Short History of Executive Compensation

Up until the beginning of this century, the problem of executive compensation did not really exist. People who ran corporations made money the old fashioned Marxist way — they owned the means of production. Early in this century, however, the development of large and relatively efficient capital markets, particularly in London and New York, enabled budding entrepreneurs and established businessmen to raise capital through the public sale of stocks. The result was the familiar separation of ownership and control in the public corporation.

This separation created a very great possibility that corporate officers could, in effect, steal corporate assets by obtaining compensation packages which exceeded the fair rate that they would have been paid for their services by a single shareholder owner. The main regulatory effort to restrain such conduct has been to encourage certain procedural safeguards like the delegation of all compensation decisions to a committee composed solely of outside directors.

As the corporate world changed over the last few decades, the concept of appropriate executive compensation changed as well. The sixties were the time of the great conglomerate mergers, when Harold Geneen at ITT and Charles Bluhdorn at Gulf & Western created vast corporate empires based on friendly acquisitions of disparate companies to create an impressive but frequently unmanageable whole. Not coincidentally, the captains of these corporate Titanics also led the way in compensation packages. In Forbes' first survey of the highest paid corporate executives in 1971, Harold Geneen of ITT finished first, earning what now seems a measly $767,000 ($3,221,400 in current dollars).

After a major recession in the U.S. in the early 1970s, the era of conglomerate mergers was replaced in the late 1970s and early 1980s by the era of hostile takeovers. Executives might wake up and read in the morning paper that some very rich but often vaguely disreputable corporate raider was making a tender offer for control of their company (note the possessive). The price being offered to shareholders through the tender offer was invariably at a premium well above the stock's prevailing market price.

In addition to posing a major practical problem for corporate managers, the growth and apparent success of many hostile takeovers posed an interesting theoretical problem for corporate academics: If, as is generally assumed, the capital markets are reasonably efficient, how was it possible for corporate raiders to make money by purchasing stock at well above market prices? The consensus answer, first expressed in the work of Professors Michael Jensen and William Meckling, was that hostile takeovers allowed vigilant corporate raiders to identify good companies with underperforming managers and replace them with stronger managers more responsive to shareholder concerns.[1] The increase in value created by such managerial changes could cause an increase in corporate value sufficient not only to justify the takeover premium, but to provide handsome profits for the raider as well. An underlying premise of this argument, you will note, was that before hostile takeovers became popular, there were a lot of underperforming corporate managers out there.

---

1. Michael C. Jensen & William H. Meckling, *Theory of the Firm: Managerial Behavior, Agency Costs and Ownership Structure*, 3 J. Fin. Econ. 305 (1976).

In the 1980s an even more theoretically puzzling phenomenon emerged: the MBO, or management buyout. Some officers of publicly held corporations, sometimes in response to or in anticipation of a hostile takeover bid, would make their own offer to shareholders. They sought to take their companies private by purchasing all the publicly traded stock, using borrowed funds which would later become corporate debt secured against the assets of the company. The MBO, if successful, would leave the management group as the sole equity holders and the company with very large debt obligations. Like the hostile raiders, these management groups also offered to buy out existing shareholders at a substantial premium above market price.

The MBO phenomenon seemed to pose a major problem for the theoretical understanding of control transactions. If the value created by hostile takeovers was primarily due to the raider's ability to replace underperforming managers, were managers who sponsored an MBO paying a premium to, in effect, replace themselves? Perhaps surprisingly, that was indeed what the theoreticians argued. Executives of publicly traded companies might well be underperforming, said the academics, not because they were lazy or lacked management skills, but simply because, as unmonitored agents, they lacked incentives to maximize shareholder value to the utmost. Quite the contrary, being rational profit maximizers, managers would have powerful incentives to utilize corporate cash flows in ways that would be most personally beneficial, like well furnished offices and corporate jets. Once an MBO occurs, however, that same management must generate sufficient corporate cash flows to pay the whopping interest bills on the debt it incurred to buy the company. Indeed, to make any money out of an MBO, management must generate cash flow that exceeds both operating costs and interest charges to create a profit. All the profit that gets created, however, goes into the pockets of the new owner managers. Many MBOs did succeed in creating such profits (although many also failed). The lesson to corporate academics, however, was that incentives were the crucial variable in managerial performance.

The stage was now set for a fundamental reconceptualization of the problem of executive compensation. Its popular expression came in a 1990 article in the Harvard Business Review titled *CEO Incentives — It's Not How Much You Pay, But How.*[2] In that article, Professors Jensen and Murphy argued that the problem of CEO compensation was not a matter of excess compensation over some fair or reasonable rate, but rather a misalignment of incentives. In a study of CEO pay over an extended period, Jensen and Murphy showed that there had been little correlation over the last thirty years between executive compensation and corporate performance. Rather, the primary determinant of the size of the executive's compensation was the size of the corporation, not its profitability. They argued that appropriate regulation of executive compensation would not involve reducing total pay or curbing specific abuses, but encouraging performance-based forms of compensation, like options and restricted stock, which more closely aligned the executive's interests with those of shareholders.

Jensen and Murphy's article was extremely influential. It fit well with both current theories of corporate governance and the prior experience of American business. It helped explain the empire building of the conglomerate mergers of the 1960s, since in making their companies bigger, even at the expense of profitability, those CEOs had been able to justify ever greater compensation. It explained why hostile takeovers, by replacing such managers and dismantling their corporate empires, could increase shareholder returns

---

2. Michael C. Jensen & Kevin J. Murphy, *CEO Incentives — It's Not How Much You Pay, But How*, HARV. BUS. REV., May–June 1990, at 138.

and profitability. It suggested that investors in all companies should do what managers of MBOs had already done for themselves — align the interests of management and shareholders so as to maximize profitability.

As a public policy matter, viewing executive compensation as an incentive alignment problem rather than as a breach of fiduciary duty had major advantages. It avoided having to ask courts, compensation committees, or anyone else to answer the difficult questions of how much compensation was reasonable for a CEO, or whether the process by which the compensation was set was fair. It substituted the far easier question of whether the form of the compensation was structured so as to provide incentives for shareholder wealth maximization. To the extent they did not, the solution was also easy — simply add such incentives as additional compensation above the executive's basic salary.

Accordingly, by the early 1990s the old concern about compensation as a breach of fiduciary duty had been largely replaced by the concern about compensation as a misalignment of incentives. This reconceptualization was embraced by virtually all the participants in the process. For institutional investors, it offered the prospect of increased managerial incentives to boost shareholder returns. For policy makers, it offered a tractable definition of the problem, clear policy objectives, and a viable regulatory program. For corporate executives and compensation consultants, it offered a powerful new set of arguments to justify increases in executive compensation.

Not surprisingly, the two major changes in U.S. legal regulation of executive compensation in the 1990s reflect this new emphasis on performance-based compensation. The first change was the adoption by the SEC of expanded disclosure rules regarding executive compensation. The disclosure required of public companies concerning the compensation paid to their directors and most highly compensated corporate officers was made much more detailed and specific. Compensation committees were required to set forth the basis on which their compensation decisions had been made, and comparative data was required relating the company's stock performance to that of other companies in its industry and to the market as a whole. The second major change was tax legislation prohibiting corporations from deducting any compensation paid to a corporate officer in excess of $1 million unless the additional compensation was performance-based. When Bill Clinton ran for the Presidency in 1992, he pledged to limit corporate deductibility of "excessive executive pay," which many interpreted as a cap on total pay. The legislation that actually passed, however, instead creates strong incentives for incentive-based pay. In the Section that follows, we will see these new rules in action.

II. Disney Dollars: A Case Study of Compensation Issues in Recent Disney Proxy Statements

... Like all the best media stories, the Disney saga implicates serious policy concerns while providing a vivid cast of characters and a direct connection to show business.

The focus of the story is Michael D. Eisner, Chairman of the Board and CEO of Walt Disney Company. Eisner, who had previously been President of Paramount Pictures, was recruited in 1984 to be Disney's CEO. He is one of the most highly paid chief executives of a publicly traded company. Between 1993 and 1996 he received $228 million in compensation as the CEO of Disney. In 1997, he negotiated a new employment contract.

Also making a significant appearance in the 1997 Disney Proxy Statement was Michael Ovitz. Ovitz had been a leading Hollywood agent and entertainment business entrepreneur. In 1995, when [Jeffrey] Katzenberg (the President and number two man at Disney) resigned after a falling out with Eisner, Ovitz was recruited to take his place. Ovitz negotiated a five-year employment contract for himself, which included one million dollars in base salary, discretionary bonuses, and five million dollars in stock options exercisable at market price on the date of issuance. The agreement also provided that, if Ovitz's employment with the company was terminated, most of these payment provisions would accelerate, giving him a hefty severance bonus. Ovitz also seems to have had a falling out with Mr. Eisner, and his employment was terminated by mutual agreement as of December 31, 1996. He received termination benefits valued at up to $140 million for slightly over one year of work. By January 6, 1997, derivative suits had been filed in California and Delaware state courts challenging the payments to Ovitz as a breach of fiduciary duty.[3]

There was also an intriguing cast of supporting characters, including Roy Disney, nephew of founder Walt Disney, who is the largest shareholder on the Disney board, owning 1.4% of the outstanding shares, Sidney Poitier, the actor, who sits on Disney's board and its compensation committee, and Reveta F. Bowers, Disney board member and principal of the private elementary school that Eisner's children once attended.

The major theme of the 1997 Disney Proxy Statement is, without a doubt, executive compensation. Of its thirty-five pages, twenty-one are devoted directly to the subject. These include a four page report of the Compensation Committee, another two pages summarizing the employment agreements of Eisner and Ovitz, and six more pages of summary charts and graphs relating to executive compensation. Although these sections might have been a little shorter in proxy statements for companies with less compensation to report, all of this information is basically required by the current rules of the SEC governing executive compensation. The heart of those rules are summary charts and graphs delineating and analyzing the compensation of the five most highly compensated corporate officers.

The Summary Compensation Table in the 1997 Disney Proxy succeeds (mostly) in giving us a pretty good idea of what is going on with Disney's compensation practices. Clearly Eisner is first among equals. Although his $750,000 base salary doesn't seem far beyond that of his colleagues, the seven to eight million dollar annual bonus he received during each of the three prior years clearly puts him in a different category from the rest. Even these amounts, however, were dwarfed by the eight million stock options Eisner received in 1996 in connection with his new employment agreement. That is eight million options, not eight million dollars....

At the time a stock option is granted, assuming that its exercise price is at or above fair market value on the date of issuance, it can be argued that the option has no value whatsoever.... [However,] stock options and their equivalents confer on their owners the right to benefit from future stock increases with no additional investment and no downside risk. Accordingly, the right provided by the typical option — to purchase company shares at a fixed price for an extended period (generally five to ten years) — is a valuable right, even on the day it is granted. How valuable, however, depends on the future performance of the company's stock, and that is a notoriously difficult thing to predict.

Because of these difficulties in valuation, the American accounting profession [did] not require companies to take any charge to earnings when they issue[d] options as executive compensation [until 2005]....

---

3. *See* In Re The Walt Disney Company Derivative Litigation, *excerpted in this chapter. — Ed.*

While the valuation of such stock-based incentives may be uncertain, in recent years, financial analysts, with the aid of sophisticated financial models and some very powerful computers, have become quite adept at making reasonable estimates concerning the present value of options based on certain assumptions about the stock's volatility, dividend yield, and prevailing risk-free interest rates. The most popular and prominent of these valuation techniques is the Black-Scholes option pricing model.

To get a sense of the value of the options granted to Eisner, one must turn to the table, "Option Grants During Fiscal 1996." In that table, Disney used the Black-Scholes model to compute the present value for Eisner's options at over $195 million.

One final question before we leave these basic disclosures regarding executive compensation: where, on these tables, is Michael Ovitz? Ovitz, you recall, obtained cash and options worth $140 million from Disney in 1996 as a result of getting fired and triggering the severance provisions in his employment contract. That would seem to place him at least second among Disney executives for 1996 compensation. Why isn't he on any of the tables? It appears that under the SEC regulations his termination benefits do not count as "compensation." Accordingly, the 1997 Proxy Statement blandly states that Ovitz was not in the top five because he "did not receive a bonus for fiscal 1996." The failure of the SEC to require any specific disclosure concerning severance or termination benefits in connection with its executive compensation disclosure appears to be a deficiency in those rules.

Nonetheless, the 1997 Disney Proxy enables us to determine that Eisner received a great deal of compensation in 1996, and it even gives us a fair idea as to how much. Does it give us any information as to whether he was worth it? The only objective data provided on that subject are two graphs which appear on pages nineteen and twenty of the Disney Proxy Statement. These are designed to enable shareholders to evaluate Disney's corporate performance in both absolute and relative terms. The first graph shows how much $100 worth of Disney stock purchased five years ago was worth at the end of fiscal 1996. It then compares that with the performance of the shares of a group of companies Disney has selected as its "peers" and with a broader-based index, the Standard and Poor's 500 (S&P 500). Although this graph may not seem to have much to do with executive compensation, it is in fact mandated by the SEC as part of the 1992 revisions of its executive compensation disclosure rules. The concept, clearly a product of the performance-based movement of the 1990s, was that if executives were being awarded above-average compensation, their companies should show above-average performance. On this basis, the five-year performance graph for Disney is a bit of a disappointment. It shows Disney doing no better than its peer companies over the relevant period and only slightly better than the broad based index.

Perhaps for that reason, Disney has included a second performance graph. This provides the same information, but provides it for a twelve-year period beginning in 1984. Here Disney is clearly the leader of the pack. Someone who invested in Disney in 1984 would have earned about three times as much from this investment as someone who bought the peer companies on the S&P 500. Unlike the five year graph that was mandated by SEC rules, this graph is not required by the SEC, although providing such additional information is certainly not prohibited. It is also probably not a coincidence that the performance period years begin in 1984, the year Eisner became CEO. But Disney's great performance over the first seven years of Eisner's stewardship and merely average performance during the next five raises further questions about his current compensation. It could be used to argue that Eisner should not seek to be paid for recent years at the same levels he received in the eighties. The alternative argument, of course, is that his drop in performance shows that he needs more incentives.

This, in essence, is the argument of the Disney Compensation Committee, whose report is also contained in the 1997 Disney Proxy Statement. There is much language in the report praising incentives generally and the performance-based nature of most of the compensation the committee has awarded. There is no attempt to justify the actual amounts being paid to Eisner.

This lack of justification was even more surprising in light of the fact that Disney shareholders were actually being asked to vote on Eisner's new compensation package. Such a vote was itself reflective of recent changes in executive compensation law. Under 162(m) of the Internal Revenue Code, passed in the first year of the Clinton administration, compensation to an executive of more than one million dollars per year is not deductible by the corporation unless it is "performance-based." The statute goes on to identify compensation as performance-based where: (i) it is based on performance goals set by a compensation committee composed solely of outside directors; (ii) the material terms, including the performance goals, have been disclosed to shareholders and "approved by a majority of the vote in a separate shareholder vote before the payment of such remuneration"; and (iii) the committee certifies that the performance goals have in fact been met.

Accordingly, in the 1997 Proxy, Disney shareholders were being asked for the first time to approve the performance-based bonus plans described in the Proxy Statement. In the absence of such approval, the future bonuses paid by Disney would not be deductible. The description of the plan the shareholders were being asked to approve, however, was surprisingly short on detail.

One of the few poignant moments in the 1997 Disney Proxy Statement appears in the shareholders proposals section, where a proposal submitted by a number of Roman Catholic organizations contrasts the pay scales of Michael Eisner with both those of the average U.S. worker and the reported wages of Haitian apparel workers who make clothes for Disney and asks the Board to consider "whether a cap should be placed on compensation packages for officers to prevent our company from paying excessive compensation." The Disney board recommends a vote "against." Its rationale, which somewhat misses the point of the critique, is that Eisner's compensation is justified because nearly ninety-eight percent of it is performance-based. The issue of income inequality raised by the proposal is left unaddressed.

The Disney shareholder meeting to which this proxy statement was addressed was held on February 25, 1997 in Anaheim, California, the home of Disneyland. Despite the fact that the meeting was held at a freezing cold ice hockey rink and that the stockholders who attended had all received free passes to Disneyland, the meeting lasted over four hours. Eisner, who attended, received a substantial amount of criticism from shareholders about his pay package as well as the Ovitz termination. (He publicly admitted that the Ovitz agreement had been a "mistake.") Nonetheless, even before he went into the meeting, Eisner knew he had more than enough votes to approve the compensation agreements. The eight percent of the voting shares that were voted against approval of Eisner's employment agreement, however, and the additional three percent who abstained were considered an "unusually strong rebuke" of the company's compensation practices. Of course, the fact that approval of an executive compensation agreement by slightly less than ninety percent of the voting shares is considered a "rebuke" may also tell us something about the effectiveness of shareholder voting as a curb on excessive compensation.

The 1998 Disney Proxy Statement and Annual Meeting were a bit of a letdown after the fireworks of the prior year. Eisner did not receive any more options, although his $9.9

million performance-based bonus on top of his $750,000 salary represented an increase in cash compensation of twenty-three percent. Certain efforts appear to have been taken to avoid some of the criticism Disney had received the previous year, particularly from its institutional shareholders. For one thing, the site of the meeting was changed from Anaheim to Kansas City (no more free tickets to Disneyland), and space limitations permitted shareholders to bring only one guest. More substantively, the 1998 Proxy Statement sought authority to abolish the classified nature of Disney's board and have each member stand for reelection each year.

In any event, institutional investors were clearly not placated. The College Retirement Equities Fund (CREF), an institutional investor which often takes public stands on corporate governance issues, submitted a shareholder proposal which, in effect, attacked the Disney board for not being sufficiently independent of management. It proposed that a majority of the board and all members of the Audit, Compensation, and Nominating Committees consist of directors with no "significant personal or financial ties" to the company or its management. While never mentioning Eisner or compensation issues expressly, there is little doubt that the CREF proposal was a reaction to Disney's problems of the previous year and reflected the view of many observers that the Disney board has been a little lax in exercising managerial oversight.

The CREF proposal received over thirty-five percent of the vote, an extremely strong showing for a proposal opposed by management, and appeared to have received support from almost all of Disney's institutional shareholders. To be sure, the proposal was not a direct attack on Eisner or his compensation, but rather a vote in favor of greater board independence. Nonetheless, the vote on the CREF resolution does seem to reflect a growing unease in many parts of the business community over the failure of boards or anyone else to impose effective limits on executive compensation. As Graef Crystal, a compensation consultant to the Disney board put it, in discussing compensation trends generally, "It can't go on like this forever."

III. Weighing Options: The Policy Implications of Performance-Based Pay

The foibles and excesses of the rich are always amusing, but the big policy question raised by these proxies is whether they actually raise a big policy question. Are current corporate remuneration practices, and the regulation that encourages them, a serious cause for concern? Or do critics of Eisner and his ilk merely have a bad case of options envy?

The Disney story illustrates well both the progress and problems in the field of executive compensation. Current SEC disclosure rules succeed fairly well in providing clear and detailed information to shareholders concerning the compensation practices of publicly traded firms, though a few problematic areas such as termination and severance pay remain. (Remember Michael Ovitz's curious absence from the Disney proxy?) ...

Who is hurt by excessive executive pay? Certainly those shareholders are hurt whose earnings are diminished or whose shares are diluted by options grants to CEOs. Investors as a group are hurt if more deals are being structured to meet performance goals or compensation concerns of incumbent management rather than to maximize shareholder returns, or if fewer talented managers are interested in starting or investing in new businesses because equally great and far less risky returns are available to them from managing established ones. And society as a whole is likely to be hurt if an increasing number of its brightest and most talented people feel obligated to pursue managerial careers but become frustrated by their failure to make it to the lucrative top of an increasingly unequal "winner take all society."

A. Shareholder Concerns

As the recent Disney vote indicates, even shareholders of fairly successful companies are beginning to realize that giving CEOs whatever they want so long as it is "performance-based" is not in the best interests of shareholders. In the first place, what CEOs mostly want is lots of compensation for very little risk. Shareholders, even if willing to pay lots of compensation, want it to be at risk to provide the appropriate incentives. Second, all of that compensation has to come from somewhere, and that somewhere is the shareholder's earnings per share, either through diminished profits or dilution of outstanding shares. Finally, managerial overreaching and directorial acquiescence may be tolerable in good financial times, but may create habits that are difficult to break when economic times turn bad. The possibility of wealth transfers from shareholders to managers has existed for a long time. Performance-based pay, however, provides new and audacious ways to accomplish such transfers.

All of these concerns come together in two of the most troubling aspects of current compensation practices—megagrants of stock options and options repricing. Excessive performance-based pay can result from either excessive amounts of compensation or insufficient performance requirements.... [T]he trend toward showering CEOs with options has become so pronounced that even many of the shareholder advocates who were prime movers of the pay for performance bandwagon are expressing some second thoughts.

Their concern, not surprisingly, is with diminution in risk and loss of incentives. If the CEO is handed an options package with a present value of one hundred million dollars, an average or even below average rise in market price of the underlying stock will be enough to make him quite rich. About the only thing he really has to worry about is a major sell off or crash, and even that can be solved by a little option repricing. In short, while large grants of stock options are generally considered performance-based pay, they often involve large payments with very little risk attached.

Granting large blocks of options not only reduces the CEOs' risk, but potentially dilutes the wealth of existing shareholders. Institutional investors talk about the "overhang" effect created when options relating to ten percent or more of a company's shares are held by executives and waiting to be exercised. The point is not that such megagrants are always a bad idea and should be prohibited, but that they impose heavy and often hidden costs on existing shareholders and should therefore not be granted by boards lightly or as a matter of course.

A similar point can be made about another recent focus of shareholder concern— options repricing. Critical to the idea of performance-based pay is that managers must have a credible fear that poor corporate performance will decrease their compensation.... Some managers have indeed accepted the downs as wells as the ups of incentives, taking sharply reduced, even zero pay when stock prices have dipped, but there are also a disturbing number of cases in which failed performance-based plans have simply been replaced with new, richer plans with easier targets....

An exclusive focus on repricing, however, reflects a misunderstanding of the basic problem, which is not about the use of certain forms of pay, but the acquiescence of boards in pay packages that provide CEOs with little incentive or downside risk. The critical issue is not the repricing itself, but whether the CEO knows, or has a reasonable expectation, that a poor stock performance will result in a repricing. Obviously, such expectations will destroy any incentive effect the options plan might have had. But viewed as a compensation decision, repricing a CEO's options may be a reasonable compensation strategy if offered by a board to create new incentives for a CEO, where the prior downturn is not seen as a CEO's fault and where the repricing creates no expectation of further repricings....

A final and serious danger for shareholders is the increased incentive performance-based pay gives CEOs to manipulate the timing of reports about corporate performance and perhaps to manipulate the substance of those reports as well. This is not traditional insider trading, but the harder to detect and police problem of CEOs delaying or accelerating disclosure of information because of the effect it may have on a personal compensation issue. Announcements of bad corporate news will tend to come after, rather than before, the date a CEO has exercised his options. CEOs have all the traditional informational advantages of intimate knowledge of the company, as well as power over the timing of such public announcements.

Even more troubling may be the effect on corporate performance. Most compensation is tied to earnings either directly, (through performance goals), or indirectly, through stock price. There is a growing concern, both at the SEC and among investors, about the increasing use of accounting gimmicks to inflate corporate earnings. Some have even suggested that the increased use of stock options and other performance-based CEO compensation may be a factor in the increased use of such tricks.

B. Concerns about Economic Incentives

... [T]here is something vaguely anti-capitalist in performance-based compensation that gives managers all the benefits of successful stock investments while removing most of the downside risk. Traditionally, there have been significant differences in the risk/reward structures of owners and managers. Entrepreneurs and venture capitalists investing in start up or small companies took large risks in the hope of obtaining even larger rewards. Corporate raiders and LBO (leveraged buyout) specialists were also willing to put their (admittedly often borrowed) money where their mouths were. Managers of established corporations, who took much smaller risks, could not expect to receive the same levels of income as a successful entrepreneur, investor, or corporate raider.

The levels of compensation that are now becoming available to successful CEOs threaten to erode this distinction between managers and owners. One effect may be on the kind of deals CEOs pursue.... Some entrepreneurs, most famously Ted Turner, have been willing to give up control in exchange for a managerial position in a larger publicly held company. Many of the mega-deals of the 1990s not only provide enormous payouts to the option-holding managers of the merged companies, but more ominously, hold out the prospect of even larger pay packages to the managers of the larger, newly created entity. Perhaps these new corporate giants really need to pay such amounts to attract the top level managerial talent to exploit the synergistic potential of these new mega-firms, but the trend seems disturbingly reminiscent of the conglomerate mergers of the 1960s.

Equally troubling are the incentive effects of a corporate world in which CEOs of existing companies make as much as top entrepreneurs and investors. The problem is not that Bill Gates deserves to make more than Michael Eisner in any deep moral sense, or even that he has a harder job. But people who try to emulate Bill Gates and create moderately successful new businesses are an important source of jobs and economic growth. It is not at all clear that the same is true for people who try to emulate Michael Eisner and wind up stuck in middle management.

C. Equality Concerns

... In their [1995] book, *The Winner-Take-All Society*, Professors Robert Frank and Philip Cook describe both the changes they see as leading to the increase in income inequality in America and the policy arguments for seeking to limit and reverse that trend.... ... [I]t must be conceded that CEO pay has little to do with the income gap between rich and poor, which is much more a function of disparities in education, decline in the labor movement, and changes in the job market.

CEO pay is much more directly involved in the growing disparity of incomes within the top twenty percent. This is the concern to which Frank and Cook's book is primarily addressed, and they make a persuasive argument that in a society in which the vast majority of benefits go to the lucky few, there will be a great deal of inefficient utilization of resources as people fail to accurately assess their chances of hitting the big time. Such people will waste time, energy, and resources struggling to become, say, unhappy and not very successful executives, corporate lawyers, or basketball players, when, if pay scales for other jobs had been a little closer to those of top CEOs, lawyers or ball players, they might have found more satisfying careers as teachers, carpenters, or engineers. Thus, Frank and Cook argue, the growth of income inequality violates norms, not only of fairness, but of efficiency as well.

But what about the argument that these folks are worth it—that they create enormous value for the people who pay them? Unlike the older critics of executives and others who earn similar amounts, Frank and Cook do not deny that they may well be "worth it" in the narrow sense that existing markets make it rational for owners or investors in certain enterprises to pay enormous amounts for the services of certain individuals. But markets themselves are artificial things, constantly changing due to developments in technology, regulation, and taste. Clearly, if motion pictures and television had not been invented, Mel Gibson and Michael Jordan, even with precisely the same skills, would not command the compensation they get in today's markets. The public corporation itself, as we noted previously, is the product of the legal development of capital markets in early twentieth century. In short, the fact that highly paid executives may be "worth it" given the market in which they sell their services does not make them any more normatively entitled to such compensation than a lottery winner.

But even if excessive executive compensation poses all these problems, and even if a little more board oversight and restraint in approving CEO pay packages would be a good thing generally, this does not mean that additional regulation is advisable. The increased regulation may create more problems than it solves, or the problem may be self-correcting. We consider these issues and a modest proposal for change in the next Section.

D. The Three Million Dollar Solution—Deductibility Caps and Performance-Based Pay

Ideally, under the American system of corporate governance, the primary source of restraint and deliberation with respect to executive compensation decisions should be the board of directors, particularly its compensation committee. In practice, directors rarely have reasons to negotiate hard on CEO salaries, but they often do have powerful incentives to give the CEO what he wants. In addition to the intangible ties of friendship and admiration that frequently unite directors with the CEO who may have been responsible for their appointment, there is the sound managerial judgment that a happy CEO is likely to be a maximally productive CEO. Accordingly, if that CEO thinks he needs eight million options to perform his best, who wants to try to bargain him down to four million, thereby running the risk he may feel resentful or unloved and spend more time either at the golf course or looking for another job. Moreover, there is undoubtedly a compensation consultant standing by, assuring the board that the compensation package requested by the CEO is easily justifiable in light of general rises in compensation levels, the fact that most of it is performance-based, etc. In short, once the board has decided that their current CEO is the right person for the job (and that tends to be the attitude of most incumbent boards), they have little incentive to exercise restraint in negotiating his compensation package.

Is there anyone else who might encourage limits on executive compensation? Institutional investors are obvious candidates, but they operate under many of the same constraints as directors. It may well be worthwhile for relational investors with sizable stakes in a company to seek to remove CEOs who are underperforming or opposed to value-enhancing corporate restructurings. But if a relational investor basically approves of current management and is looking to the CEO to increase corporate earnings and share value, such an investor has little incentive to pick a fight over a few million dollars of CEO compensation.

At one time I had hoped that corporate gadflies and investor activists, by publicizing and bringing lawsuits against the worst abuses, might impose a general restraining influence on compensation decisions. But this has not come to pass.

In the absence of any other likely sources of limits on the ever upward trend of compensation decisions, I submit it is time to rethink the idea of a deductibility cap. I know the idea of governmental limits on the amounts someone can earn seem anathema to many on ideological grounds. But a deductibility cap is far from a prohibition or any sort of wage or price control. It simply says that for every dollar above the cap which the board decides to pay to its CEO as compensation, it must also pay thirty-five cents to the federal government. Indeed, it is precisely the extreme reluctance of American business people to pay extra amounts of corporate tax, in contrast to their general willingness to pay extra amounts of executive compensation, which makes the deductibility cap a potentially effective restraint on excessive compensation. It provides a marker, a signpost, at which boards and compensation committees are likely to stop and consider the compensation decision more closely, with their reluctance to incur the double corporate tax bite acting as a counterweight to their general inclination to give the CEO whatever he wants.

It should be remembered, of course, that there already is a deductibility cap in the current tax law, but by applying only to nonperformance-based pay, the message it sends is that there are no limits with respect to performance-based pay. As we have seen, it is this same attitude which underlies the philosophy of many compensation committees and has the pernicious effect of causing them to abdicate any efforts at restraint. A deductibility cap on total pay (performance-based as well as not) would have a salutary effect of reminding boards that all forms of compensation must meet criteria of reasonableness.

It is not difficult to design a deductibility cap that would apply to all forms of compensation while retaining strong incentives toward performance-based pay. One could keep the current one million dollar cap on nonperformance-based compensation, but give corporations a right to deduct an additional amount, I would propose an additional two million dollars, in performance-based pay. The fact that companies can pay up to three million dollars to their executives in performance-based form while only one million dollars in straight salary should still provide a powerful incentive for most companies and executives to prefer performance-based pay.

Another incentive to performance-based pay would be to compute the deductibility cap on the present value of the options or other performance-based pay at the time of its issuance.... Valuing such pay on a risk discounted basis ... might channel the natural competition among CEOs into more shareholder-beneficial forms. It is likely that the push for ever higher levels of executive compensation is at least as much the result of competition among CEOs for recognition and reward as it is a reflection of CEO demands for a living wage. Valuing compensation on a risk discounted present-value basis would mean that a CEO could get more compensation, within the deductibility cap, if he were willing to accept more risk. For example, a CEO who was willing to accept options with a strike price ten percent above market could receive more such options than a CEO who demanded a strike price equal to market on the day of issuance and still qualify under the deductibility cap. A CEO who took options set at twenty-five percent over market could receive even more. There are indications that many CEOs would be inclined to take such riskier compensation, which represents a vote of confidence in both their own managerial skills and their company's prospects. If the Forbes and Business Week surveys focused not merely on which CEOs made the most, but on which CEOs realized the most total value from securities with an initial risk discounted present value of three million dollars, they would provide a closer alignment between CEO success and shareholder benefit.

What are the likely objections to a revised deductibility cap? The most predictable is a general ideological objection to governmental interference in the market for executive compensation. If superstar CEOs can command multi-million dollar bonuses in today's market, more power to them, and the government has no business poking its nose into the compensation-setting process....

The [most] cogent objection to this line of argument is to question its premise that, absent governmental regulation, the CEO compensation-setting process would be an efficient one, characterized by arms length bargaining and a rational assessment by the board of the value the CEO creates for the firm. As we have seen, compensation decisions rarely resemble arms length bargains but involve inherent tensions and conflicts of interest, and the results often raise questions as to the board's impartiality and objectivity. But all big CEO pay packages are not inherently breaches of fiduciary duty either. Rather, an honest assessment of the compensation-setting process in American public companies would recognize, as the Delaware Supreme Court put it in another context, "the omnipresent specter that a board [and management] may be acting primarily in its own interests" when determining CEO pay. Such concerns, as the Delaware Supreme Court also recognized, call not for a flat prohibition on the questionable conduct, but for higher levels of consideration and review, such as those a deductibility cap might promote.

The above considerations also respond to a more sophisticated version of the prior objection, which is "Why single out CEOs?" Lots of people are earning enormous compensation these days, yet only CEO pay is subject to these special tax rules. The answer, of course, is that only CEOs are likely to have the kind of intimate relationships with the people who are setting their salaries, which inherently raise concerns. In addition to the fact that CEO compensation is more likely to involve excessive wealth transfers than corporate payments to movie stars or investment bankers, a restraint on CEO compensation may have salutary effects on other spiraling pay scales. If, as seems likely, most people judge appropriate compensation levels in comparison with their own pay, a limit on their own compensation may make CEOs a little more reluctant to approve big corporate payments to others when the benefits of such payments to the company are not clearly apparent.

Aside from these philosophical objections, there are various technical concerns that might be raised. Present valuations of uncertain future returns is not an exact science. There are certainly dangers that companies will "massage" the computations to bring their present value calculations within the deductibility cap. Exotic forms of compensation might be concocted for which relatively standard valuation methods like the Black-Scholes model do not exist, giving companies greater leeway to avoid the rules. All these points boil down to the concern that some companies will cheat and others will hire high priced experts to help them beat the system. In short, a deductibility cap will be treated like any other restrictive tax rule. But the nice thing about the deductibility cap is that it does not have to be perfect to work well. Even if companies can find ways to pay their CEO compensation with a value of somewhat more than three million dollars, the fact that boards focus on and feel constrained by the three million dollar limit would mean that the deductibility cap was performing its function, which is simply to promote restraint on executive pay levels.

A greater concern is that the deductibility cap might actually raise compensation levels by turning the maximum level of pay into a minimum. There is some indication of such a tendency in connection with the present one million dollar salary cap. Given current trends in executive pay, however, it is hard to imagine that incentives to boost pay will be increased by a three million dollar deductibility cap. Three million dollars is already at or close to median total pay according to many of the surveys. Compensation committees that feel their companies are too small or too poor to pay that level of compensation are unlikely to change their views as a result of a deductibility limit. Even if they do, the limit would remain as a restraint on future increases....

Mark J. Loewenstein, *The Conundrum of Executive Compensation**

....

I. Are American CEOs Overpaid?

No serious consideration of solutions to the "problem" of executive compensation should proceed before determining whether, in fact, CEOs are overpaid. Many articles and books simply assume that to be the case, in part because the data regarding CEO pay seems so compelling. The conclusion that U.S. CEOs are paid excessively is generally based on one or more of these arguments: first, that the differential between CEO pay and that of blue collar workers has increased "exponentially" in the past two decades; second, that U.S. CEOs earn dramatically more than their counterparts in Europe and Japan, who head companies that compete with U.S. firms; and third, that CEO pay is not correlated to corporate performance, particularly increases in shareholder wealth. Overlaying all of these arguments is the structural argument—corporate boards are "captured" by the CEO and thus incapable of bargaining with the CEO. Under this scenario, CEOs use their leverage over these captive boards to extract excessive compensation. These arguments

---

* Originally published in 35 WAKE FOREST LAW REVIEW 1 (2000). Reprinted with permission.

do not, however, prove the premise, no matter how forcefully (or indignantly) they are stated.

A. *Comparisons with Rank and File Workers and Foreign CEOs*

The first two arguments are not persuasive, and for similar reasons. Much of the increase in CEO pay is directly attributable to the increase in stock prices over the past two decades, as the portion of CEO pay in stock options has risen dramatically in the past several years. Had the stock market declined over this period, the change in the differential between CEO and average worker compensation would look quite different, as the average worker is not paid in stock options. Similarly, stock options have not been common overseas. One compensation consultant has noted that CEO pay differences are not that dramatic between Europe and the United States unless long-term incentives—typically stock options—are taken into account. In other countries, various obstacles, including unfavorable tax treatment, have limited the use of stock options as compensation. More importantly, whether comparison is to the average worker or the foreign CEO, neither of these arguments addresses the normal market forces, either as they affect the average worker or as they affect U.S. and foreign CEOs.

One legitimate question in this area, rarely considered in reference to CEO pay, is why the wages of average workers have risen so slowly. The answer, of course, relates to the supply and demand for workers. Less skilled workers are increasingly competing with workers in foreign countries, where wages are low. This has reduced the bargaining power of U.S. workers to demand wage increases, as such workers face the threat of plant closings or technological replacement. While a more thorough analysis of this question is beyond the scope of this Article, there is little dispute that economic forces are holding down the wages of the average worker relative to CEO pay. These same economic forces may explain the rise in CEO pay, as the demand for highly skilled corporate chieftains may be outstripping the supply. Indeed, recent stories in the Wall Street Journal note the extreme shortage of talent in this market. Notably, while CEO pay has risen much faster than the pay of average workers, CEO pay has risen much slower than the pay of professional athletes. During the period 1980–95, the pay of the average worker increased 60%, that of CEOs 380%, National Basketball Association players 640%, National Football League players 800%, and Major League Baseball players 1000%. Again, market forces are likely at work in all cases.

When comparing pay across borders, one must consider first that, outside of the United States, Canada, and Great Britain, data on executive pay is very difficult to obtain and comparisons often depend on estimates. Of equal importance, critics of CEO pay rarely discuss many factors that may account for pay disparities. For instance, German companies may pay executives a second salary in a tax haven, which is not reported. In many countries overseas, perquisites are an important component of compensation and do not appear on comparison tables. In addition to their monetary value, perquisites may have an important non-monetary component. For instance, Japanese executives place a greater value than U.S. CEOs on the prestige of being a chief executive and, therefore, may be willing to accept a lower salary. Similarly, tax rates and purchasing power vary from country to country and should be considered in cross-country comparisons.

B. *Comparisons with Corporate Performance*

The final argument—that CEO pay is not correlated to performance—is the most forceful of these arguments, but it is still unpersuasive as a basis to conclude that CEOs are overpaid. Part of the problem in this area relates to what constitutes "performance." Critics of CEO pay tend to compare changes in CEO pay to changes in shareholder wealth, that is, dividends paid and increases in share prices. There is some logic to this comparison, as increasing share prices are the primary way that shareholders can benefit from their investments and, therefore, the CEO should be focused on that goal. On the other hand, CEOs have no control over the stock market, which is affected by factors such as general economic conditions, politics, and a wide array of other factors. Consequently, firms often correlate CEO pay to other performance measures, such as profits, return on equity, earnings per share, etc., that the CEO and management team presumably can influence. In the long term, achieving these financial goals should redound to the benefit of shareholders, but, given the vagaries of the stock markets, these accomplishments might not be immediately reflected in share prices.

In addition to oversimplifying the pay-performance issue, critics often explain increases in CEO pay as a function of the tendency of compensation committees to rely on salary surveys and peg the pay of their CEO in the top quadrant of the survey. This practice results in a "ratcheting up" effect as firms leap frog one another in fixing pay. Critics then argue that the market becomes distorted and that pay is more rational if related to performance, again narrowly defined. While the use of salary surveys seems to be widespread and their effect inflationary, as a practical matter, boards and compensation committees cannot set pay without regard to the pay of executives in comparable firms. Relying, at least in part, on pay surveys accommodates a firm's important motivational, recruitment, and retention concerns. Moreover, critics assume that use of the surveys results in an increase in compensation that otherwise would not have occurred. There is, however, reason to doubt this. The theory suggests that, in the absence of surveys, directors would bargain harder with the CEO, with the result of lower compensation, and that surveys somehow make the directors less effective bargainers. The executive finding himself or herself below the median may be motivated to seek higher compensation, but then why is the board not similarly motivated to hold down compensation when it discovers it is paying well above the median? Finally, executive pay has informational attributes: in light of disclosure, a firm may wish to convey information about its success or prospects through its CEO pay.

More to the point, much of the dramatic increase in CEO compensation is a direct result of the increase in incentive compensation in the form of stock options, which, in turn, were implemented by corporate boards in response to demands that CEO compensation be more closely linked to shareholder returns. This linkage is a justified measure to address the agency cost that shareholders otherwise bear: corporate executives have natural incentives to devote less than their greatest efforts to corporate business and to consume more leisure and other perquisites than is in the best interests of shareholders. Aligning executive and shareholder interests reduces this agency cost and provides a justification for granting large stock options to executives.

While generous stock plans are not the only means to reduce agency costs, they do provide some unique efficiencies. An alternative is to more closely monitor corporate executives; the board, presumably, could do this.... [I]f the CEO's compensation scheme does not provide the right incentives, the board must somehow be motivated to provide the close monitoring that would serve as a substitute, and that would come at a cost. Charles Elson has suggested that this motivation could be provided if individual directors had significant stock ownership in the companies they direct.[4] ...

---

4. *See Professor Elson's article in this volume. — Ed.*

Elson's proposal, however, is costly. He acknowledges that directors would have to receive "substantial" stock ownership and assumes that five years' worth of director fees paid in stock "should" be enough. However, judging how much stock is sufficient and whether stock acquired by the director in partial payment of a director's fee has the same motivational effects as stock purchased by the director is difficult. As to the former, a director with a multimillion-dollar portfolio of his or her own may not be highly motivated to enhance the value of $175,000 worth of stock to $250,000. In addition, all of the directors would have to receive substantial amounts of stock. The aggregate of these stakes may well exceed the stake that would properly motivate the CEO to perform in the shareholders' interests. Put differently, minimizing agency costs is not free, and a properly structured executive compensation package may be the least expensive means of accomplishing it.

More fundamentally, the important empirical question is the relationship between firm performance and ownership structure. If the board owns a significant stake in the firm, intuitively it would have incentives to monitor effectively. However, those incentives might be offset by an entrenchment effect. Indeed, one study found that firm value initially rises with increases in inside ownership and then falls, presumably due to the entrenchment effect. One recent empirical study, examining the relationship between corporate governance, executive pay, and firm performance was unable to find evidence that greater equity ownership by outside directors results in improved governance systems....

The alternative to a properly structured long-term incentive plan and active board-based monitoring is an active market for corporate control; that is, monitoring by the market. If a corporation is under-performing in the product market, or inefficiently employing its capital, this should be reflected in its stock market price. In theory, therefore, the market for corporate control would act as a monitor of excessive compensation. If resources are wasted on executive compensation, fewer resources are devoted to generating income and profits, and the corporation should be vulnerable to a takeover. There are several reasons why the market for corporate control is not a viable option, however. First, the amounts devoted to CEO compensation are, on average, immaterial. For instance, Kevin Murphy calculated that, in 1992, the 1000 largest U.S. corporations, whose total market capitalization was $3.4 trillion, paid their CEOs a total of $2.2 billion.[5] Had these CEOs worked without compensation that year, shareholder returns, which averaged 24%, would have increased by only 0.06 percentage points. This sort of increase in returns would hardly justify a 30–40% premium over market price, which is typical in a hostile tender offer.

Second, the barriers in the market for corporate control are substantial. The financial, legal, regulatory, and other expenses of a takeover are considerable. Judicial approval of poison pills and other corporate-developed defenses to takeovers, combined with widespread adoption of state antitakeover statutes, have made corporations much less vulnerable to hostile takeovers than they were in the 1980s. Finally, it is somewhat ironic to think of a takeover bid being motivated by a perception that the corporation can be operated more efficiently with a "cheaper" CEO. Indeed, the opportunity to receive a generous compensation package often motivates (at least in part) a takeover and justifies the premium the purchaser is willing to pay. In any case, the amount that can be saved in CEO compensation, standing alone, is unlikely to justify the considerable expenses of such a transaction.

---

5. Kevin J. Murphy, *Politics, Economics, and Executive Compensation*, 63 U. CIN. L. REV. 713, 726 (1995).

In sum, it would appear that performance-based pay plans that compensate managers with stock or stock options are an appropriate way to address the agency problem and award performance....

II. Structural Deficiencies of the Board as an Explanation for CEO Pay

Regardless of what comparative measure of evaluating CEO pay the critic chooses, the overarching explanation, or story, is that the CEO essentially controls the process by which his or her compensation is determined. The CEO, presumably, "hand picks" the outside directors for board service, including service on a compensation committee. The committee, in turn, is advised by a consultant selected by, and beholden to, the CEO. The analysis concludes that the "captured committee" and the "captured board" are simply incapable of bargaining hard with the CEO and, as a result, inevitably overcompensate the CEO. A variant of this story posits that the board and compensation committee consist of CEOs of other companies who have an interest in high CEO pay. Challenges to this story, whether empirical or theoretical, are rare. There are, however, grounds to doubt it.

As a preliminary matter, boards are far more independent of CEOs today than they were, say, twenty years ago when concerns about CEO pay became newsworthy, and this is particularly so since the early 1990s. Independent nominating and compensation committees are now common, particularly on stock exchange listed companies. If anything, the story is based on a somewhat outdated view of corporate governance. Second, the story does not at all account for the pay packages of incoming CEOs, who, by definition, could not have captured the board yet receive large pay packages. The oft-cited example of Michael Eisner's pay package at Disney illustrates some of these factors. His reported pay in 1993 of $203 million (which nearly equaled his combined pay for the preceding five years) astounded many people but reflected the value of options granted over nearly a decade at Disney, during which time Disney's stock price rose more than six-fold. Eisner negotiated this with a board he did not control, and it was the sort of deal that shareholders should applaud.

Third, the story depends on overbearing CEOs and timid boards in literally hundreds of public companies. The CEO must be able to: a) cause the nominating committee to nominate only individuals favorable to him, b) cause the board to appoint patsies to the compensation committee, and then c) dominate the compensation committee. Is this plausible? Are corporate boards heavily populated by individuals who simultaneously have the credentials to direct multibillion-dollar corporations but no capacity to exercise independent judgment when the issue is CEO compensation? ...

... [A] recent empirical study failed to confirm the hypothesis that "captured" directors or the presence of other CEOs on a compensation committee are correlated with higher levels or changes in CEO pay.[6] This study examined "multiple measurements of board interdependence at the committee level and multiple measurements of CEO compensation over several years." The authors studied a random sample of 200 manufacturing companies on the 1992 Fortune 500 list. The study was unique because the authors looked at changes in both contingent and non-contingent compensation over a three-year period on the theory that the decisions of a compensation committee with respect to contingent compensation (and, to some degree, non-contingent compensation) are only apparent over time. The results were surprising:

---

6. Catherine M. Daily, et al., *Compensation Committee Composition as a Determinant of CEO Compensation*, 41 ACAD. MGMT. J. 209 (1998).

1. Higher proportions of affiliated directors on the compensation committee did not necessarily mean higher levels of CEO pay. (The authors define "affiliated directors" as directors with personal and/or professional relationships with the firm or its management.)

2. There was weak statistical support for the hypothesis that a higher proportion of "captured directors" on a compensation committee leads to higher CEO pay. (The authors did not use the term "captured directors;" instead, they employed the term "interdependent directors," which they defined as "directors appointed during the tenure of an incumbent CEO.")

3. Counter to expectations, "[a] high proportion of CEOs on a compensation committee was associated with a lower level of change" in total compensation.

Assessing these findings, the authors concluded: "In sum, these findings suggest that the presence on compensation committees of high proportions of the directors most implicated in discussions of excessive executive compensation does not result in higher levels of CEO compensation in subsequent years." One can only speculate on why this is so. One obvious explanation is that directors take their responsibilities seriously and act in the shareholders' interests, not the interest of the CEO. Regardless of the explanation, however, this study suggests caution in mandating reforms to corporate boards. If the relationship between a director and the CEO does not explain the directors' actions on compensation matters, then specifying the characteristics of directors who might serve on a compensation committee or board, with the expectation that a change will occur in CEO compensation, is unwarranted.

III. Some Evidence that the Market is Functioning

To this point, I have considered the arguments that CEOs are overcompensated and tried to demonstrate that neither the theoretical arguments nor the data unambiguously support the proposition that CEOs are overpaid. This analysis, of course, does not prove that there is an efficient and functioning market setting CEO pay at an appropriate level. There are, however, some indications that a market is functioning. For instance, several studies have found that CEO pay is positively correlated to the complexity of the organization that the CEO is managing. One recent study focused on the relationship between, among other things, the degree of a firm's internationalization and the level and structure of CEO compensation. Building on earlier work, the authors described the increased complexity of managing an international firm, noting the spatial complexity associated with geographic dispersion of sales, assets, and personnel. It is also more difficult and costly for the board to monitor the firm. The authors hypothesized and demonstrated that the pay of CEOs in such firms is higher because the skills needed are a "scarce and valuable resource" and because pay reflects a higher proportion of long-term compensation, indicating the difficulty in monitoring the CEO's performance. These findings suggest that market factors may be operating: firms face a smaller pool of qualified executives and therefore offer a more attractive pay package to attract an acceptable CEO. The captured board story does not explain why companies with complex businesses and organizations pay their CEOs more.

There are other indications that the market is operating. A study of data from 120 firms in 1977–81 disclosed that CEOs recruited from outside of the firms are paid significantly more than CEOs recruited internally. We would expect this sort of result in a competitive market. In fact, in the market for professional athletes, the athletes are frequently paid significantly more when they become "free agents." Another indication that CEOs are not overcompensated comes from a 1985 study of the stock price reaction to the unexpected death of a firm's CEO. This study demonstrated that, on average, the market reacted negatively to the news, suggesting that investors view the CEO as adding value to the firm. If the CEO could be replaced with someone earning less or performing more effectively, we would expect the stock price, on average, to rise. It did not.

Against this empirical research—which does not resolve the question of whether CEOs are overcompensated—I next consider the reforms recommended to deal with the supposed problem. The important inquiry here is whether reforms will accomplish their intended purpose and, if so, at what cost to the corporation.

IV. Attempts at Reform

A. Judicial Activism

The foregoing discussion, which suggests the difficulty of determining whether CEOs are paid excessively, highlights the problem that courts would face were this a litigated issue. In part for this reason, the courts have shied away from cases alleging excessive compensation, instead deferring to the judgment of the directors under the business judgment rule. Nonetheless, from time to time, academics have called on the judiciary to play a role. Professor Detlev Vagts, after describing the roles that directors and shareholders might play in "keeping compensation from getting out of control," recommended that, when they fail, the courts should step in and, using "comparative data," adjust the level of compensation.[7] The problem with this approach is, of course, that the use of comparative data may be a source of the problem and not its solution. [*This contention is based on the theory that comparative data causes executive pay to "ratchet up" as corporations try to keep their pay packages competitive with those of other corporations.*] Were courts to rely on such data, they likely would not be comfortable setting compensation and, if they were, they would be deluged with litigation. In any case, judicial involvement in cases involving excessive compensation typically has been limited to cases involving stock option grants, golden parachutes, and pension grants, where the legal issues were limited to consideration or contract interpretation, matters that the courts feel competent to handle.

A recent example of such involvement was *Sanders v. Wang*,[8] a highly publicized Delaware Court of Chancery case involving Computer Associates. The corporation, in a plan approved by its shareholders, authorized the board to grant up to 6,000,000 shares of the company's common stock to three key officers of the company if certain performance goals were attained. Interestingly, these goals related to the company's stock price, just the sort of incentive plan that pay-for-performance advocates favor. The problem arose because the plan did not provide for an adjustment of the number of shares that might be granted in the event of a stock split, which occurred here. The board, acting under a general provision of the plan that authorized it to interpret and administer the plan, increased the stock award to take the splits into account, so that the officers received 20.25 million shares worth over $1.08 billion.

Shareholders, in a derivative action, challenged the board's action as a breach of the plan (which the court characterized as a contract between the board and the shareholders)

---

7. Detlev Vagts, *Challenges to Executive Compensation: For the Markets or the Courts?*, 8 J. CORP. L. 231, 275 (1983).
8. No. 16640, 1999 WL 1044880 [1999 DEL. CH. LEXIS 203] (Del. Ch. Nov. 8. 1999).

and a violation of the board's fiduciary duties. The court held in favor of the plaintiffs on the theory that the plan's terms were plain and unambiguous: it authorized grants of up to 6,000,000 shares and no more. Defendants' arguments that the intent of the plan was to award the participating officers 3.75% of the company's equity if the performance goals were obtained was rejected by the court. Similarly, the court found no inconsistency between the provision specifying the number of shares and the provision empowering the board to administer and interpret the plan.

The court likely was influenced by the sheer size of the award, noting that "even under the strictest reading of the Plan, the three Participants will together still receive nearly $320 million. $320 million is no mere bagatelle." If the size of the award influenced the court, then the outcome is unfortunate. The defendants pointed out that, had there been a reverse stock split, surely the directors would have been obliged to adjust downward the number of shares that might be awarded under the plan, but the court did not think such considerations relevant in light of the plain meaning rule. While an examination of the plain meaning rule is beyond the scope of this Article, its application often frustrates the intent of the parties, prompting many courts and commentators to view it with skepticism. The effect of the court's ruling may be to jeopardize other similar plans where the drafters failed to include an adjustment clause, even if the intent was to protect the beneficiaries of the plan from the adverse effects of a stock split.

Finally, the court's characterization of the plan as a "contract" between the board and the shareholders is strained. The plan seems better characterized as a contract between the corporation and the participants under the plan. As such, the board clearly was granted broad authority to interpret and administer the plan to act in place of the shareholders who, having approved the plan, delegated the implementation of the plan to the board on their behalf. In other words, the responsibility of the board with respect to the plan does not differ from its normal responsibilities to manage the business and affairs of the firm in the interests of the shareholders, as the firm's residual claimants. The courts typically defer to business judgments of the board when it acts in that capacity. By characterizing the plan as something different, the court was able to consider the merits of the board's decision, which it found lacking.

My point is not just that *Sanders* is a questionable decision, although it is that. Rather, my concern is that judicial review of compensation decisions is troublesome when undertaken directly or indirectly. Courts should resist the temptation to weigh in on these issues because doing so jeopardizes other prudential concerns. *Sanders* may have created an unfortunate precedent under the business judgment rule.

B. Increased Disclosure

Another reform calls for increased disclosure of executive compensation. The Securities and Exchange Commission ("SEC") has dealt with this issue more than once, most recently in 1992. The current rules require disclosure of a good deal of information, as much as any conscientious shareholder is likely to want. The rules were promulgated in an atmosphere of intense public interest over executive compensation and, thus, may reflect a political attempt at limiting compensation. Some commentators have speculated that disclosure has caused directors to limit performance-based compensation plans and levels of compensation out of fear that the resulting compensation would generate criticism....

On the other hand, there is reason to believe that disclosure may have the effect of increasing compensation levels. Remember, one of the intended effects of disclosure is to encourage boards to make pay plans more sensitive to, and thus contingent upon, performance. Boards or compensation committees negotiating with the CEO are motivated to increase the contingent portion of the compensation package, possibly at the expense of the fixed, non-contingent portion of the package, but the CEO is likely to be risk-averse. This risk aversion makes the CEO resistant to lowering the fixed portion of his or her compensation to substitute an equally valuable, but more risky, performance-based plan. The result is that disclosure pushes firms to more contingent pay (without a corresponding reduction in non-contingent pay), and the contingent pay, if it does what it is supposed to do, motivates the CEO to manage the firm in a way that increases its return to shareholders. Thus, higher compensation is inevitable and should occur without regard to the "ratcheting effect" discussed above. Professor Murphy put it well: "Satisfying shareholders by increasing pay-performance sensitivities ultimately implies higher, not lower, levels of pay"... Moreover, as most contingent pay is in the form of stock options, the value of which is reported when exercised, the list of "top earners" is skewed as their compensation reflects options granted and share gains over a period of time. Finally, the effect is enhanced during periods of broad stock market increases like [*that of the late 1990s*].

The possibility that increased disclosure increases compensation levels is an example of the potentially unintended effects of regulation. While the SEC is unlikely to reverse itself and lessen the amount of disclosure, it is clear that disclosure should not be regarded as an effective limitation on compensation.

C. Tax Reform

Tax reform reflects another governmental response to the "executive compensation" crisis. At about the time the SEC increased disclosure requirements, Congress amended the tax code to limit the deductibility of compensation in excess of $1,000,000 paid to executive officers of publicly-held companies unless the excess compensation is paid pursuant to performance-based plans meeting certain criteria. As in the case of disclosure reform, tax reform is unlikely to limit compensation, and it may fuel the increase of compensation. Boards are encouraged to adopt incentive plans tied to stock price. Generally, this means stock option plans with large option grants provide incentives and align executive and shareholder interests. Again, if the plans do what they are supposed to do — motivate management — compensation should rise. Moreover, if these plans are on top of existing compensation plans, compensation may well rise dramatically, particularly if stock prices generally are rising. Indeed, that appears to be the case.

The law also has another feature likely to cause an increase in compensation. Under the legislation, a plan qualifies as performance-based only if, among other things, the plan's performance goals are non-discretionary. However, IRS regulations permit discretion to reduce, but not increase, a performance bonus. Consequently, to approximate its pre-legislation discretion, compensation plans may provide a larger bonus pool than they otherwise might have prior to the legislation and then provide that individual awards may, in the committee's discretion, be reduced. Having created a larger pool, however, there will be pressure on the committee to award the entire pool or, at least, to award more than it would have under prior plans. Thus, compensation may be increased, and there is some evidence that this is occurring. In short, Congressional efforts to limit compensation through the tax code are proving to be weak and ineffectual, at best.

D. Shareholder Involvement

Shareholders can express their concern over executive compensation in several different ways. First, they can sell their stock or refuse to invest in companies that, in their view, overcompensate their executives (or any employees, for that matter). Increasingly, however, institutional shareholders are finding this option unattractive. If one believes that excessive pay is pervasive in corporate America, then exiting one company would logically mean exiting the market. For institutions whose charter or announced investment policy includes the equities of large U.S. companies, or for individual investors who view the market as an integral part of their investment plans, this obviously is not an option.

Second, shareholders can communicate with their boards or fellow shareholders either directly or through formal proposals. The latter can take the form of proposals under Rule 14a-8 of the federal proxy rules. These proposals would not be self-executing and only constitute recommendations to the board, or bylaw amendments, which would become part of the governance structure of the corporation. Bylaw amendments, especially those dealing with pay issues, are a relatively recent phenomenon. In 1998, the SEC took the view that shareholders could use Rule 14a-8 to propose bylaw amendments related to pay practices. In 1992, the SEC had reached a similar view with respect to non-binding shareholder proposals dealing with senior executive compensation. In each case, the issue was whether such proposals would be excludable as relating to the ordinary business operations of the corporation. Now, depending on the applicable state law and the corporation's articles of incorporation, shareholders can use either means to affect pay practices.

Whether as bylaw amendments or non-binding recommendations, shareholder proposals in this area generally have not fared well. The Investor Responsibility Research Center tracked ninety-two shareholder proposals dealing with compensation issues, including director compensation, in 1998.[9] For present purposes, only three categories of proposals are of particular interest. These categories deal with the amount or manner of payment of executive compensation: proposals that restrict executive compensation, proposals that require approval of executive compensation, and proposals that would restrict repricing of options without shareholder approval. The average vote for these proposals was 9.2%, 13.6%, and 27.6%, respectively. Except for the third category, dealing with repricing of options, the average vote indicates that shareholder concern about the level of executive compensation is not high. The paucity of proposals among shareholders also is reflective of a general malaise; there were only fifteen proposals to restrict executive compensation, down from twenty-nine proposals in 1997. While the repricing issue reflects some shareholder concern, there were only three proposals raising the issue, and they may have related to situations in which repricing was particularly abusive, at least in the eyes of activist shareholders.

The apparent inconsistency between the outrage expressed in the popular press and the lack of shareholder voice may have several explanations. The obvious explanation is that, except for a few instances in which poorly performing companies repriced the stock options of their executives, shareholders generally are pleased with the compensation policies of their companies. Alternatively, one might argue that shareholders are apathetic and often fail to open their proxy materials, much less take the time to complete a proxy card and mail it back to the company. Thus, one should not infer much from the low

---

9. INVESTOR RESPONSIBILITY RESEARCH CENTER, SUMMARY OF 1998 U.S. SHAREHOLDER RESOLUTIONS 2 (Feb. 3, 1999).

vote totals or the lack of proposals. While there is truth to this explanation—public companies often struggle to get a quorum at their meetings—there is also reason to doubt the explanation. Some corporate governance proposals frequently are proposed and well received. For instance, there were seven proposals in 1998 recommending the repeal of classified boards, receiving, on average, a 47.3% approval. There were thirteen proposals to repeal or vote on poison pills, receiving, on average, 57.4% approval. This suggests that, when shareholders perceive an issue as affecting the value of their investment, they will take the time to express their preferences even if, as is the case in shareholder proposals, their preferences are not binding. If true, this means that shareholders do not perceive executive compensation issues as affecting share values.

I have recommended elsewhere that shareholders should vote annually on CEO pay, in the form of a non-binding advisory vote. The concept is that much of the speculation of shareholder discontent can be confirmed or denied if there is a shareholder vote. While the sparse data available, as noted above, suggests that shareholders are not discontented, this proposal would provide more convincing data. My guess is that shareholders understand the relationship between pay and performance and will not vote against a package that provides the right incentives, irrespective of the potential size of the proposal. If shareholders do vote not to ratify, then a significant message is sent to the board, which would be difficult to ignore. This is especially so if, as a matter of practice, shareholders generally ratify the package. If the shareholders fail to ratify what is otherwise a sound plan, in the sense that it provides the right incentives to management, then they will bear the burden of their decision.

In any event, there is some reason to believe that management pays attention to shareholder votes on compensation matters. A recent article by Randall S. Thomas and Kenneth J. Martin examined the effect that shareholder votes on compensation proposals had on future compensation practices.[10] They found that companies targeted with compensation proposals tend to increase CEO pay the following year much less than comparable firms not receiving proposals. This suggests that boards are sensitive to shareholder concerns and that an annual advisory vote might influence corporate policies.

V. Conclusion

A review of the now voluminous research on executive compensation suggests a number of unresolved conundrums:

1. Do the empirical studies of CEO compensation establish that CEOs are overpaid, or is the market functioning?

2. Does the relatively higher pay of U.S. CEOs, in comparison to their foreign counterparts, reflect an economically efficient solution to the agency problem?

3. Does greater disclosure of executive compensation result in an increase or decrease in compensation?

4. Does correlating CEO pay to accounting goals add to long-term shareholder wealth more effectively than correlating pay to share prices?

5. If CEOs exercise undue influence over their boards, why are these same boards capable of removing poor performing CEOs, but incapable of compensating them within reasonable limits?

---

10. Randall S. Thomas & Kenneth J. Martin, *The Effect of Shareholder Proposals on Executive Compensation*, 67 U. Cin. L. Rev. 1021 (1999).

6. Do tax laws that encourage performance-based pay provide the proper incentives for their participants?

7. Have performance-based plans shifted too much equity to management?

8. If CEO pay is excessive, why do shareholders, when given the opportunity, fail to express dissatisfaction?

The controversy that accompanies each of these problems indicates both that further research is in order and that governmental solutions are not. While many empirical studies that I reviewed in preparing this Article had suggestions for further empirical studies, none suggested that the principal actors be interviewed to determine what boards were trying to achieve with their compensation plans, why they chose the plans that they did, and how they tested the effectiveness of their plans. What seems to be lacking in this area is an anthropological type of study, in which researchers would study the firm from the inside, discussing with the compensation committee and other directors how they arrived at their decisions, examining what sorts of negotiations took place, and how various performance measures influenced pay decisions.

Some theories are only, or at least best, verified by such research. For instance, some researchers have speculated that boards set CEO compensation very high to create a "tournament effect." The theory is that to motivate lower level managers, CEO pay is set disproportionately high in relation to the next tier of managers. The chance of winning the "lottery," that is, the CEO pay, motivates managers and is an efficient means to address the agency problem. Researchers tested this theory by hypothesizing that, if the tournament effect explained compensation, then one would expect that the larger the number of vice presidents in a firm, the greater the difference between average CEO and vice president pay levels. The hypothesis was easily tested, using data on executive compensation. While one can doubt the soundness of the hypothesis, the very nature of the problem seems to compel an entirely different sort of methodology. Asking compensation committees about the extent to which concepts like the tournament effect influenced their thinking would seem to be far more revealing than an empirical study of pay differentials.

There is some precedent for this type of work; two legal anthropologists studied how pension funds make investment decisions, in part to test the conventional wisdom that money managers were short-term oriented. Their work was interesting and valuable. Unhappily, this type of research, which can lead to valuable insights, is not only ignored, but terribly out of fashion. Indeed, the trend in corporate law is heavily in the direction of empirical work, and law reviews increasingly are looking like quantitative management journals. The area of executive compensation is one, however, that would benefit from the use of other means of analysis, as traditional tools are unable to tell us the extent to which comparative tables or tax considerations influence compensation decisions, or resolve many of the other questions in this area....

Troy A. Paredes, *Too Much Pay, Too Much Deference: Behavioral Corporate Finance, CEOs, and Corporate Governance**

... My theory is that CEOs are emboldened and more confident as a result of the great deal of corporate control concentrated in their hands, as well as the fact that their business

* Originally published in 32 FLORIDA STATE UNIVERSITY LAW REVIEW 673 (2005). Reprinted with permission of the copyright holder, the Florida State University Law Review.

judgment is deferred to and their exercise of control is for the most part unchallenged. In sum, my hypothesis is that deference to the CEO can bolster CEO confidence....

I. Analytic Framework: An Overview of Corporate Decisionmaking

A. *A Brief Introduction to Corporate Decisionmaking*

It is inescapable in business that managers will make decisions that turn out poorly. Running a company requires taking risks and acting on the basis of imperfect information. Waiting for certainty is not workable. Further, most companies face stiff competition. Sometimes a single tough competitor can squeeze a company, as companies as diverse as Home Depot and Lowe's, on the one hand, and AMD and Intel, on the other, can attest. Stated differently, ill-advised business decisions and business failures are common occurrences in a free-market system.

The agency model of managerial decisionmaking illuminates problems other than the inherent risk of business and the need for companies to withstand competitive pressures.... [T]he central theme of the agency model is that when the interests of managers and shareholders diverge, managers, if unchecked, will place their own self-interests before the best interests of the corporation and its shareholders. Three brief examples, centering on overinvestment (that is, the undertaking of negative net present value projects), illustrate this concern.

First, even if a business decision is ill-advised on a net present value basis but ultimately pays off, it can result in the promotion of the managers who were behind the project in the first place.... In short, risk neutrality, let alone conservatism, typically is not a blueprint for personal success if one hopes to climb the corporate ranks. A manager who factors in the private benefits of taking risks is more likely to overinvest in negative net present value projects.

The second example is closely related to the first one.... In the view of [the] well-known "empire-building hypothesis," managers are motivated to grow the business to boost their personal reputation, to entrench themselves, or to position themselves for future opportunities, even if the company's diversification and growth come at the expense of shareholder value.

Third, the psychic payoff of taking risks—namely, the excitement that accompanies undertaking a challenge and doing a big deal—might lead managers to engage in excessively risky business strategies....

Not only do managers have an incentive to take risks, but managers (with the possible exception of CEOs), as well as the directors who oversee them, have an incentive not to dissent when projects are proposed. For example, a small minority of dissenters might simply be ignored or, worse yet from a dissenter's perspective, rebuked—the "shoot-the-messenger" idea. By dissenting, an individual might signal that he lacks confidence in himself or in the firm and its managers, and he might be seen by others as disloyal and not a team player....

Because of the challenges and costs shareholders face in coordinating and keeping adequately informed about the corporation's business and affairs, it is difficult for shareholders to monitor and discipline the kind of managerial conduct that the agency model of corporate decisionmaking contemplates.... [T]o the extent that the challenged conduct is a business decision—such as the choice to move forward with a merger or to launch a new product line—as opposed to director or officer disloyalty, the challenged conduct will escape any hard look by the courts under the business judgment rule. Courts are much better at policing the kind of corrupt conduct that L. Dennis Kozlowski engaged in at Tyco and Richard Scrushy engaged in at HealthSouth than at monitoring substantive business judgments. Recognizing the limitations of shareholders and courts as accountability mechanisms, the agency model relies on contracts (for example, incentive-based executive compensation) and markets (for example, an active market for corporate control and capital markets) to discipline managers to maximize firm value....

Managerial motives are not the only concern, however. Managerial psychology is just as important to managerial decisionmaking as the incentives underlying the agency model. The behavioral model of corporate decisionmaking—sometimes referred to as "behavioral corporate finance"—sets aside the assumption of rationality and takes account of human psychology by focusing on how a range of well-documented cognitive biases affect how executives make business decisions. CEO overconfidence is of singular interest given the dominant position chief executives hold in firms, even after the recent spate of corporate governance reforms. Notably, unlike the agency model, behavioral corporate finance, to my knowledge, has not been an emphasis of corporate governance and has had no real impact on corporate law.

The essence of the overconfidence problem is that managers tend to overvalue projects and therefore to overinvest. In other words, managers take excessive risks by investing in negative net present value projects, even when they are acting in good faith and trying to maximize shareholder value. Not surprisingly, business decisions are likely to turn out poorly when managers err by overestimating a project's benefits, which then never materialize, and underestimating its costs, which then come in higher than projected. This situation is exacerbated because managers end up facing unrealistic expectations as a result of overly optimistic projections. An important second-order effect of overconfidence, then, is that managers might strain to satisfy investors' expectations, such as by taking even greater risks in hopes of a big payoff or by managing the business with an eye toward the next quarter instead of the long run, creating distortions and inefficiencies in how the business is run. Some managers might simply manage earnings, if not engage in outright fraud, to avoid missing earnings or revenue targets.

The challenge is to craft corporate governance regimes that address not only traditional agency problems but also account for the psychology of well-meaning managers....

B. CEO Overconfidence

A vast literature shows that people tend to be overconfident. People overestimate their abilities, believe that they know more than they in fact do, and suffer from an "illusion of control," believing that they exert more control over results than they actually do. The psychology literature also shows that a closely related self-attribution bias affects judgment. Individuals tend to take credit for success but to blame other factors for failure or underperformance. In other words, people are prone to mistake skill for luck. For example, a CEO might exaggerate the contribution of his vision and skill as a manager to his company's successful entry into a new market, especially if others have failed pursuing similar strategies; yet, if the venture turns out poorly, the CEO will likely blame other factors....

Another side to the overconfidence coin is also worth noting. At the same time that individuals overestimate their own abilities, they have been shown to neglect their competitors' skills and to underestimate their competitors' strategic countermoves. These so-called "blind spots" in a manager's evaluation of the competitive landscape might, in and of themselves, lead to overinvestment, such as excess entry into markets, overpayment in acquisitions, or imprudent capacity expansions.

The commitment bias exacerbates the consequences of overconfidence. People are prone to commit increasingly to a course of action once a decision has been made. The irrational escalation of commitment leads to what may be thought of as a sort of path dependence in decisionmaking, or throwing good money after bad. Relatedly, people are biased toward searching for and welcoming evidence that confirms their choice, while resisting and explaining away disconfirming evidence that recommends some different course of action.... A CEO has a strong incentive to engage in this sort of strategic overcommitment to protect his reputation, particularly if the CEO otherwise would have to backtrack publicly from a particular decision or overall business strategy....

... Studies show that certain types of clear feedback can debias overconfidence, at least to some extent. But for the most part, learning from experience cannot be relied on to remedy CEO overconfidence. In short, the feedback indicating that a CEO is prone to err is usually too noisy and too delayed to send a sufficiently clear signal....

For example, plenty of factors other than a bad business decision—such as rising interest rates, an economic downturn, turf battles among key management members, bad lawyers, or an unforeseen regulatory change—can plausibly be blamed for a bad business outcome, when in fact the principal culprit is a bad business decision or its poor execution. In addition, it can take years before a business decision is identified as a failure....

Managers who do take responsibility for having made a bad decision are unlikely to attribute it to cognitive bias. Therefore, any steps that are taken to improve corporate decisionmaking are unlikely to involve strategies for rooting out overconfidence, overcommitment, or other psychological factors affecting managerial judgment. To the extent that the response is simply to try harder the next time a decision is made, studies show that managers might do even worse....

The extent to which markets can constrain overconfidence ... is limited. First, a company usually has to underperform for a prolonged period of time before the CEO is replaced, although studies have found that boards are quicker to replace the CEO in the post-Enron era. A Booz Allen Hamilton study of CEO turnover at the world's 2500 largest public companies (as measured by market capitalization) found that the forced turnover rate due to poor performance was only 3.0% in 2003 for North American. (U.S. and Canadian) firms, slightly less than the 3.2% forced turnover rate for poor performance for the entire period 1997–2003....

[Second,] capital market discipline ultimately is tied to a company's financing needs— that is, to how frequently a company borrows or issues stock. When an underperforming company raises money, it will do so on less favorable terms than if the business were more profitable. However, the reality is that many companies need to raise capital infrequently. Further, even a poorly performing company will almost always be able to raise funds if needed, so capital market discipline is only so tough. Many companies can simply fund operations out of cash on hand and future cash flows, which further erodes the discipline of capital markets....

Third, boards of directors can adopt defensive tactics to fend off a hostile bidder, thereby undercutting the disciplining effects of an active takeover market and enabling the board and the management team to entrench themselves. Nor is running a proxy contest a realistic option for effecting a change in control because of the cost of running a proxy contest and the practical difficulties galvanizing shareholders to support nominees to challenge the incumbent directors the CEO favors. More generally, it is difficult to unwind the decisions of a prior management team, even after a change in control....

... The lopsided view that has been depicted so far needs to be balanced, because there is a bright side to CEO confidence, even overconfidence. Managerial overconfidence may be adaptive and ultimately serve the long-run best interests of the corporation. The managerial clarity, commitment, and charisma that arise from CEO confidence might best be realized when the CEO is overconfident, as opposed to rationally so. A rationally confident and committed CEO might be too tentative and deliberate....

It is important to stress that, unlike agency theory, the behavioral model of managerial decisionmaking assumes that managers are loyal and act in what they honestly believe to be the best interests of the corporation and its shareholders. The behavioral model might particularly resonate as an explanation of managerial mistakes with those who believe that most CEOs act in good faith and are well-intentioned.

II. Does Corporate Governance Cause Overconfidence?

Now that we have a better sense of how overconfidence can influence managerial decisionmaking, a more elusive question is raised: What might cause CEO overconfidence? It is likely that individuals who vie for the top job are highly confident to start with. My hypothesis, though, which remains to be tested empirically, is that CEO overconfidence is itself a product of corporate governance.

A. Too Much Pay

1. The Conventional Story

... [A]cademic work on executive compensation tries to explain the why, when, how, and how much of executive pay—in other words, its size and design. Two leading explanations are the so-called "optimal contracting approach" and the "managerial power approach." ...

In the optimal contracting view, compensation packages are designed to reduce agency problems that arise when there is a conflict of interest between managers and shareholders and when ownership and control are separated. The challenge of executive pay is to devise payment practices that encourage managers to maximize firm value, recognizing managers' tendency to act in their own self-interests. The primary focus is on creating the right link between executive pay and corporate performance. In emphasizing the need to create the right incentives for managers, adherents to this view worry more about the "how" than the "how much" of executive pay. Although imperfect, stock options are perhaps the best-known contracting technique for linking executive pay and corporate performance. There have, in fact, been a number of notable changes to stock options—such as minimum holding periods for shares received upon exercise and so-called premium-priced options—in response to the stark criticism of stock options following the wave of scandals beginning with Enron. Still other companies, such as Microsoft, have switched to granting restricted stock to executives and employees. The redesign of options and the switch to restricted stock is the very kind of executive compensation innovation that the optimal contracting approach anticipates.

The managerial power approach is an alternative model of executive compensation. Bebchuk, Fried, and Walker offer the most complete development of the model. They have summarized the model this way:

Analysis from this perspective focuses on the ability of executives to influence their own compensation schemes. According to the [managerial power] approach, compensation arrangements approved by boards often deviate from optimal contracting because directors are captured or subject to influence by management, sympathetic to management, or simply ineffectual in overseeing compensation. As a result ... executives can receive pay in excess of the level that would be optimal for shareholders; this excess pay constitutes rents.[11]

...

2. The Behavioral Approach

When considering the link between managerial behavior and executive pay, the emphasis typically is on incentives and agency costs. The question of managerial motives, for example, is central to both the optimal contracting and managerial power approaches. Both approaches view executive pay through the agency lens in trying to understand managers' motives and how to channel managers toward improving corporate performance and maximizing firm value.

The behavioral approach to executive compensation advanced here views executive pay through the lens of cognitive psychology. This approach emphasizes the potential impact of executive pay on the cognitive biases of CEOs. Instead of focusing on the details of why, when, how, and how much chief executives are paid, the behavioral approach is principally concerned with the consequences of executive compensation for CEO confidence and the impact of growing CEO confidence on corporate behavior. The behavioral approach to executive compensation theorizes that high levels of executive compensation can bolster CEO confidence and, accordingly, worsen the CEO overconfidence problem described earlier.

Notwithstanding significant advancements in the study of human behavior, there is always guesswork in understanding how people think and behave. It is tough enough to measure CEO confidence, let alone its origins. That said, an extensive literature indicates that past success, as well as other forms of positive feedback and reward, builds a person's confidence and self-esteem and can therefore exacerbate overconfidence. This link between success and "kudos," on the one hand, and overconfidence, on the other, has intuitive appeal—whose confidence is not bolstered after they have been validated?—and stems in part from a person's self-attributing tendency to take too much credit for positive results, while deflecting blame for poor outcomes. People who are successful or who receive kudos tend to become more confident in their skills and abilities and, consequently, are said to overestimate the likelihood of future success....

CEOs enjoy many successes, whether it is the profitable launch of a new product, a high-profile acquisition, or an effective expansion into a new market. Even a rising stock price in a rising market might be seen as validating the CEO's talent, as opposed to the result of an overheated market that might have more to do with investor irrationality than fundamentals. Not only are CEOs likely to give themselves too much credit for such successes, but others are also likely to credit disproportionately a CEO's skill and judgment. In general, CEOs receive much praise and recognition throughout their careers from the media, other executives, charitable organizations they support, politicians, and the like....

---

11. Lucian A. Bebchuk, Jesse M. Fried and David I. Walker, *Managerial Power and Rent Extraction in the Design of Executive Compensation*, 69 U. Chi. L. Rev. 751, 754 (2002).

... Not only is high CEO pay in and of itself success, but it also gives positive feedback on the chief executive's performance in running the company and more generally confers special status. Numerous studies, for example, rank CEOs according to their pay every year, and compensation has repeatedly been characterized as an important "scorecard" by which CEOs gauge themselves.... .Perhaps the link between CEO compensation and confidence would be broken if CEOs did not believe they actually deserved their pay but viewed it as a windfall or even as excessive. This does not seem to be the case, however. To the contrary, there is reason to believe that chief executives, perhaps because of self-attribution tendencies or perhaps because of ego, believe that they are worth their pay.

The link between pay and confidence is not only about the absolute level of CEO pay but also about relative pay. In their study of sources of CEO hubris, Hayward and Hambrick assumed that CEOs exert influence over what they and other managers are paid, and thus they concluded that a large pay gap between a company's CEO and its other senior executives likely reflects the CEO's perception of himself as important and therefore deserving of considerably more compensation than other top executives.... They found that a company was more likely to pay a higher acquisition premium—an indicator of hubris—the greater the gap was between CEO pay and the pay of other executives.[12]

Pay differentials, however, may not only reflect CEO self-importance but may actually breed it. When a chief executive is paid several hundred times what a rank-and-file employee receives and substantially more than other senior executives, including the next most senior manager, the CEO may see the pay spread as another sign of success that validates his worth and value to the business. The self-confidence boost that arises out of this sort of positive self-reflection is the flip side of the demoralization effects that social comparison theory predicts for individuals who believe they are unfairly underpaid....

The focus so far has been on a person's compensation after becoming CEO. But the very process of becoming CEO can breed confidence too. The process of climbing the corporate ranks to become the chief executive has been described in terms of a tournament where the winner takes all. The winners of each round are promoted until finally senior managers emerge, including the individual who is chosen to fill the top post. By definition, any person who is even considered for the CEO position will have a history of important successes, with the crowning achievement going to a single individual who is awarded the CEO title, as well as, in many cases, the title of chairman of the board....

Instead of choosing its CEO from its own ranks, a company may look to outside candidates. These outside candidates also have strong track records of success and perhaps are already CEOs elsewhere. The wooing of the outsider can further feed the target individual's sense of self-worth....

B. Too Much Deference

Large executive compensation packages are paid to chief executives against the backdrop of a corporate governance system that is characterized by deference to the CEO and his business judgment. This leads to the second reason CEO overconfidence is a likely product of corporate governance: CEOs receive too little criticism and too much affirmation....

---

12. Mathew L.A. Hayward & Donald C. Hambrick, *Explaining the Premiums Paid for Large Acquisitions: Evidence of CEO Hubris*, 42 ADMIN. SCI. Q. 103 (1997).

1. Subordinate Officers

Perhaps the most obvious deferential group is subordinate officers. Although there are always exceptions, such as an influential chief operating officer, managers who report to the CEO can be expected to quiet their dissent, or at least not to push hard in second-guessing the chief executive....

The reluctance of subordinate executives to step up and challenge the CEO creates an interesting coordination problem. Safety exists in numbers. If the senior vice president in charge of marketing or the CFO, for example, were vigorously to press the CEO at a meeting about some proposal, it might open the door for other executives to express more freely their skepticism or even flatly to object to the proposed course of action. It might also foster a norm of frank discussion, constructive criticism, and dissent. Nobody, however, wants to find himself alone out on a limb. Instead, too commonplace is a sort of herd behavior among subordinate officers to go along with the CEO. This in turn has collateral consequences, discussed below, for the information that is ultimately brought to the board's attention when exercising its business judgment.

2. Gatekeepers

The gatekeepers—attorneys, accountants, investment bankers, credit rating agencies, and securities analysts—are another quiescent group, as the wave of corporate scandals at Enron and elsewhere showed....

To the extent that lawyers, bankers, and other gatekeepers treat the CEO with kid gloves and, in particular, do not press as hard as they could when it comes to the wisdom of a particular transaction or the company's business strategy, the CEO's confidence is likely reinforced or at least not shaken. One could imagine an alternative norm whereby gatekeepers are more willing to challenge management....

3. Boards of Directors

The primary check on CEO power is the board of directors, in particular independent outside directors. Accordingly, when directors defer to the CEO, it might singularly boost a CEO's confidence. Additionally, deferential and passive boards have been routinely criticized as a reason executives are paid so much, which has prompted the NYSE and Nasdaq to require the independent directors of listed companies to set executive pay....

Boards have been criticized, especially after the scandals at Enron, WorldCom, Tyco, and elsewhere, as too quiescent and deferential to the CEO. It is easy to see why inside directors might defer to the CEO. But why do outside directors defer? Outside directors often lack the time, information, and expertise needed to challenge the CEO on business matters, let alone to block a course of action the CEO supports, and may see little reason to doubt a CEO who can point to a track record of success. Being an outside director is a part-time job. A recent study of *Fortune 1000* companies by Korn/Ferry International reports that in 2003 forty-four percent of boards met quarterly, while only nine percent of boards met monthly, and that directors spent an average of nineteen hours per month on company matters, including review and preparation time, attending meetings, and travel. Further, CEOs have control over the board's agenda and, therefore, can set what the board considers at its meetings. Routinely, important matters are slated for little discussion. Many directors complain that they have relatively little say over what is brought before them and that scripted management presentations consume most of the time allotted to an agenda item, affording directors little opportunity to ask questions and to discuss the matter during the formal meeting.

Directors often do not have (or have simply forgotten) valuable information or, in the alternative, are sent so much information that they become overloaded and unable to distinguish what is important. One constant, already alluded to, is that board members generally do not have enough time to consider fully the information they do have, and they lack the requisite knowledge and insight into the company to evaluate critically matters before them. Moreover, outside directors have limited access to various personnel, such as junior officers, office heads, plant managers, and managers of business units, who might help them vet issues; and outside directors have no appreciable contact with suppliers, customers, creditors, or rank-and-file employees. For all intents and purposes, outside directors depend on the information the CEO and the other top executives provide.

McKinsey & Company recently surveyed 150 directors who serve on the boards of more than 300 public companies. The study reported that approximately 56% of the directors polled said that they only "moderately" know what is going on at the companies where they serve, while 14% of the directors polled responded "partially" when asked to what degree they really know what is going on at their companies. Of the directors McKinsey & Company surveyed, 76% said that the CEO "largely" "controls and shapes what directors learn about the company."

Given the realities of board service, directors may understandably conclude that they are not equipped to exercise better judgment than the CEO. Accordingly, the rational choice for members of the board often is to go along with the insiders who have the best information and insight into the business.... More to the point, many directors simply believe it is not their job to run the business. Asking outside directors to be more actively engaged in corporate decision-making might be counterproductive in terms of further straining the limited resources of directors and in deterring qualified individuals from serving, concerns already raised in a post-Sarbanes-Oxley era.

The accommodating stance boards historically have taken toward their CEOs is more often attributed to a lack of director independence than a lack of director competence. An inside director may be beholden to the CEO because his job may be at risk if he dissents. An outside director may also be beholden, compromising his independence, because the director's renomination may be similarly jeopardized if he opposes the CEO, although the conflict may be less severe than for inside directors. Even if the prestige and director fees that accompany sitting on a board do not squelch dissent and lead to relative appeasement of the CEO, an outside director may be conflicted because of lucrative consulting arrangements or other business dealings he has with the company. Still other independence problems may arise when the company, if not the CEO personally, makes significant contributions to charities or other organizations important to the outside director.

Key regulatory reforms enacted in the aftermath of Enron were directed toward shoring up board independence by rooting out these types of conflicts. But not only financial conflicts and economic ties compromise independence. Social and personal relationships between a director and the CEO can also undercut a director's independence. Whatever the relationship might be at the start of a directorship, the very process of working closely for a number of years can create affinities that over time cloud a director's independent judgment. Furthermore, an outside director, who himself is a CEO at another company, might be biased toward going along with the CEO on whose board he sits, identifying with and deferring to the chief executive, just as he hopes his board will defer to him; or the director might simply believe that CEOs generally know what is best for the business and should be afforded wide discretion.

In addition, an outsider may feel indebted to the CEO who put him on the board and might therefore give the chief executive the benefit of the doubt. Relatedly, the board may become highly committed to, and therefore highly supportive of, the CEO it has decided to retain or possibly selected as part of a management transition. Indeed, the board may have actually transferred control to the CEO as part of the bargain to keep or hire him. As a background point, directors may be biased toward preserving the status quo and may seek to avoid the dissension associated with CEO criticism and especially CEO turnover. Board commitment to the CEO could also explain the ratcheting up of CEO compensation, as a board routinely tries to pay its CEO in the top half of the relevant executive pay scale....

Aside from its implications for chief executive confidence, board deference to the CEO undercuts the purpose of group corporate decisionmaking. Corporations have boards of directors for a reason. A conventional explanation for why boards exist is that groups often make better decisions than an individual actor. The benefits of group decisionmaking, though, depend on open and frank group deliberation. In terms of boards, this requires that directors, at the very least, consider a wide range of information and possibilities, develop competing ideas, and challenge each other as well as management. In other words, effective group decisionmaking requires constructive tension within the group and the willingness of individuals to share information and to express their independent views. When boards instead defer to the CEO, the deliberative process of boards is compromised as the CEO's view prevails unscathed. To put it in slightly different terms, groupthink negates the benefits of deliberation and group decisionmaking.

There are two important background points that underpin board deference to the CEO. First, just beneath the surface of the discussion has been the question of CEO power. The extent of board deference depends in part on a CEO who has power that he is willing to cultivate and use. Not all CEOs have the same power bases, so the extent of CEO power and, accordingly, board deference is likely to vary from firm to firm. The management and leadership literatures have explored in depth several sources of CEO power. I will mention just a few, some of which have already been alluded to. First, as a corporation's most senior executive, the CEO has far-reaching legal authority under corporate law and agency principles, and a CEO's authority extends further when he is also chairman of the board. CEO charisma is another important source of power that has received a great deal of attention in both the academic literature and the popular press. An aspect of charisma is self-confidence. Individuals are more likely to follow a CEO who shows self-confidence and appears to be in control. The mere fact that a CEO decisively makes a bold and risky move might persuade others to go along with him. Past success is another important power base. Understandably, people interpret prior achievement as a sign of ability. Even high CEO compensation may be a source of power and not just a product of it. The symbolism of CEO pay matters....

The second point underpinning board deference is that outside directors face only a slight risk of legal liability under state corporate law for failing to satisfy their responsibility to act with due care, even when they are relatively passive and essentially go along with management's recommendations for the business. Accordingly, there is little upside if directors oppose or even seriously challenge the CEO, and yet there are downside risks for doing so....

4. Shareholders

Shareholders' legal authority over the firm's operation is typically limited to voting on directors and on a small number of fundamental corporate changes, such as mergers or a sale of all or substantially all of the corporation's assets. Shareholders do not have control over ordinary business matters. Further, they have limited access to the company's proxy materials to make proposals that relate to the company's business. Accordingly, shareholders are constrained in their ability to express dissatisfaction with some course of action or to encourage the CEO to take certain steps in managing the business. To be sure, shareholders can solicit their own proxies. But the cost and challenge of coordinating dispersed shareholders frustrates shareholder action. Plus, the shareholder vote would not, in any event, be binding on the board or management....

5. Courts

... Courts do not acquiesce to the CEO in the way boards have come under fire for doing in recent years or in the way subordinate officers might defer to their boss. Nonetheless, it is telling that as part of the overall climate in which a CEO heads his business, a chief executive faces little, if any, judicial scrutiny of his substantive decisions, as courts intentionally take a hands-off approach and do not pass judgment on the merits of business decisions. At the very least, judicial deference, operationalized by the business judgment rule, does nothing to undercut CEO confidence, and as described above, directors face only a minimal risk of legal sanction for failing to press management in exercising the board's responsibilities....

III. Managing CEO Overconfidence

Starting from the premise that CEOs are overconfident, what can be done about it? ...

A. Metacognition

The first of the three options I consider concerns "metacognition"—that is, thinking about and understanding how one thinks. The point is straightforward. Making managers aware of their cognitive tendencies and how they process and interpret information (that is, teaching executives how they deviate from perfect rationality) can mitigate cognitive bias. Put simply, recognizing the overconfidence problem can help solve it. A CEO, for example, who is aware of his biases can discipline himself by adopting decisionmaking techniques—such as seeking dissenting viewpoints, searching for disconfirming evidence, and interrogating his own assumptions and analysis more rigorously—to guard against his overconfidence, as well as any other cognitive bias or unconscious heuristic that might lead to suboptimal decisions. Because of competitive pressures, the CEO has an incentive to discipline his decisionmaking once he is aware of his flawed judgment. Educating directors about how corporate managers make decisions and about directors' own biases is also helpful, because the board can then implement processes and controls designed to improve corporate decisionmaking.

A virtue of the kind of director and manager education envisioned here is that it skirts the need for more intrusive regulatory or judicial intervention into business and corporate governance. The only requirement is to teach the CEO, along with the board and other officers, about decisionmaking and judgment, including instructing them that corporate governance concerns should not be limited to addressing disloyalty and shirking but should include the psychology of decisionmaking as well.

B. *"Chief Naysayer"*

Studies show that explicitly considering the opposite—that is, considering arguments against a course of action, such as by asking probing questions and follow-ups, challenging key assumptions, focusing on counterfactuals, or developing other options— can reduce overconfidence. The consider-the-opposite strategy is thought to work because explicitly emphasizing contrary arguments and what could go wrong makes risks more salient to the decisionmaker. It also impresses upon a decisionmaker that he exerts less control over outcomes than he might believe, and emphasizing con arguments can overcome blind spots in considering likely competitor responses. Moreover, forcing an individual to wrestle with uncertainty can arrest a person's tendency to reconcile conflicting information in order to avoid the unpleasantness of cognitive dissonance. Pressing a consider-the-opposite strategy denies a person the luxury of arguing away or simply assuming away the risks and costs of a project. At bottom, considering the opposite results in a more balanced and presumably more accurate assessment of a course of conduct.

Negative feedback is a complementary debiasing technique that has also been shown to reduce overconfidence. A strategy of negative feedback turns on its head the notion that past success boosts confidence. To overcome a person's tendency to deflect blame, negative feedback should be clear and specific. A respected director or a trusted lieutenant, for example, could point out to the CEO concrete examples of when he has been wrong, highlighting, if possible, particular mistakes the CEO made and how those mistakes contributed to the bad outcomes.

Although not urged with CEO psychology in mind, a number of features of post-Enron corporate governance—such as more independent directors, more involved institutional investors, and more independent securities analysts—can have the effect of forcing a CEO to consider why he might be wrong, or to at least explain himself more fully and to consider alternatives more carefully. Perhaps the most promising possibility is that corporate cultures will continue to evolve so that directors routinely press the CEO and other managers with tough questioning. It may simply take the board asking the CEO, What are the top five reasons why we should reject your proposal? Consider, for example, what might have happened if this question had been asked when AMR Corp., the parent of American Airlines, took steps to shore up the retirement packages of its top executives in the event of bankruptcy, while at the same time slashing costs at the carrier, including negotiating pay and benefits cuts with its unions. The move seems inexplicable in hindsight and quickly cost AMR CEO and Chairman Donald Carty his job....

C. *Tougher Fiduciary Obligations*

... Once the psychology of CEO decisionmaking is taken into account, gaps in the coverage of the law of fiduciary duty seem even larger. As described above, corporate law focuses on policing and rooting out two sources of corporate mismanagement: (1) disloyalty and bad faith; and (2) inadequate care and shirking by directors and officers in exercising their responsibilities.... Corporate law receives more credit for promoting effective management that it deserves. Because it does not account for "good-faith mismanagement" rooted in the psychology of corporate decisionmaking, corporate law is less effective than recognized in rooting out mismanagement by imposing liability.

One possibility, then, for addressing CEO overconfidence is for courts to take a tougher stance when enforcing fiduciary obligations under the duty of care and, in so doing, to account expressly for the one-two punch of CEO overconfidence and board deference. It is easier to say that courts should take a harder look at managerial and director conduct than to explain what this might mean in practice, especially since managers and directors need flexibility to run the business and the costs of chilling entrepreneurialism and risk-taking, as a result of greater accountability and judicial second-guessing, can be substantial. A governance system characterized by overconfident CEOs, quiescent directors, and a hands-off judiciary may result in better corporate performance than one characterized by self-doubting CEOs, an aggressive and hostile board, and intrusive judges who are willing to substitute their business judgment for the judgment of management and the board.

Presently, it takes a near abdication of responsibility before courts find a breach of the duty of care. Given their active involvement on a day-to-day basis in running the company, officers will not be found liable for breach of the duty of care in practice. When it comes to directors, who are much less involved in the day-to-day business, so long as there is a modicum of process in board decisionmaking, board conduct routinely passes muster under the business judgment rule. To enhance judicial review, courts might focus more carefully on the nature of the deliberations of the board and management by more skeptically assessing whether there in fact was a fulsome consideration of the matter at hand. In applying the duty of care, for example, courts could scrutinize the decisionmaking process to look for indications that the board and management considered arguments against a course of action and to verify that the CEO and other key managers supporting a project did not go unchallenged. After all, the formality of process is not an end in itself but is intended to ensure that there is a rich and frank debate before some course of action is agreed to. Although the law of fiduciary duty should not insulate investors from business risk, it can help protect investors from a flawed decisionmaking process by requiring corporate decisionmakers to engage in the dutiful deliberation of business matters....

One particular possibility is for courts to stress that corporations must have improved internal information and reporting systems that ensure the proper flow of information to the board and that directors are in a proper position, with appropriate information, to weigh a project's pros and cons. If adequate reporting systems are in place, less of a burden is placed on individual directors to inquire proactively, as better information flows about both the company's ongoing operations and new projects become an institutionalized part of corporate decisionmaking....

Instead of intervening more directly into how corporations are run, it might be preferable for courts to leverage the law's expressive function by simply exhorting directors and management to adjust their decisionmaking processes to address the risk of overconfidence. Rock, for example, has explained that judges can inculcate good corporate practices by stressing in their opinions, which he describes as "corporate law sermons," how directors and officers *should* act, while at the same time refusing to hold parties liable for failing to live up to these aspirations....[13]

---

13. *See Edward Rock's article in this volume.* — Ed.

D. Greater Shareholder Say

To the extent corporate law takes any account of managerial bias, perhaps greater authority should be handed down to shareholders, as opposed to courts (or lawmakers) shouldering any additional responsibility for disciplining business decisions....

For example, shareholder choice could be advanced in a takeover setting by placing greater limits on the use of defensive tactics, as a number of commentators have urged over the years. Reversing course in the derivative-litigation setting requires perhaps a more novel solution, such as the one recently offered by Thompson and Thomas. Some threshold number of shareholders—such as a shareholder or group of related shareholders that holds between one and five percent of a company's outstanding shares—could be excused automatically from the demand requirement without showing demand futility or could override a board's refusal to bring a suit for fiduciary breach when demand is made.[14] Giving shareholders greater say in selling their shares to a hostile bidder or in enforcing fiduciary duties might better discipline how the business is run. This would encourage managers and directors to pay more attention to the risks of various projects.

If shareholders were handed more control, perhaps the strongest case can be made for giving shareholders more control over acquisitions. Managerial overconfidence is usually studied in the context of bidder overpayment in acquisitions, and major acquisitions can have a particularly significant and immediate impact that is difficult and costly to unwind if it goes bad. Although shareholders generally have the right to vote on mergers, triangular merger structures can cut shareholders out of the approval process. Shareholders generally do not have the right to approve an asset acquisition or a tender offer launched by their company. An acquiring company's shareholders could be given greater say by granting them the right to vote on non-merger acquisitions, or at least those that cross some threshold as measured, for example, by the impact of the deal on the acquirer's balance sheet, the aggregate purchase price in relation to the acquirer's own market capitalization, or the relation between the acquirer's and the target's respective operating revenues. Such reforms presumably could not be effected by the courts, but would have to come from the legislature or perhaps the NYSE and Nasdaq for listed companies....

Supreme Court of Delaware, *In re The Walt Disney Company Derivative Litigation**

JACOBS, Justice:

In August 1995, Michael Ovitz ("Ovitz") and The Walt Disney Company ("Disney" or the "Company") entered into an employment agreement under which Ovitz would serve as President of Disney for five years. In December 1996, only fourteen months after he commenced employment, Ovitz was terminated without cause, resulting in a severance payout to Ovitz valued at approximately $130 million.

---

14. *See* Robert B. Thompson & Randall S. Thomas, *The Public and Private Faces of Derivative Lawsuits*, 57 VAND. L. REV 1747, 1790 (2004).

* 906 A.2d 27 (Del. 2006).

In January 1997, several Disney shareholders brought derivative actions in the Court of Chancery, on behalf of Disney, against Ovitz and the directors of Disney who served at the time of the events complained of (the "Disney defendants"). The plaintiffs claimed that the $130 million severance payout was the product of fiduciary duty and contractual breaches by Ovitz, and breaches of fiduciary duty by the Disney defendants, and a waste of assets. After the disposition of several pretrial motions and an appeal to this Court, the case was tried before the Chancellor over 37 days between October 20, 2004 and January 19, 2005. In August 2005, the Chancellor handed down a well-crafted 174 page Opinion and Order, determining that "the director defendants did not breach their fiduciary duties or commit waste." The Court entered judgment in favor of all defendants on all claims alleged in the amended complaint.

The plaintiffs have appealed from that judgment, claiming that the Court of Chancery committed multitudinous errors. We conclude, for the reasons that follow, that the Chancellor's factual findings and legal rulings were correct and not erroneous in any respect. Accordingly, the judgment entered by the Court of Chancery will be affirmed.

I. The Facts

... In 1994 Disney lost in a tragic helicopter crash its President and Chief Operating Officer, Frank Wells, who together with Michael Eisner, Disney's Chairman and Chief Executive Officer, had enjoyed remarkable success at the Company's helm. Eisner temporarily assumed Disney's presidency, but only three months later, heart disease required Eisner to undergo quadruple bypass surgery. Those two events persuaded Eisner and Disney's board of directors that the time had come to identify a successor to Eisner.

Eisner's prime candidate for the position was Michael Ovitz, who was the leading partner and one of the founders of Creative Artists Agency ("CAA"), the premier talent agency whose business model had reshaped the entire industry. By 1995, CAA had 550 employees and a roster of about 1400 of Hollywood's top actors, directors, writers, and musicians. That roster generated about $150 million in annual revenues and an annual income of over $20 million for Ovitz, who was regarded as one of the most powerful figures in Hollywood.

Eisner and Ovitz had enjoyed a social and professional relationship that spanned nearly 25 years....

A. Negotiation of the Ovitz Employment Agreement

Eisner and Irwin Russell, who was a Disney director and chairman of the compensation committee, first approached Ovitz about joining Disney. Their initial negotiations were unproductive, however, because at that time MCA [Music Corporation of America] had made Ovitz an offer that Disney could not match. The MCA-Ovitz negotiations eventually fell apart.... Ovitz became receptive to the idea of joining Disney. Eisner learned of these developments and re-commenced negotiations with Ovitz in earnest. By mid-July 1995, those negotiations were in full swing.

Both Russell and Eisner negotiated with Ovitz, over separate issues and concerns. From his talks with Eisner, Ovitz gathered that Disney needed his skills and experience to remedy Disney's current weaknesses, which Ovitz identified as poor talent relationships and stagnant foreign growth. Seeking assurances from Eisner that Ovitz's vision for Disney was shared, at some point during the negotiations Ovitz came to believe that he and Eisner would run Disney, and would work together in a relation akin to that of junior and senior partner. Unfortunately, Ovitz's belief was mistaken, as Eisner had a radically different view of what their respective roles at Disney should be.

Russell assumed the lead in negotiating the financial terms of the Ovitz employment contract. In the course of negotiations, Russell learned ... that Ovitz owned 55% of CAA and earned approximately $20 to $25 million a year from that company. From the beginning Ovitz made it clear that he would not give up his 55% interest in CAA without "downside protection." Considerable negotiation then ensued over downside protection issues. During the summer of 1995, the parties agreed to a draft version of Ovitz's employment agreement (the "OEA") modeled after Eisner's.... As described by the Chancellor, the draft agreement included the following terms:

> Under the proposed OEA, Ovitz would receive a five-year contract with two tranches of options. The first tranche consisted of three million options ... and if the value of those options at the end of the five years had not appreciated to $50 million, Disney would make up the difference [the "$50 million guarantee"]. The second tranche consisted of two million options that would vest immediately if Disney and Ovitz opted to renew the contract.

> The proposed OEA sought to protect both parties in the event that Ovitz's employment ended prematurely, and provided that absent defined causes, neither party could terminate the agreement without penalty. If Ovitz, for example, walked away, for any reason other than those permitted under the OEA, he would forfeit any benefits remaining under the OEA and could be enjoined from working for a competitor. Likewise, if Disney fired Ovitz for any reason other than gross negligence or malfeasance, Ovitz would be entitled to a non-fault payment (Non-Fault Termination or "NFT"), which consisted of his remaining salary, $7.5 million a year for unaccrued bonuses, the immediate vesting of his first tranche of options and a $10 million cash out payment for the second tranche of options.

As the basic terms of the OEA were crystallizing, Russell prepared and gave Ovitz and Eisner a "case study" to explain those terms. In that study, Russell also expressed his concern that the negotiated terms represented an extraordinary level of executive compensation. Russell acknowledged, however, that Ovitz was an "exceptional corporate executive" and "highly successful and unique entrepreneur" who merited "downside protection and upside opportunity." ... Russell shared this original case study only with Eisner and Ovitz. He also recommended another, additional study of this issue.

To assist in evaluating the financial terms of the OEA, Russell recruited Graef Crystal, an executive compensation consultant, and Raymond Watson, a member of Disney's compensation committee and a past Disney board chairman who had helped structure Wells' and Eisner's compensation packages.... [Watson and Crystal] discussed and generated a set of values using different and various inputs and assumptions, accounting for different numbers of options, vesting periods, and potential proceeds of option exercises at various times and prices.... Two days later, Crystal faxed to Russell a memorandum concluding that the OEA would provide Ovitz with approximately $23.6 million per year for the first five years, or $23.9 million a year over seven years if Ovitz exercised a two year renewal option. Those sums, Crystal opined, would approximate Ovitz's current annual compensation at CAA.

... The next day, August 13, Eisner met with Ovitz, Russell, Sanford Litvack (an Executive Vice President and Disney's General Counsel), and Stephen Bollenbach (Disney's Chief Financial Officer) to discuss the decision to hire Ovitz. Litvack and Bollenbach were unhappy with that decision, and voiced concerns that Ovitz would disrupt the cohesion that existed between Eisner, Litvack and Bollenbach. Litvack and Bollenbach were emphatic that they would not report to Ovitz, but would continue to report to Eisner....

On August 14, Eisner and Ovitz signed a letter agreement (the "OLA"), which outlined the basic terms of Ovitz's employment, and stated that the agreement (which would ultimately be embodied in a formal contract) was subject to approval by Disney's compensation committee and board of directors. [Russell, Watson and Eisner] contacted each of the..board members ... to inform them of the impending new hire....

That same day, a press release made the news of Ovitz's hiring public. The reaction was extremely positive: Disney was applauded for the decision, and Disney's stock price rose 4.4% in a single day, thereby increasing Disney's market capitalization by over $1 billion.

Once the OLA was signed, ... Disney's legal department ... concluded that the $50 million guarantee created negative tax implications for Disney, because it might not be deductible. Concluding that the guarantee should be eliminated, Russell initiated discussions on how to compensate Ovitz for this change. What resulted were several amendments to the OEA to replace the back-end guarantee. The ... $50 million guarantee would be replaced by: (i) a reduction in the option strike price ... (ii) a $10 million severance payment if the Company did not renew Ovitz's contract; and (iii) an alteration of the renewal option....

On September 26, 1995, the Disney compensation committee ... met for one hour to consider, among other agenda items, the proposed terms of the OEA. A term sheet was distributed at the meeting, although a draft of the OEA was not.... Watson testified that he provided the compensation committee with the spreadsheet analysis that he had performed in August, and discussed his findings with the committee. Crystal did not attend the meeting, although he was available by telephone to respond to questions if needed, but no one from the committee called. After Russell's and Watson's presentations, Litvack also responded to substantive questions. At trial [directors and compensation committee members] Poitier and Lozano testified that they believed they had received sufficient information from Russell's and Watson's presentations to exercise their judgment in the best interests of the Company. The committee voted unanimously to approve the OEA terms, subject to "reasonable further negotiations within the framework of the terms and conditions" described in the OEA.

Immediately after the compensation committee meeting, the Disney board met in executive session. The board was told about the reporting structure to which Ovitz had agreed, but the initial negative reaction of Litvack and Bollenbach to the hiring was not recounted. Eisner led the discussion relating to Ovitz, and Watson then explained his analysis, and both Watson and Russell responded to questions from the board. After further deliberation, the board voted unanimously to elect Ovitz as President....

B. Ovitz's Performance as President of Disney

.... When Ovitz took office, the initial reaction was optimistic, and Ovitz did make some positive contributions while serving as President of the Company. By the fall of 1996, however, it had become clear that Ovitz was "a poor fit with his fellow executives." By then the Disney directors were discussing that the disconnect between Ovitz and the Company was likely irreparable and that Ovitz would have to be terminated....

C. Ovitz's Termination at Disney

... During this period Eisner was also working with Litvack to explore whether they could terminate Ovitz under the OEA for cause. If so, Disney would not owe Ovitz the NFT payment. From the very beginning, Litvack advised Eisner that he did not believe there was cause to terminate Ovitz under the OEA. Litvack's advice never changed.

... Although the Chancellor was critical of Litvack and Eisner for lacking sufficient documentation to support his conclusion and the work they did to arrive at that conclusion, the Court found that Eisner and Litvack "did in fact make a concerted effort to determine if Ovitz could be terminated for cause, and that despite these efforts, they were unable to manufacture the desired result."

... Ovitz met with Eisner on December 3, to discuss his termination. Ovitz asked for several concessions, all of which Eisner ultimately rejected. Eisner told Ovitz that all he would receive was what he had contracted for in the OEA.

... Eisner met with Ovitz to agree on the wording of a press release to announce the termination, and to inform Ovitz that he would not receive any of the additional items that he requested. By that time it had already been decided that Ovitz would be terminated without cause and that he would receive his contractual NFT payment, but nothing more. Eisner and Ovitz agreed that neither Ovitz nor Disney would disparage each other in the press, and that the separation was to be undertaken with dignity and respect for both sides....

Ovitz's termination was memorialized in a letter, dated December 12, 1996, that Litvack signed on Eisner's instruction. The board was not shown the letter, nor did it meet to approve its terms. A press release announcing Ovitz's termination was issued that same day. Before the press release was issued, Eisner attempted to contact each of the board members by telephone to notify them that Ovitz had been officially terminated. None of the board members at that time, or at any other time, objected to Ovitz's termination, and most, if not all, of them thought it was the appropriate step for Eisner to take....

II. Summary of Appellants' Claims of Error

... The appellants' claims of error are most easily analyzed in two separate groupings: (1) the claims against the Disney defendants and (2) the claims against Ovitz. The first category encompasses the claims that the Disney defendants breached their fiduciary duties to act with due care and in good faith by (1) approving the OEA, and specifically, its NFT provisions; and (2) approving the NFT severance payment to Ovitz upon his termination—a payment that is also claimed to constitute corporate waste. It is notable that the appellants do *not* contend that the Disney defendants are directly liable as a consequence of those fiduciary duty breaches. Rather, appellants' core argument is indirect, *i.e.*, that those breaches of fiduciary duty deprive the Disney defendants of the protection of business judgment review, and require them to shoulder the burden of establishing that their acts were entirely fair to Disney. That burden, the appellants contend, the Disney defendants failed to carry. The appellants claim that by ruling that the Disney defendants did not breach their fiduciary duty to act with due care or in good faith, the Court of Chancery committed reversible error in numerous respects. Alternatively, the appellants claim that even if the business judgment presumptions apply, the Disney defendants are nonetheless liable, because the NFT payout constituted corporate waste and the Court of Chancery erred in concluding otherwise.

Falling into the second category are the claims being advanced against Ovitz. Appellants claim that Ovitz breached his fiduciary duties of care and loyalty to Disney by (i) negotiating for and accepting the NFT severance provisions of the OEA, and (ii) negotiating a full NFT payout in connection with his termination....

III. The Claims Against Ovitz

...

A. Claims Based upon Ovitz's Conduct Before Assuming Office at Disney

... [A]ppellants argue [that] even though Ovitz did not formally assume the title of President until October 1, 1995, he became a *de facto* fiduciary before then. As a result, the entire OEA negotiation process became subject to a fiduciary review standard. That conclusion is compelled, appellants urge, because Ovitz's substantial contacts with third parties, and his receipt of confidential Disney information and request for reimbursement of expenses before October 1, prove that Eisner and Disney had already vested Ovitz with at least apparent authority before his formal investiture in office.... [T]he *de facto* officer argument lacks merit, both legally and factually.... Here, Ovitz did not assume, or purport to assume, the duties of the Disney presidency before October 1, 1995. In his post-trial Opinion, the Chancellor found as fact that all of Ovitz's pre-October 1 conduct upon which appellants rely to establish *de facto* officer status, represented Ovitz's preparations to assume the duties of President after he was formally in office....

B. Claims Based upon Ovitz's Conduct During His Termination as President

The appellants' second claim is that the Court of Chancery erroneously concluded that Ovitz breached no fiduciary duty, including his duty of loyalty, by receiving the NFT payment upon his termination as President of Disney....

... The record establishes overwhelmingly that Ovitz did not leave Disney voluntarily. Nor did Ovitz arrange beforehand with Eisner to structure his departure as a termination without cause.... As the trial court found, "Ovitz did not engage in a transaction with the corporation—rather, the corporation imposed an unwanted transaction upon him." ... At trial the plaintiff-appellants attempted to prove that Ovitz had colluded with Eisner and others to obtain an NFT payment to which he was not entitled. The Chancellor found the facts to be otherwise....

IV. The Claims Against the Disney Defendants

We next turn to the claims of error that relate to the Disney defendants. Those claims are subdivisible into two groups: (A) claims arising out of the approval of the OEA and of Ovitz's election as President; and (B) claims arising out of the NFT severance payment to Ovitz upon his termination....

A. Claims Arising from the Approval of the OEA and Ovitz's Election as President

1. The Due Care Determinations

.... The appellants claim that the Chancellor erred by: ... [*i.*] ruling that the old board was not required to approve the OEA; [*ii.*] concluding that the compensation committee members did not breach their duty of care in approving the NFT provisions of the OEA; and [*iii.*] holding that the remaining members of the old board (*i.e.*, the directors who were not members of the compensation committee) had not breached their duty of care in electing Ovitz as Disney's President.

...

i. Ruling That the Full Disney Board Was Not Required to Consider and Approve the OEA

The appellants next challenge the Court of Chancery's determination that the full Disney board was not required to consider and approve the OEA....

As the Chancellor found, under the Company's governing documents the board of directors was responsible for selecting the corporation's officers, but under the compensation committee charter, the committee was responsible for establishing and approving the salaries, together with benefits and stock options, of the Company's CEO and President. The compensation committee also had the charter-imposed duty to "approve employment contracts, or contracts at will" for "all corporate officers who are members of the Board of Directors regardless of salary." That is exactly what occurred here. The full board ultimately selected Ovitz as President, and the compensation committee considered and ultimately approved the OEA, which embodied the terms of Ovitz's employment, including his compensation.

The Delaware General Corporation Law (DGCL) expressly empowers a board of directors to appoint committees and to delegate to them a broad range of responsibilities, which may include setting executive compensation. Nothing in the DGCL mandates that the entire board must make those decisions....

ii. Holding That the Compensation Committee Members Did Not Fail to Exercise Due Care in Approving the OEA

The appellants next challenge the Chancellor's determination that although the compensation committee's decision-making process fell far short of corporate governance "best practices," the committee members breached no duty of care in considering and approving the NFT terms of the OEA.... [T]he overall thrust of that claim is that the compensation committee approved the OEA with NFT provisions that could potentially result in an enormous payout, without informing themselves of what the full magnitude of that payout could be....

In our view, a helpful approach is to compare what actually happened here to what would have occurred had the committee followed a "best practices" (or "best case") scenario, from a process standpoint. In a "best case" scenario, all committee members would have received, before or at the committee's first meeting on September 26, 1995, a spreadsheet or similar document prepared by (or with the assistance of) a compensation expert (in this case, Graef Crystal). Making different, alternative assumptions, the spreadsheet would disclose the amounts that Ovitz could receive under the OEA in each circumstance that might foreseeably arise. One variable in that matrix of possibilities would be the cost to Disney of a non-fault termination for each of the five years of the initial term of the OEA. The contents of the spreadsheet would be explained to the committee members, either by the expert who prepared it or by a fellow committee member similarly knowledgeable about the subject. That spreadsheet, which ultimately would become an exhibit to the minutes of the compensation committee meeting, would form the basis of the committee's deliberations and decision.

Had that scenario been followed, there would be no dispute (and no basis for litigation) over what information was furnished to the committee members or when it was furnished. Regrettably, the committee's informational and decisionmaking process used here was not so tidy. That is one reason why the Chancellor found that although the committee's process did not fall below the level required for a proper exercise of due care, it did fall short of what best practices would have counseled.

The Disney compensation committee met twice: on September 26 and October 16, 1995. The minutes of the September 26 meeting reflect that the committee approved the terms of the OEA (at that time embodied in the form of a letter agreement), except for the option grants, which were not approved until October 16 — after the Disney stock incentive plan had been amended to provide for those options. At the September 26 meeting, the compensation committee considered a "term sheet" which, in summarizing the material terms of the OEA, relevantly disclosed that in the event of a non-fault termination, Ovitz would receive: (i) the present value of his salary ($1 million per year) for the balance of the contract term, (ii) the present value of his annual bonus payments (computed at $7.5 million) for the balance of the contract term, (iii) a $10 million termination fee, and (iv) the acceleration of his options for 3 million shares, which would become immediately exercisable at market price.

... [T]he issue may be framed as whether the compensation committee members knew, at the time they approved the OEA, that the value of the option component of the severance package could reach the $92 million order of magnitude if they terminated Ovitz without cause after one year. The evidentiary record shows that the committee members were so informed.

On this question the documentation is far less than what best practices would have dictated. There is no exhibit to the minutes that discloses, in a single document, the estimated value of the accelerated options in the event of an NFT termination after one year. The information imparted to the committee members on that subject is, however, supported by other evidence, most notably the trial testimony of various witnesses about spreadsheets that were prepared for the compensation committee meetings.

... Ovitz's options were set at 75% of parity with the options previously granted to Eisner and to Frank Wells. Because the compensation committee had established those earlier benchmark option grants to Eisner and Wells and were aware of their value, a simple mathematical calculation would have informed them of the potential value range of Ovitz's options. Also, in August and September 1995, Watson and Russell met with Graef Crystal to determine (among other things) the value of the potential Ovitz options.... [Watson's] spreadsheets were shared with, and explained to, the committee members at the September meeting.... [The committee also knew that Ovitz had forgone over $150 million in commissions at CAA, and had demanded to be guaranteed at least that amount in case the Disney position did not work out; thus the committee had an idea of how valuable the options would have had to be to satisfy Ovitz.]

It is on this record that the Chancellor found that the compensation committee was informed of the material facts relating to an NFT payout. If measured in terms of the documentation that would have been generated if "best practices" had been followed, that record leaves much to be desired. The Chancellor acknowledged that, and so do we. But, the Chancellor also found that despite its imperfections, the evidentiary record was sufficient to support the conclusion that the compensation committee had adequately informed itself of the potential magnitude of the entire severance package....

... [T]he appellants stress that Crystal did not make a report in person to the compensation committee at its September 26 meeting.... The Court of Chancery noted (and we agree) that although it might have been the better course of action, it was "not necessary for an expert to make a formal presentation at the committee meeting in order for the board to rely on that expert's analysis...." The Chancellor correctly applied Section 141(e) in upholding the reliance of [compensation committee members] Poitier and Lozano upon the information that Crystal, Russell and Watson furnished to them.

Finally, the appellants contend that Poitier and Lozano did not review the spreadsheets generated by Watson at the September 26 meeting. The short answer is that even if Poitier and Lozano did not review the spreadsheets themselves, Russell and Watson adequately informed them of the spreadsheets' contents. The Court of Chancery explicitly found, and the record supports, that Poitier and Lozano "were informed by Russell and Watson of all *material* information reasonably available, even though they were not privy to every conversation or document exchanged amongst Russell, Watson, Crystal, and Ovitz's representatives."

iii. Holding That the Remaining Disney Directors Did Not Fail to Exercise Due Care in Approving the Hiring of Ovitz as the President of Disney

... The only properly reviewable action of the entire board was its decision to elect Ovitz as Disney's President....

... [W]ell in advance of the September 26, 1995 board meeting the directors were fully aware that the Company needed—especially in light of Wells' death and Eisner's medical problems—to hire a "number two" executive and potential successor to Eisner. There had been many discussions about that need and about potential candidates who could fill that role even before Eisner decided to try to recruit Ovitz. Before the September 26 board meeting Eisner had individually discussed with each director the possibility of hiring Ovitz, and Ovitz's background and qualifications. The directors thus knew of Ovitz's skills, reputation and experience, all of which they believed would be highly valuable to the Company. The directors also knew that to accept a position at Disney, Ovitz would have to walk away from a very successful business—a reality that would lead a reasonable person to believe that Ovitz would likely succeed in similar pursuits elsewhere in the industry....

The board was also informed of the key terms of the OEA (including Ovitz's salary, bonus and options). Russell reported this information to them at the September 26, 1995 executive session, which was attended by Eisner and all non-executive directors. Russell also reported on the compensation committee meeting that had immediately preceded the executive session. And, both Russell and Watson responded to questions from the board. Relying upon the compensation committee's approval of the OEA 89 and the other information furnished to them, the Disney directors, after further deliberating, unanimously elected Ovitz as President.

Based upon this record, we uphold the Chancellor's conclusion that, when electing Ovitz to the Disney presidency the remaining Disney directors were fully informed of all material facts, and that the appellants failed to establish any lack of due care on the directors' part.

2. The Good Faith Determinations

The Court of Chancery held that the business judgment rule presumptions protected the decisions of the compensation committee and the remaining Disney directors, not only because they had acted with due care but also because they had not acted in bad faith....

... [T]he duty to act in good faith is, up to this point relatively uncharted. Because of the increased recognition of the importance of good faith, some conceptual guidance to the corporate community may be helpful....

The precise question is whether the Chancellor's articulated standard for bad faith corporate fiduciary conduct—intentional dereliction of duty, a conscious disregard for one's responsibilities—is legally correct. In approaching that question, we note that the Chancellor characterized that definition as "*an* appropriate (*although not the only*) standard for determining whether fiduciaries have acted in good faith." ... [A]t least three different categories of fiduciary behavior are candidates for the "bad faith" pejorative label.

The first category involves so-called "subjective bad faith," that is, fiduciary conduct motivated by an actual intent to do harm.... [N]o such conduct is claimed to have occurred, or did occur, in this case.

The second category of conduct, which is at the opposite end of the spectrum, involves lack of due care—that is, fiduciary action taken solely by reason of gross negligence and without any malevolent intent.... Although the Chancellor found, and we agree, that the appellants failed to establish gross negligence, to afford guidance we address the issue of whether gross negligence (including a failure to inform one's self of available material facts), without more, can also constitute bad faith. The answer is clearly no.

... Both our legislative history and our common law jurisprudence distinguish sharply between the duties to exercise due care and to act in good faith, and highly significant consequences flow from that distinction.

The Delaware General Assembly has addressed the distinction between bad faith and a failure to exercise due care (*i.e.*, gross negligence) in two separate contexts. The first is Section 102(b)(7) of the DGCL, which authorizes Delaware corporations, by a provision in the certificate of incorporation, to exculpate their directors from monetary damage liability for a breach of the duty of care.... but not for conduct that is not in good faith. To adopt a definition of bad faith that would cause a violation of the duty of care automatically to become an act or omission "not in good faith," would eviscerate the protections accorded to directors by the General Assembly's adoption of Section 102(b)(7). [Similarly, Section 145 permits corporations to indemnify directors and officers for legal expenses and judgments for actions taken in "good faith" in the corporation's best interests; as with 102(b)(7), the provision appears to distinguish between "bad faith" and breach of the duty of care.]

That leaves the third category of fiduciary conduct, which falls in between the first two.... This third category is what the Chancellor's definition of bad faith—intentional dereliction of duty, a conscious disregard for one's responsibilities—is intended to capture. The question is whether such misconduct is properly treated as a non-exculpable, non-indemnifiable violation of the fiduciary duty to act in good faith. In our view it must be, for at least two reasons.

First, the universe of fiduciary misconduct is not limited to either disloyalty in the classic sense (*i.e.*, preferring the adverse self-interest of the fiduciary or of a related person to the interest of the corporation) or gross negligence. Cases have arisen where corporate directors have no conflicting self-interest in a decision, yet engage in misconduct that is more culpable than simple inattention or failure to be informed of all facts material to the decision. To protect the interests of the corporation and its shareholders, fiduciary conduct of this kind, which does not involve disloyalty (as traditionally defined) but is qualitatively more culpable than gross negligence, should be proscribed. A vehicle is needed to address such violations doctrinally, and that doctrinal vehicle is the duty to act in good faith. The Chancellor implicitly so recognized in his Opinion, where he identified different examples of bad faith as follows:

> The good faith required of a corporate fiduciary includes not simply the duties of care and loyalty, in the narrow sense that I have discussed them above, but all actions required by a true faithfulness and devotion to the interests of the corporation and its shareholders. A failure to act in good faith may be shown, for instance, where the fiduciary intentionally acts with a purpose other than that of advancing the best interests of the corporation, where the fiduciary acts with the intent to violate applicable positive law, or where the fiduciary intentionally fails to act in the face of a known duty to act, demonstrating a conscious disregard for his duties. There may be other examples of bad faith yet to be proven or alleged, but these three are the most salient.

Those articulated examples of bad faith are not new to our jurisprudence. Indeed, they echo pronouncements our courts have made throughout the decades. Second, the legislature has also recognized this intermediate category of fiduciary misconduct, which ranks between conduct involving subjective bad faith and gross negligence. Section 102(b)(7)(ii) of the DGCL expressly denies money damage exculpation for "acts or omissions not in good faith or which involve intentional misconduct or a knowing violation of law." By its very terms that provision distinguishes between "intentional misconduct" and a "knowing violation of law" (both examples of subjective bad faith) on the one hand, and "acts ... not in good faith," on the other. Because the statute exculpates directors only for conduct amounting to gross negligence, the statutory denial of exculpation for "acts ... not in good faith" must encompass the intermediate category of misconduct captured by the Chancellor's definition of bad faith.

For these reasons, we uphold the Court of Chancery's definition as a legally appropriate, although not the exclusive, definition of fiduciary bad faith. We need go no further. To engage in an effort to craft (in the Court's words) "a definitive and categorical definition of the universe of acts that would constitute bad faith" would be unwise and is unnecessary to dispose of the issues presented on this appeal.

Having sustained the Chancellor's finding that the Disney directors acted in good faith when approving the OEA and electing Ovitz as President, we next address the claims arising out of the decision to pay Ovitz the amount called for by the NFT provisions of the OEA.

B. Claims Arising from the Payment of the NFT Severance Payout to Ovitz

The appellants['] ... overall thrust is that even if the OEA approval was legally valid, the NFT severance payout to Ovitz pursuant to the OEA was not. Specifically, the appellants contend that: (1) only the full Disney board with the concurrence of the compensation committee—but not Eisner alone—was authorized to terminate Ovitz; (2) because Ovitz could have been terminated for cause, Litvack and Eisner acted without due care and in bad faith in reaching the contrary conclusion; and (3) the business judgment rule presumptions did not protect the new Disney board's acquiescence in the NFT payout, because the new board was not entitled to rely upon Eisner's and Litvack's contrary advice. Appellants urge that in rejecting these claims the Court of Chancery committed reversible error. We disagree.

1. Was Action by the New Board Required to Terminate Ovitz as the President of Disney?

The Chancellor determined that although the board as constituted upon Ovitz's termination (the "new board") had the authority to terminate Ovitz, neither that board nor the compensation committee was required to act, because Eisner also had, and properly exercised, that authority. The new board, the Chancellor found, was not required to terminate Ovitz under the company's internal documents. Without such a duty to act, the new board's failure to vote on the termination could not give rise to a breach of the duty of care or the duty to act in good faith....

Article Tenth of the Company's certificate of incorporation in effect at the termination plainly states that:

> The officers of the Corporation shall be chosen in such a manner, shall hold their offices for such terms and shall carry out such duties as are determined solely by the Board of Directors, subject to the right of the Board of Directors to remove any officer or officers at any time with or without cause.

Article IV of Disney's bylaws provided that the Board Chairman/CEO "shall, subject to the provisions of the Bylaws and the control of the Board of Directors, have general and active management, direction, and supervision over the business of the Corporation and over its officers...."

... The issue is whether the Chancellor's interpretation of these instruments, as giving the board and the Chairman/CEO concurrent power to terminate a lesser officer, is legally permissible.... If the certificate of incorporation vested the power of removal exclusively in the board, then absent an express delegation of authority from the board, the presiding officer would have not have a concurrent removal power. If, on the other hand, the governing instruments expressly placed the power of removal in both the board and specified officers, then there would be concurrent removal power.... Read together, the governing instruments do not yield a single, indisputably clear answer, and could reasonably be interpreted either way....

Where corporate governing instruments are ambiguous, our case law permits a court to determine their meaning by resorting to well-established legal rules of construction, which include the rules governing the interpretation of contracts. One such rule is that where a contract is ambiguous, the court must look to extrinsic evidence to determine which of the reasonable readings the parties intended.

Here, the extrinsic evidence clearly supports the conclusion that the board and Eisner understood that Eisner, as Board Chairman/CEO had concurrent power with the board to terminate Ovitz as President. In that regard, the Chancellor credited the testimony of new board members that Eisner, as Chairman and CEO, was empowered to terminate Ovitz without board approval or intervention; and also Litvack's testimony that during his tenure as general counsel, many Company officers were terminated and the board never once took action in connection with their terminations. Because Eisner possessed, and exercised, the power to terminate Ovitz unilaterally, we find that the Chancellor correctly concluded that the new board was not required to act in connection with that termination, and, therefore, the board did not violate any fiduciary duty to act with due care or in good faith....

2. In Concluding That Ovitz Could Not Be Terminated for Cause, Did Litvack or Eisner Breach Any Fiduciary Duty?

It is undisputed that Litvack and Eisner (based on Litvack's advice) both concluded that if Ovitz was to be terminated, it could only be without cause, because no basis existed to terminate Ovitz for cause. The appellants argued in the Court of Chancery that the business judgment presumptions do not protect that conclusion, because by permitting Ovitz to be terminated without cause, Litvack and Eisner acted in bad faith and without exercising due care. Rejecting that claim, the Chancellor determined independently, as a matter of fact and law, that (1) Ovitz had not engaged in any conduct as President that constituted gross negligence or malfeasance—the standard for an NFT under the OEA; and (2) in arriving at that same conclusion in 1996, Litvack and Eisner did not breach their fiduciary duty of care or their duty to act in good faith.

... At the trial level, the appellants attempted to show, as a factual matter, that Ovitz's conduct as President met the standard for a termination for cause, because (i) Ovitz intentionally failed to follow Eisner's directives and was insubordinate, (ii) Ovitz was a habitual liar, and (iii) Ovitz violated Company policies relating to expenses and to reporting gifts he gave while President of Disney. The Court found the facts contrary to appellants' position....

Despite their inability to show factual or legal error in the Chancellor's determination that Ovitz could not be terminated for cause, appellants contend that Litvack and Eisner breached their fiduciary duty to exercise due care and to act in good faith in reaching that same conclusion. The Court of Chancery scrutinized the record to determine independently whether, in reaching their conclusion, Litvack and Eisner had separately exercised due care and acted in good faith. The Court determined that they had properly discharged both duties. Appellants' attack upon that determination lacks merit, because it is also without basis in the factual record.

After considering the OEA and Ovitz's conduct, Litvack concluded, and advised Eisner, that Disney had no basis to terminate Ovitz for cause and that Disney should comply with its contractual obligations. Even though Litvack personally did not want to grant a NFT to Ovitz, he concluded that for Disney to assert falsely that there was cause would be both unethical and harmful to Disney's reputation. As to Litvack, the Court of Chancery held:

> I do not intend to imply by these conclusions that Litvack was an infallible source of legal knowledge. Nevertheless, Litvack's less astute moments as a legal counsel do not impugn his good faith or preparedness in reaching his conclusions with respect to whether Ovitz could have been terminated for cause....

... The Chancellor [also] found that ... Eisner had breached no duty and had exercised his business judgment:

> ... I conclude that Eisner's actions in connection with the termination are, for the most part, consistent with what is expected of a faithful fiduciary. Eisner unexpectedly found himself confronted with a situation that did not have an easy solution. He weighed the alternatives, received advice from counsel and

then exercised his business judgment in the manner he thought best for the corporation. Eisner knew all the material information reasonably available when making the decision, he did not neglect an affirmative duty to act (or fail to cause the board to act) and he acted in what he believed were the best interests of the Company, taking into account the cost to the Company of the decision and the potential alternatives. Eisner was not personally interested in the transaction in any way that would make him incapable of exercising business judgment, and I conclude that the plaintiffs have not demonstrated by a preponderance of the evidence that Eisner breached his fiduciary duties or acted in bad faith in connection with Ovitz's termination and receipt of the NFT.

... Even though the Chancellor found much to criticize in Eisner's "imperial CEO" style of governance, nothing has been shown to overturn the factual basis for the Court's conclusion that, in the end, Eisner's conduct satisfied the standards required of him as a fiduciary.

3. Were the Remaining Directors Entitled to Rely upon Eisner's and Litvack's Advice That Ovitz Could Not Be Fired for Cause?

The appellants' third claim of error challenges the Chancellor's conclusion that the remaining new board members could rely upon Litvack's and Eisner's advice that Ovitz could be terminated only without cause. The short answer to that challenge is that, for the reasons previously discussed, the advice the remaining directors received and relied upon was accurate. Moreover, the directors' reliance on that advice was found to be in good faith. Although formal board action was not necessary, the remaining directors all supported the decision to terminate Ovitz based on the information given by Eisner and Litvack....

V. The Waste Claim

... [A] plaintiff who fails to rebut the business judgment rule presumptions is not entitled to any remedy unless the transaction constitutes waste.... To recover on a claim of corporate waste, the plaintiffs must shoulder the burden of proving that the exchange was "so one sided that no business person of ordinary, sound judgment could conclude that the corporation has received adequate consideration." A claim of waste will arise only in the rare, "unconscionable case where directors irrationally squander or give away corporate assets." This onerous standard for waste is a corollary of the proposition that where business judgment presumptions are applicable, the board's decision will be upheld unless it cannot be "attributed to any rational business purpose."

... The payment of a contractually obligated amount cannot constitute waste, unless the contractual obligation is itself wasteful.... Appellants claim that the NFT provisions of the OEA were wasteful because they incentivized Ovitz to perform poorly in order to obtain payment of the NFT provisions. The appellants urge that although the OEA may have induced Ovitz to join Disney as President, no contractual safeguards were in place to retain him in that position. In essence, appellants claim that the NFT provisions of the OEA created an irrational incentive for Ovitz to get himself fired.

That claim does not come close to satisfying the high hurdle required to establish waste. The approval of the NFT provisions in the OEA had a rational business purpose: to induce Ovitz to leave CAA, at what would otherwise be a considerable cost to him, in order to join Disney.... To suggest that at the time he entered into the OEA Ovitz would engineer an early departure at the cost of his extraordinary reputation in the entertainment industry and his historical friendship with Eisner, is not only fanciful but also without proof in the record. Indeed, the Chancellor found that it was "patently unreasonable to assume that Ovitz intended to perform just poorly enough to be fired quickly, but not so poorly that he could be terminated for cause." ...

VI. Conclusion

For the reasons stated above, the judgment of the Court of Chancery is affirmed.

Omari Scott Simmons, *Taking the Blue Pill: The Imponderable Impact of Executive Compensation Reform**

I. Introduction

"The [Matrix is the] world that has been pulled over your eyes to blind you from the truth."[15]

....

No corporate governance issue captures the imagination and frustration of the American public and politicians more than executive compensation. Next to the decision to sell or merge a company, the selection of a CEO is perhaps the most important decision a board will make. In some instances, hiring a highly touted CEO can boost a company's market valuation by fifteen percent or more. Despite the importance of the decision to hire a CEO, the amount of attention executive compensation receives exceeds its impact on corporate performance. This overemphasis is due, in large part, to lawmaker opportunism upon which this Article focuses.

Whereas most of the corporate law literature on executive compensation has focused on rent extraction by wayward corporate managers, this Article uses a moderate form of public choice theory to examine the impact of lawmaker opportunism on the shape of executive compensation reform. Public choice theory generally assumes that political actors, like private market actors, are mainly self-interested and that the pursuit of lawmaker self-interest may result in government failure, that is, inefficient policies. Thus, corporate lawmaker self-interest and opportunism, just like wayward corporate managers, can be a source of rent extraction, inefficiency, and welfare loss. The existing legal literature, however, fails to capture the complexity of the executive compensation issue from a political perspective. This Article fills a critical gap in the legal literature by arguing lawmaker motivations, in large part, explain the inconsistencies, inefficiencies, perceived bias, and symbolism characterizing executive compensation reform for almost two decades....

---

* Originally appearing in 62 SOUTHERN METHODIST UNIVERSITY LAW REVIEW No. 1, 299–365 (2009). Reprinted with permission from the SMU Law Review and the Southern Methodist University Dedman School of Law.

15. THE MATRIX (Warner Bros. & Vill. Roadshow Pictures 1999). Due to the popularity of the 1999 film "The Matrix," the terms "blue pill" and "red pill" have become a popular metaphor for the choice between blissful ignorance or the examined life, respectively. In the film, the protagonist Neo is given the choice between (i) a blue pill preserving the status quo of blissful ignorance or (ii) a red pill revealing the deeper truth of the Matrix....

In the midst of a severe economic recession and the contentious 2008 presidential election, presidential candidates indiscriminately invoked excessive executive compensation as a key corporate governance issue that reflected social inequities and demanded a regulatory response. The advent of the Obama Administration reflects an even greater preoccupation with executive compensation reform. Irrespective of political rhetoric and posturing, the reduction of executive pay for a few individuals at the top of the wealth pyramid may ameliorate populist outrage, but does not necessarily put money back into the hands of ordinary Americans. Similarly, occasional disgorgements and reductions of pay for underperforming CEOs and other senior executives provide only negligible benefits to certain corporate constituencies.

In the broader political context, the overemphasis on executive compensation is a diversion from other pertinent socio-economic issues like the minimum wage, health insurance, social security, pension protection, and the sub-prime mortgage crisis that are more relevant to ordinary Americans and often addressed outside of the realm of traditional corporate law. Lawmakers often link executive compensation, albeit tenuously, to broader economic turmoil, such as plant closings, unemployment, outsourcing domestic jobs, and income inequality. For lawmakers, the matrix of executive compensation reforms operates like a blue pill, keeping corporate constituencies, especially populist groups, in a state of blissful ignorance, foregoing a deeper analysis that reveals the reality of lawmaker opportunism and manipulation. This Article contends that corporate constituents and legal commentators, by ignoring the political construction of the executive compensation issue, are in essence taking a blue pill that threatens the prospect of optimal reform.

As executive compensation levels continue to rise despite decades of lawmaker reforms (or multiple blue pills), the impact of such reforms is in question. For some corporate constituents, qualitative assessments of corporate reform prove difficult because corporate reform exhibits credence characteristics. Credence characteristics are service attributes whose quality cannot be fully determined even after significant use. Consumers of services with substantial credence characteristics (for example, automobile repair services, medical treatments, and corporate law) are never sure about the optimum amount (and even type) of the service needed.

Consider the following scenario: In the act of treating an ailing patient a doctor recommends an invasive surgical procedure, a regimen of prescription medication (that is, five blue pills daily), plus exercise and rest. Assuming the patient's ailment improves, will the patient ever know whether the surgical procedure was necessary or superfluous? Would the blue pills and exercise regimen effectively cure the ailment? Or would the body's natural healing response over time, without the intervention of a doctor and medication, suffice? The patient in this scenario has limited information and relies on the doctor's expertise for both the diagnosis and treatment. Even after the medical services have been provided, the patient still may have limited ability to evaluate the quality of the services rendered. Given the bounded rationality of the patient, the doctor, with informational advantages, has perverse incentives to provide excessive treatment or withhold treatment where profitable....

In the corporate law context, corporate lawmakers—for example, the state of Delaware and the federal government—not only provide reform services but also act as experts and diagnose corporate governance problems. The coupling of diagnosis and treatment, as well as information asymmetries between lawmakers and various corporate constituencies (for example, managers, shareholders, and populist groups), create incentives for opportunistic lawmaker behavior.... Given the credence characteristics of executive compensation reform, there is an enhanced risk that lawmakers may mitigate political backlash and promote acquiescence without actually addressing fundamental flaws in the corporate governance system or foregoing more effective redistributive policies and interventions....

II. Limitations of Existing Theories Addressing Executive Compensation

A. The Executive Pay Decision

The board is ultimately responsible for hiring the CEO, often with the assistance of an executive search firm. Similarly, the board sets CEO compensation, often via a compensation committee aided by consultants. The decision to hire a CEO is one of the most important decisions a board is likely to make. When hiring a new CEO, boards choose between external and internal candidates exhibiting a wide array of traits and competencies, such as: integrity, operational skills, financial acumen, persuasion, communication, accountability, and energy. The board's primary concern in the competitive marketplace is securing the top candidate. This aggressive quest for top talent is analogous to the free agency market in professional sports promoting high compensation levels. In the executive search process for most large companies, compensation is most likely a secondary concern. The CEO compensation decision can coincide with hiring a new CEO or negotiating with an incumbent CEO. In either case, the CEO compensation decision is generally protected under the business judgment rule.

In theory, executive compensation, when used effectively, can reduce agency costs and promote an array of predetermined corporate goals. These performance goals generally fall into two categories: financial and operational objectives. Examples of financial objectives include: net income; earnings before interest, taxes, depreciation, and amortization (EBITDA); earnings per share (EPS); and share price. In addition to the standard financial performance-based compensation metrics such as share price, a firm's management, in their discretion, may also establish operational performance-based metrics such as customer service, product development, environmental stewardship, legal compliance, and diversity. Independent of performance-based objectives, firms have additional concerns such as recruitment and retention of top executive talent that inevitably raise pay levels. When setting compensation performance goals and criteria, some degree of subjectivity is unavoidable. Despite the existence of complex formulaic approaches to determine executive compensation, it is virtually impossible to discern the exact value that a CEO confers on an organization. In this sense, the imponderability of CEO impact resembles the imponderable impact of executive compensation reform.

B. Elements of Executive Compensation

Executive compensation has many moving parts that further complicate its regulation. Accordingly, "even with enhanced SEC disclosure requirements, quantifying and evaluating executive compensation today is a much more difficult proposition than it was twenty years ago." Common elements of executive compensation include: (i) a fixed base salary; (ii) variable remuneration or bonus schemes, such as long term incentive plans (LTIPs) and stock options; (iii) perquisites, such as pensions, deferred compensation, insurance schemes, company cars, corporate jet usage, subsidized mortgages, box seats, and relocation costs; (iv) severance payments, such as golden parachutes and handshakes; and (v) charitable contributions. In addition to these examples of recognized modes of compensation, new modes of remuneration are always developing. While most executive pay derives from a managerial services contract (usually five years or less in duration), discretionary or highly subjective forms of remuneration are neither uncommon nor uncontroversial. Whether executive compensation is contractual or discretionary, equity-based or non equity-based, the link to actual executive performance is never precise. David Walker describes the difficulty presented by multiple compensation elements:

> Today executive stock options have supplanted cash salary as the largest single component of the average large company CEO's pay package, but options are only a small part of the picture. Modern CEO compensation packages include cash, options, restricted stock, phantom stock and options, a wide variety of bonus opportunities, not to mention an ever-expanding array of benefits and perks, many of which, such as SERPs and deferred compensation plans, represent significant financial commitments by shareholders.

To be fair, new Financial Accounting Standards Board (FASB) rules require companies to disclose "fair value" expenses "for all forms of equity compensation, including options, in their financial statements." Prior to these rules, "stock options were the most common equity vehicle due to their favorable accounting treatment." As a result of the new FASB rules, companies are reevaluating whether to use a greater mix of equity incentives (for example, restricted stock). However, an added effect of "dividing compensation between salary, bonuses, perks, golden parachutes, and the like tends to reduce salience and outrage and permit greater overall [managerial] appropriation." ...

III. Credence Characteristics in the Corporate Reform Context

A. *Public Choice Theory and the Political Support Maximization Model*

The political support maximization model of public choice theory is a useful paradigm to analyze executive compensation reforms in context, and also to predict when the interests of certain corporate constituencies are likely to prevail in regulatory outcomes. Public choice theorists generally assume political actors, like private market actors, are mainly self-interested and that the pursuit of lawmaker self-interest may result in government failure, that is, inefficient policies. The analysis of credence services supplements the public choice framework by analyzing how the unobservable impact of regulatory output facilitates greater lawmaker discretion.

The federal government and Delaware, both arguably monopolist lawmakers, supply credence characteristic-laden services to various corporate constituents (for example, managers, shareholders, employees, and other populist groups) in the form of corporate regulation. Despite the ability of public choice theory to predict which groups are likely to wield more influence over lawmakers, there often is no clear answer to how much a specific corporate regulation benefits various corporate constituencies. The answer to the substantive question of quality is complicated because it depends on a number of contextual variables, including (i) the type of corporate decision at issue—ownership, enterprise, or oversight; (ii) the corporate constituent's vantage point—management, shareholders, or populist groups; (iii) the desired policy value—efficiency or fairness; (iv) inter-temporal considerations—short-term versus long-term impact on business value; and (v) the degree of legal enforcement. In addition to these factors, the corporate reform quality inquiry is further constrained by credence characteristics. At a minimum, an adequate assessment of impact necessitates: (i) clear objectives for reform (that is, what executive compensation reform should accomplish); and (ii) empirical validation. In the executive compensation context, the first condition is a political decision that lawmakers have continually muddled and failed to satisfy, sometimes at the expense of vulnerable corporate constituents. Without clear objectives, empirical validation is a speculative exercise.

1. The Market for Political Capital

In the market for political capital there is an exchange between corporate constituents on the demand-side and lawmakers on the supply-side. Similar to other markets, the group with the most effective demand is most likely to receive the political spoils. Nobel Prize winner George J. Stigler is credited with laying the groundwork for the economic theory of regulation. Before embarking on a description of Stigler's supply-demand apparatus, it is useful to describe the historical antecedents to the economic theory of regulation developed by Stigler and others. Public interest theory contends that lawmakers regulate in response to market inefficiency and inequity. This approach assumes that regulation is efficient as well as costless and that lawmakers are motivated by the public interest. The so-called capture theory reaches the opposite conclusion. It holds that lawmakers maximize private wealth instead of social welfare and are captured by private interests. Both the public interest and capture theories understate the complexity of the political process.

Stigler's economic theory of regulation asserts that the state has a monopoly on coercive power and may use it to transfer wealth from one group to another.[16] For Stigler, "the problem of regulation is the problem of discovering when and why an industry (or other group of like-minded people) is able to use the state for its purposes, or is singled out by the state to be used for alien purposes." The two major constituent groups in Stigler's economic theory of regulation are producers and consumers, but in the corporate regulation context, groups are more diverse and pluralistic, involving managers, shareholders, employees, activist groups, and communities. The dominant, although not universal, view has been that corporate managers prevail in this tournament or auction for political spoils. A "rational regulator will not … [aim to] distribute benefits equally" but "will seek a structure of costs and benefits that maximizes political returns." This, however, does not necessarily mean lawmakers will invariably favor the groups with the greatest political muscle or those who can or desire to incur the transaction costs of mobilization. The "government as order-taker" analogy is too simplistic to account for the complex relationship between lawmakers and corporate constituents.…

2. Exogenous Factors Shifting Political Balance

The important question is not simply whether a supply-demand framework or interest group dynamics act as a constraint on lawmaker behavior, but instead, what are the conditions under which corporate managers are not likely to prevail? Corporate scandals and "economic disruptions often change the distribution of political power and create opportunities for public policy entrepreneurs to rearrange things to their advantage." Diffuse constituencies, despite lacking organization, may nonetheless participate in the political process when they are provided with "free (and easy to digest, perhaps entertaining) information" and "political saliency, a major national issue that commands attention and motivates action in the absence of political organization." Executive compensation is the most politically salient corporate governance issue. Rationally ignorant voters, concerned about macro economic performance" may respond by favoring executive pay reform policies, even if such policies have a trivial impact on the national economy or their own personal circumstances. This scenario results in modest cyclical quick fixes—a band-aid instead of stitches or vice versa.

For lawmakers, the pragmatic outcome to this scenario is a compromise among various interests, albeit slanted to preserve a broad coalition of support, thereby maximizing

---

16. *See* George J. Stigler, *The Theory of Economic Regulation*, 2 BELL J. ECON. 3 (1971).

lawmaker utility. As a consequence of these dynamics, the corporate regulatory framework with respect to executive compensation is laden with policies that seem economically inefficient and resemble a placebo rather than a cure. Efficient regulation may lack political appeal, and at times, merely symbolic or inefficient policies have more political utility....

IV. Supply-Side Inefficiencies: Law Makers as Suppliers of Credence Characteristic-Laden Services

A. *Maximizing Political Capital*

Corporate constituents pay with votes and other indirect forms of political support. Political capital is an important form of currency that is exchanged between lawmakers and corporate constituents, and its importance is not undermined by the fact that it is less transparent than prices in the actual buyer-seller context. Thus, "the currency with which the demanders bid is obviously a bit more complex than the stuff reported in the monetary aggregates"; political capital "includes votes delivered in support of politicians, campaign contributions, jobs in the political afterlife, and so forth." For corporate constituents like corporate managers, political capital is an "intangible asset that provides corporations with long term value extending beyond an isolated policy issue [or dispute]." Similarly, lawmakers seek to maximize political capital by generating broad political support.

At first glance, it seems rational for lawmakers to target the most valuable consumer segment. Yet the credence characteristics of corporate reform allow lawmakers to satisfy multiple constituencies simultaneously, providing lawmakers with a broader set of options to address populist outrage and market instability. Because credence characteristics make lawmaker motivations easier to camouflage, corporate constituents, particularly those with greater informational constraints, find it difficult to determine clear winners and losers. By the time these corporate constituents discern the impact of a particular regulation, public outrage has waned, only to reappear in the future. Here, political incentives and short-termism may hinder earnest exploration of issues, resulting in modest, incremental, or superficial change. Executive compensation reform tracks this pattern.

Lawmakers may camouflage unnecessary or superficial reforms, lack of expertise, incompetence, short-term commitment to an issue, and responsibility. Interestingly, this creates several dilemmas for corporate constituents. Perhaps the most important dilemma is the enhanced risk that regulators may manipulate corporate constituents in order to mitigate political backlash, promote acquiescence, and silence critics without addressing fundamental flaws or root causes of a particular issue. This raises the question of how corporate constituents can limit the risk of manipulation and constrain lawmaker opportunism that leads to suboptimal reform.

1. *Is Executive Compensation Reform a Matter of Agency Costs and Internal Abuses of Corporate Power?*

The pay-for-performance perspective on executive compensation is consistent with traditional agency cost analysis.... Yet aligning pay with performance may not necessarily lower compensation—indeed, it may do the exact opposite. If the idea is to provide incentives for performance, a perfectly plausible outcome is an increase or ratcheting-up of pay. A number of commentators assert that the crux of the issue is not the actual level of compensation, but rather the tenuous link between pay and performance and the lack of effective procedural mechanisms to constrain abuses of director discretion.

The only way to effectively constrain the absolute level of pay is to establish a cap. However, the agency cost or pay-for-performance debate perspective sidesteps the inquiry into substantive measures, such as capping pay to constrain executive compensation, and instead defaults to the presence of procedural safeguards like shareholder voting, director independence, and disclosure. This perspective usually does not question absolute levels of pay provided that fair procedures exist for determining pay. But according to a joint study by Heidrick & Struggles and the University of Southern California Marshall School of Business, approximately forty percent of directors think executive pay is too high in most cases, although over seventy-five percent think their own company's CEO compensation program is effective. The virtual impossibility of determining the correct absolute pay levels, in part, explains the preference among many legal scholars for procedures and the reluctance to acknowledge the impact of extremely high pay levels, in an absolute sense, on firm performance.

Excessive pay levels, however, can lower the size of dividends paid to shareholders, reduce earnings per share, and lead to other forms of organizational inefficiency. For example, intra-firm salary comparisons between employees throughout an organization may relate to firm efficiency goals. Organizational theory acknowledges how the perceived unfairness of executive pay (stemming from large pay discrepancies) may have a negative impact on employee morale, turnover, competitiveness, and profitability. On the other hand, the realistic prospect of higher pay and rewards most likely increases worker productivity. Finally, poor pay practices may signal broader deficiencies within the firm, such as a lack of board independence and objectivity. The underlying issue in the above-mentioned examples, however, remains agency costs. Despite the indisputable benefits of aligning pay with performance, it is unrealistic to expect the removal of all "slack" from executive pay decisions. A more realistic target is a palatable amount of slack in light of contextual constraints.

2. Is Executive Compensation Reform a Matter of Public Accountability and the External Abuse of Corporate Power?

From the prevailing shareholder protection perspective, as long as CEO pay is adequately linked to performance measures, there is no excessive pay problem. This perspective, however, does not adequately capture the range of lawmaker motivations or the politically constructed meaning of executive compensation reform. Another key dimension of the executive pay problem maintains that excessive pay is about fairness to broader non-shareholder constituencies such as employees. At a basic level, people interpret fairness by looking at the pay of others, and when they witness a gap they perceive unfairness, irrespective of how rational the sentiment. This dimension of executive compensation reform is an outgrowth of the external perception of corporations as quasi-public institutions that should be subject to accountability measures resembling those found in government, such as transparency, accountability, and the participation of external voices. With respect to executive compensation reform, "it is entirely possible that deeper instincts about the modern corporation as a politically accountable institution played a role" in the adoption of various measures. The accountability of corporate power to external non-shareholder constituencies is an undeniable undercurrent of executive compensation reform. This stakeholder-oriented perspective is often criticized because the more stakeholder concerns are implicated, the less discipline it arguably exerts on managers....

Executive compensation has an important symbolic link to discussions of broader economic turmoil, such as the wage gap, unemployment, and outsourcing, as well as the sub-prime mortgage crisis and stock market bubbles. Executive compensation, like the wage gap, is often invoked as a societal litmus test for fairness. Indeed, statistics demonstrating that Fortune 500 executives make 364 times that of the average worker undeniably raise eyebrows and a range of emotions from envy to disdain. Such headlines heighten populist concern that large corporations are self-perpetuating plutocracies accountable only to themselves at the expense of workers and other populist constituencies. From a broad social perspective, some commentators contend that societal rewards are warped and that CEOs are overcompensated when one compares his or her societal contribution to entrepreneurs, such as Bill Gates, who promote job creation, while other CEOs do not. Furthermore, these commentators argue that excessive executive compensation has broader negative economic impacts because an unreasonable amount of talented people will flock to business schools instead of pursuing other professions, thereby reducing the talent pool for other professions.

Linking the executive pay debate closely to worker or populist interests highlights the tension between a more libertarian view of the corporation versus the corporation as a quasi-public institution. Every company, including nonprofits, has the goal of controlling expenses, and senior managers have discretion to pursue multiple cost reduction strategies, such as layoffs, retraction of employee benefits, outsourcing, and industry exit. Ironically, a CEO's pursuit of cost reduction strategies, such as layoffs and the achievement of cost reduction targets, often lead to greater compensation. In most major companies, job creation is not a direct goal and labor is merely viewed as a factor of production.... Despite public accountability concerns, the prevailing trend reflects a more libertarian corporation.

B. Lawmaker Reform Services

Despite the difficulties with diagnosing the executive pay problem presented in the preceding Sections, corporate lawmakers undoubtedly find the diagnosis of executive pay problems significantly easier than designing effective policies and reforms. The matrix of current executive compensation reform policies is a prime example of this difficulty....

1. Judicial Arbitration Services

Generally, courts are reluctant to weigh-in on executive pay issues except where payment constitutes waste and bears little relationship to performance. Judges recognize the difficulty of articulating a concise set of rules and the ex post second guessing of business decisions with a strong operational component, like executive compensation. Where the board is sufficiently independent and disinterested, the business judgment rule provides significant managerial discretion. The epic Disney litigation reflects this judicial reluctance to second guess executive compensation despite significant board dysfunction....[17]

2. Procedural Reforms and Mandates to Create Independence

The 1990s witnessed the emergence of the compensation committee role. The increased focus on the compensation committee was driven in part by executive compensation scandals, IRS executive pay regulations, judicial inquiry, and enhanced disclosure surrounding compensation committee procedures. Today, stock exchanges provide specific procedural and structural requirements for compensation committees of listed companies.

---

17. *See* In re The Walt Disney Co. Derivative Litigation, *in this chapter.* — Ed.

In general, the listing rules emphasize pay-for-performance and independence. Yet procedural requirements mandating that remuneration committees be composed of non-executive directors do not necessarily mean diversity of thought on executive pay. Arguably, non-executive directors, many of whom are former CEOs or other high-level executives, maintain a similar world view. Moreover, CEOs may exert power over directors, undermining arms-length bargaining. Stock exchange rules are helpful, but not completely effective. As Lucian Bebchuk notes: "While procedural requirements may mitigate problems arising from carelessness and insufficient attention, however, they do not address those arising from directors' incentives and tendencies to use their discretion in ways that favor executives." With the assistance of consultants and lawyers, directors experience little trouble providing justifications for their decisions, "sometimes by merely using boilerplate language."[18]

3. Disclosure-Related Reforms

Since 1938, the SEC has promulgated rules on compensation disclosure to give investors a meaningful impression of executive compensation in corporate reports, proxy statements, and registration statements. These rules have emphasized tabular disclosure, narrative disclosure, and a mixture of the two. Despite these disclosure enhancements, the ability of corporate directors and executives to circumvent these regulations and award significant non-performance-based compensation remains. In 1992, SEC disclosure regulations helped make the activities of the compensation committee highly visible to corporate constituencies. The purpose of these regulations was to give shareholders more meaningful information concerning the pay of top executives.

In 2006, the SEC adopted new regulations prescribing more extensive requirements for disclosure of executive compensation, related party transactions, and compensation committee procedures.[19] Companies must disclose compensation for their top five executives in their annual disclosure documents and include a detailed compensation discussion and analysis (CD&A). The CD&A is management's disclosure, rather than the compensation committee's. The purpose behind the CD&A is to discourage boilerplate disclosures that fail to provide meaningful company specific information. The CD&A explains in detail the information contained in the compensation tables. But, even with the existing disclosure requirements, significant elements of pay, such as non-contractual severance payments and charitable contributions, remain excluded.

Without question, enhanced disclosure requirements act as a constraint on managers and improve the monitoring capabilities of corporate constituents. But, if past history is any indication of future performance, disclosure rules cannot fully curb abuses or pay levels. In certain instances, enhanced disclosure may actually lead to higher pay levels [*as CEOs demand to be paid on par with other CEOs' disclosed compensation*], and it can give rise to more opaque forms of compensation [*to circumvent disclosure*]....

To be fair, the quality of disclosures regarding equity compensation, the metrics used, and greater transparency concerning perquisites have improved over time in conjunction with financial statement treatment of equity compensation. These enhancements move toward providing corporate constituents a bottom-line snap shot of executive compensation.

---

18. LUCIAN BEBCHUK & JESSE FRIED, PAY WITHOUT PERFORMANCE: THE UNFILLED PROMISE OF EXECUTIVE COMPENSATION 195 (2004).

19. *See* Regulation S-K, Items 402 and 407, 17 C.F.R. §§ 229.402, 229.407.

An additional benefit of disclosure is that it may also lead companies to revisit compensation practices, not to simply comply with regulations but also to avoid public embarrassment.

4. *Reforms Targeting Shareholder Input and Voting*

a. Approval of Equity Compensation Plans

In 2003, the SEC approved new self-regulatory organization (SRO) rules mandating shareholder approval of equity compensation plans. The NYSE and NASDAQ shareholder approval requirements for equity compensation plans require shareholder approval for equity compensation plans and for the material alteration of such plans subject to certain exceptions. Approval of a plan, however, is not synonymous with approvals of grants to specific individuals under a plan. Shareholders may lobby their dissatisfaction with equity compensation plans, but they have little control over executive pay. Such plans are often broadly worded to leave the board significant discretion. A broadly worded plan, once approved by shareholders, allows directors to make changes, year after year, without triggering an additional shareholder voting requirement. Moreover, shareholders do not approve the specific number of options given to a particular executive. Therefore, these requirements alone cannot ensure that equity-based compensation serves shareholder interests....

b. "Say-on-Pay"

In an attempt to create greater shareholder input on the specific issue of executive compensation, a number of legislators have proposed "say on-pay" legislation. On March 1, 2007, Massachusetts Congressman Barney Frank introduced House Bill 1257, "The Shareholder Vote on Compensation Act." This legislation requires public companies to provide detailed executive compensation plans for shareholder approval at each annual meeting of shareholders, and it also requires separate shareholder approval for executive compensation related to a merger, acquisition, or disposition. The House of Representatives approved this bill with a vote of 269 to 134, and the bill was referred to the Senate in accordance with legislative procedures. On April 20, 2007, Senator Barack Obama introduced the "Shareholder Vote on Executive Compensation Act" in the U.S. Senate. This bill is virtually identical to the bill that Congressman Barney Frank introduced in the House of Representatives. [*No further action was taken on either bill. — Ed.*]

The above-mentioned say-on-pay proposals are advisory and non-binding. Thus, shareholders can articulate dissatisfaction, but cannot veto pay packages. Say-on-pay measures may have a modest impact, but will not "prevent headline-grabbing paydays" nor "further political outrage, and more red-faced bosses coming under fire." Without the actual ability to veto pay packages, is there any value to say-on-pay measures? Certainly. Say-on-pay votes, although advisory, provide a warning signal to wayward management, who may rethink future actions to avoid being voted out. The adoption of advisory say-on-pay measures may also provide a benefit to management by ameliorating shareholder and non-shareholder constituency outrage by signaling democratic virtues with which corporate constituencies may identify. In other words, even if advisory say-on-pay measures are merely symbolic, they may have a tangible impact on shareholder satisfaction and director discretion. However, the hidden costs of these mandatory one-size-fits-all proposals are unknown.

In addition to legislation, shareholders, via shareholder resolutions, have attempted to amend corporate by-laws to provide for advisory votes on executive pay. RiskMetrics predicts nearly "70 'say on pay' resolutions will be tabled in 2008..., up from 52 in 2007." While some companies have adopted such resolutions, the majority of companies still have not.

5. Tax-related Reforms

The Internal Revenue Code (IRC) and tax-related regulations have often been used to influence executive compensation. These tax-related reforms targeting executive pay have been the subject of significant controversy and criticism. Congress enacted tax laws to stem perceived abuses of executive compensation in two primary areas: (i) the level of compensation; and (ii) change-in-control agreements.

a. Tax Deductibility Limits on Non-Performance-Based Pay

In 1993, Congress passed legislation with the express purpose of containing the level of executive compensation in response to widespread public "scrutiny." Despite these intentions, the legacy of Section 162(m) has more to do with escalation of pay than its limitation. Section 162(m) of the Internal Revenue Code limits tax deductions for executive pay over $1 million; however, there is an important exception for qualified performance-based compensation for which companies are allowed to receive deductibility. Despite the deductibility cap under 162(m), most large public companies continue to pay CEOs and senior executives total compensation in excess of $1 million and have little difficulty claiming tax deductibility for compensation well in excess of $1 million. In essence, 162(m) stipulates that as long as pay is loosely tied to performance metrics and certain procedural requirements are met (for example, independent compensation committee), companies can escape the deductibility cap. As a consequence of 162(m), there was a seismic shift from fixed base pay to the award of share options based upon performance. The stated goals of 162(m) are unrealized, as executive compensation has risen to all-time highs. The failure of 162(m) rests on a faulty premise that performance-based compensation incentives will reduce overall pay. But another plausible outcome is for such incentives to ratchet-up overall pay.

b. Change-in-control Golden Parachute Limitations

In addition to 162(m), "golden parachute" tax laws under the IRC seek to limit excessive parachute payments in the event of a change of control. These provisions impose a twenty percent tax penalty on "excessive parachute payments." Not unexpectedly, there are multiple exceptions that limit the regulation's effectiveness. For example, companies can avoid the regulation by showing that pay reflects (i) personal services to be offered on or after the date of change in control or (ii) services already rendered before such date. These golden parachute tax measures, however, led to another unintended consequence known as the excise tax gross-up. A gross-up operates when companies make an agreement that, in the event an executive becomes liable for excise taxes under the golden parachute provisions, the company will compensate the executive for any resulting taxes. According to one study, excise tax gross-ups can cost companies over three dollars for every dollar of tax paid, operating as a hidden merger cost.

6. Clawback Provisions: Sarbanes Oxley Act Section 304
Forfeiture of Bonuses

Section 304 of the Sarbanes-Oxley Act of 2002 (SOX) requires the CEO and CFO of a firm required to restate earnings due to material non-compliance of financial reporting requirements under the securities laws to repay to their company any bonus or other incentive or equity-based compensation received during the 12 months following the filing of the misleading financial statement, or any profits realized from the sale of stock within that 12-month period, if the restatement results from misconduct. The statute, however, does not specify what degree of misconduct or whose misconduct is necessary to trigger the regulation. In the first six years following passage of Section 304, there have been clawbacks in only a small number of cases.

All of these cases involved a corporate officer who personally committed fraud and misconduct. Although the statute does not expressly require the officer from whom the clawback is sought to personally engage in misconduct, the statute has been construed narrowly. The ultimate impact of the SOX clawback provisions hinges on their enforcement.

V. How Can Corporate Constituencies Identify the Quality of Regulation?

A. *Procedures as a Default Heuristic for Legitimacy*

Procedures are at the heart of the legitimacy of U.S. corporate governance reforms and the executive compensation debate. Some public choice theorists contend that "the basic desire to give voters [or constituents] more control of the mechanism is not [necessarily] based on any false idea of how well the voters are informed." Instead, the issue is "simply that the voters are the only people in the whole process [even if ignorant] who do not have an element of systematic bias in their decision process." This approach is too simplistic. From this perspective, even if the average layperson is misinformed regarding the executive compensation issue, they are still actively pursuing their own perceived well-being. This perspective further assumes that if a primary goal of lawmakers is to promote the well-being of citizens, lawmakers should allow greater say and influence from the common man. This increase in participation may contribute to greater inefficiency or indeterminacy in regulatory outcomes, but it is also "likely to make the government more in accord with the preferences of the common man; *i.e.*, it brings us a little closer to the objective of popular rule which is supposed to be what democracy is about." This perspective, however, does not adequately account for credence characteristics and lawmaker opportunism, and is therefore misplaced in the corporate reform context. Participation alone is not sufficient. Informed participation is necessary to hold lawmakers accountable.

Even assuming there are laws and institutional structures reflecting democratic accountability, a serious question lingers concerning corporate constituent information asymmetries. Lawmakers, in their own self interest, may exploit these information asymmetries without risk of detection. The public's demand for democratic procedures and the seemingly earnest lawmaker response may not solve the issue but could serve as subterfuge masking the actual problem. Failure to address such information asymmetries can have perverse consequences. The executive compensation issue is a model illustration of this effect. The tenor of executive pay reform efforts may appear to enhance participation and promote democratic norms, but such participation may have little impact on setting a particular executive's pay or realigning the power dynamics within the firm. Solving executive compensation problems is not simply a matter of constituent input; rather, it involves constituents, equipped with sufficient information, making the most of their participation.

Equipped with limited knowledge concerning the impact of a particular reform, corporate constituencies by default look to procedures as a proxy for quality. The legitimacy of corporate reforms is often viewed through a procedural lens as opposed to a substantive one. There is simply too much disagreement concerning the shape of substantive reforms. And extensive substantive reforms may prove too risky for lawmakers. Not surprisingly, the majority of executive compensation reforms are procedural.

Multiple constituencies can coalesce around procedures that, irrespective of their tangible impact, symbolize elements of fairness. Shareholder voting mechanisms, independent committees, and disclosure requirements all reflect democratic procedures that the various corporate constituencies are familiar with in the governmental context. Transplanting the same democratic features and rhetoric in the corporate context provides reassurance to corporate constituencies who have asymmetric information. Democratic procedures are much easier to understand than markets and the plethora of executive compensation elements and reform measures that are constantly evolving. Whereas there are procedural mechanisms to hold governmental power accountable to the general populace, such accountability procedures are often absent in the corporate context, especially beyond the shareholder constituency. As the past two decades of executive compensation reform reveal, the presence of these procedural features, despite their reassurance, does not eliminate rising executive compensation levels or abuses. Nonetheless, democratic procedures, such as shareholder say-on-pay and a contest between corporate constituents, may signal public legitimacy, but not necessarily investor legitimacy.

VI. Conclusion and Implications

A. *The Analysis of Credence Characteristics Provides a Novel Assessment of Political Effects on Executive Compensation Reform and Corporate Reform in the Broader Context*

The analysis of credence characteristics in the executive compensation reform context has implications for Wall Street, K Street, and Main Street. At the political level, executive compensation reforms are inextricably tied to agency costs and public accountability. The credence characteristics analysis requires looking beyond laws on the books and managerial appropriation to consider lawmaker motivations and corporate constituent information asymmetries. Just like a reform's impact is difficult to decipher, lawmaker intent is difficult to discern. This situation inevitably leaves crude mechanisms upon which corporate constituents must rely to discern the quality of executive compensation reform. In a positive sense, these mechanisms have the potential to reduce information asymmetries, promote informed participation, constrain lawmaker discretion, supplement lawmaker expertise, and bolster the legitimacy of the corporate governance regime. The downside, however, is that such mechanisms are imprecise and may reflect a particular bias or distortion. The credence characteristics of executive compensation reform underscore the important roles that third-party opinions (for example, executive search firms, compensation consultants, academics, and institutional investors) and intangible mechanisms (for example, credible commitment, branding, and symbolic procedures) play in U.S. corporate governance as a check on lawmaker opportunism and, in some cases, lawmaker incompetence.

Lawmaker incentives are a key underpinning of the credence characteristic analysis. Therefore, it is necessary to make the distinction between lawmaker opportunism involving the concealment of information concerning reforms and lawmaker incompetence involving poor information quality. In either scenario, the corporate constituent faces similar risks and costs, but the potential resolution differs. The reduction of lawmaker opportunism may not necessarily require more government resources, "but only a [lawmaker] decision to stop." The mere threat of losing political capital may constrain lawmaker opportunism, provided the decision-making heuristics available to corporate constituents are reliable.... [C]ombating lawmaker deficits in expertise requires more than third party mechanisms exposing lawmaker incompetence. It may also require significant government (that is, supply-side) expenditures....

The analysis of the credence characteristics of executive compensation reform is only part of a larger conversation that might sensitize researchers to the impact of credence characteristics and political effects on corporate reform in a broader sense. Instead of proffering an in-depth analysis regarding the substantive merits of existing executive pay reforms or a clear vision of the optimal shape of such reforms, the preceding analysis illustrates the impact of political behavior (that is, lawmaker opportunism) on executive pay reforms. Without accounting for political impact on the shape of corporate reform, corporate constituents as well as legal commentators are, in essence, taking a blue pill that may ultimately displace the prospect of optimal reform. Credence characteristics, in the broader corporate reform context, highlight the need to discipline lawmaker behavior, enhance lawmaker competence, and address the informational asymmetries of corporate constituents.

B. The Credence Characteristics of Corporate Reform Allow for Incremental and Moderate Change Even in the Face of Crisis

Credence characteristics in the executive compensation context provide lawmakers with greater latitude to maintain political capital without making significant change. In other words, credence characteristics allow lawmakers to straddle the fence between political symbolism and conscientious resolution.

A number of legal commentators have expressed concern over corporate lawmakers' "crisis-mode" regulation or "knee-jerk" reform responses during periods of economic turmoil. This concern, although relevant, is overstated in the executive compensation context. Even during periods of economic turmoil, corporate lawmakers have considerable discretion to respond in a moderate fashion due to the credence characteristics of corporate reform. Corporate constituents, particularly those with information asymmetries, usually will not discern the quality or impact of the reform until after the period of economic crisis has passed and constituent outrage wanes, only to reappear again with the next economic downturn or cycle. Accordingly, corporate lawmakers will exercise their added discretion to act in a moderate or conservative fashion. Thus, executive compensation reform will continue to evolve incrementally without substantial shifts, despite corporate scandals and economic turmoil. Massive reforms are too risky. Substantial lawmaker movements could cause broad constituent backlash, expose ineptitude, and make lawmakers blameworthy. In fact, many executive compensation reforms simply formalize best practices already adopted by a significant portion of the corporate community. There is always a gap between what the law requires and what constitutes a well run company. Corporate lawmakers are reluctant to upset the internal power relationships between shareholders and management, and instead will either: (i) outsource reform to the vagaries of the market and third-parties; or (ii) regulate business activity indirectly or outside of the traditional corporate law context (for example, tax, antitrust, and labor laws). Best practice codes are an example of the former alternative. The latter alternative of indirect regulation is more likely to be populist in substance. These situational factors promote conservatism among corporate lawmakers, who wish to avoid corporate manager backlash and responsibility for failed reform efforts.

C. Executive Pay Reform Operates as a Blue Pill—A Mechanism for Lawmaker Diversion and Responsibility-Shifting

Corporate lawmaker opportunism partially explains the prominence of executive pay compared to other, arguably more pressing, corporate law issues—ownership-related decisions involving mergers, takeovers, and even certain operational decisions, such as asset divestitures, product development, and raising capital. At most, excessive executive pay, at the firm level, is merely a symptom of the greater agency cost problem. On average, executive pay for the top five executives at Fortune 500 companies in 2006 constituted 1.82 percent of profits. For large companies, the actual impact of executive compensation is minimal.

The overemphasis on executive compensation functions as a blue pill or diversion from other pertinent socio-economic issues, like the minimum wage, health insurance, retirement accounts, education, and social security, that are more relevant to ordinary Americans. This diversion of populist outrage has negative consequences for populist corporate constituencies. By singling out and seeking to limit pay for a few executives at the top of the wealth pyramid, lawmakers may divert pressure from improving the plight of those at the bottom via increasing the minimum wage or other redistributive policies and interventions. Despite the theoretical emphasis on limiting the costs of managerial appropriation and executive pay, slack in compensation practices extends beyond the CEO to employees throughout an organization and merits evaluation. But this particular aspect of compensation reform has received less attention from legal commentators as well as politicians. A reason for the enhanced focus on executive pay versus the pay of other employees is that executive pay involves greater potential for self-dealing.

Another interesting question is whether corporate managers should be overly concerned about the emphasis on executive pay. Perhaps not. Certainly no director or CEO enjoys public embarrassment like the shaming Michael Eisner received before the Delaware courts. However, the political salience of executive pay may also divert populist outrage and, to a degree, shareholder attention away from other corporate governance issues that are more problematic for managers (for example, altering internal power relationships or the balance between state and federal law). As illustrated above, executive compensation reform is often moderate and will not upset the internal affairs of the corporation nor displace business judgment. Therefore, managers should not be overly distressed about the focus on executive pay because it averts more substantial intrusions that upset existing power relationships.

D. The Positive Side of Politics?: Averting Future Backlash and Inefficiency

Notwithstanding the costs of lawmaker opportunism, there are potential positive benefits associated with incorporating political effects into the discussion of executive compensation reform and, in broader terms, corporate governance reform. Politics has the ability to disrupt markets, but it also has the power to mediate economic turmoil.... Strategic inefficiency may, on balance, be a net positive. Thus, in order to prevent greater future inefficiency, lawmakers may create moderately inefficient rules, for example, executive compensation reforms. The political value of strategic inefficiency is not diminished by the fact that one cannot measure with any degree of precision the amount of political backlash averted or the necessary amount of political accommodation. Whereas the general tendency is to ascribe negative value to interest group dynamics and politics, the interaction of inefficiency with backlash may reflect a brighter side. Lawmaker pursuit of self-interest may actually benefit shareholder and non-shareholder constituencies alike.

Discussion Questions

1. What are the advantages and drawbacks of rewarding executives for increased company earnings or share price? Recall Bratton's discussion of option compensation at Enron in Chapter 1. What is the significance of the fact, noted by Loewenstein, that "CEOs have no control over the stock market"?

2. Recall Charles Elson's argument that directors should be paid with stock in order to improve their incentive to perform. Do the same arguments apply to executive officers? Why or why not?

3. Until a rule change in 2005, accounting rules did not require corporations to count option compensation as an expense at the time it was granted. That rule was often blamed for the explosion in option compensation in the preceding decade. In a 2007 survey by the *Journal of Accountancy*, however, only 39 percent of responding companies reported reducing the use of options in response to the 2005 rule change. In addition to accounting treatment, might there be other sound economic reasons why boards that compensate executives with options do so with extremely large numbers of options? *See* Kevin J. Murphy, *Explaining Executive Compensation,* 69 U. Chi. L. Rev. 847, 868–69 (2002). Can you think of other factors that might cause the practice of option compensation to decrease?

4. Yablon proposes tax policy as the best way to respond to excessive executive compensation. What advantages and disadvantages does tax-based regulation have in comparison to direct substantive regulations on executive pay, or more traditional corporate governance tools, such as market forces, shareholder suits, or disclosure requirements? Is there something special about executive compensation that makes tax policy appropriate?

What considerations should determine whether a given area of corporate behavior should be shaped by deregulated markets, tax incentives, or direct regulation? Consider, for example, executive compensation, fair labor standards, high employment levels, product safety, and environmental responsibility.

5. Loewenstein cites a study by Daily *et al.* that found no correlation between the proportion of inside directors on a corporation's compensation committee and larger increases in its CEO's pay. Nor did a higher proportion of CEOs on the committee correlate with larger pay increases. As Loewenstein suggests, one obvious explanation for this result is that inside directors are good agents for corporate shareholders. Are there any other possible explanations?

6. The Daily study cited by Loewenstein focused on the composition of compensation committees, on the theory that the committee has a greater impact on compensation than the composition of the board as a whole. Nonetheless, might the identity of other board members still be relevant? How?

7. As Loewenstein points out at the end of his article, directors are rarely asked why they do what they do. Do you agree with his argument that asking compensation committees about their decisionmaking processes would be more illuminating than conventional quantitative studies of pay packages? What are the benefits and limitations of performing such research?

Do you think it could be useful to institute an SEC rule requiring boards to provide specific justifications for executive pay packages?

8. Loewenstein proposes that directors put executive compensation to an *advisory* vote of shareholders. In 2003, the New York Stock Exchange adopted a listing standard requiring

shareholder approval of equity compensation for "any employee, director, or service provider." The rule also requires shareholder approval of the repricing of options granted as such compensation, unless the terms of the option specifically permit repricing. How does this rule differ from Loewenstein's proposal? Is it better or worse?

9. As Loewenstein notes, Disney CEO Michael Eisner did not "control" the board that approved his large compensation packages and the termination package for Michael Ovitz that Eisner supported. But as Yablon points out in a footnote to the article excerpted in this chapter,

> Disney [had, in 1999] many board members who, while not currently employed by Disney, have personal or financial ties to Eisner or the company. These include former Disney executives (E. Cardon Walker, Gary L. Wilson), Father Leo J. Donovan, the President of Georgetown University, which one of Eisner's sons attended and to which he has donated over one million dollars, Reveta Bowers, principal of a private school previously attended by Eisner's children, George Mitchell, former Senator and special counsel to a law firm that has done work for Disney and has also consulted personally for the company, and Robert A.M. Stern, an architect, whose firm has completed multi-million dollar projects for Disney and one for Eisner himself.

On the one hand, this catalog of connections makes one suspect the board's independence. On the other hand, this "six degrees of separation" phenomenon is not unusual among corporate boards. *See* Gerald F. Davis, Mina Yoo, and Wayne E. Baker, *The Small World of the American Corporate Elite, 1982–2001,* 1 STRATEGIC ORG. 301 (2003). Does this prevalence make it seem more or less important to eliminate such connections? How would one craft and enforce a definition of director independence that would eliminate these varied and subtle connections? Should director candidates be required to disclose all their civic and personal acquaintances?

10. The popular critique of executive compensation focuses on the inequity and wastefulness of "excessive" compensation. Loewenstein, Simmons and Paredes, however, are relatively unconcerned with these arguments. What is the primary concern of each author? What are their differences and similarities? With whom do you agree?

Do you think executive pay reform is important? Why or why not?

11. Consider the following two attempts to regulate executive compensation. In 2007, federal bills giving shareholders advisory "say-on-pay" votes were introduced in the U.S. House and Senate. The bill passed in the House but stalled in the Senate Committee on Banking, Housing, and Urban Affairs. Beginning in 2008, the U.S. government's Troubled Asset Relief Program (TARP) gave financial assistance to distressed banks. It later imposed restrictions on executive compensation at firms that accepted TARP funds. In 2009, many banks repaid their TARP funds ahead of schedule specifically to escape those rules.

Do these seem like good rules? More generally, does it seem appropriate to regulate executive compensation through federal law?

12. As Simmons notes, issues involving the fairness and efficiency of pay practices are not limited to top executives, but extend to all reaches of the company. Nonetheless, law, politics, and popular discourse focus on executive pay. One reason, according to Simmons, is that executive pay presents more potential for self-dealing. Does this seem like a sufficient justification? Should there be more focus on pay practices below the executive level? Why or why not?

As a general matter, state corporate law pays much more attention to conflicts of interest than to efficiency or fairness. Why do you suppose this is so? Does this emphasis seem appropriate?

13. Economics presumes rationality, but psychology documents the prevalence of irrationality. The overwhelming trend in regulatory theory has been to assume rationality. Does the psychological approach suggest new approaches to regulation, or does it simply show that the rationality assumption is mistaken?

14. The shareholder plaintiffs in *In re Walt Disney Company Derivative Litigation* framed their complaint in terms of procedural duty of care. In fact, it took several years of dismissed complaints, appeals, and amended complaints before the Chancery Court even agreed that the plaintiffs had properly stated a claim. Their real concern, of course, was a substantive one: the generosity of the pay package. Why wasn't that sufficient to support a cause of action? Should it be?

15. Does the *Disney* opinion provide a useful deterrent to excessive executive compensation in the future? Does the case provide a clear legal rule with respect to what constitutes "excessive" executive compensation? Does it state what board procedures satisfy the duty of care in approving compensation packages? How might boards respond to *Disney*? What are the pros and cons of regulating executive compensation through procedural duties of due care?

16. Is the *Disney* opinion an example of the excessive "judicial activism" that Loewenstein criticizes? Does its treatment of statutory exculpation provisions under the Delaware Code (§ 102(b)(7)) weaken the statute excessively?

17. How well does the *Disney* opinion fit the model of Delaware jurisprudence suggested by Edward Rock's article in Chapter 3? How well does it fit Ehud Kamar's more cynical view?

18. The shareholders' original complaint in the *Disney* case accused the company of poor governance practices. For example, the directors did not own significant amounts of stock, they did not meet regularly outside the presence of the company's top executives such as CEO Michael Eisner, and they failed to provide Eisner with written evaluations. In *Brehm v. Eisner*, 746 A.2d 244 (Del. 2000), the Delaware Supreme Court upheld the dismissal of that original complaint. The court pointed out that allegations of poor corporate governance practices do not constitute allegations that the directors violated their legal duties:

> This is a case about whether there should be personal liability of the directors of a Delaware corporation to the corporation for lack of due care in the decisionmaking process and for waste of corporate assets. This case is not about the failure of the directors to establish and carry out ideal corporate governance practices.

> All good corporate governance practices include compliance with statutory law and case law establishing fiduciary duties. But the law of corporate fiduciary duties and remedies for violation of those duties are distinct from the aspirational goals of ideal corporate governance practices. Aspirational ideals of good corporate governance practices for boards of directors that go beyond the minimal legal requirements of the corporation law are highly desirable, often tend to benefit stockholders, sometimes reduce litigation and can usually help directors avoid liability. But they are not required by the corporation law and do not define standards of liability.

Why not? Why does the law set the "minimal ... requirements" on directors lower than the "ideals of good corporate governance practices"? Does this leave shareholders without recourse when management fails to meet the "ideals of good corporate governance"?

19. The *Disney* opinion reprinted in this chapter came twelve years after the plaintiffs filed their original complaint. In 2000, the Delaware Supreme Court affirmed the dismissal of that complaint, calling it a "pastiche of prolix invective" lacking particularized allegations of fact. The supreme court admonished plaintiffs to amend their complaint with specific facts by using their state-law right of access to the corporate books and records under Del. G.C.L. § 220. After the plaintiffs did so, the opinion that appears in this chapter finally found the pleadings sufficient.

A common criticism of strict pleading standards like those in the Delaware Court of Chancery's Rule 23.1 and the PSLRA (see Chapter 5) is that they require plaintiffs to allege specific facts before they have had the opportunity for discovery. Does the state-law right of access to books and records alleviate this concern?

20. The government bailout of troubled financial firms in 2008 imposed restrictions on the compensation that bailed-out firms could pay their executives. What are the pros and cons of such restrictions?

Chapter 11

The Role of the Board in the Hostile Takeover Context

The "market for corporate control" may provide a partial solution to the separation of ownership and control in the large modern corporation.[1] Under this theory, directors and officers must run corporations effectively or face the prospect of losing their jobs and control of the corporation in a hostile takeover. Incumbent directors have selfish incentives to reject all unsolicited takeover bids in order to protect themselves, even when the takeover would be in the best interest of shareholders. But not every potential takeover would be in the best interest of shareholders (or other corporate constituents). An acquirer, after all, is concerned primarily with getting the best deal for itself. Thus directors may have justification, if not an obligation, to resist at least some takeovers. As a result, the law has struggled to define how much discretion management should have when facing a hostile takeover attempt.

As Professor Rock pointed out in Chapter 3 with respect to management buyouts, the law often finds itself reacting to changes in corporate and financial practices. The readings in this chapter discuss how courts responded to innovations in the context of hostile takeovers and takeover defenses, such as the "poison pill" defense.[2] Ronald Gilson and Lucian Bebchuk argue that shareholders, and not the board, should have the ultimate say over whether to accept or reject an acquisition bid. Gilson argues that Delaware case law giving directors wide latitude to use poison pills to block hostile takeover attempts is the outdated product of economic conditions (and corporate lawyers' tactics) of the 1980s.

Bebchuk presents and critiques, from various perspectives, the common justifications for management's authority to reject takeovers. Martin Lipton, the corporate lawyer credited with inventing the poison pill, responds to Bebchuk's article with a defense of management control over takeover decisions. He argues that management can bargain effectively with acquirers on behalf of shareholders, but must retain ultimate control in order to do so.

---

1. Henry Manne pioneered this influential concept in his article, *Mergers and the Market for Corporate Control*, 73 J. POL. ECON. 110 (1965). Larry Ribstein advocates this view in Chapter 4.

2. *"Poison pill" is Wall Street jargon for a type of shareholder right that matures upon the occurrence of certain triggering conditions involving a hostile takeover. For example, a board that wishes to discourage takeovers might cause the corporation to issue to each share a right to purchase additional stock at a steep discount in the event that a would-be acquirer were to obtain a certain percentage of shares in the corporation: the shareholders' exercise of such rights would vastly increase the number of shares required to control the corporation (and disperse them widely), effectively preventing the would-be-acquirer from obtaining a controlling stake. Poison pills are typically structured so that the board of directors retains the right to "redeem" (i.e., cancel) them, so a would-be-acquirer must either convince the board to redeem the pill or obtain control of the board in a proxy contest. —Ed.*

The chapter concludes with the Delaware Supreme Court's 2009 opinion in *Lyondell Chemical Co. v. Ryan*, which explains Delaware's existing case law on takeover defenses in light of the court's subsequent jurisprudence on "good faith" (represented in this volume by *In Re The Walt Disney Company Derivative Litigation*).

Ronald J. Gilson, *Unocal Fifteen Years Later (And What We Can Do About It)*[*]

... [T]he fifteenth anniversary of the Delaware Supreme Court's announcement in *Unocal Corp. v. Mesa Petroleum Co.*[3] of a new approach to takeover law provides an appropriate occasion to step back and evaluate a remarkable experiment in corporate law — the Delaware Supreme Court's development of an intermediate standard for evaluating defensive tactics.

This experiment began with, and was surely a response to, an earlier and extremely controversial takeover wave. But these transactions were remarkable for more than just their scope, goal, and method. They also were remarkable as a social phenomenon, the studied indifference to which by sociologists remains a remarkable disciplinary failure. The emergence of junk bond financing — I prefer the period term "junk bond" to the more dignified label of "high yield" because the difference in the terms capture the distance in attitude that we've covered in the last fifteen years — opened the market for corporate control to a range of acquirers who were hardly members of the corporate establishment. During much of this period, I was a reporter for the ALI Corporate Governance Project and had special responsibility for the part of the project dealing with transactions in control.[4] As I sat in what seemed an endless series of meetings, only part of the debate was about the right legal rules; the remainder, *sotto voce*, was over who — the new raiders or the ALI members' clients — were going to control some of the most significant actors in our economy.

Finally, and here we return to the realm of law from that of economics and sociology, the Delaware courts ultimately placed themselves at the center of the maelstrom. As de Tocqueville noted about the United States some 175 years ago, lawyers are at the core of our economic and political life. In the 1980s the Delaware courts were squarely in the middle of the largest and most contentious business transactions in history.

We now have sufficient perspective, both on that takeover wave and on the Delaware courts' response, to reassess the motivation and the efficacy of this effort at modernizing corporate law to cope with the emergence of hostile tender offers, a phenomenon which then existing corporate law was both technically and conceptually inadequate to address. While acknowledging the difficult circumstances in which the Delaware Supreme Court found itself in 1985, I will argue that *Unocal* ultimately has developed into an unexplained and, I think, inexplicable preference that control contests be resolved through elections rather than market transactions.... I will also maintain that the current debate over

---

    * Originally published in 26 DELAWARE JOURNAL OF CORPORATE LAW 491 (2001). Reprinted with permission.
    3. 493 A.2d 946 (Del. 1985).
    4. *The American Law Institute's Corporate Governance Project of the 1970s and 1980s ultimately produced the* ALI Principles of Corporate Governance: Analysis and Recommendations *in 1992.* — Ed.

shareholder-adopted bylaws that repeal or amend director-adopted poison pill plans provides a vehicle to reposition Delaware takeover law for a new millennium. In the end, takeovers are just an equilibrating mechanism that is triggered by changes in the real economic environment. It is a noncontroversial prediction that the pace of change will continue to accelerate, and that transactional responses will continue to pressure corporate law. Delaware's current pro-election, anti-market bias is not suited to meet that challenge....

I. Setting the Stage

Over the last fifteen years the Delaware courts have been at the center of a process that was far larger than the law. Starting in the 1970s and accelerating through the 1980s, the United States has undergone one of the most remarkable industrial restructurings in our history. The organizational calm of the early 1970s was shattered by an unprecedented wave of hostile takeovers whose goal was quite explicit: to reshape the structure of American industry. Powered by an increase in pension fund assets and an increased capacity of the capital markets to fund control transactions, takeovers enforced a new level of financial and operational discipline. Some transactions drove an industrial movement back to focus—a strategy based on specialization in industries whose demands fit a company's experience and skills by dissipating the excess cash flow that oil companies and others were diverting to a bizarre range of diversification and unprofitable expansion, and by breaking up 1960s conglomerates. Others eliminated excess capacity by holding up all activities to the cost of the capital committed to them.

At the time, however, the industrial logic of the new takeover phenomenon was less clear. The combination of the rate of change and the vehicle of change—hostile takeovers launched by a new class of entrepreneurs who had no access to the business arena in which their targets contended until the application of junk bond financing to acquisitions — generated an extreme reaction. Many prominent commentators, some—like Martin Lipton—with a stake in resisting the takeover movement, and others—like Peter Drucker— without an ax to grind, thought junk bond financed, bust-up takeovers a threat to the very Republic. The chairman of Deutsche Bank was rather more direct. In a hyperbole the extent of whose overstatement has been made clear by recent events in Russia, characterized the takeover wave simply as "gangster capitalism."

The Delaware courts had little choice but to intercede in this controversy. Only three institutions were in a position to act effectively in response to this good faith but overheated debate, but two were unlikely candidates. Congress seemed to have exhausted its energy a decade before with the Williams Act.[5] And the Securities Exchange Commission increasingly voiced a decidedly pro-takeover position. If there was to be a balanced assessment, which given the shrillness of the debate must have seemed attractive if only for its softer tone, it would have had to come from Delaware.

Unfortunately, Delaware law was not then up to the task. As I have described the phenomenon elsewhere, the hostile takeover wave of the 1980s subjected the traditional structure of corporate law to the equivalent of a stress test. Driven by one of "the most significant corporate restructuring[s] in history, serious doctrinal cracks appeared, the most important of which concerned allocating final decision rights in the face of a hostile tender offer." Corporate law provided two general standards of review of management conduct: the business judgment rule, applicable to claims that management violated its

---

5. *The Williams Act of 1968 imposed disclosure and procedural requirements on tender offers.*

duty of care; and the intrinsic fairness test, applicable to claims that management violated its duty of loyalty. Hostile takeovers drove in a wedge at their point of tangency, leaving a yawning doctrinal chasm. On the one hand, evaluating the desirability of a target's acquisition is the quintessential business judgment. On the other hand, target management faces an inherent conflict of interest in confronting a transaction that directly threatens both their positions and their egos. Deploying defensive tactics thus resembles an interested transaction that calls for review under the rigorous entire fairness standard. As a matter of corporate law, existing doctrine left wide open the critical functional question: who should make the decision concerning the outcome of a hostile takeover bid? As a matter of public policy, the resolution of this question would significantly influence who would govern the largest and most powerful private institutions in our society.

Two contending interest groups advanced quite different answers with equal vigor. Takeover defense lawyers argued that board decisions with respect to tender offers should be treated like board decisions concerning any other acquisition proposal: the business judgment rule should operate to allocate the primary decision-making role to management. Academics took a very different view. From their perspective, tender offers are themselves an important corporate governance device. Academics therefore urged that the shareholders should be allocated the final decision-making role. In this view, the market for corporate control served to displace inefficient managers both directly through a particular transaction, and indirectly through the general deterrence resulting from the threat of a takeover. Efficient operation of the market for corporate control necessitated that shareholders make the ultimate decision concerning the success of a hostile bid.

Interestingly, the pro-management takeover defense lawyers and the pro-shareholder academics implicitly agreed on an important common premise: courts should not determine the outcome of the largest business transactions in history. . . .

In *Unocal*, the Delaware Supreme Court chose the middle ground that had been championed by no one. The court unveiled an intermediate standard of review, somewhere between the duty of care and the duty of loyalty. What was especially notable about what came to be called the proportionality test — did the hostile offer present a threat and, if so, was the target's response proportional — was the role of the court itself. In assessing the balance between threat and response, the court cast itself as an arbitrator of the substantive merit of target company behavior. As *Unocal* was originally framed, the court functions, in effect, as a regulatory agency, deciding for itself between good defensive tactics — those reasonable in relation to the threat — and bad defensive tactics, those that go beyond what the bid requires. Unusually for Delaware law, *Unocal* committed the court, in appropriate circumstances, to substitute its judgment for that of the board. And lest anyone doubt that the court had set itself up to regulate defensive conduct, the decision in *Moran v. Household International, Inc.*,[6] coming directly on the heels of *Unocal*, made matters absolutely clear. Despite the supreme court's quite activist stance in approving a board of directors' adoption of a poison pill without shareholder approval, it reserved to itself an intermediate level of review of a board's decision not to redeem the pill after an offer actually was made. The court — and plainly not the board in the exercise of its business judgment — would decide whether declining to pull the pill was a proportionate response.

---

6. 500 A.2d 1346 (Del. 1985).

II. The Chancery Court's Development of *Unocal*: Allocating Decision-Making Roles Between Shareholders and Directors

At this point, the supreme court largely retired from the field, leaving the court of chancery to work out the profile of the new regulatory role implicit in the proportionality test. In deference to Delaware's traditional respect for the business judgment rule and the limited judicial role the business judgment role dictates, the chancery court responded by recasting *Unocal* in terms of an allocation of decision-making roles not between the board and the court, but between the board and the shareholders. And it was at this point in the drama that Reinier Kraakman and I [expressed] the fear, well-placed as it turned out, that despite the bold words of *Unocal* and *Household International*, the Delaware Supreme Court could not sustain the regulatory function of directly assessing the merits of target company defensive tactics.[7]

Perhaps because it also doubted the supreme court's resolve, the chancery court in a series of cases[8] ... developed a thoughtful doctrinal framework that focused not on judicial assessment of the wisdom of director decisions, but on allocating decision responsibility between shareholders and directors. In the face of a non-coercive hostile offer, directors could respond to a belief that the price offered was too low—"substantive coercion" in today's inaccurate use of the term—by using a pill to secure the time to negotiate or seek a better offer. In the end, however, after time for negotiating and investigating alternatives, the directors could not "just say no" by declining to pull the pill, and thereby blocking the shareholders from rejecting the board's strategy and accepting the hostile offer. Chancellor Allen put the matter most clearly in [*City Capital Associates Ltd. Partnership v. Interco, Inc.*]:[9]

> To acknowledge that directors may employ the recent innovation of "poison pills" to deprive shareholders of the ability effectively to accept a noncoercive offer, after the board has had a reasonable opportunity to explore or create alternatives or attempt to negotiate on the shareholders' behalf, would, it seems to me, be so inconsistent with widely shared notions of corporate governance as to threaten to diminish the legitimacy and authority of our corporate law.

Chancellor Allen applied the same approach in [*Paramount Communications, Inc. v. Time. Inc.*], an opinion that warrants careful attention despite its ill treatment by the Delaware Supreme Court on appeal.[10] Perhaps anticipating that the supreme court, one way or another, would allow Time to complete its acquisition of Warner regardless of shareholder preferences, the Chancellor allowed Time to go forward with the acquisition. Allen stressed, however, that, "because of the timing involved, the board has no need here to rely upon a self-created power designed to assure a veto on all changes in control." And to eliminate

---

7. Ronald J. Gilson & Reinier Kraakman, *Delaware's Intermediate Standard for Defensive Tactics: Is There Substance to Proportionality Review?* 44 Bus. Law. 247, 252 (1989).

8. A.C. Acquisitions Corp. v. Anderson, Clayton & Co., 519 A.2d 103 (Del. Ch. 1986); City Capital Assocs. v. Interco, Inc., 551 A.2d 787 (Del. Ch. 1988); Grand Metro. Pub. Ltd. Co. v. Pillsbury Co., 558 A.2d 1049 (Del. Ch. 1988).

9. 551 A.2d 787 (Del. Ch. 1988).

10. Paramount Communications, Inc. v. Time, Inc., No. 10,866, 1989 Del. Ch. LEXIS 77, at *88 (Del. Ch. July 14, 1989), reprinted in 15 Del. J. Corp. L. 700, 749 (1990). Recall that Paramount could not close a tender offer for Time without securing local government approvals of the transfer of cable television franchises, a timing problem that did not impede Time's offer for Warner.

[*The better-known Delaware Supreme Court opinion on appeal affirmed the Chancery Court's holding but rejected much of its reasoning. Paramount v. Time, 571 A.2d 1140 (1990).—Ed.*]

any possibility that the point might be misunderstood, Allen appended a footnote stating that the outcome might well have been different if Time were relying on a poison pill — in Allen's words, "a control mechanism and not a device with independent business purposes." ...

... Time could proceed with its acquisition of Warner even if it had the effect of blocking Paramount's hostile offer; because Time did not rely on a pill, shareholders were free to decide whether to accept a hostile offer for the combined companies should one be made. ...

And that brings us to the supreme court's development of *Unocal*, which I will argue has proven dramatically less successful than the approach taken by the chancery court. ... [T]he supreme court's effort to articulate the *Unocal* standard, most explicitly in *Unitrin v. American General Corp.*,[11] collapses into an unexplained functional preference that changes of control should occur through elections rather than courts. ...

III. The Supreme Court Decision in *Unitrin*: The Preference for Elections over Markets

... Under *Unitrin*'s elaboration of the proportionality test, a defensive tactic survives the intermediate standard of review if it is neither coercive nor preclusive and falls within a range of reasonableness. For present purposes, the critical question is whether the defensive tactic is preclusive. But the preliminary question is preclusive of what? Refusing to redeem a poison pill will always preclude a tender offer. It will not, however, necessarily preclude a proxy fight to replace the target's directors with nominees who can be expected to conclude, after careful and informed deliberation, that the offer is in the shareholders' best interests and thereafter redeem the pill. Does the presence of a poison pill allow a target company to force a bidder to have the success of its offer determined by an election rather than a tender offer?

Without confronting the issue directly, the Delaware Supreme Court appears to have simply assumed that the availability of a proxy fight renders a poison pill non-preclusive, thereby shifting the focus to the circumstances under which the proxy fight would be conducted. The court acknowledged that "[w]ithout the approval of a target's board, the danger of activating a poison pill renders it irrational for bidders to pursue stock acquisitions above the triggering level." Thus, a poison pill is preclusive of a tender offer. But under *Unitrin*, refusal to redeem the pill is not preclusive under *Unocal* unless a proxy fight is also precluded. On remand, the supreme court in *Unitrin* directed the chancery court to "determine whether Unitrin's Repurchase Program would only inhibit American General's ability to wage a proxy fight and institute a merger or whether it was, in fact, preclusive because American General's success would either be mathematically impossible or realistically unattainable."

Thus, *Unitrin* at least identifies the circumstance when *Unocal* allows a target to block a tender offer by declining to "pull the pill" — if a proxy fight is not "mathematically impossible" or "realistically unattainable." Because the poison pill has become ubiquitous — every public company either has adopted a pill or can adopt one if a hostile offer is made — the Delaware Supreme Court's analysis reduces functionally to a preference that control contests be resolved through an election, rather than a market: a target can block a tender offer so long as a stymied bidder can press its case through a proxy fight.

---

11. 651 A.2d 1361 (Del. 1995).

My purpose here is not to criticize the court's doctrinal analysis, although that task commends itself. For example, one certainly would have thought that prior doctrine dictated a somewhat more rigorous limit on defensive action in response to a proxy fight than that the action not render the proxy fight mathematically or realistically unattainable. Rather, I will focus only on the wisdom of the court's apparent conclusion however opaquely reached: that proxy contests are preferable to tender offers as a means of resolving a control contest.

IV. The Problems with a Preference for Elections

The Delaware Supreme Court's preference for elections presents three serious problems. The first poses a simple process concern: the need for transparency in setting the rules by which important business transactions must be considered. The other two are substantive. First, markets are more efficient than elections at resolving control contests; the court's preference makes the process less effective. Second, the court's rule has had the predictable effect of shifting defensive energy into proxy contests; the *Unitrin* election preference thus serves to degrade the electoral process itself.

A. *The Obligation to Provide an Explanation*

The process problem is that the court in *Unitrin* provides neither explanation nor justification for its preference for elections. A court's obligation to provide reasons for its action is more than a matter of professional craft; explaining the chosen outcome at least imposes the discipline of logic on the range of alternatives available to a court. As important, an explanation provides in equal measure not only a justification for the result in a particular case, but also guidance for the future. In *Unitrin*, the Delaware Supreme Court confronted an issue that it had managed to avoid for ten years: can a target company "just say no" by declining to pull the pill? A common law court—and most takeover law is common law and not statutory—has a professional obligation to clearly articulate the grounds for its decision. Uncertainty may preserve a court's flexibility, as some commentators have suggested in defense of the studied ambiguity of important Delaware Supreme Court opinions, but it comes at the expense of allowing parties to order their affairs. As a result, the court gets it precisely backwards: the point is to make things easier for actors in the economy to go about their business, not to make it easier for courts.

B. *Markets Are More Efficient than Elections at Mediating the Transfer of Control*

The first substantive problem concerns the direct costs of preferring elections to markets: the preference is not justified. While this is not the time to work out the argument more formally, I think it is straightforward to show that elections at best can be the equivalent of markets in determining when it is efficient for a control change to proceed, but that under more realistic circumstances, elections will be significantly worse.

The equivalency case involves making heroically simplifying assumptions of the sort common in most economic models. Assume that a bidder launches a tender offer that target management believes is substantively coercive. Further assume that because target management declines to pull the pill, shareholders are barred from accepting the tender offer unless the board of directors is replaced. In this hypothetical, however, we have an innovative election procedure. The shareholders cast their ballots for directors by checking a box on the letter of transmittal when they conditionally tender their shares. If the ballots are sufficient to replace the directors, then the pill is automatically pulled and the bidder can take down the shares. Finally, assume that all shareholders are perfectly informed about both the merits of the competing positions and the detail of the target directors' good faith belief that the market undervalues the company's stock.

Under these quite restrictive assumptions — perfect information and an election structure identical to the tender offer — the election is tautologically equivalent to a non-coercive tender offer.

The equivalence disappears, however, once the simplifying assumptions are released and some reality intrudes on the analysis. Most important, a proxy contest invites manipulation on the part of the target company to influence the outcome of the election.... [T]arget companies may succeed in manipulating the election by recourse to techniques for strategically delaying the timing of the shareholders' meeting through notice provisions, director qualification requirements, and limits on the calling and timing of special meetings. Finally, there remains the issue of staggered boards. For those companies who have won the defensive lottery by having a staggered board in place before institutional investors decided that, because of the interaction of staggered boards with poison pills, they would not vote for them, or for those companies who went public with a staggered board already in place, the election route requires a minimum of two years to change control of the board. While one may question whether independent directors will continue the defense if the would-be bidder handily wins the first proxy fight, even a small possibility of a two-year delay can be of enormous significance in today's quickly moving product markets.

Thus, once we get real, elections clearly appear a poor second to markets in assessing the benefits of a contested control change. Of course, this should come as no surprise; the SEC directly confronted the issue of the comparative efficiency of elections and markets at mediating control changes in crafting Rule 19c-4. Then, it will be recalled, the issue was whether an election could be used to shift control of a company by means of a charter amendment creating two classes of voting common stock. Consistent with the case for requiring those seeking control to buy it rather than campaign for it, the SEC adopted a rule that favored markets over elections. As adopted in July, 1988, Rule 19c-4 prohibited changing the voting rights of existing common stock by ballot, but allowed new issuances of common stock with lesser voting rights than the outstanding class of common stock.

Despite the comparative efficiency of markets compared to elections, the court might have relied on the statute to justify its preference for elections.[12] The problem, however, is that the statutory language itself provides no clear guidance. As the debate over the poison pill in *Household International* clearly demonstrates, statutory language often does not command a particular result, but is consistent with either of the conflicting results urged by both parties. The statute, like a golem, requires an animating principle to come alive. In *Household International*, the principle was the Delaware Supreme Court's commitment to review the actual operation of the pill under *Unocal* when a takeover arose. But *Unitrin's* effective abandonment of *Unocal's* regulatory function brings us back to the need for an animating justification: why should the court prefer elections to markets? And on this issue, *Unitrin* simply leaves us hanging.

---

12. *Del. Gen. Corp. L. § 157 empowers a corporation to issue shareholder rights or options, whether or not in connection with the sale of stock, subject to provisions in the corporation's charter. In* Moran v. Household International, *the Delaware Supreme Court held that § 157 constitutes statutory authority for boards to adopt poison pills. — Ed.*

C. The Supreme Court's Election Preference Serves to Degrade the Election Process

The second substantive problem with preferring elections to markets in mediating changes in control is indirect: the impact of the supreme court's preference for elections on the integrity of the electoral process itself. The predictable result of *Unitrin* has been a quickly escalating level of board-implemented barriers to contested elections. And, to be frank, judicial efforts to constrain this process have not been up to the task.

The portion of the chancery court's opinion in *Mentor Graphics* that concerned the defensively adopted bylaw illustrates the problem.[13] The bylaw, adopted by target directors to buy time in the face of a proxy contest that they believed the company could not win, authorized the directors to delay the holding of a shareholder called meeting for 90 to 100 days after it determined the validity of the initial request. The Vice-Chancellor concluded that the "the 90 to 100 day interval chosen by the target board, although it may arguably approach the outer limit of reasonableness, struck a proper balance in this specific case." It is not unfair to the Vice-Chancellor to note that there is no real discussion of why ninety days is necessary. And it is certainly to the Vice-Chancellor's credit that he was quite clearly aware of the risk that approving a 90 to 100 day delay without an animating principle that might serve to cabin the opinion's predictable expansive drift, would encourage ever more extreme measures. After all, the worst that could happen to an overly aggressive target management is that the bylaw would be struck down.

Recognizing the incentive in favor of aggressive defensive behavior, the Vice-Chancellor explicitly warned that "attorneys who represent corporate boards would best serve their clients well by counseling caution and restraint in this area, rather than seeking continually to push the time-delay envelope outwards to test its fiduciary duty limits." But while the impulse to lecture counsel on their duties is both laudable and continues the chancery court's useful technique of instructing counsel through dicta, the simple fact is that the Delaware courts' approach in this area operates to encourage attorneys to push the envelope precisely because there is no principle guiding the outcome. What factors would counsel against a delay of ninety days, said by the court to be potentially unreasonable "in other circumstances"? If, as the court suggests, "it is impossible to draw a line that categorically separates mandatory delay periods which have a basis in reason, from those that so manifestly burden or impede the election process that they can be characterized as intended to entrench the incumbent board," then how can the ambiguity do other than encourage clients "continually to push the time-delay envelope outwards," precisely the behavior we have observed with the poison pill. Certainly, respected counsel's assistance in the adoption of slow-hand and dead-hand pills[14] gives one little reason to anticipate professional self-control.

Nor should the onus be placed entirely on the chancery court. The standard on remand in *Unitrin*—that a tactic not render a proxy fight "mathematically impossible or realistically unattainable"—itself invites extreme measures since the formulation implies that the process can be drastically skewed in management's favor so long as it is not impossible for a bidder to win the proxy fight.

In the end, the absence of a guiding principle restricting director manipulation of election contests is the greatest irony of all. While the Delaware courts plainly recognize

---

13. Mentor Graphics Corp. v. Quickturn Design Sys., 728 A.2d 25 (Del. Ch. 1998).
14. These types of poison pills slow or discourage takeovers by imposing long delays on the redemption of the pill.

that elections are all that legitimate directors' power over assets that belong to others, the shifting of control contests into the electoral process has served to degrade the electoral process itself. It is difficult to imagine an electoral process that can both confer legitimacy on the victor and still leave the incumbent very substantial discretion to manipulate the process....

V. Is There a Way Out? The Shareholder Adopted Bylaw Debate

However trenchant, criticism is made constructive only by providing a solution to the problem. How can the Delaware Supreme Court ameliorate the electoral bias created in *Unitrin* without simply reversing fifteen years of common law development? I think such an avenue exists and, indeed, in the context of an issue that the Delaware courts will certainly confront: the validity of shareholder-adopted bylaws to redeem poison pills.

Taken to its conclusion, this analysis calls into question not merely [*Paramount v. Time*], in which the supreme court lifted the chancery court's more erosion-resistant allocation of decision authority between directors and shareholders, but also *Household International*, which provided the mechanism by which the erosion subsequently occurred. Fifteen years experience with *Unocal* teaches that shareholders ought to decide whether to accept an offer made to them, subject to the board's efforts to secure for them a better alternative. As the chancery court explained in *Interco*, the legitimacy of our corporate law and, we now have seen, the legitimacy of the electoral process as well, depends on the shareholders' ultimate decision-making role. With the benefit of hindsight, the pill in *Household International* should have been struck down for the very reason that it was expedient to management: the absence of shareholder approval.

But what do we do now? I start with the widely shared view that the genius of Delaware corporate law and of American corporate law generally is that it is for the most part enabling—it gives the parties the freedom to choose their governance structure rather than imposing an outcome upon them. The Delaware courts' sympathetic treatment of the pill, understandably caught up in the frenzy of the 1980s, lost sight of that fact. The attraction of the pill to target management is that it can be imposed without shareholder approval, and shareholders cannot remove it without incurring the cost, in resources and opportunity, of replacing a board of directors that might in all other respects be doing an excellent job. That is hardly an enabling approach; as Chancellor Allen pointed out, ... directors are not Platonic guardians. Rather, it reflects the sense of the times, incorrect to be sure but an understandable accommodation in a moment of perceived crisis, that shareholders could not be trusted to vote for sensible defensive measures.

We are past that point now. Institutional investors quite routinely approve sensibly drafted pills, and even some not-so-sensibly drafted pills that are proposed by trusted, well performing management. In this calmer time, it would be appropriate to return to an enabling approach that allowed shareholders to choose their governance regime, including whether to have a poison pill. But how to accomplish this without entirely replanting a path now worn clear by fifteen years' experience?

Shareholder adopted bylaws are now working their way up the judicial process toward a determination of their fit under Delaware law. As I understand it, the standard response among many thoughtful Delaware lawyers, especially after *Mentor Graphics*, is that such bylaws violate [Del. Gen. Corp. L.] section 141(a)'s grant of managerial authority to the board of directors. However, section 141(a)'s grant of authority is qualified by the phrase "except as otherwise permitted in this chapter or in the certificate of incorporation."

Section 109(b) — obviously in "this chapter" — authorizes shareholders to adopt bylaws containing "any provision, not inconsistent with law or with the certificate of incorporation, relating to the business of the corporation, the conduct of its affairs, and the rights and powers of its stockholders, directors, officers, or employees."

As my colleague Jeffrey Gordon has perceptively noted, the broad grant of management authority to the directors in section 141(a), referring to the "business and affairs of the corporation," juxtaposed with the equally broad grant of authority for shareholder-adopted bylaws in section 109(b), referring to "the business of the corporation [and] the conduct of its affairs," should call to mind the Delaware doctrine of "equal dignity" or "independent legal significance."[15] This doctrine, which lets corporate participants choose among different statutory alternatives for dealing with precisely the same functional activity, is the very embodiment of Delaware's enabling approach. The board manages pursuant to section 141(a); the shareholders adopt bylaws pursuant to section 109(b). Under the equal dignity doctrine, the fact that the two sections cover the same ground results not in a conflict, but in alternative approaches to the same problem.

Allowing shareholders to redeem poison pills or replace them with less expansive versions by means of a bylaw allows the Delaware Supreme Court to back off with grace from the extreme position to which they were driven by the turmoil of the 1980s and the failure of any other institution, most notably the United States Congress, to give the governance of takeovers more than superficial attention. In particular, shareholder-adopted bylaws largely (but not entirely) returns to shareholders the decision-making role with respect to tender offers that *Household International* transferred to the board of directors, and allows shareholders to reverse [*Paramount v. Time*] by reinstating only an *Interco*-style constrained pill.

The shareholder bylaw route still leaves the balance between shareholders and management tipped toward management; absent *Household International*, it would be better to require the directors to seek shareholder approval to impose a pill in the first instance rather than requiring the shareholders to seek repeal because of our rules for who bears the cost of proxy initiatives. Nonetheless, it is a workable way out of an outcome that, because it encourages managerial manipulation of the electoral process, genuinely degrades the legitimacy of Delaware corporate law.

To be sure, one can undertake a more technical interpretive analysis concerning how the conflicting language of sections 109(b) and 141(a) might be rationalized. While it can be argued that the language of section 109(b) was hardly intended for this function, *Household International* itself provides the response. Responding to the same objection with respect to its broad reading of section 157, the supreme court quoted *Unocal*: "[O]ur corporate law is not static. It must grow and develop in response to, indeed in anticipation of, evolving concepts and needs. Merely because the General Corporation law is silent, as to a specific matter does not mean that it is prohibited." Stretching section 157 correspondingly stretches section 109(b).

Professor Coffee takes the problem more seriously, providing a careful and quite plausible exegesis of alternative approaches to limit the breadth of shareholder initiative under section 109(b), and thereby minimize the conflict with director authority under section 141(a), while still allowing shareholders to repeal poison pills.[16] In contrast, Professor

15. Jeffrey N. Gordon, *"Just Say Never?" Poison Pills, Deadhand Pills, and Shareholder-Adopted Bylaws: An Essay for Warren Buffett*, 19 Cardozo L. Rev. 511 (1997).

16. John C. Coffee, Jr., *The Bylaw Battlefield: Can Institutions Change the Outcome of Corporate Control Contests?*, 51 U. Miami L. Rev. 605, 617–18 (1997).

Hamermesh concludes after a lengthy analysis that traditional and non-traditional tools of statutory interpretation, the public choice problems associated with shareholder voting, and especially the difficulty of identifying of defining a "poison pill," counsel in favor of stopping section 109(b) short of poison pill repeal.[17]

My goal here is not to resolve the scope of section 109(b) as a matter of technical interpretation beyond expecting the Delaware Supreme Court to hew to its equal dignity canon, in no small measure because I am enough of a realist to be skeptical both of the power of technical arguments to drive as opposed to rationalize outcomes, especially in Delaware, and of a coherent explanation that distinguishes under Delaware law when the conflict between statutory provisions must be respected—the equal dignity move—and when the conflict is explained away through interpretation. Nonetheless, two rather practical points are worth making. First, defining a poison pill presents at worst no greater difficulty than defining a defensive action under *Unocal*, a task that has been largely uncontroversial. To paraphrase a response to a different interpretative problem, the Delaware courts have known defensive tactics when they have seen them, and will know a poison pill when they see one. Second, the interpretive problem is of no grander scale than the Delaware Supreme Court's assessment in *Household International* of whether the broad language of section 157 encompassed poison pills. The outcome requires a theory of the mechanisms that govern the shifting of corporate control, an animating structural principle for the bones of the statute. *Unocal* was to provide the theory that *Household International* lacked, but the lesson of *Unocal's* first fifteen years is that the Delaware Supreme Court's march toward an unarticulated and unjustified preference for elections over markets, however understandable in its original motivation, has proven to be a failure. The chancery court had the animating principle right in the first place: the ultimate decision-makers concerning a tender offer should be the shareholders. However realistic the threat of a tidal wave of junk bond financed, two-tier, bust-up takeovers, assisted by unthoughtful shareholders, may have appeared to the Delaware courts in 1985, we know now that it was a chimera. Between bidder and target now stand large sophisticated shareholders with carefully considered views of corporate governance. Shareholder-initiated bylaws provide an imperfect, but realistic, way to turn back the clock....

Lucian Arye Bebchuk, *The Case Against Board Veto in Corporate Takeovers**

In the last thirty years, takeover law has been the subject most hotly debated by corporate law scholars. During this period, takeover law has undergone many changes and much development, receiving the frequent attention of both legislators and courts. State legislators have been busy adopting a variety of antitakeover statutes. Courts have been busy developing a rich body of takeover doctrine. And an army of lawyers and investment bankers has been busy improving and practicing techniques of takeover defense and attack.

A central issue in the debate has been whether boards should have power to block unsolicited acquisition offers. To some scholars, such power is a serious impediment to

---

17. Lawrence A. Hamermesh, *Corporate Democracy and Stockholder-Adopted By-Laws: Taking Back the Street?*, 73 Tul. L. Rev. 409, 429 (1998).

* Originally published in 69 University of Chicago Law Review 973 (2002). Reprinted with permission.

efficient corporate governance. To others, a board veto is, on the contrary, necessary for effective corporate governance. Whereas opinions on the role of boards in corporate takeovers differ greatly, there is wide agreement about the importance of this subject for corporate governance and for the allocation of corporate assets....

I. Prerequisite: Ensuring Undistorted Shareholder Choice

A. *Ensuring Undistorted Choice via Voting*

One reason that could be given for granting boards a veto power is a concern that shareholders facing a takeover bid might be unable to exercise an undistorted choice. In the absence of any restrictions on bidders, shareholders might be pressured to tender. The pressure-to-tender problem is by now familiar to students of takeovers, and it can thus be described with brevity. In deciding whether to tender, each shareholder will recognize that its decision will not determine the fate of the offer. The shareholder therefore will take into account the scenario in which the bid is going to succeed regardless of how the shareholder acts. Whenever the expected post-takeover value of minority shares is lower than the bid price, this scenario will exert pressure on the shareholder to tender. As a result, shareholders might tender, and a takeover might occur, even if most shareholders do not view a takeover as being in their collective interest.

The pressure to tender is most visible and conspicuous in the case of partial, two-tier bids. In *Unocal*, the landmark takeover case, the potential coercive effect of such a bid was held to pose a substantial threat that justified strong defensive measures.[18] Although the pressure to tender is most visible in such cases, it is in no way limited to them. It can be shown to exist also when bids are for all shares, and when no second-step, low-value freezeout is expected, as long as the expected post-takeover value of minority shares is lower than the bid price.

The approach for addressing the distorted choice problem that I favor is one based on using a voting or vote-like mechanism. Under this approach, the problem is addressed by enabling each shareholder to express separately its preferences with respect to the following two questions: (i) whether it prefers a takeover to take place; and (ii) whether it prefers that its shares be acquired in the event that a takeover takes place. The pressure-to-tender problem essentially results from the fact that even shareholders who wish to answer question (i) in the negative (that is, who prefer that a takeover not take place) might tender and thereby support the bid because of their interest in giving a positive answer to question (ii) to ensure that their shares are acquired in the event of a takeover.

A voting mechanism provides a "clean" way of enabling shareholders to express separately their preferences on issues (i) and (ii). Consider any procedure under which: (1) shareholders vote or otherwise express their preferences on whether a takeover should take place; (2) the bidder is permitted to gain control only if a majority of the shareholders express their support for a takeover; and (3) in the event that the offer wins such majority support, all shareholders — regardless of whether they supported a takeover — receive a genuine opportunity to get their pro rata fraction of the total acquisition price. Under such a procedure, because voting against the offer would impose no penalty on the voting shareholder in the event of a takeover, shareholders' votes would solely reflect their preferences concerning whether a takeover should take place. As a result, the bid will obtain the necessary vote of shareholder support only if most shareholders indeed view a takeover as beneficial....

---

18. Unocal Corp v. Mesa Petroleum, Inc, 493 A.2d 946, 956 (Del. 1985).

B. Arrangements with Voting and No Board Veto

In the presence of a voting mechanism ensuring an undistorted shareholder choice, I argue, the board should not have veto power beyond the period necessary for exploring and preparing alternatives for shareholders' consideration. I will refer to such a regime as one of shareholder voting and no board veto. The absence of board veto implies, in particular, that directors should not be able to use their powers (i) to block a bidder's access to a vote beyond the above preparatory period, (ii) to frustrate or distort the outcome of the vote, or (iii) to block a takeover that has gained the needed vote of shareholder support....

... [P]oison pills are not necessarily inconsistent with a regime of voting and no board veto. As explained, a pill might serve merely as an instrument for requiring the bidder to win a vote of shareholder support. As long as the board cannot deny the bidder access to such a vote for too long, and as long as the victory in such a vote would result in redemption of the pill, we would have a regime of shareholder voting and no board veto....

While existing pills do not generally include provisions that enable shareholders to vote to redeem the pill, board veto could be limited or eliminated by courts placing limits on how long a board may maintain a pill. As noted, a majority of publicly traded firms have staggered boards, with a majority of such staggered boards adopted before the developments in takeover jurisprudence that made them so potent. If a board with a staggered structure could maintain the pill indefinitely, a hostile bidder would have to win two elections, one year apart, to gain control. As a result, staggered boards currently provide incumbents with a great deal of power to block bids. This veto power could be much reduced by requiring boards that lose one election over a bid to redeem the pill. Such a requirement would prevent boards from using a staggered board-poison pill combination to block an offer that enjoys shareholder support beyond the next annual election....

II. The Case Against Board Veto

On the view that I label the "board veto" view, boards should have the power to block acquisition offers, at least for a significant period of time beyond what would be necessary for preparing alternative plans and communicating them to the shareholders....

A. Alternative Normative Perspectives

... An examination of the arguments by supporters of board veto reveals that more than one normative perspective has been used. Because I wish to consider the full range of possible arguments for board veto, I will examine the board veto question from each of the four different normative perspectives that have been invoked in the literature. It would be worthwhile to describe briefly at the outset each of these perspectives.

1. The Perspective of Target Shareholders

The rules governing defensive tactics are often analyzed from the perspective of target shareholders. From this perspective, the rules that should govern target boards are those that would best serve the shareholders of these companies. These rules are those that informed and rational shareholders of these companies would have wished to adopt *ex ante*. In defending board veto from this perspective, supporters have argued that such veto power benefits target shareholders.

2. The Perspective of Targets' Long-Term Shareholders

Supporters of board veto sometimes draw a distinction between short-term shareholders, which do not plan to hold shares for long and therefore focus on short-term returns, and long-term shareholders, which plan to keep holding their shares and focus on long-run returns. Target boards, supporters of board veto sometimes argue, should give greater weight to the interests of the targets' long-term shareholders. These supporters also believe that there is some divergence of interest between these two categories of investors in the takeover context.

3. The Perspective of Total Shareholder Wealth

Another normative perspective is that of aggregate shareholder wealth, which combines the wealth of targets' shareholders and acquirers' shareholders. The use of this perspective might be justified on grounds that most target shareholders hold diversified portfolios and therefore prefer rules that would maximize aggregate shareholder gains rather than gains to targets. Alternatively, the use of this perspective might be justified on grounds that, in setting takeover rules, society should not seek rules that benefit target shareholders but rather ones that increase the total value of the corporate sector.

4. The Perspective of All Corporate Constituencies

Supporters of board veto have also argued that it would serve the interests of nonshareholder constituencies, such as employees, suppliers, host communities, and so forth. Therefore, another perspective that I will use to evaluate board veto is that of the aggregate wealth of all corporate constituencies, including both shareholders and stakeholders.

Supporters of board veto have not generally taken a clear position on which perspective is the decisive one. Indeed, because they have not conceded that board veto is undesirable from any one of the above four perspectives, they have not had to make such a choice. Invoking several normative perspectives provides these supporters with fallback positions—even if board veto were identified as undesirable for target shareholders, they could retreat to the view that such veto would be justified from the perspective of long-term shareholders. And even if board veto were identified as undesirable for any significant group of target shareholders, they could still retreat to defending it on grounds of aggregate shareholder wealth or the aggregate wealth of all corporate constituencies.

I will not attempt in this Article to resolve which normative perspective should guide the design of takeover rules. Rather, my thesis is that there is no good basis for board veto from any one of the above four perspectives. . . .

B. The Target Shareholders' Perspective: Costs of Board Veto

1. Ex Post Agency Costs

Although the ex post agency problem is a serious one, it is conceptually simple and thus can be described with brevity. The takeover context is one in which managers' and shareholders' interests often diverge. Managers might lose their control and the private benefits associated with it. To use the language of *Unocal*, the takeover context confronts us with "the omnipresent specter that a board may be acting primarily in its own interests."

Thus, whenever a bid is made, the divergence of interest gives rise to potential agency costs. First and most importantly, managers might elect to block a beneficial acquisition in order to retain their independence. Secondly, managers might use their power to extract not a higher premium for their shareholders but rather personal benefits for themselves. I will refer to these problems as "ex post" agency problems because they are ones that arise after a bid is made. I will discuss later *ex ante* agency costs, that is, adverse effects on incentives and behavior prior to the making of any bids.

Lipton and Rowe recently argued that the absence of legal cases condemning incumbents' standing behind pills is evidence that directors have in fact used their powers responsibly; the absence of such cases, they believe, indicates that the "pill has been used; it has not been abused."[19] But the absence of such court cases does not indicate whether shareholders have been hurt. Once judicial standards are established, incumbents can be expected not to deviate from them. Thus, absence of violations merely indicates that incumbents and their advisers can predict what actions would withstand judicial scrutiny.

Whereas the incidence of judicial condemnation does not provide a test for the presence of agency costs, there is other evidence that these costs are significant. To start with, the evidence indicates that, in the event that incumbents use their veto power to defeat bids, shareholders end up worse off compared with the scenario in which the bid would have been accepted. Studies indicate that, when target managers defeat offers, shareholders on average experience a significant stock market loss....

It might be objected, however, that incumbents' resistance should be evaluated by its effects on shareholders' wealth in the long-term rather than short-term. In a recent empirical study on staggered boards, Coates, Subramanian, and I therefore studied how the defeat of bids affected shareholders when evaluated from a long-term perspective.[20] We examined hostile bid cases during the period 1996–2000 in which targets remained independent. We found that, evaluated thirty months after the bid's announcement, the shareholders of targets remaining independent were on average substantially worse off compared with the scenario in which the bid would have been accepted. To illustrate, in the period we studied, we estimated that the average return to target shareholders during the thirty months following the offer was 54 percent higher for targets that were acquired than for targets that remained independent....

Finally, the presence of ex post agency costs is also suggested by evidence that managers might be willing to trade off premia to shareholders for personal benefits. A recent study by Hartzell, Ofek, and Yermack found that target CEOs are willing to accept lower acquisition premia in transactions that involve an extraordinary personal treatment (such as special payments to the CEO at the time of the acquisition or high-ranking managerial post in the buyer).[21] Another study by Wulf indicated that, in merger negotiations, CEOs are willing to trade off higher acquisition premia in exchange for better managerial positions in the merged firm.[22]

---

19. Martin Lipton & Paul K. Rowe, *Pills, Polls, and Professors*, 27 DEL. J. CORP. L. 1 (2002).
20. [Lucian Bebchuk, John C. Coates IV, & Guhan Subramanian, *The Powerful Antitakeover Force of Staggered Boards: Theory, Evidence, and Policy*, 54 STAN. L. REV. 887 (2002).]
21. [Jay Hartzell, Eli Ofek, & David Yermack, *What's in It for Me? CEOs Whose Firms Are Acquired*, 17 REV. FIN. STUD. 37 (2004).]
22. Julie Wulf, *Do CEOs in Mergers Trade Power for Premium?: Evidence from "Mergers of Equals"*, [20 J. L. ECON. & ORG. 60 (2004)].

2. Ex Ante *Agency Costs*

Board veto also produces agency costs *ex ante*, before any takeover attempts occur. Management generally acts against the background of the possibility that a takeover bid will be made. In the absence of a board veto, the takeover threat provides managers with an important source of incentives to serve shareholders. Better performance by management makes it less likely that a takeover bid will be made or that it will succeed.

Conversely, by eliminating or reducing the threat posed by a takeover, board veto provides managers with security that in turn could produce significant agency costs. With a veto power, managers might contemplate that, even if they perform poorly and a takeover bid follows, their power will enable them either to retain their control or at least to extract a good deal for themselves. Either way, the presence of a board veto eliminates or much reduces any adverse effect that a takeover might otherwise have on managers' interests. As a result, the takeover threat will lose much of its disciplinary power. Board veto might thus weaken incentives to avoid managerial slack, consumption of private benefits, empire-building, and other actions that are beneficial or convenient for managers but costly to shareholders.

The evidence indicates that insulation from the threat of a takeover does indeed have such adverse effects.... Gompers, Ishii, and Metrick found that companies whose managers enjoy more protection from takeovers (as measured by a governance index taking into account both corporate arrangements and state antitakeover provisions) are associated with poorer operating performance—including lower profit margins, return on equity, and sales growth.[23]

There is also evidence that insulation from takeover threats results in greater consumption of private benefits by managers. Borokhovich, Brunarski, and Parrino found that managers with stronger antitakeover defenses enjoy higher compensation levels.... [24]

C. *The Target Shareholders' Perspective: Arguments for Board Veto*

1. *Analogies to Other Corporate Decisions*

Before examining arguments that "start from first principles," I wish to consider first a common and influential claim that is based on an analogy to other corporate law decisions. Board control, it is argued, characterizes corporate decisionmaking in general. Indeed, for most corporate decisions, boards have not merely veto power but rather the power to make the decision either way. When a corporation faces a choice, say, whether to undertake a major investment in a new plant or a new product, directors have the power to make the decision, either way, generally without any intervention from either courts or shareholders. Why should we rely on boards for other corporate choices, supporters of board veto ask, but not for decisions on takeovers? If one accepts that delegation to boards works well in other contexts, so the challenge goes, are there any good reasons to view the takeover context as sufficiently different?

In fact, there are important differences, which call for a different treatment, between the takeover context and that of corporate decisions such as the investment decisions

---

23. [Paul A. Gompers, Joy L. Ishii, & Andrew Metrick, *Corporate Governance and Equity Prices*, 118 Q. J. Econ.107 (2003).]
24. Kenneth A. Borokhovich, Kelly R. Brunarski, & Robert Parrino, *CEO Contracting and Antitakeover Amendments*, 52 J. Fin. 1495, 1515 (1997).

noted above. To begin, the concern that managers' and shareholders' interests might diverge is greater in the takeover context. Because managers' control is at stake in the takeover context, managers' preferences in this context are likely influenced by their private interests. In contrast, a divergence of interest is less likely to arise, and if it arises to be of great magnitude, in corporate contexts such as the considered investment decision. Therefore, given managers' common ownership of shares and options, as well as their general interest in making the shareholders content, managers will likely focus on enhancing shareholder value in such other corporate contexts. They might err and therefore make incorrect decisions. But their decisions are unlikely to be distorted substantially by their private interests.

Second, in other contexts, such as the investment context considered above, letting the shareholders of a publicly traded company make the decision is not a viable option. In contrast, in the takeover context, letting the shareholders decide is a viable and practical option. Experience indicates that proxy contests conducted over an acquisition offer draw heavy participation by shareholders. The question remains, of course, whether shareholders would make good decisions, and I will consider this question below. But the fact that letting the shareholders make the decision is a viable option in the takeover context clearly distinguishes it from other contexts.

Relatedly, deference to boards in the takeover context is not called for by courts' reluctance to make business decisions. In other corporate contexts, where letting the shareholders decide is not an option, complete deference to boards can be avoided only by relying on judicial scrutiny. Given courts' limited information, expertise, and resources, the business judgment rule rightly counsels courts against substantive review of the merits of board decisions. In contrast, in the takeover context, a regime of shareholder voting and no board veto does not require courts to make business decisions. Courts need only protect shareholders' rights to make decisions in certain circumstances and to prevent managers from blocking such decisions.

Thus far, I have explained why, if we look at the takeover context and the investment context each in isolation from the other, the argument for board control is substantially weaker in the former context than in the latter. But there is an important interaction between (1) the case against board control in the takeover context, and (2) the case for board control in the investment context. Not only is (1) consistent with (2), but, furthermore, (1) strengthens and reinforces (2). One of the reasons why boards can be left with control over business decisions is that the possibility of a takeover provides a safety valve and source of discipline. Thus, not having board veto over takeovers in fact contributes to the case for board control in other corporate contexts.

2. Inefficient Capital Markets

Supporters of the board veto view believe that boards would decide better whether any given offer is worth accepting. Consequently, it is argued, it would be better for shareholders if boards were to make the decision for them. The argument that boards would decide better has two variants. One variant, which I will take up first, is based on a rejection of the efficient capital markets hypothesis and a belief that stock prices might often deviate from fundamental values. The second variant ... is based on incumbents' having private information concerning the target's value.

Let us start with the claim that board veto is called for by rejection of the efficient capital markets hypothesis. On this view, board veto can address situations in which a company's stock is trading at a "depressed" level below its fundamental value. "Must we accept (and make boards accept) short-term trading value as the sole reference point in responding to takeover proposals?" supporters of board veto ask. A negative answer to this question, they believe, calls for a board veto.

There are indeed good reasons to doubt the extent to which market prices generally reflect fundamental values. The efficient capital market hypothesis has been questioned by a large body of work in financial economics. The recent burst of the Internet bubble has provided a vivid illustration that stock prices may deviate from fundamental values. As explained below, however, accepting that capital markets are not generally informationally efficient, as the Delaware courts have done, does not imply that board veto is desirable.

To be sure, the stock market's informational inefficiency undermines the passivity approach of Easterbrook and Fischel, who believe that a takeover at a premium over the pre-bid market price is bound to increase shareholder wealth and efficiency.[25] Such informational inefficiency also significantly weakens the case for the auctions approach; some of the likely causes of this inefficiency, such as limited arbitrage, might also indicate that auctions might not always fetch a price that equals or exceeds the target's independent value.

Acceptance of informational inefficiencies, however, is consistent with a regime of shareholder voting and no board veto. In such a regime, targets of hostile bids will not be necessarily acquired for the highest price that would be offered for them in a market that might be temporarily depressed. Shareholders would vote down any premium offer if they believed that, although significantly above the target's temporarily depressed price, it falls below the target's fundamental value, which would be eventually reflected in market prices if the target were to remain independent.

That shareholders' decisions might discriminate in this way is nicely illustrated by comparing shareholders' reactions to the recent hostile bids for Shorewood and Willamette, two targets that had substantial antitakeover protections.[26] In both cases, the hostile bidders offered a substantial premium over the pre-bid market price of the target, though not over its historic price. In both cases, the board rejected the offer as inadequate on grounds that the stock market was greatly undervaluing the target's shares. In the case of Shorewood, shareholders apparently shared the view that the premium bid price was below the target's value, and only 1 percent of the targets' shares were tendered to the bidder. In contrast, in the case of Willamette, shareholders took a different view, and the bidder attracted 45 percent of the shares initially and, after the bid price was raised somewhat, 64 percent of the shares.

Thus, shareholders might sometimes accept, and might sometimes reject, claims that a premium offer is inadequate because the pre-bid market price was highly depressed. Therefore, even if we do not accept short-term value "as the sole reference point in responding to takeover proposals," board veto does not necessarily follow. The question would still remain who — shareholders or directors — should decide whether a given takeover proposal is worth accepting. Accepting that capital markets might be informationally inefficient does not by itself compel or suggest an answer to this question. To be sure, supporters of board veto might take the additional position that boards would make such decisions better. This is the claim to which I shall now turn.

---

25. Frank H. Easterbrook & Daniel R. Fischel, *The Proper Role of a Target's Management in Responding to a Tender Offer*, 94 Harv. L. Rev. 1161 (1981).

26. *See* Chesapeake Corp. v. Shore, 771 A.2d 293, 296 (Del. Ch. 2000); Jim Carlton and Robin Sidel, *Willamette Agrees to Be Bought by Weyerhaeuser*, Wall St. J., Jan. 22, 2002, at A3.

3. Directors' Superior Information

a. The Threat of an Inadequate Offer

Whether a takeover would benefit shareholders depends on how the offered acquisition price compares with the target's value in the event that it remains independent at least for the time being. This "independent value" of the target includes both the value of the possibility of remaining independent for the long haul and the value of the possibility of receiving higher offers later on. Because managers might have superior information about the target, supporters of board veto suggest, managers would be in a better position to estimate the target's independent value. Accordingly, it is argued, shareholders' interests would be served by delegating the decision to the board.

That managers might sometimes be better informed has been long accepted by takeover law. The Delaware courts have viewed as plausible and legitimate directors' concern that shareholders might mistakenly view as adequate an offer that is, in fact, inadequate according to directors' superior information. The danger that imperfectly informed shareholders will accept an inadequate offer has been referred to, using a term coined by Ronald Gilson and Reinier Kraakman [in their 1989 article], as "substantive coercion."

b. Does Informational Advantage Warrant a Board Veto?

I agree that target managers often have private information, both hard and soft, that public investors do not possess. Managers also might have devoted more time and effort to assessing the body of information about the company that is publicly available. Managers' superior information might indicate to them that the target's independent value is lower or higher than the level estimated by the target's shareholders. The possibility that shareholders will overestimate the target's value cannot provide a basis for board veto. But can the possibility that shareholders will underestimate the target's value provide such a basis? As I explain below, the answer is no.

Note first that, even accepting that directors sometimes have better informational basis for comparing the bid price and the target's independent value, they do not have the best incentives for making the right decision. Thus, a regime with board veto moves decisionmaking to a party that might be better informed but also has worse incentives. Directors might use their veto power not (or not only) for the intended purpose of blocking inadequate offers, but also to block offers that would be beneficial to shareholders. This concern is real and significant because the claim of offer inadequacy is one that incumbents can generally raise, and that would be hard to falsify, whenever they prefer their independence. In contrast, if shareholders had decisionmaking power, they might sometimes be less informed, but they would never have a reason to reject an offer that they view as beneficial to shareholders....

... [R]ational shareholders can be expected to balance two considerations. On the one hand, they will recognize that directors might be better informed; that shareholders are imperfectly informed about the target's value hardly implies that they are unaware that this is the case. This consideration would weigh in shareholders' decisionmaking in favor of deferring to the directors.

On the other hand, shareholders will also take into account considerations that weigh against deferring to the directors. First, directors might have self-serving reasons for preferring independence. Furthermore, like other humans, the directors might make mistakes and might suffer from a cognitive-dissonance tendency to view favorably both their own past performance and the course of action serving their interests. As Chancellor William Allen wisely remarked in *Interco*: "Human nature may incline even one acting in subjective good faith to rationalize as right that which is merely personally beneficial." ...

In any event, after balancing the considerations for and against deferring to the directors, rational shareholders might sometimes conclude that deference would be best on an expected value basis, and might sometimes reach the opposite conclusion. Of course, shareholders might not always get it right. But given that their money is on the line, shareholders naturally would have incentives to evaluate the tradeoff as well as possible....

The substantial presence of institutional investors makes paternalistic mandating of deference especially unwarranted. Institutions are likely to be aware of the informational advantage that management might have, and they appear capable of making reasonable decisions on whether deferring to the board would be best overall. Some institutional investors conduct their own analysis, and some rely on proxy-advisory firms such as [Institutional Shareholder Services (ISS)], which researches questions put to a shareholder vote and recommends to institutions how to vote. There is little reason to believe that the decisions of institutional investors on whether to defer would be so poor that mandating deference would be preferable to letting them make such decisions.

Finally, voting shareholders can hardly be regarded as a group that is excessively reluctant to defer to managers. Indeed, the normal patterns of corporate voting indicate that shareholders, including institutions, commonly display a great deal of deference to management's views. Thus, if anything, there are grounds for concern that voting shareholders might be excessively deferential. But that is, of course, not a reason to mandate deference. When circumstances would lead shareholders to overcome the tendency to defer to management, imposing deference on them would be unlikely to be beneficial....

... [T]he important question is not who can better judge whether the company should be sold, but rather who should decide whether deference will be given to the more informed but possibly conflicted directors. Shareholders have the best incentives to make this decision in a way that would serve their interests, and they should be permitted to make it.

c. Some Evidence

It is worth noting that the case against mandated deference is supported by the existing evidence. When incumbents defeat offers, shareholders experience on average a significant decline in stock value, a pattern that is consistent with the proposition that mandating deference makes shareholders worse off.

To be sure, supporters of board veto can rightly object that this evidence does not fully respond to their claim because it refers to short-term results. On their view, investors' possible underestimation of a target's long-term value is the very reason for board veto, and short-term declines in stock price thus do not rule out the possibility that the defeat of offers by incumbents ultimately pays off. As already noted, the staggered boards study done by Coates, Subramanian, and myself examined long-term returns and found no such long-term payoff. To the contrary, we found that thirty months after the bid announcement, the shareholders of targets that remained independent obtained on average a significantly lower value than they would have obtained had the board agreed to be acquired.

d. Judicial Screening of Inadequate Offer Claims

In response to the above analysis, it might be suggested that board veto should not be allowed when directors simply assert that the offer is inadequate but should be permitted when they provide a particularized analysis in support of their view that the target's value is substantially higher than the bid price. This approach was put forward in [the] influential article by Gilson and Kraakman. Recognizing the potential for abuse from allowing board veto based on mere assertions of offer inadequacy, Gilson and Kraakman suggested allowing such veto only when such assertions are judged (by a court) to be sufficiently substantiated and weighty. On their view, requiring such a particularized and substantial showing would screen out the instances in which board veto would be undesirable.

Chancellor Allen's famous opinion in *Interco* indeed subjected claims of offer inadequacy to judicial scrutiny. In that case, Allen did not permit a board to veto an offer of $74 per share in order to pursue a business plan that an investment banker estimated would produce a value of "at least" $76 per share. Confronting these numbers, Allen found the threat of offer inadequacy to be too mild to justify a board veto. He left open, however, the possibility that the threat of substantive coercion could justify a veto in other circumstances, such as a case in which the company's investment banker would provide an estimated independent value greatly exceeding the offer price.

Consider a "screening" rule under which courts will permit a board veto if: (1) directors provide a particularized analysis—say, in the form of an investment banker opinion—of their estimated target value in the event of bid rejection; and (2) this estimated value or range of values is substantially higher than the offer price. Imposing such limits on claims of offer inadequacy clearly would eliminate some (and possibly the worst) cases of abuse. However, this rule would still provide an unnecessary "safe harbor" for offer inadequacy claims. It would be better to let shareholders rather than courts engage in the screening of such claims....

With due respect to investment bankers' opinions, their estimates are hardly money in the bank. There is substantial room for discretion in financial estimates, and two analysts who use standard and accepted methodologies may reach very different estimates. Furthermore, the investment banker hired by management might have an incentive to help it as long as the banker would not have to bear reputational costs; thus, the banker would have an incentive to come out with the highest estimate that can be justified using legitimate methodologies....

Given that courts do not have any clear advantage over shareholders in assessing offer inadequacy claims, courts should not take such decisions away from shareholders.

4. *Bargaining by Management*

a. Premia Obtained with and without Board Veto

Thus far, I have focused on the possible benefits of board veto in those cases in which it would lead to target independence. I now turn to claims that such power might produce benefits in those cases in which an acquisition takes place by increasing premia. Even if the increased likelihood of independence produced by board veto were undesirable, it might be argued, board veto could still be desirable overall because of its effect on premia.

Management's bargaining is possibly beneficial, it is argued, because target shareholders are dispersed and therefore unable to bargain effectively. If management is given veto power, it could act as a single and effective bargaining agent on behalf of the shareholders....

There are reasons, however, to doubt the presence, or at least the significance, of the bargaining advantage that a board veto regime is claimed to have. To begin, a regime of shareholder voting and no board veto is consistent with substantial bargaining by management on behalf of the shareholders. Such a regime would merely imply that shareholders would have the power, if they so chose, to take the bargaining mandate from management. Thus, the difference between a board veto regime and a regime with shareholder voting and no board veto is only that the former grants management an irreversible mandate to bargain whereas the latter gives management a mandate to bargain that is reversible.

Consider a principal who has an agent conducting some negotiations on the principal's behalf. Even if the principal retains the power to take the mandate away from the agent, as is often the case, the agent can bargain on the principal's behalf. Lawyers, for example, bargain on behalf of clients, sometimes ferociously, even though clients are generally free, if they so choose, to accept an offer from the other side against their lawyer's recommendation. That clients are free to do so, however, hardly implies that they generally would; clients can and often do refuse to accept any offer not recommended by their lawyer....

b. Some Evidence

The discussion above suggests that, at a theoretical level, it is far from clear that a board veto should be expected to increase substantially, or even at all, the acquisition premia paid to target shareholders. Given that the question cannot be fully resolved at the level of theory, let us turn to the available evidence.

Supporters of board veto argue that the evidence shows that such veto has a substantial positive effect on premia. They rely on early studies by Georgeson & Company that found an association between poison pills and higher premia in acquisitions. Comment and Schwert, in a more systematic study, also found an association between pills and premia.[27]

As recent work by Coates shows, however, the findings of the above studies provide no basis for inferring that the presence of pills produces higher premia due to the bargaining power provided by pills.[28] Because every company can install a pill overnight, having the pill already in place does not affect the power that management would have to block a hostile bid should it occur. Both companies with and without pills in place have pills available to them if needed to block a bid. Thus, the difference in premia found in the above studies between these two types of companies could not have resulted from the bargaining advantage of pills. The difference in premia presumably reflected whatever differences in characteristics and circumstances led firms to make different choices whether to install a pill or keep it on the shelf.

Because companies with a pill already installed do not stand out in terms of managers' power to block bids, they do not enable testing the impact of board veto on premia. In contrast, as noted, effective staggered boards do provide managers with especially strong defenses, and they thus present an opportunity for such testing. In our study of staggered boards, Coates, Subramanian, and I found that, controlling for other company and bid characteristics, managers armed with effective staggered boards obtained increases in premia that were small and statistically insignificant....

---

27. Robert Comment & G. William Schwert, *Poison or Placebo?: Evidence on the Deterrence and Wealth Effects of Modern Antitakeover Measures*, 39 J. FIN. ECON. 3 (1995).

28. John C. Coates IV, *Takeover Defenses in the Shadow of the Pill: A Critique of the Scientific Evidence*, 79 TEX. L. REV. 271, 337 (2000).

5. Dangers of Short-Term Focus

Thus far, I have concluded that, given that there is a bid on the table, shareholders' interests would not be well served by boards' having a veto power. But this does not end our inquiry. It remains to explore whether board veto is beneficial due to its *ex ante* effects on managers' incentives and behavior.

Supporters of board veto have suggested that the threat of hostile takeovers forces managers to focus on short-term results and thereby discourages investments, such as investments in research and development, that would bear fruit only in the longer run. Indeed, during the corporate governance debates of the 1980s, supporters of board veto argued that the short-term bias produced by takeovers was one of the reasons why the United States economy was performing less well than Germany and Japan, where corporate managers were largely insulated from unsolicited offers. This particular concern about the consequences of takeovers is presumably no longer with us, but the basic claim underlying it should be taken seriously.

At the level of theory, there is no question that, when managers' inside information is not fully observable to public investors, managers' concern about short-term results might distort their decisions. It is worth noting, however, that the direction of the distortion is ambiguous and depends on the type of information that is unobservable to investors....
... [S]hould a takeover bid occur, shareholders deciding on it would not be able to observe the level of investment in long-term projects. As a result, the threat of an unsolicited bid discourages investment in such projects.

Another model, developed by Lars Stole and myself, analyzes the case in which the level of investment in long-term projects is observable but its quality or expected profitability is not.[29] This assumption might well fit most cases of capital investments in long-term projects made by firms. Under this assumption, the threat of unsolicited offers leads to excessive investments in long-term projects. Should a control contest arise, shareholders will be able to observe such investments. Furthermore, a higher level of investment will signal managers' confidence in the profitability of this investment, and this signaling effect provides incentives to invest excessively.

In any event, whichever direction distortions are expected to take in any given set of circumstances, the prospect of a takeover bid undoubtedly can, in theory, distort the level of long-term investments. For designing legal policy, however, the important question is whether these distortions are of sufficient magnitude to justify providing boards with veto power. Neither the theory nor the available empirical evidence supply a basis for believing this to be the case. The evidence on the existence of such distortions is mixed, with ambiguous results with respect to the sign of the effect of board veto on R&D expenditures.

Furthermore, even assuming that board veto does have beneficial *ex ante* effects on investments in long-term projects, it must be taken into account that, as discussed [above] board veto also has significant *ex ante* costs....

Supporters of board veto have provided no reasons for believing that whatever *ex ante* effects board veto has on long-term investments will be sufficiently positive to outweigh the significant negative *ex ante* effects of board veto that have been discussed earlier. Indeed, as I now turn to note, the evidence that is available supports a conclusion that

---

29. Lucian Arye Bebchuk & Lars A. Stole, *Do Short-Term Managerial Objectives Lead to Under-or Over-investment in Long-Term Projects?*, 48 J. FIN. 719 (1993).

the overall effect of board veto is negative. To begin, Gompers, Ishii, and Metrick found a significant association between stronger antitakeover protections and lower stock market valuation ... throughout the 1990s ... with the effect becoming more pronounced as the decade proceeded.

Furthermore, there is evidence that the passage of the strongest antitakeover statutes—the ones most capable of significantly enhancing boards' veto power over unsolicited offers—was accompanied by a significant decline in the stock price of the companies incorporated in these states. Massachusetts companies significantly declined in value when Massachusetts adopted a statute making staggered boards the default arrangement under state law. Companies incorporated in Pennsylvania or Ohio significantly declined in value when these states passed statutes enabling a "disgorgement" of bidders' "short-term" profits. In general, the overwhelming majority of event studies on the adoption of state antitakeover statutes found either no price reactions or negative price reactions....

D. *The Perspective of Stakeholders*

Supporters of board veto also argue that it enables managers to prevent acquisitions that would harm stakeholders—nonshareholder constituencies such as employees, suppliers, or debtholders. Indeed, a majority of the states enacted statutes allowing managers responding to a takeover bid to take into account the interests of stakeholders. Supporters of board veto have used claims about stakeholder interests in the political arena, in the courts, and in the court of public opinion.

Acquisitions, whether hostile or friendly, might sometimes adversely affect the interests of stakeholders. Employees might be laid off, creditors' debt might become riskier, suppliers might be denied a valuable business partner, communities might lose a corporate headquarters or corporate operations, and so forth. It is desirable, so the argument goes, to have in place some mechanism that would ensure that stakeholders' interests would be taken into account in deciding whether to have a takeover and that these interests would be protected if a takeover does take place. On this view, having such a mechanism would not only benefit stakeholders but also would *ex ante* be in the interest of shareholders; specifically, it would encourage *ex ante* beneficial investments and participation on the part of stakeholders.

Critics of this view have argued that, although takeovers could in theory impose such harm on stakeholders, the evidence indicates that such losses are not very common and, furthermore, are small in magnitude relative to shareholders' gains when they do occur. Critics have also argued that the law generally should not provide protection to stakeholders beyond what is called for by their contracts with the corporation. On this view of the critics, protection of stakeholder interests should be left to contracts between them and the corporation or to nonlegal sanctions. Given this line of response, it is unsurprising that some observers view the board veto question as one of shareholders versus stakeholders.

Below I will assume for the purpose of discussion that (i) takeovers often impose significant negative externalities on stakeholders (possibly employees in particular), and (ii) it is desirable to have some mechanism in place that protects stakeholders in the event of an acquisition. As I explain below, even under these assumptions, the case for board veto hardly follows. That is, fully accepting in my analysis the importance and desirability of protecting stakeholders in acquisitions, I will show that a board veto is a rather poor way of pursuing this objective, and that this objective thus cannot provide a basis for a board veto regime.

1. Expanding Discretion to Benefit Stakeholders

To begin, it is worth observing that there is no assurance that, if directors are given veto power, they will exercise it to protect stakeholders. In theory, one could consider permitting boards to block offers that shareholders would like to accept only if such blocking would protect stakeholders and thereby maximize the overall welfare of all corporate constituencies. Courts, however, would be unable to enforce compliance with such a principle.

Indeed, courts are reluctant to review the merits of board decisions — even to determine whether they serve the narrower and well-defined interests of shareholders. For this reason, those opposed to board veto do not wish to limit it by having courts review board decisions but rather to replace it with shareholders making the key decisions. Clearly, if directors were instructed to maximize the joint welfare of all corporate constituencies, courts would be unable or at least unwilling to enforce compliance with such a principle. As Oliver Hart observed, a prescription to management to take the interests of all constituencies into account "is essentially vacuous, because it allows management to justify almost any action on the grounds that it benefits some group."[30]

Supporters of board veto indeed do not assume or imply that directors would have to use their power in ways that would protect stakeholders and that courts would review whether this is done. Indeed, lest there be any misunderstanding that courts are expected to ensure that directors take stakeholders' interests into account, drafters of state constituency statutes used (in all cases but one) language that authorizes (rather than requires) directors to take into account the interests of other constituencies.

In sum, supporters of board veto wish to give boards discretion with the aspiration and hope that they would use their discretion to protect stakeholder interests. In considering how likely this is to happen, we should examine whether the interests of those granted the discretion are likely to overlap with the interests of the stakeholders that are supposed to benefit from this discretion.

2. Are Boards Good Agents of Stakeholders?

Recall the agency problem that played an important role in analyzing board veto from shareholders' perspective — the concern that, in the takeover context, managers are likely to be influenced by their private interests. Even though managers' holdings of shares and options create in general some alignment of managers' and shareholders' interests, the takeover context is one in which managers' interests are likely to diverge from those of shareholders.

Do we have good reasons for expecting managers responding to a takeover bid to be better agents of stakeholders than they can be expected to be of shareholders? To begin, note that, in most other corporate contexts, managers' interests are actually more likely to be aligned with those of shareholders rather than stakeholders. Whereas managers usually have a significant fraction of their wealth in the form of shares and options, they do not usually have as much of their wealth tied to bondholder or employee wealth. And managers' private interests in the takeover context cannot be expected to be aligned with the interests of stakeholders.

---

30. Oliver Hart, *An Economist's View of Fiduciary Duties*, 43 U. Toronto L. J. 299, 303 (1993).

To be sure, some correlation between managers' and stakeholders' preferences might arise because some acquisitions might be a threat to managers (who might lose their private benefits of control) and also to employees (who might lose their jobs) or creditors (who might be harmed by an increase in leverage). But this correlation of interests is likely to be rather limited; managers' and stakeholders' interests can be expected to overlap occasionally but not in general.

There might well be acquisitions that would be beneficial to stakeholders—say, when an acquisition by a large and rich buyer would improve opportunities for employees—but that management might well disfavor for self-serving reasons. Conversely, there might well be acquisitions that would disadvantage stakeholders but that management, at least if it is offered a sufficiently good deal for itself, would favor. Finally, in cases in which an acquisition is likely to occur ultimately, management might use whatever veto power it has to bargain for better terms not for stakeholders but rather for itself or even for shareholders. In sum, given the limited overlap between managers' and stakeholders' interests, there is no basis for expecting board veto to translate into an effective protection of stakeholders.

3. *The Tenuous Link between Stakeholder Protection and Board Veto*

Protection of stakeholders is thus not an objective that a board veto regime can serve well. If one is genuinely concerned about protecting stakeholders from being harmed by corporate acquisitions, then one presumably should seek a mechanism that (i) would apply to all or most of the transactions that might have the undesired effects, and (ii) would reasonably target and address these effects. A board veto is not such a mechanism, on both counts.

First, a concern about the effects of acquisitions on stakeholders should clearly not limit itself to, or even focus on, hostile takeovers. Such takeovers, which constitute a rather limited fraction of relevant corporate transactions, are not especially or disproportionately ones that can be expected to harm stakeholders. Layoffs, for example, might result not only from hostile acquisitions but also from negotiated acquisitions of a company or of a division, from a change of course following a proxy contest victory by challengers, or from decisions by incumbents to shut down plants. Whereas hostile takeovers are very important for an analysis focusing on how power is allocated between managers and shareholders, arrangements designed to protect stakeholders in corporate transactions have no reason to focus on hostile takeovers.

Furthermore, focusing on hostile takeover cases, the effects of board veto on outcomes in such cases would have little overlap with those desirable for stakeholders. If we seek to protect stakeholders, why do so by giving discretionary power to agents that have their own, very different interests and somehow hope for the best? One truly concerned with stakeholder interests should seek remedies that are tied more systematically to the problems that need to be addressed. For example, one concerned about harms to employees from acquisition-related layoffs might consider rules that would give such employees various procedural and substantive rights in the event of such layoffs, or provide employees and their representatives some say in corporate decisionmaking in general or in plant closings or layoffs in particular, or supplement formal contracts between firms and stakeholders with implied and good faith terms....

Boards are unlikely to be good agents of stakeholders in takeovers, at least under the existing rules for board selection and operation. Support for board veto thus should not be viewed as support for protecting employees and stakeholders but rather as support for enhancing the power of boards and managers relative to shareholders.

The debate over board veto, then, does not confront us with a choice between shareholders and stakeholders, with managers as the champion of the latter. Rather, the choice is between shareholders and managers, with stakeholders as bystanders. This is what is at stake in the board veto debate.

E. Implementation within Existing Case Law

… Delaware law on takeover defenses, which the law of many other states follows, has established principles that allow boards to adopt and maintain poison pills. This law, however, also includes principles requiring a proportionate use of defensive measures and attaching much importance to the shareholder franchise as a safety valve against potential abuse of poison pills. The considerations identified by my analysis can usefully inform and guide the implementation and development of these principles. In particular, the analysis leads me to propose that, at least in the absence of explicit charter provisions to the contrary, courts should be guided by the following principles in reviewing takeover defenses:

1. Maintaining Pills to Prevent a Takeover Unsupported by a Vote

Subject to the conditions below concerning access to and consequences of shareholder voting, the board should be permitted to maintain a poison pill in the face of a takeover bid even if the bid is "structurally non-coercive."

2. Access to a Vote

After a bid is made and a period reasonably sufficient for the board's exploring and preparing alternatives for shareholder consideration passes, maintaining a pill would be consistent with fiduciary duties and thus permissible only if, within a period as short as reasonably practical, either: (a) shareholders would have or would be given an opportunity to vote (whether in a regularly scheduled meeting, a special meeting, or through written consents) to replace some or all of the directors; or (b) shareholders would have (by the terms of the rights plan) or would be given by the board an opportunity to vote to have the pill redeemed.

3. Redemption of Pills Following Electoral Defeat

When directors of a company with a staggered board lose one election fought over an acquisition offer, they should not be permitted (absent compelling corporate justification) to continue maintaining a pill.

Furthermore, dead-hand pills, delayed-redemption pills, or any other pill terms that, in the aftermath of electoral defeat by incumbents, make it impossible, costly, or difficult to redeem the pills should be prohibited.

4. Protecting the Shareholder Franchise

In the face of an unsolicited takeover bid, the highest level of judicial scrutiny should be applied to any board decisions that might frustrate or distort the outcome of shareholder votes that would have an effect on the fate of the offer. Specifically, boards should not be permitted (absent compelling corporate justification) to adopt defensive bylaws that either:

(a) impose supermajority requirements on the adoption of shareholder bylaws; or (b) reverse shareholder bylaws.

Some of the above proposals are quite close to existing case law, whereas others might require some limited change of course. But they are all ones that would be consistent with, and indeed advance, the existing principles that defenses be proportionate to the threat posed and that the shareholder franchise be well protected. They all also would move arrangements toward a regime of shareholder voting and no board veto. They all would thus operate to enhance shareholder value and to improve the allocation of corporate assets.

III. Conclusion

Supporters of board veto in corporate takeovers have long argued, with much influence on legislators and courts, that boards should have substantial power to block acquisition offers. This Article has attempted to analyze the full array of arguments that supporters of board veto have marshaled in its defense. Examining all of these arguments both at the level of theory and in light of the substantial body of evidence that has accumulated, I have concluded that board veto is undesirable. This conclusion is reached when the subject is analyzed from either the perspective of target shareholders or from any of the other normative perspectives that have been invoked by supporters of board veto. Once mechanisms to ensure undistorted shareholder choice are in place, boards should not be permitted to block offers beyond the period necessary for putting together alternatives for shareholder consideration. All those with interest in corporate governance — be they public officials, investors, or students of the subject — should recognize the substantial costs and limited benefits of board veto.

IV. Appendix: The Takeover of Willamette

In a response to this Article, Martin Lipton vigorously defends his views in favor of board veto. Lipton forcefully puts forward his concerns that shareholders not be in any way pressured to accept takeover bids, however high the premium they offer, and that tender decisions might not reflect well shareholders' preferences. As I explained, I share these concerns, which have led me to support a regime of shareholder voting.

Lipton continues to maintain, however, that shareholder voting is not sufficient and that board veto is desirable. He cautions against a regime of shareholder voting and no board veto by arguing that, whatever the merits of such a regime, it would constitute a "radical change." As I explained in this Article, however, there are different ways of obtaining a regime of shareholder voting and no board veto. Some ways would indeed require a major legislative change to establish a referendum. However, such a regime could also be largely implemented by a limited adjustment of the existing jurisprudence.

Putting aside the question of whether moves to limit board veto would constitute a radical change, Lipton maintains that such moves would be detrimental to shareholders. Most of the reasons he gives for his position are ones that he has raised in his earlier work and that my analysis in this Article already addresses in detail. Below I therefore focus on some new claims that Lipton makes in his response in connection with the recent takeover of Willamette, where incumbents stalled the bid for fourteen months. He argues that (a) the stalling in Willamette illustrates well how board veto delivers substantial value for shareholders, and that (b) in any event, such stalling raises at most a theoretical concern.

Below I argue (a) that the takeover of Willamette does not lend support to the case for board veto, and (b) that prohibiting a Willamette-type stalling would provide valuable and practically significant benefits.

A. Did Willamette's Incumbents Deliver Value for Shareholders?

My analysis has stressed the costs produced by staggered boards, which are present in about half of publicly traded companies and provide an important source of board veto. Lipton responds by offering a detailed discussion of the takeover of Willamette and inferring from it that the veto power produced by staggered boards is actually beneficial for shareholders.

The Willamette saga lasted fourteen months. In November 2000, Weyerhaeuser made an offer of $48 per share for Willamette. Weyerhaeuser raised its offer to $50 per share in May 2001 prior to conducting a proxy contest. Weyerhaeuser won this contest in June 2001, replacing a third of Willamette's board. Protected by the staggered board, however, incumbents continued to oppose the bid. In January 2002, Weyerhaeuser raised again the offered price to $55 per share and attracted 64 percent of the shares to its offer. Later that month, after encountering substantial shareholder resistance to an alternative deal with Georgia-Pacific, Willamette's incumbents agreed to be acquired by Weyerhaeuser for $55.50 per share, which was 16 percent higher than the initial $48 per share bid. Lipton suggests that this case offers a good illustration of how a staggered board delivers value for shareholders. He argues that the case is "no less than a shining example of how a staggered board and a poison pill operate to the benefit of shareholders" and that arguments against the staggered board-poison pill combination "evaporated" following the stellar success of the board in this case.

.... [However,] there is no reason to believe that a 16 percent increase from the $48 initial price required stalling for fourteen months. A bidder's initial offer is generally understood not to represent the final price that it would be willing to pay to acquire the target. Bidders generally keep something off the table for final negotiations, and they are generally willing to offer somewhat more than the initial bid to get the deal done. Such increases can be and often are obtained without the need for massive delay and a staggered board.

.... [D]espite the strong signals that investors wanted to have discussions with the hostile bidder, Willamette's incumbents kept refusing to enter such discussions, saying that "Willamette is not for sale".... Only in October 2001, eleven months after the initial bid, and two months after being defeated in a proxy contest that enabled Weyerhaeuser to replace one-third of the board, did Willamette express willingness to sit down with Weyerhaeuser to explore how much it would be willing to raise its bid. However, Willamette subsequently terminated the brief discussion it held with Weyerhaeuser. Willamette tried to advance instead a controversial deal with Georgia-Pacific—even after Weyerhaeuser raised its offer to $55 per share—but encountered strong resistance from shareholders who tendered en masse into Weyerhaeuser's offer. Willamette then agreed to sell for $55.50 per share.

It is far from clear that the above tale is a story of a board pursuing a bargaining strategy aimed at getting top dollar for shareholders. If bargaining for a higher price was the goal of the board, why did the board for eleven months not even explore with Weyerhaeuser whether it would be willing to raise its price by at least 15 percent in order to get the deal done? The facts appear to be at least consistent with a story of management seeking to remain independent, and to avoid a sale to Weyerhaeuser altogether, and agreeing to be acquired by Weyerhaeuser only under massive pressure from shareholders. Indeed, some observers have noted that a factor in Willamette's resistance to a sale to Weyerhaeuser was animosity on the part of Willamette's incumbents toward Weyerhaeuser's CEO, who previously had been an executive of Willamette.

... I wish to stress the limits to how much one can learn from an example, which might or might not represent the population from which it is drawn. Rather than look at any particular example, it would be better to focus on more systematic evidence whenever possible. The staggered boards study by Coates, Subramanian, and myself, discussed in the Article, provides such evidence for hostile bids during 1996–2000. And this study indicates that, overall, staggered boards did not operate in that period to the benefit of target shareholders.

B. Should Willamette-Type Stalling Be Permitted?

... Incumbents in a target with a staggered board like Willamette, I have argued, should not be permitted to keep blocking an offer after losing one election for a class of directors conducted over an acquisition offer. Lipton responds that, even if continued resistance after one electoral defeat were likely undesirable (which he does not accept), it would not present a concern of significance. This issue is "largely theoretical," Lipton suggests, because "in very few instances has a target with a staggered board suffered a first-round loss—had a third of the board replaced with the raider's nominees—and continued to refuse to surrender its independence." Therefore, on Lipton's view, this issue "does not in any way warrant a change in basic corporate law."

However, ... [w]hen incumbents are protected by a staggered board and have the power to keep resisting after losing one election, this power would affect outcomes not only when it is actually exercised but also when it discourages bidders from continuing to pursue the target at earlier stages of the game. Without an effective staggered board, an electoral victory guarantees that the bidder will succeed in taking over the target. When a staggered board is in place, such a victory does not assure success. Thus, when a bidder finds that incumbents are strongly opposed to a takeover, the presence of [a staggered board] might lead the bidder to withdraw without attempting to run in any election....

The proposed approach—precluding incumbents who lose one election from maintaining pills—would take away from pills the special antitakeover power that they have in the presence of a staggered board. Given that about half of public companies now have staggered boards, a development with profound effects on the market for corporate control, this approach would not address an issue that is merely theoretical. Rather, it would substantially reduce boards' ability to block offers and would restore the safety valve of an effective shareholder vote in firms with staggered boards....

Martin Lipton, *Pills, Polls, and Professors Redux**

... September of this year will mark the twentieth anniversary of the publication of my memorandum recommending that companies adopt the poison pill, which I invented in the summer of 1982 to deal with the takeover abuses that emerged in the 1970s and had become endemic by the end of the decade. The pill prevents a hostile tender offer from

* Originally published in 69 UNIVERSITY OF CHICAGO LAW REVIEW 1037 (2002). Reprinted with permission.

being consummated unless and until the board of directors of the target redeems the pill. The pill does not prevent a proxy fight to remove and replace a board of directors that refuses to redeem the pill. It was and is a fundamental aspect of the pill that a proxy fight is the only way in which a raider can override a well-founded decision of the board to reject and block a takeover bid. Now Professor Lucian Bebchuk urges, in his brilliantly presented Article, that basic state corporation law be changed to allow a raider to demand a shareholder referendum whenever a board refuses to redeem a pill. This proposal is one of several that have been advanced over the years to deny the board of a target the ability to craft a strategy to protect corporate interests in the context of a hostile takeover bid....

This Commentary discusses the development of the law—primarily Delaware law—governing takeovers, and against that background, rebuts Professor Bebchuk's referendum proposal. In a way, this Commentary is the culmination of my efforts over a twenty-year period in courts, legislatures, and academic publications to counter those who would hang a permanent "For Sale" sign on all public companies. I have sought to preserve the ability of the board of directors of a target of a hostile takeover bid to control the target's destiny and, on a properly informed basis, to conclude that the corporation remain independent. I have never been able to understand the persistent refusal of those academics who would hang a "For Sale" sign on public corporations to recognize: (i) that there are very significant costs to corporations in being managed as if they are continuously for sale; and (ii) that there is simply no evidence at all that the damage, if any, that the anti-pill academics attribute to the pill is greater than those costs.

Prior to the 1960s, there was little academic discussion or judicial or legislative focus on the legal rules that should apply to the response by a corporation to a takeover bid. With the increase in takeover activity in the 1970s, the topic became a growing concern for lawyers who advised target corporations, but there was neither direct, cogent case law nor meaningful academic debate. From the outset, it was clear that there were three constituencies with prime interests in any rule-shaping debate: (i) the shareholders, (ii) the corporation as an operating entity, and (iii) the employees and other stakeholders. Within each group, there were gradations of interests, and the groups and interests overlapped and sometimes collided. In this period, the role of the board of directors and the grounds on which it was to act in responding to a hostile takeover bid were nebulous and had yet to be definitively determined.

In an effort to distill clarity from this confusion, in 1979 I wrote what became the seminal article in the ensuing debate. In *Takeover Bids in the Target's Boardroom*,[31] I argued, based on my experience during the 1960s and 1970s in advising boards of directors of corporations that were the targets of hostile takeover bids, that the directors should be governed by the business judgment rule and that in exercising their judgment they should be able to take into account the interests of employees, communities, and other constituents, as well as the long-term (and not just the short-term) interests of the shareholders.

This position was quickly rejected by academics opposed to an active board role in the hostile takeover context, who argued for the so-called "Rule of Passivity," relegating directors to the role of passive observers proscribed from any action other than giving advice to the shareholders.[32] A classic series of articles ensued, with the courts deciding the debate in favor of the business judgment rule. This exchange of articles reflected a fierce public policy debate. The new breed of hostile bids was, on the one hand, wreaking havoc with expectations of managers, employees, and communities, and, on the other,

---

31. Martin Lipton, *Takeover Bids in the Target's Boardroom*, 35 Bus. Law. 101, 130 (1979).
32. *See, for example, the article by Easterbrook & Fischel cited above.—Ed.*

enriching the raiders and a new class on Wall Street: the bankers who advised, financed, or arbitraged takeovers. The pro-takeover forces found theoretical support for their position among a group of economists who adhered to the efficient market theory, which was argued to offer support for the proposition that shareholder wealth could be maximized by outlawing most forms of takeover defenses. Starting from the premise that share prices at all times accurately reflect the intrinsic value of a corporation, efficient market theory partisans contended that the willingness of a bidder to offer a premium price reflects the bidder's ability to manage the assets better or more efficiently. At the same time, they contended that board reluctance to accept a premium price necessarily reflects an instinct of self-preservation rather than conviction that the tender price is inadequate. Defenses, in this view, serve only to entrench incumbents and necessarily to harm shareholders.

The opponents of the efficient market theory pointed out that corporations were not chartered by the states solely to maximize shareholders' short-term gains, and that large corporations could not function in an environment where they were continuously "for sale." The aggregate costs to all shareholders of all public companies, if they had to operate on this basis, would far exceed the costs, if any, in the long-run to the shareholders of companies that successfully resist unsolicited takeovers. Those who did not accept the relevance of the efficient market theory to the regulation of takeovers also pointed out, drawing on a growing body of economic literature, that inefficiencies in the market could exist at any given point in time, meaning that share prices did not always reflect intrinsic values.

Those in favor of takeover defenses further argued that a central assumption of efficient market theory proponents—that shareholder responses to tender offers are necessarily informed decisions that rationally reflect the supposed "best" interests of all shareholders collectively—is not true. Tender offers are not the functional equivalents of free votes, since the decision not to tender (whether into an all-cash, all-shares offer or a two-tier, front-end-loaded offer) carries with it economic risks and detriments; not knowing whether the mass of other shareholders will tender or not, the individual holder faces the classic "prisoner's dilemma" and is effectively stampeded into tendering. The proponents of takeover defenses also observed that many hostile bids were opportunistic attempts to buy assets on the cheap, and that there was no empirical evidence that such takeovers were always (or ever) good for the economy. Moreover, the view that directors were only capable of acting in their self-interest was unsupported by empirical evidence and inconsistent with the assumptions underlying the structure of American corporate law.

State legislatures around the country resolved this debate squarely in favor of directorial discretion. Between 1968 and 1982, laws designed to slow or halt the wave of opportunistic takeover activity were enacted in thirty-seven states. Thus, by the early 1980s, both the legislatures and the courts had emphatically rejected the view that directors should be passive in the face of takeover bids. But in 1982, by a razor-thin margin, the United States Supreme Court invalidated the "first generation" of antitakeover statutes in *Edgar v. MITE Corp.*[33] Now there was nothing to delay the consummation of a tender offer beyond the Williams Act's twenty business days. Increasingly, boards turned to creative attempts to release short-term value by selling pieces of the business or turning to a "white knight," but these alternative transactions were often difficult to achieve on the truncated timeline of the Williams Act minimum tender period.

The *MITE* decision coincided with the decision of most institutional investors that they would not vote for charter amendments designed to deter or regulate hostile

---

33. 457 U.S. 624, 632–34 (1982) (plurality).

takeovers and with the federal courts picking up on an earlier decision by Judge Henry Friendly in which he treated with great skepticism suits brought by targets raising antitrust, disclosure, and similar claims to enjoin hostile bids. This left the playing field heavily tipped in favor of the corporate raiders and peddlers of junk bonds. In September 1982, I published a memorandum describing the "Warrant Dividend Plan." The "warrant" of the Warrant Dividend Plan was a security that could be issued by the board of directors of a target company (before or after it was faced with an unsolicited bid) that would have the effect of increasing the time available to the board to react to an unsolicited bid and allowing the board to maintain control over the process of responding to the bid. Beginning at the end of 1982, in various forms it was used successfully by targets of hostile bids to gain time and maximize shareholder value. Six months later, in 1983, the plan was given its unfortunate nickname by an investment banker who had nothing to do with its creation. When asked by a *Wall Street Journal* reporter what to call a security—modeled on the Warrant Dividend Plan—issued on my advice by Lenox, Inc. to defend against a hostile tender offer, this banker responded flippantly, "a poison pill."

By whatever name, the pill's arrival was remarkably timely. As the tide of junk-bond-financed, bootstrap bids, sometimes linked to two-tier, front-end-loaded tenders, rolled on in the mid-1980s, there was increasing recognition that something was needed to redress the balance between the corporate raider and the board of the target. The pill met precisely that need. Nevertheless, those who believed that directors should play no active role in the hostile takeover context viewed the introduction of the pill as a radical innovation, and the attacks on the pill's validity were unrelenting.

The increasing use of the pill in 1984–85 set the stage for a decisive confrontation between the forces advocating a free hand for corporate raiders and those supporting the traditional model of the corporation and the business judgment rule. The question remained: Who would act as the decisionmaker? At the federal level, Congress had shown no interest in adopting a statutory framework for regulating takeovers beyond the Williams Act; and by 1983 the federal impulse for further regulation, even at the SEC level, had petered out. The United States Supreme Court in *Santa Fe Industries, Inc. v. Green*[34] had extinguished the ability of federal judges to federalize substantive takeover law through the securities laws. On the other hand, the Court's opinion in *MITE* had limited the ability of state legislatures to impose their own statutory regulation in the area. Meanwhile, increasing corporate reliance on defensive tactics—and the increasingly shrill objections of their opponents—created a pressing practical need for dependable legal ground rules. The state courts were left as the only institutional actors with the power and will to fashion a comprehensive resolution.

In 1985, the Delaware Supreme Court decided four cases—*Smith v. Van Gorkom*,[35] *Unocal Corp. v. Mesa Petroleum Co., Revlon, Inc. v. MacAndrews & Forbes Holdings*,[36] and *Moran v. Household International, Inc.*—that created the framework that has governed takeover law ever since. The key choices Delaware made in 1985 were the following:

(1) In *Van Gorkom*, Delaware decisively rejected the efficient market theory and not only permitted, but required, directors to make takeover-related decisions based on an informed view of the "intrinsic" value of the corporation—not the value assigned by the stock market.

---

34. 430 U.S. 462 (1977).
35. 488 A.2d 858 (Del. 1985).
36. 506 A.2d 173 (Del. 1986).

(2) In *Unocal*, citing with approval a later version of my 1979 article, *Takeover Bids in the Target's Boardroom*, Delaware accepted the utility and appropriateness of "takeover defenses" and the board of directors' discretion to deploy such defenses, but announced that henceforth they would be reviewed under an enhanced business judgment rule—a tougher and objective "reasonable in relation to the threat posed" test, rather than the preexisting subjective business judgment rule.

(3) In *Revlon*, Delaware required directors to maximize short term value once they decided to sell a company for cash; and conversely, Delaware decided that it would not require directors to maximize short-term value outside this one, relatively narrow situation. Delaware companies were not required to be for sale twenty-four hours a day, seven days a week, and directors could agree to friendly stock mergers without putting the company "in play" or having to "auction" the company.

(4) In *Household*, Delaware permitted boards to adopt the poison pill as a structural defense to a takeover bid. *Household* recognized that the pill gave boards the power to "just say no" until such time as the shareholders (if they so wished) replaced the incumbent directors, and established that judicial review of a board's use of the poison pill would be subject to the enhanced business judgment rule standard of *Unocal*.

Clearly, these four crucial decisions represented a set of compromises. Delaware accepted neither the pleas of corporate constituencies for continued application of the deferential business judgment rule to takeover defense, nor endorsed the demands of corporate raiders and academics who sought to outlaw takeover defense. Instead, Delaware chose a middle ground: Takeover defenses were permitted, but they were to be judged, in common law fashion, under a fact-intensive, case-by-case analysis in which the directors would effectively bear the burden of showing not only their good faith, but also the "reasonableness" of their chosen response.

Put to the practical test during the half-decade of intense hostile takeover activity that ensued, the new Delaware paradigm has worked well. Contrary to the fears of both sides, *Unocal* and its siblings did not usher in a period in which every takeover defense was either condemned automatically or rubber-stamped. A review of some of the major cases of that period demonstrates the suppleness of the standard and the discriminating manner in which it was applied.

Of the quartet of 1985 decisions, the one that proved to have the greatest practical impact was undoubtedly *Household*. The pill changed everything. Instead of twenty business days under the Williams Act, boards now had sufficient time to consider, respond to, and craft alternatives to unsolicited bids. And, contrary to the arguments of the plaintiffs in *Household*, the pill actually revived the importance of proxy contests as a means of determining a corporation's future. Indeed, the Delaware courts rarely receive the credit they deserve for having been right in rejecting the supposed factual, empirical arguments made by the pill's opponents in *Household* as to the predicted effect of the pill on proxy contests. Professors and experts were paraded in the Court of Chancery to testify, among other things, that validation of the pill in Delaware would suppress proxy contests. Both the Court of Chancery and the Delaware Supreme Court refused to let themselves be persuaded by these "experts"—and of course with hindsight we can see that the pill simply did not usher in the parade of horribles predicted by its opponents. As the Chancery Court correctly predicted, the pill did not spell the doom of proxy contests. A recent review of the economic literature on the shareholder-wealth effects of takeover defenses was undertaken by Professor John Coates. He concluded:

Delaware courts should take some comfort from the fact that they resisted strong academic arguments and political efforts that attempted to push them to dramatically repudiate pills and other structural defenses. The empirical case against defenses remains unproven, and, without empirical support, the theoretical case against defenses is not as compelling as it might have seemed to hostile commentators [in 1989].[37]

The new rules crafted by the Delaware courts in the four 1985 decisions met with wide acceptance. Corporate raiders did not abandon the market for corporate control; corporations did not seek to reincorporate out of Delaware in order to avoid the new regime; and litigators increasingly chose the Delaware state forum over federal and non-Delaware state courts when there was a need for adjudication. Interestingly, the pill even became a standard feature in initial public offering charters, a context in which management entrenchment is virtually absent.

But the 1985 Delaware rules were controversial enough—and perceived as insufficiently sensitive to the realities of corporate life—to provoke a legislative reaction in other states. It is a signal fact that, despite Delaware's primacy as a corporate domicile and despite some academic criticism of Delaware as too protective of management, the Delaware regime has not been broadly embraced by the other states. Instead, a number of states enacted legislation that to a greater or lesser extent rejected the Delaware compromise as too favorable to corporate raiders and hostile bids, too suspicious of the motives of directors, and too unresponsive to the legitimate interests of nonshareholder constituencies such as employees and communities. No American jurisdiction went further than Delaware and adopted rules, either by statute or judge-made law, that restrict takeover defenses more tightly than Delaware. No American jurisdiction has ever adopted a framework for takeover law based on the efficient market theory or gone farther than Delaware in that direction.

If anything, after 1985 there was a growing realization that the extreme simplicity of the world view of the anti-board partisans—that there was no place for any interference with the presumed "right" of shareholders to sell the company at any time to a bidder opposed by the board, and that directors should therefore be "passive instrumentalities"—was neither an accurate description of reality nor a desirable goal. Moreover, in 1987, the United States Supreme Court, which in 1982 had rejected states' efforts to regulate takeovers through so-called "first generation" statutes, effectively switched sides and endorsed "second generation" statutes in *CTS Corp. v. Dynamics Corp of America*.[38] The 1987 market "break," and the 1990 collapse of Drexel Burnham Lambert, the most prominent financier of hostile bids in the 1980s, further damaged the prestige and persuasiveness of the efficient market theory.

It is perhaps outside the terms of academic argument, but nonetheless suggestive, to recall the subsequent careers of the bidders whose takeover proposals were opposed by boards in some of the high profile cases of the 1980s. For example, the board of Macmillan, Inc. was harshly criticized by the Delaware courts for opposing Robert Maxwell's 1988 bid for the company. But in light of the revelations of dishonesty, corporate looting, and other wrongdoing that followed Maxwell's presumed suicide in 1991, does the Macmillan board now look quite so unreasonable in preferring a 20 cent per share lower bid from Maxwell's rival Henry Kravis? While the Maxwell and Macmillan transaction is perhaps the most thought-provoking example, is there anything in the subsequent business careers of such

---

37. John C. Coates IV, *Empirical Evidence on Structural Takeover Defense: Where Do We Stand?*, 54 U. MIAMI L. REV. 783 (2000).
38. 481 U.S. 69, 94 (1987).

raider icons of the 1980s as Boone Pickens, Carl Icahn, Paul Bilzerian, and Robert Campeau that suggests that corporate law should have been redesigned to put these people in charge of important enterprises and large pools of assets?

In 1988, Delaware adopted its own "second generation" statute. This enactment is Delaware's only major legislative response to the takeover issue, and clearly represents a further rejection of the efficient market theory. Under Section 203, directors have the statutory power effectively to block potential transfers of control to substantial shareholders by refusing to approve a transaction. While this power is not absolute, it can be overridden only by a very high "supermajority" of [66 ⅔] percent of the shareholders; Section 203 is in effect a statutory pill that can be neutered by a tender offer that attracts [66 ⅔] percent of the shares. Like the 1985 cases, Section 203 is another Delaware compromise, but clearly one that recognizes that directors should have a major role in determining the corporation's fate in a takeover situation.

Events of the 1990s have further demonstrated the wisdom of the Delaware compromise. The coercive, highly leveraged, and often destructive attributes of the 1980s takeover market have faded from view. Secure in their ability to resist hostile bids, directors have used this authority to enhance shareholder value. And directors can use this same power to resist a transaction they reasonably believe to be insufficient or unduly speculative—a power of no mean significance, wielded for the protection of the interests of shareholders and, indeed, every corporate constituency. Confirming the position I first advanced in 1979 in *Takeover Bids in the Target's Boardroom*, the American Law Institute—in its *Principles of Corporate Governance*—endorsed Delaware's takeover jurisprudence as a model for the nation.

In the same vein, it warrants notice that Delaware's two major structural features with respect to takeover law—the poison pill and Section 203—have not given rise to significant case law since the *Household* case. While the *Household* Court announced in 1985 the standard—*Unocal*—under which pill decisions were to be reviewed, there have been only three Delaware Chancery Court decisions requiring a board of directors to redeem a pill, two of which were later disapproved by the Delaware Supreme Court in *[Paramount v. Time]*. The only case in which a board of directors was found to have breached its fiduciary duties in connection with its application of Section 203 involved the improper waiver of the protections of Section 203 by the directors of a majority-owned subsidiary. The absence of such case law strongly suggests that both the pill and Section 203 are being utilized responsibly by Delaware boards and that the system they uphold is a healthy one. After twenty years, I can confidently say that the pill has been used; it has not been abused.

Nevertheless, for reasons that are not supported by history or practice, the academic community and activist investors have not been satisfied with the Delaware solution and the present state of the law. The leading spokesperson for doing away with the pill, Professor Ronald Gilson, argues that shareholders should be permitted to adopt a bylaw that repeals a poison pill previously adopted by the corporation and that prohibits the corporation from adopting a pill in response to a hostile takeover bid.[39] Professor Gilson would go back to the 1979–82 debate and essentially come down on the side of the Rule of Passivity. Without the pill, there is no effective defense against a hostile takeover, and Professor Gilson would doom all targets to being acquired by a raider or a white knight. A full explication of Professor Gilson's thesis and my refutation are available in my response to his article.... [40]

Professor Bebchuk, who in 1982 was an advocate of the Rule of Passivity, modified to permit the target's board to seek a white knight, now accepts the poison pill and

---

39. *See Professor Gilson's article in this chapter.—Ed.*
40. Martin Lipton & Paul K. Rowe, *Pills, Polls, and Professors*, 27 Del. J. Corp. L. 1 (2002).

acknowledges the right of the board of directors to deploy it in defense of a hostile takeover bid. However, he rejects the fundamental premise of Delaware law and the *Household* case that if shareholders are dissatisfied with the directors' response to a takeover bid, their remedy is to vote out the incumbent board and replace it with one that will redeem the pill and sell the corporation to the raider or a white knight. Rather, his solution is to change the law to provide that whenever a corporation becomes the target of a hostile bid, the board must submit it to a shareholder referendum. He proposes that if a majority of the outstanding shares vote in favor of the bid, the board must remove the pill and all other structural takeover defenses.

As originally proposed in 1982, and as approved in the Household decision, the pill contemplated that a board of directors could not ignore the will of the shareholders with respect to a takeover offer. The pill was structured so that it would not interfere with the right of the shareholders to vote to replace the board and would not impede a raider from instituting a proxy fight to replace the board. Professor Bebchuk acknowledges in his current work that the fact that the pill requires hostile bidders to prevail in a proxy contest—what he calls the "critical consequence of the pill"—is indeed desirable. However, he wants the decision in the form of a bidder-initiated referendum on the bid, and not on the composition of the board, and at whatever time a bidder determines.

Professor Bebchuk's central position is that shareholders should have the right to vote to replace some or all of the directors or redeem a poison pill as soon as reasonably practical after a bid is made. Alternatively, he supports the enactment of bylaws that would limit the types of pills that the board may adopt, in order to achieve the same result. In effect, Professor Bebchuk would turn the clock back to Chancellor Allen's decision in *City Capital Associates Ltd. Partnership v. Interco, Inc.*,[41] and then extend the holding in order to remove a staggered board in one election instead of several, or, more directly, to obviate the need for an election at all.

For the past year, proponents of Professor Bebchuk's referendum proposal have been citing the fourteen-month resistance by Willamette to a hostile takeover bid by Weyerhaeuser as an example of abuse of the pill and staggered board combination. Weyerhaeuser's first bid was $48 per share, which it subsequently unilaterally raised to $50 per share prior to commencing a proxy fight. Willamette's position was that Weyerhaeuser was attempting to acquire it at an inadequate price that did not reflect its true value. Willamette continued to resist after shareholders replaced a third of the board with nominees of Weyerhaeuser committed to a sale of the company and after 64 percent of the shares were tendered to the all-cash, all-shares offer. This gave the pill traducers their best argument—that the combination allows a determined board to deny the will of the shareholders not for one year, but for two. However, this argument evaporated after Weyerhaeuser increased its offer from $50 per share to $55 per share and finally to $55.50 per share, which the Willamette board finally accepted as being in the best interests of its shareholders. The Weyerhaeuser-Willamette deal is no less than a shining example of how a staggered board and poison pill operate to the benefit of shareholders. The agreed upon price of $55.50 represents a 16 percent increase over Weyerhaeuser's initial bid, and an 11 percent increase in deal value even after the conclusion of the first proxy fight. Those who would credit shareholder choice for the outcome overlook the fact that in the absence of the staggered board and poison pill, Willamette shareholders would have "chosen" $48 per share before they ever had the opportunity to receive $55.50.

---

41. 551 A.2d 787 (Del. Ch. 1988).

Willamette is typical of the experience of the past twenty years, during which very few companies have remained independent after a tender offer combined with a proxy fight to replace the board. The largely theoretical possibility of continued resistance after loss of a proxy fight that worries Professor Bebchuk and his followers does not in any way warrant a change in basic corporate law, which has long permitted shareholders to enjoy a staggered-board charter that protects against changes in management predicated on short-term events. There are strong policy reasons to assure that management has sufficient time to demonstrate the validity of its strategic plan—indeed, I have argued that this period should be five years, with a referendum on the management's performance and the possibility of a hostile takeover only at the quinquennial election.

There have been a number of instances in which an unsolicited bid has been coupled with a proxy fight to remove the target's board and replace it with a board committed to redeeming the target's pill. In some cases, the target was acquired by the original bidder, and in others, the target sought a white knight and was acquired at a higher price than that offered by the raider that initiated the process. In very few instances has a target with a staggered board suffered a first-round loss—had a third of the board replaced with the raider's nominees—and continued to refuse to surrender its independence. In all other cases, after a first-round loss, or even before, when it became clear that the shareholders would vote to replace a third of the board, the target negotiated a deal. In light of this experience, there does not appear to be any compelling need to change the law to mandate a shareholder referendum whenever a raider demands it.

By contrast, Professor Bebchuk's proposal carries with it significant dangers. As a practical matter, his proposal, like Professor Gilson's and like the 1981 Rule of Passivity proposal, would put a "For Sale" sign on all public corporations. Though the difference between a bid-and-referendum and a bid-and-proxy fight may be seen as one of degree, a referendum would create the critical problem of an open invitation for unsolicited bids. The acquirer would have the assurance of a vote on the bid, with little chance for the target to do anything other than declare an auction. Further, the costs of operating as if it were always for sale would be highly detrimental to a company. In general, a company that becomes the target of an unsolicited takeover bid must institute a series of costly programs to protect its business during the period of uncertainty as to the outcome of the bid. To retain key employees, in the face of the usual rush of headhunters seeking to steal away the best employees, expensive bonus and incentive plans are put in place. To placate concerned customers and suppliers, special price and order concessions are granted. Communities postpone or reconsider incentives to retain facilities or obtain new facilities. The company itself postpones major capital expenditures and new strategic initiatives. Creditors delay commitments and seek protection for outstanding loans. All of this imposes enormous costs on the target, which are not recovered no matter what the outcome of the takeover bid; if the bidder is successful, the bidder and its shareholders bear these costs; if the target remains independent, the target and its shareholders bear them. The poison pill alleviates some, but not all, of these concerns and related costs. To change the law to remove the protections of the pill and not protect the target against these costs is unthinkable....

As the law now stands, when faced with a takeover bid, a board has the duty to determine whether such bid is at a fair price and in the shareholders' best interests. This is not a burden to be taken lightly. Under *Unocal* and *Unitrin v. American General Corp.*,[42] a board of directors may not merely "assert" that the underlying long-term value of the corporation

---

42. 651 A.2d 1361 (Del. 1995).

exceeds the bid on the table; in the two cases in which a "just say no" defense was actually tried in court, the directors were required to show, through detailed presentations and expert testimony, that their position was reasonable and based on appropriate information[43]....

There is simply no reason to take the diametric turn in the law urged by Professor Bebchuk. And even if there were, Professor Bebchuk drastically underestimates the number and complexity of the conditions that would need to be applicable to such a referendum in order to protect the corporation and its shareholders from abusive bids. First, there would have to be assurance that the purpose of the bid is to acquire the target rather than to put it in play to profit from a topping bid. This could be accomplished by requiring that the bid represent a premium over the current market price equal to not less than the average of recent comparable acquisition premiums as set forth in an opinion of a recognized financial advisor. Here there would also be two subsidiary issues: Should the target be able to dispute the premium analysis, and should the referendum be denied to a bidder that has acquired more than 1 percent of the outstanding shares of the target within the twelve months prior to the bid?

Second, the bid could not be overly conditional. Here the principal question is the degree of material adverse change that would warrant the bidder's terminating the bid and walking away. This is a matter that has recently been contested in connection with negotiated takeovers. To protect the target and its shareholders, the adverse change condition would have to be triggered only for truly material, unforeseen events that have a long-term impact and that are company-specific as distinguished from industry-wide or macroeconomic events.

Third, the obviously necessary condition that the bidder obtain regulatory approval raises another difficult issue: How far should the bidder have to go to obtain regulatory approval, and how much time should be allowed for it to do so? Since the bidder initiates a unilateral process that it knows will be very disruptive and costly to the target, the bidder would have to be required to use its best efforts, including agreeing to any divestitures, business restrictions, or expenditures that are necessary to obtain regulatory approval. If it failed to do so, the bidder would be obligated to the target for liquidated damages in an amount equal to a percentage of the offer price sufficient to compensate for the damages caused by the disruption. This could, for example, equal 5 percent of the aggregate bid. If the time period during which regulatory approval is being sought is more than six months, and thereafter the raider fails to get the approval, the liquidated damages could be increased by, say, one percent per month to compensate for the greater damage inflicted on the target by the longer period of disruption from uncertainty as to the future of the target. Even with further compensation, it would be necessary to specify a final expiration date that could not be greater than, say, nine months. A related issue is the limitation on the bidder's ability to negotiate with regulators, who would be aware of the strictures imposed by the statutory referendum procedure.

A fourth set of issues involves the proposed consideration. Where all or part of the bid consideration is cash, the bidder would be required to furnish assurance that it has the cash on hand or a loan commitment from a major financial institution that is not qualified by a material adverse change condition that is different from the material adverse change condition in the bid.

---

43. See Moore v. Wallace, 907 F. Supp. 1545, 1549 (D. Del. 1995) (noting the three day preliminary injunction record and the voluminous record); Amanda Acquisition Corp. v. Universal Foods Corp., 708 F. Supp. 984, 1008–16 (E. D. Wis. 1989).

Where all or part of the bid consideration is securities, the bidder would be required to make the bid through a registered securities dealer. The securities dealer would have "underwriter" liability under Section 11 of the Securities Act and would be expected to perform customary due diligence. Underwriter's liability and due diligence are not perfect safeguards, but they represent the minimum protection that should be afforded to the target's shareholders against the pitfalls of Professor Bebchuk's argument that the market effectively determines the value of the bid to the target's shareholders, who need only compare the prebid share price and the value of the bid. After all, in almost every case, it would be impossible for all the target's shareholders to convert all the securities received in the bid into cash at the price on the day the tender offer is consummated. Moreover, shareholders lack information that careful due diligence might reveal; a year ago, for example, Enron stock providing a 20 percent or better premium would have been considered a "great deal" by the shareholders of most target companies.

Bidders and the banks that finance and advise them will undoubtedly have trouble with these protections for the target and its shareholders. The difficulty of achieving an appropriate balance between the interests of a bidder and those of the target and its shareholders in designing such a bid and referendum structure illustrates that mergers, acquisitions, takeovers, and proxy fights and the legal rules applicable to them are complex, with many interdependent variables. As Professors Marcel Kahan and Edward Rock demonstrate in their current work, the relationship between corporate law and private ordering is highly dynamic, with each change resulting in numerous and often unforeseen responses.[44] That is why, instead of a system of inflexible statutory rules, we have developed a system of negotiation—with the target board and the bidder as the primary negotiating counterparties. It is important to preserve the board's role as the best negotiator on behalf of the shareholders and not leap headlong into a new regime that has the potential to be seriously disruptive to business and the economy. But to be an effective negotiator—and the record shows that, on balance, boards have been—the board needs the fundamental power of any successful negotiator: the ability to "just say no" and walk away. The poison pill provides that power, which is why the pill is legal and why it enables directors to do their job effectively....

Supreme Court of Delaware, *Lyondell Chemical Co. v. Ryan**

BERGER, Justice:

We accepted this interlocutory appeal to consider a claim that directors failed to act in good faith in conducting the sale of their company. The Court of Chancery decided that "unexplained inaction" permits a reasonable inference that the directors may have consciously disregarded their fiduciary duties. The trial court expressed concern about the speed with which the transaction was consummated; the directors' failure to negotiate better terms; and their failure to seek potentially superior deals. But the record establishes that the directors were disinterested and independent; that they were generally aware of the company's value and its prospects; and that they considered the offer, under the time constraints imposed by the buyer, with the assistance of financial and legal advisors. At

---

44. Marcel Kahan & Edward D. Rock, *How I Learned to Stop Worrying and Love the Pill: Adaptive Responses to Takeover Law*, 69 U. CHI. L. REV. 871, 873 (2002).
    * 970 A.2d 235 (Del. 2009).

most, this record creates a triable issue of fact on the question of whether the directors exercised due care. There is no evidence, however, from which to infer that the directors knowingly ignored their responsibilities, thereby breaching their duty of loyalty. Accordingly, the directors are entitled to the entry of summary judgment.

Factual and Procedural Background

Before the merger at issue, Lyondell Chemical Company ("Lyondell") was the third largest independent, publicly traded chemical company in North America. Dan Smith ("Smith") was Lyondell's Chairman and CEO. Lyondell's other ten directors were independent and many were, or had been, CEOs of other large, publicly traded companies. Basell AF ("Basell") is a privately held Luxembourg company owned by Leonard Blavatnik ("Blavatnik") through his ownership of Access Industries. Basell is in the business of polyolefin technology, production and marketing.

In April 2006, Blavatnik told Smith that Basell was interested in acquiring Lyondell. A few months later, Basell sent a letter to Lyondell's board offering $26.50–$28.50 per share. Lyondell determined that the price was inadequate and that it was not interested in selling. During the next year, Lyondell prospered and no potential acquirer expressed interest in the company. In May 2007, an Access affiliate filed a Schedule 13D with the Securities and Exchange Commission disclosing its right to acquire an 8.3% block of Lyondell stock owned by Occidental Petroleum Corporation. The Schedule 13D also disclosed Blavatnik's interest in possible transactions with Lyondell.

In response to the Schedule 13D, the Lyondell board immediately convened a special meeting. The board recognized that the 13D signaled to the market that the company was "in play,"[45] but the directors decided to take a "wait and see" approach. A few days later, Apollo Management, L.P. contacted Smith to suggest a management-led LBO, but Smith rejected that proposal. In late June 2007, Basell announced that it had entered into a $9.6 billion merger agreement with Huntsman Corporation ("Huntsman"), a specialty chemical company. Basell apparently reconsidered, however, after Hexion Specialty Chemicals, Inc. made a topping bid for Huntsman. Faced with competition for Huntsman, Blavatnik returned his attention to Lyondell.

On July 9, 2007, Blavatnik met with Smith to discuss an all-cash deal at $40 per share. Smith responded that $40 was too low, and Blavatnik raised his offer to $44–$45 per share. Smith told Blavatnik that he would present the proposal to the board, but that he thought the board would reject it. Smith advised Blavatnik to give Lyondell his best offer, since Lyondell really was not on the market. The meeting ended at that point, but Blavatnik asked Smith to call him later in the day. When Smith called, Blavatnik offered to pay $48 per share. Under Blavatnik's proposal, Basell would require no financing contingency, but Lyondell would have to agree to a $400 million break-up fee and sign a merger agreement by July 16, 2007.

Smith called a special meeting of the Lyondell board on July 10, 2007 to review and consider Basell's offer. The meeting lasted slightly less than one hour, during which time the board reviewed valuation material that had been prepared by Lyondell management for presentation at the regular board meeting, which was scheduled for the following day. The board also discussed the Basell offer, the status of the Huntsman merger, and the likelihood that another party might be interested in Lyondell. The board instructed Smith to obtain a written offer from Basell and more details about Basell's financing.

---

45. On the day that the 13D was made public, Lyondell's stock went from $33 to $37 per share.

Blavatnik agreed to the board's request, but also made an additional demand. Basell had until July 11 to make a higher bid for Huntsman, so Blavatnik asked Smith to find out whether the Lyondell board would provide a firm indication of interest in his proposal by the end of that day. The Lyondell board met on July 11, again for less than one hour, to consider the Basell proposal and how it compared to the benefits of remaining independent. The board decided that it was interested, authorized the retention of Deutsche Bank Securities, Inc. ("Deutsche Bank") as its financial advisor, and instructed Smith to negotiate with Blavatnik.

Basell then announced that it would not raise its offer for Huntsman, and Huntsman terminated the Basell merger agreement. From July 12–July 15 the parties negotiated the terms of a Lyondell merger agreement; Basell conducted due diligence; Deutsche Bank prepared a "fairness" opinion; and Lyondell conducted its regularly scheduled board meeting. The Lyondell board discussed the Basell proposal again on July 12, and later instructed Smith to try to negotiate better terms. Specifically, the board wanted a higher price, a go-shop provision,[46] and a reduced break-up fee. As the trial court noted, Blavatnik was "incredulous." He had offered his best price, which was a substantial premium, and the deal had to be concluded on his schedule. As a sign of good faith, however, Blavatnik agreed to reduce the break-up fee from $400 million to $385 million.

On July 16, 2007, the board met to consider the Basell merger agreement. Lyondell's management, as well as its financial and legal advisers, presented reports analyzing the merits of the deal. The advisors explained that, notwithstanding the no-shop provision in the merger agreement, Lyondell would be able to consider any superior proposals that might be made because of the "fiduciary out" provision. In addition, Deutsche Bank reviewed valuation models derived from "bullish" and more conservative financial projections. Several of those valuations yielded a range that did not even reach $48 per share, and Deutsche Bank opined that the proposed merger price was fair. Indeed, the bank's managing director described the merger price as "an absolute home run." Deutsche Bank also identified other possible acquirer and explained why it believed no other entity would top Basell's offer. After considering the presentations, the Lyondell board voted to approve the merger and recommend it to the stockholders. At a special stockholders' meeting held on November 20, 2007, the merger was approved by more than 99% of the voted shares.

The first stockholders to litigate this merger filed suit in Texas on July 23, 2007. Walter E. Ryan, Jr., the plaintiff in this action, participated in the Texas litigation and filed suit in Delaware on August 20, 2007. The Texas court denied an application for a preliminary injunction on November 13, 2007, while the defendants in Delaware were briefing their motion for summary judgment. The Court of Chancery issued its opinion on July 29, 2008, denying summary judgment as to the "*Revlon*" and the "deal protection" claims. This Court accepted the Lyondell directors' application for certification of an interlocutory appeal on September 15, 2008.

Discussion

The class action complaint challenging this $13 billion cash merger alleges that the Lyondell directors breached their "fiduciary duties of care, loyalty and candor ... and ... put their personal interests ahead of the interests of the Lyondell shareholders." Specifically,

---

46. A "go-shop" provision allows the seller to seek other buyers for a specified period after the agreement is signed.

the complaint alleges that: 1) the merger price was grossly insufficient; 2) the directors were motivated to approve the merger for their own self-interest;[47] 3) the process by which the merger was negotiated was flawed; 4) the directors agreed to unreasonable deal protection provisions; and 5) the preliminary proxy statement omitted numerous material facts. The trial court rejected all claims except those directed at the process by which the directors sold the company and the deal protection provisions in the merger agreement.

The remaining claims are but two aspects of a single claim, under *Revlon v. MacAndrews & Forbes Holdings, Inc.*,[48] that the directors failed to obtain the best available price in selling the company. As the trial court correctly noted, *Revlon* did not create any new fiduciary duties. It simply held that the "board must perform its fiduciary duties in the service of a specific objective: maximizing the sale price of the enterprise."[49]. The trial court reviewed the record, and found that Ryan might be able to prevail at trial on a claim that the Lyondell directors breached their duty of care. But Lyondell's charter includes an exculpatory provision, pursuant to 8 *Del. C.* § 102(b)(7), protecting the directors from personal liability for breaches of the duty of care. Thus, this case turns on whether any arguable shortcomings on the part of the Lyondell directors also implicate their duty of loyalty, a breach of which is not exculpated. Because the trial court determined that the board was independent and was not motivated by self-interest or ill will, the sole issue is whether the directors are entitled to summary judgment on the claim that they breached their duty of loyalty by failing to act in good faith.

This Court examined "good faith"[50] in two recent decisions. In *In re Walt Disney Co. Deriv. Litig.*,[51] the Court discussed the range of conduct that might be characterized as bad faith, and concluded that bad faith encompasses not only an intent to harm but also intentional dereliction of duty:

> [A]t least three different categories of fiduciary behavior are candidates for the "bad faith" pejorative label. The first category involves so-called "subjective bad faith," that is, fiduciary conduct motivated by an actual intent to do harm.... [S]uch conduct constitutes classic, quintessential bad faith....

> The second category of conduct, which is at the opposite end of the spectrum, involves lack of due care—that is, fiduciary action taken solely by reason of gross negligence and without any malevolent intent.... [W]e address the issue of whether gross negligence (including failure to inform one's self of available material facts), without more, can also constitute bad faith. The answer is clearly no.

> * * *

> That leaves the third category of fiduciary conduct, which falls in between the first two categories.... This third category is what the Chancellor's definition of bad faith—intentional dereliction of duty, a conscious disregard for one's

---

47. The directors' alleged financial interest is the fact that they would receive cash for their stock options.

48. 506 A.2d 173, 182 (Del. 1986).

49. *Malpiede v. Townson*, 780 A.2d 1075, 1083 (Del 2000).

50. Our corporate decisions tend to use the terms "bad faith" and "failure to act in good faith" interchangeably, although in a different context we noted that, "[t]he two concepts—bad faith and conduct not in good faith are not necessarily identical." *25 Massachusetts Avenue Property LLC v. Liberty Property Limited Partnership*, Del. Supr., No. 188, 2008, Order at p.5, (November 25, 2008). For purposes of this appeal, we draw no distinction between the terms.

51. 906 A.2d 27 (Del. 2006). [*Reprinted in this volume.—Ed.*]

responsibilities—is intended to capture. The question is whether such misconduct is properly treated as a non-exculpable, nonindemnifiable violation of the fiduciary duty to act in good faith. In our view, it must be....

The *Disney* decision expressly disavowed any attempt to provide a comprehensive or exclusive definition of "bad faith."

A few months later, in *Stone v. Ritter*,[52] this Court addressed the concept of bad faith in the context of an "oversight" claim. We adopted the standard articulated ten years earlier, in *In re Caremark Int'l Deriv. Litig.*:[53]

> [W]here a claim of directorial liability for corporate loss is predicated upon ignorance of liability creating activities within the corporation ... only a sustained or systematic failure of the board to exercise oversight—such as an utter failure to attempt to assure a reasonable information and reporting system exists—will establish the lack of good faith that is a necessary condition to liability.

The *Stone* Court explained that the *Caremark* standard is fully consistent with the *Disney* definition of bad faith. *Stone* also clarified any possible ambiguity about the directors' mental state, holding that "imposition of liability requires a showing that the directors knew that they were not discharging their fiduciary obligations."

The Court of Chancery recognized these legal principles, but it denied summary judgment in order to obtain a more complete record before deciding whether the directors had acted in bad faith. Under other circumstances, deferring a decision to expand the record would be appropriate. Here, however, the trial court reviewed the existing record under a mistaken view of the applicable law. Three factors contributed to that mistake. First, the trial court imposed *Revlon* duties on the Lyondell directors before they either had decided to sell, or before the sale had become inevitable. Second, the court read *Revlon* and its progeny as creating a set of requirements that must be satisfied during the sale process. Third, the trial court equated an arguably imperfect attempt to carry out *Revlon* duties with a knowing disregard of one's duties that constitutes bad faith.

Summary judgment may be granted if there are no material issues of fact in dispute and the moving party is entitled to judgment as a matter of law. The facts, and all reasonable inferences, must be considered in the light most favorable to the nonmoving party. The Court of Chancery identified several undisputed facts that would support the entry of judgment in favor of the Lyondell directors: the directors were "active, sophisticated, and generally aware of the value of the Company and the conditions of the markets in which the Company operated." They had reason to believe that no other bidders would emerge, given the price Basell had offered and the limited universe of companies that might be interested in acquiring Lyondell's unique assets. Smith negotiated the price up from $40 to $48 per share—a price that Deutsche Bank opined was fair. Finally, no other acquirer expressed interest during the four months between the merger announcement and the stockholder vote.

Other facts, however, led the trial court to "question the adequacy of the Board's knowledge and efforts...." After the Schedule 13D was filed in May, the directors apparently took no action to prepare for a possible acquisition proposal. The merger was negotiated and finalized in less than one week, during which time the directors met for a total of only seven hours to consider the matter. The directors did not seriously press Blavatnik for a better price, nor did they conduct even a limited market check. Moreover, although

---

52. 911 A.2d 362 (Del. 2006).
53. 698 A.2d 959, 971 (Del. Ch. 1996).

the deal protections were not unusual or preclusive, the trial court was troubled by "the Board's decision to grant considerable protection to a deal that may not have been adequately vetted under *Revlon*."

The trial court found the directors' failure to act during the two months after the filing of the Basell Schedule 13D critical to its analysis of their good faith. The court pointedly referred to the directors' "two months of slothful indifference despite *knowing* that the Company was in play," and the fact that they "languidly awaited overtures from potential suitors...." In the end, the trial court found that it was this "failing" that warranted denial of their motion for summary judgment:

> [T]he Opinion clearly questions whether the Defendants "engaged" in the sale process.... This is where the 13D filing in May 2007 and the subsequent two months of (apparent) Board inactivity become critical.... [T]he Directors made *no apparent effort* to arm themselves with *specific knowledge* about the present value of the Company in the May through July 2007 time period, despite *admittedly knowing* that the 13D filing..effectively put the Company "in play," and, therefore, presumably, also knowing that an offer for the sale of the Company could occur at any time. It is these facts that raise the specter of "bad faith" in the present summary judgment record ...

The problem with the trial court's analysis is that *Revlon* duties do not arise simply because a company is "in play."[54] The duty to seek the best available price applies only when a company embarks on a transaction—on its own initiative or in response to an unsolicited offer—that will result in a change of control. Basell's Schedule 13D did put the Lyondell directors, and the market in general, on notice that Basell was interested in acquiring Lyondell. The directors responded by promptly holding a special meeting to consider whether Lyondell should take any action. The directors decided that they would neither put the company up for sale nor institute defensive measures to fend off a possible hostile offer. Instead, they decided to take a "wait and see" approach. That decision was an entirely appropriate exercise of the directors' business judgment. The time for action under *Revlon* did not begin until July 10, 2007, when the directors began negotiating the sale of Lyondell.

The Court of Chancery focused on the directors' two months of inaction, when it should have focused on the one week during which they considered Basell's offer. During that one week, the directors met several times; their CEO tried to negotiate better terms; they evaluated Lyondell's value, the price offered and the likelihood of obtaining a better price; and then the directors approved the merger. The trial court acknowledged that the directors' conduct during those seven days might not demonstrate anything more than lack of due care. But the court remained skeptical about the directors' good faith—at least on the present record. That lingering concern was based on the trial court's synthesis of the *Revlon* line of cases, which led it to the erroneous conclusion that directors must follow one of several courses of action to satisfy their *Revlon* duties.

There is only one *Revlon* duty—to "[get] the best price for the stockholders at a sale of the company." No court can tell directors exactly how to accomplish that goal, because they will be facing a unique combination of circumstances, many of which will be outside their control. As we noted in *Barkan v. Amsted Industries, Inc.*, "there is no single blueprint that a board must follow to fulfill its duties.[55] That said, our courts have highlighted both

54. *Paramount Communications, Inc. v. Time, Inc.*, 571 A.2d 1140, 1151 (Del. 1989).
55. 567 A.2d 1279, 1286 (Del. 1989).

the positive and negative aspects of various boards' conduct under *Revlon*.[56] The trial court drew several principles from those cases: directors must "engage actively in the sale process," and they must confirm that they have obtained the best available price either by conducting an auction, by conducting a market check, or by demonstrating "an impeccable knowledge of the market."

The Lyondell directors did not conduct an auction or a market check, and they did not satisfy the trial court that they had the "impeccable" market knowledge that the court believed was necessary to excuse their failure to pursue one of the first two alternatives. As a result, the Court of Chancery was unable to conclude that the directors had met their burden under *Revlon*. In evaluating the totality of the circumstances, even on this limited record, we would be inclined to hold otherwise. But we would not question the trial court's decision to seek additional evidence if the issue were whether the directors had exercised due care. Where, as here, the issue is whether the directors failed to act in good faith, the analysis is very different, and the existing record mandates the entry of judgment in favor of the directors.

As discussed above, bad faith will be found if a "fiduciary intentionally fails to act in the face of a known duty to act, demonstrating a conscious disregard for his duties."[57] The trial court decided that the *Revlon* sale process must follow one of three courses, and that the Lyondell directors did not discharge that "known set of [*Revlon*] 'duties.'" But, as noted, there are no legally prescribed steps that directors must follow to satisfy their *Revlon* duties. Thus, the directors' failure to take any specific steps during the sale process could not have demonstrated a conscious disregard of their duties. More importantly, there is a vast difference between an inadequate or flawed effort to carry out fiduciary duties and a conscious disregard for those duties.

Directors' decisions must be reasonable, not perfect.[58] "In the transactional context, [an] extreme set of facts [is] required to sustain a disloyalty claim premised on the notion that disinterested directors were intentionally disregarding their duties."[59] The trial court denied summary judgment because the Lyondell directors' "unexplained inaction" prevented the court from determining that they had acted in good faith. But, if the directors failed to do all that they should have under the circumstances, they breached their duty of care. Only if they knowingly and completely failed to undertake their responsibilities would they breach their duty of loyalty. The trial court approached the record from the wrong perspective. Instead of questioning whether disinterested, independent directors did everything that they (arguably) should have done to obtain the best sale price, the inquiry should have been whether those directors utterly failed to attempt to obtain the best sale price.[60]

Viewing the record in this manner leads to only one possible conclusion. The Lyondell directors met several times to consider Basell's premium offer. They were generally aware of the value of their company and they knew the chemical company market. The directors

---

56. *See, e.g.: Barkan v Amsted Industries, Inc.*, 567 A.2d at 1287 (Directors need not conduct a market check if they have reliable basis for belief that price offered is best possible.); *Paramount Communications, Inc. v. QVC Network, Inc.*, 637 A.2d 34,49 (Del. 1994) (No-shop provision impermissibly interfered with directors' ability to negotiate with another known bidder); *In re Netsmart Technologies, Inc., Shareholders Litig.*, 924 A.2d 171, 199 (Del. Ch. 2007) (Plaintiff likely to succeed on claim based on board's failure to consider strategic buyers.)

57. *Disney* at 67.

58. *Paramount Communications, Inc. v. QVC Network, Inc.*, 637 A.2d at 45.

59. *In re Lear Corp. S'holder Litig.*, 967 A.2d 640 ... (Del. Ch. [2008]).

60. *See Stone* at 369.

solicited and followed the advice of their financial and legal advisors. They attempted to negotiate a higher offer even though all the evidence indicates that Basell had offered a "blowout" price. Finally, they approved the merger agreement, because "it was simply too good not to pass along [to the stockholders] for their consideration." We assume, as we must on summary judgment, that the Lyondell directors did absolutely nothing to prepare for Basell's offer, and that they did not even consider conducting a market check before agreeing to the merger. Even so, this record clearly establishes that the Lyondell directors did not breach their duty of loyalty by failing to act in good faith. In concluding otherwise, the Court of Chancery reversibly erred.

Conclusion

Based on the foregoing, the decision of the Court of Chancery is reversed and this matter is remanded for entry of judgment in favor of the Lyondell directors. Jurisdiction is not retained.

Discussion Questions

1. Henry Butler and Fred McChesney's article in Chapter 1 argued that corporate philanthropy constitutes a routine example of a potential management conflict of interest, not a special case. Takeovers, however, are almost uniformly considered to be a special case. Why?

Can directors make the best decisions for shareholders when the directors' self-interest may affect their judgment? Is judicial review of those decisions an appropriate safeguard? What other devices could monitor directors in this context?

What might Blair and Stout's team production theory say about the choice between board veto and shareholder control? Reconsider, in the takeover context, the following question from Chapter 2: Are directors "referees" or members of the corporate "team"? If they are team members, shouldn't their interests be one factor to be weighed in making decisions that maximize the joint team product? If they are neutral referees, what gives them incentive to maximize the team product?

2. Like many commentators, Gilson does not trust courts to conduct substantive review of takeover defenses. He praises the rule developed by the Delaware Court of Chancery in the *Interco* line of cases. Do you agree with that rule? How does it differ from "substantive" review?

3. Gilson asks: "How can the Delaware Supreme Court ameliorate the electoral bias created in *Unitrin* without simply reversing fifteen years of common law development?" He suggests allowing shareholders to redeem or revise poison pills through binding bylaw amendments. Are shareholder-adopted bylaws an appropriate device in this context? Should shareholder-adopted bylaws be allowed in other areas of corporate decisionmaking? If not, what limits should be placed on shareholder bylaws, and how could such limits be imposed? See the articles by Coffee, Gordon, and Hamermesh cited in Gilson's article.

Is the problem of entrenched case law that Gilson identifies mitigated (as Rock suggests) when judges employ more flexible judicial "standards" instead of specific rules? What are the pros and cons of using case law to make rules regarding complex new transactional devices like poison pills? See Edward Rock's article in Chapter 3.

4. With respect to *Mentor Graphics*, Gilson praises the court's "impulse to lecture," but warns that lecturing without articulating rules "operates to encourage attorneys to push the envelope precisely because there is no principle guiding the outcome." Compare and contrast this view with Rock's model of judicial "preaching."

5. Lipton argues that in bargaining with an acquirer, management must hold the ultimate say over whether the corporation accepts or rejects a takeover bid in order to represent shareholders effectively. Bebchuk argues that management can bargain just as effectively if shareholders hold the ultimate say. With whom do you agree? Is directors' representation of shareholders analogous to lawyers representing clients, as Bebchuk argues?

6. Bebchuk's proposal raises important questions, which he has addressed elsewhere: Should the proposed voting rule be imposed at the state or local level? *See Federalism and the Corporation: The Desirable Limits on State Competition in Corporate Law*, 105 HARV. L. REV. 1435 (1992). Should corporations be allowed to opt out of the default voting rule? *See* Bebchuk and Assaf Hamdani, *Optimal Defaults for Corporate Law Evolution*, 96 Nw. U. L. REV. 489 (2002).

7. What are the pros and cons of elections and of the "market for corporate control" as mechanisms for disciplining management? As Lipton notes, he has elsewhere proposed an extreme version of his preference for elections over the market for corporate control. Under that proposal, hostile acquisitions and proxy fights would be replaced with elections that would subject all directors to open, competitive elections every five years. *See* Lipton and Steven A. Rosenblum, *A New System of Corporate Governance: The Quinquennial Election of Directors*, 58 U. CHI. L. REV. 187 (1991).

8. Lipton argues that unsolicited takeover bids are counterproductive in that a target corporation must adopt "costly programs to protect its business during the period of uncertainty as to the outcome of the bid." Consider the response to Oracle Corporation's hostile takeover bid in 2003–04 for PeopleSoft, a smaller company that made a competing software product. Oracle had stated that if its bid were to succeed, it would eventually discontinue production and support of PeopleSoft's software products. PeopleSoft responded by inserting into all its sales contracts a guarantee to give the customer a 300% refund of the purchase price if PeopleSoft or any successor corporation were to discontinue support of the software.

In what ways does the plan resemble a poison pill? Might a pill be preferable, as Lipton suggests? Are the existing rules on takeovers equipped to deal with this kind of defensive action? Should the law regulate such actions?

9. Lipton argues that managers can and should protect stakeholder interests in the takeover context. Bebchuk argues that managers' self-interest in resisting takeovers will only "occasionally" overlap with the interests of those stakeholders, such as employees, who favor stability and predictability over acquisition premia. What kind of empirical evidence might be useful to help settle this issue?

Assume the overlap of interests is minimal, or nonexistent. As Bebchuk points out, board veto is a poor way of protecting stakeholder interests, and there are, at least in theory, better ways of protecting employees from layoffs. But do his arguments show that shareholder voting on hostile takeovers is better for employees (or other stakeholders) than a board veto?

10. Lipton points to the costs of being a corporate target, which Bebchuk does not consider. Recall Professor Fisch's argument in Chapter 9 about the management and

monitoring functions of the board. Does an active market for corporate control compromise managerial effectiveness in exchange for more aggressive monitoring?

Would Bebchuk's proposal necessarily require every corporation to operate "as if it were always for sale," as Lipton contends? What kind of empirical research could help resolve this issue?

11. How well does the story of Lipton's 1982 "Warrant Dividend Plan" memo fit Professor Rock's theories in Chapter 3 about law firms' memoranda to their clients?

12. Does legal approval of "management veto" devices (such as the poison pill) necessarily mean that management will selfishly reject lucrative takeover offers? What other corporate governance features might affect whether the board serves shareholder interests when it responds to takeovers? *See* Marcel Kahan and Edward Rock, *How I Learned to Stop Worrying and Love the Pill: Adaptive Responses to Takeover Law*, 69 U. Chi. L. Rev. 871 (2002).

13. Do you agree with *Lyondell*'s use of the "good faith" standard to evaluate whether a board fulfilled its *Revlon* duty? Does it seem consistent with the intent of *Revlon*? Does it seem more consistent with the Gilson/Bebchuk view or the Lipton view of the judicial role? If you disagree with *Lyondell*, what standard should a court use instead of "good faith"?

14. Around the years 2004–05, many companies dismantled their poison pills or allowed them to lapse, often in response to shareholder proposals. Some observers thought this marked a permanent change in corporate governance. In 2008, however, pill adoptions and re-adoptions increased dramatically. What do you think accounts for this pattern?

Chapter 12

The Corporate Lawyer and Other "Gatekeepers"

As we have seen, internal corporate monitoring by shareholders and directors is supplemented by external monitoring by regulators, capital markets, and the market for corporate control. Professionals such as corporate lawyers, auditors, and stock analysts also have potential to serve as external monitors. Reinier Kraakman has referred to such professionals as "gatekeepers": their access to confidential corporate information gives them the ability to discover corporate misconduct and their ability to withhold crucial business services gives them the opportunity to stop their clients from engaging in such conduct.[1] Similarly, the SEC sometimes refers to these professionals as gatekeepers to the securities markets because of their role in maintaining the quality of their clients' disclosures. A key problem for gatekeepers is the conflict between their monitoring role and their professional loyalty to their clients. This problem is exacerbated when "the client" is not an individual, but a publicly traded corporation—a complex organization with multiple layers of conflicting interests.

A popular view of the lawyer's role holds that her duty is to single-mindedly pursue the client's interests using all legal means available. Deborah DeMott argues in this chapter, however, that lawyers owe duties not only to their clients, but also to the law and to the standards of the profession. Tanina Rostain examines the consequences of such a view, under which lawyers are not bound solely to their clients' instructions, but exercise independent judgment to achieve justice. Rostain argues that because lawyers often lack independence from their clients, this type of nominal autonomy would not necessarily advance social interests. In contrast, John Coates focuses on the ways that the autonomy of transactional lawyers may translate into a failure to serve the *client's* best interests.

William Bratton argues that conflicts of interest pervaded the accounting industry so severely that nominally independent auditors appear to have countenanced significant fraud at Enron. Lawrence Mitchell praises the Sarbanes-Oxley Act of 2002, passed largely in response to Enron, as a significant step toward bringing the major gatekeepers—accountants, lawyers and analysts—more explicitly into the corporate governance system. Larry Ribstein, in contrast, argues that the Act is mistaken in attempting to transform auditors and lawyers into monitors of their clients.

Frank Partnoy critically examines a category of gatekeeper that is often overlooked: the credit ratings agencies. His article, originally published in 2006, identifies many problems that eventually contributed to the meltdown of the financial sector two years later.

---

1. Reinier H. Kraakman, *Gatekeepers: The Anatomy of a Third-Party Enforcement Strategy*, 2 J.L. ECON. & ORG. 53 (1986); Reinier H. Kraakman, *Corporate Liability Strategies and the Costs of Legal Controls*, 93 YALE L.J. 857, 888–91 (1984).

The chapter ends with an excerpt from the SEC rules for lawyers promulgated under Section 307 of the Sarbanes-Oxley Act, which dramatize the conflicting expectations placed on professional gatekeepers. The rules require securities lawyers to report corporate misconduct to higher authorities within the corporation and permit them, in certain circumstances, to report their clients' misconduct to the SEC.

Deborah A. DeMott, *The Lawyer as Agent**

... The law of agency provides the foundational structure for many of the legal consequences that follow from the relationship between a lawyer and a client, as well as the relationship between an individual lawyer and a law firm. Definitional precision in the law aside, the lawyer-client relationship is a commonsensical illustration of agency. A lawyer acts on behalf of the client, representing the client, with consequences that bind the client. Lawyers act as clients' agents in transactional settings as well as in litigation. Moreover, a lawyer who is a member of a law firm acts as an agent of the firm in firm-related activity, as does an associate employed by a law firm and in-house counsel for a client organization. It is unsurprising, then, that the legal consequences of these relationships parallel the legal consequences of agency generally, even when they are not identical. In any agency relationship, for example, the agent's loyalty to the interests of the principal is a dominant concern, as is the loyalty of a lawyer to the client.

Despite its foundational significance, the law of agency does not by itself capture all of the legal consequences of relationships between lawyers and clients and between lawyers and others to whom the lawyer owes duties. In this context, agency is roughly comparable to the structural steel members that support a building and define its size and basic shape but do not govern how the building functions and looks. Lawyers are agents, but lawyers perform functions that distinguish them from most other agents. That a lawyer is an agent is sometimes irrelevant to the legal consequences of what the lawyer has done or has failed to do, making an unswerving focus on agency misleading. It is not surprising, then, that courts on occasion differentiate among agency's consequences, rather than according agency a monolithic or inexorable set of consequences.

Lawyers are more than their clients' agents. Lawyers are officers of the court, thus subjecting themselves to the court's supervision and to duties geared to protect the vigor, fairness, and integrity of processes of litigation. Furthermore, as members of a profession, lawyers are subject to duties not neatly captured by the consequences of agency.

Although this essay is far from comprehensive, its objective is to illustrate both the significance of agency and its limitations. A helpful starting point is to clarify the content and legal consequences of agency. Courts and commentators at times use the language of agency but do not fully address the consequences that agency concepts may carry. Moreover, the widespread use of agency terminology in academic disciplines like economics, philosophy, and literary studies does not necessarily parallel the content of the common law of agency. I undertake first to survey the definition and basic legal consequences of agency to illustrate its foundational significance as applied to lawyers. I turn next to a few illustrations of divergence between the general law of agency and the duties of lawyers. I conclude with an analysis of the circumstances under which a lawyer might be liable in connection with fraud perpetrated by the lawyer's client. This illustration brings to bear

---

* Originally published in 67 FORDHAM LAW REVIEW 301 (1998). Reprinted with permission.

principles of agency law to test their applicability and meaning as applied to relationships that involve lawyers.

I. Definition and Legal Consequences

A. *Agency Defined*

It is important to distinguish between the elements that must be present in a relationship to characterize it as one of agency and the legal consequences that follow from this characterization. Confusion and circularity result if analysis proceeds in the opposite direction. As defined by the Restatement (Second) of Agency, "agency is the fiduciary relation which results from the manifestation of consent by one person to another that the other shall act on his behalf and subject to his control, and consent by the other so to act." Thus, the defining elements of the relationship are mutual manifestation of consent, the agent's undertaking to act on behalf of the principal, and the principal's right to control the agent. The relationship between a lawyer and a client is generally assumed by courts and commentators to be an agency relationship and therefore a relationship in which these defining elements are present....

To be sure, the client's right of control does not trump the consequences of the lawyer's position as an officer of the court and a professional subject to profession-defined norms and discipline. To some extent, lawyers are no different from other agents in this respect. Acting as an agent is not a privilege to commit torts, crimes, and other forms of misconduct. That is, all agents are subject to legal limits on acts that may be done rightfully on behalf of a principal. Particular types of agents are subject to legal and professional constraints specific to defined agency roles. Lawyers are comparable in this respect to securities brokers and real estate agents, agents who act on behalf of clients subject to significant regulatory and legal constraints.

What is open to serious dispute is the import of the duties a lawyer owes to the court, coupled with the consequences of the court's power to supervise and sanction lawyers. In contrast to regulatory regimes applicable to other types of agents, like securities brokers and real estate agents, in the litigation context the relationship between a lawyer and the court is direct and immediate. Concurrently with the lawyer's representation of the client, the lawyer owes duties directly to the court, such as the duty to disclose controlling authority directly adverse to the client's position that is not disclosed by opposing counsel. This dimension of the lawyer's position is beyond the explanatory framework that agency supplies. Moreover, although the lawyer owes duties to both the client and the court, the lawyer is not a dual agent. The lawyer is not the court's agent, even metaphorically, because the lawyer's acts do not bind the court. Additionally, much of the justification for the duties any agent owes the principal stems from the mutual consent of the parties to the relationship. In contrast, the duties the lawyer owes the court, as well as the court's inherent sanctioning powers, are grounded in the nature of judicial institutions.

Furthermore, lawyers are distinctive as agents as a consequence of the robust professional culture and standards that define a lawyer's professional identity. Professional standards create duties that are not necessarily enforceable by the lawyer's client. Additionally, the self-regulatory nature of the legal profession distinguishes lawyers from many other types of agents because it situates significant monitoring within institutions constituted by the profession, distinct from state-created regulatory bodies, and distinct from courts. Like the lawyer's relationship to the court, the lawyer's membership in a self-regulating profession limits the reach of the lawyer's agency relationship with the client as the source of the client's rights and the lawyer's obligations. In any event, most of the time, the lawyer's responsibilities are harmonious regardless of their source....

II. The Author, the Tout, and the Scrivener

Within agency relationships, liability, like knowledge, [is imputed] upward from the agent to the principal. When wrongful conduct toward a third party occurs in connection with an agency relationship, the dispute often focuses on whether a principal is liable for the agent's wrongful conduct. In contrast, consider circumstances under which an agent might in some sense be accountable for a wrong committed at least in part by the principal. These circumstances are relatively unusual. Suppose the agent innocently repeats a defamatory statement made to the agent by the principal, a statement that the principal knows to be false. Suppose that the agent is not a lawyer and, in any event, does not repeat the principal's statement as a witness or a party in a judicial or quasi-judicial proceeding. As noted above, agency does not impute the principal's knowledge downward to the agent. The agent is the instrument of the principal's defamation, but lacks the requisite state of mind that is a defining element of the tort. When the question is the agent's individual liability for wrongful conduct, the law of agency itself does not fully answer the question, except by making it clear that the agent's position as an agent does not constitute a defense to conduct that is tortuous or criminal. An agent who repeats the principal's defamatory statement, knowing it to be false, is not immune from liability for defamation simply by virtue of being an agent. In addition, the agent does not acquire immunity by acting in a relatively ministerial capacity, such as serving as a secretary or scrivener to the principal.

It is important to have these basic points in mind in assessing the circumstances under which lawyers are accountable for their clients' fraudulent misrepresentations. Current controversy focuses on the accountability of securities lawyers in this connection.... Suppose the lawyer's work encompasses drafting a registration statement and a prospectus on behalf of an issuer of securities for an offering subject to the Securities Act of 1933. If the registration statement misstates or omits material facts, then section 11 of the statute imposes strict liability on the issuer, regardless of the identity of the person who drafted the registration statement and regardless of that person's state of mind or moral culpability. Thus, the lawyer's lack of authority to commit the client to contracts, or to negotiate with third parties on the client's behalf, does not mean that the lawyer's acts carry no legal consequences for the client. Moreover, information or knowledge that a lawyer acquires in connection with a representation [is imputed] to the client for many, if not all, purposes, even when the lawyer lacks authority to commit the client to contracts.... The lawyer's liability ... does not turn on whether the lawyer is an agent, but on whether the lawyer's conduct and state of mind suffice to constitute fraud. What the constituent elements might be for fraud under the federal securities laws is open to some question after the Supreme Court's opinion in *Central Bank of Denver v. First Interstate Bank*.[2]

In *Central Bank*, the Court held that neither the language of section 10(b) of the Securities Exchange Act nor the overall legislative scheme supported liability in private actions for collateral participants in fraud whose role was characterized as simply aiding and abetting the acts of the primary violator. The court emphasized "that the statute prohibits only the making of a material misstatement (or omission) or the commission of a manipulative act."

---

2. 511 U.S. 164 (1994).

Recent cases illustrate the variety of scenarios in which the dispositive question is whether a lawyer's conduct should be characterized as making a misrepresentation for purposes of liability in a private action for securities fraud. In *Klein v. Boyd*,[3] the lawyer had a significant role in drafting offering documents, determining what to include and what to exclude, and knew that the documents did not contain information that would be important to prospective investors. The investor-plaintiffs, however, were unaware of the lawyer's role because the lawyer did not sign or endorse the documents. *Klein* thus raises the question of how visible the lawyer's role must be to constitute a misrepresentation that the lawyer makes to investors. Otherwise, *Klein* illustrates a lawyer in an authorial role, deciding what the client's statement to investors shall contain.

Lawyers' efforts in securities transactions are not necessarily confined to generating written documentation. In *Rubin v. Schottenstein, Zox & Dunn*,[4] the client referred prospective investors with questions about the client's financial stability to the lawyer, having dissuaded the prospective investors from making direct contact with the client's lender. The lawyer assured the prospective investors that the client was financially sound and that it had no problems with the lender, which according to the lawyer would increase funding following a cash infusion from the investors. The lawyer also dissuaded the investors from contacting the lender directly and subsequently asked the investors' lawyer not to do so, repeating assurances of the client's financial health to the investors' lawyer. The lawyer, however, told neither the investors nor their lawyer that his client was already in default under its loan agreement with the lender and that the proposed investment would itself constitute a default under the agreement. The court held that these omissions made the lawyer's statements misleading. This conclusion does not conflict with the lawyer's duties of confidentiality to the client. The lawyer had no right or duty to volunteer information about his client, but once having undertaken to speak, the lawyer's duty was to provide complete and nonmisleading information. In *Rubin*, the lawyer was the author of the statements he made, functioning almost as a tout on behalf of the client.

Securities lawyers have on occasion argued that they function, not as authors or touts, but as the client's mere scriveners, drafting the substantive content of the prospectus virtually at the client's dictation, papering the deal but not independently making statements or representations to investors. In *Schatz v. Rosenberg*,[5] the court endorsed the "mere scrivener" doctrine, stating that "lawyers do not vouch for the probity of their clients when they draft documents reflecting their clients' promises, statements, or warranties." As agents, the court held, lawyers are not automatically liable for the client's misrepresentations. *Schatz* preceded *Central Bank*, which more broadly excluded rationales for liability that did not involve direct acts of misstatement or commission by a particular defendant. In any event, whether a lawyer-as-scrivener is liable for fraud is not answered by agency principles, which establish only that an agent's position is in itself not a defense.

It may be helpful to consider the other context in which the lawyer-as-scrivener argument surfaces. In *Griffith v. Taylor*,[6] an associate lawyer in a law firm prepared quitclaim deeds for property at the request of a grantee, A. The firm subsequently prepared deeds for the initial grantor, B, deeding the property to him. After the deeds to B were found to be invalid, the initial grantee, A, sued the firm for malpractice, alleging that its work for

---

3. 949 F.Supp. 280 (E.D.Pa. Jul 17, 1996); aff'd, Fed. Sec. L. Rep. (CCH) ¶ 90,136 (3d Cir. Feb. 12, 1998); opinion vacated on grant of reh'g en banc, 1998 WL 55245 (3d Cir. Mar. 9, 1998).
4. 143 F.3d 263, 266 (6th Cir. 1998) (en banc).
5. 943 F.2d 485 (4th Cir. 1991).
6. 937 P.2d 297 (Alaska 1997).

both A and B constituted a conflict of interest and a breach of its duty of loyalty to him. The court held that, although the trial court erred in granting summary judgment for the firm on the point, the firm might be protected by a scrivener's exception to its general duty of loyalty to its clients. The exception is available when a lawyer "merely fashions a statutory form of deed, or performs other clerical or ministerial tasks." The exception becomes unavailable, however, if the lawyer furnishes any legal advice to the client, in any way makes use of legal skills, or receives any confidences from the client. Even a narrowly-drawn scrivener's exception is vulnerable to the argument that it conflicts with the loyalty that all lawyers owe to clients, however humble the specific task that the lawyer is engaged to perform. The exception may reflect an era of limited literacy in which lawyers commonly served as amanuenses for people who could not use language in any written form. . . .

In contrast, the work of securities lawyers, however technical, is neither ministerial nor rote in nature. Drafting a prospectus involves making judgments and giving advice, both tasks that require access to confidential information. Nor is it the case that the lawyer has no choice other than to draft a prospectus to include statements that the lawyer knows to be false. A lawyer is not a piece of computer hardware that, functioning properly, always obeys correctly-formulated commands. Instead, recall the best-known legal scrivener, the fictional Bartleby in Herman Melville's short story ["Bartleby, the Scrivener"]. Bartleby responded to his employer's requests by stating that he "would prefer not to." Sad though Bartleby's situation is revealed to be as the story plays out, he is not an automaton.

III. Conclusion

Although lawyers serve their clients as agents, the general law of agency is often just a starting point for analyzing the legal consequences of lawyer-client relationships. Lawyers owe duties to a cast of characters wider than that defined by general agency principles, while the content of duties that lawyers owe their clients is distinctive. Moreover, the fact that a lawyer acts as the client's agent is irrelevant when the question is the lawyer's individual liability for the lawyer's personal participation in fraud, including fraud implicating the lawyer's client.

Tanina Rostain, *Waking Up from Uneasy Dreams: Professional Context, Discretionary Judgment, and* The Practice of Justice[*]

When an associate at a large corporate firm was interviewed several years ago about potential conflicts between his personal values and his work assignments, he chuckled at the quaintness of the inquiry. "Are you kidding?" he responded, "My work doesn't raise questions of conscience, it's just a fight over which big corporation is going to get a bigger chunk of the pie." By all reports, this associate's experience is typical. According to common lore, personal ethics, considerations of justice, and other ideals are far removed from the daily concerns of lawyering. Under the accepted understanding of the role of lawyers, their fundamental commitment is to advancing clients' interests. In this view, broader normative commitments have no place in practice.

* Originally published in 51 STANFORD LAW REVIEW 955 (1999). Reprinted with permission.

To William Simon, the radical disconnect between broader professional ideals and lawyers' work is a sign that something is very wrong with the practice of law. As he notes, although lawyers devote their lives to working within the system of justice, they are routinely implicated in injustice. This contradiction, Simon argues, is experienced by lawyers as profoundly alienating. With [his 1998 book] *The Practice of Justice*, Simon offers a diagnosis of lawyers' professional estrangement and an antidote. Simon locates the roots of lawyers' malaise in the dominant categorical norms of the profession, which hold that a lawyer's fundamental allegiance is to her clients and leave no room for complex contextualized decisionmaking. The cure for lawyers' alienation, according to Simon, is to replace the categorical mandates of legal ethics with a discretionary approach centered on considerations of justice....

Under the prevailing account, enunciated in bar codes, decisional law, and standard legal ethics discourse, lawyers' ethics involve the mechanical application of rules and leave no room for complex discretionary judgment. In substance, moreover, the governing norms of practice pay little or no attention to ideals of justice. Under the "Dominant View," as Simon calls it, a lawyer may—indeed must—pursue any goal of a client, through any arguably legal means. In their single-minded dedication to furthering client interests, lawyers are expected to relinquish any responsibility for the harmful effects of their conduct on others.

Simon devotes the early chapters of *The Practice of Justice* to a devastating critique of the arguments traditionally marshaled to support the Dominant View. As Simon shows, these arguments are built on questionable premises and are riddled with internal inconsistencies. Simon groups these claims into two categories: claims that clients are entitled to lawyers' zealous partisanship as a matter of right and claims that zealous partisanship results in justice in the long run. Simon demonstrates that the argument that clients are entitled to lawyers' unrestrained zeal is premised on libertarian and positivist assumptions that do not amount to a defensible theory of law. Simon also takes apart the consequentialist arguments offered for the Dominant View, which maintain that despite all its short-term unjust effects, unmitigated partisanship leads to greater justice overall. As he points out, such arguments rely on unverifiable and implausible empirical assumptions about human conduct. The factually and logically tenuous presuppositions of the consequentialist thesis are inadequate to justify the injustices that flow from lawyers' compliance with the Dominant View.

Having made short shrift of the arguments underlying the Dominant View, Simon turns to the difficult challenge of describing an alternative vision of legal ethics. With his account of contextual judgment, Simon hopes not only to avoid the weaknesses that beset the Dominant View, but also, and perhaps more importantly, to offer an approach that speaks to the legal profession's alienated circumstances. Put simply, lawyers are alienated from their work because it affords them neither an opportunity for creative expression nor for meaningful social participation. As Simon argues, the remedy is to put complex discretionary judgments based on considerations of justice at the center of legal ethics and practice.

Pursuing this logic, Simon proposes that lawyers adopt a style of reasoning to address ethical dilemmas fashioned after judicial decisionmaking processes. Just as judges make reasoned discretionary judgments to further justice, so should lawyers engage in contextual reasoning to decide what actions they should take to promote justice....

In invoking an analogy to judicial reasoning, Simon anticipates and answers an expected objection to his approach, which argues that discretionary decisionmaking by lawyers will result in ad hoc results. Simon responds that even though law is indeterminate, we nevertheless look to courts to make reasonably good judgments about what outcomes will further justice. The fact that courts often make mistakes and that judicial decisions routinely occasion controversy and disagreement does not mean that judging is an arbitrary and meaningless activity. The same logic, he argues, applies to discretionary judgments by lawyers. If lawyers are fundamentally committed to furthering justice in practice, they will generally advance justice, even if on occasion they get the analysis wrong.

With his discretionary approach, Simon's ambition is to restore a place for complex professional decisionmaking in the practice of law. Simon's is a strikingly original and attractive proposal. It invites lawyers to re-envision their practices so that they are deeply and intimately involved in articulating norms of justice. Unlike other proposals for reform, moreover, Simon's proposal does not urge lawyers to import norms of common morality into practice, but to locate the ideals that should animate their work within the law itself. According to Simon, lawyers should determine the dictates of justice on the basis of norms internal to law, legal institutions, and law practice. Simon's account thus reserves to lawyers a distinct sphere within which to exercise sophisticated professional judgment based on their unique engagement with law.

According to Simon, "lawyers should take those actions that, considering the relevant circumstances of the particular case, seem likely to promote justice." Stated at this level of generality, of course, this maxim provides no guidance to lawyers as to how to proceed. Simon accordingly devotes significant attention to fleshing out the standards that apply in a discretionary approach. Simon's standards reflect a jurisprudence that combines both substantive and positivist strands. Although Simon rejects strong legal positivism as a fundamentally incoherent account of law, he refuses to embrace wholeheartedly a substantive view, under which all law gets collapsed into morality. Instead, he seeks to articulate an account of legal ethics that maintains a commitment to the integrity of legal norms, processes, and institutions. Simon's standards for discretionary judgment accordingly recognize the deference traditionally accorded institutionalized decisionmaking and procedures, and reflect generally accepted norms of legal interpretation....

Having laid out the basic principles that should underlie discretionary judgment, Simon walks his reader through a series of examples. He offers us an insurance defense lawyer considering whether she should, to the detriment of her client, educate opposing counsel about the correct standard of the law, a tax lawyer who has conjured up a legally questionable tax avoidance device, a trial lawyer debating whether to impeach a truthful witness, a second tax lawyer faced with another legally questionable tax avoidance scheme, a legal services lawyer in a parallel situation arising under a welfare statute, and counsel on two sides of a heated labor dispute. In each case, the dilemma is given: May the lawyer depend on the existence of reliable decisionmaking procedures to press her client's advantage or should she take substantive responsibility for the outcome? May a lawyer manipulate the form of legislation to benefit a client or should she take the statute's underlying purpose into account? May a lawyer frame an issue narrowly consistent with a client's interests or should she consider a broader range of factors as relevant?

These are all important dilemmas, and Simon's analysis of these problems is profound and often persuasive. But is providing lawyers with a broad justice-based approach to deal with such questions sufficient? Will arming lawyers with such an approach ensure that they act to promote justice?

I fear not. Throughout *The Practice of Justice*, Simon invokes the ideal of judicial reasoning as his benchmark for discretionary judgment. But lawyers are not situat[ed] like judges. Whereas the ideal conditions of judicial decisionmaking are established to enhance a judge's capacity to be independent and disinterested, the conditions of law practice tend to have different effects....

I. Social and Organizational Influences on Lawyers' Attitudes and Values: Some Tentative Lessons from Sociolegal Studies

... In this day of practice and client specialization, lawyers are exposed to a fairly limited and homogeneous perspective reflecting the concerns of the clients they represent and the views of their colleagues at their firms. As a consequence, they may simply not have the capacity for independent judgment on which the success of Simon's approach depends.

The potential impact of work environment on lawyers' professional values is suggested by a study conducted by Robert Nelson of lawyers in the Chicago corporate bar in the early 1980s.[7] Nelson interviewed approximately 250 lawyers working in several large corporate firms to investigate their political, legal, and professional attitudes. Nelson sought to explore the extent to which these lawyers' orientation to issues that arise in ordinary practice was determined by their clients' interests. His conclusion, simply put, was that corporate clients' interests tended to shape their lawyers' attitudes in the fields in which they work—a problematic result for the viability of Simon's approach.

The corporate lawyers studied by Nelson were not just ideological clones of their clients. On broad political and social issues, Nelson found that the views of the lawyers diverged in important ways from those of the business elite they represented. Although Nelson's sample was drawn from only a handful of law firms, it exhibited some degree of demographic diversity. The respondents' political affiliations were pretty evenly spread across the mainstream political spectrum, with a slight tilt to left of center. These lawyers, moreover, were far more favorably disposed generally to an active regulatory state than the clients they routinely represented. More than two-thirds favored government regulation through antitrust laws, securities regulations, banking law, and consumer protection....

When it came to these lawyers' views on specific legal issues in the fields in which they practiced, however, any tension between their normative judgments and their clients' interests tended to disappear. Lawyers in the sample were questioned about what improvements they would make in the area of law in which they specialized. As Nelson explains, they were asked "to play king—to tell what they would change about the law that they practice if they had the necessary legislative and judicial power." The responses exhibited great substantive variation and included changes in court procedure, the IRS, the SEC, the EEOC [Equal Employment Opportunity Commission], civil litigation, criminal law, labor law, antitrust law, tax law, and banking law. In orientation, however, the proposals by and large reflected a pro-client perspective. The suggestions were anti-IRS, anti-SEC, and more generally anti-government, as well as pro-management, pro-bank and creditor, pro-wealthy taxpayer, and pro-civil defendant. Their biases in favor of client interests were acknowledged by the respondents after the fact: When subsequently asked open-ended questions about how their proposals would affect their clients, 80% of the responses suggested a beneficial effect on clients. In contrast, only 8% of the responses saw a potentially negative impact on any client, with the remaining seeing no

---

7. Robert Nelson, *Ideology, Practice, and Professional Autonomy: Social Values and Client Relationships in the Large Law Firm*, 37 STAN. L. REV. 503, 537 (1985).

effect on clients either way. Nelson observes: "If there is a distance between large-firm lawyers and their corporate clientele over general social and political questions, there is not much disparity between client concerns and the lawyers' agenda for change in the legal fields in which they actually practice." As Nelson concludes, "the results show such a strong identification with the interests of clients'—even to the point of putting clients long-term interests above their own short-term interests—that it is unrealistic to think of corporate lawyers as neutral professionals who are detached from the substantive interests of their clients."

What accounts for the apparent synchronicity between these lawyers' normative views in the areas in which they practice and the interests of their clients? As Nelson suggests, professional socialization is the most plausible explanation. In practice, these lawyers specialized in representing a set of clients with a common set of interests, problems, and concerns. And they did it in firms with other like-minded lawyers who represented the same clients. The professional context in which these corporate lawyers worked—their daily interactions with their clients and colleagues—was a significant determinant of their attitudes about the legal issues that arose in their work.

Nelson's evidence raises a troubling possibility for Simon's proposal: Under current conditions of practice, lawyers may become so identified with their clients that they are unable to tell when considerations of justice dictate a result at odds with their clients' interests....

II. Attitude Formation: Some Tentative Lessons from Social Psychology

Recent research in social and cognitive psychology has established the profound influence that social interactions have on individual attitudes, beliefs, and values. Social psychologists have described various processes that are relevant to understanding lawyers' views of their clients and the work they do on their behalf. As research in cognitive psychology has suggested, people tend to get their cues about the propriety of their conduct from others.... In law practice, the existence of conformist psychological processes will lead a lawyer faced with questions about the propriety of her actions to rely heavily on perceptions of how others around her behave.

A second psychological mechanism that is relevant in understanding the process of professional socialization is self-justification.... Traditionally interpreted in terms of the reduction of cognitive dissonance, this phenomenon is particularly pronounced in situations in which a person violates her concept of self, for example, in situations in which she engages in behavior that hurts another person. In such circumstances, the need to "justify" one's self, to find explanations that are consistent with one's self-conception as a decent person, is very powerful. In law practice, the phenomenon of self-justification translates into being convinced that one is representing the "right side" and finding ways of rationalizing one's conduct in any given case as consistent with a just result. As research has further established, self-justification effects are cumulative over time. The more one becomes committed to a course of action, the more entrenched is one's insistence on interpreting that conduct as ethically appropriate. Whatever lingering doubts might remain in a lawyer's mind after arguing for the first time that smoking cigarettes does not cause cancer, they begin to disappear as she repeatedly makes the same argument.

Conformist and self-justification tendencies together provide a plausible account of the psychological processes that may underlie professional socialization. In particular, they suggest how context might shape lawyers' concrete normative commitments. Consider a new lawyer who has just decided to join a law firm.... [F]rom the moment she walks into the firm, she will assimilate its culture, including the firm's normative narratives about the ethical propriety of representing a given clientele, the work it does, and the area of law in which it practices. And the more time she spends at the firm, the more deeply ingrained the firm's normative narratives will become in her professional self-conception.

These collective normative commitments, in turn, engender specific interpretive commitments. A new associate learns to interpret the law that she practices from the lawyers with whom she works, and the readings she develops will be of a piece with the core justificatory accounts these lawyers give of themselves and their clients. A lawyer who joins the tax department of a firm, for example, will be exposed to accounts emphasizing the legitimacy of their clientele's legal needs, the propriety of the tax advice the firm routinely gives, and, on the other hand, the illegitimacy of specific governmental incursions into clients' affairs. These narratives will inform her interpretation of the provisions of the code with which she works and new provisions that she encounters....

III. Implications for Simon's Discretionary Approach: The Devil in the Details

I have suggested that even if lawyers are convinced to discard the Dominant View and embrace the practice of justice along the lines proposed by Simon, their assessments of appropriate conduct in specific situations may not change. To put Simon's approach into practice, a lawyer first has to perceive that her work presents dilemmas—between substance and procedure, purpose and form, or broad and narrow framing—and then engage in reasonably reliable evaluations of the factors involved. Given current trends toward specialization, both in terms of area of law and especially type of client served, lawyers may be incapable of the type of discernment required.

To begin with, lawyers may not experience many of the situations in which they find themselves as even giving rise to the types of ethical dilemmas that concern Simon. The corporate lawyers who were studied by Nelson could recognize the legitimacy of the larger regulatory framework and still maintain a strong substantive slant that favored their clients' interests in the areas of law they practiced. Their law reform proposals further indicated that they perceived individual regulatory agencies—such as the IRS or SEC— as routinely engaging in inappropriate, intrusive, or unfair actions *vis-à-vis* their clients. In such circumstances, they might not perceive aggressive tactics to thwart such agency action as presenting any dilemma at all: Such tactics further justice by preventing agency abuse of power even as they further clients' interests....

The same sorts of issues arise in purpose/form dilemmas. Having routinely represented "one side" in a given area of law, a lawyer will accord disproportionate weight to purposes that reflect her clients' concerns and, on the other hand, fail to take sufficient account of those purposes that run counter to clients' interests. Consider, for example, a lawyer who specializes in counseling and litigation on behalf of employers in discrimination related matters. Suppose that the lawyer is consulted by a small employer, whose history suggests a tendency to discriminate against women. Under Title VII, an employer must have a minimum of fifteen employees to be subject to its requirements. The lawyer is considering the propriety under a discretionary approach of advising the client, given its small size, to do some creative restructuring of the workplace so that it ends up with less than fifteen employees as defined by the statute. As the lawyer is aware, the prohibition against discrimination in employment on the basis of gender is a fundamental purpose of the statute. From her specialized practice, however, she is particularly sensitive to a competing concern reflected in the jurisdictional statutory floor: The prevention of federal government intrusion into the affairs of businesses with very small workforces. Because this lawyer perceives the statute as a compromise among these different purposes, she is justified in a formal reading of the statute under Simon's analysis. Following Simon's approach, her advice to the small employer to restructure is appropriate—a result that, under these circumstances, does not appear likely to promote justice.

As this example suggests, which purposes are clear and which are problematic will often depend on the perspective of the actor making the interpretation.... Law's indeterminacy does not necessarily lead to the conclusion that law is just an arbitrary and illegitimate exercise of power. It does suggest, however, that the context in which the interpretive activity is taking place becomes a central site of critical empirical inquiry.

The role of context in shaping lawyers' attitudes and values has several implications for the viability of Simon's approach. First, it suggests that a theoretical shift away from the Dominant View, in and of itself, may be insufficient to effect a change in lawyers' practices. In neglecting social and organizational factors, Simon's argument reflects a weakness common throughout traditional scholarship in the area, which takes for granted that norms of legal ethics develop from the "top down." As Professor David Wilkins has emphasized, "the actual content that lawyers give to the [formal commands of legal ethics codes] is forged in the contexts in which lawyers learn, live, and work."[8]

It highlights, moreover, the need for further sociolegal research to understand the social and institutional determinants of lawyers' beliefs and values. One important site in which lawyers' attitudes are formed is law school. This process may not be exclusively, or even primarily, through the formal lessons imparted through traditional classroom pedagogy. Clinical education, for example, may play a significant role in shaping lawyers' normative perspectives. In addition, in their informal interactions with teachers, other law students and other participants, law students receive a wealth of signals about professional norms, commitments and values. Deciphering the messages transmitted in law school is a critical part of this project.

Sociolegal investigations are also necessary to develop a much richer account of the role of professional environment in shaping lawyers' commitments and beliefs. My own suspicion is that professionalization in legal practice soon eclipses the influence of legal education. In any case, research into the effects of specialization by area, client and task, firm culture and organization, and a host of other factors is necessary to understand the process of value and attitude formation in lawyers. Investigating "law talk in lawyers' offices" is a critical component of this work. Without this kind of research, there is no way of knowing under what conditions a discretionary approach might be meaningfully implemented in practice.

IV. Conclusion: Waking Up from Uneasy Dreams

... If [Franz Kafka's novel] *The Trial* describes alienation from the law, [his short story] "The Metamorphosis" describes alienation from the self. At once a powerful and

---

8. David B. Wilkins, *Everyday Practice* Is *the Troubling Case*, in EVERYDAY PRACTICES AND TROUBLE CASES 68, 97 (Austin Sarat, Marianne Constable, David Engel, Valerie Hans & Susan Lawrence eds., 1998).

disturbing commentary on the modern human condition, the story also illuminates the specific social forces that may lead human beings to degenerate into enormous, unattractive insects. Not surprisingly, work—exhausting, stressful, repetitive, boring, and relentlessly oppressive—plays a key role.

"As Gregor Samsa awoke one morning from uneasy dreams he found himself transformed in his bed into a gigantic insect." Gregor's initial reaction to this dramatic change in circumstances is remarkable for its mundaneness: Although he seems unaccustomed to his new state, he does not seem particularly surprised or distressed. In a character suddenly turned into a large insect, the expected action is profound terror and shock, perhaps accompanied by some metaphysical meditation on the grotesque meaninglessness of the human condition. Instead, Gregor's thoughts immediately go to his dreadful job as a traveling salesperson, to which he attributes his overnight transformation. These initial internal musings lead him to notice that he has overslept. Notably, Gregor's first expression of genuine anxiety comes with his realization that he will not be able to make it to work on time. The pages that follow are devoted to the drama of Gregor's pathetic and increasingly frantic efforts to get to work and save his job. (Since he is lying on his hard back with his many tiny legs waiving uselessly in the air, getting out of bed presents the first and most formidable challenge.) Gregor only manages to get out of bed and open the door to respond to the chief clerk at his office, who already by a quarter past seven, has arrived at his home and is accusing him of insubordination, dishonesty, and incompetence. Gregor's appearance, of course, costs him his job.

Two related themes in the opening section of "The Metamorphosis" are relevant to the problem of professional alienation. One is that work, at least in its more dehumanizing versions, can generate a profound transformation in the self. The second is that though one may come to realize that something has gone wrong, the implications of the change may be inaccessible. Put simply, work risks turning a person into an extremely unattractive creature and one whose sights are so narrowed that she is blind to the depth of the transformation. Popular depictions of lawyers routinely play on these themes, emphasizing the dehumanizing nature of law practice. Practice not only transforms lawyers into morally unattractive human beings, but makes them incapable of understanding what it is they have lost.

Not all practice, though, is as dehumanizing and alienating as my reading of Kafka's "The Metamorphosis" would imply. Significant diversity exists among practice settings. For one, not all lawyers work in law firms. Large numbers are in government practice and a significant number are also to be found in corporate counsel offices, public interest organizations, and other alternative settings. In addition, there is extraordinary variation among firms, which an emphasis on large corporate firm practice tends to eclipse. Even among firms that "look" the same—specialize in the same areas of law and serve the same types of clients—there can be significant differences in the normative and interpretive commitments that the lawyers in them bring to practice.

The broad diversity in lawyers' practices renders a host of new questions ethically relevant. What kind of practice a lawyer joins, who her clients are, and how her colleagues understand themselves and their work may turn out to have greater ethical import than the manner in which she approaches and resolves any given dilemma. In standard discussions in legal ethics, which involve elaborations and modifications of the Dominant View, the ethical relevance of these broader questions is eclipsed. By insisting on a vision that puts justice at the center of a practicing lawyer's concerns, *The Practice of Justice* takes an important step away from the formal analyses of standard legal ethics. A next step is to explore the normative dimensions of developing professional identity, which now becomes a legitimate focus of legal ethics.

John C. Coates IV, *Explaining Variation in Takeover Defenses: Blame the Lawyers**

I. Takeover Defenses at the IPO Stage

In 1994, IBM made a $3.3 billion hostile takeover bid for Lotus. Despite a determination to remain independent, management of Lotus capitulated within a week of IBM's bid. At roughly the same time, Moore Co. made a $1.3 billion hostile bid for Wallace Computer. After thirteen months of bitter battle, Moore Co. dropped its bid, leaving Wallace independent. What accounts for these strikingly different bid outcomes? Hostile takeover defenses do, defenses chosen by the targets years before, prior to the moment they became public companies. Defenses have become difficult if not impossible to adopt once a company's shares are sold to the public. Choice of governance structure at the initial public offering ("IPO") stage, in other words, turns out to have a large effect on whether target companies can remain independent in the face of a hostile bid. Systematic analysis of hostile bids bears out the contrast between the Lotus and Wallace bids: targets (such as Wallace) with one type of defense, classified boards, were in the 1990s three times more likely to remain independent than targets (such as Lotus) that lacked classified boards.

Understanding that takeover defenses determine bid outcomes, however, only pushes the inquiry back one step: what determines whether firms adopt takeover defenses, and in particular why do defenses vary at the IPO stage? If, on the one hand, defenses reduce firm value (by increasing agency costs between shareholders and managers), as Easterbrook and Fischel argued,[9] then why do half of companies adopt substantial defenses prior to IPOs ...? If, on the other hand, defenses have largely positive effects on firm value (by increasing bargaining power or overcoming some market failure), why do only half of companies adopt defenses prior to IPOs? The challenge, in other words, is not simply to explain the presence of defenses at the IPO stage, but to explain the variation in defense adoption.

In this Article, I present evidence from two large samples of IPOs that suggests that takeover defenses are chosen at the IPO stage primarily based on the takeover experience of the corporate lawyers working for the company at the time of the IPO. The characteristics of the lawyers working on the IPO were more predictive of defenses being adopted (or not adopted) than were testable company characteristics, such as a company's size, location, or industry. Lawyers, in other words, represent largely autonomous actors making decisions for corporate clients and determining corporate control structures, which in turn have large effects on hostile bid outcomes years later. Corporate lawyers, at least at the IPO stage, appear to be working relatively free of market, ethical, or other constraints, and many appear to be making choices, and mistakes, without determining whether such choices are in the long-term interests of their clients (that is, pre-IPO owner-managers).

Put more formally, this Article explains variation in takeover defenses at the IPO stage, hypothesizing that the quality of legal services provided to entrepreneurs and other pre-IPO shareholder-managers varies significantly, depending on the experience, size, and location of law firms serving as company counsel at the time of an IPO ("law firm hypotheses"). In competition with the claims advanced in this Article are two categories of explanations for the IPO defense puzzle. First, one might maintain that investment

* Originally published in 89 CALIFORNIA LAW REVIEW 1301 (2001). Reprinted with permission.
9. *The Proper Role of a Target's Management in Responding to a Tender Offer*, 94 HARV. L. REV. 1161 (1981).

banker advice about the effect of defenses on IPO prices varies in quality, and it is this variation that explains why companies adopt different defenses ("banker hypotheses").[10] Second, the efficiency of defenses may vary with company or pre-IPO shareholder characteristics, so that defenses are optimal at some companies, but not others ("variable efficiency hypotheses").

This Article describes the law firm hypotheses, analyzes empirical implications of the competing theories, and empirically tests each theory, to the extent feasible, as an alternative to the law firm hypotheses. Data from a sizeable sample (n=162) of IPOs from 1991–92, and a second large sample from 1998–99 (n=195), are used to test explanations for the IPO defense puzzle. Firm charters, bylaws, and prospectuses are reviewed, and summary data on the number, type, and strength of defenses are presented. These data are regressed against data on law firms to test the law firm hypotheses, and against data on underwriters to test the banker hypotheses. Also included in the regressions are variables that proxy for different variable efficiency hypotheses (specifically, agency costs, bargaining power, market myopia, and private benefits of control).

The empirical analysis produces three striking results. First, strong evidence is found that key terms in the "corporate contract," a company's suite of pre-IPO defenses, are determined by lawyers. The takeover experience, size, and location of law firms strongly correlate with the number and strength of pre-IPO takeover defenses adopted by companies they advise. Companies advised by larger law firms with more takeover experience adopt more defenses. In 1991–92, companies advised by lawyers located in Silicon Valley adopted fewer defenses, but by 1998, Silicon Valley law firms were just as likely to recommend defenses as law firms elsewhere.

Second, companies represented by high-quality underwriters or with venture capital backing are more likely to adopt defenses,[11] and the rate of defense adoption increased during the 1990s. While open to interpretation, these findings are more consistent with theories that hold it is generally optimal for pre-IPO owner-managers to adopt defenses than conventional agency-cost theories that hold it is uniformly a bad idea for defenses to be adopted. These correlations are important because underwriters, and to a lesser extent venture capitalists, are critical sources of information for pre-IPO owner-managers about the IPO prices, and in all prior writing about defenses, scholars have reasoned that if defenses are bad for pre-IPO owner-managers, it must be because defenses reduce IPO prices. Yet the correlations between defenses and underwriter reputation, and between defenses and VC-backing, both suggest that if defenses reduce IPO prices, pre-IPO owner-managers know about the effect on prices and are choosing to adopt defenses anyway. The evidence thus

---

10. *Investment banks "underwrite" IPOs, a function somewhat analogous to a retailer purchasing goods from a manufacturer and reselling them to the public. Immediately before the IPO, the underwriter and the issuer typically agree on the price at which the stock will be offered to the public. A variety of factors (including the existence of any takeover defenses) will affect this pricing analysis. When the public offering occurs, the underwriter buys the shares from the issuer at a slight discount from the agreed public offering price and immediately resells to the public (typically the underwriter's customers) at the agreed price. —Ed.*

11. *Because their profits depend on IPO prices, both underwriters and VCs presumably have some knowledge of how factors like takeover defenses will affect IPO prices. Underwriters' relationship to IPOs is described in the previous note. Venture capital firms, or VCs, provide intermediate "bridge financing" for companies that must grow somewhat before they are large enough to make public offerings. A VC takes stock in the company in exchange for the bridge financing and holds the stock until the company's IPO—one or two years later if all goes well. A VC's ultimate profit depends on the price of the public offering, at which point it will resell its stock holdings to the public. —Ed.*

suggests that defenses are "worth it," and (combined with evidence showing that defenses have increased in the 1990s) that defenses are generally good for pre-IPO owner-managers.

Third, ... some evidence suggests that the most extreme form of takeover defense (dual class capital structures) are distinct from other defenses and are motivated by high, primarily psychic (that is, non-pecuniary) private benefits of control. Little evidence is found to support variable efficiency hypotheses for defense adoption. Together, these findings suggest that variation in defenses is explained by lawyer choices that have little to do with the interest of their pre-IPO owner-manager clients....

II. Brief Overview of Takeover Defenses

The impetus for the development of modern takeover defenses was the emergence of the hostile tender offer. Hostile tender offers allowed anyone with the financing to gain rapid control of the largest businesses in the world by publicly committing to pay a significant premium over the target's stock market price. After emerging in the 1950s, the hostile tender offer enjoyed a stunning rise in importance after Morgan Stanley, which like other well-known, "white-shoe" investment banks had traditionally declined to work on hostile bids, broke ranks in 1974 to advise on a hostile bid for International Nickel. By the early 1980s, most U.S. public companies were vulnerable to hostile bids, and takeover defenses were developed to mitigate that threat. Through the mid-1980s, companies adopted a number of takeover defenses in the form of charter amendments. In retrospect, the most significant of these was the staggered or classified board, which (if properly implemented) imposes a year delay on efforts by shareholders to take control of a target's board.

But charter amendments require shareholder approval, which has not generally been forthcoming for defenses since institutional shareholders organized in the late 1980s. Not surprisingly, shareholders have been unwilling to approve defenses once a high-premium offer has been put on the table, as after IBM's 85% premium bid for Lotus, since defenses may enable target managers to defeat the bid and deprive shareholders of the bid premium. But even when a bid is not on the table, shareholders have been unwilling to approve defenses. The one significant defense that can still be adopted "midstream" (that is, after ownership is dispersed following an IPO) is the poison pill, which does not require shareholder approval. But the pill can be eliminated via proxy fight, and for a large percentage of public companies with poison pills, proxy fights take little longer than tender offers. Despite adoption of pills by 60% of the S&P 1500, there were almost seventy hostile bids in 1995, nearly as many as the peak of the takeover boom of the 1980s, and over forty hostile bids were launched in 2000.

Because midstream defenses have been constrained by legal rules and skeptical investors, the moment prior to going public is the one time at which U.S. companies have been able with certainty to reduce their legal takeover vulnerability. After an IPO is complete and ownership dispersed, the takeover defenses of a public company in the U.S. in the 1990s have generally been fixed. Only at the IPO stage does a company continue to have the ability to choose different types and amounts of defenses that will regulate hostile bids for the life of the company. For that reason, the legal advice a company receives about defenses just prior to its IPO is particularly important.

... [S]cholars have long debated the effects of defenses on companies and their shareholders, and the evidence to date is at best inconclusive. Many believe defenses harm shareholders by making it harder for takeovers to discipline managers and increasing the "agency costs" between shareholders and managers caused by the separation of ownership from corporate control. Others believe defenses may be privately beneficial by providing targets with "bargaining power," by ameliorating the effects of "market myopia," or by allowing some shareholders to preserve "private benefits of control." ... [O]ne feature of such theories should be noted: prior scholarship on defenses has uniformly made the simplifying assumption that if defenses are good for a given company, they will be adopted by that company; if they are bad, they will not be adopted. The theory of this Article, however, is that reality is more complex. Defenses may be adopted even if they are harmful, or omitted even if beneficial, because the decision to adopt defenses is made not by "companies" or by the owners or managers of those companies, but by lawyers.

III. Blame the Lawyers

Companies about to go public for the first time employ two sorts of specialized agents: investment bankers and lawyers. Generally, bankers provide advice about the pricing and timing of the IPO, and manage the sales process itself. Lawyers provide advice about securities laws and disclosure obligations, and manage the Securities Exchange Commission ("SEC") registration process. Each professional may influence the takeover defenses a firm adopts prior to the IPO. Without legal advice, the firm is unlikely to adopt defenses. Without financial advice, the firm will not know whether or how a given defense will affect the IPO price. Companies are dependent on their specialized agents for information and advice that bears directly on what defenses are likely to be adopted during the IPO process.

Given that background, variation in defenses at the IPO stage can be explained by positing inefficiencies in the provision of either financial or legal advice. If defenses are generally inefficient and the IPO pricing process itself is efficient, companies will pay a pricing penalty for adopting them. But if bankers provide poor advice to companies about the price effects of defenses, then companies may adopt defenses despite such a pricing penalty. If, on the other hand, defenses are generally optimal for pre-IPO owner-managers, either because they increase company value or decrease it by less than the control they provide is worth to initial owner-managers, then companies should adopt them. But companies may still not adopt defenses if the lawyers on whom they depend fail to advise adoption or if bankers fail to provide good advice about their price effects.

For reasons discussed [below in subsection G, "The Market for Lawyers Versus the Market for Bankers"], it seems more likely on a priori grounds that market inefficiencies would occur in the market for legal services before it would occur in the market for financial advice. Thus, the explanation proposed and tested in this Article for why defenses vary at the IPO stage is failure in the market for legal services. In short: blame the lawyers.

A. The Lawyer-Client Relationship and Agency Theory

Just as division of labor between shareholders and managers creates the classic agency relationship at the heart of conventional economic analysis of corporate law, so the division of labor between lawyers and clients creates a classic agency relationship, in which the client is dependent on lawyers. Lawyers write the documents in which defenses are (or are not) contained. Takeover defenses are "chosen" in the first instance not by a manager or shareholder, who focus on other, more important tasks (such as lining up investors, working with investment bankers on the "roadshow," and running the business), but by a lawyer. Charters, bylaws, stock certificates, and prospectuses are all generated by law firms, drafted by associates (or paralegals), reviewed by partners (or associates), and only cursorily (if at all) reviewed by nonlawyers during the IPO process.

Given this dependency on lawyers by corporate clients and their owner-managers, basic economic theory of agency provides a simple explanation of why lawyers might not do what is in the best interests of their clients. Put simply, principals (clients) have little information about what their agents are doing and about the effects of agents' actions, which makes it possible that agents will not always act in their principals' best interests. Clients can monitor their lawyers by asking questions, scrutinizing documents, and thinking about defenses themselves. But most clients will be ill-equipped to monitor implementation and will defer to the advice of the lawyer for the same reasons the client has retained the lawyer to begin with (lack of expertise, division of labor).

Gaining proficiency with defenses, providing good advice about defenses, and implementing clients' decisions based on that advice all require effort on the part of lawyers. Were clients able to perfectly monitor lawyers, this is the type of effort in which clients would want lawyers to engage. Since clients cannot easily tell if lawyers are expending that effort, lawyers have little incentive to do so. As such, lawyers will only undertake that minimal level of effort that can be easily monitored by clients. Lawyers will devote the rest of their time and energy to other activities, such as the solicitation of other potential clients, "grandstanding" activities (effort that produces highly visible and impressive results), or the pursuit of leisure activities.

The possibility that lawyers shirk their obligation to act with due care is supported by direct evidence of mistakes by lawyers found in the sample . . . , which suggest that a significant number of attorneys are not paying much attention to basic corporate documents. [*The mistakes Coates found included charter provisions that violate state law, conflicts between the charter and the bylaws, and "functional mistakes," such as attempting to protect incumbent boards by staggering terms, but undermining this protection by empowering shareholders to remove directors by written consent. — Ed.*] Somewhat astonishingly, several companies in the sample also used "form" charters and bylaws published by third-party service providers (for example, Blumberg) for generic corporations, with no effort to tailor the forms to the firm or the fact that it was going public.

B. Takeover Advice as a Credence Good

Standard economic theories of agency also suggest that the potential for mischief in the relationship between lawyers and clients is particularly large. Information asymmetries between lawyer and client in the IPO context are likely to be serious, and will be exacerbated by uncertainty and time: any effect takeover defenses have is unlikely to emerge for years, at which point the lawyers involved may no longer have a relationship with the client. But agency problems with legal advice about takeover defenses are still worse than other types of legal advice because of the particular character of advice concerning takeover defenses.

Evaluating legal services is more difficult than evaluating other types of goods or services. Economists distinguish three types of goods or services: search goods, consumption goods, and credence goods. Search goods are those whose quality can be readily ascertained by inspection prior to consumption, as with postcards. Experience goods are those whose quality can generally be learned only after they are purchased and consumed, as with a meal at a restaurant. Credence goods are those whose quality may never be fully known by the consumer, as with automobile parts, for example. Legal services rarely fall into the category of search goods. Instead, legal services often fall into the category of "experience goods." Experience goods obviously pose a risk of deception and raise special contracting problems. Legal advice often, however, is a "credence good," for which quality may never be fully known. Legal advice about defenses is certainly not a search good. Few legal consumers, even sophisticated consumers, can fully know the quality of legal services to be provided simply by meeting a lawyer or reviewing the lawyer's public record. Nor will consumers usually know the quality of legal services after they are received, since legal advice often involves questions of judgment under conditions of uncertainty that will persist even after a trial or negotiation or other legal event is completed.

What constitutes the "best" legal advice about defenses at the IPO stage is unclear for two reasons. First, the costs and benefits remain theoretically controversial and empirically uncertain. Second, takeovers are sufficiently uncommon so that a particular company may never encounter one. Although [the empirical findings of this study are] consistent with the view that defenses are generally optimal for pre-IPO owner-managers, even that evidence is far from conclusive, and it remains possible that defenses are good only for some companies, or for none at all. As a result of deep and continuing uncertainty about the "merits" of defenses, it is unlikely that clients will be able to know for certain whether the advice about defenses they received at the time of IPOs in the 1990s was good, bad, or indifferent. Knowing this, lawyers were and are even more likely than agents in other contexts to exert suboptimal effort in learning or advising about defenses. Clients, in turn, can be expected to anticipate lawyer behavior in this respect, with the upshot being a socially inefficient level of legal advice being provided, relative to first-best welfare, as with credence goods generally.

The possibility that there is a socially inefficient level of effort being exerted by lawyers is supported by the fact that in surveys, lawyers themselves acknowledge frequently making mistakes, a phenomenon that extends to the largest and most reputable law firms. A recent American Lawyer survey of partners at firms in the AmLaw 100 finds that over half (52%) of partners surveyed who worked sixty-or-more-hour workweeks "worked so fast they made mistakes." Among partners working less than fifty-five hours per week on average, 35% admitted they made mistakes. Anyone who has worked in a law firm knows that, on average, partners work shorter workweeks than associates, so these figures understate errors among lawyers at law firms generally. Partners also increasingly delegate important legal tasks. Self-reporting also underestimates errors, not only because lawyers may be worried about their reputations (researcher promises of anonymity notwithstanding), but also because lawyers will not always notice their own mistakes as they make them, particularly in areas where they are not expert.

C. The Market for Lawyers in the IPO Context

Making matters worse for clients in need of advice about takeover defenses are characteristics of the market for lawyers in the IPO context. IPO lawyers do not specialize in takeovers or takeover defense, for the most part. The legal market has been sufficiently segmented for the past fifteen years that most lawyers who routinely work on hostile takeovers do not routinely advise companies going public for the first time, and vice versa. It is rare for companies going public to be advised by lawyers who have current proficiency in takeovers. Even whole firms specialize in one or the other. Leading takeover firms, such as Wachtell Lipton, do not handle a high volume of IPOs; and leading IPO firms, such as Wilson Sonsini, do not (or did not during the early 1990s) handle a high volume of takeovers.

In addition, lawyers representing start-up companies often have multiple relationships with pre-IPO financiers and managers. Unlike investors as a class and many pre-IPO shareholders, owner-managers are often not repeat players in the IPO market.... Bernstein notes that Valley lawyers "may have a strong financial incentive to draft contractual provisions that favor ... [venture capital] funds at the expense of ... entrepreneurs."[12] Regarding defenses, in particular, IPO law firms may correctly anticipate that while their relations with venture capitalists will persist after the IPO, their relations with managers may diminish or disappear after the IPO if the company fails. Even if the company succeeds, it may become active in merger activity and need a new law firm with proficiency in that area. Relative to VC interests, the interests of owner-managers may get short shrift from IPO lawyers. Even if there is no direct conflict between VC and manager interests, IPO law firms may allocate effort and attention to the former rather than the latter. Since VCs typically sell stakes in start-up companies shortly after an IPO, they have little ongoing interest in whether the company is well-protected from takeover bids. This is not to say VCs would oppose defenses. Still, in general, VCs, and lawyers looking out primarily for VC interests, would not care as much about defenses as well-informed or well-advised owner-managers.

D. Barriers to Competition in the Market for Lawyers

The market for legal services is also protected from full and free competition by a variety of barriers to entry. Law firms have long been protected by regulatory barriers to entry, in the form of the bar exam, a three-year professional degree, and no access to public capital markets, which make the establishment of new law firms more difficult than otherwise would be the case. In addition, such regulations generally prevent other businesses (such as accounting firms or for-profit corporations) from providing third-party legal services, and thereby restrict the number of people providing legal services. Lack of access to the public capital markets has meant that law firms have not historically invested in systems and technology to the same extent as other professional service firms, which constrains competition among lawyers in providing technology-based services.

Lawyers also enjoy a large amount of "natural" (that is, nonregulatory) protection from vigorous competition. The supply of individuals with the talents and inclination to succeed as top-tier corporate lawyers may be inherently (or "naturally") limited. Clients also have reasons to avoid switching to new lawyers at the IPO stage. The clients' pre-IPO lawyers are likely to be needed during and after the IPO, simply because they will be more knowledgeable about many aspects of the clients' legal affairs than new lawyers will be, particularly arrangements with VCs or other pre-IPO outside shareholders, lenders, suppliers, and customers. Pre-IPO law firms play an important role in controlling access to capital providers and other third parties, which can give them significant market power, at least in the short run. Long-standing personal relationships, a sense of debt or gratitude if lawyers provided below-market fees during the start-up period, concerns about confidentiality, and relationship-specific information all deter clients from switching law firms. Gilson and Mnookin characterize the lawyer-client relationship as "approaching" a "bilateral monopoly."[13] Switching costs may partly explain the appearance of small law firms (fewer than twenty-five lawyers) as corporate counsel in 10% of the IPO sample..., despite the general trend toward large size in the corporate law firm market. At times, the costs of switching may be worth it, as when an actual takeover bid appears on a

---

12. Lisa E. Bernstein, *The Silicon Valley Lawyer as Transaction Cost Engineer?*, 74 Or. L. Rev. 239, 248 n.43 (1995).

13. Ronald J. Gilson & Robert H. Mnookin, *Sharing Among the Human Capitalists: An Economic Inquiry into the Corporate Law Firm and How Partners Split Profits*, 37 Stan. L. Rev. 313, 359 (1985)

company's doorstep. But at the time of an IPO, the remoteness of takeover bids may make retention of new counsel with takeover proficiency a negative net present value proposition.

E. The Mechanics of the Production of Takeover Defenses

If takeover proficiency were distributed widely among and within law firms, including down to the lowest-level associates, the lawyer-client agency problems might not be serious. But as noted above, IPO lawyers often lack firsthand experience in takeover fights. They thus lack takeover-law proficiency (1) to decide what defenses to advise a client to adopt, or (2) to implement the decision once made. Nonexpert lawyers have three general methods of handling these two tasks. First, lawyers might research the issue and arrive at their own answers. Second, they might talk to lawyers with takeover expertise, either in their own firm if possible or at other firms. Third, they might rely on "boilerplate," form documents used in prior IPOs.

1. What if the Lawyer Researches the Issue?

Having lawyers research the issue and arrive at their own conclusion is expensive and error-prone. Initially, theories about defenses are highly contentious and unresolved..., and empirical evidence on what defenses are best remains uncertain. Even if the decision of whether to adopt defenses were simple at the highest level of generality, defense analysis is complex when it comes to specifics. Laws vary from state to state, and even if a company sticks to conventional terms and does not try to innovate, it will need to make three choices for each of at least eleven terms: whether to include a given term; whether to include the term in its charter or its bylaws; and under what circumstances and by whom the term can be modified in the future. Together, the number of possible configurations for even a "plain vanilla" set of corporate documents runs into the hundreds of thousands. Over 75% of the companies [in the sample] had a set of fifteen governance terms that were unique within the sample, and no one set accounted for more than 4% of the sample.

Although defense advice also involves questions of judgment, at least on its face, little to no guidance can be found in the most relevant practical literature. A review of the best legal treatises available to assist practitioners, for example, suggests that experienced corporate attorneys pay little attention to defenses during the IPO process. One treatise in particular, Venture Capital and Public Offering Negotiation, has been highly successful since its first publication in 1983. Now in a third edition, the treatise runs over 1,300 pages in thirty-seven chapters, and is coauthored by the pantheon of the venture capital bar, including lead author Michael Halloran of Pillsbury Madison; Larry Sonsini, name partner of Wilson Sonsini; Lee Benton, managing partner of Cooley Godward; Robert Gunderson, founder of Gunderson Dettmer; and Richard Testa, founder of Testa Hurwitz. Topics include the range of legal issues that arise in IPOs. However, in contrast to a carefully annotated form of charter to be used at the time venture capitalists first invest, before the IPO, the treatise provides no good advice about (or models for) takeover defenses for a company about to go public. Other treatises or practitioner outlines addressing IPOs are no more useful to the nonexpert lawyer.

2. What if the Lawyer Speaks to a Takeover Specialist?

If the lawyer turns to another lawyer with some proficiency in takeovers, she faces different difficulties. Clients may be unwilling to foot two lawyers' bills for the same work, so bringing in another lawyer may reduce the IPO lawyer's profit. Worse, a second lawyer may steal the first lawyer's business. A client may (wrongly but understandably) expect that "a corporate lawyer" handling its IPO should have proficiency in a "corporate law" topic like takeover defense. If the IPO lawyer must go to another firm, the second firm may be able to bundle both types of legal advice together, or appear to, for so long as necessary to capture the relationship. If, on the other hand, the first lawyer minimizes contact between the second lawyer and the client, to minimize the risk of relationship capture, the second lawyer will not have good incentives to provide optimal advice. Those lawyers with "free" time to perform such tasks may not be the best lawyers for the job; expert takeover specialists, after all, make large amounts of money, and face large opportunity costs for their time.

3. What if the Lawyer Uses Boilerplate?

If research and consultation are not effective ways for a lawyer to provide a client with good advice about defenses, that leaves boilerplate as a source of information about what defenses are best for lawyer to advise a client to adopt. But inexpert reliance on boilerplate can be dangerous. Boilerplate can either be developed internally or borrowed from at least three sources, of which two are ready-at-hand and very cheap. First, the lawyer can rely on documents used by private companies (private company boilerplate). However, private company boilerplate will leave companies vulnerable to takeover. Private companies do not need defenses, and in fact benefit from having terms that would facilitate hostile takeovers if used by public companies. The cheapest and easiest boilerplate of all then, a company's own pre-IPO documents, which remain in force if no effort is made to change them, will generally make takeovers quite easy.

Second, boilerplate (of a sort) can be developed by simply keeping documents to an absolute minimum, so that "gap-filler" default terms supplied by corporate statutes and case law are implicitly adopted (default law). Default law in all fifty states, however, makes takeovers easy: Delaware default law permits shareholder action by written consent, and default law in states that follow the Revised Model Business Corporation Act ("RMBCA") permits special meetings of shareholders to be called by as few as 10% of the shareholders, which can also greatly facilitate a hostile takeover bid. IPO lawyers who borrow the language of corporate statutes to write governance terms, or who leave documents silent where they are unsure of the correct choice, will generally choose terms that make takeovers fairly easy. Thus, a bias against defenses is built into the legal system, and to the extent that IPO lawyers lack proficiency in the choice of defenses, the companies they advise will tend to go public with minimal defenses in place.

The third source from which a law firm can borrow boilerplate are public companies, which fall into three categories: (1) companies that have recently gone public with law firms that have takeover proficiency; (2) companies that have recently gone public with law firms prominent in the IPO; or (3) other public companies. If an IPO lawyer borrows from a random public company, or one randomly chosen from its own industry or locale, defenses will vary but will on average be fewer in number than is a full set of defenses installed by an expert lawyer. Existing public companies do not have the ability to adopt some midstream defenses even if they would benefit shareholders if adopted pre-IPO. In addition, at least some law firms will have allowed inertia to determine their clients' governance terms (by relying on private company boilerplate or default law). Thus, the IPO population, too, will on average be biased toward fewer defenses. Only if the source is a public company that relied on lawyers proficient in takeovers will the boilerplate be based on expert advice, and even then idiosyncratic client needs or unusual features of the company's state of incorporation or ownership structure may make such a company's defenses a poor model.

Finally, suppose a law firm develops its own boilerplate and encourages its lawyers to use it in all IPOs the firm handles. Results will tend to be fairly uniform: firms that encourage lawyers to use standard forms will tend to produce IPO documents that track each other more closely than they will track IPO documents in general. While results will be consistent for that firm, they may be consistently good or consistently bad, from the perspective of advice on defenses. If the firm does a poor job of "reinventing the wheel," if it bases its internal boilerplate on a private company model or relies on default law, or if it borrows from another inapt model, resulting documents will reflect that choice and consistently contain few defenses.

4. Implementation Once the Decision Has Been Made

After the decision of what defenses to adopt has been made, lawyers must still implement that decision. Implementation is not intrinsically difficult: writing a provision to classify a board, for example, is hardly rocket science. Yet as long as clients cannot easily monitor implementation, and few nonlawyers have the patience or training to read and evaluate charters or bylaws, a risk remains that lawyers will shirk implementation. Anyone with firsthand experience in large corporate law firms will attest that senior partners at successful law firms rarely directly perform the tedious and time-consuming task of drafting or even reading basic legal documents. Instead, such tasks are delegated to junior partners, or, increasingly, associates or even paralegals. Such individuals may lack the training to draft even straightforward provisions effectively. More important than training, however, is the fact that the same agency problem that exists between the client and the most senior lawyer also exists between the most senior lawyer and next most senior lawyer, and so on down the chain. As long as the person actually charged with drafting corporate documents does not have a significant fear of being double-checked, that person will have the same agency-based incentive to shirk on the drafting job.

F. Potential Constraints on IPO Lawyer Autonomy

Lawyers may face constraints in advising clients on takeover defenses in IPOs, and in exercising effort and care in implementing client decisions. In principle, for example, a lawyer is ethically obliged to let a client make important decisions about goals, which might mean that a lawyer has a duty to facilitate monitoring by clients. But a lawyer's ability to frame a complex choice for a client, and to decide (in the course of providing advice) what information to give the client, will so shape the choice that client autonomy is the exception and not the rule for defenses, at least in the context of small-and mid-sized companies.

With respect to defenses, ethically conscientious but inexperienced lawyers may even make matters worse, if they lack confidence to provide strong advice about what defenses to adopt. That is because they may be tempted to frame the question as a choice along a continuum: no defenses, some defenses, all (standard) defenses. A client faced with that choice and neutral advice from the lawyer about what to do may often be tempted to mimic Goldilocks, and adopt defenses that are neither too strong nor too weak. Because of the ways defenses interact, however, such a choice will tend to produce a net set of defenses much closer to the "weak" end of the continuum than the middle. In any event, it seems highly unlikely that ethical duties, which are rarely enforced in this context, constrain corporate lawyers fully.

Clients can in theory try to double-check advice by turning to another lawyer, but this generally works only if advice is simple and discrete. Otherwise the second lawyer may provide unverifiably bad advice designed to make the initial lawyer look bad, and the initial lawyer can dismiss any dispute with the second lawyer as competitively motivated or representing a simple difference in judgment. Further, the client must have some knowledge about the matter in question to even realize that his attorneys may be making a mistake and to seek a second opinion. As in the litigation context, second opinions in the corporate advisory context are of uncertain value, and rare.

The value and importance of reputation also no doubt serves to constrain lawyers to a degree. However, reputation will only constrain lawyers to the extent that the quality of services is observable by third parties and reputational information can be produced and used by others for profit. The third parties best able to evaluate law firm error and use those assessments to their advantage are other law firms, and law firms do occasionally compete by trumpeting each others' mistakes. Yet clients face similar problems evaluating such claims as they do in seeking second opinions.

In theory, to overcome some of these problems, a third-party reputational intermediary not engaged in legal practice might evaluate law firms neutrally, and sell rankings. No pure intermediary of that sort exists, however. The closest substitutes are investment banks, boards, and venture capitalists; they are again likely to impose some constraint on IPO lawyers, but the constraints are likely to be far from complete. Bankers, for example, have their own lawyers, who review firm charter and bylaws and securities. But underwriter lawyers have two fairly narrowly defined roles: most important, they must see to it that the disclosure documents, for which underwriters bear potential liability, accurately describe what the firm documents say; and second, they alert underwriters to any terms that are likely to have price effects. For the latter task, the lawyers rely on shared experience with underwriters about what terms are "standard," and generally will only raise questions if the firm is adopting some novel or unusual term. Defenses of the sort studied in this Article are neither novel nor unusual, and would generally be accepted without much discussion by underwriters' counsel. More important, the absence of a standard defense would not be itself a reason for an underwriter lawyer to object on behalf of underwriters, as the omission would not plausibly have any effect on the underwriters. Some underwriters' counsel with M&A [mergers and acquisitions] proficiency may point out missing defenses anyway (to look good in front of the underwriters, or to try to edge out company counsel for future business), so some constraint is imposed on company counsel in this way. But many omissions could easily go uncorrected.

A final and more general set of potential constraints on company counsel in an IPO are legally informed participants in the process, who may provide "curbside" advice to clients or company counsel about what defenses to adopt. These participants include in-house counsel, as well as managers, VCs, directors, investment bankers, or accountants who have legal training or takeover experience. Again, these participants will impose some constraint on company counsel in the IPO process. Still, it is unusual for these participants to have sufficient proficiency, interest, and responsibility for monitoring pre-IPO choice of legal terms to provide more than a weak constraint on company counsel.

G. The Market for Lawyers Versus the Market for Bankers

Considering that the other possible source of advice on defenses are bankers, it might be useful to contrast the legal and banking industries to show why it seems plausible that the latter would do a better job of providing good advice on a novel or difficult question. The legal industry is so fragmented as to suggest serious barriers to competition; the banking industry is much more concentrated, yet not so much so as to suggest oligopoly. Thus, competition among lawyers is likely to be weaker than competition among bankers, with the result that the latter are likely to provide better services, on average, to their clients. Likewise, relative law firm reputations fluctuate, making reputation a less reliable constraint on lawyers, whereas banker reputation does not. Lawyers are generally paid flat time or task-based rates; underwriters get paid more if the IPO price is higher. Lawyers are still mostly local, and even today few firms are truly national; top investment banks have long served the entire U.S., and are increasingly global. Law firms can be owned only by lawyers, and cannot raise outside equity to invest in technology or growth; investment banks can be owned by anyone, raise capital easily, and invest massively in technology and product development. Relative to banks, law firms are egalitarian and inflexible, whereas banks are hierarchical and restructure frequently. Lawyers traditionally resisted new lines of business; bankers rapidly fill client demand. Lawyers are apt to resist expansion for fear of recession and layoffs; bankers do not blink at layoffs, and banks balloon in booms. As a result, bankers are less likely to oversell services during lean times, or to cut corners during boom times. Again, the likely result is better services from bankers than lawyers, on average. If we had no other evidence and had to choose a likely source of inefficiency to explain the IPO defense puzzle, would we blame the bankers for providing bad advice about the IPO price effects of defenses? Or would we blame the lawyers for providing bad advice about the advantages that takeover defenses can provide?

William W. Bratton, *Enron and the Dark Side of Shareholder Value**

....

I. Enron, Generally Accepted Accounting Principles, and Auditor Independence

In addition to being the largest bankruptcy reorganization in American history (as of December 2, 2001), Enron undoubtedly also was the biggest audit failure....

A. *The Violations*

... As to the first class of Enron accounting violation, concerning SPE consolidation,[14] welcome improvements to the rules can be expected. But it nonetheless should be noted that the central problem here lay not with the rules themselves but Enron's failure to follow them. As to the second Enron accounting problem, nondisclosure of contingent liability on SPE and equity affiliate obligations, GAAP does not seem to be in need of repair. Guarantees are supposed to be disclosed fully in footnotes....

---

* Originally published in 76 TULANE LAW REVIEW 1275–1361 (2002). Reprinted with the permission of the Tulane Law Review Association, which holds the copyright.
14. *See the previous excerpt from this article in Chapter 1.—Ed.*

B. *Incentive Incompatibility at Arthur Andersen*[15]

We already have a case of audit failure here, only its extent remains to be ascertained. The question is not whether GAAP was violated, but how a firm with substantial reputational capital staked on avoiding significant audit failures could have rendered a favorable opinion on the subject financials. Why did Andersen's audit team not pick up the sham in the swaps that weren't? Why did they let the watered stock pass? Was there no review of the guaranty contracts? We must await the results of the many investigations for the detailed factual account.

A broad brush explanation can be offered presently, however. We turn to Enron's 2001 proxy statement, which reports $25 million of auditor fees and $27 million of other consulting fees to Andersen.... Enron, in fact, was Andersen's second biggest client, nationwide. In addition, the top Enron officers in charge of accounting matters were former Andersen accountants. Enron hired away Andersen employees on a routine basis. Meanwhile, numerous Andersen auditors and consultants were permanently posted in offices at Enron. In 1993, Andersen experts had designed Enron's internal compliance system.

The inference of capture is overwhelming. To protect the flow of consulting fees and the value of their long-term relationship with Enron, Andersen's auditors permitted actors at Enron to bully them into signing off on dubious financials. Indeed, so cooperative was the Andersen-Enron relationship that no bullying may have been needed. Andersen's auditors simply mimicked the actions of Enron's managers. As residents of the Enron tower, they no doubt began to internalize the firm culture, becoming risk-prone.

Such assimilation of a risk-prone firm culture is absolutely unacceptable in an auditor. As a primary gatekeeper, the auditor's job is not to collaborate but to bring an objective check to the managers' reports. That check should be not only objective but normatively counterbalancing, introducing a conservatism that reins in the risk-prone tendencies of firm culture. The check should also correct results distorted by cognitive bias. With that accomplished, the information goes to the investment community so that it, rather than the firm's managers, can make the best possible risk assessment....

In theory, the auditor's reputational interest plus a backstop threat of legal liability should import the requisite adverseness to the auditor-client relationship. Until recently, such was the case. In the 1990s, two factors changed. First, ... the liability system was adjusted to make accounting firms less susceptible to liability to private plaintiffs. [*As discussed below and in DeMott's article above, the Supreme Court held in* Central Bank of Denver v. First Interstate Bank *that Rule 10b-5 does not support a private cause of action for aiding and abetting a securities fraud, a common theory of auditor liability. Further, under the Private Securities Litigation Reform Act of 1995, securities plaintiffs must "state with particularity facts giving rise to a strong inference that the defendant acted with the required state of mind." 15 U.S.C.A. 78u-4(b)(2). Many courts interpret this to mean that a complaint must allege specific facts showing the defendant's motive to commit fraud. It is particularly difficult to identify facts showing an auditor's motive.*] Second, Big Five revenues for nonaudit or "management advisory" services grew to fifty percent of total revenues in 2000, where twenty years earlier they had constituted only thirteen percent of total revenues....

---

15. *Arthur Andersen was the accounting firm that served as Enron's outside auditor. Andersen collapsed after being convicted of obstruction of justice in connection with federal authorities' investigation of Enron.* — Ed.

C. Reform

....

1. Blaming the Rules

The [major accounting firms'] first response to Enron was business as usual. Even with his firm's reputation on the line, Joe Berardino, the managing partner of Arthur Andersen, joined Enron's officers in pointing fingers elsewhere. The real failure, he said, lay in the accounting rules themselves, which after all permit off-balance sheet financing through SPEs....

Andersen and the other big accounting firms [wrote a joint letter asking the SEC to formulate clear accounting rules.] To restore confidence, the SEC should supply "immediate guidance" to public companies respecting disclosure of off-balance sheet transactions, over-the-counter derivative contracts, and related party transactions in time to impact MD&A in 2001 reports. In particular, the SEC should require issuers to provide more details respecting off-balance sheet guarantees, commitments, lease, and debt arrangements which could impact on credit ratings, earnings, cash flow, or stock price....

It is true that openness in the framework of GAAP makes it harder for accounting firms to say no to big clients. But how open is GAAP's framework? Significantly, in the wake of Enron-related stock market reverses of early 2002, commentators began voicing the opposite complaint. The problem with GAAP, they said, is that it presents an exhaustive check-the-box system of rules. The auditors apply the rules mechanically, ignoring the substance of the clients' transactions....

From all of this there arises a question: Wherein lies the problem with GAAP—too many rules, as these commentators assert, or too many standards, as the Big Five asserted?

The answer is that the problem lies in neither place. There can never be a 100% directive rulebook in accounting anymore than there is in any other regulatory context. Nor can slavish rule application ever be trusted to yield perfect results. There is always a moment of judgment. Accordingly, GAAP, of necessity, mixes rules and standards and always will do so. Meanwhile, if we return to the application of GAAP to the facts of this case in this Article's previous Part, we see that the rules, applied in good faith, were more than adequate to pick up every material event in the story of Enron's collapse.... Standards only work when the actor authorized to apply them is ready to take responsibility for a judgment call....

If GAAP is not fundamentally flawed, then the solution to the Enron problem lies on the enforcement side, where we encounter some highly problematic institutional arrangements.

D. Audits and Shareholder Value Maximization

... [Former SEC Chair Arthur Levitt criticized Wall Street's accounting system in a 1998 address.]. Levitt's warnings respecting the institutional framework and operations of the accounting system covered most of the salient points in the Enron disclosure disaster—the compromise of auditor independence, the tendency of issuers to manage their net earnings so as to meet analyst's growth expectations, and material nondisclosures justified under the percentage-based materiality principle. Most of all, Levitt warned that the entire financial community followed perverse short-term incentives:

I'm challenging corporate management and Wall Street to re-examine our current environment. I believe we need to embrace nothing less than a cultural change. For corporate managers, remember, the integrity of the numbers in the financial reporting system is directly related to the long-term interests of a corporation. While the temptations are great, and the pressures strong, illusions in numbers are only that—ephemeral, and ultimately self-destructive.[16]

... In theory, the auditor-client relationship should have a significant adversarial aspect. Management chooses the accounting policies and practices and the auditor conducts a critical review. If management's choices fall outside the accounting profession's substantive parameters, the auditor imposes compliance with GAAP, wielding the threat of an unfavorable opinion. In today's practice context, the threat has become idle.

The accounting profession has drifted into the role of friendly service provider, lured by management bribes characterized as consultancy fees. When Enron caused everybody to wake up and ask for an enforcer, the accountants at first asked us to hand the regulatory club to someone else. The only entity equipped to pick it up was the government, acting in the guise of exhaustive rulemaker. Thus did the Big Five entreat the SEC to take over the articulation of GAAP, ready to abandon their own profession's historic assumption of responsibility respecting rulemaking. And they requested more than a transfer of the legislative function. They asked for legislation in the form of rules. This is because imposition of a standard implies voluntary analysis and judgment in which imposition of a rule may be ascribed to the rulemaker's will. The request signifies a profession in wretched decline.

II. Aiding and Abetting and Private Litigation

Of all the subjects we have considered, private rights of action are most outside the control of the SEC, being mainly the province of the courts and (lately) Congress. However, they are closely connected to the SEC's work. Unless there is a vastly enlarged SEC, private actions inevitably must serve as an enforcement substitute for deterrence purposes, as well as their more traditional role as an avenue for appropriate compensation of victims. This paper is not the place to revisit the debates of 1995 over what reforms should or should not be adopted with respect to private securities litigation. The current system, both before and after reform, bears so little resemblance to the ideal that I would be tempted simply to start anew in crafting the appropriate rules.

Here, I want to focus simply on two areas where private actions touch closely on the integrity of the financial reporting process. If private actions are to be a useful deterrence supplement to SEC enforcement, then—just like the SEC—they have to be able to reach not only issuers but also the human beings and firms that actually engineer the fraud. Here, we come to the Supreme Court's *Central Bank of Denver v. First Interstate Bank* case,[17] barring private aiding and abetting liability under Rule 10b-5 and, presumably, some other kinds of secondary agency-based or vicarious theories of liability. Imagine that a second-in-command financial officer devises some fraudulent accounting scheme, in which some investment-banking firm plays a key role in structuring the transaction. Both the manager and the investment bank should be liable, surely. But, as is well known,

---

16. "The Numbers Game," Remarks of SEC Chairman Arthur Levitt at the N.Y.U. Center for Law and Business (Sept. 28, 1998), available at http://www.sec.gov/news/speech/speecharchive/1998/spch220.txt.

17. [511 U.S. 164 (1994).]

many lower courts have followed *Central Bank* to an illogical conclusion, demanding that the fraud be visibly attributable to the person or firm before "primary" liability attaches. [*The Supreme Court affirmed this "illogical conclusion" in* Stoneridge v. Scientific-Atlanta, *552 U.S. 148 (2008).—Ed.*] Behind the scenes actors gain immunity for that reason alone, even if they are the primary authors or architects of the fraud. Other courts disagree, but it has created a mess. *Central Bank* should be overruled legislatively [*in* Central Bank (*and* Stoneridge), *the Court based its holdings on legislative intent*], leaving to other winnowing mechanisms the task of assuring that secondary actors are not named as defendants when they had no responsibility for the fraud at all.

But that probably will not occur, and hence the SEC has to step in with its explicit statutory authority. Reading the various press accounts of Enron, I have a strong suspicion (though not the facts to be sure) that much of the fraud was engineered by Enron insiders with substantial help from investment bankers and others who gave not only technical assistance in deal structuring and financing but actively marketed strategies of evasion under circumstances where there was enough awareness of Enron's desire to mislead to satisfy at least the recklessness test. If so, then one of the strongest tests of the SEC's political will in responding to the mess will be how aggressively it pursues that matter, and whether it will insist on penalties sufficient to take away far more than the profits the banks earned from these practices.

Lawrence E. Mitchell, *The Sarbanes-Oxley Act and the Reinvention of Corporate Governance?*

The Sarbanes-Oxley Act (the Act), signed into law by President Bush in July 2002, creates the need to re-think the way we approach our study of corporate governance in two ways and has the potential (depending upon the results of, and actions taken in response to, various studies that are required to be completed under that Act during the next year) dramatically to change the way we think about, write about and teach corporate law. The Act makes three specific changes in the way we think about corporate governance: first, it brings into the realm of internal governance the gatekeepers that once stood outside the box, including auditors, analysts and lawyers. Second, it significantly enhances the legal status of, and centrality of corporate governance to, the chief executive officer and the audit committee, two constituents that have received very little recognition in the law and its literature. Third, both in doing this and in other respects (like the prohibition of loans to officers and certain other conflict of interest transactions), it federalizes an important dimension of the internal laws of corporate governance, creating a new (albeit arguably narrow) duty of care for the CEO and audit committee and reintroducing serious prohibitions on conflict of interest transactions that have eroded to nothingness in the hands of the Delaware judiciary and legislature....

These insights are necessarily speculative. The Act is new. Regulations are in the process of being adopted. We have hardly begun to sort through the various causes of the corporate crisis of 2002. Moreover, corporate managers, investment bankers, accountants and lawyers have shown themselves to be enormously adept at evading the substance of regulation even as they may comply with its form. In the absence of detailed regulation and vigorous enforcement, the Act could turn out to be so much sound and fury signifying

* Originally published in 48 VILLANOVA LAW REVIEW 1189 (2003). Reprinted with permission.

nothing. I therefore present these observations in the spirit of suggesting what the Sarbanes-Oxley Act can be at its best. Whether in practice it achieves these results remains to be seen.

I. The Foxes in the Henhouse

The traditional function of the gatekeepers of our corporate system — auditors, lawyers and analysts — was to stand outside the corporate structure and evaluate, from the perspective of their respective expertise, the financial condition, legal conduct and business prospects of the corporation. Each of these gatekeepers had, and continues to have, a different relationship with the corporation than the others. Auditors, for example, have been charged with an independent role in verifying the corporation's financial reporting compliance with generally accepted accounting principles. Lawyers, consistent with their professional obligations, are more closely identified with the corporation, its secrets and interests, appearing in the public interest only indirectly to help keep the corporation's behavior within the boundaries of the law and, rarely, directly in the case of major corporate criminal behavior. Both of these gatekeepers are compensated by the corporation for their services, although in the case of the auditor that fact has always created some conflict in the auditor's independence and leaves it subject to pressure by the audited corporation. Analysts have no direct relationship to the corporation, serving instead as their clients the brokerage houses for which they work and, indirectly, the commission-paying clients of those houses who rely upon the analysts' independent financial and business evaluations of the corporation's health and prospects in making investment decisions.

Each of these gatekeepers has, of course, its own body of regulation with which it must comply. That of the accounting industry is, perhaps, most Byzantine. The accounting profession has been, until the Act, an entirely self-regulating one — except to the extent that the SEC has disciplinary jurisdiction over accountants practicing before it and the statutory authority to set substantive accounting rules (as to which it typically defers to the accounting profession). Auditing standards have been generally promulgated by the Accounting Standards Board of the American Institute of Certified Public Accountants (AICPA); auditing rules and principles by the Financial Accounting Standards Board (FASB). As a result, and despite the inchoate regulatory authority of the Commission, accounting rules and standards [were] promulgated by accountants, and therefore subject to the influence and pressure of paying clients. [Prior to the Act, p]olicing of accounting standards [was] left to the accounting firms which, on a rotating basis, sample[d] and test[ed] each others' work. [*The Sarbanes-Oxley Act replaced the self-regulation of accounting with the Public Company Accounting Oversight Board (PCAOB), an independent, private corporation charged with overseeing the auditors of public companies. — Ed.*] ...

Lawyers are in a somewhat different position. As I noted earlier, their job is not to protect the public interest, at least not directly, but to protect the interest of the corporation. While lawyers, like industry, can lobby Congress and state legislatures, the rules they apply are the output of the legislative process and, even recognizing the insights of public choice theory, less manipulable by lawyers for their clients' interests than are the accounting rules and standards. To the extent the creation of these laws is manipulable, they are theoretically more likely to be manipulated by lawyers in the interests of their corporate clients than against them.

But here is the rust in the hinges of the gate kept by lawyers. While we know, and while ethics rules recognize, that the corporate lawyer's client is the corporation, and it is the interests of the corporate body the lawyer is obligated to represent, we also know (and especially those of us that have practiced corporate law know) that the interest of the corporation is expressed by a body of humans: the board of directors. But even that expression of corporate interest is more exceptional than typical, occurring only in the cases of major corporate decisions and transactions which are, by definition, infrequent, but which are the grist for the corporate lawyer's daily practice.

As a practical matter, the lawyers handling a corporation's problems, whether in-house or outside counsel, are likely to take their orders (and thus the expression of corporate interest) from a variety of human beings, ranging from the chief executive officer to, in the case of lower level in-house counsel, middle-level managers. While each in their respective capacities, and subject to the levels of authority granted to them, these actors speak for the corporation, they all also have their own self-interests to pursue, self-interests regulated in part by the traditional state rules of corporate law. The problem, of course, is that while the lawyer is conscious of his role as representing the corporation's interest, it is also the case (as any practicing lawyer knows) that it becomes easy to identify with an individual or individuals representing that client. Thus, it is easy for those individuals to rationalize the reconciliation of corporate interest and their own interest, and it is often difficult, except in the most blatant of cases, for the lawyer to determine where one ends and the other begins—and even more so to challenge the individual when the lawyer believes that the orders he is given serve the individual's interest at the expense of the corporation.

Lawyers also self-regulate through state supreme courts and bar associations, subject to the individual states' rules of professional responsibility. (The Commission also has disciplinary power over lawyers practicing before it who violate its rules.) Those rules, mired in a tradition of fiduciary loyalty to clients' interests, are far less subject to manipulative pressure than accountants' rules because they are, for the most part and unlike the accountants' rules, designed to align the lawyers' behavior with the clients' interests. But this, too, presents a problem. To the extent that lawyers come to identify with the individuals with whom they daily deal, instead of the intangible corporation they are bound to represent, they too are subjected to tangible and psychological pressures to conform their advice and behavior to the interests of those individuals. Thus another aspect of our gatekeeper system, while not quite the Maginot Line presented by the regulatory structure of the accounting profession is, at a minimum, seriously weakened.

The third major barrier is the community of securities analysts. Unlike accountants and lawyers, analysts are neither retained by nor paid by the corporation. In fact, they choose or are assigned the corporations on which they focus. But they serve an important gate-keeping function for all that.

Analysts are hired by brokerage firms to analyze the financial past, present and future of each of the corporations they follow, compare their assessments with the market price of their respective stock, evaluate the quality of that corporation as an investment, and provide that information to their firms' brokers who, in consideration of the commissions charged to investors in trades, will recommend investments based on the analysts' conclusions. While analysts are financially trained in a manner that is usually superior to that of the average client, their work is nothing that the client could not do himself or herself if he or she had the time. The analysts' principal value lies in saving the investor that time, thus allowing the investor more broadly to diversify the investor's portfolio. Analysts also, as a practical matter and because of their access to company officials, can obtain soft information that otherwise would not be available to the average investor. In that respect, the analyst is capable of giving a more nuanced assessment of the investment merits of a particular corporation than even well-trained average investors willing to put in the time.

But the analysts' importance goes well beyond providing advice to their firms' clients. As the central players in the financial analysis of corporate America in an age of diversification, they are the actors best situated to evaluate the veracity of a corporation's public information as well as the actors who, by position and training, ought to be the first line of skepticism. As recent events have shown, in those respects they have dismally failed.

Analysts are not a self-regulating profession. They, or at least the brokers they serve, are subject to the broker-dealer rules promulgated by the Commission, and to the rules of the various stock exchanges. They are also regulated by the National Association of Securities Dealers, whose rules are designed to prevent bad practices like churning accounts, at the same time as they work to encourage analysts (and the brokers who use their information) to, at a relatively low level of intensity, work in the clients' interests. Nonetheless, analysts are subject to pressures and perverse incentives of their own. In the first place, to the extent that they are rewarded with valuable, nonpublic information (soft information, that is, not the material information that would be the subject of insider trading), they have incentives to keep their corporate contacts happy which, presumably, means recommending stock. Moreover, to the extent that their compensation is dependent upon the success of the brokerage firm for which they work, analysts have an incentive to ensure that brokers are able to generate commissions, and thus to ensure a steady flow of information that justifies stock trading. Third, as has become a central act in the corporate follies of 2002, to the extent that they work for firms that also do investment banking, they have incentives to say nice things about corporations that might become investment banking clients of their firms and thus enrich them. In the face of these pressures, the relatively weak rules that regulate analysts clash with their financial incentives and further weaken the gates our legal and financial systems have erected to keep corporations honest.

Students of corporate governance have not traditionally treated any of these three groups as relevant to their subject of study, the relationship among boards, officers and stockholders. To the extent they intersect with corporate governance issues in the context of securities regulation, which itself has largely been treated as peripheral to corporate governance, lawyers and accountants in particular have received some attention, but not much. The Sarbanes-Oxley Act changes that. By directly connecting the functions of these gatekeepers to the traditional corporate governance machinery (and by creating the potential for even further connections), it compels us to recognize these actors as centrally involved in the processes of corporate governance. And by creating (or authorizing the creation of) substantive rules to govern their outputs and behavior, it serves not only to alter the ways in which we look at the corporation but also to strengthen the relatively weak rules state law provides to regulate corporate governance, much in the way that an earlier generation of reformist scholars hoped that the securities laws themselves would.

II. Bringing the Barbarians Inside the Gate

A. Accountants and the Federalization of Corporate Governance

[*This portion of the article, excerpted in above in Chapter 9, explains how the Sarbanes-Oxley Act "connects auditors with the board and management" by requiring the board to have an independent audit committee and requiring the CEO and CFO to certify the corporation's financial reporting. — Ed.*]

... The regulations under the Act take matters still further. First, as I noted above, is the virtual requirement of a designated financial expert on the board whose responsibility for the integrity of the corporation's financial condition follows as a corollary from her public identification and accountability.

But it does far more. In the first place, … the Commission requires that certification not be just of compliance of the corporation's financial statements with GAAP, but include a requirement that these officers certify that the corporation's financial statements "and other financial information included in the report, fairly present in all material respects the financial condition, results of operations and cash flows of the issuer.…" Thus, the CEO and CFO are required to represent that any financial information presented (which presumably includes pro forma financial statements not in accordance with GAAP) give a fair picture of the corporation's financial status. Moreover, while the Act does not require this certification to cover cash flows, the Commission has added this requirement as consistent with the need for fair presentation. The certification responsibilities of the CEO and CFO impose upon them a greater centrality in the corporate governance process (at least with regard to finance) than the law of corporate governance now contemplates.

This is further illustrated by additional certification requirements (which meet up with disclosure requirements; that which is to be certified must also be disclosed.) Among the disclosures to be made are the issuer's "disclosure controls and procedures," a new concept introduced in the regulations. Disclosure controls and procedures are designed to ensure that information the issuer is required to disclose in its filings with the Commission is properly collected and processed so that disclosure occurs in a timely manner. Moreover, the CEO and CFO are required to certify that they not only are responsible for designing and maintaining those controls, but that they also have evaluated their effectiveness and disclosed their evaluations. With respect to the issuer's internal controls, CFOs and CEOs must further certify that they have identified any "significant" deficiencies to the corporation's auditors and audit committee, as well as any fraud, whether or not material, involving employees who have a role in the issuer's internal controls. Moreover, these reports are to be included in the issuer's Commission filings. It seems clear that, at least as to the presentation of financial information and the corporation's internal processes both for SEC reporting and for auditing, these two officers have been burdened with what is, in effect, a federal duty of care.

But there is more that goes to issues traditionally thought of within the context of governance. Among the disclosures the corporation is required to make is whether it has adopted a code of ethics governing the corporation's "principal executive officer, principal financial officer, [and] principal accounting officer or controller" and an explanation, in the absence of such a code, of such absence. The Act defines "code of ethics" to mean standards "reasonably necessary to promote honest and ethical conduct, including the ethical handling of actual or apparent conflicts of interest between personal and professional relationships; [and] full, fair, accurate, timely, and understandable disclosure in the periodic reports required to be filed by the issuer.…" The Commission, in its regulations, goes beyond the Act and requires such a code to focus on senior financial officers and adds "principal executive officer." Moreover, whereas the Act's definition of code of ethics is largely that presented above, the rules add that such a code also must be a "codification of standards that is reasonably designed to deter wrongdoing" and promote "avoidance of conflicts of interest" in the first place and "prompt internal reporting" of violations of the code, as well as disclosure of "accountability for adherence to the code."

While the Commission (rightly, at least in form) claims that its approach to codes of ethics is consistent with the general securities law policy of disclosure, the claim is somewhat disingenuous in two respects. First is the definition of codes of ethics noted above, which clearly specifies the substance that such a code of ethics is required to address. Second (and this is the formal truth) is the fact that the requirement that such a code of ethics be disclosed and filed more or less assures that every reporting company will adopt such a code or something that is substantially similar. In these respects, and given the fairly rigorous substantive requirements of the code (standards "preventing" conflicts of interest), the Act and regulations rather clearly impart substantive governing principles into the corporation, and indeed, when added to the certification requirement, seem to establish a rather rigorous federal duty of care.

Compare what the Act does in this respect to the incredibly weak system of corporate monitoring approved by the Delaware Chancery Court in that most disingenuous of opinions, *In re Caremark*.[18] In that case, Chancellor Allen gave a great deal of lip service to Delaware's standards of supervision and the extent to which they were met by Caremark's cosmetic policies in a case in which it was obvious, to the even marginally sophisticated observer, that Caremark's compensation system and management structure were set up in every way possible to create incentives for employees to ... defraud the Medicare program. The Act actually creates serious incentives for executives to ensure that an effective internal monitoring standard exists. The teeth behind the Act are that it makes the CEO and CFO subject not only to securities law violations, but also to disgorgement of potentially substantial portions of their compensation, if they fail to fulfill those standards. Thus is a federal duty of care clearly introduced by the Act, tied in large measure to the motivating ideal of accounting reform.

The Act also provides its own duty of loyalty rules which are far more stringent than the flabby rules that dominate state law. Section 402 severely restricts the circumstances under which corporations can make loans to insiders such that only loans of a certain type and under standards made in the ordinary course of business by that corporation (which, for the most part, means credit card companies, banks and brokerage houses) are permitted. This is something that responsible state corporate governance should already have dealt with. After all, the only "fair" basis upon which loans can truly be said to be made to insiders are those as to which the interest rate is equal to the corporation's average rate of return on its business projects. Of course this is often not the case. To the extent that such loans are, as they clearly are, a form of compensation, the fact that such compensation is made in the form of loans makes it more difficult for stockholders to value. State law disclosure requirements as to such loans are, at best, insipid.

Again, we can look to one of the more disingenuous opinions of the Delaware Chancery Court, Chancellor Allen's opinion in *Lewis v. Vogelstein*,[19] for confirmation. There the issue was disclosure of an admittedly difficult to value grant of stock options. The Chancellor, noting that the options were not susceptible to valuation under the commonly used Black-Scholes model, concluded that no disclosure was required. According to the Chancellor, disclosure might, after all, mislead or confuse stockholders. But unmentioned in the opinion is a simple fact that the Chancellor had to have known: the directors who were the recipients of those options had some opinion as to their value. How could they not? After all, nobody accepts an offer of compensation without some clear sense of what it is worth. Nonetheless, the Chancellor did not require the directors' own estimates (clearly material information) to be disclosed to the stockholders. Moreover, there is another indication that the directors had to have had some sense of the value of the

---

18. In re Caremark International Derivative Litigation, 698 A.2d 959 (Del. Ch. 1996).
19. 699 A.2d 327 (Del. Ch. 1997).

options. Surely to approve compensation in amounts that were indeterminable would be uninformed compensation and thus, without such knowledge (or at least opinion), the directors would have been unable to satisfy even Delaware's minimal requirements of the business judgment rule. The Act dispenses with such nonsense by, at least in the case of publicly held corporations, supplanting substantive state law rules with federal rules of internal corporate governance.

B. Lawyers

The next category of gatekeeper brought by the Act within the corporate governance system is the lawyer, and the Act potentially radically changes the lawyer's role. Not surprisingly, this has proven to be perhaps the most controversial portion of the Act....

The Act makes the lawyer, in a meaningful way, a coordinate constituent of the corporate governance process. The Commission follows this conception of the lawyer as a coordinate part of the corporate governance machinery rather explicitly: "Attorneys ... play an important and expanding role in the internal processes and governance of issuers...."

... [T]he Act brings within the governance structure an actor almost wholly ignored in corporate governance scholarship—the outside counsel.

But the way in which the Act does this is striking and has significant implications for the federalization of corporate law. Not only are lawyers required to "rat out" material violations of the securities laws by the corporation or its agents, they are also required to report "breaches of fiduciary duty or similar violations,"[20] violations which the Supreme Court has told us in no uncertain terms are the exclusive province of state law and have no business in federal securities legislation. Well, now they do. The Commission defines "breach of fiduciary duty" as "any breach of fiduciary or similar duty recognized under an applicable federal or state statute or at common law," including, but not limited to, misfeasance, nonfeasance, abdication of duty, abuse of trust, and approval of unlawful transactions." In creating this requirement, the Act not only makes the lawyer a central actor in the monitoring function of corporate governance with which we, as a profession, have been centrally concerned, but it also links that role directly to state substantive law. The potential either is for better corporate governance through an additional monitoring organ or, as I fear in my more cynical moments, a further watering-down of state law fiduciary duty to protect corporate lawyers, especially in their counseling role.

The implications are more significant than even these very significant effects might appear at first blush. For while lawyers have always counseled corporate clients with respect to fiduciary obligations, as instruments of the corporation's interest informed by boards and officers, the lawyer is frequently asked to counsel action and design transactions in ways that may come close to fiduciary breaches (and, sometimes, arguably are fiduciary breaches.) This is likely to be changed by the Act, or at least the incentives for changed behavior and more finely conscientious counseling are clear. For now the lawyer is obligated to report breaches of fiduciary obligation, and is subject to Commission sanctions for failing to do so. With their own liability and professional well-being on the line, it seems reasonable to expect that lawyers will be less aggressive in fiduciary counseling than they might have been—that is, less aggressive in counseling close to the line—and certainly

---

20. *See section 307; excerpts from the SEC rules promulgated thereunder are excerpted in this chapter.*

more likely to see breaches of fiduciary obligation where they might have been overlooked before....

C. Analysts

Finally we come to a group that has traditionally been completely beyond the Pale of corporate governance—securities analysts. Just as the credit rating agencies (as to which the Act demands an efficacy study) have served bondholders by providing supposedly objective advice on the investment quality of corporate bonds, the even less visible securities analysts fed their research to brokers and clients in what one might have hoped was an effort to provide an objective assessment of the financial condition and business prospects of the companies they followed. While we now know (if we had not already suspected) that their collective performance in this endeavor was deeply flawed, we have, as a profession, relied heavily upon analysts as a major mechanism in creating the efficient securities markets we assumed we had, … permitting investors to rely upon the integrity of stock prices in general and rationally diversify their portfolios without a great deal of need to perform such research functions themselves. Clearly we were wrong....

The Act works to correct this in two ways. Outside of the parameters of traditional corporate governance, it requires the Commission to adopt rules protecting analysts from any sort of penalty or retaliation from their employers because of their recommendations and requires, as a legal matter, separation of investment banking functions from brokerage and analyst functions. It also requires analysts to publicly disclose conflicts of interest. These protections and rules are clearly designed to increase the objectivity of analysts' reports and, therefore, the efficiency of the market.

At the same time, however, albeit less directly than in the case of auditors and lawyers, the effect of the Act is to improve the quality of monitoring by creating legal incentives and penalties encouraging analysts to more thoroughly and carefully examine the corporations they follow, thus providing an important adjunct to boards, auditors and lawyers in corporate monitoring. While less direct and more modest in scope than the ways in which the Act interjects auditors and lawyers into the corporate governance structure, and while not providing substantive standards of reporting or performance as it does in the case of auditors, CEOs, CFOs and audit committees, the Act nonetheless imports another measure of federal law into the corporate governance structure.

What should be clear from the preceding discussion is the extent to which the Act expands, or potentially expands, the scope of corporate governance rather dramatically by directly assigning governance responsibilities to actors who previously had stood aloof from matters of governance (although their actions clearly played a role in corporate governance). At least as important, these roles are part of a new federal scheme, largely detailed and enforced by the Commission, which significantly intrudes upon, if it does not necessarily supplant (or at least not supplant completely) the role of state corporate governance law.

Thus, the Act potentially serves as a declaration that our monitoring model of corporate governance, in which we principally relied upon a weak system of monitoring by the board (governed by laws that allowed it to abrogate much of its responsibility) and the market is a failure, as demonstrated by the events of 2002. It serves, to some extent, as an assertion that the corrective lies in the federal takeover of substantive aspects of state corporate law, as well as the mandated inclusion within the governance machinery, the responsibilities of which are directed toward ensuring the integrity of the monitoring and disclosure necessary to ensure that our corporate system works effectively. While not quite the federal corporate law envisioned by Bill Cary,[21] it has the potential to rock the preeminence of Delaware as the font of all things corporate and ensure some degree of uniformity in standards of care and loyalty in public corporations.

Larry E. Ribstein, *Market vs. Regulatory Responses to Corporate Fraud: A Critique of the Sarbanes-Oxley Act of 2002*[*]

....

I. Auditors and Other Detectives

Public accountants undoubtedly contributed to the recent corporate frauds by certifying financial statements that ultimately proved to be fraudulent or at least defective. Lax accounting standards, as in the case of the three percent equity rule for moving liabilities to off balance sheet entities,[22] arguably contributed to the problem. These rules could be tightened, but this might lead to excess conservatism that causes as many problems as excessively lax standards, including misleading the market and inviting evasion. In any event, standards could not have been the whole problem because as long as the basic transactions are recorded, the market ultimately can see through how the transactions are reported. This was certainly the case with Sunbeam, in which most of the bad accounting was uncovered by a Barron's reporter based almost entirely on the company's own disclosures, and to some extent was the case even with Enron....

Even if the sale of nonaudit services affected auditors' reporting of fraud, it is not clear that restricting accounting firms' sale of such services, as under Sarbanes-Oxley, will solve the problem. Such a restriction, standing alone, probably cannot reverse the strong profit-oriented culture that now seems to pervade accounting firms. In any event, the restriction is porous. Although the Act forbids the sale of nonaudit services "contemporaneously" with audit services by the same accounting firm, clients may still have some leverage over auditors that hope to sell nonaudit services to them in the future or to others with whom clients have contractual or ownership ties.

For present purposes, the more serious issue is whether even strong regulation will change auditors' practical ability to find corporate fraud when determined corporate insiders want to hide it. In the wake of the WorldCom disclosure, an accounting expert pointed out that accountants do not do "forensic audits" designed to uncover wrongdoing, but rather only sampling audits that may entirely miss the problem. The AICPA draft standard on auditing for fraud observes that "identifying individuals with the requisite attitude to commit fraud, or recognizing the likelihood that management or other employees will rationalize to justify committing the fraud, is difficult." The draft notes that "characteristics of fraud include concealment through (a) collusion by both internal and third parties; (b) withheld, misrepresented, or falsified documentation; and (c) the ability of management to override or instruct others to override what otherwise appear to be effective controls."

---

21. *In* Federalism and Corporate Law: Reflections upon Delaware, *83 YALE L.J. 663 (1974), Professor Cary argued that the federal government should implement "minimum corporate law provisions" as a check on the "race to the bottom" in state corporate law (see Chapter 3 of this volume). —Ed.*

   * Originally published in 28 JOURNAL OF CORPORATION LAW 1 (2002). Reprinted with permission.

22. *I.e., "special purpose entities" (SPEs). See Professor Bratton's article in Chapter 1. —Ed.*

To be sure, there is much auditors can do to spot fraud, including developing cross-check procedures and identifying risky situations.... However, requiring auditors to do significantly more than they are doing now may involve more than just changing their incentives and making them more independent, but also may involve changing the basic scope of what they do. The benefits of increased auditing may not exceed the costs.

If investors cannot rely on auditors to find fraud, it is even less realistic for them to rely on government regulators. Sarbanes-Oxley establishes a Public Company Accounting Oversight Board to scrutinize auditors. However, as indicated by the controversy over picking the chair of the board, simply designating a new regulatory overseer is unlikely to be a panacea. Sarbanes-Oxley also instructs the SEC to increase its review of financial statements and increases the SEC's budget. However, the SEC faces formidable problems in monitoring for fraud. The SEC is charged with a wide range of tasks in addition to spotting fraud in financial statements, including oversight of securities firms, exchanges, investment advisors, and mutual funds, and of market trading, including insider trading. Its staff is perennially too small for these mammoth tasks....

II. Collateral Organizational Effects

... [Section 307 of Sarbanes-Oxley instructs the SEC to promulgate rules] requiring lawyers to "report evidence of a material violation of securities law or breach of fiduciary duty or similar violation by the company or any agent thereof."[23] [This requirement] raises ... serious questions. The rule obviously inhibits conversations between lawyers and the firm's agents at all levels. In this respect, ... there is a tradeoff between the need to encourage the flow of information among the firm's agents and the need to ensure that the information flows to the right place.

The rule also imposes new risks on lawyers, with further consequences for legal representation of publicly traded corporations. The rule requires the lawyer to report "evidence" of wrongdoing whether or not the lawyer concludes that such wrongdoing has occurred. It also reaches beyond securities law violations to fiduciary breaches and "similar" violations, whatever that means. Lawyers concerned about losing their privilege to practice before the SEC, and thereby their livelihoods, will be inclined to interpret these requirements liberally. The potential breadth of the requirement increases the risks, and therefore the costs, of corporate legal representation....

[*In 2003, the ABA Model Rules of Professional Conduct were revised to agree with Sarbanes-Oxley and the new SEC rules. Prior to this revision, Model Rule 1.13's requirements on lawyers were somewhat similar to, but less demanding than, Sarbanes-Oxley and the new SEC Rules. — Ed.*] [The former] Rule 1.13(b) require[d] disclosure within the organization only where the act relate[d] to that organization and the lawyer "knows" of a potential act that "is likely to result in substantial injury to the organization." [*Compare this with the new SEC rule at 17 CFR § 205.3(b)(1). — Ed.*] [The former Rule 1.13(b) also] require[d] the lawyer to "proceed as is reasonably necessary in the best interest of the organization" giving

> due consideration to the seriousness of the violation and its consequences, the scope and nature of the lawyer's representation, the responsibility in the organization and the apparent motivation of the person involved, the policies

---

23. *Excerpts from the SEC rules promulgated pursuant to this section,* 17 C.F.R. § 205, *appear later in this chapter. — Ed.*

of the organization concerning such matters and any other relevant considerations. Any measures taken shall be designed to minimize disruption of the organization and the risk of revealing information relating to the representation to persons outside the organization.

This language require[d] lawyers to exercise professional judgment about reporting facts. [*Neither the new SEC rules nor the revised Model Rule 1.13 includes this language. — Ed.*] Moreover, rather than simply being required to report the act to a senior officer or director as under section 307, the lawyer [could] consider "asking reconsideration of the matter" or "advising that a separate legal opinion on the matter be sought for presentation to appropriate authority in the organization."

[The former] Rule 1.13 was the product of a long debate within the bar.... When a group of forty law professors wrote the SEC in the spring of 2002 urging adoption of an attorney duty to report illegal conduct to the board, the SEC rejected the move. Sarbanes-Oxley went further not only than Rule 1.13, but even the rule proposed by the law professors, by requiring report of "evidence" of misconduct that is not necessarily illegal. Thus, in the heat of a market and regulatory panic, Sarbanes-Oxley leapt over both the ABA and the SEC toward radically changing the relationship between lawyers and their corporate clients....

Frank Partnoy, *How and Why Credit Rating Agencies are Not Like Other Gatekeepers*[*]

... Credit rating agencies clearly belong within the broad classification of financial market gatekeepers. They play a verification function in the fixed-income markets by designating alphabetical ratings of debt. They have a substantial stock of resources to pledge as reputational capital in the event that they are found to have performed poorly. They act as agents, not principals, and are paid only a fraction of the proceeds of debt issues.

However, credit rating agencies differ from other gatekeepers in several important ways. Although they have performed at least as poorly as other gatekeepers during the [Enron era], their market values skyrocketed. Since 2002, as securities firms have restructured their approach to rating shares in response to a wave of private litigation and government prosecution (and to the general decline in the reputation of the ratings of securities analysts), the credit rating process has remained largely intact and credit ratings have become more prominent, important, and valuable.

In addition, credit rating agencies continue to face conflicts of interest that are potentially more serious that those of other gatekeepers: they continue to be paid directly by issuers, they give unsolicited ratings that at least potentially pressure issuers to pay them fees, and they market ancillary consulting services related to ratings. Credit rating agencies increasingly focus on structured finance and new complex debt products, particularly credit derivatives, which now generate a substantial share of credit rating agencies' revenues and profits. With respect to these new instruments, the agencies have become more like "gate openers" than gatekeepers; in particular, their rating methodologies for collateralized debt obligations (CDOs) have created and sustained that multi-trillion-dollar market.

* Adapted from Partnoy, Frank. "How and Why Credit Rating Agencies Are Not Like Other Gatekeepers," from Yasuyuki Fuchita and Robert E. Litan, eds., FINANCIAL GATEKEEPERS: CAN THEY PROTECT INVESTORS? © 2006 Brookings Institution and the Nomura Institute of Capital Markets Research. Used with permission.

Why are credit rating agencies so different from other gatekeepers? Part of the reason is that the most successful credit rating agencies have benefited from an oligopoly market structure that is reinforced by regulations that depend exclusively on credit ratings issued by Nationally Recognized Statistical Ratings Organizations (NRSROs). These regulatory benefits—which I call "regulatory licenses"—generate economic rents for NRSROs that persist even when they perform poorly and otherwise would lose reputational capital. Until [2003], there were only three NRSROs: Moody's, Standard & Poor's, and Fitch. [*As of 2009, there were ten NRSROs.*]

Another reason that credit rating agencies differ from other gatekeepers is that they have been largely immune to civil and criminal liability for malfeasance. Some rule specifically exempt credit rating agencies from liability. More important, several lower-court judges have accepted—wrongly, in my opinion—the rating agencies' argument that ratings are opinions protected by the First Amendment.

… Credit ratings continue to present an unusual paradox: rating changes are important, yet they possess little informational value. Credit ratings do not help parties manage risk, yet parties increasingly rely on ratings. Credit rating agencies are not widely respected among sophisticated market participants, yet their franchise is increasingly valuable. The agencies argue that they are merely financial journalists publishing opinions, yet ratings are far more valuable that the opinions of even the most prominent and respected financial publishers.

In this chapter I argue that optimal policy with respect to credit rating agencies should account for the ways in which agencies differ from other gatekeepers, and explain some of the reasons why these differences have persisted and in some cases widened. I next assess various policy proposals and argue that an ideal policy should both reduce the value of regulatory licenses and increase the threat of rating agency liability. Simply put, the best proposals would help resolve the paradox of credit ratings by creating incentives for credit rating agencies to generate greater informational value while reducing the impact of ratings on markets.

I. How Credit Rating Agencies Differ from Other Gatekeepers

The differences between credit rating agencies and other gatekeepers are stark. Credit rating agencies are more profitable that other gatekeepers, they face different and potentially more serious conflicts of interest, and they are uniquely active in structured finance, particularly with regard to collateralized debt obligations.

A. Profitability

The profitability of credit rating agencies can be considered from two perspectives, one historical, the other more recent. A brief examination of the history of these agencies reveals that the business of rating bonds generally was not highly profitable. A close look at the performance of the agencies over the past five years, however, reveals an extraordinary increase in their profitability. The performance of credit rating agencies is precisely the opposite of that of other gatekeepers, which, although they were consistently profitable during the twentieth century, have experienced difficulties during the past five years.

To put the profitability of modern credit rating agencies in context, it is worth remembering that before the 1970s, the agencies' business model was radically different from what it is today. Before the 1970s, when the Securities and Exchange Commission created the NRSRO designation and various regulations began to depend on NRSRO ratings, credit rating agencies made money by charging subscription fees to investors, not rating fees to issuers. In contrast, today roughly 90 percent of credit rating agencies' revenues are from issuer fees.

The modern credit rating industry grew out of various American firms that began classifying bonds, primarily railroad bonds, during the late nineteenth century. By 1980, Poor's Publishing Company, predecessor of today's S&P, was publishing *Poor's Manual*, an analysis of bonds. During the following two decades, numerous analysts issued railroad industry reports with elaborate statistics and details about operating and financial data for individual companies.

John Moody collected these details, believing that investors would pay for a service that synthesized the mass of information into an easily digestible format. He published his first rating scheme for bonds in 1909, in a book entitled *Analysis of Railroad Investments*, but there was not much demand for his ratings until the market boom of the 1920s. By 1924, the market for bond ratings was more competitive than it is today: in addition to John Moody's rating company, Poor's Standard Statistics Company, Inc., Fitch Publishing Company, and others published ratings. These early agencies made money by charging investors subscription fees; they did not charge issuers.

Following the 1929 stock market crash, the credit rating industry went into a general decline. Investors were no longer very interested in purchasing ratings, particularly given the agencies' poor track record in anticipating the sharp drop in bond values beginning in late 1929....

The rating business remained stagnant for decades. According to a study of 207 corporate bond rating changes from 1950 to 1972, credit rating changes generated information of little or no value. The changes merely reflected information already incorporated into stock market prices—and indeed lagged that information by as much as eighteen months. Concern about the failure of the rating agencies to generate accurate and reliable information led to public arguments for regulation of the credit rating industry.

Yet the agencies were not regulated, in part because regulators perceived that they did not play a prominent role in the financial system. During the early 1970s, the SEC decided that instead of regulating the credit rating industry, it would begin relying on the ratings of a handful of major credit rating agencies in making certain regulatory determinations, beginning with the calculation of net capital requirements for broker dealers. [*SEC Rule 15c3-1(c)(2), the so-called "Net Capital Rule," requires each securities broker dealer to maintain a certain amount of liquid capital as a cushion against its debts. In calculating a broker's capital for this purpose, securities owned by the broker are counted at less than market value, to account for the inherent volatility of securities. This markdown is commonly known as a "haircut." Under the Rule, the haircut is less severe for certain securities that are favorably rated by at least two NRSROs.—Ed.*] In adopting its net capital rules, the SEC created the NRSRO concept, although it neither defined the term nor indicated which agencies qualified as NRSROs. During the following years, the SEC suggested through a series of no-action letters that the major established credit rating agencies qualifies for NRSRO designation but that the smaller agencies did not. [*In 2007, the SEC adopted formal rules for NRSRO status, as directed by Congress in the Credit Rating Agency Reform Act of 2006 —Ed.*]

Over time, the SEC—and then other administrative agencies, as well as Congress— established additional legal rules that depended on NRSRO ratings. This shift in regulatory approach corresponded to a change in the economics of the credit rating industry. In particular, credit rating agencies abandoned their historical practice of charging investors for subscriptions and instead began charging issuers for ratings on the basis of the size of the issue. As additional regulations came to depend more on NRSRO ratings, those ratings became more important and more valuable. Despite those changes, during the 1980s the business of rating bonds grew only modestly. In 1980, there had been just thirty professionals working in the S&P Industrials group; by 1986, there were only forty.

The number of bonds that the major agencies rated increased dramatically during the 1990s. By 1997, Moody's was rating 20,000 public and private issuers in the United States and about 1,200 non-U.S. issuers, including both corporations and sovereign states. S&P rated slightly fewer in each category. Moody's rated $5 trillion worth of securities; S&P rated $2 trillion. Both companies' operating margins were thought to be in the range of 30 percent....

As of early September 2005, Moody's market capitalization was more than $15 billion, roughly the same as Bear Stearns Companies, Inc., a major investment bank. Yet Bear Stearns had 11,000 employees and $7 billion of revenue, whereas Moody's had 2,500 employees and $1.6 billion of revenue. Moody's operating margins have consistently been more than 50 percent since 2000, even higher that they were during the 1990s....

In financial terms, the credit rating agencies and other gatekeepers have been moving in opposite directions. While the value of Moody's shares increased by more than 300 percent [from 2000 to 2004], most banks' shares declined in value. Accounting firm profits also have declined, at least until the Sarbanes-Oxley Act of 2002 generated new opportunities. Arthur Andersen is gone, and KPMG barely survived. Most gatekeepers experienced high volatility [from 2000 to 2004]. But Moody's shares steadily increased during that period....

In sum, credit rating agencies have been more profitable than other gatekeepers. Unlike the "opinions" of other gatekeepers, the ratings of NRSROs are increasingly important and valuable. That is true notwithstanding the abysmal performance of credit rating agencies [in the Enron era].

B. Conflicts of Interest

All of the major gatekeepers have been accused of serious conflicts of interest. However, the conflicts at credit rating agencies are different from those at other gatekeepers and potentially more serious, not only because agencies are paid directly by the issuers that they rate, but also because the vast majority of rating agencies' revenues are from those fees. In addition, those credit rating agencies with market power, specifically S&P and Moody's, have been developing ancillary businesses, including consulting, that other non-credit rating agency gatekeepers are now restricting in developing.

The SEC recently conducted formal examinations of three major NRSROs and reported serious concerns about conflicts of interest. The first and most obvious conflict arises from the fact that issuers pay NRSROs for their ratings. This conflict has existed since the 1970s, when the SEC began implementing NRSRO-dependent rules and rating agencies switched from charging investors to charging issuers for ratings. However, the SEC has pointed to an increase in potential conflicts in recent years....

The rating agencies recognize that conflicts arise from having issuers pay for ratings, but they say that historically they have been able to manage those conflicts. For example, S&P has adopted procedures designed to ensure that no individual is able to link credit rating opinions to fees. Of course, credit rating agencies and other gatekeepers face some of the same actual and potential conflicts. For example, credit rating agency board members serve in various capacities for companies that the credit rating agencies rate. For example, WorldCom shared a director with Moody's and received favorable ratings even after its bonds were trading at non-investment grade credit spreads. Unlike other financial intermediaries, credit rating agencies have not been pressured to eliminate such conflicts.

To illustrate the differences between credit rating agencies and other gatekeepers with respect to conflicts, I have focused on two areas of conflict—ancillary services and unsolicited ratings—where credit rating agencies have not been subject to as much regulatory intervention as other gatekeepers. First, with respect to ancillary services, credit rating agencies market pre-rating assessments and corporate consulting. For an additional fee, issuers present hypothetical scenarios to the rating agencies to understand how a particular transaction—such as a merger, asset sale, or stock repurchase—might affect their ratings. Although the rating agencies argue that fees from ancillary services are not substantial, there is evidence that they are increasing.

In addition, Moody's, S&P, and Fitch each offer risk management consulting services. According to the SEC, the products and services offered include public and private firm credit scoring models, internal ratings systems services, and empirical data on default incidence, loss severity, default correlations, and rating transitions. The SEC found that these marketing activities exacerbated the conflicts of interests at the agencies.

These ancillary services resemble consulting services offered by accounting firms. Just as an issuer might feel pressured by its auditor to use the auditor's consulting services, they might similarly feel pressure to use a credit agency's consulting services....

Obviously, the primary difference between credit rating agencies and other gatekeepers with respect to conflicts related to ancillary services is that regulators have not restricted credit rating agencies' consulting services. In contrast, accounting firms and corporate boards face new rules regarding conflicts of interest and research analysts at investment banks must comply with restrictions on their activities and compensation. Yet no such rules govern credit rating agencies.

A second area of conflict arises from the unsolicited ratings that the agencies give to some issuers. Unsolicited credit ratings, which are highly controversial, have been the subject of ongoing litigation and scrutiny but no new regulations. Moody's has estimated in the past that 1 percent of its ratings have been unsolicited; S&P and Fitch have not publicly stated how frequently they issue unsolicited ratings, although they admit to engaging in the practice....

The controversy surrounding the practice of unsolicited ratings began in 1993, when the Jefferson County (Colorado) school district decided to issue new bonds to take advantage of lower interest rates. Although it had hires Moody's for previous bond issues, it decided to hire S&P and Fitch instead for those particular bonds. On October 20, 1993, the school district priced the bonds, and initially they were selling well. However, two hours after the pricing, Moody's issued a "negative outlook" on the bonds. Several buyers immediately canceled their orders, and the school district was forced to reprice the bonds and pay a higher rate. It sued Moody's, alleging that this "negative outlook" contained falsehoods and had increased the cost of issuing the bonds by $769,000. Moody's defense was that its evaluation of the school district's bonds was a constitutionally protected "opinion." The court agreed, and its dismissal of the claims was upheld on appeal. For now, I want to set aside the First Amendment implications of this case (and others), which I address later, and focus on the implications of unsolicited ratings.

... With respect to unsolicited ratings, the credit rating agencies are unique among gatekeepers. In particular, the conflicts involving securities analysts are the reverse of those associated with credit ratings: the allegation is that analysts give unduly favorable ratings to persuade issuers to pay additional fees for other services, not that they give unduly favorable ratings to persuade issuers to pay for the ratings. In other words, the securities analyst conflicts are "pull" conflicts in which the analyst dangles the prospect of favorable ratings to obtain future fees, whereas the rating agency conflicts are "push" conflicts in which the agency threatens the issuer with unfavorable ratings to obtain fees now.

With respect to other gatekeepers, such as auditors, the notion of unsolicited ratings makes little sense. An accounting firm would not likely give an audit opinion to a non-client; indeed, it likely would find doing so cost prohibitive. It is interesting that credit rating agencies believe that they are capable of publishing accurate unsolicited ratings even if they have no access to management or inside information and are merely making judgments based on publicly available information....

C. Structured Finance

Perhaps the starkest difference between credit rating agencies and other gatekeepers in recent years has been the increasingly substantial role that the agencies play in rating new structured finance issues, particularly credit derivatives. Financial institutions first began using credit derivatives during the mid-1990s as a mechanism to transfer credit risk, primarily because it enabled them to hedge the risk associated with their lending operations and to reduce balance sheet capital requirements.

The simplest form of credit derivative—the credit default swap (CDS)—facilitates the transfer of credit risk and does not directly implicate or involve credit rating agencies. In a CDS, one party agrees to pay money to another party if a specified "credit event" occurs, typically a default on a specified bond: one party is "selling" protection against default and will pay in the event of a default; the other party is "buying" protection against default and will be paid if a default occurs. In other words, in exchange for a payment or premium, protection buyers transfer credit risk to protection sellers, either up front or over time. The CDS market has been controversial, in part because banks used CDSs to transfer hundreds of billions of dollars of credit risk to insurance companies, pension funds, and other institutions prior to the recent wave of corporate defaults. There is an active policy debate about the costs and benefits of CDSs, but it does not directly involve credit rating agencies.

Credit rating agencies enter the picture with respect to a second form of credit derivative, known as a collateralized debt obligation. CDOs are structured, leveraged transactions backed by one or more classes of fixed-income assets. In the mid-1990s, CDOs typically were based on portfolios of high-yield corporate bonds. During the past several years, CDOs have been based on other assets, including asset-backed securities, CDSs, and even other CDOs.

At the core of a typical CDO is a special purpose entity (SPE) that issues securities to investors in several different classes, or tranches, most of which are rated by a credit rating agency. The SPE's proceeds are used to purchase a portfolio of fixed-income assets [*such as, for example, the mortgage-backed securities that contributed to the financial crash of 2008.*] If some of the assets default, the most junior of the SPE's securities takes the first loss. Payments to each tranche are governed by a stipulated priority of payments. [*In this type of arrangement, junior tranches are riskier, but dramatic failures of the underlying assets will harm even the senior tranches. Failure to appreciate this risk seems to have contributed to the financial meltdown of 2008. Even where the underlying assets were risky ones, such as subprime mortgages, senior tranches were considered to be safe investments (and were often highly rated by the credit rating agencies) because they were insulated by junior tranches that would absorb losses first. But when the housing bubble burst in 2008, the rate of mortgage default was so high that even the senior tranches incurred losses.—Ed.*]

... According to S&P, "rating agencies played an important role in the development of the market since they were able to develop criteria to size default risk based on rates of the underlying obligors." In other words, the rating agencies have developed methodologies for rating CDOs that result in the combination of the tranches being worth more than the cost of the underlying assets. The difference between the price that the investors in aggregate pay for CDO tranches and the cost of the underlying assets must be substantial, because it covers the high fees the various participants charge for structuring and arranging a CDO and for managing the underlying assets.

So how does such "arbitrage" arise? There are two views. The first is that actual value is created during the CDO process, wither because the underlying assets are mispriced or because market segmentation otherwise prevents parties from buying the types of portfolios that CDOs create. It is difficult to test this view, but there are reasons to be skeptical. Investors who want to own diversified portfolios of fixed-income assets are not prohibited from doing so.... Economists know that arbitrage opportunities rarely persist unless there is a dominant information asymmetry or regulatory explanation. The purchasers of CDO tranches typically are sophisticated, and the regulatory rationales do not apply to synthetic CDOs. Moreover, the cost of this so-called arbitrage is enormous: if a trillion dollars of CDOs have been sold, financial intermediaries have earned billions of dollars in fees.

A second view is that because the methodologies used for rating CDOs are complex, arbitrary, and opaque, they create opportunities for parties to create a ratings "arbitrage" opportunity without adding any actual value. It is difficult to test this view, too, although there are reasons to find it persuasive. Essentially, the argument is that once the rating agencies fix a given set of formulas and variables for rating CDOs, financial market participants will be able to find a set of fixed-income assets that, when run through the relevant models, generate a CDO whose tranches are more valuable that the underlying assets. Such a result might be due to errors in rating the assets themselves (that is, the assets are cheap relative to their ratings), errors in calculating the relationship between those assets and the tranche payouts (that is, the correlation and expected payout of the assets appear to be higher and therefore support higher ratings of tranches), or errors in rating the individual CDO tranches (that is, the tranches receive a higher rating than they deserve, given the ratings of the underlying assets). [*This appears to have been the problem with many mortgage-based CDOs. The massive mortgage default rates, which decimated even the senior tranches, indicate that the senior tranches were overvalued.—Ed.*]

... Perhaps surprisingly, it is the investment bank structuring the CDO, not the rating agency, that typically performs these complex calculations. The process of rating CDOs becomes a mathematical game that smart bankers know that they can win. A person who understands the details of the model can tweak the inputs, assumptions, and underlying assets to produce a CDO that appears to add value, though in reality it does not.

The mathematical precision of the models is illusory, because numerous subjective factors enter the process as well. For example, the rating agency evaluates the CDO asset manager, who has discretion to engage in trading....

Thus, with respect to structured finance, credit rating agencies have been functioning more like "gate openers" rather than gatekeepers. The agencies are engaged in a business, the rating of CDOs, which is radically different from the core business of other gatekeepers. No other gatekeeper has created a dysfunctional multi-trillion-dollar market, built on its own errors and limitations.

II. Why Credit Rating Agencies are Not Like Other Gatekeepers

Given the differences between credit rating agencies and other gatekeepers, the next question is "Why?" Are there substantive economic differences between the function of rating credit and other gatekeeping functions that would lead one to expect credit rating agencies to differ from other gatekeepers in the way that they do? Or, are the differences due to other factors?

The first reason for the differences between credit rating agencies and other gatekeepers is that many regulations depend on NRSRO ratings.... A second reason for the differences is that credit rating agencies generally are not subject to civil liability for malfeasance. It is not surprising that the credit rating agencies would prefer to compare themselves not to gatekeepers such as securities analysts and auditors but to publishing companies....

A. *Regulatory Licenses*

... [T]he paradox of credit ratings—that they can be so valuable yet lack informational content—can be resolved by understanding the regulatory framework in which credit rating agencies operate.... In particular, credit ratings are valuable not because they contain valuable information but because they grant issuers "regulatory licenses." In simple terms, a good rating entitles the issuer (and the investors in a particular issue) to certain advantages related to regulation. [*For example, the Investment Company Act Rule 2a-7 uses NRSRO ratings to determine money market funds' permissible investments. Thus, rating agencies affect the regulatory status of a fund and the marketability of both the fund and the securities it invests in. Also as noted above, a good rating allows a security to count more toward a broker's net capital, presumably making that security more attractive for a broker to hold.—Ed.*] The regulatory license view of credit ratings illuminates some of the unique aspects of the role of credit rating agencies. Once regulation is passed that incorporates ratings, rating agencies will begin to sell not only information but also the valuable property rights associated with compliance with that regulation.

Moreover, if regulation enables only a few raters to acquire and transfer regulatory licenses or if it imposes costs on new raters, so raising the barriers to entry, the rating agencies will acquire market power in the sale if regulatory licenses. Unlike rating agencies selling information in a competitive market, rating agencies selling regulatory licenses under oligopolistic (or even monopolistic) conditions will be able to earn abnormal profits.

The regulatory license view can be generalized beyond credit ratings, and it applies to a certain extent to other gatekeepers. For example, securities regulations set forth in great detail the minimal qualifications for certified and public accountants and for accountants' reports. Federal regulations also require registered companies to file audited financial statements for the previous three fiscal years. Other regulations cover the content and quality of accountant reports. Section 404 of the Sarbanes-Oxley Act now requires certification of gatekeepers' internal controls.

Since 1973 credit ratings have been incorporated into hundreds of rules, releases, and regulatory decisions, in various substantive areas including securities, pension, banking, real estate, and insurance regulation. As noted above, the cascade of regulations began after the credit crises of the early 1970s, when the SEC adopted broker-dealer net capital requirements in rule 15c3-1, the first securities rule that formally incorporated NRSRO ratings. I have noted elsewhere the extensive credit rating-dependent rules and regulations promulgated under Securities Act of 1933, the Securities Exchange Act of 1934, the Investment Company Act of 1940, various banking and insurance regulations and statutes, and other regulatory schemes. More recently, international regulatory standards, including the Basel II capital accords,[24] have depended on credit ratings.

Such extensive regulatory dependence on credit ratings is unique. For example, investors do not receive differential regulatory treatment when they purchase stocks with "buy" ratings from securities analysts. Investors might not buy the securities of an issuer without the relevant opinion letters from an audit firm, but that audit firms' opinion typically does not determine the level of the investors' compliance with government regulations.

To the extent that other gatekeepers are selling regulatory licenses, the problems are similar to those associated with credit ratings. Investment banking fairness opinions are unduly expensive, in part because they provide support for a due diligence defense for company directors who approve a merger or sale. The same is true of audit opinions, which similarly provide a legal defense. The very high fees associated with complying with Sarbanes-Oxley section 404 do not reflect the intrinsic market value of an accounting firm's substantive controls review, but rather the expense associated with being in compliance with the new law.

The overriding message is that regulatory licenses are costly. They create oligopolistic pressure and exacerbate rent seeking among already concentrated industries. They might be necessary when a regulator is unwilling to or cannot make substantive decisions on its own and the risk of market failure is sufficiently serious to justify the cost. But as a general matter, regulators should be very careful not to create regulatory licenses, and once licenses are created regulators should take great care in policing them.

Unfortunately, regulators have taken no such care with respect to NRSRO ratings. Once NRSRO-based regulation became standard, market participants began to frame decisions in terms of ratings much more frequently. To the extent that financial market behavior is path-dependent [*i.e., determined by inertia rather than efficiency—Ed.*], regulatory licenses have started parties down a suboptimal path, where dependence on ratings has generated behavioral influences. Once legal rules approve of reliance on credit ratings, it is only natural that individuals would come to rely heavily on such ratings as well.

B. Liability

The unique problems associated with credit rating agencies as gatekeepers stem from a second source: their lack of exposure to civil and criminal liability. Unlike other gatekeepers, rating agencies are explicitly immune to prosecution for certain violations

---

24. The Basel II accords are an international agreement recommending international banking standards.

of securities law, including section 11 of the Securities Act of 1933 and Regulation FD[25]. Moreover, rating agencies have been unique among gatekeepers in their ability to argue that their function is merely to provide "opinions," which are protected by the First Amendment. Because of these differenced, rating agencies have not paid substantial judgments or settlements resulting from the recent wave of corporate fraud.

The credit rating agencies claim that their core business is financial publishing. Specifically NRSROs have long argued that their core activities are purely journalistic pursuits: gathering information on matters of public concern, analyzing that information, forming opinions about it, and then broadly disseminating those opinions to the public. They have had some limited success in putting forth that argument in litigation.

As noted previously, Moody's financial statements show that it actually is engaged in a business that is entirely different from publishing, one that is much more profitable.... But even if one accepts the argument that credit rating agencies are financial publishers, that does not end the inquiry. Whether holding such a publisher or speaker liable for malfeasance would affect its freedom of expression remains a question. The securities laws are predicated on the assumption that corporate speech can be regulated to the Supreme Court has clearly indicated that "commercial speech" can be regulated to the extent that it is false or misleading. Moreover, the securities laws provide for liability for false and misleading statements even if those statements are not made with the kind of malicious intent that is required to hold speakers liable for other forms of speech. If speech by an issuer can be regulated, it should follow that speech by an agent of the issuer, whom the issuer has paid to speak, also can be regulated.

The Supreme Court has never ruled directly on the issue of whether gatekeepers are entitled to First Amendment protection of their opinions, and it is not clear what position it would take if it did....

In lower courts, both S&P and Moody's have persuaded some judges to dismiss claims against them (Fitch has had less success) and to note that credit ratings were protected expressions of opinions. However, the courts have distinguished situations in which credit rating agencies were merely acting as journalists or information gatherers from situations in which the agencies were playing a more significant role in the transaction....

III. Proposals

It follows from the preceding discussion that policy solutions should address the reasons why credit rating agencies are not like other gatekeepers. The ideal proposals would reduce the benefits associated with regulatory licenses and impose a real threat of liability on credit rating agencies for malfeasance.

A. *Reduce the Benefits of Regulatory Licenses*

There are various ways to reduce the benefits associated with regulatory licenses. The simplest would be to remove the NRSRO designation. One preliminary question is whether the markets could function properly without the designation. They operated

---

25. Rule 436(g)(1) of the Securities Act of 1933, 17 C.F.R. § 230.436(g)(1) provides for exemption of liability for NRSROs.... .NRSROs generally are shielded from liability under the securities laws for all conduct except fraud....

reasonably well prior to the 1970s, so there is reason to think that the markets and regulators could adapt to a system without NRSROs. It might be a difficult transition, as regulators would be forced to make the kinds of decisions that they made previously with respect to substantive regulation of financial market participants. They would no longer be able to delegate significant authority and responsibility to NRSROs. For example, the SEC would need to decide how to assess the net capital requirements of broker-dealers.[26] Regulators would need to determine which bonds were appropriate for money market funds. The Basel II accords suggest that some regulators might have the ability to perform such tasks. Although Basel II relies in part on credit ratings, it also contains alternative mechanisms for determining bank capital requirements without reference to credit ratings.

However while it might be a good idea to eliminate the NRSRO designation, it seems politically unlikely. A more plausible possibility is to find a replacement for NRSROs. There are three alternatives to the current regime. First, regulators could open the market to new NRSROs. Second, regulators could replace NRSROs with a market-based measure such as credit spreads[27] or credit default swaps—or even an equity-based measure of credit risk. Third, regulators could replace the concept of recognition in the NRSRO regime with the concept of "registration," which is more familiar in securities regulation more generally. [*The Credit Rating Agency Reform Act of 2006 and SEC Rules passed thereunder established registration requirements and opened the NRSRO ranks to increased competition. —Ed.*] ...

B. Create a Threat of Liability for Rating Malfeasance

The final policy proposal is simple: make credit rating agencies liable for malfeasance and limit the extent to which the First Amendment is deemed to protect their "opinions." This could be done in two ways. First, courts could reject the agencies' argument that their ratings are constitutionally protected speech. Here the trends seem to be promising....

The courts or Congress might mark the distinction emerging in some cases between agencies that play an active role and those that take a passive role, simply publishing an opinion. The argument for constitutional protection is strongest with respect to unsolicited ratings, for which an agency is not paid, and when the agency is not actively involved in either the structuring of an issue or an investigation of the issuer. In contrast, the agencies' role in the CDO market is far less likely to be protected speech. Agencies play an active role in structuring CDOs, and their "opinions" with respect to CDOs are less public.

Overall, this policy prescription is simple: treat credit rating agencies like other gatekeepers. During the past decade, credit rating agencies have become unique in various ways. That should not have happened. The simplest way to reverse course would be to amend section 11 and Regulation FD to include NRSROs and make it clear—whether through legislation or judicial decision—that credit rating agencies' "opinions" are no different from the "opinions" of other gatekeepers....

---

26. In 2008, the SEC proposed removing explicit references to NRSROs from the net-capital rules, but the proposal would permit credit ratings to be considered in net-capital determinations.

27. A bond's credit spread is the difference between that bond's yield and the yield on Treasury bonds of the same maturity. Treasuries have no risk of default; in theory, the larger the spread for a bond, the greater the market's estimation of the bond's default risk.

Code of Federal Regulations, Title 17, Chapter II, Part 205 — Standards of Professional Conduct for Attorneys Appearing and Practicing Before the Commission in the Representation of an Issuer (2004)*

17 C.F.R. § 205.2 Definitions

For purposes of this part, the following definitions apply:

Appearing and practicing before the Commission [means]:

(i) Transacting any business with the Commission, including communications in any form;

(ii) Representing an issuer in a Commission administrative proceeding or in connection with any Commission investigation, inquiry, information request, or subpoena;

(iii) Providing advice in respect of the United States securities laws or the Commission's rules or regulations thereunder regarding any document that the attorney has notice will be filed with or submitted to ... the Commission ... ; or

(iv) Advising an issuer as to whether information or a statement, opinion, or other writing is required under the United States securities laws or the Commission's rules or regulations thereunder to be filed with or submitted to ... the Commission

....

Material violation means a material violation of an applicable United States federal or state securities law, a material breach of fiduciary duty arising under United States federal or state law, or a similar material violation of any United States federal or state law.

17 C.F.R. § 205.3 Issuer as client.

(a) *Representing an issuer.* An attorney appearing and practicing before the Commission in the representation of an issuer owes his or her professional and ethical duties to the issuer as an organization. That the attorney may work with and advise the issuer's officers, directors, or employees in the course of representing the issuer does not make such individuals the attorney's clients.

(b) *Duty to report evidence of a material violation.*

(1) If an attorney, appearing and practicing before the Commission in the representation of an issuer, becomes aware of evidence of a material violation by the issuer or by any officer, director, employee, or agent of the issuer, the attorney shall report such evidence to the issuer's chief legal officer (or the equivalent thereof) or to both the issuer's chief legal officer and its chief executive officer (or the equivalents thereof) forthwith. By communicating such information to the issuer's officers or directors, an attorney does not reveal client confidences or secrets or privileged or otherwise protected information related to the attorney's representation of an issuer.

(2) The chief legal officer (or the equivalent thereof) shall cause such inquiry into the evidence of a material violation as he or she reasonably believes is appropriate to determine whether the material violation described in the report has occurred,

---

* [*The SEC promulgated these rules pursuant to Section 307 of the Sarbanes-Oxley Act.* —Ed.]

is ongoing, or is about to occur. If the chief legal officer (or the equivalent thereof) determines no material violation has occurred, is ongoing, or is about to occur, he or she shall notify the reporting attorney and advise the reporting attorney of the basis for such determination. Unless the chief legal officer (or the equivalent thereof) reasonably believes that no material violation has occurred, is ongoing, or is about to occur, he or she shall take all reasonable steps to cause the issuer to adopt an appropriate response, and shall advise the reporting attorney thereof. In lieu of causing an inquiry under this paragraph (b), a chief legal officer (or the equivalent thereof) may refer a report of evidence of a material violation to a qualified legal compliance committee ... if the issuer has duly established a qualified legal compliance committee prior to the report of evidence of a material violation.

(3) Unless an attorney who has made a report under paragraph (b)(1) of this section reasonably believes that the chief legal officer or the chief executive officer of the issuer (or the equivalent thereof) has provided an appropriate response within a reasonable time, the attorney shall report the evidence of a material violation to:

(i) The audit committee of the issuer's board of directors;

(ii) Another committee of the issuer's board of directors consisting solely of directors who are not employed, directly or indirectly, by the issuer ... (if the issuer's board of directors has no audit committee); or

(iii) The issuer's board of directors (if the issuer's board of directors has no committee consisting solely of directors who are not employed, directly or indirectly, by the issuer ...)

... (8) An attorney who receives what he or she reasonably believes is an appropriate and timely response to a report he or she has made pursuant to ... this section need do nothing more under this section with respect to his or her report....

.... (d) *Issuer confidences.*

... (2) An attorney appearing and practicing before the Commission in the representation of an issuer may reveal to the Commission, without the issuer's consent, confidential information related to the representation to the extent the attorney reasonably believes necessary:

(i) To prevent the issuer from committing a material violation that is likely to cause substantial injury to the financial interest or property of the issuer or investors;

(ii) To prevent the issuer, in a Commission investigation or administrative proceeding from committing perjury ... ; suborning perjury ... ; or committing any act ... that is likely to perpetrate a fraud upon the Commission; or

(iii) To rectify the consequences of a material violation by the issuer that caused, or may cause, substantial injury to the financial interest or property of the issuer or investors in the furtherance of which the attorney's services were used.

Discussion Questions

1. Does the lawyer's duty of loyalty and "zealous advocacy" translate from the courtroom setting to the corporate context? What issues may arise in translation?

First, consider zealous advocacy in the corporate litigation context. Consider the examples of a lawyer defending a corporation from charges that its top officers committed criminal securities law violations, or defending a corporation in a shareholder derivative lawsuit.

Second, consider zealous advocacy in the transactional context. Consider the examples of a lawyer negotiating a takeover bid (for the target and, alternatively, for the acquirer), drafting a registration statement for a securities offering, or drafting a management proxy statement.

2. Recall the arguments in Chapters 9 and 10 about board composition and equity compensation. What are the advantages and disadvantages of corporate counsel serving on the board of directors? See MARC I. STEINBERG, LAWYERING AND ETHICS FOR THE BUSINESS ATTORNEY 131–148 (2002).

What are the advantages and disadvantages of corporate counsel being compensated with an equity interest in the corporation?

3. Coates describes many factors that may give lawyers incentive to give clients poor quality advice about takeover defenses. (Indeed, similar incentives are present in almost all kinds of legal advice and representation.) Do you agree that corporate lawyers (in the context of advising clients about takeover defenses, or in other contexts) are more likely to engage in slacking than other kinds of agents? Do you agree that poor-quality legal service is the result of rationally-motivated slacking, or might there be other explanations? Do you share Coates' skepticism of constraints such as ethical duties and professional reputation? If so, are there any other existing factors, or potential reforms, that might improve the quality of legal advice?

4. Coates points out that there is considerable theoretical and empirical debate over what constitutes the "best" approach to takeover defenses. What does Coates mean by the "best" approach? Is the lawyer's role in advising an IPO to determine the "best" approach in this sense? What if the board of directors disagrees with the lawyer's definition of the "best" approach?

5. Bratton argues that accountants have a professional duty to act as aggressive monitors of their clients' conduct. Lawyers are not normally asked to perform such a monitoring role; this is why the new SEC rules for lawyers generated such controversy. Are there significant differences between lawyers and accountants that would justify these differing expectations?

Note, for example, that under Section 10A of the Securities Exchange Act of 1934, an auditor has a duty to report illegal conduct to senior management. There is a significant difference between this duty and the lawyer's duty under Sarbanes-Oxley, however: if management does not take appropriate action, the auditor must report the conduct to both the board of directors *and* the SEC.

6. Section 201 of Sarbanes-Oxley Act prohibits accounting firms from performing non-audit services for an audited company "contemporaneously" with the audit of that company. The section provides a list of prohibited services. Section 202 of the Act states that an accounting firm may provide audited companies with "any non-audit service, including tax services" that is not specifically prohibited in section 201, if the service is approved in advance by the audit committee of the audited company.

How effective will this law be in addressing the problem of auditors' conflicts of interest discussed in Bratton's article? How might this rule be improved?

7. Bratton's article in Chapter 1 pointed out the role of corporate culture in a firm's attitude toward risk-taking and law-breaking. Rock's article in Chapter 3 pointed out the

role of non-enforceable norms in guiding managerial conduct. In this chapter, Tanina Rostain points out that the corporate lawyer is similarly influenced by the culture of his or her firm. If lawyers' independent discretion is compromised "under current conditions of practice," as Rostain argues, what is to be done?

Economic concerns are leading firms to dispense with broad-based education in skills and ethics. Billable hours determine the earnings of partners and the advancement of associates, and sophisticated clients will not allow firms to bill them for the professional development of new lawyers. Thus firms economize by training new lawyers only enough "to complete the tasks at hand." *See* Robert W. Hillman, *Professional Partnerships, Competition, and the Evolution of Firm Culture: The Case of Law Firms,* 26 J. CORP. L. 1061 (2001); *see also* David B. Wilkins, *Everyday Practice* Is *the Troubling Case,* in EVERYDAY PRACTICES AND TROUBLE CASES 68, 97 (Austin Sarat, Marianne Constable, David Engel, Valerie Hans & Susan Lawrence eds., 1998).

What reforms could firms make to stem this trend? If neither clients nor firms wish to pay the cost of training ethical lawyers, should the law intervene?

Can the law reform law practice and firm culture to increase lawyers' cognitive independence? Should it? Can the profession reform itself? If ethical, independent lawyers are vanishing, might there be merit in acknowledging this fact and abandoning lawyer discretion for the "Dominant View"?

8. A common concern about government regulations on lawyers' professional conduct is that lawyers will act cautiously to avoid disciplinary sanctions rather than advocate zealously on behalf of their clients.

One commentator argues that while this concern may be warranted with respect to individual clients, it is less relevant with respect to corporate clients:

> ... [C]orporate clients, with their superior ability to monitor and control lawyer conduct, have the power both to press their lawyers to act in ways that jeopardize systemic norms and the rights of third parties, and to protect themselves against any loss of zealous advocacy or individual autonomy that might otherwise follow from an increase in external regulation.

David B. Wilkins, *Who Should Regulate Lawyers?* 105 HARV. L. REV. 801, 872 (1992).

If Wilkins is correct, and Rostain is also correct that corporate lawyers identify too closely with their clients' interests, what does that suggest about the SEC rules under Sarbanes-Oxley regarding the internal and external reporting of "material violations"? By extension, can the corporate legal profession be trusted to regulate itself?

The Sarbanes-Oxley Act established a new private, nonprofit corporation, the Public Company Accounting Oversight Board (PCAOB), to monitor the accounting profession under SEC oversight. Should corporate lawyer conduct continue to be regulated by state bar associations and state courts, as has traditionally been the case? Or does the practice of corporate law require special regulation, such as the SEC rules reprinted in this chapter, or an oversight body like the PCAOB? *See* Wilkins, *Who Should Regulate Lawyers?, supra.*

9. As Ribstein points out, the comments to ABA Model Rule 1.13(b) used to state that when a lawyer decides whether to report misconduct, "[a]ny measures taken shall be designed to minimize disruption of the organization and the risk of revealing information relating to the representation to persons outside the organization." After Sarbanes-Oxley, this language was deleted. Do you agree with Ribstein that the old language was preferable?

10. Consult the SEC's rules for attorneys reprinted in this chapter (17 C.F.R. § 205; the SEC passed these rules under the authority of the Sarbanes-Oxley Act, § 307) as you consider the following hypothetical:

You are a junior partner at a large law firm. The general counsel of EndRun Corporation, a friend of your firm's managing partner, has hired your firm to represent EndRun as outside counsel. Your job is to help EndRun prepare the SEC registration statement for a new securities offering.

In the course of preparing the registration statement, you become aware of "aggressive" internal accounting practices by EndRun that, in your view, overstate EndRun's annual earnings over the last two years.

Are you required to do anything about this?

11. Suppose you tell EndRun's general counsel (i.e., its Chief Legal Officer) about the accounting issue. She directs an assistant to recirculate a company memo reminding all accountants to abide by generally accepted accounting principles. She tells you, "There. It's taken care of. Now, as your client, I'm instructing you to finish the registration statement and forget about this little issue."

Do the SEC rules require you to do anything further?

12. Suppose you do report the accounting practices to the audit committee of EndRun's board of directors. The chair of the committee thanks you for the information and instructs you not to discuss it with anyone else.

Three weeks elapse, and you now have one week to complete the SEC filing. The firm's internal accountants insist on continuing to use the accounting practices you questioned. You ask the audit committee chair about the status of the issue. She tells you, "Thank you for raising the issue. I do not believe the practice is a problem, but I am looking into it."

Should you report EndRun's accounting practices to the SEC? What legal, ethical and practical grounds are relevant to your decision? Before going to the SEC, would it be proper for you to use the threat of exposure to demand that the corporation reform its accounting?

In 2009, an attorney for the Stanford Financial Group, a company accused of conducting an immense Ponzi scheme, withdrew from representation of the company and told the SEC he disavowed representations he had previously made to the SEC about the company. (Presumably, he had spoken in favor of his client, then had a change of heart or discovered new information.) His disavowal almost certainly revealed, at least implicitly, confidential client information; if so, what would justify revealing such information under Sarbanes-Oxley § 307 and the SEC rules in 17 C.F.R. § 205?

13. One commentator has expressed support for the so-called "Dominant View" of lawyers' duties on the following grounds:

> ... lawyers, working within the messy world of competing factual claims and arguments, rarely can be sufficiently confident about empirical facts to justify blunt betrayal of their clients. Moral activism, if it is to change the way that the professional behaviors manifest in public, means, at its core, betrayal of client trust.

Paul R. Tremblay, *Moral Activism Manqué*, 44 S. Tex. L. Rev. 127 (2002).

In the EndRun hypothetical, is it a betrayal of the client to:

a. report the accounting practices to the general counsel?

b. report to the audit committee?

    c.   report to the SEC?

Would your answers to the questions in the EndRun hypothetical change if the accounting practice in question were:

    a.   clearly illegal;

    b.   arguably legal but not in your opinion;

    c.   legal in your opinion, but potentially misleading

14. Would you, as a shareholder, prefer a rule that *prohibits* the corporation's lawyers from revealing client confidences for the protection of third parties, a rule that *requires* them to do so, or a rule, like the SEC rules for attorneys (17 C.F.R. §205.3(d)(2)), that gives them *discretion* to do so? Would you, as a director, have different preferences? As a corporate lawyer?

15. The SEC rules for attorneys define "material violation" to include not only breaches of securities law, but also breaches of fiduciary duty. Evaluate this broad definition in light of Professor Coffee's concerns about the criminalization of civil infractions (see Chapter 6) and Romano & Ribstein's preference for state over federal regulation of corporate law (see Chapters 3 & 4).

16. Many commentators believe the now-defunct accounting firm, Arthur Andersen, contributed to the misconduct and ultimate bankruptcy of Enron. As discussed in this chapter, the U.S. Supreme Court has eliminated the private cause of action for aiding and abetting securities fraud under 10b-5. Some courts have interpreted this very strictly, rejecting private actions against lawyers, accountants, and other gatekeepers unless fraud can be visibly attributed to them. The SEC can still pursue actions for aiding and abetting, but the SEC's enforcement resources are of course limited.

Should Congress reverse the effect of *Central Bank* with a law specifically allowing private suits against gatekeepers who aid and abet 10b-5 violations? Why or why not? Recall the discussion of the PSLRA in Chapter 5. What kind of limitations on private actions could strike a balance between private suits and excessive litigation in the aiding-and-abetting context?

17. The SEC rules for attorneys specifically state that they are not intended to create private causes of action. But should they?

Suppose the attorney in the EndRun hypothetical reported suspected misconduct to the board and received no response. She then chose not to report EndRun's conduct to the SEC. When the misconduct became known, the company went into a downward spiral that ended in bankruptcy. Should shareholders whose stock lost value have a private cause of action against the attorney for her failure to report to the SEC? Should creditors? What further facts might be relevant?

18. Why do you suppose the gatekeeper reforms of Sarbanes-Oxley failed to prevent the financial meltdown of 2008?

Some of Partnoy's suggested reforms to the regulation of credit rating agencies, such as NRSRO registration requirements and increased competition, had been implemented by 2008. Why do you suppose these reforms, like Sarbanes-Oxley, failed to prevent the meltdown?

19. Partnoy describes the role of special purpose entities (SPEs) in the structured-finance products (mortgage-backed securities, CDOs, and the like) that figured prominently in the financial meltdown of 2008. As Bratton points out, SPEs also played a major role in the Enron scandal. What is the difference between an SPE and a more conventional

business entity? Can the law discourage the former while encouraging the latter? Should it?

20. Partnoy says credit rating agencies and other gatekeeper "sell regulatory licenses" by approving transactions. Can corporate lawyers be said to provide regulatory licenses? Consider the role legal advice played in *In Re Walt Disney Derivative Litigation* (reprinted in Chapter 10).

Notes on Contributing Authors

JENNIFER ARLEN is the Norma Z. Paige Professor of Law at New York University School of Law.

JOHN ARMOUR is the Lovells Professor of Law and Finance in the Faculty of Law, University of Oxford.

STEPHEN M. BAINBRIDGE is the William D. Warren Professor of Law at the UCLA School of Law.

DOUGLAS G. BAIRD is the Harry A. Bigelow Distinguished Service Professor of Law at the University of Chicago Law School.

LEONARD M. BAYNES is a Professor of Law and Director of the Ronald H. Brown Center for Civil Rights and Economic Development at St. John's University School of Law.

LUCIAN ARYE BEBCHUK is the William J. Friedman and Alicia Townsend Friedman Professor of Law, Economics and Finance and Director of the Program on Corporate Governance at Harvard Law School.

BERNARD S. BLACK is a Professor of Law and Hayden W. Head Regents Chair for Faculty Excellence at the University of Texas Law School, Professor of Finance at the McCombs School of Business, and Director of the Center for Law, Business and Economics at the University of Texas.

MARGARET M. BLAIR is a Professor of Law at Vanderbilt Law School.

CHERYL D. BLOCK is a Professor of Law at the Washington University in St. Louis School of Law.

WILLIAM W. BRATTON is the Peter P. Weidenbruch, Jr., Professor of Business Law at Georgetown University Law Center.

PAMELA H. BUCY is the Bainbridge-Mims Professor of Law at the University of Alabama School of Law.

HENRY N. BUTLER is a Senior Lecturer and the Executive Director of the Searle Center on Law, Regulation, and Economic Growth at Northwestern University School of Law.

BRIAN R. CHEFFINS is the S.J. Berwin Professor of Corporate Law in the Faculty of Law, University of Cambridge.

JOHN C. COATES IV is the John F. Cogan, Jr., Professor of Law and Economics and Research Director of the Program on the Legal Profession at Harvard Law School.

JOHN C. COFFEE, JR. is the Adolf A. Berle Professor of Law and Director of the Center on Corporate Governance at Columbia Law School.

JAMES D. COX is the Brainerd Currie Professor of Law at Duke University School of Law.

LYNNE L. DALLAS is a Professor of Law at the University of San Diego School of Law.

DEBORAH A. DeMOTT is the David F. Cavers Professor of Law at Duke University School of Law.

CHARLES M. ELSON is the Edgar S. Woolard, Jr., Chair in Corporate Governance and Director of the John L. Weinberg Center for Corporate Governance at the University of Delaware, Lerner College of Business and Economics.

JILL E. FISCH is the T.J. Maloney Professor of Business Law and Director of the Center for Corporate, Securities and Financial Law at Fordham University School of Law.

RONALD J. GILSON is the Charles J. Meyers Professor of Law and Business at Stanford Law School and the Marc and Eva Stern Professor of Law and Business at Columbia Law School.

KENT GREENFIELD is a Professor of Law and Law Fund Research Scholar at Boston College Law School.

DANIEL J.H. GREENWOOD is a Professor of Law at Hofstra University School of Law.

MARILYN F. JOHNSON is an Associate Professor of Accounting and Information Systems at Michigan State University, Eli Broad College of Business.

THOMAS W. JOO is a Professor of Law at the University of California, Davis, School of Law.

EHUD KAMAR is a Professor of Law at the University of Southern California, Gould School of Law.

ROBERTA S. KARMEL is the Centennial Professor of Law and Co-Director of the Dennis J. Black Center for the Study of International Business Law at Brooklyn Law School.

DONALD C. LANGEVOORT is the Thomas Aquinas Reynolds Professor of Law and Co-Director of the Joint Degree Program in Law and Business Administration at Georgetown University Law Center.

MARTIN LIPTON is a founding partner of the law firm of Wachtell, Lipton, Rosen & Katz.

MARK LOEWENSTEIN is the Monfort Professor of Commercial Law at the University of Colorado School of Law.

JONATHAN R. MACEY is the Sam Harris Professor of Corporate Law, Corporate Finance and Securities Law at Yale University and Professor in the Yale School of Management.

TIMOTHY F. MALLOY is a Professor of Law and Co-Director of the Frank G. Wells Environmental Law Clinic at the UCLA School of Law.

FRED S. McCHESNEY is the Class of 1967 James B. Haddad Professor of Law at Northwestern University School of Law.

LAWRENCE E. MITCHELL is the Theodore Rinehart Professor of Business Law at the George Washington University Law School.

KAREN K. NELSON is a Professor of Accounting at Rice University, Jesse H. Jones Graduate School of Business.

MARLEEN A. O'CONNOR-FELMAN is a Professor of Law at Stetson University College of Law.

TROY A. PAREDES is currently a Commissioner of the United States Securities and Exchange Commission. At the time he wrote his contribution to this volume, he was a Professor of Law at the Washington University in St. Louis School of Law.

FRANK PARTNOY is the George E. Barrett Professor of Law and Finance and Director of the Center on Corporate and Securities Law at the University of San Diego School of Law.

ADAM C. PRITCHARD is the Frances and George Skestos Professor of Law at the University of Michigan Law School.

STEVEN A. RAMIREZ is a Professor of Law and Director of the Business Law Center at Loyola University Chicago School of Law.

ROBERT K. RASMUSSEN is the Dean, Carl Mason Franklin Chair in Law and Professor of Law and Political Science at the University of Southern California, Gould School of Law.

LARRY E. RIBSTEIN is the Mildred Van Voorhis Jones Chair in Law and a Professor of Law at the University of Illinois College of Law.

EDWARD B. ROCK is the Saul A. Fox Distinguished Professor of Business Law and Co-Director of the Institute for Law and Economics at the University of Pennsylvania Law School.

MARK J. ROE is the David Berg Professor of Law at Harvard Law School.

ROBERTA ROMANO is the Oscar M. Ruebhausen Professor of Law and Director of the Center for the Study of Corporate Law at Yale Law School.

TANINA ROSTAIN is a Professor of Law and co-director of the Center for Professional Values and Practice at New York Law School.

HILLARY A. SALE is the Walter D. Coles Professor of Law and a Professor of Management at Washington University in St. Louis.

DAMON SILVERS is an Associate General Counsel for the American Federation of Labor and Congress of Industrial Organizations (AFL-CIO) and Deputy Chair of the Congressional Oversight Panel overseeing the Treasury Department's implementation of the Emergency Economic Stabilization Act of 2008.

OMARI SCOTT SIMMONS is an Associate Professor of Law at Wake Forest University School of Law.

DAVID A. SKEEL, JR. is the S. Samuel Arsht Professor of Corporate Law at the University of Pennsylvania Law School.

HEATHER SLAVKIN is the Senior Legal and Policy Advisor for the American Federation of Labor and Congress of Industrial Organizations (AFL-CIO) Office of Investment.

THOMAS A. SMITH is a Professor of Law at the University of San Diego School of Law.

LYNN A. STOUT is the Paul Hastings Professor of Corporate and Securities Law at the UCLA School of Law.

LEO E. STRINE, JR. is a Vice Chancellor of the Delaware Court of Chancery.

ROBERT B. THOMPSON is the New York Alumni Chancellor's Professor of Law at Vanderbilt University Law School and Professor of Management at Vanderbilt University.

FREDERICK TUNG is the Robert T. Thompson Professor of Law and Business at Emory University School of Law.

CHERYL L. WADE is the Dean Harold F. McNiece Professor of Law at St. John's University School of Law.

CHARLES K. WHITEHEAD is an Associate Professor of Law at Cornell University Law School.

CYNTHIA WILLIAMS is a Professor of Law at the University of Illinois College of Law.

CHARLES YABLON is a Professor of Law at Yeshiva University, Benjamin N. Cardozo School of Law.

Table of Cases

Table of Statutes

(References are to specific sections or rules; for general references, see subject matter index)

Index